Y0-CAW-929

9. Prepare a post-closing trial balance.

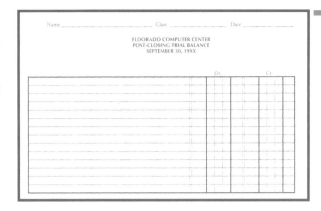

4. Prepare a trial balance.

Trial Balance	Dr.	Cr.
Asset	X	
Contra Assets		X
Liabilities		X
Capital		X
Withdrawals	X	
Revenues		X
Expenses	X	

5. Prepare a worksheet.

WORKSHEET

CLARK'S WORD PROCESSING SERVICES
WORKSHEET
FOR MONTH ENDING MAY 31, 19XX

Account Titles	Trial Balance Dr.	Trial Balance Cr.	Adjustments Dr.	Adjustments Cr.	Adjusted Trial Balance Dr.	Adjusted Trial Balance Cr.	Income Dr.
Cash	6 1 5 5 00						
Accounts Receivable	5 0 0 0 00						
Office Supplies	6 0 0 00						
Prepaid Rent	1 2 0 0 00						
Word Processing Equipment	6 0 0 0 00						
Accounts Payable		3 3 5 0 00					
Brenda Clark, Capital		1 0 0 0 0 00					
Brenda Clark, Withdrawals	6 2 5 00						
Word Processing Fees		8 0 0 0 00					
Office Salaries Expense	1 3 0 0 00						
Advertising Expense	2 5 0 00						
Telephone Expense	2 2 0 00						
	21 3 5 0 00	21 3 5 0 00					

8. Journalize and post closing entries from worksheet.

6. Prepare the financial statements from worksheet.

Income Statement	Statement of Owner's Equity	Balance Sheet
Revenues	Beginning Capital	Assets Liabilities
- expenses	+ net income	
= net income	- withdrawals	Owner's Equity
	= Ending Capital	Ending Capital

(7) Adjustments from the worksheet are journalized in the SAME JOURNAL as Step 2 and posted to SAME ledger as Step 3.

(8) All closing entries are recorded in SAME JOURNAL (Step 2) and posted to SAME LEDGER (Step 3).

(9) After closing entries have been journalized and posted, only PERMANENT accounts will have balances left in the ledger to carry over to the next.

COLLEGE ACCOUNTING

A PRACTICAL APPROACH

CHAPTERS 1–26

EIGHTH EDITION

COLLEGE ACCOUNTING

A PRACTICAL APPROACH

CHAPTERS 1–26

EIGHTH EDITION

Jeffrey Slater

**North Shore Community College
Danvers, Massachusetts**

Prentice Hall
Upper Saddle River, New Jersey 07458

Library of Congress Cataloging-in-Publication Data

Slater, Jeffery, 1947-
    College accounting : a practical approach, chapters 1-26 / Jeffery Slater. -- 8th ed.
        p. com.
    Includes index.
    ISBN 0-13-091142-9
        1. Accounting. I. Title

HF5635 .S6315 2001
657'.044 -- dc21   2001021618

Acquisitions Editor: Alana Bradley
Editor-in-Chief: P. J. Boardman
Senior Editorial Assistant: Jane Avery
Media Project Manager: Nancy Welcher
Executive Marketing Manager: Beth Toland
Marketing Assistant: Brian Rapplefeld
Managing Editor (Production): Cynthia Regan
Production Editor: Michael Reynolds
Production Assistant: Dianne Falcone
Permissions Supervisor: Suzanne Grappi
Associate Director, Manufacturing: Vincent Scelta
Design Director: Patricia Smythe
Art Director: Kevin Kall
Interior Design: Jill Wood
Cover Design: Joseph DiPinto
Cover Illustration/Photo: Corbis Images
Associate Director, Multimedia Production: Karen Goldsmith
Manager, Multimedia Production: Christy Mahon
Composition: Progressive Information Technologies
Full-Service Project Management: Progressive Publishing Alternatives
Printer/Binder: R. R. Donnelley, Willard

Credits and acknowledgments borrowed from other sources and reproduced, with permission, in this
textbook appear on page P1.

© 2002, 1999, 1996, by Prentice-Hall, Inc.

10 9 8 7 6 5 4 3 2
ISBN 0-13-091142-9

TO   Shelley
     Gracie
     Molly
     Maggie
     Amber
          With love, JEFF

Brief Contents

Contents

Dunkin' Donuts Boxes

Dunkin' Donuts Boxes

Peachtree™ Computer Workshops

Preface

E-Business via the internet is expanding quickly today. Today's accounting students are learning the skills that will help them succeed in business and technology. The eighth edition of *College Accounting: A Practical Approach* by Jeffrey Slater helps students integrate these skills by infusing the tried-and-true Slater system with real-world applications. Each chapter begins with an E-Business application that introduces students to Internet activities and accounting. A "Continuing Problem" at the end of each chapter lets students apply their skills to a practical case. Throughout the book, students read about real accounting applications in twelve Dunkin' Donuts boxes that feature both local franchise operations and corporate support functions. And students are taught computer accounting skills using *Peachtree. Supplements for Quickbooks* and *Simply Accounting* are also available.

THE REAL WORLD

Whether students will keep the books for their own small business or function within a corporation, developing an understanding of how accounting procedures are applied in a business setting is crucial to their success. That is why the eighth edition of *College Accounting: A Practical Approach* now brings the real world to the classroom through the following **NEW features**.

NEW CHAPTER OPENERS

To help prepare accounting students in real world applications. This new feature applies accounting theory and procedures to Internet activities.

Based on interviews with members of the accounting department at Dunkin' Donuts corporate headquarters, thirteen boxes have been specially crafted to illustrate how accounting procedures are used at both franchise stores and corporate headquarters. By reading about how useful the worksheet is to a shop owner throughout the year (Chapter 4), or how new IBM point-of-sale terminals help store owners generate more accurate Cash Summaries (Chapter 6), students will see how the skills they learn in class are applied by this well-known company.

The Computer Workshops following Chapters 3, 4, 5, 8, 10, 13 and 16 have been updated for Peachtree Complete 8.0. This commercial software package is used by small- to medium-sized businesses to keep their books and the Computer Workshops teach students to set up the manual systems they learn in the book in a computerized format.

Many businesses use computers in some way to manage their accounting records, so students that possess computer skills are a very valuable asset!

SIMPLY ACCOUNTING

▼ "Getting Started with Simply Accounting Release 8.0" guidebook may be shrink-wrapped with new copies of any Slater text **FREE** of charge.
▼ Simply Accounting Software release 8.0 may may be shrink-wrapped with new copies of any Slater text for a nominal cost.

QUICK BOOKS

▼ "Getting Started with QuickBooks Pro 2001" guidebook may be shrink-wrapped with new copies of any Slater text **FREE** of charge.

E-NOTES FROM JEFF SLATER

To keep your class as current as possible, Jeff Slater will e-mail articles and insights on e-Business to adopting faculty approximately every 4-6 weeks per semester. Interested faculty will be invited to share their insights as well so that a variety of perspectives can be used to enrich the student's learning environment.

THE SLATER SYSTEM

Jeffrey Slater developed his renowned teaching system through 30 years of classroom experience. Broad goals are presented at the start of each chapter. Students are then presented with material in small, manageable units followed by immediate self-checks and feedback. Each chapter is limited to a small number of units, so students review and apply concepts before they move on.

NEW! ON-LINE COURSE

Our FREE on-line course includes:

▼ On-Line Testing
▼ Course Management, Page Tracking, & Gradebook
▼ Communication (Bulletin Board, Chat Rooms, and e-Mail)
▼ Course Information
▼ Calendar

Available in your choice of Standard WebCT, Blackboard, or Course Compass.

Textbook Options

You can use the Slater System in several configurations of *College Accounting: A Practical Approach:*
On the Website (www.prenhall.com/slater) you will find resources for Students and Instructors.
Student Resources will consist of:
An On-line Study Guide containing the following items:
True/False, Multiple Choice, and Essay Questions all with "hints" and scoring. In addition, there will be Internet Exercises that expand the end of chapter Exploring Ebiz exercises in the text. Practice Quizzes will also be available for students to take as an assessment of how well they understand the text material. These Practice Quizzes were written by Jeff Slater and have been class tested for

many years. All of these features will include the option to e-mail the results to faculty or other designee. This Study Guide is in addition to the Study Guide available in Print.

Instructor Resources include the following:

Instructor Solutions Manual, PowerPoints, downloadable solutions to the Peachtree Computer Workshops, Solutions to the Who Dun It Bookstore Practice Set. In addition the downloadable solutions to the Getting Started Series may be found here as well. These resources are password protected and may be accessed using the code available from your Prentice Hall Representative.

EIGHTH EDITION HIGHLIGHTS AND CHANGES

The Slater System The eighth edition retains the proven pedagogy that has made *College Accounting* a classic.

New Chapter Opener with new screenshots and chapter opening vignettes introduce student to e-business applications.

Continuing Problem A Continuing Problem runs through Chapters 1–16, asking students to apply skills to the business scenario set in the Big Picture. It is based on Eldorado Computer Company.

Dunkin' Donuts Boxes The real-world accounting issues facing franchise owners and corporate staff are presented in boxed features based on research of the nationally known company. Discussion questions tie the boxes to chapter concepts.

Quiz Tips "Quiz Tips" provide additional guidance to help students complete the self-review activities at the end of each learning unit.

Check Figures "Check Figures" provide quick feedback for students to monitor progress in all A and B problems.

Coverage of Perpetual Inventory for merchandise inventory and special journals. New appendix in Chapter 9 that uses the general journal approach to teach entries for merchandise company using perpetual inventory. New appendix in Chapter 10 shows how all the special journals in Chapters 9 and 10 would look like in a perpetual system. New appendix in Chapter 12 shows how a worksheet for a merchandise company would look like in a perpetual inventory system.

Peachtree Computer Workshops These popular workshop activities are updated for Peachtree Complete 8.0.

One-On One Videotapes These videotapes produced by the author recreate the Self-Review Quizzes at the end of each learning unit.

Real-World Applications End-of-chapter materials, including "You Make the Call" sections, offer short cases that require critical thinking and cover ethical issues while stressing oral and written communications.

Extensive End-of-Chapter Framework Each chapter offers extensive learning aides, including:

▼ Discussion Questions
▼ Mini Exercises
▼ Exercises
▼ Problem sets A and B
▼ Real World Applications
▼ New! Exploring E-Biz Internet exercises that put your students on the Web.

▼ Continuing Problem: a cumulative problem that runs through Chapters 1–16, asking students to work through the entire business cycle for Eldorado Computer Center.

SUPPLEMENTS

For the Student

▼ Study Guide and Working Papers, Chs. 1–15 (*0-13-091790-7*)
▼ Study Guide and Working Papers, Chs. 16–26 (*0-13-091799-0*)
▼ A-1 Photography Practice Set — Manual (*0-13-080310-3*)
▼ A-1 Photography Practice Set — Computerized (*0-13-080319-7*)
▼ Who-Dun-It Bookstore Practice Set — Manual (*0-13-091803-2*)
▼ Runners Corporation Practice Set — Manual (*0-13-080316-2*)
▼ Runners Corporation Practice Set — Computerized (*0-13-080315-4*)

For the Instructor

▼ Instructor's Resource and Solutions Manual, Chs 1–15 (*0-13-091811-3*)
▼ Instructor's Resource and Solutions Manual, Chs 16–26 (*0-13-091800-8*)
▼ Solutions and Teaching Transparencies, Chapters 1–15 (*0-13-092203-X*)
▼ Solutions and Teaching Transparencies, Chapters 16–26 (*0-13-091809-1*)
▼ Solutions Manual for Who-Dun-It Bookstore Practice Set (*0-13-091801-6*)
▼ Solutions Manual for A-1 Photography/Runners Corporation Practice Sets (*0-13-080314-6*)
▼ Test Item File with Achievement Tests, Chs. 1–15 (*0-13-092002-9*)
▼ Test Item File with Achievement Tests, Chs. 16–26 (*0-13-091796-6*)
▼ Windows PH Custom Test (*0-13-091808-3*)
▼ Tips on Teaching College Accounting Video (*0-13-091806-7*)
▼ Instructors Resource CD-ROM (*0-13-091807-5*)

ACKNOWLEDGMENTS

Writers and Checkers

Tim Carse, CPA (SunGard EBS) — His work on Chapters 7 and 8

Bill Reynolds (St. Charles Community College) Revised Chapter 22

Errol Osteraa (Heald College) Salinas, Peachtree Computer Workshops

Mary McGarry — Dunkin' Donuts boxes

Beth M. Woods — Solution checking the text, Study Guide and Working Papers, and Instructor's Resource and Solutions Manual, TestBank, Who Dun It Bookstore Practice Set and the OnLine Study Guide

Jann Underwood (Eldorado College) — The Big Picture and the Continuing Problem

Nancy Brandwein, E-biz Today

Roger Dimick, (Del Mar Techinical College), Exploring E-biz

Reviewers

Rick Block, Heald College

Paul Concilio, McLennan Community College

Richard Howden, Delta College

Dolores G. Huerta, DelMar College

Marvin F. Mai, Empire College

Paul Muller, Western Nevada Community College
Sandra O'Meara, Santa Barabara City College
Bill Reynolds, St Charles County Community College
Stephen J. Wehner, Columbia College, Marysville

Supplement Authors

Errol Osteraa, (Heald College) Getting Started with Peachtree

Janet Horne (Los Angeles Peirce College) Getting Started with Quickbooks

Jean Insinga (Middlesex Community & Technical College) Getting Started with Simply Accounting

Shari L. DeMarco (Bryant & Stratton Business College) Who Dun it Bookstore Practice Set & Solutions

Patti Holmes (Des Moines Area Community College) Test Banks

Olga Quintana (University of Miami, FL) PowerPoints

Lou Procopio (North Shore Community College) Videos

Prentice Hall Staff

In addition to the people mentioned above, I would like to thank the dedicated Prentice Hall staff members who worked on this project and who did a tremendous amount of work in pulling together *both* the text and the supplements package: Beth Toland, Marketing Manager; Cheryl Clayton, Asssistant Editor; Amy Whitaker, Supplements Coordinator; Alana Bradley, Managing Editor; Michael Reynolds, Production Editor; Kevin Kall, Designer, and Walter Mendez, Accounting Customer Service Representive. Thank you all for a job well done!

—Jeff Slater

The Accounting Cycle for a Service Company

Accounting Concepts and Procedures

AN INTRODUCTION

There has been tremendous excitement surrounding the rise of the "dot.coms," the Internet businesses fueling the new economy. Electronic auctions allow customers to call the shots when it comes to price. Business-to-business cyber-exchanges enable businesses to sell products and services to other businesses seamlessly, without using paper invoices. Even specialized services like *accounting* are offered over the Internet.

In the fervor of trying to woo investors and project optimism, however, e-businesses are bending some longstanding rules of accounting. One of these rules is that **revenue**—the money a company earns for selling a product or service—should be recognized when it is earned, not when it is due. In this chapter, you'll see how the **accounting equation** can change dramatically if future revenue is counted as earned revenue. Revenue is considered part of **owner's equity** and the basic accounting equation states that **assets = liabilities + owner's equity.** If owner's equity is based on inflated revenue figures, the company's financial statement will give investors a skewed picture of the company's value.

A case in point is Microstrategy, a 10-year-old Vienna, VA, company that specializes in datamining software and services. When Microstrategy began offering its services over the Internet its reported revenues soared. In 12 months the stock rose from $7.34 to $33 a share and turned its 35-year-old CEO, Michael Saylor, into one of the nation's youngest billionaires. Then, boom, on March 20, 2000, Saylor announced a change in accounting practices and the stock lost 60% of its value in one day. Suddenly, a previously announced 1999 profit of $12.6 million turned into a loss of up to $40 million, all because the company decided to comply with Securities and Exchange Commission (SEC) guidelines. Microstrategy had been booking revenue for service contracts in hand even though the revenue would be spread out over a multi-year period. Expect to hear more about the issue of overstatement of revenues from the SEC. "Think about a bottle of fine wine," says SEC chairman Arthur Levitt. "You wouldn't pop the cork on that bottle before it was ready. But some companies are doing this — recognizing revenues before a sale is complete, before the product is delivered, or a time when the customer still has options to terminate, void or delay the sale." MicroStrategy popped the cork prematurely, but it certainly alerted its dot.com cousins to the consequences.

Sources: Based on Adam Zagorin, "The E-numbers game," *Time,* April 3, 2000, p. 66. Sandra Sugawara, "SEC unit targets accounting tricks; New team to focus on cooked books," *The Washington Post,* May 26, 2000, p. E5. James Lardner, "A tech highflier's day of reckoning: How Michael Saylor went from 'boy visionary' to poster boy for dot-com shenanigans," *U.S. News & World Report,* April 10, 2000, pp. 42–43. Robert J. Samuelson, "A high-tech accounting?" *Newsweek,* April 3, 2000, p. 37.

LEARNING OBJECTIVES

▼ Defining and listing the functions of accounting. (p. 6)

▼ Recording transactions in the basic accounting equation. (p. 7)

▼ Seeing how revenue, expenses, and withdrawals expand the basic accounting equation. (p. 13)

▼ Preparing an income statement, a statement of owner's equity, and a balance sheet. (p. 18)

Accounting is the language of business; it provides information to managers, owners, investors, governmental agencies, and others inside and outside the organization. Accounting provides answers and insights to questions like these:

▼ Should I invest in Amazon.com?

▼ Will Internet companies show good return in the future?

▼ Can American Airlines pay its debt obligations?

▼ What percentage of IBM's marketing budget is for e-Business? How does that percentage compare with the competition? What is the overall financial condition of IBM?

> The Internet is creating many new opportunities and challenges for all forms of business organizations.

Smaller businesses also need answers to their financial questions:

▼ Did business increase enough over the last year to warrant hiring a new assistant?

▼ Should we spend more money to design, produce, and send out new brochures in an effort to create more business?

▼ What role should the Internet play in our business?

Accounting is as important to individuals as it is to businesses; it answers questions like these:

▼ Should I take out a loan for a new car or wait until I can afford to pay cash for it?
▼ Would my money work better in a savings bank or in the stock market?

Accounting is the process that analyzes, records, classifies, summarizes, reports, and interprets financial information to decision makers — whether individuals, small businesses, large corporations, or governmental agencies — in a timely fashion. It is important that students understand the "whys" of the accounting process. Just knowing the mechanics is not enough.

There are three main categories of business organization: (1) sole proprietorships, (2) partnerships, and (3) corporations. Let's define each of them and look at their advantages and disadvantages. This information also appears in Table 1-1.

Sole Proprietorship

A **sole proprietorship,** such as Sam's Hair Salon, is a business that has one owner. That person is both the owner and the manager of the business. An advantage of a sole proprietorship is that the owner makes all the decisions for the business. A disadvantage is that if the business cannot pay its obligations, the business owner must pay them, which means that the owner could lose some of his or her personal assets (e.g., house or savings).

Sole proprietorships are easy to form. They end if the business closes or when the owner dies.

Partnership

A **partnership,** such as Miller and Jones, is a form of business ownership that has at least two owners (partners). Each partner acts as an owner of the company, which is an advantage because the partners can share the decision making and the risks of the business. A disadvantage is that, as in a sole proprietorship, the partners' personal assets could be lost if the partnership cannot meet its obligations.

Partnerships are easy to form. They end when a partner dies or leaves the partnership.

TABLE 1-1   TYPES OF BUSINESS ORGANIZATIONS

	Sole Proprietorship	Partnership	Corporation
Ownership	Business owned by one person.	Business owned by more than one person.	Business owned by stockholders.
Formation	Easy to form.	Easy to form.	More difficult to form.
Liability	Owner could lose personal assets to meet obligations of business.	Partners could lose personal assets to meet obligations of partnership.	Limited personal risk. Stockholders' loss is limited to their investment in the company.
Closing	Ends with death of owner or closing of business.	Ends with death of partner or exit of a partner.	Can continue indefinitely.

eBay is an example of a corporation.

Corporation

A **corporation,** such as Microsoft, is a business owned by stockholders. The corporation may have only a few stockholders, or it may have many stockholders. The stockholders are not personally liable for the corporation's debts, and they usually do not have input into the business decisions.

Corporations are more difficult to form than sole proprietorships or partnerships. Corporations can exist indefinitely.

CLASSIFYING BUSINESS ORGANIZATIONS

Whether we are looking at a sole proprietorship, a partnership, or a corporation, the business can be classified by what the business does to earn money. Companies are categorized as service, merchandise, or manufacturing businesses.

A local cab company is a good example of a **service company** because it provides a service. The first part of this book focuses on service businesses.

Macy's and J.C. Penney sell products. They are called merchandise companies. **Merchandise companies** can either make their own products or sell products that are made by another supplier. Companies like Mattel and Ford Motor Company that make their own products are called **manufacturers.** (See Table 1-2.)

DEFINITION OF ACCOUNTING

Accounting (also called the accounting process) is a system that measures the activities of a business in financial terms. It provides various reports and financial statements that show how the various transactions the business undertook (e.g., buying and selling goods) affected the business. It does this by performing the following functions:

▼ **Analyzing:** Looking at what happened and how the business was affected.

▼ **Recording:** Putting the information into the accounting system.

▼ **Classifying:** Grouping all the same activities (e.g., all purchases) together.

▼ **Summarizing:** Explaining the results.

▼ **Reporting:** Issuing the statements that tell the results of the previous functions.

▼ **Interpreting:** Examining the statements to determine how the various pieces of information they contain relate to each other.

The system communicates the reports and financial statements to people who are interested in the information, such as the business's decision makers, investors, creditors, and governmental agencies (e.g., the Internal Revenue Service).

As you can see, a lot of people use these reports. A set of procedures and guidelines were developed to make sure that everyone prepares and interprets

TABLE 1-2 EXAMPLES OF SERVICE, MERCHANDISE, AND MANUFACTURING BUSINESSES		
Service Businesses	**Merchandise Businesses**	**Manufacturing Businesses**
eBay	Macy's	Mattel
Jane's Painting Co.	J.C. Penney	Ford
Dr. Wheeler, M.D.	Amazon.com	Toro
Accountemps	Home Depot	Levi's
CellularOne Paging Services	Staples	Intel

them the same way. These guidelines are known as **generally accepted accounting principles (GAAP).**

Now let's look at the difference between bookkeeping and accounting. Keep in mind that we use the terms *accounting* and the *accounting process* interchangeably.

DIFFERENCE BETWEEN BOOKKEEPING AND ACCOUNTING

Confusion often arises concerning the difference between bookkeeping and accounting. **Bookkeeping** is the recording (recordkeeping) function of the accounting process; a bookkeeper enters accounting information in the company's books. An accountant takes that information and prepares the financial statements that are used to analyze the company's financial position. Accounting involves many complex activities. Often, it includes the preparation of tax and financial reports, budgeting, and analyses of financial information.

Today, computers are used for routine bookkeeping operations that used to take weeks or months to complete. The text takes this into consideration by explaining how the advantages of the computer can be applied to a manual accounting system by using hands-on knowledge of how accounting works. Basic accounting knowledge is needed even though computers can do routine tasks. QuickBooks and Peachtree are two popular software packages in use today.

LEARNING UNIT 1-1   THE ACCOUNTING EQUATION

ASSETS, LIABILITIES, AND EQUITIES

Let's begin our study of accounting concepts and procedures by looking at a small business: Cathy Hall's law practice. Cathy decided to open her practice at the end of August. She consulted her accountant before she made her decision. The accountant told her some important things before she made this decision. First, he told her the new business would be considered a separate business entity whose finances had to be kept separate and distinct from Cathy's personal finances. The accountant went on to say that all transactions can be analyzed using the basic accounting equation: Assets = Liabilities + Owner's Equity.

Cathy had never heard of the basic accounting equation. She listened carefully as the accountant explained the terms used in the equation and how the equation works.

Assets

Cash, land, supplies, office equipment, buildings, and other properties of value *owned* by a firm are called **assets.**

Equities

The rights of financial claim to the assets are called **equities.** Equities belong to those who supply the assets. If you are the only person to supply assets to the firm, you have the sole rights, for financial claims, to them. For example, if you supply the law firm with $5,000 in cash and $4,000 in office equipment, your equity in the firm is $9,000.

Relationship between Assets and Equities

The relationship between assets and equities is

Assets	=	Equities
(Total value of items *owned* by business)		(Total claims against the assets)

The total dollar value of the assets of your law firm will be equal to the total dollar value of the financial claims to those assets, that is, equal to the total dollar value of the equities.

The total dollar value is broken down on the left-hand side of the equation to show the specific items of value owned by the business and on the right-hand side to show the types of claims against the assets owned.

Liabilities

A firm may have to borrow money to buy more assets; when this occurs it means the firm is *buying assets on account* (buy now, pay later). Suppose the law firm purchases a new computer for $2,300 on account from Gateway, and the company is willing to wait 10 days for payment. The law firm has created a **liability:** an obligation to pay that comes due in the future. Gateway is called the **creditor.** This liability — the amount owed to Gateway — gives the store the right, or the financial claim, to $2,300 of the law firm's assets. When Gateway is paid, the store's rights to the assets of the law firm will end, because the obligation has been paid off.

Basic Accounting Equation

To best understand the various claims to a business's assets, accountants divide equities into two parts. The claims of creditors — outside persons or businesses — are labeled *liabilities.* The claim of the business's owner are labeled **owner's equity.** Let's see how the accounting equation looks now.

Assets =	Equities
	1. Liabilities: rights of creditors
	2. Owner's equity: rights of owner

Assets = Liabilities + Owner's Equity

The total value of all the assets of a firm equals the combined total value of the financial claims of the creditors (liabilities) and the claims of the owners (owner's equity). This is known as the **basic accounting equation.** The basic accounting equation provides a basis for understanding the conventional accounting system of a business. The equation records business transactions in a logical and orderly way that shows their impact on the company's assets, liabilities, and owner's equity.

Importance of Creditors

Another way of presenting the basic accounting equation is

Assets − Liabilities = Owner's Equity

This form of the equation stresses the importance of creditors. The owner's rights to the business's assets are determined after the rights of the creditors are subtracted. In other words, creditors have first claim to assets. If a firm has no liabilities — and therefore no creditors — the owner has the total rights to assets. Another term for the owner's current investment, or equity, in the business's assets is **capital.**

Elements of basic accounting equation

| Assets |
| − Liabilities |
| = Owner's Equity |

| In accounting, capital does not mean cash. Capital is the owner's current investment, or equity, in the assets of the business. |

As Cathy Hall's law firm engages in business transactions (paying bills, serving customers, and so on), changes will take place in the assets, liabilities, and owner's equity (capital). Let's analyze some of these transactions.

> **Transaction A   Aug. 28:** Cathy invests $7,000 in cash and $800 of office equipment into the business.

On August 28, Cathy withdraws $7,000 from her personal bank account and deposits the money in the law firm's newly opened bank account. She also invests $800 of office equipment in the business. She plans to be open for business on September 1. With the help of her accountant, Cathy begins to prepare the accounting records for the business. We put this information into the basic accounting equation as follows:

ASSETS		=	LIABILITIES +	OWNER'S EQUITY
Cash	+ Office Equipment	=		Cathy Hall, Capital
$7,000 +	$800	=		$7,800
	$7,800 = $7,800			

> Note: Capital is part of owner's equity; it is not an asset.
> In our analyses, assume that any number without a sign in front of it is a +.

Note that the total value of the assets, cash, and office equipment—$7,800—is equal to the combined total value of liabilities (none, so far) and owner's equity ($7,800). Remember, Hall has supplied all the cash and office equipment, so she has the sole financial claim to the assets. Note how the heading "Cathy Hall, Capital" is written under the owner's equity heading. The $7,800 is Cathy's investment, or equity, in the firm's assets.

> **Transaction B   Aug. 29:** Law practice buys office equipment for cash, $900.

From the initial investment of $7,000 cash, the law firm buys $900 worth of office equipment (such as a computer desk), which lasts a long time, whereas **supplies** (such as pens) tend to be used up relatively quickly.

ASSETS		=	LIABILITIES +	OWNER'S EQUITY	
Cash	+ Office Equipment	=		Cathy Hall, Capital	
$7,000 +	$800	=		$7,800	BEGINNING BALANCE
−900	+900				TRANSACTION
$6,100 +	$1,700	=		$7,800	ENDING BALANCE
	$7,800 = $7,800				

Shift in Assets

As a result of the last transaction, the law office has less cash but has increased its amount of office equipment. This is called a **shift in assets;** the makeup of the assets has changed, but the total of the assets remains the same.

Suppose you go food shopping at Wal-Mart with $90 and spend $60. Now you have two assets, food and money. The composition of the assets has been *shifted*—you have more food and less money than you did—but the *total* of the assets has not increased or decreased. The total value of the food, $60, plus the cash, $30, is still $90. When you borrow money from the bank, on the other hand, you have an increase in cash (an asset) and an increase in liabilities; overall there is an increase in assets, not just a shift.

An accounting equation can remain in balance even if only one side is updated. The key point to remember is that the left-hand-side total of assets must always equal the right-hand-side total of liabilities and owner's equity.

The law firm purchases an additional $400 worth of chairs and desks from Wilmington Company. Instead of demanding cash right away, Wilmington agrees to deliver the equipment and to allow up to 60 days for the law practice to pay the invoice (bill).

This liability, or obligation to pay in the future, has some interesting effects on the basic accounting equation. Wilmington Company has accepted as payment a partial claim against the assets of the law practice. This claim exists until the law firm pays off the bill. This unwritten promise to pay the creditor is a liability called **accounts payable.**

	ASSETS	=	LIABILITIES	+ OWNER'S EQUITY
	Cash + Office Equipment	=	Accounts Payable	+ Cathy Hall, Capital
BEGINNING BALANCE	$6,100 + $1,700	=		$7,800
TRANSACTION	+400		+$400	
ENDING BALANCE	$6,100 + $2,100	=	$400	$7,800
		$8,200 = $8,200		

When this information is analyzed, we can see that the law practice has increased what it owes (accounts payable) as well as what it owns (office equipment) by $400. The law practice gains $400 in an asset but has an obligation to pay Wilmington Company at a future date.

The owner's equity remains unchanged. This transaction results in an increase of total assets from $7,800 to $8,200.

Finally, note that after each transaction the basic accounting equation remains in balance.

LEARNING UNIT 1-1 REVIEW

AT THIS POINT you should be able to

▼ Define and explain the differences between sole proprietorships, partnerships, and corporations. (p. 5)
▼ List the functions of accounting. (p. 6)
▼ Compare and contrast bookkeeping and accounting. (p. 7)
▼ Explain the role of the computer as an accounting tool. (p. 7)
▼ State the purpose of the accounting equation. (p. 7)
▼ Explain the difference between liabilities and owner's equity. (p. 8)
▼ Define capital. (p. 9)
▼ Explain the difference between a shift in assets and an increase in assets. (p. 9)

To test your understanding of this material, complete Self-Review Quiz 1-1. The blank forms you need are in the *Study Guide and Working Papers* for Chapter 1. The solution to the quiz immediately follows here in the text. If you have difficulty doing the problems, review Learning Unit 1-1 and the solution to the quiz. Videotapes are available to review these quizzes. Be sure to check the Slater website for student study aids. Check with your instructor on availability.

Keep in mind that learning accounting is like learning to type: the more you practice, the better you become. You will not be an expert in one day. Be patient. It will all come together.

SELF-REVIEW QUIZ 1-1

(The blank forms you need are on page 1 of the *Study Guide and Working Papers.*)

Record the following transactions in the basic accounting equation:

1. Gracie Ryan invests $17,000 to begin a real estate office.
2. The real estate office buys $600 of computer equipment from Wal-Mart for cash.
3. The real estate company buys $800 of additional computer equipment on account from Circuit City.

Solution to Self-Review Quiz 1-1

ASSETS			=	LIABILITIES	+	OWNER'S EQUITY	
Cash	+	Computer Equipment	=	Accounts Payable	+	Gracie Ryan, Capital	
+$17,000					+	$17,000	1.
17,000			=			17,000	BALANCE
−600		+$600					2.
16,400	+	600	=			17,000	BALANCE
		+800		+$800			3.
$16,400	+	$1,400	=	$800	+	$17,000	ENDING BALANCE

$$\$17,800 = \$17,800$$

> *Quiz Tip:* Note that transaction 2 below is a shift in assets, whereas transaction 3 is an increase in assets. Keep asking yourself, What did the business get and who supplied it to the business? Remember, capital is not cash. Cash is an asset, whereas capital is part of owner's equity.

LEARNING UNIT 1-2   THE BALANCE SHEET

In the first learning unit, the transactions for Cathy Hall's law firm were recorded in the accounting equation. The transactions we recorded occurred before the law firm opened for business. A statement called a **balance sheet** or **statement of financial position** can show the history of a company before it opened. The balance sheet is a formal statementt that presents the information from the ending balances of both sides of the accounting equation. Think of the balance sheet as a snapshot of the business's financial position as of a particular date.

Let's look at the balance sheet of Cathy Hall's law practice for August 31, 200X, shown in Figure 1-1. The figures in the balance sheet come from the ending balances of the accounting equation for the law practice as shown in Learning Unit 1-1.

Note in Figure 1-1 that the assets owned by the law practice appear on the left-hand side and that the liabilities and owner's equity appear on the right-hand side. Both sides equal $8,200. This *balance* between left and right gives the balance sheet its name. In later chapters we look at other ways to set up a balance sheet.

> The balance sheet shows the company's financial position as of a particular date. (In our example, that date is at the end of August.)

POINTS TO REMEMBER IN PREPARING A BALANCE SHEET

The Heading

The heading of the balance sheet provides the following information:

▼ The company name: Cathy Hall, Attorney-at-Law.
▼ The name of the statement: Balance Sheet.
▼ The date for which the report is prepared: August 31, 200X.

> Do you remember the three elements that make up a balance sheet? Assets, liabilities, and owner's equity.

FIGURE 1-1. The Balance
Sheet

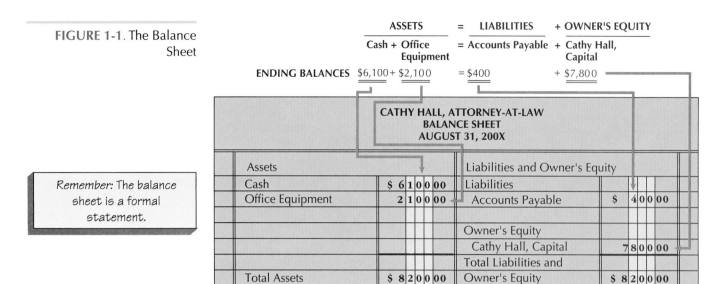

Remember: The balance
sheet is a formal
statement.

Use of the Dollar Sign

Note that the dollar sign is not repeated each time a figure appears. As shown in the balance sheet for Cathy Hall's law practice, it usually is placed to the left of each column's top figure and to the left of the column's total.

CATHY HALL, ATTORNEY-AT-LAW BALANCE SHEET AUGUST 31, 200X		
Assets		
Cash		$ 6 1 0 0 00
Office Equipment		2 1 0 0 00
Total Assets		$ 8 2 0 0 00

A single line means
the numbers above it
have been added or
subtracted.

A double line indicates
a total.

Distinguishing the Total

When adding numbers down a column, use a single line before the total and a double line beneath it. A single line means that the numbers above it have been added or subtracted. A double line indicates a total. It is important to align the numbers in the column; many errors occur because these figures are not lined up. These rules are the same for all accounting reports.

The balance sheet gives Cathy the information she needs to see the law firm's financial position before it opens for business. This information does not tell her, however, whether or not the firm will make a profit.

LEARNING UNIT 1-2 REVIEW

AT THIS POINT you should be able to

▼ Define and state the purpose of a balance sheet. (p. 11)
▼ Identify and define the elements making up a balance sheet. (p. 12)
▼ Show the relationship between the accounting equation and the balance sheet. (p. 12)
▼ Prepare a balance sheet in proper form from information provided. (p. 12)

SELF-REVIEW QUIZ 1-2

(The blank forms you need are on page 2 of the *Study Guide and Working Papers*.)

The date is November 30, 200X. Use the following information to prepare in proper form a balance sheet for Janning Company:

Accounts Payable	$40,000
Cash	18,000
A. Janning, Capital	9,000
Office Equipment	31,000

Quiz Tip: The heading of a balance sheet answers the questions *who, what,* and *when.* November 30, 200X is the particular date.

Solution to Self-Review Quiz 1-2

JANNING COMPANY
BALANCE SHEET
NOVEMBER 30, 200X

Assets		Liabilities and Owner's Equity	
Cash	$18 000 00	Liabilities	
Office Equipment	31 000 00	Accounts Payable	$40 000 00
		Owner's Equity	
		A. Janning, Capital	9 000 00
		Total Liabilities and	
Total Assets	$49 000 00	Owner's Equity	$49 000 00

Capital does not mean cash. The capital amount is the owner's current investment of assets in the business.

LEARNING UNIT 1-3

THE ACCOUNTING EQUATION EXPANDED: REVENUE, EXPENSES, AND WITHDRAWALS

As soon as Cathy Hall's office opened, she began performing legal services for her clients and earning revenue for the business. At the same time, as a part of doing business, she incurred various expenses, such as rent.

When Cathy asked her accountant how these transactions fit into the accounting equation, he began by defining some terms.

Revenue A service company earns **revenue** when it provides services to its clients. Cathy's law firm earned revenue when she provided legal services to her clients for legal fees. When revenue is earned, owner's equity is increased. In effect, revenue is a subdivision of owner's equity.

Assets are increased. The increase is in the form of cash if the client pays right away. If the client promises to pay in the future, the increase is called **accounts receivable.** When revenue is earned, the transaction is recorded as an increase in revenue and an increase in assets (either as cash and/or as accounts receivable, depending on whether it was paid right away or will be paid in the future).

Expenses A business's **expenses** are the cost the company incurs in carrying on operations in its effort to create revenue. Expenses are also a subdivision of owner's equity; when expenses are incurred, they *decrease* owner's equity. Expenses can be paid for in cash or they can be charged.

Net Income/Net Loss When revenue totals more than expenses, **net income** is the result; when expenses total more than revenue, **net loss** is the result.

Accounts receivable is an asset. The law firm expects to be able to receive amounts owed from customers at a later date.

Remember: Accounts receivable results from earning revenue even when cash is not yet received.

Record an expense when it is incurred, whether it is paid then or is to be paid later.

FIGURE 1-2. Owner's Equity

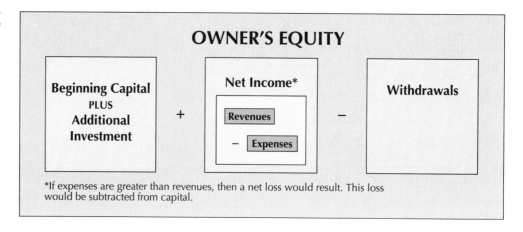

OWNER'S EQUITY

Beginning Capital
PLUS
Additional
Investment

+

Net Income*

Revenues
− Expenses

−

Withdrawals

*If expenses are greater than revenues, then a net loss would result. This loss
would be subtracted from capital.

Withdrawals At some point Cathy Hall may need to withdraw cash or other
assets from the business to pay living or other personal expenses that do not
relate to the business. We will record these transactions in an account called
withdrawals. Sometimes this account is called the *owner's drawing account.*
Withdrawals is a subdivision of owner's equity that records personal expenses
not related to the business. Withdrawals decrease owner's equity (see Fig. 1-2).

It is important to remember the difference between expenses and withdrawals. Expenses relate to business operations; withdrawals are the result of
personal needs outside the normal operations of the business.

Now let's analyze the September transactions for Cathy Hall's law firm
using an **expanded accounting equation** that includes withdrawals, revenues,
and expenses.

EXPANDED ACCOUNTING EQUATION

> Transaction D   Sept. 1–30: Provided legal services for
> cash, $3,000.

Transactions A, B, and C were discussed earlier, when the law office was
being formed in August. See Learning Unit 1-1.

	ASSETS			= LIABILITIES +		OWNER'S EQUITY			
	Cash	+ Accts. Rec.	+ Office Equip.	= Accts. Pay.	+ C. Hall, Capital	− C. Hall, Withdr.	+ Revenue	− Expenses
BALANCE FORWARD	$6,100		+ $ 2,100	= $ 400	+ $7,800			
TRANSACTION	+3,000						+$3,000	
ENDING BALANCE	$9,100		+ $ 2,100	= $ 400	+ $7,800		+ $3,000	
			$11,200 = $11,200					

In the law firm's first month of operation, a total of $3,000 in cash was
received for legal services performed. In the accounting equation, the asset
Cash is increased by $3,000. Revenue is also increased by $3,000, resulting in
an increase in owner's equity.

A revenue column was added to the basic accounting equation. Amounts
are recorded in the revenue column when they are earned. They are also
recorded in the assets column, either under Cash and/or under Accounts
Receivable. Do not think of revenue as an asset. It is part of owner's equity. It
is the revenue that creates an inward flow of cash and accounts receivable.

Transaction E   Sept. 1–30: Provided legal services on account, $4,000.

	ASSETS		= LIABILITIES +		OWNER'S EQUITY			
Cash +	Accts. Rec. +	Office Equip.	= Accts. Pay.	+ C. Hall, Capital	− C. Hall, Withdr.	+ Revenue	− Expenses	
$9,100		+ $ 2,100	= $ 400	+ $7,800		+ $3,000		BAL. FOR.
	+4,000					+4,000		TRANS.
$9,100	+ $4,000	+ $ 2,100	= $ 400	+ $7,800		+ $7,000		END. BAL.
		$15,200 = $15,200						

Cathy's law practice performed legal work on account for $4,000. The firm did not receive the cash for these earned legal fees; it accepted an unwritten promise from these clients that payment would be received in the future.

Transaction F   Sept. 1–30: Received $700 cash as partial payment from previous services performed on account.

During September some of Cathy's clients who had received services and promised to pay in the future decided to reduce what they owed the practice by $700 when their bills came due. This is shown as follows on the expanded accounting equation.

	ASSETS		= LIABILITIES +		OWNER'S EQUITY			
Cash +	Accts. Rec. +	Office Equip.	= Accts. Pay.	+ C. Hall, Capital	− C. Hall, Withdr.	+ Revenue	− Expenses	
$9,100 +	$4,000 +	$ 2,100	= $ 400	+ $7,800		+ $7,000		BAL. FOR.
+700	−700							TRANS.
$9,800 +	$3,300 +	$ 2,100	= $ 400	+ $7,800		+ $7,000		END. BAL.
		$15,200 = $15,200						

The law firm increased the asset Cash by $700 and reduced another asset, Accounts Receivable, by $700. The *total* of assets does not change. The right-hand side of the expanded accounting equation has not been touched because the total on the left-hand side of the equation has not changed. The revenue was recorded when it was earned, and the *same revenue cannot be recorded twice.* This transaction analyzes the situation *after* the revenue has been previously earned and recorded. Transaction F shows a shift in assets: more cash and less accounts receivable.

Transaction G   Sept. 1–30: Paid salaries expense, $600.

	ASSETS		= LIABILITIES +		OWNER'S EQUITY			
Cash +	Accts. Rec. +	Office Equip.	= Accts. Pay.	+ C. Hall, Capital	− C. Hall, Withdr.	+ Revenue	− Expenses	
$9,800 +	$3,300 +	$ 2,100	= $ 400	+ $7,800		+ $7,000		BAL. FOR.
−600							+$600	TRANS.
$9,200 +	$3,300 +	$ 2,100	= $ 400	+ $7,800		+ $7,000	− $600	END. BAL.
		$14,600 = $14,600						

As expenses increase, they decrease owner's equity. This incurred expense of $600 reduces the cash by $600. Although the expense was paid, the total of our expenses to date has *increased* by $600. Keep in mind that owner's equity decreases as expenses increase, so the accounting equation remains in balance.

Transaction H   Sept. 1–30: Paid rent expense, $700.

	ASSETS			= LIABILITIES +		OWNER'S EQUITY			
	Cash +	Accts. + Rec.	Office = Equip.	Accts. Pay.	+ C. Hall, Capital	− C. Hall, Withdr.	+ Revenue	− Expenses
BAL. FOR. TRANS.	$9,200 + −700	$3,300 +	$ 2,100 =	$ 400	+ $7,800		+ $7,000	− $ 600 +700
END. BAL	$8,500 +	$3,300 +	$ 2,100 =	$ 400	+ $7,800		+ $7,000	− $1,300
			$13,900 = $13,900					

During September the practice incurred rent expenses of $700. This rent was not paid in advance; it was paid when it came due. The payment of rent reduces the asset Cash by $700 as well as increases the expenses of the firm, resulting in a decrease in owner's equity. The firm's expenses are now $1,300.

Transaction I   Sept. 1–30: Incurred advertising expenses of $300, to be paid next month.

	ASSETS			= LIABILITIES +		OWNER'S EQUITY			
	Cash +	Accts. + Rec.	Office = Equip.	Accts. Pay.	+ C. Hall, Capital	− C. Hall, Withdr.	+ Revenue	− Expenses
BALANCE FORWARD TRANSACTION	$8,500 +	$3,300 +	$ 2,100 =	$ 400 +300	+ $7,800		+ $7,000	− $1,300 +300
ENDING BALANCE	$8,500 +	$3,300 +	$ 2,100 =	700	+ $7,800		+ $7,000	− $1,600
			$13,900 = $13,900					

Cathy ran an ad in the local newspaper and incurred an expense of $300. This increase in expenses caused a corresponding decrease in owner's equity. Because Cathy has not paid the newspaper for the advertising yet, she owes $300. Thus her liabilities (Accounts Payable) increase by $300. Eventually, when the bill comes in and is paid, both Cash and Accounts Payable will be decreased.

Transaction J Sept. 1–30: Cathy withdrew $200 for personal use.

	ASSETS			= LIABILITIES +		OWNER'S EQUITY			
	Cash +	Accts. + Rec.	Office = Equip.	Accts. Pay.	+ C. Hall, Capital	− C. Hall, Withdr.	+ Revenue	− Expenses
BAL. FOR. TRANS.	$8,500 + −200	$3,300 +	$ 2,100 =	$ 700	+ $7,800	+$200	+ $7,000	− $1,600
END. BAL	$8,300 +	$3,300 +	$ 2,100 =	$ 700	+ $7,800 −	$200	+ $7,000	− $1,600
			$13,700 = $13,700					

By taking $200 for personal use, Cathy has *increased* her withdrawals from the business by $200 and decreased the asset Cash by $200. Note that as withdrawals increase, the owner's equity *decreases*. Keep in mind that a withdrawal is *not* a business expense. It is a subdivision of owner's equity that records money or other assets an owner withdraws from the business for *personal* use.

Subdivision of Owner's Equity

Take a moment to review the subdivisions of owner's equity:

▼ As capital increases, owner's equity increases (see Transaction A).
▼ As withdrawals increase, owner's equity decreases (see Transaction J).
▼ As revenue increases, owner's equity increases (see Transaction D).
▼ As expenses increase, owner's equity decreases (see Transaction G).

Cathy Hall's Expanded Accounting Equation

The following is a summary of the expanded accounting equation for Cathy Hall's law firm.

CATHY HALL
ATTORNEY-AT-LAW
EXPANDED ACCOUNTING EQUATION: A SUMMARY

ASSETS			= LIABILITIES +		OWNER'S EQUITY				
Cash +	Accts. Rec. +	Office Equip. =	Accts. Pay. +	C. Hall, Capital −	C. Hall, Withdr. +	Revenue −	Expenses		
$7,000		+$800 =		+$7,800					A.
									BALANCE
7,000		+ 800 =		7,800					B.
−900		+900							BALANCE
6,100		+ 1,700 =		7,800					C.
		+400	+$400						BALANCE
6,100		+ 2,100 =	400 +	7,800					D.
+3,000						+$3,000			BALANCE
9,100		+ 2,100 =	400 +	7,800		+ 3,000			E.
	+$4,000					+4,000			BALANCE
9,100 +	4,000 +	2,100 =	400 +	7,800		+ 7,000			F.
+700	−700								BALANCE
9,800 +	3,300 +	2,100 =	400 +	7,800		+ 7,000			G.
−600							+$600		BALANCE
9,200 +	3,300 +	2,100 =	400 +	7,800		+ 7,000 −	600		H.
−700							+700		BALANCE
8,500 +	3,300 +	2,100 =	400 +	7,800		+ 7,000 −	1,300		I.
			+300				+300		BALANCE
8,500 +	3,300 +	2,100 =	700 +	7,800		+ 7,000 −	1,600		J.
−200					+$200				END
$8,300 +	$3,300 +	$ 2,100 =	$ 700 +	$7,800 −	$200 +	$7,000 −	$1,600		BALANCE
		$13,700 =	$13,700						

LEARNING UNIT 1-3 REVIEW

AT THIS POINT you should be able to

▼ Define and explain the difference between revenue and expenses. (p. 13)
▼ Define and explain the difference between net income and net loss. (p. 14)
▼ Explain the subdivision of owner's equity. (p. 17)

- ▼ Explain the effects of withdrawals, revenue, and expenses on owner's equity. (p. 17)
- ▼ Record transactions in an expanded accounting equation and balance the basic accounting equation as a means of checking the accuracy of your calculations. (p. 17)

SELF-REVIEW QUIZ 1-3

(The blank forms you need are on page 3 of the *Study Guide and Working Papers*.)

Record the following transactions into the expanded accounting equation for the Bing Company. Note that all titles have a beginning balance.

1. Received cash revenue, $4,000.
2. Billed customers for services rendered, $6,000.
3. Received a bill for telephone expenses (to be paid next month), $125.
4. Bob Bing withdrew cash for personal use, $500.
5. Received $1,000 from customers in partial payment for services performed in transaction 2.

> *Quiz Tip:* Think of expenses and withdrawals as increasing. As they increase, they will reduce the owner's rights. For example, transaction 4 withdrawals increased by $500, resulting in withdrawals increasing from $800 to $1,300. This represents a $500 decrease to owner's equity.

Solution to Self-Review Quiz 1-3

	ASSETS			= LIABILITIES +		OWNER'S EQUITY		
	Cash +	Accts. Rec. +	Cleaning = Equip.	Accts. Pay.	+ B. Bing, Capital	− B. Bing, Withdr.	+ Revenue	− Expenses
BEG. BALANCE	$10,000 +	$ 2,500 +	$ 6,500 =	$ 1,000	+ $11,800 −	$ 800 +	$ 9,000 −	$2,000
1.	+4,000						+4,000	
BALANCE	14,000 +	2,500 +	6,500 =	1,000	+ 11,800 −	800 +	13,000 −	2,000
2.		+6,000					+6,000	
BALANCE	14,000 +	8,500 +	6,500 =	1,000	+ 11,800 −	800 +	19,000 −	2,000
3.				+125				+125
BALANCE	14,000 +	8,500 +	6,500 =	1,125	+ 11,800 −	800 +	19,000 −	2,125
4.	−500					+500		
BALANCE	13,500 +	8,500 +	6,500 =	1,125	+ 11,800 −	1,300 +	19,000 −	2,125
5.	+1,000	−1,000						
END BALANCE	$14,500 +	$ 7,500 +	$ 6,500 =	$ 1,125	+ $11,800 −	$1,300 +	$19,000 −	$2,125
				$28,500 =	$28,500			

LEARNING UNIT 1-4

PREPARING FINANCIAL STATEMENTS

Cathy Hall would like to be able to find out whether her firm is making a profit, so she asks her accountant whether he can measure the firm's financial performance on a monthly basis. Her accountant replies that there are a number of financial statements that he can prepare, such as the income statement, which shows how well the law firm has performed over a specific period of time. The accountant can use the information in the income statement to prepare other reports.

> The income statement is prepared from data found in the revenue and expense columns of the expanded accounting equation.

THE INCOME STATEMENT

An **income statement** is an accounting statement that shows business results in terms of revenue and expenses. If revenues are greater than

FIGURE 1-3. The Income Statement

CATHY HALL, ATTORNEY-AT-LAW INCOME STATEMENT FOR MONTH ENDED SEPTEMBER 30, 200X		
Revenue:		
Legal Fees		$ 7 0 0 0 00
Operating Expenses:		
Salaries Expense	$ 6 0 0 00	
Rent Expense	7 0 0 00	
Advertising Expense	3 0 0 00	
Total Operating Expenses		1 6 0 0 00
Net Income		$ 5 4 0 0 00

expenses, the report shows net income. If expenses are greater than revenues, the report shows net loss. An income statement can cover one, three, six, or twelve months. It cannot cover more than one year. The statement shows the result of all revenues and expenses throughout the entire period and not just as of a specific date. The income statement for Cathy Hall's law firm is shown in Figure 1-3.

Points to Remember in Preparing an Income Statement

Heading The heading of an income statement tells the same three things as all other accounting statements: the company's name, the name of the statement, and the period of time the statement covers.

The Setup As you can see on the income statement, the inside column of numbers ($600, $700, and $300) is used to subtotal all expenses ($1,600) before subtracting them from revenue ($7,000 − $1,600 = $5,400).

Operating expenses may be listed in alphabetical order, in order of largest amounts to smallest, or in a set order established by the accountant.

> The inside column of numbers ($600, $700, $300) is used to subtotal all expenses ($1,600) before subtracting from revenue.

THE STATEMENT OF OWNER'S EQUITY

As we said, the income statement is a business statement that shows business results in terms of revenue and expenses, but how does net income or net loss affect owner's equity? To find that out we have to look at a second type of statement, the **statement of owner's equity**.

The statement of owner's equity shows for a certain period of time what changes occurred in Cathy Hall, Capital. The statement of owner's equity is shown in Figure 1-4, p. 20.

The capital of Cathy Hall can be

> If this statement of owner's equity is omitted, the information will be included in the owner's equity section of the balance sheet.

Increased by:	Owner Investment
	Net Income (Revenue − Expenses)
Decreased by:	Owner Withdrawals
	Net Loss (Expenses Greater than Revenue)

Remember, a withdrawal is *not* a business expense and thus is not involved in the calculation of net income or net loss on the income statement. It appears on the statement of owner's equity. The statement of owner's equity summarizes the effects of all the subdivisions of owner's equity (revenue, expenses, withdrawals) on beginning capital. The ending capital figure ($13,000) will be the beginning figure in the next statement of owner's equity.

CATHY HALL, ATTORNEY-AT-LAW STATEMENT OF OWNER'S EQUITY FOR MONTH ENDED SEPTEMBER 30, 200X		
Cathy Hall, Capital, September 1, 200X		$ 7 8 0 0 00
Net Income for September	$ 5 4 0 0 00	
Less Withdrawals for September	2 0 0 00	
Increase in Capital		5 2 0 0 00
Cathy Hall, Capital, September 30, 200X		$ 13 0 0 0 00

Comes from Income Statement

FIGURE 1-4. Statement of Owner's Equity

Suppose Cathy's law firm had operated at a loss in the month of September. Suppose instead of net income there was a $600 net loss, and an additional investment of $800 was made on September 15. This is how the statement would look if that had happened.

CATHY HALL, ATTORNEY-AT-LAW STATEMENT OF OWNER'S EQUITY FOR MONTH ENDED SEPTEMBER 30, 200X		
Cathy Hall, Capital, September 1, 200X		$ 7 8 0 0 00
Additional Investment, September 15, 200X		8 0 0 00
Total Investment for September		$ 8 6 0 0 00
Less: Net Loss for September	$ 6 0 0 00	
Withdrawals for September	2 0 0 00	
Decrease in Capital		8 0 0 00
Cathy Hall, Capital, September 30, 200X		$ 7 8 0 0 00

THE BALANCE SHEET

Now let's look at how to prepare a balance sheet from the expanded accounting equation (see Fig. 1-5). As you can see, the asset accounts (cash, accounts receivable, and office equipment) appear on the left side of the balance sheet.

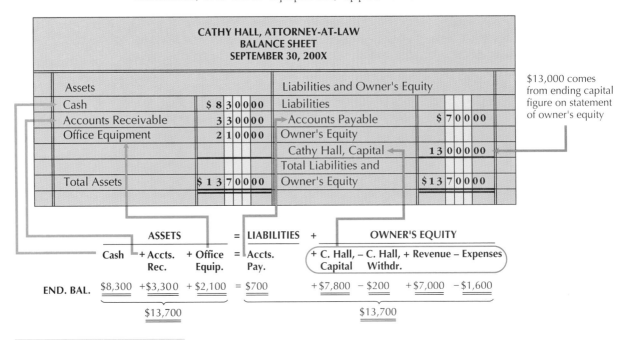

$13,000 comes from ending capital figure on statement of owner's equity

FIGURE 1-5. The Accounting Equation and the Balance Sheet

CHAPTER 1 ... ACCOUNTING CONCEPTS AND PROCEDURES

TABLE 1-3   WHAT GOES ON EACH FINANCIAL STATEMENT

	Income Statement	Statement of Owner's Equity	Balance Sheet
Assets			X
Liabilities			X
Capital* (beg.)		X	
Capital (end)		X	X
Withdrawals		X	
Revenues	X		
Expenses	X		

*Note: Additional Investments go on the Statement of Owner's Equity.

Accounts payable and Cathy Hall, Capital appear on the right side. Notice that the $13,000 of capital can be calculated within the accounting equation or can be read from the statement of owner's equity.

MAIN ELEMENTS OF THE INCOME STATEMENT, THE STATEMENT OF OWNER'S EQUITY, AND THE BALANCE SHEET

In this chapter we have discussed three financial statements: the income statement, the statement of owner's equity, and the balance sheet. A fourth statement, called the statement of cash flows, will not be covered at this time. Let us review what elements of the expanded accounting equation go into each statement and the usual order in which the statements are prepared. Figure 1-5 presents a diagram of the accounting equation and the balance sheet. Table 1-3 summarizes the following points:

▼ The income statement is prepared first; it includes revenues and expenses and shows net income or net loss. This net income or net loss is used to update the next statement, the statement of owner's equity.

▼ The statement of owner's equity is prepared second; it includes beginning capital and any additional investments, the net income or net loss shown on the financial statement, withdrawals, and the total, which is the **ending capital**. The balance in Capital comes from the statement of owner's equity.

▼ The balance sheet is prepared last; it includes the final balances of each of the elements listed in the accounting equation under Assets and Liabilities. The balance in Capital comes from the statement of owner's equity.

LEARNING UNIT 1-4 REVIEW

AT THIS POINT you should be able to

▼ Define and state the purpose of the income statement, the statement of owner's equity, and the balance sheet. (p. 19)

▼ Discuss why the income statement should be prepared first. (p. 20)

▼ Show what happens on a statement of owner's equity if there is a net loss. (p. 20)

▼ Compare and contrast these three financial statements. (p. 21)

▼ Calculate a new figure for capital on the statement of owner's equity and the balance sheet. (p. 21)

Time to make the Donuts

Remember the TV ad in which Fred the Baker stumbles out of bed in the dark and drives to work, stopping only to wake up a rooster on the way? Fred is dedicated to making donuts (and coffee and bagels) fresh for the early morning customers at his Dunkin' Donuts store. Fred Baker, one of Dunkin' Donuts' newest shop owners, smiled as he thought of this commercial while he drove to work early one morning. Fred's name had been the source of lots of jokes—thousands of them—about his choice of companies, because it was also the name of the character in Dunkin' Donuts' long-running ad campaign. Like everyone else, Fred Baker was fond of Fred the Baker.

So what has this to do with accounting? Plenty, as it turns out. As one of Dunkin' Donuts' shop owners, Fred Baker wears two hats, his baker's cap and an accountant's green eyeshade. He makes the donuts, and he manages the accounts for his store. To learn how to do his job, Fred attended Dunkin' Donuts University. We'll share the financial lessons he learned there with you, but not the baking lessons!

When you look at Fred's store, you are really seeing two businesses. Fred is the owner of his store, and he is a sole proprietor. He operates under an agreement with Dunkin' Donuts Inc. of Randolph, Massachusetts. Dunkin' Donuts Inc. supplies the business know-how and support (like training, national advertising, and recipes). Fred supplies capital (his investment) and his baking, management, and effort. Dunkin' Donuts Inc. and Fred operate interdependent businesses, and both rely on accounting information for their success.

Dunkin' Donuts Inc., in business since 1950, has grown dramatically over the years, to the point that it now has stores in 43 states and 20 countries. To manage this enormous service business requires very careful control of each of its 4,139 stores. At Dunkin' Donuts headquarters,

Dwayne Goulding, business consultant for Fred's zone, monitors Fred's reports closely. It's his job to see that Fred makes money at making donuts, which in turn results in Dunkin' Donuts Inc. making money too.

Why does headquarters require accounting reports? Accounting reports give the information both Fred and the company need to make business decisions in a number of vital areas. For example:

1. Before Fred could buy his Dunkin' Donuts store, the company needed to know how much cash Fred had and his assets and liabilities. Fred prepared a personal Balance Sheet to give them this information.
2. Fred needs to know if his store is making a profit. He prepares an Income Statement to tell him that.
3. Dwayne needs to know if Fred's store is profitable and well run compared with other shops in the zone. He compares the Income Statements of all shops to learn this. He also looks at competing businesses.
4. Fred must have the right amount of supplies on hand. If he has too few, he can't make the donuts. If he has too many, some may spoil. The Balance Sheet tells him what supplies are on hand. It also alerts Dwayne to potential problems Fred may have.
5. How often do Dunkin' Donuts stores report accounting information? Fred prepares a monthly Income Statement and Balance Sheet. He also prepares a daily Sales Report, which he summarizes and sends to national headquarters every Saturday. In addition, Fred does a weekly Payroll Report, which Dwayne reviews.

Discussion Questions

1. What makes Fred a sole proprietor?
2. Why are Fred and Dunkin' Donuts interdependent businesses?
3. Why did Fred have to share his personal Balance Sheet with Dunkin' Donuts? Do you think most interdependent businesses do this?
4. What does Dunkin' Donuts learn from Fred's Income Statement and Balance Sheet?

SELF-REVIEW QUIZ 1-4

(The blank forms you need are on pages 4 and 5 of the *Study Guide and Working Papers*.)

From the following balances for Rusty Realty prepare:

1. Income statement for the month ended November 30, 200X.
2. Statement of owner's equity for the month ended November 30, 200X.

3. Balance sheet as of November 30, 200X.

Cash	$4,000	R. Rusty, Capital	
Accounts Receivable	1,370	November 1, 200X	$5,000
Store Furniture	1,490	R. Rusty, Withdrawals	100
Accounts Payable	900	Commissions Earned	1,500
		Rent Expense	200
		Advertising Expense	150
		Salaries Expense	90

Solution to Self-Review Quiz 1-4

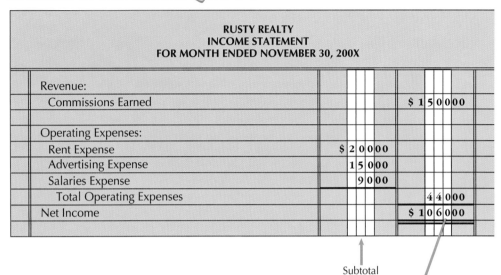

RUSTY REALTY
INCOME STATEMENT
FOR MONTH ENDED NOVEMBER 30, 200X

Revenue:		
Commissions Earned		$ 1 5 0 0 00
Operating Expenses:		
Rent Expense	$ 2 0 0 00	
Advertising Expense	1 5 0 00	
Salaries Expense	9 0 00	
Total Operating Expenses		4 4 0 00
Net Income		$ 1 0 6 0 00

Quiz Tip: Note that the inside column is only used for subtotaling.

Subtotal
Columns

RUSTY REALTY
STATEMENT OF OWNER'S EQUITY
FOR MONTH ENDED NOVEMBER 30, 200X

R. Rusty, Capital, November 1, 200X		$ 5 0 0 0 00
Net Income for November	$ 1 0 6 0 00	
Less Withdrawals for November	1 0 0 00	
Increase in Capital		9 6 0 00
R. Rusty, Capital, November 30, 200X		$ 5 9 6 0 00

The net income from the income statement is used to help build the statement of owner's equity.

RUSTY REALTY
BALANCE SHEET
NOVEMBER 30, 200X

Assets		Liabilities and Owner's Equity	
Cash	$ 4 0 0 0 00	Liabilities	
Accounts Receivable	1 3 7 0 00	Accounts Payable	$ 9 0 0 00
Store Furniture	1 4 9 0 00		
		Owner's Equity	
		R. Rusty, Capital	5 9 6 0 00
		Total Liabilities and	
Total Assets	$ 6 8 6 0 00	Owner's Equity	$ 6 8 6 0 00

The new figure for capital from the statement of owner's equity is used as the capital figure on the balance sheet.

COMPREHENSIVE DEMONSTRATION PROBLEM WITH SOLUTIONS TIPS

(The blank forms you need are on pages 6 and 7 of the *Study Guide and Working Papers.*)

Michael Brown opened his law office on June 1, 200X. During the first month of operations, Michael conducted the following transactions:

1. Invested $6,000 in cash into the law practice.
2. Paid $600 for office equipment.
3. Purchased additional office equipment on account, $1,000.
4. Performed legal services for clients receiving cash, $2,000.
5. Paid salaries, $800.
6. Performed legal services for clients on account, $1,000.
7. Paid rent, $1,200.
8. Withdrew $500 from his law practice for personal use.
9. Received $500 from customers in partial payment for legal services performed, transaction 6.

Assignment

a. Record these transactions in the expanded accounting equation.
b. Prepare the financial statements at June 30 for Michael Brown, Attorney-at-Law.

Solution to Comprehensive Demonstration Problem

	ASSETS			=	LIABILITIES	+			OWNER'S EQUITY			
A.	Cash	+ Accts. Rec.	+ Office Equip.	=	Accounts Payable	+	M. Brown, Capital	−	M. Brown, Withdr.	+	Legal Fees	− Expenses
1.	+$6,000						+$6,000					
BAL.	6,000			=			6,000					
2.	−600		+$600									
BAL.	5,400		+ 600	=			6,000					
3.			+1,000		+$1,000							
BAL.	5,400		+ 1,600	=	1,000	+	6,000					
4.	+2,000										+$2,000	
BAL.	7,400		+ 1,600	=	1,000	+	6,000			+	2,000	
5.	−800											+$800
BAL.	6,600		+ 1,600	=	1,000	+	6,000			+	2,000 −	800
6.		+$1,000									+1,000	
BAL.	6,600 +	1,000	+ 1,600	=	1,000	+	6,000			+	3,000 −	800
7.	−1,200											+1,200
BAL.	5,400 +	1,000	+ 1,600	=	1,000	+	6,000			+	3,000 −	2,000
8.	−500								+$500			
BAL.	4,900 +	1,000	+ 1,600	=	1,000	+	6,000	−	500	+	3,000 −	2,000
9.	+500	−500										
END. BAL.	$5,400 +	$ 500	+ $1,600	=	$1,000	+	$6,000	−	$500	+	$3,000 −	$2,000
					$7,500 =		$7,500					

Solution Tips to Expanded Accounting Equation

A.

▼ **Transaction 1:** The business increased its cash by $6,000. Owner's Equity (capital) increased when Michael supplied the cash to the business.

▼ **Transaction 2:** There was a shift in assets when the equipment was purchased. The business lowered its cash by $600, and a new column — Equipment — was increased for the $600 of equipment that was bought. The amount of capital is not touched because the owner did not supply any new funds.

▼ **Transaction 3:** When creditors supply $1,000 of additional equipment, the business Accounts Payable shows the debt. The business had increased what it *owes* the creditors.

▼ **Transaction 4:** Legal Fees, a subdivision of owner's equity, is increased when the law firm provides a service even if no money is received. The service provides an inward flow of $2,000 cash, an asset. Remember, that legal fees are *not* an asset. As legal fees increase, owner's equity increases.

▼ **Transaction 5:** The salary paid by Michael shows an $800 increase in expenses and a corresponding decrease in owner's equity.

▼ **Transaction 6:** Michael did the work and earned the $1,000. That $1,000 is recorded as revenue. This time the legal fees create an inward flow of assets called Accounts Receivable for $1,000. Remember that legal fees are *not* an asset. They are a subdivision of owner's equity.

▼ **Transaction 7:** The $1,200 rent expense reduces owner's equity as well as cash.

▼ **Transaction 8:** Withdrawals are for personal use. Here, business decreases cash of $500 while Michael increases $500. Withdrawals decrease the owner's equity.

▼ **Transaction 9:** This transaction does not reflect new revenue in the form of legal feels. It is only a shift in assets: more cash and less Accounts Receivable.

B-1.

MICHAEL BROWN, ATTORNEY-AT-LAW
INCOME STATEMENT
FOR MONTH ENDED JUNE 30, 200X

Revenue:		
Legal Fees		$3,000
Operating expenses:		
Salaries expense	$ 800	
Rent expense	1,200	
Total operating expenses		2,000
Net income		$1,000

B-2.

MICHAEL BROWN, ATTORNEY-AT-LAW
STATEMENT OF OWNER'S EQUITY
FOR MONTH ENDED JUNE 30, 200X

Michael Brown, Capital, June 1, 200X		$6,000
Net income for June	$1,000	
Less withdrawals for June	500	
Increase in Capital		500
Michael Brown, Capital, June 30, 200X		$6,500

B-3.

MICHAEL BROWN, ATTORNEY-AT-LAW
BALANCE SHEET
JUNE 30, 200X

Assets		Liabilities and Owner's Equity	
Cash	$5,400	Liabilities	
Accounts Receivable	500	Accounts Payable	$1,000
Office equipment	1,600	Owner's Equity	
		M. Brown, Capital	6,500
		Total Liabilities and	
Total Assets	$7,500	Owner's Equity	$7,500

Solution Tips to Financial Statements

B-1. Income statement lists only Revenues and Expenses for a period of time. The inside column is for subtotaling. Withdrawals are not listed here.

B-2. The statement of Owner's Equity takes the net income figure of $1,000 and adds it to Beginning Capital less any withdrawals. This new capital figure of $6,500 will go on the balance sheet. This statement shows changes in Capital for a period of time.

B-3. The $5,400, $500, $1,600, and $1,000 came from the totals of the expanded accounting equation. The Capital figure of $6,500 came from the statement of Owner's Equity. This balance sheet reports Assets, Liabilities, and a new figure for Capital at a specific date.

SUMMARY OF KEY POINTS

Learning Unit 1-1

1. The functions of accounting involve analyzing, recording, classifying, summarizing, reporting, and interpreting financial information.

2. A sole proprietorship is a business owned by one person. A partnership is a business owned by two or more persons. A corporation is a business owned by stockholders. All forms of business organizations are found in Internet businesses.

3. Bookkeeping is the recording part of accounting.

4. The computer is a tool to use in the accounting process.

5. Assets = Liabilities + Owner's Equity is the basic accounting equation that aids in analyzing business transactions.

6. Liabilities represents amounts owed to creditors, whereas capital represents what is invested by the owner.

7. Capital does not mean cash. Capital is the owner's current investment. The owner could have invested equipment that was purchased before the new business was started.

8. In a shift of assets, the composition of assets changes, but the total of assets does not change. For example, if a bill is paid by a customer, the firm increases cash (an asset) but decreases accounts receivable (an asset), so there is no overall increase in assets; total assets remain the same. When you borrow money from a bank, you have an increase in cash (an asset) and an increase in liabilities; overall there is an increase in assets, not just a shift.

Learning Unit 1-2

1. The balance sheet is a statement written as of a particular date. It lists the assets, liabilities, and owner's equity of a business. The heading of the balance sheet answers the questions *who, what*, and *when* (as of a specific date).

2. The balance sheet is a formal statement of a financial position.

1. Revenue generates an inward flow of assets. Expenses generate an outward flow of assets or a potential outward flow. Revenue and expenses are subdivisions of owner's equity. Revenue is not an asset.

2. When revenue totals more than expenses, net income is the result; when expenses total more than revenue, net loss is the result.

3. Owner's equity can be subdivided into four elements: capital, withdrawals, revenue, and expenses.

4. Withdrawals decrease owner's equity, revenue increases owner's equity, and expenses decrease owner's equity. A withdrawal is not a business expense; it is for personal use.

Learning Unit 1-4

1. The income statement is a statement written for a specific period of time that lists earned revenue and expenses incurred to produce the earned revenue. The net income or net loss will be used in the statement of owner's equity.

2. The statement of owner's equity reveals the causes of a change in capital. This statement lists any investments, net income (or net loss), and withdrawals. The ending figure for capital will be used on the balance sheet.

3. The balance sheet uses the ending balances of assets and liabilities from the accounting equation and the capital from the statement of owner's equity.

4. The income statement should be prepared first because the information on it about net income or net loss is used to prepare the statement of owner's equity, which in turn provides information about capital for the balance sheet. In this way one builds upon the next, and it begins with the income statement.

KEY TERMS

Accounting A system that measures the business's activities in financial terms, provides written reports and financial statements about those activities, and communicates these reports to decision makers and others.

Accounts payable Amounts owed to creditors that result from the purchase of goods or services on account: a liability.

Accounts receivable An asset that indicates amounts owed by customers.

Assets Properties (resources) of value owned by a business (cash, supplies, equipment, land).

Balance sheet A statement, as of a particular date, that shows the amount of assets owned by a business as well as the amount of claims (liabilities and owner's equity) against these assets.

Basic accounting equation Assets = Liabilities + Owner's Equity.

Bookkeeping The recording function of the accounting process.

Capital The owner's investment of equity in the company.

Corporation A type of business organization that is owned by stockholders. Stockholders usually are not personally liable for the corporation's debts.

Creditor Someone who has a claim to assets.

Ending capital Beginning Capital + Additional Investments + Net Income − Withdrawals = Ending Capital. Or: Beginning Capital + Additional Investments − Net Loss − Withdrawals = Ending Capital.

Equities The interest or financial claim of creditors (liabilities) and owners (owner's equity) who supply the assets to a firm.

Expanded accounting equation Assets = Liabilities + Capital − Withdrawals + Revenue − Expenses.

Expense A cost incurred in running a business by consuming goods or services in producing revenue; a subdivision of owner's equity. When expenses increase, there is a decrease in owner's equity.

Generally accepted accounting principles (GAAP) The procedures and guidelines that must be followed during the accounting process.

Income statement An accounting statement that details the performance of a firm (revenue minus expenses) for a specific period of time.

Liabilities Obligations that come due in the future. Liabilities result in increasing the financial rights or claims of creditors to assets.

Manufacturer Business that makes a product and sells it to its customers.

Merchandising company Business that buys a product from a manufacturing company to sell to its customers.

Net income When revenue totals more than expenses, the result is net income.

Net loss When expenses total more than revenue, the result is net loss.

Owner's equity Rights or financial claims to the assets of a business (in the accounting equation, assets minus liabilities).

Partnership A form of business organization that has at least two owners. The partners usually are personally liable for the partnership's debts.

Revenue An amount earned by performing services for customers or selling goods to customers; it can be in the form of cash and/or accounts receivable. A subdivision of owner's equity: as revenue increases, owner's equity increases.

Service company Business that provides a service.

Shift in assets A shift that occurs when the composition of the assets has changed, but the total of the assets remains the same.

Sole proprietorship A type of business ownership that has one owner. The owner is personally liable for paying the business's debts.

Statement of financial position Another name for a balance sheet.

Statement of owner's equity A financial statement that reveals the change in capital. The ending figure for capital is then placed on the balance sheet.

Supplies One type of asset acquired by a firm; it has a much shorter life than equipment.

Withdrawals A subdivision of owner's equity that records money or other assets an owner withdraws from a business for personal use.

BLUEPRINT: FINANCIAL STATEMENTS

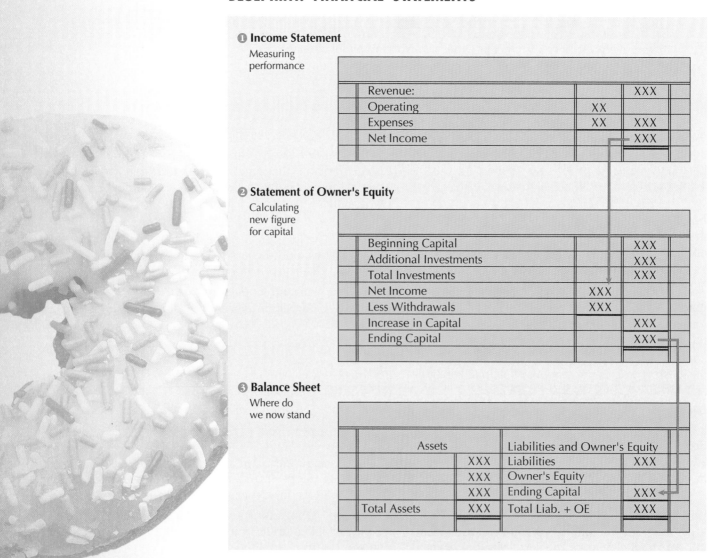

❶ Income Statement
Measuring performance

Revenue:		XXX
Operating	XX	
Expenses	XX	XXX
Net Income		XXX

❷ Statement of Owner's Equity
Calculating new figure for capital

Beginning Capital		XXX
Additional Investments		XXX
Total Investments		XXX
Net Income	XXX	
Less Withdrawals	XXX	
Increase in Capital		XXX
Ending Capital		XXX

❸ Balance Sheet
Where do we now stand

Assets		Liabilities and Owner's Equity	
	XXX	Liabilities	XXX
	XXX	Owner's Equity	
	XXX	Ending Capital	XXX
Total Assets	XXX	Total Liab. + OE	XXX

QUESTIONS, MINI EXERCISES, EXERCISES, AND PROBLEMS

Discussion Questions

1. What are the functions of accounting?
2. Define, compare, and contrast sole proprietorships, partnerships, and corporations.
3. How are businesses classified?
4. What is the relationship of bookkeeping to accounting?
5. List the three elements of the basic accounting equation.
6. Define capital.
7. The total of the left-hand side of the accounting equation must equal the total of the right-hand side. True or false? Please explain.
8. A balance sheet tells a company where it is going and how well it will perform. True or false? Please explain.
9. Revenue is an asset. True or false? Please explain.
10. Owner's equity is subdivided into what categories?
11. A withdrawal is a business expense. True or false? Please explain.
12. As expenses increase they cause owner's equity to increase. Defend or reject.
13. What does an income statement show?
14. The statement of owner's equity only calculates ending withdrawals. True or false? Please explain.

Mini Exercises

(The blank forms you need are on page 9 of the *Study Guide and Working Papers*.)

Classifying Accounts

1. Classify each of the following items as an Asset (A), Liability (L), or Part of Owner's Equity (OE).
   a. Computers   _____
   b. Accounts Payable   _____
   c. P. Jean, Capital   _____
   d. Office Supplies   _____
   e. Cash   _____
   f. Office Equipment   _____

The Accounting Equation

2. Complete the following statements.
   a. A _____ _____ _____ results when the total of the assets remain the same but the makeup of the assets has changed.
   b. Assets − _____ = Owner's Equity.
   c. Capital does not mean _____.

Shift versus Increase in Assets

3. Identify which transaction results in a shift in assets (S) and which transaction causes an increase in assets (I).
   a. Staples bought computer equipment for cash.
   b. Sears bought office equipment on account.

The Balance Sheet

4. From the following, calculate what would be the total of assets on the Balance Sheet.

H. Anna, Capital	$9,000
Word Processing Equipment	1,000
Accounts Payable	2,000
Cash	10,000

The Accounting Equation Expanded

5. From the following, which are subdivisions of Owner's Equity?

a. Land	_____	e. Accounts Payable	_____
b. B. Flynn, Capital	_____	f. Rent Expense	_____
c. Accounts Receivable	_____	g. Office Equipment	_____
d. B. Flynn, Withdrawals	_____	h. Hair Salon Fees Earned	_____

Identifying Assets

6. Identify which of the following are *not* assets.

a. Supplies	_____	c. Legal Fees Earned	_____
b. Accounts Payable	_____	d. Accounts Receivable	_____

The Accounting Equation Expanded

7. Which of the following statements are false?

a. _____ Revenue is an asset.

b. _____ Revenue is a subdivision of Owner's Equity.

c. _____ Revenue provides an inward flow of Cash and/or Accounts Receivable.

d. _____ Withdrawals are part of Total Assets.

Preparing Financial Statements

8. Indicate whether the following items would appear on the Income Statement (IS), Statement of Owner's Equity (OE), or Balance Sheet (BS).

a. _____ B. Clo, Withdrawals		e. _____ Commission Fees Earned	
b. _____ Supplies		f. _____ Salaries Expense	
c. _____ Accounts Payable		g. _____ B. Clo, Capital (Beg.)	
d. _____ Computer Equipment		h. _____ Accounts Receivable	

Preparing Financial Statements

9. Indicate next to each statement whether it refers to the Income Statement (IS), Statement of Owner's Equity (OE), or Balance Sheet (BS).

a. _____ Calculate new figure for Capital

b. _____ Prepared as of a particular date

c. _____ Statement that is prepared first

d. _____ Statement listing Revenues and Expenses

Exercises

(The forms you need are on pages 10–12 of the *Study Guide and Working Papers*.)

1-1. Complete the following table:

> The accounting equation.

ASSETS = LIABILITIES + OWNER'S EQUITY

a. $ 8,000 =   ?   + $2,000

b. ? = $6,000 + $8,000

c. $10,000 = $4,000 + ?

1-2. Record the following transactions in the basic accounting equation. Treat each one separately.

Recording transactions into the expanded accounting equation.

ASSETS = LIABILITIES + OWNER'S EQUITY

a. Ralph invests $80,000 in company.

b. Bought equipment for cash, $600.

c. Bought equipment on account, $900.

Preparing a balance sheet.

1-3. From the following, prepare a balance sheet for Avon's Cleaners at the end of November 200X: Cash, $40,000; Cleaning Equipment, $8,000; Accounts Payable, $19,000; A. Avon, Capital.

1-4. Record the following transactions into the expanded accounting equation. The running balance may be omitted for simplicity.

Recording transactions into the accounting equation.

ASSETS	= LIABILITIES +		OWNER'S EQUITY			
Cash + Accounts + Computer =	Accounts	+ B. Wong,	− B. Wong,	+ Revenues − Expenses		
Receivable Equipment	Payable	Capital	Withdrawals			

a. Bill invested $60,000 in a computer company.

b. Bought computer equipment on account, $7,000.

c. Bill paid personal telephone bill from company checkbook, $200.

d. Received cash for services rendered, $14,000.

e. Billed customers for services rendered for month, $30,000.

f. Paid current rent expense, $4,000.

g. Paid supplies expense, $1,500.

Preparing the income statement, statement of owner's equity, and balance sheet.

1-5. From the following account balances, prepare in proper form for June (a) an income statement, (b) a statement of owner's equity, and (c) a balance sheet for French Realty.

Cash	$3,310	S. French, Withdrawals	$ 40
Accounts Receivable	1,490	Professional Fees	2,900
Office Equipment	6,700	Salaries Expense	500
Accounts Payable	2,000	Utilities Expense	360
S. French, Capital, June 1, 200X	8,000	Rent Expense	500

Group A Problems

(The forms you need are on pages 13–19 of the *Study Guide and Working Papers.*)

1A-1. Gracie Wall decided to open Wall's Hair Salon. Gracie completed the following transactions:

The accounting equation.

a. Invested $17,000 cash from her personal bank account into the business.

b. Bought equipment for cash, $4,000.

c. Bought additional equipment on account, $1,000.

d. Paid $400 cash to partially reduce what was owed from Transaction C.

Check Figure: Total Assets $17,600

Based on the above information, record these transactions into the basic accounting equation.

Preparing a balance sheet.

1A-2. Joyce Hill is the accountant for Green's Advertising Service. From the following information, her task is to construct a balance sheet as of September 30, 200X, in proper form. Could you help her?

Building	$35,000	Cash	$10,000
Accounts Payable	30,000	Equipment	14,000
Green, Capital	29,000		

Check Figure: Total Assets $59,000

1A-3. At the end of November, Rick Fox decided to open his own typing service. Analyze the following transactions he completed by recording their effects on the expanded accounting equation.

    a. Invested $10,000 in his typing service.

    b. Bought new office equipment on account, $4,000.

    c. Received cash for typing services rendered, $500.

    d. Performed typing services on account, $2,100.

    e. Paid secretary's salary, $350.

    f. Paid office supplies expense for the month, $210.

    g. Rent expenses for office due but unpaid, $900.

    h. Withdrew cash for personal use, $400.

1A-4. Jane West, owner of West Stenciling Service, has requested that you prepare from the following balances (a) an income statement for June 200X, (b) a statement of owner's equity for June, and (c) a balance sheet as of June 30, 200X.

Cash	$2,300	Stenciling Fees	$3,000
Accounts Receivable	400	Advertising Expense	110
Equipment	685	Repair Expense	25
Accounts Payable	310	Travel Expense	250
J. West, Capital, June 1, 200X	1,200	Supplies Expense	190
J. West, Withdrawals	300	Rent Expense	250

1A-5. John Tobey, a retired army officer, opened Tobey's Catering Service. As his accountant, analyze the transactions listed below and present in proper form.

    a. The analysis of the transactions by using the expanded accounting equation.

    b. A balance sheet showing the position of the firm before opening for business on October 31, 200X.

    c. An income statement for the month of November.

    d. A statement of owner's equity for November.

    e. A balance sheet as of November 30, 200X.

200X

Oct. 25 John Tobey invested $20,000 in the catering business from his personal savings account.

    27 Bought equipment for cash from Munroe Co., $700

    28 Bought additional equipment on account from Ryan Co., $1,000.

    29 Paid $600 to Ryan Co. as partial payment of the October 28 transaction.

(You should now prepare your balance sheet as of October 31, 200X)

Nov. 1 Catered a graduation and immediately collected cash, $2,400.

    5 Paid salaries of employees, $690.

    8 Prepared desserts for customers on account, $300.

    10 Received $100 cash as partial payment of November 8 transaction.

    15 Paid telephone bill, $60.

    17 Paid his home electric bill from the company's checkbook, $90.

    20 Catered a wedding and received cash, $1,800.

    25 Bought additional equipment on account, $400.

    28 Rent expense due but unpaid, $600.

    30 Paid supplies expense, $400.

Group B Problems

(The forms you need are on pages 13–19 of the *Study Guide and Working Papers*.)

    1B-1. Gracie Wall began a new business called Wall's Hair Salon. The following transactions resulted:

a. Gracie invested $20,000 cash from her personal bank account into the hair salon.

b. Bought equipment on account, $1,800.

c. Paid $800 cash to partially reduce what was owed from Transaction B.

d. Purchased additional equipment for cash, $3,000.

Record these transactions into the basic accounting equation.

Check Figure:
Total Assets $21,000

1B-2. Joyce Hill Accountant has asked you to prepare a balance sheet as of September 30, 200X, for Green's Advertising Service. Could you assist Joyce?

Preparing a balance sheet.

R. Green, Capital	$19,000
Accounts Payable	70,000
Equipment	41,000
Building	16,000
Cash	32,000

Check Figure:
Total Assets $89,000

1B-3. Rick Fox decided to open his own typing service company at the end of November. Analyze the following transactions by recording their effects on the expanded accounting equation.

Recording transactions in the expanded accounting equation.

a. Rick invested $9,000 in the typing service.

b. Purchased new office equipment on account, $3,000.

c. Received cash for typing services rendered, $1,290.

d. Paid secretary's salary, $310.

e. Billed customers for typing services rendered, $2,690.

f. Paid rent expense for the month, $500.

g. Rick withdrew cash for personal use, $350.

h. Advertising expense due but unpaid, $100.

Check Figure:
Total Assets $14,820

1B-4. Jane West, owner of West Stenciling Service, has requested that you prepare from the following balances (a) an income statement for June 200X, (b) a statement of owner's equity for June, and (c) a balance sheet as of June 30, 200X.

Preparing an income statement, statement of owner's equity, and balance sheet.

Cash	$2,043	Stenciling Fees	$1,098
Accounts Receivable	1,140	Advertising Expense	135
Equipment	540	Repair Expense	45
Accounts Payable	45	Travel Expense	90
J. West, Capital, June 1, 200X	3,720	Supplies Expense	270
J. West, Withdrawals	360	Rent Expense	240

Check Figure:
Total Assets $3,723

1B-5. John Tobey, a retired army officer, opened Tobey's Catering Service. As his accountant, analyze the transactions and present the following information in proper form:

Comprehensive problem.

a. The analysis of the transactions by using the expanded accounting equation.

b. A balance sheet showing the financial position of the firm before opening on November 1, 200X.

c. An income statement for the month of November.

d. A statement of owner's equity for November.

e. A balance sheet as of November 30, 200X.

Check Figure:
Total Assets,
Nov. 30 $25,005

200X
Oct. 25 John Tobey invested $17,500 in the catering business.
27 Bought equipment on account from Munroe Co., $900.
28 Bought equipment for cash from Ryan Co., $1,500.
29 Paid $300 to Munroe Co. as partial payment of the October 27 transaction.

Nov.
1 Catered a business luncheon and immediately collected cash, $2,000.
5 Paid salaries of employees, $350.
8 Provided catering services to Northwest Community College on account, $4,500.
10 Received from Northwest Community College $1,000 cash as partial payment of November 8 transaction.
15 Paid telephone bill, $95.
17 John paid his home mortgage from the company's checkbook, $650.
20 Provided catering services and received cash, $1,800.
25 Bought additional equipment on account, $300.
28 Rent expense due but unpaid, $750.
30 Paid supplies expense, $600.

REAL-WORLD APPLICATIONS

1R-1.

You have just been hired to prepare, if possible, an income statement for the year ended December 31, 200X, for Ron's Window Washing Company. The problem is that Ron Smith kept only the following records (on the back of a piece of cardboard).

> Money in:
> My investment $ 1,200
> Window cleaning   11,376
> Loan from brother-in-law   4,000
>
> Money out:
> Salaries $5,080
> Withdrawals   6,200
> Supplies expense   1,400
>
> What I owe or they owe me
> A. People who work for me but I still owe salaries to $1,800
> B. Owe bank interest of $300
> C. Work done but clients still owe me $2,900
> D. Advertising bill due but not paid $95

Assume that Ron's Window Washing Company records all revenues when earned and all expenses when incurred.

You feel that it is part of your job to tell Ron how to organize his records better. What would you tell him?

1R-2.

While Jon Lune was on a business trip, he asked Abby Slowe, the bookkeeper for Lune Co., to try to complete a balance sheet for the year ended December 31, 200X. Abby, who had been on the job only two months, submitted the following:

LUNE CO. FOR THE YEAR ENDED DECEMBER 31, 200X				
Building	$44 600 00	Accounts Payable	$127 604 00	
Land	72 935 00	Accounts Receivable	104 337 00	
Notes Payable	75 328 00	Auto	14 268 00	
Cash	100 160 0	Desks	6 825 00	
J. Lune, Capital	?	Total Equity	$250 034 00	

1. Could you help Abby fix as well as complete the balance sheet?

2. What written recommendations would you make about the bookkeeper? Should she be retained?

3. Suppose that (a) Jon Lune invested an additional $20,000 in cash as well as additional desks with a value of $8,000 and (b) Lune Co. bought an auto for $6,000 that was originally marked $8,000, paying $2,000 down and issuing a note for the balance. Could you prepare an updated balance sheet?

YOU make the call

Critical Thinking/Ethical Case

(The forms you need are on page 8 of the *Study Guide and Working Papers*.)

1R-3.

Paul Kloss, Accountant for Lowe & Co., traveled to New York on company business. His total expenses came to $350. Paul felt that because the trip extended over the weekend he would "pad" his expense account with an additional $100 of expenses. After all, weekends represent his own time, not the company's. What would you do? Write your specific recommendations to Paul.

INTERNET EXERCISES

EX-1. [www.microstrategy.com]   In the financial statements for Microstrategy, amounts received from customers for service policies are reported in two dimensions. One dimension is actual revenue, or amounts earned from providing a service or a product to its customers. The other dimension is that of receiving cash, which represents services to be provided in future accounting periods. Suppose that, in 2000, Microstrategy received $200,000 from customers. That $200,000 represented $125,000 that was amounts for products sold or, services actually rendered. The remaining $75,000 represents services to be provided later.

1. What is the company's addition to revenue if the full amount is recorded all in one year?

2. How is the revenue number different if the amount for future services is recorded as a liability?

3. What is the justification of reporting these amounts in two separate segments?

4. Explains how reporting the revenue all at one time could mislead the reader of the company's financial statements.

EX-2. [www.microstrategy.com]   In this chapter you have been introduced to the basic concepts of assets and liabilities. Go to the Microstrategy Web site and read about the company and its operations. After reading about the company, consider these questions:

1. What are three assets you would expect them to have, other than cash?

2. What are three liabilities you would expect them to have, other than accounts payable?

3. How do liabilities represent equities, or claims?

4. In the accounting equation, why do you think the liabilities (claims of creditors) are listed before the stockholders' equity (claims of owners)?

CONTINUING PROBLEM

The following problem continues from one chapter to the next, carrying the balances forward of each month. Each chapter focuses on the learning experience of the chapter and adds additional information as the business grows. Forms are on page 23 of the *Study Guide and Working Papers*.

Assignment

1. Set up an expanded accounting equation spreadsheet using the following accounts:

Assets	Liabilities	Owner's Equity
Cash	Accounts Payable	Freedman, Capital
Supplies		Freedman, Withdrawal
Computer Shop Equipment		Service Revenue
Office Equipment		Expenses (notate type)

2. Analyze and record each transaction in the expanded accounting equation.

3. Prepare the financial statements ending July 31 for Eldorado Computer Center.

On July 1, 200X, Tony Freedman decided to begin his own computer service business. He named the business the Eldorado Computer Center. During the first month Tony conducted the following business transactions:

a. Invested $4,500 of his savings into the business.

b. Paid $1,200 (check #8095) for the computer from Multi Systems, Inc.

c. Paid $600 (check # 8096) for office equipment from Office Furniture, Inc.

d. Set up a new account with Office Depot and purchased $250 in office supplies on credit.

e. Paid July rent, $400 (check # 8097).

f. Repaired a system for a customer; collected $250.

g. Collected $200 for system upgrade labor charge from a customer.

h. Electric bill due but unpaid, $85.

i. Collected $1,200 for services performed on Taylor Golf computers.

j. Withdrew $100 (check # 8098) to take his wife, Carol, out in celebration of opening the new business.

Debits
and Credits

ANALYZING AND RECORDING BUSINESS TRANSACTIONS

"UAL Expects Loss for Third Quarter." "Ebay Earnings Beat Estimates." "Yahoo! Posts Strong Earnings." "Priceline Stock Plunges on Revenue Warning." As each quarter of the fiscal year draws to a close, you can expect to see headlines like these in the business pages of your local newspaper. Investors wait with baited breath for the quarterly financial statements of the companies in which they hold shares. Will revenue be up or down and, hence, will the value of their stocks go up or down?

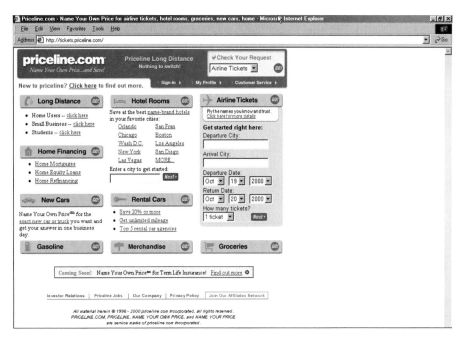

In this chapter you learn the key steps that go into generating a financial statement. When you analyze a business transaction — such as when a customer pays online with her credit card or you pay a fee to have your Web site hosted — you not only decide which accounts change in value, but also whether they increase or decrease. You'll see how to use a **T Account** to write the value of a transaction as a credit or a debit in a standard format and total the account at any time. Then, you'll use the ending balances on each side of every T account to prepare a **trial balance,** a test of the quality of debits in all your accounts. You can then use the account balances to generate financial statements that you can compare month to month. And by comparing financial statements, you can estimate how the financials will look at the end of each quarter.

In the financial pages, companies make news when they overturn predictions. Take Priceline.com, for instance, the pioneering Internet service that allows customers to literally name their price for airline tickets, hotel rooms and long distance telephone calls. In March of 2000, the company was valued higher than an airline, at $104 a share. Yet by September 2000, shares of Priceline had fallen to an all time low of $10.75 a share due to warnings that third quarter revenue would be about $40 million less than predicted. In addition, the company posted a loss when it had expected to turn its first profit ever. With its core business in airline ticket sales, Priceline is getting pummeled by competition from the airlines, which are offering their own bargain fares for more flexible tickets. Analysts and investors now wonder whether Priceline can ever reach profitability with a business model that targets bargain hunters. To see Priceline's most current financial results, go to www.Priceline.com and click on investor relations.

Based on: Jennifer Rewick, "Priceline's Stock Plunges on Revenue Warning," *Wall Street Journal,* September 28, 2000, p. B, 10:3. Saul Hansell, "Priceline Shares Fall on word Sales Won't Meet Forecasts," *New York Times,* September 28, 2000, p. C, 10:2. Anonymous, "Priceline issues earnings warning/Stock drops 42 percent after it says airline-ticket sales are down," Houston Chronicle, September 28, 2000, p. 3.

LEARNING OBJECTIVES

▼ Setting up and organizing a chart of accounts. (p. 42)

▼ Recording transactions in T accounts according to the rules of debit and credit. (p. 43)

▼ Preparing a trial balance. (p. 52)

▼ Preparing financial statements from a trial balance. (p. 53)

In Chapter 1 we used the expanded accounting equation to document the financial transactions performed by Cathy Hall's law firm. Remember how long it was: the cash column had a long list of pluses and minuses, and there was no quick system of recording and summarizing the increases and decreases of cash or other items. Can you imagine the problem Wendy's or Holiday Inn would have if they used the expanded accounting equation to track the thousands of business transactions they do each day?

LEARNING UNIT 2-1   THE T ACCOUNT

Let's look at the problem a little more closely. Each business transaction is recorded in the accounting equation under a specific **account.** There are different accounts for each of the subdivisions of the accounting equation: asset accounts, liabilities accounts, expense accounts, revenue accounts, and so on. What is needed is a way to record the increases and decreases in specific account *categories* and yet keep them together in one place. The answer is the **standard account** form (see Fig. 2-1). A standard account is a formal account that includes columns for date, explanation, posting reference, debit, and credit. Each account has a separate form, and all transactions affecting that account are recorded on the form. All the business's account forms (which often are referred to as *ledger accounts*) are then placed in a **ledger.** Each page of the ledger contains one account. The ledger may be in the form of a bound or a loose-leaf book. If computers are used, the ledger may be part of a computer printout. For simplicity's sake, we use the **T account** form. This form got

FIGURE 2-1. The Standard
Account Form Is the Source of
the T Account's Shape

Account Title								Account No.	
Date	Item	PR	Debit	Date	Item	PR	Credit		

its name because it looks like the letter T. Generally, T accounts are used for demonstration purposes.

Each T account contains three basic parts:

1

Title of Account

2   **Left side** | **Right side**   **3**

All T accounts have this structure. In accounting, the left side of any T account is called the **debit** side.

Left side
Dr. (debit) |

Just as the word *left* has many meanings, the word *debit* for now in accounting means a position, the left side of an account. Do not think of it as good (+) or bad (−).

Amounts entered on the left side of any account are said to be *debited* to an account. The abbreviation for debit, Dr., is from the Latin *debere*.

The right side of any T account is called the **credit** side.

| **Right side**
| **Cr. (credit)**

Amounts entered on the right side of an account are said to be *credited* to an account. The abbreviation for credit, Cr., is from the Latin *credere*.

At this point do not associate the definition of debit and credit with the words *increase* or *decrease*. Think of debit or credit as only indicating a *position* (left or right side) of a T account.

> *Debit* defined:
> 1. The left side of any T account.
> 2. A number entered on the left side of any account is said to be *debited* to an account.

> *Credit* defined:
> 1. The right side of any T account.
> 2. A number entered on the right side of any account is said to be *credited* to an account.

BALANCING AN ACCOUNT

No matter which individual account is being balanced, the procedure used to balance it is the same.

	Dr.	Cr.	
Entries → {	**4,000**		**300**
	500		**400**
Footings →	4,500		700
Balance	3,800		

In the "real" world, the T account would also include the date of the transaction. The date would appear to the left of the entry:

		Dr.	Cr.	
4/2		**4,000**		**300**
4/20		**500**		**400**
		4,500		700
Bal		3,800		

> Footings aid in balancing an account. The ending balance is the difference between the footings.

> If the balance is greater on the credit side, that is the side the ending balance would be on.

Note that on the debit (left) side the numbers add up to $4,500. On the credit (right) side the numbers add up to $700. The $4,500 and the $700 written in small type are called **footings.** Footing help in calculating the new (or ending) balance. The **ending balance** ($3,800) is placed on the debit or left side, because the balance of the debit side is greater than that of the credit side.

Remember that the ending balance does not tell us anything about increase or decrease. It only tells us that we have an ending balance of $3,800 on the debit side.

LEARNING UNIT 2-1 REVIEW

AT THIS POINT you should be able to

▼ Define ledger. (p. 38)
▼ State the purpose of a T account. (p. 38)
▼ Identify the three parts of a T account. (p. 39)
▼ Define debit. (p. 39)
▼ Define credit. (p. 39)
▼ Explain footings and calculate the balance of an account. (p. 39)

SELF-REVIEW QUIZ 2-1

(The blank forms you need are on page 25 of the *Study Guide and Working Papers.*)
Respond True or False to the following:

1.

Dr.	Cr.
3,000	200
200	600

The balance of the account is $2,400 Cr.

2. A credit always means increase.
3. A debit is the left side of any account.
4. A ledger can be prepared manually or by computer.
5. Footings replace the need for debits and credits.

> Quiz Tip:
> Dr. + Dr. → Add to get Dr. balance
> Cr. + Cr. → Add to get Cr. balance
> Dr. − Cr. → Subtract to get balance for the larger side.

Solutions to Self-Review Quiz 2-1

1. False   2. False   3. True   4. True   5. False

LEARNING UNIT 2-2

RECORDING BUSINESS TRANSACTIONS: DEBITS AND CREDITS

Can you get a queen in checkers? In a baseball game does a runner rounding first base skip second base and run over the pitcher's mound to get to third? No; most of us don't do such things because we follow the rules of the game. Usually we learn the rules first and reflect on the reasons for them afterward. The same is true in accounting.

Instead of first trying to understand all the rules of debit and credit and how they were developed in accounting, it is easier to learn the rules by "playing the game."

T ACCOUNT ENTRIES FOR ACCOUNTING IN THE ACCOUNTING EQUATION

Have patience. Learning the rules of debit and credit is like learning to play any game: the more you play, the easier it becomes. Table 2-1 shows the rules for the side on which you enter an increase or a decrease for each of the separate accounts in the accounting equation. For example, an increase is entered on the debit side in the asset account but on the credit side for a liability account.

It might be easier to visualize these rules of debit and credit if we look at them in the T account form, using + to show increase and − to show decrease.

ASSETS	=	LIABILITIES	+			OWNER'S EQUITY			
Dr. | Cr.		Dr. | Cr.	+	Capital	− Withdrawals	+ Revenue	− Expenses		
+ | −		− | +		Dr. | Cr.	Dr. | Cr.	Dr. | Cr.	Dr. | Cr.		
				− | +	+ | −	− | +	+ | −		

Rules for Assets Work in the Opposite Direction to Those for Liabilities When you look at the equation you can see that the rules for assets work in the opposite direction to those for liabilities. That is, for assets the increases appear on the debit side and the decreases are shown on the credit side; the opposite is true for liabilities. As for the owner's equity, the rules for withdrawals and expenses, which *decrease* owner's equity, work in the opposite direction to the rules for capital and revenue, which *increase* owner's equity.

Assets	+ Withdrawals	+ Expenses	= Liabilities	+ Capital	+ Revenue
Dr. | Cr.	Dr. | Cr.	Dr. | Cr.	Dr. | Cr.	Dr. | Cr.	Dr. | Cr.
+ | −	+ | −	+ | −	− | +	− | +	− | +

This setup may help you visualize how the rules for withdrawals and expenses are just the opposite of those for capital and revenue.

A **normal balance of an account** is the side that increases by the rules of debit and credit. For example, the balance of cash is a debit balance, because an asset is increased by a debit. We discuss normal balances further in Chapter 3.

Balancing the Equation It is important to remember that any amount(s) entered on the debit side of a T account or accounts also must be on the credit side of another T account or accounts. This ensures that the total amount added to the debit side will equal the total amount added to the credit side, thereby keeping the accounting equation in balance.

Normal Balance	
Dr.	Cr.
Assets	Liabilities
Expenses	Capital
Withdrawals	Revenue

Be sure to follow the rules of debits and credits when recording accounts. They were designed to keep the accounting equation in balance.

TABLE 2-1   RULES OF DEBIT AND CREDIT

Account Category	Increase (Normal Balance)	Decrease
Assets	Debit	Credit
Liabilities	Credit	Debit
Owner's Equity		
Capital	Credit	Debit
Withdrawals	Debit	Credit
Revenue	Credit	Debit
Expenses	Debit	Credit

TABLE 2-2 CHART OF ACCOUNTS FOR CATHY HALL, ATTORNEY-AT-LAW

Balance Sheet Accounts

Assets
111   Cash
112   Accounts Receivable
121   Office Equipment

Liabilities
211   Accounts Payable

Owner's Equity
311   Cathy Hall, Capital
312   Cathy Hall, Withdrawals

Income Statement Accounts

Revenue
411   Legal Fees

Expenses
511   Salaries Expense
512   Rent Expense
513   Advertising Expense

> The chart of accounts aids in locating and identifying accounts quickly.

> Large companies may have up to four digits assigned to each title.

Chart of Accounts   Our job is to analyze Cathy Hall's business transactions — the transactions we looked at in Chapter 1 — using a system of accounts guided by the rules of debits and credits that will summarize increases and decreases of individual accounts in the ledger. The goal is to prepare an income statement, statement of owner's equity, and balance sheet for Cathy Hall. Sound familiar? If this system works, the rules of debits and credits and the use of accounts will give us the same answers as in Chapter 1, but with greater ease.

Cathy's accountant developed what is called a **chart of accounts.** The chart of accounts is a numbered list of all of the business's accounts. It allows accounts to be located quickly. In Cathy's business, for example, 100s are assets, 200s are liabilities, and so on. As you see in Table 2-2, each separate asset and liability has its own number. Note that the chart may be expanded as the business grows.

THE TRANSACTION ANALYSIS: FIVE STEPS

We will analyze the transactions in Cathy Hall's law firm using a teaching device called a *transaction analysis chart* to record these five steps. (Keep in mind that the transaction analysis chart is not a part of any formal accounting system.) There are five steps to analyzing each business transaction:

> Steps to analyze and record transactions. Steps 1 and 2 will come from the chart of accounts.

Step 1: Determine which accounts are affected. Example: cash, accounts payable, rent expense. A transaction always affects at least two accounts.

Step 2: Determine which categories the accounts belong to: assets, liabilities, capital, withdrawals, revenue, or expenses. Example: Cash is an asset.

Step 3: Determine whether the accounts increase or decrease. Example: If you receive cash, that account is increasing.

Step 4: What do the rules of debits and credits say (Table 2-1)?

Step 5: What does the T account look like? Place amounts into accounts either on the left or right side depending on the rules in Table 2-1.

> Remember that the rules of debit and credit only tell us on which side to place information. Whether the debit or credit represents increases or decreases depends on the account category: assets, liabilities, capital, and so on. Think of a business transaction as an exchange: you get something and you give or part with something.

This is how the five-step analysis looks in chart form:

1 Accounts Affected	2 Category	3 ↓ or ↑ (decrease)(increase)	4 Rules of Dr. and Cr.	5 Appearance of T Accounts

Let us emphasize a major point: *Do not try to debit or credit an account until you have gone through the first three steps of the transaction analysis.*

APPLYING THE TRANSACTION ANALYSIS TO CATHY HALL'S LAW PRACTICE

> **Transaction A**   August 28: Cathy Hall invests $7,000 cash and $800 of office equipment in the business.

1 Accounts Affected	2 Category	3 ↓ ↑	4 Rules of Dr. and Cr.	5 Appearance of T Accounts
Cash	Asset	↑	Dr.	**Cash 111** (A) 7,000 |
Office Equipment	Asset	↑	Dr.	**Office Equipment 121** (A) 800 |
Cathy Hall, Capital	Capital	↑	Cr.	**Cathy Hall, Capital 311** | 7,800 (A)

> Note in column 3 of the chart that it doesn't matter if both arrows go up, as long as the sum of the debits equals the sum of the credits in the T accounts in column 5.

Note again that every transaction affects at least two T accounts and that the total amount added to the debit side(s) must equal the total amount added to the credit side(s) of the T accounts of each transaction.

Analysis of Transaction A

Step 1:   Which accounts are affected? The law firm receives its cash and office equipment, so three accounts are involved: Cash, Office Equipment, and Cathy Hall, Capital. These account titles come from the chart of accounts.

Step 2:   Which categories do these accounts belong to? Cash and Office Equipment are assets. Cathy Hall, Capital, is capital.

Step 3:   Are the accounts increasing or decreasing? The Cash and Office Equipment, both assets, are increasing in the business. The rights or claims of Cathy Hall, Capital, are also increasing, because she invested money and office equipment in the business.

Step 4:   What do the rules say? According to the rules of debit and credit, an increase in assets (Cash and Office Equipment) is a debit. An increase in Capital is a credit. Note that the total dollar amount of debits will equal the total dollar amount of credits when the T accounts are updated in column 5.

Step 5:   What does the T account look like? The amount for Cash and Office Equipment is entered on the debit side. The amount for Cathy Hall, Capital, goes on the credit side.

A transaction that involves more than one credit or more than one debit is called a **compound entry.** This first transaction of Cathy Hall's law firm is a compound entry; it involves a debit of $7,000 to Cash and a debit of $800 to Office Equipment (as well as a credit of $7,800 to Cathy Hall, Capital).

There is a name for this double-entry analysis of transactions, where two or more accounts are affected and the total of debits and credits is equal. It is called **double-entry bookkeeping.** This double-entry system helps in checking the recording of business transactions.

> Double-entry bookkeeping system: The total of all debits is equal to the total of all credits.

As we continue, the explanations will be brief, but do not forget to apply the five steps in analyzing and recording each business transaction.

> **Transaction B Aug. 29: Law practice bought office equipment for cash, $900.**

1 Accounts Affected	2 Category	3 ↓ ↑	4 Rules of Dr. and Cr.	5 T Account Update
Office Equipment	Asset	↑	Dr.	**Office Equipment 121** (A) 800 (B) 900
Cash	Asset	↓	Cr.	**Cash 111** (A) 7,000 | 900 (B)

Analysis of Transaction B

Step 1: The law firm paid cash for the office equipment it received. The accounts involved in the transaction are Cash and Office Equipment.

Step 2: The accounts belong to these categories: Office Equipment is an asset; Cash is an asset.

Step 3: The asset Office Equipment is increasing. The asset Cash is decreasing; it is being reduced to buy the office equipment.

Step 4: An increase in the asset Office Equipment is a debit; a decrease in the asset Cash is a credit.

Step 5: When the amounts are placed in the T accounts, the amount for Office Equipment goes on the debit side and the amount for Cash on the credit side.

> **Transaction C Aug. 30: Bought more office equipment on account, $400.**

1 Accounts Affected	2 Category	3 ↓ ↑	4 Rules of Dr. and Cr.	5 T Account Update
Office Equipment	Asset	↑	Dr.	**Office Equipment 121** (A) 800 (B) 900 (C) 400
Accounts Payable	Liability	↑	Cr.	**Accounts Payable 211** | 400 (C)

Analysis of Transaction C

Step 1: The law firm receives office equipment by promising to pay in the future. An obligation or liability, Accounts Payable, is created.

Step 2: Office Equipment is an asset. Accounts Payable is a liability.

Step 3: The asset Office Equipment is increasing; the liability Accounts Payable is increasing because the law firm is increasing what it owes.

Step 4: An increase in the asset Office Equipment is a debit. An increase in the liability Accounts Payable is a credit.

Step 5: Enter the amount for Office Equipment on the debit side of the T account. The amount for the Accounts Payable goes on the credit side.

Transaction D   Sept. 1–30: Provided legal services for cash, $3,000.

1 Accounts Affected	2 Category	3 ↓ ↑	4 Rules of Dr. and Cr.	5 T Account Update
Cash	Asset	↑	Dr.	**Cash 111** (A) 7,000 | 900 (B) (D) 3,000 |
Legal Fees	Revenue	↑	Cr.	**Legal Fees 411** | 3,000 (D)

Analysis of Transaction D

Step 1: The firm has earned revenue from legal services and receives $3,000 in cash.

Step 2: Cash is an asset. Legal Fees are revenue.

Step 3: Cash, an asset, is increasing. Legal Fees, or revenue, are also increasing.

Step 4: An increase in Cash, an asset, is debited. An increase in Legal Fees, or revenue, is credited.

Step 5: Enter the amount for Cash on the debit side of the T account. Enter the amount for Legal Fees on the credit side.

Transaction E   Sept. 1–30: Provided legal services on account, $4,000.

1 Accounts Affected	2 Category	3 ↓ ↑	4 Rules of Dr. and Cr.	5 T Account Update
Accounts Receivable	Asset	↑	Dr.	**Accounts Receivable 112** (E) 4,000 |
Legal Fees	Revenue	↑	Cr.	**Legal Fees 411** | 3,000 (D) | 4,000 (E)

Analysis of Transaction E

Step 1: The law practice has earned revenue but has not yet received payment (cash). The amounts owed by these clients are called Accounts Receivable. Revenue is earned at the time the legal services are provided, whether payment is received then or will be received sometime in the future.

Step 2: Accounts Receivable is an asset. Legal Fees are revenue.

Step 3: Accounts Receivable is increasing because the law practice has increased the amount owed to it for legal fees that have been earned but not paid. Legal Fees, or revenue, are increasing.

Step 4: An increase in the asset Accounts Receivable is a debit. An increase in Revenue is a credit.

Step 5: Enter the amount for Accounts Receivable on the debit side of the T account. The amount for Legal Fees goes on the credit side.

Transaction F   Sept. 1–30: Received $700 cash from clients for services rendered previously on account.

1 Accounts Affected	2 Category	3 ↓ ↑	4 Rules of Dr. and Cr.	5 T Account Update
Cash	Asset	↑	Dr.	**Cash 111** (A) 7,000 | 900 (B) (D) 3,000 (F) 700
Accounts Receivable	Asset	↓	Cr.	**Accounts Receivable 112** (E) 4,000 | 700 (F)

Analysis of Transaction F

Step 1: The law firm collects $700 in cash from previous revenue earned. Because the revenue is recorded at the time it is earned, and not when the payment is made, in this transaction we are concerned only with the payment, which affects the Cash and Accounts Receivable accounts.

Step 2: Cash is an asset. Accounts Receivable is an asset.

Step 3: Because clients are paying what is owed, Cash (asset) is increasing and the amount owed (Accounts Receivable) is decreasing (the total amount owed by clients to Hall is going down). This transaction results in a shift in assets, more Cash for less Accounts Receivable.

Step 4: An increase in Cash, an asset, is a debit. A decrease in Accounts Receivable, an asset, is a credit.

Step 5: Enter the amount for Cash on the debit side of the T account. The amount for Accounts Receivable goes on the credit side.

Transaction G   Sept. 1–30: Paid salaries expense, $600.

1 Accounts Affected	2 Category	3 ↓ ↑	4 Rules of Dr. and Cr.	5 T Account Update
Salaries Expense	Expense	↑	Dr.	**Salaries Expense 511** (G) 600 |
Cash	Asset	↓	Cr.	**Cash 111** (A) 7,000 | 900 (B) (D) 3,000 | 600 (G) (F) 700 |

Analysis of Transaction G

Step 1: The law firm pays $600 worth of salaries expense by cash.

Step 2: Salaries Expense is an expense. Cash is an asset.

Step 3: The Salaries Expense of the law firm is increasing, which results in a decrease in Cash.

Step 4: An increase in Salaries Expense, an expense, is a debit. A decrease in Cash, an asset, is a credit.

Step 5: Enter the amount for Salaries Expense on the debit side of the T account. The amount for Cash goes on the credit side.

Transaction H Sept. 1–30: Paid rent expense, $700.

1 Accounts Affected	2 Category	3 ↓ ↑	4 Rules of Dr. and Cr.	5 T Account Update
Rent Expense	Expense	↑	Dr.	Rent Expense 512 (H) 700 |
Cash	Asset	↓	Cr.	Cash 111 (A) 7,000 | 900 (B) (D) 3,000 | 600 (G) (F) 700 | 700 (H)

Analysis of Transaction H

Step 1: The law firm's rent expenses are paid in cash.

Step 2: Rent is an expense. Cash is an asset.

Step 3: The Rent Expense increases the expenses, and the payment for the Rent Expense decreases the cash.

Step 4: An increase in Rent Expense, an expense, is a debit. A decrease in Cash, an asset, is a credit.

Step 5: Enter the amount for Rent Expense on the debit side of the T account. Place the amount for Cash on the credit side.

Transaction I Sept. 1–30: Received a bill for Advertising Expense (to be paid next month), $300.

1 Accounts Affected	2 Category	3 ↓ ↑	4 Rules of Dr. and Cr.	5 T Account Update
Advertising Expense	Expense	↑	Dr.	Advertising Expense 513 (I) 300 |
Accounts Payable	Liability	↑	Cr.	Accounts Payable 211 | 400 (C) | 300 (I)

Analysis of Transaction I

Step 1: The advertising bill has come in and payment is due but has not yet been made. Therefore, the accounts involved here are Advertising Expense and Accounts Payable; the expense has created a liability.

Step 2: Advertising Expense is an expense. Accounts Payable is a liability.

Step 3: Both the expense and the liability are increasing.

Step 4: An increase in an expense is a debit. An increase in a liability is a credit.

Step 5: Enter the amount for Advertising Expense on the debit side of the T Account. Enter the amount for Accounts Payable on the credit side.

Transaction J Sept. 1–30: Hall withdrew cash for personal use, $200.

1 Accounts Affected	2 Category	3 ↓ ↑	4 Rules of Dr. and Cr.	5 T Account Update
Cathy Hall, Withdrawals	Withdrawals	↑	Dr.	**Cathy Hall, Withdrawals, 312** (J) 200 |
Cash	Asset	↓	Cr.	**Cash 111** (A) 7,000 | 900 (B) (D) 3,000 | 600 (G) (F) 700 | 700 (H) | 200 (J)

Analysis of Transaction J

Step 1: Cathy Hall withdraws cash from business for *personal* use. This withdrawal is not a business expense.

Step 2: This transaction affects Withdrawal and Cash accounts.

Step 3: Cathy has increased what she has withdrawn from the business for personal use. The business cash has been decreased.

Step 4: An increase in withdrawals is a debit. A decrease in cash is a credit. (*Remember:* Withdrawals go on the statement of owner's equity; expenses go on the income statement.)

Step 5: Enter the amount for Cathy Hall, Withdrawals on the debit side of the T account. The amount for Cash goes on the credit side.

> Withdrawals are always increased by debits.

SUMMARY OF TRANSACTIONS FOR CATHY HALL

ASSETS	=	LIABILITIES	+	OWNER'S EQUITY				
				Capital	− Withdrawals	+ Revenue	− Expenses	

ASSETS = **LIABILITIES** + **OWNER'S EQUITY**

Cash 111
(A) 7,000 | 900 (B)
(D) 3,000 | 600 (G)
(F) 700 | 700 (H)
| 200 (J)

= **Accounts Payable 211**
| 400 (C)
| 300 (I)

+ **Capital** − **Withdrawals** + **Revenue** − **Expenses**

Cathy Hall, Capital 311
| 7,800 (A)

− **Cathy Hall, Withdrawals 312**
(J) 200 |

+ **Legal Fees 411**
| 3,000 (D)
| 4,000 (E)

− **Salaries Expense 511**
(G) 600 |

Accounts Receivable 112
(E) 4,000 | 700 (F)

Office Equipment 121
(A) 800 |
(B) 900 |
(C) 400 |

− **Rent Expense 512**
(H) 700 |

− **Advertising Expense 513**
(I) 300 |

LEARNING UNIT 2-2 REVIEW

AT THIS POINT you should be able to

▼ State the rules of debit and credit. (p. 41)
▼ List the five steps of a transaction analysis. (p. 42)
▼ Show how to fill out a transaction analysis chart. (p. 43)
▼ Explain double-entry bookkeeping. (p. 43)

SELF-REVIEW QUIZ 2-2

(The blank forms you need are on pages 25 and 26 of the *Study Guide and Working Papers*.)

King Company uses the following accounts from its chart of accounts: Cash (111), Accounts Receivable (112), Equipment (121), Accounts Payable (211), Jamie King, Capital (311), Jamie King, Withdrawals (312), Professional Fees (411), Utilities Expense (511), and Salaries Expense (512).

Record the following transactions into transaction analysis charts.

a. Jamie King invested in the business $1,000 cash and equipment worth $700 from his personal assets.

b. Billed clients for services rendered, $12,000.

c. Utilities bill due but unpaid, $150.

d. Withdrew cash for personal use, $120.

e. Paid salaries expense, $250.

Solution to Self-Review Quiz 2-2

A.

1 Accounts Affected	2 Category	3 ↓ ↑	4 Rules of Dr. and Cr.	5 T Account Update
Cash	Asset	↑	Dr.	**Cash 111** (A) 1,000
Equipment	Asset	↑	Dr.	**Equipment 121** (A) 700
Jamie King, Capital	Capital	↑	Cr.	**Jamie King, Capital 311** 1,700 (A)

> *Quiz Tip:*
> Column 1: Row titles must come from the chart of accounts. The order doesn't matter as long as the total of all debits equals the total of all credits.

B.

1 Accounts Affected	2 Category	3 ↓ ↑	4 Rules of Dr. and Cr.	5 T Account Update
Accounts Receivable	Asset	↑	Dr.	**Accounts Receivable 112** (B) 12,000
Professional Fees	Revenue	↑	Cr.	**Professional Fees 411** 12,000 (B)

> When a business bills a client, it creates an asset, a claim for payment called an "account receivable."

C.

Record an expense when it happens, whether it is paid for or not.

1 Accounts Affected	2 Category	3 ↓ ↑	4 Rules of Dr. and Cr.	5 T Account Update
Utilities Expense	Expense	↑	Dr.	Utilities Expense 511 (C) 150 |
Accounts Payable	Liability	↑	Cr.	Accounts Payable 211 | 150 (C)

D.

Think of withdrawals as always increasing.

1 Accounts Affected	2 Category	3 ↓ ↑	4 Rules of Dr. and Cr.	5 T Account Update
Jamie King, Withdrawls	Withdrawals	↑	Dr.	Jamie King, Withdrawals 312 (D) 120 |
Cash	Asset	↓	Cr.	Cash 111 (A) 1,000 | 120 (D)

E.

Think of expenses as always increasing.

1 Accounts Affected	2 Category	3 ↓ ↑	4 Rules of Dr. and Cr.	5 T Account Update
Salaries Expense	Expense	↑	Dr.	Salaries Expense 512 (E) 250 |
Cash	Asset	↓	Cr.	Cash 111 (A) 1,000 | 120 (D) | 250 (E)

LEARNING UNIT 2-3

THE TRIAL BALANCE AND PREPARATION OF FINANCIAL STATEMENTS

Let us look at all the transactions we have discussed, arranged by T accounts and recorded using the rules of debit and credit. (See the equation at the top of page 51.) This grouping of accounts is much easier to use than the expanded accounting equation because all the transactions that affect a particular account are in one place.

As we saw in Learning Unit 2-2, when all the transactions are recorded in the accounts, the total of all the debits should be equal to the total of all the credits. (If they are not, the accountant must go back and find the error by checking the numbers and adding every column again.)

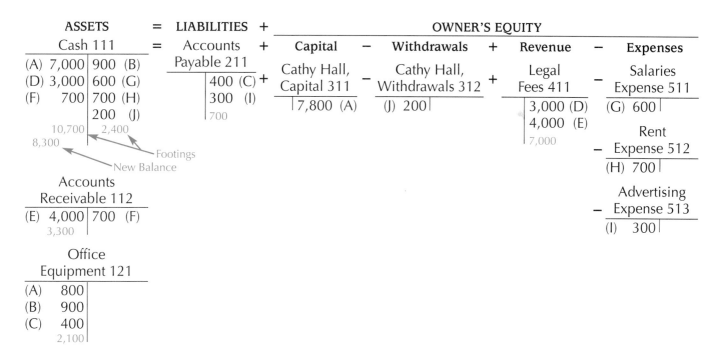

THE TRIAL BALANCE

Footings are used to obtain the balance of each side of every T account that has more than one entry. The footings are used to find the ending balance. The ending balances are used to prepare a **trial balance.** The trial balance is not a financial statement, although it is used to prepare financial statements. The trial balance lists all the accounts with their balances in the same order as they appear in the chart of accounts. It proves the accuracy of the ledger. For example, look at the Cash account above. The footing for the debit side is $10,700,

> Footings are used to obtain the balance of each side of the T account. They are not needed if there is only one entry in the account.

Time to Put the Debits on the Left . . .

Dunkin' Donuts shop owners have many accounts to deal with: food costs, payroll, rent, utilities, supplies, advertising, promotion, and —biggest of all—cash. It's critical for them to keep debits and credits straight. If not, both they and Dunkin' Donuts Inc. could lose a lot of money, quickly.

Many owners of Dunkin' Donuts smaller shops keep their own accounts, whereas most of the larger shops use accountants. In some areas of the United States, some accountants actually specialize in handling Dunkin' Donuts accounts for individual shop owners. Many shop owners, however, especially those with just one shop, handle the books themselves, both to save money and to keep a finger on the pulse of their business.

The Balance Sheet for each shop must be submitted to the zone's business consultant on the last Saturday of each month at noon. Fred had once been late in sending the Balance Sheet because he mistakenly debited both cash and

supplies when he paid for an order of paper cups. Fred had been angry at himself for having made such a basic error. Dwayne had been understanding, but had encouraged him to review the rules for recording debits and credits.

"It's only going to get harder, Fred," Dwayne had said. "Once you computerize your accounts, debits and credits are not as visible as they are with your paper system. You will only enter the payables, and the computer does the other side of the Balance Sheet. So a thorough knowledge of debits and credits is critical to understanding the [computerized] system. And the way you're growing the business, it won't be long before you'll want to switch to the computer."

Discussion Questions

1. Why is the cash account so important in Fred's business?
2. Why do you think that most owners of the larger shops use accountants to do their books instead of doing them themselves?
3. Is the difference between debits and credits important to shop owners who don't do their own books?

FIGURE 2-2. Trial Balance for Cathy Hall's Law Firm

CATHY HALL, ATTORNEY-AT-LAW TRIAL BALANCE SEPTEMBER 30, 200X		
	Dr.	Cr.
Cash	8 3 0 0 00	
Accounts Receivable	3 3 0 0 00	
Office Equipment	2 1 0 0 00	
Accounts Payable		7 0 0 00
Cathy Hall, Capital		7 8 0 0 00
Cathy Hall, Withdrawals	2 0 0 00	
Legal Fees		7 0 0 0 00
Salaries Expense	6 0 0 00	
Rent Expense	7 0 0 00	
Advertising Expense	3 0 0 00	
Totals	15 5 0 0 00	15 5 0 0 00

Because this is not a formal statement, there is no need to use dollar signs; the single and double lines under subtotals and final totals, however, are still used for clarity.

As mentioned earlier, the ending balance of cash, $8,300, is a normal balance because it is on the side that increases the asset account.

Only the ending balance of each account is listed.

and the footing for the credit side is $2,400. Because the debit side is larger, we subtract $2,400 from $10,700 to arrive at an *ending balance* of $8,300. Now look at the Rent Expense account. There is no need for a footing because there is only one entry. The amount itself is the ending balance. When the ending balance has been found for every account, we should be able to show that the total of all debits equals the total of all credits.

In the ideal situation, businesses would take a trial balance every day. The larger number of transactions most businesses conduct each day makes this impractical. Instead, trial balances are prepared periodically.

Keep in mind that the figure for capital might not be the beginning figure if any additional investment has taken place during the period. You can tell this by looking at the capital account in the ledger.

A more detailed discussion of the trial balance is provided in the next chapter. For now, notice the heading, how the accounts are listed, the debits in the left column, the credits in the right, and that the total of debits is equal to the total of credits.

A trial balance of Cathy Hall's accounts is shown in Figure 2-2.

PREPARING FINANCIAL STATEMENTS

The trial balance is used to prepare the financial statements. The diagram in Figure 2-3 on page 53 shows how financial statements can be prepared from a trial balance. Statements do not have debit or credit columns. The left column is used only to subtotal numbers.

LEARNING UNIT 2-3 REVIEW

AT THIS POINT you should be able to

▼ Explain the role of footings. (p. 51)
▼ Prepare a trial balance from a set of accounts. (p. 52)
▼ Prepare financial statements from a trial balance. (p. 53)

SELF-REVIEW QUIZ 2-3

(The blank forms you need are on page 27 of the *Study Guide and Working Papers*.)

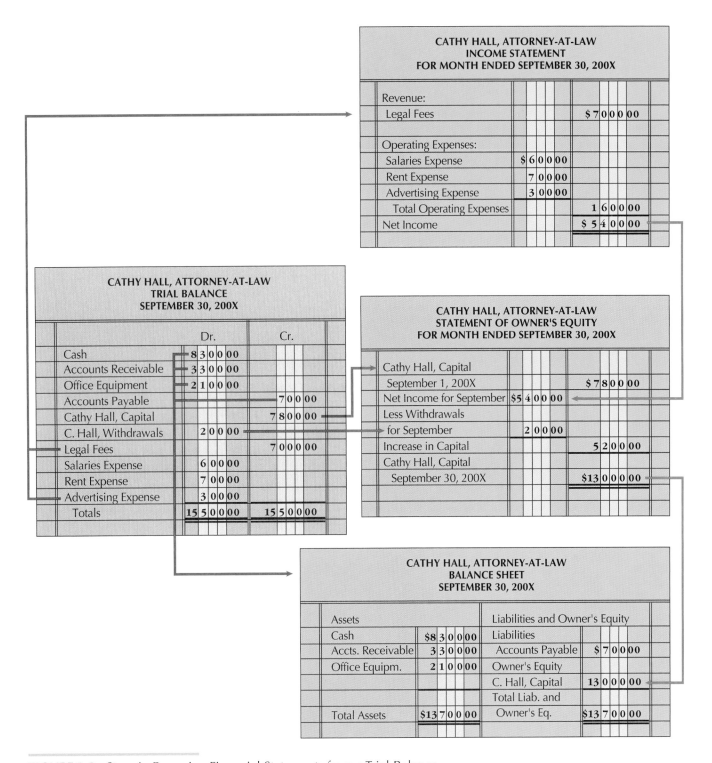

FIGURE 2-3. Steps in Preparing Financial Statements from a Trial Balance.

As the bookkeeper of Pam's Hair Salon, you are to prepare from the following accounts on June 30, 200X (1) a trial balance as of June 30, (2) an income statement for the month ended June 30, (3) a statement of owner's equity for the month ended June 30, and (4) a balance sheet as of June 30, 200X.

Cash 111		Accounts Payable 211		Salon Fees 411	
4,500	300	300	700		3,500
2,000	100				1,000
1,000	1,200				
300	1,300				
	2,600				

(Ledger continues on p. 54)

Accounts Receivable 121	Pam Jay, Capital 311	Rent Expense 511
1,000 | 300	| 4,000*	1,200 |

Salon Equipment 131	Pam Jay, Withdrawals 321	Salon Supplies Expense 521
700 |	100 |	1,300 |

		Salaries Expense 531
		2,600 |

*No additional investments.

Solution to Self-Review Quiz 2-3

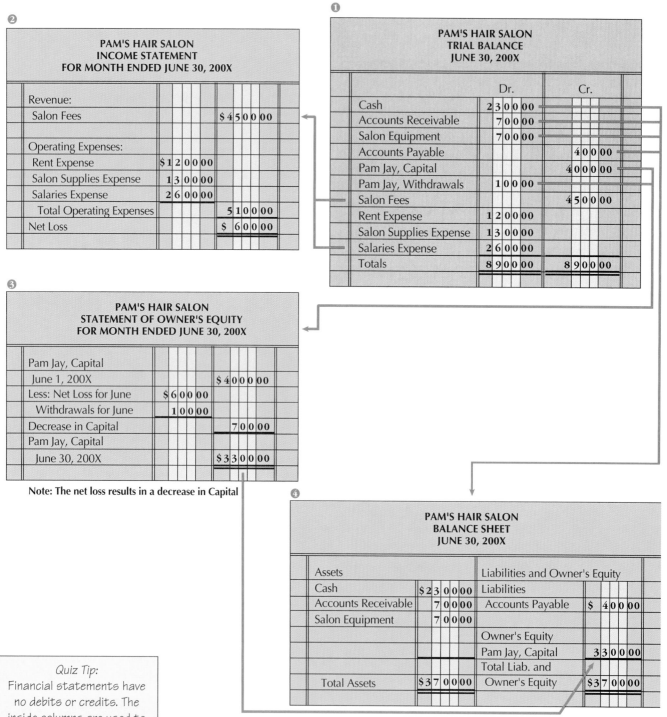

❷

PAM'S HAIR SALON
INCOME STATEMENT
FOR MONTH ENDED JUNE 30, 200X

Revenue:		
Salon Fees		$4 5 0 0 00
Operating Expenses:		
Rent Expense	$1 2 0 0 00	
Salon Supplies Expense	1 3 0 0 00	
Salaries Expense	2 6 0 0 00	
Total Operating Expenses		5 1 0 0 00
Net Loss		$ 6 0 0 00

❶

PAM'S HAIR SALON
TRIAL BALANCE
JUNE 30, 200X

	Dr.	Cr.
Cash	2 3 0 0 00	
Accounts Receivable	7 0 0 00	
Salon Equipment	7 0 0 00	
Accounts Payable		4 0 0 00
Pam Jay, Capital		4 0 0 0 00
Pam Jay, Withdrawals	1 0 0 00	
Salon Fees		4 5 0 0 00
Rent Expense	1 2 0 0 00	
Salon Supplies Expense	1 3 0 0 00	
Salaries Expense	2 6 0 0 00	
Totals	8 9 0 0 00	8 9 0 0 00

❸

PAM'S HAIR SALON
STATEMENT OF OWNER'S EQUITY
FOR MONTH ENDED JUNE 30, 200X

Pam Jay, Capital		
June 1, 200X		$4 0 0 0 00
Less: Net Loss for June	$6 0 0 00	
Withdrawals for June	1 0 0 00	
Decrease in Capital		7 0 0 00
Pam Jay, Capital		
June 30, 200X		$3 3 0 0 00

Note: The net loss results in a decrease in Capital

❹

PAM'S HAIR SALON
BALANCE SHEET
JUNE 30, 200X

Assets		Liabilities and Owner's Equity	
Cash	$2 3 0 0 00	Liabilities	
Accounts Receivable	7 0 0 00	Accounts Payable	$ 4 0 0 00
Salon Equipment	7 0 0 00		
		Owner's Equity	
		Pam Jay, Capital	3 3 0 0 00
		Total Liab. and	
Total Assets	$3 7 0 0 00	Owner's Equity	$3 7 0 0 00

Quiz Tip:
Financial statements have no debits or credits. The inside columns are used to subtotal the numbers.

If there were more than one liability we would have two columns, one to subtotal the liabilities (inside column) and one to total the liabilities (right column).

CHAPTER 2 ... DEBITS AND CREDITS

COMPREHENSIVE DEMONSTRATION PROBLEM WITH SOLUTION TIPS

(The blank forms you need are on pages 30–32 of the *Study Guide and Working Papers*.)

The chart of accounts of Mel's Delivery Service includes the following: Cash, 111; Accounts Receivable, 112; Office Equipment, 121; Delivery Trucks, 122; Accounts Payable, 211; Mel Free, Capital, 311; Mel Free, Withdrawals, 312; Delivery Fees Earned, 411; Advertising Expense, 511; Gas Expense, 512; Salaries Expense, 513; and Telephone Expense, 514. The following transactions resulted for Mel's Delivery Service during the month of July:

Transaction A: Mel invested $10,000 in the business from his personal savings account.
Transaction B: Bought delivery trucks on account, $17,000.
Transaction C: Advertising bill received but unpaid, $700.
Transaction D: Bought office equipment for cash, $1,200.
Transaction E: Received cash for delivery services rendered, $15,000.
Transaction F: Paid salaries expense, $3,000.
Transaction G: Paid gas expense for company trucks, $1,250.
Transaction H: Billed customers for delivery services rendered, $4,000.
Transaction I: Paid telephone bill, $300.
Transaction J: Received $3,000 as partial payment of transaction H.
Transaction K: Mel paid home telephone bill from company checkbook, $150.

Assignment

As Mel's newly employed accountant, you must do the following:

1. Set up T accounts in a ledger.
2. Record transactions in the T accounts. (Place the letter of the transaction next to the entry.)
3. Foot the T accounts where appropriate.
4. Prepare a trial balance at the end of July.
5. Prepare from the trial balance, in proper form, (a) an income statement for the month of July, (b) a statement of owner's equity, and (c) a balance sheet as of July 31, 200X.

Solution to Comprehensive Demonstration Problem

1,2,3.   **GENERAL LEDGER**

Cash 111		
(A) 10,000	1,200	(D)
(E) 15,000	3,000	(F)
(J) 3,000	1,250	(G)
28,000	300	(I)
22,100	150	(K)
	5,900	

Acc. Payable 211		
	17,000	(B)
	700	(C)
	17,700	

Advertising Expense 511	
(C) 700	

Acc. Receivable 112		
(H) 4,000	3,000	(J)
1,000		

Mel Free, Capital 311	
	10,000 (A)

Gas Expense 512	
(G) 1,250	

Office Equipment 121	Mel Free, Withdrawals 312	Salaries Expense 513
(D) 1,200	(K) 150	(F) 3,000

Delivery Trucks 122	Delivery Fees Earned 411	Telephone Expense 514
(B) 17,000	15,000 (E) 4,000 (H) 19,000	(I) 300

Solution Tips to Recording Transactions

A.	Cash	A	↑	Dr.		F.	Salaries Expense	Exp.	↑	Dr.
	Mel Free, Capital	Cap.	↑	Cr.			Cash	A	↓	Cr.

B.	Delivery Trucks	A	↑	Dr.		G.	Gas Expense	Exp.	↑	Dr.
	Acc. Payable	L	↑	Cr.			Cash	A	↓	Cr.

C.	Advertising Expense	Exp.	↑	Dr.		H.	Acc. Receivable	A	↑	Dr.
	Acc. Payable	L	↑	Cr.			Del. Fees Earned	Rev.	↑	Cr.

D.	Office Equipment	A	↑	Dr.		I.	Tel. Expense	Exp.	↑	Dr.
	Cash	A	↓	Cr.			Cash	A	↓	Cr.

E.	Cash	A	↑	Dr.		J.	Cash	A	↑	Dr.
	Del. Fees Earned	Rev.	↑	Cr.			Acc. Receivable	A	↓	Cr.

K.	Mel Free, Withd.	Withd.	↑	Dr.
	Cash	A	↓	Cr.

4.

MEL'S DELIVERY SERVICE
TRIAL BALANCE
JULY 31, 200X

	Dr.	Cr.
Cash	22,100	
Accounts Receivable	1,000	
Office Equipment	1,200	
Delivery Trucks	17,000	
Accounts Payable		17,700
Mel Free, Capital		10,000
Mel Free, Withdrawals	150	
Delivery Fees Earned		19,000

(continued on p. 57)

Advertising Expense	700	
Gas Expense	1,250	
Salaries Expense	3,000	
Telephone Expense	300	
TOTALS	46,700	46,700

Solution Tips to Footings and Preparation of a Trial Balance

3. Footings: Cash Add left side, $28,000.
Add right side, $5,900.
Take difference, $22,100, and stay on side that is larger.

Accounts Payable Add $17,000 + $700 and stay on same side.
Total is $17,700.

4. Trial balance is a list of the ledger's ending balances. The list is in the same order as the chart of accounts. Each title has only one number listed either as a debit or credit balance.

5a.
MEL'S DELIVERY SERVICE
INCOME STATEMENT
FOR MONTH ENDED JULY 31, 200X

Revenue:		
Delivery Fees Earned		$19,000
Operating Expenses:		
Advertising Expense	$700	
Gas Expense	1,250	
Salaries Expense	3,000	
Telephone Expense	300	
Total Operating Expenses		5,250
Net Income		$13,750

b.
MEL'S DELIVERY SERVICE
STATEMENT OF OWNER'S EQUITY
FOR MONTH ENDED JULY 31, 200X

Mel Free, Capital July 1, 200X		$10,000
Net Income for July	$13,750	
Less Withdrawals for July	150	
Increase in Capital		13,600
Mel Free, Capital, July 31, 200X		$23,600

c.
MEL'S DELIVERY SERVICE
BALANCE SHEET
JULY 31, 200X

Assets		Liabilities and Owner's Equity	
Cash	$22,100	Liabilities	
Accounts Receivable	1,000	Accounts Payable	$17,700
Office Equipment	1,200		
Delivery Trucks	17,000	Owner's Equity	
		Mel Free, Capital	23,600
		Total Liabilities and	
Total Assets	**$41,300**	**Owner's Equity**	**$41,300**

Solution Tips to Prepare Financial Statements from a Trial Balance

Trial Balance

		Dr.	Cr.
Balance Sheet	⟨ Assets	X	
	⟨ Liabilities		X
Statement of Equity	⟨ Capital		X
	⟨ Withdrawals	X	
Income Statement	⟨ Revenues		X
	⟨ Expenses	X	
		XX	XX

Net income on the income statement of $13,750 goes on the statement of owner's equity.

Ending capital of $23,600 on the statement of owner's equity goes on the balance sheet as the new figure for capital.

Note: There are no debits or credits on Financial Statements. The inside column is used for subtotaling.

SUMMARY OF KEY POINTS

Learning Unit 2-1

1. A T account is a simplified version of a standard account.
2. A ledger is a group of accounts.
3. A debit is the left-hand position (side) of an account, and a credit is the right-hand position (side) of an account.
4. A footing is the total of one side of an account. The ending balance is the difference between the footings.

Learning Unit 2-2

1. A chart of accounts lists the account titles and their numbers for a company.
2. The transaction analysis chart is a teaching device, not to be confused with standard accounting procedures.
3. A compound entry is a transaction involving more than one debit or credit.

Learning Unit 2-3

1. In double-entry bookkeeping, the recording of each business transaction affects two or more accounts, and the total of debits equals the total of credits.
2. A trial balance is a list of the ending balances of all accounts, listed in the same order as on the chart of accounts.
3. Any additional investments during the period result in capital on the trial balance not being the beginning figure for capital.
4. There are *no* debit or credit columns on the three financial statements.

KEY TERMS

Account An accounting device used in bookkeeping to record increases and decreases of business transactions relating to individual assets, liabilities, capital, withdrawals, revenue, expenses, and so on.

Chart of accounts A numbering system of accounts that lists the account titles and account numbers to be used by a company.

Compound entry A transaction involving more than one debit or credit.

Credit   The right-hand side of any account. A number entered on the right side of any account is said to be credited to an account.

Debit   The left-hand side of any account. A number entered on the left side of any account is said to be debited to an account.

Double-entry bookkeeping   An accounting system in which the recording of each transaction affects two or more accounts and the total of the debits is equal to the total of the credits.

Ending balance   The difference between footings in a T account.

Footings   The totals of each side of a T account.

Ledger   A group of accounts that records data from business transactions.

Normal balance of an account   The side of an account that increases by the rules of debit and credit.

Standard account   A formal account that includes columns for date, explanation, posting reference, debit, and credit.

T account   A skeleton version of a standard account, used for demonstration purposes.

Trial balance   A list of the ending balances of all the accounts in a ledger. The total of the debits should equal the total of the credits.

BLUEPRINT: PREPARING FINANCIAL STATEMENTS FROM A TRIAL BALANCE

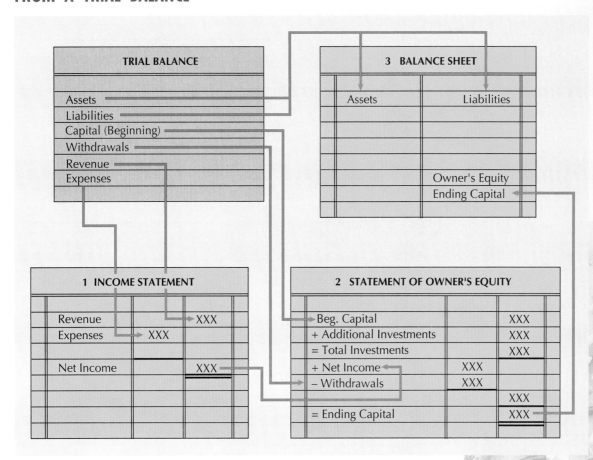

QUESTIONS, MINI EXERCISES, EXERCISES, AND PROBLEMS

Discussion Questions

1. Define a ledger.
2. Why is the left-hand side of an account called a debit?
3. Footings are used in balancing all accounts. True or false? Please explain.
4. What is the end product of the accounting process?
5. What do we mean when we say that a transaction analysis chart is a teaching device?
6. What are the five steps of the transaction analysis chart?

7. Explain the concept of double-entry bookkeeping.

8. A trial balance is a formal statement. True or false? Please explain.

9. Why are there no debit or credit columns on financial statements?

10. Compare the financial statements prepared from the expanded accounting equation with those prepared from a trial balance.

Mini Exercises

(The blank forms you need are on page 34 in the *Study Guide and Working Papers.*)

The T Account

1. From the following, foot and balance each account.

Cash 110					B. Angel, Capital 311		
4/8	3,000	4/4	2,000			3/7	6,000
4/12	6,000					3/9	3,000
						4/12	6,000

Transaction Analysis

2. Complete the following:

Account	Category	↑	↓	Normal Balance
A. Land				
B. Prepaid Rent				
C. Accounts Payable				
D. R. Snow, Capital				
E. R. Snow, Withdrawals				
F. Legal Fees				
G. Salary Expense				

Transaction Analysis

3. Record the following transaction into the transaction analysis chart: Provided legal services for $4,000, receiving $3,000 cash with the remainder to be paid next month.

Accounts Affected	Category	↓	↑	Rules of Dr. and Cr.	T Accounts

Trial Balance

4. Rearrange the following titles in the order they would appear on a Trial Balance:

Selling Expense
Accounts Receivable
Accounts Payable
D. Cope, Capital
Computer Equipment

Legal Fees
D. Cope, Withdrawals
Rent Expense
Advertising Expense
Cash

Trial Balance/Financial Statements

5. From the following Trial Balance, identify which statement each title will appear on:

▼ Income Statement (IS)
▼ Statement of Owner's Equity (OE)
▼ Balance Sheet (BS)

LOGAN CO.
TRIAL BALANCE
SEPT. 30, 200X

		Dr.	Cr.
A. _____	Cash	390	
B. _____	Supplies	100	
C. _____	Office Equipment	200	
D. _____	Accounts Payable		100
E. _____	D. Heath, Capital		450
F. _____	D. Heath, Withdrawals	160	
G. _____	Fees Earned		290
H. _____	Hair Salon Fees		300
I. _____	Salaries Expense	130	
J. _____	Rent Expense	120	
K. _____	Advertising Expense	40	
	TOTALS	1,140	1,140

Exercises

(The blank forms you need are on page 35 in the *Study Guide and Working Papers*.)

2-1. From the following, prepare a chart of accounts, using the same numbering system used in this chapter.

DVD Players	Professional Fees
Rent Expense	A. Sting, Capital
Accounts Payable	Cash
Accounts Receivable	Salaries Expense
Repair Expense	A. Sting, Withdrawals

> Preparing a chart of accounts.

2-2. Record the following transaction into the transaction analysis chart: Lois Lony bought a new piece of office equipment for $14,000, paying $3,000 down and charging the rest.

> Preparing a transaction analysis chart.

2-3. Complete the following table. For each account listed on the left, fill in what category it belongs to, whether increases and decreases in the account are marked on the debit or credit sides, and which financial statement the account appears on. A sample is provided.

> Accounts categorizing, rules, and on which reports they appear.

Accounts Affected	Category	↑	↓	Appears on which Financial Statements
Supplies	**Asset**	**Dr.**	**Cr.**	**Balance Sheet**
Legal Fees Earned				
P. Rey, Withdrawals				
Accounts Payable				
Salaries Expense				
Auto				

2-4. Given the following accounts, complete the table by inserting appropriate numbers next to the individual transaction to indicate which account is debited and which account is credited.

1. Cash
2. Accounts Receivable
3. Equipment
4. Accounts Payable
5. B. Baker, Capital

6. B. Baker, Withdrawals
7. Plumbing Fees Earned
8. Salaries Expense
9. Advertising Expense
10. Supplies Expenses

		Rules	
	Transaction	**Dr.**	**Cr.**
Example:	**A.** Paid salaries expense.	8	1
	B. Bob paid personal utilities bill from the company checkbook.		
	C. Advertising bill received but unpaid.		
	D. Received cash from plumbing fees.		
	E. Paid supplies expense.		
	F. Bob invested additional equipment into the business.		
	G. Billed customers for plumbing services rendered.		
	H. Received one-half the balance from transaction G.		
	I. Bought equipment on account.		

2-5. From the following trial balance of Hall's Cleaners, prepare the following:
▼ Income Statement
▼ Statement of Owner's Equity
▼ Balance Sheet

HALL'S CLEANERS
TRIAL BALANCE
JULY 31, 200X

	Dr.	Cr.
Cash	5 5 0 00	
Equipment	6 9 2 00	
Accounts Payable		4 5 5 00
J. Hall, Capital		8 0 0 00
J. Hall, Withdrawals	1 9 8 00	
Cleaning Fees		4 5 8 00
Salaries Expense	1 6 0 00	
Utilities Expense	1 1 3 00	
Totals	1 7 1 3 00	1 7 1 3 00

Group A Problems

(The forms you need are on pages 38–45 of the *Study Guide and Working Papers.*)

2A-1. The following transactions occurred in the opening and operation of Gail's Bookkeeping Service.

a. Gail Smith opened the bookkeeping service by investing $7,000 from her personal savings account.

b. Purchased store equipment on account, $3,000.

c. Rent expense due but unpaid, $600.

d. Received cash for bookkeeping services rendered, $800.

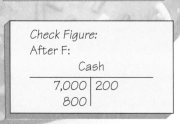

e. Billed a client on account, $500.

f. Gail withdrew cash for personal use, $200.

Complete the transaction analysis chart in the *Study Guide and Working Papers.* The chart of accounts includes Cash; Accounts Receivable; Store Equipment; Accounts Payable; Gail Smith, Capital; Gail Smith, Withdrawals; Bookkeeping Fees Earned; and Rent Expense.

2A-2. Carol Miller opened a travel agency, and the following transactions resulted:

a. Carol invested $30,000 in the travel agency.

b. Bought office equipment on account, $4,000.

c. Agency received cash for travel arrangements that it completed for a client, $3,000.

d. Carol paid a personal bill from the company checkbook, $50.

e. Paid advertising expense for the month, $700.

f. Rent expense for the month due but unpaid, $900.

g. Paid $800 as partial payment of what was owed from transaction B.

As Carol Miller's accountant, analyze and record the transactions in T account form. Set up the T accounts and label each entry with the letter of the transaction.

Recording transactions into ledger accounts.

Check Figure:
After G:

	Cash		
(A)	30,000	50	(D)
(C)	3,000	700	(E)
		800	(G)

Chart of Accounts	
Assets	**Revenue**
Cash 111	Travel Fees Earned 411
Office Equipment 121	**Expenses**
Liabilities	Advertising Expense 511
Accounts Payable 211	Rent Expense 512
Owner's Equity	
C. Miller, Capital 311	
C. Miller, Withdrawals 312	

2A-3. From the following T accounts of Mike's Window Washing Service, (a) record and foot the balances in the *Study Guide and Working Papers* where appropriate, and (b) prepare a trial balance in proper form for May 31, 200X.

Preparing a trial balance from the T accounts.

Check Figure:
Trial Balance Total $12,700

Cash 111			
5,000	(A)	100	(D)
3,500	(G)	200	(E)
		400	(F)
		200	(H)
		900	(I)

Accounts Payable 211			
100	(D)	1,300	(C)

Fees Earned 411	
	6,500 (B)

Accounts Receivable 112			
6,500	(B)	3,500	(G)

Mike Frank, Capital 311	
	5,000 (A)

Rent Expense 511	
400	(F)

Office Equipment 121	
1,300	(C)
200	(H)

Mike Frank, Withdrawals 312	
900	(I)

Utilities Expense 512	
200	(E)

Preparing financial statements from the trial balance.

2A-4. From the trial balance of Gracie Lantz, Attorney-at-Law, prepare (a) an income statement for the month of May, (b) a statement of owner's equity for the month ended May 31, and (c) a balance sheet as of May 31, 200X.

Check Figure:
Total Assets $6,400

GRACIE LANTZ, ATTORNEY-AT-LAW TRIAL BALANCE MAY 31, 200X		
	Dr.	Cr.
Cash	5 0 0 0 00	
Accounts Receivable	6 5 0 00	
Office Equipment	7 5 0 00	
Accounts Payable		4 3 0 0 00
Salaries Payable		6 7 5 00
G. Lantz, Capital		1 2 7 5 00
G. Lantz, Withdrawals	3 0 0 00	
Revenue from Legal Fees		1 3 5 0 00
Utilities Expense	3 0 0 00	
Rent Expense	4 5 0 00	
Salaries Expense	1 5 0 00	
Totals	7 6 0 0 00	7 6 0 0 00

Comprehensive problem

2A-5. The chart of accounts for Angel's Delivery Service is as follows:

Check Figure:
Total Trial Balance $38,100

Chart of Accounts

Assets
Cash   111
Accounts Receivable   112
Office Equipment   121
Delivery Trucks   122

Liabilities
Accounts Payable   211

Owner's Equity
Alice Angel, Capital   311
Alice Angel, Withdrawals   312

Revenue
Delivery Fees Earned   411

Expenses
Advertising Expense   511
Gas Expense   512
Salaries Expense   513
Telephone Expense   514

Angel's Delivery Service completed the following transactions during the month of March:

Transaction A: Alice Angel invested $16,000 in the delivery service from her personal savings account.
Transaction B: Bought delivery trucks on account, $18,000.
Transaction C: Bought office equipment for cash, $600.
Transaction D: Paid advertising expense, $250.
Transaction E: Collected cash for delivery services rendered, $2,600.
Transaction F: Paid drivers' salaries, $900.
Transaction G: Paid gas expense for trucks, $1,200.
Transaction H: Performed delivery services for a customer on account, $800.
Transaction I: Telephone expense due but unpaid, $700.
Transaction J: Received $300 as partial payment of transaction H.
Transaction K: Alice withdrew cash for personal use, $300.

As Alice's newly employed accountant, you must:

1. Set up T accounts in a ledger.
2. Record transactions in the T accounts. (Place the letter of the transaction next to the entry.)
3. Foot the T accounts where appropriate.
4. Prepare a trial balance at the end of March.
5. Prepare from the trial balance, in proper form, (a) an income statement for the month of March, (b) a statement of owner's equity, and (c) a balance sheet as of March 31, 200X.

Group B Problems

The forms you need are on pages 38–45 of the *Study Guide and Working Papers*.)

2B-1. Gail Smith decided to open a bookkeeping service. Record the following transactions into the transaction analysis charts:

> **Transaction A:** Gail invested $1,500 in the bookkeeping service from her personal savings account.
> **Transaction B:** Purchased store equipment on account, $900.
> **Transaction C:** Rent expense due but unpaid, $250.
> **Transaction D:** Performed bookkeeping services for cash, $1,200.
> **Transaction E:** Billed clients for bookkeeping services rendered, $700.
> **Transaction F:** Gail paid her home heating bill from the company checkbook, $275.

The chart of accounts for the shop includes Cash; Accounts Receivable; Store Equipment; Accounts Payable; Gail Smith, Capital; Gail Smith, Withdrawals; Bookkeeping Fees Earned; and Rent Expense.

2B-2. Carol Miller established a new travel agency. Record the following transactions for Carol in T account form. Label each entry with the letter of the transaction.

> **Transaction A:** Carol invested $18,000 in the travel agency from her personal bank account.
> **Transaction B:** Bought office equipment on account, $6,000.
> **Transaction C:** Travel agency rendered service to Jensen Corp. and received cash, $1,200.
> **Transaction D:** Carol withdrew cash for personal use, $200.
> **Transaction E:** Paid advertising expense, $600.
> **Transaction F:** Rent expense due but unpaid, $500.
> **Transaction G:** Paid $400 in partial payment of transaction B.

The chart of accounts includes Cash, 111; Office Equipment, 121; Accounts Payable, 211; C. Miller, Capital, 311; C. Miller, Withdrawals, 312; Travel Fees Earned, 411; Advertising Expense, 511; and Rent Expense, 512.

2B-3. From the following T accounts of Mike's Window Washing Service, (a) record and foot the balances in the *Study Guide and Working Papers* where appropriate and (b) prepare a trial balance for May 31, 200X.

Use of a transaction analysis chart.

Check Figure:
After F:

Cash

| (A) | 1,500 | 275 | (F) |
| (D) | 1,200 | | |

Recording transactions into ledger accounts.

Check Figure:
After G:

Cash

(A)	18,000	200	(D)
(C)	1,200	600	(E)
		400	(G)

Preparing a trial balance from the T accounts.

Cash 111

10,000	(A)	4,000	(C)
4,000	(F)	310	(D)
2,000	(G)	50	(E)
		600	(H)

Accounts Receivable 112

| 2,000 | (G) |

Office Equipment 121

| 2,000 | (B) |
| 4,000 | (C) |

(continued on p. 66)

Accounts Payable 211		
	2,000	(B)

Mike Frank, Capital 311		
	10,000	(A)

Mike Frank, Withdrawals 312		
600	(H)	

Fees Earned 411		
	4,000	(F)
	4,000	(G)

Rent Expense 511		
310	(D)	

Utilities Expense 512		
50	(E)	

2B-4. From the trial balance of Gracie Lantz, Attorney-at-Law, prepare (a) an income from the statement for the month of May, (b) a statement of owner's equity for the month ended May 31, and (c) a balance sheet as of May 31, 200X.

GRACIE LANTZ, ATTORNEY-AT-LAW
TRIAL BALANCE
MAY 31, 200X

	Debit	Credit
Cash	6 0 0 0 00	
Accounts Receivable	2 4 0 0 00	
Office Equipment	2 4 0 0 00	
Accounts Payable		2 0 0 00
Salaries Payable		6 0 0 00
G. Lantz, Capital		4 0 0 0 00
G. Lantz, Withdrawals	2 0 0 0 00	
Revenue from Legal Fees		8 8 0 0 00
Utilities Expense	1 0 0 00	
Rent Expense	3 0 0 00	
Salaries Expense	4 0 0 00	
Totals	13 6 0 0 00	13 6 0 0 00

2B-5. The chart of accounts of Angel's Delivery Service includes the following: Cash, 111; Accounts Receivable, 112; Office Equipment, 121; Delivery Trucks, 122; Accounts Payable, 211; Alice Angel, Capital, 311; Alice Angel, Withdrawals, 312; Delivery Fees Earned, 411; Advertising Expense, 511; Gas Expense, 512; Salaries Expense, 513; and Telephone Expense, 514. The following transactions resulted for Angel's Delivery Service during the month of March:

Transaction A: Alice invested $40,000 in the business from her personal savings account.

Transaction B: Bought delivery trucks on account, $25,000.

Transaction C: Advertising bill received but unpaid, $800.

Transaction D: Bought office equipment for cash, $2,500.

Transaction E: Received cash for delivery services rendered, $13,000.

Transaction F: Paid salaries expense, $1,850.

Transaction G: Paid gas expense for company trucks, $750.

Transaction H: Billed customers for delivery services rendered, $5,500.

Transaction I: Paid telephone bill, $400.

Transaction J: Received $1,600 as partial payment of transaction H.

Transaction K: Alice paid her home telephone bill from company checkbook, $88.

As Alice's newly employed accountant, you must

1. Set up T accounts in a ledger.
2. Record transactions in the T accounts. (Place the letter of the transaction next to the entry.)
3. Foot the T accounts where appropriate.
4. Prepare a trial balance at the end of March.
5. Prepare from the trial balance, in proper form, (a) an income statement for the month of March, (b) a statement of owner's equity, and (c) a balance sheet as of March 31, 200X.

REAL-WORLD APPLICATIONS

2R-1.

Andy Leaf is a careless bookkeeper. He is having a terrible time getting his trial balance to balance. Andy has asked for your assistance in preparing a correct trial balance. The following is the incorrect trial balance.

RANCH COMPANY TRIAL BALANCE JUNE 30, 200X		
	Dr.	Cr.
Cash	5 1 0 00	
Accounts Receivable		6 3 5 00
Office Equipment	3 6 0 00	
Accounts Payable	1 1 0 00	
Wages Payable	1 0 00	
H. Clo, Capital	6 3 5 00	
H. Clo, Withdrawals	1 4 4 0 00	
Professional Fees		2 2 4 0 00
Rent Expense		2 4 0 00
Advertising Expense	2 5 00	
Totals	3 0 9 0 00	3 1 1 5 00

Facts you have discovered:

▼ Debits to the Cash account were $2,640; credits to the Cash account were $2,150.
▼ Amy Hall paid $15 but was not updated in Accounts Receivable.
▼ A purchase of office equipment for $5 on account was never recorded in the ledger.
▼ Revenue was understated in the ledger by $180.

Show how these errors affected the ending balances for the accounts involved, and explain how the trial balance will indeed balance once they are corrected.

Tell Ranch Company how it can avoid this problem in the future. Write your recommendations.

2R-2.

Cookie Mejias, owner of Mejias Company, asked her bookkeeper how each of the following situations will affect the totals of the trial balance and individual ledger accounts.

1. An $850 payment for a desk was recorded as a debit to Office Equipment, $85, and a credit to Cash, $85.

2. A payment of $300 to a creditor was recorded as a debit to Accounts Payable, $300, and a credit to Cash, $100.

3. The collection on an Accounts Receivable for $400 was recorded as a debit to Cash, $400, and a credit to C. Mejias, Capital, $400.

4. The payment of a liability for $400 was recorded as a debit to Accounts Payable, $40, and a credit to Supplies, $40.

5. A purchase of equipment of $800 was recorded as a debit to Supplies, $800, and a credit to Cash, $800.

6. A payment of $95 to a creditor was recorded as a debit to Accounts Payable, $95, and a credit to Cash, $59.

What did the bookkeeper tell her? Which accounts were overstated, and which were understated? Which were correct? Explain in writing how mistakes can be avoided in the future.

YOU make the call

Critical Thinking/Ethical Case

2R-3.
Audrey Flet, the bookkeeper of ALN Co., was scheduled to leave on a three-week vacation at 5 o'clock on Friday. She couldn't get the company's trial balance to balance. At 4:30, she decided to put in fictitious figures to make it balance. Audrey told herself she would fix it when she got back from her vacation. Was Audrey right or wrong to do this? Why?

INTERNET EXERCISES

EX-1. [www.priceline.com]   In this chapter you have learned about debits and credits and their place in creating financial statements. Go to the website for Priceline, click on Investor Relations, and look for filings with the Securities and Exchange Commission (SEC). Find the 9/15/99 filing of Form 10Q and prepare a trial balance as of September 30, 1999.

EX-2. [www.priceline.com]   Use your knowledge of debits and credits in this exercise. Look at the solution for exercise and answer these questions:

1. Explain why the balance in the "Accumulated Deficit" account, an Owner's Equity account, has a debit balance, rather than the expected credit balance.

2. Calculate Total Assets, Total Liabilities, and Total Stockholders' Equity.

3. Use the accounting equation and calculate the balance of Stockholders' Equity (the Owner's Equity equivalent of a corporation), using the totals of Assets and Liabilities.

CONTINUING PROBLEM

The Eldorado Computer Center created its chart of accounts as follows:

Chart of Accounts
as of July 1, 200X

Assets
1000   Cash
1020   Accounts Receivable
1030   Supplies
1080   Computer Shop Equipment
1090   Office Equipment

Liabilities
2000   Accounts Payable

Owner's Equity
3000   Freedman, Capital
3010   Freedman, Withdrawals

Revenue
4000   Service Revenue
Expenses
5010   Advertising Expense
5020   Rent Expense
5030   Utilities Expense
5040   Phone Expense
5050   Supplies Expense
5060   Insurance Expense
5070   Postage Expense

You will use this chart of accounts to complete the Continuing Problem.

The following problem continues from Chapter 1. The balances as of July 31 have been brought forward in your *Study Guide and Working Papers* on page 49.

Assignment

1. Set up T accounts in a ledger.
2. Record transactions k through q in the appropriate T accounts.
3. Foot the T accounts where appropriate.
4. Prepare a trial balance at the end of August.
5. Prepare from the trial balance an income statement, statement of owner's equity, and a balance sheet for the two months ending with August 31, 200X.

k. Received the phone bill for the month of July, $155.
l. Paid $150 (check #8099) for insurance for the month.
m. Paid $200 (check #8100) of the amount due from transaction d in Chapter 1.
n. Paid advertising expense for the month, $1,400 (check #8101).
o. Billed a client (Jeannine Sparks) for services rendered, $850.
p. Collected $900 for services rendered.
q. Paid the electric bill in full for the month of July (check #8102, transaction h, Chapter 1).
r. Paid cash (check #8103) for $50 in stamps.
s. Purchased $200 worth of supplies from Computer Connection on credit.

Beginning the Accounting Cycle

JOURNALIZING, POSTING, AND THE TRIAL BALANCE

When you go on your Spring Break vacation to Cancun, Mexico or Jamaica's Negril*, will you buy your airline ticket online or go to a traditional neighborhood travel agency? Chances are, you'll go online to buy your ticket, or, at the very least, to research your trip and compare vacation packages. In 1999 16.5

million consumers bought air tickets online, up 146% from 1998. The huge increase in online ticketing—via sites like expedia.com, travelocity.com or orbitz.com—and lowered commissions from airlines are threatening to put traditional storefront travel agencies out of business. In fact, the ranks of traditional agencies have been thinned by 16% in the last six years.

The travel agencies that survive do so by exploiting niches and the very technology that's putting their colleagues out of business. For instance, STA Travel (statravel.com) caters to students around the world who seek low fares and often exotic locales. Students can browse offerings on STA's Web site (www.statravel.com) and even book a trip online. Yet, they must still call STA or come in to pay for their trip at one of its 200 franchises. The Web site offers a wealth of instant information on everything from popular travel destinations to tips on avoiding pickpockets and getting passports and visas. At an STA office, students can get personal treatment and hand-holding as they plan to venture off to Bangkok or Buenos Aires.

Just as savvy travel agencies like STA combine high-tech and "high-touch", so do savvy accountants who hope to thrive in the new economy. Most likely, you will accomplish all the activities in the **accounting cycle** automatically on a computer. Yet, in order to help your client or company—let's say its STA travel—you'll need to be familiar with every step so you can explain the results and correct errors. In this chapter you'll learn how to perform the first activities in the accounting cycle: keeping a **journal** of business transactions, transferring journal information to a **ledger,** and preparing a **trial balance.** Whether you do it manually or via your computer, however, step number one of the accounting cycle is the same; business transactions occur and generate source documents. At STA travel customers pay with credit card, cash, money orders or checks. Source documents will run the gamut from credit card receipts to calculator tapes and deposit slips. All must be recorded accurately as business transactions in either a computerized "journal" or with ink in an actual journal. Accuracy is extremely important since recording business transactions incorrectly will throw the rest of the accounting cycle off.

---

*Cancun and Negril are two of STA Travel's Spring Break "Hot Spots."

Based on: E. Scott Reckard, "Threatened by Web, Travel Agents Adopt New Tactics: consumer services: Despite rise in self-booked trips, industry pros are creating niches by exploiting the power of the Internet and offering a personal touch," *The Los Angeles Times,* April 30, 2000, p. C, 1. Anonymous, "Travel agents feel doubly squeezed Commission cuts, online competition makes it tougher to turn a profit," *The Atlanta Journal,* November 16, 1999, p. E, 6. Information about STA Travel is from www.statravel.com.

LEARNING OBJECTIVES

▼ Journalizing: analyzing and recording business transactions into a journal. (p. 72)

▼ Posting: transferring information from a journal to a ledger. (p. 80)

▼ Preparing a trial balance. (p. 87)

The normal accounting procedures that are performed over a period of time are called the **accounting cycle.** The accounting cycle takes place in a period of time called an **accounting period.** An accounting period is the period of time covered by the income statement. Although it can be any time period up to one year (e.g., one month or three months), most businesses use a one-year accounting period. The year can be either a **calendar year** (January 1 through December 31) or a **fiscal year.**

A fiscal year is an accounting period that runs for any 12 consecutive months, so it can be the same as a calendar year. A business can choose any fiscal year that is convenient. For example, some retailers may decide to end their fiscal year when inventories and business activity are at a low point, such as after the Christmas season. This period is called a **natural business year.** Using a natural business year allows the business to count its year-end inventory when it is easiest to do so.

Businesses would not be able to operate successfully if they only prepared financial reports at the end of their calendar or fiscal year. That is why most businesses prepare **interim statements** on a monthly, quarterly, or semiannual basis.

In this chapter, as well as in Chapters 4 and 5, we follow Brenda Clark's new business, Clark's Word Processing Services. We follow the normal accounting procedures that the business performs over a period of time. Clark has chosen to use a fiscal period of January 1 to December 31, which also is the calendar year.

Take a moment to look at the four-color road map of the accounting cycle on inside front cover. Use this map as a reference for Chapters 3, 4, and 5. It will help you to answer the question, When do I do what?

This chapter covers steps 1 to 4 of the accounting cycle. (See the road map on inside front cover.)

LEARNING UNIT 3-1

ANALYZING AND RECORDING BUSINESS TRANSACTIONS INTO A JOURNAL: STEPS 1 AND 2 OF THE ACCOUNTING CYCLE

THE GENERAL JOURNAL

A business uses a journal to record transactions in chronological order. A ledger accumulates information from a journal. The journal and the ledger are in two different books.

Chapter 2 taught us how to analyze and record business transactions into T accounts, or ledger accounts. Recording a debit in an account on one page of the ledger and recording the corresponding credit on a different page of the ledger, however, can make it difficult to find errors. It would be much easier if all the business's transactions were located in the same place. That is the function of the **journal** or **general journal.** Transactions are entered in the journal in chronological order (January 1, 8, 15, etc.), and then this recorded information is used to update the ledger accounts. In computerized accounting, a journal may be recorded on disk or tape.

We will use a general journal, the simplest form of a journal, to record the transactions of Clark's Word Processing Services. A transaction [debit(s) + credit(s)] that has been analyzed and recorded in a journal is called a **journal entry.** The process of recording the journal entry into the journal is called **journalizing.**

Journal: book of original entry.

The journal is called the **book of original entry,** because it contains the first formal information about the business transactions. The ledger is known as the **book of final entry,** because the information the journal contains will be transferred to the ledger. Like the ledger, the journal may be a bound or loose-leaf book. Each of the journal pages looks like the one in Figure 3-1. The pages of the journal are numbered consecutively from page 1. Keep in mind that the journal and the ledger are separate books.

Relationship between the Journal and the Chart of Accounts

The accountant must refer to the business's chart of accounts for the account name that is to be used in the journal. Every company has its own "unique" chart of accounts.

The chart of accounts for Clark's Word Processing Services appears on page 73. By the end of Chapter 5, we will have discussed each of these accounts.

Note that we will continue to use transaction analysis charts as a teaching aid in the journalizing process.

FIGURE 3-1. The General Journal

CLARK'S WORD PROCESSING SERVICES					
GENERAL JOURNAL					
					Page 1
Date	Account Titles and Description	PR	Dr.	Cr.	

Clark's Word Processing Services
Chart of Accounts

Assets (100–199)
111   Cash
112   Accounts Receivable
114   Office Supplies
115   Prepaid Rent
121   Word Processing Equipment
122   Accumulated Depreciation,
        Word Processing Equipment

Liabilities (200–299)
211   Accounts Payable
212   Salaries Payable

Owner's Equity (300–399)
311   Brenda Clark, Capital
312   Brenda Clark, Withdrawals
313   Income Summary

Revenue (400–499)
411   Word Processing Fees

Expenses (500–599)
511   Office Salaries Expense
512   Advertising Expense
513   Telephone Expense
514   Office Supplies Expense
515   Rent Expense
516   Depreciation Expense,
        Word Processing Equipment

Journalizing the Transactions of Clark's Word Processing Services

Certain formalities must be followed in making journal entries:

▼ The debit portion of the transaction always is recorded first.
▼ The credit portion of a transaction is indented one-half inch and placed below the debit portion.
▼ The explanation of the journal entry follows immediately after the credit and one inch from the date column.
▼ A one-line space follows each transaction and explanation. This makes the journal easier to read, and there is less chance of mixing transactions.
▼ Finally, as always, the total amount of debits must equal the total amount of credits. The same format is used for each of the entries in the journal.

May 1, 200X: Brenda Clark began the business by investing $10,000 in cash.

1 Accounts Affected	2 Category	3 ↓ ↑	4 Rules of Dr. and Cr.
Cash	**Asset**	↑	**Dr.**
Brenda Clark, Capital	**Capital**	↑	**Cr.**

CLARK'S WORD PROCESSING SERVICES
GENERAL JOURNAL

Page 1

Date			Account Titles and Description	PR	Dr.	Cr.
200X May	1		Cash		10 0 0 0 00	
			Brenda Clark, Capital			10 0 0 0 00
			Initial investment of cash by owner			

For now the PR (posting reference) column is blank; we discuss it later.

Let's now look at the structure of this journal entry. The entry contains the following information:

1. Year of the journal entry   200X
2. Month of the journal entry   May
3. Day of journal entry   1
4. Name(s) of accounts debited   Cash
5. Name(s) of accounts credited   Brenda Clark, Capital
6. Explanation of transaction   Investment of cash
7. Amount of debit(s) $10,000
8. Amount of credit(s) $10,000

May 1: Purchased word processing equipment from Ben Co. for $6,000, paying $1,000 and promising to pay the balance within 30 days.

1 Accounts Affected	2 Category	3 ↓ ↑	4 Rules of Dr. and Cr.
Word Processing Equipment	Asset	↑	Dr.
Cash	Asset	↓	Cr.
Accounts Payable	Liability	↑	Cr.

This transaction affects three accounts. When a journal entry has more than two accounts, it is called a **compound journal entry**.

Note that in this compound entry we have one debit and two credits, but the total amount of debits equals the total amount of credits.

		1	Word Processing Equipment		6 0 0 0 00	
			Cash			1 0 0 0 00
			Accounts Payable			5 0 0 0 00
			Purchase of equipment from Ben Co.			

A journal entry that requires three or more accounts is called a compound journal entry.

In this entry, only the day is entered in the date column, because the year and month were entered at the top of the page from the first transaction. There is no need to repeat this information until a new page is needed or a change of months occurs.

May 1: Rented office space, paying $1,200 in advance for the first three months.

1 Accounts Affected	2 Category	3 ↓ ↑	4 Rules of Dr. and Cr.
Prepaid Rent	Asset	↑	Dr.
Cash	Asset	↓	Cr.

In this transaction Clark gains an asset called prepaid rent and gives up an asset, cash. The prepaid rent does not become an expense until it expires.

> Rent paid in advance is an asset.

	1	Prepaid Rent			1 2 0 0 00		
		Cash				1 2 0 0 00	
		Rent paid in advance—3 mos.					

May 3: Purchased office supplies from Norris Co. on account, $600.

1 Accounts Affected	2 Category	3 ↓ ↑	4 Rules of Dr. and Cr.
Office Supplies	Asset	↑	Dr.
Accounts Payable	Liability	↑	Cr.

Remember, supplies are an asset when they are purchased. Once they are used up or consumed in the operation of business, they become an expense.

> Supplies become an expense when used up.

	3	Office Supplies			6 0 0 00		
		Accounts Payable				6 0 0 00	
		Purchase of supplies on account					
		from Norris					

May 7: Completed sales promotion pieces for a client and immediately collected $3,000.

1 Accounts Affected	2 Category	3 ↓ ↑	4 Rules of Dr. and Cr.
Cash	Asset	↑	Dr.
Word Processing Fees	Revenue	↑	Cr.

	7	Cash			3 0 0 0 00		
		Word Processing Fees				3 0 0 0 00	
		Cash received for services rendered					

May 13: Paid office salaries, $650.

1 Accounts Affected	2 Category	3 ↓ ↑	4 Rules of Dr. and Cr.
Office Salaries Expense	Expense	↑	Dr.
Cash	Asset	↓	Cr.

		13	Office Salaries Expense		6 5 0 00	
			Cash			6 5 0 00
			Payment of office salaries			

Remember, expenses are recorded when they are incurred, no matter when they are paid.

May 18: Advertising bill from Al's News Co. comes in but is not paid, $250.

1 Accounts Affected	2 Category	3 ↓ ↑	4 Rules of Dr. and Cr.
Advertising Expense	Expense	↑	Dr.
Accounts Payable	Liability	↑	Cr.

		18	Advertising Expense		2 5 0 00	
			Accounts Payable			2 5 0 00
			Bill in but not paid from Al's News			

Keep in mind that as withdrawals increase, owner's equity decreases.

May 20: Brenda Clark wrote a check on the bank account of the business to pay her home mortgage payment of $625.

1 Accounts Affected	2 Category	3 ↓ ↑	4 Rules of Dr. and Cr.
Brenda Clark, Withdrawals	Withdrawals	↑	Dr.
Cash	Asset	↓	Cr.

		20	Brenda Clark, Withdrawals		6 2 5 00	
			Cash			6 2 5 00
			Personal withdrawal of cash			

May 22: Billed Morris Company for a sophisticated word processing job, $5,000.

1 Accounts Affected	2 Category	3 ↓ ↑	4 Rules of Dr. and Cr.
Accounts Receivable	Asset	↑	Dr.
Word Processing Fees	Revenue	↑	Cr.

	22	Accounts Receivable		5 0 0 0 00	
		Word Processing Fees			5 0 0 0 00
		Billed Morris Co. for fees earned			

May 27: Paid office salaries, $650.

1 Accounts Affected	2 Category	3 ↓ ↑	4 Rules of Dr. and Cr.
Offices Salaries Expense	Expense	↑	Dr.
Cash	Asset	↓	Cr.

CLARK'S WORD PROCESSING SERVICES
GENERAL JOURNAL

Page 2

Date		Account Titles and Description	PR	Dr.	Cr.
200X May	27	Office Salaries Expense		6 5 0 00	
		Cash			6 5 0 00
		Payment of office salaries			

May 28: Paid half the amount owed for word processing equipment purchased May 1 from Ben Co., $2,500.

1 Accounts Affected	2 Category	3 ↓ ↑	4 Rules of Dr. and Cr.
Accounts Payable	Liability	↓	Dr.
Cash	Asset	↓	Cr.

	28	Accounts Payable		2 5 0 0 00	
		Cash			2 5 0 0 00
		Paid half the amount owed Ben Co.			

May 29: Received and paid telephone bill, $220.

1 Accounts Affected	2 Category	3 ↓ ↑	4 Rules of Dr. and Cr.
Telephone Expense	Expense	↑	Dr.
Cash	Asset	↓	Cr.

		29	Telephone Expense			2 2 0 00		
			Cash				2 2 0 00
			Paid telephone bill				

This concludes the journal transactions of Clark's Word Processing Services. (See page 82 for a summary of all the transactions.)

LEARNING UNIT 3-1 REVIEW

AT THIS POINT you should be able to

▼ Define an accounting cycle. (p. 71)
▼ Define and explain the relationship of the accounting period to the income statement. (p. 71)
▼ Compare and contrast a calendar year to a fiscal year. (p. 71)
▼ Explain the term *natural business year.* (p. 71)
▼ Explain the function of interim reports. (p. 72)
▼ Define and state the purpose of a journal. (p. 72)
▼ Compare and contrast a book of original entry to a book of final entry. (p. 72)
▼ Differentiate between a chart of accounts and a journal. (p. 73)
▼ Explain a compound entry. (p. 74)
▼ Journalize a business transaction. (p. 74)

SELF-REVIEW QUIZ 3-1

(The blank forms you need are on pages 52 – 53 of the *Study Guide and Working Papers.*)

The following are the transactions of Lowe's Repair Service. Journalize the transactions in proper form. The chart of accounts includes Cash; Accounts Receivable; Prepaid Rent; Repair Supplies; Repair Equipment; Accounts Payable; A. Lowe, Capital; A. Lowe, Withdrawals; Repair Fees Earned; Salaries Expense; Advertising Expense; and Supplies Expense.

200X
June   1   A. Lowe invested $7,000 cash and $5,000 of repair equipment in the business.
         1   Paid two months' rent in advance, $1,200.
         4   Bought repair supplies from Melvin Co. on account, $600. (These supplies have not yet been consumed or used up.)
        15   Performed repair work, received $600 in cash, and had to bill Doe Co. for remaining balance of $300.
        18   A. Lowe paid his home telephone bill, $50, with a check from the company.

CHAPTER 3 ... BEGINNING THE ACCOUNTING CYCLE

20 Advertising bill for $400 from Jones Co. received but payment not due yet. (Advertising has already appeared in the newspaper.)
24 Paid salaries, $1,400.

Solution to Self-Review Quiz 3-1

LOWE'S REPAIR SERVICE
GENERAL JOURNAL

Page 1

Date			Account Titles and Description	PR	Dr.	Cr.
200X June	1		Cash		7 0 0 0 00	
			Repair Equipment		5 0 0 0 00	
			A. Lowe, Capital			12 0 0 0 00
			Owner investment			
	1		Prepaid Rent		1 2 0 0 00	
			Cash			1 2 0 0 00
			Rent paid in advance—2mos.			
	4		Repair Supplies		6 0 0 00	
			Accounts Payable			6 0 0 00
			Purchase on account from Melvin Co.			
	15		Cash		6 0 0 00	
			Accounts Receivable		3 0 0 00	
			Repair Fees Earned			9 0 0 00
			Performed repairs for Doe Co.			
	18		A. Lowe, Withdrawals		5 0 00	
			Cash			5 0 00
			Personal withdrawal			
	20		Advertising Expense		4 0 0 00	
			Accounts Payable			4 0 0 00
			Advertising bill from Jones Co.			
	24		Salaries Expense		1 4 0 0 00	
			Cash			1 4 0 0 00
			Paid salaries			

Quiz Tip: All titles for the debits and credits come from the chart of accounts, debits against the date column and credits indented. The PR column is left blank in the journalizing process.

LEARNING UNIT 3-2

POSTING TO THE LEDGER: STEP 3 OF THE ACCOUNTING CYCLE

The general journal serves a particular purpose: it puts every transaction the business does in one place. There are things it cannot do, though. For example, if you were asked to find the balance of the cash account from the general

FIGURE 3-2. Four-Column
Account

Accounts Payable							Account No. 211
Date	Explanation	Post. Ref.	Debit	Credit	Balance Debit	Balance Credit	
200X May 1		GJ1		5 0 0 0 00		5 0 0 0 00	
3		GJ1		6 0 0 00		5 6 0 0 00	
18		GJ1		2 5 0 00		5 8 5 0 00	
28		GJ2	2 5 0 0 00			3 3 5 0 00	

journal, you would have to go through the entire journal and look for only the cash entries. Then you would have to add up the debits and credits for the cash account and determine the difference between the two.

What we really need to do to find balances of accounts is to transfer the information from the journal to the ledger. This is called **posting.** In the ledger we will accumulate an ending balance for each account so that we can prepare financial statements.

In Chapter 2 we used the T account form to make our ledger entries. T accounts are very simple, but they are not used in the real business world; they are only used for demonstration purposes. In practice, accountants often use a **four-column account** form that includes a column for the business's running balance. Figure 3-2 shows a standard four-column account. We use that format in the text from now on.

> Footings are not needed in four-column accounts.

POSTING

Now let's look at how to post the transactions of Clark's Word Processing Service from its journal. The diagram in Figure 3-3 shows how to post the cash line from the journal to the ledger. The steps in the posting process are numbered and illustrated in the figure.

Step 1: In the Cash account in the ledger, record the date (May 1, 200X) and the amount of the entry ($10,000).

Step 2: Record the page number of the journal "GJ1" in the posting reference (PR) column of the Cash account.

Step 3: Calculate the new balance of the account. You keep a running balance in each account as you would in your checkbook. To do so you take the present balance in the account on the previous line and add or subtract the transaction as necessary to arrive at your new balance.

Step 4: Record the account number of Cash (111) in the posting reference (PR) column of the journal. This is called **cross-referencing.**

The same sequence of steps occurs for each line in the journal. In a manual system like Clark's, the debits and credits in the journal may be posted in the order they were recorded, or all the debits may be posted first and then all the credits. If Clark used a computer system, the program menu would post at the press of a button.

Using Posting References

The posting references are very helpful. In the journal, the PR column tells us which transactions have or have not been posted and also to which accounts

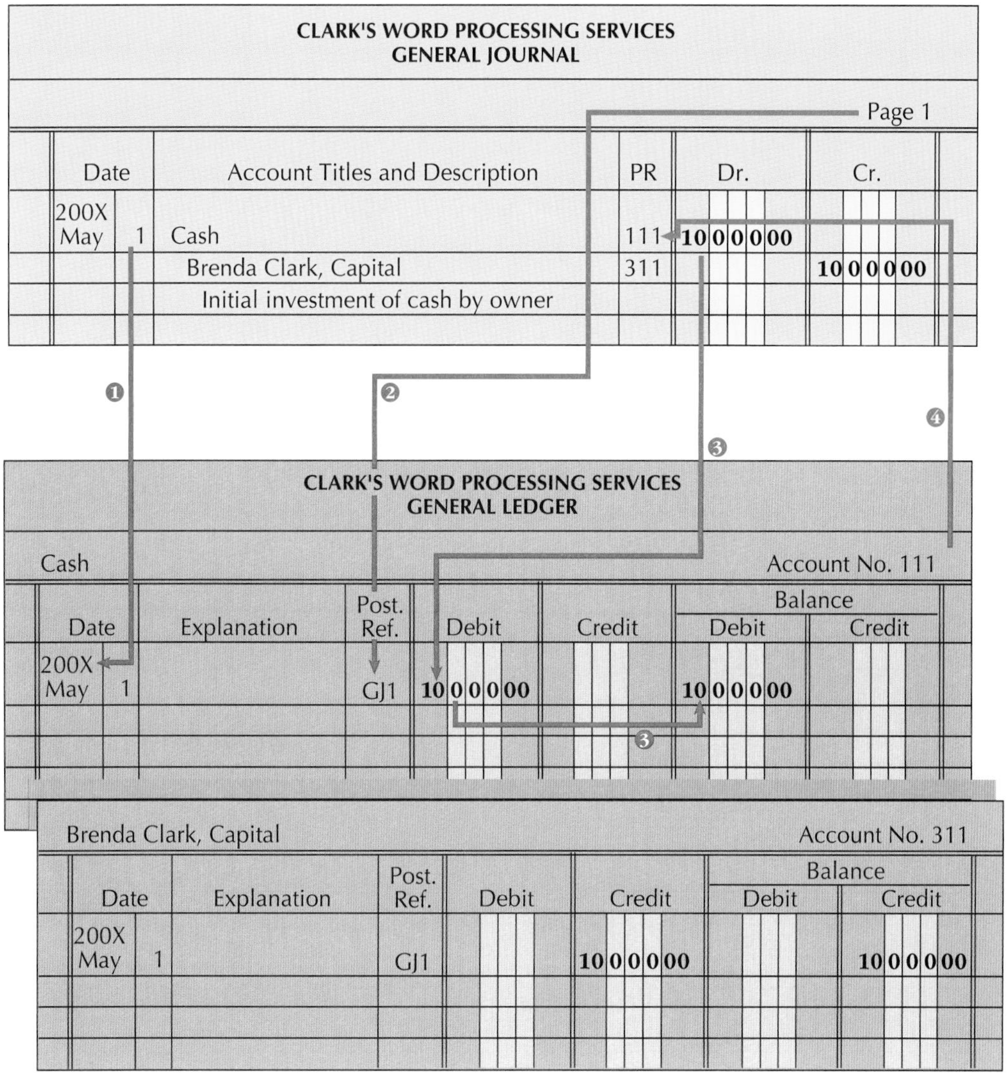

FIGURE 3-3. How to Post from Journal to Ledger

they were posted. In the ledger the posting reference leads us back to the original transaction in its entirety, so that we can see why the debit or credit was recorded and what other accounts were affected. (It leads us back to the original transaction by identifying the journal and the page in the journal from which the information came.)

LEARNING UNIT 3-2 REVIEW

AT THIS POINT you should be able to

▼ State the purpose of posting. (p. 80)
▼ Discuss the advantages of the four-column account. (p. 80)
▼ Identify the elements to be posted. (p. 81)
▼ From journalized transactions, post to the general ledger. (p. 81)

SELF-REVIEW QUIZ 3-2

(The blank forms you need are on pages 54 – 59 of the *Study Guide and Working Papers.*)

The following are the journalized transactions of Clark's Word Processing Services. Your task is to post information to the ledger. The ledger in your workbook has all the account titles and numbers that were used from the chart of accounts.

CLARK'S WORD PROCESSING SERVICES **GENERAL JOURNAL**							
							Page 1
Date			Account Titles and Description	PR	Dr.	Cr.	
200X May	1		Cash		10 0 0 00		
			Brenda Clark, Capital			10 0 0 00	
			Initial investment of cash by owner				
	1		Word Processing Equipment		6 0 0 00		
			Cash			1 0 0 00	
			Accounts Payable			5 0 0 00	
			Purchase of equip. from Ben Co.				
	1		Prepaid Rent		1 2 0 00		
			Cash			1 2 0 00	
			Rent paid in advance (3 months)				
	3		Office Supplies		6 0 00		
			Accounts Payable			6 0 00	
			Purchase of supplies on acct. from Norris				
	7		Cash		3 0 0 00		
			Word Processing Fees			3 0 0 00	
			Cash received for services rendered				
	13		Office Salaries Expense		6 5 0 00		
			Cash			6 5 0 00	
			Payment of office salaries				
	18		Advertising Expense		2 5 0 00		
			Accounts Payable			2 5 0 00	
			Bill received but not paid from Al's News				
	20		Brenda Clark, Withdrawals		6 2 5 00		
			Cash			6 2 5 00	
			Personal withdrawal of cash				
	22		Accounts Receivable		5 0 0 00		
			Word Processing Fees			5 0 0 00	
			Billed Morris Co. for fees earned				

CLARK'S WORD PROCESSING SERVICES
GENERAL JOURNAL

Page 2

Date		Account Titles and Description	PR	Dr.	Cr.
200X May	27	Office Salaries Expense		650 00	
		Cash			650 00
		Payment of office salaries			
	28	Accounts Payable		2500 00	
		Cash			2500 00
		Paid half the amount owed Ben Co.			
	29	Telephone Expense		220 00	
		Cash			220 00
		Paid telephone bill			

Solution to Self-Review Quiz 3-2

CLARK'S WORD PROCESSING SERVICES
GENERAL JOURNAL

Page 1

Date		Account Titles and Description	PR	Dr.	Cr.
200X May	1	Cash	111	10000 00	
		Brenda Clark, Capital	311		10000 00
		Initial investment of cash by owner			
	1	Word Processing Equipment	121	6000 00	
		Cash	111		1000 00
		Accounts Payable	211		5000 00
		Purchase of equip. from Ben Co.			
	1	Prepaid Rent	115	1200 00	
		Cash	111		1200 00
		Rent paid in advance (3 months)			
	3	Office Supplies	114	600 00	
		Accounts Payable	211		600 00
		Purchase of supplies on acct. from Norris			
	7	Cash	111	3000 00	
		Word Processing Fees	411		3000 00
		Cash received from services rendered			
	13	Office Salaries Expense	511	650 00	
		Cash	111		650 00
		Payment of office salaries			

Remember, the PR column remains empty until the entries have been posted.

(page 1, Clark's General Journal, cont. at top of p. 84)

	Date	Account Titles and Description	PR	Dr.	Cr.
	18	Advertising Expense	512	250 00	
		Accounts Payable	211		250 00
		Bill received but not paid from Al's News			
	20	Brenda Clark, Withdrawals	312	625 00	
		Cash	111		625 00
		Personal withdrawal of cash			
	22	Accounts Receivable	112	5000 00	
		Word Processing Fees	411		5000 00
		Billed Morris Co. for fees earned			

CLARK'S WORD PROCESSING SERVICES
GENERAL JOURNAL

Page 2

	Date		Account Titles and Description	PR	Dr.	Cr.
200X May	27		Office Salaries Expense	511	650 00	
			Cash	111		650 00
			Payment of office salaries			
	28		Accounts Payable	211	2500 00	
			Cash	111		2500 00
			Paid half the amount owed Ben Co.			
	29		Telephone Expense	513	220 00	
			Cash	111		220 00
			Paid telephone bill			

CLARK'S WORD PROCESSING SERVICES
PARTIAL GENERAL LEDGER

Cash   Account No. 111

Date		Explanation	Post. Ref.	Debit	Credit	Balance Debit	Balance Credit
200X May	1		GJ1	10000 00		10000 00	
	1		GJ1		1000 00	9000 00	
	1		GJ1		1200 00	7800 00	
	7		GJ1	3000 00		10800 00	
	15		GJ1		650 00	10150 00	
	20		GJ1		625 00	9525 00	
	27		GJ2		650 00	8875 00	
	28		GJ2		2500 00	6375 00	
	29		GJ2		220 00	6155 00	

Accounts Receivable — Account No. 112

Date	Explanation	Post. Ref.	Debit	Credit	Balance Debit	Balance Credit
200X May 22		GJ1	5 000 00		5 000 00	

Office Supplies — Account No. 114

Date	Explanation	Post. Ref.	Debit	Credit	Balance Debit	Balance Credit
200X May 3		GJ1	6 00 00		6 00 00	

Prepaid Rent — Account No. 115

Date	Explanation	Post. Ref.	Debit	Credit	Balance Debit	Balance Credit
200X May 1		GJ1	1 2 00 00		1 2 00 00	

Word Processing Equipment — Account No. 121

Date	Explanation	Post. Ref.	Debit	Credit	Balance Debit	Balance Credit
200X May 1		GJ1	6 000 00		6 000 00	

Accounts Payable — Account No. 211

Date	Explanation	Post. Ref.	Debit	Credit	Balance Debit	Balance Credit
200X May 1		GJ1		5 000 00		5 000 00
3		GJ1		6 00 00		5 600 00
18		GJ1		2 50 00		5 850 00
28		GJ2	2 500 00			3 350 00

Brenda Clark, Capital — Account No. 311

Date	Explanation	Post. Ref.	Debit	Credit	Balance Debit	Balance Credit
200X May 1		GJ1		10 000 00		10 000 00

Brenda Clark, Withdrawals — Account No. 312

Date		Explanation	Post. Ref.	Debit	Credit	Balance Debit	Balance Credit
200X May	20		GJ1	625 00		625 00	

Word Processing Fees — Account No. 411

Date		Explanation	Post. Ref.	Debit	Credit	Balance Debit	Balance Credit
200X May	7		GJ1		3000 00		3000 00
	22		GJ1		5000 00		8000 00

Office Salaries Expense — Account No. 511

Date		Explanation	Post. Ref.	Debit	Credit	Balance Debit	Balance Credit
200X May	13		GJ1	650 00		650 00	
	27		GJ2	650 00		1300 00	

Advertising Expense — Account No. 512

Date		Explanation	Post. Ref.	Debit	Credit	Balance Debit	Balance Credit
200X May	18		GJ1	250 00		250 00	

Telephone Expense — Account No. 513

Date		Explanation	Post. Ref.	Debit	Credit	Balance Debit	Balance Credit
200X May	29		GJ2	220 00		220 00	

Quiz Tip: The Post Reference column in the ledger tells which page of the journal the information came from. The Post Reference column in the journal (the last to be filled in) tells what account number in the ledger the information was posted to.

LEARNING UNIT 3-3

PREPARING THE TRIAL BALANCE: STEP 4 OF THE ACCOUNTING CYCLE

Did you note in Quiz 3-2 how each account had a running balance figure? Did you know the normal balance of each account in Clark's ledger? As we discussed in Chapter 2, the list of the individual accounts with their balances taken from the ledger is called a **trial balance.**

CLARK'S WORD PROCESSING SERVICE TRIAL BALANCE MAY 31, 200X				
		Debit		Credit
Cash		6 1 5 5 00		
Accounts Receivable		5 0 0 0 00		
Office Supplies		6 0 0 00		
Prepaid Rent		1 2 0 0 00		
Word Processing Equipment		6 0 0 0 00		
Accounts Payable				3 3 5 0 00
Brenda Clark, Capital				10 0 0 0 00
Brenda Clark, Withdrawals		6 2 5 00		
Word Processing Fees				8 0 0 0 00
Office Salaries Expense		1 3 0 0 00		
Advertising Expense		2 5 0 00		
Telephone Expense		2 2 0 00		
Totals		21 3 5 0 00		21 3 5 0 00

The trial balance lists the accounts in the same order as in the ledger. The $6,155 figure of cash came from the ledger, p. 84.

Figure 3-4. Trial Balance

The trial balance shown in Figure 3-4 was developed from the ledger accounts of Clark's Word Processing Services that were posted and balanced in Quiz 3-2. If the information is journalized or posted incorrectly, the trial balance will not be correct.

There are some things the trial balance will not show:

▼ The capital figure on the trial balance may not be the beginning capital figure. For instance, if Brenda Clark had made additional investments during the period, the additional investment would have been journalized and posted to the capital account. The only way to tell if the capital balance on the trial balance is the original balance is to check the ledger capital account to see whether any additional investments were made. This will be important when we make financial reports.

▼ There is no guarantee that transactions have been properly recorded. For example, the following errors would remain undetected: (1) a transaction that may have been omitted in the journalizing process, (2) a transaction incorrectly analyzed and recorded in the journal, and (3) a journal entry journalized or posted twice.

> The totals of a trial balance can balance and yet be incorrect.

WHAT TO DO IF A TRIAL BALANCE DOESN'T BALANCE

The trial balance of Clark's Word Processing Services shows that the total of debits is equal to the total of credits. What happens, however, if the trial balance is in balance, but the correct amount is not recorded in each ledger account? Accuracy in the journalizing and posting process will help ensure that no errors are made.

Even if there is an error, the first rule is "don't panic." Everyone makes mistakes, and there are accepted ways of correcting them. Once an entry had been made in ink, correcting an error in it must always show that the entry has been changed and who changed it. Sometimes the change has to be explained.

SOME COMMON MISTAKES

If the trial balance does not balance, the cause could be something relatively simple. Here are some common errors and how they can be fixed:

Correcting the trial balance: What to do if your trial balance doesn't balance.

Did you clear your adding machine?

▼ If the difference (the amount you are off) is 10, 100, 1,000, and so forth, there is probably a mathematical error in addition.

▼ If the difference is equal to an individual account balance in the ledger, the amount could have been omitted. It is also possible the figure was not posted from the general journal.

▼ Divide the difference by 2, then check to see if a debit should have been a credit and vice versa in the ledger or trial balance. Example: $150 difference ÷ 2 = $75. This means you may have placed $75 as a debit to an account instead of a credit or vice versa.

▼ If the difference is evenly divisible by 9, a **slide** or transposition may have occurred. A slide is an error resulting from adding or deleting zeros in writing numbers. For example, $4,175.00 may have been copied as $41.75. A **transposition** is the accidental rearrangement of digits of a number. For example, $4,175 might have been accidentally written as $4,157.

▼ Compare the balances in the trial balance with the ledger accounts to check for copying errors.

▼ Recompute balances in each ledger account.

▼ Trace all postings from journal to ledger.

If you cannot find the error after you have done all this, take a coffee break. Then start all over again.

MAKING A CORRECTION BEFORE POSTING

Before posting, error correction is straightforward. Simply draw a line through the incorrect entry, write the correct information above the line, and write your initials near the change.

Correcting an Error in an Account Title   The following illustration shows an error and its correction in an account title:

1	Word Processing Equipment		6 0 0 0 00		
	Cash			1 0 0 0 00	
	~~Accounts Receivable~~ Accounts Payable *amp*			5 0 0 0 00	
	Purchase of equipment from Ben Co.				

Correcting a Numerical Error   Numbers are handled the same way as account titles, as the next change from 520 to 250 shows:

18	Advertising Expense		2 5 0 00	
	Accounts Payable		*amp* ~~5 2 0 00~~ 2 5 0 00	
	Bill from Al's News			

Correcting an Entry Error   If a number has been entered in the wrong column, a straight line is drawn through it. The number is then written in the correct column:

1	Word Processing Equipment		6 0 0 0 00	
	Cash			1 0 0 0 00
	Accounts Payable	*amp* ~~5 0 0 0 00~~		5 0 0 0 00
	Purchase of equip. from Ben Co.			

MAKING A CORRECTION AFTER POSTING

It is also possible to correct an amount that is correctly entered in the journal but posted incorrectly to the ledger of the proper account. The first step is to draw a line through the error and write the correct figure above it. The next step is changing the running balance to reflect the corrected posting. Here, too, a line is drawn through the balance and the corrected balance is written above it. Both changes must be initialed.

			Post.			Balance	
Date	Explanation		Ref.	Debit	Credit	Debit	Credit
200X May	7		GJ1		2 5 0 0 00		2 5 0 0 00
	22		GJ1		~~1 0 0 00~~ 4 0 00 *dmp*		~~2 6 0 0 00~~ 2 6 0 0 00 *dmp*

Word Processing Fees — Account No. 411

CORRECTING AN ENTRY POSTED TO THE WRONG ACCOUNT

Drawing a line through an error and writing the correction above it is possible when a mistake has occurred within the proper account, but when an error involves a posting to the wrong account, the journal must include a correction accompanied by an explanation. In addition, the correct information must be posted to the appropriate ledgers.

Suppose, for example, as a result of tracing postings from journal entries to ledgers you find that a $180 telephone bill was incorrectly debited as an advertising expense. The following illustration shows how this is done.

Step 1: The journal entry is corrected and the correction is explained:

GENERAL JOURNAL   Page 3

Date	Account Titles and Description	PR	Dr.	Cr.
200X May 29	Telephone Expense	513	1 8 0 00	
	Advertising Expense	512		1 8 0 00
	To correct error in which			
	Advertising Exp. was debited			
	for charges to Telephone Exp.			

Step 2: The Advertising Expense ledger account is corrected:

Advertising Expense   Account No. 512

			Post.			Balance	
Date	Explanation		Ref.	Debit	Credit	Debit	Credit
200X May	18		GJ1	1 7 5 00		1 7 5 00	
	23		GJ1	1 8 0 00		3 5 5 00	
	29	Correcting entry	GJ3		1 8 0 00	1 7 5 00	

Step 3: The Telephone Expense ledger is corrected:

	Date	Explanation	Post. Ref.	Debit	Credit	Balance Debit	Balance Credit
	200X May 29		GJ3	1 8 0 00		1 8 0 00	

LEARNING UNIT 3-3 REVIEW

AT THIS POINT you should be able to

▼ Prepare a trial balance with a ledger, using four-column accounts. (p. 87)
▼ Analyze and correct a trial balance that doesn't balance. (p. 88)
▼ Correct journal and posting errors. (p. 88)

SELF-REVIEW QUIZ 3-3

(The blank forms you need are on page 60 of the *Study Guide and Working Papers.*)

1.

MEMO

To: Al Vincent

From: Professor Jones

Re: Trial Balance

You have submitted to me an incorrect trial balance. Could you please rework and turn in to me before next Friday?

Note: Individual amounts look OK.

A. RICE
TRIAL BALANCE
OCTOBER 31, 200X

	Dr.	Cr.
Cash		8 0 6 0 00
Operating Expenses		1 7 0 0 00
A. Rice, Withdrawals		4 0 0 00
Service Revenue		5 4 0 0 00
Equipment	5 0 0 0 00	
Accounts Receivable	3 5 4 0 00	
Accounts Payable	2 0 0 0 00	
Supplies	3 0 0 00	
A. Rice, Capital		11 6 0 0 00

2. An $8,000 debit to office equipment was mistakenly journalized and posted on June 9, 200X to office supplies. Prepare the appropriate journal entry to correct this error.

Solution to Self-Review Quiz 3-3

1.

<table>
<tr><td colspan="3" align="center">A. RICE
TRIAL BALANCE
OCTOBER 31, 200X</td></tr>
<tr><td></td><td>Dr.</td><td>Cr.</td></tr>
<tr><td>Cash</td><td>8 0 6 0 00</td><td></td></tr>
<tr><td>Accounts Receivable</td><td>3 5 4 0 00</td><td></td></tr>
<tr><td>Supplies</td><td>3 0 0 00</td><td></td></tr>
<tr><td>Equipment</td><td>5 0 0 0 00</td><td></td></tr>
<tr><td>Accounts Payable</td><td></td><td>2 0 0 0 00</td></tr>
<tr><td>A. Rice, Capital</td><td></td><td>11 6 0 0 00</td></tr>
<tr><td>A. Rice, Withdrawals</td><td>4 0 0 00</td><td></td></tr>
<tr><td>Service Revenue</td><td></td><td>5 4 0 0 00</td></tr>
<tr><td>Operating Expenses</td><td>1 7 0 0 00</td><td></td></tr>
<tr><td>Totals</td><td>19 0 0 0 00</td><td>19 0 0 0 00</td></tr>
</table>

Quiz Tip: Items in a trial balance are listed in the same order as in the ledger or the chart of accounts. Expect each account to have its normal balance (either debit or credit).

2.

<table>
<tr><td colspan="6" align="center">GENERAL JOURNAL</td><td>Page 4</td></tr>
<tr><td colspan="2">Date</td><td>Account Titles and Description</td><td>PR</td><td>Dr.</td><td>Cr.</td></tr>
<tr><td>200X
June</td><td>9</td><td>Office Equipment</td><td></td><td>8 0 0 0 00</td><td></td></tr>
<tr><td></td><td></td><td>Office Supplies</td><td></td><td></td><td>8 0 0 0 00</td></tr>
<tr><td></td><td></td><td>To correct error in which office supplies</td><td></td><td></td><td></td></tr>
<tr><td></td><td></td><td>had been debited for purchase of</td><td></td><td></td><td></td></tr>
<tr><td></td><td></td><td>office equipment</td><td></td><td></td><td></td></tr>
</table>

COMPREHENSIVE DEMONSTRATION PROBLEM WITH SOLUTION TIPS

(The blank forms you need are on pages 61 – 65 in the *Study Guide and Working Papers.*)

In March, Abby's Employment Agency had the following transactions:

200X
Mar.
1. Abby Todd invested $5,000 in the new employment agency.
4. Bought equipment for cash, $200.
5. Earned employment fee commission, $200, but payment from Blue Co. will not be received until June.
6. Paid wages expense, $300.
7. Abby paid her home utility bill from the company checkbook, $75.
9. Placed Rick Wool at VCR Corporation, receiving $1,200 cash.
15. Paid cash for supplies, $200.
28. Telephone bill received but not paid, $180.
29. Advertising bill received but not paid, $400.

The chart of accounts includes Cash, 111; Accounts Receivable, 112; Supplies, 131; Equipment, 141; Accounts Payable, 211; A. Todd, Capital, 311; A. Todd, Withdrawals, 321; Employment Fees Earned, 411; Wage Expense, 511; Telephone Expense, 521; and Advertising Expense, 531.

Your task is to:

a. Set up a ledger based on the chart of accounts.

b. Journalize (all page 1) and post transactions.

c. Prepare a trial balance for March 31.

Solution to Comprehensive Demonstration Problem

b.

		ABBY'S EMPLOYMENT AGENCY			Page 1
Date		Account Titles and Description	PR	Dr.	Cr.
200X Mar.	1	Cash	111	5 0 0 0 00	
		A. Todd, Capital	311		5 0 0 0 00
		Owner investment			
	4	Equipment	141	2 0 0 00	
		Cash	111		2 0 0 00
		Bought equipment for cash			
	5	Accounts Receivable	112	2 0 0 00	
		Employment Fees Earned	411		2 0 0 00
		Fees on account from Blue Co.			
	6	Wage Expense	511	3 0 0 00	
		Cash	111		3 0 0 00
		Paid wages			
	7	A. Todd, Withdrawals	321	7 5 00	
		Cash	111		7 5 00
		Personal withdrawals			

(Abby's Employment Agency, cont. at top of page 93)

				Dr.	Cr.
	9	Cash	111	1 2 0 0 00	
		Employment Fees Earned	411		1 2 0 0 00
		Cash fees			
	15	Supplies	131	2 0 0 00	
		Cash	111		2 0 0 00
		Bought supplies for cash			
	28	Telephone Expense	521	1 8 0 00	
		Accounts Payable	211		1 8 0 00
		Telephone bill owed			
	29	Advertising Expense	531	4 0 0 00	
		Accounts Payable	211		4 0 0 00
		Advertising bill received			

a.

GENERAL LEDGER

Cash   111

Date		PR	Dr.	Cr.	Balance Dr.	Balance Cr.
200X Mar.	1	GJ1	5,000		5,000	
	4	GJ1		200	4,800	
	6	GJ1		300	4,500	
	7	GJ1		75	4,425	
	9	GJ1	1,200		5,625	
	15	GJ1		200	5,425	

Accounts Receivable   112

Date		PR	Dr.	Cr.	Balance Dr.	Balance Cr.
200X Mar.	5	GJ1	200		200	

Supplies   131

Date		PR	Dr.	Cr.	Balance Dr.	Balance Cr.
200X Mar.	15	GJ1	200		200	

Equipment   141

Date		PR	Dr.	Cr.	Balance Dr.	Balance Cr.
200X Mar.	4	GJ1	200		200	

A. Todd, Capital   311

Date		PR	Dr.	Cr.	Balance Dr.	Balance Cr.
200X Mar.	1	GJ1		5,000		5,000

A. Todd, Withdrawals   321

Date		PR	Dr.	Cr.	Balance Dr.	Balance Cr.
200X Mar.	7	GJ1	75		75	

Employment Fees Earned   411

Date		PR	Dr.	Cr.	Balance Dr.	Balance Cr.
200X Mar.	5	GJ1		200		200
	9	GJ1		1,200		1,400

Wage Expense   511

Date		PR	Dr.	Cr.	Balance Dr.	Balance Cr.
200X Mar.	6	GJ1	300		300	

Telephone Expense   521

Date		PR	Dr.	Cr.	Balance Dr.	Balance Cr.
200X Mar.	28	GJ1	180		180	

(General Ledger cont. at top of page 94)

Accounts Payable					211
				Balance	
Date	PR	Dr.	Cr.	Dr.	Cr.
200X Mar. 28	GJ1		180		180
29	GJ1		400		580

Advertising Expense					531
				Balance	
Date	PR	Dr.	Cr.	Dr.	Cr.
200X Mar. 29	GJ1	400		400	

Solution Tips to Journalizing

1. When journalizing, the PR column is not filled in.
2. Write the name of the debit against the date column. Indent credits and list them below debits. Be sure total debits for each transaction equal total credits.
3. Skip a line between each transaction.

The Analysis of the Journal Entries

March 1	Cash	A	↑	Dr.	$5,000
	A. Todd, Capital	Capital	↑	Cr.	$5,000
4	Equipment	A	↑	Dr.	$ 200
	Cash	A	↓	Cr.	$ 200
5	Acc. Receivable	A	↑	Dr.	$ 200
	Empl. Fees Earned	Rev.	↑	Cr.	$ 200
6	Wage Expense	Exp.	↑	Dr.	$ 300
	Cash	A	↓	Cr.	$ 300
7	A. Todd, Withdrawals	Withd.	↑	Dr.	$ 75
	Cash	A	↓	Cr.	$ 75
9	Cash	A	↑	Dr.	$1,200
	Empl. Fees Earned	Rev.	↑	Cr.	$1,200
15	Supplies	A	↑	Dr.	$ 200
	Cash	A	↓	Cr.	$ 200
28	Telephone Expense	Exp.	↑	Dr.	$ 180
	Accounts Payable	L	↑	Cr.	$ 180
28	Advertising Expense	Exp.	↑	Dr.	$ 400
	Accounts Payable	L	↑	Cr.	$ 400

> This analysis is what should be going through your head before determining Debit or Credit.

Solution Tips to Posting

The PR column in the ledger cash account tells you from which page a journal information came (see page 92). After the ledger cash account is posted,

Account Number 111 is put in the PR column of the journal. (This is called cross-referencing.)

Note how we keep a running balance in the cash account. A $5,000 debit balance and a $200 credit entry result in a new debit balance of $4,800 on page 93.

c.

ABBY'S EMPLOYMENT AGENCY
TRIAL BALANCE
MARCH 31, 200X

	Dr.	Cr.
Cash	5,425	
Accounts Receivable	200	
Supplies	200	
Equipment	200	
Accounts Payable		580
A. Todd, Capital		5,000
A. Todd, Withdrawals	75	
Employment Fees Earned		1,400
Wage Expense	300	
Telephone Expense	180	
Advertising Expense	400	
Totals	**6,980**	**6,980**

Solution Tip to Trial Balance

The trial balance lists the ending balance of each title in the order in which they appear in the ledger. The total of $6,980 on the left equals $6,980 on the right.

SUMMARY OF KEY POINTS

Learning Unit 3-1

1. The accounting cycle is a sequence of accounting procedures that are usually performed during an accounting period.
2. An accounting period is the time period for which the income statement is prepared. The time period can be any period up to one year.
3. A calendar year is from January 1 to December 31. The fiscal year is any 12-month period. A fiscal year could be a calendar year but does not have to be.
4. Interim statements are statements that are usually prepared for a portion of the business's calendar or fiscal year (e.g., a month or a quarter).
5. A general journal is a book that records transactions in chronological order. Here debits and credits are shown together on one page. It is the book of original entry.
6. The ledger is a collection of accounts where information is accumulated from the postings of the journal. The ledger is the book of final entry.
7. Journalizing is the process of recording journal entries.
8. The chart of accounts provides the specific titles of accounts to be entered in the journal.
9. When journalizing, the post reference (PR) column is left blank.
10. A compound journal entry occurs when more than two accounts are affected in the journalizing process of a business transaction.

Learning Unit 3-2

1. Posting is the process of transferring information from the journal to the ledger.
2. The journal and ledger contain the same information but in a different form.
3. The four-column account aids in keeping a running balance of an account.
4. The normal balance of an account will be located on the side that increases it according to the rules of debits and credits. For example, the normal balances of liabilities occur on the credit side.
5. The mechanical process of posting requires care in transferring to the appropriate account the dates, post references, and amounts.

Learning Unit 3-3

1. A trial balance can balance but be incorrect. For example, an entire journal entry may not have been posted.
2. If a trial balance doesn't balance, check for errors in addition, omission of postings, slides, transpositions, copying errors, and so on.
3. Specific procedures should be followed in making corrections in journals and ledgers.

KEY TERMS

Accounting cycle For each accounting period, the process that begins with the recording of business transactions or procedures into a journal and ends with the completion of a postclosing trial balance.

Accounting period The period of time for which an income statement is prepared.

Book of final entry Book that receives information about business transactions from a book of original entry (a journal). Example: a ledger.

Book of original entry Book that records the first formal information about business transactions. Example: a journal.

Calendar year January 1 to December 31.

Compound journal entry A journal entry that affects more than two accounts.

Cross-referencing Adding to the PR column of the journal the account number of the ledger account that was updated from the journal.

Fiscal year The 12-month period a business chooses for its accounting year.

Four-column account A running balance account that records debits and credits and has a column for an ending balance (debit or credit). Replaces the standard two-column account we used earlier.

General journal The simplest form of a journal, which records information from transactions in chronological order as they occur. This journal links the debit and credit parts of transactions together.

Interim reports Financial statements that are prepared for a month, quarter, or some other portion of the fiscal year.

Journal A listing of business transactions in chronological order. The journal links on one page the debit and credit parts of transactions.

Journal entry The transaction (debits and credits) that is recorded into a journal once it is analyzed.

Journalizing The process of recording a transaction entry into the journal.

Natural business year A business's fiscal year that ends at the same time as a slow seasonal period begins.

Posting The transferring, copying, or recording of information from a journal to a ledger.

Slide The error that results in adding or deleting zeros in the writing of a number. Example: 79,200 → 7,920.

Transposition The accidental rearrangement of digits of a number. Example: 152 → 125.

Trial balance An informal listing of the ledger accounts and their balances in the ledger that aids in proving the equality of debits and credits.

BLUEPRINT OF FIRST FOUR STEPS OF ACCOUNTING CYCLE

See inside front cover for road map of entire accounting cycle.

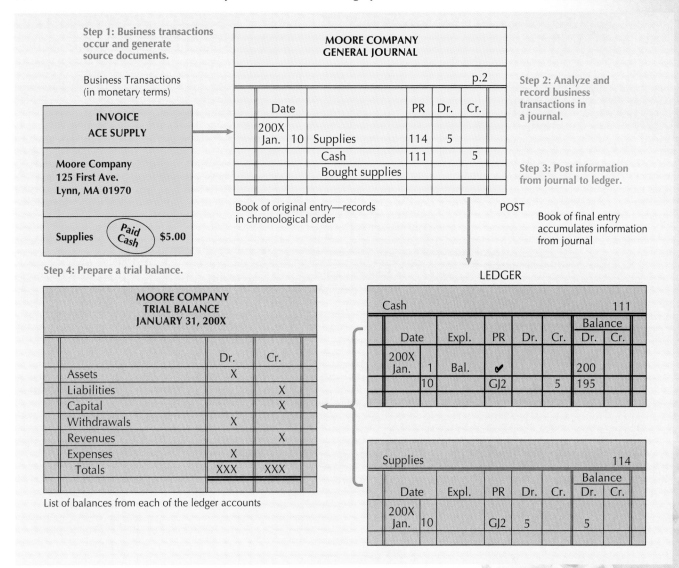

QUESTIONS, MINI EXERCISES, EXERCISES, AND PROBLEMS

Discussion Questions

1. Explain the concept of the accounting cycle.
2. An accounting period is based on the balance sheet. Agree or disagree.
3. Compare and contrast a calendar year versus a fiscal year.
4. What are interim statements?
5. Why is the ledger called the book of final entry?
6. How do transactions get "linked" in a general journal?
7. What is the relationship of the chart of accounts to the general journal?
8. What is a compound journal entry?
9. Posting means updating the journal. Agree or disagree. Please comment.
10. The side that decreases an account is the normal balance. True or false?
11. The PR column of a general journal is the last item to be filled in during the posting process. Agree or disagree.

12. Discuss the concept of cross-referencing.

13. What is the difference between a transposition and a slide?

Mini Exercises

(The blank forms you need are on page 67 of the *Study Guide and Working Papers.*)

General Journal

1. Complete the following from the general journal of Ranger Co.

<table>
<tr><td colspan="7" align="center">**RANGER COMPANY**
GENERAL JOURNAL</td><td align="right">Page 1</td></tr>
<tr><td colspan="2">Date</td><td>Account Titles and Descriptions</td><td>PR</td><td colspan="2">Dr.</td><td colspan="2">Cr.</td></tr>
<tr><td>200X
Sept.</td><td>19</td><td>Cash</td><td></td><td colspan="2">8 0 0 00</td><td colspan="2"></td></tr>
<tr><td></td><td></td><td>Equipment</td><td></td><td colspan="2">2 0 00</td><td colspan="2"></td></tr>
<tr><td></td><td></td><td> B. Ranger, Capital</td><td></td><td colspan="2"></td><td colspan="2">8 2 0 00</td></tr>
<tr><td></td><td></td><td> Initial Investment by Owner</td><td></td><td colspan="2"></td><td colspan="2"></td></tr>
<tr><td></td><td></td><td></td><td></td><td colspan="2"></td><td colspan="2"></td></tr>
</table>

a. Year of Journal Entry _____

b. Month of Journal Entry _____

c. Day of Journal Entry _____

d. Name(s) of Accounts Debited _____

e. Name(s) of Accounts Credited _____

f. Explanation of Transaction _____

g. Amount of Debit(s) _____

h. Amount of Credit(s) _____

i. Page of Journal _____

General Journal

2. Provide the explanation for each of these general journal entries.

<table>
<tr><td colspan="7" align="center">**GENERAL JOURNAL**</td><td align="right">Page 4</td></tr>
<tr><td colspan="2">Date</td><td>Account Titles and Descriptions</td><td>PR</td><td colspan="2">Debit</td><td colspan="2">Credit</td></tr>
<tr><td>200X
July</td><td>9</td><td>Cash</td><td></td><td colspan="2">8 0 0 00</td><td colspan="2"></td></tr>
<tr><td></td><td></td><td>Office Equipment</td><td></td><td colspan="2">5 0 0 00</td><td colspan="2"></td></tr>
<tr><td></td><td></td><td> J. Walsh, Capital</td><td></td><td colspan="2"></td><td colspan="2">13 0 0 00</td></tr>
<tr><td></td><td></td><td> (A)</td><td></td><td colspan="2"></td><td colspan="2"></td></tr>
<tr><td></td><td></td><td></td><td></td><td colspan="2"></td><td colspan="2"></td></tr>
<tr><td></td><td>15</td><td>Cash</td><td></td><td colspan="2">3 0 00</td><td colspan="2"></td></tr>
<tr><td></td><td></td><td>Accounts Receivable</td><td></td><td colspan="2">6 0 00</td><td colspan="2"></td></tr>
<tr><td></td><td></td><td> Hair Fees Earned</td><td></td><td colspan="2"></td><td colspan="2">9 0 00</td></tr>
<tr><td></td><td></td><td> (B)</td><td></td><td colspan="2"></td><td colspan="2"></td></tr>
<tr><td></td><td></td><td></td><td></td><td colspan="2"></td><td colspan="2"></td></tr>
<tr><td></td><td>20</td><td>Advertising Expense</td><td></td><td colspan="2">4 0 00</td><td colspan="2"></td></tr>
<tr><td></td><td></td><td>Accounts Payable</td><td></td><td colspan="2"></td><td colspan="2">4 0 00</td></tr>
<tr><td></td><td></td><td> (C)</td><td></td><td colspan="2"></td><td colspan="2"></td></tr>
<tr><td></td><td></td><td></td><td></td><td colspan="2"></td><td colspan="2"></td></tr>
</table>

Posting and Balancing

3. Balance this four-column account. What function does the PR column serve? When will the Account 111 be used in the journalizing and posting process?

	Cash				Acct. 111 Balance	
Date	Explanation	PR	Dr.	Cr.	Dr.	Cr.
200X						
June 4		GJ 1	15			
5		GJ 1	6			
9		GJ 2		4		
10		GJ 3	1			

The Trial Balance

4. The following Trial Balance was prepared *incorrectly*.
   a. Rearrange the accounts in proper order.
   b. Calculate the total of the Trial Balance. (Small numbers are used intentionally so that you can do the calculations in your head.) Assume each account has a normal balance.

LARKIN CO.
TRIAL BALANCE
OCTOBER 31, 200X

	Dr.	Cr.
B. Larkin, Capital	14	
Equipment	9	
Rent Expense		4
Advertising Expense		3
Accounts Payable		8
Taxi Fees	16	
Cash	17	
B. Larkin, Withdrawals	—	5
Totals	56	19

Correcting Entry

5. On May 1, 2001, a telephone expense for $180 was debited to Repair Expense. On June 12, 2002, this error was found. Prepare the corrected Journal Entry. When would a correcting entry *not* be needed?

Exercises

(The forms you need are on pages 68–73 of the *Study Guide and Working Papers*.)

3-1. Prepare journal entries for the following transactions that occurred during October:

Preparing journal entries.

200X
Oct.
1 Lee Clinton invested $30,000 cash and $1,000 of equipment into her new business.
3 Purchased building for $60,000 on account.
12 Purchased a truck from Lange Co. for $18,000 cash.
18 Bought supplies from Green Co. on account, $700.

Preparing journal entries.

3-2. Record the following into the general journal of Fay's Repair Shop.

200X

Jan.
1 Fay Hope invested $15,000 cash in the repair shop.
5 Paid $7,000 for shop equipment.
8 Bought from Lowell Co. shop equipment for $6,000 on account.
14 Received $900 for repair fees earned.
18 Billed Sullivan Co. $900 for services rendered.
20 Fay withdrew $300 for personal use.

Posting.

3-3. Post the following transactions to the ledger of King Company. The partial ledger of King Company is Cash, 111; Equipment, 121; Accounts Payable, 211; and A. King, Capital, 311. Please use four-column accounts in the posting process.

									Page 4	
Date 200X			PR	Dr.			Cr.			
April	6	Cash		15 0 0 0 00						
		A. King, Capital					15 0 0 0 00			
		Cash investment								
	14	Equipment		9 0 0 0 00						
		Cash					4 0 0 0 00			
		Accounts Payable					5 0 0 0 00			
		Purchase of equipment								

Journalizing, posting, and preparing a trial balance.

3-4. From the following transactions for Lowe Company for the month of July, (a) prepare journal entries (assume that it is page 1 of the journal), (b) post to the ledger (use a four-column account), and (c) prepare a trial balance.

200X

July
1 Joan Lowe invested $6,000 in the business.
4 Bought from Lax Co. equipment on account, $800.
15 Billed Friend Co. for services rendered, $4,000.
18 Received $5,000 cash for services rendered.
24 Paid salaries expense, $1,800.
28 Joan withdrew $400 for personal use.

A partial chart of accounts includes Cash, 111; Accounts Receivable, 112; Equipment, 121; Accounts Payable, 211; J. Lowe, Capital, 311; J. Lowe, Withdrawals, 312; Fees Earned, 411; and Salaries Expense, 511.

3-5. You have been hired to correct the following trial balance that has been recorded improperly from the ledger to the trial balance.

Correcting the trial balance.

SUNG CO. TRIAL BALANCE MARCH 31, 200X			
	Dr.	Cr.	
Accounts Payable	2 0 0 0 00		
A. Sung, Capital		6 5 0 0 00	
A. Sung, Withdrawals		3 0 0 00	
Services Earned		4 7 0 0 00	
Concessions Earned	2 5 0 0 00		
Rent Expense	4 0 0 00		
Salaries Expense	2 5 0 0 00		
Miscellaneous Expense		1 3 0 0 00	
Cash	10 0 0 0 00		
Accounts Receivable		1 2 0 0 00	
Totals	17 4 0 0 00	14 0 0 0 00	

3-6. On February 6, 200X, Mike Sullivan made the following journal entry to record the purchase on account of office equipment priced at $1,400. This transaction had not yet been posted when the error was discovered. Make the appropriate correction.

			GENERAL JOURNAL					
Date			Account Titles and Description	PR	Dr.		Cr.	
200X Feb.	6		Office Equipment		9 0 0 00			
			Accounts Payable				9 0 0 00	
			Purchase of office equip. on account					

Correcting an entry.

Group A Problems

(The forms you need are on pages 74–85 of the *Working Papers and Study Guide*.)

Journalizing.

3A-1. Misty Roy operates Roy's Dog Grooming Center. As the bookkeeper, you have been requested to journalize the following transactions:

200X
July
1	Paid rent for two months in advance, $4,000.
3	Purchased grooming equipment on account from Leek's Supply House, $2,500.
10	Purchased grooming supplies from Angel's Wholesale for $600 cash.
12	Received $1,400 cash from grooming fees earned.
20	Misty withdrew $600 for her personal use.
21	Advertising bill received from *Daily Sun* but unpaid, $120.
25	Paid cleaning expense, $90.
28	Paid salaries expense, $500.
29	Performed grooming work for $1,700, but payment will not be received from Rick's Kennel until May.
30	Paid Leek's Supply House half the amount owed from July 3 transaction.

Check Figure:
July 21
Dr. Advertising expense $120
Cr. Accounts Payable $120

Your task is to journalize the above transactions. The chart of accounts for Misty's Dog Grooming Center is as follows:

Chart of Accounts

Assets
111 Cash
112 Accounts Receivable
114 Prepaid Rent
116 Grooming Supplies
121 Grooming Equipment

Liabilities
211 Accounts Payable

Owner's Equity
311 Misty Roy, Capital
312 Misty Roy, Withdrawals

Revenue
411 Grooming Fees Earned

Expenses
511 Advertising Expense
512 Salaries Expense
514 Cleaning Expense

3A-2. On June 1, 200X, Molly Taylor opened Taylor's Dance Studio. The following transactions occurred in June:

Comprehensive problem: Journalizing, posting, and preparing a trial balance.

200X
June
1	Molly Taylor invested $9,000 in the dance studio.
1	Paid three months' rent in advance, $1,000.

3   Purchased $700 of equipment from Astor Co. on account.
5   Received $900 cash for fitness-training workshop for dancers.
8   Purchased $300 of supplies for cash.
9   Billed Lester Co. $2,100 for group dance lesson for its employees.
10   Paid salaries of assistants, $400.
15   Molly withdrew $150 from the business for her personal use.
28   Paid electrical bill, $125.
29   Paid telephone bill for June, $190.

Your task is to

a. Set up the ledger based on the charts of accounts below.

b. Journalize (journal is page 1) and post the June transactions.

c. Prepare a trial balance as of June 30, 200X.

The chart of accounts for Taylor's Dance Studio is as follows:

Check Figure:
Trial Balance Total $12,700

Chart of Accounts

Assets		Owner's Equity	
111	Cash	311	Molly Taylor, Capital
112	Accounts Receivable	312	Molly Taylor, Withdrawals
114	Prepaid Rent	**Revenue**	
121	Supplies	411	Fees Earned
131	Equipment	**Expenses**	
Liabilities		511	Electrical Expense
211	Accounts Payable	521	Salaries Expense
		531	Telephone Expense

Comprehensive problem: Journalizing, posting, and preparing a trial balance.

3A-3. The following transactions occurred in June 200X for A. French's Placement Agency:

200X
June

1   A. French invested $9,000 cash in the placement agency.
1   Bought equipment on account from Hook Co., $2,000.
3   Earned placement fees of $1,600, but payment will not be received until July.
5   A. French withdrew $100 for his personal use.
7   Paid wages expense, $300.
9   Placed a client on a local TV show, receiving $600 cash.
15   Bought supplies on account from Lyon Co., $500.
28   Paid telephone bill for June, $160.
29   Advertising bill from Shale Co. received but not paid, $900.

The chart of accounts for A. French Placement Agency is as follows:

Check Figure:
Trial Balance Total $14,600

Chart of Accounts

Assets		Owner's Equity	
111	Cash	311	A. French, Capital
112	Accounts Receivable	312	A. French, Withdrawals
131	Supplies	**Revenue**	
141	Equipment	411	Placement Fees Earned
Liabilities		**Expenses**	
211	Accounts Payable	511	Wage Expense
		521	Telephone Expense
		531	Advertising Expense

Your task is to

a. Set up the ledger based on the chart of accounts.

b. Journalize (page 1) and post the June transactions.

c. Prepare a trial balance as of June 30, 200X.

Group B Problems

(The forms you need are on pages 74–85 of the *Study Guide and Working Papers*.)

3B-1. In April Misty Roy opened a new dog grooming center. Please assist her by journalizing the following business transactions:

| Journalizing. |

200X

Apr. 1 Misty Roy invested $4,000 of grooming equipment as well as $6,000 cash in the new business.

3 Purchased grooming supplies on account from Rex Co., $500.

10 Purchased office equipment on account from Ross Stationery, $400.

12 Misty paid her home telephone bill from the company checkbook, $60.

20 Received $600 cash for grooming services performed.

21 Advertising bill received but not paid, $75.

25 Cleaning bill received but not paid, $90.

28 Performed grooming work for Jay Kennels, $700, but payment will not be received until May.

29 Paid salaries expense, $400.

30 Paid Ross Stationery half the amount owed from April 10 transaction.

Check Figure:
April 21
Dr. Advertising expense $75
Cr. Accounts payable $75

The chart of accounts for Roy's Dog Grooming Center includes Cash, 111; Accounts Receivable, 112; Prepaid Rent, 114; Grooming Supplies, 116; Office Equipment, 120; Grooming Equipment, 121; Accounts Payable, 211; Misty Roy, Capital, 311; Misty Roy, Withdrawals, 312; Grooming Fees Earned, 411; Advertising Expense, 511; Salaries Expense, 512; and Cleaning Expense, 514.

3B-2. In June the following transactions occurred for Taylor's Dance Studio:

Comprehensive problem:
Journalizing, posting, and
preparing a trial balance.

200X

June 1 Molly Taylor invested $6,000 in the dance studio.

1 Paid four months rent in advance, $1,200.

3 Purchased supplies on account from A.J.K., $700.

5 Purchased equipment on account from Reese Company, $900.

8 Received $1,300 cash for dance-training program provided to Northwest Junior College.

9 Billed Long Co. for dance lessons provided, $600.

10 Molly withdrew $400 from the dance studio to buy a new chain saw for her home.

15 Paid salaries expense, $400.

28 Paid telephone bill, $118.

29 Electric bill received but unpaid, $120.

Check Figure:
Total Trial Balance $9,620

Your task is to

a. Set up a ledger.

b. Journalize (all page 1) and post the June transactions.

c. Prepare a trial balance as of June 30, 200X.

The chart of accounts includes Cash, 111; Accounts Receivable, 112; Prepaid Rent, 114; Supplies, 121; Equipment, 131; Accounts Payable, 211; M. Taylor, Capital, 311; M. Taylor, Withdrawals, 321; Fees Earned, 411; Electrical Expense, 511; Salaries Expense, 521; and Telephone Expense, 531.

3B-3. In June A. French's Placement Agency had the following transactions:

200X

June
1   A. French invested $6,000 in the new placement agency.
2   Bought equipment for cash, $350.
3   Earned placement fee commission, $2,100, but payment from Avon Co. will not be received until July.
5   Paid wages expense, $400.
7   A. French paid his home utility bill from the company checkbook, $69.
9   Placed Jay Diamond on a national TV show, receiving $900 cash.
15   Paid cash for supplies, $350.
28   Telephone bill received but not paid, $185.
29   Advertising bill received but not paid, $200.

The chart of accounts includes Cash, 111; Accounts Receivable, 112; Supplies, 131; Equipment, 141; Accounts Payable, 211; A. French, Capital, 311; A. French, Withdrawals, 312; Placement Fees Earned, 411; Wage Expense, 511; Telephone Expense, 521; and Advertising Expense, 531.

Your task is to

a. Set up a ledger based on the chart of accounts.

b. Journalize (all page 1) and post transactions.

c. Prepare a trial balance for June 30, 200X.

REAL-WORLD APPLICATIONS

3R-1.

Paul Regan, bookkeeper of Hampton Co., has been up half the night trying to get his trial balance to balance. Here are his results:

HAMPTON CO.
TRIAL BALANCE
JUNE 30, 200X

	Dr.	Cr.
Office Sales		5 7 2 0 00
Cash in Bank	3 2 6 0 00	
Accounts Receivable	5 6 6 0 00	
Office Equipment	8 4 0 0 00	
Accounts Payable		4 1 6 0 00
D. Hole, Capital		11 5 6 0 00
D. Hole, Withdrawals		7 0 0 00
Wage Expense	2 6 0 0 00	
Rent Expense	9 4 0 00	
Utilities Expense	2 6 00	
Office Supplies	1 2 0 00	
Prepaid Rent	1 8 0 00	

Ken Small, the accountant, compared Paul's amounts in the trial balance with those in the ledger, recomputed each account balance, and compared postings. Ken found the following errors:

1. A $200 debit to D. Hole, Withdrawals, was posted as a credit.

2. D. Hole, Withdrawals, was listed on the trial balance as a credit.

3. A Note Payable account with a credit balance of $2,400 was not listed on the trial balance.

4. The pencil footings for Accounts Payable were debits of $5,320 and credits of $8,800.

5. A debit of $180 to Prepaid Rent was not posted.

6. Office Supplies bought for $60 was posted as a credit to Supplies.

7. A debit of $120 to Accounts Receivable was not posted.

8. A cash payment of $420 was credited to Cash for $240.

9. The pencil footing of the credits to Cash was overstated by $400.

10. The Utilities Expense of $260 was listed in the trial balance as $26.

Assist Paul Regan by preparing a correct trial balance. What advice could you give Ken about Paul? Can you explain the situation to Paul? Put your answers in writing.

3R-2.

Lauren Oliver, an accountant lab tutor, is having a debate with some of her assistants. They are trying to find out how each of the following five unrelated situations would affect the trial balance:

1. A $5 debit to cash in the ledger was not posted.

2. A $10 debit to Computer Supplies was debited to Computer Equipment.

3. An $8 debit to Wage Expense was debited twice to the account.

4. A $4 debit to Computer Supplies was debited to Computer Sales.

5. A $35 credit to Accounts Payable was posted as a $53 credit.

Could you indicate to Lauren the effect that each situation will have on the trial balance? If a situation will have no effect, indicate that fact. Put in writing how each of these situations could be avoided in the future.

YOU make the call

Critical Thinking/Ethical Case

3R-3.

Jay Simons, the accountant of See Co., would like to buy a new software package for his general ledger. He couldn't do it because all funds were frozen for the rest of the fiscal period. Jay called his friend at Joor Industries and asked whether he could copy their software. Why should or shouldn't Jay have done that?

INTERNET EXERCISES

EX-1. [www.statravel.com] Travel agencies like STAtravel operate on the principal of buying travel packages, such as cruises, from cruise ship owners, then marking up the cost and selling it to STA customers. When they do this, the two transactions require two journal entries, just like the ones you learned in this chapter. Each customer sale generates two journal entries. The first represents STA's purchase of the cruise (an expense) from the cruise ship owner. The second represents the STA customer's buying the package from STA (a sale).

Suppose that you purchase a spring break cruise for $1,500 from STA and pay them with a check. They in turn will record the other transaction with the cruise ship owner for $1,200. The $300 difference is STA's profit.

1. Write the journal entry STA would make showing your booking the cruise for $1,500 with STA.

2. Write the journal entry showing, from STA's prespective, STA's purchase of your cruise for $1,200 from the cruise ship owner.

EX-2. [www.statravel.com] Suppose STA has the following accounts in their accounting system:

Accounts Receivable	Cash
Airline Revenue	Cruise Ship Packages Payable
Airline Tickets Payable	Cruise Ship Package Purchase Expense
Airline Ticket Purchase Expense	Cruise Ship Revenue

1. List accounts in proper order with account numbers (you make them up).
2. Draw a table showing account name, account number, category, normal balance and which financial statement found on.

CONTINUING PROBLEM

Tony's computer center is picking up in business, so he has decided to expand his bookkeeping system to a general journal/ledger system. The balances from August have been forwarded to the ledger accounts. The forms are in the *Study Guide and Working Papers,* pages 89–99.

Assignment

1. Use the chart of accounts provided in Chapter 2 to record the following transactions.

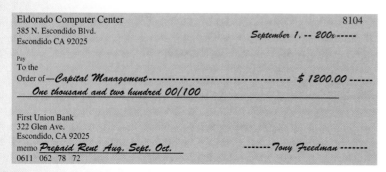

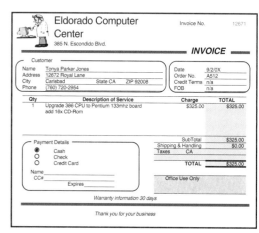

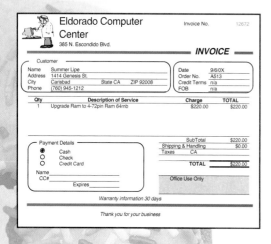

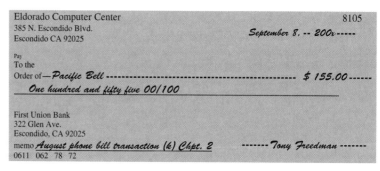

Refer back to Chapter 2 transaction k.

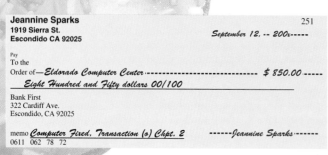

Refer back to Chapter 2, transaction o.   Refer back to Chapter 2 transaction s.

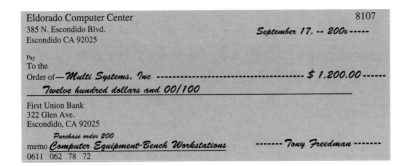

Eldorado Computer Center   8107
385 N. Escondido Blvd.   *September 17, -- 200x -----*
Escondido CA 92025

Pay
To the
Order of— *Multi Systems, Inc* ----------------------------- $ *1,200.00* ------
        Twelve hundred dollars and 00/100

First Union Bank
322 Glen Ave.
Escondido, CA 92025
        Purchase order 200
memo *Computer Equipment-Bench Workstations*   ------- *Tony Freedman* -------
0611 062 78 72

Purchased computer shop equipment.

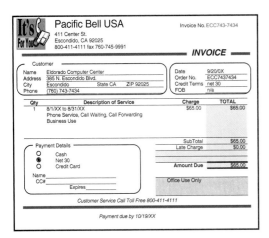

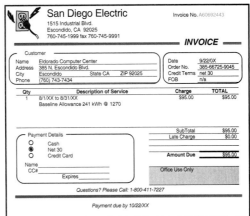

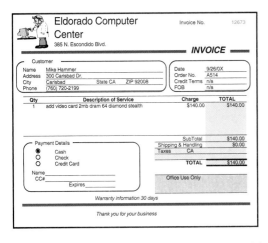

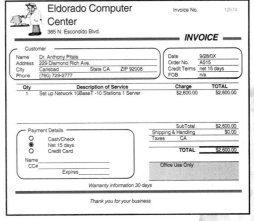

2. Post all transactions to the general ledger accounts (the Prepaid Rent Account #1025 has been added to the chart of accounts).

3. Prepare a trial balance for September 30, 200X.

4. Prepare the financial statements for the three months ended September 30, 200X.

Computerized Accounting Application for Chapter 3

*Journalizing, Posting, General Ledger, Trial Balance,
and Chart of Accounts*

Before starting on this assignment, read and complete the tasks discussed in Parts A, B, and F of the Computerized Accounting appendix at the back of this book.

> **How to open
> the company
> data files**

1. Click on the Start button. Point to Programs; point to the Peachtree folder and select Peachtree Complete Accounting. Your desktop may have the Peachtree icon allowing for a quicker entrance into the program by double clicking it.

2. Follow the "Open a File" instructions in Part A of the Computerized Accounting appendix at the back of this book to open **The Atlas Company.** You may be initially presented with the Peachtree Today window. If so, simply close it. Your screen should then look something like the illustration below:

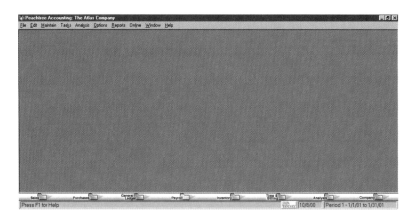

If you are missing the navigation aids at the bottom of the screen, you can activate them under the **Options** menu. Select **View Navigation Aid.** It will remain on until you turn it off. This feature offers an alternative way to access the different features of Peachtree.

> **How to add your
> name to the
> company name**

3. Click on the **Maintain** menu option. Then select **Company Information.** The program will respond by bringing up a dialogue box allowing the user to edit/add information about the company.

4. It is important for you to be able to identify the specific reports that you print for each assignment as your own, particularly if you are using a computer that shares a printer with other computers. Peachtree Complete Accounting 8.0 prints the name of the company you are working with at the top of each report. To personalize your reports so that you can identify both the company and your printed reports, the company name needs to be modified to include your name:

   a. Click in the **Company Name** entry field at the end of **The Atlas Company.** If it is already highlighted, press the right arrow key.

   b. Add a dash and your name **"-Student Name"** to the end of the company name. Your screen will look similar to the one shown following:

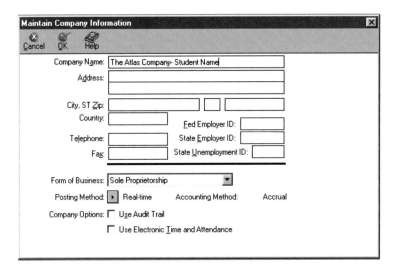

c. Click on the OK button to return to the Menu Window.

5. The owner of The Atlas Company has invested $10,000 in the business. Select **General Journal Entry** from the **Tasks** menu to open the General Journal dialog box. Enter the date 1/1/01 into the **Date** field; press the TAB key; enter "Memo" into the **Reference** field and press TAB.

   The **Date** text box is used to record the date the transaction occurred. The **Reference** text box can be used for any reference number or notation you wish to associate with a general journal entry and/or the source document that authorizes the entry. Pressing the TAB key will take you to the General Journal's **Account** field. Note that pressing ENTER will also move you from field to field.

6. With the flashing insertion point positioned in the **Account No** field, click on the pull down menu (magnifying glass icon) and double click on "1110 Cash". The program will enter the account number and name into the **Account No** field and the flashing insertion point will move to the **Description** field. Enter "Initial investment of cash by owner" into this field and press TAB to move to the **Debit** field.

7. Enter "10000" into the **Debit** field. Dollar amounts can be entered in several ways. For example, to enter $10,000.00, type 10000, or 10,000.00 or 10,000. The comma separator is always optional while the decimal point is optional when dealing with whole dollar amounts. To enter an amount containing a decimal point, type the decimal point as part of the amount. For example, enter five dollars and twenty-five cents as 5.25. Press the TAB key three times to move through the **Credit** and **Job** fields.

8. With the flashing insertion points positioned in the **Account No** field, click on the pull down menu. Double click on "3110 Owner's Capital". Use the scroll bar if the account is not visible in the pull dowm menu. Press TAB to move to the **Description** field. This should repeat the information entered in step 6 by default.

9. Press the TAB key twice to move to the **Credit** field. Enter "10000" as you did in step 7. Hit TAB twice to move the cursor back to the **Account No** field. This completes the data you need to enter into the General Journal dialog box to record the journal entry for the initial investment of cash by the owner. Your screen should look like the following:

How to record a general journal entry

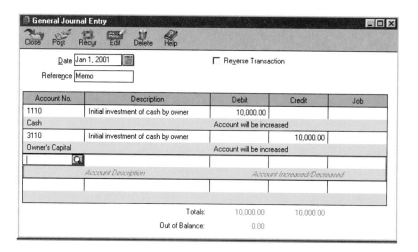

General Journal Entry

Date Jan 1, 2001
Reference Memo

☐ Reverse Transaction

Account No.	Description	Debit	Credit	Job
1110	Initial investment of cash by owner	10,000.00		
Cash		Account will be increased		
3110	Initial investment of cash by owner		10,000.00	
Owner's Capital		Account will be increased		
Account Description		*Account Increased/Decreased*		

	Totals:	10,000.00	10,000.00
	Out of Balance:		0.00

Review the journal entry before posting.

10. Before posting this transaction, you should verify that the transaction data are correct by reviewing the journal entry. Review the journal entry for accuracy, noting any errors.

11. If you have made an error, use the following editing techniques to correct the error.

How to edit an entry prior to posting.

Editing a General Journal Entry

▼ Using your mouse, click in the field that contains the error. This will highlight the selected text box information so that you can change it.

▼ Type the correct information; then press the TAB key to enter it. You may then either TAB to other fields needing corrections or again use the mouse to click in the proper field.

▼ If you have selected an incorrect account, use the pull down menu to select the correct account. This will replace the incorrect account with the correct account.

▼ Note that even though the **Post** icon will be available if the entry is out of balance, Peachtree will not allow you to post until the entry is in balance.

▼ To discard an entry and start over, click on the **Delete** icon. You will not be given the opportunity to verify this step so be sure you want to delete the transaction before selecting this option.

▼ Review the journal entry for accuracy after any editing corrections.

How to post an entry.

12. After verifying that the journal entry is correct, click on the **Post** icon to post this transaction. A blank General Journal dialog box is displayed, ready for additional General Journal transactions to be recorded. Peachtree has added a 1 to our memo in the **Reference** field and will do so as long as we remain in this input box. To keep the same reference for multiple entries on the same day, do not post between transactions.

Record additional transactions

13. Record the following additional journal entries. Enter the **Date** listed for each transaction (you may use the "+" key to advance the date or use the calendar icon next to the field to select the date from a calendar). Enter "Memo" into the **Source** text box for each transaction or accept Peachtree's additional number added to memo by pressing TAB:

2001
Jan.

1   Paid rent for two months in advance, $400.
3   Purchased office supplies on account, $100.
9   Billed a customer for fees earned, $1,500.
13   Paid telephone bill, $180.
20   Owner withdrew $500 from the business.
27   Received $450 for fees earned.
31   Paid salaries expense, $700.

CHAPTER 3 ... BEGINNING THE ACCOUNTING CYCLE

14. After you have posted the additional journal entries, click on the close button to close the General Journal dialog box. This will restore the menu window.

15. Select **General Ledger** from the **Reports** menu to bring up reports associated with the general ledger such as the **General Journal** and the **Trial Balance.** Select **General Journal** from the report selection window to bring up the report. You may also use the General Ledger navigation folder at the bottom of your screen to provide you with General Ledger options including reports. Single click on the **General Ledger** folder at the bottom of your screen and then single click **General Journal.** You will be taken to an options screen for the report. Accept all defaults by clicking on the **OK** button. Your screen should display something similar to this:

How to display and print a general journal.

The Atlas Company- Student Name
General Journal
For the Period From Jan 1, 2001 to Jan 31, 2001
Filter Criteria includes: Report order is by Date. Report is printed in Detail Format.

Date	Account ID	Reference	Trans Description	Debit Amt	Credit Amt
1/1/01	1110	Memo	Initial investment of cash by owner	10,000.00	
	3110		Initial investment of cash by owner		10,000.00
	1140		Prepaid two months rent	400.00	
	1110		Prepaid two months rent		400.00
1/3/01	1150	Memo1	Purchased office supplies on account	100.00	
	2110		Purchased office supplies on account		100.00
1/9/01	1120	Memo2	Performed services on account	1,500.00	
	4110		Performed services on account		1,500.00
1/13/01	5150	Memo3	Paid telephone bill	180.00	
	1110		Paid telephone bill		180.00
1/20/01	3120	Memo4	Owner withdrew cash from business	500.00	
	1110		Owner withdrew cash from business		500.00
1/27/01	1110	Memo5	Received cash for services performed	450.00	
	4110		Received cash for services performed		450.00
1/31/01	5120	Memo6	Paid salaries to employees	700.00	
	1110		Paid salaries to employees		700.00
		Total		13,830.00	13,830.00

16. The scroll bars can be used to advance the display to view other portions of the report. Note: You may display the entire General Journal Display window by clicking the maximize icon.

17. Click on the **Print** icon to print the General Journal. If you experience any difficulties with your printer (for example, the type size is too small), refer to Part F of the Computerized Accounting appendix for information on how to adjust the print and display settings.

18. Review your printed General Journal. If you note an error at this point, it can be easily fixed. With the General Journal report on your screen, place your cursor over the incorrect entry (it will resemble a magnifying glass with a "z" in the center). Double click on the entry you wish to correct and you will be taken to the **General Journal Entry** window that contains the entry. You may edit it using the same procedures as editing an unposted entry in step 11. After making the necessary changes, click on the **Post** icon to save your changes. You will be returned to your report where you can view the changes made.

What to do if you posted an incorrect entry

19. Click on the **Close** icon to close the General Journal report. If you originally used the menu method to bring up the General Journal report, you are taken back to the report selection window where you can select **General Ledger.** If you originally used the navigation aid folder to bring up the report, you must again select the **General Ledger** folder and select **General Ledger** from the report options given to you. Your screen will look something like the following:

How to display and print a general ledger report

```
                                              The Atlas Company- Student Name
                                                      General Ledger
                                              For the Period From Jan 1, 2001 to Jan 31, 2001
       Filter Criteria includes: Report order is by ID. Report is printed with Truncated Transaction Descriptions and in Detail Format.

       Account ID        Date        Reference   Jrnl    Trans Description       Debit Amt     Credit Amt      Balance
       Account Description

       1110              1/1/01                           Beginning Balance
       Cash              1/1/01      Memo        GENJ     Initial investment of cash by   10,000.00
                         1/1/01      Memo        GENJ     Prepaid two months rent                     400.00
                         1/13/01     Memo3       GENJ     Paid telephone bill                         180.00
                         1/20/01     Memo4       GENJ     Owner withdrew cash from b                  500.00
                         1/27/01     Memo5       GENJ     Received cash for services p    450.00
                         1/31/01     Memo6       GENJ     Paid salaries to employees                  700.00

                                                          Current Period Change   10,450.00    1,780.00      8,670.00
                         1/31/01                          Ending Balance                                     8,670.00


       1120              1/1/01                           Beginning Balance
       Accounts Receivable 1/9/01    Memo2       GENJ     Performed services on accou     1,500.00

                                                          Current Period Change    1,500.00                  1,500.00
                         1/31/01                          Ending Balance                                     1,500.00
```

20. You will not see the entire report on the screen. The scroll bars can be used to advance the display to view other portions of the report. You may also double click your mouse on any transaction to bring up the entry window for that transaction.

21. Click on the **Print** icon to print the General Ledger report.

22. Click on the close button to close the General Ledger report and return to the reports selection window. Click on the General Ledger Trial Balance option from this window. Your screen will look something like this:

How to display and print a trial balance

```
                                         The Atlas Company-Student Name
                                         General Ledger Trial Balance
                                                As of Jan 31, 2001
       Filter Criteria includes: Report order is by ID. Report is printed in Detail Format.

       Account ID     Account Description          Debit Amt        Credit Amt

       1110           Cash                         8,670.00
       1120           Accounts Receivable          1,500.00
       1140           Prepaid Rent                   400.00
       1150           Office Supplies                100.00
       2110           Accounts Payable                                 100.00
       3110           Owner's Capital                               10,000.00
       3120           Owner's Withdrawals            500.00
       4110           Fees Earned                                    1,950.00
       5120           Salaries Expense               700.00
       5150           Telephone Expense              180.00

                      Total:                      12,050.00        12,050.00
```

23. The scroll bar can be used to advance the display to view other portions of the report. You may also display zero balance accounts by clicking on the **Options** icon and clicking the box next to **Include Accounts with Zero Amounts**. Clicking on **OK** will return you to the report.

24. Click on the **Print** icon to print the Trial Balance.

How to display and print a chart of accounts

25. Again click on the close button to close the Trial Balance report. Select **Chart of Accounts** from the report selection window. Your screen will look something like the following:

```
                    The Atlas Company- Student Name
                           Chart of Accounts
                          As of Jan 31, 2001
Filter Criteria includes: Report order is by ID. Report is printed with Accounts having Zero Amounts and in Detail Format.

Account ID   Account Description        Active   Account Type

1110         Cash                       Yes      Cash
1120         Accounts Receivable        Yes      Accounts Receivable
1140         Prepaid Rent               Yes      Other Current Assets
1150         Office Supplies            Yes      Other Current Assets
1210         Office Equipment           Yes      Fixed Assets
1221         Accum. Depr- Office Equipment  Yes  Accumulated Depreciation
1230         Automobile                 Yes      Fixed Assets
1241         Accum. Depr- Automobile    Yes      Accumulated Depreciation
1250         Store Equipment            Yes      Fixed Assets
1261         Accum Depr- Store Equipment  Yes    Accumulated Depreciation
2110         Accounts Payable           Yes      Accounts Payable
3110         Owner's Capital            Yes      Equity-doesn't close
3120         Owner's Withdrawals        Yes      Equity-gets closed
3129         Beginning Balance Equity   Yes      Equity-doesn't close
3130         Retained Earnings          Yes      Equity-Retained Earnings
4110         Fees Earned                Yes      Income
5110         Rent Expense               Yes      Expenses
5120         Salaries Expense           Yes      Expenses
5150         Telephone Expense          Yes      Expenses
```

26. Click on the close button to close the Chart of Accounts window and return to the Menu Window.

27. Click on the Menu Window **File** menu; then click on Exit to end the current work session and return to your Windows desktop. Your work will automatically be saved.

28. You can exit from Peachtree Complete Accounting 8.0 at any time during a current work session from any window that offers the **File** menu. You may be asked if you wish to save any unposted work.

29. There is no need to save your work in Peachtree. Each time you make a change and click post, your work is automatically saved. You should back up your work after each session. This will be discussed in Chapter 4.

> How to exit from the program

> How to save your work during a current work session

The Accounting Cycle Continued

PREPARING WORKSHEETS AND FINANCIAL STATEMENTS

It's a fact of life: as soon as you start pulling in a paycheck, you have to give a portion of your money to the U.S. Government in the form of taxes. The government then spends your money on everything from national parks to military bases. Just as businesses must tell their shareholders how their money is spent, each government department must prepare financial reports to tell you how *your* money is spent. As you may know by now, even Uncle Sam makes mistakes—big ones. In 1999, Department of Defense Pentagon money managers required almost $7 trillion of accounting adjustments to make their books balance. Each **adjustment** represents an accoutant's correction of a discrepancy.

In this chapter you'll learn how to analyze accounts on a 10-column worksheet and identify which accounts must be **adjusted** to bring it up to date. Using your worksheet, you will then prepare financial statements to give a better picture of "how well the business is doing" than day-to-day receipts. But don't worry. Because we will be using the example of a small business, your adjustments will be in hundreds—not trillions—of dollars!

Part of the Defense Department's problem is the sheer volume of money it spends and must keep track of. The military spent $275.5 billion in 1999 alone (to see more on The Department of Defense's spending go to www.defenselink.mil), and it acquires billions more in supplies. As you'll see in this chapter, when supplies are used up, they are moved

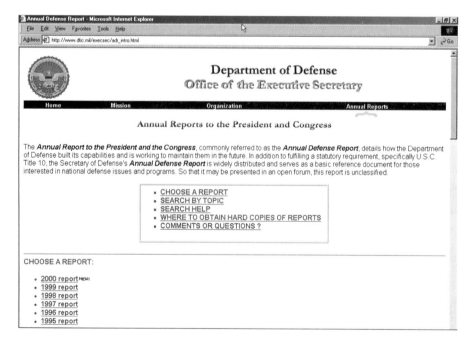

from the asset column to the expense column on the worksheet. But what if you don't have an accurate documentation of what you spent for your supplies? The General Accounting Office (GAO) found that the Defense Department lacked documentation to verify almost $120 billion in military equipment and property. Government departments, like every business, should have accurate records from which to prepare their financial statements. If they don't, the consequences effect us all. Without accurate financial information, taxpayers like you cannot determine whether the government is carrying out the will of Congress or not.

Based on: Julia Malone, "Auditors cite failings in 11 of 24 agencies," *The Atlanta Constitution*, March 31, 2000, p. A; 20. John M. Donnelly, "Pentagon's Finances Just Don't Add Up; Audit: Hundreds of computer systems fail to keep running totals of income and outgo. Last year, the Defense Department's bookkeeping errors totaled more than the entire federal budget," *The Los Angeles Times*, March 5, 2000, p. 8. Ralph Vartabedian, "Thefts Reveal Flawed Pentagon Contract System," *The Los Angeles Times*, September 28, 1998, p. 1.

LEARNING OBJECTIVES

▼ Adjustments: prepaid rent, office supplies, depreciation on equipment, and accrued salaries. (p. 117)

▼ Preparation of adjusted trial balance on the worksheet. (p. 124)

▼ The income statement and balance sheet sections of the worksheet. (p. 125)

▼ Preparing financial statements from the worksheet. (p. 130)

In the accompanying diagram, steps 1 – 4 show the parts of the manual accounting cycle that were completed for Clark's Word Processing Services in the last chapter. This chapter continues the cycle with steps 5 – 6: the preparation of a worksheet and the three financial statements. Be sure to check inside front cover for a complete ROAD MAP of the Accounting Cycle.

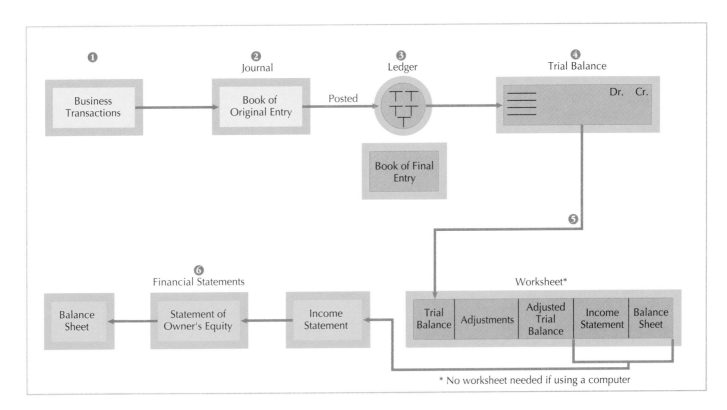

* No worksheet needed if using a computer

An accountant uses a **worksheet** to organize and check data before preparing financial statements necessary to complete the accounting cycle. The most important function of the worksheet is to allow the accountant to find and cor-

CLARK'S WORD PROCESSING SERVICES
WORKSHEET
FOR MONTH ENDING MAY 31, 200X

Account Titles	Trial Balance Dr.	Trial Balance Cr.	Adjustments Dr.	Adjustments Cr.	Adjusted Trial Balance Dr.	Adjusted Trial Balance Cr.	Income Statement Dr.	Income Statement Cr.
Cash	6 1 5 5 00							
Accounts Receivable	5 0 0 0 00							
Office Supplies	6 0 0 00							
Prepaid Rent	1 2 0 0 00							
Word Processing Equipment	6 0 0 0 00							
Accounts Payable		3 3 5 0 00						
Brenda Clark, Capital		10 0 0 0 00						
Brenda Clark, Withdrawals	6 2 5 00							
Word Processing Fees		8 0 0 0 00						
Office Salaries Expense	1 3 0 0 00							
Advertising Expense	2 5 0 00							
Telephone Expense	2 2 0 00							
	21 3 5 0 00	21 3 5 0 00						

FIGURE 4-1. Sample Worksheet

> The worksheet is not a formal report, so no dollar signs appear on it. Because it is a form, there are no commas, either.

> As is true for all accounting statements, the heading includes the name of the company, the name of the report, the date, and the length of the accounting period.

> Worksheets can be completed on excel spreadsheets

rect errors before financial statements are prepared. In a way, a worksheet acts as the accountant's scratch pad. No one sees the worksheet once the formal reports are prepared. A sample worksheet is shown in Figure 4-1.

The accounts listed on the far left of the worksheet are taken from the ledger. The rest of the worksheet has five sections: the trial balance, adjustments, adjusted trial balance, income statement, and balance sheet. Each of these sections is divided into debit and credit columns.

THE TRIAL BALANCE SECTION

We discussed how to prepare a trial balance in Chapter 2. Some companies prepare a separate trial balance; others, such as Clark's Word Processing Services, prepare the trial balance directly on the worksheet. A trial balance is taken on every account listed in the ledger that has a balance. Additional titles from the ledger are added as they are needed. (We will show this later.)

THE ADJUSTMENTS SECTION

Chapters 1–3 discussed transactions that occurred with outside suppliers and companies. In a real business, though, inside transactions also occur during the accounting cycle. These transactions must be recorded, too. At the end of the worksheet process, the accountant will have all of the business's accounts up-to-date and ready to be used to prepare the formal financial reports. By analyzing each of Clark's accounts on the worksheet, the accountant will be able to identify specific accounts that must be **adjusted,** to bring them up to date. The accountant for Clark's Word Processing Services needs to adjust the following accounts:

A. Office Supplies   C. Word Processing Equipment

B. Prepaid Rent   D. Office Salaries Expense

Let's look at how to analyze and adjust each of these accounts.

A. Adjusting the Office Supplies Account

On May 31, the accountant found out that the company had only $100 worth of office supplies on hand. When the company had originally purchased the $600 of office supplies, they were considered an asset. But as the supplies were used up, they became an expense.

▼ Office supplies available, $600 on trial balance.
▼ Office supplies left or on hand as of May 31, $100 will end up on adjusted trial balance.
▼ Office supplies used up in the operation of the business for the month of May, $500 is shown in the adjustments column.

As a result, the asset Office Supplies is too high on the trial balance (it should be $100, not $600). At the same time, if we don't show the additional expense of supplies used, the company's *net income* will be too high.

If Clark's accountant does not adjust the trial balance to reflect the change, the company's net income would be too high on the income statement and both sides (assets and owner's equity) of the balance sheet would be too high.

Now let's look at the adjustment for office supplies in terms of the transaction analysis chart.

Will go on income statement

Accounts Affected	Category	↓	↑	Rules
Office Supplies Expense	Expense		↑	Dr.
Office Supplies	Asset	↓		Cr.

Will go on balance sheet

The office supplies expense account comes from the Chart of Accounts on page 73. Since it is not listed in the account titles, it must be listed below the trial balance. Let's see how we enter this adjustment on the worksheet on the following page.

Place $500 in the debit column of the adjustments section on the same line as Office Supplies Expense. Place $500 in the credit column of the adjustments section on the same line as Office Supplies. The numbers in the adjustment column show what is used, *not* what is on hand.

B. Adjusting the Prepaid Rent Account

Back on May 1, Clark's Word Processing Services paid three months' rent in advance. The accountant realized that the rent expense would be $400 per month ($1,200 ÷ 3 months = $400).

Remember, when rent is paid in advance, it is considered an asset called *prepaid rent.* When the asset, prepaid rent, begins to expire or be used up it becomes an expense. Now it is May 31, and one month's prepaid rent has become an expense.

How is this handled? Should the account be $1,200, or is there really only $800 of prepaid rent left as of May 31? What do we need to do to bring prepaid rent to the "true" balance? The answer is that we must increase Rent Expense by $400 and decrease Prepaid Rent by $400.

Note: Amount "used up" for supplies $500 goes in adjustments column.

CLARK'S WORD PROCESSING SERVICES
WORKSHEET
FOR MONTH ENDED MAY 31, 200X

Account Titles	Trial Balance Dr.	Trial Balance Cr.	Adjustments Dr.	Adjustments Cr.
Cash	6 1 5 5 00			
Accounts Receivable	5 0 0 0 00			
Office Supplies	6 0 0 00			(A) 5 0 0 00
Prepaid Rent	1 2 0 0 00			
Word Processing Equipment	6 0 0 0 00			
Accounts Payable		3 3 5 0 00		
Brenda Clark, Capital		1 0 0 0 0 00		
Brenda Clark, Withdrawals	6 2 5 00			
Word Processing Fees		8 0 0 0 00		
Office Salaries Expense	1 3 0 0 00			
Advertising Expense	2 5 0 00			
Telephone Expense	2 2 0 00			
	2 1 3 5 0 00	2 1 3 5 0 00		
Office Supplies Expense			(A) 5 0 0 00	

A decrease in Office Supplies, $500.

An increase in Office Supplies Expense, $500.

"Used up"

Adjusting Prepaid Rent: On p. 116 the trial balance showed a figure for Prepaid Rent of $1,200. The amount of rent expired is the adjustment figure used to update Prepaid Rent and Rent Expense.

Rent Expense 515
400

Prepaid Rent 115
1200 | 400 Adj.
800

Original cost of $6,000 for word processing equipment remains unchanged after adjustments.

Without this adjustment, the expenses for Clark's Word Processing Services for May will be too low, and the asset Prepaid Rent will be too high. If unadjusted amounts were used in the formal reports, the net income shown on the income statement would be too high, and both sides (assets and owner's equity) would be too high on the balance sheet. In terms of our transaction analysis chart, the adjustment would look like this:

Will go on income statement

Accounts Affected	Category	↓	↑	Rules
Rent Expense	**Expense**		↑	**Dr.**
Prepaid Rent	**Asset**	↓		**Cr.**

Will go on balance sheet

Like the Office Supplies Expense account, the Rent Expense account comes from the chart of accounts on page 73.

The worksheet on page 119 shows how to enter an adjustment to Prepaid Rent.

C. Adjusting the Word Processing Equipment Account for Depreciation

The life of the asset affects how it is adjusted. The two accounts we discussed above, Office Supplies and Prepaid Rent, involved things that are used up relatively quickly. Equipment—like word processing equipment—is expected to last much longer. Also, it is expected to help produce revenue over a longer period. That is why accountants treat it differently. The balance sheet reports the **historical cost,** or original cost, of the equipment. The original cost also is reflected in the ledger. The adjustment shows how the cost of the equipment is allocated (spread) over its expected useful life. This spreading is called **depreciation.** To depreciate the equipment, we have to figure out how much its cost goes down each month. Then we have to keep a running total of how that

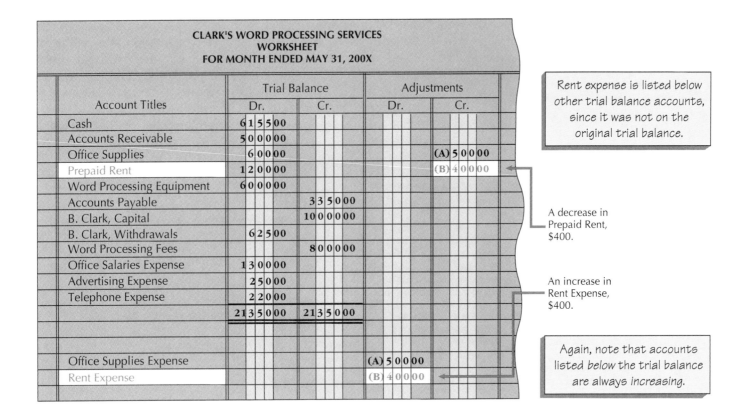

CLARK'S WORD PROCESSING SERVICES
WORKSHEET
FOR MONTH ENDED MAY 31, 200X

Account Titles	Trial Balance Dr.	Trial Balance Cr.	Adjustments Dr.	Adjustments Cr.
Cash	6 1 5 5 00			
Accounts Receivable	5 0 0 0 00			
Office Supplies	6 0 0 00			(A) 5 0 0 00
Prepaid Rent	1 2 0 0 00			(B) 4 0 0 00
Word Processing Equipment	6 0 0 0 00			
Accounts Payable		3 3 5 0 00		
B. Clark, Capital		10 0 0 0 00		
B. Clark, Withdrawals	6 2 5 00			
Word Processing Fees		8 0 0 0 00		
Office Salaries Expense	1 3 0 0 00			
Advertising Expense	2 5 0 00			
Telephone Expense	2 2 0 00			
	21 3 5 0 00	21 3 5 0 00		
Office Supplies Expense			(A) 5 0 0 00	
Rent Expense			(B) 4 0 0 00	

Rent expense is listed below other trial balance accounts, since it was not on the original trial balance.

A decrease in Prepaid Rent, $400.

An increase in Rent Expense, $400.

Again, note that accounts listed *below* the trial balance are always increasing.

depreciation mounts up over time. The Internal Revenue Service (IRS) issues guidelines, tables, and formulas that must be used to estimate the amount of depreciation. Different methods can be used to calculate depreciation (see the Appendix at the end of the text). We will use the simplest method—straight-line depreciation—to calculate the depreciation of Clark's Word Processing Services' equipment. Under the straight-line method, equal amounts are taken over successive periods of time.

The calculation of depreciation for the year for Clark's Word Processing Services is as follows:

$$\frac{\text{cost of equipment} - \text{residual value}}{\text{estimated years of usefulness}}$$

According to the IRS, word processing equipment has an expected life of five years. At the end of that time, the property's value is called its "residual value." Think of **residual value** as the estimated value of the equipment at end of the fifth year. For Clark, the equipment has an estimated residual value of $1,200.

Assume equipment has a 5-year life.

$$\frac{\$6,000 - \$1,200}{5 \text{ years}} = \frac{\$4,800}{5} = \$960 \text{ depreciation per year}$$

Our trial balance is for one month, so we must determine the adjustment for that month:

Clark will record $960 of depreciation each year.

$$\frac{\$960}{12 \text{ months}} = \$80 \text{ depreciation per month}$$

This $80 is known as *Depreciation Expense* and will be shown on the income statement.

Next, we have to create a new account that can keep a running total of the depreciation amount apart from the original cost of the equipment. That account is called **Accumulated Depreciation.**

Depreciation is an expense reported on the income statement.

Accumulated Depreciation	
Dr.	Cr.

is a contra-asset account found on the balance sheet.

At end of June the accumulated depreciation will be $160, but historical cost will stay at $6,000.

Remember, book value is not the same as market value.

The Accumulated Depreciation account shows the relationship between the original cost of the equipment and the amount of depreciation that has been taken or accumulated over a period of time. This is a *contra-asset* account; it has the opposite balance of an asset such as equipment. Accumulated Depreciation will summarize, accumulate, or build up the amount of depreciation that is taken on the word processing equipment over its estimated useful life.

This is how this would look on a partial balance sheet of Clark's Word Processing Services.

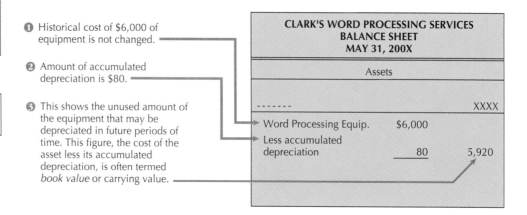

❶ Historical cost of $6,000 of equipment is not changed.

❷ Amount of accumulated depreciation is $80.

❸ This shows the unused amount of the equipment that may be depreciated in future periods of time. This figure, the cost of the asset less its accumulated depreciation, is often termed *book value* or carrying value.

CLARK'S WORD PROCESSING SERVICES
BALANCE SHEET
MAY 31, 200X

Assets		
-------		XXXX
Word Processing Equip.	$6,000	
Less accumulated depreciation	80	5,920

Let's summarize the key points before going on to mark the adjustment on the worksheet:

1. Depreciation Expense goes on the income statement, which results in
   - ▼ An increase in total expenses.
   - ▼ A decrease in net income.
   - ▼ Therefore, less to be paid in taxes.
2. Accumulated depreciation is a contra-asset account found on the balance sheet next to its related equipment account.
3. The original cost of equipment is not reduced; it stays the same until the equipment is sold or removed.
4. Each month the amount in the Accumulated Depreciation account grows larger, while the cost of the equipment remains the same.

Now, let's analyze the adjustment on the transaction analysis chart:

Taking depreciation does not result in any new payment of cash. The result of depreciation provides some tax savings.

Dep. Expense, W. P. 516	
80	

Accum. Dep., W. P. 122	
	80

Will go on income statement

Accounts Affected	Category	↓	↑	Rules
Depreciation Expense, Word Processing Equipment	Expense		↑	Dr.
Accumulated Depreciation, Word Processing Equipment	Contra Asset		↑	Cr.

Will go on balance sheet

Note that the original cost of the equipment on the worksheet has *not* been changed ($6,000).

Remember, the original cost of the equipment never changes: (1) the equipment account is not included among the affected accounts because the original cost of equipment remains the same; and (2) the original cost does not change. Even though the Accumulated Depreciation increases (as a credit), the equipment's **book value** decreases.

The worksheet on page 121 shows how we enter the adjustment for depreciation of word processing equipment.

CLARK'S WORD PROCESSING SERVICES
WORKSHEET
FOR MONTH ENDED MAY 31, 200X

Account Titles	Trial Balance Dr.	Trial Balance Cr.	Adjustments Dr.	Adjustments Cr.
Cash	6 1 5 5 00			
Accounts Receivable	5 0 0 0 00			
Office Supplies	6 0 0 00			(A) 5 0 0 00
Prepaid Rent	1 2 0 0 00			(B) 4 0 0 00
Word Processing Equipment	6 0 0 0 00			
Accounts Payable		3 3 5 0 00		
B. Clark, Capital		1 0 0 0 0 00		
B. Clark, Withdrawals	6 2 5 00			
Word Processing Fees		8 0 0 0 00		
Office Salaries Expense	1 3 0 0 00			
Advertising Expense	2 5 0 00			
Telephone Expense	2 2 0 00			
	2 1 3 5 0 00	2 1 3 5 0 00		
Office Supplies Expense			(A) 5 0 0 00	
Rent Expense			(B) 4 0 0 00	
Depreciation Exp., W. P. Equip.			(C) 8 0 00	
Accum. Deprec., W. P. Equip.				(C) 8 0 00

An increase in Depreciation Expense, W. P. Equipment.

An increase in Accumulated Depreciation, W. P. Equipment.

Because this is a new business, neither account had a previous balance. Therefore, neither is listed in the account titles of the trial balance. We need to list both accounts below Rent Expense in the account titles section. On the worksheet, put $80 in the debit column of the adjustments section on the same line as Depreciation Expense, W. P. Equipment, and put $80 in the credit column of the adjustments section on the same line as Accumulated Depreciation, W. P. Equipment.

Next month, on June 30, $80 would be entered under Depreciation Expense, and Accumulated Depreciation would show a balance of $160. Remember, in May, Clark's was a new company, so no previous depreciation was taken.

Now let's look at the last adjustment for Clark's Word Processing Services.

D. Adjusting the Salaries Accrued Account

Clark's Word Processing Services paid $1,300 in Office Salaries Expense (see the trial balance of any previous worksheet in this chapter). The last salary checks for the month were paid on May 27. How can we update this account to show the salary expense as of May 31?

Next month (June in our example), accumulated depreciation will appear listed in the original trial balance.

Accumulated Depreciation

Dr.	Cr.
	History of amount of depreciation taken to date

Adjusting Salaries

May

S	M	T	W	T	F	S
						1
2	3	4	5	6	7	8
9	10	11	12	13	14	15
16	17	18	19	20	21	22
23	24	25	26	27	28	29
30	31					

John Murray worked for Clark on May 28, 29, 30, and 31, but his next paycheck is not due until June 3. John earned $350 for these four days. Is the $350 an expense to Clark in May, when it was earned, or in June when it is due and is paid?

Think back to Chapter 1, when we first discussed revenue and expenses. We noted then that revenue is recorded when it is earned, and expenses are recorded when they are incurred, not when they are actually paid off. This principle will be discussed further in a later chapter; for now it is enough to remember that we record revenue and expenses when they occur, because we want to match earned revenue with the expenses that resulted in earning those revenues. In this case, by working those four days, John Murray created some revenue for Clark in May. Therefore, the office salaries expense must be shown in May — the month the revenue was earned.

The results are:

Office Salaries Expense is increased by $350. This unpaid and unrecorded expense for salaries for which payment is not yet due is called **accrued salaries.** In effect, we now show the true expense for salaries ($1,650 instead of $1,300):

Office Salaries Expense

| 1,300 | |
| 350 | |

The second result is that salaries payable is increased by $350. Clark's has created a liability called Salaries Payable, meaning that the firm owes money for salaries. When the firm pays John Murray, it will reduce its liability, Salaries Payable, as well as decrease its cash.

In terms of the transaction analysis chart, the following would be done:

Accounts Affected	Category	↓	↑	Rules
Office Salaries Expense,	**Expense**		↑	**Dr.**
Salaries Payable	**Liability**		↑	**Cr.**

How the adjustment for accrued salaries is entered is shown at the top of page 123.

The account Office Salaries Expense is already listed in the account titles, so $350 is placed in the debit column of the adjustments section on the same line as Office Salaries Expense. However, because the Salaries Payable is not listed in the account titles, it is added below the trial balance under Accumulated Depreciation, W. P. Equipment. Also, $350 is placed in the credit column of the adjustments section on the same line as Salaries Payable.

Now that we have finished all the adjustments that we intended to make, we total the adjustments section, as shown in Figure 4-2.

THE ADJUSTED TRIAL BALANCE SECTION

The adjusted trial balance is the next section on the worksheet. To fill it out, we must summarize the information in the trial balance and adjustments sections, as shown in Figure 4-3 on page 124.

Note that when the numbers are brought across from the trial balance to the adjusted trial balance, two debits will be added together and two credits will be added together. If the numbers include a debit and a credit, take the difference between the two and place it on the side that is larger.

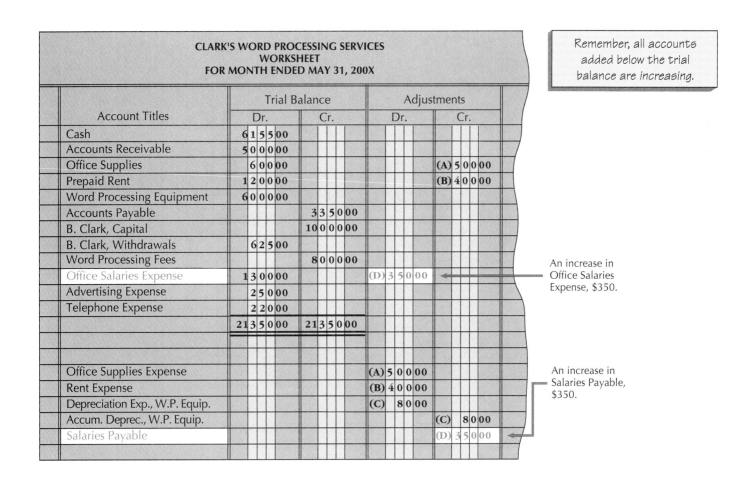

CLARK'S WORD PROCESSING SERVICES
WORKSHEET
FOR MONTH ENDED MAY 31, 200X

Remember, all accounts added below the trial balance are increasing.

An increase in Office Salaries Expense, $350.

An increase in Salaries Payable, $350.

FIGURE 4-2. The Adjustments Section of the Worksheet

CLARK'S WORD PROCESSING SERVICES
WORKSHEET
FOR MONTH ENDED MAY 31, 200X

Account Titles	Trial Balance Dr.	Trial Balance Cr.	Adjustments Dr.	Adjustments Cr.
Cash	6155 00			
Accounts Receivable	5000 00			
Office Supplies	600 00			(A) 500 00
Prepaid Rent	1200 00			(B) 400 00
Word Processing Equipment	6000 00			
Accounts Payable		3350 00		
B. Clark, Capital		10000 00		
B. Clark, Withdrawals	625 00			
Word Processing Fees		8000 00		
Office Salaries Expense	1300 00		(D) 350 00	
Advertising Expense	250 00			
Telephone Expense	220 00			
	21350 00	21350 00		
Office Supplies Expense			(A) 500 00	
Rent Expense			(B) 400 00	
Depreciation Exp., W.P. Equip.			(C) 80 00	
Accum. Deprec., W.P. Equip.				(C) 80 00
Salaries Payable				(D) 350 00
			1330 00	1330 00

CLARK'S WORD PROCESSING SERVICES
WORKSHEET
FOR MONTH ENDED MAY 31, 200X

Account Titles	Trial Balance Dr.	Trial Balance Cr.	Adjustments Dr.	Adjustments Cr.	Adjusted Trial Balance Dr.	Adjusted Trial Balance Cr.
Cash	6155 00				6155 00	
Accounts Receivable	5000 00				5000 00	
Office Supplies	600 00			(A) 500 00	100 00	
Prepaid Rent	1200 00			(B) 400 00	800 00	
Word Processing Equipment	6000 00				6000 00	
Accounts Payable		3350 00				3350 00
Brenda Clark, Capital		10000 00				10000 00
Brenda Clark, Withdrawals	625 00				625 00	
Word Processing Fees		8000 00				8000 00
Office Salaries Expense	1300 00		(D) 350 00		1650 00	
Advertising Expense	250 00				250 00	
Telephone Expense	220 00				220 00	
	21350 00	21350 00				
Office Supplies Expense			(A) 500 00		500 00	
Rent Expense			(B) 400 00		400 00	
Depreciation Exp., W.P. Equip.			(C) 80 00		80 00	
Accum. Deprec., W.P. Equip.				(C) 80 00		80 00
Salaries Payable				(D) 350 00		350 00
			1330 00	1330 00	21780 00	21780 00

Callouts:

If no adjustment is made, just carry over amount from trial balance on same side.

Supplies were $600 but we used up $500, leaving us with a $100 balance (on hand) in supplies. Note: If there are a debit and a credit, take the difference between the two and place it on the side that is larger.

Note: Equipment is not adjusted here.

Two debits are added together. If two credits, they also would have been added together.

Carry these amounts over to adjusted trial balance in the same positions.

Note: The total of the left (debit) must equal the total of the right (credit) ($21,780).

FIGURE 4-3. The Adjusted Trial Balance Section of the Worksheet

TABLE 4-1   NORMAL BALANCES AND ACCOUNT CATEGORIES

Account Titles	Category	Normal Balance on Adjusted Trial Balance	Income Statement Dr.	Income Statement Cr.	Balance Sheet Dr.	Balance Sheet Cr.
Cash	Asset	Dr.			X	
Accounts Receivable	Asset	Dr.			X	
Office Supplies	Asset	Dr.			X	
Prepaid Rent	Asset	Dr.			X	
Word Proc. Equip.	Asset	Dr.			X	
Accounts Payable	Liability	Cr.				X
Brenda Clark, Capital	Capital	Cr.				X
Brenda Clark, Withdrawals	Withdrawal	Dr.			X	
Word Proc. Fees	Revenue	Cr.		X		
Office Salaries Exp.	Expense	Dr.	X			
Advertising Expense	Expense	Dr.	X			
Telephone Expense	Expense	Dr.	X			
Office Supplies Exp.	Expense	Dr.	X			
Rent Expense	Expense	Dr.	X			
Dep. Exp., W. P. Equip.	Expense	Dr.	X			
Acc. Dep., W. P. Equip.	Contra Asset	Cr.				X
Salaries Payable	Liability	Cr.				X

Now that we have completed the adjustments and adjusted trial balance sections of the worksheet, it is time to move on to the income statement and the balance sheet sections. Before we do that though, look at the chart shown in Table 4-1. This table should be used as a reference to help you in filling out the next two sections of the worksheet.

Keep in mind that the numbers from the adjusted trial balance are carried over to one of the last four columns of the worksheet before the bottom section is completed.

THE INCOME STATEMENT SECTION

As shown in Figure 4-4 on page 126, the income statement section lists only revenue and expenses from the adjusted trial balance. Note that accumulated depreciation and salaries payable do not go on the income statement. Accumulated depreciation is a contra-asset found on the balance sheet. Salaries payable is a liability found on the balance sheet.

The revenue ($8,000) and all the individual expenses are listed in the income statement section. The revenue is placed in the credit column of the income statement section because it has a credit balance. The expenses have debit balances, so they are placed in the debit column of the income statement section. The following steps must be taken after the debits and credits are placed in the correct columns:

Step 1: Total the debits and credits.
Step 2: Calculate the balance between the debit and credit columns and place the difference on the smaller side.
Step 3: Total the columns.

The worksheet in Figure 4-4 shows that the label Net Income is added in the account title column on the same line as $4,900. When there is a net income, it will be placed in the debit column of the income statement section of the worksheet. If there is a net loss, it is placed in the credit column. The $8,000 total indicates that the two columns are in balance.

> In the worksheet, net income is placed in the debit column of the income statement. Net loss goes on the credit column.

> The difference between $3,100 Dr. and $8,000 Cr. indicates a net income of $4,900. Do not think of the Net Income as a Dr. or Cr. The $4,900 is placed in the debit column to balance both columns to $8,000. Actually, the credit side is larger by $4,900.

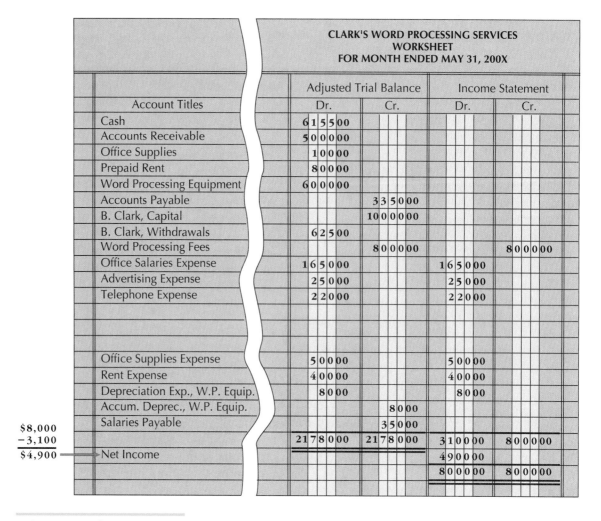

FIGURE 4-4. The Income Statement Section of the Worksheet

THE BALANCE SHEET SECTION

Remember: The ending figure for capital is not on the worksheet.

To fill out the balance sheet section of the worksheet, the following are carried over from the adjusted trial balance section: assets, contra-assets, liabilities, capital, and withdrawals. Because the beginning figure for capital* is used on the worksheet, the net income is brought over to the credit column of the balance sheet so both columns balance.

To see whether additional investments occurred for the period you must check the capital account in the ledger.

Let's now look at the completed worksheet in Figure 4-5 to see how the balance sheet section is completed. Note how the net income of $4,900 is brought over to the credit column of the worksheet. The figure for capital is also on the credit column, while the figure for withdrawals is on the debit column. By placing the net income in the credit column both sides total $18,680. If a net loss were to occur it would be placed in the debit column of the balance sheet column.

Now that we have completed the worksheet, we can go on to the three financial reports. But first let's summarize our progress.

The amounts come from the adjusted trial balance, except the $4,900, which was carried over from the income statement section.

*We assume no additional investments during the period.

Original cost of $6,000 is *not* adjusted   "used up"   "on hand"

CLARK'S WORD PROCESSING SERVICES
WORKSHEET
FOR MONTH ENDED MAY 31, 200X

Account Titles	Trial Balance Dr.	Trial Balance Cr.	Adjustments Dr.	Adjustments Cr.	Adjusted Trial Balance Dr.	Adjusted Trial Balance Cr.	Income Statement Dr.	Income Statement Cr.	Balance Sheet Dr.	Balance Sheet Cr.
Cash	615500				615500				615500	
Accounts Receivable	500000				500000				500000	
Office Supplies	60000			(A) 50000	10000				10000	
Prepaid Rent	120000			(B) 40000	80000				80000	
Word Processing Equipment	600000				600000				600000	
Accounts Payable		335000				335000				335000
B. Clark, Capital		1000000				1000000				1000000
B. Clark, Withdrawals	62500				62500				62500	
Word Processing Fees		800000				800000		800000		
Office Salaries Expense	130000		(D) 35000		165000		165000			
Advertising Expense	25000				25000		25000			
Telephone Expense	22000				22000		22000			
	2135000	2135000								
Office Supplies Expense			(A) 50000		50000		50000			
Rent Expense			(B) 40000		40000		40000			
Depreciation Exp., W. P. Equip.			(C) 8000		8000		8000			
Accum. Deprec., W. P. Equip.				(C) 8000		8000				8000
Salaries Payable				(D) 35000		35000				35000
			133000	133000	2178000	2178000	310000	800000	1868000	1378000
Net Income							490000			490000
							800000	800000	1868000	1868000

contra asset

FIGURE 4-5. The Completed Worksheet

CHAPTER 4 ... THE ACCOUNTING CYCLE CONTINUED: PREPARING WORKSHEETS AND FINANCIAL STATEMENTS

LEARNING UNIT 4-1 REVIEW

AT THIS POINT you should be able to

▼ Define and explain the purpose of a worksheet. (p. 116)
▼ Explain the need as well as the process for adjustments. (p. 117)
▼ Explain the concept of depreciation. (p. 118)
▼ Explain the difference between depreciation expense and accumulated depreciation. (p. 119)
▼ Prepare a worksheet from a trial balance and adjustment data. (p. 127)

SELF-REVIEW QUIZ 4-1

From the accompanying trial balance and adjustment data, complete a worksheet for P. Logan Co. for the month ended Dec. 31, 200X. (You can use the blank fold-out worksheet located at the end of the *Study Guide and Working Papers*.)

Note: The numbers used on this quiz may seem impossibly small, but we have done that on purpose, so that at this point you don't have to worry about arithmetic, just about preparing the worksheet correctly.

P. LOGAN TRIAL BALANCE DECEMBER 31, 200X		
	Dr.	Cr.
Cash	15 00	
Accounts Receivable	3 00	
Prepaid Insurance	3 00	
Store Supplies	5 00	
Store Equipment	6 00	
Accumulated Depreciation, Store Equipment		4 00
Accounts Payable		2 00
P. Logan, Capital		14 00
P. Logan, Withdrawals	3 00	
Revenue from Clients		25 00
Rent Expense	2 00	
Salaries Expense	8 00	
	45 00	45 00

Adjustment Data:

a. Depreciation Expense, Store Equipment, $1.
b. Insurance Expired, $2
c. Supplies on hand, $1.
d. Salaries owed but not paid to employees, $3.

Solution to Self-Review Quiz 4-1

Don't adjust this line! Store Equipment always contains the historical cost.

Amount used up

Note on hand ends up on the adjusted trial balance

P. LOGAN COMPANY
WORKSHEET
FOR MONTH ENDED DECEMBER 31, 200X

Account Titles	Trial Balance Dr.	Trial Balance Cr.	Adjustments Dr.	Adjustments Cr.	Adjusted Trial Balance Dr.	Adjusted Trial Balance Cr.	Income Statement Dr.	Income Statement Cr.	Balance Sheet Dr.	Balance Sheet Cr.
Cash	1500				1500				1500	
Accounts Receivable	300				300				300	
Prepaid Insurance	300			(B) 200	100				100	
Store Supplies	500			(C) 400	100				100	
Store Equipment	600				600				600	
Accum. Depr., Store Equipment		400		(A) 100		500				500
Accounts Payable		200				200				200
P. Logan, Capital		1400				1400				1400
P. Logan, Withdrawals	300				300				300	
Revenue from Clients		2500				2500		2500		
Rent Expense	200				200		200			
Salaries Expense	800		(D) 300		1100		1100			
	4500	4500								
Depr. Exp., Store Equipment			(A) 100		100		100			
Insurance Expense			(B) 200		200		200			
Supplies Expense			(C) 400		400		400			
Salaries Payable				(D) 300		300				300
			1000	1000	4900	4900	2000	2500	2900	2400
Net Income							500			500
							2500	2500	2900	2900

Note that Accumulated Depreciation is listed in trial balance, since this is not a new company. Store Equipment has already been depreciated $4.00 from an earlier period.

The formal financial statements can be prepared from the worksheet completed in Learning Unit 4-1. Before beginning, we must check that the entries on the worksheet are correct and in balance. To do this, we have to be sure that (1) all entries are recorded in the appropriate column, (2) the correct amounts are entered in the proper places, (3) the addition is correct across the columns (i.e., from the trial balance to the adjusted trial balance to the financial statements), and (4) the columns are added correctly.

PREPARING THE INCOME STATEMENT

The first statement to be prepared for Clark's Word Processing Services is the income statement. When preparing the income statement, it is important to remember that:

1. Every figure on the formal statement is on the worksheet. Figure 4-6 shows where each of these figures goes on the income statement.
2. There are no debit or credit columns on the formal statement.
3. The inside column on financial statements is used for subtotaling.
4. Withdrawals do not go on the income statement; they go on the statement of owner's equity.

Take a moment to look at the income statement in Figure 4-6. Note which items go where from the income statement section of the worksheet onto the formal statement.

PREPARING THE STATEMENT OF OWNER'S EQUITY

Figure 4-7 is the statement of owner's equity for Clark's. The figure shows where the information comes from on the worksheet. It is important to remember that if there were additional investments, the figure on the worksheet for capital would not be the beginning figure for capital. Checking the ledger account for capital will tell you whether the amount is correct. Note how net income and withdrawals aid in calculating the new figure for capital.

PREPARING THE BALANCE SHEET

In preparing the balance sheet (p. 132), remember that the balance sheet section totals on the worksheet ($18,680) do *not* match the totals on the formal balance sheet ($17,975). This is because information is grouped differently on the formal statement. First, in the formal report Accumulated Depreciation ($80) is subtracted from Word Processing Equipment, reducing the balance. Second, Withdrawals ($625) are subtracted from Owner's Equity, reducing the balance further. These two reductions ($-\$80 - \$625 = -\$705$) represent the difference between the worksheet and the formal version of the balance sheet ($\$17,975 - \$18,680 = -\$705$). Figure 4-8 on page 132 shows how to prepare the balance sheet from the worksheet.

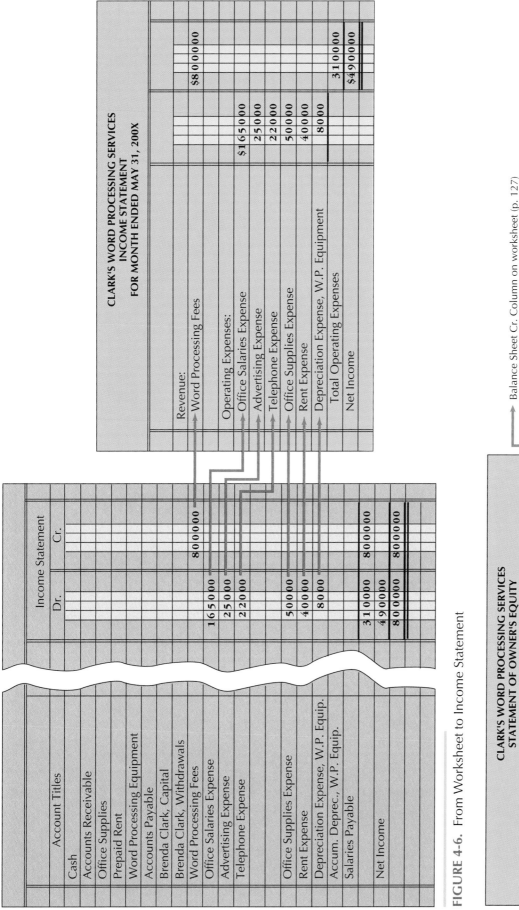

FIGURE 4-6. From Worksheet to Income Statement

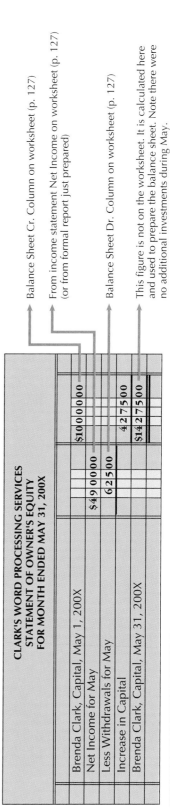

FIGURE 4-7. Completing a Statement of Owner's Equity

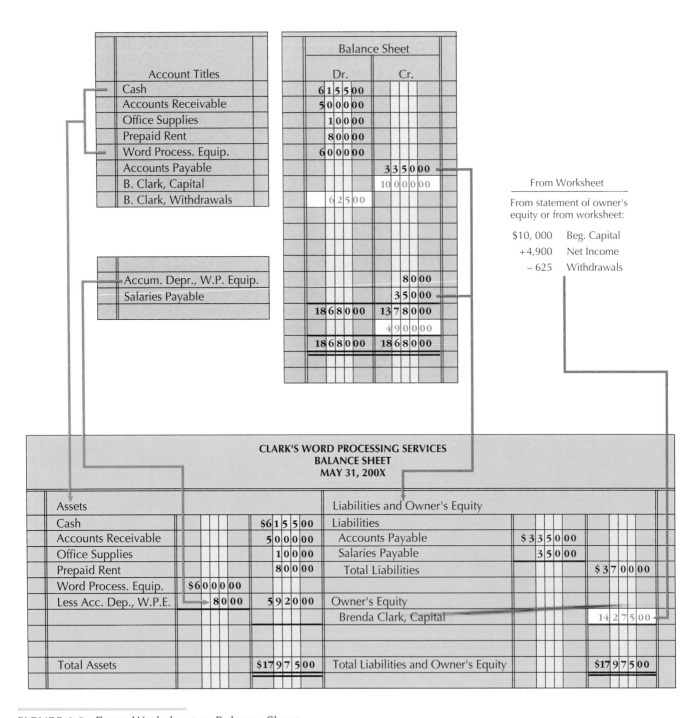

FIGURE 4-8. From Worksheet to Balance Sheet

"I've Been Working on the Worksheet . . ."

Fred has dreams. Big ones. He wants to grow his business to the point where he can start another Dunkin' Donuts shop. To do that, Fred realizes that he will have to manage his current shop more efficiently. His donuts and muffins are widely praised, and his bagel line is so successful that he has hired more help. But along with this success has come more paperwork. Fred now spends hours on his accounts. What to do?

Dunkin' Donuts' Business Consultant knows that Fred needs to reduce the time he spends handling his accounts. The business consultant has suggested that Fred hire an accountant, or that he switch to a computerized accounting system, as many owners have done recently. Fred has been hesitant to do either, because he wants to control the finances himself. And save money. And he fears computers. What to do?

Seeing Fred's dilemma, the business consultant encourages him to contact his zone's Advisory Council. This Advisory Council, like hundreds across the country, offers fellow Dunkin' Donuts shop owners from the same zone a chance to get together to share ways to improve their operations and discuss common problems. They work with the business consultant and the rest of the Dunkin' Donuts managerial team to keep their interdependent businesses running smoothly and profitably.

When Fred approaches the Council, they are very supportive. "I've been there, Fred, so I know how you feel," said Joe Franklin, from two towns away. "First, you're on the right track when you prepare a worksheet. It's too easy to mess up if you try to skip this step. Next, you might want to try keeping a clean copy of last month's worksheet. Even though you don't have to submit it to the business consultant, you frequently have to go back and refer to it when questions come up on your Income Statement or Balance Sheet. When your worksheet is all crossed out and doodled on, like this one is, you can't find info fast. Also, you may need your worksheets at tax time. I sure found that out the hard way!"

Discussion Questions

1. What is an Advisory Council? Why do you think that the business consultant recommended that Fred seek their advice?
2. Why do you think that some small business owners fear computerization and equate it with a loss of financial control?
3. Why is a clear worksheet helpful even after that month's statements have been prepared?

LEARNING UNIT 4-2 REVIEW

AT THIS POINT you should be able to

▼ Prepare the three financial statements from a worksheet. (p. 130)
▼ Explain why totals of the formal balance sheet don't match totals of balance sheet columns on the worksheet. (p. 130)

SELF-REVIEW QUIZ 4-2

(The forms you need are located on pages 101 and 102 of the *Study Guide and Working Papers.*)

From the worksheet on page 129 for P. Logan, please prepare (1) an income statement for December; (2) a statement of owner's equity; and (3) a balance sheet for December 31, 200X. No additional investments took place during the period.

Solution to Self-Review Quiz 4-2

P. LOGAN
INCOME STATEMENT
FOR THE MONTH ENDED DECEMBER 31, 200X

Revenue:			
Revenue from clients			$2500
Operating Expenses:			
Rent Expense		$200	
Salaries Expense		1100	
Depreciation Expense, Store Equipment		100	
Insurance Expense		200	
Supplies Expense		400	
Total Operating Expenses			2000
Net Income			$500

Quiz Tips:
The income statement is made up of revenue and expenses. Use the inside column for subtotaling.

The $5 on the income statement is used to update the statement of owner's equity.

P. LOGAN
STATEMENT OF OWNER'S EQUITY
FOR THE MONTH ENDED DECEMBER 31, 200X

P. Logan, Capital, December 1, 200X			$1400
Net Income for December		$500	
Less Withdrawals for December		300	
Increase in Capital			200
P. Logan, Capital, December 31, 200X			$1600

P. LOGAN
BALANCE SHEET
DECEMBER 31, 200X

Assets			Liabilities and Owner's Equity		
Cash		$1500	Liabilities		
Accounts Receivable		300	Accounts Payable	$200	
Prepaid Insurance		100	Salaries Payable	300	
Store Supplies		100	Total Liabilities		$500
Store Equipment	$600		Owner's Equity		
Less Acc. Dep., St. Eq.	500	100	P. Logan, Capital		1600
			Total Liabilities and		
Total Assets		$2100	Owner's Equity		$2100

The ending capital figure on the statement of owner's equity ($16) is used as the capital figure on the balance sheet.

COMPREHENSIVE DEMONSTRATION PROBLEM WITH SOLUTION TIPS

(The blank forms you need are on pages 103 and 104 of the *Study Guide and Working Papers*.)

From the following trial balance and additional data complete (1) a worksheet and (2) the three financial statements (numbers are intentionally small so you may concentrate on the theory).

FROST COMPANY
TRIAL BALANCE
DECEMBER 31, 200X

	Dr.	Cr.
Cash	14	
Accounts Receivable	4	
Prepaid Insurance	5	
Plumbing Supplies	3	
Plumbing Equipment	7	
Accumulated Depreciation, Plumbing Equipment		5
Accounts Payable		1
J. Frost, Capital		12
J. Frost, Withdrawals	3	
Plumbing Fees		27
Rent Expense	4	
Salaries Expense	5	
Totals	45	45

Adjustment Data:

a. Insurance Expired — $3
b. Plumbing Supplies on Hand — $1
c. Depreciation Expense, Plumbing Equipment — $1
d. Salaries owed but not paid to employees — $2

Solution Tips to Building a Worksheet

1. Adjustments

a.

Insurance Expense	Expense	↑	Dr.	$3
Prepaid Insurance	Asset	↓	Cr.	$3

Expired means used up

b.

Plumbing Supplies Expense	Expense	↑	Dr.	$2
Plumbing Supplies	Asset	↓	Cr.	$2

$3 − 1 = $2 *used up*
on hand

(cont. on p. 137)

Solution to Worksheet

FROST COMPANY
WORKSHEET
FOR MONTH ENDED DECEMBER 31, 200X

Original cost not adjusted *"used up"* *"on hand"*

Account Titles	Trial Balance Dr.	Trial Balance Cr.	Adjustments Dr.	Adjustments Cr.	Adjusted Trial Balance Dr.	Adjusted Trial Balance Cr.	Income Statement Dr.	Income Statement Cr.	Balance Sheet Dr.	Balance Sheet Cr.
Cash	1400				1400				1400	
Accounts Receivable	400				400				400	
Prepaid Insurance	500			(A) 300	200				200	
Plumbing Supplies	300			(B) 200	100				100	
Plumbing Equipment	700				700				700	
Accum. Depr., Plumb. Equip.		500		(C) 100		600				600
Accounts Payable		100				100				100
J. Frost, Capital		1200				1200				1200
J. Frost, Withdrawals	300				300				300	
Plumbing Fees		2700				2700		2700		
Rent Expense	400				400		400			
Salaries Expense	500		(D) 200		700		700			
	4500	4500								
Insurance Expense			(A) 300		300		300			
Plumbing Supplies Expense			(B) 200		200		200			
Depr. Exp. Plumb. Equip.			(C) 100		100		100			
Salaries Payable				(D) 200		200				200
			800	800	4800	4800	1700	2700	3100	2100
Net Income							1000			1000
							2700	2700	3100	3100

c.

Depreciation Expense, Plumbing Equipment	Expense	↑	Dr.	$1
Contra Asset Accumulated Depreciation, Plumbing Equipment	Contra Asset	↑	Cr.	$1

The original cost of equipment of $7 is not "touched."

d.

Salaries Expense,	Expense	↑	Dr.	$2
Salaries Payable	Liability	↑	Cr.	$2

2. Last four columns of worksheet prepared from adjusted trial balance.

3. Capital of $12 is the old figure. Net income of $10 (revenue − expenses) is brought over to same side as capital on the balance sheet Cr. column to balance columns.

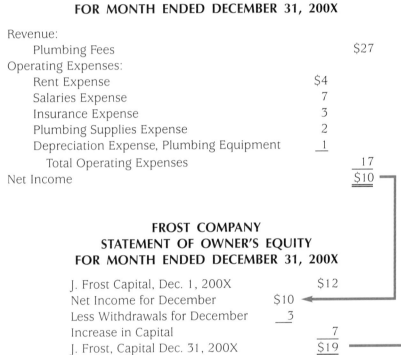

FROST COMPANY
INCOME STATEMENT
FOR MONTH ENDED DECEMBER 31, 200X

Revenue:
  Plumbing Fees $27
Operating Expenses:
  Rent Expense $4
  Salaries Expense 7
  Insurance Expense 3
  Plumbing Supplies Expense 2
  Depreciation Expense, Plumbing Equipment 1
    Total Operating Expenses 17
Net Income $10

FROST COMPANY
STATEMENT OF OWNER'S EQUITY
FOR MONTH ENDED DECEMBER 31, 200X

J. Frost Capital, Dec. 1, 200X $12
Net Income for December $10
Less Withdrawals for December 3
Increase in Capital 7
J. Frost, Capital Dec. 31, 200X $19

FROST COMPANY
BALANCE SHEET
DECEMBER 31, 200X

Assets		**Liabilities and Owner's Equity**		
Cash	$14	Liabilities		
Accounts Receivable	4	Accounts Payable	$1	
Prepaid Insurance	2	Salaries Payable	2	
Plumbing Supplies	1	Total Liabilities		$3
Original Cost				
Plumbing Equipment $7				
Less Accumulated Dep. 6	1	Owner's Equity		
		J. Frost, Capital		19
		Total Liabilities and		
Total Assets	$22	Owner's Equity		$22

Solution Tips for Preparing Financial Statements from a Worksheet

Inside columns of the three financial statements are used for subtotal. There are no debits or credits on the formal statements.

STATEMENTS

Income Statement	From Income Statement columns of worksheet for revenue and expenses.
Statement of Owner's Equity	From Balance Sheet Cr. column for old figure for Capital. Net Income from Income Statement. From Balance Sheet Dr. Column for Withdrawal figure.
Balance Sheet	From Balance Sheet Dr. column for Assets. From Balance Sheet Cr. Column for liabilities and Accumulated Depreciation. New Figure for Capital from Statement of Owner's Equity.

Note how plumbing equipment $7 and Accumulated Depreciation $6 are rearranged on the formal balance sheet. The total assets of $22 is not on the worksheet. Remember there are no debits or credits on formal statements.

SUMMARY OF KEY POINTS

Learning Unit 4-1

1. The worksheet is not a formal statement.
2. Adjustments update certain accounts so that they will be up to their latest balance before financial statements are prepared. Adjustments are the result of internal transactions.
3. Adjustments will affect both the income statement and the balance sheet.
4. Accounts listed *below* the account titles on the trial balance of the worksheet are *increasing*.
5. The original cost of a piece of equipment is not adjusted, historical cost is not lost.
6. Depreciation is the process of spreading the original cost of the asset over its expected useful life.
7. Accumulated depreciation is a contra-asset on the balance sheet that summarizes, accumulates, or builds up the amount of depreciation that an asset has accumulated.
8. Book value is the original cost less accumulated depreciation.
9. Accrued salaries are unpaid and unrecorded expenses that are accumulating but for which payment is not yet due.
10. Revenue and Expenses go on income statement sections of the worksheet. Assets, contra-assets, liabilities, capital, and withdrawals go on balance sheet sections of the worksheet.

Learning Unit 4-2

1. The formal statements prepared from a worksheet do not have debit or credit columns.
2. Revenue and expenses go on the income statement. Beginning capital plus net income less withdrawals (or: beginning capital minus net loss, less withdrawals) go on the statement of owner's equity. Be sure to check capital account in ledger to see if any additional investments took place. Assets, contra-assets, liabilities, and the new figure for capital go on the balance sheet.

KEY TERMS

Accrued salaries Salaries that are earned by employees but unpaid and unrecorded during the period (and thus need to be recorded by an adjustment) and will not come due for payment until the next accounting period.

Accumulated depreciation A contra-asset account that summarizes or accumulates the amount of depreciation that has been taken on an asset.

Adjusting The process of calculating the latest up-to-date balance of each account at the end of an accounting period.

Book value Cost of equipment less accumulated depreciation.

Depreciation The allocation (spreading) of the cost of an asset (such as an auto or equipment) over its expected useful life.

Historical cost The actual cost of an asset at time of purchase.

Residual value Estimated value of an asset after all the allowable depreciation has been taken.

Worksheet A columnar device used by accountants to aid them in completing the accounting cycle. It is not a formal report. Often called a spreadsheet.

BLUEPRINT OF STEPS 5 AND 6 OF THE ACCOUNTING CYCLE

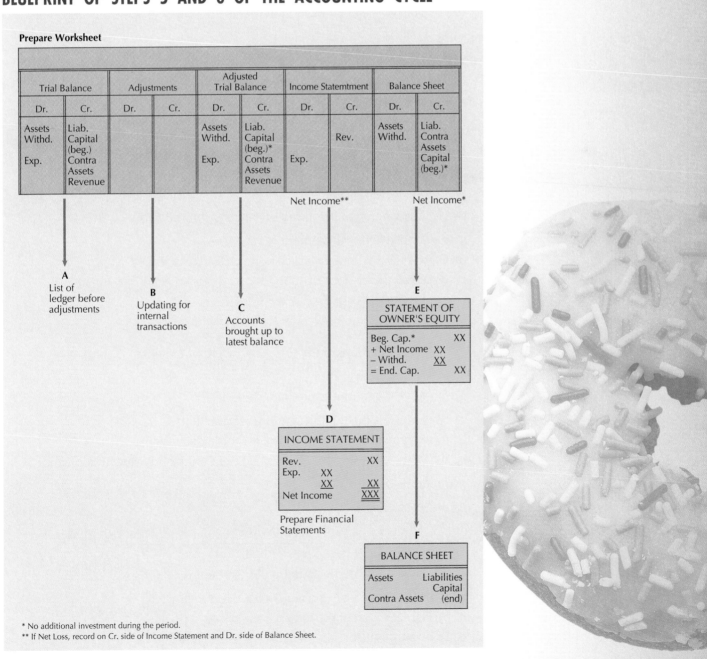

* No additional investment during the period.
** If Net Loss, record on Cr. side of Income Statement and Dr. side of Balance Sheet.

QUESTIONS, MINI EXERCISES, EXERCISES, AND PROBLEMS

Discussion Questions

1. Worksheets are required in every company's accounting cycle. Please agree or disagree and explain why.
2. What is the purpose of adjusting accounts?
3. What is the relationship of internal transactions to the adjusting process?
4. Explain how an adjustment can affect both the income statement and balance sheet. Please give an example.
5. Why do we need the accumulated depreciation account?
6. Depreciation expense goes on the balance sheet. True or false. Why?
7. Each month the cost of accumulated depreciation grows while the cost of equipment goes up. Agree or disagree. Defend your position.
8. Define accrued salaries.
9. Why don't the formal financial statements contain debit or credit columns?
10. Explain how the financial statements are prepared from the worksheet.

Mini Exercises

(The blank forms you need are on pages 106–107 of the *Study Guide and Working Papers*.)

Adjustment for Supplies

1. *Before Adjustment*

Supplies	Supplies Expense
600	

Given: At year end an inventory of supplies showed $100.

   a. How much is the adjustment for supplies?
   b. Draw a transaction analysis box for this adjustment.
   c. What will the balance of supplies be on the Adjusted Trial Balance?

Adjustment for Prepaid Rent

2. *Before Adjustment*

Prepaid Rent	Rent Expense
700	

Given: At year end rent expired is $300.

   a. How much is the adjustment for Prepaid Rent?
   b. Draw a transaction analysis box for this adjustment.
   c. What will be the balance of Prepaid Rent on the Adjusted Trial Balance?

Adjustment for Depreciation

3. *Before Adjustment*

Equip.	Acc. Dep., Equip.	Dep. Exp., Equip.
6,000	1,000	

Given: At year end depreciation on Equipment is $1,000.

   a. Which of the three T Accounts above is not affected?
   b. Which Title is a contra-asset?
   c. Draw a transaction analysis box for this adjustment.

d. What will be the balance of these three accounts on the Adjusted Trial Balance?

Adjustment for Accrued Salaries

4. *Before Adjustment*

Salaries Expense	Supplies Payable
900	

Given: Accrued Salaries, $200.

a. Draw a transaction analysis box for this adjustment.

b. What will be the balance of these two accounts on the Adjusted Trial Balance?

Worksheet

5. From the following Adjusted Trial Balance titles of a worksheet identify in which column each account will be listed on the last four columns of the worksheet.
(ID) Income Statement Dr. Column
(IC) Income Statement Cr. Column
(BD) Balance Sheet Dr. Column
(BC) Balance Sheet Cr. Column

	ATB	IS	BS
A. Supplies			
B. Acc. Receivable			
C. Cash			
D. Prepaid Rent			
E. Equipment			
F. Acc. Depreciation			
G. B., Capital			
H. B., Withdrawals			
I. Taxi Fees			
J. Advertising Expense			
K. Off. Supplies Expense			
L. Rent Expense			
M. Depreciation Expense			
N. Salaries Payable			

6. From the following Balance Sheet (which was made from the worksheet and other financial statements) explain why the lettered numbers were not found on the worksheet. *Hint:* There are no debits or credits on the formal financial statements.

H. WELLS
BALANCE SHEET
DECEMBER 31, 200X

Assets			Liabilities and Owner's Equity		
Cash		$ 6	Liabilities		
Acc. Receivable		2	Accounts Payable	$2	
Supplies		2	Salaries, Payable	1	
Equipment	$10		Total Liabilities		$ 3 (B)
Less Acc. Dep.	4	6	Owner's Equity		
			H. Wells, Capital		13 (C)
			Total Liability and		
(A) Total Assets		$16	Owner's Equity		$16 (D)

Exercises

(The blank forms you need are on pages 108–110 of the *Study Guide and Working Papers.*)

4-1. Complete the following table.

Categorizing accounts.

Account	Category	Normal Balance	Which Financial Statement(s) Found
Accounts Payable			
Prepaid Insurance			
Equipment			
Accumulated Depreciation			
A. Jax, Capital			
A. Jax, Withdrawals			
Salaries Payable			
Depreciation Expense			

Reviewing adjustments and the transaction analysis charts.

4-2. Use transaction analysis charts to analyze the following adjustments:

a. Depreciation on equipment, $500.

b. Rent expired, $200.

4-3. From the following adjustment data, calculate the adjustment amount and record appropriate debits or credits:

Recording adjusting entries.

a. Supplies purchased, $600.
   Supplies on hand, $200.

b. Store equipment, $10,000.
   Accumulated depreciation before adjustment, $900.
   Depreciation expense, $100.

Preparing a worksheet.

4-4. From the following trial balance and adjustment data, complete a worksheet for J. Trent as of December 31, 200X:

a. Depreciation expense, equipment	$2.00
b. Insurance expired	1.00
c. Store supplies on hand	4.00
d. Wages owed, but not paid for (they are an expense in the old year)	5.00

J. TRENT
TRIAL BALANCE
DECEMBER 31, 200X

	Dr.	Cr.
Cash	9 00	
Accounts Receivable	2 00	
Prepaid Insurance	7 00	
Store Supplies	6 00	
Store Equipment	7 00	
Accumulated Depreciation, Equipment		2 00
Accounts Payable		4 00
J. Trent, Capital		17 00
J. Trent, Withdrawals	6 00	
Revenue from Clients		24 00
Rent Expense	4 00	
Wage Expense	6 00	
	47 00	47 00

4-5. From the completed worksheet in Exercise 4-4, prepare

    a. An income statement for December.

    b. A statement of owner's equity for December.

    c. A balance sheet as of December 31, 200X.

Preparing financial statements from a worksheet.

Group A Problems

(The blank forms you need are on pp. 111–114 of the *Study Guide and Working Papers*.)

4A-1.

Completing a partial worksheet up to the adjusted trial balance.

GRACIE'S FITNESS CENTER
TRIAL BALANCE
DECEMBER 31, 200X

	Debit	Credit
Cash in Bank	6 0 0 0 00	
Accounts Receivable	5 0 0 0 00	
Gym Supplies	5 4 0 0 00	
Gym Equipment	7 2 0 0 00	
Accumulated Depreciation, Gym Equipment		4 0 0 0 00
G. Lang, Capital		12 3 5 0 00
G. Lang, Withdrawals	3 0 0 0 00	
Gym Fees		11 3 0 0 00
Rent Expense	9 0 0 00	
Advertising Expense	1 5 0 00	
	27 6 5 0 00	27 6 5 0 00

Check Figure:
Total of Adjusted Trial Balance $28,550

Given the following adjustment data on December 31:

    a. Gym supplies on hand, $1,000.

    b. Depreciation taken on gym equipment, $900.

Complete a partial worksheet up to the adjusted trial balance.

4A-2. On the next page is the trial balance for Fred's Plumbing Service for December 31, 200X.

Adjustment data to update the trial balance:

    a. Rent expired, $500.

    b. Plumbing supplies on hand (remaining), $100.

    c. Depreciation expense, plumbing equipment, $200.

    d. Wages earned by workers but not paid or due until January, $350.

Your task is to prepare a worksheet for Fred's Plumbing Service for the month of December.

FRED'S PLUMBING SERVICE
TRIAL BALANCE
DECEMBER 31, 200X

	Dr.	Cr.
Cash in Bank	3 6 0 6 00	
Accounts Receivable	7 0 0 00	
Prepaid Rent	8 0 0 00	
Plumbing Supplies	7 4 2 00	
Plumbing Equipment	1 4 0 0 00	
Accumulated Depreciation, Plumbing Equipment		1 0 6 0 00
Accounts Payable		4 4 2 00
Fred Jack, Capital		3 2 5 0 00
Plumbing Revenue		4 3 5 6 00
Heat Expense	4 0 0 00	
Advertising Expense	2 0 0 00	
Wage Expense	1 2 6 0 00	
	9 1 0 8 00	9 1 0 8 00

4A-3. The following is the trial balance for Kevin's Moving Co.

KEVIN'S MOVING CO.
TRIAL BALANCE
OCTOBER 31, 200X

	Dr.	Cr.
Cash	5 0 0 0 00	
Prepaid Insurance	2 5 0 0 00	
Moving Supplies	1 2 0 0 00	
Moving Truck	11 0 0 0 00	
Accumulated Depreciation, Moving Truck		9 0 0 0 00
Accounts Payable		2 7 6 8 00
K. Hoff, Capital		5 4 4 2 00
K. Hoff, Withdrawals	1 4 0 0 00	
Revenue from Moving		9 0 0 0 00
Wage Expense	3 7 1 2 00	
Rent Expense	1 0 8 0 00	
Advertising Expense	3 1 8 00	
	26 2 1 0 00	26 2 1 0 00

Adjustment data to update trial balance:

a. Insurance expired, $700.

b. Moving supplies on hand, $900.

c. Depreciation on moving truck, $500.

d. Wages earned but unpaid, $250.

Your task is to

1. Complete a worksheet for Kevin's Moving Co. for the month of October.

2. Prepare an income statement for October, a statement of owner's equity for October, and a balance sheet as of October 31, 200X.

4A-4.

Adjustment data to update trial balance:

a. Insurance expired, $700.

b. Repair supplies on hand, $3,000.

c. Depreciation on repair equipment, $200.

d. Wages earned but unpaid, $400.

Your task is to

1. Complete a worksheet for Dick's Repair Service for the month of November.

2. Prepare an income statement for November, a statement of owner's equity for November, and a balance sheet as of November 30, 200X.

Comprehensive Problem

DICK'S REPAIR SERVICE TRIAL BALANCE NOVEMBER 30, 200X	Dr.	Cr.
Cash	3 2 0 0 00	
Prepaid Insurance	4 0 0 0 00	
Repair Supplies	4 6 0 0 00	
Repair Equipment	3 0 0 0 00	
Accumulated Depreciation, Repair Equipment		7 0 0 00
Accounts Payable		5 5 7 0 00
D. Horn, Capital		3 8 0 0 00
Revenue from Repairs		7 0 0 0 00
Wages Expense	1 8 0 0 00	
Rent Expense	3 6 0 00	
Advertising Expense	1 1 0 00	
	17 0 7 0 00	17 0 7 0 00

Check Figure:
Net Income $1,830

Group B Problems

(The blank forms you need are on pages 111–114 of the *Study Guide and Working Papers*.)

4B-1.

GRACIE'S FITNESS CENTER TRIAL BALANCE DECEMBER 31, 200X	Dr.	Cr.
Cash	2 0 0 0 00	
Accounts Receivable	2 0 0 0 00	
Gym Supplies	4 2 0 0 00	
Gym Equipment	8 0 0 0 00	
Accumulated Depreciation, Gym Equipment		5 7 0 0 00
G. Lang, Capital		11 0 0 0 00
G. Lang, Withdrawals	1 0 0 0 00	
Gym Fees		1 4 0 0 00
Rent Expense	8 0 0 00	
Advertising Expense	1 0 0 00	
	18 1 0 0 00	18 1 0 0 00

Completing a partial worksheet up to adjusted trial balance.

Check Figure:
Total of Adjusted Trial Balance $18,600

Please complete a partial worksheet up to the adjusted trial balance using the following adjustment data:

a. Gym supplies on hand, $2,600.

b. Depreciation taken on gym equipment, $500.

4B-2. Given the following trial balance and adjustment data of Fred's Plumbing Service, your task is to prepare a worksheet for the month of December.

FRED'S PLUMBING SERVICE
TRIAL BALANCE
DECEMBER 31, 200X

	Dr.	Cr.
Cash in Bank	396 00	
Accounts Receivable	284 00	
Prepaid Rent	400 00	
Plumbing Supplies	310 00	
Plumbing Equipment	1000 00	
Accumulated Depreciation, Plumbing Equipment		200 00
Accounts Payable		346 00
Fred Jack, Capital		456 00
Plumbing Revenue		4680 00
Heat Expense	632 00	
Advertising Expense	1200 00	
Wage Expense	1460 00	
Total	5682 00	5682 00

Adjustment data:

a. Plumbing supplies on hand, $60.

b. Rent expired, $150.

c. Depreciation on plumbing equipment, $200.

d. Wages earned but unpaid, $115.

4B-3. Using the following trial balance and adjustment data of Kevin's Moving Co., prepare

1. A worksheet for the month of October.

2. An income statement for October, a statement of owner's equity for October, and a balance sheet as of October 31, 200X.

KEVIN'S MOVING CO.
TRIAL BALANCE
OCTOBER 31, 200X

	Dr.	Cr.
Cash	3920 00	
Prepaid Insurance	3288 00	
Moving Supplies	1400 00	
Moving Truck	10658 00	
Accumulated Depreciation, Moving Truck		3660 00
Accounts Payable		1312 00
K. Hoff, Capital		17482 00
K. Hoff, Withdrawals	4240 00	
Revenue from Moving		8162 00
Wages Expense	5712 00	
Rent Expense	1080 00	
Advertising Expense	318 00	
	30616 00	30616 00

Adjustment Data:

a. Insurance expired $600
b. Moving supplies on hand $310
c. Depreciation on moving truck $580
d. Wages earned but unpaid $410

4B-4. As the bookkeeper of Dick's Repair Service, use the information that follows to prepare

1. A worksheet for the month of November.
2. An income statement for November, a statement of owner's equity for
November, and a balance sheet as of November 30, 200X.

Comprehensive Problem

Check Figure:
Net Income $1,012

DICK'S REPAIR SERVICE
TRIAL BALANCE
NOVEMBER 30, 200X

	Dr.	Cr.
Cash	3 2 0 4 00	
Prepaid Insurance	4 0 0 0 00	
Repair Supplies	7 7 0 00	
Repair Equipment	3 1 0 6 00	
Accumulated Depreciation, Repair Equipment		6 5 0 00
Accounts Payable		1 9 0 4 00
D. Horn, Capital		6 2 5 8 00
Revenue from Repairs		5 6 3 4 00
Wages Expense	1 6 0 0 00	
Rent Expense	1 5 6 0 00	
Advertising Expense	2 0 6 00	
	14 4 4 6 00	14 4 4 6 00

Adjustment Data:

a. Insurance expired $300
b. Repair supplies on hand $170
c. Depreciation on repair equipment $250
d. Wages earned but unpaid $106

REAL-WORLD APPLICATIONS

4R-1.

MEMO

To: Hal Hogan, Bookkeeper

From: Pete Tennant, V. P.

Re: Adjustments for year ended December 31, 200X

Hal, here is the information you requested. Please supply me with the adjustments
needed ASAP. Also, please put in writing why we need to do these adjustments.

Thanks.

Attached to memo:

a. Insurance data:

Policy No.	Date of Policy Purchase	Policy Length	Cost
100	November 1 of previous year	4 years	$480
200	May 1 of current year	2 years	600
300	September 1 of current year	1 year	240

b. Rent data: Prepaid rent had a $500 balance at beginning of year. An additional $400 of rent was paid in advance in June. At year end, $200 of rent had expired.

c. Revenue data: Accrued storage fees of $500 were earned but uncollected and unrecorded at year end.

4R-2.

> **Hint: Unearned Rent is a liability on the balance sheet.**

On Friday, Harry Swag's boss asks him to prepare a special report, due on Monday at 8:00 A.M. Harry gathers the following material in his briefcase:

	Dec. 31	
	2001	**2002**
Prepaid Advertising	$300	$600
Interest Payable	150	350
Unearned Rent	500	300
Cash paid for: Advertising	$1,900	
Interest	1,500	
Cash received for: Rent	2,300	

As his best friend, could you help Harry show the amounts that are to be reported on the income statement for (a) Advertising Expense, (b) Interest Expense, and (c) Rent Fees Earned. Please explain in writing why unearned rent is considered a liability.

YOU make the call

Critical Thinking/Ethical Case

4R-3.

Janet Fox, President of Angel Co., went to a tax seminar. One of the speakers at the seminar advised the audience to put off showing expenses until next year because doing so would allow them to take advantage of a new tax law. When Janet returned to the office, she called in her accountant, Frieda O'Riley. She told Frieda to forget about making any adjustments for salaries in the old year so more expenses could be shown in the new year. Frieda told her that putting off these expenses would not follow generally accepted accounting procedures. Janet said she should do it anyway. You make the call. Write your specific recommendations to Frieda.

INTERNET EXERCISES

EX-1. [www.officemax.com] On the website look for "General Information", then click on "Corporate Information". Under "Investor Information" look for the "Fiscal 1999 Form 10K" filed with the Securities and Exchange Commission for 1999. Go to page 39 and find the Consolidated Balance Sheets.

1. Under the caption "other current assets", what accounts do you think could be there that required end-of-period adjustments?

2. If OfficeMax rented the property where its stores are located, and paid the rent in advance for 24 months, how would adjustments have been made in its financial statements?

3. What effect did these adjustments have on (a) Total Assets, and (b) Net Income?

4. Look at "current liabilities" in the balance sheet. Which accounts there seem most susceptible to the adjustment process, and why did you choose these accounts?

EX-2. [www.officemax.com] When you arrive at the website look for the information on "The Affiliate Program". Click on that link and a full explanation of this program will be on your screen. Read through the program information and relate the information to that of the accounting cycle that you learned about in Chapter 4.

Assume that you signed on to this affiliate program with Office Max and placed a link on your home page to that of Office Max. As an entrepreneur, you are now fully immersed in the accounting cycle. Your friend visits your website and while there notices your link to Office Max, and orders office supplies from them while on your site. Because of this, you will receive a commission from Office Max.

Explain how that event triggers the first four steps of the accounting cycle. Include in your discussion events beginning with the transaction and ending with your receipt of cash from Office Max.

CONTINUING PROBLEM

At the end of September, Tony took a complete inventory of his supplies and found the following:

5 dozen $1/4''$ screws at a cost of $8.00 a dozen

2 dozen $1/2''$ screws at a cost of $5.00 a dozen

2 cartons of computer inventory paper at a cost of $14 a carton

3 feet of coaxial cable at a cost of $4.00 per foot

After speaking to his accountant, he found that a reasonable depreciation amount for each of his long-term assets is as follows:

Computer purchased July 5, 200X	Depreciation $33 a month
Office Equipment purchased July 17, 200X	Depreciation $10 a month
Computer Workstations purchased Sept. 17, 200X	Depreciation $20 a month

Tony uses the straight-line method of depreciation and declares no salvage value for any of the assets. If any long-term asset is purchased in the first fifteen days of the month, he will charge depreciation for the full month. If an asset is purchased on the sixteenth of the month, or later, he will not charge depreciation in the month it was purchased.

August and September's rent has now expired.

Assignment:

Use your trial balance from the completed problem in Chapter 3 and the above adjusting information to complete the worksheet for the three months ended September 30, 200X. From the worksheets prepare the financial statements. (See pp. 119–120 in your *Study Guide and Working Papers*.)

Computerized Accounting Application for Chapter 4

PART A: Compound Journal Entries, Adjusting Entries, and Financial Reports

PART B: Backup Procedures

Before starting on this assignment, read and complete the tasks discussed in Parts A, B, and F of the Computerized Accounting appendix at the back of this book and complete the Computerized Accounting Application assignment at the end of Chapter 3.

PART A: Compound Journal Entries, Adjusting Entries, and Financial Reports

1. Click on the Start button. Point to Programs; point to the Peachtree folder and select Peachtree Complete Accounting. Your desktop may have the Peachtree icon allowing for a quicker entrance into the program.

2. Follow the "Open a File" instructions in Part A of the Computerized Accounting appendix at the back of this book to open **The Zell Company**. You may be initially presented with the Peachtree Today window. If so, simply close it. If you are missing the navigation aids at the bottom of the screen, you can activate them under the **Options** menu. Select **View Navigation Aid**. It will remain on until you turn it off. This feature offers an alternative way to access the different features of Peachtree.

3. Click on the **Maintain** menu option. Then select **Company Information**. The program will respond by bringing up a dialogue box allowing the user to edit/add information about the company.

4. Click on the **Company Name** entry field at the end of **The Zell Company**. If it is already highlighted, press the right arrow key. Add a dash and your name **"-Student Name"** to the end of the company name. Click on the OK button to return to the Menu Window.

5. In the Computerized Accounting Application assignment in Chapter 3 you learned how to record journal entries in the General Journal dialog box. Compound journal entries can also be recorded in the General Journal dialog box. The owner of The Zell Company has made an investment in the business consisting of $5,000 in cash and an automobile valued at $12,000. Select **General Journal Entry** from the **Tasks** menu to open the General Journal dialog box. Enter the date 1/1/01 into the **Date** field; press the TAB key; enter "Memo" into the **Reference** field and press TAB.

6. With the flashing insertion point positioned in the **Account No** field, click on the pull down menu (magnifying glass icon) and double click on "1110 Cash". The program will enter the account number and name into the **Account No** field and the flashing insertion point will move to the **Description** field. Enter "Initial investment of cash by owner" into this field and press TAB to move the **Debit** field. Enter "5000" and press TAB three times to move back to the **Account No** field.

7. With the flashing insertion point positioned in the **Account No** field, click on the pull down menu (magnifying glass icon) and double click on "1230 Automobile". Press TAB to move to the **Description** field. This should repeat the information entered in step 6 by default. Press the TAB key again to move to the **Debit** field. Enter "12000". Hit TAB three times to move the cursor back to the **Account No** field. You should now have two debit entries.

8. With the flashing insertion point positioned in the **Account No** field, click on the pull down menu and double click on "3110 Owner's Capital". Press TAB to move to the **Description** field. This should repeat the information entered in step 6 by default. Press the TAB key again twice to move to the **Credit** field.

How to Open the Company Data Files

How to Add Your Name to the Company Name

How to Record a Compound Journal Entry

Enter "17000". Hit TAB twice to move the cursor back to the **Account No** field. This completes the data you need to enter into the General Journal dialog box to record the compound journal entry for the initial investment by the owner. Your screen should look like this:

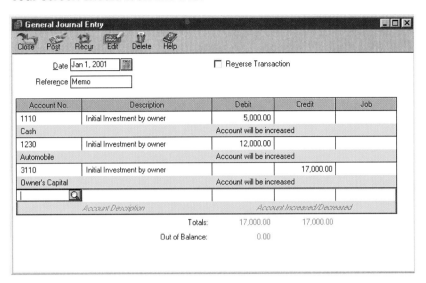

9. Review the compound journal entry for accuracy, noting any errors and making any editing corrections required.

10. After verifying that the compound journal entry is correct, click on the **Post** icon to post this transaction.

Review the Compound Journal Entry

11. Record the following additional journal entries. Enter the **Date** listed for each transaction (you may use the "+" key to advance the date or use the calendar icon next to the field to select the date from a calendar). Enter "Memo" into the **Source** text box for each transaction or accept Peachtree's additional number added to memo by pressing TAB:

Post the Entry

2001

Jan.
- 1   Paid rent for two months in advance, $500.
- 3   Purchased office supplies ($200) and office equipment ($1,100) both on account.
- 9   Billed a customer for fees earned, $2,000.
- 13   Paid telephone bill, $150.
- 20   Owner withdrew $475 from the business for personal use.
- 27   Received $600 for fees earned.
- 31   Paid salaries expense, $800.

Record Additional Transactions

12. After you have posted the additional journal entries, close the General Journal dialogue box and print the following reports accepting all defaults:

  a. General Journal (Totals = 22,825.00)

  b. General Ledger Trial Balance (Totals = 20,900)

13. Review your printed reports. If you have made an error in a posted journal entry, see step 18 from the Chapter 3 assignment.

Display and Print a General Journal and Trial Balance

14. Open the General Journal dialogue box; then record adjusting journal entries based on the following adjustment data (*Date*: 1/31/01; *Reference*: Memo). You may enter all of the adjustments on the same page before posting:

  a. One month's rent has expired.

  b. An inventory shows $25 of office supplies remaining.

  c. Depreciation on office equipment, $50.

  d. Depreciation on automobile, $150.

How to Record Adjusting Journal Entries

15. After you have posted the adjusting journal entries, close the General Journal

dialogue box and print the following reports from the **General Ledger** option of the **Reports** menu:

a. General Journal
b. General Ledger Report
c. General Ledger Trial Balance

16. Review your printed reports. If you have made an error in a posted journal entry, see step 18 from the Chapter 3 assignment.

17. Select the **Financial Statements** option of the **Reports** menu. Select Income Stmnt. An Options dialog box will appear asking you to define the information you want displayed. Press the **OK** button to accept the defaults and display the report on your screen. Your screen will look something like this:

The Zell Company- Student Name
Income Statement
For the One Month Ending January 31, 2001

	Current Month		Year to Date	
Revenues				
Fees Earned	$ 2,600.00	100.00	$ 2,600.00	100.00
Total Revenues	2,600.00	100.00	2,600.00	100.00
Cost of Sales				
Total Cost of Sales	0.00	0.00	0.00	0.00
Gross Profit	2,600.00	100.00	2,600.00	100.00
Expenses				
Rent Expense	250.00	9.62	250.00	9.62
Salaries Expense	800.00	30.77	800.00	30.77
Telephone Expense	150.00	5.77	150.00	5.77
Office Supplies Expense	175.00	6.73	175.00	6.73
Depr. Expense- Office Equip.	50.00	1.92	50.00	1.92
Depr. Expense- Automobile	150.00	5.77	150.00	5.77
Total Expenses	1,575.00	60.58	1,575.00	60.58
Net Income	$ 1,025.00	39.42	$ 1,025.00	39.42

18. The scroll bars can be used to advance the display to view other portions of the report as needed.

19. Click on the **Print** icon to print the Income Statement.

20. Close the Income Statement window. This should return you to the Select a Report dialogue box. Select Balance Sheet. An Options dialogue box will appear asking you to define the information you want displayed. Press the **OK** button to accept the defaults and display the report on your screen. Your screen will look something like this:

The Zell Company- Student Name
Balance Sheet
January 31, 2001

ASSETS

Current Assets		
Cash	$ 3,675.00	
Accounts Receivable	2,000.00	
Prepaid Rent	250.00	
Office Supplies	25.00	
Total Current Assets		5,950.00
Property and Equipment		
Office Equipment	1,100.00	
Accum. Depr- Office Equipment	<50.00>	
Automobile	12,000.00	
Accum. Depr- Automobile	<150.00>	
Total Property and Equipment		12,900.00
Other Assets		
Total Other Assets		0.00
Total Assets		$ 18,850.00

21. Use the scroll bars to advance the display to the Owner's Equity section of the Balance Sheet. Note that the program has included the Statement of Owner's Equity information directly in the Owner's Equity section of the Balance Sheet.

22. Click on Print to print the Balance Sheet and then close the Balance Sheet window.

23. Click on the Menu Window **File** menu; then click on Exit to end the current work session and return to your Windows desktop. Your work will automatically be saved.

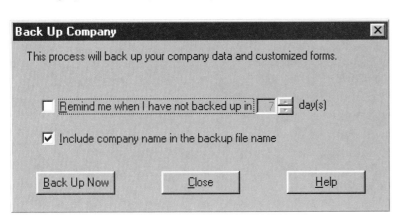

Exit from the Program

PART B: Backup Procedures

Companies that use computerized accounting systems make frequent backup copies of their accounting data for two major reasons:

1. To ensure that they have a copy of the accounting data in case the current data becomes damaged.

2. To permit the printing of historical reports after the Using date has been advanced to a new month.

The methods used to make backup copies of company data files vary greatly. Large companies may backup daily using sophisticated high-speed tape backup devices while small companies may backup weekly on floppy disk using the backup program supplied with their operating system or applications software.

Normally all backup copies of a company's data files are stored on a secondary storage medium separate from the original data files in case the original secondary storage medium becomes damaged. Your instructor will provide specific instructions on where you will store your backup files.

1. If you are not still in Peachtree Complete Accounting 8.0, start the program again and open The Zell Company.

2. While in the Menu Window, select **Back Up** from the **File** menu option. This will bring up the Back Up Company dialogue box as follows:

How to Make a Backup Copy of a Company's Data Files

Back Up Company ☒

This process will back up your company data and customized forms.

☐ Remind me when I have not backed up in [7] day(s)

☑ Include company name in the backup file name

[Back Up Now]   [Close]   [Help]

3. Click on the box next to **Include company name in the backup file name**. This will make Peachtree use Zell in the filename it selects for the backup. You could also use this dialogue box to have Peachtree provide a reminder at periodic intervals but we will leave this option alone for now. Press **Back Up Now** to continue.

4. You are now presented with a Save Back Up for the Zell Company as: dialogue box:

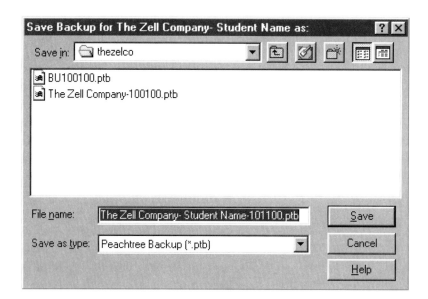

5. Peachtree will save your data files into one compressed .ptb file to any drive or path you specify. It defaults to the location where the program files are stored. Use the **Save in** pull down menu to save the files to a location specified by your instructor. Click **Save** and then **Ok** to complete the process. You now have a back up of your data.

6. For more information on making and using backup copies of a company's data files, see Parts D & E of the Computerized Accounting appendix in the back of this book.

CHAPTER 5

The Accounting Cycle Completed

ADJUSTING, CLOSING, AND POST-CLOSING TRIAL BALANCE

Accountants have traveled far from the old stereotype of the "bean counter" — the grim figure with a green eyeshade who poured over a cloth-bound ledger in a back room. In fact, today's accountants are just as likely to be cozily ensconced at home overlooking the Pacific Ocean while they serve clients as far afield as Boston or Tulsa via the Internet. At least that's what life is like for Lance and Deanna Gildea, founders of an "online" or "virtual" accounting service. The Accounting Department (TAD) is based in both San Diego, CA and Vashon Island, WA.

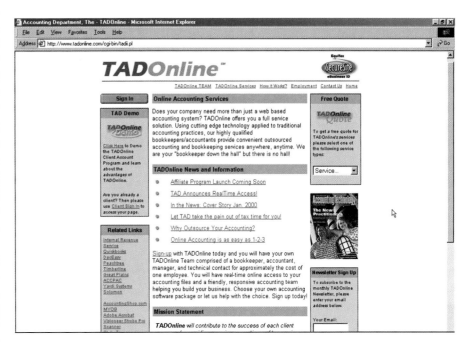

TAD accomplishes the entire accounting cycle using the accounting software of the client's choice. For the first step of the accounting cycle, which you learned in Chapter 3, TAD gets clients to scan their invoices, bank statements and other source documents into their computers. TAD even provides the scanner free-of-charge to high-end clients. Scanned documents are then transmitted to TAD, and within minutes, TAD updates the client's accounts. One of the big benefits of using TAD is that clients get real-time, 24-hour access to their accounting data. They simply use a Web browser to sign in to their home page (prepared by TAD), where they can view, print, and download reports, checks and other information.

In addition to becoming full-service outsourcing operations like TAD, accountants are morphing into accounting software consultants. Harried entrepreneurs or CEOs of small to mid-size companies often don't know how to do more than boot up their MYOB or Quickbooks accounting software. They don't have time to learn how to use it, much less use it correctly. Many also can't afford to pay a full-time accountant to do their books. Enter the new Accounting Software Consultant. These accountants are forming different kinds of relationships with clients, even to the extent of teaching them what has historically been the job of the accountant. For instance, Brian Price of Price and Associates has built a $400,000 business by consulting on low-end or small business accounting software. The typical client for a business like Price's could be anyone from the mom-and-pop business, bringing in $100,000 – $200,000 a year to a $2 million services firm.

Whether you end up being an online accountant or an accounting software consultant, you still need a thorough grounding in accounting basics. After all, in order to teach your clients how to do their books, as Brian Price does, you must be knowledgeable enough to explain each process clearly. In this chapter, as you learn how to complete the accounting cycle and close the books, think how you would explain the process to a client. How will you explain the process of posting **adjusting** and **closing entries** and preparing a **post-closing trial balance?**

_____

Based on: Antoinette Alexander, "Pioneers on the virtual frontier," Accounting Technology, Jan/Feb 2000, pp. 18 – 24. Jeff Stimpson, "The new consultant," _The Practical Accountant,_ September 1999, pp. 325 – 42. Antoinette Alexander, "The Web: Giving life to a new generation," _Accounting Technology,_ March 2000, pp. 26 – 34.

LEARNING OBJECTIVES

▼ Journalizing and posting adjusting entries. (p. 157)
▼ Journalizing and posting closing entries. (p. 160)
▼ Preparing a post-closing trial balance. (p. 171)

> Remember, for ease of presentation we are using a month as the accounting cycle for Clark. In the "real" world, the cycle can be any time period that does not exceed one year.

In Chapters 3 and 4 we completed these steps of the manual accounting cycle for Clark's Word Processing Services:

Step 1: Business transactions occurred and generated source documents.
Step 2: Business transactions were analyzed and recorded into a journal.
Step 3: Information was posted or transferred from journal to ledger.
Step 4: A trial balance was prepared.
Step 5: A worksheet was completed.
Step 6: Financial statements were prepared.

This chapter covers the following steps. This will complete Clark's accounting cycle for the month of May:

Step 7: Journalizing and posting adjusting entries.
Step 8: Journalizing and posting closing entries.
Step 9: Preparing a post-closing trial balance.

Be sure to check inside front cover of text for the ROAD MAP to the accounting cycle.

RECORDING JOURNAL ENTRIES FROM THE WORKSHEET

The information in the worksheet is up to date. The financial reports prepared from that information can give the business's management and other interested parties a good idea of where the business stands as of a particular date. The problem is that the worksheet is an informal report. The information concerning the adjustments has not been placed into the journal, or posted to the ledger accounts. This means that the books are not up to date and ready for the next accounting cycle to begin. For example, the ledger shows $1,200 of prepaid rent (p. 85), but the balance sheet we prepared in Chapter 4 shows an $800 balance. Essentially, the worksheet is a tool for preparing financial statements. Now we must use the adjustment columns of the worksheet as a basis for bringing the ledger up to date. We do this by **adjusting journal entries** (see Figs. 5-1, 5-2). Again, the updating must be done before the next accounting period starts. For Clark's Word Processing Services, the next period begins on June 1.

> At this point, many ledger accounts are not up to date.

Figure 5-2 shows the adjusting journal entries for Clark taken from the adjustments section of the worksheet. Once the adjusting journal entries are posted to the ledger, the accounts making up the financial statements that were prepared from the worksheet will equal the updated ledger. (Keep in mind that this is the same journal we have been using.) Let's look at some simplified T accounts to show how Clark's ledger looked before and after the adjustments were posted (see Adjustments A – D on pp. 158 – 159).

> Purpose of adjusting entries.

Account Titles	Trial Balance Dr.	Trial Balance Cr.	Adjustments Dr.	Adjustments Cr.
Cash	6 1 5 5 00			
Accounts Receivable	5 0 0 0 00			
Office Supplies	6 0 0 00			(A) 5 0 0 00
Prepaid Rent	1 2 0 0 00			(B) 4 0 0 00
Word Processing Equipment	6 0 0 0 00			
Accounts Payable		3 3 5 0 00		
Brenda Clark, Capital		10 0 0 0 00		
Brenda Clark, Withdrawals	6 2 5 00			
Word Processing Fees		8 0 0 0 00		
Office Salaries Expense	1 3 0 0 00		(D) 3 5 0 00	
Advertising Expense	2 5 0 00			
Telephone Expense	2 2 0 00			
	21 3 5 0 00	21 3 5 0 00		
Office Supplies Expense			(A) 5 0 0 00	
Rent Expense			(B) 4 0 0 00	
Depreciation Exp., W.P. Equip.			(C) 8 0 00	
Accum. Deprec., W.P. Equip.				(C) 8 0 00
Salaries Payable				(D) 3 5 0 00
			1 3 3 0 00	1 3 3 0 00

FIGURE 5-1. Journalizing and Posting Adjustments from the Adjustments Section of the Worksheet

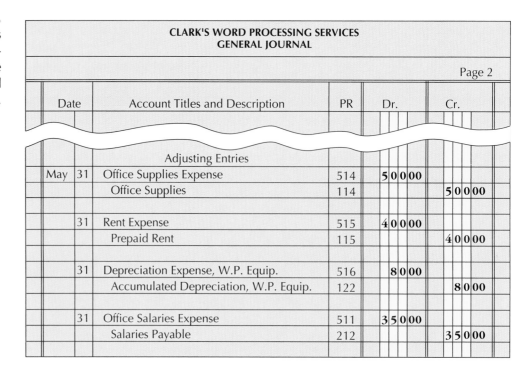

FIGURE 5-2. Adjustments A–D in the adjustments section of the worksheet must be recorded in the journal and posted to the ledger.

CLARK'S WORD PROCESSING SERVICES
GENERAL JOURNAL

Page 2

Date		Account Titles and Description	PR	Dr.	Cr.
		Adjusting Entries			
May	31	Office Supplies Expense	514	50000	
		Office Supplies	114		50000
	31	Rent Expense	515	40000	
		Prepaid Rent	115		40000
	31	Depreciation Expense, W.P. Equip.	516	8000	
		Accumulated Depreciation, W.P. Equip.	122		8000
	31	Office Salaries Expense	511	35000	
		Salaries Payable	212		35000

Adjustment (A)

Before Posting:

Office Supplies 114	Office Supplies Expense 514
600	

After Posting:

Office Supplies 114	Office Supplies Expense 514
600	500	500	

Adjustment (B)

Before Posting:

Prepaid Rent 115	Rent Expense 515
1,200	

After Posting:

Prepaid Rent 115	Rent Expense 515
1,200	400	400	

Adjustment (C)

Before Posting:

Word Processing Equipment 121	Depreciation Expense, W. P. Equipment 516	Accumulated Depreciation, W. P. Equipment 122
6,000		

After Posting:

Word Processing Equipment 121	Depreciation Expense, W. P. Equipment 516	Accumulated Depreciation, W. P. Equipment 122
6,000	80	80

The first adjustment in (C) shows the same balances for Depreciation Expense and Accumulated Depreciation. However, in subsequent adjustments the Accumulated Depreciation balance will keep getting larger, but the debit to Depreciation Expense and the credit to Accumulated Depreciation will be the same. We will see why in a moment.

Adjustment (D)

Before Posting:

Office Salaries Expense 511	Salaries Payable 212
650 650	

After Posting:

Office Salaries Expense 511	Salaries Payable 212
650 650 350	350

LEARNING UNIT 5-1 REVIEW

AT THIS POINT you should be able to

- ▼ Define and state the purpose of adjusting entries. (p. 157)
- ▼ Journalize adjusting entries from the worksheet. (p. 158)
- ▼ Post journalized adjusting entries to the ledger. (p. 158)
- ▼ Compare specific ledger accounts before and after posting of the journalized adjusting entries. (p. 158)

SELF-REVIEW QUIZ 5-1

(The blank forms you need are on pages 121–122 of the *Study Guide and Working Papers*.)

Turn to the worksheet of P. Logan (p. 129) and (1) journalize and post the adjusting entries and (2) compare the adjusted ledger accounts before and after the adjustments are posted. T accounts are provided in your study guide with beginning balances.

Solution to Self-Review Quiz 5-1

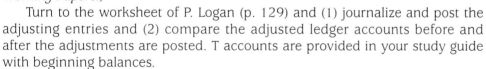

								Page 2
Date		Account Titles and Description	PR	Dr.		Cr.		
		Adjusting Entries						
Dec.	31	Depreciation Expense, Store Equip.	511	1	00			
		Accumulated Depreciation, Store Equip.	122			1	00	
	31	Insurance Expense	516	2	00			
		Prepaid Insurance	116			2	00	
	31	Supplies Expense	514	4	00			
		Store Supplies	114			4	00	
	31	Salaries Expense	512	3	00			
		Salaries Payable	212			3	00	

> *Quiz Tip:* These journalized entries come from the Adjustments column of the worksheet.

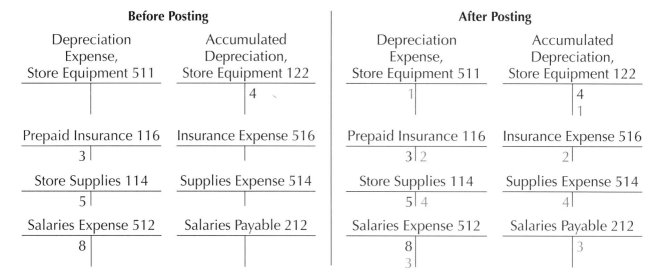

LEARNING UNIT 5-2

JOURNALIZING AND POSTING CLOSING ENTRIES: STEP 8 OF THE ACCOUNTING CYCLE

To make recording of the next period's transactions easier, a mechanical step, called *closing,* is taken by Clark's accountant. Closing is intended to end — or close off — the revenue, expense, and withdrawal accounts at the end of the accounting period. The information needed to complete closing entries will be found in the income statement and balance sheet sections of the worksheet.

To make it easier to understand this process, we will first look at the difference between temporary (nominal) accounts and permanent (real) accounts.

Here is the expanded accounting equation we used in an earlier chapter:

Assets = Liabilities + Capital − Withdrawals + Revenues − Expenses

> Permanent accounts are found on the balance sheet.

Three of the items in that equation — assets, liabilities, and capital — are known as **real** or **permanent accounts** because their balances are carried over from one accounting period to another. The other three items — withdrawals, revenue, and expenses — are called **nominal** or **temporary accounts,** because their balances are not carried over from one accounting period to another. Instead, their "balances" are set at zero at the beginning of each accounting period. This allows us to accumulate new data about revenue, expenses, and withdrawals, in the new accounting period. The process of closing summarizes the effects of the temporary accounts on capital for that period using **closing journal entries.** When the closing process is complete, the accounting equation will be reduced to:

> After all closing entries are journalized and posted to the ledger; all temporary accounts have a zero balance in the ledger. Closing is a step-by-step process.

Assets = Liabilities + Ending Capital

If you look back to page 132 in Chapter 4, you will see that we already calculated the new capital on the balance sheet to be $14,275 for Clark's Word Processing Services. But before the mechanical closing procedures are journalized and posted, the capital account of Clark in the ledger is only $10,000 (Chapter 3, p. 85). Let's look now at how to journalize and post closing entries.

HOW TO JOURNALIZE CLOSING ENTRIES

There are four steps to be performed in journalizing closing entries:

Step 1: Clear the revenue balance and transfer it to Income Summary. **Income Summary** is a temporary account in the ledger needed for closing. At the end of the closing process there will be no balance in Income Summary.

Revenue ⟶ Income Summary

Step 2: Clear the individual expense balances and transfer them to Income Summary.

Expenses ⟶ Income Summary

Step 3: Clear the balance in Income Summary and transfer it to Capital.

Income Summary ⟶ Capital

Step 4: Clear the balance in Withdrawals and transfer it to Capital.

Withdrawals ⟶ Capital

Figure 5-3 is a visual representation of these four steps. Keep in mind that this information must first be journalized and then posted to the appropriate ledger accounts. The worksheet presented in Figure 5-4 on page 162, contains all the figures we will need for the closing process.

Step 1: Clear Revenue Balance and Transfer to Income Summary

Here is what is in the ledger before closing entries are journalized and posted:

Word Processing Fees 411	Income Summary 313
8,000	

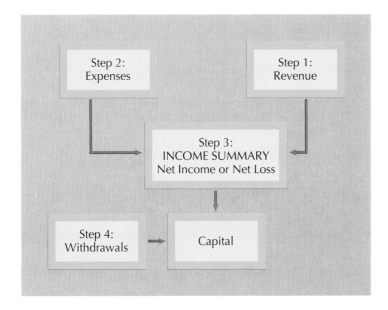

FIGURE 5-3. Four Steps in Journalizing Closing Entries. All numbers can be found on the worksheet in Figure 5-4.

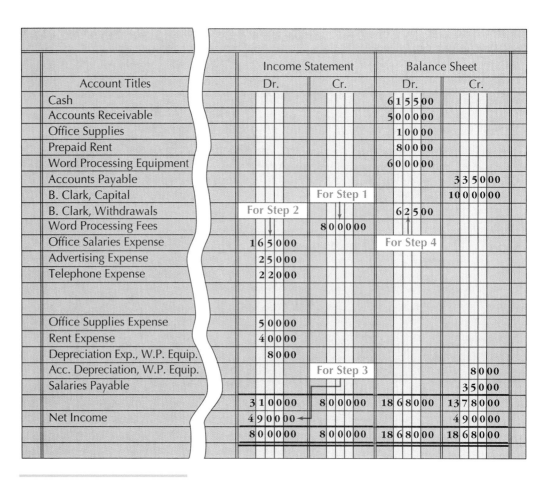

Account Titles	Income Statement Dr.	Income Statement Cr.	Balance Sheet Dr.	Balance Sheet Cr.
Cash			6 1 5 5 00	
Accounts Receivable			5 0 0 0 00	
Office Supplies			1 0 0 00	
Prepaid Rent			8 0 0 00	
Word Processing Equipment			6 0 0 0 00	
Accounts Payable				3 3 5 0 00
B. Clark, Capital		For Step 1		10 0 0 0 00
B. Clark, Withdrawals	For Step 2		6 2 5 00	
Word Processing Fees		8 0 0 0 00	For Step 4	
Office Salaries Expense	1 6 5 0 00			
Advertising Expense	2 5 0 00			
Telephone Expense	2 2 0 00			
Office Supplies Expense	5 0 0 00			
Rent Expense	4 0 0 00			
Depreciation Exp., W.P. Equip.	8 0 00			
Acc. Depreciation, W.P. Equip.		For Step 3		8 0 00
Salaries Payable				3 5 0 00
	3 1 0 0 00	8 0 0 0 00	18 6 8 0 00	13 7 8 0 00
Net Income	4 9 0 0 00			4 9 0 0 00
	8 0 0 0 00	8 0 0 0 00	18 6 8 0 00	18 6 8 0 00

FIGURE 5-4. Closing Figures on the Worksheet

The income statement section on the worksheet above shows that the Word Processing Fees have a credit balance of $8,000. To close or clear this to zero, a debit of $8,000 is needed. But if we add an amount to the debit side, we must also add a credit — so we add $8,000 on the credit side of the Income Summary.

The following is the journalized closing entry for Step 1:

May	31	Word Processing Fees	411	8 0 0 0 00	
		Income Summary	313		8 0 0 0 00

This is what Word Processing Fees and Income Summary should look like in the ledger after the first step of closing entries is journalized and posted:

Word Processing Fees 411		Income Summary 313	
8,000	8,000		8,000
Closing	Revenue		Revenue

Note that the revenue balance is cleared to zero and transferred to Income Summary, a temporary account also located in the ledger.

Step 2: Clear Individual Expense Balances and Transfer the Total to Income Summary

Here is what is in the ledger for each expense before Step 2 of closing entries is journalized and posted. Each expense is listed on the worksheet in the debit column of the income statement section on page 162.

Office Salaries Expense 511	Advertising Expense 512
650	250
650	
350	

Telephone Expense 513	Office Supplies Expense 514
220	500

Rent Expense 515	Depreciation Expense, W. P. Equipment 516
400	80

> Remember, the worksheet is a tool. The accountant realizes that the information about the total of the expenses will be transferred to the Income Summary.

The income statement section of the worksheet lists all the expenses as debits. If we want to reduce each expense to zero, each one must be credited. The following is the journalized closing entry for Step 2:

	31	Income Summary	313	3 1 0 0 00	
		Office Salaries Expense	511		1 6 5 0 00
		Advertising Expense	512		2 5 0 00
		Telephone Expense	513		2 2 0 00
		Office Supplies Expense	514		5 0 0 00
		Rent Expense	515		4 0 0 00
		Depreciation Expense, W.P.Equip.	516		8 0 00

> The $3,100 is the total of the expenses on the worksheet.

The following is what individual expenses and Income Summary should look like in the ledger after Step 2 of closing entries is journalized and posted:

Office Salaries Expense 511		Advertising Expense 512	
650	Closing 1,650	250	Closing 250
650			
350			

Telephone Expense 513		Office Supplies Expense 514	
220	Closing 220	500	Closing 500

Rent Expense 515		Depreciation Expense, W. P. Equipment 516	
400	Closing 400	80	Closing 80

Income Summary 313		
Expenses	Revenue	
Step 2 3,100	8,000	Step 1

Step 3: Clear Balance in Income Summary (Net Income) and Transfer It to Capital

This is how the Income Summary and B. Clark, Capital, accounts look before Step 3:

Income Summary 313		B. Clark, Capital 311	
3,100	8,000		10,000
	4,900		

Note that the balance of Income Summary (Revenue minus Expenses or $8,000 − $3,100) is $4,900. That is the amount we must clear from the Income Summary account and transfer to the B. Clark, Capital, account.

In order to transfer the balance of $4,900 from Income Summary (check the bottom debit column of the income statement section on the worksheet in Fig. 5-4) to Capital, it will be necessary to debit Income Summary for $4,900 (the difference between the revenue and expenses) and credit or increase Capital of B. Clark for $4,900.

This is the journalized closing entry for Step 3:

> The opposite would take place if the business had a net loss.

	31	Income Summary	313	4 9 0 0 00	
		B. Clark, Capital	311		4 9 0 0 00

This is what the Income Summary and B. Clark, Capital, accounts will look like in the ledger after Step 3 of closing entries is journalized and posted:

> At the end of these three steps, the Income Summary has a zero balance. If we had a net loss the end result would be to decrease capital. Entry would be debit capital and credit income summary for the loss.

	Income Summary 313			B. Clark, Capital 311	
Total of Expenses →	3,100	8,000	← Revenue		10,000
Debit to close account →	4,900	4,900	← Net Income		4,900 ← Net Income

Step 4: Clear the Withdrawals Balance and Transfer it to Capital

Next, we must close the withdrawals account. The B. Clark, Withdrawals, and B. Clark, Capital, accounts now look like this:

B. Clark, Withdrawals 312		B. Clark, Capital 311	
625			10,000
			4,900

To bring the Withdrawals account to a zero balance, and summarize its effect on Capital, we must credit Withdrawals and debit Capital.

Remember, withdrawals are a nonbusiness expense and thus not transferred to Income Summary. The closing entry is journalized as follows:

				Dr.	Cr.
	31	B. Clark, Capital	311	625 00	
		B. Clark, Withdrawals	312		625 00

At this point the B. Clark, Withdrawals, and B. Clark, Capital, accounts would look like this in the ledger.

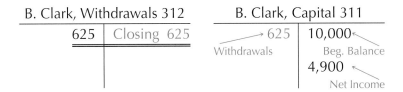

B. Clark, Withdrawals 312

625	Closing 625

B. Clark, Capital 311

→ 625 Withdrawals	10,000 Beg. Balance
	4,900 Net Income

Note that the $10,000 is a beginning balance since no additional investments were made during the period.

Now let's look at a summary of the closing entries.

		SUMMARY OF **CLOSING ENTRIES**			
Date		Account Titles and Description	PR	Dr.	Cr.
		Closing Entries			
200X					
May	31	Word Processing Fees	411	8000 00	
		Income Summary	313		8000 00
	31	Income Summary	313	3100 00	
		Office Salaries Expense	511		1650 00
		Advertising Expense	512		250 00
		Telephone Expense	513		220 00
		Office Supplies Expense	514		500 00
		Rent Expense	515		400 00
		Depreciation Expense, W.P. Equip.	516		80 00
	31	Income Summary	313	4900 00	
		B. Clark, Capital	311		4900 00
	31	B. Clark, Capital	311	625 00	
		B. Clark, Withdrawals	312		625 00

The following is the complete ledger for Clark's Word Processing Services (see Fig. 5-5). Note how the word "adjusting" or "closing" is written in the explanation column of individual ledgers, as for example in the one for Office Supplies. If the goals of closing have been achieved, only permanent accounts will have balances carried to the next accounting period. All temporary accounts should have zero balances.

FIGURE 5-5. Complete Ledger

CLARK'S WORD PROCESSING SERVICES
GENERAL LEDGER

Cash Account No. 111

Date	Explanation	Post. Ref.	Debit	Credit	Balance Debit	Balance Credit
200X May 1		GJ1	10 000 00		10 000 00	
1		GJ1		1 000 00	9 000 00	
1		GJ1		1 200 00	7 800 00	
7		GJ1	3 000 00		10 800 00	
15		GJ1		650 00	10 150 00	
20		GJ1		625 00	9 525 00	
27		GJ2		650 00	8 875 00	
28		GJ2		2 500 00	6 375 00	
29		GJ2		220 00	6 155 00	

Accounts Receivable Account No. 112

Date	Explanation	Post. Ref.	Debit	Credit	Balance Debit	Balance Credit
200X May 22		GJ1	5 000 00		5 000 00	

Office Supplies Account No. 114

Date	Explanation	Post. Ref.	Debit	Credit	Balance Debit	Balance Credit
200X May 3		GJ1	600 00		600 00	
31	Adjusting	GJ2		500 00	100 00	

(Fig. 5.5 cont.)

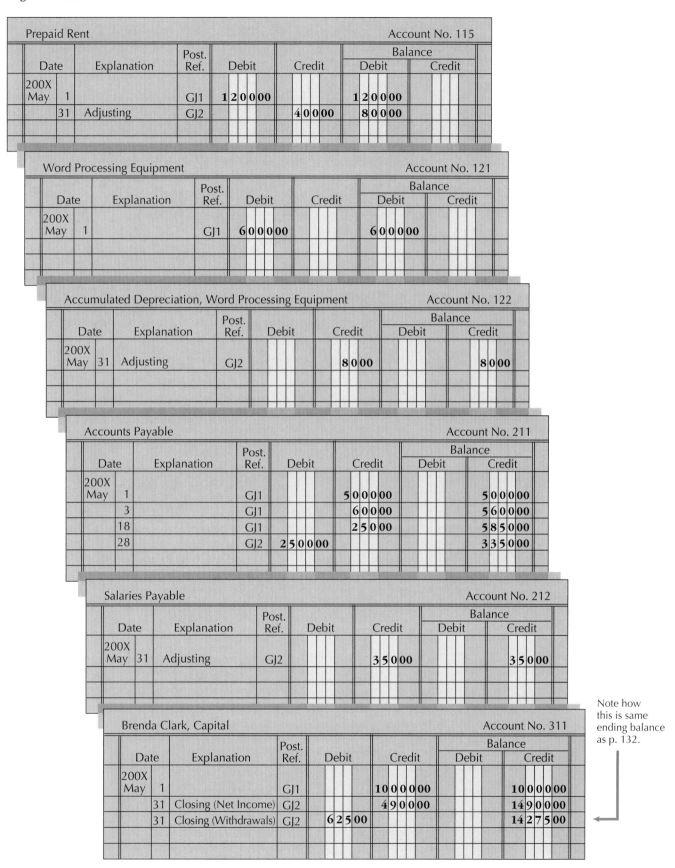

Prepaid Rent   Account No. 115

Date		Explanation	Post. Ref.	Debit	Credit	Balance Debit	Balance Credit
200X May	1		GJ1	1 2 0 0 00		1 2 0 0 00	
	31	Adjusting	GJ2		4 0 0 00	8 0 0 00	

Word Processing Equipment   Account No. 121

Date		Explanation	Post. Ref.	Debit	Credit	Balance Debit	Balance Credit
200X May	1		GJ1	6 0 0 0 00		6 0 0 0 00	

Accumulated Depreciation, Word Processing Equipment   Account No. 122

Date		Explanation	Post. Ref.	Debit	Credit	Balance Debit	Balance Credit
200X May	31	Adjusting	GJ2		8 0 00		8 0 00

Accounts Payable   Account No. 211

Date		Explanation	Post. Ref.	Debit	Credit	Balance Debit	Balance Credit
200X May	1		GJ1		5 0 0 0 00		5 0 0 0 00
	3		GJ1		6 0 0 00		5 6 0 0 00
	18		GJ1		2 5 0 00		5 8 5 0 00
	28		GJ2	2 5 0 0 00			3 3 5 0 00

Salaries Payable   Account No. 212

Date		Explanation	Post. Ref.	Debit	Credit	Balance Debit	Balance Credit
200X May	31	Adjusting	GJ2		3 5 0 00		3 5 0 00

Brenda Clark, Capital   Account No. 311

Date		Explanation	Post. Ref.	Debit	Credit	Balance Debit	Balance Credit
200X May	1		GJ1		1 0 0 0 0 00		1 0 0 0 0 00
	31	Closing (Net Income)	GJ2		4 9 0 0 00		1 4 9 0 0 00
	31	Closing (Withdrawals)	GJ2	6 2 5 00			1 4 2 7 5 00

Note how this is same ending balance as p. 132.

(Fig. 5.5 cont. on p. 168)

(Fig. 5.5 cont.)

Brenda Clark, Withdrawals — Account No. 312

Date	Explanation	Post. Ref.	Debit	Credit	Balance Debit	Balance Credit
200X May 20		GJ1	625 00		625 00	
31	Closing	GJ2		625 00	—	—

Income Summary — Account No. 313

Date	Explanation	Post. Ref.	Debit	Credit	Balance Debit	Balance Credit
200X May 31	Closing (Revenue)	GJ2		8000 00		8000 00
31	Closing (Expenses)	GJ2	3100 00			4900 00
31	Closing (Net Income)	GJ2	4900 00		—	

Word Processing Fees — Account No. 411

Date	Explanation	Post. Ref.	Debit	Credit	Balance Debit	Balance Credit
200X May 7		GJ1		3000 00		3000 00
22		GJ1		5000 00		8000 00
31	Closing	GJ2	8000 00		—	

Office Salaries Expense — Account No. 511

Date	Explanation	Post. Ref.	Debit	Credit	Balance Debit	Balance Credit
200X May 13		GJ1	650 00		650 00	
27		GJ2	650 00		1300 00	
31	Adjusting	GJ2	350 00		1650 00	
31	Closing	GJ2		1650 00	—	—

Advertising Expense — Account No. 512

Date	Explanation	Post. Ref.	Debit	Credit	Balance Debit	Balance Credit
200X May 18		GJ1	250 00		250 00	
31	Closing	GJ2		250 00	—	—

(Fig. 5.5 cont.)

Telephone Expense   Account No. 513

Date		Explanation	Post. Ref.	Debit	Credit	Balance Debit	Balance Credit
200X May	29		GJ2	2 2 0 00		2 2 0 00	
	31	Closing	GJ2		2 2 0 00		

Office Supplies Expense   Account No. 514

Date		Explanation	Post. Ref.	Debit	Credit	Balance Debit	Balance Credit
200X May	31	Adjusting	GJ2	5 0 0 00		5 0 0 00	
	31	Closing	GJ2		5 0 0 00	—	—

Rent Expense   Account No. 515

Date		Explanation	Post. Ref.	Debit	Credit	Balance Debit	Balance Credit
200X May	31	Adjusting	GJ2	4 0 0 00		4 0 0 00	
	31	Closing	GJ2		4 0 0 00	—	—

Depreciation Expense, Word Processing Equipment   Account No. 516

Date		Explanation	Post. Ref.	Debit	Credit	Balance Debit	Balance Credit
200X May	31	Adjusting	GJ2	8 0 00		8 0 00	
	31	Closing	GJ2		8 0 00	—	—

LEARNING UNIT 5-2 REVIEW

AT THIS POINT you should be able to

- ▼ Define closing. (p. 160)
- ▼ Differentiate between temporary (nominal) and permanent (real) accounts. (p. 160)
- ▼ List the four mechanical steps of closing. (p. 161)
- ▼ Explain the role of the Income Summary account. (p. 161)
- ▼ Explain the role of the worksheet in the closing process. (p. 162)

SELF-REVIEW QUIZ 5-2

(The blank forms you need are on pages 123–124 of the *Study Guide and Working Papers*.)

Go to the worksheet for P. Logan on p. 129. Then (1) journalize and post the closing entries and (2) calculate the new balance for P. Logan, Capital.

Solution to Self-Review Quiz 5-2

		Closing Entries			
Dec.	31	Revenue from Clients	410	25 00	
		Income Summary	312		25 00
	31	Income Summary	312	20 00	
		Rent Expense	518		2 00
		Salaries Expense	512		11 00
		Depreciation Expense, Store Equip.	510		1 00
		Insurance Expense	516		2 00
		Supplies Expense	514		4 00
	31	Income Summary	312	5 00	
		P. Logan, Capital	310		5 00
	31	P. Logan, Capital	310	3 00	
		P. Logan, Withdrawals	311		3 00

PARTIAL LEDGER

P. Logan, Capital 310	Revenue from Clients 410	Supplies Expense 514
3 | 14	25 | 25	4 | 4
5		
| 16		

P. Logan, Withdrawals 311	Dep. Exp., Store Equip. 510	Insurance Expense 516
3 | 3	1 | 1	2 | 2

Income Summary 312	Salaries Expense 512	Rent Expense 518
20 | 25	11 | 11	2 | 2
5 | 5		

Quiz Tip: No calculations are needed in the closing process. ALL numbers come from the worksheet. Income summary is a temporary account in the ledger.

P. Logan, Capital		$14
Net Income	$5	
Less Withdrawals	3	
Increase in Capital		2
P. Logan, Capital (ending)		$16

Closing Time

The doorbell rang at 1 A.M. "The cavalry has arrived!" said the giant in the doorway.

"You're a real friend in need, Lou," said Fred gratefully, as he opened the door. "I've been over and over this, and I can't get it to balance. And my monthly closing is due to the business consultant at noon tomorrow! I hate to bother you so late, but . . ." Fred had called Lou Jacobs, his roommate at Dunkin' Donuts University. Lou had ridden hard to the rescue—one and a half hours on the Expressway.

"You look as if you haven't slept in days, Fred," interrupted Lou. "This is what friends are for. Let me at those accounts! You put a pot of coffee on. I'll start with payroll, because you hired someone this month."

Dunkin' Donuts company policy calls for a closing every month, on the last Saturday, before noon. This way comparisons between shops are most valid. Dunkin' Donuts University stresses to all shop owners that the monthly closing grows more difficult as the year progresses. Errors get harder to find, and accuracy becomes ever more critical. There is, unfortunately, no set way to find errors, and even no set place to start. Lou chose payroll because it is one of the largest expenses and because of the new hire.

At 2:45 A.M. Lou woke Fred, who was dozing. "I think I've got it, Fred! It looks like you messed up on adjusting the Salaries Expense account. I looked at the Payroll Register and compared the total to the Salaries Payable account. It didn't match! Remember, you hired Mary Smith on the 26th, so you have to increase *both* the Salaries Expense *and* the Salaries Payable lines, because she has accrued wages. Salaries Expense is a debit and Salaries Payable is a credit. You skipped the payable. Now, if you make this adjusting entry in the General Journal, the worksheet will balance."

Fred's sigh of relief turned into a big yawn, and they both laughed. "Thank heavens *you* stayed awake in Accounting class!," said Fred, with another huge yawn.

Discussion Questions

1. How would the adjustment be made if Mary Smith received $6.50 per hour and worked 25 hours? Where would you place her accrued wages?
2. Fred bought six new uniforms for Mary Smith for $72 each, but forgot to post it to the Uniforms account. How much will the closing balance be off? In what way will it be off?
3. Why does Dunkin' Donuts require a monthly closing from each shop, no matter how much—or little—business each does?

LEARNING UNIT 5-3

THE POST-CLOSING TRIAL BALANCE: STEP 9 OF THE ACCOUNTING CYCLE AND THE CYCLE REVIEWED

PREPARING A POST-CLOSING TRIAL BALANCE

The last step in the accounting cycle is the preparation of a **post-closing trial balance,** which lists only permanent accounts in the ledger and their balances after adjusting and closing entries have been posted. This post-closing trial balance aids in checking whether the ledger is in balance. This checking is important to do because so many new postings go to the ledger from the adjusting and closing process.

The procedure for taking a post-closing trial balance is the same as for a trial balance, except that, since closing entries have closed all temporary accounts, the post-closing trial balance will contain only permanent accounts (balance sheet). Keep in mind, however, that adjustments have occurred.

> The post-closing trial balance helps prove the accuracy of the adjusting and closing process. It contains the true ending figure for capital.

THE ACCOUNTING CYCLE REVIEWED

Table 5-1 below lists the steps we completed in the manual accounting cycle for Clark's Word Processing Services for the month of May:

Insight   Most companies journalize and post adjusting and closing entries only at the end of their fiscal year. A company that prepares interim statements may complete only the first six steps of the cycle. Worksheets allow the preparation of interim reports without the formal adjusting and closing of the books. If this happens, footnotes on the interim report will indicate the extent to which adjusting and closing were completed.

Insight   To prepare a financial statement for April, the data needed can be obtained by subtracting the worksheet accumulated totals from the end of March from the worksheet prepared at the end of April. In this chapter, we chose a month that would show the completion of an entire cycle for Clark's Word Processing Services.

Remember no worksheet is needed in a computerized cycle.

TABLE 5-1   STEPS OF THE MANUAL ACCOUNTING CYCLE

Steps	Explanation
1. Business transactions occur and generate source documents.	Cash register tape, sales tickets, bills, checks, payroll cards.
2. Analyze and record business transactions into a journal.	Called journalizing.
3. Post or transfer information from journal to ledger.	Copying the debits and credits of the journal entries into the ledger accounts.
4. Prepare a trial balance.	Summarizing each individual ledger account and listing those accounts to test for mathematical accuracy in recording transactions.
5. Prepare a worksheet.	A multicolumn form that summarizes accounting information to complete the accounting cycle.
6. Prepare financial statements.	Income statement, statement of owner's equity, and balance sheet.
7. Journalize and post adjusting entries.	Use figures in the adjustment columns of worksheet.
8. Journalize and post closing entries.	Use figures in the income statement and balance sheet sections of worksheet.
9. Prepare a post-closing trial balance.	Prove the mathematical accuracy of the adjusting and closing process of the accounting cycle.

LEARNING UNIT 5-3 REVIEW

AT THIS POINT you should be able to

▼ Prepare a post-closing trial balance. (p. 171)
▼ Explain the relationship of interim statements to the accounting cycle. (p. 172)

SELF-REVIEW QUIZ 5-3

(The blank forms you need are on page 124 of the *Study Guide and Working Papers*.)

From the ledger on page 166, prepare a post-closing trial balance.

Solution to Self-Review Quiz 5-3

CLARK'S WORD PROCESSING SERVICES POST-CLOSING TRIAL BALANCE MAY 31, 200X		
	Dr.	Cr.
Cash	6 1 5 5 00	
Accounts Receivable	5 0 0 0 00	
Office Supplies	1 0 0 00	
Prepaid Rent	8 0 0 00	
Word Processing Equipment	6 0 0 0 00	
Accumulated Depreciation, Word Processing Equip.		8 0 00
Accounts Payable		3 3 5 0 00
Salaries Payable		3 5 0 00
Brenda Clark, Capital		14 2 7 5 00
Totals	18 0 5 5 00	18 0 5 5 00

Quiz Tip: The post-closing trial balance contains only permanent accounts because all temporary accounts have been closed. All temporary accounts are summarized in the capital account.

COMPREHENSIVE DEMONSTRATION PROBLEM WITH SOLUTION TIPS

(The blank forms you need are on pages 125–133 of the *Study Guide and Working Papers.*)

From the following transactions for Rolo Co. complete the entire accounting cycle. The Chart of Accounts includes:

Assets		Owner's Equity	
111	Cash	311	Rolo Kern, Capital
112	Accounts Receivable	312	Rolo Kern, Withdrawals
114	Prepaid Rent	313	Income Summary
115	Office Supplies	**Revenue**	
121	Office Equipment	411	Fees Earned
122	Accumulated Depreciation, Office Equipment	**Expenses**	
Liabilities		511	Salaries Expense
211	Accounts Payable	512	Advertising Expense
212	Salaries Payable	513	Rent Expense
		514	Office Supplies Expense
		515	Depreciation Expense, Office Equipment

We will use unusually small numbers to simplify calculation and emphasize the theory.

200X
Jan.
1 Rolo Kern invested $1,200 cash and $100 of office equipment to open Rolo Co.
1 Paid rent for three months in advance, $300
4 Purchased office equipment on account, $50
6 Bought office supplies for cash, $40
8 Collected $400 for services rendered
12 Rolo paid his home electric bill from the company checkbook, $20
14 Provided $100 worth of services to clients who will not pay till next month
16 Paid salaries, $60
18 Advertising bill received for $70 but will not be paid until next month

Adjustment Data on January 31

a.	Supplies on hand	$6
b.	Rent Expired	$100
c.	Depreciation, Office Equipment	$20
d.	Salaries Accrued	$50

Solutions to Demonstration Problem

JOURNALIZING TRANSACTIONS AND POSTING TO LEDGER, ROLO COMPANY

General Journal					Page 1
Date	Account Titles and Description	PR	Dr.	Cr.	
200X Jan 1	Cash	111	1 2 0 0 00		
	Office Equipment	121	1 0 0 00		
	R. Kern, Capital	311		1 3 0 0 00	
	Initial Investment				
1	Prepaid Rent	114	3 0 0 00		
	Cash	111		3 0 0 00	
	Rent Paid in Advance—3 mos.				
4	Office Equipment	121	5 0 00		
	Accounts Payable	211		5 0 00	
	Purchased Equipment on Account				
6	Office Supplies	115	4 0 00		
	Cash	111		4 0 00	
	Supplies purchased for cash				
8	Cash	111	4 0 0 00		
	Fees Earned	411		4 0 0 00	
	Services rendered				
12	R. Kern, Withdrawals	312	2 0 00		
	Cash	111		2 0 00	
	Personal payment of a bill				
14	Accounts Receivable	112	1 0 0 00		
	Fees Earned	411		1 0 0 00	
	Services rendered on account				
16	Salaries Expense	511	6 0 00		
	Cash	111		6 0 00	
	Paid salaries				
18	Advertising Expense	512	7 0 00		
	Accounts Payable	211		7 0 00	
	Advertising bill, but not paid				

Solution Tips to Journalizing and Posting Transactions

Jan 1	Cash	Asset	↑	Dr.	$1,200
	Office Equipment	Asset	↑	Dr.	$ 100
	R. Kern, Capital	Capital	↑	Cr.	$1,300

2	Prepaid Rent	Asset	↑	Dr.	$ 300
	Cash	Asset	↓	Cr.	$ 300

| 4 | Office Equipment | Asset | ↑ | Dr. | $ 50 |
| | Accounts Payable | Liability | ↑ | Cr. | $ 50 |

| 6 | Office Supplies | Asset | ↑ | Dr. | $ 40 |
| | Cash | Asset | ↓ | Cr. | $ 40 |

| 8 | Cash | Asset | ↑ | Dr. | $ 400 |
| | Fees Earned | Revenue | ↑ | Cr. | $ 400 |

| 12 | R. Kern, Withdrawals | Withdrawals | ↑ | Dr. | $ 20 |
| | Cash | Asset | ↓ | Cr. | $ 20 |

| 14 | Accounts Receivable | Asset | ↑ | Dr. | $ 100 |
| | Fees Earned | Revenue | ↑ | Cr. | $ 100 |

| 16 | Salaries Expense | Expense | ↑ | Dr. | $ 60 |
| | Cash | Asset | ↓ | Cr. | $ 60 |

| 18 | Advertising Expense | Expense | ↑ | Dr. | $ 70 |
| | Accounts Payable | Liability | ↑ | Cr. | $ 70 |

Note All account titles come from the chart of accounts. When journalizing, the PR column of the general journal is blank. It is in the posting process that we update the ledger. The PR column in the ledger accounts tells us from what journal page the information came. After the title in ledger is posted to, we fill in the PR column of the journal telling us to what account number the information was transferred.

COMPLETING THE WORKSHEET

See worksheet on page 177.

Solution Tips to the Trial Balance and Completion of the Worksheet

After the posting process is complete from the journal to the ledger, we take the ending balance in each account and prepare a Trial Balance on the worksheet. If a title has no balance, it is not listed on the trial balance. New titles on the worksheet will be added below as needed.

ROLO CO
WORKSHEET
FOR MONTH ENDED JANUARY 31, 200X

Account Titles	Trial Balance Dr.	Trial Balance Cr.	Adjustments Dr.	Adjustments Cr.	Adjusted Trial Balance Dr.	Adjusted Trial Balance Cr.	Income Statement Dr.	Income Statement Cr.	Balance Sheet Dr.	Balance Sheet Cr.
Cash	118000				118000				118000	
Accounts Receivable	10000				10000				10000	
Prepaid Rent	30000			(B) 10000	20000				20000	
Office Supplies	4000			(A) 3400	600				600	
Office Equipment	15000				15000				15000	
Accounts Payable		12000				12000				12000
R. Kern, Capital		130000				130000				130000
R. Kern, Withdrawals	2000				2000				2000	
Fees Earned		50000				50000		50000		
Salaries Expense	6000		(D) 5000		11000		11000			
Advertising Expense	7000				7000		7000			
	192000	192000								
Office Supplies Expense			(A) 3400		3400		3400			
Rent Expense			(B) 10000		10000		10000			
Depr. Exp., Office Equip.			(C) 2000		2000		2000			
Acc. Dep., Office Equip.				(C) 2000		2000				2000
Salaries Payable				(D) 5000		5000				5000
			20400	20400	199000	199000	33400	50000	165600	149000
Net Income							16600			16600
							50000	50000	165600	165600

ADJUSTMENTS

On hand of $6 is not the Adjustment. Need to calculate amount used up.	**Office Supplies Expense**	**Expense**	↑	**Dr.**	$ 34	($40 − $6)
	Office Supplies	**Asset**	↓	**Cr.**	$ 34	

Expired.	**Rent Expense**	**Expense**	↑	**Dr.**	$100
	Prepaid Rent	**Asset**	↓	**Cr.**	$100

Do not touch original cost of equipment.	**Depr. Exp., Office Equip.**	**Expense**	↑	**Dr.**	$ 20
	Accum. Dep., Office Equip.	**Contra-Asset**	↑	**Cr.**	$ 20

Owed but not paid.	**Salaries Expense**	**Expense**	↑	**Dr.**	$ 50
	Salaries Payable	**Liability**	↑	**Cr.**	$ 50

Note This information is on the worksheet but has *not* been updated in the ledger. (This will happen when we journalize and post adjustments at end of cycle.)

Note that the last four columns of the worksheet come from numbers on the Adjusted Trial Balance.

We move the Net Income of $166 to the Balance Sheet credit column since the capital figure is the old one on the worksheet.

PREPARING THE FORMAL FINANCIAL STATEMENTS

ROLO CO.
INCOME STATEMENT
FOR MONTH ENDED JANUARY 31, 200X

Revenue:			
Fees Earned			$ 5 0 0 00
Operating Expenses			
Salaries Expense	$ 1 1 0 00		
Advertising Expense	7 0 00		
Office Supplies Expense	3 4 00		
Rent Expense	1 0 0 00		
Depreciation Expense, Office Equipment	2 0 00		
Total Operating Expenses		3 3 4 00	
Net Income		$ 1 6 6 00	

ROLO CO.
STATEMENT OF OWNER'S EQUITY
FOR MONTH ENDED JANUARY 31, 200X

R. Kern, Capital, January 1, 200X			$ 1 3 0 0 00
Net Income for January	$ 1 6 6 00		
Less Withdrawals for January	2 0 00		
Increase in Capital		1 4 6 00	
R. Kern, Capital, January 31, 200X		$ 1 4 4 6 00	

ROLO CO.
BALANCE SHEET
JANUARY 31, 200X

Assets			Liabilities & Owner's Equity		
Cash		$1 1 8 0 00	Liabilities		
Accounts Receivable		1 0 0 00	Accounts Payable	$1 2 0 00	
Prepaid Rent		2 0 0 00	Salaries Payable	5 0 00	
Office Supplies		6 00	Total Liabilities		$ 1 7 0 00
Office Equipment	$1 5 0 00		Owner's Equity		
Less Accum. Depr.	2 0 00	1 3 0 00	R. Kern, Capital		1 4 4 6 00
			Total Liabilities &		
Total Assets		$1 6 1 6 00	Owner's Equity		$1 6 1 6 00

Solution Tips to Preparing the Financial Statements

The statements are prepared from the worksheet. (Many of the ledger accounts are not up to date.) The Income Statement lists revenue and expenses. The net income figure of $166 is used to update the Statement of Owner's Equity. The Statement of Owner's Equity calculates a new figure for Capital, $1,446 (Beginning Capital + Net Income − Withdrawals). This new figure is then listed on the Balance Sheet (Assets, Liabilities, and a new figure for Capital).

JOURNALIZING AND POSTING ADJUSTING AND CLOSING ENTRIES

See journal at top of page 180.

Solution Tips to Journalizing and Posting Adjusting and Closing Entries

ADJUSTMENTS

The adjustments from the worksheet are journalized (same journal) and posted to the ledger. Now ledger accounts will be brought up to date. Remember, we have already prepared the financial statements from the worksheet. Our goal now is to get the ledger up to date.

CLOSING

Note Income Summary is a temporary account located in the ledger.

Goals:

1. Wipe out all temporary accounts in the ledger to zero balances.
2. Get a new figure for capital in the ledger.

General Journal						Page 2
Date		Account Titles and Description	PR	Dr.	Cr.	
		ADJUSTING ENTRIES				
Jan.	31	Office Supplies Expense	514	3 4 00		
		Office Supplies	115		3 4 00	
	31	Rent Expense	513	1 0 0 00		
		Prepaid Rent	114		1 0 0 00	
	31	Depr. Expense, Office Equipment	515	2 0 00		
		Accum. Depr., Office Equip.	122		2 0 00	
	31	Salaries Expense	511	5 0 00		
		Salaries Payable	212		5 0 00	
		CLOSING ENTRIES				
	31	Fees Earned	411	5 0 0 00		
		Income Summary	313		5 0 0 00	
	31	Income Summary	313	3 3 4 00		
		Salaries Expense	511		1 1 0 00	
		Advertising Expense	512		7 0 00	
		Office Supplies Expense	514		3 4 00	
		Rent Expense	513		1 0 0 00	
		Depr. Expense, Office Equip.	515		2 0 00	
	31	Income Summary	313	1 6 6 00		
		R. Kern, Capital	311		1 6 6 00	
	31	R. Kern, Capital	311	2 0 00		
		R. Kern, Withdrawals	312		2 0 00	

Step 1 →
Step 2 →
Closing
Step 3 →
Step 4 →

Where do I get my information for closing?

STEPS IN THE CLOSING PROCESS

Step 1: Close revenue to Income Summary.

Step 2: Close individual expenses to Income Summary.

Step 3: Close balance of Income Summary to capital. (This really is the net income figure on the worksheet.)

Step 4: Close balance of withdrawals to capital.

All the journal closing entries (no new calculations needed since all figures are on the worksheet) are posted. The result in the ledger is that all temporary accounts have a zero balance.

Cash					111
				Balance	
Date	PR	Dr.	Cr.	Dr.	Cr.
1/1	GJ1	1,200		1,200	
1/1	GJ1		300	900	
1/6	GJ1		40	860	
1/8	GJ1	400		1,260	
1/12	GJ1		20	1,240	
1/16	GJ1		60	1,180	

Accounts Receivable					112
				Balance	
Date	PR	Dr.	Cr.	Dr.	Cr.
1/14	GJ1	100		100	

Prepaid Rent					114
				Balance	
Date	PR	Dr.	Cr.	Dr.	Cr.
1/1	GJ1	300		300	
1/31Adj.	GJ2		100	200	

Office Supplies					115
				Balance	
Date	PR	Dr.	Cr.	Dr.	Cr.
1/6	GJ1	40		40	
1/31Adj	GJ2		34	6	

Office Equipment					121
				Balance	
Date	PR	Dr.	Cr.	Dr.	Cr.
1/1	GJ1	100		100	
1/4	GJ1	50		150	

Accumulated Depreciation, Equipment					122
				Balance	
Date	PR	Dr.	Cr.	Dr.	Cr.
1/31Adj.	GJ2		20		20

Accounts Payable					211
				Balance	
Date	PR	Dr.	Cr.	Dr.	Cr.
1/4	GJ1		50		50
1/18	GJ1		70		120

Salaries Payable					212
				Balance	
Date	PR	Dr.	Cr.	Dr.	Cr.
1/31Adj.	GJ2		50		50

Rolo Kern, Capital					311
				Balance	
Date	PR	Dr.	Cr.	Dr.	Cr.
1/1	GJ1		1,300		1,300
1/31Clos.	GJ2		166		1,466
1/31Clos.	GJ2	20			1,446

Rolo Kern, Withdrawals					312
				Balance	
Date	PR	Dr.	Cr.	Dr.	Cr.
1/12	GJ1	20		20	
1/31Clos.	GJ2		20	—	

Income Summary					313
				Balance	
Date	PR	Dr.	Cr.	Dr.	Cr.
1/31Clos.	GJ2		500		500
1/31Clos.	GJ2	334			166
1/31Clos.	GJ2	166		—	

(General Ledger cont. on p. 182)

Fees Earned					411
Date	PR	Dr.	Cr.	Balance Dr.	Balance Cr.
1/8	GJ1		400		400
1/14	GJ1		100		500
1/31 Clos.	GJ2	500			—

Rent Expense					513
Date	PR	Dr.	Cr.	Balance Dr.	Balance Cr.
1/31 Adj.	GJ2	100		100	
1/31 Clos.	GJ2		100	—	

Salaries Expense					511
Date	PR	Dr.	Cr.	Balance Dr.	Balance Cr.
1/16	GJ1	60		60	
1/31 Adj.	GJ2	50		110	
1/31 Clos.	GJ2		110	—	

Office Supplies Expense					514
Date	PR	Dr.	Cr.	Balance Dr.	Balance Cr.
1/31 Adj.	GJ2	34		34	
1/31 Clos.	GJ2		34	—	

Advertising Expense					512
Date	PR	Dr.	Cr.	Balance Dr.	Balance Cr.
1/18	GJ1	70		70	
1/31 Clos.	GJ2		70	—	

Depreciation Expenses Office Equipment					515
Date	PR	Dr.	Cr.	Balance Dr.	Balance Cr.
1/31 Adj.	GJ2	20		20	
1/31 Clos.	GJ2		20	—	

These are all permanent accounts.

ROLO CO.
POST-CLOSING TRIAL BALANCE
JANUARY 31, 200X

	Dr.	Cr.
Cash	1 1 8 0 00	
Accounts Receivable	1 0 0 00	
Prepaid Rent	2 0 0 00	
Office Supplies	6 00	
Office Equipment	1 5 0 00	
Accum. Dep., Office Equipment		2 0 00
Accounts Payable		1 2 0 00
Salaries Payable		5 0 00
R. Kern, Capital		1 4 4 6 00
TOTAL	1 6 3 6 00	1 6 3 6 00

Solution Tips for the Post-Closing Trial Balance

The Post-Closing Trial Balance is a list of the ledger *after* adjusting and closing entries have been completed. Note the figure for capital $1,446 is the new figure.

Beginning Capital	$1,300
+ Net Income	166
− Withdrawals	20
= Ending Capital	$1,446

Next accounting period we will enter new amounts in the Revenues, Expenses, and Withdrawal accounts. For now, the post-closing trial balance is only made up of permanent accounts.

SUMMARY OF KEY POINTS

Learning Unit 5-1

1. After formal financial statements have been prepared, the ledger has still not been brought up to date.
2. Information for journalizing adjusting entries comes from the adjustments section of the worksheet.

Learning Unit 5-2

1. Closing is a mechanical process that aids the accountant in recording transactions for the next period.
2. Assets, liabilities, and capital are permanent (real) accounts; their balances are carried over from one accounting period to another. Withdrawals, revenue, and expenses are temporary (nominal) accounts; their balances are *not* carried over from one accounting period to another.
3. Income Summary is a temporary account in the general ledger and does not have a normal balance. It will summarize revenue and expenses and transfer the balance to capital. Withdrawals do not go into Income Summary, because they are *not* business expenses.
4. All information for closing can be obtained from the worksheet or ledger.
5. When closing is complete, all temporary accounts in the ledger will have a zero balance, and all this information will be updated in the capital account.
6. Closing entries are usually done only at year end. Interim reports can be prepared from worksheets that are prepared monthly, quarterly, etc.

Learning Unit 5-3

1. The post-closing trial balance is prepared from the ledger accounts after the adjusting and closing entries have been posted.
2. The accounts on the post-closing trial balance are all permanent titles.

KEY TERMS

Adjusting journal entries   Journal entries that are needed in order to update specific ledger accounts to reflect correct balances at the end of an accounting period.

Closing journal entries   Journal entries that are prepared to (a) reduce or clear all temporary accounts to a zero balance, or (b) update capital to a new balance.

Income Summary   A temporary account in the ledger that summarizes revenue and expenses and transfers its balance (net income or net loss) to capital. Does not have a normal balance.

Permanent accounts (real)   Accounts whose balances are carried over to the next accounting period. Examples: assets, liabilities, capital.

Post-closing trial balance   The final step in the accounting cycle that lists only permanent accounts in the ledger and their balances after adjusting and closing entries have been posted.

Temporary accounts (nominal)   Accounts whose balances at end of an accounting period are not carried over to the next accounting period. These accounts—revenue, expenses, withdrawals—help summarize a new or ending figure for capital to begin the next accounting period. Keep in mind that Income Summary is also a temporary account.

BLUEPRINT OF CLOSING PROCESS FROM THE WORKSHEET

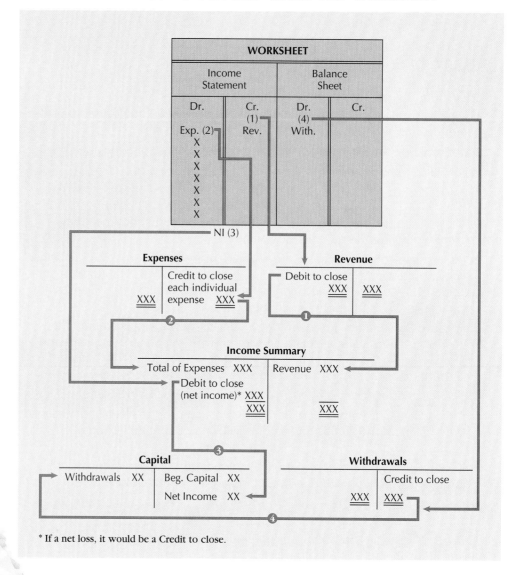

* If a net loss, it would be a Credit to close.

THE CLOSING STEPS

1. Close revenue balance to Income Summary.
2. Close each *individual* expense and transfer *total* of all expenses to Income Summary.
3. Transfer balance in Income Summary (Net Income or Net Loss) to Capital.
4. Close Withdrawals to Capital.

QUESTIONS, MINI EXERCISES, EXERCISES, AND PROBLEMS

Discussion Questions

1. When a worksheet is completed, what balances are found in the general ledger?
2. Why must adjusting entries be journalized even though the formal statements have already been prepared?

3. "Closing slows down the recording of next year's transactions." Defend or reject this statement with supporting evidence.

4. What is the difference between temporary and permanent accounts?

5. What are the two major goals of the closing process?

6. List the four steps of closing.

7. What is the purpose of Income Summary and where is it located?

8. How can a worksheet aid the closing process?

9. What accounts are usually listed on a post-closing trial balance?

10. Closing entries are always prepared once a month. Agree or disagree. Why?

Mini Exercises

(The blank forms you need are on pages 135–136 of the *Study Guide and Working Papers*.)

Journalizing and Posting Adjusting Entries

1. Post the following Adjusting Entries (be sure to cross-reference back to Journal) that came from the Adjustment columns of the worksheet.

Ledger Accounts Before Adjusting Entries Posted

Prepaid Insurance 115	Insurance Expense 510
12	

Store Supplies 116	Dep. Exp., Store Equip. 512
15	

Acc. Dep., Store Equip. 119	Supplies Expense 514
12	

Salaries Payable 210	Salaries Expense 516
	7

	General Journal				Page 3	
Date	Account Titles and Description	PR	Dr.		Cr.	
Dec. 31	Insurance Expense		4 00			
	Prepaid Insurance				4 00	
31	Supplies Expense		3 00			
	Store Supplies				3 00	
31	Depr. Exp., Store Equipment		7 00			
	Accum. Depr., Store Equipment				7 00	
31	Salaries Expense		4 00			
	Salaries Payable				4 00	

Steps of Closing and Journalizing Closing Entries

2.

Worksheet			
IS		BS	
Dr. (2)	Cr. Rev. (1)	Dr. Withd.	Cr. (4)
E X P E N S E S			

NI (3)

Goals of Closing:

1. Temporary accounts in the ledger should have a zero balance.
2. New figure for capital in closing.

Note All closing can be done from the worksheet. Income Summary is a temporary account in the ledger.

From the above worksheet explain the four steps of closing. Keep in mind that each *individual* expense normally would be listed in the closing process.

Journalizing Closing Entries

3. From the following accounts, journalize the closing entries (assume December 31).

Mel Blanc, Capital 310		Gas Expense 510	
	30	5	

Mel Blanc, Withdr. 312		Advertising Exp. 512	
6		4	

Income Summary 314		Dep. Exp., Taxi 516	
		6	

Taxi Fees 410	
	18

Posting to Income Summary

4. Draw a T Account of Income Summary and post to it all entries from Question 3 that affect it. Is Income Summary a temporary or permanent account?

Posting to Capital

5. Draw a T Account for Mel Blanc, Capital, and post to it all entries from Question 3 that affect it. What is the final balance of the capital account?

Exercises

(The blank forms you need are on pages 137–139 of the *Study Guide and Working Papers*.)

5-1. From the adjustments section of a worksheet presented here, prepare adjusting journal entries for end of December.

Journalize adjusting entries.

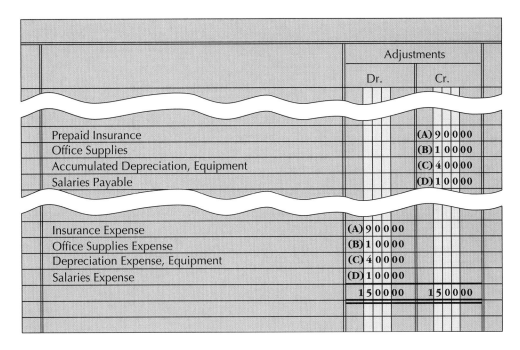

	Adjustments	
	Dr.	Cr.
Prepaid Insurance		(A) 9 0 0 00
Office Supplies		(B) 1 0 0 00
Accumulated Depreciation, Equipment		(C) 4 0 0 00
Salaries Payable		(D) 1 0 0 00
Insurance Expense	(A) 9 0 0 00	
Office Supplies Expense	(B) 1 0 0 00	
Depreciation Expense, Equipment	(C) 4 0 0 00	
Salaries Expense	(D) 1 0 0 00	
	1 5 0 0 00	1 5 0 0 00

5-2. Complete the following table by placing an X in the correct column.

	Temporary	Permanent	Will be Closed
Ex. Accounts Receivable		X	
1. Income Summary			
2. Melissa Bryant, Capital			
3. Salary Expense			
4. Melissa Bryant, Withdrawals			
5. Fees Earned			
6. Accounts Payable			
7. Cash			

Temporary vs. permanent accounts.

5-3. From the following T accounts, journalize the four closing entries on December 31, 200X.

Closing entries.

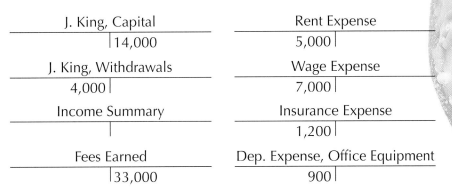

J. King, Capital	
	14,000

Rent Expense	
5,000	

J. King, Withdrawals	
4,000	

Wage Expense	
7,000	

Income Summary	

Insurance Expense	
1,200	

Fees Earned	
	33,000

Dep. Expense, Office Equipment	
900	

5-4. From the following posted T accounts, reconstruct the closing journal entries for December 31, 200X.

Reconstructing closing entries.

M. Foster, Capital			Insurance Expense	
Withdrawals 100	2,000 (Dec. 1)		50	Closing 50
	700 Net income			

M. Foster, Withdrawals		Wage Expense	
100	Closing 100	100	Closing 100

Income Summary			Rent Expense	
Expenses	600	Revenue 1,300	200	Closing 200
	700	Net Income 700		

Salon Fees			Depreciation Expense, Equipment	
Closing	1,300	1,300	250	Closing 250

> Post-closing trial balance.

5-5. From the following accounts (not in order), prepare a post-closing trial balance for Wey Co. on December 31, 200X. **Note:** These balances are **before** closing.

Accounts Receivable	$18,875	Salaries Expense	1,275
Legal Supplies	14,250	P. Wey, Capital	63,450
Office Equipment	59,700	P. Wey, Withdrawals	1,500
Repair Expense	2,850	Legal Fees Earned	12,000
		Accounts Payable	45,000
		Cash	22,000

Group A Problems

(The blank forms you need are on pages 140–157 of the *Study Guide and Working Papers.*)

5A-1. Given the following data for Lou's Consulting Service:

> Review in preparing a worksheet and journalizing adjusting and closing entries.

> Check Figure:
> Net Income $4,600

LOU'S CONSULTING SERVICE
TRIAL BALANCE
JUNE 30, 200X

	Dr.	Cr.
Cash	20 0 0 0 00	
Accounts Receivable	6 5 0 0 00	
Prepaid Insurance	4 0 0 00	
Supplies	1 5 0 0 00	
Equipment	3 0 0 0 00	
Accumulated Depreciation, Equipment		1 9 0 0 00
Accounts Payable		11 0 0 0 00
Lou Dobbs, Capital		12 8 0 0 00
Lou Dobbs, Withdrawals	3 0 0 00	
Consulting Fees Earned		9 0 0 0 00
Salaries Expense	1 4 0 0 00	
Telephone Expense	1 0 0 0 00	
Advertising Expense	6 0 0 00	
	34 7 0 0 00	34 7 0 0 00

Adjustment Data:

a.	Insurance expired	$300.
b.	Supplies on hand	$700.
c.	Depreciation on equipment	$100.
d.	Salaries earned by employees but not to be paid until July	$200.

Your task is to

1. Prepare a worksheet.
2. Journalize adjusting and closing entries.

5A-2. Enter beginning balance in each account in your working papers from the trial balance columns of the worksheet. From the worksheet on page 190, (1) journalize and post adjusting and closing entries after entering beginning balance in each account in the ledger, and (2) prepare from the ledger a post-closing trial balance for the month of March.

> *Journalizing and posting adjusting and closing entries. Preparing a post-closing trial balance.*

5A-3. As the bookkeeper of Pete's Plowing, you have been asked to complete the entire accounting cycle for Pete from the following information:

200X

Jan.
1 Pete invested $7,000 cash and $6,000 worth of snow equipment into the plowing company.
1 Paid rent for three months in advance for garage space, $2,000.
4 Purchased office equipment on account from Ling Corp., $7,200.
6 Purchased snow supplies for $700 cash.
8 Collected $15,000 from plowing local shopping centers.
12 Pete Mack withdrew $1,000 from the business for his own personal use.
20 Plowed North East Co. parking lots, payment not to be received until March, $5,000.
26 Paid salaries to employees, $1,800.
28 Paid Ling Corp. one-half amount owed for office equipment.
29 Advertising bill received from Bush Co. but will not be paid until March, $900.
30 Paid telephone bill, $210.

> *Check Figure:*
> *Post-closing Trial Balance*
> *$3,504*

> *Comprehensive review of the entire accounting cycle, Chapters 1–5.*

> *Check Figure:*
> *Net Income $15,780*

Adjustment Data:

a. Snow supplies on hand $400.

b. Rent expired $600.

c. Depreciation on office equipment $120.
   ($7,200 ÷ 5 yr. = $1,440/12 = $120)

d. Depreciation on snow equipment $100.
   ($6,000 ÷ 5 = $1,200/12 mo. = $100)

e. Accrued salaries $190.

POTTER CLEANING SERVICE
WORKSHEET
FOR MONTH ENDED MARCH 31, 200X

Account Titles	Trial Balance Dr.	Trial Balance Cr.	Adjustments Dr.	Adjustments Cr.	Adjusted Trial Balance Dr.	Adjusted Trial Balance Cr.	Income Statement Dr.	Income Statement Cr.	Balance Sheet Dr.	Balance Sheet Cr.
Cash	40000				40000				40000	
Prepaid Insurance	52000			(A) 18000	34000				34000	
Cleaning Supplies	14400			(B) 10000	4400				4400	
Auto	272000				272000				272000	
Accum. Depr. Auto		86000		(C) 15000		101000				101000
Accounts Payable		22400				22400				22400
B. Potter, Capital		54000				54000				54000
B. Potter, Withdrawals	46000				46000				46000	
Cleaning Fees		468000				468000		468000		
Salaries Expense	144000		(D) 16000		160000		160000			
Telephone Expense	26400				26400		26400			
Advertising Expense	19600				19600		19600			
Gas Expense	16000				16000		16000			
	630400	630400								
Insurance Expense			(A) 18000		18000		18000			
Cleaning Supplies Expense			(B) 10000		10000		10000			
Depr. Expense Auto			(C) 15000		15000		15000			
Salaries Payable				(D) 16000		16000				16000
			59000	59000	661400	661400	265000	468000	396400	193400
Net Income							203000			203000
							468000	468000	396400	396400

Chart of Accounts

Assets
111   Cash
112   Accounts Receivable
114   Prepaid Rent
115   Snow Supplies
121   Office Equipment
122   Accumulated Depreciation,
        Office Equipment
123   Snow Equipment
124   Accumulated Depreciation,
        Snow Equipment

Liabilities
211   Accounts Payable
212   Salaries Payable

Owner's Equity
311   Pete Mack, Capital
312   Pete Mack, Withdrawals
313   Income Summary

Revenue
411   Plowing Fees

Expenses
511   Salaries Expense
512   Advertising Expense
513   Telephone Expense
514   Rent Expense
515   Snow Supplies Expense
516   Depreciation Expense,
        Office Equipment
517   Depreciation Expense,
        Snow Equipment

Group B Problems

(The blank forms you need are on pages 140–157 of the *Study Guide and Working Papers.*)

5B-1.

> MEMO
>
> To: Ron Ear
> From: Sue French
> Re: Accounting Needs

Review in preparing a work-sheet and journalizing and closing entries.

Please prepare ASAP from the following information (attached) (1) a worksheet along with (2) journalized adjusting and closing entries.

Check Figure:
Net Income $3,530

LOU'S CONSULTING SERVICE TRIAL BALANCE JUNE 30, 200X	Dr.	Cr.
Cash	10 15 0 00	
Accounts Receivable	5 0 0 0 00	
Prepaid Insurance	7 0 0 00	
Supplies	3 0 0 00	
Equipment	12 9 5 0 00	
Accumulated Depreciation, Equipment		4 0 0 0 00
Accounts Payable		5 7 5 0 00
L. Dobbs, Capital		15 1 5 0 00
L. Dobbs, Withdrawals	4 0 0 00	
Consulting Fees Earned		5 2 0 0 00
Salaries Expense	4 5 0 0 00	
Telephone Expense	7 0 00	
Advertising Expense	8 0 00	
	30 1 0 0 00	30 1 0 0 00

Adjustment Data:

a. Insurance expired $100.
b. Supplies on hand $20.
c. Depreciation on equipment $200.
d. Salaries earned by employees but not due to be paid until July $490.

5B-2. Enter beginning balance in each account in your working papers from the trial balance columns of the worksheet. From the worksheet on page 193, (1) journalize and post adjusting and closing entries after entering beginning balances in each account in the ledger, and (2) prepare from the ledger a post-closing trial balance at end of March.

5B-3. From the following transactions as well as additional data, please complete the entire accounting cycle for Pete's Plowing (use the chart of accounts on page 191).

200X

Jan.
- 1 To open the business, Pete invested $8,000 cash and $9,600 worth of snow equipment.
- 1 Paid rent for five months in advance, $3,000.
- 4 Purchased office equipment on account from Russell Co., $6,000.
- 6 Bought snow supplies, $350.
- 8 Collected $7,000 for plowing during winter storm emergency.
- 12 Pete paid his home telephone bill from the company checkbook, $70.
- 20 Billed Eastern Freight Co. for plowing fees earned but not to be received until March, $6,500.
- 24 Advertising bill received from Jones Co. but will not be paid until next month, $350.
- 26 Paid salaries to employees, $1,800.
- 28 Paid Russell Co. one-half of amount owed for office equipment.
- 29 Paid telephone bill of company, $165.

Adjustment Data:

a. Snow supplies on hand	$200.
b. Rent expired	$600.
c. Depreciation on office equipment ($6,000/4 yr = $1,500 ÷ 12 = $125)	$125.
d. Depreciation on snow equipment ($9,600 ÷ 2 = $4,800 ÷ 12 = $400)	$400.
e. Salaries accrued	$300.

REAL-WORLD APPLICATIONS

5R-1.

Ann Humphrey needs a loan from the Charles Bank to help finance her business. She has submitted to the Charles Bank the following unadjusted trial balance. As the loan officer, you will be meeting with Ann tomorrow. Could you make some specific written suggestions to Ann regarding her loan report?

Cash in Bank	770	
Accounts Receivable	1,480	
Office Supplies	3,310	
Equipment	7,606	
Accounts Payable		684
A. Humphrey, Capital		8,000
Service Fees		17,350
Salaries	11,240	

Journalizing and posting adjusting and closing entries. Preparing a post-closing trial balance.

Check Figure:
Post-closing Trial Balance
$3,294

Comprehensive review of entire accounting cycle. Review of Chapters 1–5.

Check Figure:
Net Income $9,610

POTTER CLEANING SERVICE
WORKSHEET
FOR MONTH ENDED MARCH 31, 200X

Account Titles	Trial Balance Dr.	Trial Balance Cr.	Adjustments Dr.	Adjustments Cr.	Adjusted Trial Balance Dr.	Adjusted Trial Balance Cr.	Income Statement Dr.	Income Statement Cr.	Balance Sheet Dr.	Balance Sheet Cr.
Cash	172400				172400				172400	
Prepaid Insurance	35000			(A) 20000	15000				15000	
Cleaning Supplies	80000			(B) 60000	20000				20000	
Auto	122000				122000				122000	
Accumulated Depreciation, Auto		66000		(C) 15000		81000				81000
Accounts Payable		67400				67400				67400
B. Potter, Capital		248000				248000				248000
B. Potter, Withdrawals	60000				60000				60000	
Cleaning Fees		370000				370000		370000		
Salaries Expense	200000		(D) 17500		217500		217500			
Telephone Expense	28400				28400		28400			
Advertising Expense	27600				27600		27600			
Gas Expense	26000				26000		26000			
	751400	751400								
Insurance Expense			(A) 20000		20000		20000			
Cleaning Supplies Expense			(B) 60000		60000		60000			
Depreciation Expense, Auto			(C) 15000		15000		15000			
Salaries Payable				(D) 17500		17500				17500
			112500	112500	783900	783900	394500	370000	389400	413900
Net Loss								24500	24500	
							394500	394500	413900	413900

Utilities Expense	842	
Rent Expense	360	
Insurance Expense	280	
Advertising Expense	146	
Totals	26,034	26,034

5R-2.

Janet Smother is the new bookkeeper who replaced Dick Burns, owing to his sudden illness. Janet finds on her desk a note requesting that she close the books and supply the ending capital figure. Janet is upset, since she can only find the following:

a. Revenue and expense accounts all were zero balance.

b. Income Summary

$$14,360 \mid 19,300$$

c. Owner withdrew $8,000.

d. Owner beginning capital was $34,400.

Could you help Janet accomplish her assignment? What written suggestions should Janet make to her supervisor so that this situation will not happen again?

YOU make the call

Critical Thinking/Ethical Case

5R-3.

Todd Silver is the purchasing agent for Moore Co. One of his suppliers, Gem Co., offers Todd a free vacation to France if he buys at least 75 percent of Moore's supplies from Gem Co. Todd, who is angry because Moore Co. has not given him a raise in over a year, is considering the offer. Write your recommendation to Todd.

INTERNET EXERCISES

EX-1. [www.tadonline.com]   At the beginning of your accounting education is a good time to begin formulating your philosophy of how to do accounting work. By studying and learning you are also learning good work habits. The TADOnline website presents a section on "Why Outsource Your Accounting". The discussion presents some good suggestions and may also cause you to reflect on how people choose an accounting or bookkeeping firm.

Use that discussion as a springboard and discuss what factors you believe affect a client's choice for someone to help them with their vital accounting records. TADOnline is not "just around the corner". Is location an important factor in deciding who will do a business's accounting?

EX-2. [www.peachtree.com]; [www.quickbookscom]   Most businesses today are employing some type of computerized accounting system. Some business' requirements are simple, and they use only a general ledger program. Others are much more complex and employ inventory modules, payroll modules, in addition to accounts receivable and accounts payable modules for tracking customer and vendor information.

1. Browse the two websites in this exercise. Compare and contrast the products by looking at information like these suggestions:
   a. What kind of output is available?
   b. How are the input systems similar?
   c. Does the program have an inventory module?
   d. At each site are there different products for different complexities in accounting systems?
   e. What online help is available?
2. Set up a visit to a local accounting firm. In addition to the two sample programs in this exercise ask them what they use in their offices.

CONTINUING PROBLEM

Tony has decided to end the Eldorado Computer Center's first year as of September 30, 200X. Below is an updated chart of accounts.

Assets
1000 Cash
1020 Accounts Receivable
1025 Prepaid Rent
1030 Supplies
1080 Computer Shop Equip.
1081 Accum. Depr. CS Equip.
1090 Office Equipment
1091 Accum. Depr. Office Equip.

Liabilities
2000 Accounts Payable

Owner's Equity
3000 T. Freedman, Capital
3010 T. Freedman, Withdrawals
3020 Income Summary

Revenue
4000 Service Revenue

Expenses
5010 Advertising Expense
5030 Utilities Expense
5050 Supplies Expense
5070 Postage Expense
5090 Depr. Exp. Office Equip.
5020 Rent Expense
5040 Phone Expense
5060 Insurance Expense
5080 Depr. Exp. C.S. Equip.

Assignment:

(See pp. 162–169 in your *Study Guide and Working Papers*.)

1. Journalize the adjusting entries from Chapter 4.
2. Post the adjusting entries to the ledger.
3. Journalize the closing entries.
4. Post the closing entries to the ledger.
5. Prepare a post-closing trial balance.

VALDEZ REALTY

Reviewing the Accounting Cycle TWICE

This comprehensive review problem requires you to complete the accounting cycle for Valdez Realty twice. This will allow you to review Chapters 1–5 while reinforcing the relationships between all parts of the accounting cycle. By completing two cycles, you will see how the ending June balances in the ledger are used to accumulate data in July. (The blank forms you need are on pages 170–190 of the *Study Guide and Working Papers.*)

Take a moment to review ROAD MAP of the accounting cycle on inside front cover of text.

First, let's look at the chart of accounts for Valdez Realty below.

On June 1 Juan Valdez opened a real estate office called Valdez Realty. The following transactions were completed for the month of June:

200X

June

1	Juan Valdez invested $7,000 cash in the real estate agency along with $3,000 of office equipment.
1	Rented office space and paid three months rent in advance, $2,100.
1	Bought an automobile on account, $12,000.
4	Purchased office supplies for cash, $300.
5	Purchased additional office supplies on account, $150.
6	Sold a house and collected a $6,000 commission.
8	Paid gas bill, $22.
15	Paid the salary of the office secretary, $350.
17	Sold a building lot and earned a commission, $6,500. Payment is to be received on July 8.
20	Juan Valdez withdrew $1,000 from the business to pay personal expenses.

(cont. on p. 197)

Valdez Realty
Chart of Accounts

Assets
111   Cash
112   Accounts Receivable
114   Prepaid Rent
115   Office Supplies
121   Office Equipment
122   Accumulated Depreciation, Office Equipment
123   Automobile
124   Accumulated Depreciation, Automobile

Liabilities
211   Accounts Payable
212   Salaries Payable

Owner's Equity
311   Juan Valdez, Capital
312   Juan Valdez, Withdrawals
313   Income Summary

Revenue
411   Commissions Earned

Expenses
511   Rent Expense
512   Salaries Expense
513   Gas Expense
514   Repairs Expense
515   Telephone Expense
516   Advertising Expense
517   Office Supplies Expense
518   Depreciation Expense, Office Equipment
519   Depreciation Expense, Automobile
524   Miscellaneous Expense

21 Sold a house and collected a $3,500 commission.
22 Paid gas bill, $25.
24 Paid $600 to repair automobile.
30 Paid the salary of the office secretary, $350.
30 Paid the June telephone bill, $510.
30 Received advertising bill for June, $1,200. The bill is to be paid on July 2.

Required Work for June:

1. Journalize transactions and post to ledger accounts.

2. Prepare a trial balance in the first two columns of the worksheet and complete the worksheet using the following adjustment data:

   a. One month's rent had expired.

   b. An inventory shows $50 of office supplies remaining.

   c. Depreciation on office equipment, $100.

   d. Depreciation on automobile, $200.

3. Prepare a June income statement, statement of owner's equity, and balance sheet.

4. From the worksheet, journalize and post adjusting and closing entries (p. 3 of journal).

5. Prepare a post-closing trial balance.

During July, Valdez Realty completed these transactions:

200X

July
1 Purchased additional office supplies on account, $700.
2 Paid advertising bill for June.
3 Sold a house and collected a commission, $6,600.
6 Paid for gas expense, $29.
8 Collected commission from sale of building lot on June 17.
12 Paid $300 to send employees to realtors' workshop.
15 Paid the salary of the office secretary, $350.
17 Sold a house and earned a commission of $2,400. Commission to be received on August 10.
18 Sold a building lot and collected a commission of $7,000.
22 Sent a check for $40 to help sponsor a local road race to aid the poor. (This is not to be considered an advertising expense, but it is a business expense.)
24 Paid for repairs to automobile, $590.
28 Juan Valdez withdrew $1,800 from the business to pay personal expenses.
30 Paid the salary of the office secretary, $350.
30 Paid the July telephone bill, $590.
30 Advertising bill for July, $1,400. The bill is to be paid on August 2.

Required Work for July:

1. Journalize transactions in a general journal (p. 4) and post to ledger accounts.

2. Prepare a trial balance in the first two columns of the worksheet and complete the worksheet using the following adjustment data:

   a. One month's rent had expired.

   b. An inventory shows $90 of office supplies remaining.

   c. Depreciation on office equipment, $100.

   d. Depreciation on automobile, $200.

3. Prepare a July income statement, statement of owner's equity, and balance sheet.

4. From the worksheet, journalize and post adjusting and closing entries (p. 6 of journal).

5. Prepare a post-closing trial balance.

Computerized Accounting Application for Valdez Realty Mini Practice Set for Chapter 5

Closing Process and Post-Closing Trial Balance

Before starting on this assignment, read and complete the tasks discussed in Parts A, B, and F of the Computerized Accounting appendix at the back of this book and complete the Computerized Accounting Application assignments for Chapters 3 and 4.

   This comprehensive review problem requires you to complete the accounting cycle for Valdez Realty twice. This will allow you to review Chapters 1–5 while reinforcing the relationships between all parts of the accounting cycle. By completing two cycles, you will see how the ending June balances in the ledger are used to accumulate data in July.

PART A: The June Accounting Cycle

On June 1, Juan Valdez opened a real estate office called Valdez Realty.

> Open the
> Company Data
> Files

1. Click on the Start button. Point to Programs; point to Peachtree folder and select Peachtree Complete Accounting. Your desktop may have the Peachtree icon allowing for a quicker entrance into the program.

2. Follow the "Open a File" instructions in Part A of the Computerized Accounting appendix at the back of this book to open **Valdez Realty**.

3. Click on the **Maintain** menu option. Then select **Company Information**. The program will respond by bringing up a dialogue box allowing the user to edit/add information about the company.

> How to Add Your
> Name to the
> Company Name

4. Click on the **Company Name** entry field at the end of **Valdez Realty.** If it is already highlighted, press the right arrow key. Add a dash and your name "-**Student Name**" to the end of the company name. Click on the OK button to return to the Menu Window.

> Record June
> Transactions

5. Record the following journal entries. Enter the **Date** listed for each transaction (you may use the "+" key to advance the date or use the calendar icon next to the field to select the date from a calendar). Enter "Memo" into the **Source** text box for each transaction or accept Peachtree's additional number added to memo by pressing TAB:

2001

Jun.	1	Juan Valdez invested $7,000 cash in the real estate agency along with $3,000 in office equipment.
	1	Rented office space and paid three months' rent in advance, $2,100.
	1	Bought an automobile on account, $12,000.
	4	Purchased office supplies for cash, $300.
	5	Purchased additional office supplies on account, $150.
	6	Sold a house and collected a $6,000 commission.
	8	Paid gas bill, $22.
	15	Paid the salary of the office secretary, $350.
	17	Sold a building lot and earned a commission, $6,500. Expected receipt 7/8/01.
	20	Juan Valdez withdrew $1,000 from the business to pay personal expenses.
	21	Sold a house and collected a $3,500 commission.
	22	Paid gas bill, $25.

24   Paid $600 to repair automobile.

30   Paid the salary of the office secretary, $350.

30   Paid the June telephone bill, $510.

30   Received advertising bill for June, $1,200. The bill is to be paid on 7/2/01.

6. After you have posted the journal entries, close the General Journal; then print the following reports:

   a. General Journal -(check figure debit = $44,607)

   b. Trial Balance -(check figure debit = $39,350)

Review your printed reports. If you have made an error in a posted journal entry, correct the error before proceeding.

> Print Working Reports

7. Open the General Journal; then record adjusting journal entries based on the following adjustment data using "Adj" in the reference field:

   a. One month's rent has expired.

   b. An inventory shows $50 of office supplies remaining.

   c. Depreciation on office equipment, $100.

   d. Depreciation on automobile, $200.

> Record June Adjusting Entries

8. After you have posted the adjusting journal entries, close the General Journal then print the following reports accepting all defaults offered by Peachtree:

   a. General Journal -(check figure debit = $46,007)

   b. Trial Balance -(check figure debit = $39,650)

   c. General Ledger Report -(check figure cash = $11,243)

   d. Income Statement -(Net Income = $11,543)

   e. Balance Sheet -(Total Capital = $20,543)

> Print Final Statements

Review your printed reports. If you have made an error in a posted journal entry, use the procedures detailed in step 18 from chapter 3 to make any necessary corrections. Reprint all reports if corrections are made.

9. Computerized Accounting systems maintain all of it's input in compartments called periods. Some systems identify these periods with the name of the month or with a simple numeric designation such as 1, 2, 3, et. al. Peachtree currently has Valdez Realty in Period 6, the June period. You can see this in the status bar at the bottom of the screen. This is because Valdez has elected to use the calendar year for his Fiscal year. We will need to change the current period to the July period prior to inputting the July transactions in part B of this workshop. You must always tell Peachtree to move to the next accounting period when starting on the transactions for a new month. This process is the equivalent of "Closing" in a manual accounting system although the temporary accounts are not really closed until the end of the month.

> Closing the Accounting Records

10. It is always wise to backup accounting data at the end of each month, saving it into a file that will be saved until the end of the year. We will use Peachtree's Backup feature to do this. Click on the Company Window **File** menu; select **Backup,** use a filename such as "ValdezJun" to make sure you can recognize what the backup represents. Click on **Ok.**

> Make a Backup Copy of June Accounting Records

11. We must now advance the period to prepare Peachtree for the July transactions.

   ▼ Using your mouse, click on **System** from the **Tasks** menu. Select **Change Accounting Periods.** You are presented with the following:

> Advancing the Period

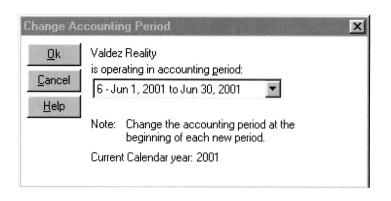

Using the pull down menu, select period 7 - Jul 1, 2001 to Jul 31, 2001 and click on "Ok"

▼ You will be asked whether you wish to print reports before continuing. Since we have already printed our reports, we can answer "No".

▼ Note that the status bar at the bottom of the screen now reflects that you are in period 7.

Exit the Program

12. Click on the Company Window File menu; then click on Exit to end the current work session and return to your Windows desktop or continue with step 3 below.

PART B: The July Accounting Cycle

1. Start Peachtree Complete Accounting.

Open the Company Data Files

2. Open **Valdez Realty.**

3. Record the following journal entries. Enter the **Date** listed for each transaction (you may use the "+" key to advance the date or use the calendar icon next to the field to select the date from a calendar). Enter "Memo" into the **Source** text box for each transaction or accept Peachtree's additional number added to memo by pressing TAB:

Record July Transactions

2001

July		
	1	Purchased additional office supplies on account, $700.
	2	Paid advertising bill for June, $1,200.
	3	Sold a house and collected a commission, $6,600.
	6	Paid for gas expense, $29.
	8	Collected commission from sale of building lot on 6/17/01 (collected our accounts receivable).
	12	Paid $300 to send employees to realtor's workshop.
	15	Paid the salary of the office secretary, $350.
	17	Sold a house and earned a commission of $2,400. Expected receipt on 8/10/01.
	18	Sold a building lot and collected a commission of $7,000.
	22	Sent a check for $40 to help sponsor a local road race to aid the public (This is not to be considered an advertising expense, but it is a business expense.)
	24	Paid for repairs to automobile, $590.
	28	Juan Valdez withdrew $1,800 from the business to pay personal expenses.
	30	Paid the salary of the office secretary, $350.
	30	Paid the July telephone bill, $590.
	30	Advertising bill for July, $1,400. The bill is to be paid on 8/2/01.

Print Working Reports

4. After you have posted the journal entries, close the General Journal; then print the following reports:

   a. General Journal -(check figure debit = $29,849)

   b. Trial Balance -(Check figure debit = $56,550)

Review your printed reports. If you have made an error in a posted journal entry, correct the error before proceeding.

5. Open the General Journal; then record adjusting journal entries based on the following adjustment data using "Adj" in the reference field:

Record July Adjusting Entries

   a. One month's rent has expired.

   b. An inventory shows $90 of office supplies remaining.

   c. Depreciation on office equipment, $100.

   d. Depreciation on automobile, $200.

6. After you have posted the adjusting journal entries, close the General Journal then print the following reports accepting all defaults offered by Peachtree:

Print Final Statements

   a. General Journal -(check figure debit = $31,509)

   b. Trial Balance -(check figure debit = $56,850)

   c. General Ledger Report -(check figure cash = $26,094)

   d. Income Statement -(Net Income = $10,691)

   e. Balance Sheet -(Total Capital = $29,434)

   Review your printed reports. If you have made an error in a posted journal entry, use the procedures detailed in step 18 from chapter 3 to make any necessary corrections. Reprint all reports if corrections are made.

7. Computerized Accounting systems maintain all of it's input in compartments called periods. Some systems identify these periods with the name of the month or with a simple numeric designation such as 1, 2, 3, et. al. Peachtree currently has Valdez Realty in Period 7, the July period. You can see this in the status bar at the bottom of the screen. This is because Valdez has elected to use the calendar year for his Fiscal year. We will need to change the current period to the August period prior to inputting the next month's transactions. You must always tell Peachtree to move to the next accounting period when starting on the transactions for a new month. This process is the equivalent of "Closing" in a manual accounting system although the temporary accounts are not really closed until the end of the month.

Closing the Accounting Records

8. It is always wise to backup accounting data at the end of each month, saving it into a file that will be saved until the end of the year. We will use Peachtree's Backup feature to do this. Click on the Company Window **File** menu; select **Backup,** use a filename such as "ValdezJuly" to make sure you can recognize what the backup represents.

Make a Backup Copy of July Accounting Records

9. We must now advance the period to prepare Peachtree for the August transactions.

Advancing the Period

   ▼ Using your mouse, click on **System** from the **Tasks** menu. Select **Change Accounting Periods.**

   ▼ Using the pull down menu, select period 8 - Aug 1, 2001 to Aug 31, 2001 and click on "Ok"

   ▼ You will be asked whether you wish to print reports before continuing. Since we have already printed our reports, we can answer "No".

   ▼ Note that the status bar at the bottom of the screen now reflects that you are in period 8.

10. Click on the Company Window File menu; then click on Exit to end the current work session and return to your Windows desktop.

Exit the Program

PART 2

Banking and Payroll

CHAPTER 6

Banking Procedures and Control of Cash

One of the fundamental principles of controlling and monitoring cash in a business—from the smallest mom n' pop grocery to the largest conglomerate—is separation of duties. For instance, the person who takes the money can't be the same as the person who counts it. Yet, as obvious as this dictum would seem, there have been astounding instances of companies ignoring this ground rule, and with disastrous consequences.

Perhaps you've heard of the Barings Bank debacle of 1995, in which a fresh-faced 28-year-old trader brought a venerable 233-year-old British bank to its knees? Barings fell because it lacked sufficient **internal controls,** a system of procedures and methods to control a firm's assets as well as monitor its operations. Since 1992, Nick Leeson had worked as a trader in Barings' Singapore office. While there Leeson was allowed to execute cross *trades,* transactions in which he acted as both buyer and seller. Leeson's transactions were not arms' length, where the seller tries to get the highest price, and the buyer tries to pay the lowest price. Without arms' length trading, the amount of the transaction could be anything Leeson entered into the system. Amazingly, the bank had not required Leeson give up his job as head of selling when he became head of buying.

While almost totally unsupervised in Singapore, Leeson bought $27 billion worth of securities on Japan's Nikkei stock market. When the Nikkei plunged, the Bank lost $27 billion and collapsed. Perhaps more surprising than the bank's ignorance of Leeson's financial shenanigans was its refusal to heed its own internal auditors. Several months before the collapse Barings' internal auditors had warned against the danger of Leeson's dual role as a buyer and seller. Yet, Barings' higher-ups viewed Leeson as a golden boy and ignored the audit report.

In all likelihood, you will not have to monitor billions of dollars and complicated securities trades, like Leeson's, in your first stint as an accountant. In this chapter you'll learn how to accomplish basic banking procedures — such as depositing, writing and endorsing checks and reconciling a bank statement — and how to control cash through a petty cash fund.

Based on: Lillian Chew, "Not Just One Man," http://www.risk.ifci.ch/137560.htm. Robert D. Allen, "Managing internal audit conflicts," *The Internal Auditor,* August 1996, p. 58. Anonymous, "The Collapse of Barings: A fallen star," *The Economist,* March 4, 1995, p. 19.

LEARNING OBJECTIVES

▼ Depositing, writing, and endorsing checks for a checking account. (p. 207)

▼ Reconciling a bank statement. (p. 212)

▼ Establishing and replenishing a petty cash fund; setting up an auxiliary petty cash record. (p. 219)

▼ Establishing and replenishing a change fund. (p. 220)

▼ Handling transactions involving cash short and over. (p. 222)

> The internal control policies of a company will depend on things such as number of employees, company size, sources of cash, and usage of the Internet.

In the first five chapters of this book, we analyzed the accounting cycle for businesses that perform personal services (for example, word processing or legal services). In this chapter, we turn our attention to Debbie's Wholesale Stationery Company, a merchandising company that earns revenue by selling goods (or merchandise) to customers. When Debbie found that her business was increasing, she became concerned that she was not monitoring the business's cash closely enough. To remedy the situation, Debbie and her accountant decided to develop a system of **internal controls.**

After studying the situation carefully, Debbie began a series of procedures that were to be followed by all company employees. The new company policies that Debbie's Wholesale Stationery Company put into place are as follows:

1. Responsibilities and duties of employees will be divided. For example, the person receiving the cash, whether at the register or by opening the mail, will not record this information into the accounting records. The accountant will not be handling the cash receipts.

2. All cash receipts of Debbie's Wholesale will be deposited into the bank the same day they arrive.

3. All cash payments will be made by check (except petty cash, which is discussed later in this chapter).

4. Employees will be rotated. This change allows workers to become acquainted with the work of others as well as to prepare for a possible changeover of jobs.

5. Debbie Lawrence will sign all checks after receiving authorization to pay from the departments concerned.

6. At time of payment, all supporting invoices or documents will be stamped paid. The stamp will show when the invoice or document is paid as well as the number of the check used.

7. All checks will be prenumbered. This change will control the use of checks and make it difficult to use a check fraudulently without its being revealed at some point.

8. Use of online Banking will be continually evaluated.

Now let's look at how Debbie's Wholesale implemented these policies.

LEARNING UNIT 6-1

BANK PROCEDURES, CHECKING ACCOUNTS, AND BANK RECONCILIATIONS

Before Debbie's Wholesale opened on April 1, 200X, Debbie had a meeting at Security National Bank to discuss the steps in opening up and using a checking account for the company.

OPENING A CHECKING ACCOUNT

The bank manager gave Debbie a signature card to fill out. The signature card included space for signature(s), business and home addresses, references, type of account, and so forth. Because Debbie would be signing all the checks for her company, she was the only employee who had to sign the card. The bank keeps the signature card in its files. When checks are presented for payment, the bank checks it to validate Debbie's signature. Such checking helps avoid possible forgeries.

> Purpose of a signature card.

Once the account was opened, Debbie received a set of checks and **deposit tickets** that were preprinted with the business's name, address, and account number (see Fig. 6-1). Debbie's Wholesale was to use the deposit tickets when it received cash or checks from any source and deposited them into the checking account.

On a deposit ticket, check amounts are listed separately along with the code number of city and bank on which they are drawn. The code can be found in the upper right corner of a check (see Fig. 6-3 on p. 210). The top part of the fraction (53-393) is known as the *American Bankers' Association Transit Number:* 53 identifies the large city or state the bank is located in; 393 identifies the bank.

The lower part of the fraction (113) is split in two; 1 represents the First Federal Reserve District; 13 is a routing number used by the Federal Reserve Bank. This is the way the code number appears on a check.

Deposit tickets usually come in duplicate. The bank keeps one copy and the company keeps the other so it can verify that the items making up the deposit have actually been deposited correctly. The bank manager told Debbie that she could give the deposits to a bank teller or she could use an automated teller machine **(ATM).** The ATM could also be used for withdrawing cash, transferring funds, or paying bills.

Often, Debbie makes her deposits after business hours, when the bank is closed. At those times, she puts the deposit into a locked bag (provided by the bank) and places the bag in the night depository. The bank will credit Debbie's

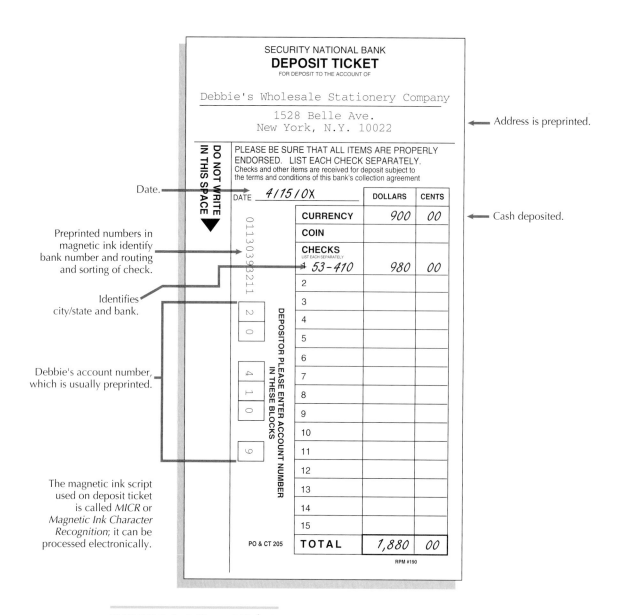

FIGURE 6-1. A Deposit Ticket

account in the morning, when the deposit is processed. All payments of money are by written check (except petty cash), and all money (checks) received is deposited in the bank account.

Many checking accounts earn interest. For our purposes, however, we assume that the checking account for Debbie's Wholesale does not pay interest. Also assume that the checking account has a monthly service charge and that there is no individual charge for each check written.

> When a bank credits your account, it is increasing the balance.

CHECK ENDORSEMENT

Checks have to be *endorsed* (signed) by the person to whom the check is made out before they can be deposited or cashed. **Endorsement** is the signing or stamping of one's name on the back left-hand side of the check.

> Endorsements can be made by using a rubber stamp instead of a handwritten signature.

This signature means that the drawer has transferred the right to deposit or cash the check to someone else (the bank). The bank can then collect the money from the person or company that issued the check.

Three different types of endorsement can be used (see Fig. 6-2). The first is a *blank endorsement*. A blank endorsement does not specify that a particular person or firm must endorse it. It can be further endorsed by someone else.

Blank Endorsement

A signature on the back left side of a check of the person or firm the check is payable to. This check can be *further* endorsed by someone else; the bank will give the money to the last person who signs the check. This type of endorsement is not very safe. If the check is lost, anyone who picks it up can sign it and get the money.

Pay to the order of
Security National Bank.
Debbie's Wholesale Stationery Co.
204109

Full Endorsement

This type of endorsement is safer than a simple signature, because the person or company signing (or stamping) the back of the check indicates the name of the company or person to whom the check is to be paid. Only the person or company named in the endorsement can transfer the check to someone else.

Payable to the order of
Security National Bank
for deposit only.
Debbie's Wholesale Stationery Co.
204109

Restrictive Endorsement

This endorsement is the safest for businesses. Debbie's Wholesale stamps the back of the check so that it must be deposited in the firm's account. This endorsement limits any further use to the check (it can only be deposited in the specified account).

FIGURE 6-2. Types of Check Endorsement

The bank will pay the last person who signs the check. This type of endorsement is not very safe. If the check is lost, the person who finds it can sign it and get the money.

The second type of endorsement is a *full endorsement*. The person or company signing (or stamping) the back of the check indicates the name of the company or the person to whom the check is to be paid. Only the person or company named in the endorsement can transfer the check to someone else.

Restrictive endorsements are the third type of endorsement. This endorsement is the safest one for businesses. Debbie's Wholesale stamps the back of the check so that it must be deposited in the firm's account. This stamp limits any further use of the check.

The regulations require the endorsement to be within the top $1\frac{1}{2}$ inches to speed up the check clearing process.

THE CHECKBOOK

When Debbie opened her business's checking account, she received checks. These checks could be used to buy things for the business or to pay bills or salaries.

A **check** is a written order signed by a **drawer** (the person who writes the check) instructing a **drawee** (the person who pays the check) to pay a specific sum of money to the **payee** (the person to whom the check is payable). Figure 6-3 shows a check issued by Debbie's Wholesale Stationery Company. Debbie Lawrence is the drawer, Security National Bank is the drawee, and Joe Francis Company is the payee.

Look at the check in Figure 6-3. Notice that certain things, such as the company's name and address and the check number, are preprinted. Other things you should notice are (1) the line drawn after $\frac{XX}{100}$ is to fill up the empty space and ensure that the amount cannot be changed and (2) the word "and" should be used only to differentiate between dollars and cents.

Drawer: One who writes the check.

Drawee: One who pays money to payee.

Payee: One to whom the check is payable.

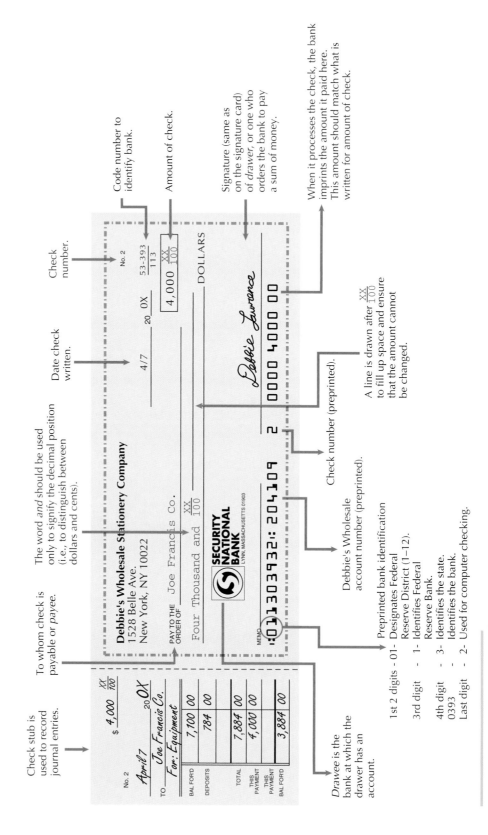

FIGURE 6-3. A Company Check

Check stub is used to record journal entries.

To whom check is payable or *payee*.

The word *and* should be used only to signify the decimal position (i.e., to distinguish between dollars and cents).

Date check written.

Check number.

Code number to identify bank.

Amount of check.

Signature (same as on the signature card) of *drawer*, or one who orders the bank to pay a sum of money.

When it processes the check, the bank imprints the amount it paid here. This amount should match what is written for amount of check.

A line is drawn after $\frac{XX}{100}$ to fill up space and ensure that the amount cannot be changed.

Check number (preprinted).

Debbie's Wholesale account number (preprinted).

Preprinted bank identification

1st 2 digits - 01- Designates Federal Reserve District (1–12).

3rd digit - 1- Identifies Federal Reserve Bank.

4th digit - 3- Identifies the state.

0393 - Identifies the bank.

Last digit - 2- Used for computer checking.

Drawee is the bank at which the drawer has an account.

No. 2

April 7 20 0X

TO Joe Francis Co.

$ 4,000 $\frac{XX}{100}$

For: Equipment

BAL FOR'D	7,100	00
DEPOSITS	784	00
TOTAL	7,884	00
THIS PAYMENT	4,000	00
THIS PAYMENT BAL FOR'D	3,884	00

Debbie's Wholesale Stationery Company
1528 Belle Ave.
New York, NY 10022

No. 2

53-393
113

4/7   20 0X

PAY TO THE ORDER OF   Joe Francis Co. $ 4,000 $\frac{XX}{100}$

Four Thousand and $\frac{XX}{100}$ DOLLARS

SECURITY NATIONAL BANK
LYNN, MASSACHUSETTS 01903

MEMO   Debbie Lawrence

⑆011303932⑈ 204109 2   0000 4000 00

Figure 6-3 includes a check stub. The check stub is used to record transactions, and it is kept for future reference. The information found on the stub includes the beginning balance ($7,100), the amount of any deposits ($784), the total amount in the account ($7,884), the amount of the check being written ($4,000), and the ending balance ($3,884). The check stub should be filled out before the check is written.

If the written amount on the check does not match the amount expressed in figures, Security National Bank may either pay the amount written in words, return the check unpaid, or contact the drawer to see what was meant.

Many companies use checkwriting machines to type out the information on the check. These machines prevent people from making fraudulent changes on handwritten checks.

During the same time period, in-company records must be kept for all transactions affecting Debbie's Wholesale Stationery Company's checkbook balance. Figure 6-4 (below) shows these records. Note that the bank deposits ($14,324) minus the checks written ($6,994) give an ending checkbook balance of $7,330.

Banking on the Internet is expanding rapidly.

MONTHLY RECORDKEEPING: THE BANK'S STATEMENT OF ACCOUNT AND IN-COMPANY RECORDS

Each month, Security National Bank will send Debbie's Wholesale Stationery Company a Statement of Account. This statement reflects all the activity in the account during that period. It begins with the beginning balance of the account at the start of the month, along with the checks the bank has paid and any deposits received (see Fig. 6-5). Any other charges or additions to the bank balance are indicated by codes found on the statement. All checks that have been paid by the bank are sent back to Debbie's Wholesale. These are called **cancelled checks** because they have been processed by the bank and are no longer negotiable. The ending balance in Figure 6-5 is $6,919.

Figure 6.5 shows one format for a bank statement. Different banks use different formats.

BANK DEPOSITS MADE FOR APRIL

Date of Deposit	Amount	Received From
Apr. 1	$ 8,000	Debbie Lawrence, Capital
4	784	Check — Hal's Clothing
16	1,880	Cash sales/Check — Bevans Company
22	1,960	Check — Roe Company
27	500	Sale of equipment
30	1,200	Cash sales
Total deposits for month:	$14,324	

CHECKS WRITTEN FOR MONTH OF APRIL

Date	Check No.	Payment To	Amount	Description
Apr. 2	1	Peter Blum	$ 900	Insurance paid in advance
7	2	Joe Francis Co.	4,000	Paid equipment
9	3	Rick Flo Co.	800	Cash purchases
12	4	Thorpe Co.	594	Paid purchases
28	5	Payroll	700	Salaries
		Total amount of checks written:	$6,994	

Cash/checks deposited	$14,324
Checks paid	− 6,994
Balance in company checkbook	$ 7,330

FIGURE 6-4. Transactions Affecting Checkbook Balance

SECURITY NATIONAL BANK

Debbie's Wholesale Stationery Company
1528 Belle Ave.
New York, New York 10022

ACCOUNT
NUMBER   20   410   9

CLOSING
PERIOD   4/30/0X

AMOUNT
ENCLOSED $ _____

RETURN THIS PORTION WITH YOUR PAYMENT IF YOU ARE NOT USING OUR AUTOMATIC PAYMENT PLAN   Address Correction on Reverse Side ☐

CHECKING ACCOUNT

ON	YOUR BALANCE WAS	NO.	WE SUBTRACTED CHECKS TOTALING	LESS SERVICE CHARGE	NO.	WE ADDED DEPOSITS OF	MAKING YOUR PRESENT BALANCE
	0	3	5,700.00	5.00	5	12,624.00	6,919.00

DATE	CHECKS • WITHDRAWALS • PAYMENTS	DEPOSITS • INTEREST • ADVANCES	BALANCE
4/1		8,000.00	8,000.00
4/2	900		7,100.00
4/4		784.00	7,884.00
4/7	4,000		3,884.00
4/9	800		3,084.00
4/16		1,880.00	4,964.00
4/22		1,960.00	6,924.00
4/25	5.00 SC		6,919.00

FIGURE 6-5. A Bank Statement

THE BANK RECONCILIATION PROCESS

The problem is that the ending bank balance of $6,919 does not agree with the amount in Debbie's checkbook, $7,330, or the balance in the cash amount in the ledger, $7,330. Such differences are caused partly by the time a bank takes to process a company's transactions. A company records a transaction when it occurs. A bank cannot record a deposit until it receives the funds, and it cannot pay a check until the check is presented by the payee. In addition, the bank statement will report fees and transactions that the company did not know about.

Debbie's accountant has to find out why there is a $411 difference between the balances and how the records can be brought into balance. The process of reconciling the bank balance on the bank statement versus the company's checkbook balance is called a **bank reconciliation.** Bank reconciliations involve several steps, including calculating the deposits in transit and the outstanding checks. The bank reconciliation usually is done on the back of the **bank statement** (see Fig. 6-6). It can also be done by computer software, however.

> Online banking has made the reconciliation process even easier.

Deposits in Transit

In comparing the list of deposits received by the bank with the checkbook, the accountant notices that the two deposits made on April 27 and 30 for $500 and $1,200 were not on the bank's statement. The accountant realizes that to prepare this statement, the bank only included information about Debbie's Wholesale Stationery up to April 25. These two deposits made by Debbie were not shown on the monthly bank statement, because they arrived at the bank after the statement was printed. Thus, timing becomes a consideration in the

FIGURE 6-6. Bank Reconciliation Using the Back of the Bank Statement

CHECKS OUTSTANDING		
NUMBER	AMOUNT	
4	594	00
5	700	00
TOTAL OF CHECKS OUTSTANDING	1,294	00

1. Enter balance shown on this statement	6,919	00
2. If you have made deposits since the date of this statement add them to the above balance.	1,700	00
3. SUBTOTAL	8,619	00
4. Deduct total of checks outstanding	1,294	00
5. ADJUSTED BALANCE This should agree with your checkbook.	7,325	00

TO VERIFY YOUR CHECKING BALANCE

1. Sort checks by number or by date issued and compare with your check stubs and prior outstanding list. Make certain all checks paid have been recorded in your checkbook. If any of your checks were not included with this statement, list the numbers and amounts under "CHECKS OUTSTANDING."

2. Deduct the Service Charge as shown on the statement from your checkbook balance.

3. Review copies of charge advices included with this statement and check for proper entry in your checkbook.

IF THE ADJUSTED BALANCE DOES NOT AGREE WITH YOUR CHECKBOOK BALANCE, THE FOLLOWING SUGGESTIONS ARE OFFERED FOR YOUR ASSISTANCE.

• Recheck additions and subtractions in your checkbook and figures to the left.

• Make certain checkbook balances have been carried forward properly.

• Verify deposits recorded on statement against deposits entered in checkbook.

• Compare amount on each checkbook stub.

> Keep in mind that both the bank and the depositor can make mistakes that will not be discovered until the reconciliation process.

reconciliation process. The deposits not yet added onto the bank balance are called **deposits in transit.** These two deposits need to be added to the bank balance shown on the bank statement. Debbie's checkbook is not affected, because the two deposits have already been added to its balance. The bank has no way of knowing that the deposits are coming until they are received.

> Deposits in transit: These unrecorded deposits could result if a deposit were placed in a night depository on the last day of the month.

Outstanding Checks

The first thing the accountant does when the bank statement is received is put the checks in numerical order (1, 2, 3, etc.). In doing so, the accountant notices that two payments were not made by the bank and two checks, no. 4 and no. 5, were not returned by the bank.

> Checks #4 and #5 are outstanding.

Debbie's books showed that these two checks had been deducted from the checkbook balance. These **outstanding checks,** however, were not yet presented to the bank for payment or deducted from the bank balance. When these checks do reach the bank, the bank will reduce the amount of the balance.

> Checks outstanding are checks drawn by the depositor but not yet presented to the bank for payment by the payee.

Service Charges

Debbie's accountant also notices a bank service charge of $5. Thus, Debbie's checkbook balance should be lowered by $5.

Nonsufficient Funds

An **NSF (nonsufficient funds)** check is a check that has been returned because the drawer did not have enough money in its account to pay the check. Accountants are continually on the lookout for NSF (nonsufficient funds) checks. If there is an NSF check, it means that there is less money in the checking account than was thought. Debbie's Wholesale will have to (1) lower the checkbook balance and (2) try to collect the amount from the customer. The bank would notify Debbie's Wholesale of an NSF (or other deductions) check by a **debit memorandum.** Think of a debit memorandum as a deduction from the depositor's balance.

> Debit memorandum:
> Deducted from balance

If the bank acts as a collecting agent for Debbie's Wholesale, say in collecting notes, it will charge Debbie a small fee and the net amount collected will be added to Debbie's bank balance. The bank will send to Debbie a **credit memorandum** verifying the increase in the depositor's balance.

A journal entry is also needed to bring the ledger accounts of cash and service charge expense up to date. Any adjustment to the checkbook balance results in a journal entry. The following entry was made to accomplish this step:

Apr.	30	Service Charge Expense		5 00		
		Cash				5 00
		Bank service charge for April				

Example of a More Comprehensive Bank Reconciliation

The bank reconciliation of Debbie's Stationery was not as complicated as it is for many other companies. Let's take a moment to look at the bank reconciliation for Monroe Company, which is based on the following:

Checkbook balance: $3,978.

Balance reported by bank: $5,230.

Recorded in journal check no. 108 for $54 *more* than amount of check when store equipment was purchased.

Bank collected a note ($2,000) for Monroe, charging a collection fee of $10.

A bounced check for $252 (NSF) has to be covered by Monroe. The bank has lowered Monroe's balance by $252 (see Fig. 6-7).

Bank service charge of $10.

Deposits in transit, $1,084.

Checks not yet processed by the bank:

Check	Amount
191	$204
198	250
201	100

MONROE COMPANY
BANK RECONCILIATION AS OF JUNE 30, 200X

Checkbook Balance			Balance per Bank			
Checkbook Balance			Bank Statement Balance			$5,230
Add:		$3,978	Add:			
Error in recording			Deposits in Transit			1,084
check no. 108	$54					$6,314
Proceeds of a note						
less collection						
charge by bank	1,990	2,044	Deduct:			
		$6,022	Check no.	191	$204	
				198	250	
Deduct:				201	100	554
NSF Check	$252					
Bank Service						
Charge	10	262				
Reconciled Balance		$5,760	Reconciled Balance			$5,760

FIGURE 6-7. Sample Debit Memorandum

	Debit:	Monroe Co.		Valley Bank
		170 Roe Rd.		
		Dallas, TX 75208		

2/4–10–60811 Date: 6/30/0X

NSF Check—Alvin Sooth	$252.00

Approved
JS

Note that every time an adjustment is made in the reconciliation process to the checkbook balance, a journal entry is needed. Monroe Company has to make the following journal entries:

Date		Account Title and Description	PR	Dr.	Cr.
200X June	30	Cash		1 9 9 0 00	
		Collection Expense		1 0 00	
		Notes Receivable*			2 0 0 0 00
		Note collected			
	30	Cash		5 4 00	
		Store Equipment			5 4 00
		Error recording check no. 108			
	30	Accounts Receivable		2 5 2 00	
		Cash			2 5 2 00
		Alvin Sooth NSF check			
	30	Miscellaneous Expense		1 0 00	
		Cash			1 0 00
		Bank service charge			

* We discuss Notes Receivable in a later chapter. For now, think of it as a kind of written Accounts Receivable.

TRENDS IN BANKING

Electronic Funds Transfer

Many financial institutions have developed or are developing ways to transfer funds electronically, without the use of paper checks. Such systems are called **electronic funds transfers (EFT).** Most EFTs are established to save money and avoid theft.

Automatic payroll deposits are an example of an EFT. It works as follows: The company asks its employees if they would like their paychecks deposited automatically into their checking accounts. Employees who agree to do so are asked to sign an authorization form. The bank, upon receiving computer-coded payroll data, adds each worker's payroll amount to his or her checking account. Employees who do not sign the authorization continue to get paper checks that they must cash themselves.

Another good example is the automatic teller machine (ATM). In some states, ATMs now issue postage stamps, railroad tickets, and grocery coupons. **Debit cards** are still another example of an EFT. If a customer buys a service or a product with a debit card, the amount of the purchase is deducted directly from the customer's bank account. The Internet continues to expand online Banking.

Check Truncation (Safekeeping)

Some banks do not return cancelled checks to the depositor but use a procedure called **check truncation** or **safekeeping.** The bank holds a cancelled check for a specific period of time (usually 90 days) and then keeps a microfilm copy handy and destroys the original check. In Texas, for example, some credit unions and savings and loan institutions do not send back checks. Instead, the check date, number, and amount are listed on the bank statement. If the customer needs a copy of a check, the bank will provide the check or a photocopy for a small fee. (Photocopies are accepted as evidence in Internal Revenue Service tax returns and audits.)

Truncation cuts down on the amount of "paper" that is returned to customers and thus provides substantial cost savings. It is estimated that over 80 million checks are written each day in the United States.

LEARNING UNIT 6-1 REVIEW

AT THIS POINT you should be able to

- ▼ Define and explain the need for deposit tickets. (p. 207)
- ▼ Explain where the American Bankers' Association transit number is located on the check and what its purpose is. (p. 207)
- ▼ List as well as compare and contrast the three common types of check endorsement. (p. 209)
- ▼ Explain the structure of a check. (p. 210)
- ▼ Define and state the purpose of a bank statement. (p. 212)
- ▼ Explain deposits in transit, checks outstanding, service charge, and NSF. (p. 213)
- ▼ Explain the difference between a debit memorandum and a credit memorandum. (p. 213)
- ▼ Explain how to do a bank reconciliation. (p. 214)
- ▼ Explain electronic funds transfer and check truncation. (p. 215)

SELF-REVIEW QUIZ 6-1

(The blank forms you need are on page 191 of the *Study Guide and Working Papers.*)

Indicate, by placing an X under it, the heading that describes the appropriate action for each of the following situations:

Situation	Add to Bank Balance	Deduct from Bank Balance	Add to Checkbook Balance	Deduct from Checkbook Balance
1. Check printing charge				
2. Deposits in transit				
3. NSF check				
4. A $75 check was written and recorded by the company as $85				
5. Proceeds of a note collected by the bank				
6. Check outstanding				
7. Forgot to record ATM withdrawal				
8. Forgot to record direct deposit of a payroll check				

Solution to Self-Review Quiz 6-1

Situation	Add to Bank Balance	Deduct from Bank Balance	Add to Checkbook Balance	Deduct from Checkbook Balance
1				X
2	X			
3				X
4			X	
5			X	
6		X		
7				X
8			X	

Quiz Tip: Deposits in transit are added to the bank balance, whereas checks outstanding are subtracted from the bank balance.

LEARNING UNIT 6-2

THE ESTABLISHMENT OF PETTY CASH AND CHANGE FUNDS

Debbie realized how time-consuming and expensive it would be to write checks for small amounts to pay for postage, small supplies, and so forth, so she set up a **petty cash fund.** Similarly, she established a *change fund* to make cash transactions more convenient. This unit explains how to manage petty cash and change funds.

Petty Cash is an asset on the balance sheet.

Setting up the Petty Cash Fund

The *petty cash fund* is an account dedicated to paying small day-to-day expenses. These petty cash expenses are recorded in an auxiliary record and later summarized, journalized, and posted. Debbie estimated that the company would need a fund of $60 to cover small expenditures during the month of May. This petty cash was not expected to last longer than one month. She gave one of her employees responsibility for overseeing the fund. This person is called the *custodian*.

Debbie named her office manager, John Sullivan, as custodian. In other companies the cashier or secretary may be in charge of petty cash. Check no. 6 was drawn to the order of the custodian and cashed to establish the fund. John keeps the petty cash fund in a small tin box in the office safe.

Shown here is the transaction analysis chart for the establishment of a $60 petty cash fund, which would be journalized on May 1, 200X, as follows:

> The check for $60 is drawn to the order of the custodian and is cashed, and the proceeds are turned over to John Sullivan, the custodian.

> Petty Cash is an asset, which is established by writing a new check. The Petty Cash account is debited only once unless a greater or lesser amount of petty cash is needed on a regular basis.

Accounts Affected	Category	↑ ↓	Rules
Petty Cash	Asset	↑	Dr.
Cash (checks)	Asset	↓	Cr.

GENERAL JOURNAL						Page 1
Date		Account Title and Description	PR	Dr.	Cr.	
200X May	1	Petty Cash		60 00		
		Cash			60 00	
		Establishment				

Note that the new asset called *Petty Cash,* which was created by writing check no. 6, reduced the asset Cash. In reality, the total assets stay the same; what has occurred is a shift from the asset Cash (check no. 6) to a new asset account called Petty Cash.

The Petty Cash account is not debited or credited again if the size of the fund is not changed. If the $60 fund is used up quickly, the fund should be increased. If the fund is too large, the Petty Cash account should be reduced. We take a closer look at this when we discuss replenishment of petty cash.

MAKING PAYMENTS FROM THE PETTY CASH FUND

John Sullivan has the responsibility for filling out a **petty cash voucher** for each cash payment made from the petty cash fund. The petty cash vouchers are numbered in sequence.

Note that when the voucher (shown in Fig. 6-8) is completed, it will include:

▼ The voucher number (which will be in sequence).
▼ The date.
▼ The person or organization to whom the payment was made.
▼ The amount of payment.
▼ The reason for payment: cleaning.
▼ The signature of the person who approved the payment.
▼ The signature of the person who received the payment from petty cash.
▼ The account to which the expense will be charged.

FIGURE 6-8. Petty Cash Voucher

Petty Cash Voucher No. 1

Date: May 2, 200X   Amount: $3.00

Paid To: Al's Cleaning

For: Cleaning

Approved By: *John Sullivan*

Payment Received By: *Debbie Lawrence*

Debit Account No.: 619

The completed vouchers are placed in the petty cash box. No matter how many vouchers John Sullivan fills out, *the total of (1) the vouchers in the box and (2) the cash on hand should equal the original amount of petty cash with which the fund was established ($60).*

Assume that at the end of May the following items are documented by petty cash vouchers in the petty cash box as having been paid by John Sullivan:

200X

May   2   Cleaning package, $3.00.

         5   Postage stamps, $9.00.

         8   First-aid supplies, $15.00.

         9   Delivery expense, $6.00.

      14   Delivery expense, $15.00.

      27   Postage stamps, $6.00.

John records this information in the **auxiliary petty cash record** shown in Figure 6-9. It is not a required record but an aid to John, an auxiliary record that is not essential but is quite helpful as part of the petty cash system. You may want to think of the auxiliary petty cash record as an optional worksheet. Let's look at how to replenish the petty cash fund.

Date	Voucher No.	Description	Receipts	Payments	Postage Expense	Delivery Expense	Sundry Account	Sundry Amount
200X May 1		Establishment	60 00					
2	1	Cleaning		3 00			Cleaning	3 00
5	2	Postage		9 00	9 00			
8	3	First Aid		15 00			Misc.	15 00
9	4	Delivery		6 00		6 00		
14	5	Delivery		15 00		15 00		
27	6	Postage		6 00	6 00			
		Total	60 00	54 00	15 00	21 00		18 00

FIGURE 6-9. Auxiliary Petty Cash Record

HOW TO REPLENISH THE PETTY CASH FUND

No postings are done from the auxiliary book because it is not a journal. At some point the summarized information found in the auxiliary petty cash record is used as a basis for a journal entry in the general journal and eventually posted to appropriate ledger accounts to reflect up-to-date balances.

This $54 of expenses (see Fig. 6-9) is recorded in the general journal (Fig. 6-10 on p. 221) and a new check, no. 17, for $54 is cashed and returned to John Sullivan. In replenishment, old expenses are updated in journal and ledger to show where money has gone. The order is auxiliary before replenishment. The petty cash box now once again reflects $60 cash. The old vouchers that were used are stamped to indicate that they have been processed and the fund replenished.

> A new check is written in the replenishment process, which is payable to the custodian, and is cashed by John, and the cash is placed in the petty cash box.

Note that in the replenishment process the debits are a summary of the totals (except sundry, because individual items are different) of expenses or other items from the auxiliary petty cash record. Posting these specific expenses will ensure that the expenses will not be understated on the income statement. The credit to cash allows us to draw a check for $54 to put money back in the petty cash box. The $60 in the box now agrees with the petty cash account balance. The end result is that our petty cash box is filled, and we have justified for which accounts the petty cash money was spent. Think of replenishment as a single, summarizing entry.

Remember that if at some point the petty cash fund is to be greater than $60, a check can be written that will increase Petty Cash and decrease Cash. If the Petty Cash account balance is to be reduced, we can credit or reduce Petty Cash. For our present purpose, however, Petty Cash will remain at $60.

The auxiliary petty cash record after replenishment would look as follows (keep in mind no postings are made from the auxiliary):

											Category of Payments					
															Sundry	
Date		Voucher No.	Description	Receipts		Payments		Postage Expense		Delivery Expense		Account		Amount	
200X May	1		Establishment	60 00											
	2	1	Cleaning			3 00						Cleaning		3 00	
	5	2	Postage			9 00		9 00							
	8	3	First Aid			15 00						Misc.		15 00	
	9	4	Delivery			6 00				6 00					
	14	5	Delivery			15 00				15 00					
	27	6	Postage			6 00		6 00							
			Total	60 00		54 00		15 00		21 00				18 00	
			Ending Balance			6 00									
				60 00		60 00									
			Ending Balance	6 00											
	31		Replenishment	54 00											
	31		Balance (New)	60 00											

AUXILIARY PETTY CASH RECORD

Figure 6-11 may help you put the sequence together.

Before concluding this unit, let's look at how Debbie will handle setting up a change fund and problems with cash shortages and overages.

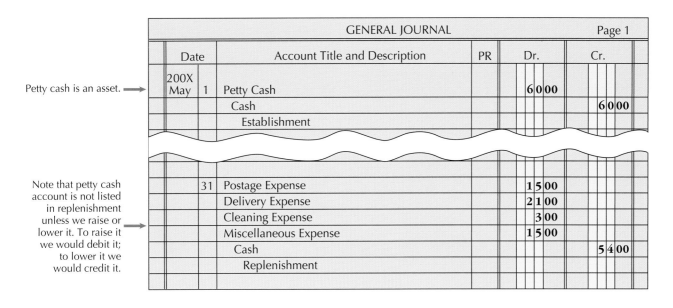

GENERAL JOURNAL					Page 1	
Date	Account Title and Description	PR	Dr.		Cr.	
200X May 1	Petty Cash		60 00			
	Cash				60 00	
	Establishment					
31	Postage Expense		15 00			
	Delivery Expense		21 00			
	Cleaning Expense		3 00			
	Miscellaneous Expense		15 00			
	Cash				54 00	
	Replenishment					

Petty cash is an asset. →

Note that petty cash account is not listed in replenishment unless we raise or lower it. To raise it we would debit it; to lower it we would credit it.

FIGURE 6-10. Establishment and Replenishment of Petty Cash Fund

SETTING UP A CHANGE FUND AND INSIGHT INTO CASH SHORT AND OVER

If a company like Debbie's Stationery expects to have many cash transactions occurring, it may be a good idea to establish a **change fund.** This fund is placed in the cash register drawer and used to make change for customers who pay cash. Debbie decides to put $120 in the change fund, made up of various denominations of bills and coins. Let's look at a transaction analysis chart and the journal entry (on p. 222) for this sort of procedure.

Date	Description	New Check Written	Petty Cash Voucher Prepared	Recorded in Auxiliary Petty Cash Record	
200X Jan. 1	Establishment of petty cash for $60	X		X	Dr. petty cash Cr. cash
2	Paid salaries, $2,000	X			
10	Paid $10 from petty cash for Band-Aids		X	X	No journal entries
19	Paid $8 from petty cash for postage		X	X	
24	Paid light bill, $200	X			
29	Replenishment of petty cash to $60	X		X	Dr. individual expenses Cr. cash

Has nothing to do with petty cash (amounts too great).

In this step the old expenses are listed in general journal and a new check is written to replenish. All old vouchers removed from the petty cash box.

FIGURE 6-11. Which Transactions Involve Petty Cash and How to Record Them

Time to Check That Cash

Dunkin' Donuts is urging its shop owners to get rid of their cash registers and switch to a new IBM point-of-sale terminal. With these new machines, clerks just use a touch screen to punch in the number and type of items bought. This method is faster than using the old cash registers and easier to learn. Training staff to handle cash is a critical component of a cash business like Dunkin' Donuts. Every sale must be recorded, and recorded correctly. Cash control is built into the new IBM system, which also provides the owners with information that will help them spot problems and track trends.

Fred was pleased when he heard about the new system at the company's annual convention in Orlando, Florida. Register training was a recurring problem for him and for most store owners. Now the terminals in the store would be easier to learn. They are linked, so he would be able to see consolidated data quickly. The chore of closing out the cash drawer at the end of a shift remained, however, and it was still a critical control point.

"I have to remember that," said Fred, thinking back to the convention, "when I explain to Sally how to close out

her cash register drawer again. Even though she messes up my Cash Summary almost every day, getting mad sure hasn't helped. Maybe I should go through it with her step by step." Fred had spent hours figuring out a discrepancy between the cash in the drawer and the register tape. Sally had forgotten to void a mistaken entry for $99.99. Fred had first suspected that Sally had made a huge error in counting change.

Nodding happily to himself, Fred treated himself to one of his glazed donuts. Doing the daily Cash Summary normally gave Fred a sense of accomplishment (when Sally wasn't working). And the monthly chore of reconciling the shop's bank account had been no problem. The cash on the monthly financials that he submitted to Dwayne were right on the money.

Discussion Questions

1. How would Fred catch a discrepancy in the cash account?
2. How would Fred record a loss?
3. Why is cash register training so important to a service business like Fred's?
4. Why does Dunkin' Donuts invest time, money, and effort in investigating new cash handling systems like the IBM point-of-sale terminals?

Accounts Affected	Category	↑ ↓	Dr./Cr.
Change Fund	Asset	↑	Dr.
Cash	Asset	↓	Cr.

Apr.	1	Change Fund		1 2 0 00		
		Cash			1 2 0 00
		Establish change fund			

At the close of the business day, Debbie will place the amount of the change fund back in the safe in the office. She will set up the change fund (the same $120) in the appropriate denominations for the next business day. She will deposit in the bank the *remainder* of the cash taken in for the day.

In the next section, we look at how to record errors that are made in making change, called **cash short and over.**

Cash Short and Over

In a local pizza shop the total sales for the day did not match the amount of cash on hand. Errors often happen in making change. To record and summarize the differences in cash, an account called *cash short and over* is used. This

Beg. change fund
+ Cash register total
= Cash should have on hand
− Counted cash
= Shortage or overage of cash

account will record both overages (too much money) and shortages (not enough money). Lets first look at the account (in T account form).

Cash Short and Over

Dr.	Cr.
shortage	overage

All shortages will be recorded as debits and all overages will be recorded as credits. This account is temporary. If the ending balance of the account is a debit (a shortage), it is considered a miscellaneous expense that would be reported on the income statement. If the balance of the account is a credit (an overage), it is considered as other income reported on the income statement. Let's look at how the cash short and over account could be used to record shortages or overages in sales as well as in the petty cash process.

Example 1: Shortages and Overages in Sales

On December 5 a pizza shop rang up sales of $560 for the day but only had $530 in cash.

Accounts Affected	Category	↑ ↓	Dr./Cr.
Cash	Asset	↑	Debit $530
Cash Short and Over	Misc. Exp.	↑	Debit $30
Sales	Revenue	↑	Credit $560

The journal entry would be as follows:

Dec.	5	Cash			530 00				
		Cash Short and Over			30 00				
		Sales					560 00		
		Cash shortage							

Note that the shortage $30 is a debit and would be recorded on the income statement as a miscellaneous expense.

What would the entry look like if the pizza shop showed a $50 overage?

Accounts Affected	Category	↑ ↓	Dr./Cr.
Cash	Asset	↑	Debit $610
Cash Short and Over	Other Income	↑	Credit $50
Sales	Revenue	↑	Credit $560

The journal entry would be as follows:

Dec.	5	Cash			610 00				
		Cash Short and Over					50 00		
		Sales					560 00		
		Cash shortage							

Note that the cash short and over account would be reported as other income on the income statement. Now let's look at how to use this cash short and over account to record petty cash transactions.

Example 2: Cash Short and Over in Petty Cash

A local computer company had established petty cash for $200. Today, November 30, the petty cash box had $160 in vouchers as well as $32 in coin and currency. What would be the journal entry to replenish petty cash? Assume the vouchers were made up of $90 for postage and $70 for supplies expense.

If you add up the vouchers and cash in the box, cash is short by $8.

Accounts Affected	Category	↑	↓	Dr./Cr.
Postage Expense	Expense	↑		Debit $90
Supplies Expense	Expense	↑		Debit $70
Cash Short and Over	Misc. Expense	↑		Debit $8
Cash	Asset		↓	Credit $168

The journal entry is as follows:

Nov.	8	Postage Expense		9 0 00			
		Supplies Expense		7 0 00			
		Cash Short and Over		8 00			
		Cash				1 6 8 00	

If there had been an overage, the cash short and over would be a credit as other income. The solution to Self-Review Quiz 6-2 shows how a fund shortage would be recorded in the auxiliary record.

LEARNING UNIT 6-2 REVIEW

AT THIS POINT you should be able to

▼ State the purpose of a petty cash fund. (p. 217)
▼ Prepare a journal entry to establish a petty cash fund. (p. 218)
▼ Prepare a petty cash voucher. (p. 219)
▼ Explain the relationship of the auxiliary petty cash record to the petty cash process. (p. 219)
▼ Prepare a journal entry to replenish Petty Cash to its original amount. (p. 220)
▼ Explain why individual expenses are debited in the replenishment process. (p. 221)
▼ Explain how a change fund is established. (p. 221)
▼ Explain how Cash Short and Over could be a miscellaneous expense. (p. 223)

SELF-REVIEW QUIZ 6-2

(The blank forms you need are on pages 191 – 192 of the *Study Guide and Working Papers.*)

As the custodian of the petty cash fund, it is your task to prepare entries to establish the fund on October 1 as well as to replenish the fund on October 31. Please keep an auxiliary petty cash record.

200X

Oct.
- 1 Establish petty cash fund for $90, check no. 8.
- 5 Voucher 11, delivery expense, $21.
- 9 Voucher 12, delivery expense, $15.
- 10 Voucher 13, office repair expense, $24.
- 17 Voucher 14, general expense, $12.
- 30 Replenishment of petty cash fund, $78, check no. 108. (Check would be payable to the custodian.)

> *Quiz Tip:*
> How to calculate shortage:
> $21 + $15 + $24 + $12 = $72
> of vouchers. Replenished with $78 check. Thus there was a $6 shortage.
> Note how cash short and over was entered in the auxiliary petty cash record.

Solution to Self-Review Quiz 6-2

GENERAL JOURNAL				Page 6	
Date	Account Title and Description	PR	Dr.	Cr.	
200X Oct. 1	Petty Cash		90 00		
	Cash			90 00	
	Establishment, Check 8				

31	Delivery Expense		36 00		
	General Expense		12 00		
	Office Repair Expense		24 00		
	Cash Short and Over		6 00		
	Cash			78 00	
	Replenishment, Check 108				

AUXILIARY PETTY CASH RECORD							Catagory of Payments			
Date	Voucher No.	Description	Receipts	Payments	Delivery Expense	General Expense	Sundry			
							Account	Amount		
200X Oct. 1		Establishment	90 00							
5	11	Delivery		21 00	21 00					
9	12	Delivery		15 00	15 00					
10	13	Repairs		24 00			Office Repair	24 00		
17	14	General		12 00		12 00				
25		Fund Shortage		6 00			Cash Short and Over	6 00		
		Totals	90 00	78 00	36 00	12 00		30 00		
		Ending Balance		12 00						
				90 00						
30		Ending Balance	12 00							
31		Replenishment	78 00							
Nov. 1		New Balance	90 00							

SUMMARY OF KEY POINTS

Learning Unit 6-1

1. Restrictive endorsement limits any further negotiation of a check.

2. Check stubs are filled out before a check is written.

3. The payee is the person to whom the check is payable. The drawer is the one who orders the bank to pay a sum of money. The drawee is the bank with which the drawer has an account.

4. The process of reconciling the bank balance with the company's balance is called the bank reconciliation. The timing of deposits, when the bank statement was issued, and so forth, often result in differences between the bank balance and the checkbook balance.

5. Deposits in transit are added to the bank balance.

6. Checks outstanding are subtracted from the bank balance.

7. NSF means that a check has nonsufficient funds to be credited (deposited) to a checking account; therefore, the amount is not included in the bank balance and thus the checking account balance is lowered.

8. When a bank debits your account they are deducting an amount from your balance. A credit to the account is an increase to your balance.

9. All adjustments to the checkbook balance require journal entries.

10. The Internet has expanded online Banking options.

Learning Unit 6-2

1. Petty Cash is an asset found on the balance sheet.

2. The auxiliary petty cash record is an auxiliary book; thus no postings are done from this book. Think of it as an optional worksheet.

3. When a petty cash fund is established, the amount is entered as a debit to Petty Cash and a credit to Cash.

4. At time of replenishment of the petty cash fund, all expenses are debited (by category) and a credit to Cash (a new check) results. This replenishment, when journalized and posted, updates the ledger from the journal.

5. The only time the Petty Cash account is used is to establish the fund initially or to bring the fund to a higher or lower level. If the petty cash level is deemed sufficient, all replenishments will debit specific expenses and credit cash (new check written). The asset Petty Cash account balance will remain unchanged.

6. A change fund is an asset that is used to make change for customers.

7. Cash Short and Over is an account that is either a miscellaneous expense or miscellaneous income, depending on whether the ending balance is shortage or overage.

KEY TERMS

ATM   Automatic teller machine.

Auxiliary petty cash record   A supplementary record for summarizing petty cash information.

Bank reconciliation   The process of reconciling the checkbook balance with the bank balance given on the bank statement.

Bank statement   A report sent by a bank to a customer indicating the previous balance, individual checks processed, individual deposits received, service charges, and ending bank balance.

Cancelled check   A check that has been processed by a bank and is no longer negotiable.

Cash Short and Over   The account that records cash shortages and overages. If ending balance is a debit, it is recorded on the income statement as a miscellaneous expense; if it is a credit, it is recorded as miscellaneous income.

Change fund   Fund made up of various denominations that are used to make change for customers.

Check   A form used to indicate a specific amount of money that is to be paid by the bank to a named person or company.

Check truncation (safekeeping)   Procedure whereby checks are not returned to drawer with the bank statement but are instead kept at the bank for a certain amount of time before being first transferred to microfilm and then destroyed.

Credit memorandum   Increase in depositor's balance.

Debit card   A card similar to a credit card except that the amount of a purchase is deducted directly from the customer's bank account.

Debit memorandum   Decrease in depositor's balance.

Deposits in transit   Deposits that were made by customers of a bank but did not reach, or were not processed by, the bank before the preparation of the bank statement.

Deposit ticket   A form provided by a bank for use in depositing money or checks into a checking account.

Drawee   Bank that drawer has an account with.

Drawer   Person who writes a check.

Electronic funds transfer (EFT)   An electronic system that transfers funds without the use of paper checks.

Endorsement   *Blank:* Could be further endorsed. *Full:* Restricts further endorsement to only the person or company named. *Restrictive:* Restricts any further endorsement.

Internal control   A system of procedures and methods to control a firm's assets as well as monitor its operations.

NSF (nonsufficient funds)   Notation indicating that a check has been written on an account that lacks sufficient funds to back it up.

Outstanding checks   Checks written by a company or person that were not received or not processed by the bank before the preparation of the bank statement.

Payee   The person or company to whom the check is payable.

Petty cash fund   Fund (source) that allows payment of small amounts without the writing of checks.

Petty cash voucher   A petty cash form to be completed when money is taken out of petty cash.

BLUEPRINT: A BANK RECONCILIATION

Checkbook Balance		Balance Per Bank		
Ending Balance per Books	$XXX	Ending Bank Statement Balance (last figure on bank statement)	$XXX	
Add:		Add:		
Recording of errors that understate balance	$XXX	Deposits in transit (amount not yet credited by bank)	$XXX	
Proceeds of notes collected by bank or other items credited (added) by bank but not yet updated in checkbook (Interest earned is an example)	XXX	Bank errors	XXX	XXX
	XXX			

(Cont. on p. 228)

Deduct:			Deduct:		
Recording of errors that over-state balance	XXX		List of outstanding checks (amount not yet debited by bank)	XXX	
Service charges	XXX		Bank errors	XXX	
Printing charges	XXX				XXX
NSF, check, or other items debited (charged) by bank but not yet updated in checkbook (ATM withdrawal not recorded is a good example)	XXX				
		XXX			
Reconciled Balance (Adjusted Balance)		$XXX	Reconciled Balance (Adjusted Balance)		$XXX

QUESTIONS, MINI EXERCISES, EXERCISES, AND PROBLEMS

Discussion Questions

1. What is the purpose of internal control?
2. What is the advantage of having preprinted deposit tickets?
3. Explain the difference between a blank endorsement and a restrictive endorsement.
4. Explain the difference between payee, drawer, and drawee.
5. Why should check stubs be filled out first, before the check itself is written?
6. A bank statement is sent twice a month. True or false? Please explain.
7. Explain the end product of a bank reconciliation.
8. Why are checks outstanding subtracted from the bank balance?
9. An NSF check results in a bank issuing the depositor a credit memorandum. Agree or disagree. Please support your response.
10. Why do adjustments to the checkbook balance in the reconciliation process need to be journalized?
11. What is EFT?
12. What is meant by check truncation or safekeeping?
13. Petty cash is a liability. Accept or reject. Explain.
14. Explain the relationship of the auxiliary petty cash record to the recording of the cash payment.
15. At time of replenishment, why are the totals of individual expenses debited?
16. Explain the purpose of a change fund.
17. Explain how Cash Short and Over can be a miscellaneous expense.

Mini Exercises

(The blank forms you need are on page 194 in the *Study Guide and Working Papers*.)

Bank Reconciliation

1. Indicate what effect each situation will have on the bank reconciliation process:

    1. Add to bank balance.
    2. Deduct from bank balance.

3. Add to checkbook balance.

4. Deduct from checkbook balance.

_____ a. $12 bank service charge.

_____ b. $300 deposit in transit.

_____ c. $162 NSF check.

_____ d. A $15 check was written and recorded as $25.

_____ e. Bank collected a $1,000 note less $50 collection fee.

_____ f. Check no. 111 was outstanding for $88.

Journal Entries in Reconciliation Process

2. Which of the transactions in Mini Exercise 1 would require a journal entry?

Bank Reconciliation

3. From the following, construct a bank reconciliation for June Co. as of May 31, 200X.

Checkbook balance	$20
Bank statement balance	30
Deposits in transit	10
Outstanding checks	30
Bank service charge	10

Petty Cash

4. Indicate what effect each situation will have:

1. New check written.

2. Recorded in general journal.

3. Petty cash voucher prepared.

4. Recorded in auxiliary petty cash record.

_____ a. Established petty cash.

_____ b. Paid $1,000 bill.

_____ c. Paid $2 for Band-Aids from petty cash.

_____ d. Paid $3.00 for stamps from petty cash.

_____ e. Paid electric bill, $250.

_____ f. Replenished petty cash.

Replenishment of Petty Cash

5. Petty cash was originally established for $20. During the month, $5 was paid out for Band-Aids and $6 for stamps. During replenishment, the custodian discovered that the balance in petty cash was $8. Record, using a general journal entry, the replenishment of petty cash back to $20.

Increasing Petty Cash

6. In Mini Exercise 5, if the custodian decided to raise the level of petty cash to $30, what would be the journal entry to replenish (use a general journal entry)?

Exercises

(The blank forms you need are on pages 195–196 of the *Study Guide and Working Papers*.)

6-1. From the following information, construct a bank reconciliation for Lang Co. as of July 31, 200X. Then prepare journal entries if needed.

Checkbook balance	$1,260	Outstanding checks	285
Bank statement balance	900	Bank service charge	45
Deposits (in transit)	600	(debit memo)	

Bank reconciliation.

6-2. In general journal form, prepare journal entries to establish a petty cash fund on July 1 and replenish it on July 31.

Establishing and replenishing petty cash.

200X

July   1   A $40 petty cash fund is established.

31   At end of month $12 cash plus the following paid vouchers exist: donations expense, $10; postage expense, $7; office supplies expense, $7; miscellaneous expense, $4.

Cash shortage in replenishment.

6-3. If in Exercise 6-2 cash on hand is $11, prepare the entry to replenish the petty cash on July 31.

Cash overage in replenishment.

6-4. If in Exercise 6-2 cash on hand is $13, prepare the entry to replenish the petty cash on July 31.

Calculate cash shortage with Change Fund.

6-5. At the end of the day the clerk for Pete's Variety Shop noticed an error in the amount of cash he should have. Total cash sales from the sales tape were $1,100, whereas the total cash in the register was $1,056. Pete keeps a $30 change fund in his shop. Prepare an appropriate general journal entry to record the cash sale as well as reveal the cash shortage.

Group A Problems

(The blank forms you need are on pages 197–204 of the *Study Guide and Working Papers*.)

Preparing a bank reconciliation including collection of a note.

6A-1. Royal.com received a bank statement from Morris Bank indicating a bank balance of $7,100. Based on Royal.com's check stubs, the ending checkbook balance was $5,700. Your task is to prepare a bank reconciliation for Royal.com as of July 31, 200X, from the following information (journalize entries as needed):

Check Figure: Reconciled Balance $6,410

   a. Checks outstanding: no. 122, $800; no. 130, $1,000.

   b. Deposits in transit $1,110.

   c. Bank service charges $93.

   d. Morris Bank collected a note for Royal.com, $810, less a $7 collection fee.

Preparing a bank reconciliation with NSF using back side of a bank statement.

6A-2. From the bank statement below, please (1) complete the bank reconciliation for Rick's Deli found on the reverse of the bank statement and (2) journalize the appropriate entries as needed.

Check Figure: Reconciled Balance $6,270

   a. A deposit of $3,000 is in transit.

   b. Rick's Deli has an ending checkbook balance of $6,600.

   c. Checks outstanding: no. 111, $600; no. 119, $1,200; no. 121, $330.

   d. Jim Rice's check for $300 bounced due to lack of sufficient funds.

LOWELL NATIONAL BANK
RIO MEAN BRAND
BUGNA, TEXAS

RICK'S DELI
8811 2ND ST,
BUGNA, TEXAS

Old Balance	Checks in Order of Payment		Deposits	Date	New Balance
6,000				2/2	6,000
	90.00	210.00		2/3	5,700
	150.00		300.00	2/10	5,850
	600.00		600.00	2/15	5,850
	300.00	NSF	300.00	2/20	5,850
	1,200.00		1,200.00	2/24	5,850
	600.00	30.00 SC	180.00	2/28	5,400

6A-3. The following transactions occurred in April for Merry Co.:

200X

April

1 Issued check no. 14 for $80 to establish a petty cash fund.
5 Paid $5 from petty cash for postage, voucher no. 1.
8 Paid $10 from petty cash for office supplies, voucher no. 2.
15 Issued check no. 15 to Reliable Corp. for $200 from past purchases on account.
17 Paid $8 from petty cash for office supplies, voucher no. 3.
20 Issued check no. 16 to Roger Corp., $600 from past purchases on account.
24 Paid $4 from petty cash for postage, voucher no. 4.
26 Paid $9 from petty cash for local church donation, voucher no. 5 (a miscellaneous payment).
28 Issued check no. 17 to Roy Kloon to pay for office equipment, $700.
30 Replenish petty cash, check no. 18.

Establishment and replenishment of petty cash.

Check Figure: Cash Replenishment $36

Your tasks are to

1. Record the appropriate entries in the general journal as well as the auxiliary petty cash record as needed.

2. Be sure to replenish the petty cash fund on April 30 (check no. 18).

6A-4. From the following, record the transactions into Logan's auxiliary petty cash record and general journal (p. 2) as needed:

200X

Oct.

1 A check was drawn (no. 444) payable to Roberta Floss, petty cashier, to establish a $100 petty cash fund.
5 Paid $14 for postage stamps, voucher no. 1.
9 Paid $12 for delivery charges on goods for resale, voucher no. 2.
12 Paid $8 for donation to a church (Miscellaneous Expense), voucher no. 3.
14 Paid $9 for postage stamps, voucher no. 4.
17 Paid $8 for delivery charges on goods for resale, voucher no. 5.
27 Purchased computer supplies from petty cash for $8, voucher no. 6.
28 Paid $4 for postage, voucher no. 7.
29 Drew check no. 618 to replenish petty cash and a $3 shortage.

Establishing and replenishing petty cash including a cash shortage.

Check Figure: Cash Replenishment $66

Group B Problems

(The blank forms you need are on pages 197–204 of the *Study Guide and Working Papers.*)

6B-1. As the bookkeeper of Royal.com, you received the bank statement from Morris Bank indicating a balance of $9,185. The ending checkbook balance was $8,215. Prepare the bank reconciliation for Royal.com as of July 31, 200X, and prepare journal entries as needed based on the following:

a. Deposits in transit, $3,600.

b. Bank service charges, $29.

c. Checks outstanding: no. 111, $590; no. 115, $1,255.

d. Morris Bank collected a note for Royal.com, $2,760, less a $6 collection fee.

6B-2. Based on the following, please (1) complete the bank reconciliation for Rick's Deli found on the reverse of the bank statement on the following page and (2) journalize the appropriate entries as needed.

a. Checks outstanding: no. 110, $80; no. 116, $160; no. 118, $52.

b. A deposit of $416 is in transit.

c. The checkbook balance of Rick's Deli shows an ending balance of $798.

d. Jim Rice's check for $40 bounced due to lack of sufficient funds.

Preparing a bank reconciliation including collection of a note.

Check Figure: Reconciled Balance $10,940

Preparing a bank reconciliation with NSF using the back side of a bank statement.

Check Figure: Reconciled Balance $756

LOWELL NATIONAL BANK
RIO MEAN BRAND
BUGNA, TEXAS

RICK'S DELI
8811 2ND ST,
BUGNA, TEXAS

Old Balance	Checks in Order of Payment		Deposits	Date	New Balance
718.00				4/2	718.00
	12.00	36.00		4/3	670.00
	20.00		40.00	4/10	690.00
	80.00		80.00	4/15	690.00
	40.00	NSF	40.00	4/20	690.00
	160.00		160.00	4/24	690.00
	80.00	2.00 SC	24.00	4/28	632.00

6B-3. From the following transactions, (1) record the entries as needed in the general journal of Merry Co. as well as the auxiliary petty cash record and (2) replenish the petty cash fund on April 30 (check no. 8).

200X
Apr.
1 Issued check no. 4 for $60 to establish a petty cash fund.
5 Paid $9 from petty cash for postage, voucher no. 1.
8 Paid $12 from petty cash for office supplies, voucher no. 2.
15 Issued check no. 5 to Reliable Corp. for $400 from past purchases on account.
17 Paid $7 from petty cash for office supplies, voucher no. 3.
20 Issued check no. 6 to Roger Corp, $300 from past purchases on account.
24 Paid $6 from petty cash for postage, voucher no. 4.
26 Paid $12 from petty cash for local church donation, voucher no. 5 (a miscellaneous payment).
28 Issued check no. 7 to Roy Kloon to pay office equipment, $800.
30 Replenish petty cash, check no. 8.

6B-4. From the following, record the transactions into Logan's auxiliary petty cash record and general journal (p. 2) as needed:

200X
Oct.
1 Roberta Floss, the petty cashier, cashed a check, no. 444, to establish a $90 petty cash fund.
5 Paid $16 for postage stamps, voucher no. 1.
9 Paid $14 for delivery charges on goods for resale, voucher no. 2.
12 Paid $6 for donation to a church (Miscellaneous Expense), voucher no. 3.
14 Paid $10 for postage stamps, voucher no. 4.
17 Paid $7 for delivery charges on goods for resale, voucher no. 5.
27 Purchased computer supplies from petty cash for $9, voucher no. 6.
28 Paid $3 for postage, voucher no. 7.
29 Drew check no. 618 to replenish petty cash and a $4 shortage.

REAL-WORLD APPLICATIONS

6R-1.
Claire Montgomery, the bookkeeper of Angel Co., has appointed Mike Kaminsky as the petty cash custodian. The following transactions occurred in November:

200X
Nov.
25 Check no. 441 was written and cashed to establish a $50 petty cash fund.
27 Paid $8.50 delivery charge for goods purchased for resale.

29 Purchased office supplies for $12 from petty cash.

30 Purchased postage stamps for $15 from petty cash.

On December 3, Mike received the following internal memo:

MEMO

To: Mike Kaminsky
FROM: Claire Montgomery
RE: Petty Cash

Mike, I'll need $5 for postage stamps. By the way, I noticed that our petty cash account seems to be too low. Let's increase its size to $100.

Could you help Mike replenish petty cash on December 3 by providing him with a general journal entry? Support your answer and indicate in writing whether Claire was correct.

6R-2.

Lee Company has the policy of depositing all receipts and making all payments by check. On receiving the bank statement, Bill Free, a new bookkeeper, is quite upset that the balance in cash in the ledger is $4,209.50, whereas the ending bank balance is $4,440.50. Bill is convinced the bank has made an error. Based on the following facts, is Bill's concern warranted? What other written suggestions could you offer Bill in the bank reconciliation process?

a. The Nov. 30 cash receipts, $611, had been placed in the bank's night depository after banking hours and consequently did not appear on the bank statement as a deposit.

b. Two debit memorandums and a credit memorandum were included with the returned check. None of the memorandums had been recorded at the time of the reconciliation. The first debit memorandum had a $130 NSF check written by Abby Ellen. The second was a $6.50 debit memorandum for service charges. The credit memorandum was for $494 and represented the proceeds less a $6 collection fee from a $500 non-interest-bearing note collected for Lee Company by the bank.

c. It was also found that checks no. 942 for $71.50 and no. 947 for $206.50, both written and recorded on Nov. 28, were not among the cancelled checks returned.

d. Bill found that check no. 899 was correctly drawn for $1,094, in payment for a new cash register. This check, however, had been recorded as though it were for $1,148.

e. The October bank reconciliation showed two checks outstanding on September 30, no. 621 for $152.50 and no. 630 for $179.30. Check no. 630 was returned with the November bank statement, but check no. 621 was not.

YOU make the call

Critical Thinking/Ethical Case

6R-3.

Sean Nah, the bookkeeper of Revell Co., received a bank statement from Lone Bank. Sean noticed a $250 mistake made by the bank in the company's favor. Sean called his supervisor, who said that as long as it benefits the company, he should not tell the bank about the error. You make the call. Write your specific recommendations to Sean.

INTERNET EXERCISES

EX-1. **[www.dallasfed.org]** This site will provide you details of the operation of the Federal Reserve Bank of Dallas, Texas. The Federal Reserve System, nicknamed "the Fed" has member banks in 13 cities. Each provides a wealth of economic information on the region it serves. The Dallas Fed website contains an article on "dot com" banking.

1. Read that article and answer these questions:

   a. Do "dot com" banks present a challenge to local banks in your city?

   b. What do you believe is the future of "dot com" banks? Will they be scrutinized more closely than traditional banking institutions?

2. Gather with a group of your fellow students and compare paper money. Use the money you have to determine the location of other Federal Reserve Banks. Look at the circular seal on the left side of the bills to determine these locations.

3. What services does the Fed offer to member banks?

EX-2. **[www.e-analysis.com/bonds/fed20.htm]** Checks that you write on your bank eventually return to your bank and the amount of the check is deducted from your account. In between the time you write the check and it comes back, you have use of the funds because of a phenomenon called "float". Individual checking accounts are handled much the same way this paragraph describes. Float is described as the period of time that two banks have the funds on their books. Suppose you pay your bill for a magazine subscription. You write the check on your bank, and mail it to the magazine company. When they deposit it, it is then "float" because your bank has not yet paid the check.

The Federal Reserve System handles float for large commercial accounts, in a method which is detailed in this article.

1. How does the Federal Reserve System handle checks from its member banks?

2. What is the impact of float on monetary policy of the United States?

CONTINUING PROBLEM

The books have been closed for the first year of business for Eldorado Computer Center. The company ended up with a marginal profit for the first three months in operation. Tony expects faster growth as he enters into a busy season.

Following is a list of transactions for the month of October. Petty Cash Account #1010 and Miscellaneous Expense Account #5100 have been added to the chart of accounts.

Assignment:

(See pages 208–218 in the *Study Guide and Working Papers*.)

1. Record the transactions in general journal or petty cash format.

2. Post the transactions to the general ledger accounts.

3. Prepare a trial balance.

Oct. 1 Paid rent for November, December, and January, $1,200 (check #8108).

2 Established a petty cash fund for $100.

4 Collected $3,600 from a cash customer for building five systems.

5   Collected $2,600, the amount due from A. Pitale's invoice #12674, customer on account.
6   Purchased $25 worth of stamps, using petty cash voucher #101.
7   Withdrew $2,000 (check #8109) for personal use.
8   Purchased $22 worth of supplies, using petty cash voucher #102.
12   Paid the newspaper carrier $10, using petty cash voucher #103.
16   Paid the amount due on the September phone bill, $65 (check #8110).
17   Paid the amount due on the September electric bill, $95 (check #8111).
22   Performed computer services for Taylor Golf; billed the client $4,200 (invoice #12675).
23   Paid $20 for computer paper, using petty cash voucher #104.
30   Took $15 out of petty cash for lunch, voucher #105.
31   Replenished the petty cash. Coin and currency in drawer total $8.00.

Because Tony was so busy trying to close his books, he forgot to reconcile his last three months of bank statements. What follows on pages 235 and 236 is a list of all deposits and checks written for the past three months (each entry is identified by chapter, transaction date, or transaction letter) and bank statements for July through September. The statement for October won't arrive until the first week of November.

ELDORADO COMPUTER CENTER SUMMARY OF DEPOSITS AND CHECKS

Chapter	Transaction	Payor/Payee	Amount
		DEPOSITS	
1	a	Tony Freedman	$4,500
1	f	Cash customer	250
1	i	Taylor Golf	1,200
1	g	Cash customer	200
2	p	Cash customer	900
3	Sept. 2	Tonya Parker Jones	325
3	Sept. 6	Summer Lipe	220
3	Sept. 12	Jeannine Sparks	850
3	Sept. 26	Mike Hammer	140

Chapter	Transaction	Check #	Payor/Payee	Amount
			CHECKS	
1	b	8095	Multi Systems, Inc.	$1,200
1	c	8096	Office Furniture, Inc.	600
1	e	8097	Capital Management	400
1	j	8098	Tony Freedman	100
2	l	8099	Insurance Protection, Inc.	150
2	m	8100	Office Depot	200
2	n	8101	Computer Edge Magazine	1,400
2	q	8102	San Diego Electric	85
2	r	8103	U.S. Postmaster	50
3	Sept. 1	8104	Capital Management	1,200
3	Sept. 8	8105	Pacific Bell USA	155
3	Sept. 15	8106	Computer Connection	200
3	Sept. 16	8107	Multi Systems, Inc.	1,200

BANK STATEMENT
First Union Bank 322 Glen Ave. Escondido, CA 92025

Eldorado Computer Center   Statement Date: July 22, 200X

Checks Paid:

Date paid	Number	Amount	Date received	Amount
			Deposits and Credits:	
7–4	8085	1,200.00	7–1	4,500.00
7–7	8096	600.00	7–10	250.00
7–15	8097	400.00	7–20	1,200.00
			7–21	200.00
			Total Deposits	$6,150.00

Total 3 checks paid for $2,200.00
Ending balance on July 22 —
$3,950.00

Received Statement July 29, 200X.

BANK STATEMENT
First Union Bank 322 Glen Ave. Escondido, CA 92025

Eldorado Computer Center   Statement Date: August 21, 200X

Checks Paid:

Date paid	Number	Amount	Date received	Amount
			Deposits and Credits:	
8–2	8098	100.00	8–12	900.00
8–3	8099	150.00		
8–10	8100	200.00		
8–15	8101	1,400.00		
8–20	8102	85.00		

Total 5 checks paid for $1,935.00   Total Deposits $900.00
Beginning balance on July 22 —   Ending balance on August 21 —
$3,950.00 $2,915.00

Received statement August 27, 200X.

BANK STATEMENT
First Union Bank 322 Glen Ave. Escondido, CA 92025

Eldorado Computer Center   Statement Date: September 20, 200X

Checks Paid:

Date paid	Number	Amount	Date received	Amount
			Deposits and Credits:	
9–2	8103	50.00	9–4	325.00
9–6	8104	1,200.00	9–7	220.00
9–12	8105	155.00	9–14	850.00

Total 3 checks paid for $1,405.00   Total Deposits $1,395.00
Beginning balance on August 21   Ending balance on September 20
$2,915.00 $2,905.00

Received statement September 29, 200X.

Assignment:

1. Compare the Computer Center's deposits and checks with the bank statements and complete a bank reconciliation as of September 30, 200X.

Payroll Concepts and Procedures

Coffee isn't the only thing perking at Starbucks, the Seattle-based coffee retailer that jump-started the nationwide espresso craze. "Perks," such as bonus pay, a hefty discount on merchandise and a free pound of coffee a week, are part of what have put this company on Fortune's list of "The Hundred Best Companies to Work For" for several years running.

Whether they are part-time *baristas*—the front-line employees who pull espresso for your latté— or full time financial executives are all "partners" in the Starbucks enterprise. And every single partner receives full medical and dental coverage and stock options— the opportunity to purchase company stock at bargain prices— after three months on the job. In addition, if a partner hankers to be a coffee connoisseur or marketing dynamo, Starbucks will enroll her in the appropriate training program. Finally, it can't hurt morale to be given a pound of fresh java for free each week and a 30% discount on company merchandise. For all these reasons in addition to a pleasing, youth-oriented culture, the turnover rate (the rate at which

employees leave the company) is only 16% compared to the restaurant industry average of 300%.

With 35,000 partners in all, the cost of payroll alone could easily amount to more than half of Starbuck's total expenses. At Starbucks, a partner's total pay package is called "Your Special Blend." While the blend varies depending upon who you are and what you do for the company, it has up to six major "ingredients." And these are base pay, bonuses, benefits (including health, life and disability insurance), savings programs, stock and stock options, and "extra shots" like company recognition and award programs.

Beyond the cost of all these "ingredients," Starbucks, like all businesses, is responsible for complying with rules that govern payroll deductions. In this chapter you'll learn how to calculate both hourly wages and overtime. You'll also learn the basic rules and procedures for making payroll deductions, withholding taxes, and paying taxes. And, if you want to learn more about the job opportunities available at Starbucks just go to www.starbucks.com and click on "job center."

Based on: information from Starbucks Web site, www.starbucks.com. Carla Joinson, "The cost of doing business?" *HRMagazine*, December 1999, pp. 86–92. Stephanie Armour, "Part-timers reap benefits of tight market Employers offer them same perks as full-time workers," *USA Today*, November 1, 1999.

LEARNING OBJECTIVES

▼ Calculating overtime pay, FICA deductions for Social Security and Medicare, and federal income tax withholding. (p. 240)

▼ Preparing a payroll register. (p. 246)

▼ Journalizing and posting the payroll entry from the payroll register. (p. 253)

▼ Maintaining an individual employee earnings record. (p. 255)

An essential part of running a business is hiring and paying employees. Whether a business is a small mom-and-pop grocery store in your own town or a huge nationwide corporation, the rules for payroll are really the same. That's why it's important to know how to calculate and record a payroll.

In this chapter we take a close look at the employees of Gradesoft.com, a company that programs and sells teacher grading software to see how a payroll is figured and recorded. We look at how a payroll is affected by federal, state, and local taxes and how the accountant at Gradesoft.com handles a payroll for the company.

LEARNING UNIT 7-1

INTRODUCTION TO PAYROLL ACCOUNTING

Ernie Goldman is the accountant for Gradesoft.com. This new company creates software that allows teachers to track and calculate students' grades electronically using a personal computer. Ernie has the responsibility of calculating and recording each payroll for the company. Several key parts of Ernie's job in working with payroll need mention here. First, Ernie *must be accurate* in everything he does, because any mistake he makes in working with the payroll may affect both the employee and the company. Second, Ernie needs to be *on time* when working on the company's payroll so that the employees get their paychecks when they are due. Third, Ernie must at all times *comply with the appropriate federal, state, and local laws governing payroll matters*. Fourth, Ernie always needs to keep everything *confidential* when working on the payroll.

Ernie must first calculate the earnings for Gradesoft.com employees. For Ernie to make the correct calculations, he must know how each employee has been classified for payroll purposes. As a rule, a company will classify each employee as either "hourly" or "salaried" when it comes to paying earnings. If an employee is an *hourly employee,* that employee will only be paid for the hours he or she worked. If an employee is classified as a *salaried employee,* he or she will receive a set dollar amount for the hours worked.

Gradesoft.com has classified three of its six employees as hourly. For these employees, Ernie must compute the hours they have worked during a specific period of time known as a *pay period.* A pay period is important because Ernie uses it to determine how much each hourly employee has earned. For payroll purposes, pay periods are defined as daily, weekly, biweekly (every two weeks), semimonthly (twice each month), monthly, quarterly, or annual. A pay period can start on any day of the week and must end after the specified period of time has past. Most companies use weekly, biweekly, semimonthly, or monthly pay periods when calculating their payrolls.

Gradesoft.com uses a biweekly pay period for its hourly employees and a monthly pay period for its three salaried employees. The biweekly pay period starts on Monday and ends 14 days (two weeks) later on a Sunday. The monthly pay period starts on the first day of the calendar month and ends on the last day.

Now that Ernie knows the pay period for Gradesoft.com's hourly employees, he must calculate their total or *gross earnings.* The gross earnings amount for an employee is composed of two amounts; regular earnings and overtime earnings (if any).

Overtime earnings must be figured according to federal (and in some cases, state) law. This federal law is known as the **Fair Labor Standards Act** (also known as Federal Wage and Hour Law). For most employers, the law states that an hourly employee must be paid more per hour for any hours worked over 40 during a period of time called a *work week.* A work week is a time period that can start at any time on any given day, but it must end 168 hours later (or seven calendar days of 24 hours each). One work week follows another, and the starting time must be the same time each week. For rules of the Fair Labor Standards Act to apply to an employer, the employer must be involved in interstate commerce.

For the hourly employees of Gradesoft.com, there are two work weeks in each biweekly pay period. Gradesoft.com's work week starts on Monday morning at 12:01 A.M. and ends the following Sunday evening at 12:00 midnight (168 hours later). Thus, Ernie must figure any overtime pay if any employee has worked more than 40 hours during each week of the two weeks (that is, biweekly) pay period.

The federal law also set the minimum standard for overtime pay. It is one and a half times the regular hourly rate of pay for an employee. Let's look at Lee Jackson, one of the hourly employees of Gradesoft.com who worked overtime hours during the biweekly pay period starting on August 7 and ending on August 20 (remember that there are 14 days in the biweekly pay period, and two work weeks in the same pay period for figuring overtime earnings).

Lee worked 45 hours for the week of August 7 to August 13 and 39 for the week of August 14 to August 20. How many regular and overtime hours did Lee work for this biweekly pay period? First, Ernie must look at each work week separately from the next. Thus, Lee worked 40 regular and 5 overtime hours for the first work week and 39 regular and 0 overtime hours for the second work week. Note that Ernie did not take any overtime hours from the first work week and apply them to the second work week to pay Lee for 40 hours.

Remember that each work week stands independently of another, even if during another work week the employee worked fewer than 40 hours.

There are two ways of figuring the regular and overtime hours for Lee during this pay period. Ernie notes here that Lee makes $10.80 per hour. Now let's look at each way to figure the total hours Lee must be paid.

Method One

$$\begin{array}{ll} \text{Total hours} \times \text{regular rate} & = 84 \text{ hours} \times \$10.80/\text{hour} = \$907.20 \\ \quad \text{worked} \qquad \text{of pay} & \\ + \text{Overtime} \times \tfrac{1}{2} \text{ regular rate} & = 5 \text{ hours} \quad \times \$5.40/\text{hour} \ = \$\ 27.00 \\ \quad \text{hours} \qquad \text{of pay} & \end{array}$$

Total pay for Lee Jackson	$934.20

Method Two

$$\begin{array}{l} \text{Regular hours} \times \text{regular rate of pay} = 79 \text{ hours} \times \$10.80/\text{hour} = \$853.20 \\ + \text{Overtime hours} \times 1\tfrac{1}{2} \text{ regular rate of pay} = 5 \text{ hours} \times \$16.20 = \$\ 81.00 \end{array}$$

Total pay for Lee Jackson	$934.20

As you can see, Ernie can use either way to arrive at the total or gross earnings for Lee Jackson for the pay period. Method One clearly shows Ernie how much Lee is being paid in overtime. Because Method Two is more commonly used to figure gross earnings, we use it to figure gross earnings for Gradesoft.com employees in this chapter.

EMPLOYEE FEDERAL AND STATE INCOME TAX WITHHOLDING

After Ernie has figured Lee Jackson's gross earnings, he must now start figuring out how much Lee will receive in pay after several different taxes have been withheld. These taxes, known as **payroll taxes** or **income tax withholding,** must be paid by each employee based on how much was earned each pay period. Gradesoft.com is required to withhold payroll taxes for each employee and pay them to the government according to a special timetable. The amount paid by Gradesoft.com for payroll taxes is known as a **payroll tax deposit.** We discuss how payroll tax deposits work in Chapter 8.

For Ernie to determine how much to withhold from Lee's check in payroll taxes, Lee must complete a form known as a Form W-4, Employee's Withholding Allowance Certificate. This form contains information Ernie needs to calculate Lee's federal income tax (FIT) withholding for the pay period. Ernie will use the information from Form W-4, along with special tax withholding tables supplied by the Internal Revenue Service (IRS), to determine how much to withhold in FIT from Lee's check. Lee Jackson is actually paying the government the amount that he would owe in federal income taxes by having Gradesoft.com take it at the time he is paid. In this way Lee pays his taxes on a "pay-as-you-go" basis, which is based on how much he earns each pay period.

Notice in Figure 7-1 p. 241 that Lee's Form W-4 shows his marital status and total number of allowances he is claiming for federal income tax purposes. In general, an employee is granted one allowance (also known as an exemption) for himself or herself, one for a spouse (unless the spouse works and claims his or her own allowance), and one for each of his or her dependents (e.g., children) for whom the employee provides more than one-half support during a year. Employees who wish to have more withheld from their paychecks can elect to claim fewer allowances than they actually have on Form W-4.

| Form **W-4**
Department of the Treasury
Internal Revenue Service | **Employee's Withholding Allowance Certificate**
For Privacy Act and Paperwork Reduction Act Notice, see page 2. | OMB No. 1545-0010
20⬡X |

| 1 Type or print your first name and middle initial
LEE | Last name
JACKSON | 2 Your social security number
923 85 1316 |

| Home address (number and street or rural route)
1225 HIGHTOWN STREET | 3 ☒ Single ☐ Married ☐ Married, but withhold at higher Single rate.
Note: *If married, but legally separated, or spouse is a nonresident alien, check the Single box.* |

| City or town, state, and ZIP code
SOUTHSIDE, MA 01945 | 4 If your last name differs from that on your social security card, check
here. **You must call 1-800-772-1213 for a new card** . . . ☐ |

5	Total number of allowances you are claiming (from line **H** above **OR** from the applicable worksheet on page 2)	**5**	1
6	Additional amount, if any, you want withheld from each paycheck	**6** $	
7	I claim exemption from withholding for 2000, and I certify that I meet **BOTH** of the following conditions for exemption: Last year I had a right to a refund of **ALL** Federal income tax withheld because I had **NO** tax liability **AND** This year I expect a refund of **ALL** Federal income tax withheld because I expect to have **NO** tax liability. If you meet both conditions, write "EXEMPT" here	**7**	

Under penalties of perjury, I certify that I am entitled to the number of withholding allowances claimed on this certificate, or I am entitled to claim exempt status.

Employee's signature
(Form is not valid
unless you sign it) ▶ *Lee Jackson*   Date ▶ JANUARY 3, 200X

| 8 Employer's name and address (Employer: Complete lines 8 and 10 only if sending to the IRS.) | 9 Office code
(optional) | 10 Employer identification number |

Cat. No. 10220Q

FIGURE 7-1. Form W-4, Employee's Withholding Allowance Certificate

Ernie will use Lee's marital status and number of allowances claimed from his Form W-4 along with Lee's gross earnings for the pay period to look up the amount of federal tax to withhold using an IRS wage bracket table (see Fig. 7-2). These tables can be found in an IRS publication known as **Circular E, Employer's Tax Guide,** also known as Publication 15. Note in Figure 7-2 (p. 242) that the wage bracket table has been grouped according to pay period and marital status. *Circular E* contains tables for daily, weekly, biweekly, semi-monthly, monthly, quarterly, and annual pay periods. For each pay period there are separate "single" and "married" tables. Finally, each individual table is organized according to the gross earnings of the employee for the pay period.

Let's look at how Ernie will use the Single Biweekly Payroll Period table in *Circular E* to see how he arrived at the amount of FIT to be withheld from Lee Jackson's check. First, Ernie knows that Lee is paid biweekly (once every two weeks). Ernie has also figured Lee's gross earnings for the last biweekly pay period Lee worked ($934.20). Ernie can then look at Lee's form W-4 and see that Lee has claimed one allowance (for himself) and has indicated that he is single (look at Fig. 7-1 again). It is now easy for Ernie to look up the FIT amount from the table by going down the left-hand column labeled "If the wages are." Ernie will stop at the line "At least $920 But less than $940." Ernie stops at this line because Lee's earnings are $934.20, which is an amount within that range of earnings. Now Ernie will move to the right until he finds the amount in the column labeled "1," which indicates the number of with-holding allowances per Lee's Form W-4. Where the row and the column meet, Ernie finds an amount of $108, the amount of FIT that Ernie will withhold from Lee's paycheck.

Now what would happen if Lee actually earned $940 for the pay period? Ernie would go to the next line below in the table because the first column reads "At least $940." The amount Lee would owe in FIT withholding would be

If the wages are—		And the number of withholding allowances claimed is—										
At least	But less than	0	1	2	3	4	5	6	7	8	9	10
		The amount of income tax to be withheld is—										
$800	$820	106	90	74	58	42	25	9	0	0	0	0
820	840	109	93	77	61	45	28	12	0	0	0	0
840	860	112	96	80	64	48	31	15	0	0	0	0
860	880	115	99	83	67	51	34	18	2	0	0	0
880	900	118	102	86	70	54	37	21	5	0	0	0
900	920	121	105	89	73	57	40	24	8	0	0	0
920	940	124	108	92	76	60	43	27	11	0	0	0
940	960	127	111	95	79	63	46	30	14	0	0	0
960	980	130	114	98	82	66	49	33	17	1	0	0
980	1,000	133	117	101	85	69	52	36	20	4	0	0
1,000	1,020	136	120	104	88	72	55	39	23	7	0	0
1,020	1,040	139	123	107	91	75	58	42	26	10	0	0
1,040	1,060	142	126	110	94	78	61	45	29	13	0	0
1,060	1,080	145	129	113	97	81	64	48	32	16	0	0
1,080	1,100	151	132	116	100	84	67	51	35	19	3	0
1,100	1,120	156	135	119	103	87	70	54	38	22	6	0
1,120	1,140	162	138	122	106	90	73	57	41	25	9	0
1,140	1,160	167	141	125	109	93	76	60	44	28	12	0
1,160	1,180	173	144	128	112	96	79	63	47	31	15	0
1,180	1,200	179	149	131	115	99	82	66	50	34	18	2
1,200	1,220	184	154	134	118	102	85	69	53	37	21	5
1,220	1,240	190	160	137	121	105	88	72	56	40	24	8
1,240	1,260	195	165	140	124	108	91	75	59	43	27	11
1,260	1,280	201	171	143	127	111	94	78	62	46	30	14
1,280	1,300	207	177	146	130	114	97	81	65	49	33	17
1,300	1,320	212	182	152	133	117	100	84	68	52	36	20
1,320	1,340	218	188	158	136	120	103	87	71	55	39	23
1,340	1,360	223	193	163	139	123	106	90	74	58	42	26
1,360	1,380	229	199	169	142	126	109	93	77	61	45	29
1,380	1,400	235	205	174	145	129	112	96	80	64	48	32
1,400	1,420	240	210	180	150	132	115	99	83	67	51	35
1,420	1,440	246	216	186	155	135	118	102	86	70	54	38
1,440	1,460	251	221	191	161	138	121	105	89	73	57	41
1,460	1,480	257	227	197	167	141	124	108	92	76	60	44
1,480	1,500	263	233	202	172	144	127	111	95	79	63	47
1,500	1,520	268	238	208	178	148	130	114	98	82	66	50
1,520	1,540	274	244	214	183	153	133	117	101	85	69	53
1,540	1,560	279	249	219	189	159	136	120	104	88	72	56
1,560	1,580	285	255	225	195	164	139	123	107	91	75	59
1,580	1,600	291	261	230	200	170	142	126	110	94	78	62
1,600	1,620	296	266	236	206	176	145	129	113	97	81	65
1,620	1,640	302	272	242	211	181	151	132	116	100	84	68
1,640	1,660	307	277	247	217	187	157	135	119	103	87	71
1,660	1,680	313	283	253	223	192	162	138	122	106	90	74
1,680	1,700	319	289	258	228	198	168	141	125	109	93	77
1,700	1,720	324	294	264	234	204	173	144	128	112	96	80
1,720	1,740	330	300	270	239	209	179	149	131	115	99	83
1,740	1,760	335	305	275	245	215	185	155	134	118	102	86
1,760	1,780	341	311	281	251	220	190	160	137	121	105	89
1,780	1,800	347	317	286	256	226	196	166	140	124	108	92
1,800	1,820	352	322	292	262	232	201	171	143	127	111	95
1,820	1,840	358	328	298	267	237	207	177	147	130	114	98
1,840	1,860	363	333	303	273	243	213	183	152	133	117	101
1,860	1,880	369	339	309	279	248	218	188	158	136	120	104
1,880	1,900	375	345	314	284	254	224	194	164	139	123	107
1,900	1,920	380	350	320	290	260	229	199	169	142	126	110
1,920	1,940	386	356	326	295	265	235	205	175	145	129	113
1,940	1,960	391	361	331	301	271	241	211	180	150	132	116
1,960	1,980	397	367	337	307	276	246	216	186	156	135	119
1,980	2,000	403	373	342	312	282	252	222	192	161	138	122
2,000	2,020	408	378	348	318	288	257	227	197	167	141	125
2,020	2,040	414	384	354	323	293	263	233	203	173	144	128
2,040	2,060	419	389	359	329	299	269	239	208	178	148	131
2,060	2,080	425	395	365	335	304	274	244	214	184	154	134
2,080	2,100	431	401	370	340	310	280	250	220	189	159	137

$2,100 and over — Use Table 2(a) for a **SINGLE person** on page 34. Also see the instructions on page 32.

FIGURE 7-2. Wage Bracket Tables—Single Persons

$111; Lee would owe a little more in tax because he made a little more in gross earnings. Had Lee earned $939 instead of $940, his earnings would have still been "Less than $940." Ernie would use the same line of the table and would find that Lee would owe $108 in FIT.

Lee will probably owe state income tax (or SIT) as well as FIT. Many states allow payroll people to use the federal Form W-4 for state income tax withholding as well. Other states have their own versions of Form W-4 that employees must fill out. Many states have their own version of the IRS *Circular E* that can be used to look up SIT withholding. These states also require an employer to withhold and collect the state income taxes and then make state payroll tax deposits according to state rules. Forty-one states currently tax an employee's gross earnings; nine do not and do not require SIT withholding.

EMPLOYEE WITHHOLDING FOR SOCIAL SECURITY TAXES

Another tax that Ernie must compute and withhold from employee checks is known as Social Security Tax or FICA (FICA stands for Federal Insurance Contributions Act, a 1935 federal law that has required workers to pay this tax since 1937). The proceeds of this tax support federal payments for (1) monthly retirement benefits for those over 62 years old, (2) medical benefits for those over 65 years old, (3) benefits for workers who have become disabled, and (4) benefits for families of deceased workers who were covered by this law. Both employees of companies as well as self-employed individuals must pay FICA taxes.

There are two special things to know about Social Security (or FICA) tax. First, Social Security tax is really two taxes. One of these taxes is called Social Security (or OASDI, which stands for old age, survivors, and disability insurance), and the other is known as Medicare (or HI, which stands for health insurance). Usually, people group both taxes together and call them Social Security (or FICA) tax. Second, the rate of Social Security tax and the maximum dollar amount of earnings upon which the tax can be computed may change each year. The maximum dollar amount of earnings upon which the tax is computed is known as an earnings, or wage-base limit. Note that the wage-base limit applies only to the Social Security (or OASDI) part of the tax because there is no limit for Medicare (or HI) tax.

Let's look at how Ernie computes the Social Security tax on Lee's earnings to give you a better idea of how this tax is calculated. First, Ernie knows both the current year's tax rate and the wage-base limit for the Social Security portion of the tax. Here are the rates and limit he will use:

> Current year's rate for Social Security (OASDI) tax = 6.20 percent
>
> Current year's rate for Medicare (HI) tax = 1.45 percent
>
> Current year's Wage-base limit for Social Security (OASID) tax = $76,200

Note again that these rates and wage-base limit may change each year. In general, the wage-base limit will increase from year to year, as may the rate of taxes. Therefore, we use the term *current* when referring to these tax rates and wage-base limit.

Once Ernie knows the rates and limit he is ready to begin making calculations. First, Ernie needs to look at how much Lee has earned for the year *prior* to his current pay-period earnings. He will use this information to determine whether Lee's earnings are under or more than the current wage-base limit for Social Security tax. Ernie finds that Lee's year-to-date (abbreviated YTD) gross earnings before this pay period equal $20,872.65. This dollar amount is below the wage-base limit of $76,200 for the year, so Lee's total gross earnings of $934.20 will be taxed at a rate of 6.20% for Social Security purposes. Ernie will withhold $57.92 in Social Security taxes (or $934.20 × .062 = $57.92).

What if Lee had made close to or more than $76,200 for the year before his current pay-period earnings? Let's suppose that Lee's prior year-to-date earnings are $75,818.95. If we add $934.20 to this amount, Lee's new year-to-date earnings will be $76,753.15 ($75,818.95 + $934.20), which is more than the current $76,200 wage-base limit. In this situation Ernie must withhold Social Security tax *on only the portion of Lee's current gross earnings that will not exceed the $76,200 wage-base limit.* Ernie must make the following calculation to determine this amount by subtracting Lee's prior year-to-date earnings from the wage base-limit: $76,200 − $75,818.95 = $381.05. Thus, only $381.05 of Lee's $934.20 in current gross earnings will be subject to Social Security tax at a rate of 6.20%. The remaining $553.15 of Lee's current pay (or $934.20 − $381.05) will not be taxed for Social Security (OASDI) purposes. Therefore, whatever Lee earns for the rest of the current calendar year will not be subject to this tax because Lee has exceeded the wage-base limit for the year.

It is important to know that all these calculations apply only to each current calendar year. An employee's year-to-date earnings in one year will never be carried over and used in the next year for the purpose of looking at the Social Security wage-base limit. Every employee starts the new year on January 1 with $0.00 in year-to-date earnings for wage-base limit analysis.

It is easier to figure Medicare (or HI) tax because there is no wage-base limit connected with this tax. Ernie will simply figure Medicare tax at a rate of 1.45 percent of Lee's earnings no matter how much he earns during the year. Ernie will withhold $13.55 in Medicare (or HI) tax on Lee's gross earnings for the pay period ($934.20 × .0145 = $13.55).

Another important fact about Social Security tax is that the amount withheld and paid by each employee must be matched and paid by the employer, using the same rules we have discussed. In Chapter 8 we look at the employer's side of Social Security and Medicare taxes.

OTHER INCOME TAX WITHHOLDING

We pointed out previously that employees will have state income taxes withheld from their paychecks if they live in one of the 41 states that tax income. In addition, many cities and counties tax employee earnings. Sometimes the tax will be a certain percentage of gross earnings, or it may be a flat dollar amount withheld every pay period. Such cities and counties will have their own rules regarding payroll tax deposits and tax reports for this type of withholding.

WORKERS' COMPENSATION INSURANCE

Workers' compensation insurance provides protection for employees from any loss they may incur due to injury or death while on the job. Each employer (working with an insurance agent or a state agency) must estimate the cost of this insurance. The premium must be paid in advance. In the majority of states, this tax is paid by the employer, not the employee. California is one exception where employees pay state disability insurance via withholding from their paychecks. In Chapter 8 we look at how the premium is figured and what responsibility the employer has in paying this tax.

LEARNING UNIT 7-1 REVIEW

AT THIS POINT you should be able to

- ▼ Explain the purpose of the Federal Wage and Hour Law. (p. 239)
- ▼ Calculate overtime pay. (p. 240)
- ▼ Complete a W-4 form. (p. 241)
- ▼ Discuss the term *claiming an allowance.* (p. 241)
- ▼ Use a wage-bracket tax table to arrive at the withholding amount for federal income tax. (p. 241)
- ▼ Define the purposes of Social Security (FICA) tax. (p. 243)
- ▼ Calculate the deductions for Social Security and Medicare taxes. (p. 243)
- ▼ Understand the purpose of workers' compensation insurance. (p. 244)

SELF-REVIEW QUIZ 7-1

(The forms you need are found on page 219 of the *Study Guide and Working Papers.*)

John Small is a software engineer who is paid biweekly. He earned $2,064 in the currently biweekly pay period. To date this year, *before* the current payroll, John has earned a total $75,000 in salary. Please calculate the amount of tax for Social Security and Medicare, federal income tax, and state income tax deducted for the pay period.

- ▼ Social security tax is 6.20 percent with a wage-base limit of $76,200 for the year.
- ▼ Medicare tax is 1.45 percent with no wage-base limit.
- ▼ John is single and claims two withholding allowances.
- ▼ The state income tax rate is 8 percent.
- ▼ No other deductions are taken out of John's paycheck by his employer.

Solution to Self-Review Quiz 7-1

- ▼ Social Security tax: $74.40 ($1,200 × .062). The $1,200 was found by taking $76,200 − $75,000.
- ▼ Medicare tax: $29.93 ($2,064 × .0145). Remember that there is no wage-base limit for this tax.
- ▼ State income tax: $165.12 ($2,064 × .08).
- ▼ Federal income tax: $365. Found by looking at where the "At least $2,060" line meets the "Two withholding allowance" column.

LEARNING UNIT 7-2   THE PAYROLL PROCESS

Ernie Goldman will now enter the payroll information for the three hourly employees of Gradesoft.com into a worksheet known as a Payroll Register. Figure 7-3 (p. 246) shows a completed payroll register for the biweekly pay period from August 7 through August 20. We refer to this figure in both Chapters 7 and 8.

This multicolumn form is used specifically for the purpose of tracking the earnings of employees for any given pay period. Note that Gradesoft.com will have both biweekly and monthly payroll registers

GRADESOFT.COM INC.
PAYROLL REGISTER
AUGUST 7–20, 200X

Employee Name	Allowances and Marital Status	Cumulative Earnings (YTD)	Salary for Pay Period	No. of Hours Worked	Wages per Hour	Earnings Regular	Earnings Overtime	Earnings Gross	Cumulative Earnings (YTD)	Taxable Earnings Federal Unemployment	Taxable Earnings Soc. Sec. Tax	Taxable Earnings Medicare
Jackson, L.	S-1	20 87 26 5	—	84 00	10 80	8 53 20	81 00	9 34 20	21 80 685	—	9 34 20	9 34 20
Stowe, S.	S-0	48 50 25	—	80 00	24 50	19 60 00	—	19 60 00	6 81 025	19 60 00	19 60 00	19 60 00
Regan, P.	S-2	46 58 70 5	—	81 50	21 75	17 40 00	48 94	17 88 94	48 37 599	—	17 88 94	17 88 94
TOTALS		72 30 995	—			45 53 20	1 29 94	46 83 14	76 99 309	19 60 00	46 83 14	46 83 14
Discussions in this chapter are keyed to these letters	(A)	(B)	(C)	(C)	(C)	(D)	(E)	(F)	(G)	(H)	(I)	(J)

FIGURE 7-3. Payroll Register for Gradesoft.com

FIGURE 7-3. (Cont.)

GRADESOFT.COM INC.
PAYROLL REGISTER
AUGUST 7–20, 200X

FICA		Deductions			Net Pay	Check No.	Distribution of Expense Accounts	
Soc. Sec.	Medicare	Federal Income Tax	State Income Tax	Medical Insurance			Business Analyst Expense	Program. Develop. Expense
5792	1355	10800	7474	2200	65799	506	93420	
12152	2842	39700	15680	4400	121226	507		196000
11091	2594	28600	14312	2200	120097	508		178894
29035	6791	79100	37466	8800	307122		93420	374894
(K)	(L)	(M)	(N)	(O)	(P)	(Q)	(R)	(S)

Discussions in this chapter are keyed to these letters

Note: Sheila Stowe's medical insurance is $44.00 because she pays to cover both herself and her daughter.

because it tracks its hourly employees on a biweekly basis and its salaried employees on a monthly basis. (We only show the biweekly register here.) Let's look closely at each column in the register to see how the numbers were generated.

(A) ALLOWANCES AND MARITAL STATUS

The information in column A comes from the completed Form W-4 that each employee has completed. You will recall that this form (see Fig. 7-1) indicates the employee's marital status and number of withholding allowances (or exemptions) that is used to arrive at the correct amount of federal income tax (column M) to be withheld for the pay period.

Example: Sheila Stowe is single and provides total support for her nine-year-old daughter. Even though she can claim two withholding allowances, she claims zero allowances because she wants to have more taken out of her paycheck each pay period. If she has paid too much in FIT, she can claim a refund after the end of the year when filing her individual income tax return.

(B) CUMULATIVE (YTD) EARNINGS

Column B shows the employee's year-to-date (or cumulative) earnings for the year *before* the current pay period earnings have been added to it. Ernie will look at the amount in this column to determine if the employee is over or under the Social Security wage-base limit.

Example: Lee Jackson has earned $20,872.65 before the current biweekly pay period.

(C) SALARY FOR PAY PERIOD, NUMBER OF HOURS WORKED, AND WAGES PER HOUR

Specific columns are used to record the amount any salaried employees have earned for the pay period, the hours worked by hourly employees, and the hourly rate of pay for nonsalaried employees.

Example: Because this payroll register is used only for hourly employees, no amounts are entered in the Salary for Pay Period column. Please note that Lee Jackson is paid $10.80 per hour, and he worked 84 total hours for the pay period.

(D) "REGULAR" EARNINGS

To get an amount for column D, Ernie must multiply the total regular earnings by the hourly rate of pay for each employee.

Example: Sheila Stowe has earned $1,960.00 for the pay period.

Hours Worked		Rate of Pay per Hour		Regular Earnings
80	×	$24.50	=	$1,960.00

(E) OVERTIME EARNINGS

After 40 hours each work week, hourly employees are entitled to receive overtime pay at a rate of one and one-half times their regular hourly rate of pay.

Example: Pat Regan worked 81.5 hours, of which 80 were regular and 1.5 hours were classified as overtime. Pat is paid overtime at a rate of $32.625 per hour.

Hourly Rate		Time and a Half		Overtime Rate of Pay
$21.75	×	1.5	=	$32.625

Overtime Hours Worked		Overtime Rate		Overtime Earnings
1.5	×	$32.625	=	$48.94

(F) GROSS EARNINGS

Gross earnings is the total amount that an employee has earned (regular earnings plus any overtime earnings). These amounts will be used to fill in columns R and S.

Example: Pat Regan's gross earnings are $1,788.94.

Regular Earnings		Overtime Earnings		Gross Earnings
$1,740.00	+	$48.94	=	$1,788.94

(G) CUMULATIVE EARNINGS (YTD)

Column G shows the employee's year-to-date earnings after the current pay period earnings have been computed. This amount will be "carried over" to the next payroll register column B for the next pay period.

Example: Sheila Stowe has earned $6,810.25 as of August 20.

Cumulative Earnings before the Pay Period		Gross Earnings for the Pay Period		Cumulative Earnings YTD as of August 20
$4,850.25	+	$1,960.00	=	$6,810.25

(H) TAXABLE EARNINGS: UNEMPLOYMENT INSURANCE

In Chapter 8 we talk about certain payroll taxes that are only paid by employers. Federal unemployment taxes (per the Federal Unemployment Tax Act, or FUTA) are paid according to a wage-base limit (like Social Security tax). The current wage-base limit for FUTA tax is the first $7,000 that each employee earns during a calendar year. Note that this column shows the FUTA wage-base limit for each employee, not the amount of FUTA tax that Gradesoft.com has paid.

> **Example:** Before this pay period, Sheila Stowe's cumulative year-to-date earnings are $4850.25. For the pay period ending on August 20, Sheila earned $1,960. Her new cumulative year-to-date earnings now amount to $6,810.25, which is under the $7,000 FUTA wage-base limit. Gradesoft.com will pay FUTA tax on the $1,960.00 that Sheila earned for the pay period.

During the next pay period, Gradesoft.com will pay FUTA tax only on $189.75 of Sheila's earnings (assuming Sheila earns at least this much during the next pay period) because Sheila's earnings will meet the FUTA wage-base limit of $7,000 in this pay period.

> **Example:**
>
> | | |
> |---|---|
> | Total taxable earnings for FUTA tax | $7,000.00 |
> | Cumulative earnings for Sheila Stowe before the new pay period | 6,810.25 |
> | Taxable earnings for FUTA tax | $ 189.75 |

(I) TAXABLE EARNINGS FOR SOCIAL SECURITY (OASDI) TAX

All employees pay Social Security tax until they reach each current year's wage-base limit. Our current limit for this example is $76,200. Column I shows the amount of earnings that will be taxed. It does not show that amount of Social Security tax the employee or employer pays. None of the three hourly employees has reached the wage-base limit as of the August 20 pay period. Keep in mind this column is *not* the tax, it is amount subject to the tax.

(J) TAXABLE EARNINGS FOR MEDICARE TAX

Column J shows the amount of earnings subject to Medicare tax. Remember that there is no wage-base limit for Medicare tax, so this column will match the amount found in column G, cumulative year-to-date earnings. Keep in mind this column is *not* the tax, it is amount subject to the tax.

(K) FICA DEDUCTION — SOCIAL SECURITY TAX

The current rate for Social Security tax is 6.20 percent up to $76,200. The amount in column I is multiplied by the 6.20 percent rate to arrive at the tax for each employee in this column.

> **Example:** Lee Jackson's Social Security tax for the pay period is $57.92.
>
> | Column I Amount | | Current Social Security Rate | Column K Social Security Tax |
> |---|---|---|---|
> | $934.20 | × | .062 | $57.92 |

(L) FICA DEDUCTION — MEDICARE TAX

The current rate for Medicare tax is 1.45 percent on all employee earnings with no wage-base limit.

Example: Sheila Stowe's gross earnings of $1,960.00 is multiplied by 1.45 percent to arrive at $28.42 in Medicare tax.

Gross Earnings		Medicare Tax Rate		Medicare Tax
$1,960.00	×	.0145	=	$28.42

(M) FEDERAL INCOME TAX (FIT)

Recall that federal income tax does not have any wage-base limit. Employees pay FIT on their gross earnings each pay period throughout the year. The amount of tax withheld depends on the employee's (1) income for the pay period, (2) marital status, and (3) number of withholding allowances claimed on Form W-4. (Fig. 7-1)

Ernie has used the IRS table found in *Circular E* (see Fig. 7-2) to find the amount of FIT to withhold from the three employees for the August 20 pay period. Look at Figure 7-2 again and use the information found in column A to verify the amounts Ernie has listed in column M of the payroll register.

(N) STATE INCOME TAX (SIT)

Ernie uses a rate of 8 percent to calculate and withhold state income tax for the August 20 pay period. Like federal income tax, there is no wage-base limit for state income tax, so all employee gross earnings for the pay period will be taxed.

Example: Pat Regan's state income tax is $143.12.

Gross Earnings		Tax Rate		State Income Tax
$1,788.94	×	.08	=	$143.12

(O) MEDICAL INSURANCE

Gradesoft.com deducts an amount to pay for medical insurance coverage for its employees. The rate is $22.00 per pay period for coverage for an employee only and $44.00 per pay period for coverage of an employee and his or her dependents.

(P) NET PAY

Net pay, or take-home pay, is the employee's gross earnings minus taxes withheld and any other deductions, such as medical insurance. Gross pay is what all employees wish they had; net pay is what employees are left with!

Ernie will subtract all withholding taxes and medical insurance premiums from all employees' gross earnings to arrive at their net pay.

Example: Lee Jackson's net pay is $657.99, computed as follows:

Gross earnings		$934.20
Less: FICA — Social Security tax	$ 57.92	
FICA — Medicare tax	13.55	
Federal income tax	108.00	
State income tax	74.74	
Medical insurance	22.00	
Net pay		$657.99

(Q) CHECK NUMBER

When Ernie prepares the paychecks, he records each check number in column Q of the payroll register.

(R AND S) DISTRIBUTION OF EXPENSE ACCOUNTS

The gross earnings for each employee is an expense of Gradesoft.com. Ernie uses columns R and S to identify the specific expense account to which each employee's earnings will be posted. This identification will help him make the journal entry to record the August 20 payroll. Note that Lee Jackson's earnings will be posted to the Business Analyst Expense account whereas Sheila's and Pat's earnings will be posted to the Programming Development Expense account.

LEARNING UNIT 7-2 REVIEW

AT THIS POINT you should be able to

▼ Explain and prepare a payroll register (p. 248)
▼ Explain the purpose of the taxable earnings columns and how they relate to the cumulative earnings columns (p. 250)

SELF-REVIEW QUIZ 7-2

(The forms you need are on page 219 of the *Study Guide and Working Papers.*)

Mike Henley is an hourly employee who is paid biweekly. He is paid overtime at a rate of 1.5 times his hourly rate of pay for any hours he works over 40 in a work week. Mike has worked many overtime hours this year to develop a new software program, and as of December 10 he has cumulative earnings of $74,978.06. For the pay period ending on December 24, Mike's gross earnings are $1,940.85. Calculate Mike's net pay based on the following facts:

▼ The Social Security tax rate is 6.2 percent with a wage-base limit of $76,200 for the year; the Medicare rate is 1.45 percent with no wage-base limit.
▼ Mike is single and claims three withholding allowances per his Form W-4. Use the tax table in Figure 7-2 to find Mike's federal income tax withholding amount.
▼ The state income tax rate is 8 percent with no wage-base limit.
▼ Mike pays $44.00 for medical insurance for the pay period.

Solution to Self-Review Quiz 7-2

1. FICA — Social Security tax is $75.76 ($1,221.94 × .062. Remember to subtract the cumulative year-to-date earnings from the wage-base limit when the employee's earnings approach the limit ($76,200 − $74,978.06). FICA — Medicare tax is $28.14 ($1,940.85 × .0145).
2. Federal income tax is $301 by the table (see Fig. 7-2).
3. State income tax is $155.27 ($1,940.85 × .08).

Mike Henley's net pay is $1,336.68 ($1,940.85 − $75.76 − $28.14 − $301.00 − $155.27 − $44.00).

Quiz Tip: Only the first $1,221.94 of Mike's wages is subject to social security tax ($76,200 − $74,978.06).

After Ernie Goldman has completed the payroll register for the August 20 pay period, he must next take the summary total amounts (found at the bottom of the columns of the payroll register) and post them to specific accounts in the general ledger. Refer back to the payroll register in Figure 7-3.

For Gradesoft.com, the payroll for the biweekly pay period ending on August 20 is recorded in the general journal as follows:

General Journal					
200X					
Aug.	20	Business Analyst expense	934 20		
		Programming Development expense	3748 94		
		FICA—Social Security tax payable			290 35
		FICA—Medicare tax payable			67 91
		Federal income tax payable			791 00
		State income tax payable			374 66
		Medical insurance payable			88 00
		Wages and salaries payable			3071 22
		To record payroll for August 20, 200X			

Note that the amounts recorded in the Gradesoft.com general journal come from the August 20 payroll register. Look back at Figure 7-3 and note that the two expense account amounts (Business Analyst and Programming Development Expense) are the same figures found in columns R and S. The credit amounts to the various tax payable and medical insurance accounts come from the totals found in columns K through O. The amount of the net pay comes from column P. The ledger (Figure 7-4) of Gradesoft.com will look as follows *after* the posting process has been completed.

Wages and Salaries Payable 202	FICA—Social Security Payable 203	FICA—Medicare Payable 204
	3,071.23		290.35		67.91
Liability on the balance sheet	Liability on the balance sheet	Liability on the balance sheet

Federal Income Tax Payable 205	State Income Tax Payable 206	Medical Insurance Payable 207
	791.00		374.65		88.00
Liability on the balance sheet	Liability on the balance sheet	Liability on the balance sheet

Business Analyst Expense 601	Programming Development Expense 602
934.20		3,748.94	
Expense on the income statement	Expense on the income statement

Figure 7-4 on page 254 summarizes this process.

FIGURE 7-4. The Payroll Recording and Posting Process

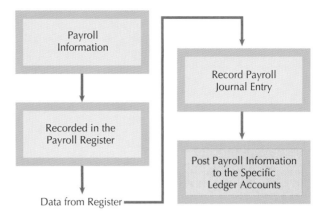

PAYROLL CHECKING ACCOUNTS: PAYING THE PAYROLL

Gradesoft.com, like the vast majority of companies, uses a special checking account for pay checks. This account is called Payroll Checking Cash. A company with a medium to a large payroll will use this account to clear paychecks because (1) the company has much better internal control over the funds deposited to pay employees and (2) it is easier for the payroll person to reconcile the account each month and determine if someone has not cashed his or her paycheck for some reason.

A deposit for the total net amount of the payroll is placed in this separate checking account. When all the checks are written, the payroll checking account balance should be zero. The following journal entries would result in paying the payroll.

Payroll Checking Cash
    Cash   ←—— Separate account for payroll setup.

Wages and Salaries Payable
    Payroll Checking Cash ←—— Payroll paid and balance in Payroll Checking is zero.

The checks that Gradesoft.com uses for payroll purposes provide a detail accounting of an employee's gross earnings as well as all deductions withheld, as shown in Figure 7-5.

Remember that if a payroll checking account is not used by a business, its payroll can be paid by debiting Wages and Salaries Payable and crediting Cash. In this instance the company's regular checking account would be used to pay employees.

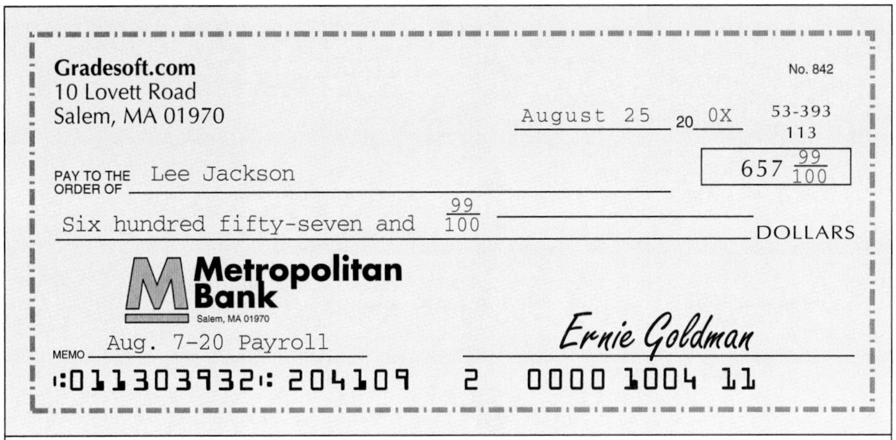

Gradesoft.com
10 Lovett Road
Salem, MA 01970

No. 842

August 25 20 0X

53-393
113

PAY TO THE ORDER OF Lee Jackson

657 $\frac{99}{100}$

Six hundred fifty-seven and $\frac{99}{100}$ DOLLARS

Metropolitan Bank
Salem, MA 01970

MEMO Aug. 7-20 Payroll

Ernie Goldman

⑆011303932⑆ 204109 2 0000 1004 11

	Totals:	Year-to-date:
Gross Pay:	$934.20	$21,806.85
FICA–Social Security:	$57.92	$1,352.03
FICA–Medicare:	$13.55	$316.20
Federal Income Tax:	$108.00	$1,744.55
State Income Tax:	$74.74	$1,308.20
Medical Insurance:	$22.00	$374.00
Net Pay:	$657.99	$16,711.87

FIGURE 7-5. Check from Gradesoft.com

THE INDIVIDUAL EMPLOYEE EARNINGS RECORD

Ernie has yet another task to attend to when it comes to payroll record keeping. Individual employee earnings records must be maintained by Gradesoft.com to meet federal and state employment laws and regulations.

The employee earnings record (see Fig. 7-6 on p. 256) provides a summary of each employee's earnings, deductions, net pay, and cumulative earnings during each calendar year. The information summarized in this record will be used by Ernie to prepare quarterly and annual payroll tax reports (which we discuss in Chapter 8). Thus, the employee earnings record is broken into calendar quarters (each calendar quarter is 13 weeks in length).

Figure 7-7 on p. 257 shows the payroll function for Gradesoft.com. Note that the payroll function begins with recording the hours worked by employees each biweekly and monthly pay period. The flow of information is the same for each pay period during the calendar year.

INDIVIDUAL EMPLOYEE EARNINGS RECORD
FOR PAT REGAN
FOURTH QUARTER, 200X

Pay Period No. and Pay Dates	Hours Worked			Total Earnings	Deductions					Net Pay	Check No.	Cumulative Earnings
	Week #	Regular	Overtime		Soc. Sec.	Medicare	Fed. Inc. Tax	State Inc. Tax	Med. Ins.			
10/02–10/15	20	80	4.5	188681	11698	2736	31400	15094	2200	125553	511	5599457
10/16–10/29	21	80	3.75	186234	11546	2700	30900	14899	2200	123988	525	5785691
10/30–11/12	22	80	5.25	191128	11850	2771	32000	15290	2200	127017	530	5976819
11/13–11/26	23	80	6	193575	12002	2808	32600	15486	2200	128480	544	6170394
11/27–12/10	24	80	8.75	202547	12558	2937	35400	16204	2200	133248	565	6372941
12/11–12/24	25	77	0	167475	10383	2428	25300	13398	2200	113766	574	6540416
12/25–12/31	26*	48	0	104400	6473	1514	11000	8352	2200	74861	590	6644816
Total 4th Quarter				1234040	76510	17894	198600	98723	15400	826913		
YTD Total				6644816	411979	96350	826500	531585	57200	4721202		

*Note the last biweekly pay period will end in the next calendar year (January 8); Ernie will only use Pat's hours worked this year to complete her employee earnings record for this year.

FIGURE 7-6. Individual Employee Earnings Record

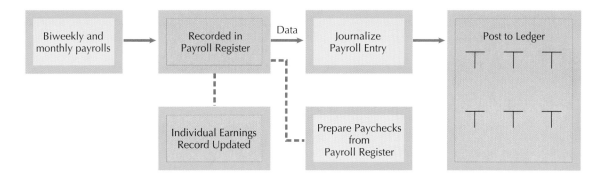

FIGURE 7-7. Payroll Function for Gradesoft.com

LEARNING UNIT 7-3 REVIEW

AT THIS POINT you should be able to

▼ Explain how to enter payroll information into the general journal from the payroll register (p. 253)
▼ Journalize entries to pay a payroll. (p. 253)
▼ Update an individual employee earnings record (p. 255)

SELF-REVIEW QUIZ 7-3

(The forms you need are on page 220 of the *Study Guide and Working Papers.*) Indicate which of the following statements are false.

1. The use of a payroll register to record a company's payroll is optional.
2. FICA — Social Security Payable is a liability on the income statement.
3. Wages and Salaries Expense has a normal credit balance.
4. Individual employee earnings records are used by employees to keep track of their wages.
5. Every calendar quarter has 13 weeks.

Solution to Self-Review Quiz 7-3

1. False   2. False   3. False   4. False   5. True

> *Quiz Tip:* There are four quarters in a year.

Time After Time: Stuck on Payroll Records

Each Dunkin' Donuts shop keeps a master file of employee information, containing every employee's name, address, phone number, Social Security number, rate of pay, hours worked per week, and W-4 form. Different shop owners offer different rates of pay, depending on local conditions. They offer different benefits as well. They employ mostly part-time workers, usually with a core of full-time employees. Fred, for example, pays clerks with less than one year's experience the minimum wage. He offers health and dental insurance. Some of the bigger shop owners also offer profit sharing to employees with a minimum of five years of service. The frequency of pay varies by state and sometimes by city or county. So, of course, do tax rates.

All this information must be recorded and reported to the various state, local, and federal authorities, and to Dunkin' Donuts headquarters through the zone's business consultant.

Scheduling workers and keeping payroll records are Fred's least-favorite jobs. He was pleased to hear the business consultant announce at an Advisory Council meeting that the company's new IBM terminals will offer an electronic scheduling package.

"Wow! That will really help, the business consultant!" said Fred joyously. "No more different colors of ink just to keep track of who will work when! Now we can plan around the exam schedules of the part-time workers without a hassle! Scheduling will be my favorite module in the new system!"

"Sure," said Molly Harris, another shop owner. "Now you can concentrate on payroll records. What fun!"

Fred groaned.

Discussion Questions

1. What payroll records does Fred need to keep for his donut shop?
2. What other information might Fred want so as to schedule working hours for each employee?
3. How does the payroll register help Fred prepare the payroll? Consult the process outlined on page 257.

SUMMARY OF KEY POINTS

Learning Unit 7-1

1. The Fair Labor Standards Act states that a worker (1) will receive a minimum hourly rate of pay and (2) will work a maximum of 40 hours during the week at the regular rate of pay with time and a half after 40 hours.

2. For the rules of the Fair Labor Standards Act to apply to an employer, the employer must be involved in interstate commerce.

3. The employee and employer equally contribute to Social Security tax an amount that is based on a given yearly rate and wage base for a calendar year. Only Social Security tax has a wage-base limit of $76,200 as of this writing. Medicare has no wage-base limit, so an employee and employer will pay this tax on all the employee's earnings during the calendar year.

4. Tax tables for federal income tax withholding can be found in IRS *Circular E, Employer's Tax Guide* (also known as Publication 15).

Learning Unit 7-2

1. Gross pay less deductions equals net pay.

2. The taxable earnings columns do not show the tax. They show amount of earnings to be taxed for unemployment taxes, Social Security, and Medicare. Note that FICA is made up of two taxes, Social Security and Medicare.

Learning Unit 7-3

1. A payroll register provides the data for journalizing the payroll entry in the general journal.

2. Deductions for payroll represent liabilities for the employer until paid.

3. The account distribution columns of the payroll register indicate which accounts will be debited to record the total payroll wages and salaries expense when a journal entry is prepared.

4. The accounts FICA — Social Security Payable and FICA — Medicare Payable accumulate the tax liabilities of both the employer and the employee for Medicare and Social Security.

5. Paying a payroll results in debiting Wages and Salaries Payable and crediting Cash (or Payroll Checking Cash).

6. The individual employee earnings records are updated soon after the payroll register is prepared.

KEY TERMS

Allowance (also called exemption) A certain dollar amount of a person's income that will be considered nontaxable for income tax withholding purposes.

Calendar year A one-year period beginning on January 1 and ending on December 31. Employers must use a calendar year for payroll purposes, even if the employer uses a fiscal year for financial statements and for any other reasons.

Circular E An IRS tax publication of tax tables.

Fair Labor Standards Act (Federal Wage and Hour Law) A law the majority of employers must follow that contains rules stating the minimum hourly rate of pay and the maximum number of hours a worker will work before being paid time and a half for overtime hours worked. This law also has other rules and regulations that employers must follow for payroll purposes.

Federal income tax withholding Amount of federal income tax withheld by the employer from the employee's gross pay; the amount withheld is determined by the employee's gross pay, the pay period, the number of allowances claimed by the employee on the W-4 form, and the marital status indicated on the W-4 form.

FICA (Federal Insurance Contributions Act) Part of the Social Security Act of 1935, this law requires that a tax be levied on both the employer and employee up to a certain maximum rate and wage base for Social Security tax purposes. Furthermore, there is a tax for Medicare purposes with no employer or employee wage-base maximum.

FICA — Medicare Payable A liability account that accumulates tax for Medicare.

FICA — Social Security Payable A liability account that accumulates tax for Social Security.

Gross earnings Amount of pay received before any deductions.

Individual employee earnings record An accounting document that summarizes the total amount of wages paid and the deductions for the calendar year. It aids in preparing governmental reports. A new record is prepared for each employee each year.

Interstate commerce A test that is applied to determine whether an employer must follow the rules of the Fair Labor Standards Act. If an employer communicates or does business with another business in some other state it is usually considered to be involved in interstate commerce.

Market Wages Expense An account that records from the payroll register gross wages earned by employees of a market (grocery) outlet.

Medical insurance A deduction from employee's paycheck for health insurance.

Net pay Gross pay less deductions. Net pay (or *take-home pay*) is what the worker actually takes home.

Office Salaries Expense An account that records from the payroll gross salaries earned by employees of an office.

Pay (or payroll) period A length of time used by an employer to calculate the amount of an employee's earnings. Pay periods can be weekly, biweekly (once every two weeks), semimonthly (twice each month), monthly, quarterly or annual.

Payroll register A multicolumn form that can be used to record payroll data. The data in the payroll register are then used to prepare the general journal entry to record the paying of employees for a pay period.

Payroll tax deposits Amounts an employer pays to the government for payroll taxes. We discuss these deposits in more detail in Chapter 8.

Payroll tax Amount of federal tax withheld from each employees' gross pay.

State income tax withholding Amount of state income tax withheld by the employer from the employee's gross pay.

Taxable earnings Shows amount of earnings subject to a tax. The tax itself is not shown.

W-4 (Employee's Withholding Allowance Certificate) A form filled out by employees used by employers to supply needed information about the number of allowances claimed, marital status, and so forth. The form is used for payroll purposes to determine federal income tax withholding from an employee's paycheck.

Wage bracket tables Various charts in IRS *Circular E* providing information about deductions for federal income tax based on earnings and data supplied on the W-4 form.

Wages and Salaries Payable A liability account that shows net pay for payroll before employees are paid. Account zeros out after employees are paid.

Workers' compensation insurance Insurance required by employers to protect their employees against losses due to injury or death incurred while on the job.

Work week A seven-day (168-hour) period used to determine overtime hours for employees. A work week can begin on any given day, but must end seven days later.

QUESTIONS, MINI EXERCISES, EXERCISES, AND PROBLEMS

Discussion Questions

1. What is the purpose of the Fair Labor Standards Act (also called Federal Wage and Hour Law)?
2. Explain how to calculate overtime.
3. Define and state the purpose of completing a W-4 form (called the Employee's Withholding Allowance Certificate).
4. The more allowances an employee claims on a W-4 form, the more take-home pay the employee gets with each paycheck. True or false.

(cont. on p. 262)

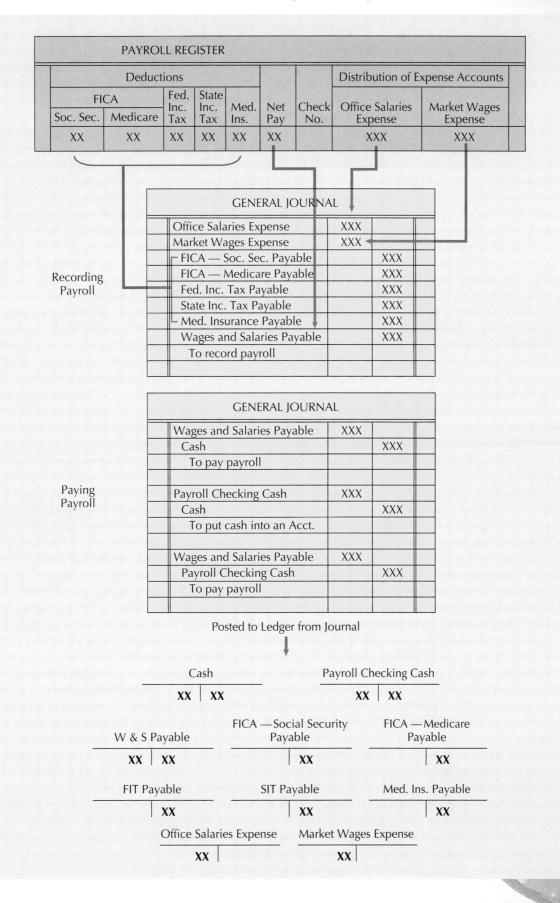

5. Why should a business prepare a payroll register before employees are paid? Please explain.

6. The taxable earnings column of a payroll register records the amount of tax due. True or false?

7. Define and state the purpose of FICA taxes.

8. Explain how to calculate Social Security and Medicare taxes.

9. The employer doesn't have to contribute to Social Security. Agree or disagree. Please explain.

10. Explain how federal and state income tax withholding are determined.

11. What is a calendar year?

12. An employer must always use a calendar year for payroll purposes. True or false?

13. What purpose does the individual employee earnings record serve?

14. Why does payroll information center on 13-week quarters?

15. Please draw a diagram showing how the following items relate to each other: (a) a weekly payroll, (b) a payroll register, (c) individual employees' earnings, (d) general journal entries for payroll, (e) a payroll checking account.

16. If you earned $130,000 this year, you would pay more Social Security and Medicare taxes than your partner who earned $75,000. Do you agree or disagree? Please provide calculations to support your answer.

Mini Exercises

(The forms you need are on page 222 of the *Study Guide and Working Papers*.)

Calculating Gross Earnings

1. Calculate the total wages earned (assume an overtime rate of time and a half over 40 hours).

Employee	Hourly Rate	No. of Hours Worked
A. Dawn Slow	$10	37
B. Jill Jones	12	50

FICA

2. Pete Martin, single claiming 1, has cumulative earnings before this biweekly pay period of $80,000. Assuming he is paid $2,000 this week, what will his deduction be for FIT and FICA (Medicare and Social Security)? Use tables and rates in text.

Net Pay

3. Calculate Pete's Net Pay from Mini Exercise 2 above. State income tax is 5 percent and death insurance is $40.

Payroll Register

4. From the following identify:
   1. Total of gross pay (comes from distribution of expense accounts).
   2. A deduction.
   3. Net Pay.
      _____ a. Office Salaries Expense and Wages Expense
      _____ b. FICA — Social Security Payable
      _____ c. FICA — Medicare Payable
      _____ d. Federal Income Tax Payable
      _____ e. Medical Insurance Payable
      _____ f. Wages and Salaries Payable

Payroll Account

5. From the following, indicate if the title is:
   1. An asset.   4. Appears on the Income Statement.
   2. A liability.   5. Appears on the balance sheet.
   3. An expense.

   _____ **a.** FICA — Social Security Payable
   _____ **b.** Office Salaries Expense
   _____ **c.** Federal Income Tax Payable
   _____ **d.** FICA — Medicare Payable
   _____ **e.** Wages and Salaries Payable

Exercises

(The forms you need are on pages 223–224 of the *Study Guide and Working Papers*.)

7-1. Calculate the total wages earned for each employee (assume an overtime rate of time and a half over 40 hours).

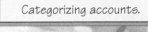

Calculating wages with overtime.

Employee	Hourly Rate	No. of Hours Worked
Bob Role	$ 8	35
Jill West	12	44
Dale Aster	11	46

Tax table.

7-2. Compute the Net Pay for each employee using the federal income tax withholding tables in Figure 7-2. (Assume the following for FICA: Social Security tax is 6.2 percent on a wage-base limit of $76,200; Medicare is 1.45 percent on all earnings; the payroll is paid biweekly; there is no state income tax.)

Employee	Status	Claiming	Cumulative Pay	This Week's Pay
Alvin Cell	Single	1	$50,000	$1,190
Angel Lowe	Single	0	$64,300	$1,200

7-3. Complete the table.

Categorizing accounts.

	Category	↑	Normal Balance	Account Appears on Which Financial Statements
Medical Insurance Payable				
Wages and Salaries Payable				
Office Salaries Expense				
Market Wages Expense				
FICA — Social Security Payable				
Federal Income Tax Payable				
State Income Tax Payable				

7-4. The following weekly payroll journal entry was prepared by Luster Company from its payroll register. Which columns of the payroll register have the data come from? How does the *taxable earnings* column of the payroll register relate to this entry?

Payroll register and the journal entry.

	Oct.	7	Shop Salaries Expense		4 0 0 0 00		
			Factory Wages Expense		2 0 0 0 00		
			FICA—Social Security Payable				3 7 2 00
			FICA—Medicare Payable				8 7 00
			Federal Income Tax Payable			1 2 0 0 00	
			State Income Tax Payable			1 2 5 6 00	
			Union Dues Payable			1 1 0 00	
			Wages and Salaries Payable			2 9 7 5 00	

7-5. The following amounts have been taken from the weekly payroll register for the Debra Company on October 9, 200X. Using the same account title headings that we have used in this chapter, please prepare the general journal entry to record the payroll for Debra Company for October 9.

Recording payroll by journal entry.

Factory Wages Expense	$3,579.00
Office Salaries Expense	1,597.00
Deduction for FICA — Social Security	296.15
Deduction for FICA — Medicare	75.05
Deduction for federal income tax	1,112.84
Deduction for state income tax	258.80
Deduction for union dues	350.00

Group A Problems

(The forms you need are on pages 225–229 of the *Study Guide and Working Papers*.)

7A-1. From the following information, please complete the chart for gross earnings for the week. (Assume an overtime rate of time and one half over 40 hours.)

Calculating gross earnings with overtime.

Check Figure:
d. $660   Gross Earnings

		Hourly Rate	No. of Hours Worked	Gross Earnings
a.	Joe Jackson	$ 6	40	
b.	Edna Kane	8	47	
c.	Dick Wall	10	42	
d.	Pat Green	12	50	

7A-2. March Company has five salaried employees. Your task is to record the following information into a payroll register.

Completing a payroll register.

Employee	Allowance and Marital Status	Cumulative Earnings before This Payroll	Biweekly Salary	Department
Kool, Alice	S-1	$42,000	$1,200	Sales
Lose, Bob	S-1	30,000	800	Office
Moore, Linda	S-2	59,200	1,240	Office
Relt, Rusty	S-3	75,100	1,270	Sales
Veel, Larry	S-0	29,000	820	Sales

CHAPTER 7 ... PAYROLL CONCEPTS AND PROCEDURES

Assume the following:

1. FICA — Social Security: 6.2 percent on $76,200; FICA — Medicare: 1.45 percent on all earnings.
2. Each employee contributes $25 biweekly for union dues.
3. State income tax is 6 percent of gross pay.
4. FIT is calculated from Figure 7-2.

Check Figure:
Net Pay $3,867.99

Completing a payroll register and journalizing the payroll entry.

7A-3. The bookkeeper of Gore Co. gathered the following data from individual employees' earnings records and daily time cards. Your tasks are to (1) complete a payroll register on December 12 and (2) journalize the appropriate entry to record the payroll.

Employee	Allowance and Marital Status	Cumulative Earnings before This Payroll	M	T	W	T	F	Hourly Rate of Pay	FIT	Department
Boy, Pete	M-1	$64,100	5	11	9	8	8	$18	86	Sales
Heat, Donna	S-0	15,000	8	10	9	9	4	16	113	Office
Pyle, Ray	M-3	66,000	8	10	10	10	10	16	86	Sales
Vent, Joan	S-1	19,000	8	8	8	8	8	20	145	Office

Assume the following:

1. FICA — Social Security: 6.2 percent on $76,200; FICA — Medicare: 1.45 percent on all earnings.
2. Federal income tax has been calculated from a weekly table for you.
3. Each employee contributes $25 biweekly for health insurance.
4. Overtime is paid at a rate of time and a half over 40 hours.

Check Figure:
Net Pay $2,258.06

Payroll register completed; journalizing and posting.

7A-4. Gary Nelson, Accountant, has gathered the following data from the time cards and individual employee earnings records. Your tasks are as follows:

1. On December 5, 200X, prepare a payroll register for this biweekly payroll.
2. Journalize (p. 4) in the general journal and post to the general ledger accounts.

Check Figure:
Net Pay $3,332.07

Employee	Allowance and Marital Status	Cumulative Earnings before This Payroll	Biweekly Salary	Check No.	Department
Aulson, Andy	S-3	$30,000	$ 950	30	Factory
Flynn, Jacki	S-1	50,000	1,000	31	Office
Moore, Jeff	S-2	60,000	1,200	32	Factory
Sullivan, Alison	S-1	65,000	1,300	33	Office

Assume the following:

1. FICA — Social Security: 6.2 percent on $76,200; FICA — Medicare: 1.45 percent on all earnings.
2. Federal income tax is calculated from Figure 7-2.
3. State income tax is 5 percent of gross pay.
4. Union dues are $10 biweekly.

Group B Problems

(The forms you need are on pages 225–229 in the *Study Guide and Working Papers.*)

7B-1. From the following information, please complete the chart for gross earnings for the week. (Assume an overtime rate of time and one half over 40 hours.)

Calculating gross earnings with overtime.

	Hourly Rate	No. of Hours Worked	Gross Earnings
a. Joe Jackson	$ 5	40	
b. Edna Kane	9	47	
c. Dick Wall	12	36	
d. Pat Green	14	55	

Check Figure:
d. Gross Pay $875

Completing a payroll register.

7B-2. March Company has five salaried employees. Your task is to record the following information into a payroll register.

Employee	Allowance and Marital Status	Cumulative Earnings before This Payroll	Biweekly Salary	Department
Kool, Alice	S-1	$45,150	$1,290	Sales
Lose, Bob	S-1	22,575	800	Office
Moore, Linda	S-2	59,300	1,240	Office
Relt, Rusty	S-3	75,300	1,300	Sales
Veel, Larry	S-0	21,875	860	Sales

Check Figure:
Net Pay $3,985.41

Assume the following:

1. FICA—Social Security: 6.2 percent up to $76,200: FICA—Medicare: 1.45 percent on all earnings.
2. Each employee contributes $25 biweekly for union dues.
3. State income tax is 6 percent of gross pay.
4. FIT is calculated from Figure 7-2.

Completing a payroll entry and journalizing the payroll entry.

7B-3. The bookkeeper of Gore Co. gathered the following data from individual employees' earnings records and daily time cards. Your tasks are to (1) complete a payroll register on December 12 and (2) journalize the appropriate entry to record the payroll.

Employee	Allowance and Marital Status	Cumulative Earnings before This Payroll	M	T	W	T	F	Hourly Rate of Pay	FIT	Department
Boy, Pete	S-1	$64,900	12	11	7	7	7	$16	125	Sales
Heat, Donna	S-0	19,000	8	9	9	9	5	16	113	Office
Pyle, Ray	M-3	76,550	10	10	10	10	5	20	105	Sales
Vent, Joan	S-1	13,500	6	8	8	8	8	19	122	Office

Assume the following:

1. FICA—Social Security: 6.2 percent on $76,200; FICA—Medicare: 1.45 percent on all earnings.
2. Federal income tax has been calculated from a table for you.
3. Each employee contributes $25 biweekly for health insurance.
4. Overtime is paid at a rate of time and a half over 40 hours.

Check Figure:
Net Pay $2,308.73

Payroll entry completed; journalizing and posting.

7B-4. Gary Nelson, Accountant, has gathered the following data from the time cards and individual employee earnings records. Your task is to
1. On December 5, 200X, prepare a payroll register for this biweekly payroll.
2. Journalize (p. 4) in the general journal and post to the general ledger accounts.

Employee	Allowance and Marital Status	Cumulative Earnings before This Payroll	Biweekly Salary	Check No.	Department
Aulson, Andy	S-3	$30,000	$ 800	30	Factory
Flynn, Jacki	S-1	50,000	1,100	31	Office
Moore, Jeff	S-2	60,000	1,050	32	Factory
Sullivan, Alison	S-1	65,000	1,200	33	Office

Assume the following:

1. FICA—Social Security: 6.2 percent on $76,200; FICA—Medicare: 1.45 percent on all earnings.
2. Federal income tax is calculated from Figure 7-2.
3. State income tax is 6 percent of gross pay.
4. Union dues are $15 biweekly.

REAL-WORLD APPLICATIONS

7R-1.

Small Company, a sole proprietorship, has two employees, Jim Roy and Janice Alter. The owner of Small Co. is Bert Ryan. During the current pay period, Jim worked 48 hours and Janice 56. The reason for these extra hours is that both Jim and Janice worked their regular 40-hour work week, plus Jim worked 8 extra hours on Sunday and Janice worked 8 extra hours on Saturday and Sunday. Their contract with Small Co. is that they are each paid an hourly rate of $8 per hour with all hours over 40 to be time and a half and double time on Sunday. Bert, the owner, feels he is also entitled to a salary, because he works as many hours. He plans to pay himself $425.

As the accountant for Small Co., (1) calculate the gross pay for Jim and Janice and (2) write a letter to Bert Ryan with your recommendations regarding his salary.

7R-2.

Marcy Moore works for Moose Company during the day and GTA Company at night. Both her employers have deducted FICA taxes for Social Security and Medicare. At year end Marcy has earned $72,000 at her job at Moose Company and $8,000 at GTA.

At a party she tells Bill Barnes, an accountant, who tells her she has paid too much Social Security tax and that she is entitled to a refund or credit on her tax return she files for the year. Bill suggests that she call the Internal Revenue Service's toll-free number and ask for taxpayer assistance. Assume Social Security of 6.2 percent on $76,200 and Medicare of 1.45 percent on all Marcy's earnings during the year.

As Marcy's friend, (1) check to see if indeed she has overpaid any FICA tax and (2) write a brief note to her and show her your calculations to support your answer.

YOU make the call

Critical Thinking/Ethical Case

7R-3.

Russ Todd works for a delicatessen. As the bookkeeper Russ has been asked by the owner to keep two separate books for meals tax. The owner has asked

Todd to hire someone on the weekends to punch in false tapes that can be submitted to the state. These tapes would show low sales and thus less liability for meals tax payments. You make the call. Write down your specific recommendations to Russ.

INTERNET EXERCISES

EX-1. [www.tei-employment.com] Suppose that Starbucks decided to follow one of the great trends in American employment, that of "leasing" employees from a temporary agency. One such agency is Temporary Employees, Inc. in Houston, Texas. When a business employs temporary workers, they supervise the temps just like they do their own employees. What they do not have to do is the everyday administrative work that accompanies having employees.

1. Visit their website and describe how Starbucks, or any other employer, could save money by hiring temporary employees.
2. While there are advantages to hiring temporary workers there are also disadvantages. List some of the disadvantages.

EX-2. [www.americanpayroll.org/mission.html] The American Payroll Association (APA) is an organization of payroll professionals, and it provides a semiannual certification examination. APA provides an avenue for payroll professionals to support others, and to assist in meeting common problems encountered in this important profession.

1. From your viewing of their website discuss how this organization fills a niche in the field of Human Resources and payroll administration.
2. What would be the organization's advantage to you if you were to pursue a career in payroll administration?

CONTINUING PROBLEM

In preparing for next year, Tony Freedman has hired two employees to work hourly, assisting with some troubleshooting and repair work.

Assignment

(See pages 232–241 in the *Study Guide and Working Papers.*)

1. Record the following transactions in general journal format and post to the general ledger.
2. Prepare a payroll register.
3. Prepare a trial balance as of November 30, 200X.

Assume the following transactions:

a. The following accounts have been added to the chart of accounts: Wage Expense #5110, FICA — Social Security Payable #2020, FICA — Medicare Payable #2030, FIT Payable #2040, State Income Tax Payable #2050, and Wages Payable #2010.

b. FICA — Social Security is taxed at 6.2 percent up to $76,200 in earnings, and Medicare at 1.45 percent on all earnings.

c. State income tax is 2 percent of gross pay.

d. Both employees have no federal income tax taken out of their pay.

e. Each employee earns $10 an hour and is paid $1\frac{1}{2}$ times salary for hours worked in excess of 40 weekly.

Nov.	1	Billed Vita Needle Company $6,800; invoice #12675 for services rendered.
	3	Billed Accu Pac, Inc. $3,900; invoice #12676 for services rendered.
	5	Purchased new shop benches $1,400 on account from System Design Furniture.
	7	Paid the two employee wages: Lance Kumm, 38 hours, and Anthony Hall, 42 hours.
	9	Received the phone bill, $150.
	12	Collected $500 of the amount due from Taylor Golf.
	14	Paid the two employee wages: Lance Kumm, 25 hours, and Anthony Hall, 36 hours.
	18	Collected $800 of the amount due from Taylor Golf.
	20	Purchased a fax machine for the office from Multi Systems, Inc. on credit, $450.
	21	Paid the two employee wages: Lance Kumm, 26 hours, and Anthony Hall, 35 hours.

The Employer's Tax Responsibilities

PRINCIPLES AND PROCEDURES

To fuel rapid growth and, at the same time, keep headcount low, Microsoft has engaged in practices that have not only raised eyebrows at the Internal Revenue Service (IRS) but also raised the ire of local technical workers.

In 1990, the IRS noticed that the Seattle software giant was employing loads of independent contractors (freelance employees) for long periods of time and was not taking taxes from their paychecks. When it became clear that the jobs of the independent contractors and of Microsoft full-timers were not substantially different, the IRS asked the company to change its policies so that *all* employees would be giving the government its fair share of their paychecks every two weeks. Yet, the IRS left the decision on just how to handle that change up to Microsoft.

Microsoft's solution to this taxing dilemma has once again put the company in an unwelcome spotlight. Microsoft required their independent contractors to sign up with local temporary agencies that are responsible for paying the independent contractors' payroll and health benefits. As a result, Microsoft continues to maintain a two-tier workforce of full-timers and "permatemps," so called because these temporary workers have often worked at

Microsoft several years. As they work alongside full-timers who receive better health benefits and who have grown rich from company stock options, a growing number of permatemps have become disgruntled. They are filing class action suits, and they are winning: federal courts have ruled that a 10,000 person class of "permatemp" workers now stand to collect as much as $100 million from Microsoft in back benefits.

The reason Microsoft and other technology companies have been loath to turn independent contractors into employees is because of the heavy expenses involved. After studying Chapter 8, you will have a full grasp of these expenses. They include employer **payroll taxes** and **worker's compensation insurance,** which the law requires the employer to pay. In addition, benefits such as medical and health insurance become an additional operating expense.

Then, too, when employers take on employees rather than independent contractors, they must spend time complying with state and local government regulations. They must submit quarterly and annual federal tax returns, similar to the personal income tax return you are required to submit each April. And most states require the employer to pay state unemployment insurance (SUTA) for each employee. When permatemps' projects are over at Microsoft, they don't get any unemployment insurance. In fact, their projects may end sooner than they thought. In order to avoid costly permatemp problems the company now limits all temp employment to one year and requires a 100-day break between temporary engagements at Microsoft.

Based on: Ron Lieber, "The Permatemps Contretemps," *Fast Company,* August 2000, pp. 198+. Gilbert Nicholson, "Get your benefit ducks in a row," *Workforce,* September 2000, pp. 78–84. Anonymous, "Microsoft Moves to Curb Use of Temporary Workers," *Wall Street Journal,* July 3, 2000, p. B2.

LEARNING OBJECTIVES

▼ Calculating and journalizing employer payroll tax expenses. (p. 272)

▼ Completing the Employer's Quarterly Federal Tax Return and Deposit Coupon (Forms 941 and 8109) and paying tax obligations for FICA tax (Social Security and Medicare) and federal income tax. (p. 277)

▼ Preparing Forms W-2, W-3 and 940-EZ and estimates of workers' compensation insurance premiums. (p. 285)

In Chapter 7 we looked at how Gradesoft.com computed and recorded payroll data about its employees. This chapter focuses on specific tax responsibilities of the employer.

LEARNING UNIT 8-1

THE EMPLOYER'S PAYROLL TAX EXPENSE

When opening a business, every employer must get a federal **employer identification number** (also known as an **EIN**) for purposes of reporting earnings, taxes, and so forth. When Gradesoft.com began, Ernie Goldman filled out **Form SS-4** to obtain the company's EIN. The SS-4 form asks for the following information:

1. Name of applicant.
2. Trade name of business.
3. Address or place of business.
4. County in which business is located.
5. Name of the principle officer or owner of the business.
6. Type of business (sole proprietor, partnership, etc.).
7. The reason for applying for an EIN.
8. The date the business began.
9. The closing month of the accounting year.
10. First date that the business will pay its employees.
11. The potential number of employees in the coming year.
12. Main activity or nature of the business.

Gradesoft.com's payroll tax obligations are recorded in the general journal when the payroll is recorded. Gradesoft.com is responsible for (1) Social Security and Medicare tax (or FICA), (2) federal unemployment tax, and (3) state unemployment tax. The total of these taxes are recorded in the **Payroll Tax Expense** account in the general ledger.

Let's look at how Ernie calculates the amount of each tax.

CALCULATING THE EMPLOYER'S PAYROLL TAXES

FICA (Federal Insurance Contributions Act)

It is the responsibility of Gradesoft.com to match whatever its employees pay into the **Federal Insurance Contributions Act (FICA)** on a dollar-for-dollar basis each pay period. The accounts in the ledger, *FICA — Social Security Payable* and *FICA — Medicare Payable,* record the tax for *both* the employee and the employer. To determine the amount of FICA Gradesoft.com owes, we must use the FICA taxable earnings columns for Social Security and Medicare from the payroll register discussed in Chapter 7 and reproduced here for your convenience as Figure 8-1.

The payroll register shows that $4,683.14 (column I) of wages is subject to Social Security tax, and in column J we also see $4,683.14 of wages is subject to tax for Medicare.

$$\text{Social Security} \quad \$4{,}683.14 \times .062 = \$290.36$$
$$\text{Medicare} \quad \$4{,}683.14 \times .0145 = \$\ 67.91$$

The employer must match the FICA contribution of the employee for Social Security *and* Medicare taxes.

FICA — Social Security Payable 203	FICA — Medicare Payable 204
290.36 (employee)	67.91 (employee)
290.36 (employer)	67.91 (employee)

FUTA (Federal Unemployment Tax Act)

Unemployment insurance is a joint effort on the part of the federal government, all 50 states, the District of Columbia, and U.S. territories. Each state is required to run its own unemployment program for its unemployed workers. The state programs are approved and monitored by the federal government.

To raise money for these unemployment programs, the federal government levies taxes on employers under a law called the **Federal Unemployment Tax Act (FUTA).** This law (1) induces states to create their own unemployment programs and (2) allows the federal government to monitor

GRADESOFT.COM INC.
PAYROLL REGISTER
AUGUST 7–20, 200X

Employee Name	Allowances and Marital Status	Cumulative Earnings (YTD)	Salary for Pay Period	No. of Hours Worked	Wages per Hour	Earnings Regular	Earnings Overtime	Earnings Gross	Cumulative Earnings (YTD)	Taxable Earnings Unemployment	Taxable Earnings Soc. Sec. Tax	Taxable Earnings Medicare
Jackson, L.	S-1	2087265		84.00	1080	85320	8100	93420	2180685		93420	93420
Stowe, S.	S-0	4850025		80.00	2450	196000	—	196000	6810025	196000	196000	196000
Regan, P.	S-2	4658705		81.50	2175	174000	4894	178894	4837599	—	178894	178894
TOTALS		72309995				455320	12994	468314	7699309	196000	468314	468314
Discussions in this chapter are keyed to these letters	(A)	(B)	(C)			(D)	(E)	(F)	(G)	(H)	(I)	(J)

FIGURE 8-1. Partial Payroll for Gradesoft.com

state programs. As mentioned in Chapter 7, the FUTA tax currently is 6.2 percent of wages paid during the year, and the wage-base limit is $7,000.

Usually, the federal government allows employers a credit against FUTA tax as long as the employer has paid all monies due to the state unemployment fund on time. This credit, called the **normal FUTA tax credit,** cannot exceed 5.4 percent. So, an employer who is entitled to the normal FUTA credit will pay a net amount of eight-tenths of 1 percent, as shown below:

6.2%	FUTA tax
− 5.4%	normal FUTA tax credit
.8%	net FUTA tax for federal purposes

In effect, the federal law says to employees, "Comply with your state's unemployment tax laws and your total tax will not exceed a maximum of 6.2 percent: 0.8 percent to the federal government and a state rate that will vary up to a maximum of 5.4 percent." Remember that employers alone are responsible for paying FUTA tax; it is never deducted from employees' wages.

In Learning Unit 8-3, we look at how to complete the federal report and the deposit requirements for FUTA tax. For now, let's calculate the amount of accumulated federal unemployment tax for Gradesoft.com based on the unemployment column under taxable earnings in the payroll register. Remember that the $1,960.00 in column H represents the amount of earnings taxable for federal unemployment.

To calculate the FUTA tax, we multiply the FUTA taxable earnings times the net FUTA tax rate.

Taxable FUTA Earnings	×	FUTA Rate	=	FUTA Tax	FUTA Tax Payable 209
$1,960.00		.008		$15.68	⎸15.68

FUTA tax is paid after the end of a calendar year if the total tax owed is less than $100 for the year. If the amount owed is more than $100, the tax is paid on a quarterly basis, no later than the end of the month following the end of the quarter.

SUTA (State Unemployment Tax Acts)

To support state unemployment programs, all states charge employers a certain percent in taxes under the **State Unemployment Tax Act (SUTA).** Usually, employers pay more in SUTA tax than FUTA tax.

Each state has its own state unemployment wage-base limit. Currently, these limits range from a low of $7,000 to a high of $27,500. The limits vary according to the needs of each state unemployment fund and are subject to change. For the current rate in your state, check with the state department of labor and employment.

The states vary the percentage rates charged to employers. The differences are based on the total amount of contributions the employer makes into the state fund and the dollar amount of unemployment claim money paid out of the fund to former employees of the employer. For example, employers who do not lay off employees during slack seasons (such as after the Christmas season or at the end of a ski resort season) owe a smaller percentage for state unemployment tax purposes. The variance, which is called an **experience** or **merit rating,** motivates employers to stabilize their workforce.

Gradesoft.com's current state unemployment tax rate is 5.4 percent of the first $7,000 paid to each of Fred's employees during the calendar year. From the taxable earnings column (column H) of the payroll register in Figure 8-1, we multiply $1,960.00 by the SUTA tax rate of 5.4 percent.

Taxable Earnings	×	SUTA Rate	=	SUTA Tax	SUTA Tax Payable 208
$1,960.00		.054		$105.84	⎸105.84

SUTA taxes are paid after the end of each **calendar quarter.** Employers are required to complete a state unemployment tax report and pay any SUTA tax due at this time.

JOURNALIZING PAYROLL TAX EXPENSE

Before showing the general journal entry to record Gradesoft.com's payroll tax expense, let's review the categories and rules that affect the specific payroll ledger accounts used to record this expense.

Accounts Affected	Category	↑ ↓	Rules
Payroll Tax Expense	Expense	↑	Dr.
FICA—Social Security Payable	Liability	↑	Cr.
FICA—Medicare Payable	Liability	↑	Cr.
State Unemployment Tax Payable (SUTA)	Liability	↑	Cr.
Federal Unemployment Tax Payable (FUTA)	Liability	↑	Cr.

The total of employer's portion of FICA for Social Security and Medicare tax, FUTA tax, and SUTA tax equals the total of Gradesoft.com's payroll tax expense.

The Journal Entry

The following is the general journal entry recording Gradesoft.com's payroll tax expense for the biweekly payroll ending August 20. (We look carefully at the general ledger entries in Learning Unit 8-2.)

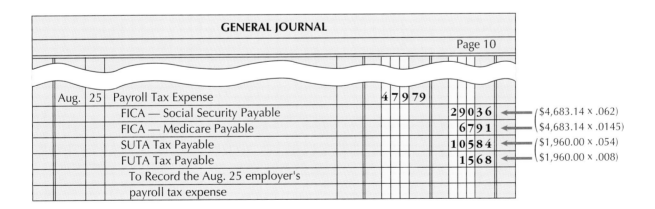

In Learning Unit 8-2 we see how to complete the form that goes with the payment of FICA tax (Social Security and Medicare) of the employee *and* the employer along with the amounts of federal income tax deducted from employees' paychecks. It is important to keep in mind that FUTA and SUTA taxes also have separate report forms to be completed, which we look at in Learning Unit 8-3.

LEARNING UNIT 8-1 REVIEW

AT THIS POINT you should be able to

- ▼ Explain the purpose of the Form SS-4. (p. 271)
- ▼ Explain the use of the taxable earnings column in calculating the employer's payroll tax expense. (p. 272)
- ▼ Calculate the employer's payroll taxes. (p. 272)
- ▼ Explain the difference between FUTA and SUTA taxes. (p. 274)
- ▼ Explain when FUTA and SUTA taxes are paid. (p. 274)
- ▼ Journalize the employer's payroll tax expense. (p. 275)

SELF-REVIEW QUIZ 8-1

(The forms you need are on page 242 of the *Study Guide and Working Papers.*)

Given the following, prepare the general journal entry to record the payroll tax expense for Bill Co. for the weekly payroll of July 8. Assume the following: (a) SUTA tax is paid at a rate of 5.6 percent on the first $7,000 of earnings; (b) FUTA tax is paid at the net rate of .8 percent on the first $7,000 of earnings; (c) FICA tax rate for Social Security is 6.2 percent on $76,200, and Medicare is 1.45 percent on all earnings.

Employee	Cumulative Pay before This Week's Payroll	Gross Pay for Week
Bill Jones	$6,000	$800
Julie Warner	6,600	400
Al Brooks	7,900	700

Solution to Self-Review Quiz 8-1

July	8	Payroll Tax Expense			2 2 2 15		
		FICA — Social Security Payable				1 1 7 80	
		FICA — Medicare Payable				2 7 55	
		SUTA Tax Payable				6 7 20	
		FUTA Tax Payable				9 60	
		Record employer's payroll tax					

Quiz Tip: Al Brooks earned more than $7,000; thus his employer takes no SUTA or FUTA tax on the $700 of Al's gross pay.

FICA:
- SS: $1,900 × .062 = $117.80
- Med: 1,900 × .0145 = 27.55
- SUTA: 1,200 × .056 = 67.20
- FUTA: 1,200 × .008 = 9.60

  $222.15

LEARNING UNIT 8-2

FORM 941: COMPLETING THE EMPLOYER'S QUARTERLY FEDERAL TAX RETURN AND PAYING TAX OBLIGATIONS FOR FICA TAX AND FEDERAL INCOME TAX

In this unit we look at Gradesoft.com's last calendar quarter (October, November, and December). Our goals are (1) determining the timing for paying FICA (for both the employees and the employer) and federal income tax (or FIT) and (2) completing **Form 941,** the **Employer's Quarterly Federal Tax Return.**

Before getting into specific deposit rules and form completions, let's look at Figure 8-2, a worksheet that Ernie prepared to monitor Gradesoft.com's deposit requirements for the taxes reported on Form 941: Social Security, Medicare, and federal income taxes. These so-called **Form 941 taxes** are discussed later in this Learning Unit. (The worksheet in Figure 8-2 has nothing to do with unemployment taxes, which follow different rules.)

Do note on the worksheet that the quarter is 13 weeks. Because Form 941 requires FICA information to be separated into Social Security and Medicare, you can see how helpful the worksheet can be. Note that for the December 31 monthly payroll some wages are not taxable for Social Security because the $76,200 wage-base limit was met. *All* wages for Medicare are taxable, however, because there is no wage-base limit for this tax. This worksheet can be built from the information in each individual's employee's earnings record and the weekly payroll registers.

Now let's look at the deposit rules Gradesoft.com must follow regarding Form 941 taxes (which are FICA and FIT).

Payroll Period		Pay Check Date	Earnings	FIT	Taxable FICA Wages for		FICA		Total Tax	Cumulative Tax
					Soc. Sec.	Medicare	Soc. Sec. EE + ER	Medicare EE + ER		
October	2–15	Oct. 20	4892 75	778 00	4892 75	4892 75	606 70	141 89	1526 59	1526 59
October	16–29	Nov. 3	5013 25	810 00	5013 25	5013 25	621 64	145 38	1577 03	3103 62
October	31	Oct. 31	16231 84	3895 00	16231 84	16231 84	2012 75	470 72	6378 47	9482 09
Oct./Nov.	30–12	Nov. 17	5007 15	809 00	5007 15	5007 15	620 89	145 21	1575 09*	11057 18
November	13–26	Dec. 1	5152 50	832 00	5152 50	5152 50	638 91	149 42	1620 33	12677 52
November	30	Nov. 30	16231 84	3895 00	16231 84	16231 84	2012 75	470 72	6378 47	19055 99
Nov./Dec.	27–10	Dec. 15	5629 00	909 00	5629 00	5629 00	698 00	163 24	1770 24	20826 22
December	11–24	Dec. 29	5700 75	921 00	5700 75	5700 75	706 89	165 32	1793 21	22619 44
December	25–31	Dec. 29	2105 68	367 00	2105 68	2105 68	261 10	61 06	689 17	23308 61
December	31	Dec. 29	16231 83	3895 00	11354 75	16231 83	1407 99	470 72	5773 71	29082 32
Totals for the Quarter			82196 59	17111 00	77319 51	82196 59	9587 62	2383 70	29082 32	29082 32
			(A)	(B)	(C)	(D)	(E)	(F)	(G)	(H)

*Off 1 cent due to rounding ($1,575.10)

FIGURE 8-2. Worksheet to monitor deposit requirements

DEPOSITING FORM 941 TAXES

The amount of tax due must be deposited in what is called an authorized depository in Gradesoft's area or a Federal Reserve bank. Authorized depositories are banks that have been authorized by the Federal Reserve system to accept payroll tax deposits from their own checking account customers. A Federal Reserve bank can accept payroll tax deposits from any business, no matter where the business maintains its checking account.

Types of Payroll Tax Depositors*

For payroll tax deposit purposes, employers are classified as either **monthly** or **semiweekly depositors.** A monthly depositor is an employer who only has to deposit Form 941 taxes on the fifteenth day of every month. Semiweekly depositors must deposit their Form 941 taxes once or twice each week.

The employer's classification depends on the dollar amount of the Form 941 taxes it has paid in the past. The IRS has developed a rule known as the **look-back period** rule to determine how to classify an employer for payroll tax deposits. Under this rule, the IRS will *look back* to a one-year time period that begins on July 1 and ends the following June 30. (For example, to determine the employer's status for 2003, the IRS will look at the period between July 1, 2001, and June 30, 2002.) If, during this look-back period, the employer has paid under $50,000 of Form 941 taxes, the IRS considers the employer to be a *monthly depositor.* If the employer has paid $50,000 or more during this period, it is considered to be a *semiweekly depositor.* Figure 8-3 shows how the look-back period works for payroll purposes.

Gradesoft.com is a semiweekly depositor because it made in excess of $50,000 in FICA and FIT deposits during the look-back period. If Gradesoft.com had made less than $50,000 in payroll tax deposits during the look-back period, it would have been classified as a monthly depositor.

New employers are automatically classified as monthly depositors until they have been in business long enough to have a look-back period for evaluation purposes. The employer's status is reevaluated every year.

Rules for Monthly Depositors   The rules for monthly depositors are fairly simple. They are:

1. The employee and employer Social Security and Medicare taxes and the employees' FIT accumulated during any month must be deposited by the fifteenth of the next month.

> The IRS examines the amount of Form 941 taxes paid during the period beginning July 1 and ending June 30 of the following year to determine whether the employer is a monthly depositor or a semiweekly depositor. This examination is called the look-back period rule.

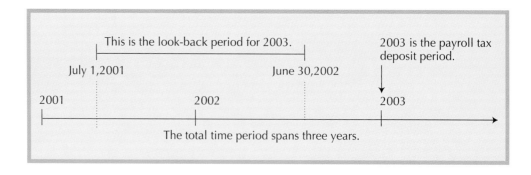

FIGURE 8-3. The level of payroll taxes paid during the look-back period determines how often the employer deposits payroll taxes

---

*Effective Jan. 1, 2001 IRS ends monthly employment-tax deposit requirements for those that owe less than $2,500 compared to the past $1,000.

	Monday	Tuesday	Wednesday	Thursday	Friday	Saturday	Sunday
The payday occurs this week →			■ If the payday occurs on one of these days, the deposit will be due Wednesday of the next week.			★ If the payday occurs on Saturday or Sunday, or...	
	★...Monday or Tuesday, then payroll tax deposit will be due and payable on Friday of this week.		■ Deposit day for Wednesday–Friday payday		★ Deposit day for Saturday–Tuesday payday		

FIGURE 8-4. The payday determines when the tax deposit is due

2. If the fifteenth of the month is a Saturday, Sunday, or bank holiday, the employer must make the payroll tax deposit on the next banking day.

Rules for Semiweekly Depositors   Semiweekly depositors like Gradesoft.com may have to make up to two payroll tax deposits every week, depending on when employees are   paid. For this purpose, each seven-day week begins on Wednesday and ends on the following Tuesday. The seven-day week is broken into two payday time periods: Wednesday through Friday and Saturday through Tuesday. In addition, the following rules apply:

1. If the company's payday occurs on Wednesday, Thursday, or Friday, the payroll tax deposit is due on the following Wednesday. If the company's payday occurs on Saturday, Sunday, Monday, or Tuesday, the payroll tax deposit is due on the following Friday. Thus, if an employer pays its employees on a Thursday and a Monday, it must make two payroll tax deposits — one on Wednesday for the Thursday payday, and one on Friday for the Monday payday.

2. If a bank holiday occurs after the end of the payday time-period but before the day the payroll tax deposit is due, the employer gets one extra day in which to make the deposit. So, a deposit due on a Wednesday will be due on Thursday, and a Friday deposit will be due on the following Monday.

As a general rule, the depositor always has three banking days in which to make the payroll tax deposit. The diagram in Figure 8-4 shows how these rules are applied.

Here is how the rules apply to Gradesoft.com. First, look back at Figure 8-2 (p. 277) to locate the dates of each weekly payday. Next, look at Figure 8-5, which shows a calendar for the last quarter of the year.

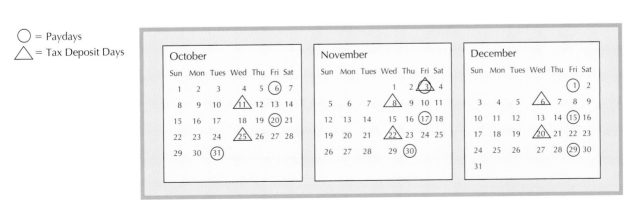

FIGURE 8-5. Last calendar quarter for Gradesoft.com shows paydays falling on Fridays

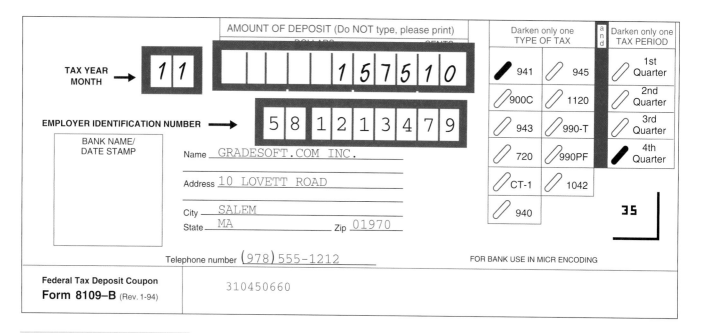

FIGURE 8-6. Form 8109

Note that each payday falls on a Friday. Because Fred's Market is a semi-weekly payroll tax depositor, its Form 941 payroll tax deposits are due on the following Wednesday. Fred's first payday in October falls on October 7. Its first payroll tax deposit will be due on October 12. Another deposit will be due on every Wednesday from that date until the end of the year. However, if we look at week 51 in Figure 8-2 (p. 277), the payday for this week is December 23, which is two days before Christmas. Christmas is a bank holiday, but in looking at the December calendar in Figure 8-5, we see that it falls on a Sunday. Under the law, Monday, December 26 then becomes the legal holiday. Ernie must then apply the rule regarding a holiday that falls between a payday and the tax deposit day, and will make the Form 941 tax deposit on Thursday, December 29.

Completion of Form 8109 to Accompany Deposits

To make Gradesoft.com's payroll tax deposits properly, Ernie must write a check for the total amount of the Form 941 tax deposit after each pay period. The deposits must also be accompanied by IRS **Form 8109, Federal Tax Deposit Coupon,** as shown in Figure 8-6.

Ernie received a book of coupons when he got the EIN for Gradesoft.com. Figure 8-6 shows Form 8109 completed for the October 30/November 12 pay period Form 941 payroll tax deposit. Note that the dollar amount found at the top of the form ($1,575.10) is the same as the amount found in the "Total Tax" column for the pay period in Figure 8-2.

In Figure 8-6, in the upper-right-hand corner the "Type of Tax" and "Tax Period" must be indicated by darkening the appropriate oval using a No. 2 pencil. Ernie has darkened the "941" and "4th Quarter" ovals for the October 30/November 12 payday.

Journalizing and Posting Payroll Tax Deposits

Payment of the payroll tax deposit for October 30/November 12 is made in the general journal as follows:

Accounts Affected	Category	↑ ↓	Rules
FICA—Social Security Payable	Liability	↓	Dr.
FICA—Medicare Payable	Liability	↓	Dr.
Federal Income Tax Payable	Liability	↓	Dr.
Cash	Asset	↓	Cr.

GRADESOFT.COM
GENERAL JOURNAL

				Dr.	Cr.
Nov	22	FICA — Social Security Payable	203	6 2 0 89	
		FICA — Medicare Payable	204	1 4 5 21	
		Federal Income Tax Payable	205	8 0 9 00	
		Cash	111		1 5 7 5 10
		To record the Form 941 tax deposit for the			
		biweekly payroll on November 17, 200X			

Now let's look at the partial general ledger of Gradesoft.com to get a better understanding of how specific payroll accounts in the ledger are updated regarding FICA (Social Security and Medicare) and FIT. Note in the *FICA—Social Security* and *Medicare Payable* accounts how the posting came from the general journal for the employees' and employer's share of FICA tax.* The general journal is also used when the payroll tax deposit is made, recording a debit to the *FICA—Social Security* and *Medicare Payable* accounts as well as the *Federal Income Tax Payable* account.

Under the Form 941 payroll tax deposit rules, the general journal entries to record the payroll are made biweekly on Friday, whereas the entries to record the payment of the payroll taxes are made the Wednesday after each biweekly payday. Check Figure 8-2 (p. 277) to see how the Form 941 tax liability has been recorded and then paid in the partial general ledger accounts shown below.

FICA—Social Security Payable					203
Date	PR	Dr.	Cr.	Cr. Bal.	
200X					
Nov. 17	GJ28		6 2 0 89	6 2 0 89	
22	GJ28	6 2 0 89		0	
30	GJ28		2 0 1 2 75	2 0 1 2 75	
Dec. 1	GJ29		6 3 8 91	2 6 5 1 66	
6	GJ29	2 6 5 1 66		0	
15	GJ29		6 9 8 00	6 9 8 00	
20	GJ29	6 9 8 00		0	

FICA—Medicare Payable					204
Date	PR	Dr.	Cr.	Cr. Bal.	
200X					
Nov. 17	GJ28		1 4 5 21	1 4 5 21	
22	GJ28	1 4 5 21		0	
30	GJ28		4 7 0 42	4 7 0 42	
1	GJ29		1 4 9 42	6 1 9 84	
6	GJ29	6 1 9 84		0	
15	GJ29		1 6 3 24	1 6 3 24	
20	GJ29	1 6 3 24		0	

FORM 941: EMPLOYER'S QUARTERLY FEDERAL TAX RETURN

Ernie Goldman, the controller for Gradesoft.com, used the worksheet in Figure 8-2 in preparing Form 941 for the last quarter of the year (see Fig. 8-7). The top section of the form identifies the taxpayer (Gradesoft.com), its address, the date the quarter ended, and Gradesoft's EIN. The two-letter U.S. Postal Service abbreviation for the state where Gradesoft is located ("MA" for Massachusetts) is filled in on the left-hand side of the form.

---

*Note: Each credit would actually be 2 credits: one from the employee and one from the employer.

Employer's Quarterly Federal Tax Return

► See separate instructions for information on completing this return.

Please type or print.

OMB No. 1545-0029

Enter state code for state in which deposits were made ONLY if different from state in address to the right ► M:A (see page 2 of instructions).

Name (as distinguished from trade name)

Trade name, if any
Gradesoft.com Inc.

Address (number and street)
10 Lovett Road

Date quarter ended
Dec. 31, 200X

Employer identification number
58-12134791

City, state, and ZIP code
Salem, MA 01970

T	
FF	
FD	
FP	
I	
T	

If address is different from prior return, check here ►

IRS Use

1 1 1 1 1 1 1 1 1   2   3 3 3 3 3 3 3   4 4 4   5 5 5

6   7   8 8 8 8 8 8 8   9 9 9   10 10 10 10 10 10 10 10 10 10

If you do not have to file returns in the future, check here ► ☐ and enter date final wages paid ►

If you are a seasonal employer, see **Seasonal employers** on page 1 of the instructions and check here ► ☐

1	Number of employees in the pay period that includes March 12th . ► 1			
2	Total wages and tips, plus other compensation	**2**	82,196	59
3	Total income tax withheld from wages, tips, and sick pay	**3**	17,111	00
4	Adjustment of withheld income tax for preceding quarters of calendar year	**4**		
5	Adjusted total of income tax withheld (line 3 as adjusted by line 4—see instructions) . . .	**5**	17,111	00

6	Taxable social security wages	**6a**	77,319	51	× 12.4% (.124) =	**6b**	9,587	62
	Taxable social security tips	**6c**			× 12.4% (.124) =	**6d**		
7	Taxable Medicare wages and tips . . .	**7a**	82,196	59	× 2.9% (.029) =	**7b**	2,383	70

8	Total social security and Medicare taxes (add lines 6b, 6d, and 7b). Check here if wages are not subject to social security and/or Medicare tax . . . . ► ☐	**8**	11,971	32
9	Adjustment of social security and Medicare taxes (see instructions for required explanation) Sick Pay $ _____ ± Fractions of Cents $ _____ ± Other $ _____ =	**9**		
10	Adjusted total of social security and Medicare taxes (line 8 as adjusted by line 9—see instructions)	**10**	11,971	32
11	**Total taxes** (add lines 5 and 10)	**11**	29,082	32
12	Advance earned income credit (EIC) payments made to employees	**12**		
13	Net taxes (subtract line 12 from line 11). **If $1,000 or more, this must equal line 17, column (d) below (or line D of Schedule B (Form 941))**	**13**	29,082	32
14	Total deposits for quarter, including overpayment applied from a prior quarter . . .	**14**	29,082	32
15	**Balance due** (subtract line 14 from line 13). See instructions	**15**	— 0 —	

16 **Overpayment.** If line 14 is more than line 13, enter excess here ► $ _____
and check if to be: ☐ Applied to next return **OR** ☐ Refunded.

• **All filers:** If line 13 is less than $1,000, you need not complete line 17 or Schedule B (Form 941).

• **Semiweekly schedule depositors:** Complete Schedule B (Form 941) and check here . . . . ► ☒

• **Monthly schedule depositors:** Complete line 17, columns (a) through (d), and check here . . . . . ► ☐

17	**Monthly Summary of Federal Tax Liability.** Do not complete if you were a semiweekly schedule depositor.		
(a) First month liability	**(b)** Second month liability	**(c)** Third month liability	**(d)** Total liability for quarter

Sign Here

Under penalties of perjury, I declare that I have examined this return, including accompanying schedules and statements, and to the best of my knowledge and belief, it is true, correct, and complete.

Signature ► **Ernie Goldman**

Print Your Name and Title ► **Controller**

Date ► **1-31-200X**

For Privacy Act and Paperwork Reduction Act Notice, see back of Payment Voucher.   Cat. No. 17001Z   Form **941**

FIGURE 8-7. Employer's Quarterly Federal Tax Return

Ernie filled out Form 941 using the dollar amounts from Figure 8-2 as follows. Please refer back to the particular column identified by letter (A, B, C, etc.) to see where Ernie obtained the amounts used in preparing the form:

Line   1a: This line is only filled in for the first quarter of the year. It is left blank for the last quarter.

2:   Total gross pay: $82,196.59 (the total for the quarter). See column A.

3:   Total income tax: $17,111.00. See column B.

4:   No adjustment needed here: this line is used only for special situations.

5:   Because there was no adjustment amount on line 4, this amount is the same as found on line 3: $17,111.00.

6a: The wages subject to Social Security tax are multiplied by 12.4 percent (6.2 percent for the employee and 6.2 percent for the employer). Total taxable wages are $77,319,51. Note that this line is different from line 2 because of the Social Security wage-base limit of $76,200 for the year. The tax is $9,587.62. See column E.

6b: Ernie leaves this line blank because no employee of Gradesoft.com receives any tip income (for example, as do employees in restaurants).

7a: The taxable wages for Medicare tax are $82,196.59 (see column D). Please note that this line will be the same as line 2 because there is no wage-base limit for Medicare tax. The tax amount is $2,383.70 (1.45 percent for the employee and 1.45 percent for the employer). See column F.

8:   The total of Social Security and Medicare taxes is $11,971.32 ($9,587.62 + $2,383.70).

9:   Due to the rounding of individual FICA amounts calculated and pay period total FICA amounts paid, there may be a difference between the total taxes shown in a general ledger and the actual payroll tax deposits. Line 9 can be used to reconcile these differences (called "fractions of cents") to account for rounding. Ernie's amounts do not need adjustment, so no amount is entered on line 9.

> Fraction of cents: If there is a difference between the total tax on Line 8 and the total deducted from your employees' wages or tips because of fractions of cents added or dropped in collecting the tax, report the difference on Line 9. Use the center column on Line 9 with a + or − sign to show the amount of the adjustment.

10:   This line is the sum of lines 8 and 9.

11:   This line is the sum of lines 5 and 10 added together. See columns G and H.

12:   If Gradesoft.com advanced any earned income credit to its employees, it would deduct the amount on this line.

13:   This line is the net of line 11 as adjusted by any amount found on line 12. See columns G and H.

14:   The total of the deposits made by Ernie for Gradesoft.com for the last quarter is $29,082.32. Remember that Gradesoft.com uses the semiweekly deposit rules. Note that the last Form 941 deposit is made after the year ends but is allowed to be taken as a last quarter deposit because it applies to the December 31 biweekly and monthly payrolls.

15:   There is no balance due to Gradesoft.com.

16:   There is no overpayment for Gradesoft.com. Note that directly below line 16 are two boxes that are checked only under certain circumstances. Ernie will check the box for semiweekly depositors and prepare Form 941 Schedule B. This schedule is an itemized listing of the semiweekly deposits made for the last quarter. It is not shown here.

17:   This line is filled in only if the employer has been classified as a monthly depositor of employment taxes. Please note that the line is broken into four sections. The first three sections — (a), (b), and (c) — are the monthly Form 941 tax liabilities. The sum of sections (a), (b), (c), must equal the section (d) amount. Likewise, the section (d) amount on line 17 must equal the amount found on line 13 of the return. Ernie does not complete this line because Gradesoft.com has been classified as a semiweekly depositor.

AT THIS POINT you should be able to

▼ Explain which taxes are reported on Form 941. (p. 277)
▼ Understand how employers are classified as payroll tax depositors. (p. 278)
▼ Explain the summary of Form 941 payroll tax deposit rules for monthly depositors. (p. 279)
▼ Explain the summary of Form 941 payroll tax deposit rules for semiweekly depositors. (p. 279)
▼ Prepare and explain the purpose of Form 8109. (p. 280)
▼ Record the general journal entry to pay FICA (Social Security and Medicare) and federal income taxes when a payroll tax deposit is made. (p. 281)
▼ Review how the general journal entries are posted into the general ledger to record the paying of employees and the paying of payroll taxes. (p. 281)
▼ Complete an Employer's Quarterly Federal Tax Return from a worksheet. (p. 282)

SELF-REVIEW QUIZ 8-2

(The blank forms you need are on page 243 of the *Study Guide and Working Papers.*)

Carol Ann's Import Chalet is a business that employs five full-time employees and four part-time employees. The accountant for Carol Ann's has determined that the business is a monthly depositor. The accountant prepared a worksheet showing the following payroll tax liabilities for the month of October:

Date	Social Security (EE + ER)	Medicare (EE + ER)	FIT
10/7	$ 486.56	$169.05	$ 829.00
10/14	632.15	165.01	901.00
10/21	579.43	131.05	734.00
10/28	389.99	142.24	765.00
Totals	$2,088.13	$607.35	$3,229.00

1. What is the dollar amount of the Form 941 tax deposit and when must it be made under the monthly deposit rule? Use Figure 8-5 (p. 279) for the date.

2. Assume that Carol Ann's is classified as a semiweekly depositor. Please calculate the amount of each Form 941 tax deposit and when it would be made by completing the table on the next page (use Fig. 8-5 for the dates):

Payday Date	Date of Deposit	Amount of Deposit
10/7	?	?
10/14	?	?
10/21	?	?
10/28	?	?

Solutions to Self-Review Quiz 8-2

1. As a monthly depositor, Carol Ann's deposit date is Tuesday, November 15. The total amount of the deposit is $5,924.48 ($2,088.13 + $607.35 + $3,229.00).

2. As a semiweekly depositor, Carol Ann's deposit schedule is completed as follows:

Payday Date	Date of Deposit	Amount of Deposit
10/7	10/12	$1,484.61
10/14	10/19	1,698.16
10/21	10/26	1,444.48
10/28	11/2*	1,297.23*

LEARNING UNIT 8-3

W-2, W-3, FORM 940-EZ, AND WORKERS' COMPENSATION

W-2: WAGE AND TAX STATEMENT

Form W-2, Wage and Tax Statement is a multipart form that is prepared by the employer each year. Gradesoft.com is required to give (or mail) copies of Form W-2 to each person who was employed in the past year. These forms must be distributed by January 31 of the following year. Employees use the figures on Form W-2 to compute the amount of income tax they must pay. One copy of the form must be attached to his or her federal income tax return; other copies must be attached to state and local tax returns.

Anyone who stopped working for Gradesoft.com before the end of that year may be given a Form W-2 at any time after the employment ends. If the former employee asks for it, the employer must supply completed copies within 30 days of the request or the final wage payment, whichever is later.

Additional copies of Form W-2 are sent to the Social Security Administration and state and local governments. The employer retains a copy of the W-2 form for each employee for its records.

Figure 8-8 on p. 286 shows the W-2 that James T. Zott received from Gradesoft.com. The information was obtained from his individual employee earnings record. Note that Social Security wages and taxes are shown separately from the amounts reported for Medicare wages and taxes because there is a wage base limit for the Social Security tax, but not for the Medicare tax.

W-3: TRANSMITTAL OF INCOME AND TAX STATEMENTS

Form W-3, Transmittal of Income and Tax Statements, is prepared and sent by the employer to the Social Security Administration along with copies of each employees' Form W-2. Form W-3 reports the total amounts of wages, tips, and compensation paid to employees; the total federal income tax withheld; the total Social Security and Medicare taxes withheld; and some other information.

Employers are required to send Form W-3 and Form W-2 to the Social Security Administration for FICA tax purposes. The Social Security

---

*Note that this deposit will be made in November given the calendar dates found in Figure 8-5.

a Control number	22222	Void ☐	For Official Use Only OMB No. 1545-0008		
b Employer identification number 58-12134791				**1** Wages, tips, other compensation 77,587.00	**2** Federal income tax withheld 19,818.00
c Employer's name, address, and ZIP code Gradesoft.com 10 Lovett Road Salem, MA 01940				**3** Social security wages 76,200.00	**4** Social security tax withheld 4,724.40
				5 Medicare wages and tips 77,587.00	**6** Medicare tax withheld 1,125.01
				7 Social security tips	**8** Allocated tips
d Employee's social security number 922-80-1250				**9** Advance EIC payment	**10** Dependent care benefits
e Employee's name (first, middle initial, last) James T. Zott 80 Garfield Street Marblehead, MA 01945				**11** Nonqualified plans	**12** Benefits included in box 1
				13 See instrs. for box 13	**14** Other
f Employee's address and ZIP code				**15** Statutory employee ☐ Deceased ☐ Pension plan ☐ Legal rep. ☐ Deferred compensation ☐	

16 State	Employer's state I.D. no.	**17** State wages, tips, etc.	**18** State income tax	**19** Locality name	**20** Local wages, tips, etc.	**21** Local income tax
MA	6 21-8966-4	77,587.00	6,206.96			

W-2 Wage and Tax Statement   **200X**

Copy A For Social Security Administration— Send this entire page with Form W-3 to the Social Security Administration; photocopies are **not** acceptable.

Cat. No. 10134D

Department of the Treasury—Internal Revenue Service

For Privacy Act and Paperwork Reduction Act Notice, see separate instructions.

Do NOT Cut, Fold, or Staple Forms on This Page — Do NOT Cut, Fold, or Staple Forms on This Page

FIGURE 8-8. Completed Form W-2

Administration, under a special agreement with the IRS, makes all information found on individual W-2 forms electronically available to the IRS so that it can check to verify the accuracy of the employer's 941 forms and individual employees' federal income tax returns.

The information used to complete Form W-3 in Figure 8-9 came from a summary of the individual employee earnings records that Ernie prepared after the end of the year (see Fig. 8-10 on p. 287).

FORM 940-EZ: EMPLOYER'S ANNUAL FEDERAL UNEMPLOYMENT TAX RETURN

There are two types of federal unemployment tax returns. **Form 940-EZ, Employer's Annual Federal Unemployment Tax Return,** is used by a business that only employs workers in one state. Businesses that employ workers in several states (multistate employers) must file a **Form 940, Employer's Annual Federal Unemployment Tax Return.** Form 940 asks for additional information that is not required on Form 940-EZ.

Gradesoft.com must file Form 940-EZ. After the first year it files this form, the IRS will send Ernie a preaddressed Form 940-EZ, near the close of each calendar year. Form 940-EZ must be filed no later than January 31 unless all required FUTA deposits have been made during the year, in which case

DO NOT STAPLE OR FOLD

a Control number	33333	For Official Use Only ▶ OMB No. 1545-0008		

b Kind of Payer ▶	941 ☒ CT-1 ☐	Military ☐ Hshld. emp. ☐	943 ☐ Medicare govt. emp. ☐	1 Wages, tips, other compensation 316,994.82	2 Federal income tax withheld 61,996.00

				3 Social security wages 316,032.82	4 Social security tax withheld 19,346.04
c Total number of Forms W-2 6		d Establishment number		5 Medicare wages and tips 316,994.82	6 Medicare tax withheld 4,596.43
e Employer identification number 58-12134791				7 Social security tips	8 Allocated tips
f Employer's name Gradesoft.com Inc.				9 Advance EIC payments	10 Dependent care benefits
10 Lovett Road Salem, MA 01970				11 Nonqualified plans	12 Deferred compensation
				13	
				14	
g Employer's address and ZIP code					
h Other EIN used this year				15 Income tax withheld by third-party payer	
i Employer's state I.D. no. 6 21-8966-4					

Contact person E. Goldman	Telephone number (617) 555-1212	Fax number (617) 555-1213	E-mail address egoldman@gradesoft.com

Under penalties of perjury, I declare that I have examined this return and accompanying documents, and, to the best of my knowledge and belief, they are true, correct, and complete.

Signature ▶ _Ernie Goldman_   Title ▶ _Controller_   Date ▶ 1/31/200X

Form **W-3** **Transmittal of Wage and Tax Statements**   **200X**   Department of the Treasury Internal Revenue Service

Send this entire page with the entire Copy A page of Form(s) W-2 to the Social Security Administration. Photocopies are NOT acceptable.
Do NOT send any remittance (cash, checks, money orders, etc.) with Forms W-2 and W-3.

FIGURE 8-9. Completed Form W-3

Employee	Total Earnings	FICA Taxable Earnings		FICA Tax		FIT
		Soc. Sec.	Medicare	Soc. Sec.	Medicare	
Jackson, Lee	34,812 55	34,812 55	34,812 55	2,158 38	504 78	3,984 00
Sheila Stowe	19,872 11	19,872 11	19,872 11	1,232 07	288 15	2,290 00
Regan, Pat	66,448 16	66,448 16	66,448 16	4,119 79	963 50	8,265 00
Goldman, Ernie	38,500 00	38,500 00	38,500 00	2,387 00	558 25	5,989 00
Zott, Jim	77,587 00	77,200 00	77,587 00	4,724 40	1,125 01	19,818 00
Nguyen, Vince	79,775 00	79,200 00	79,775 00	4,724 40	1,156 74	21,650 00
	316,994 82	316,032 82	316,994 82	19,346 04	4,596 43	61,996 00

FIGURE 8-10. Employee Earnings Record Summary

Form 940-EZ

Department of the Treasury
Internal Revenue Service

Employer's Annual Federal Unemployment (FUTA) Tax Return

► See separate **Instructions for Form 940-EZ** for information on completing this form.

OMB No. 1545-1110

200**X**

T	
FF	
FD	
FP	
I	
T	

Name (as distinguished from trade name)

Trade name, if any
Gradesoft.com Inc.

Address and ZIP code
10 Lovett Road, Salem, MA 01970

Calendar year
200X

Employer identification number
58 12134791

Answer the questions under **Who May Use Form 940-EZ** *on page 2. If you cannot use Form 940-EZ, you must use Form 940.*

A Enter the amount of contributions paid to your state unemployment fund. (See separate instructions.) . . . ► $ *1,890.00*

B (1) Enter the name of the state where you have to pay contributions . . . . ► .... *MASSACHUSETTS* ....
   (2) Enter your state reporting number as shown on your state unemployment tax return ► *281-615*

If you will not have to file returns in the future, check here (see **Who Must File** in separate instructions), **and complete and sign the return.** ► ☐

If this is an Amended Return, check here . . . . ► ☐

Part I   Taxable Wages and FUTA Tax

1	Total payments (including payments shown on lines 2 and 3) during the calendar year for services of employees	**1**	316,994 82
2	Exempt payments. (Explain all exempt payments, attaching additional sheets if necessary.) ►	**2**	
3	Payments of more than $7,000 for services. Enter only amounts over the first $7,000 paid to each employee. Do not include any exempt payments from line 2. The $7,000 amount is the Federal wage base. Your state wage base may be different. **Do not use your state wage limitation**	**3** 274,994 82	
4	Total exempt payments (add lines 2 and 3)	**4**	274,994 82
5	**Total taxable wages** (subtract line 4 from line 1) . . . . ►	**5**	42,000 00
6	**FUTA tax.** Multiply the wages on line 5 by .008 and enter here. (**If the result is over $100, also complete Part II.**)	**6**	336 00
7	Total FUTA tax deposited for the year, including any overpayment applied from a prior year	**7**	336 00
8	**Balance due** (subtract line 7 from line 6). Pay to the "United States Treasury" . . . . ►	**8**	– 0 –
	If you owe more than $100, see **Depositing FUTA tax** in separate instructions.		
9	**Overpayment** (subtract line 6 from line 7). Check if it is to be: ☐ **Applied to next return or** ☐ **Refunded** ►	**9**	

Part II   Record of Quarterly Federal Unemployment Tax Liability (Do not include state liability.) **Complete only if line 6 is over $100.**

Quarter	First (Jan. 1 – Mar. 31)	Second (Apr. 1 – June 30)	Third (July 1 – Sept. 30)	Fourth (Oct. 1 – Dec. 31)	Total for year
Liability for quarter	198.00	– 0 –	114.00	24.00	336.00

Under penalties of perjury, I declare that I have examined this return, including accompanying schedules and statements, and, to the best of my knowledge and belief, it is true, correct, and complete, and that no part of any payment made to a state unemployment fund claimed as a credit was, or is to be, deducted from the payments to employees.

Signature ► *Ernie Goldman*   Title (Owner, etc.)► *Controller*   Date ► *2/10/200X*

For Privacy Act and Paperwork Reduction Act Notice, see separate instructions.   Cat. No. 10983G   Form **940-EZ**

FIGURE 8-11. Completed Form 940-EZ

the return can be filed by February 10. The completed form is shown in Figure 8-11.

FUTA   As we saw earlier, the FUTA tax rate is .8 percent (or eight tenths of one percent) on the first $7,000 of each employee's gross pay. If Gradesoft.com's accumulated FUTA tax liability is $100 or more during the calendar year, Ernie must make a FUTA tax deposit with a Federal Reserve bank or a bank authorized to take payroll tax deposits. The FUTA tax deposit rule is quite simple: If the amount of FUTA tax owed is $100 or more during any calendar quarter, the employer must deposit the amount due no later than one month after the quarter ends.

At the end of the first quarter Gradesoft.com owes $198 for FUTA taxes. Ernie has prepared a schedule showing how the tax was computed. (See Table 8-1 below for the calculations.) If an employee earned over the $7,000 FUTA wage base limit, only the first $7,000 will be taxable for FUTA purposes. Note that only one of Gradesoft.com's employees earned over the $7,000 FUTA limit during the first quarter of the year. Please see Part II of the Form 940-EZ in Figure 8-11.

Because Gradesoft.com owes $198 in FUTA taxes, Ernie will make the FUTA tax deposit on April 30 to comply with the FUTA deposit rule. The general journal entry is prepared as shown below.

			GRADESOFT.COM GENERAL JOURNAL					
*	April	30	FUTA Payable	212	198 00		
			SUTA Payable	213	1336 48		
			Cash	111		1534 48
			To record the FUTA and SUTA tax				
			deposits for the first quarter of the year.				

*Note: This entry could be two separate entries.

SUTA Gradesoft.com must also pay state unemployment tax to Massachusetts. The SUTA tax is also due one month after the quarter ends, on April 30. Ernie will pay out $1,336.48 in tax, based on a SUTA percentage rate of 5.4 percent on the first $7,000 that each of the employees has earned ($24,749.62 × .054 = $1,336.48).

The amount of SUTA Ernie pays is shown on lines A and B of Form 940-EZ.

WORKERS' COMPENSATION INSURANCE

Gradesoft.com is required to have **workers' compensation insurance** to insure its employees against losses due to accidental injury or death incurred while on the job. Ernie is required to estimate the cost of this insurance and pay the premium in advance.

The premium for workers' compensation insurance is based on the total estimated gross payroll, and the rate is calculated per $100 of weekly payroll. At year end, the actual payroll is compared with the estimated payroll, and Fred will either receive credit for overpayment or be responsible for paying additional premiums.

TABLE 8-1   COMPUTATION OF FUTA TAX FOR THE FIRST QUARTER OF 200X

Employee	Amount Earned in First Quarter	Amount Taxable for FUTA
Lee, Jackson	$ 4,703.56	$ 4,703.56
Stowe, Sheila*	0	0
Regan, Pat	$ 4,512.14	$ 4,512.14
Goldman, Ernie[†]	$ 3,208.33	$ 3,208.33
Zott, James T.[†]	$ 5,325.59	$ 5,325.59
Nguyen, Vince	$19,943.75	$ 7,000.00
		$24,749.62 × .008 = $197.99

*Sheila Stowe was not hired until the third quarter of the year.
[†]Ernie Goldman and James T. Zott were hired in March of the year (one month's earnings for quarter).

These are the facts on which Gradesoft.com's insurance cost was calculated:

1. Estimated payroll: $320,000.
2. Two grades of workers: Developers and Managers.
3. Rate per $100 of payroll: Developers, $1.90; Managers $.14.
4. Estimated payroll: Developers, $120,000; Managers, $200,000.

The estimated premium was, calculated as follows:

Developers: $120,000/$100 = 1,200 × $1.90 = $2,280
Managers: $200,000/$100 = 2,000 × $.14 =   280
                          Total Estimated Premium: $2,560

Accounts Affected	Category	↑ ↓	Dr./Cr.
Prepaid Insurance, Worker's Compensation	Asset	↑	Dr.
Cash	Asset	↓	Cr.

Gradesoft.com would have to pay $2,560 in advance. At the end of the year, records show that the developer payroll was $121,114 and the manager payroll was $195,862.

Given those amounts, Gradesoft.com's actual premium should be $2,575.16 calculated as follows:

Developers: $121,114/$100 = 1,211 × $1.90 = $2,300.90
Managers: $195,862/$100 = 1,959 × $.14 =   274.26
                          Total Estimated Premium: $2,575.16

Because the actual premium is $15.16 higher than the estimate, Ernie must pay this amount in January together with the estimated premium for the next year.

The $15.16 adjustment takes place on December 31 by debiting *Workers' Compensation Insurance Expense* and crediting *Workers' Compensation Insurance Payable*.

Accounts Affected	Category	↑ ↓	Dr./Cr.
Workers' Compensation Insurance Expense	Expense	↑	Dr.
Workers' Compensation Insurance Payable	Liability	↑	Cr.

LEARNING UNIT 8-3 REVIEW

AT THIS POINT you should be able to

▼ Prepare a W-2 form. (p. 286)
▼ Explain the difference between a W-2 form and a W-3 form. (p. 286)
▼ Prepare a 940-EZ form. (p. 288)
▼ Explain the difference between a Form 940-EZ and a Form 940. (p. 288)

▼ Calculate estimated premium for workers' compensation insurance. (p. 290)

▼ Prepare journal entries to record as well as adjust the premiums for workers' compensation insurance. (p. 290)

SELF-REVIEW QUIZ 8-3

(The forms you need are on page 243 of the *Study Guide and Working Papers.*) Are the following questions true or false?

1. W-4s must be received by employees by January 31 of the following year.
2. Form W-3 is sent to the Social Security Administration yearly.
3. A Form 940 is prepared by a business that employs workers in only one state.
4. The Employer's Annual Federal Unemployment Tax Return records the employer's FICA and FIT tax liabilities.
5. A FUTA tax liability of $100 must be paid 10 days after the quarter ends.
6. Premiums for workers' compensation insurance may be adjusted based on actual payroll figures.

A Taxing Time

As an employer, Fred, what are your tax responsibilities?" asked George Olsen, president of the local Kiwanis club. They were at one of the luncheons sponsored by the club every month. Fred had been asked to join a panel discussion on the Role of Small Business in Our Local Economy. Luckily, George had told the panelists the questions in advance, so Fred had his answers ready.

"Well, of course, I pay city, state, and U.S. government taxes myself. I also have to file city, state, and federal withholding taxes for each of my employees. I have to withhold state unemployment taxes, as well as FICA, which is another name for Social Security and Medicare taxes, for each of them. I pay workers' compensation, too," said Fred quickly.

"That's funny," said a voice from the audience. "My brother-in-law has a Dunkin' Donuts shop in the southern part of the state, and he doesn't pay any city taxes. What's going on here?"

"Naturally, the situation is slightly different for Dunkin' Donuts shop owners in different cities and towns in our state," said Fred confidently. "Not all cities have city income taxes. Different states have different regulations about worker's comp, as well."

"Oh, right," said the voice, sounding embarrassed.

"What happens at the corporate level at Dunkin' Donuts, Fred?" asked George Olsen, shifting the topic diplomatically.

"That's a really big operation, as you can imagine," said Fred. "We have corporate employees in some 20 states and countries, so a portion of the payroll function is not handled in-house. Instead it is outsourced to ADP, an international payroll processing service. They generate the checks and handle the tax reporting to the various cities, states, and countries. The corporate employees manage all the other aspects of the payroll process, from collecting information on hours worked to analysis of the labor dollars."

"Thanks, Fred," said George, "Now let's move on to Eva Jonet, who is going to tell us about advertising her new nail salon."

Fred nodded and breathed a sigh of relief as Eva took the microphone from him. He much preferred baking to public speaking!

Discussion Questions

1. George had warned Fred not to use technical language in preparing his remarks, so Fred didn't mention Form 941 taxes. Define Form 941 taxes.
2. Fred is classified as a monthly depositor of Form 941 taxes. Why?
3. Assume Fred owed $2,679.90 in Form 941 taxes for November. When would it be due? What would happen if that day were a Sunday?

Solutions to Self-Review Quiz 8-3

Quiz Tip: If you are getting refunds for FIT, you may want to change your withholding.

1. False. W-2 forms must be sent to each employee by January 31 of the next year. The W-4 form is filled out by a new employee and is used for calculating federal and state income taxes.

2. True.

3. False. Form 940 will be prepared by a business that employs workers in more than one state. Form 940-EZ will be prepared by an employer with workers in only one state.

4. False. The Employer's Annual Federal Unemployment Tax Return records and reports the FUTA tax liability. Form 941 records and reports the FICA and FIT tax liabilities.

5. False. A FUTA tax liability of $100 must be paid one month after the quarter ends.

6. True.

SUMMARY OF KEY POINTS

Learning Unit 8-1

1. The Payroll Tax Expense for the employer is made up of FICA tax (Social Security and Medicare) and the state and federal unemployment insurance taxes.

2. The maximum amount of credit given for state unemployment taxes paid against the FUTA tax is 5.4 percent. This figure is known as the normal FUTA tax credit.

3. The Payroll Tax Expense is recorded at the time the payroll is recorded.

Learning Unit 8-2

1. Federal Form 941 is prepared and filed no later than one month after the calendar quarter ends. It reports the amount of Social Security, Medicare, and federal income taxes withheld from employees and the Social Security and Medicare taxes due from the employer during the quarter.

2. Social Security, Medicare, and federal income taxes are known as *Form 941 taxes.*

3. The total amount of Form 941 taxes paid by a business during a specific period of time determines how often the business will have to make its payroll tax deposits. This time period is called a *look-back period.*

4. Businesses will make their payroll tax deposits either monthly or semi-weekly when paying Form 941 taxes.

5. Different deposit rules apply to monthly and semiweekly depositors.

6. Form 941 payroll tax deposits must be made using Form 8109 known as the Federal Tax Deposit Coupon.

Learning Unit 8-3

1. Information to prepare W-2 forms can be obtained from the individual employee earnings records.

2. Form W-3 is used by the Social Security Administration in verifying that taxes have been withheld as reported on individual employee W-2 forms.

3. 940-EZ is prepared by January 31, after the end of the previous calendar year. This form can be filed by February 10 if all required deposits have been made by January 31.

4. If the amount of FUTA taxes is equal to or more than $100 during any calendar quarter, the deposit must be made no later than one month after the quarter ends. If the amount is less than $100, no deposit is required until the liability reaches the $100 point.

5. Workers' Compensation Insurance (the estimated premium) is paid at the beginning of the year by the employer to protect against potential losses to its employees due to accidental death or injury incurred while on the job.

KEY TERMS

Calendar quarter   A three-month time period. There are four calendar quarters in a calendar year (January 1 through December 31). The first quarter is January through March, the second is April through June, the third is July through September, and the fourth is October through December.

Employer identification number (EIN)   This number assigned by the IRS is used by an employer when recording and paying payroll and income taxes.

Experience/merit rating   A percentage rate that is assigned to a business by the state in calculating state unemployment taxes. The rate is based on the employment record and amount of contributions paid into the state unemployment fund. The lower the rating, the less tax that must be paid.

Federal Insurance Contributions Act (FICA)   Part of the Social Security law that requires employees and employers to pay Social Security taxes and Medicare taxes.

Federal Unemployment Tax Act (FUTA)   A tax paid by employers to the federal government. The current rate is .8 percent after applying the normal FUTA tax credit on the first $7,000 of earnings of each employee.

Form 940, Employer's Annual Federal Unemployment Tax Return   One version of the form used by employers at the end of the year to report the amount of unemployment tax due for the calendar year. This version of the form is used by an employer with workers in more than one state. If more than $100 is cumulatively owed in a quarter, it should be paid quarterly, one month after the end of the quarter. Normally, payment is due January 31 after the calendar year, or February 10 if deposits have already been made by an employer.

Form 940-EZ, Employer's Annual Federal Unemployment Tax Return   The other version of the form used by employers at the end of the year to report the amount of unemployment tax due for the calendar year. The "EZ" version of this form is used by an employer with workers in only one state.

Form 941, Employer's Quarterly Federal Tax Return   A tax report that a business will complete after the end of each calendar quarter indicating the total FICA (Social Security and Medicare) owed plus the amount of federal income tax withheld from employees' pay for the quarter. If federal tax deposits have been made timely, the total amount deposited should equal the amount due on Form 941. If there is a difference, a payment may be due.

Form 941 taxes   Another term used to describe Social Security, Medicare, and federal income taxes. This name comes from the form used to report these taxes.

Form 8109, Federal Tax Deposit Coupon   A coupon that is completed and sent along with payments of tax deposits relating to either Forms 940-EZ or 941. This form can also be used to deposit other types of taxes a business may owe the federal government.

Form SS-4   The form filled out by an employer to get an employer identification number. The form is sent to the IRS, who assigns the number to the business.

Form W-2, Wage and Tax Statement   A form completed by the employer at the end of the calendar year to provide a summary of gross earnings and deductions to each employee. At least two copies go to the employee, one copy to the IRS, one copy to any state where employees' income taxes have been withheld, one copy to the Social Security Administration, and one copy into the records of the business.

Form W-3, Transmittal of Income and Tax Statements   A form completed by the employer to verify the number of W-2s and amounts withheld as shown on them. This form is sent to a Social Security Administration data processing center along with copies of each employee's W-2 forms.

Look-back period   A period of time used to determine if a business will make its Form 941 tax deposits on a monthly or semiweekly basis. The IRS has defined this period as July 1 through June 30 of the year prior to the year in which Form 941 tax deposits will be made.

Monthly depositor   A business classified as a monthly depositor will make its payroll tax deposits only once each month for the amount of Form 941 due from the prior month.

Normal FUTA Tax Credit   A credit given to employers who pay their state unemployment taxes on time. The credit is usually 5.4 percent, which is applied against a 6.2 percent rate. The result is a net FUTA tax of .8 percent.

Payroll Tax Expense   The general ledger account that records the total of the employer's FICA (Social Security and Medicare), SUTA, and FUTA tax responsibilities.

Semiweekly depositor   A business classified as a semiweekly depositor may make its payroll tax deposits up to twice in one week. Semiweekly depositors will make a minimum of one Form 941 payroll tax deposit each week.

State Unemployment Tax Act (SUTA)   A tax usually paid only by employers to the state for employee unemployment insurance.

Workers' compensation insurance   Insurance paid for, in advance, by an employer to protect its employees against loss due to injury or death incurred during employment.

BLUEPRINT: FORM 941 TAX DEPOSIT RULES

10 Frequently Asked Questions and Answers about Depositing Social Security, Medicare, and Federal Income Taxes to the Government

Here is a summary of questions and answers to help you understand the payroll tax deposit rules for Form 941 taxes.

1. **What are Form 941 taxes?** The term Form 941 taxes is used to describe the amount of Social Security, Medicare, and federal income tax paid by employees and the amount of Social Security and Medicare taxes that are matched and paid by an employer. The total of these taxes are known as Form 941 taxes because they are reported on Form 941 each quarter.

2. **When does an employer deposit Form 941 taxes?** How often an employer deposits Form 941 taxes depends on how the employer is classified for this purpose. The IRS classifies an employer as either a *monthly* or *semiweekly depositor* based on the amount of Form 941 taxes paid during a time period known as a *look-back period.*

3. **When is a look-back period?** A look-back period is a fiscal year that begins on July 1 and ends on June 30 of the year before the calendar year when the deposits will be made. For example, for the 2003 calendar year, an employer's look-back period will begin on July 1, 2001, and end June 30, 2002.

4. **What is the dollar amount used to classify an employer for Form 941 tax deposits?** The key dollar amount used to determine if an employer is a *monthly* or *semiweekly depositor* is $50,000 in Form 941 taxes. Two rules apply here:

    a. If the total amount deposited in Form 941 taxes is less than $50,000 during the look-back period, the employer is considered a *monthly tax depositor.*

    b. If the total amount deposited in Form 941 taxes is $50,000 or more during the look-back period, the employer is considered a *semiweekly tax depositor.*

5. **How do employers deposit Form 941 taxes?** An employer fills out a Form 8109 (Federal Tax Deposit Coupon) and gives this form with a check to a bank authorized to receive payroll tax deposits or to a Federal Reserve bank. Usually, authorized banks will only take checks written from an account maintained at that same bank. Therefore, an employer usually cannot make a Form 941 deposit at bank A using a check written from an account maintained at bank B. A Federal Reserve bank will accept a check from any U.S. bank for payroll tax deposit purposes.

6. **When do monthly depositors make their deposits?** A monthly depositor will figure the total amount of Form 941 taxes owed in a calendar month and then pay this amount by the fifteenth of the next month. If an employer owes $3,125 in Form 941 taxes for the month of June, it will deposit this same amount no later than July 15 of the same year.

7. **When do semiweekly depositors make their deposits?** The rules for making deposits are a little more complicated. A semiweekly depositor may have to make up to two Form 941 deposits each week. When a tax deposit is due depends on when the employees are paid. To keep the rules consistent, the IRS has taken a calendar week and divided it into two payday time periods. It is easiest to think of a two-week period of time when discussing these time periods: *Wednesday, Thursday, and Friday* of week one, and *Saturday and Sunday* of week one and *Monday and Tuesday* of week two.

    Two deposit rules apply to these two time periods. We can call these rules the Wednesday and Friday rules.

    a. **Wednesday rule:** If employees are paid during the week one

Wednesday–Friday period, the tax deposit will be due on Wednesday of week two.

b. Friday rule: If employees are paid anytime from Saturday or Sunday of week one or Monday or Tuesday of week two, the tax deposit will be due on Friday of week two.

These rules mean that the payroll tax deposit will be due three banking days after the payday time period ends. For the Wednesday rule, the deposit is due three banking days after Friday of week one, on the following Wednesday (in week two). For the Friday rule, the deposit is due three banking days after Tuesday of week two, on Friday of week two.

8. What is a banking day? The term *banking day* refers to any day that a bank is open to the public for business. Saturdays, Sundays, and legal holidays are not banking days.

9. How do legal holidays affect payroll tax deposits? If a legal holiday occurs after the last day of a payday time period, the employer will get one extra day to make its Form 941 tax deposit as follows:

a. For monthly depositors: If the fifteenth of the month is a Saturday, Sunday, or legal holiday, the deposit will be due and payable on the next banking day.

b. For semiweekly depositors: A deposit due on Wednesday will be due on Thursday of the same week, and a Friday deposit will be due on Monday of the following week. Remember that the employer will always have three banking days after the last day of either payday time period to make its payroll tax deposit.

10. What happens if an employer is late with its Form 941 tax deposit? If a Form 941 tax deposit is not made the day it should be deposited, the employer may be assessed a fine for lateness and may even be charged interest, depending on how late the deposit is.

QUESTIONS, MINI EXERCISES, EXERCISES, AND PROBLEMS

Discussion Questions

1. What taxes make up *Payroll Tax Expense?*

2. Explain how an employer can receive a credit against the FUTA tax due.

3. Explain what an experience or merit rating is and how it affects the amount paid by an employer for state unemployment insurance.

4. How is an employer classified as a monthly or semiweekly depositor for Form 941 tax purposes?

5. What is the purpose of Form 8109?

6. How often is Form 941 completed?

7. Please comment on the following statement: The amount found on line 17(d) of Form 941 must always be the same amount found on line 13 of the form.

8. Bill Smith leaves his job on July 9. He requests a copy of his W-2 form when he leaves. His boss tells him to wait until January of next year. Please discuss whether Bill's boss is correct in making this statement.

9. Why would one employer prepare a Form 940 but another would prepare a 940-EZ?

10. Employer A has a FUTA tax liability of $67.49 on March 31 of the current year. When does the employer have to make the deposit for this liability?

11. Employer B has a FUTA tax liability of $553.24 on January 31 of the current year. When does the employer have to make the deposit for this liability?

12. is the year-end adjusting entry needed for workers' compensation insurance?

Mini Exercises

(The forms you need are on page 245 of the *Study Guide and Working Papers*.)

Account Classifications

1. Complete the following table:

Accounts Affected	Category	↑	Rules
a. Payroll Tax Expense			
b. FICA—Social Security Payable			
c. FICA—Medicare Payable			
d. State Unemployment Tax Payable			
e. Federal Unemployment Tax Payable			

Exempt Wages

2. Pete Bole's cumulative earnings before this pay period were $6,800; his gross pay for this week's $500. How much of *this* week's pay will be subject to taxes for: FICA — Medicare, FICA — Social Security, SUTA, and FUTA. Assume base and rates in the text.

Look-Back Periods

3. Label the following look-back periods for 200C by months.

A	B	C	D
200A		200B	

Monthly versus Semiweekly Depositor

4. In November 200B, Pete is trying to find out if he is a monthly or semi-weekly depositor for FICA (Social Security and Medicare) and federal income tax for 200C. Please advise based on the following taxes owed:

200A	Quarter 3	$28,000
	Quarter 4	12,000
200B	Quarter 1	3,000
	Quarter 2	10,000

Paying the Tax

5. Complete the following table:

Depositor	Four-Quarter Look-Back Period Tax Liability	Payroll Paid	Tax Paid by
Monthly	$28,000	Nov.	A
Semiweekly	$66,000	On Wednesday	B
		On Thursday	C
		On Friday	D
		On Saturday	E
		On Sunday	F
		On Monday	G

Exercises

(The forms you need are on pages 246–248 of the *Study Guide and Working Papers*.)

Journalizing the payroll tax.

8-1. From the following information, prepare a general journal entry to record the payroll tax expense for Asty Company for the payroll of August 9:

Employee	Cumulative Earnings before Weekly Payroll	Gross Pay for Week
J. Kline	$3,500	$900
A. Met	6,600	750
D. Ring	7,900	300

The FICA tax rate for Social Security is 6.2 percent on $76,200, and Medicare is 1.45 percent on all earnings. Federal unemployment tax is .8 percent (.008 when expressed as a decimal) on the first $7,000 earned by each employee. The experience or merit rating for Asty is 5.6 percent on the first $7,000 of employee earnings for state unemployment purposes.

Change in merit rating.

8-2. Using Exercise 8-1, the state changed Asty's experience/merit rating to 4.9 percent. What effect would this change have on the total payroll tax expense?

Change in payroll tax expense.

8-3. Using Exercise 8-1, if D. Ring earned $2,000 for the week instead of $300, what effect would this change have on the total payroll tax expense?

Journalizing payment of deposit.

8-4. At the end of January 200X, the total amount of Social Security, $610, and Medicare, $200, was withheld as tax deductions from the employees of Cornfield Acres Inc. Federal income tax of $3,000 was also deducted from their paychecks. Cornfield Acres has been classified as a monthly depositor of Form 941 taxes. Indicate when this payroll tax deposit is due and provide a general journal entry to record the payment.

Calculating total payroll tax expense.

8-5. The total wage expense for Howie Co. was $150,000. Of this total, $30,000 was beyond the Social Security wage-base limit and not subject to this tax. All earnings are subject to Medicare tax, and $60,000 was beyond the federal and state unemployment wage base limits and not subject to unemployment taxes. Please calculate the total payroll tax expense for Howie Co. given the following rates and wage-base limits:

a. FICA tax rate: Social Security, 6.2 percent; Medicare, 1.45 percent.

b. State unemployment tax rate: 5.9 percent.

c. Federal unemployment tax rate (after credit): .8 percent.

Determining when tax deposits are due.

8-6. Carol's Grocery Store made the following Form 941 payroll tax deposits during the look-back period of July 1, 200A, through June 30, 200B:

Quarter Ended	Amount Paid in 941 Taxes
September 30, 200A	$13,783.26
December 31, 200A	14,893.22
March 31, 200B	14,601.94
June 30, 200B	15,021.01

Should Carol's Grocery Store make Form 941 tax deposits monthly or semiweekly for 200C?

Determining when tax deposits are due.

8-7. If Carol's Grocery Store downsized its operation during the second quarter of 200B and as a result paid only $6,121.93 in Form 941 taxes for the quarter that ended on June 30, 200B, should Carol's Grocery make its Form 941 payroll tax deposits monthly or semiweekly for 200C?

8-8. From the following accounts, record the payment of (a) the July 3 payment for FICA (Social Security and Medicare) and federal income taxes, (b) the July 30 payment of state unemployment tax, and (c) the July 30 deposit of FUTA tax that may be required. Please prepare general journal entries from the following T accounts:

Journal entry to record payment of taxes.

FICA—Social Security Payable 203	
	June 30 400 (EE)
	400 (ER)

FICA—Medicare Payable 204	
	June 30 100 (EE)
	100 (ER)

FIT Payable 205	
	June 30 3,005

FUTA Tax Payable 206	
	June 30 119

SUTA Tax Payable 207	
	June 30 411

FUTA.

8-9. At the end of the first quarter of 200X, you have been asked to determine the FUTA tax liability for Oscar Company as well as to record any payment of tax liability. The following information has been supplied to you; the FUTA tax rate is .8 percent on the first $7,000 each employee earns during the year.

Employee	Gross Pay per Week
J. King	$400
A. Lane	500
B. Move	600
C. Slade	900

Workers' compensation.

8-10. From the following data, estimate the annual premium and record it by preparing a general journal entry:

Type of Work	Estimated Payroll	Rate per $100
Office	$15,000	$ .17
Sales	42,000	1.90

Group A Problems

(The forms you need are on pages 249–255 of the *Study Guide and Working Papers.*)

8A-1. For the biweekly pay period ending on April 8 at Kane's Hardware, the partial payroll summary shown below is taken from the individual employee earnings records.

Journal entry to record payroll tax expense.

Your Tasks Are to

1. Complete the table.
2. Prepare a journal entry to record the payroll tax expense for Kane's. Use the federal income tax withholding table in Figure 7-2 (p. 242) to figure the amount of income tax withheld. Please show the calculations for FICA taxes.

Check Figure:
Payroll Tax Expense
$593.58

Employee	Allowance and Marital Status	Gross	FICA Social Security	Medicare	Federal Income Tax
Al Jones	S-1	$ 850			
Janice King	S-0	900			
Alice Long	S-2	800			
Jill Reese	S-0	1,060			
Jeff Vatack	S-2	1,365			

Assume the FICA tax rate for Social Security is 6.2 percent up to $76,200 in earnings (no one has earned this much as of April 8) and Medicare is 1.45 percent on all earnings. The state unemployment tax rate is 5.1 percent on the first $7,000 of earnings, and the federal unemployment tax rate is .8 percent of the first $7,000 of earnings. (Only Jeff Vatack has earned more than $7,000 as of April 8.) In cases where the amount of FICA tax calculates to one-half cent, round up to the next cent.

8A-2. The following is the monthly payroll of Hogan Company, owned by Dean Hogan. Employees are paid on the last day of each month.

Employer's tax responsibilities.

JANUARY

Employee	Monthly Earnings	Year-to-Date Earnings	FICA Social Security	Medicare	Federal Income Tax
Sam Koy	$1,800	$1,800	$ 111.60	$ 26.10	$ 241
Joy Lane	3,150	3,150	195.30	45.68	361
Amy Hess	4,100	4,100	254.20	59.45	500
	$9,050	$9,050	$561.10	$131.23	$1,102

FEBRUARY

Employee	Monthly Earnings	Year-to-Date Earnings	FICA Social Security	Medicare	Federal Income Tax
Sam Koy	$1,975	$ 3,775	$122.45	$ 28.64	$ 265
Joy Lane	2,900	6,050	179.80	42.05	325
Amy Hess	3,775	7,875	234.05	54.74	426
	$8,650	$17,700	$536.30	$125.43	$1,016

Check Figure:
Deposit of SUTA Tax
$1,195.58

MARCH

Employee	Monthly Earnings	Year-to-Date Earnings	FICA Social Security	Medicare	Federal Income Tax
Sam Koy	$ 3,200	$ 6,975	$198.40	$ 46.40	$ 608
Joy Lane	4,080	10,130	252.96	59.16	558
Amy Hess	4,250	12,125	263.50	61.63	545
	$11,530	$29,230	$714.86	$167.19	$1,711

Hogan Company is located at 2 Roundy Road, Marblehead, MA 01945. Its employer identification number is 29-3458821. The FICA tax rate for Social Security is 6.2 percent up to $76,200 in earnings during the year and Medicare is 1.45 percent on all earnings. The SUTA tax rate is 5.7 percent on the first $7,000. The FUTA tax rate is .8 percent on the first $7,000 of earnings. Hogan Company is classified as a monthly depositor for Form 941 taxes.

Your Tasks Are to

1. Journalize entries to record the employer's payroll tax expense for each pay period in the general journal.

2. Journalize entries for the payment of each tax liability including SUTA tax in the general journal.

Journal entries and Form 941.

8A-3. Ed Ward, accountant of Hogan Company, has been requested to complete Form 941 for the first quarter of the current year. Using Problem 8A-2, Ed gathers the needed data. Ed has suddenly been called away to an urgent budget meeting and has requested you to assist him by preparing the Form 941 for the first quarter. Please note that the difference in the tax liability, a few cents, should be adjusted in the middle column of line 9; this difference is due to the rounding of FICA tax amounts.

Check Figure:
Total Liability for Quarter
$8,301.22

8A-4. The following is the monthly payroll for the last three months of the year for Henson's Sporting Goods Shop, 1 Roe Road, Lynn, MA 01945. The shop is a sole proprietorship owned and operated by Bill Henson. The employer ID number for Henson's Sporting Goods is 28-93118921.

Journal entries and Form 941.

The employees at Henson's are paid once each month on the last day of the month. Pete Avery is the only employee who has contributed the maximum into Social Security. None of the other employees will reach the Social Security wage-base limit by the end of the year. Assume the rate for Social Security to be 6.2 percent with a wage-base maximum of $76,200, and the rate for Medicare to be 1.45 percent on all earnings. Henson's is classified as a monthly depositor for Form 941 payroll tax deposit purposes.

Check Figure:
Dec. 31 Payroll Tax Expense $736.67

OCTOBER

| Employee | Monthly Earnings | Year-to-Date Earnings | FICA | | Federal Income Tax |
			Social Security	Medicare	
Pete Avery	$ 2,950	$ 72,250	$182.90	$ 42.78	$ 530
Janet Lee	3,590	40,150	222.58	52.06	427
Sue Lyons	3,800	43,900	235.60	55.10	536
	$10,340	$156,300	$641.08	$149.94	$1,493

NOVEMBER

| Employee | Monthly Earnings | Year-to-Date Earnings | FICA | | Federal Income Tax |
			Social Security	Medicare	
Pete Avery	$ 3,180	$ 75,430	$197.16	$ 46.11	$ 597
Janet Lee	3,772	43,922	233.86	54.69	468
Sue Lyons	3,891	47,791	241.24	56.42	559
	$10,843	$167,143	$672.26	$157.22	$1,624

DECEMBER

| Employee | Monthly Earnings | Year-to-Date Earnings | FICA | | Federal Income Tax |
			Social Security	Medicare	
Pete Avery	$ 4,250	$ 79,680	$ 47.74	$ 61.63	$ 902
Janet Lee	3,800	47,722	235.60	55.10	479
Sue Lyons	4,400	52,191	272.80	63.80	704
	$12,450	$179,593	$556.14	$180.53	$2,085

Your Tasks Are to

1. Journalize entries to record the employer's payroll tax expense for each pay period in the general journal.

2. Journalize entries for the payment of each tax for FICA tax (Social Security and Medicare) and federal income tax given that Henson's is a monthly Form 941 tax depositor.

3. Complete Form 941 for the fourth quarter of the current year.

8A-5. Using the information from Problem 8A-4, please complete a Form 940-EZ for Henson's Sporting Goods for the current year. Additional information needed to complete the form is as follows:

Form 940-EZ.

a. FUTA tax deposit for first quarter: $168.00.

b. SUTA rate: 5.7 percent.

c. State reporting number: 025-319-2.

Check Figure:
Total Exempt Payments $158,593

Please note that there were no FUTA tax deposits for the second, third, or fourth quarters of the year. Henson's has three employees for the year who all earned over $7,000.

Group B Problems

(The forms you need are on pages 249–255 of the *Study Guide and Working Papers.*)

(The forms you need are on pages 249–255 of the *Study Guide and Working Papers.*)

8B-1. For the biweekly pay period ending on April 8 at Kane's Hardware, the following partial payroll summary is taken from the individual employee earnings records. Both Jill Reese and Jeff Vatack have earned more than $7,000 before this payroll.

Your Tasks Are to

1. Complete the table.
2. Prepare a journal entry to record the payroll tax expense for Kane's. Use the federal income tax withholding tables in Figures 7-2 and 7-3 to figure the amount of income tax withheld. Please show the calculations for FICA taxes.

Employee	Allowance and Marital Status	Gross	FICA Social Security	FICA Medicare	Federal Income Tax
Al Jones	S-1	$ 820			
Janice King	S-2	890			
Alice Long	S-0	850			
Jill Reese	S-1	1,100			
Jeff Vatack	S-2	1,340			

Assume the FICA tax rate for Social Security is 6.2 percent up to $76,200 in earnings (no one has earned this much as of April 8) and Medicare is 1.45 percent on all earnings. The state unemployment tax rate is 5.2 percent on the first $7,000 of earnings, and the federal unemployment tax rate is .8 percent of the first $7,000 of earnings. In cases where the FICA tax calculates to one-half cent, round up to the next cent.

8B-2. The following is the monthly payroll of Hogan Company owned by Dean Hogan. Employees are paid on the last day of each month.

JANUARY

Employee	Monthly Earnings	Year-to-Date Earnings	FICA Social Security	FICA Medicare	Federal Income Tax
Sam Koy	$1,675	$1,675	$103.85	$ 24.29	$217
Joy Lane	3,000	3,000	186.00	43.50	343
Amy Hess	3,590	3,590	222.58	52.06	396
	$8,265	$8,265	$512.43	$119.85	$956

FEBRUARY

Employee	Monthly Earnings	Year-to-Date Earnings	FICA Social Security	FICA Medicare	Federal Income Tax
Sam Koy	$1,975	$ 3,650	$122.45	$ 28.64	$ 265
Joy Lane	2,900	5,900	179.80	42.05	325
Amy Hess	3,775	7,365	234.05	54.74	426
	$8,650	$16,915	$536.30	$125.43	$1,016

Journal entry to record payroll tax expense.

Check Figure:
Payroll Tax Expense
$536.11

Employer's tax responsibilities.

CHAPTER 8 ... THE EMPLOYER'S TAX RESPONSIBILITIES: PRINCIPLES AND PROCEDURES

| Employee | Monthly Earnings | Year-to-Date Earnings | FICA | | Federal Income Tax |
			Social Security	Medicare	
Sam Koy	$ 3,220	$ 6,870	$199.64	$ 46.69	$ 608
Joy Lane	4,000	9,900	248.00	58.00	535
Amy Hess	4,300	11,665	266.60	62.35	556
	$11,520	$28,435	$714.24	$167.04	$1,699

Hogan Company is located at 2 Roundy Road, Marblehead, MA 01945. Its employer identification number is 29-3458821. The FICA tax rate for Social Security is 6.2 percent up to $76,200 in earnings during the year, and Medicare is 1.45 percent on all earnings. The SUTA tax rate is 5.7 percent on the first $7,000. The FUTA tax rate is .8 percent on the first $7,000 of earnings. Hogan Company is classified as a monthly depositor for Form 941 taxes.

Your Tasks Are to

1. Journalize entries to record the employer's payroll tax expense for each pay period in the general journal.

2. Journalize entries for the payment of each tax liability including SUTA tax in the general journal.

> Journal entries and Form 941.

8B-3. Ed Ward, accountant of Hogan Company, has been requested to complete Form 941 for the first quarter of the current year. Using Problem 8B-2, Ed gathers the needed data. Ed has suddenly been called away to an urgent budget meeting and has requested you to assist him by preparing the Form 941 for the first quarter. Please note that the difference in the tax liability, a few cents, should be adjusted in the middle column of line 9; this difference is due to the rounding of FICA tax amounts.

> Check Figure:
> Liability for Quarter
> $8,021.58

8B-4. The following is the monthly payroll for the last three months of the year for Henson's Sporting Goods Shop, 1 Roe Road, Lynn, MA 01945. The shop is a sole proprietorship owned and operated by Bill Henson. The employer ID number for Henson's Sporting Goods is 28-93118921.

> Journal entries and Form 941.

The employees at Henson's are paid once each month on the last day of the month. Pete Avery is the only employee who has contributed the maximum into Social Security. None of the other employees will reach the Social Security wage-base limit by the end of the year. Assume the rate for Social Security to be 6.2 percent with a wage base maximum of $76,200 and the rate for Medicare to be 1.45 percent on all earnings. Henson's is classified as a monthly depositor for Form 941 payroll taxes.

| Employee | Monthly Earnings | Year-to-Date Earnings | FICA | | Federal Income Tax |
			Social Security	Medicare	
Pete Avery	$ 2,950	$ 73,400	$182.90	$ 42.78	$ 530
Janet Lee	3,590	41,075	222.58	52.06	427
Sue Lyons	3,800	44,000	235.60	55.10	536
	$10,340	$158,475	$641.08	$149.94	$1,493

NOVEMBER

Employee	Monthly Earnings	Year-to-Date Earnings	FICA Social Security	FICA Medicare	Federal Income Tax
Pete Avery	$ 3,000	$ 76,400	$173.60	$ 43.50	$ 552
Janet Lee	3,650	44,725	226.30	52.93	439
Sue Lyons	3,710	47,710	230.02	53.80	503
	$10,360	$168,835	$629.92	$150.23	$1,494

DECEMBER

Employee	Monthly Earnings	Year-to-Date Earnings	FICA Social Security	FICA Medicare	Federal Income Tax
Pete Avery	$ 4,250	$ 80,650	—	$ 61.63	$ 902
Janet Lee	3,850	48,575	$238.70	55.83	490
Sue Lyons	3,900	51,610	241.80	56.55	559
	$12,000	$180,835	$480.50	$174.01	$1,951

Check Figure:
Dec 31 Payroll Tax Expense
$654.51

Your Tasks Are to

1. Journalize entries to record the employer's payroll tax expense for each pay period in the general journal.

2. Journalize entries for the payment of each tax for FICA tax (Social Security and Medicare) and federal income tax.

3. Complete Form 941 for the fourth quarter of the current year.

Form 940-EZ.

8B-5. Using the information from Problem 8B-4, please complete a form 940-EZ for Henson's Sporting Goods for the current year. Additional information needed to complete the form is as follows:

a. FUTA tax deposit for first quarter: $168.

b. SUTA tax rate: 5.7 percent.

c. State reporting number: 025-319-2.

Check Figure:
Line 4 Total Exempt
Payments $149,035

Please note that there were no FUTA tax deposits for the third or fourth quarters of the year. Henson's has three employees for the year who all earned over $7,000.

REAL-WORLD APPLICATIONS

8R-1.

Sunshine School Supplies is a leading manufacturer of back-to-school kits and other items used by students in elementary and middle schools. Each summer Sunshine needs additional help to assemble, pack, and ship school items sold in stores around the country. Sunshine's company policy has been to hire 30 additional workers for 12 weeks during the summer. Each employee works 40 hours per week and earns $6 per hour. At the end of August these additional workers are laid off.

Sunshine's state unemployment rate has risen to 5.4 percent with no experience/merit rating allowed due to these layoffs in the last few years.

Miriam Holtz, who is the president of Sunshine, asks for your help to find a way to reduce Sunshine's 5.4 state unemployment rate. When Miriam called the state department of labor and employment, she was told that Sunshine's unemployment rate could drop to 4.1 percent if it stopped laying off workers.

Miriam has thought about using temporary employment agency workers during the summer months as a way to obtain the help the company needs and at the same time stop the seasonal layoffs.

Miriam asks you if this is a good idea. She gives you the following facts to use in analyzing this idea:

1. Five hundred workers who are permanent employees of Sunshine earn in excess of $7,000 each by September of each year.

2. A temporary employment agency told Miriam it would charge Sunshine $7.00 per hour for each worker it supplied during the summer.

3. The current federal unemployment tax rate is .8 percent up to the first $7,000 each employee earns during a year.

4. The current SUTA wage base limit is the first $7,000 each employee earns during a year.

5. Sunshine pays a FICA tax rate of 6.2 percent for Social Security and 1.45 percent for Medicare. The Social Security wage-base limit is $76,200; there is no wage-base limit for Medicare.

Please write a short memo to Miriam Holtz that shows your analysis of two options: (1) Continue to hire 30 additional workers for the summer and then lay them off or (2) have the temporary employment agency provide 30 additional workers for the summer.

In your memo be sure to show the financial effect of both options in terms of the tax calculations on employee earnings for SUTA, FUTA, and FICA. For option 1 be sure to include the SUTA and FUTA tax effects for *both* the permanent and temporary workers. At the end of your memo please provide Miriam with your conclusion so she can make a good decision for her company.

8R-2.

Cathy Johnson has just been hired as a bookkeeper for the Small Fry Dog Toy Company. She recently graduated from the local community college with an associate degree in business. She took several accounting courses at school but was unable to take the school's payroll accounting course.

Cathy is confused about payroll tax forms and their purpose. She wants to learn more about the forms the business must prepare and send in to the government.

You are the accountant for Small Fry. Your boss has asked you to help teach Cathy about the forms and why they are used. The boss feels it is best to give Cathy a brief written summary about the following forms:

1. Form 941.
2. Form 940-EZ.
3. Form 8109.
4. Form W-2.
5. Form W-3.

Please write a brief report to Cathy to help her to understand the following points about these payroll tax forms:

a. The purpose of each form.
b. What is reported on each form.
c. When each form is sent to the government.
d. Where the amounts found on each form come from in the accounting system.

YOU make the call

Critical Thinking/Ethical Case

8R-3.

Abby Ross works in the Payroll Department for Lange Co. as a junior accountant. Abby is also going to school for an advanced degree in accounting. After work each day she uses the company's photocopy machine to make extra copies of her assignments. Should she be photocopying personal material on a company machine? You make the call. Write down your specific recommendations to Abby.

INTERNET EXERCISES

EX-1. [www.microsoft.com]   Microsoft is one of the growing number of American companies who hires temporary workers who are independent contractors to fill permanent spots in its labor force. These "permatemps" are not of the same status of employees who enjoy full benefits with Microsoft.

In this exercise, let us say that Microsoft hires a temporary worker and pays her $20 per hour. Assuming this employee does not go over the statutory FICA limits prescribed by the chapter, nor goes over the FUTA $7,000 ceiling, how much does the company save by having an "independent contractor" perform the work over the cost of having an "employee" do the same work?

EX-2. [http://ebs.adp.com/prod/index.html]   Automatic Data Processing, Inc. (ADP) is long-recognized leader in payroll preparation for businesses of all sizes. ADP does provide other services to businesses, but much of their professional reputation stems from their being one of the early "outsourcing" companies for payroll.

Services they provide in addition to strictly payroll calculation include benefits administration, staffing, time and attendance reporting, and assisting businesses in retaining high quality employees.

1. From information you obtain from this website, explain why ADP has an important niche in Human Relations and payroll preparation.
2. What advantage can a company of any size obtain by outsourcing its payroll preparation and tax reporting activities?

CONTINUING PROBLEM

As December comes to an end, Tony Freedman wants to take care of his payroll obligations. He will complete Form 941 for the first quarter of the current year and Form 940-EZ for federal unemployment taxes. Tony will make the necessary deposits and payments associated with his payroll.

Assignment

(See pages 260–262 in your *Study Guide and Working Papers.*)

1. Record the payroll tax expense entry in general journal format for the quarter, using the information in the Chapter 7 problem.
2. Journalize entries for the payment of each tax liability including SUTA tax in the general journal. Eldorado Computer Center is classified as a quarterly depositor.
3. Prepare Form 941 for the first quarter. Eldorado Computer Center's employer identification number is 35-41325881.
4. Complete Form 940 for Eldorado Computer Center. The FUTA tax ceiling is $7,000, and the SUTA tax ceiling is $10,000 in cumulative wages for each employee. The Eldorado Computer Center's FUTA rate is .8 percent, and the SUTA rate is 2.7 percent. No deposits have been made.

Hint: Sometimes the amount of Social Security taxes paid by the employee for the quarter will not equal the employee's tax liability because of rounding. Any overage or difference should be reported on line 9 of Form 941.

PETE'S MARKET

Completing Payroll Requirements for First Quarter and Preparing Form 941

This Mini Practice Set aids in putting the pieces of payroll together. In this project you are the bookkeeper and have the responsibility of recording payroll in the payroll register, paying the payroll, recording the employer's tax responsibilities, and paying tax deposits as well as completing the quarterly report. (The forms you need are on pages 263–268 of the *Study Guide and Working Papers*.)

Pete's Market, owned by Pete Reel, is located at 4 Sun Avenue, Swampscott, MA 01970. His employer identification number is 42-4583312. Please assume the following:

1. FICA: Social Security, 6.2 percent on $76,200; Medicare, 1.45 percent on all earnings.

2. SUTA: 4.9 percent (due to favorable merit rating) on $7,000.

3. FUTA: .8 percent on first $7,000.

4. Employees are paid monthly. The payroll is recorded the last day of each month and is paid on the first day of the next month.

5. FIT table provided with problem from IRS Circular E, *Employer's Tax Guide* (see p. 309).

6. State income tax is 8 percent.

The following are the employees of Pete's Market along with their monthly salary exemptions and other information:

SALARY PER MONTH

		January	February	March	
Fred Flynn	S-0	$2,500	$2,590	$2,475	(Sales Salaries)
Mary Jones	S-2	3,000	3,000	4,000	(Market Salaries)
Lilly Vron	S-1	3,000	3,000	4,260	(Sales Salaries)

Partial Ledger Accounts
as of December 31, 200X

FICA—Social Security Payable 210	
	410.90 (EE)
	410.90 (ER)

FICA—Medicare Payable 212	
	100 (EE)
	100 (ER)

FIT Payable 220	
	600

SIT Payable 225	
	150

FUTA Payable 230	
	88

SUTA Payable 240	
	155

Using the general journal and payroll register provided, please complete the following:

200X

Jan. 15   Record the entry for the deposit of Social Security, Medicare, and FIT from last month's payroll. (For simplicity, we will not record the payment of state income tax in this problem.)

       31   Pay state unemployment tax due from last quarter.

       31   Pay federal unemployment tax owed.

       31   Complete payroll register for January payroll, journalize payroll entry, and journalize entry for employer's payroll tax expense.

Feb. 1   Transfer cash for the January Net Pay from Cash to Payroll Checking Cash.

       1   Pay payroll.

       15   Pay taxes due for Social Security, Medicare, and FIT.

       28   Complete payroll register for February payroll. Journalize payroll entry as well as journalize entry for employer's payroll tax expense.

Mar. 1   Transfer cash for the February Net Pay from Cash to Payroll Checking Cash.

       1   Pay payroll.

       15   Pay taxes due for Social Security, Medicare, and FIT.

       31   Complete payroll register for March payroll. Journalize payroll entry as well as journalize entry for employer's payroll tax expense.

Apr. 1   Transfer cash for the March Net Pay from Cash to Payroll Checking Cash.

       1   Pay payroll.

       15   Pay taxes due for Social Security, Medicare, and FIT.

       30   Pay federal unemployment tax due for quarter 1.

       30   Pay state unemployment tax due for quarter 1.

       30   Complete Form 941 for the first quarter.

If the wages are—		And the number of withholding allowances claimed is—										
At least	But less than	0	1	2	3	4	5	6	7	8	9	10
		The amount of income tax to be withheld is—										
$2,440	$2,480	354	301	266	231	196	161	126	91	56	21	0
2,480	2,520	365	307	272	237	202	167	132	97	62	27	0
2,520	2,560	376	313	278	243	208	173	138	103	68	33	0
2,560	2,600	388	322	284	249	214	179	144	109	74	39	4
2,600	2,640	399	333	290	255	220	185	150	115	80	45	10
2,640	2,680	410	345	296	261	226	191	156	121	86	51	16
2,680	2,720	421	356	302	267	232	197	162	127	92	57	22
2,720	2,760	432	367	308	273	238	203	168	133	98	63	28
2,760	2,800	444	378	314	279	244	209	174	139	104	69	34
2,800	2,840	455	389	324	285	250	215	180	145	110	75	40
2,840	2,880	466	401	335	291	256	221	186	151	116	81	46
2,880	2,920	477	412	347	297	262	227	192	157	122	87	52
2,920	2,960	488	423	358	303	268	233	198	163	128	93	58
2,960	3,000	500	434	369	309	274	239	204	169	134	99	64
3,000	3,040	511	445	380	315	280	245	210	175	140	105	70
3,040	3,080	522	457	391	326	286	251	216	181	146	111	76
3,080	3,120	533	468	403	337	292	257	222	187	152	117	82
3,120	3,160	544	479	414	348	298	263	228	193	158	123	88
3,160	3,200	556	490	425	360	304	269	234	199	164	129	94
3,200	3,240	567	501	436	371	310	275	240	205	170	135	100
3,240	3,280	578	513	447	382	317	281	246	211	176	141	106
3,280	3,320	589	524	459	393	328	287	252	217	182	147	112
3,320	3,360	600	535	470	404	339	293	258	223	188	153	118
3,360	3,400	612	546	481	416	350	299	264	229	194	159	124
3,400	3,440	623	557	492	427	361	305	270	235	200	165	130
3,440	3,480	634	569	503	438	373	311	276	241	206	171	136
3,480	3,520	645	580	515	449	384	319	282	247	212	177	142
3,520	3,560	656	591	526	460	395	330	288	253	218	183	148
3,560	3,600	668	602	537	472	406	341	294	259	224	189	154
3,600	3,640	679	613	548	483	417	352	300	265	230	195	160
3,640	3,680	690	625	559	494	429	363	306	271	236	201	166
3,680	3,720	701	636	571	505	440	375	312	277	242	207	172
3,720	3,760	712	647	582	516	451	386	320	283	248	213	178
3,760	3,800	724	658	593	528	462	397	332	289	254	219	184
3,800	3,840	735	669	604	539	473	408	343	295	260	225	190
3,840	3,880	746	681	615	550	485	419	354	301	266	231	196
3,880	3,920	757	692	627	561	496	431	365	307	272	237	202
3,920	3,960	768	703	638	572	507	442	376	313	278	243	208
3,960	4,000	780	714	649	584	518	453	388	322	284	249	214
4,000	4,040	791	725	660	595	529	464	399	333	290	255	220
4,040	4,080	802	737	671	606	541	475	410	345	296	261	226
4,080	4,120	813	748	683	617	552	487	421	356	302	267	232
4,120	4,160	824	759	694	628	563	498	432	367	308	273	238
4,160	4,200	836	770	705	640	574	509	444	378	314	279	244
4,200	4,240	847	781	716	651	585	520	455	389	324	285	250
4,240	4,280	858	793	727	662	597	531	466	401	335	291	256
4,280	4,320	869	804	739	673	608	543	477	412	347	297	262
4,320	4,360	880	815	750	684	619	554	488	423	358	303	268
4,360	4,400	892	826	761	696	630	565	500	434	369	309	274
4,400	4,440	903	837	772	707	641	576	511	445	380	315	280
4,440	4,480	914	849	783	718	653	587	522	457	391	326	286
4,480	4,520	925	860	795	729	664	599	533	468	403	337	292
4,520	4,560	936	871	806	740	675	610	544	479	414	348	298
4,560	4,600	948	882	817	752	686	621	556	490	425	360	304
4,600	4,640	959	893	828	763	697	632	567	501	436	371	310
4,640	4,680	970	905	839	774	709	643	578	513	447	382	317
4,680	4,720	981	916	851	785	720	655	589	524	459	393	328
4,720	4,760	992	927	862	796	731	666	600	535	470	404	339
4,760	4,800	1,004	938	873	808	742	677	612	546	481	416	350
4,800	4,840	1,015	949	884	819	753	688	623	557	492	427	361
4,840	4,880	1,026	961	895	830	765	699	634	569	503	438	373
4,880	4,920	1,037	972	907	841	776	711	645	580	515	449	384
4,920	4,960	1,048	983	918	852	787	722	656	591	526	460	395
4,960	5,000	1,060	994	929	864	798	733	668	602	537	472	406
5,000	5,040	1,072	1,005	940	875	809	744	679	613	548	483	417

$5,040 and over   Use Table 4(a) for a **SINGLE person** on page 34. Also see the instructions on page 32.

Computerized Accounting Application for Pete's Market Mini Practice Set for Chapter 8

Completing Payroll Requirements for First Quarter and Preparing Form 941

Before starting on this assignment, read and complete the tasks discussed in Parts A, B, and F of the Computerized Accounting appendix at the back of this book and complete the Computerized Accounting Application assignments for Chapter 3, Chapter 4, and the Valdez Realty Mini Practice Set (Chapter 5).

Pete's Market, owned by Pete Reel, is located at 4 Sun Avenue, Swampscott, Massachusetts, 01970. His employer identification number is 42-4583312. The version of Peachtree Complete Accounting used with this text uses the state and federal tax laws in effect for calendar year 2000. Federal Income Tax (FIT), State Income Tax (SIT), Social Security, Medicare, FUTA, and SUTA are all calculated automatically by the program based on the following assumptions and built-in tax rates:

1. FICA: Social Security, 6.2 percent on $76,200; Medicare, 1.45 percent on all earnings.
2. SUTA: 4.9 percent on the first $10,800 in earnings.
3. FUTA: .8 percent on the first $7,000 in earnings.
4. Employees are paid monthly. The payroll is recorded and paid on the last day of each month. The company uses a payroll checking account and the net pay must be transferred to that account as part of the payroll process.
5. FIT is calculated automatically by the program based on the marital status and number of exemptions claimed by each employee. These have been set up already.
6. SIT for Massachusetts is calculated automatically by the program based on the marital status and number of exemptions claimed by each employee.

The Payroll module in Peachtree Complete Accounting is designed to work with the General Ledger module in an integrated fashion. When transactions are recorded in the Payroll Journal, the program automatically updates the employee records, records the journal entry, and posts all accounts affected in the general ledger.

The following are the employees of Pete's Market and their monthly wages they will earn for the first payroll quarter:

	January	February	March
Fred Flynn	$2,500	$2,590	$2,475
Mary Jones	3,000	3,000	4,000
Lilly Vron	3,000	3,000	4,260

The trial balance for Pete's Market as of 1/1/00 appears below:

		Debits	Credits
1010	Cash	84,964.04	—
1020	Payroll Checking Cash	—	—
2310	FIT Payable	—	1,415.94
2320	SIT Payable	—	535.50
2330	Social Security Tax Payable	—	1,116.00
2335	Medicare Tax Payable	—	261.00
2340	FUTA Payable	—	48.00
2350	SUTA Payable	—	1,587.60
3560	Pete Reel, Capital	—	80,000.00
		84,964.04	84,964.04

1. Click on the Start button. Point to Programs; point to the Peachtree folder and select Peachtree Complete Accounting. Your desktop may have the Peachtree icon allowing for a quicker entrance into the program.

Open the Company Data Files.

2. Follow the "Open a File" instructions in Part A of the Computerized Accounting appendix at the back of this book to open **Pete's Market**

3. Click on the **Maintain** menu option. Then select **Company Information.** The program will respond by bringing up a dialogue box allowing the user to edit/add information about the company.

Add Your Name to the Company Name.

4. Click on the **Company Name** entry field at the end of **Pete's Market.** If it is already highlighted, press the right arrow key. Add a dash and your name **"-Student Name"** to the end of the company name. Click on the OK button to return to the Menu Window.

5. Record the payment of last month's payroll liabilities using the General Journal Entry window. Enter the **Date** listed for each transaction (you may use the "+" key to advance the date or use the calendar icon next to the field to select the date from a calendar). Enter "Memo" into the **Source** text box for each transaction or accept Peachtree's additional number added to memo by pressing TAB:

Record Payment of December Payroll Liabilities and Taxes.

   2000
   Jan.   15   Record the compound journal entry for the deposit of Social Security, Medicare, and FIT from last month's payroll. (We will not record the payment of state income tax.) 941 Deposit
   31   Record the payment of SUTA from last quarter.
   31   Record the payment of FUTA tax owed. 940 Deposit

6. Close the General Journal. Peachtree has two options for paying your employees. Both are available under the **Tasks** menu. The first option is **Select for Payroll Entry** which selects all employees who meet an indicated criteria while the second, **Payroll Entry,** allows you to select the employees one by one. Since we wish to pay all of our salaried employees, we will select the first option, **Select for Payroll Entry.** This will bring up a dialogue box from which we can filter which employees to pay this period:

How to Record Payroll.

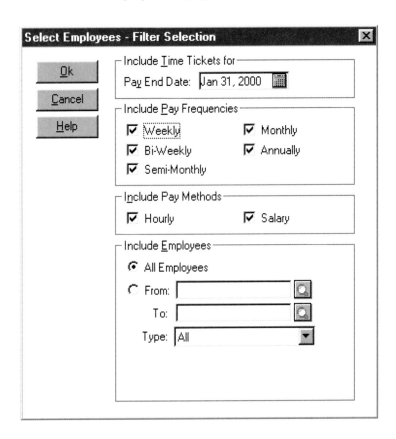

7. Since ours is a monthly payroll paid on the last day of the month, we will change the **Pay End Date:** to reflect January 31 using the small calendar to the right of the field. Click on the small calendar and then select the 31st from the calendar presented. The other filters allow us to pay only a certain frequency type employee, hourly and/or salary, or a range of employees by employee number. You can explore these options but leave them set at the default values shown in the preceding illustration.

8. Click on the **Ok** button when you are ready to continue. This will bring up a Select Employees to Pay dialogue box:

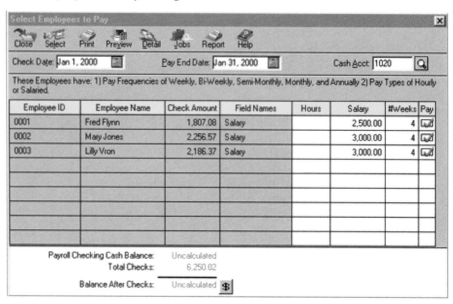

Review the Payroll.

9. Notice how Peachtree has selected all three of our employees and has automatically flagged them for payment with a red check mark. It has also calculated all of the required withholdings and payroll taxes for each employee. Since we are paying the employees on the last day of the month, we should change the **Check Date** to reflect January 31, 2000.

How to Edit a Payroll Journal Entry Prior to Posting.

10. If you want to see the detail on any of the employees, simply double click on that employee's entry to bring up a Detail dialogue box. Try selecting Fred Flynn. You can change any of the numbers presented in the white fields of this dialogue box by double clicking on the number you wish to change. We will accept all the information as given. Leave this dialogue box by clicking on **Ok** or **Cancel** since we made no changes:

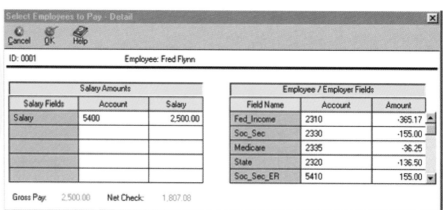

How to Post a Payroll Entry.

11. After verifying that the payroll entries are correct, click on the **Print** icon to print checks and post this transaction. A Print Forms: Payroll Checks dialogue box is presented for the user to select the proper check format. Peachtree supports many different blank check formats. Select the first option, OCR-7″ Chks Preprinted, since we are printing to a blank sheet of paper and the format will not matter.

12. You are now presented with a dialogue box to select **Real** or **Practice**. Practice would be used to make sure the checks are aligned in the printer. This is particularly important with dot matrix type printers. Select **Real** since we are not printing on real forms and do not have to worry about alignment.

13. You are now prompted for a check number to begin the numbering with. Type in "001" and select **Ok** to print the checks. You may need to tell your printer to continue since it will wait for the user to insert the check forms. Telling it to continue will print the checks on the paper currently loaded in the printer. When the checks have finished, you will be asked to confirm the printing process. This feature allows you to print them a second time if something interfered with the printing process the first time through. Upon confirming a successful run, you will be taken back to the Menu Screen of Peachtree and Peachtree will create and post all the necessary journal entries internally.

14. From the **Reports** menu, select **Payroll.** This will bring up a Select a Report dialogue box containing a list of several payroll reports available to us. Select **Payroll Register** to bring up a payroll register for the checks we just issued. We will use this report to determine the net pay for the payroll period. This amount must be transferred to our Payroll Checking account since our paychecks are drawn on that account. It must be funded prior to issuing the checks to our employees. Accept all defaults provided by Peachtree and we are presented with:

How to Display and Print a Payroll Register.

Pete's Market
Payroll Register
For the Period From Jan 1, 2000 to Jan 31, 2000

Filter Criteria includes: Report order is by Check Date. Report is printed in Detail Format.

Employee ID Employee SS No Reference Date	Pay Type	Pay Hrs	Pay Amt	Amount	Gross State SUI_ER	Fed_Income Soc_Sec_ER SDI_ER	Soc_Sec Medicare_ER	Medicare FUTA_ER
0001 Fred Flynn 001 1/31/00	Salary		2,500.00	1,807.08	2,500.00 -136.50 -122.50	-365.17 -155.00	-155.00 -36.25	-36.25 -20.00
0002 Mary Jones 002 1/31/00	Salary		3,000.00	2,256.57	3,000.00 -139.43 -147.00	-374.50 -186.00	-186.00 -43.50	-43.50 -24.00
0003 Lilly Vron 003 1/31/00	Salary		3,000.00	2,186.37	3,000.00 -144.30 -147.00	-439.83 -186.00	-186.00 -43.50	-43.50 -24.00
Summary Total 1/1/00 thru 1/31/00	Salary		8,500.00	6,250.02	8,500.00 -420.23 -416.50	-1,179.50 -527.00	-527.00 -123.25	-123.25 -68.00
Report Date Final Total 1/1/00 thru 1/31/00	Salary		8,500.00	6,250.02	8,500.00 -420.23 -416.50	-1,179.50 -527.00	-527.00 -123.25	-123.25 -68.00

15. We will now transfer cash from our regular Cash account into our Payroll Checking account in order to cover the checks we have just written. Note from the register totals, we have a total of $6,250.02 in net pay.

▼ Select **General Journal Entry** from the **Tasks** menu to open the General Journal dialog box. Enter the date 1/31/00 into the **Date** field; press the TAB key; enter "Memo" into the **Reference** field and press TAB.
▼ Select account number "1020 Payroll Checking Cash"
▼ Enter "Transfer net payroll" in the **Description** field
▼ Enter "6250.02" in the **Debit** field
▼ Tab to **Account No.** and select "1010 Cash"
▼ Tab to the **Credit** field and enter 6250.02 again
▼ Click **Post** to complete the transfer

Print Reports.

16. After you have posted the journal entry, close the General Journal Entry window and print the following reports accepting all defaults offered by Peachtree:

    a. General Journal-(check figure debit = $10,678.56)

    b. Trial Balance-(check figure debit = $83,920.23)

Review your printed reports. If you have made an error in a posted journal entry, use the procedures detailed in step 18 from chapter 3 to make any necessary corrections. Reprint all reports if corrections are made.

Make a January Backup
Copy.

17. It is always wise to backup accounting data at the end of each month, saving it into a file that will be saved until the end of the year. We will use Peachtree's Backup feature to do this. Click on the Company Window **File** menu; select **Backup,** use a filename such as "PeteJan" to make sure you can recognize what the backup represents. Click on **Ok.**

Advancing the Period.

18. We must now advance the period to prepare Peachtree for the February transactions.

    ▼ Using your mouse, click on **System** from the **Tasks** menu. Select **Change Accounting Periods.**

    ▼ Using the pull down menu, select period 2 - Feb 1, 2000 to Feb 29, 2000 and click on "**Ok**"

    ▼ You will be asked whether you wish to print reports before continuing. Since we have already printed our reports, we can answer "No".

    ▼ Note that the status bar at the bottom of the screen now reflects that you are in period 2.

Record Payment of January
Payroll Liabilities and Taxes.

19. Record the following general journal entry:

2000
Feb. 15 Record the compound journal entry for the deposit of Social Security, Medicare, and FIT from last month's payroll. Use the trial balance created in #16 above to determine the amounts owed.

Record February Payroll.

20. Record the February payroll journal entries for Fred Flynn, Mary Jones, and Lilly Vron. Remember that Fred Flynn is making more than his usual amount this month. He will earn $2,590 instead of his usual $2,500. After selecting employees to pay (See How to Record the Payroll above except use February 29), double click on Fred's Salary field and change his salary to the new amount. Everything will automatically recalculate using the new gross. Follow the same procedure for printing checks as you used in January except use the date February 29. Peachtree should select check #004 as the starting check number automatically. Be sure to transfer the net pay into the Payroll Checking Cash account.

Print Reports.

21. Print the following reports accepting all defaults:

    a. Payroll Register-(check figure Net = $6,302.66)

    b. General Journal-(check figure debit = $8,782.66)

    c. Trial Balance-(check figure debit = $84,874.34)

Make a February Backup
Copy.

22. Click on the Company Window **File** menu; select **Backup,** use a filename such as "PeteFeb" to make sure you can recognize what the backup represents. Click on **Ok.**

Advance Dates.

23. We must now advance the period to prepare Peachtree for the March transactions.

    ▼ Using your mouse, click on **System** from the **Tasks** menu. Select **Change Accounting Periods.**

    ▼ Using the pull down menu, select period 3 - Mar 1, 2000 to Mar 31, 2000 and click on "**Ok**"

    ▼ You will be asked whether you wish to print reports before continuing. Since we have already printed our reports, we can answer "No".

    ▼ Note that the status bar at the bottom of the screen now reflects that you are in period 3.

24. Record the following general journal entry:

2000
Mar. 15 Record the compound journal entry for the deposit of Social Security, Medicare, and FIT from last month's payroll.

Record Payment of February Payroll Liabilities and Taxes.

25. Record the March payroll journal entries for Fred Flynn, Mary Jones, and Lilly Vron. Note that all three will receive other than their normal salary for this pay period. Be sure to transfer the net pay into the Payroll Checking Cash account.

Record March Payroll

26. Print the following reports accepting all defaults:

a. Payroll Register-(check figure Net = $7,557.49)

b. General Journal-(check figure debit = $10,076.47)

c. Trial Balance-(check figure debit = $86,911.40)

Print Reports

27. From the **Reports** menu, select **Payroll.** This will bring up a Select a Report dialogue box containing a list of several payroll reports available to us. Select the **941** folder near the bottom to open up our 941 options. Peachtree is set up to print directly on the actual government 941 form. It can print on either the 1996/1997 version of the form or the newer 1999/2000 version. It will print both pages needed for a semi-weekly depositor as well as for either style (941 and 941B). If you have access to the blank 941 forms, you may print the report directly on the form. If not, you can still print the report on plain paper. With the **941** folder open, select **FedForm 941 1999/2000.** Accept all defaults by clicking on **Ok.**

How to Print 941 Summary Reports.

28. Close the Select a Report Window when you are finished.

29. Click on the Company Window **File** menu; select **Backup,** use a filename such as "PeteMar" to make sure you can recognize what the backup represents. Click in **Ok.**

Make a March Backup Copy.

30. We must now advance the period to prepare Peachtree for the April transactions.

Advance Dates.

▼ Using your mouse, click on **System** from the **Tasks** menu. Select **Change Accounting Periods.**

▼ Using the pull down menu, select period 4 - Apr. 1, 2000 to Apr. 30, 2000 and click on "**Ok.**"

▼ You will be asked whether you wish to print reports before continuing. Since we have already printed our reports, we can answer "No".

▼ Note that the status bar at the bottom of the screen now reflects that you are in period 4.

31. Record the following general journal entry:

2000
Apr. 15 Record the compound journal entry for the deposit of Social Security, Medicare, and FIT from last month's payroll.
 30 Record the payment of SUTA from last quarter.
 30 Record the payment of FUTA tax owed.

Record Payment of March Payroll Liabilities and Taxes.

32. Print the following reports accepting all defaults:

a. General Journal-(check figure debit = $4,979.19)

b. Trial Balance-(check figure debit = $81,932.21)

Print Reports.

The Accounting Cycle for a Merchandise Company*

*New! with special optional appendix on pages 359 and 402 for an introduction to a merchandise company using a general journal for a perpetual inventory system.

CHAPTER 9

Special Journals

SALES AND CASH RECEIPTS

Suppose you live in New York City and want to buy a Razor scooter to whiz down the sidewalk and get to your accounting class quickly. You can buy one at the local college stationery store for $99.99 plus 8.25% sales tax, bringing your purchase up to $108.25. Or you can surf the Web for an online retailer—like Etoys or Amazon—and get your Razor scooter for $8.25 cheaper. Why? The Supreme Court has ruled that only the U.S. Congress can require retailers who don't have a physical location in the state to charge sales taxes and so far congress is stalled on the issue of whether to make e-tailers charge sales tax.

It's no wonder, then, that the issue of taxing the Internet has pitted brick-and-mortar retailers against their rivals in cyberspace. For merchandise companies on main street, like the one we discuss in this chapter (Chou's Toy Shop), sales tax is a **liability** payable to the state in which they are located. Yet there is more at stake than unfair competition between retailers and e-tailers. By 2003, state and local governments may lose $20 billion in sales tax revenues if Internet sales are exempted. The sales tax you pay builds roads and pays your governor, the mayor, and other state and local employees, such as firefighters and teachers. In addition, if e-commerce takes over, there may be no downtowns left in San Antonio or Tacoma—just boarded up businesses and empty strip malls.

For the purposes of this chapter, we will assume that main street is thriving and that the states' sales tax coffers are getting their due. You will learn how to journalize an entry for **sales tax payable** as you account for sales and cash receipts. In order to keep accurate, detailed records of sales transactions, you will learn how to keep **special journals** to track sales activity and cash receipts. But what if your client is a fledgling dot.com? Will you need to

subtract "Sales Tax Payable" from "Cash" and "Accounts Receivable"? If you want up-to-the-minute news on how your dot.com clients should handle sales tax, go to EcommerceTax.com.

Based on: Peter Schrag, "loophole.com," *The Nation,* May 15, 2000, pp. 6–7. Anonymous, "United States: Offline," *The Economist,* March 25, 2000, p. 35. http://www.ecommercetax.com/doc/043000.htm.

LEARNING OBJECTIVES

▼ Journalizing sales on account in a sales journal. (p. 326)

▼ Posting from a sales journal to the general ledger. (p. 327)

▼ Recording to the accounts receivable subsidiary ledger from a sales journal. (p. 327)

▼ Preparing, journalizing, recording, and posting a credit memorandum. (p. 330)

▼ Journalizing and posting transactions using a cash receipts journal as well as recording to the accounts receivable subsidiary ledger. (p. 338)

In Chapters 9 and 10 we look at how merchandise companies operate. Chapter 9 focuses on sellers of goods; Chapter 10 discusses buyers. In both chapters companies do not keep continual track of their inventory. This is called a *periodic inventory system.* A company simply takes an inventory at the end of its accounting period of what is left. New to this edition is appendix material on pages 359 and 402 at end of Chapters 9 and 10 that looks at how a company keeps continual track of its inventory. This system is called a *perpetual inventory system.*

Let's first look at Chou's Toy Shop to get an overview of merchandise terms and journal entries. After that, we take an in-depth look at how Art's Wholesale Clothing Company keeps its books. Remember that we will first look at the periodic system (No continual track of inventory).

LEARNING UNIT 9-1

CHOU'S TOY SHOP: SELLER'S VIEW OF A MERCHANDISE COMPANY

Chou's Toy Shop, owned by Chou Li, is a **retailer.** It buys toys, games, bikes, and so forth from manufacturers and **wholesalers** and resells these goods (or **merchandise**) to its customers. The shelving, display cases, and so forth are called "fixtures" or "equipment." These items are not for resale.

GROSS SALES

> Gross sales: Revenue earned from sale of merchandise to customers.

Each cash or charge sale made at Chou's Toy Shop is rung up at the register. Suppose the shop had $3,000 in sales on July 18. Of that amount, $1,800 was cash sales and $1,200 was charges. The account that recorded those sales would be:

Sales (Gross)

Dr.	Cr.
	3,000 ← Revenue account with a credit balance

This account is a revenue account with a credit balance and will be found on the income statement. Here is the journal entry for the day. *Note:* We talk about sales tax later.

Accounts Affected	Category	↑	↓	Rules	T-Account Update
Cash	Asset	↑		Dr.	Cash 1,800 |
Accounts Receivable	Asset	↑		Dr.	Accounts Receivable 1,200 |
Sales	Revenue	↑		Cr.	Sales | 3,000

July	18	Cash		1	8	0	0	00					
		Accounts Receivable		1	2	0	0	00					
		Sales							3	0	0	0	00
		Sales for July 18											

SALES RETURNS AND ALLOWANCES

It would be great for Chou if all the customers were completely satisfied, but that rarely is the case. On July 19, Michelle Reese brought back a doll she bought on account for $50. She told Chou that the doll was defective and that she wanted either a price reduction or a new doll. They agreed on a $10 price reduction. Michelle now owes Chou $40. The account called **Sales Returns and Allowances (SRA)** would record this information.

Sales Returns and Allowances

Contra-revenue account with a debit balance ⟶

Dr.	Cr.
10	

This account is a contra-revenue account with a debit balance. It will be recorded on the income statement. This is how the journal entry would look:

Accounts Affected	Category	↑	↓	Rules	T-Account Update
Sales Returns and Allowances	Contra-revenue	↑		Dr.	Sales Ret. & Allow Dr. | Cr. 10 |
Accounts Receivable, Michelle Reese	Asset		↓	Cr.	Accounts Receivable Dr. | Cr. 1,200 | 10

Look at how the sales returns and allowances increase.

	July	19	Sales Returns and Allowances				1 0 00					
			Accounts Receivable, Michelle Reese						1 0 00		
			Issued credit memorandum								

SALES DISCOUNT

Chou gives a 2 percent **sales discount** to customers who pay their bills early. He wants his customers to know about this policy, so he posted the following sign at the cash register:

Sales Discount Policy

| 2/10, n/30 | 2% discount is allowed off price of bill if paid within the first 10 days or full amount is due within 30 days |
| n/10, EOM | No discount. Full amount of bill is due within 10 days after the end of the month. |

Note that the **discount period** is the time when a discount is granted. The discount period is less time than the **credit period,** which is the length of time allowed to pay back the amount owed on the bill.

If Michelle pays her $40 bill early, she will get an $.80 discount. This information is recorded as follows:

Sales Discount

Contra-revenue account with a debit balance ⟶

| Dr. | Cr. |
| .80 | |

Michelle's discount is calculated as follows:

$$.02 \times \$40 = \$.80$$

Michelle pays her bill on July 24. She is entitled to the discount because she paid her bill within 10 days. Let's look at how Chou would record this payment on his books.

Gross sales
− Sales discount
− SRA
= Net sales

Accounts Affected	Category	↑ ↓	Rules	T-Account Update
Cash	Asset	↑	Dr.	Cash Dr. | Cr. 39.20 |
Sales Discount	Contra-revenue	↑	Dr.	Sales Discount Dr. | Cr. .80 |
Accounts Receivable	Asset	↓	Cr.	Accounts Receivable Dr. | Cr. 1,200 | 40

July	24	Cash				39 20		
		Sales Discount				80		
		Accounts Receivable, Michelle Reese					40 00	

Although Michelle pays $39.20, her Accounts Receivable is credited for the full amount, $40.

In the examples so far we have not shown any transactions with sales tax. Note that the actual or **net sales** for Chou would be **gross sales** less sales returns and allowances less any sales discounts. Let's look at how Chou would record his monthly sales if sales tax were charged.

SALES TAX PAYABLE

None of the examples shown above shows state sales tax. Still, like it or not, Chou must collect that tax from his customers and send it to the state. Sales tax represents a liability to Chou.

Assume the state Chou's is located in charges a 5 percent sales tax. Remember that Chou's sales on July 18 were $3,000. Chou must figure out the sales tax on the purchases. For this purpose, let's assume there were only two sales on that date: the cash sale ($1,800) and the charge sale ($1,200).

The sales tax on the cash purchase is calculated as follows:

$$\$1,800 \times .05 = \$90 \text{ tax}$$
$$\$1,800 + \$90 \text{ tax} = \$1,890 \text{ cash}$$

Here is how the sales tax on the charge sale is computed:

$$\$1,200 \times .05 = \$60 \text{ tax} + \$1,200 \text{ charge} = \$1,260 \text{ Accounts Receivable}$$

It would be recorded as follows:

Accounts Affected	Category	↑	↓	Rules	T-Account Update
Cash	Asset	↑		Dr.	Cash Dr. | Cr. 1,890 |
Accounts Receivable	Asset	↑		Dr.	Accounts Receivable Dr. | Cr. 1,260 |
Sales Tax Payable	Liability	↑		Cr.	Sales Tax Payable Dr. | Cr. | 90 | 60
Sales	Revenue	↑		Cr.	Sales Dr. | Cr. | 3,000

July	18	Cash				1890 00		
		Accounts Receivable				1260 00		
		Sales Tax Payable					150 00	
		Sales					3000 00	
		July 18 Sales						

In Learning Unit 9-3 we show you how to record a credit memorandum with sales tax.

LEARNING UNIT 9-1 REVIEW

AT THIS POINT you should be able to

▼ Explain the purpose of a contra-revenue account. (p. 321)
▼ Explain how to calculate net sales. (p. 322)
▼ Define, journalize, and explain gross sales, sales returns and allowances, and sales discounts. (p. 322)
▼ Journalize an entry for sales tax payable. (p. 323)

SELF-REVIEW QUIZ 9-1

(The forms you need can be found on page 269 of the *Study Guide and Working Papers.*)

Respond true or false to the following:

1. Sales Returns and Allowances is a contra-asset account.
2. Sales Discount has a normal balance of a debit.
3. Sales Tax Payable is a liability.
4. Sales Discount is a contra-asset.
5. A periodic system of inventory keeps continual track of the merchandise.

Quiz Tip:
Sales:	Revenue	↑	Cr.
SRA:	Contra-revenue	↑	Dr.
SD:	Contra-revenue	↑	Dr.

Solutions to Self-Review Quiz 9-1

1. False   **2.** True   **3.** True   **4.** False   **5.** False

LEARNING UNIT 9-2

THE SALES JOURNAL AND ACCOUNTS RECEIVABLE SUBSIDIARY LEDGER

SPECIAL JOURNALS*

Now let's examine how Art's Wholesale Clothing Company keeps its books. Art's business conducts many transactions. The following partial general journal shows the journal entries Art's must make for these sales on account transactions.

ART'S WHOLESALE CLOTHING COMPANY GENERAL JOURNAL						
Apr.	3	Accounts Receivable, Hal's		8 0 0 00		
		Sales			8 0 0 00	
		Sales on Account				
	6	Accounts Receivable, Bevans		1 6 0 0 00		
		Sales			1 6 0 0 00	
		Sales on Account				
	18	Accounts Receivable, Roe		2 0 0 0 00		
		Sales			2 0 0 0 00	
		Sales on Account				

*Special journals for a perpetual system are shown at end of Chapter 10.

This method is not very efficient. If Art's Wholesale Clothing Company kept a **special journal** for each type of transaction he conducts, however, the number of postings and recordings required for each transaction would be reduced. After carefully looking at the situation with his accountant, Art Newner, the owner, decided to use the following special journals:

Special Journal Type	What It Records	
Sales journal (SJ)	Sale of merchandise on account	Covered in this chapter
Cash receipts journal (CRJ)	Receiving cash from any source	
Purchases journal (PJ)	Buying merchandise or other items on account	Covered in the next chapter
Cash payments journal (CPJ) (cash disbursement journal)	Paying of cash for any purpose	

SUBSIDIARY LEDGERS

In the same way Art's Wholesale Clothing Company needs more than just a general journal, the business needs more than just a general ledger. For example, so far in this text, the only title we have used for recording amounts owed to the seller has been Accounts Receivable. Art could have replaced the Accounts Receivable title in the general ledger with the following list of customers who owe him money:

▼ Accounts Receivable, Bevans Company.
▼ Accounts Receivable, Hal's Clothing.
▼ Accounts Receivable, Mel's Department Store.
▼ Accounts Receivable, Roe Company.

As you can see, this system would not be manageable if Art had 1,000 credit customers. To solve this problem, Art sets up a separate **accounts receivable subsidiary ledger.** Such a special ledger, often simply called a **subsidiary ledger,** contains a single type of account, such as credit customers. An account is opened for each customer, and the accounts are arranged alphabetically.

The diagram in Figure 9-1 on p. 326 shows how the accounts receivable subsidiary ledger fits in with the general ledger. To clarify the difference in updating the general ledger versus the subsidiary ledger, we will *post* to the general ledger and *record* to the subsidiary ledger. The word *post* refers to information that is moved from the journal to the general ledger; the word *record* refers to information that is transferred from the journal into the individual customer's account in the subsidiary ledger.

The accounts receivable subsidiary ledger, or any other subsidiary ledger, can be in the form of a card file, a binder notebook, or computer tapes or disks. It will not have page numbers. The accounts receivable subsidiary ledger is organized alphabetically based on customers' names and addresses; new customers can be added and inactive customers deleted.

When using an accounts receivable subsidiary ledger, the title Accounts Receivable in the general ledger is called the **controlling account** — Accounts Receivable because it summarizes or controls the accounts receivable subsidiary ledger. At the end of the month the total of the individual accounts in the accounts receivable ledger will equal the ending balance in Accounts Receivable in the general ledger.

> The general ledger is not in the same book as the accounts receivable subsidiary ledger.

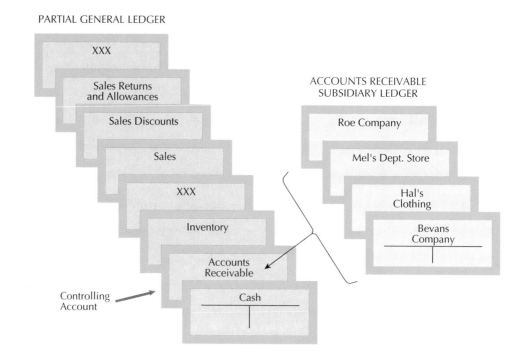

FIGURE 9-1. Partial General Ledger of Art's Wholesale Clothing Company and Accounts Receivable Subsidiary Ledger

Proving: At the end of the month, the sum of the accounts receivable subsidiary ledger will equal the ending balance in accounts receivable, the controlling account in the general ledger.

Art's Wholesale Clothing Company will use the following subsidiary ledgers:

Accounts receivable subsidiary ledger (debit balance)	Records money owed by credit customers	Covered in this chapter
Accounts payable subsidiary ledger (credit balance)	Records money owed by Art to creditors	Covered in next chapter

Let's now look closer at the sales journal, general ledger, and subsidiary ledger for Art's to see how transactions are updated in the special journal as well as posted and recorded to specific titles.

THE SALES JOURNAL

The **sales journal** for Art's Wholesale Clothing Company records all sales made on account to customers. Figure 9-2 shows the sales journal at the end of the first month in operation along with the recordings to the accounts receivable ledger and posting to the general ledger. Keep in mind that the reason the balances in the accounts receivable subsidiary ledger are *debit* balances is that the customers listed *owe* Art's Wholesale money. For some other companies, a sales journal might have multiple revenue account columns.

Look at the first transaction listed in the sales journal. It shows that on April 3, Art's Wholesale Clothing Company sold merchandise on account to Hal's Clothing for $800. The bill or **sales invoice** for this sale is shown in Figure 9-3 on p. 328.

Recording from the Sales Journal to the Accounts Receivable Subsidiary Ledger

As shown on the first line of the sales journal in Figure 9-2, the information on the invoice is recorded in the sales journal. The *PR column is left blank,* however. As soon as possible we now update the accounts receivable subsidiary ledger. To do so, we pull out the Hal's Clothing file card and update it: The debit side must show the $800 he owes Art along with the date (April 3) and page of the sales journal (p. 1). Once that is done, place a ✓ in the postreference col-

Recording to the accounts receivable subsidiary ledger occurs daily.

Hal's Clothing

Dr.	Cr.
4/3 SJ1	
800	

A ✓ means that the accounts receivable ledger has been updated.

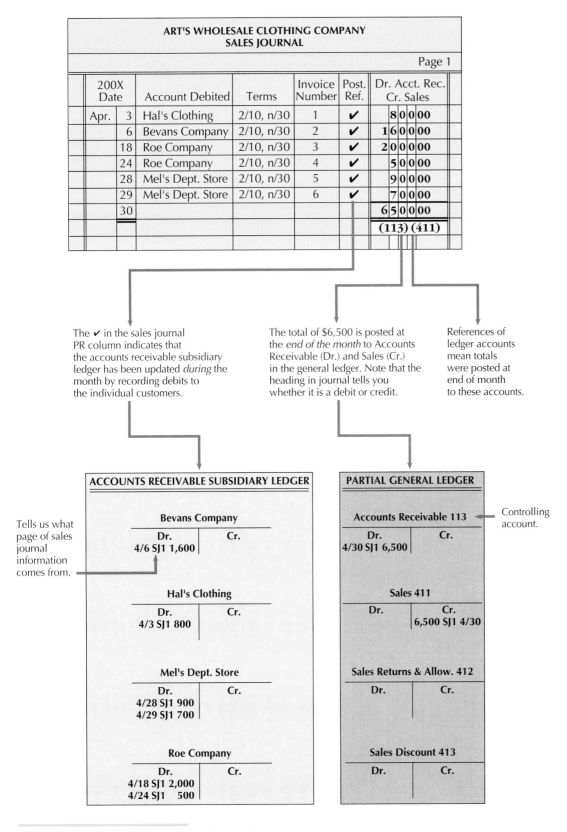

FIGURE 9-2. Sales Journal Recording and Postings

umn of the sales journal. The accounts receivable subsidiary ledger shows us Hal's outstanding balance at any moment in time. We do not have to go through all the invoices. Note how the sales journal only needs one line instead of the three lines that would have been required in a general journal.

FIGURE 9-3. Sales Invoice

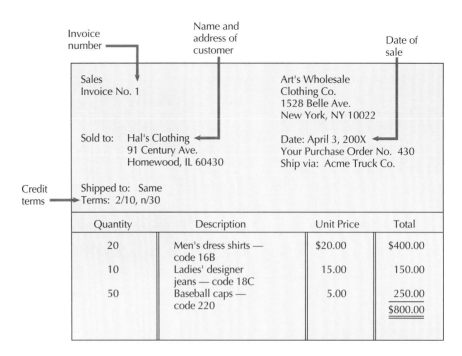

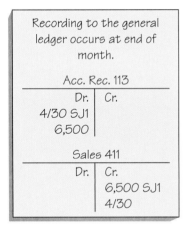

Recording to the general ledger occurs at end of month.

Acc. Rec. 113

Dr.	Cr.
4/30 SJ1	
6,500	

Sales 411

Dr.	Cr.
	6,500 SJ1
	4/30

Sales Tax Payable

	XXX

A liability in general ledger.

Posting at End of Month from the Sales Journal to the General Ledger

The sales journal is totaled ($6,500) at the end of the month. Looking back at page 327, you can see that the heading of Art's sales journal is a debit to accounts receivable and a credit to sales. Therefore, at the end of the month the $6,500 total is posted to Accounts Receivable (debit) *and* to Sales (credit) in the general ledger. In the general ledger we record the date (4/30), the initials of the journal (SJ), the page of the sales journal (1), and appropriate debit or credit ($6,500). Once the account in the general ledger is updated, we place below the totals in the sales journal the account numbers to which the information was posted (in this case, accounts 113 and 411).

Sales Tax

Art's Wholesale Clothing Company does not have to deal with sales tax because it sells goods wholesale. If Art's were a retail company, however, it would have to pay sales tax.

Let's look at how Munroe Menswear Company, a retailer, handles sales tax on a purchase made by Jones Company. Figure 9-4 shows Munroe's sales journal.

Also, a new account, **Sales Tax Payable,** must be created. That account is a liability account in the general ledger with a credit balance. The customer owes Munroe the sale amount plus the tax.

Keep in mind that if sales discounts are available, they are not calculated on the sales tax. The discount is on the selling price less any returns before the tax. For example, if Jones receives a 2 percent discount, he pays the following:

$$\begin{array}{ll} & \$5,250 \quad \text{Total owed (tax is \$250)} \\ \$5,000 \times .02 = \$100 \text{ savings} \rightarrow & \underline{-\ 100} \quad \text{Savings (discount)} \\ & \underline{\$5,150} \quad \text{Amount paid} \end{array}$$

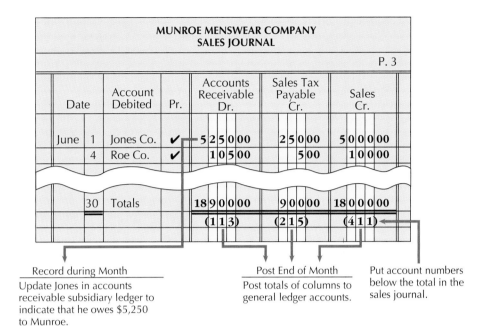

FIGURE 9-4. Munroe Sales Journal

		MUNROE MENSWEAR COMPANY SALES JOURNAL				P. 3
Date	Account Debited	Pr.	Accounts Receivable Dr.	Sales Tax Payable Cr.	Sales Cr.	
June 1	Jones Co.	✔	5 2 5 0 00	2 5 0 00	5 0 0 0 00	
4	Roe Co.	✔	1 0 5 00	5 00	1 0 0 00	
30	Totals		18 9 0 0 00	9 0 0 00	18 0 0 0 00	
			(1 1 3)	(2 1 5)	(4 1 1)	

__Record during Month__
Update Jones in accounts receivable subsidiary ledger to indicate that he owes $5,250 to Munroe.

__Post End of Month__
Post totals of columns to general ledger accounts.

Put account numbers below the total in the sales journal.

LEARNING UNIT 9-2 REVIEW

AT THIS POINT you should be able to

- ▼ Define and state the purposes of special journals. (p. 324)
- ▼ Define and state the purposes of the accounts receivable subsidiary ledger. (p. 325)
- ▼ Define and state the purpose of the controlling account, Accounts Receivable. (p. 325)
- ▼ Journalize, record, or post sales on account to a sales journal and its related accounts receivable and general ledgers. (p. 327)

SELF-REVIEW QUIZ 9-2

(The forms you need are on page 269 of the *Study Guide and Working Papers*.) Respond true or false to the following:

1. Special journals completely replace the general journal.
2. Special journals aid the division of labor.
3. The subsidiary ledger makes the general ledger less manageable.
4. The subsidiary ledger is separate from the general ledger.
5. The controlling account is located in the accounts receivable subsidiary ledger.
6. The totals of a sales journal are posted to the general ledger at the end of the month.
7. The accounts receivable subsidiary ledger is arranged in alphabetical order.
8. Transactions recorded into a sales journal are recorded only weekly to the accounts receivable subsidiary ledger.

> *Quiz Tip:* The normal balance of the accounts receivable subsidiary ledger is a debit.

Solutions to Self-Review Quiz 9-2

1. False   2. True   3. False   4. True
5. False   6. True   7. True   8. False

At the beginning of this chapter we introduced the Sales Returns and Allowances account. Merchandising businesses often use this account to handle transactions involving goods that have already been sold. For example, if a customer returns the goods he has bought, his account will be credited for the amount he paid; if a customer gets an allowance because the goods he purchased were damaged, his account will be credited for the amount of the allowance. In both these examples, the company's sales revenue decreases. Hence, the account is called a contra-revenue account: The sales revenue decreases and the normal balance is a debit.

Companies usually handle sales returns and allowances by means of a **credit memorandum.** Credit memoranda inform customers that the amount of the goods returned or the amount allowed for damaged goods has been subtracted (credited) from the customer's ongoing account with the company.

A sample credit memorandum from Art's Wholesale Clothing Company appears in Figure 9-5. It shows that on April 12 credit memo no. 1 was issued to Bevans Company for defective merchandise that had been returned. (Figure 9-2 shows that Art's Wholesale Clothing Company sold Bevans Company $1,600 of merchandise on April 6.)

Let's assume that Art's Clothing has high-quality goods and does not expect many sales returns and allowances. Based on this assumption, no special journal for sales returns and allowances will be needed. Instead, any returns and allowances will be recorded in the general journal, and all postings and recordings will be done when journalized. Let's look at a transaction analysis chart before we journalize, record, and post this transaction.

> A credit memorandum reduces accounts receivable.

> Remember: No sales tax was involved because Art's is a wholesale company.

> | Sales Returns and Allowances | |
> |---|---|
> | Dr. | Cr. |
> | + | − |
>
> A contra-revenue account.

> Note that the Sales Returns and Allowances account is increasing, which in turn reduces sales revenue and reduces amount owed by customer (accounts receivable).

Accounts Affected	Category	↑ ↓	Rules
Sales Returns and Allowances	**Contra-revenue account**	↑	**Dr.**
Accounts Receivable, Bevans Co.	**Asset**	↓	**Cr.**

FIGURE 9-5. Credit Memorandum

> Art's Wholesale
> Clothing Co.
> 1528 Belle Ave.
> New York, NY 10022
>
> Credit
> Memorandum No. 1
> Date: April 12, 200X
> Credit to Bevans Company
> 110 Aster Rd.
> Cincinnati, Ohio 45227
> We credit your account as follows:
> Merchandise returned 60 model 8 B men's dress gloves—$600

> End result is that Bevan owes Art's Wholesale less money.

JOURNALIZING, RECORDING, AND POSTING THE CREDIT MEMORANDUM

The credit memorandum results in two postings to the general ledger and one recording to the accounts receivable subsidiary ledger (see Fig. 9-6).

Note in the PR column next to Accounts Receivable, Bevans Co., that there is a diagonal line with the account number 113 above and a ✔ below. This notation is to show that the amount of $600 has been credited to Accounts Receivable in the controlling account in the general ledger *and* credited to the account of Bevans Company in the accounts receivable subsidiary ledger.

If the accountant for Art's Wholesale Clothing Company decided to develop a special journal for sales allowances and returns, the entry for a credit memorandum such as the one we've been discussing would be the following:

> *Remember: Sales discounts are not taken on returns.*

						Sales Ret. and Allow. – Dr. Accts. Rec. – Cr.	
	Date		Credit Memo No.	Account Credited	PR		
200X April	12		1	Bevans Company	✔	6 0 0 00	

SALES RETURNS AND ALLOWANCES JOURNAL

During the month the subsidiary ledger is updated

THE CREDIT MEMORANDUM WITH SALES TAX

Figure 9-4 (p. 329) shows the sales journal for Munroe Menswear Company. Remember that because Munroe is a retail company, its customers must pay sales tax. Let's assume that on June 8 Roe returns $50 worth of the $100 of merchandise he bought earlier in the month. Let's analyze and journalize the credit memo that Munroe issued. Keep in mind that the customer is no longer responsible for paying for either the returned merchandise or the tax on it.

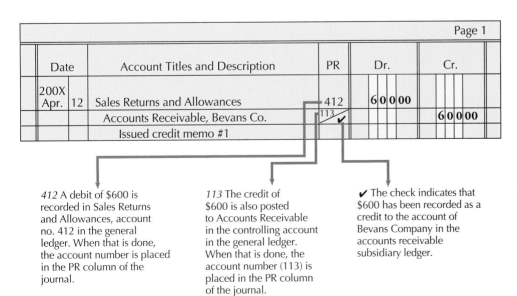

	Date	Account Titles and Description	PR	Dr.	Cr.		Page 1
200X Apr.	12	Sales Returns and Allowances	412	6 0 0 00			
		Accounts Receivable, Bevans Co.	113 ✔		6 0 0 00		
		Issued credit memo #1					

412 A debit of $600 is recorded in Sales Returns and Allowances, account no. 412 in the general ledger. When that is done, the account number is placed in the PR column of the journal.

113 The credit of $600 is also posted to Accounts Receivable in the controlling account in the general ledger. When that is done, the account number (113) is placed in the PR column of the journal.

✔ The check indicates that $600 has been recorded as a credit to the account of Bevans Company in the accounts receivable subsidiary ledger.

FIGURE 9-6. Postings and Recordings for the Credit Memorandum into the Subsidiary and General Ledger.

Accounts Affected	Category	↑	↓	Rules	T-Account Update
Sales Returns and Allowances	Contra-revenue	↑		Dr.	**Sales Ret. & Allow.** Dr. | Cr. 50 |
Sales Tax Payable ($5 tax on $100) ($2.50 tax on $50)	Liability		↓	Dr.	**Sales Tax Payable** Dr. | Cr. 2.50 |
Accounts Receivable, Roe	Asset		↓	Cr.	**Acc. Rec** Dr.|Cr. | 52.50 **Roe Co.** Dr.|Cr. 105|52.50

June	8	Sales Returns and Allowances			5 0 00			
		Sales Tax Payable			2 50			
		Accounts Receivable, Roe Co.				5 2 50		
		Received credit memo						

This journal entry requires three postings to the general ledger and one recording to Roe in the accounts receivable subsidiary ledger. Note that because Roe returned half of his merchandise he was able to reduce what he pays for sales tax by half (from $5 to $2.50).

LEARNING UNIT 9-3 REVIEW

AT THIS POINT you should be able to

▼ Explain Sales Tax Payable in relation to Sales Discount. (p. 331)
▼ Explain, journalize, post, and record a credit memorandum with or without sales tax. (p. 331)

SELF-REVIEW QUIZ 9-3

(The forms you need are on pages 269–271 of the *Study Guide and Working Papers*.)

Journalize the following transactions into the sales journal or general journal for Shoes.com. Record to the accounts receivable subsidiary ledger and post to general ledger accounts as appropriate. Use the same journal headings that we used for Art's Wholesale Clothing Company. (All sales carry credit terms of 2/10, n/30.) There is no tax.

200X

May	1	Sold merchandise on account to Jane Company, invoice no. 1, $600.
	5	Sold merchandise on account to Ralph Company, invoice no. 2, $2,500.
	20	Issued credit memo no. 1 to Jane Company for $200 due to defective merchandise returned.

Solution to Self-Review Quiz 9-3

SHOES.COM
SALES JOURNAL

Page 1

Date		Account Debited	Terms	Invoice No.	Post Ref.	Dr. Acct. Rec. Cr. Sales
200X May	1	Jane Company	2/10, n/30	1	✔	6 0 0 00
	5	Ralph Company	2/10, n/30	2	✔	2 5 0 0 00
	31					3 1 0 0 00
						(112) (411)

Quiz Tip: Total of accounts receivable subsidiary ledger $400 + $2,500 does indeed equal the balance in the controlling account, accounts receivable $2,900 at end of month, in the general ledger.

SHOES.COM
GENERAL JOURNAL

Page 1

Date		Account Titles and Description	PR	Dr.	Cr.
200X May	20	Sales Ret. and Allowances	412	2 0 0 00	
		Acct. Rec., Jane Company	112 ✔		2 0 0 00
		Issued credit memo #1			

Controlling Account

PARTIAL GENERAL LEDGER

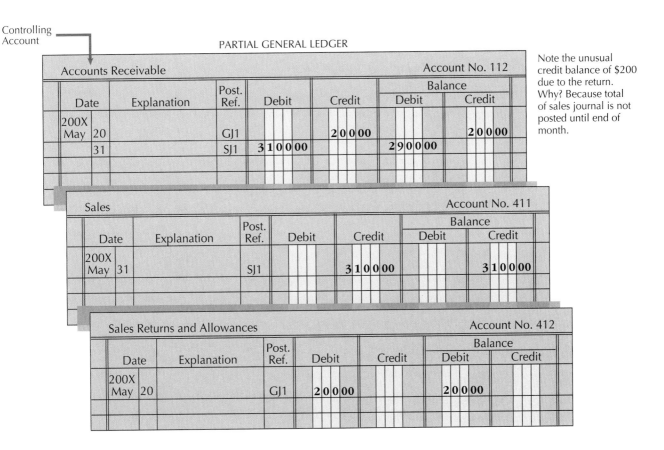

Note the unusual credit balance of $200 due to the return. Why? Because total of sales journal is not posted until end of month.

Accounts Receivable						Account No. 112	
Date	Explanation	Post. Ref.	Debit	Credit	Balance Debit	Balance Credit	
200X May 20		GJ1		2 0 0 00		2 0 0 00	
31		SJ1	3 1 0 0 00		2 9 0 0 00		

Sales						Account No. 411	
Date	Explanation	Post. Ref.	Debit	Credit	Balance Debit	Balance Credit	
200X May 31		SJ1		3 1 0 0 00		3 1 0 0 00	

Sales Returns and Allowances						Account No. 412	
Date	Explanation	Post. Ref.	Debit	Credit	Balance Debit	Balance Credit	
200X May 20		GJ1	2 0 0 00		2 0 0 00		

ACCOUNTS RECEIVABLE SUBSIDIARY LEDGER

NAME Jane Company
ADDRESS 118 Morris Rd., Boston, MA 01935

Customers owe
Shoes.com money
and thus have
a debit balance.

Date		Explanation	Post. Ref.	Debit	Credit	Dr. Balance
200X May	1		SJ1	600 00		600 00
	20		GJ1		200 00	400 00

NAME Ralph Company
ADDRESS 31 Norris Rd., Boston, MA 01935

Date		Explanation	Post. Ref.	Debit	Credit	Dr. Balance
200X May	5		SJ1	2500 00		2500 00

LEARNING UNIT 9-4

CASH RECEIPTS JOURNAL AND SCHEDULE OF ACCOUNTS RECEIVABLE

A **cash receipts journal** is another special journal often used in a merchandising operation. The cash receipts journal records the receipt of cash (or checks) from any source. The number of columns in the cash receipts journal depends on how frequently certain types of transactions occur. Figure 9-7 shows the headings in the cash receipts journal for Art's Wholesale, describes the purpose of each column, and tells when to update the accounts receivable ledger as well as general ledger.

The following transactions occurred and affected the cash receipts journal for Art's Clothing in April:

200X
Apr.
1   Art Newner invested $8,000 in the business.
4   Received check from Hal's Clothing for payment of invoice no. 1 less discount.
15   Cash sales for first half of April, $900.
16   Received check from Bevans Company in settlement of invoice no. 2 less returns and discount.
22   Received check from Roe Company for payment of invoice no. 3 less discount.
27   Sold store equipment, $500.
30   Cash sales for second half of April, $1,200.

Benefits of a Cash Receipts Journal

Before we look at how these transactions will look in the cash receipts journal, let's see how the April 4 transaction would look if it were put into a general journal. This step illustrates the benefits of using a cash receipts journal.

200X
Apr.
4   Received check from Hal's Clothing for payment of invoice no. 1 less discount. (Keep in mind the sales journal showed the invoice at $800 on April 3.)

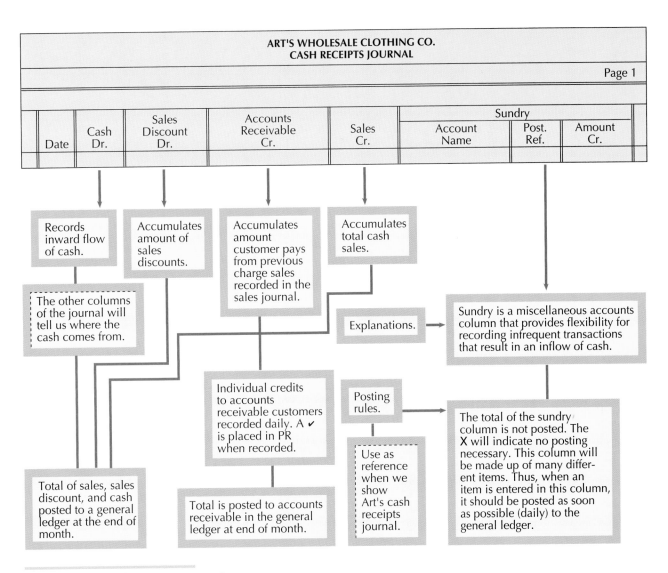

FIGURE 9-7. Cash Receipts Journal

Accounts Affected	Category	↓ ↑	Rules	T-Account Update			
Cash	Asset	↑	Dr.	**Cash**			
				Dr. 784	Cr.		
Sales Discount	Contra-revenue	↑	Dr.	**Sales Discount**			
				Dr. 16	Cr.		
Accounts Receivable, Hal's Clothing	Asset	↓	Cr.	**Acc. Rec.** Dr. 800 / Cr. 800		**Hal's Clothing** Dr. 800 / Cr. 800	

> Hal's Clothing is located in the Accounts Receivable Subsidiary Ledger.

	Apr.	4	Cash			7 8 4 00		
			Sales Discount			1 6 00		
			Accounts Receivable, Hal's Clothing				8 0 0 00	

If a general journal had been used, there would have been three postings and one recording. Using a cash receipts journal (see Fig. 9-7 on p. 335), the totals of cash sales discount and accounts receivable are not posted till the end of the month.

The diagram in Figure 9-8 shows the cash receipts journal for the end of April along with the recordings in the accounts receivable subsidiary ledger and posting to the general ledger.

JOURNALIZING, RECORDING, AND POSTING FROM THE CASH RECEIPTS JOURNAL

Now let's look at how the April 4 transaction is recorded in the cash receipts journal.

When payment is received, Art's Wholesale updates the cash receipts journal (see Fig. 9-8 on p. 338) by entering the date (April 4), cash debit of $784, sales discount debit of $16, credit to accounts receivable of $800, and which account name (Hal's Clothing) is to be credited. The terms of sale indicate that Hal's Clothing is entitled to the discount and no longer owes Art's Wholesale the $800 balance. As soon as this line is entered into the cash receipts journal, Art's Wholesale will update the card file of Hal's Clothing. Note in the accounts receivable subsidiary ledger of Hal's Clothing how the date (April 4), post reference (CRJ1), and credit amount ($800) are recorded. The balance in the accounts receivable ledger is zero. The last step of this transaction is to go back to the cash receipts journal and put a ✓ in the post reference column.

In looking back at this cash receipts journal, note the following:

▼ All totals of cash receipts journal *except* **sundry** were posted to the general ledger at the end of the month.
▼ Art Newner, Capital, and Store Equipment were posted to the general ledger when entered in the sundry column. For now in the general ledger it was assumed that the equipment account had a beginning balance of $4,000.
▼ The cash sales were not posted when entered (thus the X to show no posting is needed). The sales and cash totals are posted at the *end* of the month.
▼ A ✓ means information was recorded daily to the accounts receivable subsidiary ledger.
▼ The Account Name column was used to describe each transaction.

We can prove the accuracy of recording transactions of the cash receipts journal by totaling the columns with debit balances and credit balances. This process, called **crossfooting,** is done before the totals are posted.

If a bookkeeper were using more than one page for the cash receipts journal, the balances on the bottom of one page would be brought forward to the next page. Let's crossfoot the cash receipts journal of Art's Wholesale (Fig. 9-8, p. 338).

Debit Columns   **Credit Columns**

Cash   + Sales Discount = Accounts Receivable + Sales   + Sundry
$14,324 + $76   = $3,800   + $2,100 + $8,500
         $14,400 = $14,400

Recording Sales Tax

Consider the following situation. It involves Ryan Stationery, a retail stationer that must charge 5 percent sales tax to its customers. On July 1 Hope Co. bought $600 of equipment for cash from Ryan.

Remember: Subsidiary ledgers can be in the form of a card file, a binder notebook, or computer tapes or disks.

Sundry: Miscellaneous accounts column(s) in a special journal that record transactions that seldom occur.

The last step is to put a ✓ back in the PR of the cash receipts journal to show the accounts receivable ledger is up to date.

Crossfooting special journals makes it easier to look for journalizing or posting errors.

The total of sales tax payable would be posted to Sales Tax Payable in the general ledger at the end of the month.

Here is how the transaction would be recorded in the general journal:

Accounts Affected	Category	↑	↓	Rules	T-Account Update
Cash	Asset	↑		Dr.	Cash 630 |
Sales Tax Payable	Liability	↑		Cr.	Sales Tax Payable | 30
Sales	Revenue	↑		Cr.	Sales | 600

July	1	Cash		630 00		
		Sales Tax Payable			30 00	
		Sales			600 00	
		Cash Sale				

The transaction would be recorded in a cash receipts journal as follows:

						Sundry		
CASH RECEIPTS JOURNAL								
Date	Cash Dr.	Sales Discount Dr.	Accounts Receivable Cr.	Sales Tax Payable Cr.	Sales Cr.	Acct.	Post Ref.	Amt.
July 1	630 00			30 00	600 00		✗	

The total of the sales tax as a result of cash sales would be posted to Sales Tax Payable in the general ledger at the end of the month. It represents a liability of the merchant to forward the tax to the government. Remember that no cash discounts are taken on the sales tax.

Now let's prove the accounts receivable subsidiary ledger to the controlling account — accounts receivable — at the end of April for Art's Wholesale Clothing Company.

SCHEDULE OF ACCOUNTS RECEIVABLE

The **schedule of accounts receivable** is an alphabetical list of the companies that have an outstanding balance in the accounts receivable subsidiary ledger. This total should be equal to the balance of the accounts receivable controlling account in the general ledger at the end of the month.

Let's examine the schedule of accounts receivable for Art's Wholesale Clothing Company:

ART'S WHOLESALE CLOTHING COMPANY SCHEDULE OF ACCOUNTS RECEIVABLE APRIL 30, 200X	
Mel's Dept. Store	$1 600 00
Roe Company	500 00
Total Accounts Receivable	$ 2 100 00

Schedule is listed in alphabetical order.

The balance of the controlling account, Accounts Receivable ($2,100), in the general ledger (p. 338) does indeed equal the sum of the individual customer balances in the accounts receivable ledger ($2,100) as shown in the schedule of accounts receivable. The schedule of accounts receivable can help forecast potential cash inflows as well as possible credit and collection decisions.

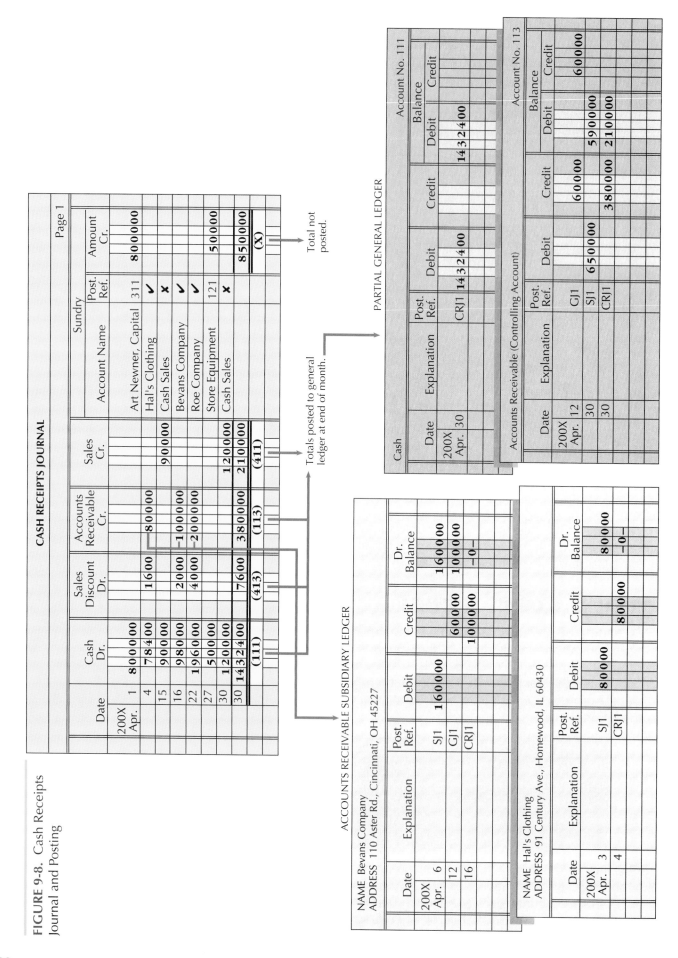

FIGURE 9-8. Cash Receipts Journal and Posting

PARTIAL GENERAL LEDGER

Store Equipment — Account No. 121

Date	Explanation	Post. Ref.	Debit	Credit	Balance Debit	Balance Credit
200X Apr. 1	Balance	✔			4000 00	
27		CRJ1		500 00	3500 00	

Art Newner, Capital — Account No. 311

Date	Explanation	Post. Ref.	Debit	Credit	Balance Debit	Balance Credit
200X Apr. 1		CRJ1		8000 00		8000 00

Sales — Account No. 411

Date	Explanation	Post. Ref.	Debit	Credit	Balance Debit	Balance Credit
200X Apr. 30		SJ1		6500 00		6500 00
30		CRJ1		2100 00		8600 00

Sales Discount — Account No. 413

Date	Explanation	Post. Ref.	Debit	Credit	Balance Debit	Balance Credit
200X Apr. 30		CRJ1	76 00		76 00	

ACCOUNTS RECEIVABLE SUBSIDIARY LEDGER

NAME Mel's Dept. Store
ADDRESS 181 Foss Rd., Swampscott, MA 01907

Date	Explanation	Post. Ref.	Debit	Credit	Dr. Balance
200X Apr. 28		SJ1	900 00		900 00
29		SJ1	700 00		1600 00

NAME Roe Company
ADDRESS 18 Rantool St., Beverly, MA 01915

Date	Explanation	Post. Ref.	Debit	Credit	Dr. Balance
200X Apr. 18		SJ1	2000 00		2000 00
22		CRJ1		2000 00	-0-
24		SJ1	500 00		500 00

LEARNING UNIT 9-4 REVIEW

AT THIS POINT you should be able to

▼ Journalize, record, and post transactions using a cash receipts journal with or without sales tax. (p. 338)
▼ Prepare a schedule of accounts receivable. (p. 337)

SELF-REVIEW QUIZ 9-4

(The forms you need are on pages 272–274 of the Study Guide and Working Papers.)

Journalize, crossfoot, record, and post when appropriate the following transactions into the cash receipts journal of Moore Co. Use the same headings as for Art's Wholesale Clothing.

ACCOUNTS RECEIVABLE SUBSIDIARY LEDGER

NAME	BALANCE	INVOICE NO.
Irene Welch	$500	1
Janis Fross	200	2

PARTIAL GENERAL LEDGER

	Acct. No.	Balance
Cash	110	$600
Accounts Receivable	120	700
Store Equipment	130	600
Sales	410	700
Sales Discount	420	

200X
May
1   Received check from Irene Welch for invoice no. 1 less 2 percent discount.
8   Cash sales collected, $200.
15   Received check from Janis Fross for invoice no. 2 less 2 percent discount.
19   Sold store equipment at cost, $300.

Solution to Self-Review Quiz 9-4

MOORE COMPANY
CASH RECEIPTS JOURNAL

Page 2

Date	Cash Dr.	Sales Discount Dr.	Accounts Receivable Cr.	Sales Cr.	Sundry Account Name	Post. Ref.	Sundry Amount Cr.
200X May 1	490 00	10 00	500 00		Irene Welch	✔	
8	200 00			200 00	Cash Sales	✗	
15	196 00	4 00	200 00		Janis Fross	✔	
19	300 00				Store Equipment	130	300 00
31	1186 00	14 00	700 00	200 00			300 00
	(110)	(420)	(120)	(410)			(X)

Crossfooting: $1,200 = $1,200

PARTIAL GENERAL LEDGER

Cash — Account No. 110

Date		Explanation	Post. Ref.	Debit	Credit	Balance Debit	Balance Credit
200X May	1	Balance	✔			600 00	
	31		CRJ2	1186 00		1786 00	

Accounts Receivable — Account No. 120

Date		Explanation	Post. Ref.	Debit	Credit	Balance Debit	Balance Credit
200X May	1	Balance	✔			700 00	
	31		CRJ2		700 00	—	

Store Equipment — Account No. 130

Date		Explanation	Post. Ref.	Debit	Credit	Balance Debit	Balance Credit
200X May	1	Balance	✔			600 00	
	19		CRJ2		300 00	300 00	

Sales — Account No. 410

Date		Explanation	Post. Ref.	Debit	Credit	Balance Debit	Balance Credit
200X May	1		✔				700 00
	31		CRJ2		200 00		900 00

Sales Discount — Account No. 420

Date		Explanation	Post. Ref.	Debit	Credit	Balance Debit	Balance Credit
200X May	31		CRJ2	14 00		14 00	

Quiz Tip: Sum of all debits equals sum of all credits.

Quiz Tip: The total of the sundry column $300 is not posted. Only individual amounts are posted to the general ledger during the month.

ACCOUNTS RECEIVABLE SUBSIDIARY LEDGER

NAME Irene Welch
ADDRESS 10 Rong Rd., Beverly, MA 01215

Date		Explanation	Post. Ref.	Debit	Credit	Dr. Balance
200X May	1	Balance	✔			500 00
	1		CRJ2		500 00	—

NAME Janis Fross
ADDRESS 81 Foster Rd., Beverly, MA 01915

Date		Explanation	Post. Ref.	Debit	Credit	Dr. Balance
200X May	1	Balance	✔			200 00
	15		CRJ2		200 00	—

341

COMPREHENSIVE DEMONSTRATION PROBLEM WITH SOLUTION TIPS

(The forms you need are on pages 275–278 of the *Study Guide and Working Papers*.)

a. Journalize, record, and post, as needed, the following transactions to the sales, cash receipts, and general journal. All terms are 2/10, n/30.

b. Prepare a schedule of Accounts Receivable.

Solution Tips to Journalizing

200X

CRJ	July	1	Walter Lantze invested $2,000 into the business.
SJ		1	Sold merchandise on account to Panda Co., invoice no. 1 for $300.
SJ		2	Sold merchandise on account to Buzzard Co., invoice no. 2 for $600.
CRJ		3	Cash sale, $400.
GJ		9	Issued Credit Memorandum no. 1 to Panda Co. for defective merchandise, $100.
CRJ		10	Received check from Panda Co. for invoice no. 1 less returns and discount.
CRJ		16	Cash sale, $500.
SJ		19	Sold merchandise on account to Panda Co., $550, invoice no. 3.

Record immediately to subsidiary ledger.

WALTER LANTZE CO.
SALES JOURNAL

Page 1

Date		Account Debited	Terms	Invoice No.	Post Ref.	Dr. Acct. Rec. Cr. Sales
200X July	1	Panda Co.	2/10, n/30	1	✔	3 0 0 00
	2	Buzzard Co.	2/10, n/30	2	✔	6 0 0 00
	19	Panda Co.	2/10, n/30	3	✔	5 5 0 00
	31					1 4 5 0 00
						(112) (411)

Total posted at end of month to General Ledger Accounts.

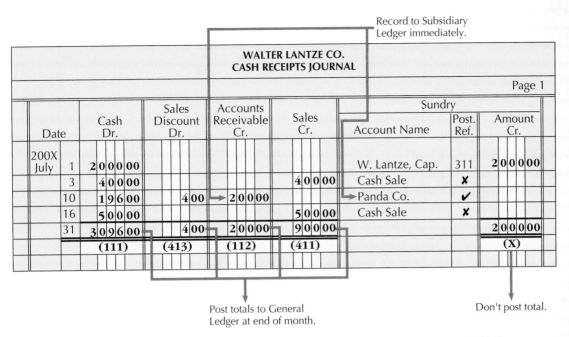

Record to Subsidiary Ledger immediately.

WALTER LANTZE CO. CASH RECEIPTS JOURNAL

Page 1

Date	Cash Dr.	Sales Discount Dr.	Accounts Receivable Cr.	Sales Cr.	Sundry — Account Name	Post. Ref.	Amount Cr.
200X July 1	2 0 0 0 00				W. Lantze, Cap.	311	2 0 0 0 00
3	4 0 0 00			4 0 0 00	Cash Sale	✗	
10	1 9 6 00	4 00	2 0 0 00		Panda Co.	✓	
16	5 0 0 00			5 0 0 00	Cash Sale	✗	
31	3 0 9 6 00	4 00	2 0 0 00	9 0 0 00			2 0 0 0 00
	(111)	(413)	(112)	(411)			(X)

Post totals to General Ledger at end of month.

Don't post total.

GENERAL JOURNAL				Page 1	
Date	Account Title and Description	PR	Dr.	Cr.	
200X July 9	Sales Returns and Allowances	412	1 0 0 00		
	Accounts Receivable, Panda Co.	112 ✓		1 0 0 00	
	Issued credit memo #1				

Post immediately to General Ledger.

Record immediately to Subsidiary Ledger.

Accounts Receivable Subsidiary Ledger is usually a debit balance.

Accounts Receivable Subsidiary Ledger

Buzzard Co.

Date	PR	Debit	Credit	Dr. Balance
200X July 2	SJ1	6 0 0 00		6 0 0 00

Panda Co.

Date	PR	Debit	Credit	Dr. Balance
200X July 1	SJ1	3 0 0 00		3 0 0 00
9	GJ1		1 0 0 00	2 0 0 00
10	CRJ1		2 0 0 00	—
19	SJ1	5 5 0 00		5 5 0 00

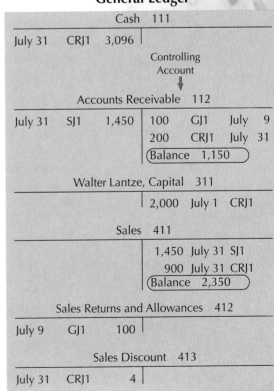

General Ledger

Cash 111

July 31	CRJ1	3,096	

Controlling Account

Accounts Receivable 112

July 31	SJ1	1,450	100	GJ1	July 9
			200	CRJ1	July 31
			Balance 1,150		

Walter Lantze, Capital 311

			2,000	July 1	CRJ1

Sales 411

			1,450	July 31	SJ1
			900	July 31	CRJ1
			Balance 2,350		

Sales Returns and Allowances 412

July 9	GJ1	100	

Sales Discount 413

July 31	CRJ1	4	

The controlling account at end of the month equals the sum of the Accounts Receivable Subsidiary Ledger.

LANTZE CO. SCHEDULE OF ACCOUNTS RECEIVABLE JULY 31, 200X		
Buzzard Co.	$ 600	00
Panda Co.	550	00
Total Accounts Receivable	$1150	00

SUMMARY OF KEY POINTS

Learning Unit 9-1

1. A periodic inventory system records the cost of ending inventory at the end of each accounting period.

2. A perpetual inventory system keeps a continual update of inventory.

3. Sales Returns and Allowances and Sales Discount are contra-revenue accounts.

4. Net Sales = Gross Sales − Sales Returns and Allowances − Sales Discounts.

5. Discounts are not taken on sales tax, freight, or goods returned. The discount period is shorter than the credit period.

Learning Unit 9-2

1. A general journal is still used with special journals.

2. A sales journal records sales on account.

3. The accounts receivable subsidiary ledger, organized in alphabetical order, is not in the same book as Accounts Receivable, the controlling account in the general ledger.

4. At the end of the month the total of all customers' ending balances in the accounts receivable subsidiary ledger should be equal to the ending balance in Accounts Receivable, the controlling account in the general ledger.

Learning Unit 9-3

1. The ✓ in the PR column of the sales journal means a customer's account in the accounts receivable ledger (or the accounts receivable subsidiary ledger) (on the debit side) has been updated (or recorded) during the month.

2. At the end of the month the totals of the sales journal are posted to general ledger accounts.

3. Sales Tax Payable is a liability found in the general ledger.

4. When a credit memorandum is issued, the result is that Sales Returns and Allowances is increasing and Accounts Receivable is decreasing. When we record this entry into a general journal, we assume all parts of the transaction will be posted to the general ledger and recorded in the subsidiary ledger when the entry is journalized.

Learning Unit 9-4

1. The cash receipts journal records receipt of cash from any source.

2. The sundry column records the credit part of a transaction that does not occur frequently. Never post the *total* of sundry. Post items in sundry column to the general ledger when entered.

3. A ✓ in the PR column of the cash receipts journal means that the accounts receivable ledger (or the accounts receivable subsidiary ledger) has been updated (recorded) with a credit.

4. An X in the cash receipts journal PR column means no posting was necessary, because the totals of these columns will be posted at the end of the month.

5. Crossfooting means proving that the total of debits and the total of credits are equal in the special journal, thus verifying the accuracy of recording.

6. A schedule of accounts receivable is a listing of the ending balances of customers in the accounts receivable subsidiary ledger. This total should be the same balance as found in the controlling account, Accounts Receivable, in the general ledger.

KEY TERMS

Accounts receivable subsidiary ledger A book or file that contains, in alphabetical order, the individual records of amounts owed by various credit customers.

Cash receipts journal A special journal that records all transactions involving the receipt of cash from any source.

Controlling account — Accounts Receivable The Accounts Receivable account in the general ledger, after postings are complete, shows a firm the total amount of money owed to it. This figure is broken down in the accounts receivable ledger, where it indicates specifically who owes the money.

Credit memorandum A piece of paper sent by the seller to a customer who has returned merchandise previously purchased on credit. The credit memorandum indicates to the customer that the seller is reducing the amount owed by the customer.

Credit period Length of time allowed for payment of goods sold on account.

Crossfooting The process of proving that the total debit columns of a special journal are equal to the total credit columns of a special journal.

Discount period A period shorter than the credit period when a discount is available to encourage early payment of bills.

Gross sales The revenue earned from sale of merchandise to customers.

Merchandise Goods brought into a store for resale to customers.

Net sales Gross sales less sales returns and allowances less sales discounts.

Periodic inventory system An inventory system that, at the *end* of each accounting period, calculates the cost of the unsold goods on hand by taking the cost of each unit times the number of units of each product on hand.

Perpetual inventory system An inventory system that keeps *continual track* of each type of inventory by recording units on hand at beginning, units sold, and the current balance after each sale or purchase.

Retailers Merchants who buy goods from wholesalers for resale to customers.

Sales discount account A contra-revenue account that records cash discounts granted to customers for payments made within a specific period of time.

Sales invoice A bill sent to customer(s) reflecting a sale on credit.

Sales journal A special journal used to record only sales made on account.

Sales Returns and Allowances (SRA) account A contra-revenue account that records price adjustments and allowances granted on merchandise that is defective and has been returned.

Sales Tax Payable account An account in the general ledger that accumulates the amount of sales tax owed. It has a credit balance.

Schedule of accounts receivable A list of the customers, in alphabetical order, that have an outstanding balance in the accounts receivable ledger (or the accounts receivable subsidiary ledger). This total should be equal to the balance of the Accounts Receivable controlling account in the general ledger at the end of the month.

Special journal A journal used to record similar groups of transactions. Example: The sales journal records all sales on account.

Subsidiary ledger A ledger that contains accounts of a single type. Example: The accounts receivable subsidiary ledger records all credit customers.

Sundry Miscellaneous accounts column(s) in a special journal, which records part of transactions that do not occur too often.

Wholesalers Merchants who buy goods from suppliers and manufacturers for sale to retailers.

QUESTIONS, MINI EXERCISES, EXERCISES, AND PROBLEMS

Discussion Questions

1. What is the difference between a perpetual inventory system and a periodic inventory system.

2. Explain the purpose of a contra-revenue account.

3. What is the normal balance of sales discount?

4. Give two examples of contra-revenue accounts.

5. What is the difference between a discount period and a credit period?

6. Explain the terms:
    a. 2/10, n/30.
    b. n/10, EOM.

7. If special journals are used; what purpose will a general journal serve?

8. Compare and contrast the controlling account Accounts Receivable to the accounts receivable subsidiary ledger.

9. Why is the accounts receivable subsidiary ledger organized in alphabetical order?

10. When is a sales journal used?

11. What is an invoice? What purpose does it serve?

12. Why is sales tax a liability to the business?

13. Sales discounts are taken on sales tax. Agree or disagree and tell why.

14. When a seller issues a credit memorandum (assume no sales tax), what accounts will be affected?

15. Explain the function of a cash receipts journal.

16. When is the sundry column of the cash receipts journal posted?

17. Explain the purpose of a schedule of accounts receivable.

Mini Exercises

(The forms you need are on pages 280–281 of the *Study Guide and Working Papers*.)

Overview

1. Complete the table below for Sales, Sales Returns and Allowances, and Sales Discounts.

Accounts Affected	Category	↓ ↑	Temporary or Permanent

Calculating Net Sales

2. Given the following, calculate net sales:

Gross sales	$30
Sales Returns and Allowances	8
Sales Discounts	2

Sales Journal and General Journal

3. Match the following to the three journal entries (more than one number can be used).

1. Journalized into sales journal.
2. Record immediately to subsidiary ledger.
3. Post totals from sales journal at end of month to general ledger.
4. Journalized in general journal.
5. Record and post immediately to subsidiary and general ledgers.

a. _____ Sold merchandise on account to Ree Co., invoice no. 1, $50.

b. _____ Sold merchandise on account to Flynn Co., invoice no. 2, $100.

c. _____ Issued credit memorandum no. 1 to Flynn Co. for defective merchandise, $25.

(continued on p. 349)

BLUEPRINT: SALES AND CASH RECEIPTS JOURNALS

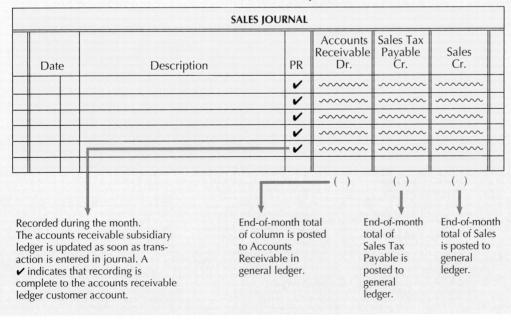

SUMMARY OF HOW TO POST AND RECORD
Single-Column Sales Journal

SALES JOURNAL					
	Date	Description	PR	Accounts Rec.: Dr. Sales: Cr.	
			✔	. . .	
			✔	. . .	
			✔	. . .	
			✔	. . .	
			✔	. . .	
				( ) ( )	

Posted End of Month
Total of column is posted to general ledger accounts. Accounts Receivable and Sales.

Recorded During the Month
Accounts receivable subsidiary ledger is updated as soon as transaction is entered in sales journal.
A ✔ indicates that recording is complete to the accounts receivable ledger customer account.

Multicolumn Sales Journal

SALES JOURNAL						
	Date	Description	PR	Accounts Receivable Dr.	Sales Tax Payable Cr.	Sales Cr.
			✔	~~~~	~~~~	~~~~
			✔	~~~~	~~~~	~~~~
			✔	~~~~	~~~~	~~~~
			✔	~~~~	~~~~	~~~~
			✔	~~~~	~~~~	~~~~
				( )	( )	( )

Recorded during the month. The accounts receivable subsidiary ledger is updated as soon as transaction is entered in journal. A ✔ indicates that recording is complete to the accounts receivable ledger customer account.

End-of-month total of column is posted to Accounts Receivable in general ledger.

End-of-month total of Sales Tax Payable is posted to general ledger.

End-of-month total of Sales is posted to general ledger.

Issuing a Credit Memo without Sales Tax Recorded in a General Journal

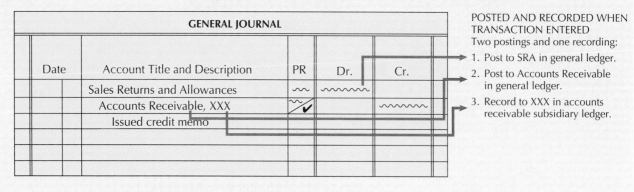

GENERAL JOURNAL

Date	Account Title and Description	PR	Dr.	Cr.
	Sales Returns and Allowances	~	~~~~~~	
	Accounts Receivable, XXX	✔		~~~~~~
	Issued credit memo			

POSTED AND RECORDED WHEN TRANSACTION ENTERED
Two postings and one recording:
1. Post to SRA in general ledger.
2. Post to Accounts Receivable in general ledger.
3. Record to XXX in accounts receivable subsidiary ledger.

Issuing a Credit Memo with Sales Tax Recorded in a General Journal

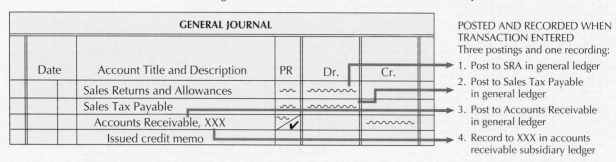

GENERAL JOURNAL

Date	Account Title and Description	PR	Dr.	Cr.
	Sales Returns and Allowances	~	~~~~~~	
	Sales Tax Payable	~	~~~~~~	
	Accounts Receivable, XXX	✔		~~~~~~
	Issued credit memo			

POSTED AND RECORDED WHEN TRANSACTION ENTERED
Three postings and one recording:
1. Post to SRA in general ledger
2. Post to Sales Tax Payable in general ledger
3. Post to Accounts Receivable in general ledger
4. Record to XXX in accounts receivable subsidiary ledger

The Cash Receipts Journal

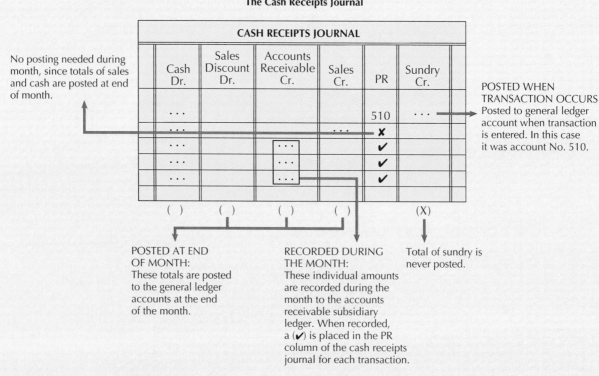

CASH RECEIPTS JOURNAL

Cash Dr.	Sales Discount Dr.	Accounts Receivable Cr.	Sales Cr.	PR	Sundry Cr.
...				510	...
...			...	✗	
...		...		✔	
...		...		✔	
...		...		✔	
( )	( )	( )	( )		(X)

No posting needed during month, since totals of sales and cash are posted at end of month.

POSTED WHEN TRANSACTION OCCURS
Posted to general ledger account when transaction is entered. In this case it was account No. 510.

POSTED AT END OF MONTH:
These totals are posted to the general ledger accounts at the end of the month.

RECORDED DURING THE MONTH:
These individual amounts are recorded during the month to the accounts receivable subsidiary ledger. When recorded, a (✔) is placed in the PR column of the cash receipts journal for each transaction.

Total of sundry is never posted.

Note: If a Sales Tax Payable column were added, total of column would be posted at end of month.

Credit Memorandum

4. Draw a transactional analysis box for the following credit memorandum: Issued credit memorandum to Met.com for defective merchandise, $200.

Sales and Cash Receipts Journal

5. Match the following to the four journal entries (a number can be used more than once).

---
1. Journalized into sales journal.
2. Journalized into cash receipts journal.
3. Record immediately to subsidiary ledger.
4. Totals of special journals will be posted at end of month (except Sundry column).
5. Post to general ledger immediately.
6. Journalize into general journal.
---

a. _____ Sold merchandise on account to Ally Co., invoice no. 10, $40.

b. _____ Received check from Moore Co., $100 less 2 percent discount.

c. _____ Cash Sales, $100.

d. _____ Issued credit memorandum no. 2 to Ally Co. for defective merchandise, $20.

6. From the following, prepare a schedule of Accounts Receivable for Blue Co., for May 31, 200X.

Accounts Receivable Subsidiary Ledger		General Ledger	
Bon Co.		**Accounts Receivable**	
5/6 SJ1 100		5/31 SJ1 140	5/31 CRJ1 10
Peke Co.			
5/20 SJ1 30	5/27 CRJ1 10		
Green Co.			
5/9 SJ1 10			

Exercises

(The forms you need are on pages 282–284 of the *Study Guide and Working Papers*.)

9-1. From the following sales journal p. 350, record to the accounts receivable subsidiary ledger and post to the general ledger accounts as appropriate.

> Recording to accounts receivable ledger and posting to general ledger.

9-2. Journalize, record, and post when appropriate the following transactions into the sales journal (same heading as Exercise 9-1) and general journal (p. 1) (all sales carry terms of 2/10, n/30):

> Journalizing, recording, and posting that includes credit memorandum.

200X

May	16	Sold merchandise on account to Ronald Co., invoice no. 1, $1,000.
	18	Sold merchandise on account to Bass Co., invoice no. 2, $1,700.
	20	Issued credit memorandum no. 1 to Bass Co. for defective merchandise, $700.

Use the following account numbers: Accounts Receivable, 112; Sales, 411; Sales Returns and Allowances, 412.

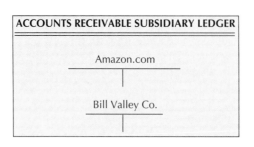

SALES JOURNAL					
					P. 1
Date	Account Debited	Invoice No.	PR	Dr. Accts. Receivable Cr. Sales	
200X Apr. 18	Amazon.com	1		5 0 0 00	
19	Bill Valley Co.	2		6 0 0 00	

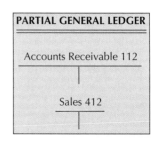

ACCOUNTS RECEIVABLE SUBSIDIARY LEDGER	PARTIAL GENERAL LEDGER
Amazon.com	Accounts Receivable 112
Bill Valley Co.	Sales 412

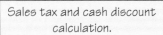

Journalizing transaction into cash receipts journal.

9-3. From Exercise 9-2, journalize in the cash receipts journal the receipt of check from Ronald Co. for payment of invoice no. 1 on May 24. Use the same headings as for Art's Wholesale Clothing (on p. 327).

Journalizing, recording, and posting sales and cash receipts journal; schedule of accounts receivable.

9-4. From the following transactions for Edna Co., when appropriate, journalize, record, post, and prepare a schedule of accounts receivable. Use the same journal headings (all p. 1) and chart of accounts (use Edna Cares, Capital) that Art's Wholesale Clothing used in the text. You will have to set up your own accounts receivable subsidiary ledger and partial general ledger as needed. All sales terms are 2/10, n/30.

200X

June 1 Edna Cares invested $3,000 in the business.
     1 Sold merchandise on account to Boston Co., invoice no. 1, $700.
     2 Sold merchandise on account to Gary Co., invoice no. 2, $900.
     3 Cash sale, $200.
     8 Issued credit memorandum no. 1 to Boston for defective merchandise, $200.
     10 Received check from Boston for invoice no. 1 less returns and discount.
     15 Cash sale, $400.
     18 Sold merchandise on account to Boston Co., invoice no. 3, $600.

Sales tax and cash discount calculation.

9-5. From the following facts calculate what Ann Frost must pay Blue Co. for the purchase of a dining room set. Sale terms are 2/10, n/30.

  a. Sales ticket price before tax, $4,000, dated April 5.

  b. Sales tax, 7 percent.

  c. Returned one defective chair for credit of $400 on April 8.

  d. Paid bill on April 13.

Group A Problems

(The forms you need are on pages 285–304 of the *Study Guide and Working Papers*.)

Multicolumn journal: Journalizing and posting to general ledger, recording to accounts receivable subsidiary ledger, and preparing a schedule of accounts receivable.

9A-1. Jill Blue has opened Food.com, a wholesale grocery and pizza company. The following transactions occurred in June:

200X
June 1 Sold grocery merchandise to Duncan Co. on account, $500, invoice no. 1.
4 Sold pizza merchandise to Sue Moore Co. on account, $600, invoice no. 2.
8 Sold grocery merchandise to Long Co. on account, $700, invoice no. 3.
10 Issued credit memorandum no. 1 to Duncan Co. for $150 of grocery merchandise returned due to spoilage.
15 Sold pizza merchandise to Sue Moore Co. on account, $160, invoice no. 4.
19 Sold grocery merchandise to Long Co. on account, $300, invoice no. 5.
25 Sold pizza merchandise to Duncan Co. on account, $1,200, invoice no. 6.

Required

1. Journalize the transactions in the appropriate journals.
2. Record to the accounts receivable subsidiary ledger and post to general ledger as appropriate.
3. Prepare a schedule of accounts receivable.

9A-2. The following transactions of Ted's Auto Supply occurred in November (your working papers have balances as of Nov. 1 for certain general ledger and accounts receivable ledger accounts):

200X
Nov. 1 Sold auto parts merchandise to R. Volan on account, $1,000, invoice no. 60, plus 5 percent sales tax.
5 Sold auto parts merchandise to J. Seth on account, $800, invoice no. 61, plus 5 percent sales tax.
8 Sold auto parts merchandise to Lance Corner on account, $9,000, invoice no. 62, plus 5 percent sales tax.
10 Issued credit memorandum no. 12 to R. Volan for $500 for defective auto parts merchandise returned from Nov. 1 transaction. (Be careful to record the reduction in sales tax payable as well.)
12 Sold auto parts merchandise to J. Seth on account, $600, invoice no. 63, plus 5 percent sales tax.

Required

1. Journalize the transactions in the appropriate journals.
2. Record to the accounts receivable subsidiary ledger and post to general ledger as appropriate.
3. Prepare a schedule of accounts receivable.

9A-3. Mark Peaker owns Peaker's Sneaker Shop. (In your working papers balances as of May 1 are provided for the accounts receivable and general ledger accounts.) The following transactions occurred in May:

200X
May 1 Mark Peaker invested an additional $12,000 in the sneaker store.
3 Sold $700 of merchandise on account to B. Dale, sales ticket no. 60, terms 1/10, n/30.
4 Sold $500 of merchandise on account to Ron Lester, sales ticket no. 61, terms 1/10, n/30.
9 Sold $200 of merchandise on account to Jim Zon, sales ticket no. 62, terms 1/10, n/30.
10 Received cash from B. Dale in payment of May 3 transaction, sales ticket no. 60, less discount.
20 Sold $3,000 of merchandise on account to Pam Pry, sales ticket no. 63, terms 1/10, n/30.

Check Figure:
Schedule of Accounts
Receivable $3,310

Multicolumn sales journal:
Use of sales tax, journalizing and posting to general ledger and recording to accounts receivable ledger, and preparing a schedule of accounts receivable.

Check Figure:
Schedule of Accounts
Receivable $13,045

Comprehensive Problem:
Recording transactions into sales, cash receipts, and general journals. Recording to accounts receivable subsidiary ledger and posting to general ledger. Preparing a schedule of accounts receivable.

22   Received cash payment from Ron Lester in payment of May 4 transaction, sales ticket no. 61.
23   Collected cash sales, $3,000.
24   Issued credit memorandum no. 1 to Pam Pry for $2,000 of merchandise returned from May 20 sales on account.
26   Received cash from Pam Pry in payment of May 20, sales ticket no. 63. (Don't forget about the credit memo and discount.)
28   Collected cash sales, $7,000.
30   Sold sneaker rack equipment for $300 cash. (Beware.)
30   Sold merchandise priced at $4,000, on account to Ron Lester, sales ticket no. 64, terms 1/10, n/30.
31   Issued credit memorandum no. 2 to Ron Lester for $700 of merchandise returned from May 30 transaction, sales ticket no. 64.

Required

1. Journalize the transactions.
2. Record to the accounts receivable subsidiary ledger and post to general ledger as needed.
3. Prepare a schedule of accounts receivable.

9A-4. Bill Murray opened Bill's Cosmetic Market on April 1. There is a 6 percent sales tax on all cosmetic sales. Bill offers no sales discounts. The following transactions occurred in April:

200X
Apr.   1   Bill Murray invested $8,000 in the Cosmetic Market from his personal savings account.
        5   From the cash register tapes, lipstick cash sales were $5,000 plus sales tax.
        5   From the cash register tapes, eye shadow cash sales were $2,000 plus sales tax.
        8   Sold lipstick on account to Alice Koy Co., $300, sales ticket no. 1, plus sales tax.
        9   Sold eye shadow on account to Marika Sanchez Co., $1,000, sales ticket no. 2, plus sales tax.
       15   Issued credit memorandum no. 1 to Alice Koy Co. for $150 for lipstick returned. (Be sure to reduce sales tax payable for Bill.)
       19   Marika Sanchez Co. paid half the amount owed from sales ticket no. 2, dated April 9.
       21   Sold lipstick on account to Jeff Tong Co., $300, sales ticket no. 3, plus sales tax.
       24   Sold eye shadow on account to Rusty Neal Co., $800, sales ticket no. 4, plus sales tax.
       25   Issued credit memorandum no. 2 to Jeff Tong Co. for $200 for lipstick returned from sales ticket no. 3, dated April 21.
       29   Cash sales taken from the cash register tape showed:
             1. Lipstick: $1,000 + $60 sales tax collected.
             2. Eye shadow: $3,000 + $180 sales tax collected.
       29   Sold lipstick on account to Marika Sanchez Co., $400, sales ticket no. 5, plus sales tax.
       30   Received payment from Marika Sanchez Co. of sales ticket no. 5, dated April 29.

Required

1. Journalize the above in the sales journal, cash receipts journal, or general journal.

2. Record to the accounts receivable subsidiary ledger and post to general ledger when appropriate.

3. Prepare a schedule of accounts receivable for the end of April.

Group B Problems

(The forms you need are on pages 285–304 of the *Study Guide and Working Papers*.)

9B-1. The following transactions occurred for Food.com for the month of June:

200X

June	1	Sold grocery merchandise to Duncan Co. on account, $800, invoice no. 1.
	4	Sold pizza merchandise to Sue Moore Co. on account, $550, invoice no. 2.
	8	Sold grocery merchandise to Long Co. on account, $900, invoice no. 3.
	10	Issued credit memorandum no. 1 to Duncan Co. for $160 of grocery merchandise returned due to spoilage.
	15	Sold pizza merchandise to Sue Moore Co. on account, $700, invoice no. 4.
	19	Sold grocery merchandise to Long Co. on account, $250, invoice no. 5.

Multicolumn journal: Journalizing and posting to general ledger, recording to accounts receivable subsidiary ledger, and preparing a schedule of accounts receivable.

Check Figure: Schedule of Accounts Receivable $3,040

Required

1. Journalize the transactions in the appropriate journals.
2. Record to the accounts receivable subsidiary ledger and post to general ledger as appropriate.
3. Prepare a schedule of accounts receivable.

9B-2. In November the following transactions occurred for Ted's Auto Supply (your working papers have balances as of Nov. 1 for certain general ledger and accounts receivable ledger accounts):

200X

Nov.	1	Sold merchandise to R. Volan on account, $4,000, invoice no. 70, plus 5 percent sales tax.
	5	Sold merchandise to J. Seth on account, $1,600, invoice no. 71, plus 5 percent sales tax.
	8	Sold merchandise to Lance Corner on account, $15,000, invoice no. 72, plus 5 percent sales tax.
	10	Issued credit memorandum no. 14 to R. Volan for $2,000 for defective merchandise returned from Nov. 1 transaction. (Be sure to record the reduction in sales tax payable as well.)
	12	Sold merchandise to J. Seth on account, $1,400, invoice no. 73, plus 5 percent sales tax.

Multicolumn sales journal: Use of sales tax, journalizing and posting to general ledger and recording to accounts receivable subsidiary ledger, and preparing a schedule of accounts receivable.

Check Figure: Schedule of Accounts Receivable $22,600

Required

1. Journalize the transactions in the appropriate journals.
2. Record to the accounts receivable subsidiary ledger and post to general ledger as appropriate.
3. Prepare a schedule of accounts receivable.

9B-3. (In your working papers all the beginning balances needed are provided for the accounts receivable subsidiary and general ledger.) The following transactions occurred for Peaker's Sneaker Shop:

200X

May	1	Mark Peaker invested an additional $14,000 in the sneaker store.
	3	Sold $2,000 of merchandise on account to B. Dale, sales ticket no. 60, terms 1/10, n/30.

Check Figure: Schedule of Accounts Receivable $8,000

4   Sold $900 of merchandise on account to Ron Lester, sales ticket no. 61, terms 1/10, n/30.

9   Sold $600 of merchandise on account to Jim Zon, sales ticket no. 62, terms 1/10, n/30.

10   Received cash from B. Dale in payment of May 3 transaction, sales ticket no. 60, less discount.

20   Sold $4,000 of merchandise on account to Pam Pry, sales ticket no. 63, terms 1/10, n/30.

22   Received cash payment from Ron Lester in payment of May 4 transaction, sales ticket no. 61.

23   Collected cash sales, $6,000.

24   Issued credit memorandum no. 1 to Pam Pry for $500 of merchandise returned from May 20 sales on account.

26   Received cash from Pam Pry in payment of May 20 sales ticket no. 63. (Don't forget about the credit memo and discount.)

28   Collected cash sales, $12,000.

30   Sold sneaker rack equipment for $200 cash.

30   Sold $6,000 of merchandise on account to Ron Lester, sales ticket no. 64, terms 1/10, n/30.

31   Issued credit memorandum no. 2 to Ron Lester for $800 of merchandise returned from May 30 transaction, sales ticket no. 64.

Required

1. Journalize the transactions in the appropriate journals.
2. Record and post as appropriate.
3. Prepare a schedule of accounts receivable.

9B-4. Bill's Cosmetic Market began operating in April. There is a 6 percent sales tax on all cosmetic sales. Bill offers no discounts. The following transactions occurred in April:

200X
Apr.

1   Bill Murray invested $10,000 in the Cosmetic Market from his personal account.

5   From the cash register tapes, lipstick cash sales were $5,000 plus sales tax.

5   From the cash register tapes, eye shadow cash sales were $3,000 plus sales tax.

8   Sold lipstick on account to Alice Koy Co., $400, sales ticket no. 1, plus sales tax.

9   Sold eye shadow on account to Marika Sanchez Co., $900, sales ticket no. 2, plus sales tax.

15   Issued credit memorandum no. 1 to Alice Koy Co. for lipstick returned, $200. (Be sure to reduce sales tax payable for Bill.)

19   Marika Sanchez Co. paid half the amount owed from sales ticket no. 2, dated April 9.

21   Sold lipstick on account to Jeff Tong Co., $600, sales ticket no. 3, plus sales tax.

24   Sold eye shadow on account to Rusty Neal Co., $1,000, sales ticket no. 4, plus sales tax.

25   Issued credit memorandum no. 2 to Jeff Tong Co. for $300, for lipstick returned from sales ticket no. 3, dated April 21.

29   Cash sales taken from the cash register tape showed:
     1. Lipstick: $4,000 + $240 sales tax collected.
     2. Eye shadow: $2,000 + $120 sales tax collected.

29　Sold lipstick on account to Marika Sanchez Co., $700, sales ticket no. 5 plus sales tax.

30　Received payment from Marika Sanchez Co. of sales ticket no. 5, dated April 29.

Required

1. Journalize, record, and post as appropriate.
2. Prepare a schedule of accounts receivable for the end of April.

REAL-WORLD APPLICATIONS

9R-1.

Ronald Howard has been hired by Green Company to help reconstruct the sales journal, general journal, and cash receipts journal, which were recently destroyed in a fire. The owner of Green Company has supplied him with the following data. Please ignore dates, invoice numbers, and so forth and enter the entries into the reconstructed sales journal, general journal, and cash receipts journal. What written recommendation should Ron make so reconstruction will not be needed in the future?

Accounts Receivable Subsidiary Ledger

	P. Bond				M. Raff		
Bal.	100	150	CRJ	Bal.	200		
SJ	150	Entitled to 2% discount		SJ	100		

	J. Smooth				R. Venner		
Bal.	300	1,000	GJ	Bal.	200	400	CRJ
SJ	2,000	1,000	CRJ	SJ	400		
SJ	1,000	500	GJ				
	Entitled to 1% discount						

Partial General Ledger

	Cash				Accounts Receivable		
Bal.	12,737			Bal.	800	1,000	GJ
				SJ	3,650	500	GJ
						1,550	CRJ

	Shelving Equipment				M. Rang, Capital		
Bal.	200	200	CRJ			1,000	Bal.
						5,000	Additional investment this month

	Sales				Sales Discount		
		800	Bal.	CRJ	13		
		6,000	CRJ ← (5,000 and 1,000)				
		3,650	SJ				

	Sales Returns and Allowances	
GJ	1,000	
GJ	500	

9R-2.
The bookkeeper of Floore Company records credit sales in a sales journal and returns in a general journal. The bookkeeper did the following:

1. Recorded an $18 credit sale as $180 in the sales journal.

2. Correctly recorded a $40 sale in the sales journal but posted it to B. Blue's account as $400 in the accounts receivable ledger.

3. Made an additional error in determining the balance of J. B. Window Co. in the accounts receivable ledger.

4. Posted a sales return that was recorded in the general journal to the Sales Returns and Allowance account and the Accounts Receivable account but forgot to record it to the B. Katz Co.

5. Added the total of the sales column incorrectly.

6. Posted a sales return to the Accounts Receivable account but not to the Sales Returns and Allowances account. The Accounts Receivable ledger was recorded correctly.

Could you inform the bookkeeper in writing as to when each error will be discovered?

YOU make the call

Critical Thinking/Ethical Case

9R-3.
Amy Jak is the National Sales Manager of Land.com. To get sales up to the projection for the old year, Amy asked the accountant to put the first two weeks of sales in January back into December. Amy told the accountant that this secret would only be between them. Should Amy move the new sales into the old sales year? You make the call. Write down your specific recommendations to Amy.

INTERNET EXERCISES

EX-1. [www.dillards.com] Special journals are designed to be excellent labor savers. Now that you have been shown the basics of the Sales Journal and the Cash Receipts Journal, you will recognize them next time you visit any large retailer. The labor saved by these journals is that transactions in them are posted monthly, rather than as they occur. Briefly explain the advantages of using them instead of merely posting transactions in a General Journal. In your explanation discuss posting differences in special journals from the General Journal.

EX-2. [www.dillards.com] Compare the process of entering transactions from source documents into a manual Sales Journal or Cash Receipts Journal with the "automatic" creation of the entries from a "point of sale terminal" you would see in a department store. Mention in your answer what different types of accounting records would be posted at the "point of sale".

CONTINUING PROBLEM

Tony will use two specialized journals for recording business transactions in the month of January. To assist you in recording the transactions, at the end of this problem is the Schedule of Accounts Receivable as of December 31 and an updated chart of accounts with the current balance listed for each account.

Assignment

(See p. 309 in the *Study Guide and Working Papers*.)

1. Journalize the transactions in the appropriate journals (cash receipts, sales journal, or general journal).

2. Record in the accounts receivable subsidiary ledger and post to the general ledger as appropriate. A partial general ledger is included in the *Working Papers*.

3. Prepare a schedule of accounts receivable as of January 31, 200X.

The January transactions are as follows:

Jan.	1	Sold $700 worth of merchandise to Taylor Golf on credit, sales invoice no. 5000; terms are 2/10, n/30.
	10	Sold $3,000 worth of merchandise on account to Anthony Pitale, sales invoice no. 5001; terms are 2/10, n/30.
	11	Received $3,000 from Accu Pac, Inc. toward payment of its balance; no discount allowed.
	12	Collected $2,000 cash sales.
	19	Sold $4,000 worth of merchandise on account to Vita Needle, sales invoice no. 5002; terms are 4/10, n/30.
	20	Collected balance in full from invoice no. 5001, Anthony Pitale.
	29	Issued credit memorandum to Taylor Golf for $400 worth of merchandise returned, invoice no. 5000.
	29	Collect full payment from Vita Needle, invoice no. 5002.

SCHEDULE OF ACCOUNTS RECEIVABLE
ELDORADO COMPUTER CENTER
DECEMBER 31, 200X

Taylor Golf	$ 2,900.00
Vita Needle	6,800.00
Accu Pac	$ 3,900.00
Total Amount Due	$13,600.00

CHART OF ACCOUNTS AND CURRENT BALANCES AS OF 12/31/0X

Account #	Account Name	Debit Balance	Credit Balance
1000	Cash	$ 3,336.65	
1010	Petty Cash	100	
1020	Accounts Receivable	13,600	
1025	Prepaid Rent	1,600	
1030	Supplies	132	
1040	Merchandise Inventory	0	
1080	Computer Shop Equipment	3,800	
1081	Accumulated Dep., CS Equip.		$ 99
1090	Office Equipment	1,050	
1091	Accumulated Dep., Office Equip.		20
2000	Accounts Payable		2,050
2010	Wages Payable		0
2020	FICA—Social Security Payable		0
2030	FICA—Medicare Payable		0
2040	FIT Payable		0
2050	SIT Payable		0

(continued on p. 358)

2060	FUTA Payable		0
2070	SUTA Payable		0
3000	Freedman Capital		7,406
3010	Freedman Withdrawals	2,015	
3020	Income Summary		0
4000	Service Revenue		18,500
4010	Sales		0
4020	Sales Returns and Allowances	0	
4030	Sales Discounts	0	
5010	Advertising Expense	0	
5020	Rent Expense	0	
5030	Utilities Expense	0	
5040	Phone Expense	150	
5050	Supplies Expense	0	
5060	Insurance Expense	0	
5070	Postage Expense	25	
5080	Dep. Exp., C.S. Equipment	0	
5090	Dep. Exp., Office Equipment	0	
5100	Miscellaneous Expense	10	
5110	Wage Expense	2,030	
5120	Payroll Tax Expense	226.35	
5130	Interest Expense	0	
5140	Bad Debt Expense	0	
6000	Purchases	0	
6010	Purchases Returns and Allowances		0
6020	Purchases Discounts		0
6030	Freight In	0	

Introduction to a Merchandise Company Using a General Journal for a Perpetual Inventory System

INTRODUCTION TO THE MERCHANDISE CYCLE

Let's use Wal-Mart as an example. We know that Wal-Mart must buy inventory from suppliers to sell to you, the customer. This inventory is called *merchandise inventory*. It is an asset sold to you for cash and/or accounts receivable and represents *sales revenue* or sales for Wal-Mart.

What did it cost Wal-Mart to bring the inventory into the store? The *cost of goods sold* is the total cost of merchandise inventory brought into the store and sold. These costs do not include any operating expenses such as heat, advertising, and salaries. To find Wal-Mart's profit before operating expenses, we take the sales revenue less cost of goods sold. This figure is called gross profit on sales.

| Wal-Mart Sales Revenue | – | Cost of Goods Sold | = | Gross Profit on Sales |

For example, if Wal-Mart sells a TV for $500 that cost them $300 to bring in the store, its gross profit is $200. To find its net income or net loss, Wal-Mart would subtract its operating expenses. Figure 11A-1 shows how a merchandiser calculates its net income or net loss.

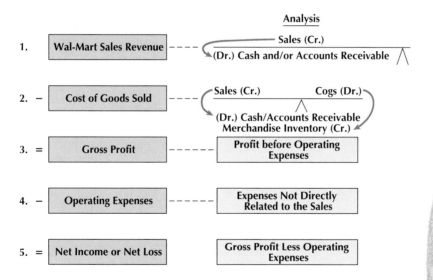

FIGURE 11A-1. Introduction to perpetual inventory for a merchandise company

Note   In step 1 the sales provide an inflow of cash and/or accounts receivable. Step 2 shows that when the inventory is sold, it is recognized as a cost (cost of goods sold). By subtracting sales less cost of goods sold, we arrive at the gross profit in step 3. Step 4 shows that operating expenses subtracted from gross profit result in a net income or net loss in step 5.

WHAT INVENTORY SYSTEM WAL-MART USES

When you pay at Wal-Mart you see the use of bar codes and optical scanners. Wal-Mart keeps detailed records of the inventory it brings into the store and what inventory is sold. This continuous updating of inventory is called a *per-*

petual inventory system. With this method, Wal-Mart keeps track of what it costs to make the sale (cost of goods sold).

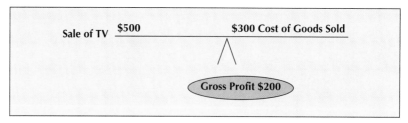

More and more companies large or small are using the perpetual inventory system due to increasing computerization. Wal-Mart knows that using the perpetual inventory system will help control stocks of inventory as well as lost or stolen goods.

RECORDING MERCHANDISE TRANSACTIONS

Now let's look at Wal-Mart as both a buyer and seller. Let's first focus on Wal-Mart the buyer.

Wal-Mart: The Buyer

When Wal-Mart brings merchandise inventory into the stores from suppliers it is recorded in the *merchandise inventory account.* Think of this account as purchases of merchandise for cash or on account that is for *resale* to customers. Each order is documented by an invoice for Wal-Mart. Keep in mind merchandise inventory is the cost of bringing the merchandise into the store, not the price at which the merchandise will be sold to customers. Let's assume on *July 9 that Wal-Mart brought flat TVs from Sony Corp. for $7,000 with terms 2/10, n/30.* Wal-Mart would record the purchase as follows:

Analysis:	Merchandise Inventory	A	↑	Dr.	$7,000
	Accounts Payable	L	↑	Cr.	$7,000

Journal Entry:	July	9	Merchandise Inventory	7 0 0 0 00	
			Accounts Payable		7 0 0 0 00
			Purchased Inventory on account		
			from Sony 2/10, n/30		

Keep in mind not all purchases will go to merchandise inventory. Wal-Mart will buy supplies, equipment and so forth that are not for resale to customers. These amounts will be debited to the specific account. For example, if Wal-Mart bought $5,000 of shelving equipment on account for its store on Nov. 9, the transaction would be recorded as follows:

Analysis:	Shelving Equipment	A	↑	Dr.	$5,000
	Accounts Payable	L	↑	Cr.	$5,000

Journal Entry:	Nov.	9	Shelving Equipment	5 0 0 0 00	
			Accounts Payable		5 0 0 0 00
			Bought equipment on account		

What happens if Wal-Mart finds a TV to be defective from its purchase from Sony?

Recording Purchases Returns and Allowances Because Wal-Mart noticed a damaged TV in the shipment on July 14 they issue a *debit memorandum*. This document notified Sony, the supplier, that Wal-Mart is reducing what is owed Sony by $600, the cost of the TV (to bring it into the store) and that the TV is being returned. On Wal-Mart's books the following analysis and journal entry resulted:

Analysis:	Accounts Payable	L	↓	Dr.	$600
	Merchandise Inventory	A	↓	Cr.	$600

Journal Entry:	July	14	Accounts Payable		6 0 0 00	
			Merchandise Inventory			6 0 0 00
			To record Debit Memo #10			

Note that the cost of merchandise inventory has been reduced by $600 due to the return. In the perpetual inventory system there is no purchases, returns, and allowances title. The savings from the return is recorded *directly* into the merchandise inventory account. Let's now look at how Wal-Mart would record any cash discounts it would receive due to payment of the Sony bill within the discount period.

Recording Purchase Discounts Let's assume Wal-Mart pays Sony within the first 10 days. Keep in mind that we take no discounts on returned goods (the $600 return). The amount of purchase discount will be recorded as a reduction to the cost of merchandise inventory. The following is the analysis and journal entry on July 16:

Analysis:	Accounts Payable	L	↓	Dr.	$6,400
	Cash	A	↓	Cr.	$6,272
	Merchandise Inventory	A	↓	Cr.	$ 128

A discount lowers the cost of inventory.

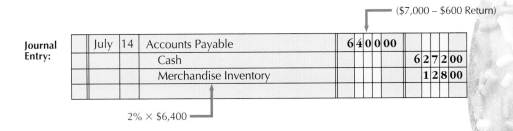

($7,000 – $600 Return)

Journal Entry:	July	14	Accounts Payable		6 4 0 0 00	
			Cash			6 2 7 2 00
			Merchandise Inventory			1 2 8 00

2% × $6,400

Keep in mind that had Wal-Mart missed the discount period it would have debited accounts payable $6,400 and credited cash for $6,400. Merchandise inventory would not be reduced.

Recording Cost of Freight The cost of freight ($300) is to be paid by Wal-Mart. When the purchaser is responsible for cost of freight, it is added to the cost of merchandise inventory. If the cost of freight is paid by the seller, it could be recorded in an operating expense account called freight-out. The following is the analysis and journal entry for freight on July 10:

Analysis:	Merchandise Inventory	A	↑	Dr.	$300
	Cash	A	↓	Cr.	$300

Freight Cost added to Merchandise Inventory

Journal Entry:	July	10	Merchandise Inventory		3 0 0	00			
			Cash					3 0 0	00
			Payment of Freight						

Wal-Mart: The Seller

Now let's look at Wal-Mart as the *seller* of merchandise.

Recording Sales at Wal-Mart   Sales revenues are earned at Wal-Mart when the goods are transferred to the buyer. The earned revenue can be for cash and or credit. Let's look at the following example of the sale of a TV at Wal-Mart for $950 on credit on Aug. 10 that cost Wal-Mart $600. Keep in mind when using the perpetual inventory systems that at time of the earned sale Wal-Mart will:

At selling price →1. **Record the sales (cash and or credit).**
At cost →   2. **Record the cost of the inventory sold and the reduction in inventory.**

First, let's analyze the transaction.

Selling Price <	Accounts Receivable	Asset	↑	Dr.	$950
	Sales	Revenue	↑	Cr.	$950
Cost to < Make sale	Cost of Goods Sold	Cost	↑	Dr.	$600
	Merchandise Inventory	Asset	↓	Cr.	$600

Note that we will have two entries, one to record the sale and one to show a new cost and less inventory on hand:

Aug.	10	Accounts Receivable		9 5 0	00			
		Sales					9 5 0	00
		Charge sales						
	10	Cost of Goods Sold		6 0 0	00			
		Merchandise Inventory					6 0 0	00
		To record cost of						
		merchandise sold on account						

Be sure to go back to steps 1 and 2 of Figure 11A-1. These two steps reinforce the above journal entries. Remember that if the sale were a cash sale, we would have debited cash instead of accounts receivable. Note also that the sales account only records sales of goods held for resale.

How Wal-Mart Records Sales Returns Allowances and Sales Discounts   Keep in mind that we are now looking at how the *seller* of merchandise records a transaction giving the customer a credit due to an allowance or a return of goods from a previous sale. Usually, the seller will issue a *credit memorandum,* a document informing the customer of the adjustment due to the return or allowance. For example, on August 15, let's look at a customer who returned a $950 TV that had been purchased at

Wal-Mart due to customer dissatisfaction. On Wal-Mart's books, the following analysis and journal entry resulted:

The Analysis: at Selling Price	Sales Returns and Allowances	Contra-Revenue	↑	Dr.	$950
	Accounts Receivable	Asset	↓	Cr.	$950
At Cost	Merchandise Inventory	Asset	↑	Dr.	$600
	Costs of Goods Sold	Cost	↓	Cr.	$600

Journal Entries:

				Debit	Credit
Aug.	15	Sales Returns and Allowances		9 5 0 00	
		Accounts Receivable			9 5 0 00
		Returned Goods			
	15	Merchandise Inventory		6 0 0 00	
		Cost of Goods Sold			6 0 0 00

The first entry records the return at the original selling price using the contra-revenue account sales returns and allowances. The second entry records putting the inventory back in Wal-Mart's books at cost and reducing its cost of goods sold because the inventory was not sold. Remember that we only record the cost of goods sold when the sale has been earned. Keep in mind that if the customer kept the TV but at a reduced price, no entry affecting merchandise inventory and cost of goods sold would be needed. Let's assume a customer on August 25 gets a 2 percent discount for paying for a $950 TV early. The following analysis and entry would result on the seller's book:

The Analysis:	Cash	Asset	↑	Dr.	$931
	Sales Discount	Contra-Revenue	↑	Dr.	$ 19
	Accounts Receivable	Asset	↓	Cr.	$950

Journal Entry:

				Debit	Credit
Aug.	25	Cash		9 3 1 00	
		Sales Discount		1 9 00	
		Accounts Receivable			9 5 0 00

Now let's summarize all the entries for both the buyer and the seller (in this case, Wal-Mart).

	Wal-Mart the Buyer			Wal-Mart the Seller	
Bought Inventory for Resale on Account	Merchandise Inventory → At		Sold Inventory on Account	Accounts Receivable → At	
	Accounts Payable Cost			Sales Selling Price	
				Cost of Goods Sold → At	
				Merchandise Inventory Cost	
Issued a Debit Memo for Merchandise Returned	Accounts Payable → At		Issued a Credit Memo for Returned Merchandise	Sales Returns and Allowances → At	
	Merchandise Inventory Cost			Accounts Receivable Selling Price	
				Merchandise Inventory → At	
				Cost of Goods Sold Cost	
Recorded a Purchase Discount	Accounts Payable		Recorded a Sales Discount	Cash	
	Cash			Sales Discount	
	Merchandise Inventory			Accounts Receivable	

Amount of discount

PROBLEM FOR APPENDIX

(The blank forms you need are on page 314 of the *Study Guide and Working Papers*.)

Pete's Clock Shops completed the following merchandise transaction in the month of June:

200X

June
1 Purchased merchandise on account from Clock Suppliers, $4,000; terms 2/10, n/30.
3 Sold merchandise on account, $2,000; terms 2/10, n/30. The cost of the merchandise sold was $1,200.
4 Received credit from Clock Suppliers for merchandise returned, $400.
10 Received collections in full, less discounts, from June 3 sales.
11 Paid Clock Suppliers in full, less discount.
14 Purchased office equipment for cash, $500.
15 Purchased $2,800 of merchandise from Abe's Distribution for cash.
16 Received a refund due to defective merchandise for supplier on cash purchase of $400.
17 Purchased merchandise from Rose Corp., $6,000 free on board shipping point (buyer pays freight); terms 2/10, n/30. Freight to be paid on June 20.
18 Sold merchandise for $3,000 cash; the cost of the merchandise sold was $1,600.
20 Paid freight on June 17 purchase, $180.
25 Purchased merchandise from Lee Co., $1,400, free on board destination (seller pays freight); terms 2/10, n/30.
26 Paid Rose Corp. in full, less discount.
27 Made refunds to cash customers for defective clock, $300. The cost of the defective clocks was $120.

Pete's Clock Shop accounts included the following:

No. 101 Cash, No. 112 Accounts Receivable,

No. 120 Merchandise Inventory, No. 124 Office Equipment, No. 201 Accounts Payable,

No. 301 P. Rings Capital, No. 401 Sales,

No. 412 Sales Discounts, No. 501 Cost of Goods Sold

Assignment

Journalize the transactions using a perpetual inventory system.

CHAPTER 10

Special Journals*

PURCHASES AND CASH PAYMENTS

In the last chapter you saw that e-retailers are currently exempt from having to charge sales tax to their customers. This gives them a leg up on their brick-and-mortar competition. However, e-businesses (and mail-order businesses) have one cost that the shop down the street from you doesn't have: shipping and handling. When you buy your Razor scooter from Etoys,** you'll have to pay $5.95 for shipping and handling if you want your scooter in 3–8 business days and $12.95 if you want it to arrive sooner. If you're impatient for your scooter, the shipping and handling charge will wipe out any savings on sales tax, so you might be better off going to your neighborhood store.

Shipping and handling is a significant expense for Etoys, Amazon, CDNow and other online merchandisers. As you'll see in this chapter, their shipping costs are considered "F.O.B. shipping point" because the buyer (you) are responsible for paying shipping costs. Yet even though you are charged for shipping on your credit card when you order from Amazon, the company pays Federal Express or another delivery company up front to have your package sent. When you are making your **purchases journal** in this chapter, you will learn that shipping costs are *not* considered when calculating net purchases. You use a purchases journal to record purchases of merchandise on account. For instance, if Amazon records its purchases of books from publishers or wholesalers, it will not deduct shipping costs to calculate net purchases. In addition to learning how to journalize transactions in a purchases journal, you will learn how to journalize and post from a **cash payments journal.**

---

*With new Appendix on what Special Journals would look like in a Perpetual Inventory System.
**At time of writing Etoys has filed for bankruptcy.

Just how the dot coms treat shipping charges is currently a matter of some controversy. Amazon.com had been accounting for it as a marketing expense. This way, shipping and fulfillment charges are not deducted from gross profit and, hence, the profit looks better to potential investors. Several accounting task forces are reviewing this matter, so it's clear that Amazon will have to change its treatment of shipping and handling soon.

Based on: Albert B. Crenshaw, "Taking the New Economy Into Account; Climate spurs Accounting Task Force To Rethink Rules on Stock Value, Options and Recognition of Revenue," *The Washington Post,* September 20, 2000, p. G18. Anonymous, "Web Retailers' 'Gross Profit' Questioned; E-commerce; The SEC may make some firms account for distribution costs, possibly turning their profits into losses," *The Los Angeles Times,* February 19, 2000, p. 2. [Alana, another source was a handout Jeannine gave me, "Chapter 5: E-business, the Internet, and your Accounting, Auditing, or Taxation Course," but I'm not sure how to cite this.] Information on shipping charges for a Razor scooter from Etoys was from www.Etoys.com.

LEARNING OBJECTIVES

▼ Calculating net purchases. (p. 368)

▼ Journalizing transactions in a purchases journal. (p. 372)

▼ Posting from a purchases journal to the accounts payable subsidiary ledger and the general ledger. (p. 372)

▼ Preparing, journalizing, recording, and posting a debit memorandum. (p. 373)

▼ Journalizing and posting from a cash payments journal. (p. 377)

▼ Preparing a schedule of accounts payable. (p. 378)

Chapter 9 focused on the sellers in merchandise companies. This chapter looks at the buyers. Many of the concepts and rules related to special journals carry over to this chapter. At the end of this chapter is a new appendix showing how all the special journals in Chapters 9 and 10 would look like in a perpetual inventory system.

LEARNING UNIT 10-1

CHOU'S TOY SHOP: BUYER'S VIEW OF A MERCHANDISE COMPANY

PURCHASES

Chou brings merchandise into his toy store for resale to customers. The account that records the cost of this merchandise is called **Purchases.** Suppose Chou buys $4,000 worth of Barbie dolls on account from Mattel Manufacturing on July 6. The Purchases account records all merchandise bought for resale. Here's how this purchase would be recorded if special journals were not used.

Purchases is a cost.
The rules work just like they were an expense.

Purchases	
Dr.	Cr.
4,000	

This account has a debit balance and is classified as a cost. Purchases represent costs that are directly related to bringing merchandise into the store for resale to customers. The July 6 entry would be analyzed and journalized as follows:

Accounts Affected	Category	↑	↓	Rules	T-Account Update
Purchases	Cost	↑		Dr.	**Purchases** Dr. | Cr. 4,000 |
Accounts Payable, Mattel	Liability	↑		Cr.	**Acc. Payable** **Mattel** Dr. | Cr. | 4,000 | 4,000

> If Chou's purchased a new display case for the store, it would not show up in the Purchase account. The case is considered equipment that is not for resale to customers.

July	6	Purchases	4 0 0 0 00		
		Accounts Payable, Mattel		4 0 0 0 00	
		Purchases on account			

Keep in mind we would have to record to Mattel in the accounts payable subsidiary ledger. We talk about the subsidiary ledger in Learning Unit 10-2.

PURCHASES RETURNS AND ALLOWANCES

Chou noticed that some of the dolls he received were defective, and he notified the manufacturer of the defects. On July 9, Mattel issued a debit memorandum indicating that Chou would get a $500 reduction from the original selling price. Chou then agreed to keep the dolls. The account that records a decrease to a buyer's cost is a contra-cost account called **Purchases Returns and Allowances.** The account lowers the cost of purchases.

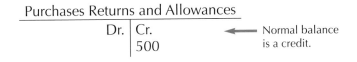

Purchases Returns and Allowances
Dr. | Cr.
     | 500   ◄——— Normal balance is a credit.

Let's analyze this reduction to cost and prepare a general journal entry.

Accounts Affected	Category	↑	↓	Rules	T-Account Update
Accounts Payable Mattel	Liability		↓	Dr.	**Acc. Payable** **Mattel** Dr. | Cr. 500 | 4,000 500 | 4,000
Purchases Returns and Allowances	Contra-cost	↑		Cr.	**Purchases Ret. & Allow.** Dr. | Cr. | 500

July	9	Accounts Payable, Mattel	5 0 0 00		
		Purchases Returns and Allowances		5 0 0 00	
		Received debit memorandum			

When posted to general ledger accounts as well as recording to Mattel in the accounts payable subsidiary ledger, Chou owes $500 less.

Purchases Discount

Now let's look at the analysis and journal entry when Chou pays Mattel. Mattel offers a 2 percent cash discount if the invoice is paid within 10 days. To take advantage of this cash discount, Chou sent a check to Mattel on July 15. The discount is taken after the allowance.

$$\begin{array}{r} \$4,000 \\ -\ 500\ \text{allowance} \\ \hline \$3,500 \times .02 = \$70\ \text{purchases discount} \end{array}$$

The account that records this discount is called **Purchases Discount**. It, too, is a contra-cost account because it lowers the cost of purchases.

Purchases Discount
Dr. | Cr.
     | 70   ← Normal balance is a credit.

Let's analyze and prepare a general journal entry:

Accounts Affected	Category	↑ ↓	Rules	T-Account Update
Accounts Payable Mattel	Liability	↓	Dr.	Acc. Payable — Dr. Cr. / 500 4,000 / 3,500 Mattel — 500 4,000 / 3,500
Purchases Discount	Contra-cost	↑	Cr.	Purchases Discount — Dr. Cr. / 70
Cash	Asset	↓	Cr.	Cash — Dr. Cr. / 3,430

July	15	Accounts Payable, Mattel		3 5 0 0 00			
		Purchases Discount				7 0 00	
		Cash				3 4 3 0 00	
		Paid Mattel balance owed					

After the journal entry is posted and recorded to Mattel, the result will show that Chou saved $70 and totally reduced what he owed to Mattel. The actual—or net—cost of his purchase is $3,430, calculated as follows:

Purchases	$4,000
− Purchases Returns and Allowances	500
− Purchases Discounts	70
= Net Purchases	$3,430

Freight charges are not taken into consideration in calculating net purchases. Still, they are very important. If the seller is responsible for paying the shipping cost until the goods reach their destination, the freight charges are **F.O.B. destination.** (**F.O.B.** stands for "free on board" the carrier.) For example, if a seller located in Boston sold goods F.O.B. destination to a buyer in New York, the seller would have to pay the cost of shipping the goods to the buyer.

If the buyer is responsible for paying the shipping costs, the freight charges are **F.O.B. shipping point.** In this situation, the seller will sometimes prepay the freight charges as a matter of convenience and will add it to the invoice of the purchaser.

F.O.B. Destination:
Seller pays freight to point
of destination.

F.O.B. Shipping Point:
Buyer pays freight from
seller's shipping point.

Example:

Bill amount ($800 + $80 prepaid freight)	$880
Less 5% cash discount (.05 × $800)	40
Amount to be paid by buyer	$840

Purchases discounts are not taken on freight. The discount is based on the purchase price.

If the seller ships goods F.O.B. shipping point, legal ownership (title) passes to the buyer *when the goods are shipped.* If goods are shipped by the seller F.O.B. destination, title will change *when goods have reached their destination.*

When does title change to
goods shipped?

LEARNING UNIT 10-1 REVIEW

AT THIS POINT you should be able to

- ▼ Explain and calculate purchases, purchases returns and allowances, and purchases discounts. (p. 366)
- ▼ Calculate net purchases. (p. 368)
- ▼ Explain why purchase discounts are not taken on freight. (p. 368)
- ▼ Compare and contrast F.O.B. destination with F.O.B. shipping point. (p. 369)

SELF-REVIEW QUIZ 10-1

(The forms you need can be found on page 316 of the *Study Guide and Working Papers.*)

Respond true or false to the following:

1. Net purchases = Purchases − Purchases Returns and Allowances − Purchases Discount.
2. Purchases is a contra-cost.
3. F.O.B. destination means the seller covers shipping cost and retains title till goods reach their destination.
4. Purchases discounts are not taken on freight.
5. Purchases Discount is a contra-cost account.

Solutions to Self-Review Quiz 10-1

1. True   **2.** False   **3.** True   **4.** True   **5.** True

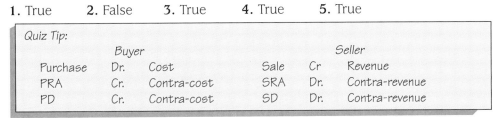

Quiz Tip:						
	Buyer				*Seller*	
Purchase	Dr.	Cost		Sale	Cr	Revenue
PRA	Cr.	Contra-cost		SRA	Dr.	Contra-revenue
PD	Cr.	Contra-cost		SD	Dr.	Contra-revenue

Merchandising companies must take specific steps when they purchase goods for resale. Let's look at the steps Art's Wholesale Clothing Company took when it ordered goods from Abby Blake Company on April 3.

Step 1: Prepare a Purchase Requisition at Art's Wholesale Clothing Company

> Authorized personnel initiate purchase requisition.

The inventory clerk notes a low inventory level of ladies' jackets for resale, so the clerk sends a **purchase requisition** to the purchasing department. A duplicate copy is sent to the accounting department. A third copy remains with the department that initiated the request, to be used as a check on the purchasing department.

Step 2: Purchasing Department of Art's Wholesale Clothing Company Prepares a Purchase Order

> Four copies of purchase order: (1) (original) to supplier, (2) to accounting department, (3) remains with department that initiated purchase requisition, and (4) to file of purchasing department.

After checking various price lists and suppliers' catalogs, the purchasing department fills out a form called a **purchase order.** This form gives Abby Blake Company the authority to ship the ladies' jackets ordered by Art's Wholesale Clothing Company (see Fig. 10-1).

Step 3: Sales Invoice Prepared by Abby Blake Company

Abby Blake Company receives the purchase order and prepares a sales invoice. The sales invoice for the seller is the **purchase invoice** for the buyer. A sales invoice is shown in Figure 10-2.

The invoice shows that the goods will be shipped F.O.B. Englewood Cliffs. Thus Art's Wholesale Clothing Company is responsible for paying the shipping costs.

The sales invoice also shows a freight charge. Thus Abby Blake prepaid the shipping costs as a matter of convenience. Art's will repay the freight charges when it pays the invoice.

FIGURE 10-1. Purchase Order

```
                    PURCHASE ORDER NO. 1
              ART'S WHOLESALE CLOTHING COMPANY
                        1528 BELLE AVE.
                      NEW YORK, NY 10022

  Purchased From:   Abby Blake Company        Date:  April 1, 200X
                    12 Foster Road            Shipped VIA:  Freight Truck
                    Englewood Cliffs, NJ 07632  Terms: 2/10, n/60
                                              FOB: Englewood Cliffs
```

Quantity	Description	Unit Price	Total
100	Ladies' Jackets Code 14-0	$50	$5,000

Art's Wholesale
By: Bill Joy

Purchase order number must appear on all invoices.

FIGURE 10-2. Sales Invoice

```
                  SALES INVOICE NO. 228
                   ABBY BLAKE COMPANY
                     12 FOSTER ROAD
                 ENGLEWOOD, CLIFFS, NJ 07632

Sold To:  Art's Wholesale              Date:  April 3, 200X
          Clothing Co.                 Shipped VIA:  Freight Truck
          1528 Belle Ave.              Terms:  2/10, n/60
          New York, NY 10022           Your Order No:  1
                                       FOB: Englewood Cliffs

    Quantity          Description        Unit Price      Total

      100       Ladies' Jackets Code 14-0    $50        $5,000
                Freight                                      50
                                                        $5,050
```

Step 4: Receiving the Goods

When goods are received, Art's Wholesale inspects the shipment and completes a **receiving report.** The receiving report verifies that the exact merchandise that was ordered was received in good condition.

Step 5: Verifying the Numbers

Before the invoice is approved for recording and payment, the accounting department must check the purchase order, invoice, and receiving report to make sure that all are in agreement and that no steps have been omitted. The form used for checking and approval is an **invoice approval form** (see Fig. 10-3).

Keep in mind that Art's Wholesale Clothing Company does not record this purchase until the *invoice is approved for recording and payment.* Abby Blake Company records this transaction in its records when the sales invoice is prepared, however.

THE PURCHASES JOURNAL AND ACCOUNTS PAYABLE SUBSIDIARY LEDGER

Let's look at how Art's Wholesale Clothing Company journalizes, posts, and records to the accounts payable subsidiary ledger. We also look at the **purchases journal,** a multicolumn special journal Art's uses to record the buying of merchandise or other items on account, and the **accounts payable subsidiary ledger,** an alphabetical list of the amounts owed to creditors from purchases on account.

FIGURE 10-3. Invoice Approval Form

```
                INVOICE APPROVAL FORM
                Art's Wholesale Clothing Co.

Purchase Order #              _____
Requisition check             _____
Purchase Order check          _____
Receiving Report check        _____
Invoice check                 _____
Approved for Payment          _____
```

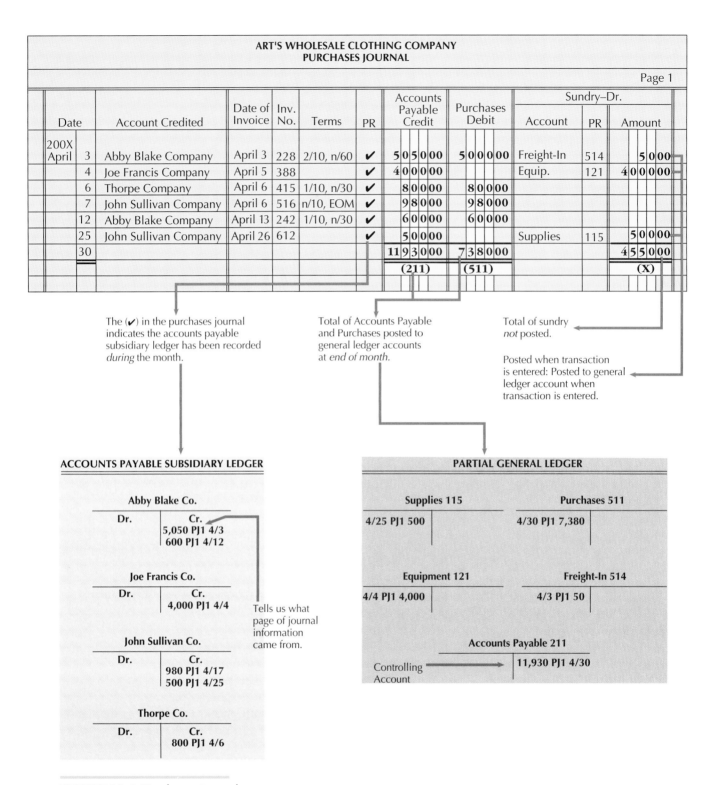

FIGURE 10-4. Purchases Journal

For example, on April 3 Art's Wholesale Clothing Company records in its purchases journal the following:

▼ Date: April 3, 200X.
▼ Account Credited: Abby Blake Company.
▼ Date of Invoice: April 3.
▼ Invoice Number: 228.
▼ Terms: 2/10, n/60.
▼ Accounts payable: $5,050; purchases: $5,000; freight-in, $50.

As soon as the information is journalized in the purchases journal (see Fig. 10-4), you should:

1. Record to Abby Blake Co. in the accounts payable subsidiary ledger to indicate that the amount owed is now $5,050. When this is complete, place a ✓ in the PR column of the purchases journal.
2. Post to Freight-In, account no. 514, in the general ledger right away. When this posting is complete, record the 514 in the PR column under Sundry in the purchases journal.

The posting and recording rules are similar to those in the previous chapter, but here we are looking at the buyer rather than at the seller.

See Figure 10-4 for a complete purchases journal.

Note that the normal balance in the accounts payable subsidiary ledger is a credit.

THE DEBIT MEMORANDUM

In Chapter 9, Art's Wholesale Clothing Company had to handle returned goods as a seller. It did so by issuing credit memoranda to customers who returned or received an allowance on the price. In this chapter, Art's must handle returns as a buyer. It does so by using debit memoranda. A **debit memorandum** is a piece of paper issued by a customer to a seller. It indicates that a return or allowance has occurred.

Suppose Art's Wholesale had purchased men's hats for $800 from Thorpe Company on April 6 (p. 372). On April 9, 20 hats valued at $200 were found to have defective brims. Art's issued a debit memorandum to Thorpe Company, as shown in Figure 10-5. At some point in the future, Thorpe will issue Art's a credit memorandum. Let's look at how Art's Wholesale Clothing Company handles such a transaction in its accounting records.

Journalizing and Posting the Debit Memo

First, let's look at a transactional analysis chart.

Accounts Affected	Category	↑	↓	Rules
Accounts Payable	Liability		↓	Dr.
Purchases Returns and Allowances	Contra-cost	↑		Cr.

Result of debit memo: "debits" or reduces Accounts Payable. On seller's books, accounts affected would include Sales Returns and Allowances and Accounts Receivable.

```
                    DEBIT MEMORANDUM                    No. 1

Art's Wholesale
Clothing Company
1528 Belle Ave.
New York, NY 10022

TO: Thorpe Company                           April 9, 200X
    3 Access Road
    Beverly, MA 01915

WE DEBIT your account as follows:

Quantity                          Unit Cost        Total
  20    Men's Hats Code 827 – defective brims  $10    $200
```

FIGURE 10-5. Debit Memorandum

A debit memo shows that Art's does not owe as much money as was indicated in the company's purchases journal.

Next, let's examine the journal entry for the debit memorandum:

Purchases Returns and Allowances	
Dr.	Cr.
−	+

A contra-cost-of-goods-sold account.

GENERAL JOURNAL

Page 1

Date		Account Titles and Description	PR	Dr.	Cr.
April	9	Accounts Payable, Thorpe Company	211 ✔	2 0 0 00	
		Purchases Returns and Allowances	513		2 0 0 00
		Debit memo #1			

The two postings and one recording are:

1. 211: Post to Accounts Payable as a debit in the general ledger account no. 211. When done, place in the PR column the account number, 211, above the diagonal on the same line as Accounts Payable in the journal.

2. ✔: Record to Thorpe Co. in the accounts payable subsidiary ledger to show that Art's doesn't owe Thorpe as much money. When done, place a ✔ in the journal in the PR column below the diagonal line on the same line as Accounts Payable in the journal.

3. 513: Post to Purchases Returns and Allowances as a credit in the general ledger (account no. 513). When done, place the account number, 513, in the PR column of the journal on the same line as Purchases Returns and Allowances. (If equipment was returned that was not merchandise for resale, we would credit Equipment and not Purchases Returns and Allowances.)

LEARNING UNIT 10-2 REVIEW

AT THIS POINT you should be able to

- Explain the relationship between a purchase requisition, a purchase order, and a purchase invoice. (p. 370)
- Explain why a typical invoice approval form may be used. (p. 371)
- Journalize transactions into a purchases journal. (p. 372)
- Explain how to record the accounts payable subsidiary ledger and post to the general ledger from a purchases journal. (p. 372)
- Explain a debit memorandum and be able to journalize an entry resulting from its issuance. (p. 373)

SELF-REVIEW QUIZ 10-2

(The forms you need are on pages 317–335 of the *Study Guide and Working Papers.*)

Journalize the following transactions into the purchases journal or general journal for Munroe Co. Record to accounts payable subsidiary ledger and post to general ledger accounts as appropriate. Use the same journal headings we used for Art's Wholesale Clothing Company.

May	5	Bought merchandise on account from Flynn Co., invoice no. 512, dated May 6, $900, terms 1/10, n/30.	
	7	Bought merchandise from John Butler Company, invoice no. 403, dated May 7, $1,000, terms n/10 EOM.	
	13	Issued debit memo no. 1 to Flynn Co. for merchandise returned, $300, from invoice no. 512.	
	17	Purchased $400 of equipment on account from John Butler Company, invoice no. 413, dated May 18.	

Solution to Self-Review Quiz 10-2

Page 2

Date		Account Credited	Date of Invoice	Inv. No.	Terms	PR	Accounts Payable Credit	Purchases Debit	Sundry–Dr.		
									Account	PR	Amount
200X May	5	Flynn Co.	May 6	512	1/10, n/30	✔	900 00	900 00			
	7	John Butler	May 7	403	n/10, EOM	✔	1000 00	1000 00			
	17	John Butler	May 18	413		✔	400 00		Equip.	121	400 00
	31						2300 00	1900 00			400 00
							(212)	(512)			(X)

MUNROE CO.
GENERAL JOURNAL

Page 1

Date		Account Titles and Description	PR	Dr.	Cr.
200X May	13	Accounts Payable, Flynn Co.	212/ ✔	300 00	
		Purchases Returns and Allowances	513		300 00

ACCOUNTS PAYABLE SUBSIDIARY LEDGER

JOHN BUTLER COMPANY
18 REED RD.
HOMEWOOD, ILLINOIS 60430

Date		Explanation	Post. Ref.	Debit	Credit	Cr. Balance
200X May	7		PJ2		1000 00	1000 00
	17		PJ2		400 00	1400 00

FLYNN COMPANY
15 FOSS AVE.
ENGLEWOOD CLIFFS, NEW JERSEY 07632

Date		Explanation	Post. Ref.	Debit	Credit	Cr. Balance
200X May	5		PJ2		900 00	900 00
	13		GJ1	300 00		600 00

Equipment   Account No. 121

Date	Explanation	Post. Ref.	Debit	Credit	Balance Debit	Balance Credit
200X May 17		PJ2	4 0 0 00		4 0 0 00	

Accounts Payable   Account No. 212

Date	Explanation	Post. Ref.	Debit	Credit	Balance Debit	Balance Credit
200X May 13		GJ1	3 0 0 00		3 0 0 00	
31		PJ2		2 3 0 0 00		2 0 0 0 00

Purchases   Account No. 512

Date	Explanation	Post. Ref.	Debit	Credit	Balance Debit	Balance Credit
200X May 31		PJ2	1 9 0 0 00		1 9 0 0 00	

Purchases, Returns, and Allowances   Account No. 513

Date	Explanation	Post. Ref.	Debit	Credit	Balance Debit	Balance Credit
200X May 13		GJ1		3 0 0 00		3 0 0 00

> *Quiz Tip:*
>
> | Buyer | Seller |
> |-------|--------|
> | Receives Credit Memo | Issues Credit Memo |
> | Issues Debit Memo | Receives Debit Memo |
> | Dr. Accounts Payable | Dr. SRA |
> | Cr. PRA | Cr. Accounts Receivable |

LEARNING UNIT 10-3

THE CASH PAYMENTS JOURNAL AND SCHEDULE OF ACCOUNTS PAYABLE

Art's Wholesale Clothing Company will record all payments made in cash (or by check) in a **cash payments journal** (also called a **cash disbursements journal**). In many ways the structure of this journal resembles that of the cash receipts journal discussed in Chapter 9. Now, however, we are looking at the outward flow of cash instead of the inward flow.

Art's conducted the following cash transactions in April:

200X

Apr.   2   Issued check no. 1 to Pete Blum for insurance paid in advance, $900.

7   Issued check no. 2 to Joe Francis Company in payment of its April 5 invoice no. 388.

9   Issued check no. 3 to Rick Flo Co. for merchandise purchased for cash, $800.

12   Issued check no. 4 to Thorpe Company in payment of its April 6 invoice no. 414 less the return and discount.

28   Issued check no. 5, $700, for salaries paid.

Figure 10-6 on p. 378 shows the cash payments journal for the end of April along with the recordings to the accounts payable subsidiary ledger and postings to the general ledger. Study the diagram; we review it in a moment.

Posting and recording rules for this journal are similar to those for the cash receipts journal in Chapter 9.

JOURNALIZING, POSTING, AND RECORDING FROM THE CASH PAYMENTS JOURNAL TO THE ACCOUNTS PAYABLE SUBSIDIARY LEDGER AND THE GENERAL LEDGER

Figure 10-6 shows how Art's Wholesale Clothing Company recorded the payment of cash on April 12 to Thorpe Company. The purchases journal shows that Art's purchased $800 of merchandise from Thorpe on account on April 6. The amount Art's owes is discounted 1 percent. The amount owed ($800 − $200 returns) is recorded in the accounts payable subsidiary ledger as soon as the entry is made in the cash payments journal. The payment reduces the balance to Thorpe to zero. Art's Wholesale Clothing Company receives a $6 purchases discount.

At the end of the month the totals of the Cash, Purchases Discount, and Accounts Payable accounts are posted to the general ledger. The total of sundry is *not* posted. The accounts Prepaid Insurance, Purchases, and Salaries Expense are posted to the general ledger at the time the entry is put in the journal.

The cash payments journal of Art's Wholesale Clothing Company can be crossfooted as follows:

As explained in Chapter 9, Sundry is a miscellaneous accounts column that provides flexibility for reporting infrequent transactions that result in an inflow of cash.

Debit = Credit Columns
Sundry + Accounts Payable = Purchases Discounts + Cash
$2,400 + $4,600   = $6   + $6,994
$7,000 = $7,000

Schedule of Accounts Payable

Now let's prove that the sum of the accounts payable subsidiary ledger at the end of the month is equal to the controlling account, Accounts Payable, at the end of April for Art's Wholesale Clothing Company. To do so, creditors with an ending balance in Art's accounts payable subsidiary ledger must be listed in the schedule of accounts payable (see Fig. 10-7). At the end of the month the total owed ($7,130) in Accounts Payable, the **controlling account** in the general ledger, should equal the sum owed the individual creditors that are listed on the schedule of accounts payable. If it doesn't, the journalizing, posting, and recording must be checked to ensure that they are complete. Also, the balances of each title should be checked.

Remember:
There is no discount on sales tax or freight.

ART'S WHOLESALE CLOTHING COMPANY SCHEDULE OF ACCOUNTS PAYABLE APRIL 30, 200X		
Abby Blake Co.	$5 6 5 0	00
John Sullivan Co.	1 4 8 0	00
Total Accounts Payable	$7 1 3 0	00

FIGURE 10-7. Schedule of Accounts Payable

FIGURE 10-6. Cash Payments Journal Recording and Posting

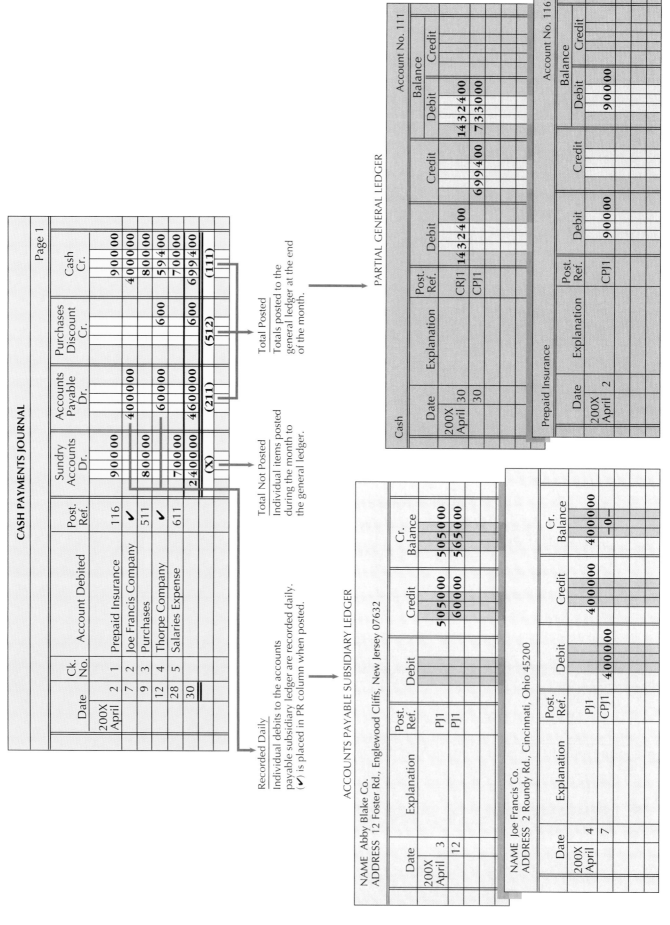

FIGURE 10-6. (Cont.)

Controlling Account →

Accounts Payable Account No. 211

Date		Explanation	Post. Ref.	Debit	Credit	Balance Debit	Balance Credit
200X April	9		GJ1	20000		20000	
	30		PJ1		1193000		1173000
	30		CPJ1	460000			713000

Purchases Account No. 511

Date		Explanation	Post. Ref.	Debit	Credit	Balance Debit	Balance Credit
200X April	9		CPJ1	80000		80000	
	30		PJ1	738000		818000	

Purchases Discount Account No. 512

Date		Explanation	Post. Ref.	Debit	Credit	Balance Debit	Balance Credit
200X April	30		CPJ1		600		600

Salaries Expense Account No. 611

Date		Explanation	Post. Ref.	Debit	Credit	Balance Debit	Balance Credit
200X April	28		CPJ1	70000		70000	

NAME John Sullivan Co.
ADDRESS 18 Print St., Wellesley, Mass. 01980

Date		Explanation	Post. Ref.	Debit	Credit	Cr. Balance
200X April	7		PJ1		98000	98000
	25		PJ1		50000	148000

NAME Thorpe Co.
ADDRESS 3 Access Rd., Chicago, Illinois 60430

Date		Explanation	Post. Ref.	Debit	Credit	Cr. Balance
200X April	6		PJ1		80000	80000
	9		GJ1	20000		60000
	12		CPJ1	60000		-0-

Trade Discounts

Trade discounts are reductions from the purchase price. Usually, they are given to customers who buy items to resell or to use to produce other salable goods.

Amount of Trade Discount = List Price − Net Price

Different trade discounts are available to different classes of customers. Often, trade discounts are listed in catalogs that contain the list price and the amount of trade discount available. Such catalogs usually are updated by discount sheets.

Trade discounts have *no relationship* to whether a customer is paying a bill early. Trade discounts and list prices are not shown in the accounts of either the purchaser or the seller. Cash discounts are not taken on the amount of trade discount.

For example, look at the following:

> Trade discounts are not reflected on the books.

▼ List price, $800.
▼ 30% trade discount.
▼ 5% cash discount.
▼ Thus: Invoice cost of $560 ($800 − $240) less the cash discount of $28 ($560 × .05) results in a final cost of $532 if the cash discount is taken.

The purchaser as well as the seller would record the invoice amount at $560.

LEARNING UNIT 10-3 REVIEW

AT THIS POINT you should be able to

◆ Journalize, post, and record transactions utilizing a cash payments journal. (p. 377)
◆ Prepare a schedule of accounts payable. (p. 377)
◆ Compare and contrast a cash discount to a trade discount. (p. 380)

SELF-REVIEW QUIZ 10-3

(The forms you need are on pages 319–322 of the *Study Guide and Working Papers*.)

Given the following information, journalize, crossfoot, and when appropriate record and post the transactions of Melissa Company. Use the same headings as used for Art's Clothing. All purchases discounts are 2/12, n/30. The cash payments journal is page 2.

ACCOUNTS PAYABLE SUBSIDIARY LEDGER

Name	Balance	Invoice No.
Bob Finkelstein	$300	488
Al Jeep	200	410

PARTIAL GENERAL LEDGER

	Account No.	Balance
Cash	110	$700
Accounts Payable	210	500
Purchases Discount	511	—
Advertising Expense	610	—

200X
June 1 Issued check no. 15 to Al Jeep in payment of its May 25 invoice no. 410 less purchases discount.

8 Issued check no. 16 to Moss Advertising Co. to pay advertising bill due, $75, no discount.

9 Issued check no. 17 to Bob Finkelstein in payment of its May 28 invoice no. 488 less purchases discount.

Solution to Self-Review Quiz 10-3

MELISSA COMPANY
CASH PAYMENTS JOURNAL

Page 2

Date		Ck. No.	Account Debited	Post. Ref.	Sundry Accounts Dr.	Accounts Payable Dr.	Purchases Discount Cr.	Cash Cr.
200X June	1	15	Al Jeep	✔		200 00	4 00	196 00
	8	16	Advertising Expense	610	75 00			75 00
	9	17	Bob Finkelstein	✔		300 00	6 00	294 00
	30				75 00	500 00	10 00	565 00
					(X)	(210)	(511)	(110)

$75 + $500 = $10 + $565
$575 = $575

ACCOUNTS PAYABLE SUBSIDIARY LEDGER

NAME Bob Finkelstein
ADDRESS 112 Flying Highway, Trenton, New Jersey 08611

Date		Explanation	Post. Ref.	Debit	Credit	Cr. Balance
200X June	1	Balance	✔			300 00
	9		CPJ2	300 00		—0—

NAME Al Jeep
ADDRESS 118 Wang Rd., Saugus, Mass. 01432

Date		Explanation	Post. Ref.	Debit	Credit	Cr. Balance
200X June	1	Balance	✔			200 00
	1		CPJ2	200 00		—0—

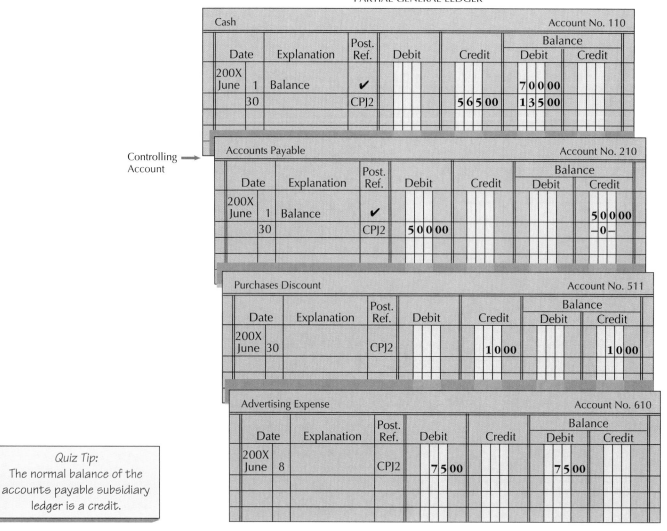

Controlling Account →

Cash — Account No. 110

Date		Explanation	Post. Ref.	Debit	Credit	Balance Debit	Balance Credit
200X June	1	Balance	✔			700 00	
	30		CPJ2		565 00	135 00	

Accounts Payable — Account No. 210

Date		Explanation	Post. Ref.	Debit	Credit	Balance Debit	Balance Credit
200X June	1	Balance	✔				500 00
	30		CPJ2	500 00			–0–

Purchases Discount — Account No. 511

Date		Explanation	Post. Ref.	Debit	Credit	Balance Debit	Balance Credit
200X June	30		CPJ2		10 00		10 00

Advertising Expense — Account No. 610

Date		Explanation	Post. Ref.	Debit	Credit	Balance Debit	Balance Credit
200X June	8		CPJ2	75 00		75 00	

> *Quiz Tip:*
> The normal balance of the accounts payable subsidiary ledger is a credit.

COMPREHENSIVE DEMONSTRATION PROBLEM WITH SOLUTION TIPS

(The forms you need are on pages 322–324 of the *Study Guide and Working Papers*.)

Record the following transactions into special or general journals. Record and post as appropriate.

Note:

All credit sales are 2/10, n/30. All merchandise purchased on account has 3/10, n/30 credit terms.

Solution Tips to Journalizing

200X

Mar.			
	1	J. Ling invested $2,000 into the business.	CRJ
	1	Sold merchandise on account to Balder Co., $500, invoice no. 1.	SJ
	2	Purchased merchandise on account from Case Co., $500.	PJ
	4	Sold $2,000 of merchandise for cash.	CRJ
	6	Paid Case Co. from previous purchases on account, check no. 1.	CPJ
	8	Sold merchandise on account to Lewis Co., $1,000, invoice no. 2.	SJ
	10	Received payment from Balder for invoice no. 1.	CRJ
	12	Issued a credit memorandum to Lewis Co. for $200 for faulty merchandise.	GJ
	14	Received payment from Lewis Co.	CRJ
	16	Purchased merchandise on account from Noone Co., $1,000.	PJ
	17	Purchased equipment on account from Case Co., $300.	PJ
	18	Issued a debit memorandum to Noone Co. for $500 for defective merchandise.	GJ
	20	Paid salaries, $300, check no. 2.	CPJ
	24	Paid Noone balance owed, check no. 3.	CPJ

Record Accounts Receivable Subsidiary Ledger immediately.

J. LING, CO.
SALES JOURNAL

Page 1

Date		Account Debited	Terms	Invoice No.	PR	Dr. Acc. Rec Cr. Sales
200X Mar.	1	Balder Co.	2/10, N/30	1	✔	5 0 0 00
	8	Lewis Co.	2/10, N/30	2	✔	1 0 0 0 00
	31					1 5 0 0 00
						(112) (410)

Total posted at end of month to these accounts.

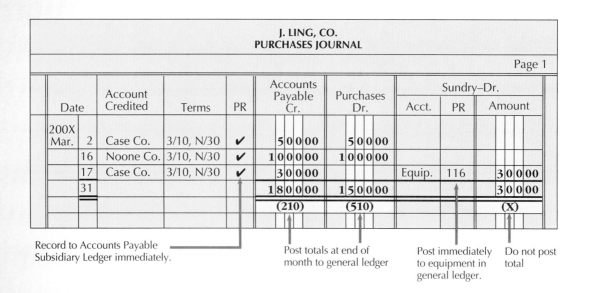

J. LING, CO.
PURCHASES JOURNAL

Page 1

Date	Account Credited	Terms	PR	Accounts Payable Cr.	Purchases Dr.	Sundry–Dr. Acct.	PR	Amount
200X Mar. 2	Case Co.	3/10, N/30	✔	50000	50000			
16	Noone Co.	3/10, N/30	✔	100000	100000			
17	Case Co.	3/10, N/30	✔	30000		Equip.	116	30000
31				180000	150000			30000
				(210)	(510)			(X)

Record to Accounts Payable Subsidiary Ledger immediately.

Post totals at end of month to general ledger

Post immediately to equipment in general ledger.

Do not post total

Post to capital immediately.

J. LING, CO.
CASH RECEIPTS JOURNAL

Page 1

Date	Cash Dr.	Sales Discount Dr.	Accts. Receivable Cr.	Sales Cr.	Sundry Account Names	PR	Amount Cr.
200X Mar. 1	200000				J. Ling, Cap.	310	200000
4	200000			200000	Cash sale	✗	
10	49000	1000	50000		Balder Co.	✔	
14	78400	1600	80000		Lewis Co.	✔	
31	527400	2600	130000	200000			200000
	(111)	(430)	(112)	(410)			(X)

Post totals at end of month to general ledger

Record immediately to Accounts Receivable Subsidiary Ledger.

Don't post total

Record immediately to Accounts Payable Subsidiary ledger.

J. LING, CO.
CASH PAYMENTS JOURNAL

Page 1

Date	Ck. No.	Account Debited	PR.	Sundry Dr.	Accounts Payable Dr.	Purchases Discount Cr.	Cash Cr.
200X Mar. 6	1	Case Co	✔		50000	1500	48500
20	2	Salaries Expense	610	30000			30000
24	3	Noone Co.	✔		50000	1500	48500
31				30000	100000	3000	127000
				(X)	(210)	(530)	(111)

Post immediately to salaries expense.

Do not post total.

Post totals at end of month to the general ledger.

GENERAL JOURNAL — Page 1

	Date	Account Titles and Description	PR	Dr.	Cr.
	200X Mar. 12	Sales Returns and Allowances	420	2 0 0 00	
		Accounts Receivable, Lewis Co.	112 ✓		2 0 0 00
		Issued Credit Memo			
	18	Accounts Payable, Noone Co.	210 ✓	5 0 0 00	
		Purchases Returns and Allowances	520		5 0 0 00
		Issued Debit Memo			

Record and post immediately to
Subsidiary and General Ledger.

ACCOUNTS RECEIVABLE SUBSIDIARY LEDGER

Balder Company

Date	PR	Dr.	Cr.	Dr. Bal.
200X 3/1	SJ1	500		500
3/10	CRJ1		500	—

Lewis Company

Date	PR	Dr.	Cr.	Dr. Bal.
200X 3/8	SJ1	1,000		1,000
3/12	GJ1		200	800
3/14	CPJ1		800	—

ACCOUNTS PAYABLE SUBSIDIARY LEDGER

Case Company

Date	PR	Dr.	Cr.	Cr. Bal.
200X 3/2	PJ1		500	500
3/6	CPJ1	500		—
3/17	PJ1		300	300

Noone Company

Date	PR	Dr.	Cr.	Cr. Bal.
200X 3/16	PJ1		1,000	1,000
3/18	GJ1	500		500
3/24	CPJ1	500		—

GENERAL LEDGER

Cash 111

3/31 CRJ1 5,274		1,270	3/31 CPJ1
Balance 4,004			

Sales 410

		1,500	3/31 SJ1
		2,000	3/31 CRJ1
		3,500	Balance

Accounts Receivable 112

3/31 SJ1 1,500		200	3/12 GJ1
Balance 0		1,300	3/31 CRJ1

Sales Returns + Allowances 420

3/12 GJ1 200	

Equipment 116

3/17 PJ1 300	

Sales Discount 430

3/31 CRJ1 26	

Accounts Payable 210		Purchases 510	
3/18 GJ1 500	1,800 3/31 PJ1	3/31 PJ1 1,500	
3/31 CPJ1 1,000	300 Balance		

J. Ling, Capital 310		Purchase Ret. + Allow. 520	
	2,000 3/1 CRJ1		500 3/18 GJ1

Purchase Discount 530	
	30 3/31 CPJ1

Salaries Expense 610	
3/20 CPJ1 300	

Summary of Solution Tips

Chapter 9: Seller

Sales Journal
Cash Receipts Journal
Accounts Receivable Subsidiary Ledger
Sales (Cr.)
Sales Returns + Allowances (Dr.)
Sales Discounts (Dr.)
Accounts Receivable (Dr.)
Issue a Credit Memo
       or
Receive a Debit Memo
Schedule of Accounts Receivable

Chapter 10: Buyer

Purchases Journal
Cash Payments Journal
Accounts Payable Subsidiary Ledger
Purchases (Dr.)
Purchase Returns + Allowances (Cr.)
Purchase Discounts (Cr.)
Accounts Payable (Cr.)
Receive a Credit Memo
       or
Issue a Debit Memo
Schedule of Accounts Payable

When Do I Do What? A Step-by-Step Walk-Through of This Comprehensive Demonstration Problem

Transaction	What to Do Step by Step

200X
Mar.

1   *Money Received:* Record in Cash Receipts Journal. Post immediately to J. Ling, Capital, because it is in Sundry.

1   *Sale on Account:* Record in Sales Journal. Record immediately to Balder Co., in accounts receivable subsidiary ledger. Place a ✓ in PR column of Sales Journal when subsidiary is updated.

2   *Buy Merchandise on Account:* Record in Purchases Journal. Record to Case Co. immediately in the accounts payable subsidiary ledger.

4   *Money In:* Record in Cash Receipts Journal. No posting needed (Put an **X** in PR column.)

6   *Money Out:* Record in Cash Payments Journal. Save $15, which is a Purchase Discount. Record immediately to Case Co. in accounts payable subsidiary ledger (the full amount of $500).

8   *Sales on Account:* Record in Sales Journal. Update immediately to Lewis in accounts receivable subsidiary ledger.

10   *Money In:* Record in Cash Receipts Journal. Because Balder pays within 10 days, it gets a $10 discount. Record immediately to Balder in the accounts receivable subsidiary ledger, the full amount.

Transaction	What to Do Step by Step
12	*Returns:* Record in general journal. Seller issues credit memo resulting in higher sales returns and customers owing less. All postings and recordings are done immediately.
14	*Money In:* Record in Cash Receipts Journal:

$$\$1,000 - \$200 \text{ returns} = \$800$$
$$\times .02$$
$$\overline{\$\ 16 \text{ discount}}$$

Record immediately the $800 to Lewis in the accounts receivable subsidiary ledger.

16	*Buy Now, Pay Later:* Record in Purchases Journal. Record immediately to Noone Co. in the accounts payable subsidiary ledger.
17	*Buy Now, Pay Later:* Record in Purchases Journal in Sundry. This item is not merchandise for resale. Record and post immediately.
18	*Returns:* Record in general ledger. Buyer issues a debit memo reducing the Accounts Payable due to Purchases Return and Allowances. Post and record immediately.
20	*Salaries:* Record in Cash Payments Journal, Sundry column. Post immediately to Salaries Expense.
24	*Money Out:* Record in Cash Payments Journal. Save 3 percent ($15), a Purchase Discount. Record immediately to accounts payable subsidiary ledger that you reduce Noone by $500.

End of Month:

Post totals (except Sundry) of Special Journal to the general ledger.

Note:

In this problem at end of month, (1) Accounts Receivable in the general ledger, the controlling account, has a zero balance, as does each title in the accounts receivable subsidiary ledger; and (2) The Balance in Accounts Payable (the controlling account) is $300. In the accounts payable subsidiary ledger, we owe Case $300. The sum of the accounts payable subsidiary ledger does equal the balance in the controlling account at the end of the month.

SUMMARY OF KEY POINTS

Learning Unit 10-1

1. Purchases are merchandise for resale. It is a cost.
2. Purchases Returns and Allowances and Purchases Discount are contra-costs.
3. *F.O.B. shipping point* means that the purchaser of the goods is responsible for covering the shipping costs. If the terms were *F.O.B. destination,* the seller would be responsible for covering the shipping costs until the goods reached their destination.
4. Purchases discounts are not taken on freight.

Learning Unit 10-2

1. The steps for buying merchandise from a company may include the following:
   a. The requesting department prepares a purchase requisition.
   b. The purchasing department prepares a purchase order.
   c. Seller receives the order and prepares a sales invoice (a purchase invoice for the buyer).

d. Buyer receives the goods and prepares a receiving report.

e. Accounting department verifies and approves the invoice for payment.

2. The purchases journal records the buying of merchandise or other items on account.

3. The accounts payable subsidiary ledger, organized in alphabetical order, is not in the same book as Accounts Payable, the controlling account in the general ledger.

4. At the end of the month the total of all creditors' ending balances in the accounts payable subsidiary ledger should equal the ending balance in Accounts Payable, the controlling account in the general ledger.

5. A debit memorandum (issued by the buyer) indicates that the amount owed from a previous purchase is being reduced because some goods were defective or not up to a specific standard and thus were returned or an allowance requested. On receiving the debit memorandum, the seller will issue a credit memorandum.

Learning Unit 10-3

1. All payments of cash (check) are recorded in the cash payments journal.

2. At the end of the month, the schedule of accounts payable, a list of ending amounts owed individual creditors, should equal the ending balance in Accounts Payable, the controlling account in the general ledger.

3. Trade discounts are deductions off the list price that have nothing to do with early payments (cash discounts). Invoice amounts are recorded *after* the trade discount is deducted. Cash discounts are not taken on trade discounts.

KEY TERMS

Accounts payable subsidiary ledger   A book or file that contains in alphabetical order the name of the creditor and amount owed from purchases on account.

Cash payments journal (cash disbursements journal)   A special journal that records all transactions involving the payment of cash.

Controlling account   The account in the general ledger that summarizes or controls a subsidiary ledger. Example: The Accounts Payable account in the general ledger is the controlling account for the accounts payable subsidiary ledger. After postings are complete, it shows the total amount owed from purchases made on account.

Debit memorandum   A memo issued by a purchaser to a seller, indicating that some Purchases Returns and Allowances have occurred and therefore the purchaser now owes less money on account.

F.O.B.   Free on board, which means without shipping charge either to the buyer or seller up to or from a specified location. In the view of one or the other, the shipment is *free* on board the carrier.

F.O.B. destination   *Seller* pays or is responsible for the cost of freight to purchaser's location or destination.

F.O.B. shipping point   *Purchaser* pays or is responsible for the shipping costs from seller's shipping point to purchaser's location.

Invoice approval form   Used by the accounting department in checking the invoice and finally approving it for recording and payment.

Purchase invoice   The seller's sales invoice, which is sent to the purchaser.

Purchase order   A form used in business to place an order for the buying of goods from a seller.

Purchase requisition   A form used within a business by the requesting department asking the purchasing department of the business to buy specific goods.

Purchases   Merchandise for resale. It is a cost.

Purchases Discount   A contra-cost account in the general ledger that records discounts offered by suppliers of merchandise for prompt payment of purchases by buyers.

Purchases journal A multicolumn special journal that records the buying of merchandise or other items on account.

Purchases Returns and Allowances A contra-cost account in the ledger that records the amount of defective or unacceptable merchandise returned to suppliers and/or price reductions given for defective items.

Receiving report A business form used to notify the appropriate people of the ordered goods received along with the quantities and specific condition of the goods.

QUESTIONS, MINI EXERCISES, EXERCISES, AND PROBLEMS

Discussion Questions

1. Explain how net purchases is calculated.
2. What is the normal balance of Purchases Discount?
3. What is a contra-cost?
4. Explain the difference between F.O.B. shipping point and F.O.B. destination.
5. F.O.B. destination means that title to the goods will switch to the buyer when goods are shipped. Agree or disagree. Why?
6. What is the normal balance of each creditor in the accounts payable subsidiary ledger?
7. Why doesn't the balance of the controlling account, Accounts Payable, equal the sum of the accounts payable subsidiary ledger during the month?
8. What is the relationship between a purchase requisition and a purchase order?
9. What purpose could a typical invoice approval form serve?
10. Explain the difference between merchandise and equipment.
11. Why would the purchaser issue a debit memorandum?
12. Explain the relationship between a purchases journal and a cash payments journal.
13. Explain why a trade discount is not a cash discount.

Mini Exercises

(The forms you need are on page 326 of the *Study Guide and Working Papers.*)

Overview

1. Complete the following table:

To the Seller		To the Buyer
Sales	↔	a. _____
Sales Returns and Allowances	↔	b. _____
Sales discount	↔	c. _____
Sales Journal	↔	d. _____
Cash Receipts Journal	↔	e. _____
Credit memorandum	↔	f. _____
Schedule of Accounts Receivable	↔	g. _____
Accounts receivable subsidiary ledger	↔	h. _____

Purchase of Merchandise or Other Items on Account

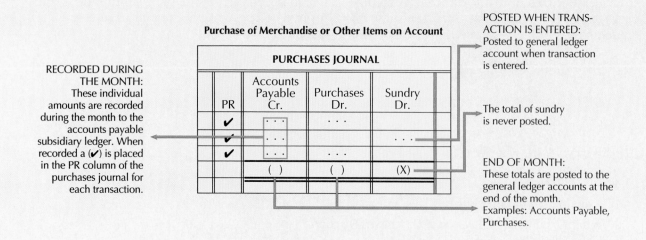

RECORDED DURING THE MONTH: These individual amounts are recorded during the month to the accounts payable subsidiary ledger. When recorded a (✔) is placed in the PR column of the purchases journal for each transaction.

POSTED WHEN TRANSACTION IS ENTERED: Posted to general ledger account when transaction is entered.

The total of sundry is never posted.

END OF MONTH: These totals are posted to the general ledger accounts at the end of the month. Examples: Accounts Payable, Purchases.

Issuing a Debit Memo (or Receiving a Credit Memo)

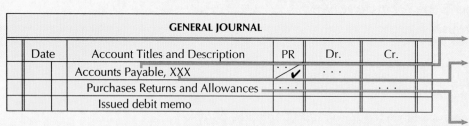

POSTED AND RECORDED WHEN TRANSACTION IS ENTERED
Two postings and one recording:
1. Posted to Accounts Payable in the general ledger.
2. Recorded to XXX in the accounts payable subsidiary ledger. A (✔) indicates recording to the accounts payable subsidiary ledger is complete.
3. Posted to Purchases Returns and Allowances in general ledger.

Outward Flow of Cash

Post to general ledger when transaction entered.

No posting needed during month, since totals of purchases and cash are posted at end of month.

The total of sundry is never posted.

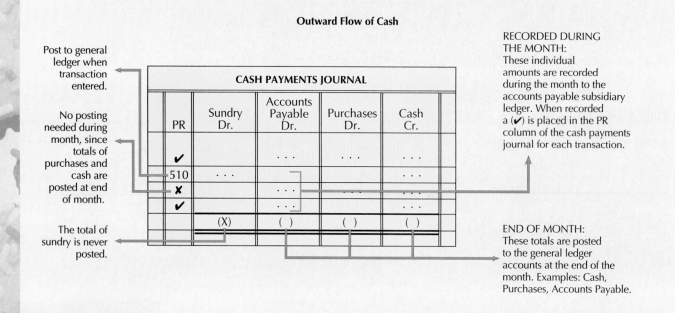

RECORDED DURING THE MONTH: These individual amounts are recorded during the month to the accounts payable subsidiary ledger. When recorded a (✔) is placed in the PR column of the cash payments journal for each transaction.

END OF MONTH: These totals are posted to the general ledger accounts at the end of the month. Examples: Cash, Purchases, Accounts Payable.

2. Complete the following table:

	Category	↑	↓	Temporary or Permanent
Purchases **Purchases Returns and Allowances** **Purchases Discount**				

Calculating Net Purchases

3. Calculate Net Purchases from the following: Purchases, $8; Purchases Returns and Allowances, $3; Purchases Discounts, $1.

Purchases Journal, General Journal, Recording, and Posting

4. Match the following to the three journal entries (more than one number can be used).

1.	Journalized into Purchases Journal.
2.	Record immediately to subsidiary ledger.
3.	Post totals from Purchases Journal (except Sundry total) at end of month to general ledger.
4.	Journalized in general journal.
5.	Record and post immediately to subsidiary and general ledgers.

    a. Bought merchandise on account from Ryan.com., invoice no. 12, $40.

    b. Bought equipment on account from Jone Co., invoice no. 13, $75.

    c. Issued debit memo no. 1 to Ryan.com for merchandise returned, $7, from invoice no. 12.

Recording Transactions in Special Journals

5. Indicate in which journal each transaction will be journalized:

    1. SJ   **4.** CPJ

    2. PJ   **5.** GJ

    3. CRJ

    _____ **a.** Issued credit memo no. 2, $29.
    _____ **b.** Cash sales, $180.
    _____ **c.** Received check from Blue Co., $50 less 3 percent discount.
    _____ **d.** Bought merchandise on account from Mel Co., $35, invoice no. 20, terms 1/10, n/30.
    _____ **e.** Cash Purchase, $15.
    _____ **f.** Issued debit memo to Mel Co., $15, for merchandise returned from invoice no. 20.

6. From the following prepare a schedule of Accounts Payable for Web.com for May 31, 200X:

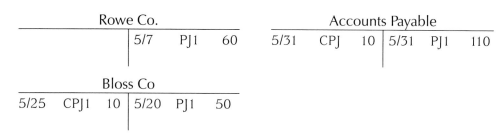

Accounts Payable Subsidiary Ledger

Rowe Co.

			5/7	PJ1	60

General Ledger

Accounts Payable

5/31	CPJ	10	5/31	PJ1	110

Bloss Co

5/25	CPJ1	10	5/20	PJ1	50

Exercises

(The forms you need are on pages 327–329 of the *Study Guide and Working Papers*.)

10-1. From the accompanying purchases journal, record to the accounts payable subsidiary ledger and post to general ledger accounts as appropriate.

PURCHASES JOURNAL

Page 1

Date	Account Credited	Date of Invoice	Terms	Post Ref.	Accounts Payable Credit	Purchases Debit	Sundry-Dr. Account	PR	Amount
200X June 3	Rey.com	May 3	1/10, n/30		8 0 0 00	8 0 0 00			
4	Lane.com	May 4	n/10, EOM		9 0 0 00	9 0 0 00			
8	Sail.com	May 8			4 0 0 00		Equipment		4 0 0 00

> Recording to the accounts payable subsidiary ledger and posting to the general ledger from a purchases journal.

Partial Accounts Payable Subsidiary Ledger

Rey.com

Lane.com

Sail.com

Partial General Ledger

Equipment 120

Accounts Payable 210

Purchases 510

> Journalizing, recording, and posting a debit memorandum.

10-2. On July 10, 200X, Aster Co. issued debit memorandum no. 1 for $400 to Reel Co. for merchandise returned from invoice no. 312. Your task is to journalize, record, and post this transaction as appropriate. Use the same account numbers as found in the text for Art's Wholesale Clothing Company. The general journal is page 1.

> Journalizing, recording, and posting a cash payments journal.

10-3. Journalize, record, and post when appropriate the following transactions into the cash payments journal (p. 2) for Morgan's Clothing. Use the same headings as found in the text (p. 378). All purchases discounts are 2/10, n/30.

ACCOUNTS PAYABLE SUBSIDIARY LEDGER

Name	Balance	Invoice No.
A. James	$1,000	522
B. Foss	400	488
J. Ranch	900	562
B. Swanson	100	821

PARTIAL GENERAL LEDGER

Account	Balance
Cash 110	$3,000
Accounts Payable 210	2,400
Purchases Discount 511	
Advertising Expense 610	

200X

Apr. 1 Issued check no. 20 to A. James Company in payment of its March 28 invoice no. 522.

8 Issued check no. 21 to Flott Advertising in payment of its advertising bill, $100, no discount.

15 Issued check no. 22 to B. Foss in payment of its March 25 invoice no. 488.

10-4. From Exercise 10-3, prepare a schedule of accounts payable and verify that the total of the schedule equals the amount in the controlling account.

> Schedule of accounts payable.

10-5. Record the following transaction in a transaction analysis chart for the buyer: Bought merchandise for $9,000 on account. Shipping terms were F.O.B. destination. The cost of shipping was $500.

> F.O.B. destination.

10-6. Angie Rase bought merchandise with a list price of $4,000. Angie was entitled to a 30 percent trade discount as well as a 3 percent cash discount. What was Angie's actual cost of buying this merchandise after the cash discount?

> Trade and cash discounts.

Group A Problems

(The forms you need are on pages 330–351 of the *Study Guide and Working Papers*.)

10A-1. Abby Kim recently opened Skates.com. As the bookkeeper of her company, please journalize, record, and post when appropriate the following transactions (account numbers are Store Supplies, 115; Store Equipment, 121; Accounts Payable, 210; Purchases, 510):

> Journalizing, recording, and posting a purchases journal.

200X

June 4 Bought $700 of merchandise on account from Mail.com., invoice no. 442, dated June 5, terms 2/10, n/30.

5 Bought $4,000 of store equipment from Norton Co., invoice no. 502, dated June 6.

8 Bought $1,400 of merchandise on account from Rolo Co., invoice no. 401, dated June 9, terms 2/10, n/30.

14 Bought $900 of store supplies on account from Mail.com., invoice no. 419, dated June 14.

> *Check Figure:*
> Total of Purchases Column $2,100

10A-2. Mabel's Natural Food Store uses a purchases journal (p. 10) and a general journal (p. 2) to record the following transactions (continued from April):

200X

May 8 Purchased $600 of merchandise on account from Aton Co., invoice no. 400, dated May 9, terms 2/10, n/60.

10 Purchased $1,200 of merchandise on account from Broward Co., invoice no. 420, dated May 11, terms 2/10, n/60.

12 Purchased $500 of store supplies on account from Midden Co., invoice no. 510, dated May 13.

14 Issued debit memo no. 8 to Aton Co. for merchandise returned, $400, from invoice no. 400.

17 Purchased $560 of office equipment on account from Relar Co., invoice no. 810, dated May 18.

24 Purchased $650 of additional store supplies on account from Midden Co., invoice no. 516, dated May 25, terms 2/10, n/30.

> Journalizing, recording, and posting a purchases journal as well as recording debit memorandum and preparing a schedule of accounts payable.

> *Check Figure:*
> Total Schedule of Accounts Payable $5,810

The food store has decided to keep a separate column for the purchases of supplies in the purchases journal. Your tasks are to

1. Journalize the transactions.
2. Post and record as appropriate.
3. Prepare a schedule of accounts payable.

**ACCOUNTS PAYABLE
SUBSIDIARY LEDGER**

Name	Balance
Aton Co.	$ 400
Broward Co.	600
Midden Co.	1,200
Relar Co.	500

PARTIAL GENERAL LEDGER

Account	Number	Balance
Store Supplies	110	$ —
Office Equipment	120	—
Accounts Payable	210	2,700
Purchases	510	16,000
Purchases Returns and Allowances	512	—

Journalizing, recording, and posting a cash payments journal. Preparing a schedule of accounts payable.

Check Figure:
Total of Schedule of
Accounts Payable $1,900

10A-3. Wendy Jones operates a wholesale computer center. All transactions requiring the payment of cash are recorded in the cash payments journal (p. 5). The account balances as of May 1, 200X, are as follows:

**ACCOUNTS PAYABLE
SUBSIDIARY LEDGER**

Name	Balance
Alvin Co.	$1,200
Henry Co.	600
Soy Co.	800
Xon Co.	1,400

PARTIAL GENERAL LEDGER

Account	Number	Balance
Cash	110	$17,000
Delivery Truck	150	—
Accounts Payable	210	4,000
Computer Purchases	510	—
Computer Purchases Discount	511	—
Rent Expense	610	—
Utilities Expense	620	—

Your tasks are to

1. Journalize the following transactions.
2. Record to the accounts payable subsidiary ledger and post to general ledger as appropriate.
3. Prepare a schedule of accounts payable.

200X
May

1 Paid half the amount owed Henry Co. from previous purchases of appliances on account, less a 2 percent purchases discount, check no. 21.

3 Bought a delivery truck for $8,000 cash, check no. 22, payable to Bill Ring Co.

6	Bought computer merchandise from Lectro Co., check no. 23, $2,900.
18	Bought additional computer merchandise from Pulse Co., check no. 24, $800.
24	Paid Xon Co. the amount owed less a 2 percent purchases discount, check no. 25.
28	Paid rent expense to King's Realty Trust, check no. 26, $2,000.
29	Paid utilities expense to Stone Utility Co., check no. 27, $300.
30	Paid half the amount owed Soy Co., no discount, check no. 28.

10A-4. Abby Ellen opened Abby's Toy House. As her newly hired accountant, your tasks are to

1. Journalize the transactions for the month of March.
2. Record to subsidiary ledgers and post to general ledger as appropriate.
3. Total and rule the journals.
4. Prepare a schedule of accounts receivable and a schedule of accounts payable.

The following is the partial chart of accounts for Abby's Toy House:

> Comprehensive Problem: All special journals and the general journal. Schedule of accounts payable and accounts receivable.

Abby's Toy House Chart of Accounts

Assets
110   Cash
112   Accounts Receivable
114   Prepaid Rent
121   Delivery Truck

Liabilities
210   Accounts Payable

Owner's Equity
310   A. Ellen, Capital

Revenue
410   Toy Sales
412   Sales Returns and Allowances
414   Sales Discounts

Cost of Goods
510   Toy Purchases
512   Purchases Returns and Allowances
514   Purchases Discount

Expenses
610   Salaries Expense
612   Cleaning Expense

> Check Figures: Total of Schedule of Accounts Receivable $7,600
> Total of Schedule of Accounts Payable $9,000

200X
Mar.

1	Abby Ellen invested $8,000 in the toy store.
1	Paid three months' rent in advance, check no. 1, $3,000.
1	Purchased merchandise from Earl Miller Company on account, $4,000, invoice no. 410, dated March 2, terms 2/10, n/30.
3	Sold merchandise to Bill Burton on account, $1,000, invoice no. 1, terms 2/10, n/30.
6	Sold merchandise to Jim Rex on account, $700, invoice no. 2, terms 2/10, n/30.
8	Purchased merchandise from Earl Miller Co. on account, $1,200, invoice no. 415, dated March 9, terms 2/10, n/30.
9	Sold merchandise to Bill Burton on account, $600, invoice no. 3, terms 2/10, n/30.
9	Paid cleaning service, check no. 2, $300.
10	Jim Rex returned merchandise that cost $300 to Abby's Toy House. Abby issued credit memorandum no. 1 to Jim Rex for $300.
10	Purchased merchandise from Minnie Katz on account, $4,000, invoice no. 311, dated March 11, terms 1/15, n/60.
12	Paid Earl Miller Co. invoice no. 410, dated March 2, check no. 3.
13	Sold $1,300 of toy merchandise for cash.
13	Paid salaries, $600, check no. 4.

14 Returned merchandise to Minnie Katz in the amount of $1,000. Abby's Toy House issued debit memorandum no. 1 to Minnie Katz.

15 Sold merchandise for $4,000 cash.

16 Received payment from Jim Rex, invoice no. 2 (less returned merchandise) less discount.

16 Bill Burton paid invoice no. 1.

16 Sold toy merchandise to Amy Rose on account, $4,000, invoice no. 4, terms 2/10, n/30.

20 Purchased delivery truck on account from Sam Katz Garage, $3,000, invoice no. 111, dated March 21 (no discount).

22 Sold to Bill Burton merchandise on account, $900, invoice no. 5, terms 2/10, n/30.

23 Paid Minnie Katz balance owed, check no. 5.

24 Sold toy merchandise on account to Amy Rose, $1,100, invoice no. 6, terms 2/10, n/30.

25 Purchased toy merchandise, $600, check no. 6.

26 Purchased toy merchandise from Woody Smith on account, $4,800, invoice no. 211, dated March 27, terms 2/10, n/30.

28 Bill Burton paid invoice no. 5, dated March 22.

28 Amy Rose paid invoice no. 6, dated March 24.

28 Abby invested an additional $5,000 in the business.

28 Purchased merchandise from Earl Miller Co., $1,400, invoice no. 436, dated March 29, terms 2/10, n/30.

30 Paid Earl Miller Co. invoice no. 436, check no. 7.

30 Sold merchandise to Bonnie Flow Company on account, $3,000, invoice no. 7, terms 2/10, n/30.

Group B Problems

(The forms you need are on pages 330–351 of the *Study Guide and Working Papers*.)

Journalizing, recording, and posting a purchases journal.

Check Figure: Total of Purchases Column $2,200

10B-1. From the following transactions of Abby Kim's Skate.com, journalize in the purchases journal and record and post as appropriate:

200X
June 4 Bought merchandise on account from Rolo Co., invoice no. 400, dated June 5, $1,800, terms 2/10, n/30.

5 Bought store equipment from Norton Co., invoice no. 518, dated June 6, $6,000.

8 Bought merchandise on account from Mail.com, invoice no. 411, dated June 5, $400, terms 2/10, n/30.

14 Bought store supplies on account from Mail.com, invoice no. 415, dated June 13, $1,200.

Journalizing, recording, and posting a purchases journal as well as recording the issuing of a debit memorandum and preparing a schedule of accounts payable.

Check Figure: Total of Schedule of Accounts Payable $6,000

10B-2. As the accountant of Mabel's Natural Food Store (1) journalize the following transactions into the purchases (p. 10) or general journal (p. 2), (2) record and post as appropriate, and (3) prepare a schedule of accounts payable. Beginning balances are in the *Study Guide and Working Papers.*

200X
May 8 Purchased merchandise on account from Broward Co., invoice no. 420, dated May 9, $500, terms 2/10, n/60.

10 Purchased merchandise on account from Aton Co., invoice no. 400, dated May 11, $900, terms 2/10, n/60.

12 Purchased store supplies on account from Midden Co., invoice no. 510, dated May 13, $700.

14 Issued debit memo no. 7 to Aton Co. for merchandise returned, $400, from invoice no. 400.

17 Purchased office equipment on account from Relar Co., invoice no. 810, dated May 18, $750.

24 Purchased additional store supplies on account from Midden Co., invoice no. 516, dated May 25, $850.

10B-3. Wendy Jones has hired you as her bookkeeper to record the following transactions in the cash payments journal. She would like you to record and post as appropriate and supply her with a schedule of accounts payable. (Beginning balances are in your workbook or Problem 10A-3, p. 394 in the text.)

Journalizing, recording, and posting a cash payments journal. Preparing a schedule of accounts payable.

200X
May

1 Bought a delivery truck for $8,000 cash, check no. 21, payable to Randy Rosse Co.

3 Paid half the amount owed Henry Co. from previous purchases of computer merchandise on account, less a 5 percent purchases discount, check no. 22.

6 Bought computer merchandise from Jane Co. for $900 cash, check no. 23.

18 Bought additional computer merchandise from Jane Co., check no. 24, $1,000.

24 Paid Xon Co. the amount owed less a 5 percent purchases discount, check no. 25.

28 Paid rent expense to Regan Realty Trust, check no. 26, $3,000.

29 Paid half the amount owed Soy Co., no discount, check no. 27.

30 Paid utilities expense to French Utility, check no. 28, $425.

Check Figure:
Total of Schedule of
Accounts Payable $1,900

10B-4. As the new accountant for Abby's Toy House, your tasks are to

1. Journalize the transactions for the month of March.

2. Record to subsidiary ledgers and post to general ledger as appropriate.

3. Total and rule the journals.

4. Prepare a schedule of accounts receivable and a schedule of accounts payable.

(Use the same chart of accounts as in Problem 10A-4, p. 395. Your *Study Guide and Working Papers* has all the forms you need to complete this problem.)

Check Figures: Total of
Schedule of Accounts
Receivable $9,900
Total of Schedule of
Accounts Payable $9,200

200X
Mar.

1 Abby invested $4,000 in the new toy store.

1 Paid two months' rent in advance, check no. 1, $1,000.

1 Purchased merchandise from Earl Miller Company, invoice no. 410, dated March 2, $6,000, terms 2/10, n/30.

3 Sold merchandise to Bill Burton on account, $1,600, invoice no. 1, terms 2/10, n/30.

6 Sold merchandise to Jim Rex on account, $800, invoice no. 2, terms 2/10, n/30.

8 Purchased merchandise from Earl Miller Company, $800, invoice no. 415, dated March 9, terms 2/10, n/30.

9 Sold merchandise to Bill Burton on account, $700, invoice no. 3, terms 2/10, n/30.

9 Paid cleaning service, $400, check no. 2.

10 Jim Rex returned merchandise that cost $200 to Abby. Abby issued credit memorandum no. 1 to Jim Rex for $200.

10 Purchased merchandise from Minnie Katz, $7,000, invoice no. 311, dated March 11, terms 1/15, n/60.

12 Paid Earl Miller Co. invoice no. 410, dated March 2, check no. 3.

13 Sold $1,500 of toy merchandise for cash.

13 Paid salaries, $700, check no. 4.

14	Returned merchandise to Minnie Katz in the amount of $500. Abby issued debit memorandum no. 1 to Minnie Katz.
15	Sold merchandise for cash, $4,800.
16	Received payment from Jim Rex for invoice no. 2 (less returned merchandise) less discount.
16	Bill Burton paid invoice no. 1.
16	Sold toy merchandise to Amy Rose on account, $6,000, invoice no. 4, terms 2/10, n/30.
20	Purchased delivery truck on account from Sam Katz Garage, $2,500, invoice no. 111, dated March 21 (no discount).
22	Sold to Bill Burton merchandise on account, $2,000, invoice no. 5, terms 2/10, n/30.
23	Paid Minnie Katz balance owed, check no. 5.
24	Sold toy merchandise on account to Amy Rose, $2,000, invoice no. 6, terms 2/10, n/30.
25	Purchased toy merchandise, $800, check no. 6.
26	Purchased toy merchandise from Woody Smith on account, $5,900, invoice no. 211, dated March 27, terms 2/10, n/30.
28	Bill Burton paid invoice no. 5, dated March 22.
28	Amy Rose paid invoice no. 6, dated March 24.
28	Abby invested an additional $3,000 in the business.
28	Purchased merchandise from Earl Miller Co., $4,200, invoice no. 436, dated March 29, terms 2/10, n/30.
30	Paid Earl Miller Co. invoice no. 436, check no. 7.
30	Sold merchandise to Bonnie Flow Company on account, $3,200, invoice no. 7, terms 2/10, n/30.

REAL-WORLD APPLICATIONS

10R-1.

Angie Co. bought merchandise for $1,000 with credit terms of 2/10, n/30. Owing to the bookkeeper's incompetence, the 2 percent cash discount was missed. The bookkeeper told Pete Angie, the owner, not to get excited. After all, it was a $20 discount that was missed, not hundreds of dollars. Could you please act as Mr. Angie's assistant and show the bookkeeper that his $20 represents a sizable equivalent interest cost? In your calculation assume a 360-day year. Make some written recommendations so that this situation will not happen again.

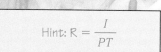

Hint: $R = \dfrac{I}{PT}$

10R-2.

Jeff Ryan completed an Accounting I course and was recently hired as the bookkeeper of Spring Co. The special journals have not been posted, nor are *Dr.* and *Cr.* used on the column headings. Please assist Jeff by marking the Dr. and Cr. headings as well as setting up and posting to the general ledger and recording to the subsidiary ledger. (Only post or record the amounts, because no chart of accounts is provided.) Make some written recommendations on how a new computer system may lessen the need for posting.

SALES JOURNAL		
Account	PR	
Blue Co.		4 8 0 0 00
Jon Co.		5 6 0 0 00
Roff Co.		6 4 0 0 00
Totals		16 8 0 0 00

PURCHASES JOURNAL		
Account	PR	
Ralph Co.		4 0 0 0 00
Sos Co.		6 0 0 0 00
Jingle Co.		8 0 0 0 00
Totals		18 0 0 0 00

GENERAL JOURNAL			
	Sales Returns and Allowances	1 6 0 0 00	
	Accounts Receivable, Jon Co.		1 6 0 0 00
	Customer returned merchandise		
	Accounts Payable, Jingle Co.	8 0 0 00	
	Purchases, Returns, and Allowances		8 0 0 00
	Returned defective merchandise		

CASH RECEIPTS JOURNAL*						
Cash Dr.	Sales Discount Dr.	Accounts Receivable Cr.	Sales Cr.	Sundry-Dr.		
				Account Name	PR	Amount Cr.
4 7 0 4 00	9 6 00	4 8 0 0 00		Blue Co.		
1 9 6 0 00	4 0 00	2 0 0 0 00		Jon Co.		
5 0 0 0 00			5 0 0 0 00	Sales		
20 0 0 0 00				Notes Payable		20 0 0 0 00
3 1 3 6 00	6 4 00	3 2 0 0 00		Roff Co.		
4 6 0 0 00			4 6 0 0 00	Sales		
39 4 0 0 00	2 0 0 00	10 0 0 0 00	9 6 0 0 00	Totals		20 0 0 0 00

* *Note:* This company's set of columns differs from that shown in the chapter.

CASH PAYMENTS JOURNAL					
Account	PR	Sundry	Accounts Payable	Purchases Discount	Cash
Sos Co.			3 0 0 0 00	6 0 00	2 9 4 0 00
Salaries Expense		2 6 0 0 00			2 6 0 0 00
Jingle Co.			4 0 0 0 00	8 0 00	3 9 2 0 00
Salaries Expense		2 6 0 0 00			2 6 0 0 00
Totals		5 2 0 0 00	7 0 0 0 00	1 4 0 00	12 0 6 0 00

YOU make the call

Critical Thinking/Ethical Case

10R-3.

Spring Co. bought merchandise from All Co. with terms 2/10, n/30. Joanne Ring, the bookkeeper, forgot to pay the bill within the first 10 days. She went to Mel Ryan, Head Accountant, who told her to backdate the check so that it looked like the bill was paid within the discount period. Joanne told Mel that she thought they could get away with it. Should Joanne and Mel backdate the check to take advantage of the discount? You make the call. Write down your specific recommendations to Joanne.

INTERNET EXERCISES

EX-1. [www.llbean.com] Each holiday season an extraordinary amount of merchandise is moved from online retailers like L. L. Bean from their warehouses to their customers. In the previous chapter you learned about the handling of sales and cash receipts transactions. In this chapter you learned about the other side of those transactions, Purchases and Cash Payments, using the related special journals.

Retailers wish to know their profits by product line or by department. From your examination of this website, suggest several columns which might appear in a Purchases Journal. For each suggestion state whether it would be a "debit" or "credit" column.

EX-2. [www.amazon.com] When merchandise for resale is paid for by the seller, the transaction is recorded in the Cash Payments Journal. At the same time an entry is made on the Subsidiary Ledger of the vendor. When all of the transactions are journalized and posted a Schedule of Accounts Payable may be prepared. In a manual accounting system individual ledger cards for vendors can become misplaced. If your coworker were to find a subsidiary ledger card but did not know whether to return it to Accounts Payable or the Accounts Receivable department, how could you assist in getting it to the right place? In which columns of the ledger card could you examine to answer this dilemma?

CONTINUING PROBLEM

Tony was very happy to see the progress made by using the specialized journals. For the month of February he will add two more journals (purchases journal and the cash payments journal). To assist you in recording the transactions, the following is an updated schedule of accounts payable as of January 31, 200X.

SCHEDULE OF ACCOUNTS PAYABLE

Office Depot	$ 50
System Design Furniture	1,400
Pac Bell	150
Multi Systems, Inc.	450
Total Accounts Payable	$2,050

Assignment

(See pages 356–361 in the *Study Guide and Working Papers*.)

1. Journalize the transactions in the appropriate journals (cash payments, purchase journal, or general journal).
2. Record in the accounts payable subsidiary ledger and post to the general ledger as appropriate. A partial general ledger is included in the Study Guide and Working Papers.
3. Prepare a schedule of accounts payable as of February 28, 200X.

The transactions for the month of February are as follows:

200X

Feb.
1	Prepaid the rent for the months of February, March, and April, $1,200, check no. 2585.
4	Bought merchandise on account from Multi Systems, Inc., purchase order no. 4010, $450; terms are 3/10, n/30.
8	Bought office supplies on account from Office Depot, purchase order no. 4011, $250; terms are n/30.
9	Purchased merchandise on account from Computer Connection, purchase order no. 4012, $500; terms are 1/30, n/60.
15	Paid purchase order no. 4010 in full to Multi Systems, Inc.; check no. 2586.
21	Issued debit memorandum no. 10 to Computer Connection for merchandise returned from purchase order no. 4012, $100.
27	Paid for office supplies, $50, check no. 2587.

What Special Journals Would Look Like in a Perpetual Accounting System

A SALES JOURNAL UNDER A PERPETUAL SYSTEM

ART'S WHOLESALE CLOTHING COMPANY
SALES JOURNAL

Page 1

Date	Account Debited	Terms	Invoice No.	Post Ref.	Dr. Acc. Rec Cr. Sales	Cost of Goods Sold Dr. Merchandise Inventory Cr.
200X Apr. 3	Hal's Clothing	2/10, n/30	1	✔	8 0 0 00	5 6 0 00
6	Bevans Company	2/10, n/30	2	✔	1 6 0 0 00	1 1 2 0 00
18	Roe Company	2/10, n/30	3	✔	2 0 0 0 00	1 4 0 0 00
24	Roe Company	2/10, n/30	4	✔	5 0 0 00	3 5 0 00
28	Mel's Dept. Store	2/10, n/30	5	✔	9 0 0 00	6 3 0 00
29	Mel's Dept. Store	2/10, n/30	6	✔	7 0 0 00	4 9 0 00
30					6 5 0 0 00	4 5 5 0 00
					(113) (411)	(510) (114)

What's new:

In journal: New columns for cost of goods sold (Dr.) and inventory (Cr.). Each time a charge sale is earned, the cost of goods sold increases and the amount of inventory at cost is reduced.

In general ledger: New ledger accounts for inventory and cost of goods sold.

Example On April 3, Art's Wholesale sold Hal's Clothing $800 of merchandise on account. This sale cost Art $560 to bring this merchandise into the store.

A CASH RECEIPTS JOURNAL UNDER A PERPETUAL SYSTEM

					ART'S WHOLESALE CLOTHING COMPANY CASH RECEIPTS JOURNAL			Page 1
Date	Cash Dr.	Sales Discount Dr.	Accounts Receivable Cr.	Sales Cr.	Sundry Account Name	Post Ref.	Amount Cr.	Costs of Goods Sold Dr. Merchandise Inventory Cr.
200X Apr. 1	8000 00				Art Newner, Capital	311	8000 00	
4	784 00	16 00	800 00		Hal's Clothing	✔		
15	900 00			900 00	Cash Sales	x		630 00
16	980 00	20 00	1000 00		Bevans Company	✔		
22	1960 00	40 00	2000 00		Roe Company	✔		
27	500 00				Store Equipment	121	500 00	
30	1200 00			1200 00	Cash Sales	x		840 00
	14324 00	76 00	3800 00	2100 00			8500 00	1470 00
	(111)	(413)	(113)	(411)			(X)	(510) (114)

What's new:

In journal: New columns for cost of goods sold (Dr.) and inventory (Cr.). Each time a cash sale is earned, the cost of goods sold increases and the amount of inventory at cost is reduced.

In general ledger: New ledger accounts for inventory and cost of goods sold.

Example: On April 15, Art's Wholesale made cash sales for $900. These sales cost Art $630 to bring them into the store.

A PURCHASES JOURNAL UNDER A PERPETUAL SYSTEM

								Sundry–Dr.		
								ART'S WHOLESALE CLOTHING COMPANY PURCHASES JOURNAL		
Date	Account Credited	Date of Invoice	Inv. No.	Terms	Post Ref.	Accounts Payable Credits	Merchandise Inventory Debit	Account	Post Ref.	Amount
200X Apr. 3	Abby Blake Company	April 3	228	2/10, n/60	✔	5050 00	5000 00	Freight-In	514	50 00
4	Joe Francis Company	April 5	388		✔	4000 00		Equip.	121	4000 00
6	Thorpe Company	April 6	415	1/10, n/30	✔	800 00	800 00			
7	John Sullivan Company	April 6	516	n/10, EOM*	✔	980 00	980 00			
12	Abby Blake Company	April 13	242	1/10, n/30	✔	600 00	600 00			
25	John Sullivan Company	April 26	612		✔	500 00		Supplies	115	500 00
30						11930 00	7380 00			4550 00
						(211)	(114)			(X)

*End of month dating

What's new:

In journal: The column for purchases is replaced with a column for inventory. The cost of all merchandise bought on account for resale is debited to inventory.

In ledger: New ledger account for inventory.

Example: On April 7, Art's Wholesale bought $980 of merchandise for resale to customers from John Sullivan Company.

A CASH PAYMENTS JOURNAL UNDER A PERPETUAL SYSTEM

ART'S WHOLESALE CLOTHING COMPANY
CASH PAYMENTS JOURNAL

Page 1

Date	Ck. No.	Account Debited	Post Ref.	Sundry Accounts Dr.	Accounts Payable Dr.	Merchandise Inventory Cr.	Cash Cr.
200X Apr. 2	1	Prepaid Insurance	116	900 00			900 00
7	2	Joe Francis Company	✔		400 00		400 00
9	3	Merchandise Inventory	114	800 00			800 00
12	4	Thorpe Company	✔		600 00	6 00	594 00
28	5	Salaries Expense	611	700 00			700 00
30							
				2400 00	4600 00	6 00	6994 00
				(X)	(211)	(114)	(111)

What's new:

In journal: New column for merchandise inventory replaces to purchase inventory replaces the purchase discount column. In the perpetual system, a purchase discount reduces the cost of merchandise inventory.

In general ledger: New ledger account for merchandise inventory.

Example: On April 12, Art's wholesale paid Thorpe Company amount owed less a 1 percent discount.

Computerized Accounting Application for Chapter 10

PART A: Recording Transactions in the Sales, Receipts, Purchases, and Payments Journals

PART B: Computerized Accounting Instructions for Abby's Toy House (Problem 10A-4)

Before starting on this assignment, read and complete the tasks discussed in Parts A, B, and F of the Computerized Accounting appendix at the back of this book and complete the Computerized Accounting Application assignments for Chapter 3, Chapter 4, the Valdez Realty Mini Practice Set (Chapter 5), and the Pete's Market Mini Practice Set (Chapter 8).

PART A: RECORDING TRANSACTIONS IN THE SALES, RECEIPTS, PURCHASES, AND PAYMENTS JOURNALS

The Sales/Invoicing and Receipts features in Peachtree Complete Accounting were designed to work with the accounts receivables and general ledger modules in an integrated fashion. When transactions are recorded in the Sales/Invoicing and Receipts windows, the program automatically posts the customer's account in the accounts receivable subsidiary ledger, records the journal entry, and posts all accounts affected in the general ledger. However, the type of transactions recorded in the Sales/Invoicing and Receipts windows in Peachtree Complete Accounting differ from the types of transactions recorded in these journals in a manual accounting system. An explanation of the differences appears in the following chart:

> Where to Record Sales and Cash Receipts

Name of Computerized Entry Window	Types of Transactions Recorded in Computerized Journal
Sales/Invoicing	Sales of merchandise on account
	Sales returns and allowances
Receipts	Cash sales and payments from credit customers on account

An Aged Receivables report (the computerized version of a schedule of accounts receivable) for The Mars Company appears below (terms of 2/10, n/30 are offered to all credit customers of The Mars Company):

> Computerized Aged Receivables

THE MARS COMPANY: CUSTOMER AGED DETAIL AS AT 3/1/01

	Total	Current	31 to 60	61 to 90	91+
John Dunbar					
909 2/25/01 Invoice	500.00	500.00	—	—	—
Kevin Tucker					
911 2/26/01 Invoice	550.00	550.00	—	—	—
	1,050.00	1,050.00	—	—	—

The Purchases and Payments windows in Peachtree Complete Accounting are designed to work with the accounts payable and general ledger modules in an integrated fashion.

> Where to Record Purchases and Cash Payments

When transactions are recorded in the Purchases and Payments windows, the program automatically posts the vendor's account in the accounts payable subsidiary ledger, records the journal entry, and posts all accounts affected in the general ledger. However, the type of transactions recorded in the Purchases and Payments windows in Peachtree Complete Accounting differ from the types of transactions recorded in these journals in a manual accounting system. An explanation of the differences appears in the following chart:

Name of Computerized Journal	Types of Transactions Recorded in Computerized Journal
Purchases Window	Purchases of merchandise and other items on account
	Purchase returns and allowances
Payments Journal	Cash payments to credit and cash vendors

Aged Payables

An Aged Payables report (the computerized version of a schedule of accounts payable) for The Mars Company appears below:

THE MARS COMPANY: VENDOR AGED DETAIL AS AT 3/1/01

	Total	Current	31 to 60	61 to 90	91+
Laurie Snyder					
567 2/27/01 Invoice	435.00	435.00	—	—	—
Young's Space Simulations					
789 2/25/01 Invoice	112.00	112.00	—	—	—
	547.00	547.00	—	—	—

Open the Company Data Files

1. Click on the Start button. Point to Programs; point to the Peachtree folder and select Peachtree Complete Accounting. Your desktop may have the Peachtree icon allowing for a quicker entrance into the program.

2. Follow the "Open a File" instructions in Part A of the Computerized Accounting appendix at the back of this book to open **Mars Company.**

3. Click on the **Maintain** menu option. Then select **Company Information.** The program will respond by bringing up a dialogue box allowing the user to edit/add information about the company. In the **Company Name** entry field at the end of **Mars Company,** add a dash and your name "**-Student Name**" to the end of the company name. Click on the OK button to return to the Menu Window.

Add Your Name to the company Name

How to Record a Sale on Account

4. On March 1, 2001 sold merchandise to Kevin Tucker on account, $800, invoice #913, terms 2/10, n/30 consisting of the following:

Stock #	Description	Quantity
001	Space Age Lamp	2
002	Solar Clock	5
005	Space Shuttle Model	1

5. Select **Sales/Invoicing** from the **Tasks** menu. Using the magnifying glass next to the **Customer ID** field, select Kevin Tucker by double clicking on his name. You are then moved to the **Invoice #** field. Type in "913". Press the TAB key that then moves you to the **Date** field. It should already reflect Mar 1, 2001

but if not, type in the date or use the calendar to the right of the field to select this date. TAB until you reach the **Quantity** field. Type in "2" and click TAB. This will move you to the **Item** field. Using the pull down menu, select the first item 001 Space Age Lamp by double clicking on it. This moves you to the **Description** field that will automatically fill in with information stored in the Inventory module. In fact, Peachtree will fill in all of the remaining fields as you tab through them until you are back to the **Quantity** field. Enter the remaining items from the previous table in the same manner as the Lamp. Your screen should look like this:

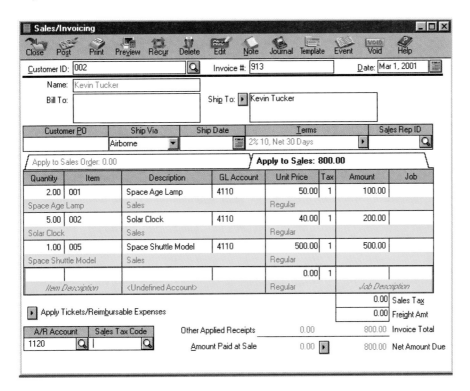

6. Before posting this transaction, you may wish to see how Peachtree will record the transaction. Click on the **Journal** icon on the tool bar. This activates a feature of Peachtree called "Accounting Behind the Screens" and allows the user a look at the workings of the program. It will bring up a Sales Journal showing exactly how it will post this invoice. That is to say, it will show you what accounts will be debited and which accounts credited. Note that Peachtree uses a perpetual inventory system and has created the entries to move the goods sold out of the Inventory account and into the Cost of Sales (COGS) account.

7. Close the Sales Journal window. If you have made an error anywhere on the invoice, simply click in the field containing the error and correct it.

8. After verifying that the journal entry is correct, click on the **Print** icon to print this invoice. You will be asked to select a form. As with the payroll checks, Peachtree supports a variety of blank invoice formats. It will also print its own format on plain paper. Select **Invoice Plain** for your printing. Peachtree will both print and post the transaction in one step. A blank invoice is displayed, ready for additional transactions to be recorded. If you wish to batch print later, you can simply hit the **Post** icon which will store the invoice for printing using the **Select a Report** option under the **Accounts Receivable** reports. We will print all our invoices as we create them.

9. On March 5, 2001 issued credit memorandum #CM14 to Kevin Tucker for the return of one of the lamps he purchased. Peachtree uses the same entry window, **Sales/Invoicing,** to record credits issued to customers. There are two primary differences. One is that quantities will be entered as negative amounts

How to Review a Sales Journal

How to Edit a Sale or Purchase Entry Prior to Posting

How to Print/Post a Sales Entry

How to Record a Credit Memo

and the second is that the printing will be accomplished with a Credit form rather than an invoice form.

10. Select **Sales/Invoicing** from the **Tasks** menu. Using the magnifying glass next to the **Customer ID** field, select Kevin Tucker by double clicking on his name. You are then moved to the **Invoice #** field. Type in "CM14". Press the TAB key that then moves you to the **Date** field. Type in the date "Mar 5, 2001" or use the calendar to the right of the field to select this date. TAB until you reach the **Quantity** field. Type in " − 1" (negative one) and click TAB. This will move you to the **Item** field. Using the pull down menu, select the first item 001 Space Age Lamp by double clicking on it. This moves you to the **Description** field which will automatically fill in with information stored in the Inventory module. In fact, Peachtree will fill in all of the remaining fields as you tab through them until you are back to the **Quantity** field. Your screen should look like this:

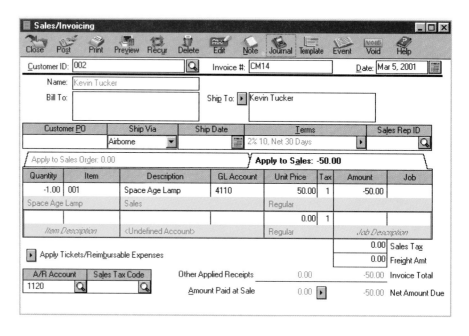

Review the Entry

11. You may again use the **Journal** icon to see what this entry will look like in the Sales Journal.

12. Close the Sales Journal window; then make any editing corrections that may be required.

Print the Credit Memo

13. After verifying that the journal entry is correct, click on the Print icon to print this transaction. Select **Credit Plain** as the form on which to print the credit memo. When you are finished, close the **Sales/Invoicing** box.

How to Record a Cash Receipt from a Credit Customer

14. On March 7, 2001 received check #1634 from Kevin Tucker in the amount of $735 in payment of invoice #913 ($800), dated March 1, less credit memorandum #CM14 ($50), less 2 percent discount ($16 − 1 = $15 net sales discount). Select **Receipts** from the **Tasks** menu. Peachtree will place the current date in the **Deposit ticket ID** field. You can accept this or change it to the date of the transaction. Using the magnifying glass, select customer Kevin Tucker. This will bring up a listing of the invoices and credits currently open in his account. The cursor will automatically move to the **Reference** field. We can enter Kevin's check number, 1634, in this field. We can now select the invoices and/or credits that are included in Kevin's payment. In the column marked **Pay** are small boxes that can be checked by clicking on them with the mouse. This marks the invoices selected for payment with the check received. We will check the boxes at the end of the lines containing invoice #913 and credit memo #CM14 which is associated with this invoice. Note that the field for **Receipt Amount** automatically reflects the amount

of his payment. Please note that if we were receiving cash as the result of a cash sale or for any other reason rather than a payment on account, we would use the **Apply to Revenues** tab instead of the **Apply to Invoices** tab. In that screen, we can use any GL account we like to offset the receipt of the cash. If you recorded this payment on account correctly, your screen should look like this:

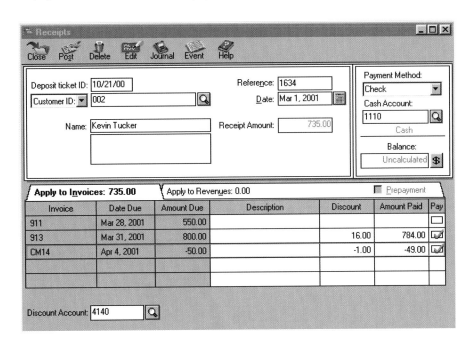

15. As before, we can preview how Peachtree will handle this transaction behind the screens by clicking on the **Journal** icon. This will bring up a Receipts Journal reflecting the accounts that will be affected by this entry.

16. Close the Sales Journal window. If you have made an error anywhere on the invoice, simply click in the field containing the error and correct it.

17. After verifying that the journal entry is correct, click on the **Post** icon to post this transaction. A blank Receipts Journal dialog box is displayed, ready for additional Receipts transactions to be recorded. Close the Receipts dialog box when you are finished.

18. On March 15, 2001 purchased merchandise from Young's Space Simulations on account, $278, invoice #796, terms 2/10, n/30 consisting of the following:

Stock #	Description	Quantity
001	Space Age Lamp	5
003	Martian Landscape Lithograph	5
004	Simulated Moon Rock	9

19. Select **Purchases/Receive Inventory** from the **Tasks** menu. Using the magnifying glass next to the **Customer ID** field, select 002 Young's Space Simulations by double clicking on his name. You are then moved to the **Invoice #** field. Type in "796". Press the TAB key that then moves you to the **Date** field. Type in the date "Mar 15, 2001" or use the calendar to the right of the field to select this date. TAB until you reach the **Quantity** field. Type in "5" and click TAB. This will move you to the **Item** field. Using the pull down menu, select the first item 001 Space Age Lamp by double clicking on it. This moves you to the **Description** field that will automatically fill in with information stored in the Inventory module. In fact, Peachtree will fill in all of the remaining

How to Review the Receipts Journal

How to Post a Receipts Entry

How to Record a Purchase on Account

fields as you tab through them until you are back to the **Quantity** field. Should your Unit Price be different than that brought up by Peachtree, you can easily change the amount rather than tabbing through that field. If we were purchasing something besides merchandise inventory, we would skip over the Quantity and Item fields and fill in the Description, GL Account and Amount fields based on what we purchased and its cost. If you entered our inventory purchase correctly, your screen should look like this:

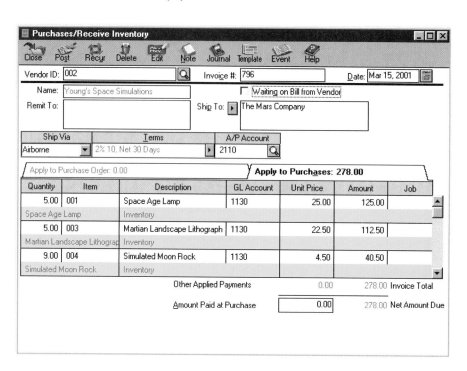

How to Review a Purchases Journal Entry

20. Before posting this transaction, you may wish to see how Peachtree will record the transaction. Click on the **Journal** icon on the tool bar. This activates a feature of Peachtree called "Accounting Behind the Screens" and allows the user a look at the workings of the program. It will bring up a Purchases Journal showing exactly how it will post this invoice. That is to say, it will show you what accounts will be debited and which accounts credited.

21. Close the Purchases Journal window. If you have made an error anywhere on the invoice, simply click in the field containing the error and correct it.

How to Post a Purchases Journal Entry

22. After verifying that the journal entry is correct, click on the **Post** icon to post this transaction. A blank Purchases screen is displayed, ready for additional Purchase transactions to be recorded.

How to Record a Debit Memo

23. On March 17, 2001 returned two of the Space Age Lamps to Young's Space Simulations with a value of $50. Issued debit memo #DM27. Select **Purchases/Receive Inventory** from the **Tasks** menu. Using the magnifying glass next to the **Customer ID** field, select 002 Young's Space Simulations by double clicking on his name. You are then moved to the **Invoice #** field. Type in "DM27". Press the TAB key that then moves you to the **Date** field. Type in the date "Mar 17, 2001" or use the calendar to the right of the field to select this date. TAB until you reach the **Quantity** field. Type in "− 2" (negative two) and click TAB. This will move you to the **Item** field. Using the pull down menu, select the first item 001 Space Age Lamp by double clicking on it. This moves you to the **Description** field that will automatically fill in with information stored in the Inventory module. In fact, Peachtree will fill in all of the remaining fields as you tab through them until you are back to the **Quantity** field. Your screen should look like this:

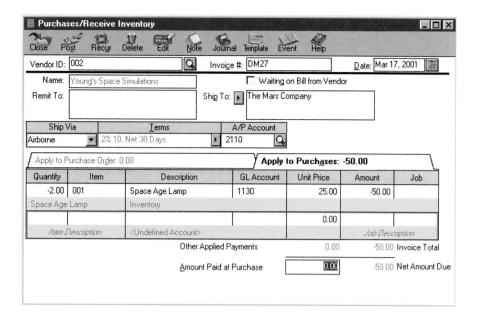

24. Before posting this transaction, you may wish to see how Peachtree will record the transaction. Click on the **Journal** icon on the tool bar. This activates a feature of Peachtree called "Accounting Behind the Screens" and allows the user a look at the workings of the program. It will bring up a Purchases Journal showing exactly how it will post this invoice. That is to say, it will show you what accounts will be debited and which accounts credited.

How to Review a Purchases Journal Entry

25. Close the Purchases Journal window. If you have made an error anywhere on the invoice, simply click in the field containing the error and correct it.

26. After verifying that the journal entry is correct, click on the **Post** icon to post this transaction; then close the Purchases window.

Post the Entry

27. On March 25, 2001 issued check #437 to Young's Space Simulations in the amount of $223.44 in payment of invoice #796 ($278), dated March 15, less debit memorandum #27 ($50), less 2 percent discount ($5.56 − 1.00 = $4.56 net purchases discount). Select **Payments** from the **Tasks** menu. Using the magnifying glass, select vendor Young's Space Simulations. This will bring up a listing of the invoices and credits currently open in this account. TAB to the **Date** field and type in "March 25, 2001" or use the calendar to select this date. In the column marked **Pay** are small boxes that can be checked by clicking on them with the mouse. This marks the invoices selected for payment with the check you are creating. We will check the boxes at the end of the lines containing invoice #796 and debit memo #DM27 which is associated with this invoice. If we need to make a payment for something that is not already recorded in our accounts payable, we can use the **Apply to Expenses** tab instead of the **Apply to Invoices** tab that we are using. We can write a check for any purpose, including prepaid expenses, using this feature. With our payment, note that the field for the amount of the check automatically reflects the amount of this payment. Also note that the **Check Number** field is left blank. This field is used only to enter a check that has already been written or printed. We will enter the check number when we print the check. Your screen should look like the following:

How to Record a Cash Payment to a Credit Vendor

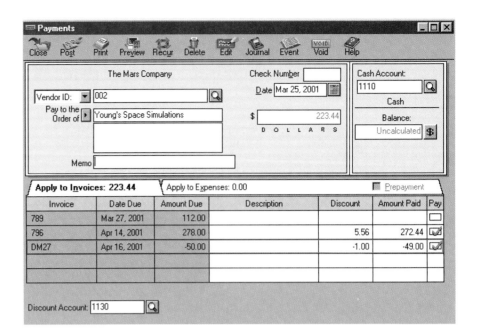

How to Review a Disburse-
ments Journal Entry

28. Before printing this check, you may wish to see how Peachtree will record the transaction. Click on the **Journal** icon on the tool bar. It will bring up a Disbursements Journal showing exactly how it will post this payment. That is to say, it will show you what accounts will be debited and which accounts credited.

29. Close the Disbursements Journal window. If you have made an error anywhere on the check, simply click in the field containing the error and correct it. If you need to change which invoice to pay, click on the red check for the incorrect invoice to deselect it and reselect the correct invoice.

How to Print a Check

30. After verifying that the check is correct, click on the **Print** icon to print this check. You will be presented with a Print Forms: Disbursement Checks selection box. As before, Peachtree has the ability to print on a variety of different blank check forms. Since we will be printing on plain white paper, it does not matter which form we choose. Select "AP Preprint 1 Stub" which is the first option. Click on **Ok** to continue. You are now asked whether this will be a real run or a practice run for alignment purposes. Click on **Real** since no alignment is needed. You are now prompted for the check number. Enter "437" and again select **Ok.** The check will now print. You may need to tell your printer to continue since it will want you to insert the blank check forms. A blank Payment window is displayed, ready for additional Payments transactions to be recorded. Close the Payments dialog box.

How to Display and Print a
Customer Aged Receivables
Report

31. From the **Reports** menu, select **Accounts Receivable.** This will bring up a Select a Report dialog box containing a list of several receivables related reports available to us. Select **Aged Receivables** to bring up the schedule of receivables still owed to Mars Company. Click on the **Print** icon to print the report.

32. Close the Aged Receivables window. From the Select A Report dialogue box, select Accounts Payable from the **Report Area** portion of the window. This will bring up a selection of payables related reports. Select **Aged Payables** to bring up the schedule of payables still owed by the Mars Company. Click on the **Print** icon to print the report.

How to Display and Print a
Vendor Aged Payables
Report

33. Close the Aged Payables window. From the Select A Report dialogue box, select General Ledger from the **Report Area** portion of the window then print the following reports:

a. General Ledger Trial Balance (Totals = 16,201.00)

b. General Ledger Report (Cash = $10,511.56)

Print Reports

34. You may wish to experiment with some of the other reports that are available in the various areas of Peachtree's report area. Some examples you might

want to see are a Sales Journal, Purchases Journal, Cash Receipts Journal, etc. Exit the program when you are finished.

PART B: COMPUTERIZED ACCOUNTING INSTRUCTIONS FOR ABBY'S TOY HOUSE (PROBLEM 10A-4)

1. Click on the Start button. Point to Programs; point to the Peachtree folder and select Peachtree Complete Accounting. Your desktop may have the Peachtree icon allowing for a quicker entrance into the program.

2. Follow the "Open a File" instructions in Part A of the Computerized Accounting appendix at the back of this book to open **Abby's Toy House.**

3. Click on the **Maintain** menu option. Then select **Company Information.** The program will respond by bringing up a dialogue box allowing the user to edit/add information about the company. In the **Company Name** entry field at the end of **Abby's Toy House,** add a dash and your name "**-Student Name**" to the end of the company name. Click on the OK button to return to the Menu Window.

4. Record the following transactions using the appropriate General(G), Sales/Invoicing(S), Receipts(R), Purchases(PU), and Payments(PA) windows. Use the same forms when printing invoices, credits and checks as in Part A changing the starting numbers as needed. The transactions for March:

2001

Mar.	1	Abby Ellen invested $8,000 in the toy store. (G)
	1	Paid three month's rent in advance, check # 1, $3,000. (G)
	2	Purchased merchandise from Earl Miller Company on account, $4,000, invoice # 410, terms 2/10, n/30 consisting of the following: 6- Mountain Bikes, 12- Bike Carriers, 8- Deluxe Bike Seats. (PU)
	3	Sold merchandise to Bill Burton on account, $1,000, invoice # 1, terms 2/10, n/30 consisting of the following: 1- Mountain Bike, 1- Bike Carrier. (S)
	6	Sold merchandise to Jim Rex on account, $700, invoice # 2, terms 2/10, n/30 consisting of the following: 3- Bike Carriers, 1- Deluxe Bike Seat. (S)
	9	Purchased merchandise from Earl Miller Co. on account, $1,200, invoice # 415, terms 2/10, n/30 consisting of the following: 2- Mountain Bikes, 4- Bike Carriers. (PU)
	9	Sold merchandise to Bill Burton on account, $600, invoice # 3, terms 2/10, n/30 consisting of the following: 3- Bike Carriers. (S)
	9	Paid cleaning service $300, check # 2. (G)
	10	Jim Rex returned merchandise that cost $300 to Abby's Toy House consisting of the following: 1- Bike Carrier, 1- Deluxe Bike Seat. Abby issued credit memorandum # 1 to Jim Rex for $300. (S) Remember to use negative quantities.
	11	Purchased merchandise from Minnie Katz on account, $4,000, invoice # 311, terms 1/15, n/60 consisting of the following: 2- Doll Houses w/Furniture, 4- Porcelain Face Dolls, 10- Yo Yo's, Designer, 10- Magic Kits. (PU)
	12	Issued check # 3 to Earl Miller Co. in the amount of $3,920 in payment of invoice # 410 ($4,000), dated March 2, less 2 percent discount ($80). (PA)
	13	Sold $1,300 of toy merchandise for cash consisting of the following: 1- Doll House w/Furniture, 1- Magic Kit. (Use the Receipts window with Customer Name and Reference fields reflecting "Cash". Change Payment Method to Cash. Use the Apply to Sales tab and list the items sold accepting all other defaults.)
	13	Paid salaries, $600, check # 4. (G)

Open the Company Data Files

Add Your Name to the company Name

Record Transactions

14 Returned merchandise to Minnie Katz in the amount of $1,000 consisting of the following: 1- Doll House w/Furniture, 2- Porcelain Face Dolls. Abby's Toy House issued debit memorandum # 1. (PU)

15 Sold merchandise for $4,000 cash consisting of the following: 3- Mountain Bikes, 3- Bike Carriers, 2- Magic Kits, 4- Yo Yo's, Designer. (R)

16 Received check # 9823 from Jim Rex in the amount of $392 in payment of invoice # 2 ($700), dated March 6, less credit memorandum # 1 ($300), less 2 percent discount ($14 − 6 = $8 net sales discount). (R)

16 Received check # 4589 from Bill Burton in the amount of $1,000 in payment of invoice # 1, dated March 2. (R) Notice how Peachtree does not factor in the discount since it is past the discount date.

16 Sold merchandise to Amy Rose on account, $4,000, invoice # 4, terms 2/10, n/30 consisting of the following: 1- Porcelain Face Doll, 3- Mountain Bikes, 4- Bike Carriers, 3- Deluxe Bike Seats.

21 Purchased delivery truck on account from Sam Katz Garage, $3,000, invoice # 111, (no discount). (PU) Since this is not an inventory item, you do not need to fill in the **Item** field. You must type in the **Description.** Peachtree will default the GL code to a truck since this vendor was set up to do so. You will need to type in the purchase price.

22 Sold to Bill Burton merchandise on account, $900, invoice # 5, terms 2/10, n/30 consisting of the following: 3- Magic Kits. (S)

23 Issued check # 5 to Minnie Katz in the amount of $2,970 in payment of invoice # 311 ($4,000), dated March 11, less debit memorandum # 1 ($1,000), less 1 percent discount ($40 − 10 = $30 net purchases discount). (PA)

24 Sold toy merchandise on account to Amy Rose, $1,100, invoice # 6, terms 2/10, n/30 consisting of the following: 1- Porcelain Face Doll, 1- Magic Kit, 3- Yo Yo's, Designer. (S)

25 Purchased toy merchandise for cash from Woody Smith while waiting for an account to be approved, $600, check # 6 consisting of the following: 2- Marionettes, Hand Carved. (Use the Payments window, Apply to Expenses tab and list the items purchased)

27 Purchased toy merchandise from Woody Smith on account, $4,800, invoice # 211, terms 2/10, n/30 consisting of the following: 16- Marionettes, Hand Carved. (PU)

28 Received check # 4598 from Bill Burton in the amount of $882 in payment of invoice # 5 ($900), dated March 22, less 2 percent discount ($18). (R)

28 Received check # 3217 from Amy Rose in the amount of $1,078 in payment of invoice # 6, dated March 24, less 2 percent discounts ($22). (R)

28 Abby invested an additional $5,000 in the business. (G)

29 Purchased merchandise from Earl Miller Co. $1,400, invoice # 436, terms 2/10, n/30 consisting of the following: 3- Mountain Bike, 2- Bike Carriers. (PU)

30 Issued check # 7 to Earl Miller Co. in the amount of $1,372 in payment of invoice # 436 ($1,400), dated March 29, less 2 percent discount ($28). (PA)

30 Sold merchandise to Bonnie Flow Company on account, $3,000 invoice # 7, terms 2/10, n/30 consisting of the following: 5- Marionettes, Hand Carved. (S)

5. Print the following reports accepting all defaults:

a. Aged Receivables

b. Aged Payables

c. General Journal

d. General Ledger Report

Print Reports

CHAPTER 11

The Combined Journal

Therapeutic pet message? Chiropractic for horses? The Bureau of Labor Statistics projected that service-producing establishments will account for

virtually all of the job growth over the next 10 years. And, in a booming economy, the more money people have to spend, the more specialty services crop up to meet their every need, often very distinct and special needs. Jonathan Rudinger's PetMassage Training and Research Clinic in Toledo Ohio is one such specialty service establishment. With more disposable income, pet owners have more money to spend on their poodles and parakeets. Hence, an increase in specialty services and products for the nation's pets—from bakeries that sell doggy treats to clinics offering equine massage therapy.

Whether he is a pet massage therapist or a computer consultant, the ultimate goal of a service provider is to increase the number of clients and, of course, to offer them high quality services. To that end, service providers would rather spend their time marketing to or serving clients than posting entries to several special journals. In fact, because service providers have fewer transactions than merchandisers or manufacturers, the special journals we introduced in the last chapter are less appropriate for their needs. In this chapter you will learn to use a **combined journal** that replaces all special journals and the general journal. It is similar to an accounting worksheet and can be used in a spreadsheet format on computer. In addition to learning how to keep a combined journal, you will learn the difference between using the cash basis of accounting, modified cash or accrual basis of accounting.

Busy service providers will want to get their combined journal up and running with a software accounting package such as Intuit's QuickBooks Pro 2000 (www.quickbooks.com), the acknowledged market leader for small accounting packages. QuickBooks offers over 100 customizable reports that you can export to an Excel spreadsheet. In addition, QuickBooks continues to expand the integration of Internet features. For instance, when you register the software online, you can step through a quick questionnaire and create a free Web site for your company using over 250 templates. What better way for a new service business to offer clients instant information? Jonathan Rudinger's Web site offers everything from tips on giving massage to your pet to an online store for his retail products, such as educational videos and spa robes for dogs. Click it out at www.petmassage.com.

Source: [BLS statistic] Anonymous, "Service sector jobs will dominate the employment landscape," *HR Focus*, April 2000, p. 8. [Quickbooks and other accounting software package information can be found in] John Hedtke, "Low-cost high-function accounting," *Accounting Technology*, May 2000, pp. 34–46 [info on chiropractic service for horses] Sandra Thompson, "Chiropractic Care is Strictly for the Animals Massage Therapist Devoted to her Four-Legged Patients," *Chicago Tribune*, July 31, 2000, p. 2DN3.

LEARNING OBJECTIVES

▼ Defining methods of accounting: accrual basis, cash basis, and modified cash basis. (p. 317)

▼ Recording, journalizing, and posting transactions for a combined journal of a professional service company using a modified cash basis. (p. 417)

▼ Recording, journalizing, and posting transactions for a combined journal of a merchandise company using an accrual basis of accounting. (p. 423)

In the first 10 chapters of this text, we used general journals and special journals to record business transactions. Often, students want to know how to set up journals for their own small businesses. They think the general journals are too simple and special journals are too detailed.

The solution is a combined journal. A combined journal is a special journal that replaces the general journal and other special journals. It has the same basic features as other special journals. Combined journals are an option for small businesses that do not have many transactions. Lawyers, doctors, dentists, and other professionals may use a combined journal, which may be modified in many ways to suit their individual needs. If the volume of transactions increases, more specialized journals may be required. For example, if a company adds bookkeepers to its accounting department, management must be prepared to provide a system of dividing the work to be done. This division of labor may play an important part in determining the types of special journals that are needed.

Before we can discuss combined journals, however, we must first learn the difference between cash basis accounting and accrual basis accounting.

The *accrual basis of accounting* is based on the matching principle, which says that revenue is recorded when it is earned (not when the money actually comes in) and expenses are recorded when they are incurred (not when they are paid). Companies often choose the accrual basis because they want to show earned revenue along with the expenses that were incurred to earn that revenue. All the businesses we have discussed so far used accrual basis accounting.

Accrual accounting:
▼ Earning revenue
▼ Incurred expenses

In the *cash basis of accounting,* revenue is recorded when cash is received and expenses are recorded when they are paid. Service companies use the cash basis because it is simpler and more convenient than the accrual basis. Companies with inventory do not use this method. Also, if this accounting method is used, the revenue and expenses may not show up in the same accounting period.

Let's look at the difference between accrual and cash basis with the following example: John Mills earned real estate commissions of $100,000, of which he received $60,000 in cash. He incurred $25,000 in expenses. Of that amount, $10,000 was paid in cash.

COMPARISON OF CASH BASIS WITH ACCRUAL BASIS FOR MONTH OF JULY 200X

Cash Basis		Accrual Basis	
Revenue (received)	$60,000	Revenue (earned)	$100,000
Expenses (paid)	10,000	Expenses (incurred)	25,000
Net income	$50,000	Net income	$ 75,000

Note how net income differs according to which system is used.

LEARNING UNIT 11-1

COMBINED JOURNAL: A MODIFIED CASH-BASIS SYSTEM FOR A PROFESSIONAL OR BUSINESS SERVICE COMPANY

This learning unit focuses on Dr. Gail Duncan, a dentist who uses a modified cash system in her professional service company. She wanted to use a strictly cash-basis system, but her accountant told her that doing so would distort her financial reports and violate IRS guidelines. The accountant said that the best system for a dentist is the **modified cash-basis** or **hybrid method,** which is a combination of the cash and accrual methods. Many professional services (e.g., attorneys, doctors, dentists, architects) and business services (e.g., real estate, insurance, dry cleaning) use this method.

Using the modified cash-basis system, Dr. Duncan will record professional fees and her expenses when cash is received. Long-lived assets (equipment, building, etc.) are depreciated (i.e., the amount paid for these items are not treated as expense of just that period). For example, Dr. Duncan must depreciate (or allocate) the cost of her dental equipment over a period of years. These items are treated the same way under cash and accrual accounting. Insurance premiums and purchases of a large amount of supplies are treated the same under cash and accrual accounting. Thus the amount consumed or used up is shown as an expense in the current year and the amount on hand is carried over into the next accounting period.

These exceptions require adjusting entries.

Chart of Accounts

The chart of accounts for Dr. Duncan is shown in Figure 11-1 on p. 418. Note that, unlike a chart of accounts on the accrual basis, there are no categories for Accounts Receivable, Accounts Payable, or Salaries Payable. This chart of

FIGURE 11-1. Chart of
Accounts

Dr. Gail Duncan
Chart of Accounts

Assets
111 Cash
113 Petty Cash Fund
131 Prepaid Insurance
141 Office Furniture
142 Accum. Dep., Office Furniture
151 Dental Equipment
152 Accum. Dep., Dental Equipment
161 Auto
162 Accum. Dep., Auto

Liabilities
211 FICA—Social Security Payable
212 FICA—Medicare Payable
213 Federal Income Tax Payable
214 Notes Payable

Owner's Equity
311 G. Duncan, Capital
312 G. Duncan, Withdrawals
313 Income Summary

Revenue
411 Professional Fees

Expenses
511 Automobile Expense
512 Rent Expense
513 Salaries Expense
514 Telephone Expense
515 Dep. Exp., Office Furniture
516 Dep. Exp., Dental Equipment
517 Dep. Exp., Auto
518 Miscellaneous Expense
519 Insurance Expense
520 Dental Supplies Expense
521 Payroll Tax Expense

*Example of a modified cash
system.*

accounts does have titles for handling the exceptions (for example, Accumulated Depreciation, Prepaid Insurance). There is no supplies account under assets, because Dr. Duncan is *not* buying a large amount of supplies, and thus all will be shown as Dental Supplies Expense without distorting the financial reports.

The transactions that occurred for the month of November are as follows:

Transactions for Dr. Gail Duncan

200X
Nov.

1	Paid $200 office rent for November, check no. 61.
1	Received checks for $3,000 from patients for dental work.
4	Paid telephone bill, $80, check no. 62.
4	Issued check no. 63 to Bill Blan Insurance Agency for premium on insurance for three years, $600.
7	Purchased dental supplies from Roe Suppliers, $150, check no. 64.
8	Received checks from patients, $1,600.
8	Calculated current cash balance.
11	Issued check no. 65 to Moe Gas for automobile expenses charged during October, $80.
11	Dr. Duncan withdrew $500 for personal use, check no. 66.
14	Issued check no. 67 to V. P. Suppliers Company for dental supplies charged during October, $250.
15	Paid office salaries for the period November 1 to November 15, $2,000, check no. 68.
15	Cash receipts from patients totaled $2,800 for the week.
15	Calculated current cash balance.
19	Collected $800 from insurance companies for patients' accounts.
21	Purchased dental supplies from J. Labs, $200, check no. 69.
22	Cash receipts for the week totaled $2,900.
22	Calculated current cash balance.
27	Issued check no. 70 for charitable contributions, $300.
27	Purchased dental supplies from J. Labs, $100, check no. 71.
28	Received checks from patients' insurance companies totaling $3,300.

29   Paid office salaries for the period November 15 to November 30, $1,500, check no. 72.

30   Calculated current cash balance and crossfooted journal.

Monthly Transactions

These transactions are recorded in the **combined journal,** the special journal that replaces the general journal. The combined journal has the same basic features as other special journals that were introduced in Chapters 9 and 10. Each business designs the headings of the combined journal to fit its individual needs. Accounts that are used most often are the ones that should have a special column, which saves time in journalizing and posting.

RECORDING TRANSACTIONS IN THE COMBINED JOURNAL

The combined journal for Dr. Duncan is shown in Figure 11-2 on p. 420. Note that the bank balance can be calculated at any time. For example, in the explanation column, note the beginning balance of $9,500. On November 8 the current balance was calculated as follows:

Beg. Balance	$ 9,500
+ Deposits	4,600
− Checks written	1,030
Ending Balance	$13,070 ← Recorded in explanation column

This combined jounal is proved this way:

	Dr.	Cr.
Cash	$14,400	$ 5,960
Sundry	5,260	
Professional Fees		14,400
Dental Sup. Exp.	700	
	$20,360	$20,360

> Proving the journal is the same method that is used for proving special journals. The sum of all the debit columns should equal the sum of all the credit columns.

POSTING THE COMBINED JOURNAL

Because this system is a modified cash-basis system, there are no subsidiary ledgers for accounts receivable or accounts payable. Companies using a modified cash-basis system usually keep information about any receivables or payables in an informal memorandum record until cash is received or paid. During the month, items entered into the sundry column can be updated in the general ledger. At end of month the totals of Cash, Professional Fees, and Dental Supplies Expense would be posted to the general ledger. The account numbers are shown at the bottom of the columns of the combined journal to show that the totals were posted. The **X** means that no posting is necessary. The total of the sundry column is not posted.

> Memorandum records can be used in a modified cash-basis system.

RECORDING PAYROLL DEDUCTIONS AND EMPLOYER'S TAX EXPENSE

Back in Chapters 7 and 8 we studied payroll. The payroll register recorded gross pay, deductions, and net pay. A general journal entry is prepared from the payroll register to record the payroll. We also discussed using a general journal to record the employer's payroll tax expense before it is paid (for FICA—Social Security Payable, FICA—Medicare Payable, FUTA, and SUTA). The recordkeeping involved in paying an employee is similar in a combined

FIGURE 11-2. The Combined Journal

DR. GAIL DUNCAN
COMBINED JOURNAL

Month: November

Cash Deposits Dr.	Checks Cr.	Check No.	Date	Explanation	PR	Sundry Dr.	Sundry Cr.	Prof. Fees Cr.	Dental Supplies Expense Dr.
			200X Nov.	Cash Balance 9,500					
	200 00	61	1	Rent Expense	512	200 00			
3 000 00			1	Professional Fees	X			3 000 00	
	80 00	62	4	Telephone Expense	514	80 00			
	600 00	63	4	Prepaid Insurance	131	600 00			
	150 00	64	7	Roe Suppliers	X				150 00
1 600 00			8	Professional Fees 13,070	X			1 600 00	
	80 00	65	11	Auto. Exp.	511	80 00			
	500 00	66	11	G. Duncan, Withdrawals	312	500 00			
	250 00	67	14	V.P. Suppliers	X				250 00
	2 000 00	68	15	Salaries Expense	513	2 000 00			
2 800 00			15	Professional Fees 13,040	X			2 800 00	
800 00			19	Professional Fees	X			800 00	
	200 00	69	21	J. Labs	X				200 00
2 900 00			22	Professional Fees 16,540	X			2 900 00	
	300 00	70	27	Miscellaneous Expense	518	300 00			
	100 00	71	27	J. Labs	X				100 00
3 300 00			28	Professional Fees	X			3 300 00	
	1 500 00	72	29	Salaries Expense 17,940	513	1 500 00			
14 400 00	5 960 00					5 260 00		14 400 00	700 00
(111)	(111)					(X)		(411)	(520)

$20,360 = $20,360

journal using the cash-basis method, but the employer's payroll tax expense is recorded differently.

The different recording methods are because the owner's share of Social Security, Medicare, FUTA, and SUTA are recorded when they are paid under the cash-basis method. In accrual accounting they are recorded when they are incurred.

Let's look at a partially completed combined journal on page 422 and explain each entry.

A. Bill Smith's gross salary of $500 is recorded as a salary expense, and the deductions for FICA—Social Security, FICA—Medicare, and FIT are listed as liabilities until the employer makes the deposit. Note that the check is written for $371.75 (net pay). The same procedure is followed for Joe Ring.

B. On June 3 the deposit for the quarterly Form 941 is assumed made. Thus the employer pays the FICA (SS and Med.) for the employee as well as the employer's matching share, along with the FIT taken out of the employees' paychecks.

The payroll tax expense is now being recorded for the employer's FICA share of Social Security and Medicare because it is now being paid. Note that the check amount is for $262.40, which includes the total of the following three taxes:

> The payroll tax expense is now being recorded for the employer's FICA share of Social Security and Medicare because it is now being paid.

Federal Income Tax Payable	$140.00
FICA — Social Security Payable	49.60
FICA — Medicare Payable	11.60
This is employer's FICA share → Payroll Tax Expense	61.20

for Social Security and Medicare

The end result is to reduce the three liabilities owed as well as record the employer's share of FICA for Social Security and Medicare as payroll tax expense. When FUTA or SUTA tax is *paid*, the employer's payroll tax expense will be recorded for these taxes.

In summary:

WHEN FICA TAX AND FEDERAL
INCOME TAX PAID

| Employee Fed. Inc. Tax Payable |
| FICA—Social Security Payable |
| FICA—Medicare Payable |
| Payroll Tax Expense |
| Cash |

WHEN FUTA TAX OR
SUTA TAX PAID

| Payroll Tax Expense |
| Cash |

Some systems will record the FICA portion of the employer when the payroll is paid instead of when the FICA tax deposit is made. Then when the deposit is made they will record the entry as follows:

| Fed. Inc. Tax Payable |
| FICA—Social Security Payable |
| FICA—Medicare Payable |
| Cash |

COMBINED JOURNAL

| | Voe Bank | | Check No. | Date | Accounts or Explanations | PR | Sundry | | Professional Fees Cr. | Salary Expense Dr. | Payroll Deduct. | | |
	Deposits Dr.	Checks Cr.					Dr.	Cr.			FICA SS. Cr.	FICA Med. Cr.	Fed. Inc. Tax Payable Cr.
(A)		371 75	33	May 5	Bill Smith	✗				500 00	31 00	7 25	90 00
		227 05	34	5	Joe Ring	✗				300 00	18 60	4 35	50 00
(B)		262 40	50	June 3	Employee FIT Payable	211	140 00						
					FICA Soc. Sec. Payable	211	49 60						
					FICA–Medicare Payable	212	11 60						
					Payroll Tax Expense	612	61 20						

LEARNING UNIT 11-1 REVIEW

AT THIS POINT you should be able to

▼ Explain the modified cash-basis system of accounting. (p. 417)
▼ Journalize transactions into a combined journal. (p. 418)
▼ Calculate the current bank balance of a combined journal. (p. 419)
▼ Prove a combined journal. (p. 419)
▼ Explain how to record payroll as well as payroll tax expense into a combined journal. (p. 421)

SELF-REVIEW QUIZ 11-1

(The forms you need are on page 362 of the *Study Guide and Working Papers.*)
Respond true or false to the following:

1. A modified cash-basis system will only have one exception, long-lived assets, in the adjustment process.
2. A cash-basis system in a chart of accounts usually has titles for FUTA and SUTA taxes.
3. Headings of combined journals can be modified to meet the needs of the user.
4. The cash balance can easily be calculated in a combined journal.
5. Payroll tax expense will be recorded when the tax (be it Social Security, Medicare, FUTA, or SUTA) is paid.

Solutions to Self-Review Quiz 11-1

1. False   **2.** False   **3.** True   **4.** True   **5.** True

LEARNING UNIT 11-2

COMBINED JOURNAL FOR ART'S WHOLESALE CLOTHING COMPANY

In Chapters 9 and 10 we developed the sales journal, cash receipts journal, purchases journal, cash payments journal, and general journal for Art's Wholesale Clothing Company. Many small businesses that are concerned with saving journalizing, recording, and posting labor, however, only have one bookkeeper. Such businesses are likely to want the advantages provided by special journals but would like to reduce the number of journals needed. This unit develops a combined journal, a book of original entry, that dispenses with the special journals yet gains their advantages in journalizing, recording, and posting for a company that uses an accrual accounting approach.

Note: To focus on the combined journal here, we save specific details of payroll for Chapter 13.

Our goal in this unit is to place all the special journals for Art's Wholesale Clothing Company into the following combined journal:

ART'S WHOLESALE CLOTHING COMPANY
COMBINED JOURNAL

Date		Explanation	Ck. No.	PR	Sundry Dr.	Sundry Cr.	Cash Dr.	Cash Cr.	Accounts Receivable Dr.	Accounts Receivable Cr.
200X Apr.	1	Art Newner, Cap.		311		8000 00	8000 00			
	2	Prepaid Ins.	1	116	900 00			900 00		
	3	Hal's Clothing		✔					800 00	
	3	Freight-In, Abby Blake		512✔	50 00					
	4	Equip., Joe Francis		121✔	4000 00					
	4	Hal's Clothing		✔			784 00			800 00
	6	Thorpe Co.		✔						
	6	Bevans Co.		✔					1600 00	
	7	J. Francis Co.	2	✔				4000 00		
	7	J. Sullivan Co.		✔						
	9	Purchases	3	✗				800 00		
	9	Pur. R&A, Thorpe Co.		514✔		200 00				
	12	Thorpe Co.	4	✔				594 00		
	12	Sales R&A, Bevans Co.		412✔	600 00					600 00
	12	Abby Blake Co.		✔						
	15	Cash Sales		✗			900 00			
	16	Bevans Co.		✔			980 00			1000 00
	18	Roe Co.		✔					2000 00	
	22	Roe Co.		✔			1960 00			2000 00
	24	Roe Co.		✔					500 00	
	25	Sup., J. Sullivan		115✔	500 00					
	27	Store Equip.		121		500 00	500 00			
	28	Salaries Expense	5	611	700 00			700 00		
	28	Mel's Dept. St.		✔					900 00	
	29	Mel's Dept. St.		✔					700 00	
	30	Cash Sales		✗			1200 00			
		Totals			6750 00	8700 00	14324 00	6994 00	6500 00	4400 00
					(X)	(X)	(111)	(111)	(113)	(113)

FIGURE 11-3. Combined Journal Completed

Proving the accuracy of the combined journal.

Account Title	Dr.	Cr.
Sundry	$ 6750 00	$ 8700 00
Cash	14324 00	6994 00
Accounts Receivable	6500 00	4400 00
Accounts Payable	4800 00	11930 00
Sales		8600 00
Sales Discount	76 00	
Purchases	8180 00	
Purchases Discount		6 00
Totals	$40630 00	$40630 00

Month: April

Accounts Payable Dr.	Accounts Payable Cr.	Sales Cr.	Sales Discount Dr.	Purchases Dr.	Purchases Discount Cr.
		800 00			
	5050 00			5000 00	
	4000 00				
			16 00		
	800 00			800 00	
		1600 00			
4000 00					
	980 00			980 00	
				800 00	
200 00					
600 00					6 00
	600 00			600 00	
		900 00			
			20 00		
		2000 00			
			40 00		
		500 00			
	500 00				
		900 00			
		700 00			
		1200 00			
4800 00	**11930 00**	**8600 00**	**76 00**	**8180 00**	**6 00**
(211)	(211)	(411)	(413)	(511)	(513)

FIGURE 11-3. (Cont.)

COMBINED JOURNAL

Month: April — Page 1

Date	Explanation	Check No.	PR	Sundry Dr.	Sundry Cr.	Cash Dr.	Cash Cr.	Acct. Rec. Dr.	Acct. Rec. Cr.	Acct. Pay. Dr.	Acct. Pay. Cr.	Sales Cr.	Sales Dis. Dr.	Pur. Dr.	Pur. Dis. Cr.

The first thing Art and his accountant must do is go over the chart of accounts. Their goal would be to set up columns in the combined journal for accounts in which transactions would occur frequently. In the case of Art's Wholesale Clothing Company, the following special columns would be needed:

▼ *Cash Dr.:* Used to record increases in cash.
▼ *Cash Cr.:* Used to record decreases in cash.

> Note that because Art uses *accrual* accounting, we now have columns for Accounts Receivable and Accounts Payable.

- ▼ *Accounts Receivable Dr.:* Used to record amounts owed from sales on account.
- ▼ *Accounts Receivable Cr.:* Used to record amounts paid by customers from past sales on account.
- ▼ *Accounts Payable Dr.:* Used to record amounts paid to creditors.
- ▼ *Accounts Payable Cr.:* Used to record amounts owed to creditors.
- ▼ *Sales Cr.:* Used to record all sales made for cash or on account.
- ▼ *Sales Discount Dr.:* Used to record the amounts of discounts taken by customers.
- ▼ *Purchases Dr.:* Used to record all purchases of merchandise for resale.
- ▼ *Purchases Discount Cr.:* Used to record the amounts of discounts Art receives by paying for purchases before the discount period expires.
- ▼ *Sundry Dr., Cr.:* Used to record transactions that do not occur very frequently. If a transaction occurs and no special columns are set up to record part or all of it, it can be recorded in the sundry columns.

Figure 11-3 on p. 424 shows the completed combined journal for the month of April for Art's Wholesale Clothing Company. The combined journal can be proved as shown on the same page.

RECORDING AND POSTING THE COMBINED JOURNAL

The recording and posting rules we learned for Art's special journals will hold true for the combined journal. Here are some key points:

- ▼ ✓: Record to accounts receivable or accounts payable subsidiary ledgers daily.
- ▼ *Sundry:* Update the general ledger account on a daily basis. Use the ledger account number as a posting reference.
- ▼ An **X** in the PR column indicates no posting, because the total is posted at the end of the month. An **X** below the total means that the total of the column is not posted.

CJ1 (Combined Journal, p. 1) will be placed in PR of ledger account, where information from journal is updated in ledger.

Adjusting and closing entries would be recorded in the sundry columns of a combined journal.

The total of each column except sundry will be posted to the general ledger at the end of the month. Note that the account number from the ledger is placed at the bottom of the column in the combined journal, indicating that the total was posted to that account.

Note the following when a combined journal is used:

1. Charge *and* cash sales are recorded in the sales column.
2. Purchases returns, sales returns, and so forth are recorded in sundry, because no general journal is used with a combined journal.
3. Adjusting and closing entries will be recorded in the sundry columns.

Whether Art uses a combined journal or a set of special journals, the schedule of accounts receivable and accounts payable will be the same, as will the trial balance.

SPECIAL SITUATIONS

If a company has many sales returns and allowances, a special column could be developed.

A sample of how a combined journal might look if it included Sales Tax Payable is shown in Figure 11-4. Note that the totals of accounts receivable, sales, and sales tax payable must be posted to the general ledger at the end of the month. Keep in mind that sales tax payable is a liability located on the general ledger.

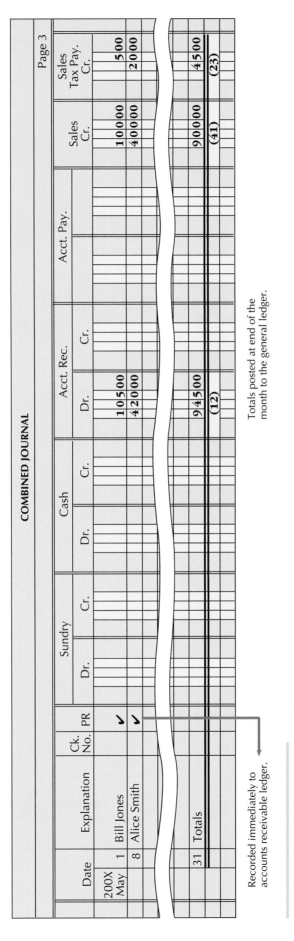

FIGURE 11-4. Combined Journal with Sales Tax Payable Column

COMBINED JOURNAL

Page 3

Date		Explanation	Ck. No.	PR	Sundry Dr.	Sundry Cr.	Cash Dr.	Cash Cr.	Acct. Rec. Dr.	Acct. Rec. Cr.	Acct. Pay.	Sales Cr.	Sales Tax Pay. Cr.
200X May	1	Bill Jones		✔					105 00			100 00	5 00
	8	Alice Smith		✔					420 00			400 00	20 00
	31	Totals							945 00			900 00	45 00
									(12)			(41)	(23)

Recorded immediately to accounts receivable ledger.

Totals posted at end of the month to the general ledger.

427

LEARNING UNIT 11-2 REVIEW

AT THIS POINT you should be able to

▼ Journalize transactions into the combined journal for a merchandise company. (p. 424)
▼ Explain how to record and post the combined journal. (p. 425)
▼ Compare special journals (cash payments, receipts, etc.) and the combined journal. (p. 426)
▼ Explain how sales tax could be recorded in a combined journal. (p. 427)

SELF-REVIEW QUIZ 11-2

(The forms you need are on page 362 of the *Study Guide and Working Papers*.)

Based on the combined journal presented in this unit, classify each statement as true or false.

1. Combined journals are less efficient than other types of special journals.
2. The total of the cash column is posted daily.
3. The total of the sundry column is not posted.
4. The total of the sales column is not posted.
5. All combined journals have the same headings.
6. Combined journals cannot be proved.
7. Subsidiary ledgers are posted from the cash column.
8. The combined journal is used for large companies.
9. A dentist could use a combined journal.
10. A lawyer will always use a combined journal.

Solutions to Self-Review Quiz 11-2

1. False	**2.** False	**3.** True	**4.** False	**5.** False
6. False	**7.** False	**8.** False	**9.** True	**10.** False

SUMMARY OF KEY POINTS

Learning Unit 11-1

1. A company with inventory will not use the cash method.

2. The modified cash-basis system is used because federal and state requirements make a strictly cash-basis system difficult to implement without distorting financial reports.

3. The modified cash-basis system requires adjustments for depreciation, insurance premiums, and large amounts of supplies purchased. Adjustments are recorded in the sundry columns of the combined journal.

4. No accounts for Accounts Payable or Accounts Receivable are used in the chart of accounts for a modified cash-basis system. Companies use memorandums to keep track of receivables or payables until money is received or paid.

5. The bank balance (cash balance) can be determined at any time when a combined journal is used.

6. A combined journal can be proved by crossfooting the totals to verify that total debits equal total credits.

7. The payroll tax expense for the employer using a cash-basis system is recorded when the tax is paid. In the cash-basis system there are no liability accounts for FUTA or SUTA; you record them when paid as part of Payroll Tax Expense.

Learning Unit 11-2

1. A combined journal for Art's Wholesale Clothing Company replaces the individual special journals (SJ, CRJ, PJ, CPJ, GJ).

2. Many small companies use a combined journal.

3. A combined journal on an accrual basis uses columns for accounts receivable and accounts payable. Subsidiary ledgers will be recorded during the month. The total of the sundry columns is not posted.

4. Adjusting and closing entries will be recorded in the sundry columns.

KEY TERMS

Combined journal A special journal that combines the features of the sales, cash payments, cash receipts, purchases, and general journals.

Modified cash-basis method (hybrid) The accounting method that records revenue when cash is received and expenses when they are paid. Adjustments to long-lived assets, as well as insurance premiums and amounts of supplies on hand, are required by state and federal laws so that financial reports will not be distorted.

QUESTIONS, MINI EXERCISES, EXERCISES, AND PROBLEMS

Discussion Questions

1. All companies with inventory must use the cash basis of accounting. Agree or disagree.

2. Why does the strictly cash-basis method tend to distort financial reports?

3. List three adjustments that may result in a modified cash system.

4. Explain how a company can change its method of accounting.

5. A modified cash system has an accounts receivable as well as accounts payable ledger. Agree or disagree. Please support your answer.

6. Explain how a cash balance can be calculated during the month when using a combined journal.

7. How is a combined journal proved?

8. Explain why there are no accounts for SUTA or FUTA in the chart of accounts in the cash-basis method.

9. What purpose would an informal memorandum serve when dealing with accounts payable and accounts receivable in a modified cash system?

10. Explain when the Payroll Tax Expense account will be updated in a modified cash system.

BLUEPRINT: A TYPICAL CHART OF ACCOUNTS FOR AN ATTORNEY USING A MODIFIED CASH BASIS (INCLUDING PAYROLL)

ASSETS

No Accounts Receivable account

Village National Bank	111
Petty Cash	112
Office Supplies	113
Prepaid Insurance	114
Office Equip.	115
Accum. Dep. Office Equip.	116
Automobiles	117
Accum. Dep., Auto	118

LIABILITIES

No Accounts Payable account

FICA — Social Security Payable	211	For payroll, note no titles for FUTA or SUTA
FICA — Medicare Payable	212	
Federal Income Tax Payable	213	
Notes Payable	214	

OWNER'S EQUITY

Jack Smith, Capital	311
Jack Smith, Withdrawals	312
Income Summary	313

Only recorded when cash received →

REVENUE

Professional Fees	411

EXPENSES

Dep. Exp., Office Equip.	511	For adjustments so financial statements will not be distorted
Dep. Exp., Auto	512	
Insurance Expense	513	
Office Supplies Expense	514	
Dues	515	
Postage	516	
Payroll Tax Expense	517	← Records the tax expense for employer when the Social Security, Medicare, FUTA, or SUTA is *paid*
Rent Expense	518	
Salary Expense	519	
Telephone Expense	520	
Miscellaneous Expense	521	

11. Explain how a combined journal for an accrual-based company will aid in reducing the number of special journals needed.

12. If a company is expanding, a combined journal could be efficient. Please respond.

Mini Exercises

(The forms you need are on page 364 of the *Study Guide and Working Papers*.)

Accounts Needing Adjustment

1. Which of the following titles may require adjusting entries using a modified cash-basis method?

	Yes	No
Cash in bank	_____	_____
Accounts Receivable	_____	_____
Computer Equipment	_____	_____
Supplies	_____	_____
Accounts Payable	_____	_____
Salaries Payable	_____	_____
Accumulated Depreciation	_____	_____
Prepaid Insurance	_____	_____

Deposit of Employee Taxes

2. Using the modified cash basis the following balances have been found in the ledger: FIT, $275; FICA — Social Security Payable, $70; FICA — Medicare Payable, $90. Prepare a journal entry to record the employees' deposit of these taxes along with the employees' payroll tax expense.

SUTA Payment

3. Grace Stafford uses a modified cash-basis system. She pays a SUTA tax of $175. Please record the general journal entry.

Combined Journal Headings

4. Match the following partial list of column headings of Pete Moore's combined journal to the statements below. Use only one number for each letter.

1. Cash   Cr.
2. Accounts Payable   Cr.
3. Sales Discounts   Dr.
4. Sundry   Dr./Cr.
5. Sales   Cr.

_____ a. Reflects amounts owed to creditors.

_____ b. Records the amounts of discounts taken by customers.

_____ c. Records transactions that do not occur very often.

_____ d. Records sales made for cash or on account.

_____ e. Records decreases in cash.

Recording to Subsidiary Ledgers

5. Indicate which of the following transactions would result in a recording to a subsidiary ledger. The company uses a combined journal with an accrual accounting approach.

a. Pete Daving invests $20,000 into the business.

b. Sold $300 of merchandise to French Co. on account.

c. Cash sales $200.

d. Received half the amount owed by French from sales on account in part b.

Exercises

(The forms you need are on page 365 of the *Study Guide and Working Papers*.)

> Identifying adjustment titles for a modified cash-basis system.

11-1. In a modified cash-basis system, which of the following titles may need adjustments?

Cash	B. Jee, Capital
Supplies	B. Jee, Withdrawals
Prepaid Insurance	Commission Sales
Equipment	Salary Expense
Notes Payable	

> Posting a combined journal using the accrual approach.

11-2. Line.com uses a combined journal with the following headings:

Sundry	Dr.	Cr.
Accounts Receivable	Dr.	Cr.
Accounts Payable	Dr.	Cr.
Commission Sales	Cr.	
Salary Expense	Dr.	
Cash	Dr.	Cr.

   a. How can the balance of cash be determined at any point in the month?

   b. Which column total will not be posted?

   c. Do you think Line.com has subsidiary ledgers? Please explain.

   d. Which columns will be used to record the payment of advertising expense?

> Preparing a chart of accounts for a modified cash-basis system.

11-3. Listed are the accounts used by Dr. Jonson, who keeps his records on strictly a cash basis. As his accountant, which titles do you think could be added to use a modified cash-basis system? Assume a large amount of supplies is bought. The accounts are Cash; Notes Payable; L. Jonson, Capital; L. Jonson, Withdrawals; Professional Fees; Auto Expense; Rent Expense; Office Furniture Expense; Insurance Expense; Medical Supplies Expense.

> Explaining postings of a combined journal for a modified cash-basis system.

11-4. Using the headings of the combined journal for Dr. Gail Duncan, p. 420, indicate when postings would occur in a modified cash-basis system.

200X
May

3	D. Hercher invested $5,000 in the dental business.
8	Paid three months' insurance premiums, $1,200.
15	Received checks from patients, $900.
19	Paid office salaries, $500.

> Explaining recordings and postings of a combined journal using an accrual approach.

11-5. Using the headings of the combined journal for Art's Wholesale Clothing Company (p. 424), indicate when recordings and postings would occur in an accrual approach.

200X
May

2	Linda Rice invested $12,000 in the business.
5	Bought $600 of merchandise for cash.
8	Cash sale, $600.
19	Received $400 less a 3 percent discount from Alvie Corp. from past sale on account.

Group A Problems

(The forms you need are on pages 366–378 of the *Study Guide and Working Papers*.)

11A-1. Dr. Joy French, M.D., uses the following chart of accounts:

Assets
111 Borne Bank
113 Petty Cash
114 Prepaid Insurance
115 Medical Supplies
121 Medical Equipment
122 Accumulated Depreciation, Medical Equipment
123 Office Furniture
124 Accumulated Depreciation, Office Furniture
125 Auto
126 Accumulated Depreciation, Auto

Liabilities
211 Notes Payable

Owner's Equity
311 Joy French, Capital
312 Joy French, Withdrawals
313 Income Summary

Revenue
411 Professional Fees

Expenses
511 Rent Expense
512 Donation Expense
513 Salaries Expense
514 Medical Supplies Expense
515 Depreciation Expense, Medical Equipment
516 Depreciation Expense, Office Furniture
517 Depreciation Expense, Automobile
518 Insurance Expense
519 Telephone Expense
610 Cleaning Expense
611 Miscellaneous Expense

The headings of the combined journal are as follows:

										Page 1	
Date	Explanation	PR	Sundry Dr.	Sundry Cr.	Medical Supplies Dr.	Joy French, Withdrawals Dr.	Cleaning Expense Dr.	Prof. Fees Cr.	Ck. No.	Borne Bank Dr.	Borne Bank Cr.

From the transactions listed below:

1. Journalize them in the combined journal for a modified cash-basis system.
2. Prove the combined journal.

200X
May
1 Dr. Joy French deposited $7,000 in the practice.
3 Paid rent for the month to Foster Realty, $800, check no. 1.
8 Bought medical equipment from Ace Supply Co., $1,500, check no. 2.
12 Bought medical supplies from Lone Co., $700, check no. 3.
15 Received cash from patients, $2,800.
18 Bought additional medical supplies from Lone Co., $1,200, check no. 4.
19 Dr. French withdrew $600 for personal use, check no. 5.
21 Paid Al's Janitorial Service, $300, check no. 6.
24 Received cash from patients, $1,900.
25 Paid for postage stamps, $40 (miscellaneous expense), check no. 7.
27 Paid salaries for month, $1,400, check no. 8.
28 Paid Al's Janitorial Service, $400, check no. 9.
29 Dr. French withdrew $400 for personal use, check no. 10.

11A-2. The following is the chart of accounts of Dr. Fox, M.D.:

Journalizing transactions of a modified cash-basis system into a combined journal with headings for payroll deductions as well as recording payroll tax expense.

Check Figure:
Crossfooting $31,534

Assets
111 Valley Blue Bank
112 Prepaid Insurance
113 Medical Supplies
121 Office Equipment
122 Accumulated Depreciation, Office Equipment

Liabilities
211 FICA—Social Security Payable
212 FICA—Medicare Payable
213 Federal Income Tax Payable

Owner's Equity
311 Al Fox, Capital
312 Al Fox, Withdrawals
313 Income Summary

Revenue
411 Professional Fees

Expenses
511 Rent Expense
512 Medical Supplies Expense
513 Salaries Expense
514 Payroll Tax Expense
515 Telephone Expense
516 Depreciation Expense, Office Equipment
517 Insurance Expense
518 Cleaning Expense
519 Miscellaneous Expense

The headings of Dr. Fox's combined journal are as follows:

Date	Explanation	PR	Valley Blue Bank Dr.	Valley Blue Bank Cr.	Ck. No.	Prof. Fees Cr.	Sal. Exp. Dr.	FICA SS. Cr.	FICA Med. Cr.	Fed. Inc. Tax Payable Cr.	Med. Supp. Dr.	Sundry Dr.	Sundry Cr.

From the transactions listed below:

1. Journalize them in the combined journal (beginning balances are provided in the *Study Guide and Working Papers.*)
2. Prove the combined journal.

200X
May
1 Received $3,000 from patients.
3 Issued check no. 480 to Lane Drug for medical supplies, $600.
5 Issued check no. 481 to A. Realty to pay three months' insurance premiums, $1,200.
9 Received checks from patients, $2,000.
12 Issued the following payroll checks to staff:

	Check No.	Gross Pay	Social Security	Medicare	FIT	Net Pay
Abby Slat	482	$ 700	$ 43	$10	$140	$ 507
Jane Reeves	483	600	38	8	120	434
Bob Swan	484	500	31	7	100	362
		$1,800	$112	$25	$360	$1,303

18 Issued check no. 485 to Lane Drug for medical supplies, $400.
25 Dr. Fox withdrew $700 for personal use, check no. 486.
28 Dr. Fox paid Social Security, Medicare, and federal income tax from payroll of May 12, check no. 487. (Don't forget Dr. Fox's share of FICA.)

11A-3. Dr. Dick Clark, a recent graduate of a medical school, has decided to open his own office. Based on the advice of his accountant, he will use a combined journal. The following is the chart of accounts for Dr. Clark's office:

Assets
111 Cash
112 Accounts Receivable
113 Prepaid Insurance
121 Office Equipment

Liabilities
211 Accounts Payable

Owner's Equity
311 D. Clark, Capital
312 Income Summary

Revenue
411 Medical Fees

Expenses
511 Telephone Expense
512 Cleaning Expense
513 Utilities Expense

Check Figure:
Total of Sundry Dr. Column
$2,060

The headings of Dr. Clark's combined journal are as follows:

COMBINED JOURNAL													
								Month				Page 1	
Date	Explanation	Ck. No.	PR	Sundry Dr.	Cr.	Cash Dr.	Cr.	Acct. Rec. Dr.	Cr.	Acct. Pay. Dr.	Cr.	Office Equip. Dr.	Medical Fees Cr.

Your Tasks Are to

1. Record the following transactions in the combined journal. Complete the PR column as if you were recording and posting.
2. Prove the combined journal.

200X
July

1   Dr. Dick Clark invested $7,000 cash and $4,000 of office equipment in the practice.

1   Paid insurance on the office for one year in advance, $1,700, check no. 1.

9   Purchased office equipment on account from Smith Stationery Co., $400.

12   Purchased office equipment on account from Vole Stationery Co., $700.

18   Completed physical examinations on each schoolchild at Salem Elementary School, $3,000 on account.

18   Received $900 cash for medical fees earned.

19   Performed a complete examination for Alvin Ray's son, $75 on account.

20   Paid Smith Stationery one-half the amount owed from July 9 transaction, check no. 2.

26   Paid telephone bill, $90, check no. 3.

27   Paid utilities, $170, check no. 4.

28   Paid Toby Cleaning Co. for cleaning service performed, $100, check no. 5.

29   Paid one-half the amount owed Vole Stationery Company from July 12 transaction, check no. 6.

11A-4. Buzzy Sullivan opened a dry-cleaning store that also sold accessories. The following is the chart of accounts for Buzzy's Cleaning Company.

Assets
111 Cash
112 Accounts Receivable
113 Prepaid Insurance
121 Cleaning Equipment

Liabilities
211 Accounts Payable
212 Note Payable

Owner's Equity
311 B. Sullivan, Capital
312 Income Summary

Revenue
411 Cleaning Sales
412 Cleaning Sales Discount

Cost of Goods Sold
511 Purchases
512 Purchases Returns and
        Allowances
513 Purchases Discounts

Expenses
611 Utilities Expense
612 Advertising Expense

Here are the transactions for the month of January:

200X

Jan.

1	Buzzy Sullivan invested $8,000 cash in the business.
8	Paid a five-year insurance policy in advance, $1,500, check no. 1.
10	Purchased merchandise on account from Role Company, $900.
12	Cleaned shirts for cash, $650.
15	Cleaned suits on account for Pete Daley, $200.
17	Purchased cleaning equipment on account from Ral Company, $900.
20	Borrowed $6,000 from Frank National Bank.
21	Cleaned shirts for Pete Daley for $50 on account.
24	Received payment from Pete Daley for $200 less a 2 percent discount from January 15 transaction.
25	Purchased merchandise on account from Bomb Company, $250.
26	Cleaned pants on account for Alice Small, $15.
27	Paid Role Company $900 less a 2 percent discount for merchandise that was purchased on January 10, check no. 2.
28	Returned $100 of cleaning equipment to Ral Company for faulty work.
29	Paid Bomb Company $250 less a 10 percent discount on purchases made on account on January 25, check no. 3.
30	Cash sales, $800.
30	Received payment from Alice Small, $15, less a 20 percent sales discount.

Your Tasks Are to

1. Set up accounts in the general ledger (some accounts may not be used in January).
2. Set up accounts in the accounts payable and accounts receivable subsidiary ledger as needed.
3. Journalize the above transactions.
4. Record to the accounts payable and accounts receivable subsidiary ledger as appropriate.
5. Post to the general ledger as appropriate.
6. Prove the sum of the subsidiary ledgers equal the controlling accounts.
7. Prove the combined journal.

The headings of the combined journal of Buzzy's Cleaning Company will be as follows:

COMBINED JOURNAL																	
				Month													
				Sundry		Cash		Acct. Rec.		Acct. Pay.		Cleaning Sales Disc.	Cleaning Sales	Purch.	Purch. Dis.		
Date	Explanation	Ck. No.	PR	Dr.	Cr.	Dr.	Cr.	Dr.	Cr.	Dr.	Cr.	Dr.	Cr.	Dr.	Cr.		

Group B Problems

(The forms you need are on pages 366–378 of the *Study Guide and Working Papers*.)

11B-1. Using the chart of accounts of Dr. Joy French from Problem 11A-1 (p. 433), record the following transactions in the combined journal and then prove the journal:

Journalizing transactions of a modified cash-basis system into a combined journal.

Check Figure: Crossfooting Total $25,280

200X

May
- 1 Dr. Joy French deposited $9,000 in the practice.
- 3 Paid rent for the month to Jane Jones Realty, $700, check no. 1.
- 8 Bought medical supplies from Able Co., $750, check no. 2.
- 12 Bought medical equipment from Jane's Supply, $4,000, check no. 3.
- 15 Received cash from patients, $3,000.
- 18 Bought additional medical supplies from Able Co., $910, check no. 4.
- 19 Dr. French withdrew $790 for personal use, check no. 5.
- 21 Paid Ron's Janitorial Service, $500, check no. 6.
- 24 Received cash from patients, $3,400.
- 25 Paid for postage stamps, $30 (miscellaneous expense), check no. 7.
- 27 Paid salaries for month, $1,600, check no. 8.
- 28 Paid Ron's Janitorial Service, $300, check no. 9.
- 29 Dr. French withdrew $300 for personal use, check no. 10.

11B-2. Using the chart of accounts for Dr. Fox from Problem 11A-2 (p. 434), record the following transactions in the combined journal and then prove the journal. (Beginning balances are in the *Study Guide and Working Papers*.)

Journalizing transactions of a modified cash-basis system into a combined journal with headings for payroll deductions and recording payroll tax expenses.

Check Figure: Crossfooting Total $34,212

200X

May
- 1 Received $4,000 from patients.
- 3 Issued check no. 400 to Lane Drug for medical supplies, $700.
- 5 Issued check no. 401 to J. Realty to pay three months' insurance premiums, $900.
- 9 Received checks from patients, $3,000.
- 12 Issued the following payroll checks:

	Check No.	Gross Pay	Social Security	Medicare	FIT	Net Pay
Amy Wand	402	$ 900	$ 56	$13	$180	$ 651
Jessie Fire	403	800	49	12	160	579
Willard Scott	404	600	37	9	120	434
		$2,300	$142	$34	$460	$1,664

- 18 Issued check no. 405 to Lane Drug for medical supplies, $900.
- 25 Dr. Fox withdrew $400 for personal use, check no. 406.
- 28 Dr. Fox paid Social Security, Medicare, and FIT from payroll of May 12, check no. 407. (Don't forget Dr. Fox's share of Social Security and Medicare.)

11B-3. Using the chart of accounts of Dr. Dick Clark from Problem 11A-3 (p. 435), journalize the following transactions and prove the combined journal. Fill

Journalizing, recording, and posting combined journal used to record transactions using the accrual basis of accounting.

Check Figure:
Total of Sundry Dr. Column $1,430

200X

July 1 Dr. Dick Clark invested $6,000 cash and $4,000 of office equipment in the practice.

1 Paid insurance on the office for one year in advance, $1,200, check no. 1.

9 Purchased office equipment on account from Smith Stationery Co., $1,400.

12 Completed physical examinations on each schoolchild at Salem Elementary School, $2,000 on account.

18 Received $700 cash for medical fees earned.

19 Performed a complete examination for Alvin Ray's son, $200 on account.

20 Paid Smith Stationery one-half the amount owed from July 9 transaction, check no. 2.

26 Paid telephone bill, $95, check no. 3.

27 Paid utilities, $60, check no. 4.

28 Paid Toby Cleaning Co. for cleaning service performed, $75, check no. 5.

11B-4. Buzzy Sullivan opened a dry-cleaning store that also sold accessories. The chart of accounts for Buzzy's Cleaning Company is given in Problem 11A-4 (p. 436). Here are the transactions for the month of January:

Check Figure: Total of
Sundry Dr. Column $1,800

200X

Jan. 1 Buzzy Sullivan invested $6,000 cash in the business.

8 Paid for a five-year company insurance policy in advance, $1,200, check no. 1.

10 Purchased merchandise on account from Role Company, $700.

12 Cleaned shirts for cash, $950.

15 Cleaned suits on account for Pete Daley, $500.

17 Purchased cleaning equipment on account from Ral Company, $600.

20 Borrowed $4,000 from Frank National Bank.

21 Cleaned shirts on account for P. Daley, $50.

24 Received payment from P. Daley for $500 less a 2 percent discount from January 15 transaction.

25 Purchased merchandise on account from Bomb Company, $90.

26 Cleaned pants on account for Alice Small, $20.

27 Paid Role Company $700 less a 2 percent discount for merchandise that was purchased on January 10, check no. 2.

28 Returned $200 of cleaning equipment to Ral Company for faulty work.

29 Paid Bomb Company $90 less a 10 percent discount on purchases made on account on January 25, check no. 3.

30 Cash sales, $700.

Your tasks are to journalize, record, post, and prove the combined journal for Buzzy.

REAL-WORLD APPLICATIONS

11R-1.

Jeff Smith has been running his business on strictly a cash basis. At a party over the weekend he met an accountant who told him that his business should use a modified cash system. Jeff has brought you his chart of accounts so that you may revise it as well as lay out a combined journal. Using the following chart of accounts, please design a combined journal for Jeff. Allow columns for payroll deductions. Tell Jeff in writing some of the benefits of a modified cash-basis system.

Jeff Smith Chart of Accounts

Assets
111 Cash
113 Petty Cash

Liabilities
211 Notes Payable

Owner's Equity
311 J. Smith, Capital
312 J. Smith, Withdrawals
313 Income Summary

Revenue
411 Professional Fees

Expenses
511 Insurance Expense
512 Furniture Expense
514 Medical Equipment Expense
515 Medical Supplies Expense
516 Salary Expense
517 Telephone Expense
518 Miscellaneous Expense

11R-2.
Margie Heaves is about to open a dry-cleaning shop. She has hired you to design a combined journal for her shop. It will definitely be a small business with a limited number of transactions that are not too complicated. After analyzing Margie's company, you develop the following chart of accounts:

1. Cash.

2. Accounts Receivable.

3. Equipment.

4. Accounts Payable.

5. Cleaning Sales.

6. Wage Expense.

7. Supplies Expense.

8. Miscellaneous Expense.

Margie has asked you to provide her, as soon as possible, a written justification for your design of the parts of the combined journal. Be prepared to support the combined journal you present to her. Please label all headings of the journal in terms of Debits and Credits. What titles are missing from the chart of accounts?

YOU make the call

Critical Thinking/Ethical Case

11R-3.
Angel Shower, the bookkeeper of Aster Company, also collects the payments of invoices by customers. Angel noticed that Rume Company paid the April 10 invoice twice. Angel, who is in need of extra cash, does not plan to inform Rume Company of the double payment. Do you agree with Angel's decision? You make the call. Write down your specific recommendations to Angel.

INTERNET EXERCISE

EX-1. [http://www.carnivalcorp.com]   Many companies have a goal of continuing to grow and develop. Some companies grow through expansion of existing operations and increased utilization of existing assets. Other firms will grow through the acquisition of other firms that may be in the same industry the firm currently operates within, or by purchasing a firm that covers new territory for the firm. No matter which method the firm selects, capital budgeting is an important part of a systematic expansion plan. Consider the expansion activities of Carnival Corporation, a firm that has expanded through acquisition, new assets and also consider asset replacement.

1. Go to the home page for Carnival Corporation at http://www.carnivalcorp.com. Select the link to the investor overview. What cruise lines does Carnival own or have an interest in? How many current ships does Carnival operate? What type of plans does the firm list for future expansion? What does this information indicate about the intent of the firm?

2. As we can see, the firm has looked ahead to buying new ships. To get additional information click on the link to the annual reports, and then select the most recent annual report and open it using Adobe Acrobat Reader. Go to the section on Management's Discussion and Analysis of Financial Condition and Results of Operations near the end of the report. Looking at the operating results summary, use the passenger cruise days and occupancy percentage to compute Carnival's capacity in passenger cruise days. How has this capacity changed over the past three years?

3. Now backtrack to the beginning of the annual report and read the CEO's letter. What does the letter tell the investor about new investment during the current year? What form did the investment/expansion take? What are the investment plans for the future?

4. While acquiring contracts for new ships and increasing ownership of other lines is noteworthy, the firm must in some manner plan to pay for this expansion. Let's look at the Statement of Cash Flows to see if we can determine where the firm got the cash to pay for the new ships. Based on your review of the cash flow statement, how much money did the firm invest in new assets? Where did Carnival generate these funds?

5. Another example of Carnival's planning for expansion is found in the footnote on Commitments and Contingencies (footnote 8 in 1999). What information does this footnote provide? How does this information indicate that Carnival has considered a capital budget of some sort?

CONTINUING PROBLEM

Using the combined journal to replace all previously used journals, record the following transactions for the month of March.

Assignment

(See pages 382–394 in the *Study Guide and Working Papers*.)
    Post all transactions to the required ledger accounts and prepare a trial balance as of March 31.

200X

Mar.		
	2	Billed Vita Needle for services performed; invoice no. 12686, $1,300.
	5	Paid a balance owed on the phone bill received in November, $150.
	6	Received the electric bill for the month, $290, due in 30 days.
	10	Collected balance in full from Taylor Golf, sales invoice no. 5000.
	11	Paid for advertising with Pacific Bell, $800.
	20	Paid the insurance premium for the month, $100.
	28	Bought postage on account for direct mail piece from Mail Boxes, Etc., $150.

CHAPTER 12

Preparing a Worksheet for a Merchandise Company

WITH SPECIAL APPENDIX ON WHAT WORKSHEETS LOOK LIKE IN A PERPETUAL INVENTORY SYSTEM

The Upside
You have six months of inventory
The downside
It will be obsolete in three

This is the copy for a United Parcel Service (UPS) ad that ran in the October 2000 issue of *eCompany Now* magazine. The copy goes on to promise UPS's business customers that the company can help them "increase inventory velocity."

It's a hallmark of today's hyperactive economy that we even consider the notion that inventory has a *speed*. Yet with the lifespan of a computer component or trendy leather handbag now measured in weeks, speed to market can matter more than product features or quality. Hence, inventory is more likely to be zipping around the world via overnight air express than gathering dust in a warehouse.

This is all good news for the air express companies, which are the benefi-ciaries and enablers of a wired, global economy. Picking up and delivering packages is just part of the total menu of products and services that the top four global express companies — Federal Express, United Parcel Service, DHL Worldwide Express, and TNT International — now offer their customers. These companies have evolved to meet customer's business needs; they are faster and more sophisticated with round the clock operations around the globe.

At the DHL Air Express hub in Brussels, Belgium, you get a snapshot of lean inventory in action. It is 3:00 A.M. and workers use forklifts to hoist Dell com-puters, Nokia cell phones, and boxes of Pashmina scarves onto planes bound for Finland, South Africa, and Argentina. And all these products just came off other planes: everything is in perpetual motion and has never seen a warehouse.

This emphasis on keeping inventory in motion calls for a more up-to-date way to track inventory costs. In the chapter's appendix we introduce a method of accounting for inventory called, appropriately, the **perpetual method.** It requires more accounting effort than the **periodic method,** which is explained in the text of the chapter. However, the perpetual method has an important advantage: key accounts of Merchandise Inventory and Cost of Goods Sold will always provide current information to managers about their investment in inventory and the cost of the merchandise sold to customers.

Based on: Lara L. Sowinski, "This isn't your father's express shipper," *World Trade,* July 2000, pp. 52–55. Andrew Tanzer, "Warehouses that fly," *Forbes,* October 18, 1999, pp. 120-124. Vanessa Drucker, "B2B boom," *Global Finance,* April 2000, pp. 46–48. Anonymous, "New Offerings: DHL considers an IPO after buyback of stake DAILY INVESTING REPORT, *The Atlanta Constitution,* December 14, 1999, p. F6.

LEARNING OBJECTIVES

▼ Figuring adjustments for merchandise inventory, unearned rent, supplies used, insurance expired, depreci-ation expense, and salaries accrued. (p. 443)

▼ Preparing a worksheet for a merchandise company. (p. 446)

In Chapters 9 and 10 we discussed the special journals and subsidiary ledgers of a merchandise company. Appendix material provided an introduction to perpetual inventory. Now we shift our attention to recording adjustments and completing a worksheet for a merchandise company. Note that the appendix at the end of the chapter shows worksheets for a perpetual system.

LEARNING UNIT 12-1

ADJUSTMENTS FOR MERCHANDISE INVENTORY AND UNEARNED RENT

Gross Sales
− Sales Ret. + Allow.
− Sales discount
= Net Sales

The Merchandise Inventory account shows the goods that a merchandise com-pany has available to sell to customers. There are several ways of keeping track of the **cost of goods sold** (the total cost of the goods sold to customers) and the quantity of inventory that a company has on hand. In this chapter we discuss the **periodic inventory system,** in which the balance in inventory is updated

FIGURE 12-1. Ending Inventory Sheet

ART'S WHOLESALE CLOTHING COMPANY ENDING INVENTORY SHEET AS OF DECEMBER 31, 20X2			
Amount	Explanation	Unit Cost	Total
20	Ladies' Jackets code 14-0	$50	$1,000
10	Men's Hats code 327	10	100
90	Men's Shirts code 423	10	900
100	Ladies' Blouses code 481	20	2,000
			$4,000
Counted by _____ Checked and priced by _____			

only at the end of the accounting period.* This system is used by companies like Art's Wholesale Clothing Company, which sell a variety of merchandise with low unit prices.

Assume Art's Wholesale Clothing Company started the year with $19,000 worth of merchandise. This merchandise is called **beginning merchandise inventory** or simply **beginning inventory.** The balance of beginning inventory never changes. Instead, all purchases of merchandise are recorded in the Purchases account. During the accounting period $52,000 worth of such purchases were made and recorded in the Purchases account.

At the end of the period, the company takes a physical count of the merchandise in stock; this amount is called **ending merchandise inventory** or simply **ending inventory.** It is calculated on an inventory sheet as shown in Figure 12-1.

This $4,000, which is the ending inventory for this period, will be the beginning inventory for the next period.

When the income statement is prepared, the cost of goods sold section requires two distinct numbers for inventory. The beginning inventory adds to the cost of goods sold, and the ending inventory is subtracted from the cost of goods sold (see margin aids at right). Remember that the two figures for beginning and ending inventory were calculated months apart. Thus combining these amounts to come up with one inventory figure would not be accurate.

Note that in the calculation (in the margin) of cost of goods sold that a new title called **Freight-in** is shown. Freight-in is a cost of goods sold account that records the shipping cost to the buyer. Note that net sales less cost of goods sold equals **gross profit.** Subtracting operating expenses from gross profits equals net income.

> Net Sales
> − Cost of goods sold
> = Gross profit
> − Operating expenses
> = Net Income

> Cost of goods sold:
> Beginning inventory
> + Net purchases
> + Freight-in
> − Ending inventory
> = Cost of goods sold

ADJUSTMENT FOR MERCHANDISE INVENTORY

Adjusting the Merchandise Inventory account is a two-step process because we must record the beginning inventory and ending inventory amounts separately. The first step deals with beginning merchandise inventory.

Given: Beginning Inventory, $19,000

Our first adjustment removes beginning inventory from the asset account (Merchandise Inventory) and transfers it to Income Summary. We do so by crediting Merchandise Inventory for $19,000 and debiting Income Summary for the same amount. This adjustment is shown on page 444 in T account form and on a transaction analysis chart:

> First adjustment transfers amount in beginning inventory from Merchandise Inventory to Income Summary.

> Note that Income Summary has no normal balance of debit or credit.

*For a discussion of the **perpetual inventory system**, see the appendix at the end of chapter 9, p. 359.

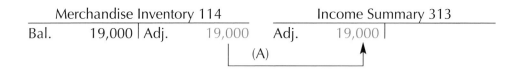

	Merchandise Inventory 114		Income Summary 313
Bal.	19,000	Adj. 19,000	Adj. 19,000	

(A)

Accounts Affected	Category	↑ ↓	Rules
Income Summary	—	—	**Dr.**
Merchandise Inventory	**Asset**	↓	**Cr.**

(The adjusting entries would be recorded first on the worksheet and then in the general journal.)

The second step is entering the amount of ending inventory ($4,000) in the Merchandise Inventory account. This step is done to record the amount of goods on hand at the end of the period as an asset and to subtract this amount from the cost of goods sold (because we have not sold this inventory yet). To do so, we debit Merchandise Inventory for $4,000 and credit Income Summary for the same amount. This adjustment is shown below in T account form and on a transaction analysis chart:

> **Second adjustment updates inventory account with a figure for ending inventory.**

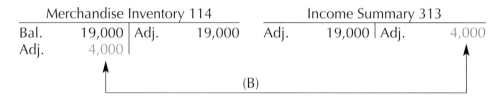

	Merchandise Inventory 114		Income Summary 313	
Bal.	19,000	Adj. 19,000	Adj. 19,000	Adj. 4,000
Adj.	4,000			

(B)

Beginning inventory	$19,000
+ Net cost of purchases	50,910
= Cost of goods available for sale	$69,910
− Ending inventory	4,000
= Cost of goods sold	$65,910

Note: If freight-in was involved, it would have been added to net cost of purchases.

Let's look at how this process or method of recording merchandise inventory is reflected in the balance sheet and income statement (see Figure 12-2). Note that the $19,000 of beginning inventory is assumed sold and is shown on the income statement as part of the cost of goods sold. The ending inventory of $4,000 is assumed not to be sold and is subtracted from the cost of goods sold on the income statement. The ending inventory becomes next month's beginning inventory on the balance sheet. When the income statement is prepared, we will need a figure for beginning inventory as well as a figure for ending inventory.

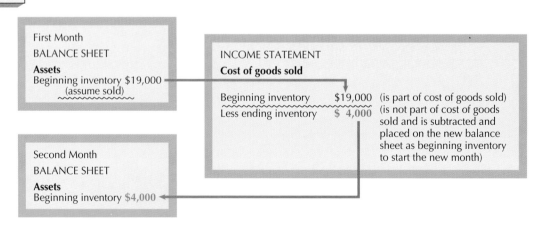

FIGURE 12-2. Recording Inventory on a Partial Balance Sheet and Income Statement

ADJUSTMENT FOR UNEARNED RENT

A second new account we have not seen before is a liability called Unearned Rent or Rent Received in Advance. This account records the amount collected for rent before the service (renting the space) has been provided.

Suppose Art's Wholesale Clothing Company is subletting a portion of its space to Jesse Company for $200 per month. Jesse Company sends Art a check for $600 for three months' rent paid in advance. This unearned rent ($600) is a liability on the balance sheet because Art's Wholesale owes Jesse Company three months' worth of occupancy.

When Art's Wholesale fulfills a portion of the rental agreement—when Jesse Company has been in the space for a period of time—this liability account will be reduced and the Rental Income account will be increased. Rental Income is another type of revenue for Art's Wholesale.

Remember that under accrual accounting, revenue is recognized when it is earned, whether payment is received then or not. Here, Art's Wholesale collected cash in advance for a service that it has not performed as yet. A liability called Unearned Rent is the result. Art's Wholesale may have the cash, but the Rental Income is not recorded until it is earned. There are other types of unearned revenue besides unearned rent. Examples are subscriptions for magazines, legal fees collected before the work is performed, and insurance.

Received cash for renting space in future.

Cash	Asset	↑	Dr.
Unearned Rent	Liab.	↑	Cr.

The adjustment when rental income is earned:

Unearned Rent	Liab.	↓	Dr.
Rental Income	Rev.	↑	Cr.

LEARNING UNIT 12-1 REVIEW

AT THIS POINT you should be able to

- ▼ Define the periodic method of inventory accounting. (p. 442)
- ▼ Explain why beginning and ending inventory are two separate figures in the cost of goods sold section on the income statement. (p. 443)
- ▼ Calculate net sales, cost of goods sold, gross profit, and net income. (p. 444)
- ▼ Show how to calculate a figure for ending inventory. (p. 444)
- ▼ Explain why unearned rent is a *liability* account. (p. 445)

SELF-REVIEW QUIZ 12-1

(The forms you need are on page 395 of the *Study Guide and Working Papers*.)

Given the following, prepare the two *adjusting* entries for Merchandise Inventory on 12/31/0X.

Merchandise Inventory, 1/1/0X	$ 8,000
Purchases	9,000
Merchandise Inventory, 12/31/0X	4,000
Cost of Goods Sold	10,000
Unearned Magazine Subscriptions	8,000

Solution to Self-Review Quiz 12-1

Dec.	31	Income Summary	8 0 0 0 00		
		Merchandise Inventory		8 0 0 0 00	
	31	Merchandise Inventory	4 0 0 0 00		
		Income Summary		4 0 0 0 00	

Quiz Tip: Note that Unearned Magazine Subscriptions is a liability and is not involved in the adjustment for Merchandise Inventory.

LEARNING UNIT 12-2

COMPLETING THE WORKSHEET

In this unit we prepare a worksheet for Art's Wholesale Clothing Company. For convenience we reproduce the company's chart of accounts in Figure 12-3.

Figure 12-4 shows the trial balance that was prepared on December 1, 200X, from the special journals of Art's Wholesale. (Note that it is placed directly on the first two columns of the worksheet.)

In looking at the trial balance, we see many new titles that have appeared since we completed a trial balance for a service company in Chapter 5. Let's look specifically at these new titles in the summary in Table 12-1.

Note the following:

▼ **Mortgage Payable** is a liability account that records the increases and decreases in the amount of debt owed on a mortgage. We discuss this account more in the next chapter, when financial reports are prepared.

▼ **Interest Expense** represents a nonoperating expense for Art's Wholesale and thus is categorized as Other Expense. The interest would be a regular expense if it were incurred for business purposes. We look at this expense in the next chapter.

▼ **Unearned Revenue** is a liability account that records receipt of payment for goods and services in advance of delivery. Unearned Rent is a particular example of this general type of account.

FIGURE 12-3. Art's Wholesale Clothing Company Chart of Accounts

CHART OF ACCOUNTS	
Assets 100–199	**Revenue 400–499**
111 Cash	411 Sales
112 Petty Cash	412 Sales Returns and Allowances
113 Accounts Receivable	413 Sales Discount
114 Merchandise Inventory	414 Rental Income
115 Supplies	**Cost of Goods Sold 500–599**
116 Prepaid Insurance	511 Purchases
121 Store Equipment	512 Purchases Discount
122 Accum. Depreciation, Store Equipment	513 Purchases Returns and Allowances
Liabilities 200–299	514 Freight-In
211 Accounts Payable	**Expenses 600–699**
212 Salaries Payable	611 Salaries Expense
213 Federal Income Tax Payable	612 Payroll Tax Expense
214 FICA—Social Security Payable	613 Depreciation Expense, Store Equipment
215 FICA—Medicare Payable	614 Supplies Expense
216 State Income Tax Payable	615 Insurance Expense
217 SUTA Tax Payable	616 Postage Expense
218 FUTA Tax Payable	617 Miscellaneous Expense
219 Unearned Rent*	618 Interest Expense
220 Mortgage Payable	619 Cleaning Expense
Owner's Equity 300–399	620 Delivery Expense
311 Art Newner, Capital	
312 Art Newner, Withdrawals	
313 Income Summary	

*Although Unearned Rent is the only term under Liabilities not using payable, it is a liability.

FIGURE 12-4. Trial Balance Section of the Worksheet

	Trial Balance	
	Dr.	Cr.
Cash	12 9 2 0 00	
Petty Cash	1 0 0 00	
Accounts Receivable	14 5 0 0 00	
Merchandise Inventory	19 0 0 0 00	
Supplies	8 0 0 00	
Prepaid Insurance	9 0 0 00	
Store Equipment	4 0 0 0 00	
Acc. Dep., Store Equipment		4 0 0 00
Accounts Payable		17 9 0 0 00
Federal Income Tax Payable		8 0 0 00
FICA-Soc. Sec. Payable		4 5 4 00
FICA-Medicare Payable		1 0 6 00
State Income Tax Payable		2 0 0 00
SUTA Tax Payable		1 0 8 00
FUTA Tax Payable		3 2 00
Unearned Rent		6 0 0 00
Mortgage Payable		2 3 2 0 00
Art Newner, Capital		7 9 0 5 00
Art Newner, Withdrawals	8 6 0 0 00	
Income Summary		
Sales		95 0 0 0 00
Sales Returns and Allowances	9 5 0 00	
Sales Discount	6 7 0 00	
Purchases	52 0 0 0 00	
Purchases Discount		8 6 0 00
Purchases Returns and Allowances		6 8 0 00
Freight-In	4 5 0 00	
Salaries Expense	11 7 0 0 00	
Payroll Tax Expense	4 2 0 00	
Postage Expense	2 5 00	
Miscellaneous Expense	3 0 00	
Interest Expense	3 0 0 00	
	127 3 6 5 00	127 3 6 5 00

We have already discussed adjustments (p. 444), which make up the two-step process involved in adjusting Merchandise Inventory at the end of the accounting period. Now we show T accounts and transaction analysis charts for some more adjustments that need to be made at this point in a merchandise firm, just as they do in a service company.

Adjustment C: Rental Income Earned by Art's Wholesale, $200

A month ago, Cash was increased by $600, as was a liability, Unearned Rent. Art's Wholesale received payment in advance but had not earned the rental income. Now, because $200 has been earned, the liability is reduced and Rental Income can be recorded for the $200. This step is shown as follows:

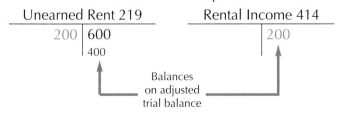

Unearned Rent	Liability	↓	Dr.	$200
Rental Income	Revenue	↑	Cr.	$200

Adjustment D: Supplies on Hand, $300

$500 worth of supplies has been used up; thus there is a need to increase Supplies Expense and decrease the asset Supplies.

Supplies Expense	Expense	↑	Dr.	$500
Supplies	Asset	↓	Cr.	$500

TABLE 12-1 SUMMARY OF NEW ACCOUNT TITLES

Title	Category	Report(s) Found on	Normal Balance	Temporary or Permanent
Petty Cash	Asset	Balance Sheet	Dr.	Permanent
Merchandise Inventory* (Beginning)	Asset	Balance Sheet from prior period	Dr.	Permanent
	Cost of Goods Sold	Income Statement of current period		
Federal Income Tax Payable	Liability	Balance Sheet	Cr.	Permanent
FICA—Social Security Payable	Liability	Balance Sheet	Cr.	Permanent
FICA—Medicare Payable	Liability	Balance Sheet	Cr.	Permanent
State Income Tax Payable	Liability	Balance Sheet	Cr.	Permanent
SUTA Tax Payable	Liability	Balance Sheet	Cr.	Permanent
FUTA Tax Payable	Liability	Balance Sheet	Cr.	Permanent
Unearned Rent†	Liability	Balance Sheet	Cr.	Permanent
Mortgage Payable	Liability	Balance Sheet	Cr.	Permanent
Sales	Revenue	Income Statement	Cr.	Temporary
Sales Returns and Allowances	Contra Revenue	Income Statement	Dr.	Temporary
Sales Discount	Contra Revenue	Income Statement	Dr.	Temporary
Purchases§	Cost of Goods Sold	Income Statement	Dr.	Temporary
Purchases Discount	Contra-Cost of Goods Sold	Income Statement	Cr.	Temporary
Purchases Returns and Allowances	Contra-Cost of Goods Sold	Income Statement	Cr.	Temporary
Freight-In	Cost of Goods Sold	Income Statement	Dr.	Temporary
Payroll Tax Expense	Expense	Income Statement	Dr.	Temporary
Postage Expense	Expense	Income Statement	Dr.	Temporary
Interest Expense	Other Expense	Income Statement	Dr.	Temporary

*The ending inventory of current period is a contra-cost of goods sold on the income statement and will be an asset on the balance sheet for next period.

†Referred to as Unearned Revenue.

§Note that the category for Purchases and Freight-In are Cost of Goods Sold, whereas Purchases Discounts and Purchases Returns and Allowances are Contra-Cost of Goods Sold.

Adjustment E: Insurance Expired, $300

Because insurance has expired by $300, Insurance Expense is increased by $300 and the asset Prepaid Insurance is decreased by $300.

Insurance Expense	Expense	↑	Dr.	$300
Prepaid Insurance	Asset	↓	Cr.	$300

Adjustment F: Depreciation Expense, $50

When depreciation is taken, Depreciation Expense and Accumulated Depreciation are both increased by $50. Note that the cost of the store equipment remains the same.

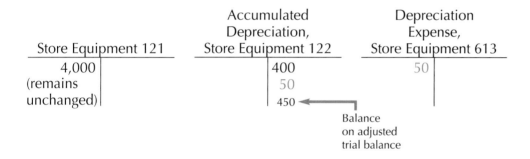

Dep. Exp., Store Equip.	Expense	↑	Dr.	$50
Acc. Dep., Store Equip.	Contra-Asset	↑	Cr.	$50

Adjustment G: Salaries Accrued, $600

The $600 in Salaries Accrued causes an increase in Salaries Expense and Salaries Payable.

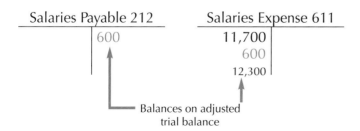

Salaries Expense	Expense	↑	Dr.	$600
Salaries Payable	Liability	↑	Cr.	$600

Remember: We do not combine the $19,000 and $4,000 in Income Summary. When we prepare the cost of goods sold section for the formal financial statement, we will need both a beginning and an ending figure for inventory.

Figure 12-5 shows the worksheet with the adjustments and adjusted trial balance column filled out. Note that the adjustment numbers in Income Summary from beginning and ending inventory are also carried over to the adjusted trial balance and are not combined.

The next step in completing the worksheet is to fill out the income statement columns from the adjusted trial balance, as shown in Figure 12-6.

	Trial Balance Dr.	Trial Balance Cr.	Adjustments Dr.	Adjustments Cr.	Adjusted Trial Balance Dr.	Adjusted Trial Balance Cr.
Cash	12,920 00				12,920 00	
Petty Cash	100 00				100 00	
Accounts Receivable	1,450 00		(B)	(A)	1,450 00	
Merchandise Inventory	19,000 00		4,000 00	19,000 00	4,000 00	
Supplies	800 00			(D) 500 00	300 00	
Prepaid Insurance	900 00			(E) 300 00	600 00	
Store Equipment	4,000 00				4,000 00	
Acc. Dep., Store Equipment		400 00		(F) 50 00		450 00
Accounts Payable		17,900 00				17,900 00
Federal Income Tax Payable		800 00				800 00
FICA-Soc. Sec. Payable		454 00				454 00
FICA-Medicare Payable		106 00				106 00
State Income Tax Payable		200 00				200 00
SUTA Tax Payable		108 00				108 00
FUTA Tax Payable		32 00				32 00
Unearned Rent		600 00	(C) 200 00			400 00
Mortgage Payable		2,320 00				2,320 00
Art Newner, Capital		7,905 00				7,905 00
Art Newner, Withdrawals	8,600 00		(A)	(B)	8,600 00	
Income Summary			19,000 00	4,000 00	19,000 00	4,000 00
Sales		95,000 00				95,000 00
Sales Returns and Allowances	950 00				950 00	
Sales Discount	670 00				670 00	
Purchases	52,000 00				52,000 00	
Purchases Discount		860 00				860 00
Purchases Returns and Allowances		680 00				680 00
Freight-In	450 00				450 00	
Salaries Expense	11,700 00		(G) 600 00		12,300 00	
Payroll Tax Expense	420 00				420 00	
Postage Expense	25 00				25 00	
Miscellaneous Expense	30 00				30 00	
Interest Expense	300 00				300 00	
	127,365 00	127,365 00				
Rental Income				(C) 200 00		200 00
Supplies Expense			(D) 500 00		500 00	
Insurance Expense			(E) 300 00		300 00	
Depreciation Expense, Store Equip.			(F) 50 00		50 00	
Salaries Payable				(G) 600 00		600 00
			24,650 00	24,650 00	132,015 00	132,015 00

FIGURE 12-5. Worksheet with Three Columns Filled Out

$19,000 of beginning inventory is assumed sold during the period and thus is part of the cost of goods sold. By placing it in the debit column of Income Summary we increase the cost of goods sold.

$4,000 is the cost of ending inventory at the end of the period. It is assumed to be unsold and therefore is not part of the cost of goods sold. By placing it in the credit column of Income Summary we reduce the cost of goods sold.

$95,000 is the credit balance of Sales. The Sales Returns and Allowances, $950, and Sales Discount, $670, are placed on the debit side, which represents a reduction to total sales:
(Cr.) Sales
(Dr.) Less: Sales Returns and Allowances
(Dr.) Less: Sales Discount

The purchases account, $52,000, is on the debit side, reflecting an increase in costs due to purchasing additional merchandise. The Purchases Discount, $860, and Purchases Returns and Allowances, $680, are on the credit side, which reduces cost of purchases:
(Dr.) Purchases
(Cr.) Less: Purchases Returns and Allowances
(Cr.) Less: Purchases Discount

Freight-In adds to the cost of goods sold.

Rental Income, which falls under the category "other income" for Art's Wholesale, is increased by $200, because the first month's rental agreement has been fulfilled.

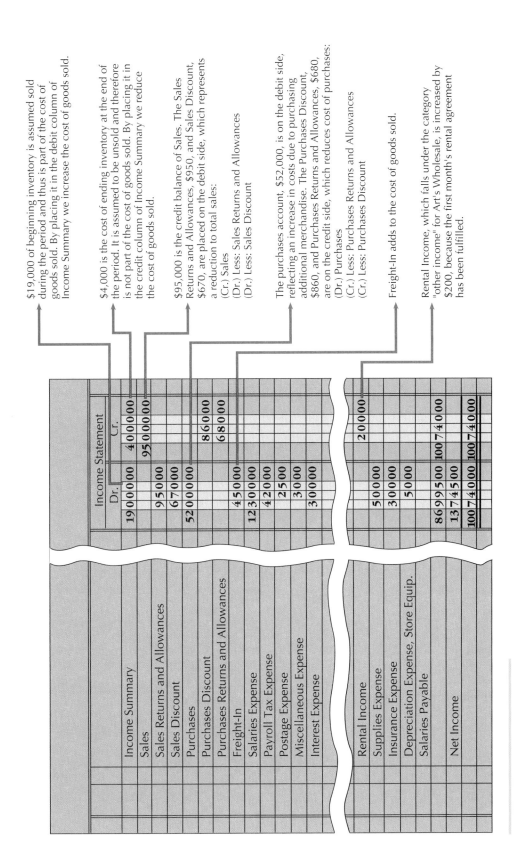

	Income Statement	
	Dr.	Cr.
Income Summary	19 000 00	4 000 00
Sales		95 000 00
Sales Returns and Allowances	9 50 00	
Sales Discount	6 70 00	
Purchases	52 000 00	
Purchases Discount		8 60 00
Purchases Returns and Allowances		6 80 00
Freight-In	4 50 00	
Salaries Expense	12 30 00	
Payroll Tax Expense	4 20 00	
Postage Expense	25 00	
Miscellaneous Expense	30 00	
Interest Expense	30 00	
Rental Income		2 00 00
Supplies Expense	5 00 00	
Insurance Expense	3 00 00	
Depreciation Expense, Store Equip.	50 00	
Salaries Payable		
	86 995 00	100 740 00
Net Income	13 745 00	
	100 740 00	100 740 00

FIGURE 12-6. Income Statement Section of the Worksheet

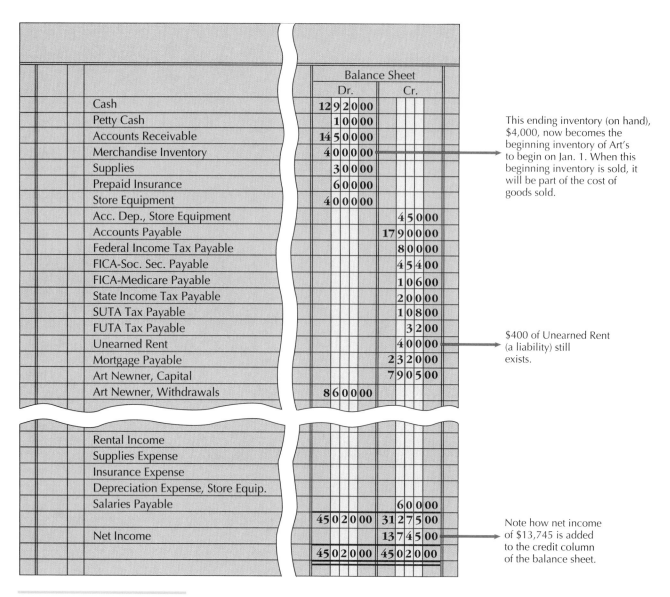

		Balance Sheet	
		Dr.	Cr.
Cash		12 9 2 0 00	
Petty Cash		1 0 0 00	
Accounts Receivable		14 5 0 0 00	
Merchandise Inventory		4 0 0 0 00	
Supplies		3 0 0 00	
Prepaid Insurance		6 0 0 00	
Store Equipment		4 0 0 0 00	
Acc. Dep., Store Equipment			4 5 0 00
Accounts Payable			17 9 0 0 00
Federal Income Tax Payable			8 0 0 00
FICA-Soc. Sec. Payable			4 5 4 00
FICA-Medicare Payable			1 0 6 00
State Income Tax Payable			2 0 0 00
SUTA Tax Payable			1 0 8 00
FUTA Tax Payable			3 2 00
Unearned Rent			4 0 0 00
Mortgage Payable			2 3 2 0 00
Art Newner, Capital			7 9 0 5 00
Art Newner, Withdrawals		8 6 0 0 00	

This ending inventory (on hand), $4,000, now becomes the beginning inventory of Art's to begin on Jan. 1. When this beginning inventory is sold, it will be part of the cost of goods sold.

$400 of Unearned Rent (a liability) still exists.

Rental Income			
Supplies Expense			
Insurance Expense			
Depreciation Expense, Store Equip.			
Salaries Payable			6 0 0 00
		45 0 2 0 00	31 2 7 5 00
Net Income			13 7 4 5 00
		45 0 2 0 00	45 0 2 0 00

Note how net income of $13,745 is added to the credit column of the balance sheet.

FIGURE 12-7. Balance Sheet Section of the Worksheet

The next step in completing the worksheet is to fill out the balance sheet columns (Fig. 12-7). Note how ending inventory is carried over to the balance sheet from the adjusted trial balance column. Take time also to look at the placement of the payroll tax liabilities as well as Unearned Rent on the worksheet. Figure 12-8, on pages 454–455, is the completed worksheet.

LEARNING UNIT 12-2 REVIEW

AT THIS POINT you should be able to

▼ Complete adjustments for a merchandise company. (p. 446)
▼ Complete a worksheet. (pp. 450–452)

(Use the foldout worksheet at the end of the *Study Guide and Working Papers.*)

From the trial balance shown here, complete a worksheet for Ray Company. Additional data include the following: (A and B) On December 31, 200X, ending inventory was calculated as $200; (C) Storage Fees Earned, $516; (D) Rent expired, $100; (E) Depreciation Expense, Office Equipment, $60; (F) Salaries Accrued, $200.

Account Title	Trial Balance Dr.	Trial Balance Cr.
Cash	2 4 8 6 00	
Merchandise Inventory	8 2 4 00	
Prepaid Rent	1 1 5 2 00	
Prepaid Insurance	6 0 00	
Office Equipment	2 1 6 0 00	
Accumulated Depreciation, Office Equipment		5 6 0 00
Unearned Storage Fees		2 5 1 6 00
Accounts Payable		1 0 0 00
B. Ray, Capital		1 9 3 2 00
Income Summary	—	—
Sales		1 1 0 4 0 00
Sales Returns and Allowances	5 4 6 00	
Sales Discount	2 1 6 00	
Purchases	5 2 5 6 00	
Purchases Returns and Allowances		1 6 8 00
Purchases Discount		1 0 2 00
Salaries Expense	2 0 1 6 00	
Insurance Expense	1 3 9 2 00	
Utilities Expense	9 6 00	
Plumbing Expense	2 1 4 00	
	1 6 4 1 8 00	1 6 4 1 8 00

Solution to Self-Review Quiz 12-2

The solution is shown on page 456.

> *Quiz Tip:* The ending inventory of $200 becomes next month's beginning inventory.

WORKSHEET
FOR YEAR ENDED DECEMBER 31, 200X

Account	Trial Balance Dr.	Trial Balance Cr.	Adjustments Dr.	Adjustments Cr.
Cash	12 920 00			
Petty Cash	100 00			
Accounts Receivable	14 500 00			
Merchandise Inventory	19 000 00		(B) 4000 00	(A) 19000 00
Supplies	800 00			(D) 500 00
Prepaid Insurance	900 00			(E) 300 00
Store Equipment	4 000 00			
Acc. Dep., Store Equipment		400 00		(F) 50 00
Accounts Payable		17 900 00		
Federal Income Tax Payable		800 00		
FICA—Social Security Payable		454 00		
FICA—Medicare Payable		106 00		
State Income Tax Payable		200 00		
SUTA Tax Payable		108 00		
FUTA Tax Payable		32 00		
Unearned Rent		600 00	(C) 200 00	
Mortgage Payable		2 320 00		
Art Newner, Capital		7 905 00		
Art Newner, Withdrawals	8 600 00			
Income Summary			(A) 19000 00	(B) 4000 00
Sales		95 000 00		
Sales Returns and Allowances	950 00			
Sales Discount	670 00			
Purchases	52 000 00			
Purchases Discount		860 00		
Purchases Returns and Allowances		680 00		
Freight-In	450 00			
Salaries Expense	11 700 00		(G) 600 00	
Payroll Tax Expense	420 00			
Postage Expense	25 00			
Miscellaneous Expense	30 00			
Interest Expense	300 00			
	127 365 00	127 365 00		
Rental Income				(C) 200 00
Supplies Expense			(D) 500 00	
Insurance Expense			(E) 300 00	
Depreciation Expense, Store Equip.			(F) 50 00	
Salaries Payable				(G) 600 00
			24 650 00	24 650 00
Net Income				

FIGURE 12-8. Completed Worksheet

Adjusted Trial Bal. Dr.	Adjusted Trial Bal. Cr.	Income Statement Dr.	Income Statement Cr.	Balance Sheet Dr.	Balance Sheet Cr.
12 92 0 00				12 92 0 00	
1 00 0 00				1 00 0 00	
14 50 0 00				14 50 0 00	
4 00 0 00				4 00 0 00	
3 00 00				3 00 00	
6 00 00				6 00 00	
4 00 0 00				4 00 0 00	
	4 50 00				4 50 00
	17 90 0 00				17 90 0 00
	8 00 00				8 00 00
	4 54 00				4 54 00
	1 06 00				1 06 00
	2 00 00				2 00 00
	1 08 00				1 08 00
	3 2 00				3 2 00
	4 00 00				4 00 00
	2 32 00				2 32 00
	7 90 5 00				7 90 5 00
8 60 0 00				8 60 0 00	
19 00 0 00	4 00 0 00	19 00 0 00	4 00 0 00		
	95 00 0 00		95 00 0 00		
9 50 00		9 50 00			
6 70 00		6 70 00			
52 00 0 00		52 00 0 00			
	8 60 00		8 60 00		
	6 80 00		6 80 00		
4 50 00		4 50 00			
12 30 0 00		12 30 0 00			
4 20 00		4 20 00			
2 5 00		2 5 00			
3 0 00		3 0 00			
3 00 00		3 00 00			
	2 00 00		2 00 00		
5 00 00		5 00 00			
3 00 00		3 00 00			
5 0 00		5 0 00			
	6 00 00				6 00 00
132 01 5 00	132 01 5 00	86 99 5 00	100 74 0 00	45 02 0 00	31 27 5 00
		13 74 5 00			13 74 5 00
		100 74 0 00	100 74 0 00	45 02 0 00	45 02 0 00

FIGURE 12-8. *(cont.)*

RAY COMPANY
WORKSHEET
FOR YEAR ENDED DECEMBER 31, 200X

Account	Trial Balance Dr.	Trial Balance Cr.	Adjustments Dr.	Adjustments Cr.	Adjusted Trial Balance Dr.	Adjusted Trial Balance Cr.	Income Statement Dr.	Income Statement Cr.	Balance Sheet Dr.	Balance Sheet Cr.
Cash	248600				248600				248600	
Merchandise Inventory	82400		(B)20000	(A)82400	20000				20000	
Prepaid Rent	115200			(D)10000	105200				105200	
Prepaid Insurance	6000				6000				6000	
Office Equipment	216000				216000				216000	
Acc. Dep., Store Equipment		56000		(E)6000		62000				62000
Unearned Storage Fees		251600	(C)51600			200000				200000
Accounts Payable		10000				10000				10000
B. Ray, Capital		193200				193200				193200
Income Summary			(A)82400	(B)20000	82400	20000	82400	20000		
Sales		1104000				1104000		1104000		
Sales Returns and Allowances	54600				54600		54600			
Sales Discount	21600				21600		21600			
Purchases	525600				525600		525600			
Purchases Returns and Allowances		16800				16800		16800		
Purchases Discount		10200				10200		10200		
Salaries Expense	201600		(F)20000		221600		221600			
Insurance Expense	139200				139200		139200			
Utilities Expense	9600				9600		9600			
Plumbing Expense	21400				21400		21400			
	1641800	1641800								
Storage Fees Earned				(C)51600		51600		51600		
Rent Expense			(D)10000		10000		10000			
Depreciation Expense, Equipment			(E)6000		6000		6000			
Salaries Payable				(F)20000		20000				20000
			190000	190000	1687800	1687800	1092000	1202600	595800	485200
Net Income							110600			110600
							1202600	1202600	595800	595800

SUMMARY OF KEY POINTS

Learning Unit 12-1

1. The periodic inventory system updates the record of goods on hand only at the *end* of the accounting period. This system is used for companies with a variety of merchandise with low unit prices.

2. In the periodic inventory system, additional purchases of merchandise during the accounting period will be recorded in the Purchases account. The amount in beginning inventory will remain unchanged during the accounting period. At the end of the period, a new figure for ending inventory will be calculated.

3. Beginning inventory at the end of the accounting period is part of the cost of goods sold, whereas ending inventory is a reduction to cost of goods sold.

4. The perpetual inventory system keeps a continuous record of inventory. It is used by companies with high amounts of inventory.

5. Net Sales less cost of goods sold equals gross profit. Gross profit less operating expenses equals Net Income.

6. Unearned Revenue is a liability account that accumulates revenue that has *not* been earned yet, although the cash has been received. It represents a liability to the seller until the service or product is performed or delivered.

Learning Unit 12-2

1. Two important adjustments in the accounting for a merchandise company deal with the Merchandise Inventory account and with the Unearned Revenue account (unearned rent).

2. When a company delivers goods or services for which it has been paid in advance, an adjustment is made to reduce the liability account Unearned Revenue and to increase an earned revenue account.

KEY TERMS

Beginning merchandise inventory (beginning inventory) The cost of goods on hand in a company to *begin* an accounting period.

Cost of goods sold Total cost of goods sold to customers.

Ending merchandise inventory (ending inventory) The cost of goods that remain unsold at the *end* of the accounting period. It is an asset on the new balance sheet.

Freight-in A cost of goods sold account that records shipping cost to buyer.

Gross profit Net sales less cost of goods sold.

Interest Expense The cost of borrowing money.

Mortgage Payable A liability account showing amount owed on a mortgage.

Periodic inventory system An inventory system that, at the *end* of each accounting period, calculates the cost of the unsold goods on hand by taking the cost of each unit times the number of units of each product on hand.

Perpetual inventory system An inventory system that keeps *continual track* of each type of inventory by recording units on hand at beginning, units sold, and the current balance after each sale or purchase.

Unearned Revenue A liability account that records receipt of payment for goods or services in advance of delivery.

BLUEPRINT: A WORKSHEET FOR A MERCHANDISE COMPANY

Account Titles	Adjustments Dr.	Adjustments Cr.	Adjusted Trial Balance Dr.	Adjusted Trial Balance Cr.	Income Statement Dr.	Income Statement Cr.	Balance Sheet Dr.	Balance Sheet Cr.
Cash			X				X	
Petty Cash			X				X	
Accounts Receivable			X				X	
Merchandise Inventory	X-E	X-B	X-E				X-E	
Supplies			X				X	
Equipment			X				X	
Acc. Dep., Store Equipment				X				X
Accounts Payable				X				X
Federal Income Tax Payable				X				X
FICA-Social Security Payable				X				X
FICA-Medicare Payable				X				X
State Income Tax Payable				X				X
SUTA Tax Payable				X				X
FUTA Tax Payable				X				X
Unearned Sales				X				X
Mortgage Payable				X				X
A. Flynn, Capital				X				X
A. Flynn, Withdrawals			X				X	
Income Summary*	X-B	X-E	X-B	X-E	X-B	X-E		
Sales				X		X		
Sales Returns and Allow.			X		X			
Sales Discount			X		X			
Purchases			X		X			
Purchases Ret. and Allow.				X		X		
Purchases Discount				X		X		
Freight-In			X		X			
Salaries Expense			X		X			
Payroll Tax Expense			X		X			
Insurance Expense			X		X			
Depreciation Expense			X		X			
Salaries Payable				X				X
Rental Income				X		X		

* Note that the figures for beginning (X-B) and ending inventory (X-E) are never combined on the Income Summary line of the worksheet. When the formal income statement is prepared, two distinct figures for inventory will be used to explain and calculate cost of goods sold. Beginning inventory adds to cost of goods sold; ending inventory reduces cost of goods sold.

QUESTIONS, MINI EXERCISES, EXERCISES, AND PROBLEMS

Discussion Questions

1. What is the function of the Purchases account?
2. Explain why Unearned Revenue is a liability account.
3. In a periodic system of inventory, the balance of beginning inventory will remain unchanged during the period. True or false?

4. What is the purpose of an inventory sheet?

5. Why do many Unearned Revenue accounts have to be adjusted?

6. Explain why figures for beginning and ending inventory are not combined on the Income Summary line of the worksheet.

Mini Exercises

(The forms you need are on page 397 of the *Study Guide and Working Papers.*)

Adjustment for Merchandise Inventory

1. Given the following, journalize the adjusting entries for merchandise inventory. Note that ending inventory has a balance of $14,000.

Merchandise Inventory 114	Income Summary 313
30,000	

Adjustment for Unearned Fees

2.
   a. Given the following, journalize the adjusting entry. By December 31, $300 of the unearned dog walking fees were earned.

Unearned Dog Walking Fees 225	Earned Dog Walking Fees 441
650 12/1/XX	4,000 12/1/XX

   b. What is the category of unearned dog walking fees?

Worksheet

3. Match the following:
   1. Located on the Income Statement debit column of the worksheet.
   2. Located on the Income Statement credit column of the worksheet.
   3. Located on the Balance Sheet debit column of the worksheet.
   4. Located on the Balance Sheet credit column of the worksheet.

   _____ a. Ending Merchandise Inventory
   _____ b. Unearned Rent
   _____ c. Sales Discount
   _____ d. Purchases
   _____ e. Rental Income
   _____ f. Petty Cash

Merchandise Inventory Adjustment on Worksheet

4. Adjustment column of a worksheet:

   | Merchandise Inventory | (A) — (B) |
   | Income Summary | (B) — (A) |

   Explain what the letters A and B represent. Why are they never combined?

Income Summary on the Worksheet

5.

	Adj.		ATB		Income Statement	
	Dr.	Cr.	Dr.	Cr.	Dr.	Cr.
Income Summary	A	B	C	D	E	F

Given a figure of Beginning Inventory of $500 and a $700 figure for Ending Inventory, place these numbers on the Income Summary line of this partial worksheet.

Exercises

(The forms you need are on page 398 of the *Study Guide and Working Papers*.)

Categorizing account titles.

12-1. Indicate the normal balance and category of each of the following accounts.

    a. Unearned Revenue

    b. Merchandise Inventory (beginning of period)

    c. Freight-In

    d. Payroll Tax Expense

    e. Purchases Discount

    f. Sales Discount

    g. FICA — Social Security Payable

    h. Purchases Returns and Allowances

Calculating net sales, cost of goods sold, gross profit, and net income.

12-2. From the following, calculate (a) net sales, (b) cost of goods sold, (c) gross profit, and (d) net income: Sales, $22,000; Sales Discount, $500; Sales Returns and Allowances, $250; Beginning Inventory, $650; Net Purchases, $13,200; Ending Inventory, $510; Operating Expenses, $3,600.

Unearned revenue.

12-3. Allan Co. had the following balances on December 31, 200X:

Cash		Unearned Janitorial Service	
2,100			600

Janitorial Service	
	7,200

The accountant for Allan has asked you to make an adjustment, because $400 of janitorial services has just been performed for customers who had paid two months. Construct a transaction analysis chart.

Calculating cost of goods sold.

12-4. Lesan Co. purchased merchandise costing $400,000. Calculate the cost of goods sold under the following different situations:

    a. Beginning inventory $40,000 and no ending inventory.

    b. Beginning inventory $50,000 and a $60,000 ending inventory.

    c. No beginning inventory and a $30,000 ending inventory.

Preparing a worksheet.

12-5. Prepare a worksheet from the following information:

    a/b. Merchandise Inventory, ending   13

    c. Store Supplies on hand   4

    d. Depreciation on Store Equipment   4

    e. Accrued Salaries   2

MOORE CO. TRIAL BALANCE DECEMBER 31, 200X		
	Dr.	Cr.
Cash	8 00	
Accounts Receivable	5 00	
Merchandise Inventory	11 00	
Store Supplies	10 00	
Store Equipment	20 00	
Accumulated Depreciation, Store Equipment		6 00
Accounts Payable		5 00
J. Moore, Capital		34 00
Income Summary	—	—
Sales		64 00
Sales Returns and Allowances	9 00	
Purchases	23 00	
Purchases Discount		3 00
Freight-In	3 00	
Salaries Expense	10 00	
Advertising Expense	13 00	
Totals	112 00	112 00

Group A Problems

(The forms you need are on page 399 of the *Study Guide and Working Papers*. You can also use the foldout worksheets at the end of the *Study Guide and Working Papers*.)

Calculating net sales, cost of goods sold, gross profit and net income.

12A-1. Based on the accounts listed below, calculate:

    a. Net sales.

    b. Cost of goods sold.

    c. Gross profit.

Check Figure:
Net Income $1,958

    d. Net income.

Accounts Payable	$ 4,800
Operating Expenses	1,500
Lang.com, Capital	18,200
Purchases	1,300
Freight-In	70
Ending Merchandise Inventory, Dec. 31, 200X	55
Sales	5,000
Accounts Receivable	400
Cash	700
Purchases Discount	40
Sales Returns and Allowances	210
Beg. Merchandise Inventory, Jan. 1, 200X	75
Purchases Returns and Allowances	66
Sales Discount	48

12A-2. From the trial balance on page 460, complete a worksheet for Jim's Hardware. Assume the following:

    a/b. Ending inventory on December 31 is calculated at $310.

    c. Insurance expired, $150.

    d. Depreciation on store equipment, $60.

    e. Accrued wages, $90.

Comprehensive Problem: Completing a worksheet for a merchandise company.

JIM'S HARDWARE
TRIAL BALANCE
DECEMBER 31, 200X

	Dr.	Cr.
Cash	786 00	
Accounts Receivable	1 152 00	
Merchandise Inventory	600 00	
Prepaid Insurance	684 00	
Store Equipment	2 160 00	
Accumulated Depreciation, Store Equipment		660 00
Accounts Payable		516 00
Jim Spool, Capital		1 632 00
Income Summary	—	
Hardware Sales		11 040 00
Hardware Sales Returns and Allowances	546 00	
Hardware Sales Discount	216 00	
Purchases	5 256 00	
Purchases Discount		168 00
Purchases Returns and Allowances		102 00
Wages Expense	1 716 00	
Rent Expense	792 00	
Telephone Expense	114 00	
Miscellaneous Expense	96 00	
	14 118 00	14 118 00

12A-3. The owner of Waltz Company has asked you to prepare a worksheet from the following trial balance.

WALTZ COMPANY
TRIAL BALANCE
DECEMBER 31, 200X

	Dr.	Cr.
Cash	5 408 00	
Petty Cash	240 00	
Accounts Receivable	2 512 00	
Beginning Merchandise Inventory, Jan. 1	5 092 00	
Prepaid Rent	616 00	
Office Supplies	944 00	
Office Equipment	9 280 00	
Accumulated Depreciation, Office Equipment		7 600 00
Accounts Payable		5 964 00
K. Waltz, Capital		5 476 00
K. Waltz, Withdrawals	4 800 00	
Income Summary	—	—
Sales		52 484 00
Sales Returns and Allowances	96 00	
Sales Discount	2 400 00	
Purchases	29 316 00	
Purchases Discount		16 00
Purchases Returns and Allowances		348 00
Office Salaries Expense	7 408 00	
Insurance Expense	2 400 00	
Advertising Expense	800 00	
Utilities Expense	576 00	
	71 888 00	71 888 00

Additional data:

a/b. Ending merchandise inventory on December 31, $1,805.

   c. Office supplies used up, $210.

   d. Rent expired, $195.

   e. Depreciation expense on office equipment, $550.

   f. Office salaries earned but not paid, $310.

12A-4. From the following trial balance and additional data, complete the worksheet for Ron's Wholesale Clothing Company.

> Comprehensive Problem:
> Completing a worksheet with payroll and unearned revenue.

RON'S WHOLESALE CLOTHING COMPANY TRIAL BALANCE DECEMBER 31, 200X		
	Dr.	Cr.
Cash	4 4 6 0 00	
Petty Cash	3 0 0 00	
Accounts Receivable	7 5 0 0 00	
Merchandise Inventory	9 0 0 0 00	
Supplies	1 0 0 0 00	
Prepaid Insurance	8 5 0 00	
Store Equipment	2 5 0 0 00	
Acc. Dep., Store Equipment		1 5 0 0 00
Accounts Payable		10 6 3 5 00
Federal Income Tax Payable		5 0 0 00
FICA—Social Security Payable		4 5 4 00
FICA—Medicare Payable		1 0 6 00
State Income Tax Payable		1 5 0 00
SUTA Tax Payable		1 0 8 00
FUTA Tax Payable		3 2 00
Unearned Storage Fees		3 2 5 00
Ron Win, Capital		12 5 0 0 00
Ron Win, Withdrawals	4 3 0 0 00	
Income Summary		
Sales		45 0 0 0 00
Sales Returns and Allowances	1 4 7 5 00	
Sales Discount	1 3 3 5 00	
Purchases	26 0 0 0 00	
Purchases Discount		5 5 0 00
Purchases Returns and Allowances		4 0 0 00
Freight-In	2 2 5 00	
Salaries Expense	12 0 0 0 00	
Payroll Tax Expense	4 2 0 00	
Interest Expense	8 9 5 00	
	72 2 6 0 00	72 2 6 0 00

> Check Figure:
> Net Loss $824

Additional data:

a/b. Ending merchandise inventory on December 31, $6,000.

   c. Supplies on hand, $400.

   d. Insurance expired, $600.

   e. Depreciation on store equipment, $400.

   f. Storage fees earned, $176.

Group B Problems

(The forms you need are on page 399 of the *Study Guide and Working Papers*.)

12B-1. From the following accounts, calculate (a) net sales, (b) cost of goods sold, (c) gross profit, and (d) net income.

Sales Discount	$ 452
Purchases Returns and Allowances	64
Beginning Merchandise Inventory, Jan 1, 200X	79
Sales Returns and Allowances	191
Purchases Discounts	42
Cash	3,895
Accounts Receivable	441
Sales	3,950
Ending Merchandise Inventory, Dec. 31, 200X	75
Freight-In	41
Purchases	1,152
R. Roland, Capital	1,950
Operating Expenses	895
Accounts Payable	129

12B-2. As the accountant for Jim's Hardware, you have been asked to complete a worksheet from the following trial balance as well as additional data.

JIM'S HARDWARE
TRIAL BALANCE
DECEMBER 31, 200X

	Dr.	Cr.
Cash	9 6 0 00	
Accounts Receivable	1 6 0 0 00	
Merchandise Inventory	7 3 6 00	
Prepaid Insurance	1 1 1 2 00	
Store Equipment	3 2 0 0 00	
Accumulated Depreciation, Store Equipment		1 6 8 0 00
Accounts Payable		1 4 0 8 00
J. Spool, Capital		2 5 7 6 00
Income Summary	—	—
Hardware Sales		1 4 8 0 0 00
Hardware Sales Returns and Allowances	7 2 8 00	
Hardware Sales Discount	6 8 8 00	
Purchases	7 0 8 8 00	
Purchases Discounts		2 4 0 00
Purchases Returns and Allowances		2 4 8 00
Wages Expense	2 3 0 4 00	
Rent Expense	1 8 4 0 00	
Telephone Expense	5 5 2 00	
Miscellaneous Expense	1 4 4 00	
	20 9 5 2 00	20 9 5 2 00

Additional data:

a/b. Cost of ending inventory on December 31, $480.

c. Insurance expired, $112.

d. Depreciation on store equipment, $90.

e. Accrued wages, $150.

12B-3. From the following, complete a worksheet for Waltz Company.

Comprehensive Problem:
Completing a worksheet.

Check Figure:
Net Income $6,850

WALTZ COMPANY TRIAL BALANCE DECEMBER 31, 200X	Dr.	Cr.
Cash	3 8 0 0 00	
Petty Cash	1 0 0 00	
Accounts Receivable	3 4 0 0 00	
Merchandise Inventory	5 2 0 4 00	
Prepaid Rent	1 2 0 0 00	
Office Supplies	1 3 6 0 00	
Office Equipment	9 6 8 0 00	
Accumulated Depreciation, Office Equipment		4 0 4 0 00
Accounts Payable		7 9 6 4 00
K. Waltz, Capital		5 4 7 6 00
K. Waltz, Withdrawals	5 0 0 0 00	
Income Summary		
Sales		52 4 6 2 00
Sales Returns and Allowances	1 1 6 00	
Sales Discount	2 2 0 0 00	
Purchases	29 2 9 6 00	
Purchases Discounts		1 2 0 8 00
Purchases Returns and Allowances		1 3 5 0 00
Office Salaries Expense	7 4 0 8 00	
Insurance Expense	2 2 0 0 00	
Advertising Expense	8 0 0 00	
Utilities Expense	7 3 6 00	
	72 5 0 0 00	72 5 0 0 00

Additional data:

a/b. Ending merchandise inventory on December 31, $1,600.

 c. Office supplies on hand, $90.

 d. Rent expired, $110.

 e. Depreciation expense on office equipment, $250.

 f. Salaries accrued, $180.

Comprehensive Problem:
Completing a worksheet with
payroll and unearned
revenue.

12B-4. From the following trial balance and additional data, complete the worksheet for Ron's Wholesale Clothing Company.

RON'S WHOLESALE CLOTHING COMPANY
TRIAL BALANCE
DECEMBER 31, 200X

	Dr.	Cr.
Cash	2 6 0 0 00	
Petty Cash	3 0 00	
Accounts Receivable	3 0 0 0 00	
Merchandise Inventory	3 6 0 0 00	
Supplies	2 7 0 00	
Prepaid Insurance	1 8 0 00	
Store Equipment	1 0 0 0 00	
Accumulated Depreciation, Store Equipment		4 9 6 00
Accounts Payable		4 5 9 0 00
FIT Payable		3 5 0 00
FICA—Social Security Payable		1 9 4 00
FICA—Medicare Payable		4 6 00
SIT Payable		1 0 0 00
SUTA Tax Payable		6 0 00
FUTA Tax Payable		1 4 00
Unearned Storage Fees		3 5 0 00
Ron Win, Capital		2 7 3 4 00
Ron Win, Withdrawals	1 8 0 0 00	
Income Summary	—	—
Sales		1 9 4 0 0 00
Sales Returns and Allowances	5 6 0 00	
Sales Discount	4 8 0 00	
Purchases	8 6 0 0 00	
Purchases Discount		2 4 0 00
Purchases Returns and Allowances		1 6 0 00
Freight-In	1 0 0 00	
Salaries Expense	6 0 0 0 00	
Payroll Tax Expense	1 9 4 00	
Interest Expense	3 2 0 00	
	28 7 3 4 00	28 7 3 4 00

Additional data:

a/b. Ending merchandise inventory on December 31, $9,000.

   c. Supplies on hand, $50.

   d. Insurance expired, $55.

   e. Depreciation on store equipment, $100.

   f. Storage fees earned, $115.

REAL-WORLD APPLICATIONS

12R-1.
Kim Andrews prepared the following income statement on a cash basis for Ed Sloan, M.D.

ED SLOAN, M.D. INCOME STATEMENT FOR YEAR ENDED DECEMBER 31, 20X2	
Professional Fees Earned	50 0 0 0 00
Expenses	18 0 0 0 00
Net Income	32 0 0 0 00

Dr. Sloan has requested written information from Kim as to what his professional fees earned would be under the accrual-basis system of accounting. Kim has asked you to provide Dr. Sloan with this information, based on the following facts that Kim ignored in the original preparation of the financial report:

	20X1	20X2
Accrued Professional Fees	$4,200	$5,300
Unearned Professional Fees	6,200	4,250

Make a written recommendation of the advantages of an accrual system to Dr. Sloan.

12R-2.

Abby Jay is having a difficult time understanding the relationship of sales, cost of goods sold, gross profit, and net income for a merchandise company. As the accounting lab tutor, you have been asked to sit down with Abby and explain how to calculate the missing amounts in each situation listed below. Keep in mind that each situation is a distinct and separate business problem.

	Sales	Beg. Inv.	Purchases	End Inv.	Cost of Goods Sold	Gross Profit	Expense	Net Income or Loss
Sit. 1	320,000	200,000	160,000	?	260,000	?	80,000	?
Sit. 2	380,000	140,000	?	180,000	200,000	?	100,000	80,000
Sit. 3	480,000	200,000	?	160,000	?	220,000	140,000	80,000
Sit. 4	?	160,000	280,000	140,000	?	160,000	140,000	?
Sit. 5	440,000	160,000	260,000	?	240,000	?	100,000	?
Sit. 6	280,000	120,000	?	140,000	160,000	?	?	40,000
Sit. 7	?	160,000	200,000	120,000	?	160,000	?	−20,000
Sit. 8	320,000	?	200,000	140,000	?	120,000	?	40,000

Explain in writing why gross profit does not always mean cash.

YOU make the call

Critical Thinking/Ethical Case

12R-3.

Jim Heary is the custodian of petty cash. Jim, who is short of personal cash, decided to pay his home electrical and phone bill from petty cash. He plans to pay it back next month. Do you feel Jim should do so? You make the call. Write down your specific recommendations to Jim.

INTERNET EXERCISES

EX-1. [www.saturnofelmhurst.com] An automobile dealer with a large inventory has a huge amount of cash invested in his product. The investment requires careful accounting to safeguard the asset from both a physically safe viewpoint, and from a safe accounting standpoint. Because each of the individual units in an automobile inventory is identifiable, automobile inventories lend themselves as excellent candidates for perpetual inventory accounting.

At the end of an accounting period what procedures would a car dealer take to determine if all of the units in its perpetual inventory are accounted for? How would you adjust the inventory for an extra unit found on the sales lot, if the unit was not in the perpetual inventory records?

EX-2. [www.saturnofelmhurst.com] In the previous example you determined what entries to make for inventory that was not on the accounting records, or for making an adjustment for inventory that was in the accounting records but not on the location.

In this exercise state how each of the following independent cases would affect Gross Profit. State whether Gross Profit is UNDERSTATED or OVERSTATED and give a reason for the answer you choose in each case.

a. One unit of inventory in the accounting records is not on the location.

b. One unit of inventory on the location is not in the accounting records.

c. One unit shown as a sale in the accounting records is on the location.

CONTINUING PROBLEM

The first six months of the year have concluded for Eldorado Computer Center, and Tony wants to make the necessary adjustments to his accounts to prepare accurate financial statements.

Assignment

(The worksheet is in the envelope at the end of the *Study Guide and Working Papers.*)

To prepare these adjustments, use the trial balance from Chapter 11 and the following inventory that Tony took at the end of March:

10 dozen $\frac{1}{4}''$ screws at a cost of $10 a dozen.

5 dozen $\frac{1}{2}''$ screws at a cost of $7 a dozen.

2 feet of coaxial cable at a cost of $5 per foot.

There was $300 worth of merchandise left in stock.

Depreciation of computer equipment:

Computer depreciates at $33 a month; purchased July 5.

Computer workstations depreciate at $20 per month; purchased September 17.

Shop benches depreciate at $25 per month; purchased November 5.

Depreciation of office equipment:

Office Equipment depreciates at $10 per month; purchased July 17.

Fax machine depreciates at $10 per month; purchased November 20.

Six months' worth of rent at a rental rate of $400 per month has expired.

Remember: If any long-term asset is purchased in the first 15 days of the month, Tony will charge depreciation for the full month. If an asset is purchased later than the 16th, he will not charge depreciation in the month it was purchased.

Complete the 10-column worksheet for the six months ended March 31, 200X.

A Worksheet for Art's Wholesale Clothing Co. Using a Perpetual Inventory System

What's New: The Merchandise Inventory account does not need to be adjusted. The $4,000 figure for merchandise is the up-to-date balance in the account. The difference between beginning inventory and ending inventory will be part of a new account called *Cost of Goods Sold* on the worksheet.

How the $65,910 of Cost of Goods Sold was calculated from a periodic setup:

	Purchases	$52,000	←	Assumed sold; part of cost
+	Merchandise Inventory	$15,000	←	Beg. Inv. − Ending Inv. $19,000 − $4,000
−	Purchases Discount	860	→	Reduces costs
−	Purchases Returns and Allowances	680	↗	
+	Freight-In	450	→	Adds to cost
		$65,910		Cost of Goods Sold

What's deleted from the Periodic Worksheet: Account titles for Purchases, Purchases Discounts, Purchases Returns and Allowances, and Freight-In.

Note: Net income is same on the periodic and the perpetual Worksheets.

Problem for Appendix

Using the solution to Self-Review Quiz 12-2 (p. 456), convert this worksheet to a perpetual inventory system worksheet. (The worksheet is in the envelope at the end of the *Study Guide and Working Papers.*)

ART'S WHOLESALE CLOTHING CO.
WORKSHEET
FOR YEAR ENDED DECEMBER 31, 200X

Account Titles	Trial Balance Dr.	Trial Balance Cr.	Adjustments Dr.	Adjustments Cr.	Adjusted Trial Balance Dr.	Adjusted Trial Balance Cr.	Income Statement Dr.	Income Statement Cr.	Balance Sheet Dr.	Balance Sheet Cr.
Cash	12 920 00				12 920 00				12 920 00	
Petty Cash	100 00				100 00				100 00	
Accounts Receivable	14 500 00				14 500 00				14 500 00	
Merchandise Inventory	4 000 00				4 000 00				4 000 00	
Supplies	800 00			(B) 500 00	300 00				300 00	
Prepaid Insurance	900 00			(C) 300 00	600 00				600 00	
Store Equipment	4 000 00				4 000 00				4 000 00	
Acc. Dep., Store Equip.		400 00		(D) 50 00		450 00				450 00
Accounts Payable		17 900 00				17 900 00				17 900 00
Federal Income Tax		800 00				800 00				800 00
FICA—Social Security		454 00				454 00				454 00
FICA—Medicare		106 00				106 00				106 00
State Income Tax		200 00				200 00				200 00
SUTA Tax		108 00				108 00				108 00
FUTA Tax Payable		32 00				32 00				32 00
Unearned Rent		600 00	(A) 200 00			400 00				400 00
Mortgage Payable		2 320 00				2 320 00				2 320 00
Art Newner, Capital		7 905 00				7 905 00				7 905 00
Art Newner, Withdrawal	8 600 00				8 600 00				8 600 00	
Sales		95 000 00				95 000 00		95 000 00		
Sales Returns and Allow.	950 00				950 00		950 00			
Sales Discount	670 00				670 00		670 00			
Cost of Goods Sold	65 910 00				65 910 00		65 910 00			
Salaries Expense	11 700 00		(E) 600 00		12 300 00		12 300 00			
Payroll Tax Expense	420 00				420 00		420 00			
Postage Expense	25 00				25 00		25 00			
Miscellaneous Expense	30 00				30 00		30 00			
Interest Expense	300 00				300 00		300 00			
	125 825 00	125 825 00								
Rental Income				(A) 200 00		200 00		200 00		
Supplies Expense			(B) 500 00		500 00		500 00			
Insurance Expense			(C) 300 00		300 00		300 00			
Dep. Exp., Store Equip.			(D) 50 00		50 00		50 00			
Salaries Payable				(E) 600 00		600 00				600 00
			1 650 00	1 650 00	126 475 00	126 475 00	81 455 00	95 200 00	45 020 00	31 275 00
Net Income							13 745 00			13 745 00
							95 200 00	95 200 00	45 020 00	45 020 00

RAY COMPANY
WORKSHEET
FOR YEAR ENDED DECEMBER 31, 200X

Account Titles	Trial Balance Dr.	Trial Balance Cr.	Adjustments Dr.	Adjustments Cr.	Adjusted Trial Balance Dr.	Adjusted Trial Balance Cr.	Income Statement Dr.	Income Statement Cr.	Balance Sheet Dr.	Balance Sheet Cr.
Cash	248600				248600				248600	
Merchandise Inventory	20000				20000				20000	
Prepaid Rent	115200			(B)10000	105200				105200	
Prepaid Insurance	6000				6000				6000	
Office Equipment	216000				216000				216000	
Accumulated Dep., Off. Equip.		56000		(C)6000		62000				62000
Unearned Storage Fees		251600	(A)51600			200000				200000
Accounts Payable		10000				10000				10000
B. Ray, Capital		193200				193200				193200
Sales		1104000				1104000		1104000		
Sales Returns and Allowances	54600				54600		54600			
Sales Discounts	21600				21600		21600			
Cogs*	561000				561000		561000			
Salaries Expense	201600		(D)20000		221600		221600			
Insurance Expense	139200				139200		139200			
Utilities Expense	9600				9600		9600			
Plumbing Expense	21400				21400		21400			
	1614800	1614800								
Storage Fees Earned				(A)51600		51600		51600		
Rent Expense			(B)10000		10000		10000			
Dep. Expense, Equip.			(C)6000		6000		6000			
Salaries Payable				(D)20000		20000				20000
			87600	87600	1640800	1640800	1045000	1155600	595800	485200
Net Income							110600			110600
							1155600	1155600	595800	595800

*$624 ($824 − $200) + $5,256 − $168 − $102.

Completion of the Accounting Cycle for a Merchandise Company

Who ever thought that a discount store, selling everything from dish detergent to cut-rate clothing, would end up being hip? Pronounced "Tar Jay" with

tongue in cheek by those in the know, Target has wowed consumers with its affordable designer tea kettles and chess sets, cheap chic clothes and classy advertising. In one TV ad models prance in front of a kaleidoscopic array of Puffs, Tide and other products lifted from the store's shelves. The company even hosted a fun fashion show at New York's Chelsea Piers, in which models paraded down a runway shaped like the company's bulls-eye logo wearing snake-printed chiffon handkerchief skirts and pumpkin-colored microfleece vests.

Target is popular with consumers, and its earnings have grown by 20–30% annually. Yet, its parent corporation, Target Corp., is in danger of being dragged down by the blighted department store division, which includes Dayton's, Mervyn's and Marshall Field. Of the $1.2 billion Target Corp. gains in profits, 75% come from Target stores. Hence, in order to boost revenue and profits, Target Corp. has decided to focus on

Target stores alone. Their plan is two-pronged: double the number of Target stores in the next ten years, from 942 to 1800, and expand Target's Internet operations.

When merchandise companies, like Target Corp., plan for the future, they need to analyze past results. At the end of each fiscal year, they close their books and generate financial reports that give them accurate information on such key accounts as **selling expenses** (such as the money Target spends for its upscale ads), **administrative expenses** (including salaries for Target's 250,000 employees) and **cost of goods sold** (including supplies Target bought through an auction on the web-based Worldwide Retail Exchange). Only by looking at the complete cycle of accounting information can Target's managers plan their expansion.

In this chapter you'll learn the steps involved in completing the accounting cycle for a merchandise company—from preparing financial statements to completing reversing entries.

Based on: Mark Borden, "Shoppers love Target, but shareholders are seeing red," *Fortune*, September 18, 2000, pp. 64–68. Anonymous, "Official of Target Says Company Was Right to Shun Web Spinoff," *Wall Street Journal*, September 11, 2000, p. A41A. Lynn Yaeger, "Target practice," *The Village Voice*, August 8, 2000, p. 14.

LEARNING OBJECTIVES

▼ Preparing financial statements for a merchandise company. (p. 476)

▼ Recording adjusting and closing entries. (p. 482)

▼ Preparing a postclosing trial balance. (p. 487)

▼ Completing reversing entries. (p. 488)

In this chapter we discuss the steps involved in completing the accounting cycle for a merchandise company. The steps involved include preparing financial reports, journalizing and posting adjusting and closing entries, preparing a postclosing trial balance, and reversing entries.

LEARNING UNIT 13-1

PREPARING FINANCIAL STATEMENTS

As we discussed in Chapter 5, when we were dealing with a service company rather than a merchandise company, the three financial statements can be prepared from the worksheet. Let's begin by looking at how Art's Wholesale Clothing Company prepares the income statement.

THE INCOME STATEMENT

Art is interested in knowing how well his shop performed for the year ended December 31, 200X. What were its net sales? Were there many returns of goods from dissatisfied customers? What was the cost of the goods brought into the store versus the selling price received? How many goods were returned to suppliers? What is the cost of the goods that have not been sold? What was the cost of the Freight-In account? The income statement in Figure 13-1 p. 476 is prepared from the income statement columns of the worksheet. Note that there are no debit or credit columns on the formal income statement; the inside columns on financial reports are used for subtotaling, not for debit and credit.

The income statement is broken down into several sections. Remembering the sections can help you set it up correctly on your own. The income statement shows:

> Net Sales
> − Cost of Goods Sold
> ──────────────
> = Gross Profit
> − Operating Expenses
> ──────────────
> = Net Income from Operations
> + Other Income
> − Other Expenses
> ──────────────
> = Net Income

Let's take these sections one at a time and see where the figures come from on the worksheet.

Revenue Section

Net Sales The first major category of the income statement shows net sales. The figure here — $93,380 — is not on the worksheet. Instead, the accountant must combine the amounts for gross sales, sales returns and allowances, and sales discount found on the worksheet to arrive at a figure for net sales. Thus these individual amounts are not summarized in a single figure for net sales until the formal income statement is prepared.

> Sales
> − Sales Ret. & Allow.
> − Sales Discount
> ──────────────
> = Net Sales

Cost of Goods Sold Section

The figures for Merchandise Inventory are shown separately on the worksheet. The $19,000 represents the beginning inventory of the period, and the $4,000, calculated from an inventory sheet, is the ending inventory. Note on the financial report that the cost of goods sold section uses two separate figures for inventory.

Note that the following numbers are not found on the worksheet but are shown on the formal income statement (they are combined by the accountant in preparing the income statement):

▼ Net Purchases: $50,460 (Purchases − Purchases Discount − Purchases Returns and Allowances)
▼ Net Cost of Purchases: $50,910 (Net Purchases + Freight-In)
▼ Cost of Goods Available for Sale: $69,910 (Beginning Inventory + Net Cost of Purchases)
▼ Cost of Goods Sold: $65,910 (Cost of Goods Available for Sale − Ending Inventory)

> Beg. Inventory
> + Net Cost of Purchases
> − Ending Inventory
> ──────────────
> = Cost of Goods Sold

> Remember:
> In the periodic inventory system, goods brought in during the accounting period are added to the Purchases account, not to the Merchandise Inventory account.

Gross Profit

Gross profit ($27,470) is calculated by subtracting the cost of goods sold from net sales ($93,380 − $65,910). The amount is not found on the worksheet.

> Net Sales
> − Cost of Goods Sold
> ──────────────
> = Gross Profit

FIGURE 13-1. Partial Worksheet and Income Statement

ART'S WHOLESALE CLOTHING COMPANY
PARTIAL WORKSHEET
FOR YEAR ENDED DECEMBER 31, 200X

	Income Statement	
	Dr.	Cr.
Income Summary	19 000 00	4 000 00
Sales		95 000 00
Sales Returns and Allowances	950 00	
Sales Discount	670 00	
Purchases	52 000 00	
Purchases Discount		860 00
Purchases Returns and Allowances		680 00
Freight-In	450 00	
Salaries Expense	12 300 00	
Payroll Tax Expense	420 00	
Postage Expense	25 00	
Miscellaneous Expense	30 00	
Interest Expense	300 00	
Rental Income		200 00
Supplies Expense	500 00	
Insurance Expense	300 00	
Depreciation Expense, Store Equip.	50 00	
Salaries Payable		
	86 995 00	100 740 00
Net Income	13 745 00	
	100 740 00	100 740 00

ART'S WHOLESALE CLOTHING COMPANY
INCOME STATEMENT
FOR YEAR ENDED DECEMBER 31, 200X

Revenue:			
Gross Sales			$95 000 00
Less: Sales Ret. and Allow.		$ 950 00	
Sales Discount		670 00	1 620 00
Net Sales			$93 380 00
Cost of Goods Sold:			
Merchandise Inventory, 1/1/0X			$19 000 00
Purchases		$52 000 00	
Less: Purch. Discount	$ 860 00		
Purch. Ret. and Allow.	680 00	1 540 00	
Net Purchases		$50 460 00	
Add: Freight-In		450 00	
Net Cost of Purchases			50 910 00
Cost of Goods Available for Sale			$69 910 00
Less: Merch. Inv., 12/31/0X			4 000 00
Cost of Goods Sold			65 910 00
Gross Profit			$27 470 00
Operating Expenses:			
Salaries Expense		$12 300 00	
Payroll Tax Expense		420 00	
Dep. Exp., Store Equip.		50 00	
Supplies Expense		500 00	
Insurance Expense		300 00	
Postage Expense		25 00	
Miscellaneous Expense		30 00	
Total Operating Expenses			13 625 00
Net Income from Operations			$13 845 00
Other Income:			
Rental Income		$ 200 00	
Other Expenses:			
Interest Expense		300 00	
Net Income			$13 745 00

Operating Expenses Section

Like the other figures we have discussed, the business's operating expenses do not appear on the worksheet. To get this figure ($13,625), the accountant adds up all the expenses on the worksheet.

Many operating companies break expenses down into those directly related to the selling activity of the company **(selling expenses)** and those related to administrative or office activity **(administrative expenses or general expenses).** Here's a sample list broken down into these two categories:

Operating Expenses

▼ Selling Expenses:
    Sales Salaries Expense
    Delivery Expense
    Advertising Expense
    Depreciation Expense, Store Equipment
    Insurance Expense
      Total Selling Expenses

▼ Administrative Expenses:
    Rent Expense
    Office Salaries Expense
    Utilities Expense
    Supplies Expense
    Depreciation Expense, Office Equipment
      Total Administrative Expenses
        Total Operating Expenses

Other Income (or Other Revenue) Section

The Other Income or Other Revenue section is used to record any revenue other than revenue from sales. For example, Art's Wholesale makes a profit from subletting a portion of a building. The $200 of rental income the company earns from this is recorded in the **Other Income** section.

Other Expenses Section

The Other Expenses section is used to record nonoperating expenses, that is, expenses that are not related to the main operating activities of the business. For example, Art's Wholesale owes $300 interest on money it has borrowed. That expense is shown in the **Other Expenses** section.

STATEMENT OF OWNER'S EQUITY

The information used to prepare the statement of owner's equity comes from the balance sheet columns of the worksheet. Keep in mind that the capital account in the ledger should be checked to see whether any additional investments have occurred during the period. The diagram on p. 478 shows how the worksheet aids in this step. The ending figure of $13,050 for Art Newner, Capital, is carried over to the balance sheet, which is the final report we look at in this chapter.

> Statement of owner's equity is the same for a merchandise business as for a service firm.

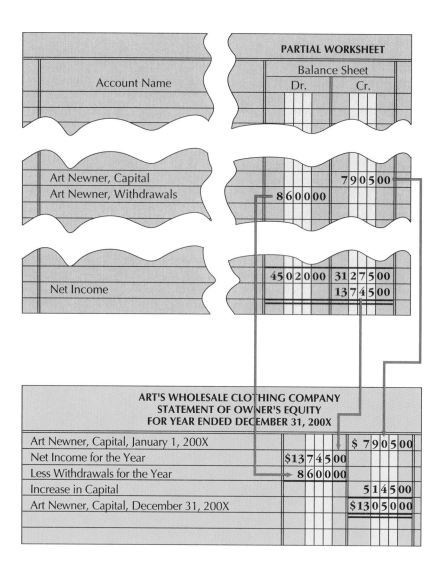

Any additional investment by the owner would be added to his or her beginning capital amount.

PARTIAL WORKSHEET

| Account Name | Balance Sheet | |
| | Dr. | Cr. |

Account Name	Dr.	Cr.
Art Newner, Capital		7 9 0 5 00
Art Newner, Withdrawals	8 6 0 0 00	

	Dr.	Cr.
	45 0 2 0 00	31 2 7 5 00
Net Income		13 7 4 5 00

ART'S WHOLESALE CLOTHING COMPANY
STATEMENT OF OWNER'S EQUITY
FOR YEAR ENDED DECEMBER 31, 200X

Art Newner, Capital, January 1, 200X		$ 7 9 0 5 00
Net Income for the Year	$13 7 4 5 00	
Less Withdrawals for the Year	8 6 0 0 00	
Increase in Capital		5 1 4 5 00
Art Newner, Capital, December 31, 200X		$13 0 5 0 00

THE BALANCE SHEET

Figure 13-2 shows how a worksheet is used to aid in the preparation of a **classified balance sheet.** A classified balance sheet breaks down the assets and liabilities into more detail. Classified balance sheets provide management, owners, creditors, and suppliers with more information about the company's ability to pay current and long-term debts. They also provide a more complete financial picture of the firm.

The categories on the classified balance sheet are as follows:

▼ **Current assets** are defined as cash and assets that will be converted into cash or used up during the normal operating cycle of the company or one year, whichever is longer. (Think of the **operating cycle** as the time period it takes a company to buy and sell merchandise and then collect accounts receivable.)

Accountants list current assets in order of how easily they can be converted into cash (called liquidity). In some cases Accounts Receivable can be turned into cash more quickly than Merchandise Inventory. For example, it can be quite difficult to sell an outdated computer in a computer store or to sell last year's model car this year.

▼ **Plant and Equipment** are long-lived assets that are used in the production or sale of goods or services. Art's Wholesale has only one plant asset, store

ART'S WHOLESALE CLOTHING COMPANY
CLASSIFIED BALANCE SHEET
FOR YEAR ENDED DECEMBER 31, 200X

Assets

Current Assets:			
Cash		$1292000	
Petty Cash		10000	
Accounts Receivable		1450000	
Merchandise Inventory		400000	
Supplies		30000	
Prepaid Insurance		60000	
Total Current Assets			$3242000
Plant and Equipment:			
Store Equipment	$400000		
Less: Accum. Depreciation	45000	355000	
Total Assets			$3597000

Liabilities

Current Liabilities:			
Mortgage Payable (current portion)	$ 32000		
Accounts Payable	1790000		
Federal Income Tax Payable	80000		
FICA-Social Security Payable	45400		
FICA-Medicare Payable	10600		
State Income Tax Payable	20000		
SUTA Tax Payable	10800		
FUTA Tax Payable	3200		
Salaries Payable	60000		
Unearned Rent	40000		
Total Current Liabilities		$2092000	
Long-Term Liabilities			
Mortgage Payable		200000	
Total Liabilities			$2292000

Owner's Equity

Art Newner, Capital, December 31, 200X			1305000
Total Liabilities and Owner's Equity			$3597000

ART'S WHOLESALE CLOTHING COMPANY
WORKSHEET
FOR YEAR ENDED DECEMBER 31, 200X

	Balance Sheet	
	Dr.	Cr.
Cash	1292000	
Petty Cash	10000	
Accounts Receivable	1450000	
Merchandise Inventory	400000	
Supplies	30000	
Prepaid Insurance	60000	
Store Equipment	400000	
Acc. Dep., Store Equipment		45000
Accounts Payable		1790000
Federal Income Tax Payable		80000
FICA-Social Security Payable		45400
FICA-Medicare Payable		10600
State Income Tax Payable		20000
SUTA Tax Payable		10800
FUTA Tax Payable		3200
Unearned Rent		40000
Mortgage Payable		232000
Art Newner, Capital		7905 00
Salaries Payable		60000
	4502000	3127500
Net Income		1374500
	4502000	4502000

FIGURE 13-2. Partial Worksheet and Classified Balance Sheet

equipment; other plant assets could include buildings and land. The assets are usually listed in order according to how long they will last; the shortest-lived assets are listed first. Land would always be the last asset listed (and land is never depreciated). Note that we still show the cost of the asset less its accumulated depreciation.

▼ **Current liabilities** are the debts or obligations of Art's Wholesale that must be paid within one year or one operating cycle. The order of listing accounts in this section is not always the same; many times companies will list their liabilities in the order they expect to pay them off. Note that the current portion of the mortgage, $320 (that portion due within one year), is listed before Accounts Payable.

▼ **Long-term liabilities** are debts or obligations that are not due and payable for a comparatively long period, usually for more than one year. For Art's Wholesale there is only one long-term liability, Mortgage Payable. The long-term portion of the mortgage is listed here; the current portion, due within one year, is listed under current liabilities.

> Mortgage Payable:
> $2,320
> − 320 current portion
> $2,000 long-term liability

LEARNING UNIT 13-1 REVIEW

AT THIS POINT you should be able to

▼ Prepare a detailed income statement from the worksheet. (p. 476)
▼ Explain the difference between selling and administrative expenses. (p. 477)
▼ Explain which columns of the worksheet are used in preparing a statement of owner's equity. (p. 477)
▼ Prepare a classified balance sheet from a worksheet. (p. 479)
▼ Explain as well as compare current assets with plant and equipment. (p. 479)
▼ Using Mortgage Payable as an example, explain the difference between current and long-term liabilities. (p. 480)

SELF-REVIEW QUIZ 13-1

(The forms you need are on pages 405–407 of the *Study Guide and Working Papers.*)

Using the worksheet on page 456 from Self-Review Quiz 12-2, prepare in proper form (1) an income statement, (2) a statement of owner's equity, (3) a classified balance sheet for Ray Company.

Solutions to Self-Review Quiz 13-1

1.

RAY COMPANY INCOME STATEMENT FOR YEAR ENDED DECEMBER 31, 200X				
Revenue:				
Sales				$11 04 0 00
Less: Sales Ret. and Allow.			$ 5 46 00	
Sales Discount			2 16 00	76 2 00
Net Sales				$10 27 8 00
Cost of Goods Sold:				
Merchandise Inventory, 1/1/0X			$ 82 4 00	
Purchases		$5 25 6 00		
Less: Pur. Ret. and Allow.	$ 1 68 00			
Purchases Discount	1 02 00	2 70 00		
Net Purchases			4 98 6 00	
Cost of Goods Available for Sale			$ 5 81 0 00	
Less: Merchandise Inv., 12/31/0X			2 00 00	
Cost of Goods Sold				5 61 0 00
Gross Profit				$ 4 66 8 00
Operating Expenses:				
Salaries Expense		$ 2 21 6 00		
Insurance Expense		1 39 2 00		
Utilities Expense		9 6 00		
Plumbing Expense		2 14 00		
Rent Expense		1 00 00		
Depreciation Exp., Equip.		6 0 00		
Total Operating Expenses				4 07 8 00
Net Income from Operations				$ 59 0 00
Other Income:				
Storage Fees				51 6 00
Net Income				$ 1 10 6 00

Quiz Tip:
Note that Cost of Goods Sold has a separate figure for Beginning Inventory and Ending Inventory.

2.

RAY COMPANY STATEMENT OF OWNER'S EQUITY FOR YEAR ENDED DECEMBER 31, 200X	
B. Ray, Capital, 1/1/0X	$ 1 93 2 00
Net Income for the Year	1 10 6 00
B. Ray, Capital, 12/31/0X	$ 3 03 8 00

3.

RAY COMPANY BALANCE SHEET DECEMBER 31, 200X			
Assets			
Current Assets:			
Cash	$ 2 4 8 6 00		
Merchandise Inventory	2 0 0 00		
Prepaid Rent	1 0 5 2 00		
Prepaid Insurance	6 0 00		
Total Current Assets		$ 3 7 9 8 00	
Plant and Equipment:			
Office Equipment	$ 2 1 6 0 00		
Less: Accumulated Depreciation	6 2 0 00	1 5 4 0 00	
Total Assets		$ 5 3 3 8 00	
Liabilities			
Current Liabilities			
Accounts Payable	$ 1 0 0 00		
Salaries Payable	2 0 0 00		
Unearned Storage Fees	2 0 0 0 00		
Total Liabilities		$ 2 3 0 0 00	
Owner's Equity			
B. Ray, Capital, December 31, 200X		3 0 3 8 00	
Total Liabilities and Owner's Equity		$ 5 3 3 8 00	

LEARNING UNIT 13-2

JOURNALIZING AND POSTING ADJUSTING AND CLOSING ENTRIES; PREPARING THE POSTCLOSING TRIAL BALANCE

JOURNALIZING AND POSTING ADJUSTING ENTRIES

From the worksheet of Art's Wholesale, repeated here in Figure 13-3 p. 484 for your convenience, the adjusting entries can be journalized from the adjustments column and posted to the ledger. Keep in mind that the adjustments have been placed only on the worksheet, not in the journal or in the ledger. At this point the journal does not reflect adjustments, and the ledger still contains only unadjusted amounts.

ART'S WHOLESALE CLOTHING CO.
GENERAL JOURNAL

Page 2

Date	Account Titles and Description	PR	Dr.	Cr.
	Adjusting Entries			
31	Income Summary	313	19 0 0 0 00	
	Merchandise Inventory	114		19 0 0 0 00
	Transferred beginning inventory			
	to Income Summary			
31	Merchandise Inventory	114	4 0 0 0 00	
	Income Summary	313		4 0 0 0 00
	Records cost of ending inventory			
31	Unearned Rent	219	2 0 0 00	
	Rental Income	414		2 0 0 00
	Rental Income earned			
31	Supplies Expense	614	5 0 0 00	
	Supplies	115		5 0 0 00
	Supplies consumed			
31	Insurance Expense	615	3 0 0 00	
	Prepaid Insurance	116		3 0 0 00
	Insurance expired			
31	Dep. Exp., Store Equipment	613	5 0 00	
	Acc. Dep., Store Equipment	122		5 0 00
	Depreciation on equipment			
31	Salaries Expense	611	6 0 0 00	
	Salaries Payable	212		6 0 0 00
	Accrued salaries			

PARTIAL LEDGER

Merchandise Inventory 114		Accum. Dep., Store Equipment 122		Income Summary 313		Dep. Expense, Store Equip. 613	
19,000	19,000		400	19,000	4,000	50	
4,000			50				

Supplies 115		Salary Payable 212		Supplies Expense 614		Salaries Exp. 611	
800	500		600	500		12,000	
						600	

Prepaid Insurance 116		Unearned Rent 219		Insurance Expense 615		Rental Income 414	
900	300	200	600	300			200

The journalized and posted adjusting entries are shown above. Note that the liability Unearned Rent is reduced by $200 and Rental Income has increased by $200.

ART'S WHOLESALE CLOTHING CO.
WORKSHEET
FOR YEAR ENDED DECEMBER 31, 200X

	Trial Balance		Adjustments	
	Dr.	Cr.	Dr.	Cr.
Cash	1292000			
Petty Cash	10000			
Accounts Receivable	1450000			
Merchandise Inventory	1900000		(B)400000	(A)1900000
Supplies	80000			(D)50000
Prepaid Insurance	90000			(E)30000
Store Equipment	400000			
Acc. Dep., Store Equipment		40000		(F)5000
Accounts Payable		1790000		
Federal Income Tax Payable		80000		
FICA—Social Security Payable		45400		
FICA—Medicare Payable		10600		
State Income Tax Payable		20000		
SUTA Tax Payable		10800		
FUTA Tax Payable		3200		
Unearned Rent		60000	(C)20000	
Mortgage Payable		232000		
Art Newner, Capital		790500		
Art Newner, Withdrawals	860000			
Income Summary			(A)1900000	(B)400000
Sales		950000		
Sales Returns and Allowances	95000			
Sales Discount	67000			
Purchases	5200000			
Purchases Discount		86000		
Purchases Returns and Allowances		68000		
Freight-In	45000			
Salaries Expense	1170000		(G)60000	
Payroll Tax Expense	42000			
Postage Expense	2500			
Miscellaneous Expense	3000			
Interest Expense	30000			
	12736500	12736500		
Rental Income				(C)20000
Supplies Expense			(D)50000	
Insurance Expense			(E)30000	
Depreciation Expense, Store Equip.			(F)5000	
Salaries Payable				(G)60000
			2465000	2465000
Net Income				

FIGURE 13-3. Completed Worksheet

	Adjusted Trial Bal.		Income Statement		Balance Sheet	
	Dr.	Cr.	Dr.	Cr.	Dr.	Cr.
	12920 00				12920 00	
	100 00				100 00	
	14500 00				14500 00	
	4000 00				4000 00	
	300 00				300 00	
	600 00				600 00	
	400 00				400 00	
		450 00				450 00
		17900 00				17900 00
		800 00				800 00
		454 00				454 00
		106 00				106 00
		200 00				200 00
		108 00				108 00
		32 00				32 00
		400 00				400 00
		2320 00				2320 00
		7905 00				7905 00
	8600 00				8600 00	
	19000 00	4000 00	19000 00	4000 00		
		9500 00		9500 00		
	950 00		950 00			
	670 00		670 00			
	52000 00		52000 00			
		860 00		860 00		
		680 00		680 00		
	450 00		450 00			
	12300 00		12300 00			
	420 00		420 00			
	25 00		25 00			
	30 00		30 00			
	300 00		300 00			
		200 00		200 00		
	500 00		500 00			
	300 00		300 00			
	50 00		50 00			
		600 00				600 00
	132015 00	132015 00	86995 00	100740 00	45020 00	31275 00
			13745 00			13745 00
			100740 00	100740 00	45020 00	45020 00

FIGURE 13-3. (cont.)

JOURNALIZING AND POSTING CLOSING ENTRIES

In Chapter 5, we discussed the closing process for a service company. The goals of closing are the same for a merchandise company. These goals are (1) to clear all temporary accounts in the ledger to zero and (2) to update capital in the ledger to its latest balance. The company must use the worksheet and the steps listed here to complete the closing process.

Step 1: Close all balances on the income statement credit column of the worksheet except Income Summary by debits.
    Then credit the total to the Income Summary account.

Step 2: Close all balances on the income statement debit column of the worksheet except Income Summary by credits.
    Then debit the total to the Income Summary account.

FIGURE 13-4. General Journal Closing Entries

	Date	Account Titles and Description	PR	Dr.	Cr.
		ART'S WHOLESALE CLOTHING CO. **GENERAL JOURNAL**			Page 2
		Closing Entries			
Step 1	31	Sales	411	95 0 0 0 00	
		Rental Income	414	2 0 0 00	
		Purchases Discount	512	8 6 0 00	
		Purchases Ret. and Allow.	513	6 8 0 00	
		Income Summary	313		96 7 4 0 00
		Transfers credit account balances			
		on income statement column of			
		worksheet to Income Summary			
Step 2	31	Income Summary	313	67 9 9 5 00	
		Sales Returns and Allowances	412		9 5 0 00
		Sales Discount	413		6 7 0 00
		Purchases	511		52 0 0 0 00
		Freight-In	514		4 5 0 00
		Salaries Expense	611		12 3 0 0 00
		Payroll Tax Expense	612		4 2 0 00
		Postage Expense	616		2 5 00
		Miscellaneous Expense	617		3 0 00
		Interest Expense	618		3 0 0 00
		Supplies Expense	614		5 0 0 00
		Insurance Expense	615		3 0 0 00
		Depreciation Expense, Store Equip.	613		5 0 00
		Transfers all expenses, and			
		deductions to Sales are			
		closed to Income Summary			
Step 3	31	Income Summary	313	13 7 4 5 00	
		A. Newner, Capital	311		13 7 4 5 00
		Transfer of net income to			
		Capital from Income Summary			
Step 4	31	A. Newner, Capital	311	8 6 0 0 00	
		A. Newner, Withdrawals	312		8 6 0 0 00
		Closes withdrawals to			
		Capital Account			

Step 3: Transfer the balance of the Income Summary account to the Capital account.

Step 4: Transfer the balance of the owner's Withdrawal account to the Capital account.

Let's look now at the journalized closing entries in Figure 13-4.

When these entries are posted, all the temporary accounts will have zero balances in the ledger, and the Capital account will be updated with a new balance.

Let's take a moment to look at the Income Summary account in T account form:

	Income Summary 313		
Adj.	19,000	4,000	Adj.
Clos.	67,995	96,740	Clos.
	86,995	100,740	
Net Income → Clos.	13,745		

Note that Income Summary before the closing process contains the adjustments for Merchandise Inventory. The end result is that the net income of $13,745 is closed to the Capital account.

THE POSTCLOSING TRIAL BALANCE

The following postclosing trial balance is prepared from the general ledger. Note first that all temporary accounts have been closed and thus are not shown on this postclosing trial balance. Note also that the ending inventory figure of the last accounting period, $4,000, becomes the beginning inventory figure on January 1, 20X3.

ART'S WHOLESALE CLOTHING COMPANY POSTCLOSING TRIAL BALANCE DECEMBER 31, 200X		
	Dr.	Cr.
Cash	12 9 2 0 00	
Petty Cash	1 0 0 00	
Accounts Receivable	14 5 0 0 00	
Merchandise Inventory	4 0 0 0 00	
Supplies	3 0 0 00	
Prepaid Insurance	6 0 0 00	
Store Equipment	4 0 0 0 00	
Accum. Depreciation, Store Equipment		4 5 0 00
Accounts Payable		17 9 0 0 00
Federal Income Tax Payable		8 0 0 00
FICA—Social Security Payable		4 5 4 00
FICA—Medicare Payable		1 0 6 00
State Income Tax Payable		2 0 0 00
SUTA Tax Payable		1 0 8 00
FUTA Tax Payable		3 2 00
Salary Payable		6 0 0 00
Unearned Rent		4 0 0 00
Mortgage Payable		2 3 2 0 00
Art Newner, Capital		13 0 5 0 00
	36 4 2 0 00	36 4 2 0 00

AT THIS POINT you should be able to

▼ Journalize and post adjusting entries for a merchandise company. (p. 483)
▼ Explain the relationship of the worksheet to the adjusting and closing process. (p. 483)
▼ Complete the closing process for a merchandise company. (p. 486)
▼ Prepare a postclosing trial balance and explain why ending merchandise inventory is not a temporary account. (p. 487)

SELF-REVIEW QUIZ 13-2

(The forms you need are on page 408 of the *Study Guide and Working Papers.*)
Using the worksheet on page 456 from Self-Review Quiz 12-2, journalize the closing entries.

Solution to Self-Review Quiz 13-2

	Date		Account Titles and Description	PR	Dr.	Cr.
			Page 2			
			Closing			
	Dec.	31	Sales		11 0 4 0 00	
			Storage Fees Earned		5 1 6 00	
			Purchases Returns and Allowances		1 6 8 00	
			Purchases Discount		1 0 2 00	
			Income Summary			11 8 2 6 00
		31	Income Summary		10 0 9 6 00	
			Sales Returns and Allowances			5 4 6 00
			Sales Discount			2 1 6 00
			Purchases			5 2 5 6 00
			Salaries Expense			2 2 1 6 00
			Insurance Expense			1 3 9 2 00
			Utilities Expense			9 6 00
			Plumbing Expense			2 1 4 00
			Rent Expense			1 0 0 00
			Depreciation Exp., Equipment			6 0 00
		31	Income Summary		1 1 0 6 00	
			B. Ray, Capital			1 1 0 6 00

Quiz Tip:
Note in the first closing entry that the four account titles (now listed as debits) were found on the worksheet as credits in the Income Statement column.

LEARNING UNIT 13-3

REVERSING ENTRIES (OPTIONAL SECTION)

Reversing entries are an option; they are not mandatory.

The accounting cycle for Art's Wholesale Clothing Company is completed. Now let's look at **reversing entries,** an optional way of handling some adjusting entries. Reversing entries are general journal entries that are the opposite of adjusting entries. Reversing entries help reduce potential errors and simplify the recordkeeping process. If Art's accountant does reversing entries, routine transactions can be done in the usual steps.

To help explain the concept of reversing entries, let's look at these two adjustments that could be reversed:

1. When there is an increase in an asset account (no previous balance).

   Example: Interest Receivable
   Interest Income

   (Interest earned but not collected is covered in later chapters.)

2. When there is an increase in a liability account (no previous balance).

   Example: Wages Expense
   Wages Payable

With the exception of businesses in their first year of operation, accounts such as Accumulated Depreciation or Inventory cannot be reduced because they have previous balances.

Art's bookkeeper handles an entry without reversing for salaries at the end of the year (see Fig. 13-5). Note that the permanent account, Salaries Payable, carries over to the new accounting period a $600 balance. Remember that the $600 was an expense of the prior year.

On January 8 of the new year the payroll to be paid is $2,000. If the optional reversing entry is *not* used, the bookkeeper must make the following journal entry:

Salaries Payable	600 00			
Salaries Expense	1 400 00			
Cash		2 000 00		

Salaries Exp.	Salaries Pay.	Cash
1,400	600 | 600	| 2,000

To do so, the bookkeeper has to refer back to the adjustment on December 31 to determine how much of the salary of $2,000 is indeed a new salary expense and what portion was shown in the old year although not paid. It is easy to see how potential errors can result if the bookkeeper pays the payroll but forgets about the adjustment in the previous year. In this way reversing entries can help avoid potential errors.

Figure 13-6 shows the four steps the bookkeeper would take if reversing entries were used. Note that steps 1 and 2 are the same whether the accountant uses reversing entries or not.

ADJUSTING JOURNAL ENTRY   T ACCOUNT UPDATE

❶ On December 31 after adjusting entry was journalized and posted for $600 of salaries incurred but not paid.

Salaries Expense	600 00		
Salaries Payable		600 00	

Salaries Exp.	Salaries Pay.
11,700	600
600	

❷ On January 1 after closing entries have been journalized and posted, Salaries expense has a zero balance.

Income Summary	XXX		
Salaries Expense		12 300 00	

Salaries Exp.		Salaries Pay.
11,700	12,300	600
600		

FIGURE 13-5. Reversing Entries Not Used

1

On December 31
adjustment for salary
was recorded.

Salaries Exp.	Salaries Pay.
11,700	600
600	

2

Closing entry on
December 31.

Salaries Exp.		Salaries Pay.
11,700	12,300	600
600		

3

On January 1 (first day of
the following fiscal period)
reverse adjusting entry
was made for salary
on December 31(a
"flipping" adjustment).

Jan.	1	Salaries Payable	600 00	
		Salaries Expense		600 00

Salaries Exp.	Salaries Pay.
600	600	600

This way, the liability is reduced to 0. We know it will be paid in this new period,
but the salaries expense has a credit balance of $600 until the payroll is paid. When the
payroll of $2,000 is paid, the following results:

4

Paid Payroll $2,000.

Jan.	1	Salaries Expense	2000 00	
		Cash		2000 00

Salaries Exp.	Cash
2,000	600	2,000

FIGURE 13-6. Reversing Entries Used

Note that the balance of Salaries Expense is indeed only $1,400, the *true*
expense in the new year. Reversing results in switching the adjustment the first
day of the new period. Also note that each of the accounts ends up with the
same balance no matter which method is chosen. Using reversing entry for
salaries, however, allows the accountant to make the normal entry when it is
time to pay salaries.

LEARNING UNIT 13-3 REVIEW

AT THIS POINT you should be able to

▼ Explain the purpose of reversing entries. (p. 488)
▼ Complete a reversing entry. (p. 489)
▼ Explain when reversing entries can be used. (p. 489)

SELF-REVIEW QUIZ 13-3

Explain which of the following situations could be reversed:

1.
Supplies Exp.	Supplies
200	800	200

2.
Wages Exp.	Wages Payable
3,200	200
200	

3.

Sales		Unearned Sales	
	4,000	50	200
	50		

Solutions to Self-Review Quiz 13-3

(The forms you need are on page 409 of the *Study Guide and Working Papers*.)

1. Not reversed: asset Supplies is decreasing, not increasing.
2. Reversed: liability is increasing and no previous balance exists.
3. Not reversed: liability is decreasing and a previous balance exists.

SUMMARY OF KEY POINTS

Learning Unit 13-1

1. The formal income statement can be prepared from the income statement columns of the worksheet.
2. There are no debit or credit columns on the formal income statement.
3. The cost of goods sold section has a figure for beginning inventory and a separate figure for ending inventory.
4. Operating expenses could be broken down into selling and administrative expenses.
5. The ending figure for capital is not found on the worksheet. It comes from the statement of owner's equity.
6. A classified balance sheet breaks assets into current and plant and equipment. Liabilities are broken down into current and long-term.

Learning Unit 13-2

1. The information for journalizing, adjusting, and closing entries can be obtained from the worksheet.
2. In the closing process all temporary accounts will be zero and the capital account is brought up to its new balance.
3. Inventory is not a temporary account. The ending inventory, along with other permanent accounts, will be listed in the postclosing trial balance.

Learning Unit 13-3

1. Reversing entries are optional. They could aid in reducing potential errors and can simplify the recordkeeping process.
2. The reversing entry "flips" the adjustment on the first day of a new fiscal period. Thus the bookkeeper need *not* look back at what happened in the old year when recording the current year's transactions.
3. Reversing entries are only used if (a) assets are increasing and have no previous balance or (b) liabilities are increasing and have no previous balance.

KEY TERMS

Administrative expenses (general expenses) Expenses such as general office expenses that are incurred indirectly in the selling of goods.

Classified balance sheet A balance sheet that categorizes assets as current or plant and equipment and groups liabilities as current or long term.

Current assets Assets that can be converted into cash or used within one year or the normal operating cycle of the business, whichever is longer.

Current liabilities Obligations that will come due within one year or within the operating cycle, whichever is longer.

Long-term liabilities Obligations that are not due or payable for a long time, usually for more than a year.

Operating cycle Average time it takes to buy and sell merchandise and then collect accounts receivable.

Other expenses Nonoperating expenses that do not relate to the main operating activities of the business; they appear in a separate section on the income statement. One example given in the text is Interest Expense, interest owed on money borrowed by the company.

Other income Any revenue other than revenue

from sales. It appears in a separate section on the income statement. Examples: Rental Income and Storage Fees.

Plant and equipment Long-lived assets such as buildings or land that are used in the production or sale of goods or services.

Reversing entries Optional bookkeeping technique in which certain adjusting entries are reversed or switched on the first day of the new accounting period so that transactions in the new period can be recorded without referring back to prior adjusting entries.

Selling expenses Expenses directly related to the sale of goods.

QUESTIONS, MINI EXERCISES, EXERCISES, AND PROBLEMS

Discussion Questions

1. Which columns of the worksheet aid in the preparation of the income statement?
2. Explain the components of cost of goods sold.
3. Explain how operating expenses can be broken down into different categories.
4. What is the difference between current assets and plant and equipment?
5. What is an operating cycle?
6. Why journalize adjusting entries *after* the formal reports have been prepared?
7. Explain the steps of closing for a merchandise company.
8. Temporary accounts could appear on a postclosing trial balance. Agree or disagree.
9. What is the purpose of using reversing entries? Are they mandatory? When should they be used?

Mini Exercises

(The forms you need are on page 411 of the *Study Guide and Working Papers*.)

Calculate Net Sales

1. From the following, calculate net sales:

Purchases	$ 80	Sales Discount	$ 5
Gross Sales	140	Operating Expenses	25
Sales Returns and Allowances	10		

Calculate Cost of Goods Sold

2. Calculate Cost of Goods Sold:

Freight-In	$ 5	Ending Inventory	$15
Beginning Inventory	20	Net Purchases	50

Calculate Gross Profit and Net Income

3. Using Mini Exercises 1 and 2, calculate

   a. Gross Profit.
   b. Net Income or Net Loss.

BLUEPRINT: FINANCIAL STATEMENTS

(1) INCOME STATEMENT					
Revenue:					
Sales				$ XXX	
Less: Sales Ret. and Allow.			$ XXX		
Sales Discount			XXX	XXX	
Net Sales				$ XXXX	
Cost of Goods Sold:					
Merchandise Inventory, 1/1/0X			$ XXX		
Purchases		$XXX			
Less: Purchases Discount	$XXX				
Purch. Ret. and Allow.	XXX	XXX			
Net Purchases		XXX			
Add: Freight-In		XXX			
Net Cost of Purchases			XXX		
Cost of Goods Avail. for Sale			$XXXX		
Less: Merch. Inv., 12/31/0X			XXX		
Cost of Goods Sold				XXXX	
Gross Profit				$XXXX	
Operating Expenses:					
~~			$XXX		
~~			XXX		
~~			XXX		
Total Operating Expenses				XXX	
Net Income from Operations				$ XXX	
Other Income:					
Rental Income			$ XXX		
Storage Fees Income			XXX		
Total Other Income			$ XXX		
Other Expenses:					
Interest Expenses			XXX	XXX	
Net Income:				$ XXX	

(2) STATEMENT OF OWNER'S EQUITY			
Beginning Capital		$XXX	
Additional Investments		XXX	
Total Investment		$XXX	
Net Income	$XXX		
Less: Withdrawals	XXX		
Increase in Capital		XXX	
Ending Capital		$XXX	

(Cont. on p. 495)

(3) BALANCE SHEET				
Assets				
Current Assets:				
Cash		$ XXXX		
Acccounts Receivable		XXXX		
Merchandise Inventory		XXXX		
Prepaid Insurance		XXX		
Total Current Assets			$ XXXX	
Plant and Equipment:				
Store Equipment	$XXXX			
Less Accumulated Depreciation	XXXX	$XXXX		
Office Equipment	$XXXX			
Less Accumulated Depreciation	XXX	XXX		
Total Plant and Equipment			XXXX	
Total Assets			$XXXX	
Liabilities				
Current Liabilities:				
Unearned Revenue		$XXX		
Mortgage Payable (current portion)		XXX		
Accounts Payable		XXX		
Salaries Payable		XX		
FICA—Social Security Payable		XX		
FICA—Medicare Payable		XX		
Income Taxes Payable		XX		
Total Current Liabilities			$XXX	
Long-Term Liabilities				
Mortgage Payable			$XXX	
Total Liabilities			$XXXX	
Owner's Equity				
Capital*			XXXX	
Total Liabilities and Owner's Equity			$XXXX	

* From statement of owner's equity

Classification of Accounts

4. Match the following categories to each account listed below:
   1. Current Asset.
   2. Plant and Equipment.
   3. Current Liabilities.
   4. Long-Term Liabilities.

   _____ **a.** Merchandise Inventory   _____ **f.** Mortgage Payable (Not Current)

   _____ **b.** Unearned Rent   _____ **g.** FUTA Payable

   _____ **c.** Prepaid Insurance   _____ **h.** Accumulated Depreciation

   _____ **d.** SUTA Payable   _____ **i.** FICA — Social Security Payable

   _____ **e.** Store Equipment   _____ **j.** Petty Cash

Reversing Entries

5. **a.** On January 1, prepare a reversing entry. On January 8, journalize the entry to record the paying of salary expense, $900.

   b. What will be the balance in Salaries Expense on January 8 (after posting)?

December 31:

Salaries Expense			Salaries Payable	
	900	1,200 closing		300 Adj.
Adj.	300			

Exercises

(The forms you need are on pages 412–447 of the *Study Guide and Working Papers*.)

13-1. From the following accounts, prepare a cost of goods sold section in proper form: Merchandise Inventory, 12/31/X1, $6,000; Purchases Discount, $900; Merchandise Inventory, 12/1/X1, $4,000; Purchases, $58,000; Purchases Returns and Allowances, $1,000; Freight-In, $300.

13-2. Give the category, the classification, and the report(s) on which each of the following appears (for example: Cash—asset, current asset, balance sheet):

   a. Salaries Payable.   **e.** SIT Payable.

   b. Accounts Payable.   **f.** Office Equipment.

   c. Mortgage Payable.   **g.** Land.

   d. Unearned Legal Fees.

13-3. From the partial worksheet on page 497, journalize the closing entries of December 31 for A. Slow Co.

13-4. From the worksheet in Exercise 13-3, prepare the assets section of a classified balance sheet.

13-5. On December 31, 20X1, $300 of salaries has been accrued. (Salaries before accrued amount totaled $26,000.) The next payroll to be paid will be on February 3, 20X2, for $6,000. Please do the following:

   a. Journalize and post the adjusting entry (use T accounts).

   b. Journalize and post the reversing entry on January 1.

   c. Journalize and post the payment of the payroll. Cash has a balance of $15,000 before the payment of payroll on February 3.

Preparing cost of goods sold section.

Categorizing and classifying account titles.

Journalizing closing entries.

Preparing partially completed balance sheet.

Reversing entry.

	A. SLOW CO. WORKSHEET FOR YEAR ENDED DECEMBER 31, 200X			
	Income Statement		Balance Sheet	
Account Titles	Dr.	Cr.	Dr.	Cr.
Cash			193 00	
Merch. Inventory			450 00	
Prepaid Advertising			561 00	
Prepaid Insurance			30 00	
Office Equipment			1080 00	
Accum. Depr., Office Equip.				210 00
Accounts Payable				258 00
A. Slow, Capital				966 00
Income Summary	362 00	450 00		
Sales		5520 00		
Sales Returns and Allowances	223 00			
Sales Discount	108 00			
Purchases	2628 00			
Purchases Returns and Allow.		34 00		
Purchases Discount		51 00		
Salaries Expense	1083 00			
Insurance Expense	696 00			
Utilities Expense	48 00			
Plumbing Expense	57 00			
Advertising Expense	15 00			
Depr. Expenses, Office Equip.	30 00			
Salaries Payable				75 00
	5250 00	6055 00	2314 00	1509 00
Net Income	805 00			805 00
	6055 00	6055 00	2314 00	2314 00

Group A Problems

(The forms you need are on pages 414–431 of the *Study Guide and Working Papers*.)

13A-1. Prepare a formal income statement from the partial worksheet for Ring.com on the next page.

13A-2. Prepare a statement of owner's equity and a classified balance sheet from the worksheet for James Company (p. 498). *Note:* Of the Mortgage Payable, $200 is due within one year.

13A-3. **a.** Complete the worksheet for Jay's Supplies on page 499.

   b. Prepare an income statement, a statement of owner's equity, and a classified balance sheet. (*Note:* The amount of the mortgage due the first year is $800.)

   c. Journalize the adjusting and closing entries.

13A-4. Using the ledger balances and additional data shown on page 499, do the following for Callahan Lumber for the year ended December 31, 200X:

   1. Prepare the worksheet.

   2. Prepare the income statement, statement of owner's equity, and balance sheet.

Check Figure: Net Income from operations $761

Check Figure: Total Assets $33,340

Check Figure: Net Income $4,340

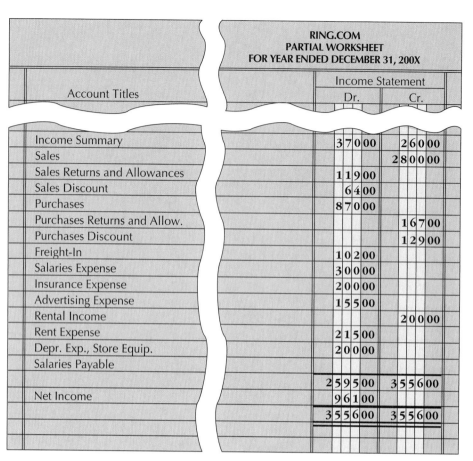

RING.COM
PARTIAL WORKSHEET
FOR YEAR ENDED DECEMBER 31, 200X

Account Titles	Income Statement Dr.	Income Statement Cr.
Income Summary	3 7 0 00	2 6 0 00
Sales		28 0 0 00
Sales Returns and Allowances	1 1 9 00	
Sales Discount	6 4 00	
Purchases	8 7 0 00	
Purchases Returns and Allow.		1 6 7 00
Purchases Discount		1 2 9 00
Freight-In	1 0 2 00	
Salaries Expense	3 0 0 00	
Insurance Expense	2 0 0 00	
Advertising Expense	1 5 5 00	
Rental Income		2 0 0 00
Rent Expense	2 1 5 00	
Depr. Exp., Store Equip.	2 0 0 00	
Salaries Payable		
	2 5 9 5 00	3 5 5 6 00
Net Income	9 6 1 00	
	3 5 5 6 00	3 5 5 6 00

JAMES COMPANY
WORKSHEET
FOR YEAR ENDED DECEMBER 31, 200X

Account Titles	Balance Sheet Dr.	Balance Sheet Cr.
Cash	23 5 0 0 00	
Petty Cash	9 0 00	
Accounts Receivable	1 3 5 0 00	
Merchandise Inv.	4 0 0 0 00	
Supplies	3 2 5 00	
Prepaid Insurance	5 0 0 00	
Store Equipment	2 8 0 0 00	
Acc. Dep., Store Eq.		7 0 0 00
Automobile	1 7 0 0 00	
Acc. Dep., Auto.		2 2 5 00
Accounts Payable		2 8 0 0 00
Taxes Payable		2 4 0 0 00
Unearned Rent		18 5 0 0 00
Mortgage Payable		4 5 0 00
H. James, Capital		12 4 0 0 00
H. James, With.	1 0 0 00	
Salaries Payable		6 0 0 00
	34 3 6 5 00	38 0 7 5 00
Net Loss	3 7 1 0 00	
	38 0 7 5 00	38 0 7 5 00

Preparing a statement of owner's equity and a classified balance sheet from a worksheet.

CHAPTER 13 ... COMPLETION OF THE ACCOUNTING CYCLE FOR A MERCHANDISE COMPANY

JAY'S SUPPLIES
WORKSHEET
FOR YEAR ENDED DECEMBER 31, 200X

Account Titles	Trial Balance Dr.	Trial Balance Cr.	Adjustments Dr.	Adjustments Cr.
Cash	2 000 00			
Accounts Receivable	3 000 00			
Merch. Inv., 1/1/XX	11 000 00	(B)	(A) 10 400 00	11 000 00 (A)
Prepaid Insurance	1 880 00			500 00 (E)
Equipment	3 400 00			
Accum. Dep., Equipment		1 080 00		400 00 (D)
Accounts Payable		5 080 00		
Unearned Training Fees		2 120 00	(C) 320 00	
Mortgage Payable		1 200 00		
P. Jay, Capital		10 560 00		
P. Jay, Withdrawals	4 280 00			
Income Summary		(A)	11 000 00	10 400 00 (B)
Sales		95 800 00		
Sales Returns and Allowances	3 200 00			
Sales Discount	2 600 00			
Purchases	63 600 00			
Purchases Returns and Allow.		1 360 00		
Purchases Discount		320 00		
Freight-In	2 680 00			
Advertising Expense	11 400 00			
Rent Expense	10 000 00			
Salaries Expense	13 600 00			
	132 640 00	132 640 00		
Training Fees Earned				320 00 (C)
Dep. Exp., Equipment			(D) 400 00	
Insurance Expense			(E) 500 00	
			22 620 00	22 620 00

3. Journalize and post adjusting and closing entries. (Be sure to put beginning balances in the ledger first.)

4. Prepare a postclosing trial balance.

5. Journalize the reversing entry for wages.

Comprehensive Problem. Worksheet preparation: preparing financial reports, journalizing and posting adjusting and closing entries, preparing a post-closing trial balance, and journalizing reversing entry.

Check Figure:
Net Income $4,336

Acct. No.

110	Cash	$ 1,340
111	Accounts Receivable	1,300
112	Merchandise Inventory	4,550
113	Lumber Supplies	269
114	Prepaid Insurance	218
121	Lumber Equipment	3,000
122	Accum. Depr., Lumber Equipment	490
220	Accounts Payable	1,160
221	Wages Payable	
330	J. Callahan, Capital	7,352
331	J. Callahan, Withdrawals	3,000
332	Income Summary	—
440	Sales	22,800
441	Sales Returns and Allowances	200

550	Purchases	14,800
551	Purchases Discount	285
552	Purchases Returns and Allowances	300
660	Wages Expense	2,480
661	Advertising Expense	400
662	Rent Expense	830
663	Dep. Expense, Lumber Equipment	
664	Lumber Supplies Expense	
665	Insurance Expense	

Additional Data

a./b.	Merchandise inventory, December 31	$4,900
c.	Lumber supplies on hand, December 31	75
d.	Insurance expired	150
e.	Depreciation for the year	250
f.	Accrued wages on December 31	95

Group B Problems

(The forms you need are on pages 435–447 of the *Study Guide and Working Papers*.)

13B-1. From the partial worksheet shown below, prepare a formal income statement.

Preparing an income statement from a worksheet.

Check Figure: Net Income from operations $845

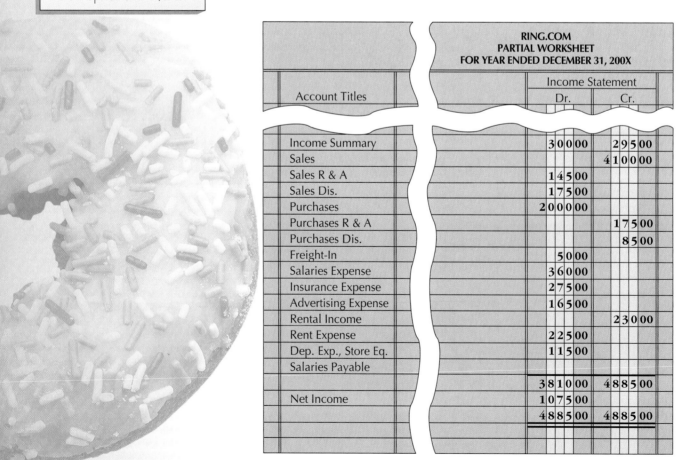

RING.COM
PARTIAL WORKSHEET
FOR YEAR ENDED DECEMBER 31, 200X

Account Titles	Income Statement Dr.	Income Statement Cr.
Income Summary	3 0 0 00	2 9 5 00
Sales		4 1 0 0 00
Sales R & A	1 4 5 00	
Sales Dis.	1 7 5 00	
Purchases	2 0 0 0 00	
Purchases R & A		1 7 5 00
Purchases Dis.		8 5 00
Freight-In	5 0 00	
Salaries Expense	3 6 0 00	
Insurance Expense	2 7 5 00	
Advertising Expense	1 6 5 00	
Rental Income		2 3 0 00
Rent Expense	2 2 5 00	
Dep. Exp., Store Eq.	1 1 5 00	
Salaries Payable		
	3 8 1 0 00	4 8 8 5 00
Net Income	1 0 7 5 00	
	4 8 8 5 00	4 8 8 5 00

13B-2. From the worksheet shown below, complete

    a. Statement of owner's equity.

    b. Classified balance sheet.

    Note: Of the Mortgage Payable, $3,000 is due within one year.

Preparing a statement of owner's equity and a classified balance sheet from a worksheet.

Check Figure:
Total Assets $28,294

JAMES COMPANY
WORKSHEET
FOR YEAR ENDED DECEMBER 31, 200X

Account Titles	Balance Sheet	
	Dr.	Cr.
Cash	2 5 0 0 00	
Petty Cash	5 0 00	
Acct. Rec.	1 3 0 0 00	
Merch. Inv.	4 2 5 0 00	
Supplies	3 4 4 00	
Prepaid Ins.	6 0 0 00	
Store Equip.	1 8 0 0 0 00	
Acc. Dep., Store Eq.		7 5 0 00
Automobile	2 5 0 0 00	
Acc. Dep., Auto.		5 0 0 00
Acct. Pay.		3 4 5 0 00
Taxes Pay.		2 1 0 0 00
Unearned Rent		1 1 0 0 0 00
Mortgage Pay.		8 0 0 0 00
H. James, Capital		1 0 5 0 0 00
H. James, Withd.	4 0 0 0 00	
Salaries Payable		1 0 0 00
	3 3 5 4 4 00	3 6 4 0 0 00
Net Loss	2 8 5 6 00	
	3 6 4 0 0 00	3 6 4 0 0 00

Completing the worksheet; preparing financial reports; and journalizing adjusting and closing entries.

Check Figure:
Net Loss $12,050

13B-3. From the partial worksheet on page 502, your tasks are to

    1. Complete the worksheet.

    2. Prepare the income statement, statement of owner's equity, and classified balance sheet. The amount of the mortgage due the first year is $800.

    3. Journalize the adjusting and closing entries.

13B-4. From the following ledger balances and additional data on pages 502–503, do the following:

    1. Prepare the worksheet.

    2. Prepare the income statement, statement of owner's equity, and balance sheet.

    3. Journalize and post adjusting and closing entries. (Be sure to put beginning balances in the ledger first.)

    4. Prepare a postclosing trial balance.

    5. Journalize the reversing entry for wages.

Comprehensive Problem: Worksheet preparation; preparing financial reports, journalizing and posting adjusting and closing entries; preparing a post-closing trial balance; and journalizing reversing entry.

Check Figure:
Net Income $2,730

JAY'S SUPPLIES
WORKSHEET
FOR YEAR ENDED DECEMBER 31, 200X

Account Titles	Trial Balance Dr.	Trial Balance Cr.	Adjustments Dr.	Adjustments Cr.
Cash	3 0 0 00			
Accounts Receivable	3 0 0 00			
Merch. Inventory, 1/1/XX	11 7 0 0 00		(B) 8 0 0 00	11 7 0 0 00 (A)
Prepaid Insurance	1 0 0 00			3 5 0 00 (E)
Equipment	5 0 0 00			
Accum. Dep., Equipment		1 9 0 0 00		5 0 0 00 (D)
Accounts Payable		2 1 0 0 00		
Unearned Training Fees		1 4 5 0 00	(C) 4 0 0 00	
Mortgage Payable		2 4 0 0 00		
P. Jay, Capital		27 7 5 0 00		
P. Jay, Withdrawals	4 0 0 0 00			
Income Summary			(A)11 7 0 0 00	8 0 0 00 (B)
Sales		100 8 0 0 00		
Sales Returns and Allowances	4 1 0 0 00			
Sales Discount	2 8 0 0 00			
Purchases	70 0 0 0 00			
Purchases Returns and Allow.		2 0 0 0 00		
Purchases Discounts		1 4 0 0 00		
Freight-In	2 7 0 0 00			
Advertising Expense	8 0 0 00			
Rent Expense	8 5 0 0 00			
Salaries Expense	16 0 0 0 00			
	139 8 0 0 00	139 8 0 0 00		
Training Fees Earned				4 0 0 00 (C)
Dep. Exp., Equipment			(D) 5 0 0 00	
Insurance Expense			(E) 3 5 0 00	
			20 9 5 0 00	20 9 5 0 00

Acct. No.

110	Cash	$ 940
111	Accounts Receivable	1,470
112	Merchandise Inventory	5,600
113	Lumber Supplies	260
114	Prepaid Insurance	117
121	Lumber Equipment	2,600
122	Acc. Dep., Lumber Equipment	340
220	Accounts Payable	1,330
221	Wages Payable	
330	J. Callahan, Capital	7,562
331	J. Callahan, Withdrawals	3,500
332	Income Summary	—
440	Sales	23,000
441	Sales Returns and Allowances	400
550	Purchases	14,700

551	Purchases Discount	440
552	Purchases Returns and Allowances	545
660	Wages Expense	2,390
661	Advertising Expense	400
662	Rent Expense	840
663	Dep. Exp., Lumber Equipment	
664	Lumber Supplies Expense	
665	Insurance Expense	

Additional Data

a./b.	Merchandise inventory, December 31	$3,900
c.	Lumber supplies on hand, December 31	60
d.	Insurance expired	50
e.	Depreciation for the year	400
f.	Accrued wages on December 31	175

REAL-WORLD APPLICATIONS

13R-1.

Chan Company recently had most of its records destroyed in a fire. The information for 20X1 was discovered by the bookkeeper.

Beg. Inv. $1,400
End. Inv. 3,000

CHAN COMPANY
GENERAL JOURNAL

Page 2

Date		Description	PR	Dr.	Cr.
Dec.	31	Income Summary	312	3 6 3 0 00	
		Sales Returns and Allowances	420		1 4 0 00
		Sales Discount	430		3 0 00
		Purchases	500		2 4 0 0 00
		Delivery Expense	600		9 0 00
		Salaries Expense	610		8 4 0 00
		Rent Expense	620		3 0 00
		Office Supplies Expense	630		5 0 00
		Advertising Expense	640		1 0 00
		Dep. Exp., Store Equipment	650		4 0 00
	31	Sales	410	5 5 4 2 00	
		Purchases Discount	510	1 2 0 00	
		Purchases Returns and Allowances	520	1 0 0 00	
		Income Summary	312		5 7 6 2 00
	31	Income Summary	312	3 7 3 2 00	
		J. Chan, Capital	310		3 7 3 2 00

Please assist the bookkeeper in reconstructing an income statement for 20X1.

13R-2.

Hope Lang, a junior accountant, has the December 31, 200X trial balance of
Gregot Company sitting on her desk. Attached is a memo from her supervisor

requesting that a classified balance sheet be prepared. Hope gathers the following data:

1. A physical inventory at December 31 showed $80,000 on hand.
2. Office supplies on hand was $600.
3. Insurance unexpired was $750.
4. Depreciation (straight-line) is based on a 25-year life.

Using the following trial balance of Gregot Co., please assist Hope with this project. *Hint:* Ending figure for capital is $115,850.

GREGOT COMPANY
TRIAL BALANCE
DECEMBER 31, 200X

	Dr.	Cr.
Cash	11 000 00	
Accounts Receivable	38 000 00	
Inventory, Jan. 1	80 000 00	
Prepaid Insurance	2 000 00	
Office Supplies	1 000 00	
Land	17 500 00	
Building	50 000 00	
Accumulated Depreciation, Building		10 000 00
Notes Payable		40 000 00
Accounts Payable		30 000 00
G. Gregot, Capital		98 400 00
G. Gregot, Withdrawals	13 000 00	
Income Summary	—	—
Retail Sales		329 000 00
Sales Returns and Allowances	21 000 00	
Sales Discount	8 000 00	
Purchases	215 500 00	
Purchases Returns and Allowances		11 600 00
Purchases Discount		4 000 00
Transportation-In	5 000 00	
Advertising Expense	2 500 00	
Wage Expense	55 000 00	
Utilities Expense	3 500 00	
	523 000 00	523 000 00

YOU make the call

Critical Thinking/Ethical Case

13R-3.

Janet Flynn, owner of Reel Company, plans to apply for a bank loan at Petro National Bank. Because the company has a lot of debt on its balance sheet, Janet does not plan to show the loan officer the balance sheet. She plans only to bring the income statement. Do you feel that this move is a sound financial move by Janet? You make the call. Write down your specific recommendations to Janet.

INTERNET EXERCISES

EX-1. [www.liquidics.com/financials.htm] Liquidics is an electronics firm which claims to be positioning itself for rapid growth in the semiconductor market. The financial statements they present are straightforward.

1. Look over the Balance Sheet and comment on its classifications, using those presented in this chapter as a guide.

2. Read the Notes to the Financial Statements and determine more information about the Prepaid License Agreement listed under Current Assets.

EX-2. [www.exxonmobil.com/shareholder publications/c annual 99/c financials.html] This is another exercise in looking at the classifications in classified balance sheets. ExxonMobil is a vastly different company than is Liquidics, from exercise 1. Observe, however, the classifications in the Balance Sheet of ExxonMobil. How does it compare to that of Liquidics? How is it different? Notice how they are basically the same as presented in this chapter.

CONTINUING PROBLEM

Using the worksheet in Chapter 12 for Eldorado Computer Center, journalize and post the adjusting entries and prepare the financial statements. (See page 435 in the *Study Guide and Working Papers*.)

THE CORNER DRESS SHOP

*Reviewing the Accounting Cycle
for a Merchandise Company*

(The forms you need are on pages 448–470 of the *Study Guide and Working Papers.* This practice set will help you review all the key concepts of a merchandise company along with the integration of payroll, including the preparation of Form 941.)

Because you are the bookkeeper of The Corner Dress Shop, we have gathered the following information for you. It will be your task to complete the accounting cycle for March.

THE CORNER DRESS SHOP POSTCLOSING TRIAL BALANCE FEBRUARY 28, 200X	1	2
Cash	2 5 0 2 90	
Accounts Receivable	2 2 0 0 00	
Petty Cash	3 5 00	
Merchandise Inventory	5 6 0 0 00	
Prepaid Rent	1 8 0 0 00	
Delivery Truck	6 0 0 0 00	
Accumulated Depreciation, Truck		1 5 0 0 00
Accounts Payable		1 9 0 0 00
FIT Payable		1 2 8 4 00
FICA—Social Security Payable		1 3 3 9 20
FICA—Medicare Payable		3 1 3 20
SIT Payable		7 5 6 00
SUTA Payable		9 7 9 20
FUTA Payable		1 6 3 20
Unearned Rent		8 0 0 00
B. Loeb, Capital		9 1 0 3 10
	18 1 3 7 90	18 1 3 7 90

Betty Loeb's dress shop is located at 1 Milgate Rd., Marblehead, MA 01945. Its identification number is 33-4158215.

Balances in subsidiary ledgers as of March 1 are as follows:

Accounts Receivable		Accounts Payable	
Bing Co.	$2,200	Blew Co.	$1,900
Blew Co.	—	Jones Co.	—
Ronald Co.	—	Moe's Garage	—
		Morris Co.	—

Payroll is paid monthly:

FICA rate	Social Security 6.2 percent on $76,200
	Medicare 1.45% on all earnings
SUTA rate	4.8 percent on $7,000
FUTA rate	.8 percent on $7,000
SIT rate	7 percent
FIT	Use table provided on page 510.

The payroll register for January and February is provided. In March salaries are as follows:

Mel Case $3,325
Jane Holl 4,120
Jackie Moore 4,760

Your tasks are to

1. Set up a general ledger, accounts receivable subsidiary ledger and accounts payable subsidiary ledger, auxiliary petty cash record and payroll register. (Be sure to update ledger accounts based on given information in postclosing trial balance for February 28 before beginning.)
2. Journalize the transactions and prepare the payroll register.
3. Update the accounts payable and accounts receivable subsidiary ledgers.
4. Post to the general ledger.
5. Prepare a trial balance on a worksheet and complete the worksheet.
6. Prepare an income statement, statement of owner's equity, and classified balance sheet.
7. Journalize the adjusting and closing entries.
8. Post the adjusting and closing entries to the ledger.
9. Prepare a postclosing trial balance.
10. Complete Form 941 and sign it as of the last day in April.

Chart of Accounts for The Corner Dress Shop

Assets
110 Cash
111 Accounts Receivable
112 Petty Cash
114 Merchandise Inventory
116 Prepaid Rent
120 Delivery Truck
121 Accumulated Depreciation, Truck

Liabilities
210 Accounts Payable
212 Salaries Payable
214 Federal Income Tax Payable
216 FICA—Soc. Sec. Payable
218 FICA—Medicare Payable
220 State Income Tax Payable
222 SUTA Tax Payable
224 FUTA Tax Payable
226 Unearned Rent

Owner's Equity
310 B. Loeb, Capital
320 B. Loeb, Withdrawals
330 Income Summary

Revenue
410 Sales
412 Sales Returns and Allowances
414 Sales Discount
416 Rental Income

Cost of Goods Sold
510 Purchases
512 Purchases Returns and Allowances
514 Purchase Discount

Expenses
610 Sales Salaries Expense
611 Office Salaries Expense
612 Payroll Tax Expense
614 Cleaning Expense
616 Depreciation Expense, Truck
618 Rent Expense
620 Postage Expense
622 Delivery Expense
624 Miscellaneous Expense

THE CORNER DRESS SHOP
PAYROLL REGISTER
JANUARY AND FEBRUARY 200X

Employees	Allow. and Marital Status	Cum. Earnings	Salary	Earnings Reg.	O/T	Gross	Cum. Earnings
Mel Case	M – 2	—	3 3 0 0 00	3 3 0 0 00		3 3 0 0 00	3 3 0 0 00
Jane Holl	M – 1	—	3 4 0 0 00	3 4 0 0 00		3 4 0 0 00	3 4 0 0 00
Jackie Moore	M – 0	—	4 1 0 0 00	4 1 0 0 00		4 1 0 0 00	4 1 0 0 00
Totals for Jan.			10 8 0 0 00	10 8 0 0 00		10 8 0 0 00	10 8 0 0 00
Mel Case	M – 2	3 3 0 0 00	3 3 0 0 00	3 3 0 0 00		3 3 0 0 00	6 6 0 0 00
Jane Holl	M – 1	3 4 0 0 00	3 4 0 0 00	3 4 0 0 00		3 4 0 0 00	6 8 0 0 00
Jackie Moore	M – 0	4 1 0 0 00	4 1 0 0 00	4 1 0 0 00		4 1 0 0 00	8 2 0 0 00
Totals for Feb.		10 8 0 0 00	10 8 0 0 00	10 8 0 0 00		10 8 0 0 00	21 6 0 0 00

PAYROLL REGISTER

Taxable Earnings Unemp.	FICA Soc. Sec.	FICA Medicare	Deductions FICA Soc. Sec.	FICA Medicare	FIT	SIT	Net Pay	Ck. No.	Distribution Office Salary Expense	Sales Salary Expense
3 3 0 0 00	3 3 0 0 00	3 3 0 0 00	2 0 4 60	4 7 85	3 4 4 00	2 3 1 00	2 4 7 2 55		3 3 0 0 00	
3 4 0 0 00	3 4 0 0 00	3 4 0 0 00	2 1 0 80	4 9 30	3 9 7 00	2 3 8 00	2 5 0 4 90			3 4 0 0 00
4 1 0 0 00	4 1 0 0 00	4 1 0 0 00	2 5 4 20	5 9 45	5 4 3 00	2 8 7 00	2 9 5 6 35			4 1 0 0 00
10 8 0 0 00	10 8 0 0 00	10 8 0 0 00	6 6 9 60	1 5 6 60	1 2 8 4 00	7 5 6 00	7 9 3 3 80		3 3 0 0 00	7 5 0 0 00
3 3 0 0 00	3 3 0 0 00	3 3 0 0 00	2 0 4 60	4 7 85	3 4 4 00	2 3 1 00	2 4 7 2 55		3 3 0 0 00	
3 4 0 0 00	3 4 0 0 00	3 4 0 0 00	2 1 0 80	4 9 30	3 9 7 00	2 3 8 00	2 5 0 4 90			3 4 0 0 00
4 1 0 0 00	4 1 0 0 00	4 1 0 0 00	2 5 4 20	5 9 45	5 4 3 00	2 8 7 00	2 9 5 6 35			4 1 0 0 00
10 8 0 0 00	10 8 0 0 00	10 8 0 0 00	6 6 9 60	1 5 6 60	1 2 8 4 00	7 5 6 00	7 9 3 3 80		3 3 0 0 00	7 5 0 0 00

200X
Mar.

1 Bing paid balance owed, no discount.

2 Purchased merchandise from Morris Company on account, $10,000, terms 2/10, n/30.

2 Paid $6 from the petty cash fund for cleaning package, voucher no. 18 (consider it a cleaning expense).

3 Sold merchandise to Ronald Company on account, $7,000, invoice no. 51, terms 2/10, n/30.

5 Paid $3 from the petty cash fund for postage, voucher no. 19.

6 Sold merchandise to Ronald Company on account, $5,000, invoice no. 52, terms 2/10, n/30.

8 Paid $10 from the petty cash fund for First Aid emergency, voucher no. 20.

9 Purchased merchandise from Morris Company on account, $5,000, terms 2/10, n/30.

9 Paid $5 for delivery expense from petty cash fund, voucher no. 21.

9	Sold more merchandise to Ronald Company on account, $3,000, invoice no. 53, terms 2/10, n/30.
9	Paid cleaning service, $300, check no. 110.
10	Ronald Company returned merchandise costing $1,000 from invoice no. 52; The Corner Dress Shop issued credit memo no. 10 to Ronald Company for $1,000.
11	Purchased merchandise from Jones Company on account, $10,000, terms 1/15, n/60.
12	Paid Morris Company invoice dated March 2, check no. 111.
13	Sold $7,000 of merchandise for cash.
14	Returned merchandise to Jones Company in amount of $2,000; The Corner Dress Shop issued debit memo no. 4 to Jones Company.
14	Paid $5 from the petty cash fund for delivery expense, voucher no. 22.
15	Paid taxes due for FICA (Social Security and Medicare) and FIT for February payroll, check no. 112.
15	Sold merchandise for $29,000 cash.
15	Betty withdrew $100 for her own personal expenses, check no. 113.
15	Paid state income tax for February payroll, check no. 114.
16	Received payment from Ronald Company for invoice no. 52, less discount.
16	Ronald Company paid invoice no. 51, $7,000.
16	Sold merchandise to Bing Company on account, $3,200, invoice no. 54, terms 2/10, n/30.
21	Purchased delivery truck on account from Moe's Garage, $17,200.
22	Sold merchandise to Ronald Company on account, $4,000, invoice no. 55, terms 2/10, n/30.
23	Paid Jones Company the balance owed, check no. 115.
24	Sold merchandise to Bing Company, $2,000, invoice no. 56, terms 1/10, n/30.
25	Purchased merchandise for $1,000, check no. 116.
27	Purchased merchandise from Blew Company on account, $6,000, terms 2/10, n/30.
27	Paid $2 postage from the petty cash fund, voucher no. 23.
28	Ronald Company paid invoice no. 55 dated March 22, less discount.
28	Bing Company paid invoice no. 54 dated March 16.
29	Purchased merchandise from Morris Company on account, $9,000, terms 2/10, n/30.
30	Sold merchandise to Blew Company on account, $10,000, invoice no. 57, terms 2/10, n/30.
30	Issued check no. 117 to replenish to the same level the petty cash fund.
30	Recorded payroll in payroll register.
30	Journalized payroll entry (to be paid on 31st).
30	Journalized employer's payroll tax expense.
31	Paid payroll checks no. 118, no. 119, and no. 120.

Additional Data

a./b. Ending merchandise inventory, $13,515.

c. During March, rent expired, $600.

d. Truck depreciated, $150.

e. Rental income earned, $200 (one month's rent from subletting).

MARRIED Persons—MONTHLY Payroll Period
(For Wages Paid in 2000)

If the wages are—		And the number of withholding allowances claimed is—										
At least	But less than	0	1	2	3	4	5	6	7	8	9	10
		The amount of income tax to be withheld is—										
$3,240	$3,280	408	373	338	303	268	233	198	163	128	93	58
3,280	3,320	414	379	344	309	274	239	204	169	134	99	64
3,320	3,360	420	385	350	315	280	245	210	175	140	105	70
3,360	3,400	426	391	356	321	286	251	216	181	146	111	76
3,400	3,440	432	397	362	327	292	257	222	187	152	117	82
3,440	3,480	438	403	368	333	298	263	228	193	158	123	88
3,480	3,520	444	409	374	339	304	269	234	199	164	129	94
3,520	3,560	450	415	380	345	310	275	240	205	170	135	100
3,560	3,600	456	421	386	351	316	281	246	211	176	141	106
3,600	3,640	462	427	392	357	322	287	252	217	182	147	112
3,640	3,680	468	433	398	363	328	293	258	223	188	153	118
3,680	3,720	474	439	404	369	334	299	264	229	194	159	124
3,720	3,760	480	445	410	375	340	305	270	235	200	165	130
3,760	3,800	486	451	416	381	346	311	276	241	206	171	136
3,800	3,840	492	457	422	387	352	317	282	247	212	177	142
3,840	3,880	498	463	428	393	358	323	288	253	218	183	148
3,880	3,920	504	469	434	399	364	329	294	259	224	189	154
3,920	3,960	510	475	440	405	370	335	300	265	230	195	160
3,960	4,000	516	481	446	411	376	341	306	271	236	201	166
4,000	4,040	522	487	452	417	382	347	312	277	242	207	172
4,040	4,080	532	493	458	423	388	353	318	283	248	213	178
4,080	4,120	543	499	464	429	394	359	324	289	254	219	184
4,120	4,160	554	505	470	435	400	365	330	295	260	225	190
4,160	4,200	565	511	476	441	406	371	336	301	266	231	196
4,200	4,240	577	517	482	447	412	377	342	307	272	237	202
4,240	4,280	588	523	488	453	418	383	348	313	278	243	208
4,280	4,320	599	534	494	459	424	389	354	319	284	249	214
4,320	4,360	610	545	500	465	430	395	360	325	290	255	220
4,360	4,400	621	556	506	471	436	401	366	331	296	261	226
4,400	4,440	633	567	512	477	442	407	372	337	302	267	232
4,440	4,480	644	579	518	483	448	413	378	343	308	273	238
4,480	4,520	655	590	524	489	454	419	384	349	314	279	244
4,520	4,560	666	601	536	495	460	425	390	355	320	285	250
4,560	4,600	677	612	547	501	466	431	396	361	326	291	256
4,600	4,640	689	623	558	507	472	437	402	367	332	297	262
4,640	4,680	700	635	569	513	478	443	408	373	338	303	268
4,680	4,720	711	646	580	519	484	449	414	379	344	309	274
4,720	4,760	722	657	592	526	490	455	420	385	350	315	280
4,760	4,800	733	668	603	537	496	461	426	391	356	321	286
4,800	4,840	745	679	614	549	502	467	432	397	362	327	292
4,840	4,880	756	691	625	560	508	473	438	403	368	333	298
4,880	4,920	767	702	636	571	514	479	444	409	374	339	304
4,920	4,960	778	713	648	582	520	485	450	415	380	345	310
4,960	5,000	789	724	659	593	528	491	456	421	386	351	316
5,000	5,040	801	735	670	605	539	497	462	427	392	357	322
5,040	5,080	812	747	681	616	551	503	468	433	398	363	328
5,080	5,120	823	758	692	627	562	509	474	439	404	369	334
5,120	5,160	834	769	704	638	573	515	480	445	410	375	340
5,160	5,200	845	780	715	649	584	521	486	451	416	381	346
5,200	5,240	857	791	726	661	595	530	492	457	422	387	352
5,240	5,280	868	803	737	672	607	541	498	463	428	393	358
5,280	5,320	879	814	748	683	618	552	504	469	434	399	364
5,320	5,360	890	825	760	694	629	564	510	475	440	405	370
5,360	5,400	901	836	771	705	640	575	516	481	446	411	376
5,400	5,440	913	847	782	717	651	586	522	487	452	417	382
5,440	5,480	924	859	793	728	663	597	532	493	458	423	388
5,480	5,520	935	870	804	739	674	608	543	499	464	429	394
5,520	5,560	946	881	816	750	685	620	554	505	470	435	400
5,560	5,600	957	892	827	761	696	631	565	511	476	441	406
5,600	5,640	969	903	838	773	707	642	577	517	482	447	412
5,640	5,680	980	915	849	784	719	653	588	523	488	453	418
5,680	5,720	991	926	860	795	730	664	599	534	494	459	424
5,720	5,760	1,002	937	872	806	741	676	610	545	500	465	430
5,760	5,800	1,013	948	883	817	752	687	621	556	506	471	436
5,800	5,840	1,025	959	894	829	763	698	633	567	512	477	442

$5,840 and over   Use Table 4(b) for a **MARRIED person** on page 34. Also see the instructions on page 32.

Computerized Accounting Application for The Corner Dress Shop Mini Practice Set for Chapter 13

Accounting Cycle for a Merchandise Company

Before starting on this assignment, read and complete the tasks discussed in Parts A, B, and F of the Computerized Accounting appendix at the end of this book and complete the Computerized Accounting Application assignments for Chapter 3, Chapter 4, Valdez Realty Mini Practice Set (Chapter 5), Pete's Market Mini Practice Set (Chapter 8), and Chapter 10.

This practice set will help you review all the key concepts of a merchandise company along with the integration of payroll, including the preparation of Form 941.

Since you are the bookkeeper on The Corner Dress Shop, we have gathered the following information for you. It will be your task to complete the accounting cycle for March.

The Corner Dress Shop: Trial Balance As at 3/1/00

		Debits	Credits
1110	Cash	2,502.90	—
1115	Petty Cash	35.00	—
1120	Accounts Receivable	2,200.00	—
1130	Inventory	5,600.00	—
1140	Prepaid Rent	1,800.00	—
1250	Delivery Truck	6,000.00	—
1251	Accum. Dep — Delivery Truck	—	1,500.00
2110	Accounts Payable	—	1,900.00
2310	Federal Income Tax Payable	—	1,284.00
2320	State Income Tax Payable	—	756.00
2330	FICA — Soc. Sec. Payable	—	1,339.20
2335	FICA — Medicare Payable	—	313.20
2340	FUTA Payable	—	163.20
2350	SUTA Payable	—	979.20
2400	Unearned Rent	—	800.00
3110	Betty Loeb, Capital	—	9,103.10
		18,137.90	18,137.90

The Corner Dress Shop: Customer Aged Detail As at 3/1/00

			Total	Current	31 to 60	61 to 90
Bing. Co.						
12	1/1/00	Invoice	2,200.00	—	2,200.00	—

The Corner Dress Shop: Vendor Aged Detail As at 3/1/00

			Total	Current	31 to 60	61 to 90
Blew Co.						
422	2/15/00	Invoice	1,900.00	1,900.00	—	—

The Corner Dress Shop, owned by Betty Loeb, is located at 1 Milgate Road, Marblehead, Massachusetts, 01945. Her employer identification number is 33-415821. Federal Income Tax (FIT), State Income Tax (SIT), Social Security,

Medicare, FUTA, and SUTA are all calculated automatically by the program based on the following assumptions and built-in tax rates:

▼ FICA: Social Security, 6.2 percent on $76,200; Medicare, 1.45 percent on all earnings.
▼ SUTA: 4.8 percent on the first $7,000 in earnings.
▼ FUTA: .8 percent on the first $7,000 in earnings.
▼ Employees are paid monthly. The payroll is recorded and paid on the last day of each month.
▼ FIT is calculated automatically by the program based on the marital status and number of exemptions claimed by each employee.
▼ SIT for Massachusetts is calculated automatically by the program based on the marital status and number of exemptions claimed by each employee. Note that since Peachtree uses a different method for calculating FIT and SIT, your answers may not match the manual practice set causing slight differences in the payroll checks.

Open the Company Data Files

1. Click on the Start button. Point to Programs; point to the Peachtree folder and select Peachtree Complete Accounting. Your desktop may have the Peachtree icon allowing for a quicker entrance into the program.

2. Follow the "Open a File" instructions in Part A of the Computerized Accounting appendix at the back of this book to open **The Corner Dress Shop.**

Add Your Name to the Company Name

3. Click on the **Maintain** menu option. Then select **Company Information.** The program will respond by bringing up a dialogue box allowing the user to edit/add information about the company. In the **Company Name** entry field at the end of **The Corner Dress Shop,** add a dash and your name "**-Student Name**" to the end of the company name. Click on the OK button to return to the Menu Window.

Printing an Inventory Valuation Report

4. To see what inventory items The Corner Dress Shop has available, let's print a listing. Select **Inventory** from the **Reports** menu. Select Inventory Valuation Report from the Reports List. Accept all defaults and print the resulting report. You will see that we have 6 items in our inventory. In addition, we can see our current cost on each item.

Maintain Inventory Items

5. Peachtree's Inventory module allows the user to easily add new items or make changes to existing items such as recording price changes. Since you will be asked to change prices later in the practice set, let's take a look at how that works now. Do not actually change any of the fields for the item we will be looking at.

▼ Select **Inventory Items** from the **Maintain** menu.
▼ In the **Item ID** field, select "6000" using the Look Up feature.
▼ In the **Description** field, you will see the current description of this inventory item. Should a change be needed, we would simply place the cursor where the change needs to be made and edit as needed.
▼ Under the **General** Tab is a field where we can select and then enter a longer description of this item that will appear on sales and/or purchase invoices when we include this item on sales or purchase invoices.
▼ The current selling price for this item is kept in the **Sales Price #1** field. Peachtree has the capability of storing multiple prices for an item. This feature can be activated by clicking on the arrow to the right of the **Sales Price #1** field. Go ahead and click on this arrow. A table is presented which allows us to enter up to 5 different selling prices. Different customers can be assigned to different price levels in this manner. Since we have only one price, we can **Cancel** the Multiple Pricing Level box to return to the Maintain Inventory Items window. When you are prompted to change prices later in the practice set, you will simply change the price in the **Sales Price #1** field rather than add multiple prices.

▼ Unit/Measure, Item Type and Location are sorting and information fields that can be used as needed and have no restrictions as to content except length.

▼ The **Cost Method** field is where we can select the cost assumption to use with this item. Using the pull down menu, you can see our selection consists of FIFO, LIFO or Average. We will leave the setting at "Average". These cost assumptions will be discussed in greater detail in chapter 16.

▼ Peachtree has used default information to select the GL accounts needed for an inventory transaction. If there is some need to change these, we can decline the defaults and select any account we may need. Since there is no need to change these accounts, we will leave them at their default settings.

▼ We could also establish a minimum stock level and have Peachtree warn us when we fall below this level. We can also establish a reorder point that Peachtree can use to generate an inventory reorder listing.

▼ We can also select the vendor from whom we would normally order this item. Peachtree uses this and all the information we can see in this window to work interactively with Peachtree's other modules and report features.

▼ Your screen should look like this:

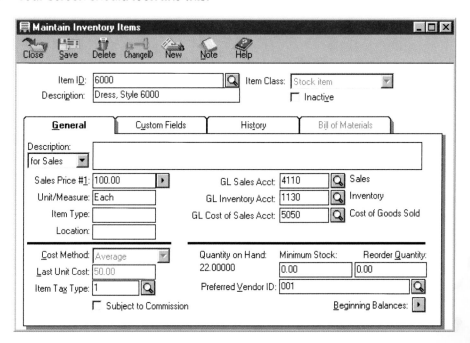

6. Record the following transactions using the appropriate General (G), Sales/Invoicing (S), Receipts (R), Purchases (PU), and Payments (PA) windows. Use the same forms when printing invoices, credits and checks as in Chapter 10 changing the starting numbers as needed. Accept defaults for any field for which you are not given data. Use the date of the transaction for the Deposit Ticket ID field. The transactions for March:

Record March Transactions

2000

Mar. 1 Received check no. 7634 from the Bing Co. in the amount of $2,200 in payment of invoice no. 12 ($2,200), dated January 1. (R)

2 Purchased merchandise from the Morris Co. on account, $10,000, invoice no. 1210, terms 2/10, n/30 consisting of 184- Style 1000 and 180- Style 2000 dresses. (P)

3 Sold merchandise to the Ronold Co. on account, $7,000, invoice no. 51, terms 2/10, n/30 consisting of 48- Style 1000, 30- Style 2000, 8- Style 3000, 9- Style 4000, 8- Style 5000 and 8- Style 6000 dresses. (S)

6 Sold merchandise to the Ronold Co. on account, $5,000, invoice no. 52, terms 2/10, n/30 consisting of 48- Style 1000, 24- Style

2000, 5- Style 3000, 3- Style 4000, 3- Style 5000 and 3- Style 6000 dresses. (S)

9 Purchased merchandise from the Morris Co. on account, $5,000, invoice no. 1286, terms 2/10, n/30 consisting of 92- Style 1000 and 90- Style 2000 dresses. (P)

9 Sold merchandise to the Ronold Co. on account, $3,000, invoice no. 53, terms 2/10, n/30 consisting of 20- Style 1000, 20- Style 2000, 4- Style 3000, 2- Style 4000, and 4- Style 5000 dresses. (S)

9 Paid cleaning service $300, check no. 110 to Ronda's Cleaning Service. In the Payments window:

▼ Enter Ronda's name in the Pay To field
▼ Enter a description of the payment in that field.
▼ Select the correct GL account for this line (Cleaning Expense)
▼ Enter the amount in the Amount column.
▼ Print the check as you did in Chapter 10. (PA)

10 Ronold Co. returned merchandise that cost $1,000 from invoice no. 52. consisting of 4- Style 1000, 5- Style 2000, 2- Style 3000, 1- Style 4000, 2- Style 5000 and 1- Style 6000 dresses. The Corner Dress Shop issued credit memorandum no. CM 10 to the Ronold Co. for $1,000. Remember to use negative quantities for returns. (S)

11 Purchased merchandise from the Jones Co. on account, $10,000, invoice no. 4639, terms 1/15, n/60 consisting of 144- Style 3000, and 124- Style 4000 dresses. (P)

12 Issued check no. 111 to the Morris Co. in the amount of $9,800 in payment of invoice no. 1210 ($10,000), dated March 2, less 2 percent discount ($200). (PA)

13 Sold $7,000 of merchandise for cash consisting of 24- Style 1000, 30- Style 2000, 24- Style 3000 and 29- Style 4000 dresses. Be sure to use CASH for the customer name and for the Reference field. (R)

14 Returned merchandise to the Jones Co. in the amount of $2,000 consisting of 32- Style 3000 and 22- Style 4000 dresses. Remember to use negative quantities for returns. Assign DM 4 as the invoice number. (P)

15 Paid FIT, Social Security, and Medicare taxes due for February payroll, check no. 112 in the amount of $2,936.40. Make the check payable to the IRS. You may wish to print a General Trial Balance first to determine how much to pay for each account. Use the procedure established with your payment on the 9th adding as many lines as you need to pay all the accounts required. (PA)

15 Due to increased operating costs, The Corner Dress Shop must raise its selling prices as follows:

Style 1000	$60.00
Style 2000	$70.00
Style 3000	$80.00
Style 4000	$90.00
Style 5000	$110.00
Style 6000	$120.00

Make these changes using the procedures discussed at the start of this practice set before continuing.

15 Sold merchandise for $29,000 cash consisting of 4- Style 1000, 5- Style 2000, 2- Style 3000, 1- Style 4000, 2- Style 5000 and 1- Style 6000 dresses. Use CASH for the Name and Reference fields. If you do not end up with $29,000 as your total, check to make sure you accomplished the price changes correctly. (R)

15 B. Loeb withdrew $100 for her own personal expenses, check no. 113. (PA)

15   Paid SIT tax for February payroll, check no. 114. Make the check payable to the State of Massachusetts. (PA)

16   Received check no. 5432 from the Ronold Co. in the amount of $3,920 in payment of invoice no. 52 ($5,000), dated March 6, less credit memo CM 10 ($1,000), less 2 percent discount ($100 − 20 = $80, net sales discount). (R)

16   Received check no. 5447 from the Ronold Co. in the amount of $7,000 in payment of invoice no. 51, dated March 3.

16   Sold merchandise to the Bing Co. on account, $3,200, invoice no. 54, terms 2/10, n/30 consisting of 12- Style 1000, 10- Style 2000, 11- Style 3000 and 10- Style 4000 dresses. Be sure to change the invoice number when printing. (S)

21   Purchased delivery truck on account from Moe's Garage, invoice no. 7113, $17,200.

   ▼ Select Moe's Garage in the Vendor ID field
   ▼ Enter the invoice number and date
   ▼ Enter a description of the payment in that field
   ▼ Select the correct GL account for this line (Delivery Truck)
   ▼ Enter the amount in the Amount column.
   ▼ Post

22   Sold merchandise to the Ronold Co. on account, $4,000, invoice no. 55, terms 2/10, n/30 consisting of 24- Style 1000, 24- Style 2000, 3- Style 3000, 2- Style 4000, 2- Style 5000 and 2- Style 6000 dresses. (S)

23   Issued check no. 115 to the Jones Co. in the amount of $7,920 in payment of invoice no. 4639 ($10,000), dated March 11, less debit memo no. DM 4 ($2,000), less 1 percent discount ($100 − 20 = $80 net purchases discount). (PA)

24   Sold merchandise to the Bing Co. on account, $2,000, invoice no. 56, terms 2/10, n/30 consisting of 1- Style 2000, 10- Style 3000, 10- Style 4000, 1- Style 5000 and 1- Style 6000 dresses. (S)

25   Purchased merchandise for $1,000, cash from the Jones Company, check no. 116, consisting of, 16- Style 3000 and 11- Style 4000 dresses. Use the Quantity and Item fields in the Payments window just as you would in the Purchases window. (PA)

27   Purchased merchandise from the Blew Co. on account, $6,000, invoice no. 437, terms 2/10, n/30 consisting of, 60- Style 5000 and 66- Style 6000 dresses. (P)

28   Received check no. 5562 from the Ronold Co. in the amount of $3,920 in payment of invoice no. 55 ($4,000), dated March 22, less 2 percent discount ($80). (R)

28   Received check no. 8127 from the Bing Co. in the amount of $3,200 in payment of invoice no. 54, dated March 16. (R)

29   Purchased merchandise from the Morris Co. on account, $9,000, invoice no. 1347, terms 2/10, n/30 consisting of, 150- Style 1000 and 150- Style 2000 dresses. The vendor has changed his prices on these items so instead of accepting Peachtree's default for the unit prices, enter $28.00 and $32.00 for the Style 1000 and style 2000 respectively. (P)

30   Sold merchandise to the Blew Co. on account, $10,000, invoice no. 57, terms 2/10, n/30 consisting of 6- Style 3000, 5- Style 4000, 41- Style 5000 and 38- Style 6000 dresses. (S)

30   The Auxiliary Petty Cash Record for March listed the following: Postage Expense, $5; Delivery Expense, $10; Cleaning Expense, $6; Miscellaneous Expense, $10. Issued check no. 117 to replenish the petty cash fund. The check should be made out to CASH. (PA)

31   Issued payroll checks for March wages as follows:

Employee	March Wages	Check no.
Case, Mel	$3,325	118
Holl, Jane	4,120	119
Moore, Jackie	4,760	120

Use **Select for <u>P</u>ayroll Entry** under the **Tas<u>k</u>s** menu. Use 31 March as the Pay End date as well as for the check date.

Print Reports

7. Print the following reports:
   a. General Ledger Trial Balance
   b. Aged Receivables
   c. Aged Payables
   d. Payroll Register
   e. 941 (FedForm 941 1999/2000) Print this report on plain paper unless you have the blank forms available.

Record March Adjusting Entries

8. Open the General Journal; then record adjusting journal entries based on the following adjustment data:
   a. During March, rent expired, $600.
   b. Truck depreciated, $150.
   c. Rental income earned, $200 (one month's rent from subletting).

Print Reports

9. After you have posted the adjusting journal entries, close the General Journal; then print the following reports:
   a. General Journal
   b. General Ledger Trial Balance
   c. General Ledger Report
   d. Balance Sheet
   e. Inventory Valuation Report

10. Compare the Inventory Valuation Report with the one created at the start of this practice set. Note that the first two items, the ones whose cost price changed when we last purchased them, have neither the original prices of $25.00 and 30.00 nor the new prices of $28.00 and $32.00 respectively. Peachtree has created a weighted-average for these items. You will study the mechanics behind this calculation in chapter 16.

Other Reports

11. Peachtree contains dozens of reports that you could examine at this time. Feel free to experiment with looking at the various report options available to you in the Reports menu.

Advance Dates

12. In order to close the accounting period we must now advance the period.

   ▼ Using your mouse, click on **System** from the **Tasks** menu. Select **Change Accounting Periods.**
   ▼ Using the pull down menu, select period 4 - Apr 1, 2000 to Apr 30, 2000 and click on **"<u>O</u>k".**
   ▼ You will be asked whether you wish to print reports before continuing. Since we have already printed our reports, we can answer "No".
   ▼ Note that the status bar at the bottom of the screen now reflects that you are in period 4. You would be ready to start recording the April transactions.

Bad Debts, Notes, Merchandise, and Equipment

CHAPTER 14

Accounting for Bad Debits

How did you pay for that CD you purchased online? Or the munchies you ordered from Kozmo.com? You punched in your credit card number and other identifying digits. Nobody saw your face. Nobody checked your signature. In fact, someone who happened across your credit card number and address could easily masquerade as you and fill up an electronic shopping cart with a host of online goods.

The anonymity of cyberspace sales transactions has paved the way for an increase in identity theft and credit card chargebacks. In the former, someone uses the identifying information of another person — name, credit card number, mother's maiden name or other personal data — to commit fraud. A chargeback occurs when customers deny charges that they actually did make. If someone denies a charge for a brick-and-

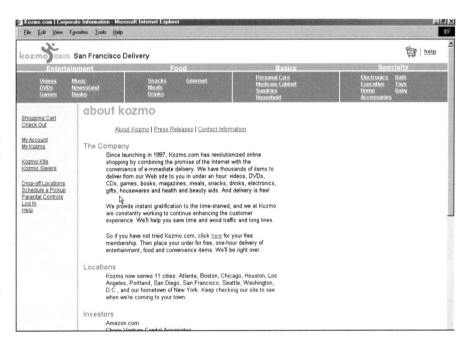

mortar transaction, the bank that issued the credit card ends up taking the hit, not the store or establishment. However, e-retailers do not have any paper trail to back themselves up, so they end up having to eat losses due to identity theft fraud and chargebacks. Online travel company Expedia Inc. was recently victimized by criminals who used stolen credit-card numbers to buy airplane tickets online. The Bellevue, WA, company had to set aside $6 million to pay for the fraud.

When customers do not or cannot pay all or part of their debt — whether due to fraud, chargebacks or the simple inability to pay — the business incurs an account that becomes uncollectible, known as **bad debt**.

In this chapter you will learn how to determine the potential bad debt a business may incur and there are a few ways to do this. For instance, some companies prefer to write off bad debt after a certain number of days; others may choose to set an allowance of what they expect to become uncollectible during the year. The allowance for bad debt can be determined by the aging of the accounts receivable or as a percentage of sales on credit. These methods usually require some history of account trends or comparison to another, similar business. Dot-com start-ups would be wise to canvass an association of e-retailers for information about the percentage of bad debt that they can expect.

Based on: Charlie Fletcher, "ID Thievery is on the rise," *Catalog Age,* June 2000, p. 57. Marcia Savage, "Online fraud: New twist on old issue," *Computer Reseller News,* March 27, 2000, p. 28. Leslie Beyer, "The Internet revolution," *Credit Card Management,* November 1999. Patricia A. Murphy, "The murky world of 'Net charge-backs." *Credit Card Management,* February 2000, pp. 54–60.

LEARNING OBJECTIVES

▼ Describing how the Bad Debts Expense account and the Allowance for Doubtful Accounts account are used to record bad debts. (p. 521)

▼ Using the income statement approach and the balance sheet approach to estimate the amount of Bad Debts Expense. (p. 523)

▼ Preparing an Aging of Accounts Receivable. (p. 525)

▼ Writing off an account using the Allowance for Doubtful Accounts account. (p. 527)

▼ Using the direct write-off method. (p. 528)

Eventually, all companies (Internet based or not) that sell goods or services on account will come upon customers that do not pay their bills. The question of these *bad debts* affects the company's credit policy. If a company extends credit too easily, it may end up with too many uncollectible accounts. On the other hand, if the credit policy is too strict, the company will end up losing customers to other firms with easier credit policies, which could also mean lost profit.

This chapter looks at how bad debts are recorded in the accrual system of accounting. It also discusses when accounts receivable turn into bad debts (or uncollectible accounts), how and what to charge them to, and how to write them off.

LEARNING UNIT 14-1

ACCRUAL ACCOUNTING AND RECORDING BAD DEBTS

As discussed in Chapter 2, the accrual system of accounting matches earned revenue with expenses that have been incurred in producing revenue during an accounting period. One expense incurred as a result of sales on credit or on account is a bad debts expense. The problem is that it may take as long as a year for the seller to realize that the debt is uncollectible. What happens in the meantime? How can the books be kept up to date?

One way is to estimate at the end of the year what percentage of sales made during that year will turn out to be bad debts. There are several ways of arriving at the percentage. At the moment, let's say Abby Ellen Company estimates that 1.6 percent of its sales of $100,000 for the year 20X1 will not be collectible; thus the company expects not to collect $1,600 of the $100,000 owed it from sales. (Other ways to estimate the amount are discussed in Learning Unit 14-2.)

Two accounts that we haven't discussed before, Bad Debts Expense and Allowance for Doubtful Accounts, are needed. **Bad Debts Expense** is an expense account whose normal balance is a debit; it is a temporary account that is closed to Income Summary at year's end. **Allowance for Doubtful Accounts** is a contra-asset account that accumulates the expected amount of bad debts as of a given date; its normal balance is a credit. It is a permanent account that is *not* closed to Income Summary at the end of the year.

In the case of Abby Ellen Company, which expects to be unable to collect $1,600 of the $100,000 owed it from sales, at the end of the year (20X1) an adjustment is made debiting Bad Debts Expense and crediting Allowance for Doubtful Accounts for $1,600. This transaction is shown below with a transaction analysis chart:

20X1					
Dec.	31	Bad Debt Expense	1 6 0 0 00		
		Allowance for Doubtful Accounts		1 6 0 0 00	
		Record estimate of bad debts.			

1 Accounts Affected	2 Category	3 ↑ ↓	4 Rules
Bad Debts Expense	**Expense**	↑	**Dr.**
Allowance for Doubtful Accounts	**Contra-Asset**	↑	**Cr.**

> Will go on income statement as an operating expense and eventually be closed to Income Summary.

The allowance account is subtracted from Accounts Receivable, leaving a **net realizable value** of $98,400. Net realizable value is the amount Abby Ellen Company expects to collect. When an account is written off, the net realizable value doesn't change, because both the Accounts Receivable and the Allowance for Doubtful Accounts are reduced (see Fig. 14-1).

Think of the Allowance for Doubtful Accounts as a reservoir that is filled before bad debts occur. The reservoir is drained when a customer's bill is declared uncollectible. Abby Ellen Company estimates that out of its $100,000

> Will go on balance sheet as a reduction to Accounts Receivable. The normal balance of the allowance account is a credit. It will not be closed at the end of the period.

FIGURE 14-1. Partial Balance Sheet

> Writing off an account. *Note:* Bad Debts Expense is not involved.

ABBY ELLEN COMPANY PARTIAL BALANCE SHEET DECEMBER 31, 20X1			
Assets			
Current Assets:			
Cash		$ 51 4 0 0 00	
Accounts Receivable	$100 0 0 0 00		
Less: Allowance for Doubtful Accounts	1 6 0 0 00	98 4 0 0 00	
Merchandise Inventory		200 0 0 0 00	
Total Current Assets		$349 8 0 0 00	

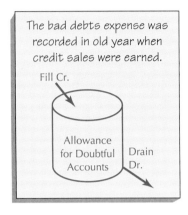

Accounts Receivable
− Allowance for Doubtful Accounts
= Net Realizable Value

The bad debts expense was recorded in old year when credit sales were earned.

Fill Cr.

Allowance for Doubtful Accounts

Drain Dr.

of credit sales, $1,600 will prove to be uncollectible, but it does not know which accounts those will be.

WRITING OFF AN ACCOUNT DEEMED UNCOLLECTIBLE

At some point a customer's bill must be written off as uncollectible. Let's look at how Abby Ellen Company would write off the account of Jones Moore on June 5, 20X2. (The $200 sale was made in 20X1.)

Remember, at end of 20X1, Abby made an adjusting entry increasing Bad Debts Expense (debit) and filling the Allowance for Doubtful Accounts (credit) with the estimate of accounts receivable that will not be collectible. The following journal entry is recorded to write off this account:

20X2 June	5	Allowance For Doubtful Accounts		2 0 0 00		
		Accounts Receivable, J. Moore			2 0 0 00	
		Writing off J. Moore account.				

Note that we did *not* debit the account Bad Debts Expense, because the estimate for this account was made on December 31, 20X1 (and applies to that year, not to 20X2). When that estimate was made, we did not know which bills would turn out to be uncollectible. Once the debt is identified as uncollectible, we reduce both the Allowance account and the controlling account Accounts Receivable and update the accounts receivable subsidiary ledger. The subsidiary ledger will be credited just as the controlling account is.

LEARNING UNIT 14-1 REVIEW

AT THIS POINT you should be able to

▼ Define and explain the purpose of Bad Debts Expense and Allowance for Doubtful Accounts. (p. 521)
▼ Explain why the subsidiary ledger account cannot be updated at the time the Bad Debts Expense is estimated. (p. 521)
▼ Prepare an adjusting entry for Bad Debts Expense. (p. 521)
▼ Prepare a partial balance sheet showing the relationship between the Allowance for Doubtful Accounts and Accounts Receivable. (p. 521)
▼ Explain net realizable value. (p. 521)
▼ Prepare a journal entry to write off a customer's debt in a year following the sale. (p. 522)

SELF-REVIEW QUIZ 14-1

(The forms you need are on page 471 of the *Study Guide and Working Papers*.) Respond true or false to the following:

1. The Bad Debts Expense account should be updated only when the customer's debt is declared to be uncollectible.

2. The Allowance for Doubtful Accounts is a contra-asset account on the balance sheet.

3. Bad Debts Expense is part of cost of goods sold.

4. Net realizable value equals Accounts Receivable less Allowance for Doubtful Accounts.

5. When a customer's debt is written off as uncollectible, the account Allowance for Doubtful Accounts is credited.

> *Quiz Tip:* The Allowance account fills with a credit and <u>Drains</u> with a debit.

Solutions to Self-Review Quiz 14-1

1. False   **2.** True   **3.** False   **4.** True   **5.** False

LEARNING UNIT 14-2

THE ALLOWANCE METHOD: TWO APPROACHES TO ESTIMATING THE AMOUNT OF BAD DEBTS EXPENSE

As mentioned earlier, at the end of each year companies must estimate what percentage of their sales for that year will turn out to be uncollectible accounts or bad debts. How is this estimate arrived at? In this unit we look at two of the most common ways of arriving at this amount: the income statement approach and the balance sheet approach. The diagram in Figure 14-2 on p. 524 outlines these methods.

THE INCOME STATEMENT APPROACH

Abby Ellen Company uses the **income statement approach** to calculate how much Bad Debts Expense will be associated with this year's sales. Based on the past several years, the company has averaged Bad Debts Expense of 1 percent of *net* credit sales. From the following facts, let's prepare an adjusting entry to record the Bad Debts Expense that is based on a percentage of net credit sales.

> Bad Debts Expense can be based on a percentage of the dollar volume of net credit sales on the income statement.

20X4	Dr.	Cr.
Sales (all credit)		$95,000
Sales Returns and Allowances	$10,000	
Sales Discount	5,000	
Accounts Receivable	7,000	
Allowance for Doubtful Accounts		100

1 Accounts Affected	2 Category	3 ↑ ↓	4 Rules
Bad Debts Expense	**Expense**	↑	**Dr.**
Allowance for Doubtful Accounts	**Contra-Asset**	↑	**Cr.**

> *Analysis:*
> | Sales | $95,000 |
> |---|---|
> | − SRA | 10,000 |
> | − Sales Discount | 5,000 |
> | Net Credit Sales | $80,000 |

	20X4						
	Dec.	31	Bad Debts Expense	8 0 0 00		
			Allowance for Doubtful Accounts		8 0 0 00
			Record estimate of bad debts		
			(.01 × $80,000)		

FIGURE 14-2. Two
approaches to Estimating
Amount of Bad Debts
Expense.

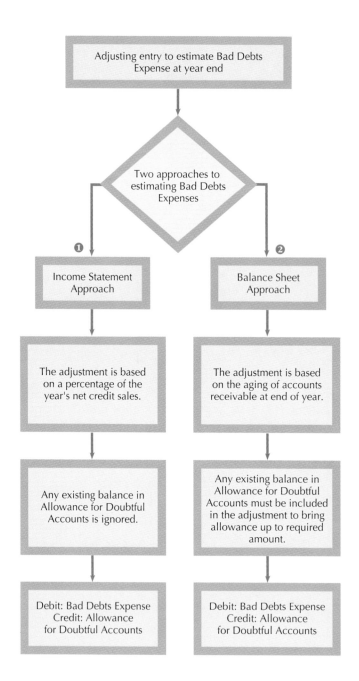

When it is posted, the Allowance account looks like the following:

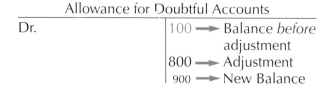

The income statement approach emphasizes the matching requirements of the income statement. The $100 in the Allowance account represents a carryover of potential bad debts from *prior* years. Thus the total of $900 represents total potential uncollectible accounts of several periods of sales. If, over the years, the estimate for Bad Debts Expense has been inaccurate, an adjusting entry can be made in the current year's Bad Debts Expense. If that happens, the company may reevaluate its percentage and use $1\frac{1}{2}$ percent instead of 1 percent.

Beginning balance in Allowance account represents potential bad debts from previous periods.

THE BALANCE SHEET APPROACH

The **balance sheet approach** bases the new total Allowance for Doubtful Accounts on the current Accounts Receivable on the balance sheet. Thus the adjustment is reduced by the old balance in Allowance for Doubtful Accounts. When the adjustment is credited, the new balance will reflect the state of Accounts Receivable. (See Fig. 14-2.) This approach focuses on the aging of Accounts Receivable.

Aging of Accounts Receivable

The longer a bill has been due and not paid, the more likely it is that it is not going to be paid. Therefore, one way of estimating the amount of bad debts for the year just past is to look at Accounts Receivable and analyze it according to how many days past due the accounts are. This process is called **aging of Accounts Receivable.**

> Aging classifies uncollected amounts of individual customers according to days past due.

Table 14-1 shows an analysis that the Abby Ellen Company did on December 31, 20X0. Note that 29 percent of the total receivables for Abby Ellen are past due from 1 to 30 days. (This analysis will also provide feedback to the credit department about how well the current credit policy is working.) Now let's look at how the company will estimate what balance in the Allowance for Doubtful Accounts is required to meet probable bad debts.

> Today, with a computer, an analysis of Accounts Receivable can be completed quickly.

The schedule shown in Table 14-2 on p. 526 is prepared to assist the company in calculating the needed balance. In this schedule Abby Ellen Company has applied a sliding scale of percents (3, 4, 10, 20, 50), based on previous experience, to the total amount of receivables due in each time period. For example, of the $3,600 not yet due, 3 percent or $108, will probably never be paid. Looking at this schedule reveals that Abby Ellen Company needs $480 to cover estimated bad debts. *Currently,* the balance in the Allowance account is $100. Thus, to reach a balance of $480, we must adjust the balance of the account by the following adjusting journal entry:

20X4				
Dec.	31	Bad Debts Expense	3 8 0 00	
		Allowance for Doubtful Accounts		3 8 0 00
		Estimate of bad debts		

> The balance in the Allowance for Doubtful Accounts is *not* ignored.

TABLE 14-1   AGING OF ACCOUNTS RECEIVABLE

Name of Customer	Total Balance	Not Yet Due	Days Past Due			
			1–30	31–60	61–90	Over 90
Jane Elliot	$ 100	$ 100				
Joshua Harras	30			$ 30		
Alan Kedbury	160	160				
John Sullivan	180				$160	$ 20
Sheri Lissan	80	80				
Others	6,450	3,260	$2,000	840	40	310
Totals	$7,000	$3,600	$2,000	$870	$200	$330
Percent of total (rounded to nearest whole percent)	100%	51% $\left(\dfrac{\$3,600}{\$7,000}\right)$	29% $\left(\dfrac{\$2,000}{\$7,000}\right)$	12% $\left(\dfrac{\$870}{\$7,000}\right)$	3% $\left(\dfrac{\$200}{\$7,000}\right)$	5% $\left(\dfrac{\$330}{\$7,000}\right)$

TABLE 14-2 **BALANCE REQUIRED TO MEET PROBABLE BAD DEBTS**

	Amount	Estimated Percent Considered to Be Bad Debts Expense	Amount Needed in Allowance for Doubtful Accounts to Cover Estimated Bad Debts Expense
Not Yet Due	$3,600	3	$108 ($3,600 × .03)
Days Past Due			
1–30	2,000	4	80
31–60	870	10	87
61–90	200	20	40
Over 90	330	50	165
Total Accounts Receivable ⟶	$7,000	Total Balance Required in ⟶ Allowance for Doubtful Accounts	$480
Less current balance			−100
Adjusting entry			$380

Bad Debits Expense		Allowance for Doubtful Accounts	
Dr.	Cr.	Dr.	Cr.
380			100 Beg. Balance
			380 Adj.
			480 New balance in Allowance

> Some companies that feel aging is too time-consuming may estimate bad debts based on a percentage of total Accounts Receivable.

The desired balance of $480 is now reached. If the Allowance had a *debit* balance of $100 before the adjustment, the amount of the adjusting entry would be $580 credit to the Allowance to arrive at the $480 balance. Once again, the adjustment *must* consider the existing balance in the Allowance account before the adjusting entry is prepared.

LEARNING UNIT 14-2 REVIEW

AT THIS POINT you should be able to

▼ Explain the two approaches to estimating Bad Debts Expense. (p. 523)
▼ Explain why the balance in the Allowance for Doubtful Accounts is ignored when an adjusting entry for bad debts is prepared in the income statement approach. (p. 524)
▼ Show how to prepare an aging of Accounts Receivable. (p. 525)
▼ Explain how the aging of Accounts Receivable is used to arrive at the balance required in the Allowance for Doubtful Accounts. (p. 525)

SELF-REVIEW QUIZ 14-2

(The forms you need are on page 471 of the *Study Guide and Working Papers*.)
From the following, prepare an adjusting journal entry for Bad Debts Expense for (1) the income statement approach and (2) the balance sheet approach.

Allowance for Doubtful Accounts	
Dr.	Cr.
	400

Income Statement Approach

Net Sales $160,000
1 % of Net Sales

Balance Sheet Approach

		Percent Considered Bad Debts
Not yet due:	$4,000	4
Days past due:		
1–30	3,000	5
31–60	400	10
Over 60	5,000	30

Solution to Self-Review Quiz 14-2

(1)	Dec.	31	Bad Debts Expense	1600 00	
			Allowance for Doubtful Accounts		1600 00
			(.01 × $160,000)		
(2)		31	Bad Debts Expense	1450 00	
			Allowance for Doubtful Accounts		1450 00
			$4,000 × .04 = $ 160		
			3,000 × .05 = 150		
			400 × .10 = 40		
			5,000 × .30 = 1,500		
			$1,850		

$1,850 is amount required.

Quiz Tip: Note allowance adjusted: $1,850 − $400 = $1,450.

LEARNING UNIT 14-3

WRITING OFF AND RECOVERING UNCOLLECTIBLE ACCOUNTS

WRITING OFF AN ACCOUNT USING THE ALLOWANCE FOR DOUBTFUL ACCOUNTS

Let's assume that on March 18, 20X7, the Abby Ellen Company determines that the account of Jill Sullivan for $900 is uncollectible. (The sale to Jill Sullivan was back in 20X6.) Thus this Accounts Receivable amount should no longer be considered an asset and should be written off. The following journal entry reduces the Allowance for Doubtful Accounts and reduces the Accounts Receivable controlling account as well as the accounts receivable subsidiary ledger.

20X7					
Mar.	18	Allowance for Doubtful Accounts	900 00	
		Accounts Receivable, Jill Sullivan		900 00
		Wrote off Sullivan account		

Key Points:

▼ This journal entry does *not* affect any expenses. Remember that Bad Debts Expense is not affected when an account is finally written off. The estimate for Bad Debts Expense was recorded in the previous year before the bad debt actually occurred.

▼ If more than one customer is written off, a compound entry can be used, debiting Allowance for the total and crediting each individual account.

▼ The net realizable value of Accounts Receivable is unchanged. Let's prove it:

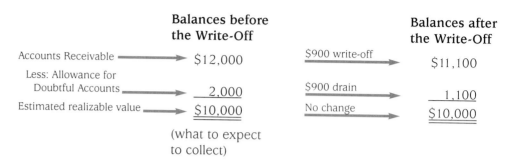

	Balances before the Write-Off		Balances after the Write-Off
Accounts Receivable	$12,000	$900 write-off	$11,100
Less: Allowance for Doubtful Accounts	2,000	$900 drain	1,100
Estimated realizable value	$10,000	No change	$10,000
	(what to expect to collect)		

Recording Recovered Debts Using Allowance for Doubtful Accounts What would happen if Jill Sullivan paid all or part of the debt after Abby Ellen Company wrote it off? Consider this situation: Assume that Jill Sullivan is able to pay off half of her debt and send a check to Abby Ellen Company on February 1, 20X8. (Keep in mind that her account was written off on March 18, 20X7, and the original sale was made in 20X6.) To record this payment, Abby Ellen Company reverses in part the entry that was made to write off the account in the amount expected to be recovered and records the amount received from Jill. The following are the journal entries to record the recovery of $450 out of the original amount of $900:

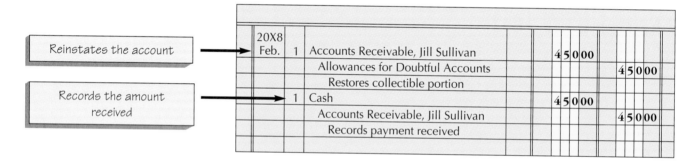

	20X8				
Reinstates the account →	Feb.	1	Accounts Receivable, Jill Sullivan	450 00	
			Allowances for Doubtful Accounts		450 00
			Restores collectible portion		
Records the amount received →		1	Cash	450 00	
			Accounts Receivable, Jill Sullivan		450 00
			Records payment received		

The reason we record both a debit and a credit to Accounts Receivable is that it provides a clear picture of the transactions involving Jill Sullivan. If the company is considering giving credit again to Jill Sullivan, these previous records could be of assistance in determining how much if any credit could be extended. Note how the first entry reinstates the account and the second entry records the cash received.

THE DIRECT WRITE-OFF METHOD

The direct write-off method does not fulfill the matching principle but is acceptable for federal income tax reporting.

When a company cannot reasonably estimate its Bad Debts Expense, it may use the **direct write-off method.** Using this method, an account that is determined to be uncollectible would be directly written off to this year's Bad Debts Expense account without regard to when the original sale was made. In this method, the Allowance for Doubtful Accounts is not used, because no adjustment is needed at the end of the year to estimate Bad Debts Expense. The Journal entry would be a debit to Bad Debts Expense and a credit to Accounts Receivable.

Recording Recovered Debts Using the Direct Method Let's suppose that Jill Sullivan repays half of her outstanding debt after Abby Ellen Company has written it off. The recovered debt would be accounted for using the direct write-off method, as follows:

20X7 Mar.	18	Bad Debts Expense	9 0 0 00		
		Accounts Receivable, Jill Sullivan		9 0 0 00	
		Wrote off account			

Writing off Jill Sullivan on March 18, 20X7. Note that Allowance account is not used. See p. 527.

A new account title, **Bad Debts Recovered,** must be created. Think of this account as a revenue account found in the Other Income section of an income statement.

20X8 Feb.	1	Acct. Rec., Jill Sullivan	4 5 0 00		
		Bad Debts Recovered		4 5 0 00	
		Restores collectible portion			
	1	Cash	4 5 0 00		
		Acct. Rec., Jill Sullivan		4 5 0 00	
		Records payment received			

Recovery of half the amount owed by Jill Sullivan on February 1, 20X8. Note that Bad Debts Recovered is used instead of Allowance for Doubtful Accounts.

In the direct write-off method, when the amount is written off, no Allowance for Doubtful Accounts is used. Instead, the debit is to Bad Debts Expense. If the debt is recovered later, the direct method credits Bad Debts Recovered (an account in the "Other Revenue" category). In effect, this method increases the revenue and puts the Accounts Receivable back on the books. If recovery is made the same year (let's say on May 1) as the debt is written off, the entry made to write off the account is reversed:

On the balance sheet, Accounts Receivable is recorded at gross. No Allowance account or realizable amount is used.

Bad Debts Recov.	Other Revenue	↑	Cr.

20X7 May	1	Accounts Receivable, Jill Sullivan	4 5 0 00		
		Bad Debts Expense		4 5 0 00	

LEARNING UNIT 14-3 REVIEW

AT THIS POINT you should be able to

▼ Write off an account using the Allowance for Doubtful Accounts method. (p. 527)

▼ Explain why net realizable value is unchanged after a write-off is complete. (p. 528)

▼ Prepare journal entries to recover entire or partial amounts that were once declared uncollectible. (p. 529)

▼ Explain the direct write-off method and prepare appropriate journal entries for write-off and recovery. (p. 529)

SELF-REVIEW QUIZ 14-3

(The forms you need are on page 472 of the *Study Guide and Working Papers*.) Respond true or false to the following:

1. When an account using the Allowance for Doubtful Accounts method is written off in a period following the sale, the result is a debit to Bad Debts Expense and a credit to Accounts Receivable.

2. The direct write-off method will sometimes use the Allowance for Doubtful Accounts.

3. When an account is written off (using the Allowance for Doubtful Accounts method), net realizable value is unchanged.

4. Bad Debts Recovered is an asset.

5. A debit balance in the Allowance for Doubtful Accounts indicates that the estimate for Bad Debts Expense was too low.

Solutions to Self-Review Quiz 14-3

1. False   2. False   3. True   4. False   5. True

SUMMARY OF KEY POINTS

Learning Unit 14-1

1. If accrual accounting is used, Bad Debts Expense should be recognized in the year the sale was earned, even though the actual write-off may not yet have taken place.

2. Bad Debts Expense is an expense found on the income statement.

3. The Allowance for Doubtful Accounts is a contra-asset account found on the balance sheet that accumulates the amount of estimated uncollectibles before they are actually written off.

4. Net realizable value equals Accounts Receivable minus Allowance for Doubtful Accounts.

5. When an account is written off, the Allowance for Doubtful Accounts is debited and Accounts Receivable is credited (along with the subsidiary ledger account).

Learning Unit 14-2

1. The two approaches to estimating Bad Debts Expense are the income statement approach and the balance sheet approach.

2. The income statement approach estimates Bad Debts Expense based on a percent of net sales. (Some companies use credit sales, some use total sales.) The balance is ignored in the Allowance for Doubtful Accounts when the Bad Debts Expense is estimated from sales of the period.

3. The balance sheet approach estimates the balance required in the Allowance for Doubtful Accounts by aging the Accounts Receivable. The balance in the Allowance account will have to be adjusted based on the aging of the receivables.

Learning Unit 14-3

1. When an account is written off (using the Allowance account) in years following the sale, the result is to debit the Allowance for Doubtful Accounts and credit Accounts Receivable. Do not debit Bad Debts Expense, because it has already been recorded in the year the sale was earned.

2. When an uncollectible account has been written off and is now recovered, the entry reverses the original write-off by debiting Accounts Receivable and crediting the Allowance for Doubtful Accounts. Then the cash received is debited and the Accounts Receivable is credited.

3. The direct write-off method will recognize the Bad Debts Expense when the customer account is declared uncollectible. The direct method does *not* use the Allowance for Doubtful Accounts, because no estimate is made for bad debts. This method does not follow the matching principle in the accrual basis of accounting.

4. Bad Debts Recovered is classified as "other revenue" when a customer account is reinstated after being written off in the direct method.

> After the write-off, net realizable value is unchanged.

KEY TERMS

Aging of Accounts Receivable The procedure of classifying accounts of individual customers by age group, where age is the number of days elapsed from due date.

Allowance for Doubtful Accounts A contra-asset account that is subtracted from the Accounts Receivable. This account accumulates the *expected* amount of uncollectibles as of a given date.

Bad Debts Expense The operating expense account that estimates the amount of credit sales that will probably not be collectible in a given accounting period when the Allowance method is used. For the direct write-off method, this account would be the actual amount written off.

Bad Debts Recovered When an Account Receivable has been written off and is recovered, this account, which is in the "Other Revenue" category, is credited in the direct write-off method if the recovery is in a year *following* the write-off.

Balance sheet approach A method used to calculate the amount *required* in the Allowance for Doubtful Accounts to cover expected uncollectibles. This method is based on the Accounts Receivable amount and the aging process. The adjustment to the Allowance for Doubtful Accounts will bring the new balance of that account to the new required level.

Direct write-off method The method of writing off uncollectibles when they occur and thus *not* using the Allowance for Doubtful Accounts. This method does not fulfill the matching principle of accrual accounting.

Income statement approach A method that estimates the amount of Bad Debts Expense that will result based on a percent of net credit sales for the period. The amount of the expected bad debt is added to the existing balance of Allowance for Doubtful Accounts.

Net realizable value The amount (Accounts Receivable – Allowance for Doubtful Accounts) that is expected to be collected.

QUESTIONS, MINI EXERCISES, EXERCISES, AND PROBLEMS

Discussion Questions

1. Explain the matching principle in relationship to recording Bad Debts Expense.
2. What is the purpose of the Allowance for Doubtful Accounts?
3. What is net realizable value?
4. When an Account Receivable is written off, Bad Debts Expense must be debited. True or false? Please discuss.
5. Explain why the Allowance for Doubtful Accounts is a contra-asset account.
6. Recording Bad Debts Expense is a closing entry. True or false? Defend your position.
7. The income statement approach used to estimate bad debts is based on Accounts Receivable on the balance sheet. Accept or reject. Why?
8. In which approach is the balance of the Allowance for Doubtful Accounts considered when the estimate of Bad Debts Expense is made? Please explain.
9. Why would a company age its Accounts Receivable?
10. Using the Allowance for Doubtful Accounts method, what journal entries would be made to write off an account as well as later record the recovery of the Accounts Receivable?
11. Why doesn't net realizable value change when an account is written off in the use of the Allowance account?
12. What is the purpose of using a direct write-off method?
13. Explain the purpose of the Bad Debts Recovered account.

Mini Exercises

(The forms you need are on page 474 of the *Study Guide and Working Papers*.)

BLUEPRINT: SUMMARY OF RECORDING BAD DEBTS EXPENSE, WRITE-OFFS, AND RECOVERY

Situation	ALLOWANCE FOR DOUBTFUL ACCOUNTS METHOD		DIRECT WRITE-OFF METHOD
	A. Income Statement Approach	B. Balance Sheet Approach	
Adjusting entry to record estimated uncollectible accounts	Bad Debts Expense XX Allowance for Doubtful Accounts XX Based on percent of net sales. Balance in Allowance account is ignored.	Bad Debts Expense XX Allowance for Doubtful Accounts XX Aging of Accounts Receivable determines amount needed in Allowance account. Balance in Allowance account is adjusted.	None
Accounts Receivable is determined to be uncollectible	Allowance for Doubtful Accounts XX Accounts Receivable, XX	Allowance for Doubtful Accounts XX Accounts Receivable, XX	Bad Debts Expense XX Accounts Receivable, XX
Bad Debts are recovered	Accounts Receivable, XX Allowance for Doubtful Accounts XX Cash XX Accounts Receivable, XX	Accounts Receivable, XX Allowance for Doubtful Accounts XX Cash XX Accounts Receivable, XX	Accounts Receivable, XX Bad Debts Recovered* XX Cash XX Accounts Receivable, XX
Balance sheet update	**Shows net realizable value**	**Shows net realizable value**	**Does not show net realizable value**

*Used if recovery is not in the same year as the sale.

Categorizing Accounts

1. **a.** Complete the following transactional analysis chart:

	Category	↑ ↓	Rules
Bad Debts Expense **Allowance for Doubtful Accounts**			

    b. On which financial statement will each title be recorded?

    c. Which account is temporary? Which account is permanent?

Allowance Method

2. Complete the table:

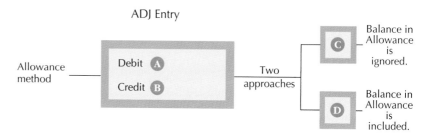

Journalize Adjusting Entries for Income Statement and Balance Sheet Approach

3. Given the balance in the Allowance for Doubtful Accounts of $200 credit, prepare Adjusting entries for Bad Debts based on the following assumptions:

    a. Bad Debts to be 5 percent of Net Credit Sales or $600.

    b. Based on Aging of Accounts Receivable, Bad Debts should be $500.

Writing Off Uncollectible Accounts and Reinstatement: Allowance Method

4. Journalize entries for the following situations (assume allowance method):

    Situation 1: Wrote off Bill Allen as a bad debt two years after the sale for $50.

    Situation 2: Reinstated Bill Allen, who sent in his past due amount.

Writing Off Uncollectible Account and Reinstatement: Direct Write-Off Method

5. Journalize entries for the following situation (assume direct write-off method):

    Situation 1: Wrote off Bill Allen as a bad debt two years after the sale of $50.

    Situation 2: Reinstated Bill Allen, who sent in his past due amount two years after it had been written off.

Exercises

(The forms you need are on pages 475–476 of the *Study Guide and Working Papers*.)

> Preparing a partial balance sheet with Allowance for Doubtful Accounts.

14-1. Bob.com has requested that you prepare a partial balance sheet on December 31, 20XX, from the following: Cash, $110,000; Petty Cash, $70; Accounts Receivable, $70,000; Bad Debts Expense, $50,000; Allowance for Doubtful Accounts, $14,000; Merchandise Inventory, $19,000.

14-2. The following information is given:

Accounts Receivable	Sales	Sales Returns and Allowances
30,000	110,000	500

	Sales Discount	Allowance for Doubtful Accounts
	9,500	5,000

Calculating Bad Debts Expense by income statement approach.

Journalize the adjusting entry on December 31, 20XX, for Bad Debts Expense, which is estimated to be 4 percent of net sales. The income statement approach is used.

14-3. Assuming that in Exercise 2 the balance sheet approach is used, prepare a journalized adjusting entry for Bad Debts Expense. Based on an aging of Accounts Receivable, an $8,000 balance in the Allowance account will be needed to cover bad debts.

Calculating Bad Debts Expense by balance sheet approach.

14-4. Austin Co., which uses an Allowance for Doubtful Accounts, had the following transactions in 20X5 and 20X6. (Use the income statement approach.)

Journalizing adjustment for Bad Debts as well as reinstatement by Allowance method; comparison with direct write-off method.

20X5
Dec. 31 Recorded Bad Debts Expense of $12,000.

20X6
Apr. 3 Wrote off Angie Ring account of $4,000 as uncollectible.
June 4 Wrote off Mike Catuc account of $3,000 as uncollectible.

20X7
Aug. 5 Recovered $500 from Mike Catuc.

a. Journalize the transactions. (The company uses the income statement approach in estimating bad debts.)

b. Journalize how Austin Co. would record the Mike Catuc bad debt situation if the direct write-off method were used.

14-5. Rowe Company had credit sales of $200,000 during 20X7. The balance in the Allowance for Doubtful Accounts is a $1,000 debit balance. Journalize the Bad Debts Expense for December 31 using each of the following methods:

a. Bad Debts Expense is estimated at $1\frac{1}{2}$ percent of credit sales.

b. The aging of Accounts Receivable indicates that $2,200 will be required in the Allowance account to cover Bad Debts Expense.

Journalizing adjustments for Bad Debts Expense (1) based on percent of sales and (2) based on aging of Accounts Receivable with balance of Allowance for Doubtful Accounts, a debit balance.

Group A Problems

(The forms you need are on pages 477–483 of the *Study Guide and Working Papers.*)

14A-1. Angel.com has requested that you prepare journal entries from the following (this company uses the Allowance for Doubtful Accounts method based on the income statement approach):

The income statement approach: journalizing Bad Debts Expense and writing accounts off.

20X7
Dec. 31 Recorded Bad Debts Expense of $12,000.

20X8
Jan. 7 Wrote off Gene Smore's account of $800 as uncollectible.
Mar. 5 Wrote off Paul Jane's account of $600 as uncollectible.
July 8 Recovered $300 from Paul Jane.
Aug. 19 Wrote off Bob Seager's account of $1,300 as uncollectible.
Aug. 24 Wrote off Jill Neuman's account of $750 as uncollectible.
Nov. 19 Recovered $400 from Bob Seager.

Check Figure:
August 24:
Dr.: Allowance for Doubtful Accounts
Cr.: Accounts Receivable, Jill Neuman

14A-2. Given the information presented below:

a. Prepare on December 31, 20X8, the adjusting journal entry for Bad Debts Expense.

The balance sheet approach: aging analysis and journalizing of Bad Debts Expense.

Check Figure: Net Realizable Value $146,650

b. Prepare a partial balance sheet on December 31, 20X8, showing how net realizable value is calculated.

c. If the balance in the Allowance for Doubtful Accounts was a $300 debit balance, journalize the adjusting entry for Bad Debts Expense on December 31, 20X8.

			ALVIE CO. DECEMBER 31, 20X8			
		Amount	Estimated Percent Considered to Be Bad Debts Expense	Estimated Amount Needed in Allowance for Doubtful Accounts		
	Not yet due	$130,000	.01			
	0–60	9,000	.05			
	61–180	8,000	.20			
	Over six months	5,000	.40			
		$152,000				

Balances: Cash, $30,000; Accounts Receivable, $152,000; Allowance for Doubtful Accounts, $300; Inventory, $12,000.

The direct write-off method.

14A-3. T. J. Rack Company uses the direct write-off method for recording Bad Debts Expense. At the beginning of 20X8, Accounts Receivable has a $119,000 balance. Journalize the following transactions for T. J. Rack:

Check Figure:
Dec. 7:
Dr.:   Bad Debt Expense
Cr.:   Acc. Rec., J. Miller

20X8

Mar. 13   Wrote off S. Rose's account for $1,800.

Apr. 14   Wrote off P. Soy's account for $750.

20X9

Nov. 8   P. Soy paid bad debt of $750 that was written off April 14, 20X8.

Dec. 7   Wrote off J. Miller's account as uncollectible, $285.

Dec. 12   Wrote off D. Lovejoy's account for $375 due from sales made on account in 20X7.

Journalizing and posting adjustments for Bad Debts Expense and write-offs and recovery based on balance sheet approach. Preparation of partial balance sheet.

14A-4. Simon Company completed the following transactions:

20X8

Jan. 9   Sold merchandise on account to Ray's Supply, $1,500.

Jan. 15   Wrote off the account of Pete Runnels as uncollectible because of his death, $600.

Mar. 17   Received $400 from Roland Co., whose account had been written off in 20X7. The account was reinstated and the collection recorded.

Apr. 9   Received 10 percent of the $4,000 owed by Lane Drug. The remainder was written off as uncollectible.

June 15   The account of Mel's Garage was reinstated for $1,200. The account was written off three years ago and collected in full today.

Oct. 18   Prepared a compound entry to write the following accounts off as uncollectible: Jane's Diner, $200; Keen Auto, $400; Ralph's Hardware, $600.

Nov. 12   Sold merchandise on account to J. B. Rug, $1,900.

Dec. 31   Based on an aging of Accounts Receivable, it was estimated that $7,000 will be uncollectible out of a total of $160,000 in Accounts Receivable.

Dec. 31   Closed Bad Debts Expense to Income Summary.

From the above as well as the following additional data:

	Acct. No.	Balance
Allowance for Doubtful Accounts	114	$4,100
Income Summary	312	—
Bad Debts Expense	612	—

Check Figure:
Total current assets
$272,360

a. Journalize the transactions.

b. Post to Allowance for Doubtful Accounts, Income Summary, and Bad Debts Expense Accounts as needed. (Be sure to record the beginning balance in the Allowance account in your *Study Guide and Working Papers.*)

c. Prepare a current assets section of the balance sheet. Ending balances needed: Cash, $13,000; Accounts Receivable, $160,000; Office Supplies, $2,110; Merchandise Inventory, $103,000; Prepaid Rent, $1,250.

Group B Problems

(The forms you need are on pages 477–483 of the *Study Guide and Working Papers.*)

14B-1. Angel.com has requested that you prepare journal entries from the following (this company uses the Allowance for Doubtful Accounts method based on the income statement approach).

> The income statement approach: journalizing Bad Debts Expense and writing accounts off.

20X7

Dec.	31	Recorded Bad Debts Expense of $14,800.

20X8

Jan.	7	Wrote off Woody Tree's Account of $1,200 as uncollectible.
Mar.	5	Wrote off Jim Lantz's account of $600 as uncollectible.
July	8	Recovered $600 from Jim Lantz.
Aug.	19	Wrote off Mabel Hest's account of $750 as uncollectible.
Aug.	24	Wrote off Jim O'Reilly's account of $950 as uncollectible.
Nov.	19	Recovered $500 from Mabel Hest.

> Check Figure:
> Aug. 24:
> Dr.: Allow for D.A.
> Cr.: Acc. Rec., Jim O'Reilly

14B-2. Given the following information and the information below: Cash, $42,000; Accounts Receivable, $173,000; Allowance for Doubtful Accounts, $400; Merchandise Inventory, $12,000:

> The balance sheet approach: aging analysis and journalizing of Bad Debts Expense.

a. Prepare on December 31, 20X8, the adjusting journal entry for Bad Debts Expense.

b. Prepare a partial balance sheet on December 31, 20X8, showing how net realizable value is calculated.

c. If the balance in the Allowance for Doubtful Accounts was a $400 debit balance, journalize the adjusting entry for Bad Debts Expense on December 31, 20X8.

> Check Figure:
> Net Realizable Value
> $166,000

ALVIE CO. DECEMBER 31, 20X8			
	Amount	Estimated Percent Considered to Be Bad Debts Expense	Estimated Amount Needed in Allowance for Doubtful Accounts
Not yet due	$150,000	.02	
0–60	10,000	.06	
61–180	9,000	.20	
Over six months	4,000	.40	
	$173,000		

14B-3. T. J. Rack Company uses the direct write-off method for recording Bad Debts Expense. At the beginning of 20X8, Accounts Receivable has an $88,000 balance. Journalize the following transactions for T. J. Rack:

> The direct write-off method.

20X8

Mar.	13	Wrote off Jill Diamond's account for $1,950.
Apr.	14	Wrote off Buffy Hall's account for $900.

20X9

Nov.	8	Buffy Hall paid debt of $900 that was written off April 14, 20X8.
Dec.	7	Wrote off Joe Francis's account as uncollectible, $880.
Dec.	12	Wrote off Joe Martin's account for $410 from sales made on account in 20X7.

14B-4. Simon Company completed the following transactions:

20X8

Jan.	9	Sold merchandise on account to Lowe's Supply, $1,900.
Jan.	15	Wrote off the account of Kevin Reese as uncollectible because of his death, $700.
Mar.	17	Received $300 from J. James whose account had been written off in 20X7. The account was reinstated and the collection recorded.
Apr.	9	Received 20 percent of the $5,000 owed by Long Drug. The remainder was written off as uncollectible.
June	15	The account of Morse's Garage was reinstated for $3,100. The account was written off three years ago and collected in full today.
Oct.	18	Prepared a compound entry to write the following accounts off as uncollectible: Sal's Diner, $800; Ring Auto, $1,300; Neel's Hardware, $800.
Nov.	12	Sold merchandise on account to Able Roy, $1,950.
Dec.	31	Based on an aging of Accounts Receivable, it was estimated that $8,000 will be uncollectible out of a total of $170,000 in Accounts Receivable.
Dec.	31	Closed Bad Debts Expense to Income Summary.

From the above as well as the following additional data:

	Acct. No.	Balance
Allowance for Doubtful Accounts	114	$3,300
Income Summary	312	—
Bad Debts Expense	612	—

a. Journalize the transactions.

b. Post to Allowance for Doubtful Accounts, Income Summary, and Bad Debts Expense Account as needed.

c. Prepare a current assets section of the balance sheet. Ending balances needed: Cash, $24,000; Accounts Receivable, $170,000; Office Supplies, $3,000; Merchandise Inventory, $94,000; Prepaid Rent, $1,200.

REAL-WORLD APPLICATIONS

14R-1.

Joan Rivers, the newly hired bookkeeper of Lyon Company, has until 5:00 P.M. today to prepare an analysis on December 31 of Accounts Receivable by age as well as record the entry for Bad Debts Expense. Please assist Joan, who has found the following invoices and balances scattered on her desk (see the top of p. 537). Terms of all sales are n/30. Explain in writing why the allowance method is used.

14R-2.

MEMO	
To: Al Jones	Sept. 30, 20XX
FROM: Peter Flynn, Pres.	
RE: Bad Debts	

At a party last night a friend of mine told me that we should not be using the direct write-off method. He told me that it doesn't fulfill the matching principle of accounting. Check the Tax Reform Act of 1986 in your Research Department to support or reject this information. Please provide me with a written report.

Jones Co. May 12 $1,500	Ron Co. Aug. 18 $700	Roger Co. Dec. 15 $1,400
Bill Co. Oct. 5 $125	Doe Co. Nov. 1 $ 900 Dec. 18 1,200	Joe Co. Sept. 5 $1,200
Francis Co. July 8 $200 July 15 $400	Balance in Allowance for Doubtful Accounts $350	Not yet due 1% 1–30 3% 31–60 8% 61–90 12% Over 90 30%

YOU make the call

Critical Thinking/Ethical Case

14R-3.

Pete Sazich, the accountant for Moore Company, feels that all bad debts will be eliminated if credit transactions are done by credit card. He also feels that the cost of the credit cards should be added to the price of the goods. Pete feels that in the future the allowance method will be totally eliminated. You make the call. Write a letter stating your opinion regarding this matter to Pete's boss.

INTERNET EXERCISES

EX-1. [www.dnb.com/english/aboutdnb/index.htm] Dun and Bradstreet is one of the world's best known names in reporting and analyzing business credit. D and B prides itself in providing credit and financial management services to businesses. From this site, look into some of the areas in which Dun and Bradstreet can help businesses.

1. Briefly state what these functions are, and how a new or existing business could be served in this manner.
2. What is D and B doing in the "new economy" based upon web businesses?

EX-2. [http://www.cccsintl.org/] The Consumer Credit Counseling Service assists individuals who have gotten into credit problems. This not-for-profit organization helps by working out problems between creditors and individuals with the hope of keeping debtors out of bankruptcy. When you arrive at this site, click on "debt counseling services" and investigate the types of help available from this organization. What is the advantage to creditors in working with this agency?

CONTINUING PROBLEM

The Eldorado Computer Center currently has an $11,900 balance in accounts receivable. Here is a current schedule of accounts receivable:

Eldorado Computer Center
Schedule of Accounts Receivable
March 31, 20XX

Taylor Golf	$ 2,900
Vita Needle	8,100
Accu Pac	900
Total	$11,900

Assignment

(See p. 487 in your *Study Guide and Working Papers.*)

Although Accu Pac's account is not 90 days past due, Freedman has determined that it is necessary to write off the entire balance because the business has foreclosed. Make the necessary journal entry using the direct write-off method.

CHAPTER 15

Notes Receivable and Notes Payable

Cartoon characters need cash too. In the summer of 2000, Harvey Entertainment Company, the LA-company that owns the rights to Casper the Friendly Ghost, Audrey, Richie Rich and several other classic cartoon characters, faced a cash shortfall. Operating results for the second quarter of 2000 revealed that Harvey had $30.6 million in **liabilities**. This is compared to total **assets** of $49.3 million. Yet, of that figure only $806,000 was in the form of cash. Included in Harvey's liabilities was $19 million in **notes payable**. This means that Harvey has borrowed $19 million from banks or other lenders.

In this chapter you will understand how to account for **notes payable** and **notes receivable**. When any person or business borrows money, there is a cost beyond the repayment of the money borrowed (principal). The borrower also pays interest. For a business, interest is usually accounted for either at the end of the accounting period or when the loan is repaid.

How will Harvey Entertainment get the cash it needs to pay back the principal and interest on its notes payable in addition to covering operating expenses for the foreseeable future? The company is actively seeking equity investors — businesses that want to own shares — as well as rights to new characters. In August of 2000 Mr. Magoo came to the rescue. The company received an investment of $26 million in cash from Classic Media LLC as well as rights to the cartoon character "Mr. Magoo."

Information on Harvey's financials from: Dwight Oestricher, "Harvey Is Facing Liquidity Shortfall in Next 12 Months, *Wall Street Journal,* August 23, 2000, p. B10. Anonymous, "Harvey to Get Cash Influx, Magoo Rights," *The Los Angeles Times,* August 25, 2000, p. 2.

LEARNING OBJECTIVES

▼ Determining interest calculations and maturity dates on notes. (p. 542)

▼ Journalizing entries to record renewal of a note, dishonoring of a note, eventual receipt of payment, and note given in exchange for equipment purchased. (p. 547)

▼ Discounting an interest-bearing note receivable and recording a discounted note that has been dishonored. (p. 551)

▼ Handling adjustments for interest expense and interest income. (p. 556)

Notes receivable: asset.
Notes payable: liability.

So far the accounts receivable and accounts payable transactions we have been discussing have involved informal promises: Purchase orders and sales receipts are not formal written promises. In this chapter we turn to transactions by buyers and sellers that require promissory notes (or notes), which are *formal written promises.* Notes receivable record amounts owed to a company by others. Notes payable record amounts the company itself owes.

Companies use notes instead of informal promises for many reasons, such as (1) recording sales of high-cost items like farm machinery or construction equipment that have long-term credit periods (usually over 60 days), (2) giving additional time to settle past due accounts, or (3) borrowing money from a bank for a fee. The fee that is charged for the use of one's money over a period of time is called **interest.** In addition, a note gives the seller or lender a stronger legal claim for collecting a past due account because the note acts as formal proof of the transaction.

LEARNING UNIT 15-1

PROMISSORY NOTES, INTEREST CALCULATIONS, AND DETERMINING MATURITY DATES

Before looking at recording notes receivable and notes payable, let's discuss the structure of a note and how to determine interest calculations and *maturity dates* (when the note comes due).

A **promissory note** (often called simply a *note*) is a written promise by a borrower to pay a certain sum of money to the lender at a fixed future date. Figure 15-1 is a promissory note that Able Company issued to Green Company. Take a moment to look at the structure of this note. The following explanation is keyed to the figure:

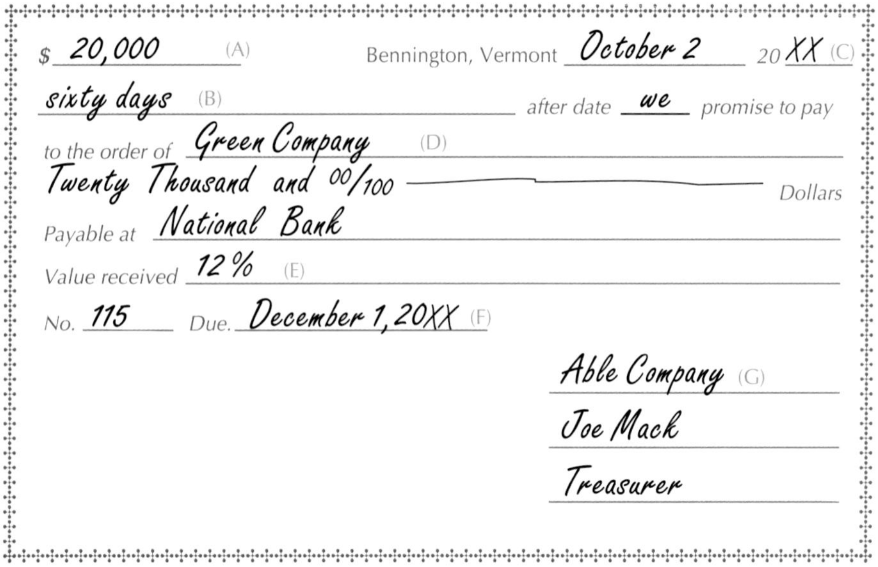
$ 20,000 (A) Bennington, Vermont October 2 20XX (C)

sixty days (B) after date we promise to pay

to the order of Green Company (D)

Twenty Thousand and 00/100 Dollars

Payable at National Bank

Value received 12% (E)

No. 115 Due. December 1, 20XX (F)

Able Company (G)

Joe Mack

Treasurer

FIGURE 15-1. A Promissory Note

a. Able Company is borrowing $20,000; this amount is called the **principal.**
b. Money is being borrowed for 60 days.
c. The note is issued on October 2, 20XX.
d. The Green Company is the **payee** to whom the note is payable.
e. The note carries a 12 percent annual interest rate. (Even though the note is for 60 days, interest is stated as a yearly rate.)
f. The date the note will come due, December 1, 20XX, is called the **maturity date.**
g. Able Company is the **maker,** or the one promising to pay the note plus interest when it comes due.

> Think of the payee as the lender.

> The maker is often also called the payor or debtor.

The maker (Able Company) is the borrower. The borrower calls this obligation a **note payable.** The payee (Green Company) views this note as an asset called a **note receivable.** Able Company's interest expense is interest income for Green Company. Remember that interest expense is classified on the income statement as "other expenses" and interest income is "other income."

> Most interest on notes will be paid on maturity date. We will cover exceptions later in chapter.

HOW TO CALCULATE INTEREST

The formula for calculating the interest on a note is

Interest = Principal × Rate × Time

- Principal ↑ The face value or amount stated on note indicating amount borrowed
- Rate ↑ Percent per year
- Time ↑ Years or fraction of year

Let's look at some illustrative situations to show specific interest calculations.

Interest calculated for one year on a $6,000 12 percent note:

$$I = P \times R \times T$$

$$12\% = .12 \text{ or } \frac{12}{100} = \$6{,}000 \times .12 \times 1$$

$$= \$720$$

Interest calculated for five months on an $8,000 10 percent note: Time is expressed in twelfths of a year; thus 5 months is

$$I = P \times R \times T$$
$$= \$8,000 \times .10 \times \tfrac{5}{12}$$
$$= \$333.33$$

Interest calculated for exact number of days based on a 360-day year, 60 days at 6 percent on a $4,000 note: When the note is given in days, the fraction for time is

$$\frac{\text{Exact Number of Days}}{360}$$

So we have

$$I = P \times R \times T$$
$$= \$4,000 \times .06 \times \tfrac{60}{360}$$
$$= \$40$$

> Some federal agencies use 365 days, but common business practice is to use 360.

TABLE 15-1 DAYS IN A YEAR

Day of Month	Jan.	Feb.*	Mar.	Apr.	May	June	July	Aug.	Sept.	Oct.	Nov.	Dec.	Day of Month
1	1	32	60	91	121	152	182	213	244	274	305	335	1
2	2	33	61	92	122	153	183	214	245	275	306	336	2
3	3	34	62	93	123	154	184	215	246	276	307	337	3
4	4	35	63	94	124	155	185	216	247	277	308	338	4
5	5	36	64	95	125	156	186	217	248	278	309	339	5
6	6	37	65	96	126	157	187	218	249	279	310	340	6
7	7	38	66	97	127	158	188	219	250	280	311	341	7
8	8	39	67	98	128	159	189	220	251	281	312	342	8
9	9	40	68	99	129	160	190	221	252	282	313	343	9
10	10	41	69	100	130	161	191	222	253	283	314	344	10
11	11	42	70	101	131	162	192	223	254	284	315	345	11
12	12	43	71	102	132	163	193	224	255	285	316	346	12
13	13	44	72	103	133	164	194	225	256	286	317	347	13
14	14	45	73	104	134	165	195	226	257	287	318	348	14
15	15	46	74	105	135	166	196	227	258	288	319	349	15
16	16	47	75	106	136	167	197	228	259	289	320	350	16
17	17	48	76	107	137	168	198	229	260	290	321	351	17
18	18	49	77	108	138	169	199	230	261	291	322	352	18
19	19	50	78	109	139	170	200	231	(262)	292	323	353	19
20	20	51	79	110	140	171	201	232	263	293	324	354	20
21	21	52	80	111	141	(172)	202	233	264	294	325	355	21
22	22	53	81	112	142	173	203	234	265	295	326	356	22
23	23	54	82	113	143	174	204	235	266	296	327	357	23
24	24	55	83	114	144	175	205	236	267	297	328	358	24
25	25	56	84	115	145	176	206	237	268	298	329	359	25
26	26	57	85	116	146	177	207	238	269	299	330	360	26
27	27	58	86	117	147	178	208	239	270	300	331	361	27
28	28	59	87	118	148	179	209	240	271	301	332	362	28
29	29		88	119	149	180	210	241	272	302	333	363	29
30	30		89	120	150	181	211	242	273	303	334	364	30
31	31		90		151		212	243		304		365	31

*For leap years, February has 29 days, and the number of each day after February 28 is one greater than the number given in the table.

HOW TO DETERMINE MATURITY DATE

Maturity Date Determined by Exact Days

To determine the maturity date of a 90-day note dated June 21, the following could be set up (or you could count on a calendar):

Number of days remaining in June (30 − 21)	9
Days in July	31
Days in August	31
Number of days at end of August	71
Days in September to reach 90	19
Term of note	90

> 30 days have September, April, June, and November; all the rest have 31, except February, which has 28 (29 during a leap year).

Thus the maturity date of the note is September 19.

Another way to calculate the maturity date is to use a table of days in a year (see Table 15-1 p. 544).

The original note is dated June 21. Look at the top of the table for June and down the left column to day 21. The point of intersection reveals that June 21 is day 172 of the year. If we add 172 and 90 (length of note) we get 262. By searching in the table for 262, we see the date of maturity is September 19.

Maturity Date Determined by Number of Months

If the note were expressed in months rather than days, the table or calendar would not be needed. The maturity date could be found by counting the months from the date the note was issued, regardless of number of days in each month.

Here are some examples:

Date of Note	Length of Note	Maturity Date	
March 31	Two months	May 31	
April 30	Three months	July 31	(last day of
July 31	Two months	September 30	month)

LEARNING UNIT 15-1 REVIEW

AT THIS POINT you should be able to

- ▼ Explain the advantages of using notes instead of informal promises. (p. 542)
- ▼ Define and explain the structure of a promissory note. (p. 543)
- ▼ Calculate interest on notes in days, monthly, or yearly. (p. 543)
- ▼ Calculate maturity date by days in the month, by special chart, or by months. (p. 545)

SELF-REVIEW QUIZ 15-1

(The forms you need are on page 488 of the *Study Guide and Working Papers*.)

1. Calculate the interest for the following:

   a. $10,000   12%   1 year

   b.   9,000   13%   7 months

   c.   7,000   10%   80 days

2. Find the maturity date of an 80-day note dated March 3 by (a) days in each month and (b) using a days-in-a-year chart.

3. Find the maturity date of a note dated March 31, due in five months.

Interest: Time is Money

Coffee by the Pound! Why that's like money in the bank! I gotta get in on that," thought Fred happily. "I've got plenty of room for the big floor display. It costs twice as much as the countertop unit, but it's worth it. I might as well get the header panel too. It's less than $40, and it really finishes off the display. Then I'll buy the coffee grinder, and some rolls of the variety stickers . . . and . . . the bags of coffee too! The bigger my order, the lower my cost. But this is adding up fast! I'd better think about getting a loan."

Fred found himself in a position not uncommon for businesses of all sizes: the need to spend money to make more money. He checked the interest rates at his bank and calculated what it would cost him to repay a note with a principal of $3,000, an interest rate of 9 percent, and a time of 120 days.

$$\$3,000 \times .09 \times \frac{120}{360} = \$90.00$$

"$90 bucks," thought Fred. "That's steep. I wonder if I could do better at another bank?" Fred then checked with Country Bank. They offered him $3,000, an interest rate of 8 3/4 percent, and a time of 90 days.

$$\$3,000 \times .0875 \times \frac{90}{360} = \$65.63$$

"$65 bucks is more like it," thought Fred. "But how can I pay it back in only 3 months? That really puts the pressure on. Is it worth the $25 difference to pay back the loan so fast? It's 30 days more or $25 more. In either case I can deduct the interest from my taxes as a business expense. So it's really less than a $25 difference. Hmmm . . ."

Discussion Questions

1. Which loan would you take if you were in Fred's place? Why?
2. Assume Fred wanted the loan on October 1. What is the maturity date for the 90-day loan? The 120-day loan?
3. Always cautious, Fred expects slow coffee-by-the-pound sales for October and November, but brisk sales by December. How might his sales expectations affect his decision to take a longer loan?

Solutions to Self-Review Quiz 15-1

1. **a.** $10,000 × .12 × 1 = $1,200.
    b. $ 9,000 × .13 × $\frac{7}{12}$ = $682.50.
    c. $ 7,000 × .10 × $\frac{80}{360}$ = $155.56.

2. **a.**

Number of days remaining in March (31 − 3)	28
Days in April	30
Number of days at end of April	58
Days in May to reach 80	22
Maturity date — May 22	80

   b. March 3   62 days
                  + 80
                 142   May 22

3. March 31, April, May, June, July, August 31 .

LEARNING UNIT 15-2   RECORDING NOTES

> *We use general journal entries to keep things simple instead of using special journals.*

To understand how notes can be used to extend credit periods and to see how a note is paid off, let's look at some illustrative transactions involving Mace Company and Jane Company.

Sale of Merchandise on Account   On August 1, 20XX, Mace Company sold $6,000 of merchandise on account to Jane Company.

ON BOOKS OF SELLER—MACE COMPANY

Aug.	1	Accounts Receivable, Jane Co.		6 0 0 0 00	
		Sales			6 0 0 0 00
		Sold merchandise on account			

ON BOOKS OF BUYER—JANE COMPANY

Aug.	1	Purchases		6 0 0 0 00	
		Accounts Payable, Mace Co.			6 0 0 0 00
		Purchased merchandise on account			

On September 1, the end of the credit period, Jane Company gave a $6,000, 60-day, 13 percent note to Mace Company to gain additional time to settle the past due account. The following entries would be made on the books of the buyer and seller.

TIME EXTENSION WITH A NOTE

SELLER—MACE COMPANY

Sept.	1	Notes Receivable		6 0 0 0 00	
		Accounts Receivable, Jane Co.			6 0 0 0 00
		Received 60-day, 13% note for			
		extension of past due account			

> Notes Receivable is a current asset on the balance sheet.

BUYER—JANE COMPANY

Sept.	1	Accounts Payable, Mace Co.		6 0 0 0 00	
		Notes Payable			6 0 0 0 00
		Issued 60-day, 13% note for			
		extension of past due account			

> Notes Payable is a current liability on the balance sheet.

When this transaction is journalized, both Accounts Receivable and Accounts Payable are reduced. With *notes* a subsidiary ledger is usually *not* needed, because the file of the notes provides all the information.

Mace might accept this note as an extension because (1) if Jane Company doesn't pay, a formal written promise is in hand, and (2) interest is accumulating on the note.

Seller →	The end result of this transaction is a shifting of assets of Mace Company from Accounts Receivable to Notes Receivable.
Buyer →	For Jane Company, the result is a shift in liabilities from Accounts Payable to Notes Payable.

NOTE DUE AND PAID AT MATURITY

Now let's look at the journal entries that will be made if Jane Company pays off the note on October 31.

It is important to emphasize that the interest is calculated on the maturity date of the note.

			SELLER—MACE COMPANY											
Oct.	31	Cash		6	1	3	0	00						
		Notes Receivable								6	0	0	0	00
		Interest Income									1	3	0	00
		Collected Jane Company note												

$$[\$6{,}000 \times .13 \times \tfrac{60}{360} = \$130 \text{ Interest Income}]$$

			BUYER—JANE COMPANY											
Oct.	31	Notes Payable		6	0	0	0	00						
		Interest Expense			1	3	0	00						
		Cash								6	1	3	0	00
		Paid note to Mace Company												

$$[\$6{,}000 \times .13 \times \tfrac{60}{360} = \$130 \text{ Interest Expense}]$$

NOTE RENEWED AT MATURITY

If Jane Company is unable to pay the $6,130 at maturity, it is possible for the company to renew all or part of the note. Let's assume that the company can pay the interest of $130 and give another note for 90 days at 13 percent. The transaction could be recorded as follows on the books of the buyer and seller:

			SELLER—MACE COMPANY											
Oct.	31	Cash			1	3	0	00						
		Notes Receivable (new)		6	0	0	0	00						
		Notes Receivable (old)								6	0	0	0	00
		Interest Income									1	3	0	00
		Interest of old note collected and												
		renewal of note for 90 days												

			BUYER—JANE COMPANY											
Oct.	31	Notes Payable (old)		6	0	0	0	00						
		Interest Expense			1	3	0	00						
		Notes Payable (new)								6	0	0	0	00
		Cash									1	3	0	00
		Interest of old note paid and												
		renewal of note recorded												

Note on the seller's books how the interest is received, the old note is canceled, and the new note is put on the books.

DISHONORED NOTE

Mace Company does not have to renew the note if Jane Company fails to pay it at maturity. In this situation the note is said to be a **dishonored note.** Another wording is to say that Jane Company has **defaulted** on its note.

On Jane's and Mace's books the amounts in Notes Receivable and Notes Payable will then be removed and transferred back to Accounts Receivable and Accounts Payable, because the note has reached the maturity date. At the same time, whether the note is paid or not, the interest expense is due and payable and should be recorded (for Mace Company this is Interest Income and for Jane Company it is Interest Expense).

Let's see what entries would look like if Jane Company first defaults and then finally pays the amount owed on December 1. To keep it simple, no additional charges will be calculated for the extra month Jane Company has taken to pay off the amount owed to Mace Company.

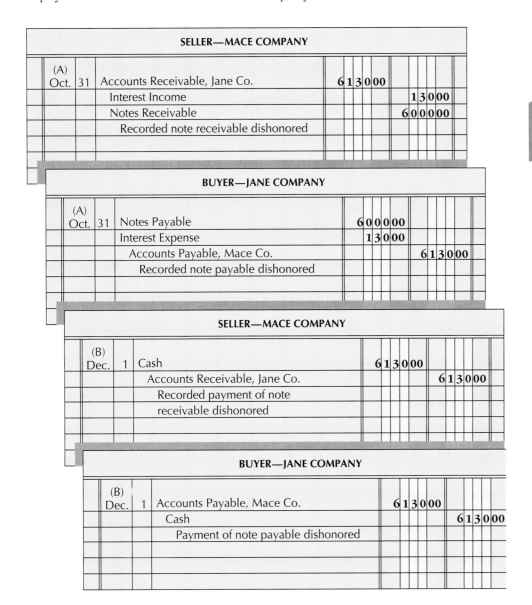

			SELLER—MACE COMPANY			
(A) Oct.	31		Accounts Receivable, Jane Co.	6 1 3 0 00		
			Interest Income		1 3 0 00	
			Notes Receivable		6 0 0 0 00	
			Recorded note receivable dishonored			

> Only unmatured notes are in the Notes Receivable account.

			BUYER—JANE COMPANY			
(A) Oct.	31		Notes Payable	6 0 0 0 00		
			Interest Expense	1 3 0 00		
			Accounts Payable, Mace Co.		6 1 3 0 00	
			Recorded note payable dishonored			

			SELLER—MACE COMPANY			
(B) Dec.	1		Cash	6 1 3 0 00		
			Accounts Receivable, Jane Co.		6 1 3 0 00	
			Recorded payment of note			
			receivable dishonored			

			BUYER—JANE COMPANY			
(B) Dec.	1		Accounts Payable, Mace Co.	6 1 3 0 00		
			Cash		6 1 3 0 00	
			Payment of note payable dishonored			

NOTE GIVEN IN EXCHANGE FOR EQUIPMENT PURCHASED

A note may be given in exchange for an asset that is purchased. For instance, suppose Jane Company decided to buy from Ronald Company some display racks for $7,000. Because the price was high, Jane Company gave a note instead of buying the racks on account. The note issued by Jane Company was a 60-day, 9 percent interest-bearing note for $7,000. This transaction is recorded on the books of the buyer and seller as follows:

			SELLER—RONALD COMPANY												
May	9		Notes Receivable	7	0	0	0	00							
			Sales							7	0	0	0	00	
			Sold display racks with a												
			60 day, 9% note												

			BUYER—JANE COMPANY												
May	9		Store Equipment	7	0	0	0	00							
			Notes Payable							7	0	0	0	00	
			Purchased display racks with a												
			60 day, 9% note												

When the note is paid at maturity, the same transactions discussed earlier would result.

LEARNING UNIT 15-2 REVIEW

AT THIS POINT you should be able to

▼ Journalize entries for buyer and seller to record the extension of a past due account by issuing a note. (p. 547)
▼ Explain why a subsidiary ledger may not be needed with Notes Payable and Notes Receivable. (p. 547)
▼ Journalize entries for the buyer and seller to record renewal of a note, dishonoring of a note, eventual receipt of payment, and a note given in exchange for equipment purchased. (p. 548)

SELF-REVIEW QUIZ 15-2

(The forms you need are on page 489 of the *Study Guide and Working Papers*.) Journalize the following transactions for Action Company:

A. Action Company sold $8,000 of merchandise on account to Brian Company.
B. Action Company received a 60-day, $8,000, 12 percent note for a time extension of past due account of Brian Company.
C. Collected the Brian Company note on the maturity date.
D. Brian Company renewed the note for 90 days and paid interest on the old note. (Alternative to step C.)
E. Assuming that Brian Company defaulted in step C, record the note receivable dishonored.
F. Brian Company paid note receivable dishonored.

Solution to Self-Review Quiz 15-2

(A)	Accounts Receivable, Brian Co.		8 0 0 0 00					
	Sales				8 0 0 0 00			
	Sold merchandise on account							
(B)	Notes Receivable		8 0 0 0 00					
	Accounts Receivable, Brian Co.				8 0 0 0 00			
	Started note at 12% for 60 days							
(C)	Cash		8 1 6 0 00					
	Interest Income				1 6 0 00			
	Notes Receivable				8 0 0 0 00			
	Collected Brian Co. note							
	($8,000 × .12 × $\frac{60}{360}$ = $160)							
(D)	Cash		1 6 0 00					
	Notes Receivable		8 0 0 0 00					
	Notes Receivable				8 0 0 0 00			
	Interest Income				1 6 0 00			
	Collected interest and renewed note							
(E)	Accounts Receivable, Brian Company		8 1 6 0 00					
	Notes Receivable				8 0 0 0 00			
	Interest Income				1 6 0 00			
	Brian Co. defaulted on note							
(F)	Cash		8 1 6 0 00					
	Accounts Receivable, Brian Company				8 1 6 0 00			
	Brian Co. paid dishonored note							

LEARNING UNIT 15-3

HOW TO DISCOUNT CUSTOMERS' NOTES

Many times a company that accepts notes from customers will not (or cannot) wait to receive its cash until the maturity date. Instead, it goes to a bank and exchanges the note for cash. This process is called **discounting a note.** The company will endorse the note and receive the **maturity value** of the note (principal plus interest) less what the bank charges for holding the note from the date of discounting until the maturity date. The time period during which the bank holds the note (until maturity) is called the **discount period.**

The amount that the bank charges the company is called the **bank discount.** It is the difference between what the company receives from the bank and the maturity value of the note. The actual amount of money the company receives when a note is discounted is called the **proceeds** (maturity value less the bank discount).

Let's see how Marvin Company discounts an interest-bearing note receivable. The best way to understand the process is to take it step by step.

> Think of the bank discount as the cost of cashing in a note before maturity.

HOW TO DISCOUNT AN INTEREST-BEARING NOTE RECEIVABLE

What Marvin Company will receive from bank is called the proceeds.

Marvin Company received an $8,000, 90-day, 12 percent note from Jee Company dated October 1. On October 31 Marvin Company needed cash to finance its inventory, so it discounted the note to Blue Bank, which charges a bank discount rate of 14 percent. An overview of the process is shown in Figure 15-2.

Step 1: Find the *maturity* value of the note:

Find maturity value.

$$\text{(a) } \$8,000 \times .12 \times \frac{90}{360} = \$240 \text{ interest}$$

$$\text{(b) Maturity Value = Principal + Interest}$$
$$= \$8,000 + \$240$$
$$= \underline{\$8,240}$$

Calculate discount period.

Step 2: Calculate the *discount* period (number of days from the date of discounting until the maturity date):

90 Days	Note
− 30 Days	Expired before Discounting (Oct. 31 − Oct. 1)
= 60 Days	That Bank Holds Note until It Comes Due

Calculate bank discount.

Step 3: Calculate the bank discount (what the bank charges Marvin Company for holding the note until maturity: To do so, we use the following formula:

$$\text{Bank Discount = Maturity Value} \times \text{Bank Discount Rate} \times \frac{\text{No. of Days Bank Holds Note until Maturity}}{\text{360 Days}}$$

$$= \$8,240 \times .14 \times \frac{60}{360}$$
$$= \$192.27$$

Note that the bank discount is based on the maturity value, because we are borrowing the maturity value for the number of days in the discount period.

Calculate proceeds.

Step 4: Calculate the proceeds (what Marvin Company receives from the bank in the discounting process):

$$\text{Proceeds = Maturity Value − Bank Discount}$$
$$= \$8,240 − \$192.27$$
$$= \$8,047.73$$

Issue Date October 1	Date of Discount October 31	Maturity Date
Oct. 31 − Oct. 1 = 30 days	90 days − 30 days = 60 days = Discount Period	
Marvin Company holds note	Bank holds note	
Face Value: $8,000		Maturity Value: $8,240

90 days

FIGURE 15-2. Discounting a Note Receivable, $8,000 at 12 percent for 90 days

If Marvin Company could have waited until the maturity date, it would have received $8,240. By discounting the note the company lost interest of $192.27, or the cost charged by the bank to hold the note until maturity. Let's look at how Marvin Company would record this item on its books (again for simplicity we use general journal entries rather than special journals).

Oct.	31	Cash	8 0 4 7 73		
		Notes Receivable		8 0 0 0 00	
		Interest Income		4 7 73	
		Discounted Jee Company's			
		90-day, 12% note at 14%			

Journalizing the discounted note receivable:

$8,047.73
− 8,000.00
$ 47.73
(Interest Income)

There is Interest Income because the proceeds Marvin Company received were more than the face value of the note ($8,000). In actuality, if the proceeds had been *less* than the $8,000, Marvin Company would have incurred an interest expense. That could have happened, for example, if Marvin Company held the note for only a short period of time and Blue Bank had a bank discount rate much higher than the original note. Suppose the note was discounted after being held only 2 days, and the bank's discount rate was 18 percent. The bank discount, or amount the bank charges, would be calculated as follows:

$$\text{Bank Discount} = \underset{\text{maturity value}}{\$8,240} \times .18 \times \underset{\text{discount period}}{\frac{88}{360}}$$
$$= \$362.56$$

Thus the proceeds to Marvin Company would be

$$\text{Proceeds} = \$8,240 - \$362.56$$
$$= \$7,877.44$$

Note that here Marvin Company is receiving less than the $8,000 face value of the note. The general journal entry of Marvin Company would thus look as follows:

Oct.	31	Cash	7 8 7 7 44		
		Interest Expense	1 2 2 56		
		Notes Receivable		8 0 0 0 00	
		To record discount of note			

PROCEDURE WHEN A DISCOUNTED NOTE IS DISHONORED

Who is liable for the note if Jee Company fails to pay the note at maturity? The answer is Marvin Company.

When Marvin Company endorsed the note to Blue Bank, it agreed to pay the note at maturity if Jee Company failed to. The potential liability is called a **contingent liability.** Until the note is paid, Marvin Company will state this contingent liability as a footnote on its balance sheet.

At some point before maturity, Jee Company is notified that Blue Bank is holding the note. Let's assume that the maturity date is reached and Jee

Note:
If Marvin Company endorsed the note without recourse, it would not have any liability. Instead, the bank would have liability if Jee Company did not pay.

Company defaults. Blue Bank notifies Marvin Company and charges Marvin Company the full amount of the note, including interest and a $5 protest fee, which is the charge made by Blue Bank for notifying Marvin Company that the note was presented to the maker for payment and was not received. Thus the bank charges Marvin Company (and Marvin will in turn charge Jee Company) the following:

Note	$8,000
Interest	240
Protest Fee	5
	$8,245

The following entry is recorded on Marvin Company's book:

Dec.	30	Accounts Receivable, Jee Co.	8 2 4 5 00	
		Cash		8 2 4 5 00
		To record default		

You can be sure that Marvin Company will try to collect this $8,245 from Jee Company. Marvin Company may charge additional interest for this delay in paying the $8,245. For simplicity we have left this step out. If the $8,245 becomes uncollectible, the account could be written off as a bad debt using the Allowance for Doubtful Accounts method discussed in Chapter 14.

LEARNING UNIT 15-3 REVIEW

AT THIS POINT you should be able to

▼ Define and explain discounting, maturity value, discount period, bank discount, and proceeds. (p. 552)
▼ Explain the four steps required in discounting an interest-bearing note receivable. (p. 552)
▼ Prepare a journal entry to record the proceeds of a note. (p. 553)
▼ Define contingent liability and compare it with an endorsement without recourse. (p. 553)
▼ Journalize the entry to record a discounted note that has been dishonored. (p. 554)

SELF-REVIEW QUIZ 15-3

(The forms you need are on pages 490–491 of the *Study Guide and Working Papers.*)

Al Gene Company received a $10,000, 60-day, 12 percent note from Broom Company dated July 5, 20XX. On August 3 Al Gene Company discounted the note to Ryan Bank, which charged a bank discount rate of 15 percent.

a. Complete the four steps to discount the note.

b. Journalize the entry to record the proceeds.

c. Journalize the entry if a default occurs, assuming a $5 protest fee.

Solution to Self-Review Quiz 15-3

a. **Step 1:** Maturity value (principal + interest)

$$I = \$10,000 \times .12 \times \frac{60}{360}$$
$$= \$200$$
$$MV = \$10,000 + \$200$$
$$= \$10,200$$

Step 2: Discount period:

July 31	
− 5	
26	Days Al Gene Held Note in July
3	Days Al Gene Held Note in August
29	Days Al Gene Held Note
60	Days
− 29	Days
31	Days Bank Holds Note

Step 3: Bank discount:

$$\text{Bank Discount} = \text{Maturity Value} \times \text{Bank Discount Rate} \times \frac{\text{No. of Days Bank Holds Note Until Maturity}}{360}$$

$$= \underset{\text{(Step 1)}}{\$10,200} \times \underset{\text{(Given in facts)}}{.15} \times \frac{31}{360}$$
$$= \$131.75$$

Step 4: Proceeds:

$$\text{Proceeds} = \text{Maturity Value} - \text{Bank Discount}$$
$$= \$10,200 - \$131.75$$
$$= \$10,068.25$$

b.

Aug.	3	Cash	10068 25		
		Notes Receivable		10000 00	
		Interest Income		68 25	
		Discounted Broom Company			
		12% note at 15%			

c.

Sept.	3	Accounts Receivable, Broom Company	10205 00		
		Cash		10205 00	
		To record default			

LEARNING UNIT 15-4

DISCOUNTING ONE'S OWN NOTE

In the last unit we looked at how a note of a customer was discounted. Now our attention shifts to Jones Company, which is borrowing $10,000 by giving Alvin Bank its own 12 percent, 60-day note on December 16, 20XX. In this case Alvin Bank deducts the interest in advance. The following is the formula to calculate the bank discount (cost of borrowing) and the proceeds (what Jones Company gets):

> Note that maturity value here is the same as the original principal, because interest is deducted in advance.

$$\text{Bank Discount} = (\text{Maturity Value}) \times (\text{Interest Rate}) \times \frac{\text{Discount Period}}{360}$$

$$= \$10,000 \quad \times \quad .12 \quad \times \quad \frac{60}{360}$$

$$= \$200$$

$$\text{Proceeds} = \text{Maturity Value} - \text{Discount}$$

$$= \$10,000 - \$200$$

$$= \$9,800$$

> Discount on Notes Payable is a contra-liability.

Thus Jones Company receives $9,800 and at the time of maturity will pay back $10,000. The $200 of interest is recorded in a new account called **Discount on Notes Payable.** This account is a contra-liability account that is subtracted from Notes Payable on the balance sheet, where it looks like the following:

Current Liabilities

Notes Payable	$10,000	
Less: Discount on		
Notes Payable	200	
		$9,800

Later in this unit, when we talk about adjustments, we see that as the note matures, the discount will be reduced and then charged to Interest Expense. For now, however, let's record the journal entry for Jones Company as it discounts its own note with interest deducted in advance:

Dec.	16	Cash	9 8 0 0 00		
		Discount on Notes Payable	2 0 0 00		
		Notes Payable		10 0 0 0 00	
		Discounted own note at 12%			

Accounts Affected	Category	↑ ↓	Rules	
Cash	**Asset**	↑	**Dr.**	$9,800
Discount on Notes Payable	**Contra-Liability**	↑	**Dr.**	$200
Notes Payable	**Liability**	↑	**Cr.**	$10,000

When the note is paid, the accountant will debit Notes Payable for $10,000 and credit Cash for $10,000.

Note: Although the bank interest rate is stated at 12 percent, the truth is that Jones Company really has the use of only $9,800. To calculate the true interest rate, which is called the **effective interest rate,** the following formula applies:

Effective interest rate: The cost of borrowing the $10,000 is not 12 percent but really almost 12 1/4 percent.

$$\text{Effective interest rate} = \frac{(\text{Maturity value of note}) \times (\text{bank interest rate})}{\text{amount of cash proceeds received from note}}$$

$$= \frac{\$10,000 \times .12}{\$9,800}$$

$$= 12.24 \text{ percent}$$

Now let's look at how adjustments will be handled for some of the transactions presented in this chapter.

INTEREST: THE NEED FOR ADJUSTMENTS

Because interest-bearing notes are often taken out and then paid off in different accounting periods, it is necessary to adjust or bring up to date Interest Income and Interest Expense. The following diagram shows why we need to adjust as well as who does the adjusting:

Accrued Interest Income	Accrued Interest Expense
Must adjust for income that has been earned during the period but has not been received or recorded because payment is not yet due.	Must adjust for interest that has been incurred during the period but has not been paid or recorded because payment is not yet due.
↓	↓
Notes Receivable *(payee)*	(A) Note Payable *(maker)*
	(B) Company's Own discounted note

The payee is the seller and the maker is the buyer.

Let's look at how to record adjustments for Interest Income and Interest Expense from the following: Bog Company receives a $24,000, 60-day, 10 percent note on December 16, 200X, from Jan Company.

Step 1: Calculate interest on the note:

$$\text{Interest} = \$24,000 \times .10 \times \frac{60}{360}$$

$$= \$400$$

Step 2: Calculate the number of days the note has already run before the end of the current period (see Fig. 15-3 p. 558):

$$\begin{array}{ll} \text{Dec. 31} & \text{(end of period)} \\ -\text{ Dec. 16} & \text{(starting date of note)} \\ \hline 15 & \text{Days} \end{array}$$

Step 3: Calculate interest incurred for this period:

$$\text{Length of note} \rightarrow \frac{15 \text{ Days}}{60 \text{ Days}} = \frac{1}{4} \times \$400$$

$$= \$100$$

FIGURE 15-3. Adjusting for Interest Accrued

Another way to calculate the interest is

$$\$24{,}000 \times .10 \times \frac{15}{360} = \$100$$

Step 4: Prepare the adjusting journal entries:

On Books of *Seller* (Holder of Note)

Dec.	31	Interest Receivable	1 0 0 00	
		Interest Income		1 0 0 00
		Adj. for int.		

On Books of *Buyer* (Debtor)

Dec.	31	Interest Expense	1 0 0 00	
		Interest Payable		1 0 0 00
		Adj. for int.		

Interest Receivable	
100	
Current Asset on balance sheet	

Interest Expense	
100	
Other Expense on income statement	

Interest Income	
	100
	Other Income on income statement

Interest Payable	
	100
	Current Liability on balance sheet

When the note is paid off on February 14, the first two entries are made, assuming that no reversing entry is used, as follows:

(No Reversing Entry)

SELLER

Feb.	14	Cash	24 4 0 0 00	
		Interest Receivable		1 0 0 00
		Notes Receivable		24 0 0 0 00
		Interest Income		3 0 0 00
		Received payment of note		

BUYER

Feb.	14	Notes Payable	24 0 0 0 00	
		Interest Expense	3 0 0 00	
		Interest Payable	1 0 0 00	
		Cash		24 4 0 0 00
		Paid off note		

Note that by not using reversing entries, the bookkeepers of the buyer and seller had to look up the amount of accrued interest that was recorded in the *old* year so that this year's interest expense or income would not be overstated.

If a reversing entry (which is optional) is used, the following entries are made:

(Reversing Entry Made)

SELLER

Feb.	14	Cash	24 40 0 00		
		Notes Receivable		24 00 0 00	
		Interest Income		4 0 0 00	
		Received payment of note			

BUYER

Feb.	14	Notes Payable	24 00 0 00		
		Interest Expense	4 0 0 00		
		Cash		24 40 0 00	
		Paid off note			

The last adjustment deals with a firm discounting its own note. Back on page 556, at the beginning of this unit, we saw Jones Company discounting its own note on December 16 for $10,000 for 60 days at 12 percent interest. Jones Company actually received $9,800 and recorded the $200 interest deducted in advance by the bank in a contra-liability account called *Discount on Notes Payable*.

Discount on Notes Payable	Interest Expense
200	

At the end of December, 15 out of the 60 days have passed. Thus one-fourth of the interest on this note should be recorded in the old year. To record this interest we reduce the amount in the Discount on Notes Payable by $50 ($\frac{1}{4} \times \$200$). The following journal entry is made:

Dec.	31	Interest Expense	5 0 00	
		Discount on Notes Payable		5 0 00
		Recognition of expense incurred		

Accounts Affected	Category	↑ ↓	Rules	
Interest Expense	**Other Expense**	↑	Dr.	$50
Discount on Notes Payable	**Contra-Liability**	↓	Dr.	$50

See p. 556 for comparison of this section before discount on note is reduced.

$$\frac{45\ days}{60\ days} \times \$200$$

The current liability on the balance sheet will look as follows:

Current Liabilities

Notes Payable	$10,000
Less: Discount on Notes Payable	150
	$9,850

When the note is paid the following journal entry will result:

Feb.	14	Notes Payable	10 0 0 0 00		
		Interest Expense	1 5 0 00		
		Discount on Notes Payable			1 5 0 00
		Cash			10 0 0 0 00
		Note paid			

LEARNING UNIT 15-4 REVIEW

AT THIS POINT you should be able to

▼ Explain the purpose of the Discount on Notes Payable account. (p. 556)
▼ Calculate the effective interest rate. (p. 557)
▼ Make adjustments for interest income and interest expense at end of period. (p. 557)
▼ Adjust the Discount on Notes Payable account. (p. 559)

SELF-REVIEW QUIZ 15-4

(The forms you need are on page 491 of the *Study Guide and Working Papers*.) Respond true or false to the following:

1. No bank deducts interest in advance.
2. Discount on Notes Payable is a contra-liability account.
3. When Discount on Notes Payable is reduced, Interest Expense results.
4. Effective rate of interest is lower than the stated rate.
5. Reversing entries are never used to adjust interest at the end of a period of time.

Solutions to Self-Review Quiz 15-4

1. False 2. True 3. True 4. False 5. False

SUMMARY OF KEY POINTS

Learning Unit 15-1

1. A promissory note is a written promise by a borrower to pay a certain sum of money to a lender at a fixed future date. The note may be interest-bearing or non-interest-bearing.

2. The payee is the party to whom the note is payable.

3. The maker is the one who will pay the promissory note.

4. Maturity date is the time when note comes due.

5. $\text{Interest} = \text{principal} \times \text{rate} \times \dfrac{\text{number of days}}{360}$.

Learning Unit 15-2

1. Notes Payable is a current liability on the balance sheet.

2. Notes do not need subsidiary ledgers.

3. Interest Income for the payee is Interest Expense for the maker.

4. A note that is not paid at maturity is said to be dishonored.

5. Notes may be renewed as well as issued to buy assets.

Learning Unit 15-3

1. Maturity value = principal + interest.

2. Discount period = number of days from date of discounting until maturity date.

3. Bank discount = what the bank charges for holding a note until the maturity date, as shown in the formula:

$$\text{Bank Discount} = \text{Maturity Value} \times \text{Bank Discount Rate} \times \frac{\text{No. of Days Bank Holds Note until Maturity}}{360 \text{ Days}}$$

4. Proceeds = what one receives from bank in the discounting process (the maturity value minus the bank discount).

5. If a discounted note is dishonored, the original holder of the note may be liable for payment unless the note was endorsed without recourse. This liability is called contingent liability.

Learning Unit 15-4

1. In discounting one's own note, the interest is usually deducted in advance.

2. The interest that is deducted in advance is recorded in a contra-liability account called Discount on Notes Payable.

3. The effective interest rate is higher than the stated rate.

4. At the end of the period, adjustments are made for Interest Income and Interest Expense that have accrued or built up. These entries can be reversed on the first day starting the next period to simplify recording when interest is paid or received in the new period.

5. The interest in the Discount on Notes Payable account is adjusted by reducing the Discount on Notes Payable and recording it as Interest Expense.

KEY TERMS

Bank discount   What the bank charges to hold a note until maturity (maturity value − proceeds).

Contingent liability   Liability on the part of one who discounts a note to pay if the maker of the note defaults at maturity date.

Default   Failure of maker to pay the maturity value of a note when due.

Discounting a note   The process or act of transferring the note to a bank before the maturity date.

Discount on Notes Payable   The amount of interest deducted in advance by the lender. This account reduces Notes Payable to actual cash value.

Discount period   The amount of time the bank holds a note that was discounted until the maturity date.

Dishonored note   A note that was not paid at maturity by the maker.

Effective interest rate   The true rate of simple interest.

Interest   The cost of using money for a period of time.

Maker   One promising to pay a note.

Maturity date   Due date of the promissory note.

Maturity value   The value of the note that is due on the date of maturity (principal + interest).

Note payable   A promissory note from the maker's point of view.

Note receivable   A promissory note from the payee's point of view.

Payee   One to whom a note is payable.

Principal   The face amount of the note.

Proceeds   Maturity value less bank discount.

Promissory note   A formal written promise by a borrower to pay a certain sum at a fixed future date.

QUESTIONS, MINI EXERCISES, EXERCISES, AND PROBLEMS

Discussion Questions

1. List three reasons why a company may use Notes Payable instead of Accounts Payable.
2. Explain the parts of a promissory note.
3. What is the difference between finding a maturity date by (a) days or (b) months?
4. Notes Receivable is a current liability on the balance sheet. Accept or reject. Why?
5. Why is a subsidiary ledger not needed for notes?
6. Only matured notes are listed in the Notes Receivable account. Please discuss.
7. Explain what will happen if a maker defaults on a note. (Assume the note has not been discounted.)
8. List the four steps to arrive at proceeds in the process of discounting a note.
9. What is meant by a contingent liability?
10. When could interest be deducted in advance by a lender?
11. What is the normal balance of the Discount on Notes Payable account?
12. How is the effective interest rate calculated?
13. How could Discount on Notes Payable be adjusted?

Mini Exercises

(The forms you need are on pages 493–494 of the *Study Guide and Working Papers*.)

Determining Maturity Date

1. Find the maturity date of the following:
   a. 120-day note dated July 8.
   b. 90-day note dated October 8.

(Cont. on p. 566)

BLUEPRINT: NOTES PAYABLE AND NOTES RECEIVABLE

	SELLER (Payee)	BUYER (Maker)
Sales of merchandise on account	Accounts Receivable, XXX Sales Sold on account	Purchases Accounts Payable, XXX Bought on account
Time extension with a note	Notes Receivable Accounts Receivable, XXX Transferred to note rec.	Accounts Payable, XXX Notes Payable Transferred to note pay.
Note due and paid	Cash Interest Income Notes Receivable Received payment	Notes Payable Interest Expense Cash Paid off note
Note renewed at maturity	Cash Notes Receivable (new) Notes Receivable (old) Interest Income Renewed note	Notes Payable Interest Expense Notes Payable (new) Cash Renewed note
Note given in exchange for equipment purchased	Notes Receivable Sales Sold on note rec.	Store Equipment Notes Payable Bought equip. for note

(Continued)

BLUEPRINT: NOTES PAYABLE AND NOTES RECEIVABLE (cont.)

SITUATIONS AFFECTING SELLER ONLY

Discounting a note—
receiving more
than face value

Cash		
Interest Income		
Notes Receivable		
Loaned discounted note		

Discounting a note—
receiving less
than face value

Cash		
Interest Expense		
Notes Receivable		
Loaned discounted note		

SITUATION BORROWING FROM BANK

Discounted note
dishonored

Accounts Receivable, XXX		
Cash		
Discounted customer note		

Discounting one's
own note

Cash		
Discount on Notes Payable		
Notes Payable		
Borrowed with a discount		

(Continued)

ADJUSTMENTS	SELLER	BUYER
Adjust interest	**20X1 Dec. 31** Interest Receivable / Interest Income / *Interest adj.*	**20X1 Dec. 31** Interest Expense / Interest Payable / *Interest adj.*
Note paid (no reversing entry was made)	**20X2 Feb. 1** Cash / Interest Receivable / Interest Income / Notes Receivable / *Received cash from note*	**20X2 Feb. 1** Interest Expense / Interest Payable / Notes Payable / Cash / *Paid cash for note*
Note paid (reversing entry was made)	**Feb. 1** Cash / Interest Income / Notes Receivable / *Received cash from note*	**Feb. 1** Interest Expense / Notes Payable / Cash / *Paid cash for note*
Recognizing interest from discount on Notes Payable	**Dec. 31** Interest Expense / Discount on Notes Payable / *Adjustment for interest*	

Calculate Maturity Value

2. Find the maturity value of the following:

    a. $6,000   6%   9 months

    b. $8,000   7%   70 days

Recording Notes for Buyer and Seller

3. For each of the following transactions for Frank Co. (the seller), journalize what the entry would be for the buyer.

    a.

Accounts Receivable, Bore Co.	7,000	
Sales		7,000
Sold on account		

    b.

Notes Receivable	7,000	
Accounts Receivable, Bore Co.		7,000
Transferred to note rec.		

    c.

Cash	7,140	
Notes Receivable		7,000
Interest Income		140

Discounting a Note

4. Pete Jones discounted a $9,000, 8 percent, 90-day note at Friend Bank. He recorded the following entry:

Cash	9,100	
Notes Receivable		9,000
Interest Income		100

How much interest did Pete Jones lose by discounting the note?

Four Steps in the Discounting Process

5. Blue Co. received a $1,000, 6 percent, 60-day note from Aluin Co. dated August 10. On August 30 Blue discounted the note at Reel Bank, which charged a discount rate of 8 percent. Calculate the following:

    a. Maturity value.

    b. Discount period.

    c. Bank discount.

    d. Proceeds.

Journal Entry for Discounting

6. Journalize the discounted note for Blue from Mini Exercise 5.

Defaulting

7. If Aluin defaults on the note from Mini Exercise 5, what would be the journal entry for Blue Co., assuming a $5 protest fee?

Discounting One's Own Note

8. Aster Co. discounts its own note at a bank. This $5,000 note results in the bank deducting $300 interest in advance. Draw a transactional analysis box for this situation.

Adjusting the Discount

9. If in Mini Exercise 8 the discount of $100 needs to be adjusted at year end, what would be the journalized adjusting entry?

Exercises

(The forms you need are on pages 495–496 of the *Study Guide and Working Papers*.)

15-1. Calculate the interest for the following:

Calculating interest.

   a. $17,000   7%   1 year

   b. $20,000   10%   7 months

   c. $ 9,000   12%   80 days

15-2. Determine the maturity date for each of the following without the use of tables:

Determining maturity date without tables.

Note Issued	Length of Time
a. January 17, 20X4	30 days
b. July 14, 20X4	90 days
c. May 31, 20X4	4 months
d. June 25, 20X4	75 days

15-3. Use the table in the text (p. 544) to prove your answers for Exercise 15-2.

Determining maturity date by tables.

15-4. On May 15, 20X4, Ralph Co. gave Blue Co. a 180-day, $9,000, 8 percent note. On July 21 Blue Co. discounted the note at 9 percent.

Discounting a note and journalizing entry for proceeds.

   a. Journalize the entry for Blue to record the proceeds.

   b. Record the entry for Blue if Ralph fails to pay at maturity.

15-5. Jamie Slater negotiated a bank loan for $30,000 for 120 days at a bank rate of 10 percent. Assuming the interest is deducted in advance, prepare the entry for Jamie to record the bank loan.

Discount on Notes Payable.

Group A Problems

(The forms you need are on pages 497–502 of the *Study Guide and Working Papers*.)

15A-1. Journalize the following entries for (1) the buyer and (2) the seller. Record all entries for the buyer first.

Journalizing Notes Receivable and Notes Payable along with note dishonored.

20X9

June	11	Lee Company sold $7,000 of merchandise on account to Rover Company.
July	11	Lee Company received a 90-day, $5,000, 8 percent note for a time extension of past due account of Rover Company.
Oct.	9	Collected the Rover Company note on the maturity date.
Oct.	9	Assume Rover Company defaulted on its July 11 note and record the dishonored note.
Oct.	15	Rover Company paid the note receivable that was dishonored on October 9 (no additional interest is charged).

Check Figure:
Oct. 9   Interest income and interest expense $100

15A-2. On May 1, 20X4, Apples Company received a $30,000, 90-day, 9 percent note from Fletcher Company dated May 1. On June 20, 20X4, Apples discounted the note at Run Bank at a discount rate of 10 percent.

Identifying steps in discounting a note along with journal entry.

   1. Calculate the following:

      a. Maturity value of the note.

      b. Number of days the bank will hold the note until maturity date.

      c. Bank discount.

      d. Proceeds.

   2. Journalize the entry to record the proceeds.

Check Figure:
Proceeds $30,334.17

15A-3. Journalize the following transactions for Joye Company:

20X1

June 18 Joye discounted its own $40,000, 90-day note at National Bank at 10 percent.

Sept. 16 Paid the amount due on the note of June 18. (Be sure to record interest expense from Discount on Notes Payable.)

Nov. 2 Joye discounted its own $20,000, 120-day note at National Bank at 11 percent.

Dec. 31 Record the adjusting entry for interest expense.

15A-4. Journalize the following transactions for Rochester Company:

> *Check Figure:*
> Nov. 2 Discount on Notes Payable $733.33

20XX

Apr. 18 Received $15,000, 80-day, 11 percent note from Mark Castle in payment of account past due.

May 9 Wrote off the Hal Balmer account as uncollectible for $600. (Rochester uses the Allowance method to record bad debts.)

July 7 Mark Castle paid Rochester the note in full.

Nov. 11 Gave Reech Company a $9,000, 30-day, 12 percent note as a time extension of account now past due.

Nov. 15 Hal Balmer paid Rochester amount previously written off on May 9.

Dec. 3 Discounted its own $5,000, 90-day note at Tree Bank at 10 percent.

Dec. 5 Received a $10,000, 60-day, 12 percent note dated December 5 from Beverly Fields in payment of account past due.

Dec. 11 Paid principal and interest due on note issued to Reech Company from November 11 note.

Dec. 16 Received a $20,000, 60-day, 11 percent note from Larry Company in payment of account past due.

Dec. 28 Discounted the Beverly Fields note to Realty Bank at 13 percent.

Dec. 31 Recorded adjusting entries as appropriate.

> Comprehensive Problem. Integration of Notes Receivable and Notes Payable with Allowance for Doubtful Accounts and discounting.

> *Check Figure:*
> Dec. 31 Interest expense $38.89

Group B Problems

(The forms you need are on pages 497–502 of the *Study Guide and Working Papers*.)

15B-1. Journalize the following entries for (1) the buyer and (2) the seller.

20X9

July 10 Lee Company sold $8,000 of merchandise on account to Connors Company.

Aug. 10 Lee Company received a 90-day, $6,000, 9 percent note for a time extension of past due account of Rover Company.

Nov. 8 Collected the Rover Company note on the maturity date.

Nov. 8 Assuming Rover Company defaulted on November 8, record the dishonored note.

Nov. 16 Rover Company paid the note receivable that was dishonored on November 8 (no additional interest is charged).

> Journalizing Notes Receivable and Notes Payable along with note dishonored.

> *Check Figure:*
> Nov. 8 Interest expense and interest income $135

15B-2. On June 2, 20X4, Apples Company received a $40,000, 90-day, 11 percent note from Fletcher Company dated June 2. On July 16, 20X4, Apples discounted the note at Run Bank at a discount rate of 12 percent.

1. Calculate the following:
   a. Maturity value of the note.
   b. Number of days the bank will hold the note until maturity date.
   c. Bank discount.
   d. Proceeds.
2. Journalize the entry to record the proceeds.

> Identifying steps in discounting a note along with journal entry.

> *Check Figure:*
> Proceeds $40,469.80

15B-3. As the bookkeeper of Joye Company, record in the general journal the following transactions:

> Discounting one's own note.

20X2

May	9	Joye discounted its own $25,000, 90-day note at National Bank at 10 percent.
Aug.	7	Paid the amount due on the note of May 9. (Be sure to record interest expense from Discount on Note Payable.)
Oct.	7	Joye discounted its own $18,000, 120-day note at National Bank at 11 percent.
Dec.	31	Record the adjusting entry for interest expense.

Check Figure:
Dec. 31 Interest expense
$467.50

15B-4. Record the following entries into the general journal of Rochester Company:

20XX

May	12	Received $13,000, 90-day, 9 percent note from Mark Castle in payment of account past due.
June	15	Wrote off the Hal Balmer account as uncollectible for $900 using the Allowance method.
Aug.	10	Mark Castle paid Rochester the note in full.
Nov.	2	Gave Reech Company a $20,000, 30-day, 8 percent note as a time extension of account now past due.
Nov.	18	Hal Balmer paid Rochester amount previously written off on June 15.
Dec.	2	Discounted its own $10,000, 90-day note at Tree Bank at 9 percent.
Dec.	2	Received a $6,000, 60-day, 11 percent note dated December 3 from Beverly Fields in payment of account past due.
Dec.	2	Paid principal and interest due on note issued to Reech Company from November 2 note.
Dec.	16	Received a $2,000, 60-day, 11 percent note from Larry Company in payment of account past due.
Dec.	28	Discounted the Beverly Fields note to Realty Bank at 12 percent.
Dec.	31	Recorded adjusting entries as appropriate.

Comprehensive Problem. Integration of Notes Receivable and Notes Payable with Allowance for Doubtful Accounts and discounting.

Check Figure:
Dec. 31 Interest income
$9.17

REAL-WORLD APPLICATIONS

15R-1.

Abby Scale, the bookkeeper of Roland Company, is having difficulty calculating the amount that is due Agent Company on March 19. Based on the following information, prepare a detailed calculation of the amount due Agent.

Roland issued Agent a $2,000, 60-day, 12 percent note dated December 19, 20X1. Roland was notified by Alvin Bank that the note had been discounted by Agent and that the note would be payable to Alvin Bank. On February 18 the bookkeeper of Roland became ill and the note wasn't paid. Alvin Bank notified Agent and charged them an additional $9 protest fee. On March 19 Abby decided to pay Agent the amount owed. Agent indicated they were charging the maturity value of the note, the protest fee, and interest on *both* for 30 days beyond maturity at 14 percent. Do you think these charges are fair? Make your recommendation in writing.

15R-2.

Moe Ring has left the following notes on your desk. As the new bookkeeper of Ryan Company you realize that no adjusting entries were made in 20X1.

Notes Receivable	
11/25/X1	$20,000
12%	150 days

Notes Payable	
12/16/X1	$33,600
15%	30 days

a. Please prepare the appropriate adjusting entries.

b. Moe would like to know whether reversing entries are needed. Prepare a set of T accounts to show what would result on the books in the year 20X2 when the notes are paid (1) if there are no reversing entries and (2) if reversing entries are made. Provide Moe with a written justification for the use of reversing entries.

YOU make the call

Critical Thinking/Ethical Case

15R-3.

Kevin Hoffaman works as a teller in Victory Bank. Yesterday he looked up confidential information concerning several friends. Kevin told his girlfriend all about the confidential information. Do you think Kevin acted appropriately? You make the call. Write down your recommendations to Kevin.

INTERNET EXERCISES

EX-1. [www.factors.net] Businesses who buy accounts receivable (thus, practicing discounting as presented in the chapter) are known as **factors.** At some time in your spending history you have probably been involved with a factor, either knowingly or unknowingly. For example, when you joined the health club and signed a note agreeing to pay monthly for the right to be a member, the health club probably sold your note to a factor. From this website, determine why it is that some companies wish to sell their accounts receivable.

EX-2. [www.gmacbc.com] When you approach this website, click on "About Us" and read about how GMAC works with businesses to provide them funding via discounting and purchasing "paper" from them. This site explains some of the considerations that a business should look at when attempting to obtain financing in this market. Apply what this chapter taught you about discounting. Navigate through the site and summarize how GMAC assists businesses with financing.

CONTINUING PROBLEM

Several banks have offered loans to the Eldorado Computer Center for their expansion, however, Freedman wants to weigh each option to determine the best financial situation for the company. Currently the Eldorado Computer Center is trying to collect from its customers to strengthen the cash flow of the business.

Assignment

(See p. 507 in your *Study Guide and Working Papers.*)

Using the information provided by each bank, determine the due date and interest amount for each.

Bank of America	A 90-day note dated April 15 for $20,000 at a 6% interest rate
Bank One	A 120-day note dated April 10 for $40,000 at a 5% interest rate
Capital One Bank	A 75-day note dated April 5 for $30,000 at a 4% interest rate

Inventory, Plant Assets, and Partnerships

CHAPTER 16

Accounting for Merchandise Inventory

"They can put a man on the moon but they can't get my children a few simple toys for Christmas," moaned Amanda Lichfield, an irate New Jersey mom who spent weeks looking for a Nintendo Game Boy and an Amazing Ally interactive doll. Every Christmas there are a few toys that gets so much pre-holiday hype that stores cannot keep them in stock. Desperate parents end up scouring the Internet to see if the toys are available at online auctions, or they pay ridiculously high prices from the now ubiquitous toy scalpers.

While it's no comfort to parents, inventory management, is, quite frankly, a headache for merchandisers in seasonal businesses, like the toy industry. During Christmas season 1999, its first year of selling toys online, Amazon.com was extremely afraid of alienating customers with out of stock toys. As a result, the company bought far too much inventory and ended up after Christmas with a 50-week supply of Kermit the Frog telephones and a $39 million charge against earnings for unsold goods.

This Christmas, Amazon doesn't want to get caught holding the bag — of Santa's unsold goods, that is — so the company has made what most analysts consider a very smart move. Amazon has teamed up with Toysrus.com, the Internet operation of Toys "Я" Us Inc. Under this agreement, the burden of purchasing and owning most of Amazon's toy inventory now lies with Toysrus.com, a company that has much more experience in dealing with the hair-raising supply and demand crises of Christmas inventories. Amazon will then handle toy sales, the toy Web site and order fulfillment.

How will Toysrus.com account for inventory? The **periodic method,** discussed in Chapter 12, would only give them a portrait of inventory at the end of each accounting period. They will use the **perpetual method,** detailed in this chapter, to update the inventory account as items are sold. In this chapter you'll not only learn how to account for inventory using the perpetual method, but you'll also learn how to track the value of inventory. Each method discussed will give you a different dollar value for the cost of inventory sold and the amount of inventory still on hand—particularly important if you are left with thousands of Kermit the Frog telephones! Then you will learn how to decide which method is the best for your type of business.

Lisa Bannon and Joseph Pereira, "E-Business: Toy Wars II: Holiday Cyber Battle Begins – Two Big Online Toy Sellers Fight Over Delivery Speed and Exclusive Products," *Wall Street Journal,* September 25, 2000, p. B1. Nick Wingfield, "Toy Wars II: Holiday Cyber Battle Begins — Amazon Vows to Avoid Mess of 1999 Christmas Rush; Too Many Kermit Phones," *Wall Street Journal,* September 25, 2000, p. B1. Jane Martinson, "e-finance: Amazon joins Toys Я Us online: Strategy aims to unite old and new economy strengths," *The Guardian,* August 11, 2000, p. 1.25. Joseph Pereira, "Where Have Game boy and Amazing Ally Gone?" *Wall Street Journal,* December 22, 1999, p. B, 1:2.

LEARNING OBJECTIVES

▼ Understanding and journalizing transactions using the perpetual inventory system and explaining the difference between perpetual and periodic inventory systems. (p. 575)

▼ Maintaining a subsidiary ledger for inventory. (p. 580)

▼ Understanding periodic methods of determining the value of the ending inventory. (p. 583)

▼ Estimating ending inventory using the retail method and gross profit method and understanding how the ending inventory amount affects financial reports. (p. 590)

Have you ever thought of the perfect present for someone at Christmas time only to find that everyone else in the world had the same idea, and the stores were out of stock? In recent years such gifts have included Elmo, Barney, Pokemon, Beanie Babies, home computers, and various video games. Having the right quantities of inventory is crucial to a retail business. It's bad to run out of stock and miss out on sales revenue, especially during the holidays, but it's also harmful to have too much of an item. A store must consider the cost of carrying inventory, and it must also worry about product obsolescence or the possibility of a fad running its course before all the products are sold. A good example is your local computer store. Models change so quickly that an inventory of old models could mean losing sales to competitors.

In Chapter 12 we discussed the periodic inventory system. A major weakness of the periodic system is that inventory is checked and counted only at the beginning and end of the accounting period and therefore managers do not know the actual amount of inventory on hand nor the actual cost of goods sold until the end of the accounting period. Today, with computers in so many businesses, the trend is toward perpetual inventory. Managers need to have *current* information about how much of their capital is tied up in inventory, and they need to have *current* information about the profitability of their sales of merchandise. The *perpetual* system of accounting for merchandise inventory provides this information on a transaction-by-transaction basis. Managers can know the balance of inventory and the profitability of sales as soon as each sale is completed. The perpetual system requires extra time and effort to gain these benefits, but, fortunately, computers can handle much of the detail. In this chapter we look at how the perpetual inventory system can be used in a merchandising business. We also compare the perpetual system to the periodic system.

In the last part of the chapter we discuss how to assign costs to inventory using the *periodic inventory system,* because many businesses with small inventories still use this system.

LEARNING UNIT 16-1

PERPETUAL INVENTORY SYSTEM

In the **perpetual inventory system*** we have two key accounts: Merchandise Inventory and Cost of Goods Sold.

The Merchandise Inventory account is an asset account that will reveal the current balance of inventory at all times (perpetually). This account is the same that was used in the previous discussion of the periodic inventory system, but in the periodic system the balance of the Merchandise Inventory was correct *only* at the end of each accounting period. In the perpetual system entries will be recorded to the Merchandise Inventory account each time the store purchases new merchandise and each time the store sells merchandise to a customer.

The other key account is the Cost of Goods Sold account. As merchandise is sold to customers, an entry will be recorded that will remove the cost of the merchandise from the Merchandise Inventory account and transfer that cost to the Cost of Goods Sold account. Thus the Merchandise Inventory account will show the correct cost for the inventory on hand, and the Cost of Goods Sold account will show the cumulative total cost of all merchandise that has been sold to customers during the accounting period.

With the perpetual inventory system the key accounts, Merchandise Inventory and Cost of Goods Sold, will always provide current information to managers about their investment in inventory and the cost of the merchandise sold to customers.

Accounts Affected	Category	↑ ↓	Rules
Merchandise Inventory	**Asset**	↑	**Dr.**
Cost of Goods Sold	**Cost of Goods Sold**	↑	**Cr.**

You have been hired to work for a software retail business called Painless Bytes. A best seller for Painless Bytes is an accounting software package called A-I-B, (<u>A</u>lways <u>I</u>n <u>B</u>alance). Let's record some transactions relating to buying and selling A-I-B software. Because most businesses buy their merchandise inventory on account, we use Accounts Payable in the transactions.

20XX
June   2   Purchased 10 packages of A-I-B software at a cost $25 per package for a total of $250.

---

*Appendix on Perpetual Inventory was introduced in Chapter 9.

	June	2	Merchandise Inventory			2 5 0 00		
			Accounts Payable				2 5 0 00	
			To record the purchase of inventory					

Note that the asset account, Merchandise Inventory, has been increased by the cost of the new merchandise we have purchased. Now let's look at a sales transaction.

20XX
June 3 Sold three software packages for cash to a customer at $50 each for a total of $150.

	June	3	Cash			1 5 0 00		
			Sales Revenue				1 5 0 00	
			To record sale of 3 packages of A-I-B					
	June	3	Cost of Goods Sold			7 5 00		
			Merchandise Inventory				7 5 00	
			To record the cost of goods sold					

Note that in the perpetual inventory system we record both the retail value of the sale (three units at $50) in the Sales Revenue account and the cost of the sale (three units at $25) in the Cost of Goods Sold account with two related transactions. What if the customer returns one of the packages? Assuming that the returned package is still in new condition, here is what we would record:

20XX
June 5 Allowed the customer to return one package for a cash refund, $50.

	June	5	Sales Returns and Allowances			5 0 00		
			Cash				5 0 00	
			To record the return of one					
			package A-I-B					

	June	5	Merchandise Inventory			2 5 00		
			Cost of Goods Sold				2 5 00	
			To record return of one package					
			A-I-B at cost					

In this transaction we must record the reduction in revenue of $50 and we must also record that we now have returned one package of software to our inventory by adding the $25 cost of that unit back to the Merchandise Inventory account.

Once in a while a business may have to return some inventory that came in damaged or for some other reason. Painless Bytes would prepare a debit memo. Let's see how this transaction is handled in a perpetual inventory system.

20XX

June   6   Returned one damaged A-I-B software package from the June 2 purchase.

June	6	Accounts Payable		2 5 00				
		Merchandise Inventory			2 5 00			
		To record return of damaged A-I-B						
		package to vendor						

This transaction reduced what is owed the vendor by $25, the cost of the package, and we reduced the Asset account – Merchandise Inventory – because we returned the item to the vendor. *Note:* We do not use a Purchases Returns and Allowances account when we are recording in a perpetual inventory system. The Asset account Merchandise Inventory is directly reduced by the amount we returned to our vendor.

Now let's look at how these transactions relate to the accounts and to the financial statements. In the T accounts that follow you can see that the Merchandise Inventory account shows the correct balance for the seven software packages remaining in inventory and that the Cost of Goods Sold account shows the correct amount for the cost of the two software packages actually sold. Asset accounts such as Merchandise Inventory are shown on the Balance Sheet, and the Sales and Cost of Goods Sold accounts appear on the Income Statement. Remember that we calculate Gross Profit when we subtract Cost of Goods Sold from Sales. In fact, we know the gross profit on each sale just as soon as the sale is completed.

GENERAL LEDGER ACCOUNTS

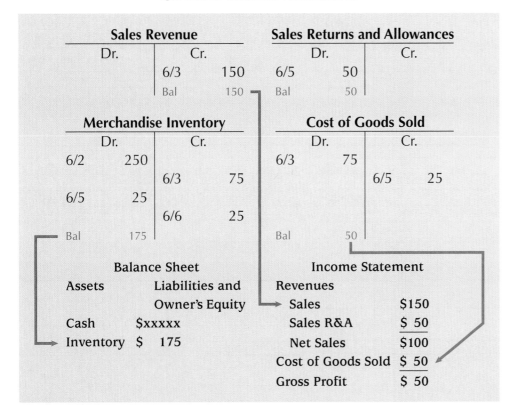

COMPARISON OF THE PERPETUAL AND PERIODIC INVENTORY SYSTEMS

In our discussion of the perpetual inventory system, the primary benefit from this system is that the value of merchandise inventory is known after every purchase and sale. The cost of goods sold is known after every sale. The merchandise inventory account becomes an active account. The Cost of Goods Sold is now an account in the general ledger rather than just an item on the Income Statement. The *periodic inventory system* does not give accurate or up-to-date information about merchandise inventory or cost of goods sold until after an ending inventory is taken.

The taking of a physical inventory at least once a year is not eliminated by a business that uses the perpetual inventory system. An inventory must be taken at least once a year to detect any inventory recording errors, shoplifting, or damages to the merchandise inventory.

The comparisons of recording of transactions in the two systems are revealed in the chart.

COMPARISON OF PERPETUAL AND PERIODIC SYSTEMS

Transaction	Perpetual System		Periodic System	
(A) Sold merchandise that cost $8,000 on account for $20,000	Acc. Receiv.	20 0 0 00	Acc. Receiv.	20 0 0 00
	Sales		20 0 0 00	Sales		20 0 0 00
	Cost of Goods Sold	8 0 0 00		
	Merch. Inventory		8 0 0 00		
(B) Purchased $900 of merchandise on account	Merch. Inventory	9 0 0 00	Purchases	9 0 0 00
	Acc. Payable		9 0 0 00	Acc. Payable		9 0 0 00
(C) Paid $50 freight charges.	Merch. Inventory	5 0 00	Freight-In	5 0 00
	Cash		5 0 00	Cash		5 0 00
(D) Customer returned $200 of merchandise. Cost of merchandise was $100	Sales Ret. & Allow.	2 0 0 00	Sales Ret. & Allow.	2 0 0 00
	Accounts Receiv.		2 0 0 00	Accts. Receiv.		2 0 0 00
	Merchandise Inv.	1 0 0 00		
	Cost of Goods Sold		1 0 0 00		
(E) Returned $400 of merchandise previously bought on account due to defects.	Acc. Payable	4 0 0 00	Acc. Payable	4 0 0 00
	Merch. Inv.		4 0 0 00	Pur. Ret. and Allow		4 0 0 00

The chart shows that in a perpetual inventory system, the Purchases, Purchases Returns and Allowances, and Freight accounts *do not* exist. Inventory and Cost of Goods Sold are updated immediately.

LEARNING UNIT 16-1 REVIEW

AT THIS POINT you should be able to

▼ Explain the perpetual inventory system. (p. 575)
▼ Journalize transactions for a perpetual inventory system. (p. 576)
▼ Explain the difference between the perpetual and periodic inventory systems. (p. 578)

SELF-REVIEW QUIZ 16-1

(The blank forms you need are on page 2 of the *Study Guide and Working Papers*.)

Journalize the following transactions for a firm that uses a perpetual inventory system:

a. Bought $200 of merchandise on account.

b. Sold $100 of merchandise on account that cost $50.

c. Allowed a customer to return for cash $30 worth of inventory. Our cost was $15.

d. We got permission from our vendor to return $30 worth of inventory.

Solutions to Self-Review Quiz 16-1

a.

Merchandise Inventory	2 0 0 00	
Accounts Payable		2 0 0 00

b.

Accounts Receivable	1 0 0 00	
Sales		1 0 0 00

Cost of Goods Sold	5 0 00	
Merchandise Inventory		5 0 00

c.

Sales Returns and Allowances	3 0 00	
Cash		3 0 00

Merchandise Inventory	1 5 00	
Cost of Goods Sold		1 5 00

d.

Accounts Payable	3 0 00	
Merchandise Inventory		3 0 00

Suppose the business Painless Bytes sells many different kinds of software packages. How can Painless Bytes keep track of the cost and balances of a variety of inventory items? How do stores such as Wal-Mart keep track of the thousands of items that they keep in inventory? The answer is found in the use of a subsidiary ledger for inventory and the use of computers to maintain the subsidiary ledger.

Do you recall from Chapters 9 and 10 that when we had a large number of account receivable or account payable accounts, we used subsidiary ledgers to maintain the details for each customer or vendor? This same accounting procedure can be used to keep track of inventory. Our Merchandise Inventory account becomes a control account keeping track of the total balance of inventory, while the details are kept in separate inventory records in a subsidiary ledger for inventory. Let's first show our existing inventory account with a subsidiary ledger and with the transactions from Learning Unit 16-1. On the left is our inventory account in T form, and on the right is an inventory record form for our A-I-B product.

General Ledger Account

Merchandise Inventory

Dr.		Cr.	
6/2	250		
		6/3	75
6/5	25		
		6/6	25
Bal	175		

Subsidiary Ledger Records

A-I-B Software

Date	Purchased	Sold	Balance
6/2	10 @ $25		$250
6/3		3 @ $25	$175
6/5		(1) @ $25	$200
6/6	(1) @ $25		$175

Notice that the inventory record form on the right contains the detail about the quantity and per unit cost for the transactions posted to the general ledger account on the left. Notice too that the return of 6/5 is recorded in the inventory record as a negative sale and that the ending balances agree. The debit memo transaction of 6/6 is entered as a negative purchase and again the ending balances agree. Try using your calculator to see if you can also calculate the running balance shown in the inventory record.

In this next transaction Painless Bytes adds R&C, (Rows and Columns), a spreadsheet software package, to the line of software it sells.

June   6   Purchased 7 packages of R&C software on account at a cost $225 per package and a total of $1,575.

	June	6	Merchandise Inventory			1	5	7	5	00					
			Accounts Payable								1	5	7	5	00
			To record the purchase of inventory												

Note that the Merchandise Inventory account has again been increased by the cost of the new merchandise we have purchased. Because we now have two products in inventory, our inventory ledger will have a new inventory record form for the R&C product. Check out the way our inventory records relate to the Merchandise Inventory account.

General Ledger Account

Merchandise Inventory

Dr.		Cr.	
6/2	250		
		6/3	75
6/5	25		
6/6	1,575	6/6	25
Bal	1,750		

Subsidiary Ledger Records

Product #1: A-I-B Software

Date	Purchased	Sold	Balance
6/2	10 @ $25		$ 250
6/3		3 @ $25	$ 175
6/5		(1) @ $25	$ 200
6/6	(1) @ $25		$ 175

Product #2: R&C Software

Date	Purchased	Sold	Balance
6/6	7 @ $225		$1,575

Does the total of the balances of the two inventory records agree with the Merchandise Inventory account?

Now let's try another sales transaction.

20XX

June   9   Sold two A-I-B packages at $50 each and three R&C packages at $295 each for a total of $985

June	9	Cash		9 8 5 00			
		Sales Revenue			9 8 5 00	
		Sold 2 A-I-B and 3 R&C				
June	3	Cost of Goods Sold		7 2 5 00		
		Merchandise Inventory			7 2 5 00	
		To record the cost of goods sold				

Again, we record both the total sales price of the transaction and the cost of the merchandise sold. Do you know how we arrived at the cost of goods sold figure of $725? A quick look at the inventory record forms will show us how we know the cost of goods sold.

General Ledger Account

Merchandise Inventory

Dr.		Cr.	
6/2	250		
		6/3	75
6/4	25		
6/6	1,575	6/6	25
		6/9	725
Bal	1,025		

Subsidiary Ledger Records

Product #1: A-I-B Software

Date	Purchased	Sold	Balance
6/2	10 @ $25		$ 250
6/3		3 @ $25	$ 175
6/4	(1) @ $25		$ 200
6/5	(1) @ $25		$ 175
6/6		2 @ $25	$ 125

Product #2: R&C Software

Date	Purchased	Sold	Balance
6/6	7 @ $225		$1,575
6/9		3 @ $225	$ 900

We obtained the cost of goods sold total when we posted the quantities sold to each of the inventory records. Two units of A-I-B at $25 each plus three units of R&C at $225 each equals a total cost of $725. Notice that the ending balances of the two products will total to the same amount as the balance shown in the Merchandise Inventory account.

In summary a business with a variety of products in inventory will use an inventory subsidiary ledger with an individual record for each different product. These records will keep the detail about the quantity and cost of inventory on hand and will allow us to calculate the cost of goods sold on each sale.

FIGURE 16-1. An Inventory Record

				Inventory Control					

Item VX113

Description Digital Clock

Location Storeroom 1

Maximum 22

Reorder Level 12

Reorder Quantity 10

	Received				Sold			Balance	
Date	Units	Cost per Unit	Total	Units	Cost per Unit	Total	Units	Cost per Unit	Total
20XX Jan. 1	Balance		FWD				14	50	$ 700
12				2	50	100	12	50	600
19	10	60	600				{12	50	
							{10	60	1,200
25				8	50	400	{ 4	50	
							{10	60	800

Computerized accounting systems can handle a perpetual inventory system with ease. You have no doubt seen such systems in operation when the clerk at your local store used a laser scanner or a bar code to enter your purchases into the cash register. The transaction put into the cash register will record the sale and update the cost of goods sold and inventory. Computerized systems keep track of inventory by many different methods. When figuring the value of the inventory, they could use average cost; first in, first out (FIFO); or last in, first out (LIFO). The example in Figure 16-1 uses the FIFO method in determining the cost of the merchandise for each sale.

LEARNING UNIT 16-2 REVIEW

AT THIS POINT you should be able to

▼ Understand how a subsidiary ledger for inventory works with a controlling account for inventory. (p. 581)
▼ Journalize and post transactions that affect the general ledger Merchandise Inventory account as well as the individual inventory records in the Merchandise Inventory Subsidiary Ledger. (p. 581)

SELF-REVIEW QUIZ 16-2

(The forms you need are on page 3 of the *Study Guide and Working Papers*.)

Journalize and post the following transactions for a firm that uses a subsidiary ledger for Merchandise Inventory. Only post to the accounts that you have.

a. Bought 3 X-Products at $3 each on account.

b. Sold one of the X-Products we purchased above for cash, $6.

c. Bought 4 more X-Products at $3 and 5 Z-Products at $10 on account.

d. Sold for cash 2 more X-Products at $6 each and 3 Z-Products at $20 each.

Solutions to Self-Review Quiz 16-2

a.

Merchandise Inventory	114 ✔		9 00					
Accounts Payable					9 00			

b.

Cash			6 00					
Sales					6 00			
Cost of Goods Sold			3 00					
Merchandise Inventory	114 ✔				3 00			

c.

Merchandise Inventory	114 ✔		6 2 00					
Accounts Payable					6 2 00			

d.

Cash			7 2 00					
Sales					7 2 00			
Cost of Goods Sold			3 6 00					
Merchandise Inventory	114 ✔				3 6 00			

General Ledger Account

Merchandise Inventory

Dr.		Cr.	
a.	9	b.	3
c.	62	d.	36
Bal.	32		

Subsidiary Ledger Records

Product #1:   X Product

Date	Purchased	Sold	Balance
a.	3 @ $3		9
b.		1 @ $3	6
c.	4 @ $3		18
d.		2 @ $3	12

Product #2:   Z Product

Date	Purchased	Sold	Balance
c.	5 @ $10		50
d.		3 @ $10	20

LEARNING UNIT 16-3

METHODS OF DETERMINING THE VALUE OF THE ENDING INVENTORY WHEN USING THE PERIODIC INVENTORY SYSTEM

For a small business or any business using the **periodic inventory system,** the method used to assign costs to ending inventory will have a direct effect on the company's cost of goods sold and gross profit. Note in the table how the ending inventory does in fact have an effect on the Gross Profit.

	Situation A		Situation B		Situation C		Situation D	
Net Sales		$50,000		$50,000		$50,000		$50,000
Beginning Inventory	$ 4,000		$ 4,000		$ 4,000		$ 4,000	
Net Purchases	20,000		20,000		20,000		20,000	
Cost of Goods Available for Sale	24,000		24,000		24,000		24,000	
Ending Inventory	5,000		6,000		7,000		8,000	
Cost of Goods Sold		19,000		18,000		17,000		16,000
Gross Profit		$31,000		$32,000		$33,000		$34,000

If all inventory brought into a store had the same cost, it would be simple to calculate the ending inventory, and we would not have to have this discussion. Unfortunately, things are not that easy; often the very same products are purchased and brought into the store at different costs during the same accounting period. Over the years, four generally accepted methods have been developed to assign a cost to ending inventory. The reason these methods are needed is that often inventory is brought in at different times. The result is that the inventory is made up of many past purchases at *different* prices. Think of the inventory methods as a way of tracing costs. These methods are (1) specific invoice; (2) first in, first out; (3) last in, first out; and (4) weighted average. Each is based on an assumed flow of costs, not on the actual physical movement of goods sold in a store.

We now look at how the four inventory cost assumptions are applied within the periodic inventory system. The following situation occurred at Jones Hardware. Jones Hardware sells rakes. The job before us is to come up with the value of the ending inventory and cost of goods sold using the four methods we have listed. The following table provides us with all the information needed to accomplish our task.

Goods Available for Sale

		Units	Cost	Total
January 1	Beginning Inventory	10	@ $10 =	$100
March 15	Purchases	9	@ 12 =	108
August 18	Purchases	20	@ 13 =	260
November 15	Purchases	5	@ 15 =	75
		44		$543

Actual inventory on December 31 revealed that 12 rakes remained in stock.

SPECIFIC INVOICE METHOD

In the **specific invoice method** the cost of ending inventory is assigned by identifying each item in that inventory by a specific purchase price and invoice number, and maybe even by serial number.

For our example of this method, let's assume that Jones Hardware knew that six of the rakes not sold were from the March 15 invoice and the other six were from the August 18 purchase. Thus $150 was assigned as the actual cost of ending inventory. If the total cost of goods available for sale is $543 and we subtract the actual cost of ending inventory ($150), this method provides a figure of $393 for cost of goods sold.

SPECIFIC INVOICE METHOD

	Goods Available for Sale			Calculating Cost of Ending Inventory		
	Units	Cost	Total	Units	Cost	Total
January 1 Beg. Inventory	10	@ $10 =	$100			
March 15 Purchased	9	@ 12 =	108	6	@ $12	$ 72
August 18 Purchased	20	@ 13 =	260	6	@ 13	78
November 15 Purchased	5	@ 15 =	75			
	44		$543	12		$150

Cost of Goods Available for Sale → $543
Less: Cost of Ending Inventory 150 ←
= Cost of Goods Sold $393

Let's look at the pros and cons of this method.

SPECIFIC INVOICE METHOD: A REFERENCE GUIDE

Pros	Cons
1. Simple to use if company has small amount of high-cost goods such as autos, jewels, boats, or antiques.	1. Difficult to use for goods with large unit volume and small unit prices such as nails at a hardware store or packages of toothpaste at a drug store.
2. Flow of goods and flow of cost are the same.	2. Difficult to use for decision-making purposes; ordinarily an impractical approach because companies usually deal with high-cost unique items.
3. Costs are matched with the sales they helped to produce.	

FIRST IN, FIRST OUT METHOD (FIFO)

In the **FIFO method,** we assume that the oldest goods are sold first. Therefore, the items in the ending inventory will be valued at the costs shown on the most recent invoices.

FIFO METHOD

	Goods Available for Sale			Calculating Cost of Ending Inventory		
	Units	Cost	Total	Units	Cost	Total
January 1 Beg. Inventory	10	@ $10 =	$100			
March 15 Purchased	9	@ 12 =	108			
August 18 Purchased	20	@ 13 =	260	7	@ $13 =	$ 91
November 15 Purchased	5	@ 15 =	75	5	@ 15 =	75
	44		$543	12		$166

Cost of Goods Available for Sale → $543
Less: Cost of Ending Inventory 166 ←
= Cost of Goods Sold $377

In our Jones Hardware example the ending inventory of 12 rakes on hand is assigned a cost from the last two purchase invoices of rakes (purchases made on November 15 and part of the purchases made on August 18), totaling $166. Think of the inventory as being taken from the bottom layer first, then the next one up. If our ending inventory is valued at $166, our cost of goods sold must be $377.

The following are the pros and cons of this method.

FIFO METHOD: A REFERENCE GUIDE

Pros	Cons
1. The cost flow tends to follow the physical flow; most businesses try to sell the old goods first (perishables such as fruit or vegetables). 2. The figure for ending inventory is made up of current costs on the balance sheet (because inventory left over is assumed to be from goods last brought into the store).	1. During periods of inflation this method will produce higher income on the income statement and thus more taxes to be paid (discussed later in the chapter.) 2. Recent costs are not matched with recent sales, because we assume *old* goods are sold first.

LAST IN, FIRST OUT METHOD (LIFO)

Under the **LIFO method,** it is assumed that the goods *most recently acquired* are sold first. Therefore, the items in the ending inventory will be valued at the invoice costs shown from the top of the list down.

For Jones Hardware this assumption means that the 12 rakes not sold were assigned costs from the 10 listed in beginning inventory and 2 from the March 15 invoice. The ending inventory totals $124 and the cost of goods sold would be $419.

LIFO METHOD

	Goods Available for Sale			Calculating Cost of Ending Inventory		
	Units	Cost	Total	Units	Cost	Total
January 1 Beg. Inventory	10 @	$10 =	$100	10 @	$10 =	$100
March 15 Purchased	9 @	12 =	108	2 @	12 =	24
August 18 Purchased	20 @	13 =	260			
November 15 Purchased	5 @	15 =	75			
	44		$543	12		$124

Cost of Goods Available for Sale $543
Less: Cost of Ending Inventory 124
= Cost of Goods Sold $419

The pros and cons of this method are as follows.

WEIGHTED-AVERAGE METHOD

The **weighted-average method** calculates an average unit cost by dividing the *total cost* of goods available for sale by the *total units* of goods available for sale. In this example the total cost of goods available for sale was $543, and the total units available for sale was 44. Taking the $543 and dividing that number by the 44 total units for the period gives a $12.34 weighted average per unit.

In this illustration Jones Hardware assumes that the 12 units left on hand are *average* units and therefore assigns an *average* cost figure of $12.34 to each of the 12 rakes left in inventory. Thus we have a fair approximation of the cost of the ending inventory at $148.08 and of the amount of cost of goods sold, $394.92.

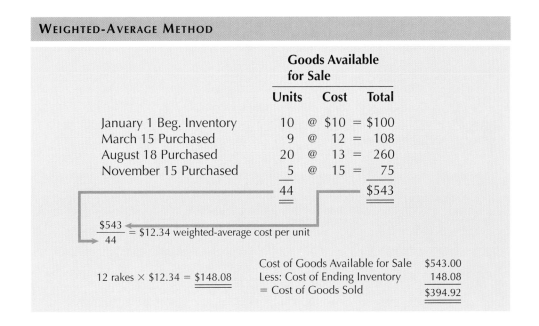

Weighted-Average Method

	Goods Available for Sale		
	Units	Cost	Total
January 1 Beg. Inventory	10 @	$10 =	$100
March 15 Purchased	9 @	12 =	108
August 18 Purchased	20 @	13 =	260
November 15 Purchased	5 @	15 =	75
	44		$543

$$\frac{\$543}{44} = \$12.34 \text{ weighted-average cost per unit}$$

12 rakes × $12.34 = $148.08

Cost of Goods Available for Sale	$543.00
Less: Cost of Ending Inventory	148.08
= Cost of Goods Sold	$394.92

The pros and cons of this method are as follows:

WEIGHTED-AVERAGE METHOD: A REFERENCE GUIDE	
Pros	**Cons**
1. Weighted-average takes into account the number of units purchased at each amount, not a simple average cost. Good for products sold in large volume, such as grains and fuels. 2. Accountant assigns an equal unit cost to each unit of inventory; thus when the income statement is prepared, net income will not fluctuate as much as with other methods.	1. Current prices have no more significance than prices of goods bought months earlier. 2. Compared with other methods, the most recent costs are *not* matched with current sales. This fact is important in financial reporting so as to provide an accurate picture of the company. 3. Cost of ending inventory is not as up to date as it could be using another method.

Remember that all four methods are acceptable accounting procedures. Management needs to select the method best suited to its business and be consistent in the application of that method.

WHEN CAN AN INVENTORY METHOD BE CHANGED

In accounting there is a principle of **consistency,** which means that once a business selects a particular accounting method, it should follow it consistently from one year to the next without switching to another method. In the previous part of this chapter we saw four methods of inventory valuations causing four different results for a business in terms of cost of goods sold and, ultimately, net income. Therefore, if a company kept switching from LIFO to FIFO each year, significant changes would result in the profit it reported. The financial reports would become undependable. Keeping with the same method, readers of the financial reports can make meaningful comparisons of the cost of ending inventory, cost of goods sold, and so forth from year to year.

The principle of consistency doesn't mean that a company can *never* change from one method of inventory valuation to another. If a change is decided upon, however, the company should fully disclose the change, the effects of the change on profit and inventory valuation, and the justification for change in a footnote on the financial report. This principle is called the **full disclosure principle** in accounting.

ITEMS THAT SHOULD BE INCLUDED IN THE COST OF INVENTORY
Goods in Transit

On the date inventory is taken, goods in transit should be added to inventory if the ownership of the inventory has been transferred to the buyer. For example, if the merchandise was purchased *F.O.B. shipping point,* the buyer becomes the owner of the merchandise when the merchandise is placed on the carrier at the shipping point. On the other hand, if the buyer purchases the merchandise *F.O.B. destination,* the seller has ownership of the merchandise until the merchandise reaches the destination, and it should not be included in the cost of the buyer's inventory.

Merchandise on Consignment

Consignment means that a business (the **consignor**) is selling its merchandise through an agent (the **consignee**) who doesn't own the merchandise but who has possession of it. Consigned merchandise belongs to the consignor and should not be included in the consignee's inventory cost.

Damaged or Obsolete Merchandise

If the merchandise is not saleable, it should *not* be added to the cost of the inventory. For merchandise that is saleable but at a lower cost, the value of that inventory should be estimated at a conservative figure and added to the cost of the inventory.

LEARNING UNIT 16-3 REVIEW

AT THIS POINT you should be able to

▼ Calculate cost of ending inventory and cost of goods sold by specific invoice: first in, first out; last in, first out; and weighted-average method. (p. 585)
▼ Explain the pros and cons of each method used to calculate cost of ending inventory and cost of goods sold. (p. 585)
▼ Explain the principles of consistency and full disclosure. (p. 588)
▼ Explain how merchandise in transit, merchandise on consignment, and damaged or obsolete merchandise are counted in calculating inventory. (p. 588)

SELF-REVIEW QUIZ 16-3

(The forms you need are on page 4 of the *Study Guide and Working Papers*.)

1. From the information given below, calculate the cost of inventory as well as the cost of goods sold, using the (a) specific invoice, (b) weighted-average, (c) first in, first out, and (d) last in, first out methods.

	Goods Available for Sale			Additional Fact: Inventory Not Sold
	Units	Cost	Total	
January 1 Beg. Inventory	40 @	$ 8 =	$ 320	40 from January 1
April 1 Purchased	20 @	9 =	180	
May 1 Purchased	20 @	10 =	200	4 from May 1
October 1 Purchased	20 @	12 =	240	4 from October 1
December 1 Purchased	20 @	13 =	260	
	120		$1,200	

2. Respond true or false to the following:
   a. It is possible for a company to change from LIFO to FIFO if the company follows specific guidelines.
   b. Goods in transit (shipped F.O.B. shipping point) will not be included as part of the inventory for the purchaser.

c. Damaged goods are always added to the cost of inventory.

Solutions to Self-Review Quiz 16-3

1. a. Total cost of goods available for sale $1,200
      Less ending inventory based on specific invoices:
      40 units from Jan. 1 purchased at $8 $320
       4 units from May 1 purchased at $10   40
       4 units from Oct. 1 purchased at $12   48
      48 units in ending inventory   408
      Cost of goods sold $ 792

   b. $1,200 ÷ 120 units = $10 weighted-average cost per unit.
      Total cost of goods available for sale $1,200
      Less ending inventory priced at weighted-
        average basis: 48 units at $10.00   480
      Cost of goods sold $ 720

   c. Total cost of goods available for sale $1,200
      Less ending inventory priced on FIFO:
      20 units from Dec. 1 at $13 $260
      20 units from Oct. 1 at $12   240
       8 units from May 1 at $10   80
      48 units in ending inventory   580
      Cost of goods sold $ 620

   d. Total cost of goods available for sale $1,200
      Less ending inventory priced on LIFO:
      40 units from Jan. 1 at $8 $320
       8 units from April 1 purchased at $9   72
      48 units in ending inventory   392
      Cost of goods sold $ 808

2. a. True   b. False   c. False

LEARNING UNIT 16-4   ESTIMATING ENDING INVENTORY

The actual taking of a physical inventory is time-consuming and expensive. Because of the time and expense involved, most businesses take a physical inventory only once a year. For the business using the periodic inventory system, the need to have an inventory cost figure more often may become necessary. That is especially true when a business makes interim financial reports. This business may find that estimating the inventory rather than taking a physical inventory is accurate enough. Another reason to estimate the ending inventory is in case of a fire when the inventory may be destroyed. The business would need an inventory cost figure when it submits a claim of loss to the insurance company.

Two common and recognized ways to estimate ending inventory are the **retail method** and the **gross profit method.**

RETAIL METHOD

To use the retail method, a business must have the following information available:

Time to Take Stock

Not again!" moaned Sally. "Didn't we just take an inventory of the stockroom last month?

My sister works at Wal-Mart, and they only take inventory once a year!"

"Yes, we did. And now we're doing it again," said Fred patiently. "We have a very different business than Wal-Mart. We have to make sure that we get enough cream cheese and milk, but not too much, or it will spoil. And I don't want to run out of Coffee Coolatta™ mix again. That special rush shipping cost extra."

"I'm selling lots of Coolatta, especially the hazelnut," said Sally. "It's my favorite, too. We can't run out of it!" With that, she sped to the stockroom and started work on the inventory.

The popularity of the new Coffee Coolatta™ had taken Dunkin' Donuts by surprise. The test marketing in 1996 had been successful, but the rollout had surpassed all expectations. Shop owners reported that their regular morning coffee and donut customers were returning in the afternoon for a Coolatta, and often another donut. Fears that the Coolatta would just replace hot coffee sales were unfounded. Instead, Coolatta sales accounted for 30 percent of all coffee sales in just six months. Hot coffee sales were unaffected.

The necessity of managing physical inventory is clear in a business that sells prepared food and drinks. In terms of physical flow, perishable inventory must be FIFO; the first inventory in is the first used, so that nothing is allowed to get stale or spoiled. If a Dunkin' Donuts shop uses the FIFO method for accounting, the cost follows the physical flow. Although every Dunkin' Donuts shop owner uses the FIFO method for physical flow, not every shop owner chooses the FIFO method of accounting. Some prefer LIFO for financial accounting, because with this method, the cost of goods sold is matched to current selling prices. In a time of inflation, when prices rise quickly, LIFO saves taxes because it lowers net income.

Dunkin' Donuts currently uses a periodic inventory system. It is encouraging the use of new computerized cash registers because they will create a perpetual inventory system, but a physical count of inventory will still be needed because spoilage and shrinkage are always possible.

Discussion Questions

1. Learning Unit 16-4 discusses the retail inventory method. Why does Fred insist on a physical count?
2. The different benefits LIFO and FIFO offer Fred are discussed above. Why might Fred choose a weighted-average method of accounting for inventory costs?
3. The price of coffee is subject to rapid changes, depending on growing conditions in Brazil, Colombia, Kenya, and other parts of the world. What effect might this changeability have on the method of financial accounting a Dunkin' Donuts shop owner chooses?

---

1. Beginning inventory at cost and at retail (selling price).
2. Cost of net purchases at both cost and at retail.
3. The net sales at retail.

Let's look at the diagram on page 592 to see how French Company estimates ending inventory at cost by the retail method.

French completed the following steps to arrive at ending inventory cost of $3,600.

Step 1: Calculate cost of merchandise available for sale at cost and retail.

Step 2: Calculate the cost ratio (cost of goods available for sale at cost divided by cost of goods available for sale at retail). It cost French Company .60, or 60 cents for each $1 of sales for the merchandise.

Step 3: Deduct net sales from retail value of merchandise available for sale to arrive at an estimated ending inventory at retail.

Step 4: Multiply cost ratio (.60 in this case) times ending inventory at retail to arrive at ending inventory at cost of $3,600.

Keep in mind that at year-end French will take a physical inventory.

THE RETAIL INVENTORY METHOD

		Cost	Retail
Goods Available for Sale:			
Beginning Inventory		$ 4,100	$ 6,900
Net Purchases		7,900	13,100
Step 1 → Cost of Goods Available for Sale		$12,000	$20,000
Step 2 → Cost Ratio (relationship between cost and retail)	$\frac{\$12,000}{\$20,000} = 60\%$		
Step 3 → Net Sales at Retail			14,000
↳ Inventory at Retail			$ 6,000
Step 4 → Ending Inventory at Cost, $6,000 × .60		$ 3,600	

GROSS PROFIT METHOD

Another method of estimating ending inventory without taking a physical count is the gross profit method. The method develops a relationship among sales, cost of goods sold, and gross profit in estimating the cost of ending inventory.

To use this method a company would have to keep track of the following:

1. Average gross profit rate.
2. Net sales, beginning inventory, and net purchases.

> Freight, if any, would be added to cost of net purchases.

The steps Moose Company takes to estimate its ending inventory are shown in the accompanying diagram. We assume a normal gross profit rate of 30 percent of net sales. If 30 cents on a dollar is profit, 70 cents on a dollar is cost.

THE GROSS PROFIT METHOD

Goods Available for Sale:		
Inventory, January 1, 20XX		$10,000
Net Purchases		4,000
Step 1 → Cost of Goods Available for Sale		$14,000
Less: Estimated Cost of Goods Sold:		
Net Sales at Retail	$6,000	
Step 2 → Cost percentage (100% − 30%)	.70	
Estimated Cost of Goods Sold		4,200
Step 3 → Estimated Inventory, January 31, 20XX		$ 9,800

Step 1: Moose determines cost of goods available for sale (beginning inventory plus net purchases).

Step 2: Moose estimates cost of goods sold by multiplying cost percentage (70 percent) times net sales.

Step 3: Moose subtracts cost of goods sold from cost of goods available for sale to arrive at an estimated inventory of $9,800.

This method, besides helping prepare financial statements, can help determine the amount of inventory on hand due to a fire or can verify at year's end the accuracy of the physical inventory.

Before concluding this unit, let's look at how an error made in calculating ending inventory will affect financial statements.

How Incorrect Calculation of Ending Inventory Affects Financial Statements

As we have stated before, assigning costs to ending inventory can have an effect on cost of goods sold, gross profit, net income, and current assets as well as owner's capital. Let's look at a diagram to see — if a mistake is in fact made — what items on the income statement will be affected and what the mistake's impact will be over time.

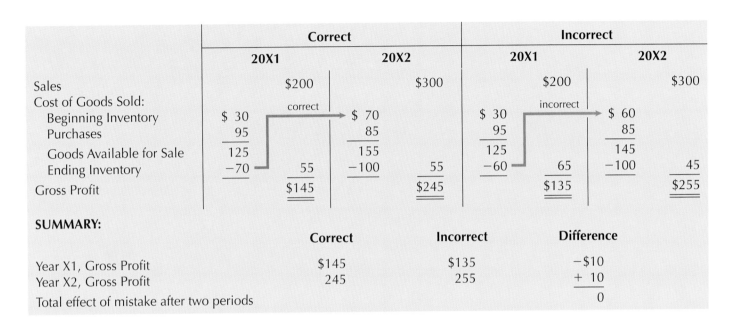

	Correct				Incorrect			
	20X1		**20X2**		**20X1**		**20X2**	
Sales		$200		$300		$200		$300
Cost of Goods Sold:		correct				incorrect		
Beginning Inventory	$ 30		$ 70		$ 30		$ 60	
Purchases	95		85		95		85	
Goods Available for Sale	125		155		125		145	
Ending Inventory	−70	55	−100	55	−60	65	−100	45
Gross Profit		$145		$245		$135		$255

SUMMARY:

	Correct	Incorrect	Difference
Year X1, Gross Profit	$145	$135	−$10
Year X2, Gross Profit	245	255	+ 10
Total effect of mistake after two periods			0

Note when the incorrect figure of $60 is used for ending inventory in 20X1, it causes cost of goods sold to be $65 instead of $55 and profit to be $135 instead of $145. In other words, when ending inventory is understated ($60 instead of $70), cost of goods sold is overstated and profit is understated.

As we look next at 20X2, we see that the ending incorrect inventory of 20X1 is carried as the beginning inventory of 20X2. The understatement of beginning inventory in 20X2 of $60 (instead of $70) causes cost of goods sold to be understated and gross profit to be overstated.

Thus at the end of 20X2, the error will be self-correcting.

To review, look at the following diagram and prove it to yourself by going back over the previous explanation.

If the Item Is	Overstated	Understated
Beginning Inventory	Profit is understated	Profit is overstated
Ending Inventory	Profit is overstated	Profit is understated

> Ending Inventory works in same direction as Profit. Beginning Inventory is inversely related.

Keep in mind that since ending inventory is recorded as a current asset on the balance sheet, any mistake will cause the assets to be under- or overstated. The statement of owner's equity will also be affected, since we have seen that the net income will be over- and understated.

LEARNING UNIT 16-4 REVIEW

AT THIS POINT you should be able to

▼ Calculate ending inventory by the retail method. (p. 591)
▼ Calculate ending inventory by the gross profit method. (p. 592)
▼ Explain how understating or overstating ending inventory will affect financial reports. (p. 593)

SELF-REVIEW QUIZ 16-4

(The forms you need are on page 5 of the *Study Guide and Working Papers*.)

1. Alon Company needs to estimate its month-end inventory. From the following, estimate the cost of ending inventory on September 30 by the retail method.

	Cost	Retail
Beginning Inventory	$ 8,000	$10,000
Net Purchases	40,000	60,000
Net Sales		30,000

(Carry out the cost ratio to nearest hundredth percent.)

2. Respond true or false to the following:

a. The retail inventory method is an estimate.
b. The cost ratio in the gross profit method represents only sales, not costs.
c. The first step in the gross profit method is to determine cost of goods available for sale.
d. If ending inventory is overstated, net income will be overstated.
e. If beginning inventory is overstated, net income will be overstated.

Solutions to Self-Review Quiz 16-4

		Cost	Retail
1.	Beginning Inventory	$ 8,000	$10,000
	Net Purchases	40,000	60,000
	Cost of Goods Available for Sale	$48,000	70,000
	Cost Ratio, $48,000/$70,000 = 68.57%		
	Net Sales at Retail		30,000
	Inventory at Retail		$40,000
	Ending Inventory at Cost,		
	$40,000 × .6857	$27,428	

2. **a.** True **b.** False **c.** True **d.** True **e.** False

SUMMARY OF KEY POINTS

Learning Unit 16-1

1. In the perpetual inventory method we have two key accounts that are kept up to date at all times. These accounts are Merchandise Inventory and Cost of Goods Sold.

2. Each purchase of merchandise is recorded by a debit to the Merchandise Inventory account.

3. Each sale requires two entries. One entry records the revenue or selling price of the merchandise, and the other entry transfers the cost of the items sold from the Merchandise Inventory account to the Cost of Goods Sold account.

4. Sales returns also require two entries. One entry is to record the reduction in revenue in a Sales Returns and Allowance account, and the other entry is to move the cost of the items returned back to the Merchandise Inventory account from the Cost of Goods Sold account.

5. When the business returns merchandise to the vendor because of damage or some other reason, the Merchandise Inventory account is credited because the merchandise is no longer available to sell.

6. The comparison of the perpetual inventory system and the periodic inventory system reveals the Purchases, Purchases Returns and Allowances, and Freight accounts do not exist in the perpetual inventory system. The accounts Merchandise Inventory and Cost of Goods Sold become active accounts in the perpetual inventory system.

Learning Unit 16-2

1. If there are many items in inventory, a subsidiary inventory ledger will be used to keep track of the details of quantities and cost for each item in inventory.

2. An inventory record form will be used for each item in the inventory. This form has columns for recording the quantities and cost of units purchased and units sold, and it provides a running balance of inventory on hand.

3. When selling an item, the inventory record form provides the cost information for the debit to Cost of Goods sold and the credit to Merchandise Inventory.

4. The total cost represented by all the inventory record forms will equal the balance of the Merchandise Inventory account in the General Ledger.

Learning Unit 16-3

1. In assigning a cost to ending inventory, the flow of goods may *not* follow the actual flow of costs.

2. The specific invoice method identifies each item in inventory with a specific invoice in assigning a cost of ending inventory. It matches costs exactly with revenues.

3. FIFO assumes the old goods are sold first. Because ending inventory is valued at most recent costs, FIFO provides the most realistic figure for ending merchandise inventory.

4. LIFO assumes the newest goods are sold first. It provides the most realistic figure for cost of goods sold. LIFO may also reduce income taxes.

5. The weighted-average method provides an average unit cost of all inventory. Weighted-average inventory value generally falls somewhere between LIFO and FIFO.

6. Accounting principles require that we be consistent in the use of the inventory method that is adopted.

7. Goods in transit should be added to the value of the inventory. Merchandise on consignment and damaged or obsolete merchandise should not be included in the value of the inventory.

Learning Unit 16-4

1. Taking a physical inventory is costly and time-consuming.

2. If a business needs to take an inventory more often than once a year, the retail method or gross profit method is used to prepare interim financial statements or in submitting a claim for insurance purposes.

3. The ending inventory amount has an effect on the financial reports, and a mistake will cause the assets to be understated or overstated. Net income will also be understated or overstated by this mistake.

KEY TERMS

Consignee A company or person to whom merchandise is consigned but who doesn't have ownership.

Consignment Sales of goods through an agent who has possession but not ownership.

Consignor The one who consigns merchandise to the consignee.

Consistency The accounting principle that requires companies to follow the same accounting methods or procedures from period to period.

FIFO (First in, First out) method Valuing of inventory assuming that the company sells the first goods received in the store.

Full disclosure principle The accounting principle that requires companies to fully disclose on their financial reports changes in accounting procedures and methods along with effects of the change as well as justification for change.

Gross profit method A method used to determine the value of the ending inventory using a predetermined gross profit rate. This method can be used to determine value of ending inventory if a loss from fire occurs.

LIFO (Last in, Last out) method Valuing of inventory with the assumption the last goods received in the store are the first to be sold.

Periodic inventory system An inventory system that does not keep continuous inventory of merchandise on hand.

Perpetual inventory system The inventory system of a company that keeps a continuous (perpetual) record of inventory on hand and of the cost of goods sold.

Retail method A method used to determine the value of the ending inventory using a cost to retail ratio. Often used for interim financial reports.

Specific invoice method Valuing of inventory where each item is identified with a specific invoice.

Weighted-average method Valuing of inventory where each item is assigned the same unit cost. This unit cost is found by dividing cost of goods available for sale by the total number of units for sale.

QUESTIONS, MINI EXERCISES, EXERCISES, AND PROBLEMS

Discussion Questions

1. Why would a manager prefer the perpetual inventory system over the periodic system of inventory?

2. What are the two key accounts in the perpetual inventory system?

3. In the perpetual system what account is debited to record the cost of merchandise purchased?

4. Why are there two entries required to record each sale in the perpetual inventory system?

5. Explain the relationship between the merchandise inventory account and the subsidiary inventory ledger.

BLUEPRINT: METHODS OF ESTIMATING INVENTORY

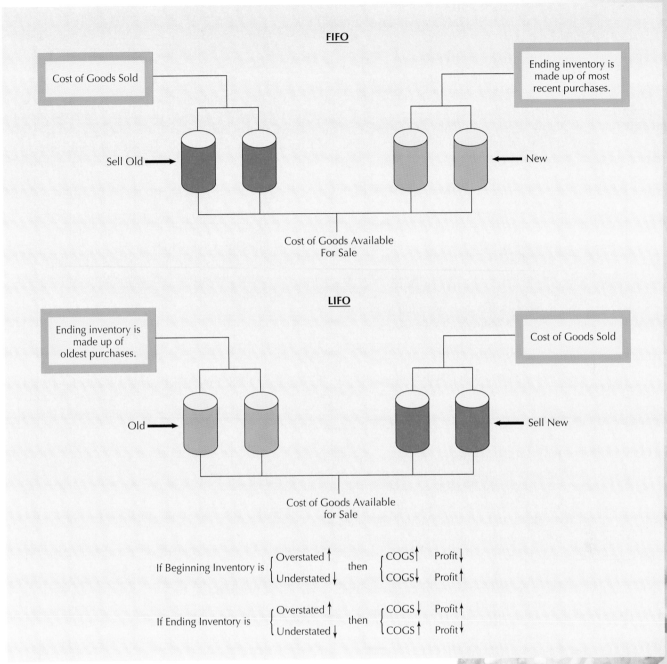

FIFO

Cost of Goods Sold

Ending inventory is made up of most recent purchases.

Sell Old →

← New

Cost of Goods Available For Sale

LIFO

Ending inventory is made up of oldest purchases.

Cost of Goods Sold

Old →

← Sell New

Cost of Goods Available for Sale

If Beginning Inventory is $\begin{cases} \text{Overstated} \uparrow \\ \text{Understated} \downarrow \end{cases}$ then $\begin{cases} \text{COGS} \uparrow \quad \text{Profit} \downarrow \\ \text{COGS} \downarrow \quad \text{Profit} \uparrow \end{cases}$

If Ending Inventory is $\begin{cases} \text{Overstated} \uparrow \\ \text{Understated} \downarrow \end{cases}$ then $\begin{cases} \text{COGS} \downarrow \quad \text{Profit} \uparrow \\ \text{COGS} \uparrow \quad \text{Profit} \downarrow \end{cases}$

 (Cont. on p. 598)

6. Must the flow of cost in inventory match the physical movement of merchandise? Please explain.

7. What are the four methods of inventory valuation? Explain each.

8. During inflation, which inventory method will provide the lowest income on the income statement?

9. Which inventory method provides the most current valuation of inventory on the balance sheet? Please explain.

10. Explain why goods in transit (F.O.B. shipping point) to buyer and goods issued on consignment are added to inventory valuations.

11. When Ending Inventory is understated, what effect will it have on cost of goods sold and net income?

	Pros	**Cons**
Specific Invoice	1. Simple to use if company has small amount of high-cost goods such as autos, jewels, boats, or antiques. 2. Flow of goods and flow of cost are the same. 3. Costs are matched with the sales they helped to produce.	1. Difficult to use for goods with large unit volume and small unit prices such as nails at a hardware store or packages of toothpaste at a drug store. 2. Difficult to use for decision-making purposes; ordinarily an impractical approach.
FIFO	1. The cost flow tends to follow the physical flow; most businesses try to sell the old goods first (perishables such as fruit or vegetables). 2. The figure for ending inventory is made up of current costs on the balance sheet (because inventory left over is assumed to be from goods last brought into the store).	1. During inflation this method will produce higher income on the income statement and thus more taxes to be paid. 2. Recent costs are not matched with recent sales, because we assume *old* goods are sold first.
LIFO	1. Cost of goods sold is stated at or near current costs, because costs of *latest* goods acquired are used. 2. Matches current costs with current selling prices. 3. During inflation this method produces the lowest net income, which is a tax advantage. (The lower cost of ending inventory means a higher cost of goods sold; with a higher cost of goods sold, gross profit and ultimately net income are smaller and thus taxes are lower.)	1. Ending inventory is valued at very old prices. 2. Doesn't match physical flow of goods (but can still be used to calculate flow of costs).
Weighted-Average Method	1. Weighted-average takes into account the number of units purchased at each amount, not a simple average cost. Good for products sold in large volume, such as grains and fuels. 2. Accountant assigns an equal unit cost to each unit of inventory; thus when the income statement is prepared, net income will not fluctuate as much as with other methods.	1. Current prices have no more significance than prices of goods bought months earlier. 2. Compared with other methods, the most recent costs are *not* matched with current sales. 3. Cost of ending inventory is not as up to date as it could be using another method.

12. Why would a company use the retail method to determine the value of the ending inventory? Why would it use the gross profit method?

Mini Exercises

(The blank forms you need are on pages 6–9 of the *Study Guide and Working Papers.*)

Transaction Analysis

1. Complete the following transaction analysis:

Accounts Affected	Category	↑ ↓	Rules
Merchandise Inventory Cost of Goods Sold		↓ ↑	

Journal Entries

Use the perpetual inventory system.

2. Journalize the following transaction in correct form:

20XX
Mar. 1   Sold merchandise on account, $500. The merchandise cost $300.

3. Journalize the following transaction in correct form:

20XX
Mar. 15   A customer returned merchandise for a cash refund of $250. The item cost the seller $125.

4. Journalize the following transaction in correct form:

20XX
Mar. 20   The business returned to the vendor a damaged inventory item that cost $150.

Estimating Inventory Value

5. From the following information calculate the cost of ending inventory and cost of goods sold using the a. FIFO, b. LIFO, and c. weighted-average methods.

		Units	Cost
January 1	Beginning Inventory	5	$1
March 6	Purchased	3	2
August 9	Purchased	2	3
December 10	Purchased	4	4

The ending inventory reveals six items unsold.

Retail Inventory Method

6. Complete the following using the retail inventory method. (Round cost ratio is nearest whole percent.)

	Cost	Retail
Goods Available for Sale		
Beginning Inventory	$50	$100
Net Purchases	70	90
Cost of Goods Available for Sale	A	B
Cost Ratio	C	
Net Sales at Retail		140
Inventory at Retail		D
Ending Inventory	E	

Gross Profit Method

7. Complete the following using the gross profit method. Assume a normal gross profit rate of 40 percent of Net Sales.

Goods Available for Sale

Inventory January 1, 20XX		$50
Net Purchases		10
Cost of Goods Available for Sale		A
Less: Estimated Cost of Goods Sold:		
Net Sales at Retail	$40	
Cost Percentage	B	
Estimated Cost of Goods Sold		C
Estimated Inventory Jan. 31, 20XX		D

Exercises

(The blank forms you need are on pages 10–13 of the *Study Guide and Working Papers*.)

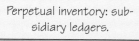

Journalizing perpetual entries.

16-1. The DMM Electric Company uses the perpetual inventory system. Record these transactions in a two-column journal.

20XX

Feb.

3   Purchased 10 model 77DX light fixtures on account from Dealer's Electric at total cost of $230, terms n/30.

5   Sold 3 model U67 light fixtures for cash for $84 total. The cost of these three fixtures amounted to $54.

6   Our customer returned 1 model U67 light fixture. We gave the customer a $28 cash refund.

10   We issued a debit memo for $23 to Dealer's Electric for 1 model 77DX light fixture that came in damaged in the shipment of February 3.

Perpetual inventory: subsidiary ledgers.

16-2. The RJM Company uses the perpetual inventory system with a subsidiary ledger for inventory. Enter the following information into the inventory record form for product U47. Be sure to keep the balance on hand up to date.

20XX

Nov.

5   Purchased 5 units at a cost of $10 each. (There were no units on hand prior to this purchase.)

6   Sold 3 units for $16 each. (*Hint:* The inventory record form only contains information about the cost of a product, not the selling price!)

7   Sold 1 unit for $15.50.

10   Purchased 12 additional units at a cost of $10 each.

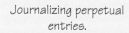

Journalizing perpetual entries.

16-3. Journalize and post the above transactions using a two-column journal.

16-4. CVR Sales uses the FIFO method with the perpetual inventory system. Enter the following information into the inventory record form for product 44BX. Be sure to keep the balance on hand up to date.

FIFO: perpetual method.

20XX

Oct.

1   Balance on hand: 3 units at a cost of $21 each.

2   Purchased 5 units at a cost of $23 each.

5   Sold 2 units for $31 each. (Remember to use cost and not selling price in the inventory record.)

6   Sold 5 units for $31 each.

8   Purchased 6 units at a cost of $24 each.

Periodic method.

16-5. The Loyola Company uses the periodic inventory system. Calculate the cost of ending inventory and cost of goods sold using the (a) FIFO,

(b) LIFO, and (c) weighted-average methods. Loyola sells only one product called SM57.

		Units	Cost per Unit
January 1	Beginning inventory	50	$ 9
March 18	Purchased	12	10
August 19	Purchased	40	12
November 8	Purchased	48	13

Ending inventory is 52 units.

16-6. From the following facts, calculate the correct cost of inventory for Ray Company.

Shipping goods.

▼ Cost of inventory on shelf, $4,000, which includes $300 of goods received on consignment.
▼ Goods in transit en route to Ray Company shipped F.O.B. shipping point, $22,000.
▼ Goods in transit en route to Ray shipped F.O.B. destination, $300. Ray Company has $600 worth of goods on consignment in Alice's Dress Shop.

16-7. Miles Company's May 1 inventory had a cost of $58,000 and a retail value of $72,000. During May, net purchases cost $255,000 with a retail value of $405,000. Net sales at retail for Miles Company during May were $225,000. Calculate the ending inventory at cost using the retail inventory method. (Round the cost ratio to the nearest hundredth percent.)

Retail inventory.

16-8. Amy Company on January 1, 20XX, had inventory costing $30,000 and during January had net purchases of $67,000. Over recent years Amy Company's gross profit has averaged 40 percent on sales. Given that the company has net sales of $106,000, calculate an estimated cost of ending inventory using the gross profit method.

Gross profit method.

Group A Problems

(The blank forms you need are on pages 14–23 of the *Study Guide and Working Papers*.)

16A-1. The Wren Company uses the perpetual inventory system. Record these transactions in a two-column journal. All credit sales are n/30.

Journalizing perpetual inventory.

20XX
Mar.
5 Purchased merchandise on account totaling $1,750. Terms n/30.
6 Sold merchandise on account to Tommy Dorsey for $85. This merchandise cost $63.
8 Returned $100 of defective merchandise purchased March 5.
9 Sold $125 of merchandise for cash. This merchandise cost $98.
9 Allowed a return for credit of $7 of merchandise sold on March 6. The cost of the returned merchandise was $5. (*Hint:* Don't forget to return the cost of the merchandise to the Merchandise Inventory account.)
10 Purchased $800 of merchandise on account from BG Supply. Terms n/30.
12 Received payment from Tommy Dorsey for the March 6 sale less the return.
13 Sold $380 of merchandise for cash. The cost was $290.

> **Check Figure:**
> Mar. 13
> Dr. Cost of goods sold $290
> Cr. Merch. inventory $290

16A-2. Mr. E. L. Best owns an electronics supply company called Best Electronics. His company uses the perpetual inventory system with a subsidiary inventory ledger to maintain control over an inventory of thousands of electronic parts. See page 602 for the quantities and costs for three of the parts in his inventory:

Journalizing perpetual inventory.

Part No.	Quantity on Hand	Cost per Unit
KT88	3	$17.50
EL34	22	16.40
12AX7	5	8.70

Your Job Is to

1. Enter the above beginning balances in the inventory record forms; beginning inventory is $456.80.

2. Journalize and post the following transactions.

20XX

Oct. 10 Purchased the following on account:

Part No.	Quantity	Cost per Unit
KT88	24	$17.50
12AX7	36	8.70

(*Hint:* Be sure to update each inventory record.)

11 Sold four number KT88 units for cash at a selling price of $27.50 each. (*Hint:* Remember to record both the revenue and the cost. The cost data will be found in the inventory record form for this part number. Don't forget to update the form.)

13 Sold the following for cash:

Part No.	Quantity	Sales price per unit
KT88	12	$27.50
EL34	8	25.00
12AX7	14	12.90

15 A customer brought back one of KT88 bought two days ago because it did not work.

16 Best Electronics sent back to the vendor the faulty KT88 that the customer brought back.

16A-3. Agree Company uses a perpetual inventory system. From the information given below, prepare an inventory record form (a) assuming that the FIFO method is in use and (b) assuming that the LIFO method is in use. Assume on January 1, 20XX, a beginning inventory of 800 units at a cost of $8 each.

RECEIVED			SOLD	
Date	Quantity	Cost per Unit	Date	Quantity
Apr. 15	220	$ 7	Mar. 8	500
Nov. 12	800	9	Oct. 5	350
Dec. 31	700	10	Nov. 30	400

16A-4. Ashley Company, using the periodic inventory system, began the year with 250 units of product B in inventory with a unit cost of $35. The following additional purchases of the product were made:

Apr. 1	300 units @ $40 each
July 5	400 units @ 50 each
Aug. 15	500 units @ 60 each
Nov. 20	150 units @ 70 each

At end of year Ashley Company had 500 units of its product unsold. Your task is to calculate cost of ending inventory as well as cost of goods sold by the (a) FIFO, (b) LIFO, and (c) weighted-average methods. (Round the weighted-average to the nearest cent.)

16A-5. Marge Company uses the retail method to estimate cost of ending inventory for its monthly interim reports. From the following facts, estimate Marge's ending inventory at cost for the end of January. (Round the cost ratio to the nearest tenth percent.)

January 1 inventory at cost	$ 16,500
January 1 inventory at retail	32,000
Net purchases at cost	110,800
Net purchases at retail	195,000
Net sales at retail	191,000

Retail inventory method.

Check Figure:
$20,196   Ending inventory
at cost

16A-6. Over the past four years the gross profit rate for Hall Company was 30 percent. Last week a fire destroyed all Hall's inventory. Luckily all the records for Hall were in a fireproof safe and indicated the following facts:

Inventory (January 1, 20XX)	$ 39,000
Sales	128,500
Sales Returns	3,200
Purchases	78,000
Purchases Returns and Allowances	3,000

Please estimate the cost of inventory that was destroyed in the fire.

Gross profit method.

Check Figure:
$26,290   Estimated
inventory

Group B Problems

(The blank forms you need are on pages 14–23 of the *Study Guide and Working Papers.*)

16B-1. The Wren Company uses the perpetual inventory system. Record these transactions in a two-column journal. All credit sales are n/30.

Journalizing perpetual
inventory.

20XX

Mar.	15	Purchased merchandise on account totaling $1,450. Terms n/30.
	16	Sold merchandise on account to Bobby Hackett for $92. This merchandise cost $71.
	18	Returned $120 of defective merchandise purchased March 15.
	19	Sold $230 of merchandise for cash. This merchandise cost $175.
	19	Allowed a return for credit of $14 of merchandise sold on March 16. The cost of the returned merchandise was $11. (*Hint:* Don't forget to return the cost of the merchandise to the Merchandise Inventory account.)
	20	Purchased $900 of merchandise on account from JT Supply. Terms n/30.
	22	Received payment from Bobby Hackett for the March 16 sale less the return.
	23	Sold $410 of merchandise for cash. The cost was $320.

Check Figure:
Mar. 23
Dr.   Cost of goods sold
$320
Cr.   Merch. inventory
$320

16B-2. Mr. E. L. Best owns an electronics supply company called Best Electronics. His company uses the perpetual inventory system with a subsidiary inventory ledger to maintain control over an inventory of thousands of electronic parts. Here are the quantities and costs for three of the parts in his inventory:

Journalizing perpetual
inventory.

Check Figure:
12AU7   Ending balance
$117

Part No.	Quantity on Hand	Cost per Unit
6L6	4	$12.50
EL84	18	9.40
12AU7	3	7.80

Your Job Is to

1. Enter the above beginning balances in the inventory record forms; beginning inventory is $242.60.

2. Journalize and post the following transactions.

20XX

Oct. 10 Purchased the following on account:

Part No.	Quantity	Cost per Unit
6L6	18	$12.50
12AU7	28	7.80

(*Hint:* Be sure to update each inventory record.)

11 Sold four number 12AU7 units for cash at a selling price of $18.50 each. (*Hint:* Remember to record both the revenue and the cost. The cost data will be found in the inventory record form for this part number. Don't forget to update the form.)

13 Sold the following for cash:

Part No.	Quantity	Sales Price per Unit
6L6	10	$18.50
EL84	9	14.00
12AU7	12	11.80

15 A customer brought back one 6L6 that was bought two days ago because it did not work.

16 Best Electronics returned to the vendor the faulty part that was returned yesterday.

Perpetual: LIFO, FIFO.

Check Figure:
$6,900

16B-3. Agree Company uses a perpetual inventory system. From the information given below, prepare an inventory record form (a) assuming that the FIFO method is in use and (b) assuming that the LIFO method is in use. Assume on January 1, 20XX, a beginning inventory of 500 units at a cost of $7 each.

RECEIVED			SOLD	
Date	Quantity	Cost per Unit	Date	Quantity
Apr. 15	200	$ 8	Mar. 8	400
Nov. 12	300	9	Oct. 5	300
Dec. 31	600	10	Nov. 30	200

Periodic inventory.

Check Figure:
LIFO $52,900   Cost of
goods sold

16B-4. On January 1, 20XX, Ashley Company, a company which uses the periodic inventory system, began with 150 units of product B in inventory with a unit cost of $20. The following additional purchases of the product were made:

Apr. 1	210 units @ $30 each
Jul. 5	500 units @ 40 each
Aug. 15	450 units @ 50 each
Nov. 20	200 units @ 60 each

At end of year Ashley Company had 400 units of its product unsold. Your task is to calculate cost of ending inventory as well as cost of goods sold by the (a) FIFO, (b) LIFO, (c) weighted-average methods. (Round the weighted-average to the nearest cent.)

Retail inventory method.

Check Figure:
$28,450   Ending inventory

16B-5. Marge Company uses the retail method to estimate cost of ending inventory for its monthly interim reports. From the facts given below, estimate Marge's ending inventory at cost for the end of January. (Round the cost ratio to the nearest hundredth percent.)

January 1 inventory at cost	$ 17,000
January 1 inventory at retail	35,000
Net purchases at cost	119,000
Net purchases at retail	204,000
Net sales at retail	189,000

16B-6. Over the past four years the gross profit rate for Hall Company was 35 percent. Last week a fire destroyed all Hall's inventory. Luckily all the records for Hall were in a fireproof safe and indicated the following facts:

Inventory (January 1, 20XX)	$ 5,400
Sales	127,000
Sales Returns	3,250
Purchases	94,900
Purchases Returns and Allowances	4,100

Using the gross profit method, estimate the cost of inventory that was destroyed in the fire.

Gross profit method.

Check Figure:
$15,762.50   Estimated inventory

REAL-WORLD APPLICATION

16R-1.

The following inventory errors were discovered during an internal audit:

a. The beginning inventory was overstated by $200.

b. The ending inventory was understated by $300.

c. $900 of purchases were unrecorded.

d. A sales return of $1,500 was not recorded.

Indicate what effect these mistakes (treat each one separately) will have on (1) the cost of goods sold, (2) the gross profit, and (3) the owner's equity. Please provide a written explanation.

YOU make the call

Critical Thinking/Ethical Case

16R-2.

Lyon Co. has used a perpetual inventory system for six months. The president of the company has issued a memo stating that the new computer system has failed to deliver acceptable standards in servicing the customers and too many goods are out of stock. Fran, Lyon's accountant, blames the Computer Department and tells the president to fire the head of that department. The president wants to return immediately to a periodic inventory system. You make the call. Write down your recommendations to the president.

INTERNET EXERCISES

EX-1. [www.conns.com]   Merchandise Inventory represents one of the major investments of a retailing business. Accounting for inventory is a much more diverse process than presented in the chapter you have just studied. In addition to FIFO, LIFO, perpetual, periodic, there are many other terms associated with inventory. The age of computers allows companies to maintain perpetual inventory records even if they are reporting inventory on a periodic basis.

LIFO achieved recognition in the United States when a major revision of the Internal Revenue Code was undertaken in 1954. LIFO provides a tax saving device for businesses who use it, by deferring the payment of taxes to future periods.

Assume that Conn's has Merchandise Available for Sale of $25,000,000. When they count their inventory and value it at $7,000,000 using FIFO and at $5,000,000 using LIFO, how does this affect their Gross Profit under each method? Which method provides the LOWER Gross Profit?

EX-2. [www.audiexchange.com/]   One method of inventory accounting discussed in the chapter is that of "specific identification." Specific identification is usually employed in companies that have a large amount of inventory, both in terms of dollars and in terms of numbers of units. An automobile dealer lends itself to specific identification. The number used to track the inventory from purchase through point of sale is the car's serial number. It is unique to each car. Pay a visit to your local shopping mall. What other types of businesses do you notice that could easily employ specific identification for inventory accounting?

CONTINUING PROBLEM

The Eldorado Computer Center had 300 pieces of merchandise inventory as of March 31, 20XX. The inventory was purchased with prices as follows:

Lot	Price Each Piece	Number of Pieces	Total Cost
First lot	$1.00	100	$100
Second lot	$1.75	100	$175
Third lot	$2.00	80	$160
Fourth lot	$2.50	100	$250
Fifth lot	$1.65	100	$165

Lot numbers represent oldest to newest.

Assignment

(See Page 27 in the *Study Guide and Working Papers.*)

Using the FIFO, LIFO, and weighted-average methods, calculate the dollar value of the Eldorado Computer Center's ending inventory.

Computerized Accounting Application for Chapter 16

Perpetual Inventory System

Before starting on this assignment, read and complete the tasks discussed in Parts A, B, and F of the Computerized Accounting appendix at the back of this book and complete the Computerized Accounting Application assignments for Chapter 3, Chapter 4, Valdez Realty Mini Practice Set (Chapter 5), Pete's Market Mini Practice Set (Chapter 8), Chapter 10, and The Corner Dress Shop Mini Practice Set (Chapter 13).

One of the most powerful features of a computerized accounting system is its ability to maintain perpetual inventory records easily and accurately. In the prior Computer Workshops this feature was demonstrated as you recorded purchases and sales of inventory. Peachtree Complete Accounting has the ability to maintain perpetual inventory records through its Inventory module. Peachtree Complete Accounting can use FIFO, LIFO or the weighted-average method as its inventory cost flow assumption. While a default assumption can be set, one can be designated for each inventory item individually.

In this Computer Workshop you will be working with the data files for a company called The Paint Place. The Paint Place uses the Sales/Invoicing, Receipts, Purchases, Payments and Inventory modules of Peachtree Complete Accounting to maintain its accounting and perpetual inventory records. The Paint Place extends terms of 2/10, n/30 to all of its credit customers. The inventory items currently stocked by The Paint Place appear below:

> Inventory List

THE PAINT PLACE
INVENTORY SYNOPSIS 3/1/00

No.	Description	Unit	Sell	Quantity	Cost	Value	Margin (%)
1	Latex Flat	Gallon	16.95	642	7.47	4,795.74	55.93
2	Latex Semi-gloss	Gallon	16.95	1,066	7.47	7,963.02	55.93
3	Latex High-gloss	Gallon	16.95	600	7.47	4,482.00	55.93
4	Oil High-gloss	Gallon	17.95	801	8.97	7,184.97	50.03
5	Oil Semi-gloss	Gallon	17.95	502	8.97	4,502.94	50.03
						28,928.67	

1. Click on the Start button. Point to Programs; point to the Peachtree folder and select Peachtree Complete Accounting. Your desktop may have the Peachtree icon allowing for a quicker entrance into the program.

   > Open the Company Data Files

2. Follow the "Open a File" instructions in Part A of the Computerized Accounting appendix at the back of this book to open **The Paint Place.**

3. Click on the **Maintain** menu option. Then select **Company Information.** The program will respond by bringing up a dialogue box allowing the user to edit/add information about the company. In the **Company Name** entry field at the end of **The Paint Place,** add a dash and your name "**-Student Name**" to the end of the company name. Click on the OK button to return to the Menu Window.

   > Add Your Name to the company Name

4. Peachtree Complete Accounting allows the user to quickly, and easily add new inventory items to the Inventory module. This is accomplished by selecting **Inventory Items** from the **Maintain** menu. From this window, we

   > Adding or Editing Inventory Items

can also obtain and edit information about items currently in our inventory. To illustrate how easily inventory items can be added, let's add a new product to **The Paint Place's** inventory module.

▼ Select **Inventory Items** from the **Maintain** menu.

▼ In the **Item ID** field, type "006" and hit TAB.

▼ In the **Description** field, type in "Oil Flat" and hit TAB.

▼ We are now in a field where we can change the type of inventory item this is. Since this will be a regular stocked item, we can accept the default of Stock Item by hitting TAB again.

▼ We are now in a field where we can select and then enter a longer description of this item that will appear on sales and/or purchase invoices when we select it. Since we do not have a longer description, we can TAB until we reach the **Sales Price #1** field.

▼ We will sell this item normally for $16.95 so enter this amount.

▼ Peachtree has the capability of storing multiple prices for an item. This feature can be activated by clicking on the arrow to the right of the **Sales Price #1** field. Go ahead and click on this arrow. A table is presented which allows us to enter up to 5 different selling prices. Different customers can be assigned to different price levels in this manner. Since we will have only one price, we can **Cancel** the Multiple Pricing Level box and TAB to Unit/Measure field.

▼ Since the paint is sold in 1 gallon cans, type in "Gallon" in this field. Hit TAB to move to the next field.

▼ Item Type and Location are sorting and information fields that we will not use at this time. TAB until you reach **Cost Method.** Here is where we can select the cost assumption to use with this item. Using the pull down menu, you can select FIFO, LIFO or Average. We will select "Average".

▼ Peachtree has used default information to select the GL accounts needed for an inventory transaction. Unless there is some need to change these, we will accept the defaults. In fact, we will accept Peachtee's default information on the rest of the accounts in this field. We will also not use the **Custom Fields** or **History** tabs in this window. Your entry should look like this:

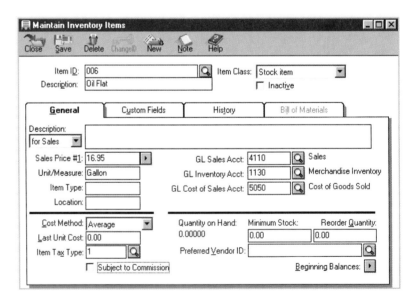

▼ Clicking on **Save** will place this item in our inventory module.

▼ We can view and edit information about items in our inventory from this window as well. We can use the magnifying glass next to the **Item ID** field to select any item from our inventory by double clicking on it. Once it is in the Maintain Inventory Items box, we can click on and change information as needed.

5. Using the procedures learned in Chapter 10 (feel free to refer back to that chapter if you need to review a procedure), record the following transactions. Accept defaults for any fields for which you are not given information. Remember to use the Plain Invoice format for sales invoices and to insert the invoice number during the printing process for all print activities:

1997

Mar.

1   Sold 5 gallons of Oil High-gloss (Item #4) at $17.95 per gallon to Elaine Anderson on account, invoice no. 5469, $89.75, terms 2/10, n/30.

2   Received invoice no. 6892 from Wholesale Paints in the amount of $1,504 for the purchase of 200 gallons of Latex High-gloss (Item #3) at $7.52 per gallon, (don't forget to change the **Unit Price**), terms 2/10, n/30.

3   Received invoice no. CC675 from the Painter's Supply in the amount of $906 for the purchase of 100 gallons of Oil High-gloss (Item #4) at 9.06 per gallon (don't forget to change the **Unit Price!**), terms 2/10, n/30.

4   Sold 5 gallons of Oil High-gloss paint (Item #4) at $17.95 per gallon to Jake Kerns on account, invoice no. 5470, $89.75, terms 2/10, n/30.

6   Received check no. 8723 from Wes Young in the amount of $3,225.13 in payment of invoice no. 5468 ($3,290.95), dated February 28, less 2 percent discount ($65.82). Enter the discount amount in the discount field next to the invoice in the Receipts window.

7   Issued check no. 2345 to Vantage Tints in the amount of $1,082.84 in payment of invoice no. 5658 ($1,116.33), dated February 28, less 3 percent discount ($33.49). Again, enter the discount amount in the discount field next to the invoice in the Payments window.

14   Sold 10 gallons of Latex Semi-gloss (Item #2) at $16.95 per gallon to Elaine Anderson on account, $169.50, invoice no. 5471, terms 2/10, n/30.

16   Received invoice no. 6943 from Wholesale Paints in the amount of $1,134 for the purchase of 150 gallons of Latex Semi-gloss (Item #2) at 7.56 per gallon (don't forget to change the **Unit Price!**), terms 2/10, n/30.

19   Received invoice no. CC691 from Painter's Supply in the amount of $1,618.75 for the purchase of 175 gallons of Oil Semi-gloss (Item #5) at 9.25 per gallon (don't forget to change the **Unit Price!**), terms 2/10, n/30.

21   Sold 10 gallons of Latex Semi-gloss (Item #2) at $16.95 per gallon to Jake Kerns on account, $169.50, invoice no. 5472, terms 2/10, n/30.

24   Sold 25 gallons of Oil Semi-gloss paint (Item #5) at $17.95 per gallon to Elaine Anderson on account, $448.75, invoice no. 5473, terms 2/10, n/30.

25   Received invoice no. CC787 from Painter's Supply in the amount of $465 for the purchase of 50 gallons of Oil Semi-gloss (Item #5) at 9.30 per gallon (don't forget to change the **Unit Price!**), terms 2/10, n/30.

31   Sold 25 gallons of Oil Semi-gloss (Item #5) at $17.95 per gallon to Jake Kerns on account, $448.75, invoice no. 5474, terms 2/10, n/30.

6. You may wish to see how active the items in your inventory have been. Peachtree has a Unit Activity Report which will summarize the units

How to Display an Inventory Activity Detail Report

bought for any selected period. Select **Inventory** from the **Reports** menu. Select Inventory Unit Activity Report. Accept all defaults. Your screen will look like this:

The Paint Place
Inventory Unit Activity Report
For the Period From Mar 1, 2000 to Mar 31, 2000
Filter Criteria includes: 1) Stock/Assembly. Report order is by ID. Report is printed with Truncated Long Descriptions.

Item ID Item Description Item Class	Beg Qty	Units Sold	Units Purc	Adjust Qty	Assembly Qty	Qty on Hand
001 Latex Flat Stock item	642.00					642.00
002 Latex Semi-Gloss Stock item	1066.00	20.00	150.00			1196.00
003 Latex High-Gloss Stock item	600.00		200.00			800.00
004 Oil High-Gloss Stock item	801.00	10.00	100.00			891.00
005 Oil Semi-Gloss Stock item	502.00	50.00	225.00			677.00
006 Oil Flat Stock item						
		80.00	675.00			

Inventory Valuation

7. An important inventory report is the Inventory Valuation Report. From the same report screen, select Inventory Valuation report and accept all defaults. Your screen will look like this:

The Paint Place
Inventory Valuation Report
As of Mar 31, 2000
Filter Criteria includes: 1) Stock/Assembly. Report order is by ID. Report is printed with Truncated Long Descriptions.

Item ID Item Class	Item Description	Unit	Cost Met	Qty on Hand	Item Value	Avg Cost	% of Inv Valu
001 Stock item	Latex Flat	Gallon	Average	642.00	4,795.74	7.47	14.16
002 Stock item	Latex Semi-Gloss	Gallon	Average	1196.00	8,947.51	7.48	26.42
003 Stock item	Latex High-Gloss	Gallon	Average	800.00	5,986.00	7.48	17.68
004 Stock item	Oil High-Gloss	Gallon	Average	891.00	8,001.22	8.98	23.63
005 Stock item	Oil Semi-Gloss	Gallon	Average	677.00	6,134.11	9.06	18.11
006 Stock item	Oil Flat	Gallon	Average				
					33,864.58		100.00

8. As you can see from the report menu, there are numerous other reports Peachtree can utilize. These are outside the scope of this class.

Print Reports

9. Print the following reports accepting all defaults:
   a. General Ledger Trial Balance
   b. Aged Receivables
   c. Aged Payables
   d. Income Statement
   e. Balance Sheet

Exit from the Program

10. Click on the File menu; then click on Exit to end the current work session and return to your Windows desktop.

Accounting for Property, Plant Equipment, and Intangible Assets

The Airbus A3XX is the largest aircraft ever built, with double decker seating designed to accommodate 555 passengers. In September 2000, Singapore International Airlines (SIA) became the first airline to order the superjumbo aircraft. They will pay $8.6 billion for 25 planes, and the new planes will be accounted for as *long-term assets* (assets held longer than one year). The secret to SIA's success has always been the impeccable quality of its long-term assets, both tangible and intangible: its fleet of 90 planes and its service on the ground and in the air.

SIA's planes are known as the most efficient in the world. The company buys new planes every five years the way most people buy new cars, keeping them well-maintained and up-to-date. SIA is already planning to devote years of research on customer preferences to determine what amenities to offer on board the new A3XX planes, scheduled to arrive by 2006. The superjumbo planes have been likened to flying cruise ships that can be kitted out with restaurants, bars and even casinos.

While the planes are the most visible sign of the airline, an airline's service is just as important, particularly in these times of increased air traffic, delays and competition. SIA credits its Terminal Services Group (SATS) with reducing the adverse effects of the Asian economic downturn. The company's YES! Campaign trains everyone — from baggage handlers to security personnel — to act like frontline staff. No wonder business travelers have chosen Singapore International Airlines as the "best airline" for eleven years running.

In today's knowledge- and technology-driven economy, the value of intangible assets — such as patents, copyrights, systems and employee knowledge — is fast surpassing the value of physical assets. You might be surprised to know, for instance, that American Airlines' electronic reservation system — Sabre — was valued at 60% of the company's assets, far more than the company's fleet of planes. In this chapter you'll learn how to allocate the cost of intangible assets over time (amortization). But first, you'll learn how to account for depreciation (loss of value) of long term physical assets, such as plants and equipment, using four different methods.

Based on: Wayne Arnold, "Airbus Wins $8 Billion Deal For Its New Jet," *New York Times,* September 30, 2000, p. C, 1:2. Leonard Hill, "Two for the Money," *Air Transport World,* May 2000, pp. 59–63. Perry Flint, "SIA's global tilt," *Air Transport World,* May 2000, pp. 50–55. Anonymous, "Business travelers select Singapore Airlines No. 1," *Houston Chronicle,* January 23, 2000, p. 5. Ben Dolven, "Profitable romance," *Far Eastern Economic Review,* December 30, 1999–January 6, 2000, pp. 78–79. Staff Reports, Companies May Be Unwittingly Ignoring The Bulk of Their Asset Value," *Investor Relations Business,* December 13, 1999, p. 4.

LEARNING OBJECTIVES

▼ Calculating the cost of an asset. (p. 613)

▼ Calculating depreciation using one of four methods: straight line, declining balance, units of production, and sum of the years' digits. (p. 614)

▼ Calculating depreciation for tax purposes using the Modified Accelerated Cost Recovery System. (p. 618)

▼ Explaining the difference between capital expenditures and revenue expenditures. (p. 622)

▼ Journalizing entries for discarding, selling, or exchanging plant assets. (p. 624)

▼ Explaining amortization and how it applies to intangible assets. (p. 629)

In Chapter 13 we classified assets as either current or plant and equipment. Current assets are those that are used up in a company's operations or converted into cash within one year or one accounting cycle, whichever is longer. Long-term assets, such as plant and equipment, provide benefits to a company for more than one year or one accounting cycle. Types of long-term assets include property (such as land), plant (such as buildings), and equipment (such as trucks and tools). Another classification of assets is called **intangible assets.** These assets are rights owned by a business that do not involve a *physical* object. Examples are patents or franchises. Intangible assets are also considered long-term assets.

In this chapter we look at how to calculate a long-term asset's overall cost and its depreciation (depreciation being the allocation of the cost of the asset over its lifetime). We also show how to record expenditures involved in improving or repairing an asset and how to account for the disposal of these assets.

LEARNING UNIT 17-1

COST OF PROPERTY, PLANT, AND EQUIPMENT

The cost of property, plant, and equipment is not just the price one pays to buy it. One must also include the cost involved in getting it into position and in condition for use in the company. Thus the cost of a machine includes freight, assembly, and all other costs that are needed to get the machine up and ready to run.

For example, Smith ordered a machine with a list price of $20,000 with terms of 3/10, n/30. There was a freight charge of $1,500 to cover transportation to the railroad station. Smith had to pay $250 to transport the machine from the railroad station to corporate headquarters. Total costs of assembling and installation amounted to $700. In addition, Smith purchased a special concrete foundation to keep the machine from tilting when operational for $900. The life of the machine is expected to be 15 years.

HOW SMITH CALCULATES COST OF MACHINE

List price	$20,000
Less: Cash discount (.03 × $20,000)	600
Net purchase price	19,400
Freight	1,500
Transportation from railroad station	250
Assembly and installation	700
Special foundation	900
Total cost of machine	$22,750

> Note that cash discount is deducted in arriving at total cost of machine. If sales tax were involved, it too would be added to the cost of the asset.

Entries to record freight, assembly, installation, and so forth would be made as a debit to the Machinery account and as a credit to Cash.

The $22,750 cost of the asset will be spread over the years the machine helps Smith produce revenue. This example is one of the matching principle. Notice, however, that all these additional costs were reasonable and necessary to get the machine *ready for use*. If the buyer causes negligence, illegal acts, or gross inefficiencies to occur, these acts would be charged to an expense and not to the cost of the asset.

> Cost of machine will be matched with revenue.

Let's look now at how to record the cost of land.

LAND AND LAND IMPROVEMENTS

When land (which has unlimited useful life) is purchased, there are usually many incidental costs that are considered part of the *cost* of the land. These costs include surveying, commissions to attorneys and real estate brokers, title searches, grading, draining, and clearing the property. If there is a special one-time assessment made for paving a street or installing sewers, it should be charged to cost of land, because it adds "permanent value" to the land.

> Land does not depreciate, because it has an unlimited life.

Now let's look at some items related to land that will not be added to cost of land. **Land Improvements** is an asset account that records improvements to land that have a *limited* useful life. Some examples are driveways, fences, shrubbery, paving of parking lots, and sprinkler systems. These improvements are subject to depreciation, and thus we need an account that is kept separate from the Land account, which does *not* depreciate.

BUILDINGS

The cost of buying a building would include the purchase price and all the cost of repairs and other expenses to get the building *ready for use.* For construction of a new building, the cost would include all reasonable and necessary payments for labor, insurance, building permits, architect's fees, legal fees, and so on to get the building ready for use.

If a building and land are purchased for one lump-sum payment, the cost must be separated (allocated) for each, because land will not depreciate, but buildings will.

LEARNING UNIT 17-1 REVIEW

AT THIS POINT you should be able to

- ▼ Explain how to classify property, plant, and equipment. (p. 613)
- ▼ Calculate the cost of an asset. (p. 613)
- ▼ Explain the difference between land and land improvements. (p. 613)

SELF-REVIEW QUIZ 17-1

(The forms you need are on page 28 of the *Study Guide and Working Papers.*)
Respond true or false to the following:

1. Land does not depreciate.
2. Total cost of acquiring an asset cannot include cost of freight.
3. Land improvements are not subject to depreciation.
4. A cash discount is added to list price.
5. Sales tax is added to cost of asset.

Solutions to Self-Review Quiz 17-1

1. True **2.** False **3.** False **4.** False **5.** True

LEARNING UNIT 17-2   DEPRECIATION METHODS

Now that students know which long-term assets are depreciable, let's look at different methods for computing depreciation. If you want to check any of the concepts of depreciation we discussed in Chapter 4, take a moment to refer back to page 118.

When a company calculates its periodic depreciation expense, different methods will produce significantly different results. Thus the method of depreciation chosen will affect the net income for current as well as future periods as well as the **book value** (cost of asset less accumulated depreciation) of the asset on the balance sheet.

Let's assume that Melvin Company purchased a truck on January 1, 20XX, for $20,000, with a **residual value (salvage value)** of $2,000 and an estimated life of five years. The following are the four common depreciation methods that Melvin Company could use:

1. Straight-line method.
2. Units-of-production method.
3. Double declining-balance method.
4. Sum-of-the-years'-digits method. (an optional section)

Think of residual value as trade-in value at end of estimated life.

STRAIGHT-LINE METHOD

The **straight-line method** is simple to use, because it allocates the cost of the asset (less residual value) evenly over its estimated useful life. (At the time an asset is acquired, an estimate is made of its usefulness or **useful life** in terms of number of years it would last, amount of output expected, and so forth.) Let's look at how Melvin Company calculates its depreciation expense for each of the estimated five years of usefulness using the straight-line method. Take a moment to read the key points in the parentheses below the accompanying table.

The formula is

$$\frac{\text{Cost} - \text{Residual Value}}{\text{Service Useful Life in Years}} = \frac{\$20,000 - \$2,000}{5} = \$3,600$$

End of Year	Cost of Delivery Truck	Yearly* Depreciation Expense	Accumulated Depreciation, End of Year	Book Value, End of Year (Cost − Accum. Dep.)
1	$20,000	$3,600	$ 3,600	$16,400
2	20,000	3,600	7,200	12,800
3	20,000	3,600	10,800	9,200
4	20,000	3,600	14,400	5,600
5	20,000	3,600	18,000	2,000
	↑	↑	↑	↑
	(Cost of machine doesn't change.)	(Note that depreciation expense is the same each year.)	(Accumulated depreciation increases by $3,600 each year.)	(Book value each year is lowered by $3,600 until residual value of $2,000 is reached.)

*The depreciation rate is 100 percent ÷ 5 years = 20 percent. The 20 percent is then multiplied times the cost minus the residual value.

UNITS-OF-PRODUCTION METHOD

With the **units-of-production method** it is assumed that *passage of time* does not determine the amount of depreciation taken. Depreciation expense is based on *use,* be it total estimated miles, tons hauled, or estimated units of production (for example, the number of shoes a machine could produce in its expected useful life). The accompanying table shows the calculations that Melvin Company makes for its truck using the units-of-production method (note that for this example the truck is assumed to have an estimated life of 90,000 miles).

The formula is

Depreciation expense is directly related to use, not to passage of time.

$$\frac{\text{Cost} - \text{Residual Value}}{\text{Estimated Units of Production}} = \frac{\$20,000 - \$2,000}{90,000 \text{ Miles}} = \$.20 \text{ per Mile}$$

$$(\$.20) \times (\text{Number of Miles Driven}) = \text{Depreciation Expense for Period}$$

End of Year	Cost of Delivery Truck	Miles Driven in Year	Yearly Depreciation, Expense	Accumulated Depreciation, End of Year	Book Value, End of Year (Cost − Accum. Dep.)
1	$20,000	$30,000	$ 6,000	$ 6,000	$14,000
2	20,000	21,000	4,200	10,200	9,800
3	20,000	15,000	3,000	13,200	6,800
4	20,000	5,000	1,000	14,200	5,800
5	20,000	19,000	3,800	18,000	2,000
		↑	↑		↑
		(After 5 years, truck has been driven 90,000 miles.)	(Depreciation expense is directly related to number of miles driven.)		(Residual value of $2,000 is reached.)

DOUBLE DECLINING-BALANCE METHOD

The **double declining-balance method** is an accelerated method in which a larger depreciation expense is taken in earlier years and smaller amounts in later years. For this reason it is called an **accelerated depreciation method.** This method depreciates at twice the straight-line rate, which is why it is called the *double* declining-balance method.

A key point in this method is that *residual value* is *not* deducted from cost in the calculations, although the asset cannot be depreciated below its residual value. To calculate depreciation, take the following steps:

1.   Calculate the straight-line rate and double it:

$$\frac{100\%}{\text{Useful Life}} \times 2$$

2.   At the *end of each year* multiply the rate times the book value of the asset at the beginning of the year.

Let's look at how Melvin Company calculates the depreciation on its truck using this method.

Note that the rate of .40 is not changed (20% × 2.)

End of Year	Cost	Accumulated Depreciation, Beg. of Year	Book Value Beg. of Year (Cost − Acc. Dep.)	Dep. Exp. (Book Value Beg. of Year × Rate)	Accumulated Depreciation, End of Year	Book Value, End of Year (Cost − Acc. Dep.)
1	$20,000		$20,000	$8,000 ($20,000 × .40)	$ 8,000	$12,000 (20,000 − 8,000)
2	20,000	$ 8,000	12,000	4,800 (12,000 × .40)	12,800 (8,000 + 4,800)	7,200
3	20,000	12,800	7,200	2,880 (7,200 × .40)	15,680	4,320
4	20,000	15,680	4,320	1,728 (4,320 × .40)	17,408	2,592
5	20,000	17,408	2,592	592	18,000	2,000
	↑			↑		↑
	(Original cost remains the same.)			(Depreciation is limited to $592, because the asset cannot depreciate below the residual value.)		(The book value now equals the residual value.)

Be sure to note the $592 in year 5 of depreciation expense. We could not take more than the $592 or we would have depreciated the asset below the residual value.

OPTIONAL SECTION: SUM-OF-THE-YEARS'-DIGITS METHOD

The **sum-of-the-years'-digits method** places more depreciation expense in the early years rather than in the later years to match revenue and expenses better, because an asset's productivity may be reduced in later years. To use it, you multiply cost minus residual times a certain fraction. This fraction is made up of the following:

1. The *denominator.* The denominator is based on how many years the asset is likely to last (say 5). You then add the sum of the digits of five years $(1 + 2 + 3 + 4 + 5)$, which equals 15; 15 is the denominator. [There is also a formula to use for the denominator: $N(N + 1)/2$, where N stands for number of years of useful life (in our case, five years). In our case the formula would give $5(5 + 1)/2 = 15$.]

2. The *numerator.* The years in reverse order are the numerator (in our case, 5, 4, 3, 2, 1).

Thus in year 1 the fraction would be $\frac{5}{15}$; in year 2, $\frac{4}{15}$; in year 3, $\frac{3}{15}$; in year 4, $\frac{2}{15}$; in year 5, $\frac{1}{15}$. In each year you would multiply this fraction times cost minus residual to find the depreciation expense. This process is shown in the following table.

End of Year	$\left(\begin{array}{c}\text{Cost} \\ \text{Minus} \\ \text{Residual}\end{array}\right) \times \left(\begin{array}{c}\text{Fraction} \\ \text{for Year}\end{array}\right)$		Yearly = Depreciation Expense	Accumulated Depreciation, End of Year	Book Value, End of Year (Cost − Accum. Dep.)
1	$18,000 (20,000	$\times \frac{5}{15}$ − 2,000)	= $ 6,000	$ 6,000	$14,000 ($20,000 − $6,000)
2	18,000	$\times \frac{4}{15}$	= 4,800	10,800	9,200
3	18,000	$\times \frac{3}{15}$	= 3,600	14,400	5,600
4	18,000	$\times \frac{2}{15}$	= 2,400	16,800	3,200
5	18,000	$\times \frac{1}{15}$	= 1,200	18,000	2,000
	↑ (Fraction for year is multiplied times cost minus residual.)		↑ (Depreciation expense in first year is highest.)	↑ (Each year depreciation accumulates by a smaller amount.)	↑ (Book value goes down each year until residual is reached.)

Take a moment to make sure you see how the figures for these calculations are arrived at before moving on to the next method.

Now let's look at how Melvin Company could handle depreciation calculations for partial years (if it bought a truck on May 4).

DEPRECIATION FOR PARTIAL YEARS

When depreciating for partial years we assume that for any asset purchased before the 15th of the month, depreciation is calculated for a full month. After the 15th of the month, the depreciation is disregarded for the month.

Straight-Line Method

Original calculation is on p. 615.

For Melvin Company, if the truck was purchased on May 4, depreciation expense would be calculated as follows:

$$\frac{\$20,000 - \$2,000}{5 \text{ Years}} \times \frac{8}{12} = \$2,400$$

We use 8 because the truck was bought on May 4. Do not count the first four months of the year in the calculation of depreciation. The following year the full yearly depreciation would be taken.

Units-of-Production Method

The units-of-production method would not be affected, because depreciation is based on usage, not passage of time.

Double Declining-Balance Method

Original calculation on p. 616.

Because Melvin has the benefit of the truck for eight months, his depreciation on year 1 would be

$$(\$20,000 \times .40) \times \tfrac{8}{12}$$

In year 2 and in future years the annual rate of 40 percent is multiplied times the *current* book value.

Sum-of-the-Years'-Digits Method (Optional Section)

Original calculation on p. 617.

If the truck is bought on May 4, Melvin would receive benefits of eight months of $4,000 ($18,000 $\times \tfrac{5}{15}$) $\times \tfrac{8}{12}$. In the following year Melvin would assume benefits of the last four months of the first year and the first eight months of the second year. Let's look at the calculation for year 2:

$$\text{Year 2} = (\$18,000 \times \tfrac{5}{15}) \times \tfrac{4}{12} + (18,000 \times \tfrac{4}{15}) \times \tfrac{8}{12}$$

Depreciation completed from old year first

DEPRECIATION FOR TAX PURPOSES: MODIFIED ACCELERATED COST RECOVERY SYSTEM (MACRS), INCLUDING THE TAX ACT OF 1989

The 1986 tax act generally overhauled the depreciation setup of property placed in service after December 31, 1986. This **Modified Accelerated Cost Recovery System** is known as MACRS.* Previous methods we have discussed have been for financial reporting, not for tax purposes. This tax law requires a business to depreciate assets placed in service after December 31, 1986. To do so, two factors must be known:

1. Recovery classification.
2. MACRS depreciation rates.

Look for a moment at Figure 17-1 at the top of page 620.

According to the 1986 act, classes 3, 5, 7, and 10 use 200 percent declining balance, switching to straight line, whereas classes 15 and 20 use 150 percent declining balance, switching to straight line. Both residential and nonresidential real property must use straight line. Note that the recovery period is $27\frac{1}{2}$ years for residential property and $31\frac{1}{2}$ years for nonresidential property.

Let's use Table 17-1 to calculate depreciation on the purchase of a nonluxury car for $5,000 on March 19, 1990.

---

*MACRS has been renamed the General Depreciation System (GDS).

TABLE 17-1 ANNUAL RECOVERY (PERCENT OF ORIGINAL DEPRECIABLE BASIS)

Recovery Year	3-Year Class (200% Depreciable Basis)	5-Year Class (200% Depreciable Basis)	7-Year Class (200% Depreciable Basis)	10-Year Class (200% Depreciable Basis)	15-Year Class (150% Depreciable Basis)	20-Year Class (150% Depreciable Basis)
1	33.00	20.00	14.28	10.00	5.00	3.75
2	45.00	32.00	24.49	18.00	9.50	7.22
3	15.00*	19.20	17.49	14.40	8.55	6.68
4	7.00	11.52*	12.49	11.52	7.69	6.18
5		11.52	8.93*	9.22	6.93	5.71
6		5.76	8.93	7.37	6.23	5.28
7			8.93	6.55*	5.90*	4.89
8			4.46	6.55	5.90	4.52
9				6.55	5.90	4.46*
10				6.55	5.90	4.46
11				3.29	5.90	4.46
12					5.90	4.46
13					5.90	4.46
14					5.90	4.46
15					5.90	4.46
16					3.00	4.46
17						

*Identifies when switch is made to the straight-line method.

When we use Table 17-1, we do not have to decide which year we should switch from the declining-balance to the straight-line method.

> Note that auto is now a five-year class.

YEAR	DEPRECIATION	
1	.20 × $5,000 =	$1,000
2	.32 × $5,000 =	1,600
3	.1920 × $5,000 =	960
4	.1152 × $5,000 =	576
5	.1152 × $5,000 =	576
6	.0576 × $5,000 =	288

THE TAX ACT OF 1989

In 1989 the Omnibus Budget Reconciliation Act was passed. One section of the act dealt with depreciation of cellular phones and similar equipment under MACRS. Because cellular phones are subject to personal use, the tax act now treats them as listed property. Thus unless business use is greater than 50 percent, the straight-line method of depreciation is required.

LEARNING UNIT 17-2 REVIEW

AT THIS POINT you should be able to

▼ Explain and calculate the four methods of depreciation. (p. 614)
▼ Calculate depreciation for partial years. (p. 617)
▼ Explain and calculate depreciation for MACRS. (p. 618)

FIGURE 17-1. Summary of Classes for the Tax Reform Act of 1986

The following classes use a 200 percent declining balance, switching to straight line:

▼ 3 year: Race horses more than 2 years old or any horse other than a race horse that is more than 12 years old at time placed into service; special tools of certain industries

▼ 5 year: Automobiles (not luxury); taxis; light general-purpose trucks, semi-conductor manufacturing equipment; computer-based telephone central office switching equipment; qualified technological equipment; property used in connection with research and experimentation

▼ 7 year: Railroad track; single-purpose agricultural (pigpens) or horticultural structure; fixtures, equipment, and furniture

▼ 10 year: The 1986 law doesn't add any specific property under this class.

The following classes use a 150 percent declining balance, switching to straight line:

▼ 15 year: Municipal wastewater treatment plants; telephone distribution plants and comparable equipment used for two-way exchange of voice and data communications

▼ 20 year: Municipal sewers

The following classes use straight line:

▼ 27.5 year: Only residential rental property
▼ 31.5 year: Only nonresidential real property

SELF-REVIEW QUIZ 17-2

(The forms you need are on pages 28 – 29 of the *Study Guide and Working Papers*.)

From the following facts complete depreciation schedules for the (a) straight-line, (b) units-of-production, (c) declining-balance methods, and (d) sum-of-the-years'-digits (optional).

Cost of equipment	$40,000
Residual value	7,000
Service life	5 years
Estimated units of output	20,000
Units produced in year 1:	8,000
2:	2,000
3:	5,000
4:	2,800
5:	2,200

> Remember: Residual value is not subtracted in the declining-balance method, although the equipment cannot be depreciated below residual value.

Solutions to Self-Review Quiz 17-2

a.

End of Year	Cost of Equipment	Yearly Depreciation Expense	Accumulated Depreciation, End of Year	Book Value, End of Year (Cost − Acc. Dep.)
1	$40,000	$6,600	$ 6,600	$33,400 ($40,000 − $6,600)
2	40,000	6,600	13,200	26,800
3	40,000	6,600	19,800	20,200
4	40,000	6,600	26,400	13,600
5	40,000	6,600	33,000	7,000 ← Book value now equals residual value.

b.

End of Year	Cost of Equipment	Units of Output in Year	Yearly Depreciation Expense	Accumulated Depreciation, End of Year	Book Value, End of Year
$\dfrac{\$40,000 - \$7,000}{20,000 \text{ units}} = \$1.65$					
1	$40,000	8,000	$13,200 (8,000 × $1.65)	$13,200	$26,800
2	40,000	2,000	3,300	16,500	23,500
3	40,000	5,000	8,250	24,750	15,250
4	40,000	2,800	4,620	29,370	10,630
5	40,000	2,200	3,630	33,000	7,000

c.

End of Year	Cost	Accumulated Depreciation, Beg. of Year	Book Value Beg. of Year (Cost − Acc. Dep.)	Dep. Exp. (B.V. Beg. of Year × Rate)	Acc. Dep., End of Year	Book Value, End of Year (Cost − Acc. (Dep.)
1	$40,000	—	$40,000	$16,000 ($40,000 × .40)	$16,000	$24,000 ($40,000 − $16,000)
2	40,000	$16,000	24,000	9,600 ($24,000 × .40)	25,600	14,400 ($40,000 − $25,600)
3	40,000	25,600	14,400	5,760	31,360	8,640
4	40,000	31,360	8,640	→ 1,640	33,000	7,000

Only $1,640 could be taken so that book value would not go below residual value.

Rate is 40 percent
$\dfrac{100\%}{5 \text{ Years}} = \dfrac{1.00}{5}$
$= .20 = 20\%$
$2 \times 20\% = 40\%$

d. (optional)

End of Year	Cost Less Residual × Rate = Yearly Depreciation Expense	Accumulated Depreciation, End of Year	Book Value, End of Year
1	$33,000 × $\dfrac{5}{15}$ = $11,000	$11,000	$29,000 ($40,000 − $11,000)
2	$33,000 × $\dfrac{4}{15}$ = 8,800	$19,800	$20,200
3	$33,000 × $\dfrac{3}{15}$ = 6,600	$26,400	$13,600
4	$33,000 × $\dfrac{2}{15}$ = 4,400	$30,800	$9,200
5	$33,000 × $\dfrac{1}{15}$ = 2,200	$33,000	$7,000

Now that we have seen depreciation calculations, let's look at capital and revenue expenditures and the disposal of plant assets.

CAPITAL EXPENDITURES

Capital expenditures include the original cost of an asset as well as payments that improve on or enlarge existing assets. Capital expenditures may be broken down into three categories: additions or enlargements, extraordinary repairs, and betterments. The differences among these three categories are based on whether or not the change will add to the value of the asset, extend the life of the asset, or only improve its efficiency. For example, adding a new wing to a school building will increase the value of the asset, so it is categorized as an **addition or enlargement.** Overhauling an aircraft engine definitely extends the life of the asset, so it is categorized as an **extraordinary repair.** Adding a CB radio to a fleet of delivery trucks improves the efficiency of the asset but does not extend its life, so it is categorized as a **betterment.** These three categories are shown in the chart in Figure 17-2.

It may be a little difficult at first to see the difference between betterments and extraordinary repairs. Betterments do not extend the life of the asset: the cost of a betterment is debited to the asset account. Extraordinary repairs do

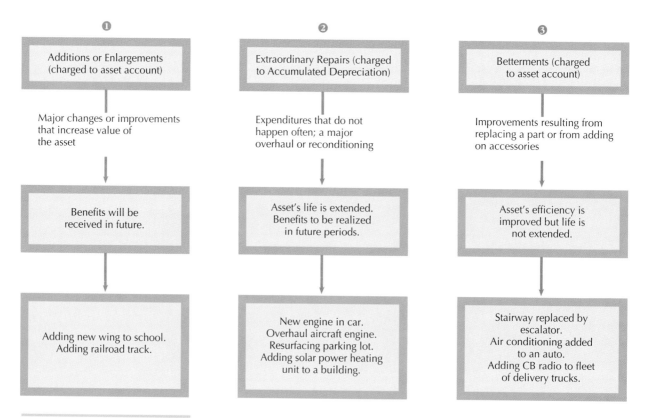

FIGURE 17-2. Three Categories of Capital Expenditures.

extend the life of the asset. The result of the extraordinary repair is to cancel some of the past depreciation.

The following is an example of how to analyze and record an extraordinary repair to a machine whose cost is $20,000, has no residual value, and has an estimated life of 10 years.

Additions or enlargements and betterments are charged to the asset account.

Machine	Accumulated Depreciation, Machine
20,000	16,000 (after 8 years)

Note that after eight years the book value of the machine is $4,000 ($20,000 − $16,000). On March 30, a major overhaul of the machine is completed for $3,000. It is believed that this overhaul will extend the machine's life by three years. Thus the journal entry to record this extraordinary repair is as follows:

Mar.	30	Accumulated Depreciation, Machine	3 0 0 0 00	
		Cash		3 0 0 0 00
		To record extraordinary repair		

Because the machine's life is extended by three years, there are now five years of depreciation to be taken. The new annual depreciation of $1,400 (instead of $1,000) is calculated as follows:

Book value before extraordinary repair	$4,000
Extraordinary repair	3,000
New book value	$7,000 ÷ 5 years = $1,400 per year

If there were an estimated residual value, it would be subtracted from the new book value.

REVENUE EXPENDITURES

Another type of expenditure occurs after an asset has been acquired. *Revenue expenditures* are payments made for ordinary maintenance of an asset or unnecessary or unreasonable situations. These expenditures occur on a regular basis and are recorded as expenses. Examples include changing oil and greasing a car, replacing window panes, changing tires on a truck, repainting a car and adding a sun roof. When an expenditure is treated as a revenue expenditure, it is recorded on the income statement as an expense and thus reduces net income in the period in which it occurred. Now let's turn our attention to the disposal of certain plant assets.

DISPOSAL OF PLANT ASSETS

We now move on to the basic accounting procedures followed when disposing of plant assets in the following ways:

a. Discarding plant assets.

b. Selling plant assets.

c. Exchanging for similar plant assets.

We present a different example for each category (A, B, or C). It is important to remember that depreciation is recorded up until the date a plant asset is disposed of. Take time to compare journal entries to T accounts in each example.

A. Disposal by Discarding Plant Assets

A company discards a plant asset when it is no longer operational (for example, machinery or a truck that no longer works). That also means that no other company is willing to buy or exchange something for the asset.

Situation 1: No Gain or Loss.   Boulder Company is disposing of a $7,000 truck with no residual value that has been fully depreciated (remember that it is possible to keep using a fully depreciated asset, but in this case the asset—the truck—is no longer in working order). Because the asset has been fully depreciated, there will be no need to bring any depreciation up to date before getting rid of it.

The following journal entry is made after disposing of the truck:

Accumulated Depreciation, Truck		7 0 0 0 00	
Truck			7 0 0 0 00

Here is how the ledger for these accounts would look after posting:

Truck		Accumulated Depreciation, Truck	
7,000	7,000	7,000	7,000

Therefore, the truck and the accumulated depreciation associated with it are off the books. Note that there was no gain or loss here.

Situation 2: Loss on Disposal.   Moore Company disposed of a partially depreciated truck. The truck costing $6,000 was considered worthless (depreciation of $5,000 to date). Because we are receiving nothing for this asset that has a book value of $1,000, the difference between the cost of the truck and the accumulated depreciation is a loss. The Loss on Disposal account is categorized as Other Expense on the income statement. Let's look at the journal entry for this loss on disposal and see how the ledger would look after posting:

Loss on Disposal of Plant Asset		1 0 0 0 00	
Accumulated Depreciation, Truck		5 0 0 0 00	
Truck			6 0 0 0 00

Truck		Accumulated Depreciation, Truck		Loss on Disposal of Plant Asset	
6,000	6,000	5,000	5,000	1,000	

Situation 3: Loss from Fire.   Missan Company received a check for $500 from an insurance company, settling a claim on a machine costing $1,500 that was damaged by fire before the end of its useful life. There was a balance in Accumulated Depreciation of $900. The following is the journal entry Missan Company records when it receives the $500 check:

Cash		5 0 0 00	
Loss from Fire		1 0 0 00	
Accumulated Depreciation, Machinery		9 0 0 00	
Machinery			1 5 0 0 00

There is a loss from the fire of $100; the book value of the machine was $600 ($1,500 − $900), and the amount received from the insurance company was $500.

Here is how the ledger would look after posting:

Machinery	Accumulated Depreciation, Machinery	Loss from Fire
1,500 | 1,500	900 | 900	100 |

Now our attention turns to situations when assets could be sold rather than discarded.

B. Disposal by Selling Plant Assets

Situation 4: Gain on Sale. Mason Company sold a truck costing $7,000 for $1,500 cash. The balance in Accumulated Depreciation is $6,000.

To see whether this sale results in a gain or loss, Mason Company must calculate whether the amount of cash received is greater or less than the book value of the truck. If the amount received is greater than the book value, there is a gain. A gain on the sale of a plant asset is categorized as Other Income on the income statement. Let's look at the calculation:

Cost of truck	$7,000	Amount received	$1,500
Less accumulated depreciation	6,000	Less book value	1,000
Book value	$1,000	Gain on sale	$ 500

Because there is a gain on the sale, the following journal entry is made:

Cash		1 5 0 0 00	
Accumulated Depreciation, Truck		6 0 0 0 00	
Truck			7 0 0 0 00
Gain on Sale of Plant Asset			5 0 0 00

Here is what the ledger would look like after posting:

Truck	Accumulated Depreciation, Truck
7,000 | 7,000	6,000 | 6,000

Gain on Sale of Plant Asset
| 500

Situation 5: Loss on Sale. Let's assume that in the previous situation Mason Company receives only $900 cash for the truck.

Now let's look at the calculation Mason Company does to see whether there is a loss or gain:

Cost of truck	$7,000
Less accumulated depreciation	− 6,000
Book value	1,000
Amount received	− 900
Loss on sale	$ 100

When price is less than book value, there is a loss. Because Mason's truck has a book value of $1,000 and the cash received is $900, the end result is a loss of $100 on the sale of the plant asset. This entry is categorized as Other Expense on the income statement. The following is the journal entry prepared by Mason to record this loss:

Cash		9 0 0 00		
Accumulated Depreciation, Truck		6 0 0 0 00		
Loss on Sale of Plant Asset		1 0 0 00		
Truck			7 0 0 0 00	

Here is what the ledger would look like after posting:

Truck		Accumulated Depreciation, Truck		Loss on Sale of Plant Asset
7,000	7,000	6,000	6,000	100

The final category of disposal is exchanging a plant asset rather than discarding or selling.

C. Disposal by Exchanging for Similar Plant Assets

Situation 6: Loss on Exchange. VTR Company trades its old machine costing $19,000 for a new one for a cash price of $22,000 less a trade-in allowance of $2,000. Accumulated Depreciation of the old machine has a balance of $16,000. A **trade-in allowance** is given when you are buying a new car, for example, and trade in your old one for a sum of money that is applied to the price of the new car. A loss on exchange will result if the book value of the old machine is greater than what is received for the trade-in allowance. Let's look at how VTR calculates its loss on this machine exchange.

Step 1: Calculate the book value of the old machine:

Cost	$19,000
− Accumulated depreciation	16,000
Book value	$ 3,000

Step 2: Compare the book value of the old machine with the trade-in:

$3,000	Book value of old
2,000	Trade-in
$1,000	Loss

Because the book value of the old machine is $3,000 and VTR receives only a $2,000 trade-in, the result is a $1,000 loss. The following is the journal entry prepared by VTR:

Machinery		22 0 0 0 00	
Loss on Exchange of Machinery		1 0 0 0 00	
Accumulated Depreciation, Machinery		16 0 0 0 00	
Machinery			19 0 0 0 00
Cash			20 0 0 0 00

The entry puts on the books the cost of the new machine as well as recording the loss on the exchange and the removal of the old machine and the related accumulated depreciation. Note that cash is reduced by $20,000 (cash price less trade-in). Here is what the ledger would look like after posting:

Machinery (Old)		Accumulated Depreciation, Machinery
19,000	19,000	16,000 16,000

Machinery (New)		Loss on Exchange of Machinery
22,000		1,000

Situation 7: Gain Is Absorbed into Cost of New Machine. The Accounting Principles Board has ruled that when a gain exists on an exchange of a similar asset it should not be recorded as a gain, but the new asset should be equal to the book value of the old asset plus cash given in the exchange. In other words, no account called Gain is used, *but the actual gain is absorbed into the cost of the new machine.* The reason behind this decision was that an exchange of similar assets is not the result of an earnings process. In this situation we assume that VTR (situation 6) will receive a $5,000 trade-in allowance (instead of the $2,000) for trading in an old machine for a new machine for a cash price of $22,000. VTR will complete the following steps to calculate the new cost of the machine (assuming a gain). Remember that a gain would be absorbed into the cost of the new machine for exchanges of similar assets.

1. Calculate the book value of the old machine.
2. Identify the cash paid (cash price less trade-in).
3. Calculate the value of the new machine as it will show up on the books. (This value is called the cash basis of the machine.) This step is done by adding steps 1 and 2.

Let's now look at VTR's actual calculation of these steps.

Step 1: Calculate the book value of the old machine:

$$\begin{aligned} \$19{,}000 \\ -\,16{,}000 \\ \hline = \$\,3{,}000 \end{aligned}$$

Step 2: Identify cash paid:

$$\$17{,}000\ (\$22{,}000 - \$5{,}000)$$

Step 3: New cash basis (step 1 + step 2):

$$\underline{\$20{,}000}\ (\$3{,}000 + \$17{,}000)$$

Note that the cash basis is $20,000, not $22,000 as stated as original cost of new equipment. Note also that the new machine shows up on the books at the value of the things that were given up for it: an old machine with a book value of $3,000 and cash of $17,000.

Now let's look at how VTR records this exchange on its books:

Machinery	20 0 0 0 00	
Accumulated Depreciation, Machinery	16 0 0 0 00	
Machinery		19 0 0 0 00
Cash		17 0 0 0 00

Note that there is no account that records the gain. The gain is absorbed into the cost of the new asset. Remember that a gain results in *less* depreciation in the future, because the cost of the machine has a value of $20,000, not $22,000. The ledger when posted would look as follows:

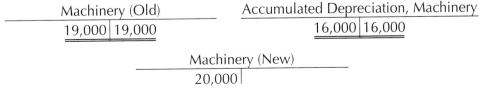

Machinery (Old)	Accumulated Depreciation, Machinery
19,000	19,000	16,000	16,000

Machinery (New)
20,000	

Income tax rules agree with accountants regarding nonrecognition of gains and absorbing them into cost of new asset (situation 7). The Internal Revenue

Service also believes losses should not be recognized and thus should be absorbed into cost of new assets.* Often two sets of records are kept. Situation 6 followed guidelines of the Accounting Principles Board. Situation 8 follows tax rules of the Internal Revenue Service. Compare the two.

Situation 8: Loss Is Absorbed in Cost of New Asset.   Let's assume that VTR receives only a $2,000 trade-in allowance instead of $5,000 (situation 7) when the old machine is traded in for the new machine for a cash price of $22,000. VTR calculates the cost basis of the new machine (assuming it uses the **income tax method** of absorbing losses into the cost of the new machine) as follows:

Cost of old machine	$19,000
− Accumulated depreciation	16,000
= Book value	3,000
+ Cash paid	20,000
($22,000 − $2,000)	
= Cost basis of new machine	$23,000

This loss of $1,000 (VTR having received $1,000 less than the book value) is *added on* to the cost of the new machine, resulting in a cost basis of $23,000. VTR records the exchange in the journal as follows:

Machinery		23 0 0 0 00	
Accumulated Depreciation, Machinery		16 0 0 0 00	
Machinery			19 0 0 0 00
Cash			20 0 0 0 00

Note that there is no Loss account. The loss has been absorbed into the cost of the equipment, the result being that more depreciation will be taken in future periods ($23,000 versus $22,000), because the cost of the new equipment is $1,000 higher.

Here is what the ledger would look like after posting:

Machinery (Old)		Accumulated Depreciation, Machinery	
19,000	19,000	16,000	16,000

Machinery (New)	
23,000	

LEARNING UNIT 17-3 REVIEW

AT THIS POINT you should be able to

▼ Compare and contrast capital and revenue expenditures. (p. 622)
▼ Prepare journal entries to record discarding, selling, or exchanging plant assets. (p. 624)
▼ Compare and contrast Internal Revenue procedures with those of the Financial Accounting Principles Board regarding gains and losses that result from exchanges of plant assets. (p. 627)

---

*Accountants will do this only if loss is considered to be immaterial.

SELF-REVIEW QUIZ 17-3

(The forms you need are on page 29 of the *Study Guide and Working Papers*.)
Respond true or false to the following:

1. In selling a plant asset, a gain results if cash received is greater than the book value of the asset sold.
2. A loss on exchange of equipment can result if the book value of the old equipment is less than the trade-in allowance.
3. The Financial Accounting Principles Board does not recognize gains on exchange of similar assets.
4. Internal Revenue Service rules are consistent with the Financial Accounting Principles Board in recognizing losses when assets are exchanged.
5. When a loss is absorbed into the cost of an asset, it allows for more depreciation in future periods.
6. Revenue expenditures extend the useful life of an asset.
7. Putting an air conditioner in a truck is an example of a betterment.

Solutions to Self-Review Quiz 17-3

1. True **2.** False **3.** True **4.** False **5.** True **6.** False **7.** True

---

LEARNING UNIT 17-4 NATURAL RESOURCES AND INTANGIBLE ASSETS

There's another type of long-term asset, natural resources, that we haven't discussed yet. Natural resources consist of natural assets such as oil, coal, or timber. The acquisition of oil wells or timber is recorded at cost, and as the oil or timber or coal is extracted from the earth, the allocation of that cost occurs through a process known as **depletion.** Depletion is similar to the units-of-production method of depreciation, discussed earlier in the chapter, and is listed as an operating expense on the income statement.

Let's take the example of a coal deposit. If a coal deposit has 200,000 tons available and was purchased for $200,000, the depletion per ton is $1. Thus if 91,000 tons were removed from the deposit in 20X1, the depletion charge that year would be recorded as follows:

20X1					
Dec.	31	Depletion of Coal Deposit	91 0 0 0 00		
		Accumulated Depletion, Coal		91 0 0 0 00	

> Accumulated Depletion is a contra-asset on the balance sheet.

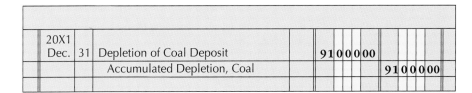

Coal Deposit	Accumulated Depreciation, Coal
200,000 |	|91,000
(on balance sheet)	(on balance sheet)

Depletion of Coal Deposit
91,000 \|
(on income statement)

INTANGIBLE ASSETS

Intangible assets are long-lived assets that have no physical existence but do represent valuable legal rights and monetary relationships that benefit a company. (In fact, Prepaid Insurance, Notes, and Accounts Receivable are intangible, but they are classified as *current* assets.) We are looking at intangible assets classified in the *long-term* asset section. Examples include patents, copyrights, franchises, and goodwill. Intangible assets are recorded at cost on the balance sheet and usually have no contra-accounts.

The process of allocating the cost of an intangible asset over all the periods it provides benefits is called amortization. The expense incurred in acquiring these assets is **amortized;** that means it is written off over a fixed number of years. **Amortization expense** is an operating expense on the income statement.

Patents

> A patent is good for 20 years but is amortized for a shorter period.

A **patent** is an exclusive right to the owner to sell or produce his or her discovery or invention. Let's assume that on January 1, 20XX, a patent costing $100,000 is amortized over 10 years. The following adjusting entry is made:

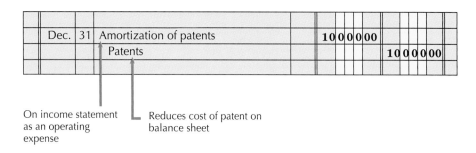

Dec.	31	Amortization of patents		10 00 0 00	
		Patents			10 00 0 00

On income statement as an operating expense

Reduces cost of patent on balance sheet

Copyrights

Copyrights are exclusive rights to publish artistic, literary, or musical work granted to owners by the federal government. In the United States a copyright is granted for the life of the creator and for 50 years thereafter. The cost of the copyright is recorded as a cost and amortized over its expected useful life in an account called Amortization Expense, Copyrights.

Franchises

A **franchise** is the result of someone purchasing an exclusive privilege or right to sell a manufacturer's product or a service in a specifically defined geographical location. Holiday Inns, for example, are franchises. The cost of obtaining a franchise is amortized over its life or 40 years, whichever is shorter.

Goodwill

> Cost of assets purchased
> − Value of assets identified
> = Goodwill

When all or part of a business is purchased, the difference between the price paid and the value of the identifiable assets is called **goodwill.** Goodwill occurs when the expected rate of future earnings is greater than the rate of earnings for the industry standard. Some considerations that may cause goodwill could include brand names, business location, and service. It is not easy to pinpoint the exact amount of goodwill in each accounting period. Thus in the accounting profession it is agreed not to put a cost on goodwill until a company is bought or sold.

LEARNING UNIT 17-4 REVIEW

AT THIS POINT you should be able to

▼ Define depletion and accumulated depletion and indicate their normal balances and on which financial reports they are located. (p. 629)
▼ Explain amortization. (p. 630)
▼ Discuss how a patent is amortized. (p. 630)
▼ Explain the life of a copyright. (p. 630)
▼ Define and explain how goodwill is calculated. (p. 630)

SELF-REVIEW QUIZ 17-4

(The forms you need are on page 29 of the *Study Guide and Working Papers*.)
Respond true or false to the following:

1. Intangible assets are depleted, not amortized.
2. The life of a patent is 12 years.
3. A copyright lasts for 25 years.
4. The cost of a franchise must be amortized over 40 years.
5. Goodwill represents excess earning power for a company.

Solutions to Self-Review Quiz 17-4

1. False   2. False   3. False   4. False   5. True

CHAPTER REVIEW

SUMMARY OF KEY POINTS

Learning Unit 17-1

1. Total cost of an asset includes all expenditures that are reasonable and necessary in acquiring it and getting it into position and in condition for use in the company.
2. Cash discounts are deducted from the cost of an asset.
3. Incidental costs related to the purchase of land and special costs that add a permanent value are added to the cost of land.
4. The Land Improvements account records improvements to land that have a limited useful life (such as driveways or fences). This account is subject to depreciation.
5. The cost of buying a building would include purchase price and all cost of repairs and other expenses to get the building ready for use. When constructing a new building, the cost would include all payments necessary to get the building ready for use.

Learning Unit 17-2

In this unit we look at four different depreciation methods.

1. Straight-line method:
   a. Depreciation expense is the same each year.
   b. Book value each year is lowered until residual value is reached.
2. Units-of-production method: Depreciation expense is directly related to output or usage of asset.
3. Double declining-balance method:
   a. Residual value is not deducted from cost.
   b. Depreciation expense is book value at beginning of year times rate.
   c. Asset cannot depreciate below book value.
4. Sum-of-the-years'-digits method (optional section):
   a. Fraction for the year is multiplied times cost less residual value.
   b. Depreciation in year 1 is highest.
5. Depreciation can be taken for partial years. If an asset is purchased in the first 15 days of the month, the whole month is considered in the depreciation calculation.
6. MACRS are for tax reporting, whereas the other four depreciation methods are used for financial reports.

Learning Unit 17-3

1. Capital expenditures include the original cost of an asset and three categories of additional payments:
   a. Additions or enlargements: major changes or improvements that increase the value of an asset.
   b. Extraordinary repairs: extend the life of the asset.
   c. Betterments: improvements that increase efficiency but do not extend the life of an asset. Additions or enlargements and betterments are charged to the asset account; extraordinary repairs are charged to Accumulated Depreciation.

2. After an asset is acquired, the expenditures for ordinary maintenance and unnecessary or unreasonable situations that do not try to extend useful life are treated as expenses of the current period and are called revenue expenditures.

3. A plant asset can be disposed of by discarding, selling, or exchanging it.

4. The Loss on Disposal account appears as Other Expense on the income statement.

5. A gain on sale of an asset occurs if the cash received is greater than the book value of the asset. Such a gain appears as Other Income on the income statement.

6. When a plant asset is exchanged, loss occurs when the trade-in allowance is less than the book value of the asset.

7. In an exchange of similar assets, the Financial Accounting Principles Board has ruled that gains are to be absorbed into the cost of the new asset.

8. Income tax rules require that gains *and losses* on exchange of assets be absorbed into the cost of the new asset. This requirement is inconsistent with the Financial Accounting Principles Board's ruling on losses.

Learning Unit 17-4

1. Natural resources, such as oil, coal, or timber, will deplete over a period of time as resources are extracted. Depletion expense is listed as an operating expense on the income statement.

2. Accumulated depletion is a contra-asset on the balance sheet.

3. Intangible assets, such as patents, copyrights, franchises, and goodwill, are also used up over a period of years. Amortization is the process of estimating and recording the charges as these intangible assets are used up.

4. Amortization expenses are operating expenses on the income statement.

5. A patent is good for 17 years; a copyright is granted for the life of the creator and 50 years thereafter.

6. The cost of obtaining a franchise is amortized over its life or 40 years, whichever is shorter.

7. Because it is not easy to put a price on goodwill in each accounting period, it is not until a company is bought or sold that a cost is placed on goodwill.

KEY TERMS

Accelerated depreciation   More depreciation taken in early years of asset's life, decreasing amounts in later years.

Additions or enlargements   Major changes or improvements that increase the value of an asset (such as adding a new wing to a school).

Amortization expense   An operating expense on the income statement relating to intangible assets.

Amortize   To charge a portion of an expenditure over a fixed number of years.

Betterments   Improvements that increase the efficiency of an asset by adding accessories or replacing parts.

Book value   Cost of asset less accumulated depreciation.

Capital expenditures   Original cost of an asset as well as additions or enlargements, extraordinary repairs, and betterments.

Copyright   The exclusive right that is granted by the federal government to sell and reproduce literary, musical, or artistic works for a period of time.

Depletion   Amount of natural resources that has been exhausted by mining, pumping, and so forth for a period of time.

Double declining-balance method   An accelerated depreciation method that uses up to twice the straight-line rate times book value of asset to calculate depreciation expense. Residual value is not subtracted from cost of asset in determining depreciation.

Extraordinary repairs   Infrequent expenditures that extend an asset's life (such as a new engine in a car).

Franchise A right granted by business or government to produce or sell goods in a specific geographic region. Examples are a Burger King or Holiday Inn.

Goodwill When a business is purchased, the difference between the price paid and the value of the identifiable assets is goodwill. Goodwill may depend on brand names, business location, service, or other elements; it is a valuable asset that plays an important part in the expected rate of future earnings of a business.

Income tax method When plant assets are exchanged, tax law says the gain or loss must be absorbed into the cost of new asset.

Intangible assets Assets having no physical substance (such as patents or franchises).

Land Improvements An asset account that records improvements made to land; such improvements have a limited life and are subject to depreciation (an example is a driveway or fences).

Modified Accelerated Cost Recovery System (MACRS) A system for businesses to calculate depreciation for tax purposes based on the Tax Laws of 1986 and 1989. Also known as the General Depreciation System (GDS).

Patent An exclusive right to sell or produce his or her discovery or invention. A patent is good for 20 years.

Residual (salvage) value The amount of the asset's cost that will be recovered when the asset is sold, traded in, or scrapped.

Straight-line method Method that allocates an equal amount of depreciation over an asset's period of usefulness.

Sum-of-the-years'-digits method An accelerated method that allocates depreciation each period of an asset's life by multiplying a fraction for that period times cost less residual value.

Trade-in allowance A value received when one asset is traded in on the purchase of another asset. For example, when you buy a new car you may trade in your old car for an amount of money that is applied toward the purchase of the new car.

Units-of-production method A depreciation method that is based on usage and not on time. An example of units of production is the numbers of shoes a machine could produce in its expected useful life.

Useful life At the time an asset is acquired an estimate is made of its usefulness in terms of years, output, and so forth.

BLUEPRINT: KEY ACCOUNTS

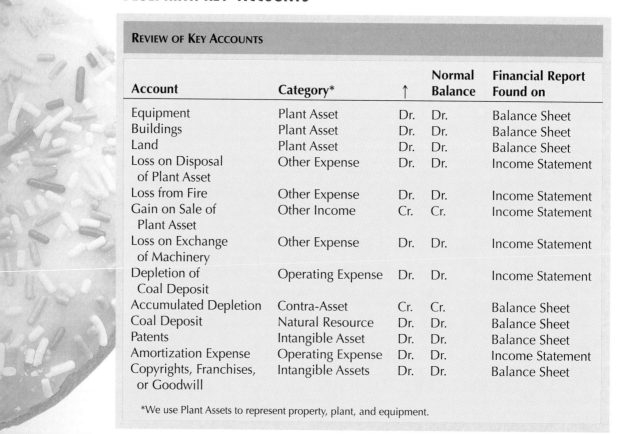

REVIEW OF KEY ACCOUNTS

Account	Category*	↑	Normal Balance	Financial Report Found on
Equipment	Plant Asset	Dr.	Dr.	Balance Sheet
Buildings	Plant Asset	Dr.	Dr.	Balance Sheet
Land	Plant Asset	Dr.	Dr.	Balance Sheet
Loss on Disposal of Plant Asset	Other Expense	Dr.	Dr.	Income Statement
Loss from Fire	Other Expense	Dr.	Dr.	Income Statement
Gain on Sale of Plant Asset	Other Income	Cr.	Cr.	Income Statement
Loss on Exchange of Machinery	Other Expense	Dr.	Dr.	Income Statement
Depletion of Coal Deposit	Operating Expense	Dr.	Dr.	Income Statement
Accumulated Depletion	Contra-Asset	Cr.	Cr.	Balance Sheet
Coal Deposit	Natural Resource	Dr.	Dr.	Balance Sheet
Patents	Intangible Asset	Dr.	Dr.	Balance Sheet
Amortization Expense	Operating Expense	Dr.	Dr.	Income Statement
Copyrights, Franchises, or Goodwill	Intangible Assets	Dr.	Dr.	Balance Sheet

*We use Plant Assets to represent property, plant, and equipment.

QUESTIONS, MINI EXERCISES, EXERCISES, AND PROBLEMS

Discussion Questions

1. What types of payment are considered "reasonable and necessary" when determining cost of an asset?
2. What is the purpose of the Land Improvements account?
3. What is the difference between revenue and capital expenditures?
4. What are four methods of calculating depreciation? Briefly explain the key points of each.
5. What is the purpose of the Modified Accelerated Cost Recovery System?
6. A betterment is a revenue expenditure. True or false? Please explain.
7. Which method of depreciation does *not* deduct residual value in its calculation?
8. When a plant asset is sold, a loss results if the cash received is greater than book value. Defend or reject. Please explain.
9. A loss on an exchange of plant assets occurs when the book value of the old machine is more than the trade-in allowance. True or false?
10. Explain how the income tax method differs from the Accounting Principles Board ruling with regard to the recording exchanges of plant assets that result in a loss.
11. What is the purpose of the accumulated depletion account?
12. List and describe three intangible assets.

Mini Exercises

(The forms you need are on pages 31 – 32 of the *Study Guide and Working Papers.*)

Cost of Property, Plant, and Equipment

1. Calculate the total cost of the machine given the following:

List price	$2,000
Cash discount	5%
Freight	$ 50
Assembly	150
Special foundation	50

Straight-Line Method

2. Mel Jones depreciates his truck by the straight-line method. Calculate the yearly depreciation expense given the following:

Cost	$6,000
Residual value	$1,000
Service of useful life	10 years

Book Value

3. If a machine had a cost of $4,000 with an accumulated depreciation of $1,000, what would be its book value?

Units-of-Production Method

4. If Mel Jones (Mini Exercise 2) depreciated his truck by the units-of-production method, calculate the first year's depreciation based on the following: Cost $6,000; residual value $1,000. Estimated mileage is 100,000. The truck was driven 8,000 miles in year 1.

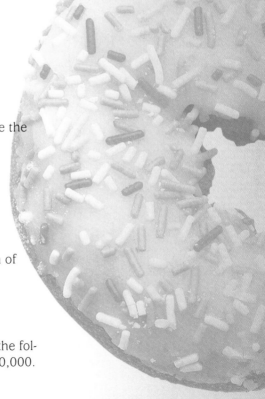

Double Declining-Balance Method

5. If Mel Jones (Mini Exercise 2) depreciated his truck by the double declining-balance method, calculate the depreciation expense for year 1.

Sum-of-the-Year's-Digits Method (Optional)

6. If Mel Jones (Mini Exercise 2) depreciated his truck by the sum-of-the-year's-digits method, calculate the first year's depreciation. Round the answer to the nearest dollar.

Capital and Revenue Expenditures

7. Identify each situation as a Capital or Revenue Expenditure.

Situation	Capital Expenditure		Revenue Expenditure
	Addition	Betterment/ Extraordinary Repair	
a. New tires			
b. New air conditioning for a car			
c. New car engine			
d. New addition on school			

Loss and Gains

8. Complete the following:

	Account	Category	Financial Statement Found on
a. Accumulated Depletion			
b. Loss on Disposal of Plant Assets			
c. Gain on Sale of Plant Assets			

Exchange with Loss

9. Pete Co. traded in an old machine costing $10,000 for a new machine for a cash price of $13,000 with a trade-in allowance of $3,000. Accumulated Depreciation on the old machine was $6,000.

    a. What is book value of the old machine? What is the loss?

    b. Provide a journal entry to record the exchange.

Exchange with Gain

10. Assume in Mini Exercise 9 the trade-in value was $5,000. Prepare a journal entry to record the exchange.

Income Tax Method

11. If in Mini Exercise 9 the income tax method was used, prepare the journal entry to record the exchange.

Exercises

(The forms you need are on pages 33 – 36 of the *Study Guide and Working Papers*.)

17-1. Mack Company incurred the following expenditures to buy a new machine:

Calculating cost of equipment.

- ▼ Invoice, $30,000 less 10 percent cash discount.
- ▼ Freight charges, $500.
- ▼ Assembly charges, $1,400.
- ▼ Special base to support machine, $505.
- ▼ Machine dropped and repaired, $350.

What is the actual cost of the machine?

17-2. From the following, prepare depreciation schedules for the first two years for (a) straight-line, (b) units-of-production, (c) double declining-balance at twice the straight-line rate, and (d) sum-of-the-years'-digits (optional) methods.

Depreciation schedules.

- ▼ Machine purchased on January 1, $1,440.
- ▼ Residual value, $240.
- ▼ Estimated useful life, five years.
- ▼ Total estimated output, 600 units.
- ▼ Output year 1, 100 units.
- ▼ Output year 2, 200 units.

17-3. Larson Co., whose accounting period ends on December 31, purchased a machine for $6,800 on January 1 with an estimated residual value of $800 and estimated useful life of 10 years. Prepare depreciation schedules for the current as well as the following year using (a) straight-line, (b) double declining-balance at twice the straight-line rate, and (c) sum-of-the-years'-digits methods (optional).

Depreciation schedules.

17-4. A machine that cost $9,000 with $3,900 of accumulated depreciation was traded in for a similar machine having a $5,800 cash price. An $800 trade-in was offered by the seller.

Loss on exchange and income tax methods.

- **a.** Calculate the book value of the old machine.
- **b.** Calculate the loss on the exchange.
- **c.** Prepare the journal entry for the exchange.
- **d.** Calculate the cost basis of the new equipment if the income tax method is used and prepare a journal entry.

17-5. On May 1, 20X1, Osgood Company bought a patent at a cost of $5,000. It is estimated that the patent will give Osgood a competitive advantage for 10 years. Record in general journal form amortization for 20X1 and 20X2. (Assume December 31 is the end of the accounting period for Osgood.)

Patent.

17-6. Pultzer Company bought a light general-purpose truck for $9,000 on March 8, 1991. Calculate the yearly depreciation using the MACRS method.

MACRS and Tax Reform Act of 1986.

Group A Problems

(The forms you need are on pages 37–42 of the *Study Guide and Working Papers*.)

17A-1. Record the following transactions into the general journal of Orange Company:

Property, plant, and equipment transactions.

20XX

Feb.	5	Purchased land for $86,000. The $86,000 included attorney's fees of $5,000.
	18	Orange Company decided to pave the parking lot for $5,400.
Mar.	24	Purchased a building for $90,000, putting down 30 percent and mortgaging the remainder.
	29	Bought equipment for $32,000. Freight and assembly were an additional $4,000.

May	10	Added a new wing for $175,000 to building that was purchased on March 24.
June	15	Performed ordinary repair work on equipment purchased March 29, $750, to maintain its normal operations.
July	1	Bought a truck for $14,000.
Oct.	15	Added a hydraulic loader to truck, $2,200.
Nov.	30	Truck purchased in July was brought in for grease and oil, $33.
Dec.	30	Overhauled truck's motor for $900, extending its life by more than one year.
Dec.	31	Changed tires on truck, $325.

17A-2. On January 1, 20X1, a machine was installed at Lavy Factory at a cost of $58,000. Its estimated residual value at the end of its estimated life of four years is $18,000. The machine is expected to produce 80,000 units with the following production schedule:

▼ 20X1: 12,000 units
▼ 20X2: 27,000 units
▼ 20X3: 15,000 units
▼ 20X4: 26,000 units

Complete depreciation schedules for (a) straight-line, (b) units-of-production, (c) double declining-balance at twice the straight-line rate, and (d) sum-of-the-years'-digits (optional) methods.

17A-3. On June 13, 20X1, Cook Company bought equipment for $4,080. Its estimated life is four years with a residual value of $240. Prepare depreciation schedules for 20X1, 20X2, and 20X3 for (a) straight-line, (b) double declining-balance at twice the straight-line rate, and (c) sum-of-the-years'-digits (optional) methods.

17A-4. Journalize the following transactions for the Robe Company and below each entry show all calculations:

20XX

Jan.	1	Sold a truck for $1,250 that cost $6,750 and had accumulated depreciation of $6,100.
Feb.	10	A machine costing $3,200 with accumulated depreciation of $2,450 was destroyed in a fire. The insurance company settled the claim for $300.
May	1	Traded in a machine costing $19,400 with $16,500 of accumulated depreciation for a new machine costing $25,100 with a trade-in allowance of $2,700. Note that depreciation is up to date. The loss is to be recognized.
July	8	Traded in a machine costing $40,000 with $34,000 of accumulated depreciation (which is up to date) for a new machine for a cash price of $45,000 and a trade-in allowance of $8,000.
Aug.	9	Journalize the May 1 transaction using the income tax method.
Sept.	12	A truck costing $7,000 and fully depreciated was disposed of.

Group B Problems

(The forms you need are on pages 37 – 42 of the *Study Guide and Working Papers*.)

17B-1. Journalize the following transactions for Orange Company.

20XX

Apr.	1	Purchased a machine for $89,500 along with an additional charge for freight and assembly of $1,500.
	8	Purchased land at a cost of $22,000. The $22,000 included attorney's fees of $2,500.
	15	Purchased a building for $90,000, putting down 10 percent and mortgaging the remainder.

29 At a cost of $1,900, cleared and graded the land purchased on April 8 (the additional cost considered as part of cost of land).

May 1 Performed regular maintenance work on machinery, $160, to maintain its normal operations.

8 Painted the building purchased on April 15, $2,900. Painting was necessary to have the building ready for proper use.

30 Purchased a second airplane for company business, $65,000.

June 30 Installed a hydraulic loader on a truck at a cost of $2,900.

July 30 First airplane's engine was overhauled for $7,900.

Sept. 30 Building is completely renovated at a cost of $30,000, which will extend its life by 10 years.

Check Figure:
May 8:
Dr. Building $2,900
Cr. Cash $2,900

17B-2. On January 1, 20X1, Lavy Factory installed a new machine at a cost of $117,000. Its estimated residual value at the end of its estimated life of four years is $9,000. The machine is expected to produce 90,000 units with the following production schedule:

▼ 20X1: 11,000 units
▼ 20X2: 9,000 units
▼ 20X3: 11,000 units
▼ 20X4: 59,000 units

Methods of computing depreciation.

Complete depreciation schedules for (a) straight-line, (b) units-of-production, (c) double declining-balance at twice the straight-line rate, and (d) sum-of-the-years'-digits (optional) methods.

Check Figure:
(d) Dep. expense 20X3
$21,600

17B-3. On April 5, 20X1, Cook Company bought equipment for $6,200. Its estimated life is five years with a residual value of $200. Prepare depreciation schedules for 20X1, 20X2, and 20X3 for (a) straight-line, (b) double declining-balance at twice the straight-line rate, and (c) sum-of-the-years'-digits (optional) methods.

Check Figure:
(c) Dep. expense 20X1
$1,500

17B-4. Journalize the following transactions for the Robe Company and below each entry show all calculations:

Disposing of plant assets.

20XX

Jan. 1 Sold a truck for $3,600 that cost $12,800 and had accumulated depreciation of $10,900.

Feb. 8 A machine costing $4,000 with accumulated depreciation of $3,390 was destroyed in a fire. The insurance company settled the claim for $150.

May 9 Traded in a machine costing $18,500 with $15,750 of accumulated depreciation (which is up to date) for a new machine costing $26,200 with a trade-in allowance of $2,600. The loss is to be recognized.

Check Figure:
May:
Loss on exchange $150 Dr.

July 10 Traded in a machine costing $39,500 with $35,700 of accumulated depreciation (depreciation is up to date) for a new machine for a cash price of $44,000 and a trade-in allowance of $11,500.

Aug. 19 Journalize the May 9 transaction using the income tax method.

Sept. 12 A truck costing $11,000 and fully depreciated was disposed of.

REAL-WORLD APPLICATIONS

17R-1.

On August 1, 20X1, Hope Co. purchased a customized light truck for $96,000 cash. On August 3, special shelving was added to the truck for $6,000. The truck has a useful life of six years with a trade-in value of $12,000 and is depreciated by the straight-line method. On January 1, 20X4, Hope Co. was trying to decide whether to overhaul the truck at a cost of $15,000 or buy a new truck for $100,000 and depreciate it by MACRS. Overhauling the truck would increase its useful life by two years, and residual value would remain at $12,000.

As the accountant of Hope Co., you have been called into a meeting with Mr. Reynolds, the vice president, to further discuss this matter. Bring all your data with you, along with a written recommendation.

17R-2.

Work up a comparison of MACRS and straight-line depreciation along with a written recommendation to help Pete Sanchez make his decision.

YOU make the call

Critical Thinking/Ethical Case

17R-3.

Pete went to an auto dealer to buy a new Jeep. The salesperson told Pete that cars really appreciate in value. He cited antique cars as a perfect example. The dealer went on to tell Pete that buying a car represents some great tax savings. He told Pete that leasing is getting less and less popular. Should Pete buy a new car? You make the call. Write down your recommendations to Pete.

INTERNET EXERCISES

EX-1. [www.boeing.com/commercial/prices/index.html] This site shows you about how much you would have to pay to have a Boeing jetliner for your weekend jaunts. The costs in the examples are for jets ready to fly away from the production line. Before you commit to deciding which model you want, you have some homework to do. Write down some of the costs that you, or the airline you own, would have to consider as part of the cost of this valuable asset. Consider the factors you learned in this chapter that are part of the cost of an asset, and consider factors like who will pay for delivery of the jet to the runway near your desert retreat. Give some examples of "revenue expenditures" that would go into operation of your plane.

EX-2. [www.lufthansa.com/dlh/en/htm/presse/bildarchiv/index.html] Many industries have special ways of depreciating their Plant and Equipment assets. One method taught in this chapter on Plant and Equipment Assets is that of "units of production." An airline is required by federal regulations to completely overhaul its engines every 2,000 flight hours. The engines are completely stripped down and rebuilt at that point. This results in a completely reconditioned engine. The cost of one of these engines is, perhaps, $5 million.

1. Using the number of flight hours, what is the "per unit" depreciation if the "unit" is one hour of operation?

2. If the engine is operated for a total of 1,500 hours this year, how much depreciation will be recorded using the "units of production" method?

CHAPTER 18

Partnerships

If you're feeling entrepreneurial, the best way to get inspired is to look at how successful companies got their start. They usually begin with nothing more than enthusiastic partners and a winning idea. Ben & Jerry's Homemade, Inc. is a classic example. The Vermont-based manufacturer of ice cream, frozen yogurt and sorbet was founded in 1978 by two childhood friends, Ben Cohen and Jerry Greenfield. They set up shop in a renovated gas station with only a $12,000 investment, $4,000 of which was borrowed. They soon became tremendously popular, not only for their innovative flavors, like Bovinity Divinity and Chunky Monkey, but for their social mission, which they carry out by donating 7.5% of profits to liberal causes. Twenty-two years later European consumer product giant, Unilever, bought this once small and homespun company for $329 million dollars!

Partnerships are now spawning thousands of dot coms, too. The story of Yahoo! Founders Jerry Yang and David Filo is now legend. In 1994, the two Stanford graduate students came up with a way to categorize Web sites. Begun as a hobby, their guide, named Yahoo!, was the first place for Web browsers to find sites easily. Now Yahoo! is a global Internet communications, commerce, and media company with over 2000 employees. Yahoo! has a global Web network of 21 properties and offices in Europe, Asia, Latin America, Canada, and the United States.

When two or more people agree to be partners in a business enterprise the result is a **partnership.** In this chapter you will learn how to calculate a partner's share of net income based on the investment in the business. You will also learn about the advantages and disadvantages of forming a partnership — and how to liquidate this type of ownership, if it should become necessary. Businesses do not stay partnerships for long. For instance, it wasn't long before Ben Cohen and Jerry Greenfield decided to incorporate their business, putting the "Inc." in Ben & Jerry's, or before David Filo and Jerry Yang

became part of Yahoo! Inc. One of the characteristics of a partnership is its **limited life.** When there is a change in membership or when someone leaves, a partnership is dissolved. Also, as businesses expand they often incorporate to protect the partners from **unlimited liability,** one of the risks of partnership that you'll learn about in this chapter.

Based on: [Yahoo!] Information from http://join.yahoo.com/chief.html and http://join.yahoo.com/overview.html. [Ben & Jerry's] Information from http://benjerry.com. David Gram, "Here's the scoop on moving, shaking in Ben & Jerry's sale," *Houston Chronicle,* May 14, 2000, p. 7. Fred Bayles, "Reviews in on Ben & Jerry's Sweet Deal," *USA Today,* April 20, 2000.

LEARNING OBJECTIVES

▼ Journalizing the entry for formation of a partnership. (p. 643)

▼ Calculating a partner's share of net income based on fractional ratio, beginning capital investment, and salary and interest allowances. (p. 646)

▼ Preparing a statement of partners' equity. (p. 650)

▼ Journalizing entries to record admitting a new partner, withdrawal of a partner, and bonuses to partners. (p. 651)

▼ Journalizing entries involved in the liquidation process and preparing a statement of liquidation. (p. 656)

Up to this point we have been using the sole proprietorship form of business organization in discussing the accounting process. We are now ready to look at another form of business organization, the **partnership.**

A partnership, as defined by the **Uniform Partnership Act,** is "an association of two or more persons to carry on as co-owners a business for profit." Examples of partnerships include service businesses and professional practitioners, such as physicians, dentists, attorneys, and accountants. Many small wholesale as well as retail companies are formed as partnerships. Your local convenience store may be a partnership.

The recording of business transactions involving assets, liabilities, revenue, and expenses is handled the same for both a sole proprietorship and a partnership. The major difference in recording business transactions for these two forms of organization lies in the capital account(s). A sole proprietorship has only one capital and withdrawals account, whereas in a partnership each owner has his or her own separate capital and withdrawals account. First we look at the characteristics of a partnership and how it is formed.

LEARNING UNIT 18-1

PARTNERSHIP CHARACTERISTICS AND FORMATION OF PARTNERSHIPS

It is quite easy to form a partnership. When two or more people agree orally or in writing to be partners, a contract results. Although the oral agreement is binding, it makes more sense to seek legal advice and have a formal written agreement prepared. Putting agreements in writing may minimize conflicts in the future. This written agreement, which formalizes the partners' relationship, is called the **articles of partnership.**

Some things that should be included in the written articles of partnership are the following:

1. Name and address of each partner, along with the date of agreement.
2. Rights and responsibilities of each partner.
3. Amount that each partner is investing.
4. Specific manner in which partners' profits or losses will be shared.
5. Provisions for one or more partners quitting the partnership.
6. How new partners will be admitted.
7. How assets will be distributed if the business is completely terminated.
8. How accounting records will be maintained.

The more partners a partnership has, (1) the easier it may be to finance the business with the owners' investments and (2) the more unique abilities may result from the different backgrounds of the owners.

CHARACTERISTICS OF PARTNERSHIPS

Limited Life

A partnership has a **limited life.** An advantage is that it does have more flexibility than some other forms of ownership to react to the marketplace because legal restrictions are minimal. When there is a change in the membership of a partnership — when someone new joins or when someone leaves — the partnership is dissolved, however. Dissolution can occur if a partner dies, becomes incapacitated, goes bankrupt, or withdraws. Admission of a new partner or expiration of the life of the partnership as stated in the articles of partnership could also result in the partnership being dissolved.

If a partnership is dissolved, a new partnership can be formed and the business can continue to operate without any interruptions.

Mutual Agency

Mutual agency means that the actions of one partner are binding on all the other partners. For example, Jill Joy, who is a partner in a merchandise business, enters into a contract with Flynn Company to lease a building. This contract is binding on all Jill's partners, because the transaction was within the scope of the business. If Jill, on the other hand, entered into a contract to provide *legal* work to another company, it would not be binding on the partners, because legal work is not in the normal scope of a merchandise company.

Mutual agency allows each partner to act for the partnership as a whole, because all the partners are agents for the business. Poor judgment on the part of one partner, however, could, through mutual agency, result in heavy losses to all partners. An advantage of a partnership is that a credit rating is usually higher because one partner is responsible for the company's debt. So this characteristic of a partnership can be both an advantage and a disadvantage.

Unlimited Liability

Unlimited liability means that if a partnership is unable to pay its obligations, each **general partner** is individually liable to cover with his or her *personal* assets the obligations the partnership cannot meet. Think of a general partner as one who risks not only his or her investment in the partnership, but also his or her own personal assets. If the personal assets of some of the partners are exhausted, the other partners have the responsibility for covering the debts outstanding. There are, however, a few exceptions to this rule. First, a partner just entering an existing partnership is not held liable for past obligations before he or she joined the partnership. Second, in some states some members of a partnership have liability only up to the amount they have invested in the partnership. These people are called **limited partners.**

Co-ownership of Property

Co-ownership of property means that all partners share all the assets of the partnership. For example, if Bill Boyd invests cash and Joyce Regan invests a building in their partnership, the assets become the property of the partnership. Joyce no longer has a specific claim to the building. Ownership is now shared by Bill and Joyce.

Taxation

The partnership itself does not pay taxes, but each partner pays taxes on his or her share of net income that has been allocated. (Note that the tax is on the net income and not on the amount that a partner has withdrawn from the partnership.) Remember that in a sole proprietorship, like a partnership, owners are not paid salaries. They take withdrawals from the company.

FORMATION OF A PARTNERSHIP

Let's look now at the journal entries that are needed when a partnership is formed. The important point is that when partners invest in a business, the assets should be recorded at their current fair value. This value is established by having the assets appraised. Partners have to agree on the amounts assigned to the noncash assets. These costs now represent the true acquisition cost to the partnership. Appraising of assets at their current fair value avoids inequities in the balances of the capital accounts of the partners.

Let's look at the following situation: On June 1, 20XX, Jane Reedy and Bill Burr enter into a partnership. Reedy invests from her old business $9,000 cash and store equipment worth $25,000 with accumulated depreciation of $5,000. The current appraised value of the equipment is $28,000. Also on the books is Accounts Receivable of $2,000 with an Allowance for Doubtful Accounts of $500. The partnership will take on the responsibility for a $6,000 note issued by Reedy. Burr invests $20,000 cash in the partnership. The following journal entries record this information:

20XX						
June	1	Cash	9 0 0 0 00		
		Accounts Receivable	2 0 0 0 00		
		Store Equipment	28 0 0 0 00		
		Allowances for Doubtful Accounts		5 0 0 00
		Notes Payable		6 0 0 0 00
		J. Reedy, Capital		32 5 0 0 00
	1	Cash	20 0 0 0 00	
		B. Burr, Capital		20 0 0 0 00

These entries could be recorded in the cash receipts journal. Note that the $32,500 is the assets minus the liabilities.

Note that the store equipment has no accumulated depreciation associated with it, because the appraised value is now the new book value. If the old book value was used, Reedy's capital would be understated. Reedy should not be penalized, because her investment has increased. Any additional investments made by the partners will result in a journal entry that debits Cash and credits the partners' capital account.

LEARNING UNIT 18-1 REVIEW

AT THIS POINT you should be able to

▼ Define a partnership and compare its equity section with that of a sole proprietorship. (p. 644)
▼ List the characteristics of a partnership. (p. 644)
▼ Journalize the formation of a partnership, recording assets of current fair value. (p. 645)

SELF-REVIEW QUIZ 18-1

(The forms you need are on page 47 of the *Study Guide and Working Papers.*)
   Respond true or false to the following:

1. Articles of partnership are required in forming a partnership.
2. Limited life means that when a partnership is dissolved, the business ceases operations.
3. Unlimited liability could result from mutual agency.
4. Co-ownership of property means each asset belongs to the person who invested it.
5. Assets invested in the formation of a partnership are recorded at current fair value.

Solutions to Self-Review Quiz 18-1

1. False   **2.** False   **3.** True   **4.** False   **5.** True

LEARNING UNIT 18-2

DIVISION OF NET INCOME AND NET LOSS AMONG PARTNERS

Partners work so as to gain a share of the net income of their partnership; they do not earn salaries as their employees do. As a matter of fact, they cannot legally hire themselves and pay themselves a salary. There are several ways to divide up net income and net loss among partners, based on partners' differing talent and abilities, time spent working for the partnership, and amount of investment in the partnership.

We need to introduce two terms to help describe how net income is divided among partners. One way is through a **salary allowance.** A salary allowance is not the same thing as the Salary Expense involved in paying employees, and it is not in fact a salary at all; it is just a way to divide net income. It is usually used to account for unequal service contributions among partners, such as if one partner worked full time for the business and the other put in only 20 hours a week. In such a case the partners might agree to pay $1,000 per week to the first partner and $500 per week to the other. This money would come out of the net income earned by the partnership.

Another way to divide net income among partners is through **interest allowance.** This method is usually used when partners have put different amounts into the partnership as an initial investment. Let's say that one has invested $5,000 and the other has invested $10,000. At the end of the accounting period, they would each get 10 percent interest on their investment: the first would get $500 ($5,000 × .10) and the second would get $1,000 ($10,000 × .10). This method is used because it would be unfair to give half of net income to the first partner when he or she invested only one-third of the capital.

Now let's look at several different situations to see how a partnership might divide its net income or net loss. These situations will be based on the following facts. Dot Alexander, John Sullivan, and Sheldon Brown invested $8,000, $6,000, and $4,000, respectively, in a partnership. The partnership in the first year had a net income of $24,300.

Situation 1

Partners could not agree on how to share net income of $24,300. The law states that if an agreement is not reached on how partners share earnings, they will be divided equally.

The Calculation: $24,300 ÷ 3 = $8,100 to each partner

The journal entry at closing to allocate net income will look like the following:

	20XX					
	Dec.	31	Income Summary	24 3 0 0 00		
			Dot Alexander, Capital		8 1 0 0 00	
			John Sullivan, Capital		8 1 0 0 00	
			Sheldon Brown, Capital		8 1 0 0 00	

> The journal entry at closing to allocate net income looks like this one.

Note that the closing process now divides the net income into the *three* capital accounts. In a sole proprietorship the net income was closed to the one capital account. If this situation involved net loss instead of net income, each capital account would be debited and the credit would be to Income Summary.

Situation 2

Partners share net income of $24,300 in the ratio of their beginning capital investments.

The Calculation:

Step 1: Find the total capital invested:

Alexander	$ 8,000
Sullivan	6,000
Brown	4,000
	$18,000

Step 2: Set up a ratio (fraction) of each partner's investment to the total of capital invested ($18,000):

ALEXANDER	SULLIVAN	BROWN
$8,000	$6,000	$4,000
$18,000	$18,000	$18,000

Step 3: Multiply the ratio in step 2 by the amount of income to be distributed.

Alexander: $\dfrac{\$8,000}{\$18,000} \times \$24,300 = \$10,800$

Sullivan: $\dfrac{\$6,000}{\$18,000} \times \$24,3000 = \$8,100$

Brown: $\dfrac{\$4,000}{\$18,000} \times \$24,300 = \$5,400$

The journal entry at closing to allocate net income will look like the following:

20XX					
Dec.	31	Income Summary	24 30 0 00	
		Dot Alexander, Capital		10 8 0 0 00
		John Sullivan, Capital		8 1 0 0 00
		Sheldon Brown, Capital		5 4 0 0 00

This ratio in step 2 may be used if the net income of the company is related only to the amount the partners have invested. Alexander has invested the most ($8,000) and thus receives the largest portion of the earnings ($10,800).

Alternative to Ratio Based on Investment Only: Some partnerships share net income according to an agreed-upon ratio. If a ratio is $3:2:1$, it means that 3/6 of net income goes to one partner, 2/6 to the next, and 1/6 to the last. Such a fractional ratio could be based on service as well as capital investment. Such ratios are called **profit and loss ratios.**

Situation 3

Partners' services and capital contributions are unequal, but net income does cover salary and interest allowance. The salary allowance is used to compensate for the partners' unequal service contributions, and the interest allowance is used to compensate for their unequal investments. One way to share net income in this situation is as follows:

a. Annual salary allowance of $6,000 to Alexander, $6,000 to Sullivan, and $9,000 to Brown.

b. Ten percent interest on each partner's capital investment.

c. Remaining net income or net loss shared equally.

		ALEXANDER		SULLIVAN		BROWN		TOTAL
a. Salary Allowance		$6,000	+	$6,000	+	$9,000	=	$21,000
b. Interest on Capital Investments								
.10 × $8,000		800						
.10 × $6,000			+	600				
.10 × $4,000					+	400		
Total Interest Allowance							=	1,800
Total Salary and Interest Allowance		$6,800	+	$6,600	+	$9,400	=	$22,800
c. Net Income	$24,300							
Less: Salary and Interest	22,800							
Income to be distributed equally	$ 1,500	500		500		500		
Share of Net Income to Partners		$7,300	+	$7,100	+	$9,900	=	$24,300

The journal entry at closing to allocate net income will look like the following:

	20XX						
	Dec.	31	Income Summary	24 3 0 0 00		
			D. Alexander, Capital		7 3 0 0 00
			J. Sullivan, Capital		7 1 0 0 00
			S. Brown, Capital		9 9 0 0 00

Note that in this case there was still net income remaining after salary and interest allowances. In the next situation we see that net income doesn't always cover all the salary and interest allowance.

Situation 4

Partners' services and capital contributions are unequal, but net income does not cover salary and interest allowance.

Assume (1) net income is $20,700 and (2) salary and interest allowance are the same as in Situation 3.

Whether net income covers the salaries and interest makes *no difference* in calculating the salary or interest allowance. As shown in the accompanying calculation, the total of salaries and allowances is $22,800. Net income is only $20,700; thus the partners must all share in a reduction of the profits allocated to them by $700 each. Remember that items (a) and (b) are calculated first *before* we consider the difference between net income and the amount that is needed to cover salary and interest allowance. There is no need to think of the $700 **deficit** as a loss; think of it as a reduction in the share of profits, because all the interest and salary allowance was not covered.

		ALEXANDER		SULLIVAN		BROWN		TOTAL
a. Salary Allowance		$6,000	+	$6,000	+	$9,000	=	$21,000
b. Interest on Capital Investments:								
.10 × $8,000		800						
.10 × $6,000			+	600				
.10 × $4,000					+	400		
Total Interest Allowance							=	1,800
Total Salary and Interest Allowance		$6,800	+	$6,600	+	$9,400	=	$22,800
c. Net Income	$20,700							
Less: Salary and Interest	22,800							
Deficit to be shared equally	< $ 2,100 >	< 700 >		< 700 >		< 700 >		
Share of Net Income to Partners		$6,100	+	$5,900	+	$8,700	=	$20,700

	20XX						
	Dec.	31	Income Summary	20 7 0 0 00		
			D. Alexander, Capital		6 1 0 0 00
			J. Sullivan, Capital		5 9 0 0 00
			S. Brown, Capital		8 7 0 0 00

PARTNERSHIP FINANCIAL STATEMENT

Just as we had a statement of owner's equity for a sole proprietorship, we can prepare a statement of partners' equity. The accompanying statement was prepared from Situation 3.

On their personal tax returns, partners are taxed on their net income in the partnership, whether they withdraw it or not. For example, Alexander would pay taxes on $7,300, even though she withdrew only $4,000.

ALEXANDER, SULLIVAN, AND BROWN
STATEMENT OF PARTNERS' EQUITY
FOR YEAR ENDED DECEMBER 31, 20XX

	Alexander	Sullivan	Brown
Capital Balances, January 1, 20XX	$ 8 0 0 0 00	$ 6 0 0 0 00	$ 4 0 0 0 00
Add: Net Income for 20XX	7 3 0 0 00	7 1 0 0 00	9 9 0 0 00
Totals	$15 3 0 0 00	$13 1 0 0 00	$13 9 0 0 00
Less: Withdrawals	4 0 0 0 00	5 0 0 0 00	8 0 0 0 00
Capital Balances, December 31, 20XX	$11 3 0 0 00	$ 8 1 0 0 00	$ 5 9 0 0 00

The ending balances for each partner would then be reported on the balance sheet. Think of the statement of partner's equity as a supporting document to arrive at a new figure for each capital account on the balance sheet.

LEARNING UNIT 18-2 REVIEW

AT THIS POINT you should be able to

▼ Explain why salary and interest allowances are not expenses when used to divide up earnings of a partnership. (p. 646)
▼ Calculate partners' earnings if shared (a) equally, (b) by ratio of beginning capital or fractional ratio, and (c) by salary and interest allowances. (p. 648)
▼ Prepare a statement of partner's equity. (p. 650)

SELF-REVIEW QUIZ 18-2

(The forms you need are on page 48 of the *Study Guide and Working Papers*.)

From the following information, calculate the partners' share of net income. J. French and J. Small receive salary allowances of $60,000 and $48,000, respectively. The interest allowance is 12 percent of their beginning balances of $160,000 and $120,000, respectively. The remainder of the net income will be divided evenly. Net income for the year was $150,000.

Solution to Self-Review Quiz 18-2

	FRENCH		SMALL	=	TOTAL
Salary Allowance	$60,000	+	$48,000	=	$108,000
Interest on Capital Investments:					
.12 × $160,000	19,200				
.12 × $120,000		+	14,400		
Total Interest Allowance				=	33,600
Total Salary and Interest Allowance	$79,200	+	$62,400	=	$141,600
Net Income	$150,000				
Less: Salary and Interest	141,600				
Income to be distributed equally	$8,400 →	4,200		4,200	
Share of Net Income to Partners	$83,400	+	$66,600	=	$150,000

LEARNING UNIT 18-3

RECORDING ADMISSIONS AND WITHDRAWALS OF PARTNERS

This unit looks at how the capital structure of a partnership may change due to (1) admission of a new partner or (2) withdrawal of a partner.

ADMISSION OF A NEW PARTNER

There are two ways to join a partnership:

1. **Purchase an equity interest** from one or more of the existing partners.
2. Make an investment into the business.

No matter what approach is taken, the admission of a new partner will technically dissolve the old partnership. Let's look at how Peter Mix bought into the partnership of Jones and Ryan.

Buying an Equity Interest from an Original Partner

The partners' balance sheet of Jones and Ryan looked as follows before Peter Mix purchased an interest in the company (there are no liabilities):

JONES AND RYAN				
Assets		**Partners' Equity**		
Cash	$ 5 0 0 0 00	Jones, Capital	$ 6 0 0 0 00	
Other Assets	7 0 0 0 00	Ryan, Capital	6 0 0 0 00	
Total Assets	$12 0 0 0 00	Total Equities	$12 0 0 0 00	

On April 3 Ryan sold Peter Mix his equity in the company for $9,000. The following entry is recorded on the books of the partnership:

Apr.	3	Ryan, Capital	6 0 0 0 00	
		Mix, Capital		6 0 0 0 00

The end result of this transaction is to transfer the $6,000 capital account of Ryan to Mix. Note that the difference in the selling price of $3,000 ($9,000 − $6,000) doesn't affect the books of the partnership, because the cash is paid directly to Ryan and not to the business. Think of it as a side transaction. All this transaction does is transfer the equity amounts. Any personal profit the former partner makes is of a personal nature and is not reflected in the accounts of the business.

Keep in mind also that Jones must agree to the equity exchange by Ryan if Mix is to become a partner. If Jones agrees, a new partnership contract is formed along with new profit or loss ratios. If Jones doesn't accept Mix as a partner, Mix still has the right to share in Ryan's profits and losses, but he will have no voice in the running of the company until he is admitted as a partner.

> Ryan cannot force Jones to accept Mix as a partner.

Investing in an Existing Partnership

As an alternative to buying equity from an existing partner, one may simply invest assets in the partnership on one's own. For example, assume Roger Foss wants to invest cash in a business on July 8 so that he will have a one-third interest in the partnership. Before Roger makes his investment, the partners' equity is as follows:

PARTNERS' EQUITY

B. Blee, Capital $3,000
A. Jarvis, Capital   1,000

Roger wants one-third interest, and the $4,000 ($3,000 + $1,000) represents two-thirds interest; therefore, Roger will have to contribute $2,000

$$\left(\begin{array}{ll} \$2,000 & \text{Roger's Contribution} \\ \$6,000 & \text{Total Capital with Roger's Contribution} \end{array} \right)$$

to gain the one-third interest. The entry to record the admission of Roger Foss would be as follows:

July	8	Cash		2 0 0 0 00	
		R. Foss, Capital			2 0 0 0 00

Recording a Bonus to the Old Partners When Admitting a New Partner

When the equity of a partnership in reality is worth more than the amounts recorded in its accounting records, the partners may require an incoming partner to pay an additional amount or **bonus.** This situation could result if a company had an outstanding earnings record with even higher expectations in the future compared with other companies in the industry. Let's see how it would work from the previous example of Roger Foss, assuming the partners Blee and Jarvis on July 8 require a payment of $3,500 (instead of $2,000) to give Foss a one-third interest.

Blee and Jarvis, Capital	$4,000
Investment of Foss	3,500
Capital of New Partnership	$7,500
$\frac{1}{3}$ interest of Foss ($\frac{1}{3}$ × $7,500)	$2,500

Foss only needed to invest $2,000 to gain a one-third interest, but the old partners required $3,500.

Note that the $1,000 ($3,500 − $2,500) difference represents the bonus the old partners will share. The old partners share all losses and gains equally. Thus the journal entry to admit Foss is as follows:

July	8	Cash		3 5 0 0 00	
		B. Blee, Capital			5 0 0 00
		A. Jarvis, Capital			5 0 0 00
		R. Foss, Capital			2 5 0 0 00

Recording a Bonus to a New Partner

A firm often is anxious to bring into the company a new partner who has special skills, business contacts, or abilities. The old partners then must accept a reduction in their capital balances to make up the difference in what the new

Having a one-third interest doesn't mean Roger has rights to one-third of the net income. The partners must agree on how to share profit and loss.

$$\frac{\$4,000}{2 \text{ parts}} = \$2,000 \text{ per part}$$
OR
$$\frac{\$4,000}{X} = \frac{2}{3}$$
$$2X = \$12,000$$
$$X = \$6,000$$

The bonus to the old partners will be shared in their profit and loss ratio.

$$\frac{\$7,500}{3 \text{ parts}} = \$2,500 \text{ per part}$$

Capital of new partner minus investment of new partner equals bonus by which old owners will reduce their capital balance, using their profit and loss ratio.

partner invests compared with his or her capital balance. Let's play back the previous example by looking at how "anxious" Blee and Jarvis are to obtain the managerial talents of Roger Foss. Now the old partners have required Foss on July 8 to invest only $1,400 to have a one-third interest in the business.

Blee and Jarvis, Capital	$4,000
Investment of Foss	1,400
Capital of New Partnership	$5,400
$\frac{1}{3}$ interest of Foss ($\frac{1}{3}$ × $5,400)	$1,800

$$\frac{\$5,400}{3 \ parts} = \$1,800 \ per \ part$$

Note that Foss invested only $1,400, while in reality he needed to invest $1,800. Thus the old partners are absorbing equally the bonus of $400 ($1,800 − $1,400) by reducing their capital balance. The journal entry to record the admitting of Foss to the partnership is as follows:

> Remember: A one-third interest in equity doesn't necessarily entitle Foss to one-third of the income. His share depends on the agreement set up by the partners.

July	8	Cash		1 4 0 0 00	
		B. Blee, Capital		2 0 0 00	
		A. Jarvis, Capital		2 0 0 00	
		R. Foss, Capital			1 8 0 0 00

RECORDING PERMANENT WITHDRAWAL OF A PARTNER

When a partnership contract is drawn up, it usually states the procedures to be followed when a partner withdraws. Often the procedures include an audit of the accounting records and the adjustment of the assets to their current fair market value. These steps are done so that the capital of the retiring partner does indeed reflect the current value of his or her equity. Let's look at (1) the balance sheet before revaluation of Ring, Rotter, and Freeze; (2) the entry made to record revaluation; (3) the new, revalued balance sheet; and (4) withdrawal of J. Freeze (assume no liabilities). Partners of Ring, Rotter, and Freeze have a profit and loss ratio of 1/2, 1/4, and 1/4, respectively.

> Any loss or gain in the revaluation is shared according to the partners' profit and loss ratio.

1. The balance sheet before revaluation is as follows:

RING, ROTTER, AND FREEZE					
Assets			**Partners' Equity**		
Cash		$ 2 2 0 0 00	A. Ring, Capital		$ 4 4 0 0 00
Merchandise Inventory		3 2 0 0 00	B. Rotter, Capital		2 0 0 0 00
Store Equipment	$ 4 0 0 0 00		J. Freeze, Capital		2 0 0 0 00
Less Acc. Dep.	1 0 0 0 00	3 0 0 0 00			
Total Assets		$ 8 4 0 0 00	Total Equities		$ 8 4 0 0 00

2. When the accountant completes the audit, it is reported that inventory, owing to market conditions, is overvalued by $400. The journal entry to record the revaluation is as follows:

Nov.	30	A. Ring, Capital		2 0 0 00	
		B. Rotter, Capital		1 0 0 00	
		J. Freeze, Capital		1 0 0 00	
		Merchandise Inventory			4 0 0 00

> Ring $= \frac{1}{2}$ × $400
> $= $200
> Rotter $= \frac{1}{4}$ × $400
> $= $100
> Freeze $= \frac{1}{4}$ × $400
> $= $100

3. Here is the new, revalued balance sheet:

RING, ROTTER, AND FREEZE						
Assets				Partners' Equity		
Cash			$ 2 2 0 0 00	A. Ring, Capital		$ 4 2 0 0 00
Merchandise Inventory			2 8 0 0 00	B. Rotter, Capital		1 9 0 0 00
Store Equipment	$ 4 0 0 0 00			J. Freeze, Capital		1 9 0 0 00
Less Acc. Dep.	1 0 0 0 00		3 0 0 0 00			
Total Assets			$ 8 0 0 0 00	Total Equities		$ 8 0 0 0 00

The withdrawal means a new partnership and a new profit and loss ratio for Ring and Rotter.

4. The entry to record the withdrawal of Freeze from the partnership is as follows:

Nov.	30	J. Freeze, Capital	1 9 0 0 00			
		Cash			1 9 0 0 00	

RECORDING PERMANENT WITHDRAWAL WHEN A PARTNER TAKES ASSETS OF LESS VALUE THAN HIS BOOK EQUITY

In the last situation Freeze received the revalued amount of his capital by taking out $1,900 in cash. Often, when a partner retires, the assets may not be revalued. In this case the partners have to agree whether the assets are overvalued and whether the withdrawing partner should settle for less than the book value of his or her equity. For example, let's look at the following balance sheet for Joll, Smoot, and Jangles to see what will happen if Smoot settles for less than his book value on July 31 (assume a profit and loss ratio of 2:2:1):

A partner who wants "out" quickly may be willing to take less than book value of his equity.

JOLL, SMOOT, AND JANGLES				
Assets		Partners' Equity		
Cash	$25 0 0 0 00	R. Joll, Capital	$28 0 0 0 00	
Merchandise Inventory	29 0 0 0 00	A. Smoot, Capital	18 0 0 0 00	
		B. Jangles, Capital	8 0 0 0 00	
Total Assets	$54 0 0 0 00	Total Equities	$54 0 0 0 00	

Smoot is extremely anxious to withdraw from the partnership and is willing to accept a cash settlement of $12,000. Joll and Jangles will share the $6,000 ($18,000 − $12,000) of capital that Smoot does not take with him in the ratio of 2:1. The journal to record the withdrawal of Smoot is as follows:

$$\frac{2:1}{}$$

2/3 for Joll

1/3 for Jangles

R. Joll $= \frac{2}{3} \times \$6,000$

$= \$4,000$

B. Jangles $= \frac{1}{3} \times \$6,000$

$= \$2,000$

July	31	A. Smoot, Capital	18 0 0 0 00			
		Cash			12 0 0 0 00	
		R. Joll, Capital			4 0 0 0 00	
		B. Jangles, Capital			2 0 0 0 00	

Now let's look at what could happen if Smoot withdrew assets valued at *more* than his book equity.

RECORDING PERMANENT WITHDRAWAL WHEN A PARTNER TAKES ASSETS OF GREATER VALUE THAN BOOK EQUITY

Using the previous example, Smoot might withdraw assets valued at *more* than book equity if:

1. Partnership assets are undervalued, and
2. Joll and Jangles are anxious to have him retire.

Assume the assets are undervalued by $12,000 and the owners want to leave them this way. Thus Smoot's capital would be increased by $4,800 ($\frac{2}{5} \times$ $12,000$), and the other owners' equity would be reduced to cover this $4,800 increase to Smoot's capital. The following entry would be recorded when Smoot leaves the partnership:

July	31	A. Smoot, Capital	18 0 0 0 00	
		R. Joll, Capital	3 2 0 0 00	
		B. Jangles, Capital	1 6 0 0 00	
		Cash		22 8 0 0 00

R. Joll $= \frac{2}{3} \times$ $4,800$
$= $3,200$

B. Jangles $= \frac{1}{3} \times$ $4,800$
$= $1,600$

Note that Smoot receives in cash the $18,000 value of his capital plus the $4,800 to reflect the capital of $22,800 agreed upon by the other owners. Note also how the capital of Joll and Jangles was reduced according to their profit and loss ratio.

Remember that when a partner dies, the partnership ends, and his or her estate is entitled to receive the proper value of the capital account of the deceased after an audit and revaluation of the assets. Journal entries for the death of a partner are similar to those for other situations when a partner leaves. To have enough cash to pay the full value of the deceased partner's capital account, partnerships often carry life insurance policies on partners.

LEARNING UNIT 18-3 REVIEW

AT THIS POINT you should be able to

▼ Explain how a new partner can be admitted in a partnership. (p. 651)
▼ Journalize the entry to record the admitting of a partner. (p. 651)
▼ Explain why a one-third interest doesn't mean that the net income is split three ways. (p. 652)
▼ Calculate as well as journalize a bonus to old partners when a new partner is admitted. (p. 652)
▼ Calculate as well as journalize a bonus to a new partner. (p. 653)
▼ Explain how assets might be revalued when a partner withdraws. (p. 654)
▼ Calculate as well as journalize entries to record withdrawal of a partner taking assets for less or more than book equity if assets are not revalued. (p. 654)

SELF-REVIEW QUIZ 18-3

(The forms you need are on page 49 of the *Study Guide and Working Papers*.) Respond true or false to the following:

1. When new partner, Cohen, buys an equity of existing partner, Lee-Ying, the cash account is always increased in the business.
2. The profit and loss ratio must be based on the capital balances of the partners.
3. A bonus to old partners is based on their profit and loss ratio.
4. A bonus to a new partner could result if the old partners are anxious to recruit the new partner.
5. Any loss or gain when assets are revalued is shared in the partners' profit and loss ratio.
6. Assets of a partnership cannot be revalued.
7. A partner, Jaworski, can never withdraw assets that are valued at less than his book equity.
8. A partner who withdraws assets of greater value than book equity causes the capital of the remaining partners to decrease when assets are not revalued.

Solutions to Self-Review Quiz 18-3

1. False   **2.** False   **3.** True   **4.** True   **5.** True   **6.** False
7. False   **8.** True

LEARNING UNIT 18-4

THE LIQUIDATION OF A PARTNERSHIP

Up to this point we have looked at the admission and withdrawal of partners. Each time this happens, a new partnership is formed and any losses or gains are shared in an agreed-upon ratio. The operations of the business continue, of course, even when the new partnership is formed. In this unit we look at three situations in which a partnership is **liquidated.** Liquidation is when the business is completely ended by converting assets into cash and paying off obligations and equity. The following steps complete a liquidation:

1. Assets are sold for cash with any loss or gain recognized.
2. Any loss or gain is divided among the partners based on their profit or loss ratio.
3. Creditors are paid off.
4. Remaining cash is distributed to the partners based on their capital balances.

We will look at three different situations based on the following information. Peters, French, and Smith are liquidating their business on May 31, 20XX. The partners have a profit and loss ratio of $3:2:1$. The following is the updated balance sheet at the end of May. Note that at this point we've closed out the temporary accounts.

PETERS, FRENCH, AND SMITH
BALANCE SHEET
MAY 31, 20XX

Assets		
Cash	$ 7 0 0 0 00	
Other Assets	138 0 0 0 00	
Total Assets	$145 0 0 0 00	
Liabilities and Partners' Equity		
Liabilities	$ 25 0 0 0 00	
Jane Peters, Capital	30 0 0 0 00	
Joe French, Capital	70 0 0 0 00	
Alan Smith, Capital	20 0 0 0 00	
Total Liabilities and Partners' Equity	$145 0 0 0 00	

Using this information, let's look at three different situations in which liquidation occurs.

Situation 1

Selling assets at a gain (assets sold for $144,000).

The Liquidation Process:

Step 1:   Record sale of assets along with any loss or gain from realization*
(gain = $144,000 − $138,000) on June 7:

June	7	Cash	144 0 0 0 00	
		Other Assets		138 0 0 0 00
		Loss or Gain from Realization		6 0 0 0 00

Step 2:   Loss or gain from realization is allocated to each partner in ratio of 3 : 2 : 1:

June	7	Loss or Gain from Realization	6 0 0 0 00	
		Jane Peters, Capital		3 0 0 0 00
		Joe French, Capital		2 0 0 0 00
		Alan Smith, Capital		1 0 0 0 00

Peters: $\frac{3}{6}$ × $6,000
French: $\frac{2}{6}$ × $6,000
Smith: $\frac{1}{6}$ × $6,000

Step 3:   Pay claims of the creditors on June 15:

June	15	Liabilities	25 0 0 0 00	
		Cash		25 0 0 0 00

---

*Realization means the conversion of noncash assets into cash as part of the liquidation process. It can result in either gain or loss. The account Loss or Gain from Realization is similar to the Cash Short and Over account discussed in Chapter 6. The account will be closed separately, because closing entries take place before liquidation. In using this account think of loss as a debit and gain as a credit.

THE LEDGER BEFORE STEP 4

J. Peters, Capital	J. French, Capital	A. Smith, Capital	Cash
30,000	70,000	20,000	7,000 | 25,000
3,000	2,000	1,000	144,000
			Bal: 126,000

Step 4: Distribute cash that is left to partners based on their capital balance. *No* profit and loss ratios are used in this step.

June	30	Jane Peters, Capital		33 0 0 0 00		
		Joe French, Capital		72 0 0 0 00		
		Alan Smith, Capital		21 0 0 0 00		
		Cash			126 0 0 0 00	

The accompanying Statement of Liquidation gives a comprehensive report of the liquidation process involved in situation 1. Keep in mind that the liquidation process takes time to complete; it isn't done overnight.

PETERS, FRENCH, AND SMITH
STATEMENT OF LIQUIDATION
FOR MONTH OF JUNE 20XX

	Cash	+ Other Assets	= Liabilities +	Capital		
				Peters	+ French +	Smith
Balances before realization	$7,000 +	$138,000	= $25,000 +	$30,000 +	$70,000 +	$20,000
Recording gain from sales of assets	+ $144,000 −	$138,000		+ 3,000	+ 2,000	+ 1,000
Balances updated	$151,000		= $25,000	$33,000 +	$72,000 +	$21,000
Paying of liabilities	− $25,000		− $25,000			
Balances updated	$126,000		=	+ $33,000 +	$72,000 +	$21,000
Distribution of cash to partners	− $126,000		=	− $33,000 −	$72,000 −	$21,000

Now let's look at what would happen if the assets were sold at a loss.

Situation 2

Selling assets at a loss (assets sold for $126,000).

The Liquidation Process:

Step 1: Record sale of assets with loss or gain from realization (loss = $138,000 − $126,000) on June 7:

June	7	Cash		126 0 0 0 00		
		Loss or Gain from Realization		12 0 0 0 00		
		Other Assets			138 0 0 0 00	

Step 2: Loss or gain from realization is allocated to each partner in ratio of 3:2:1:

June	7	J. Peters, Capital	6 0 0 0 00		
		J. French, Capital	4 0 0 0 00		
		A. Smith, Capital	2 0 0 0 00		
		Loss or Gain from Realization		12 0 0 0 00	

Step 3: Pay claims of creditors:

June	15	Liabilities	25 0 0 0 00		
		Cash		25 0 0 0 00	

THE LEDGER BEFORE STEP 4

J. Peters, Capital	J. French, Capital	A. Smith, Capital	Cash
6,000 | 30,000	4,000 | 70,000	2,000 | 20,000	7,000 | 25,000
			126,000 |
			Bal: 108,000 |

Step 4: Distribute cash that is left to partners based on their capital balances on June 30:

June	30	J. Peters, Capital	24 0 0 0 00		
		J. French, Capital	66 0 0 0 00		
		A. Smith, Capital	18 0 0 0 00		
		Cash		108 0 0 0 00	

> No profit and loss ratios are used in this step.

The accompanying Statement of Liquidation provides a comprehensive report of this liquidation process.

PETERS, FRENCH, AND SMITH
STATEMENT OF LIQUIDATION
FOR MONTH OF JUNE 20XX

	Cash	+ Other Assets	= Liabilities +	Capital		
				Peters	+ French +	Smith
Balances before realization	$7,000 +	$138,000	= $25,000 +	$30,000 +	$70,000 +	$20,000
Recording loss from sales of assets	+ $126,000 −	$138,000		− 6,000	− 4,000	− 2,000
Balances updated	$133,000		= $25,000	$24,000 +	$66,000 +	$18,000
Paying of liabilities	− $25,000		− $25,000			
Balances updated	$108,000		=	$24,000 +	$66,000 +	$18,000
Distribution of cash to partners	− $108,000		=	− $24,000 −	$66,000 −	$18,000

In the final situation the partners are unable to cover a deficit from the sale of assets.

Situation 3

Selling assets at a loss, with some partner's capital not being enough to cover the deficit (assets sold for $42,000).

The Liquidation Process:

Step 1: Record sale of assets along with any loss or gain from realization (Loss = $138,000 − $42,000) on June 7:

June	7	Cash	42 0 0 0 00			
		Loss or Gain from Realization	96 0 0 00			
		Other Assets			138 0 0 0 00	

Peters: $\frac{3}{6}$ × $96,000
French: $\frac{2}{6}$ × $96,000
Smith: $\frac{1}{6}$ × $96,000

Step 2: Loss or gain from realization is allocated to each partner in ratio 3:2:1:

June	7	J. Peters, Capital	48 0 0 00		
		J. French, Capital	32 0 0 00		
		A. Smith, Capital	16 0 0 00		
		Loss or Gain from Realization		96 0 0 00	

When the loss exceeds the capital balance of a partner and the partner cannot make up the deficit, the other partners have unlimited liability to make up the deficit.

Peters, Capital		French, Capital		Smith, Capital	
48,000	30,000	32,000	70,000	16,000	20,000

Note that Peters has a deficit of $18,000 ($48,000 − $30,000). The other partners must share this deficit in their profit and loss ratio of 2:1.

French: $\frac{2}{3}$ × $18,000
Smith: $\frac{1}{3}$ × $18,000

June	7	Joe French, Capital	12 0 0 00		
		Alan Smith, Capital	6 0 0 00		
		Jane Peters, Capital		18 0 0 00	

Peters, Capital		French, Capital		Smith, Capital	
48,000	30,000	32,000	70,000	16,000	20,000
	18,000	12,000		6,000	

Note that now *Smith* has a $2,000 deficit. French is the only partner left with a capital balance and thus is liable for this deficit.

June	7	Joe French, Capital	2 0 0 00		
		Alan Smith, Capital		2 0 0 00	

Step 3: Pay claims of creditors on June 15:

June	15	Liabilities	25 0 0 00		
		Cash		25 0 0 00	

Step 4: Distribute remaining cash on June 30:

June	30	J. French, Capital		24 00 00 0		
		Cash			24 00 00 0	

French, Capital	
32,000	70,000
12,000	
2,000	

The accompanying statement of liquidation provides a comprehensive report of this liquidation process.

PETERS, FRENCH, AND SMITH
STATEMENT OF LIQUIDATION
FOR MONTH OF JUNE 20XX

	Cash	+ Other Assets	= Liabilities	+ Peters	+ French	+ Smith
					Capital	
Balances before realization	$7,000 +	$138,000	= $25,000 +	$30,000 +	$70,000 +	$20,000
Recording loss from sale of assets	+ $42,000 −	$138,000	= −	48,000 −	32,000 −	16,000
Balances updated	$49,000		$25,000 −	$18,000 +	$38,000 +	$4,000
Deficit of Peters covered by partners in ratio 2:1			+	$18,000 −	$12,000 −	6,000
Balances updated	$49,000		= $25,000		+ $26,000 −	$2,000
Deficit of Smith covered by French					− $2,000 +	$2,000
Balances updated	$49,000		= $25,000		+ $24,000	
Paying of liabilities	− $25,000		$25,000			
Balances updated	$24,000		=		$24,000	
Distribution of cash to French	− $24,000				− $24,000	

LEARNING UNIT 18-4 REVIEW

AT THIS POINT you should be able to

▼ Explain the steps of the liquidation process. (p. 656)
▼ Explain why the profit and loss ratio is not used to pay off the partners in the liquidation process. (p. 657)
▼ Prepare a liquidation statement. (p. 658)

SELF-REVIEW QUIZ 18-4

(The forms you need are on page 50 of the *Study Guide and Working Papers*.)

From the information given below, journalize the (A) sale of assets, (B) loss or gain from realization, (C) payment of liabilities, and (D) distribution of remaining cash to the partners.

1. Cash, $4,000; Other Assets, $13,000; Liabilities, $2,000; Jay, Capital, $3,000; Joger, Capital, $5,000; and Ynet, Capital, $7,000.

2. Partners share losses or gains in a 3 : 1 : 1 ratio.

3. Assets sold for $16,000.

Jay: $\frac{3}{5} \times \$3,000$

Joger: $\frac{1}{5} \times \$3,000$

Ynet: $\frac{1}{5} \times \$3,000$

Solution to Self-Review Quiz 18-4

(A)	Cash		16 0 0 00		
	Other Assets			13 0 0 00	
	Loss of Gain from Realization			3 0 0 00	
(B)	Loss or Gain from Realization		3 0 0 00		
	Jay, Capital			1 8 0 00	
	Joger, Capital			6 0 00	
	Ynet, Capital			6 0 00	
(C)	Liabilities		2 0 0 00		
	Cash			2 0 0 00	
(D)	Jay, Capital		4 8 0 00		
	Joger, Capital		5 6 0 00		
	Ynet, Capital		7 6 0 00		
	Cash			18 0 0 00	

SUMMARY OF KEY POINTS

Learning Unit 18-1

1. Forming a partnership is quite easy and can be agreed upon in writing or orally. Having a written articles of partnership clearly spells out the "specifics" of the partnership.

2. Although the life of a partnership is limited, dissolving a partnership does not mean that the business will cease operations.

3. Mutual agency means that in most cases all partners are bound by the acts of one partner who enters in to a contract as an agent of the company.

4. In the formation of a partnership, one records assets at their current fair value.

Learning Unit 18-2

1. Salary and interest allowances are not expenses but mechanisms used to divide net income or net loss among partners. Salary is based on personal service; interest is based on a percent of each partner's capital balance.

2. Whether net income covers the salary and interest allowances makes no difference in calculating them; they are allocated, and *then* one looks to see the effect on partners' equity.

3. The statement of partners' equity is a supporting document that calculates the ending capital balance found on the balance sheet for each partner.

Learning Unit 18-3

1. When a new partner buys an equity interest from an existing partner, any personal profit belongs to the existing partner and is not recorded in the partnership. All that results on the partnership's books is a change of equity.

2. One partner cannot force other partners to accept a new partner.

3. A one-quarter equity interest doesn't necessarily mean a one-quarter share of all earnings; it would depend on the profit and loss ratio agreed upon by the partners.

4. A bonus is given to old partners if a new partner contributes more than his or her equity interest. On the other hand, a bonus is given to a new partner if he or she invests less than equity interest. The bonus is shared based on the profit and loss ratio.

5. At the time a partner leaves, a partnership may be audited and assets adjusted to their current fair market value. Revaluations are shared between the partners based on the profit and loss ratio.

6. A partner may withdraw for less than or more than book equity. The difference is then shared by the other partners based on the profit and loss ratio. If assets are not revalued, partners must agree whether assets are overstated or not, and then the equity change of the partner who is leaving is shared in profit and loss ratio by the other partners.

Learning Unit 18-4

1. Liquidation is the winding-up process involved in ending a business.

2. Liquidation steps include the following:

   a. Selling assets for cash.

   b. Dividing loss or gain for realization among partners.

   c. Paying creditors.

   d. Paying remaining cash to partners based on capital balances.

KEY TERMS

Articles of partnership   The written contract that spells out the details of the agreement among the partners.

Bonus   When a new partner is admitted, he or she may pay more or less than equity interest. If the new partner pays more, the old partners share a bonus in the profit and loss ratio. Of course, the opposite could result, and the new partner could receive a bonus if he or she invests less than equity interest.

Co-ownership of property   Each partner owns a share of the assets.

Deficit   Amount by which net income falls short of salary and interest allowance.

General partner   A partner who has unlimited liability.

Interest allowance   A mechanism for dividing earnings of a partnership based on a percent of capital balances of the partners (not an expense).

Limited life   Partnership is dissolved by admission, withdrawal, or death of a partner. Although the partnership is dissolved, the operations of the business continue.

Limited partner   The partner's liability is limited to the amount of his or her investment in the partnership.

Liquidation   Occurs when a business is terminated, the assets are sold, and liabilities and partners are paid off.

Mutual agency   Act of a single partner is binding on all members of the partnership.

Partnership   The association of two or more persons who act as co-owners of a business.

Profit and loss ratio   An agreed-upon ratio used to divide earnings or losses of a partnership.

Purchase of an equity interest   Transfer of ownership between an existing partner and a new partner.

Realization   The conversion of noncash assets into cash in the liquidation process.

Salary allowance   A mechanism for dividing earnings of a partnership based on personal services provided by the partners (not an expense).

Uniform Partnership Act   Laws enacted in most states that govern how a partnership is formed, operated, and liquidated.

Unlimited liability   Partners may be personally liable for debts of partnership.

BLUEPRINT—ADVANTAGES AND DISADVANTAGES OF A PARTNERSHIP

Advantages	Disadvantages
1. Ease of formation; legal status under Uniform Partnership Act.	1. Limited life expectancy; any changes in membership dissolve the partnership.
2. Ability to raise more capital than a sole proprietorship.	2. Mutual agency; action by one partner binds all other partners.
3. Pooled resource of talents.	3. Unlimited liability; each partner must cover partnership debts with his or her personal assets.
4. Flexibility to react to the marketplace, because legal restrictions are minimal.	4. Cannot admit a new partner without agreement of all other partners; a partner cannot withdraw without agreement of all other partners.
5. Credit rating usually higher, because more than one partner is responsible for company's debts.	

QUESTIONS, MINI EXERCISES, EXERCISES, AND PROBLEMS

Discussion Questions

1. How is the equity of a partnership different from that of a sole proprietorship?
2. List five characteristics of a partnership.
3. What is the function of the articles of partnership?

4. Explain how a company could operate even when being dissolved.

5. Mutual agency could create unlimited liability. Agree or disagree. Defend your position.

6. Explain why salary and interest allowances are not expenses for a partnership.

7. Give an example of a fractional ratio.

8. The statement of partners' capital is a required report. Accept or reject. Defend your position.

9. What is meant by a "side transaction" when a new partner is admitted by an existing partner's selling the new partner his or her equity?

10. What is meant by a "bonus" when a partner is admitted?

11. When a partner withdraws, why would a partnership revalue its assets?

12. Why would a partner who is withdrawing take more or less than his or her book equity?

13. What are the four steps of the liquidation process?

Mini Exercises

(The forms you need are on pages 52–53 of the *Study Guide and Working Papers*.)

Forming a Partnership

1. Alice Hall and Jim Brown enter into a partnership. On July 1, 200X, Alice invests $5,000 cash in the partnership. Jim invests $2,000 cash and store equipment worth $6,000 with accumulated depreciation of $2,000. The equipment has a current appraised value of $7,000. Prepare a journal entry to record this transaction.

Division of Net Income

2. James Slater, Scupper Ring, and Molly Flynn invested $2,000, $4,000, and $6,000. At the end of the first year, the company's net income was $21,000. Assuming no agreement was reached on how to share net income, prepare a journal entry at closing to allocate net income.

Division of Net Income Based on Beginning Capital Balances

3. If partners in Mini Exercise 2 share net income based on their beginning capital investments, what would be the journal entry at closing to allocate net income?

Calculating Total Salary and Interest Allowance

4. If partners in Mini Exercise 2 have the following agreement, please calculate the total salary and interest allowance.
   a. *Salary Allowance:* Slater, $7,000; Ring, $6,000; and Flynn, $4,000.
   b. 10 percent interest on capital investments.

Share of Net Income to Partners; Deficit Sharing

5. Using your answer in Mini Exercise 4, how much more income is to be distributed to the partners (assume each shares equally) after the salary and interest allowance? If net income was $17,990, how much would partners share in the deficit?

Admission of a New Partner

6. On March 8, Alan Oll sold his equity in the partnership to B. Mills for $4,000. Alan's capital account had a $3,000 balance. Record the journal entry.

Investing into an Existing Partnership

7. Pete Raul wants to have a one-third interest in a law practice that has two partners with capital balances as follows:

R. Seel, Capital $4,000
A. Pool, Capital   1,000

How much must Pete invest into the partnership?

Calculating Profit and Loss Ratio

8. From the following capital balances, calculate the profit and loss ratio for each account:

B. Bool, Capital $100
A. Jones, Capital 500
T. Pool, Capital   400

Liquidation

9. From the following journalize the (a) sale of assets and (b) loss or gain from liquidation realization. Given:

Cash $ 3,000
Other Assets $15,000
Liabilities   3,000
Moxie, Capital   4,000
Carol, Capital   6,000
Earl, Capital   5,000

Partners agreed to share losses or gains in a 4:1:2 ratio and sold assets for $19,200.

Exercises

(The forms you need are on pages 54–55 of the *Study Guide and Working Papers.*)

18-1. Earl Munroe and Carol Rogers form a partnership on May 1, 20XX. Munroe contributes $40,000. Rogers contributes $28,000 cash and land costing $18,000 with a current fair value of $29,000. A $30,000 note payable due Rogers is assumed by the new partnership. Please prepare the journal entries to record Munroe's and Rogers's investment in the partnership.

18-2. A. Lot and B. Stall have decided their partnership earnings will be shared as follows: (a) 10 percent interest allowance on capital balances at beginning of year, (b) remainder to be shared equally. Capital balances of A. Lot and B. Stall at the beginning of the year are $80,000 and $30,000, respectively. Net income is $16,000 for the year. Record the journal entry to update the capital balances of A. Lot and B. Stall on December 31.

18-3. Julie Elliott, Tami DiVito, and Abby Ellen are partners who share losses and gains in a ratio of 2:2:1. Their capital balances are $5,000, $6,000, and $4,000, respectively. The partners are anxious to have Tami retire and have paid her $12,000. Give the journal entry to record the payment to Tami along with the absorption of the amount over book equity by Julie and Abby on July 31, 20XX.

18-4. L. White, V. Slye, and E. Rothe are partners with capital balances of $90,000, $80,000, and $70,000, respectively. Rothe sells his interest in the company for $88,000 to P. Smith. White and Slye have consented to the new partner. Record the journal entry for the admission of Smith on April 8.

18-5. Sullivan, Roe, and Hinch have capital balances before liquidation of $12,000, $24,000, and $32,000, respectively. Cash balance is $48,000,

Journal entries to record investing into a partnership.

Interest allowance.

Withdrawal of partner taking assets greater than book equity.

Admission of new partner.

Liquidation.

and the principals share losses and gains in a 3:2:1 ratio. All noncash assets are sold, for a gain on realization of $24,000. In your calculations assume there are no liabilities. What will each partner receive in cash in the liquidation process?

Distributing partners' earnings.

Group A Problems

(The forms you need are on pages 57–62 of the *Study Guide and Working Papers*.)

18A-1. (a) The partnership of Bell and Shell began with the partners' investing $4,000 and $2,400, respectively. At the end of the first year the partnership earned net income of $8,200. Under each of the following independent situations, calculate how much of the $8,200 each is entitled to the following:

Check Figure:
(b) Deficit to be shared equally $1,840

Situation 1:	No agreement on how income was to be shared.
Situation 2:	Bell and Shell share income based on the beginning-of-year investment ratio.
Situation 3:	Salary allowance of $2,800 to Bell and $2,400 to Shell. Ten percent interest on beginning year's investment. Remainder split equally.

(b) In situation 3 what would the earnings to each partner be if net income were $4,000?

18A-2. Bob Kerne and Whitney Blak are partners with capital balances of $1,600 and $800, respectively. They share all profits and losses equally. From the following independent situations, journalize the admission of the new partner, Jack Ray:

Admission of a new partner under various assumptions.

Situation 1:	Ray purchased Blak's interest for $6,000, paying it personally to Blak.
Situation 2:	Ray invested an amount exactly equal to one-third interest in the partnership.
Situation 3:	Ray invested $1,800 for a one-third interest. Kerne and Blak share the bonus.
Situation 4:	Ray invested $600 for a one-third interest. Bonus is credited to Ray's account.

Check Figure:
Sit. 3: $400 Bonus to old partners

18A-3. Lane, Right, and Von are partners. On July 30, 20XX, the balance sheet was as follows:

Cash	$12,000	Lane, Capital	$ 7,500
Inventory	5,000	Right, Capital	12,500
Other Assets	8,000	Von, Capital	5,000
Total Assets	$25,000	Total Liab. + Equity	$25,000

The partners agree to share all losses and gains in a 2:2:1 ratio. Von is withdrawing from the partnership. From the following independent situations, journalize the withdrawal of Von.

Withdrawal of a partner.

Check Figure:
Sit. 1:
Dr. Von, Capital $5,000
Cr. Jones, Capital $5,000

Situation 1:	Von sells his equity to Jones for $18,000. Partners agree to admission of Jones.
Situation 2:	On withdrawal of Von, inventory is determined to be overvalued by $1,000. (Before withdrawal, assets are revalued to current fair market value.) Be sure to record entry to revalue inventory as well as the withdrawal of Von.
Situation 3:	Von is paid $3,000 out of the assets of the partnership. Because the assets are overvalued, the partners do not want to decrease the recorded asset values.
Situation 4:	Von is paid $8,500 out of the assets of the partnership. Because the assets are undervalued, the partners do not want to increase the recorded asset values.

Check Figure:
Sit. 1:
Dr. Von, Capital
                    $35,000
Cr. Jones, Capital
                    $35,000

18A-4. The partnership of Jones, Reston, and Sullivan is being liquidated. All gains and losses are shared in a 3 : 2 : 1 ratio. Before liquidation, their balance sheet looks as follows:

Cash	$22,500	Liabilities	$ 6,300
Other Assets	14,700	A. Jones, Capital	11,100
		C. Reston, Capital	18,000
		J. Sullivan, Capital	1,800
Total Assets	$37,200	Total Liab. + Equity	$37,200

Journalize the entries needed in the liquidation process under the following independent situations and assume a date of October 1, 20XX, for sale of assets and October 15 for paying off liabilities and distributing cash to partners.

Situation 1:   Sold other assets for $32,700.
Situation 2:   Sold other assets for $5,700.
Situation 3:   Sold other assets for $2,100. Sullivan cannot cover his deficit.

Group B Problems

(The forms you need are on pages 57–62 of the *Study Guide and Working Papers.*)

18B-1. (a) B. Bell and R. Shell began a partnership by investing $4,800 and $3,200, respectively. At the end of the first year the partnership earned net income of $7,600. Under each of the following independent situations, calculate how much of the $7,600 each is entitled to.

Situation 1:   No agreement on how income was to be shared.
Situation 2:   Bell and Shell share income based on the beginning-of-year investment ratio.
Situation 3:   Salary allowance of $2,480 to Bell and $2,800 to Shell. Twelve percent interest on beginning year's investment. Remainder split equally.

(b) In situation 3 what would the earnings to each partner be if net income were $5,600?

18B-2. Bob Kerne and Whitney Blak are partners with capital balances of $3,000 and $1,000, respectively. They share all profits and losses equally. From the following independent situations, journalize the admission of the new partner, Jack Ray:

Situation 1:   Ray purchases Blak's interest for $6,000, paying it personally to Blak.
Situation 2:   Ray invested an amount exactly equal to one-fifth interest in the partnership.
Situation 3:   Ray invested $2,000 for a one-fifth interest. Kerne and Blak share the bonus.
Situation 4:   Ray invested $300 for a one-fifth interest. Bonus is credited to Ray's account.

18B-3. Lane, Right, and Von are partners of LRV Repairs Service. On July 31, 20XX, the balance sheet was as follows:

Cash	$50,000	Lane, Capital	$30,000
Other Assets	20,000	Right, Capital	15,000
Other Assets	10,000	Von, Capital	35,000
Total Assets	$80,000	Total Liab. + Equity	$80,000

The partners agree to share all losses and gains in a 2 : 1 : 2 ratio. Von is withdrawing from the partnership. From the following independent situations, journalize the withdrawal of Von.

Situation 1:   Von sells his equity to Jones for $120,000. Partners agree to admission of Jones.

Situation 2:   On withdrawal of Von, inventory is determined to be overvalued by $6,000. (Before withdrawal, assets are revalued to current fair market value.)

Situation 3:   Von is paid $32,000 out of the assets of the partnership. Although the assets are overvalued, the partners do not want to decrease the recorded asset values.

Situation 4:   Von is paid $44,000 out of the assets of the partnership. Because the assets are undervalued, partners do not want to increase the recorded asset values.

18B-4. Jones, Reston, and Sullivan are liquidating their partnership. All losses and gains are shared in a 4:2:1 ratio (not based on investment). Before liquidation their balance sheet looked as follows:

> Liquidation of a partnership.

> Check Figure:
> Sit 2: Loss or gain from realization $1,400 Dr.

Cash	$ 800	Liabilities	$ 6,000
Other Assets	19,200	A. Jones, Capital	4,000
		C. Reston, Capital	8,000
		J. Sullivan, Capital	2,000
Total Assets	$20,000	Total Liab. + Equity	$20,000

Journalize the entries needed in the liquidation process under the following independent situations (assume a date of July 1, 20XX, for sale of assets and a date of July 15 to pay off liabilities and distribute cash that is left to partners).

Situation 1:   Sold other assets for $26,200.

Situation 2:   Sold other assets for $17,800.

Situation 3:   Sold other assets for $10,800; Jones cannot cover his deficit. (For simplicity round any calculations to the nearest dollar.)

REAL-WORLD APPLICATIONS

18R-1.

Al Ring and Marvin Smoy are partners who are extremely worried about the financial condition of their company. As of December 31, 20XX, their balance sheet revealed the following:

Assets		**Liabilities and Owner's Equity**	
Cash	$ 30,000	Liabilities	$ 60,000
Noncash assets	400,000	A. Ring, Capital	200,000
		M. Smoy, Capital	170,000
Total Assets	$430,000	Total Liab. + Equity	$430,000

There is a pending lawsuit that could result in a settlement of more than $400,000 against the company for negligence. Al wants out of the partnership before the case is settled. Marvin claims they are both in this together. As the accountant, could you explain in writing to Al how the situation looks? All losses and gains are shared in a 2:1 ratio.

18R-2.

On May 15 Peter Rig and Joan Fess formed a partnership in the catering business. Peter invested $30,000 in cash and $8,000 in equipment. Joan invested land worth $15,000, a building worth $24,000, and merchandise worth $8,000.

The partners decided that they would insure the building and its contents beginning June 1. On May 28 a fire broke out and destroyed half of the merchandise, the building, and the equipment. That night Rig and Fess decided to liquidate the business.

Rig told Fess that he would take his cash (which was in a fireproof safe) and Fess would take the land. Fess argued that in a partnership Rig couldn't do that. Could you settle this dispute? Make your recommendations in writing.

YOU make the call

Critical Thinking/Ethical Case

18R-3.

Jee Jones is in a partnership with Alvin Scott and Morry Flynn. Jee signed a long-term contract with a supplier without telling either partner. When Alvin heard about it he hit the roof. He told Jee the partnership could not afford this contract and he would have nothing to do with it. Do you think Alvin should be upset? You make the call. Write down your recommendations to Alvin.

INTERNET EXERCISES

EX-1. [www.wld.com/conbus/weal/wlimlpar.htm] You have now learned about general liability partnerships. Your text teaches you that a partnership shall have at least one general partner who is "generally" liable for the partnership's debts.

In recent years a new partnership device has become popular in many states. This device is called a "limited liability partnership" or LLP. Begun in Texas, the LLP is now functional in at least 21 states and the District of Columbia.

Examine this site and list some of the differences in a general partnership and a limited liability partnership. Determine if your state has a limited liability partnership law.

EX-2. [www.touchngo.com/lglcntr/akstats/Statutes/Title32/Chapter05/Section350.htm] A general guideline for states to govern partnerships is the Uniform Partnership Act. This law was presented to the states as a "model" law. Most of the states have adopted it, and most of them have modified it from its original version.

The Act states how partnerships account for transactions affecting the partners just as it specifies how to account for transactions with those outside the partnership. This website presents the State of Alaska's version of the Act. Your text presented a method of liquidating a partnership. The website shows the text of the Alaska law. Read the text of the law and comment on how its provisions compare with the liquidation procedures written in the text.

Corporations

ORGANIZATION AND CAPITAL STOCK

Suppose you are attending a sports memorabilia fair and buy a baseball signed by legendary batter Ty Cobb. If you later find out that the signature is a fake, you might want to take legal action against the dealer or the dealer and his partner. Both sole proprietors and partnerships are personally liable, so the unscrupulous dealers would stand to lose their personal assets if the judge finds in your favor. Yet, suppose you buy your baseball memorabilia from the popular Internet auction site, eBay, and the goods are not up to snuff. You will then make a suit against eBay, the **corporation,** and not against one or two individuals. As you'll see in this chapter, one of the main characteristics that sets corporations apart from sole proprietorships or partnerships is that the corporation is a separate legal entity.

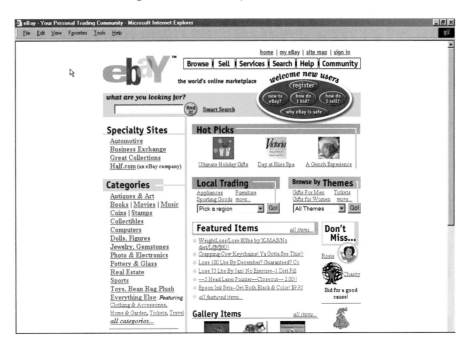

The eBay case mentioned above is not purely hypothetical. At this moment, eBay is being sued by six people who bought sports memorabilia from dealers who sold their goods via the site. The plaintiffs say fake merchandise on the site, bearing forged signatures of baseball greats such as Joe DiMaggio and Ty Cobb, fetched $10 million for unwitting buyers in thousands of online transactions. California law requires dealers to guarantee the authenticity of the sports memorabilia they sell. However, eBay, which lists about four million items for sale each day, has argued that it merely operates as a venue for buyers and sellers and cannot be held liable for fraudulent transactions.

This case will be closely watched because it could set legal precedent for the burgeoning online auction business. Auction houses like Sotheby's and Christies are held liable when fake goods are sold. While eBay claims it is just a listing service, the company *does* make a profit on sales commissions, just like its brick-and-mortar cousins. Yet, with 12 million registered users, can eBay or other cyberspace auction sites be expected to monitor and guarantee the authenticity of the millions of goods bought and sold on their sites each day? The legal complaint strikes at the heart of eBay's "we're just the middle-man" business model. The company fears that sellers won't list with them if the laws that govern brick-and-mortar auction companies are applied to the fast-paced, laissez-faire online auction industry.

You can be certain that the value of eBay's stock will go down if the six plaintiffs win their suit. Another characteristic of a corporation, like eBay, is that stockholders, such as the owners and other investors, own shares of stock in the company. In this chapter you will learn how to record entries for issuing stock, dividends, and capital gains. Day-to-day corporate accounting is exactly the same as for the other forms of ownership. The biggest difference is in the ownership itself—that is, each share of stock represents a unit of ownership, and the owners are called stockholders instead of partners.

Based on: Lisa Guernsey, "Ebay Faces Suit on Sale of Fake Goods," *New York Times,* October 16, 2000, p. 6. Lisa Guernsey, "Ebay Users Refile Lawsuit On Sale of Fake Memorabilia," *New York Times,* October 17, 2000, p. 10. Michael Liedtke, "The Cutting Edge; Critics Say Ebay Needs to Increase Safeguards; Company's hands-off policy infuriates some, who want the company to be required to patrol its online auction site more vigilantly," *The Los Angeles Times,* July 6, 2000, p. 6.

LEARNING OBJECTIVES

▼ Defining a corporation; establishing a corporation; listing the advantages and disadvantages of a corporation. (p. 672)

▼ Journalizing entries for issuing par-value stock, no-par stock, and no-par with stated value stock. (p. 676)

▼ Calculating dividends on preferred and common stock. (p. 679)

▼ Recording capital stock transactions under a stock subscription plan. (p. 687)

So far we've learned about sole proprietorships and partnerships; now we're going to learn about corporations. A **corporation,** like Cisco Systems, is a separate legal entity. We first look at how a corporation is formed, along with its main characteristics.

LEARNING UNIT 19-1

FORMING A CORPORATION; CHARACTERISTICS OF THE CORPORATE STRUCTURE

Four steps are involved in forming a corporation.

Step 1: The **incorporators,** those wishing to form the corporation, apply to a state for a charter. They do so by submitting an **articles of incorporation** drawn up by an attorney, together with a fee. The articles of incorporation consist of the following information:

1. Name of the corporation and incorporation date.
2. Purpose of business.
3. Organizational structure.

4. Expected life, usually "forever."

5. Primary location of business.

6. Types of stock to be offered. (Stock is what owners purchase to gain ownership rights in the company. We look at stock in detail in a few moments.)

Step 2: The Office of the Secretary of State reviews the application and, if deemed in order, a **charter** (often called a **certificate of incorporation**) is issued to the incorporators. Copies of the charter and the articles of incorporation are placed on file for public record.

> When the charter is issued, the corporation's legal entity is established.

Step 3: The stock is issued by the corporation to the owners (called **stockholders**).

Step 4: The stockholders meet to elect a board of **directors** and adopt the bylaws of the corporation. Often in a new corporation the stockholders become the directors. As the company grows, people are appointed to the board who are not stockholders. Records of meetings of the board of directors and stockholders are kept in a **minute book,** as directed by law. The board of directors appoints the officers to run the company; it is the board's job to oversee the overall management of the corporation, whereas the officers follow the policies set up by the board.

ADVANTAGES OF THE CORPORATE FORM OF ORGANIZATION

1. Limited Liability/Separate Legal Entity

Stockholders have **limited liability;** they are not personally liable for the obligations of the corporation, because a corporation is a separate and distinct legal entity. The corporation enters into contracts, buys or sells property, and sues or is sued in its own name. Thus the only amount the stockholders can lose is the amount of their investment in the business. Of course, stockholders can still be held liable for any fraudulent or negligent actions they perform in connection with the corporation.

2. Unlimited Life

A corporation's life is perpetual (goes on forever) except in the case of bankruptcy, mergers, or vote of the stockholders.

3. Ease of Transferring Ownership Interest

When an owner invests in a corporation, each share of ownership is represented by one or more formal documents called **stock certificates.** The stockholder can sell or transfer shares of some corporations through *brokerage firms,* companies that act as middlemen in the trading of stock. This trading occurs at various marketplaces called *stock exchanges*. On the back of the certificate is a form that the seller endorses. A key point is that when the shares of stock are sold by the stockholder, the sale has *no* effect on the company's assets and liabilities. What happens is really a *shift* in the ownership.

4. No Mutual Agency

In a corporation there is no mutual agency as there is in a partnership. For example, if John Jones is a stockholder of Passon Corporation and enters into a contract with the city of Lynn, this action by John cannot bind the corporation to complete the contract with the city of Lynn.

5. Ease of Raising Capital

With no mutual agency, with limited liability, and with the ease of transferring ownership interest, the investment in a corporation becomes attractive to many people. As a result, the corporation can raise large amounts of capital by assembling investment groups of stockholders.

DISADVANTAGES OF THE CORPORATE STRUCTURE

1. Difficulties in Forming a Corporation/Government Regulations

As we have seen, a corporation is more difficult to form than a sole proprietorship or a partnership. Incorporators must complete the articles of incorporation and pay an incorporation fee. The complexity of forming a corporation also usually means hiring a lawyer to deal with legal aspects. When granted a certificate of incorporation, corporations are required to fulfill many state and federal regulations and to file many governmental reports.

2. Corporate Taxation

Because the corporation is a separate legal entity, its income is taxed by the federal government. The corporation may also be taxed at the state and local levels. At the same time, any income that is distributed to the stockholders is taxable to the stockholders. Thus there is double taxation of a corporation's earnings.

Company Time

"But WHY can't I buy stock in Dunkin' Donuts, Fred?" asked Marv. "Well, Marv, it's a long story," said Fred. "Pull up a chair, and I'll explain. The 4,139 Dunkin' Donuts shops are individually owned businesses," Fred continued, "working under a franchise agreement with Dunkin' Donuts Inc. The shops (called franchises) may be organized as sole proprietorships, partnerships, or corporations. Most shop owners (called franchisees) have chosen the corporate form, because corporations offer the advantage of limited liability. A wage is paid to the manager, and a franchise fee is paid to Dunkin' Donuts, Inc. Then the profits are distributed to the stockholders/owners as dividends on their common stock."

"But what does Dunkin' Donuts Inc. do?" asked Marv.

"Well," Fred continued, "the corporate structure for Dunkin' Donuts Inc. is complex. Dunkin' Donuts Inc. is owned by the British conglomerate, Allied Domecq PLC, which owns a number of different kinds of companies located throughout the world. As a British corporation, Allied Domecq operates under different accounting rules than American corporations. Allied Domecq's Retailing USA Division is composed of three different companies: Dunkin' Donuts, Baskin-Robbins (the ice cream shops), and Togos (sandwich shops).

"I'll sketch it out for you," said Fred, grabbing a paper napkin. (His sketch appears to the right.)

"So that's the story, Marv," said Fred. "You can't buy stock in Dunkin' Donuts Inc., but you could buy stock in Allied Domecq, on the London Stock Exchange. Or you could buy a franchise yourself."

Discussion Questions

1. Why might Fred want to become a corporation?
2. How can Dunkin' Donuts Inc.'s profits be distributed to stockholders, if no one owns stock in Dunkin Donuts' Inc.?

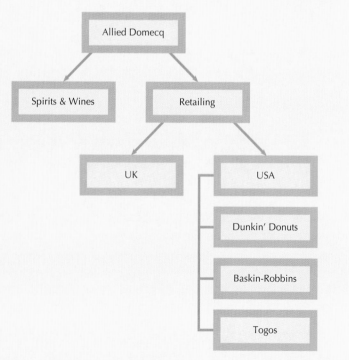

LEARNING UNIT 19-1 REVIEW

AT THIS POINT you should be able to

▼ Explain the steps in forming a corporation. (p. 672)
▼ List as well as explain the advantages and disadvantages of the corporate form of organization. (p. 673)

SELF-REVIEW QUIZ 19-1

(The forms you need are on page 66 of the *Study Guide and Working Papers.*)
Respond true or false to the following:

1. The articles of incorporation is quite easy to fill out.
2. A corporation is a separate legal entity.
3. The officers of a corporation always elect the board of directors.
4. Stocks can be transferred by stockholders without affecting the operations of a corporation.
5. Double taxation does exist in a corporate structure.

Solutions to Self-Review Quiz 19-1

1. False   **2.** True   **3.** False   **4.** True   **5.** True

LEARNING UNIT 19-2

STOCKHOLDERS' EQUITY: RETAINED EARNINGS AND CAPITAL STOCK

The equity section of a corporation differs from that of a sole proprietorship or a partnership. In the sole proprietorship we have simply a capital account and a withdrawals account. In the partnership there is a separate capital and withdrawals account for each partner. With the corporation, the stockholders' equity section is broken down into two major parts:

1. **Paid-in Capital** is the amount that stockholders have invested in the business. It is equal to the values of the assets (usually cash) that have been contributed to the business.
2. **Retained earnings** are accumulated profits that are retained or kept in the corporation. Retained earnings does not mean cash; cash is an *asset,* whereas retained earnings is part of stockholders' *equity.*

CORPORATION

$$A = L + \text{Stockholders' Equity}$$

Paid-In Capital:	**Retained Earnings:**
Capital Stock	Retained Earnings

Let's look more closely at the term *Capital Stock.*

CAPITAL STOCK

In Chapter 20, we look at the difference between issued and outstanding stock.

In return for their investment in the corporation, stockholders are issued shares of **capital stock.** Think of ownership of a corporation as being represented by shares of stock. There are two classes of capital stock, common and preferred. The charter of the corporation indicates the maximum amount of shares of each class of capital stock that a company can legally issue, but the company does not have to issue all of it. **Authorized capital stock** is the amount listed in the charter, **issued capital stock** refers to the shares sold to the stockholders, and **outstanding capital stock** means shares sold and in the stockholders' possession. Let's look at the two classes of capital stock, beginning with common stock.

CHARACTERISTICS OF COMMON STOCK

The most prevalent type of capital stock is called **common stock.** When a corporation has only one kind of capital stock, it will be common stock. When the stock is issued, the owners receive certain rights from the corporation. These rights include the following:

1. The right to vote at stockholders' meetings.
2. The right to share in profits by receiving dividends.
3. The right to dispose of or sell their stock.
4. The right to maintain their proportionate ownership interest in the company. This right is called **preemptive right.** For example, if Jill Evans owns 15 percent of the common stock of the corporation, she would have the chance to also purchase 15 percent of any *additional* common stock that is issued, before it is offered to the public at large.
5. The right, when a company is liquidated, to share in assets after creditors and others with prior claims are paid off.

CHARACTERISTICS OF PREFERRED STOCK

Another type of capital stock some corporations may issue is called **preferred stock.** It is stock that provides stockholders with prior claim to a corporation's profits and assets over holders of common stock. Corporations watch current market conditions and try to offer preferred stock that will be attractive to investors. Holders of preferred stock often give up some of the rights that go with common stock—such as voting rights, preemptive rights, or even some earnings potential—in return for their more stable earnings that come from preferred stock. In many ways preferred stock is a less risky investment than common stock.

DIVIDENDS ON COMMON AND PREFERRED STOCK

We show how to calculate dividends for preferred and common stock on pp. 683–684.

Dividends are paid to stockholders as their share of the corporation's profits. A dividend must be voted by the board of directors, and if it has been a bad year for profits, the board may refuse to vote a dividend. Keep in mind a company may decide against a dividend in a good year, feeling it may be wise to invest money in research and development, etc.

As mentioned, preferred stock gives its stockholders a prior claim to a corporation's profits over holders of common stock. There are several ways that could happen:

1. If a preferred stock is **cumulative,** the holders have a right to a certain dividend every year. If in some years the board does not issue a dividend,

the amount payable will accumulate until the earnings justify the payout. At this time the preferred stockholders will get dividends for all past years as well as the current year before the holders of common stock get any dividend.

For example, Moore Company has 3,000 shares of cumulative preferred stock that is entitled to a dividend of $3 per share. In 20X7, owing to financial problems, Moore Company decided to pay no dividend. Thus the company has **dividends in arrears** of $9,000. No dividends can be paid to common stockholders until the preferred dividends are paid off in full; the amount in arrears plus the current year's dividend. Because financial conditions improved in 20X8, Moore paid the $9,000 of dividends in arrears (3,000 shares × $3) to holders of preferred stock plus the current year's dividend of $9,000.

2. If a preferred stock is **noncumulative,** holders have a right to the current year's dividend, but there are no holdovers from past years when dividends were not declared.

3. If a preferred stock is **nonparticipating,** each year the holders of preferred stock receive a certain percent as dividend and the remainder goes to common stock. Thus if a company declared a dividend of $50,000, the preferred stockholders would get their usual percent and the common stockholders would get all the rest, even if it was a greater percent dividend than preferred got.

4. If a preferred stock is **participating,** preferred stockholders get their yearly dividend and can get a percent of what's left over, splitting it in various ways with common stockholders.

STOCK VALUE (FOR CAPITAL STOCK)

When a corporation is created, it issues a certain number of shares of stock, which are then sold to stockholders. At the time that the corporation receives its charter, the board of directors may assign a **par value** to the stock, something like $25 or $50 a share. This value is entirely arbitrary; no one can say that the stock is really worth that much. It is a way of dividing up ownership of the corporation into a number of units and putting a value on each unit. Many companies have par values of 5 or 10 cents per share. The key point par value is a value assigned arbitrarily. It is stated on the stock certificate. Figure 19-1 can be used as a summary as you read the rest of the chapter.

In most states the assigning of par value per share times the number of shares issued for a corporation represents the **legal capital,** an amount that a corporation must retain in the business for protection of creditors.

Because the concept of par value can be quite misleading, some corporations will issue **no-par stock,** stock with no par value. Thus the *entire* proceeds from selling this issue represents the legal capital (number of shares issued times amount investors paid for each share).

Most states permit (or some require) that the directors of a company set a **stated value** on the shares. This value also is arbitrary but can be changed by the board of directors. Stated value, which has the same purpose as par value, may be less confusing to investors, because it is not printed on the stock certificates.

Whether a stock is issued at par value, no par value with no stated value, or no par value with stated value, the capital stock account can be updated with entries that indicate whether investors paid more or less than par value or stated value. We look at specific examples of recording capital stock in the next unit.

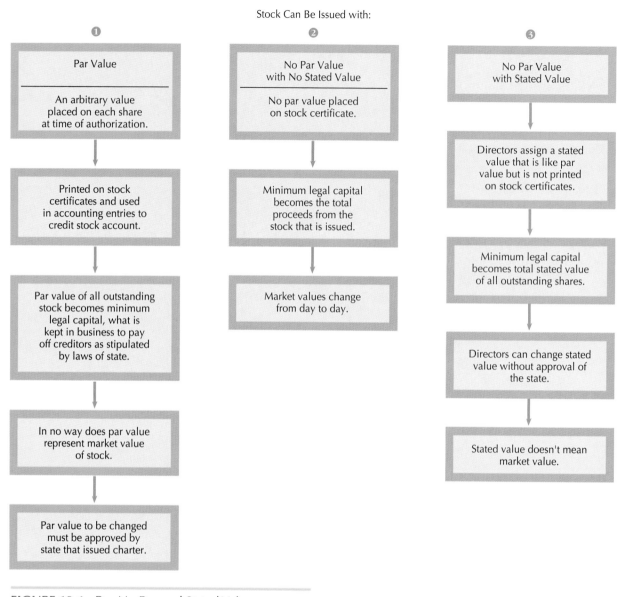

Stock Can Be Issued with:

❶

Par Value
An arbitrary value placed on each share at time of authorization.

↓

Printed on stock certificates and used in accounting entries to credit stock account.

↓

Par value of all outstanding stock becomes minimum legal capital, what is kept in business to pay off creditors as stipulated by laws of state.

↓

In no way does par value represent market value of stock.

↓

Par value to be changed must be approved by state that issued charter.

❷

No Par Value with No Stated Value
No par value placed on stock certificate.

↓

Minimum legal capital becomes the total proceeds from the stock that is issued.

↓

Market values change from day to day.

❸

No Par Value with Stated Value

↓

Directors assign a stated value that is like par value but is not printed on stock certificates.

↓

Minimum legal capital becomes total stated value of all outstanding shares.

↓

Directors can change stated value without approval of the state.

↓

Stated value doesn't mean market value.

FIGURE 19-1. Par, No Par, and Stated Value

LEARNING UNIT 19-2 REVIEW

AT THIS POINT you should be able to

▼ Explain the difference between authorized and issued stock. (p. 676)
▼ List the characteristics of common and preferred stock. (p. 676)
▼ Define and explain cumulative, noncumulative, participating, and nonparticipating preferred stock. (p. 677)
▼ Define and explain par value, legal capital, no-par stock, and stated value. (p. 677)

SELF-REVIEW QUIZ 19-2

(The forms you need are on page 66 of the *Study Guide and Working Papers.*)
Respond true or false to the following:

1. Retained Earnings is part of Paid-in Capital.
2. Preferred stock is the most prevalent type of capital stock.
3. Preemptive right allows one to maintain one's proportionate ownership interest in a company.
4. Preferred stock that is cumulative is entitled to dividends in arrears.
5. Par value doesn't represent the market value of the stock.
6. Stock cannot be issued at par value.

Solutions to Self-Review Quiz 19-2

1. False   **2.** False   **3.** True   **4.** True   **5.** True   **6.** False

LEARNING UNIT 19-3

RECORDING CAPITAL STOCK TRANSACTIONS AND CALCULATING DIVIDENDS

In this unit we look at how to record the issuing of stock that has (1) par value, (2) no par value, and (3) no par value with stated value. We also see how to record transactions in which stock is exchanged for noncash assets. We then look at how to calculate dividends for preferred and common stock.

RECORDING THE SALE OF STOCK THAT HAS PAR VALUE

Situation 1: Selling Common Stock at Par

Roger Company sells 200 shares of a $10 par value common stock at $10 per share on February 3, 20XX.

Here is an analysis of the transaction:

Accounts Affected	Category	↑ ↓	Rules	
Cash	Asset	↑	Dr. $2,000	$10 par
Common Stock	SE	↑	Cr. $2,000	× 200 shares = $2,000

Common Stock is recorded at number of shares times par value. That value represents the legal capital. The journal entry would be as follows:

20XX Feb.	3	Cash			2 0 0 0 00			
		Common Stock				2 0 0 0 00		

Situation 2: Selling Preferred Stock at Par

Roger Co. sells 300 shares of $50 par value preferred stock at $50 on March 18, 20XX.

Once again, here is an analysis of the transaction:

Accounts Affected	Category	↑ ↓	Rules	
Cash	Asset	↑	Dr. $15,000	300 shares
Preferred Stock	SE	↑	Cr. $15,000	× $50 par = $15,000

Preferred Stock is recorded at number of shares times par value. The journal entry would be as follows:

20XX Mar.	18	Cash		15 0 0 0 00		
		Preferred Stock			15 0 0 0 00	

Situation 3: Selling Common Stock at a Premium (More than Par Value)

Roger Co. sells 50 shares of $10 par value common stock at $15 on June 8, 20XX.

The Analysis: The common stock is recorded at par value. Because this stock is sold at a **premium** (more than par value), the excess of the par value will be recorded in a new account called **Paid-in Capital in Excess of Par Value—Common.** Note in the transactional analysis that follows that this account is part of stockholders' equity. On the balance sheet it will be listed below common stock in the paid-in capital section of stockholders' equity.

Accounts Affected	Category	↑ ↓	Rules	
Cash	Asset	↑	Dr. $750	→ 50 shares × $15
Common Stock	SE	↑	Cr. $500	→ 50 shares × $10 par
Paid-in Capital in Excess of Par Value—Common	SE	↑	Cr. $250	→ 50 shares × $5 excess per share over par

The journal entry will be as follows:

20XX June	8	Cash		7 5 0 00		
		Common Stock			5 0 0 00	
		Paid-in Capital in				
		Excess of Par Value—Common			2 5 0 00	

Situation 4: Selling Common Stock at a Discount (Below Par)*

Roger Co. sells 100 shares of $10 par value common stock at $8 on July 3, 20XX.

The Analysis: When a stock is sold below par, a **discount on stock** results. An account called *Discount on Common Stock* records the discount. It is a contra-

---

*This situation does not occur very often.

stockholders' equity account that will reduce the common stock account it is related to. Some states do not allow stock to be sold at a discount.

Accounts Affected	Category	↑ ↓	Rules	
Cash	Asset	↑	Dr. $800	→ 100 shares × $8
Discount on Common Stock	Contra SE	↑	Cr. $200	→ 100 shares × $2 ($10 par − $8)
Common Stock	SE	↑	Cr. $1,000	→ 100 shares × $10 par

The journal entry will be as follows:

20XX July	3	Cash		8 0 0 00		
		Discount on Common Stock		2 0 0 00		
		Common Stock			1 0 0 0 00	

Now let's look at how to record the sale of stock with no par value, with or without stated value.

RECORDING SALE OF STOCK WITH NO PAR VALUE AND STATED VALUE

Note: Corporations cannot legally sell stock at less than the stated value.

Situation 5: Selling No-Par Common Stock with No Stated Value

Moss Co. sells 300 shares of no-par common stock for $20 per share on July 19, 20XX.

The transaction analysis chart shows the following:

Accounts Affected	Category	↑ ↓	Rules	
Cash	Asset	↑	Dr. $6,000	} 300 shares × $20
Common Stock	SE	↑	Cr. $6,000	

The journal entry will be as follows:

20XX July	19	Cash		6 0 0 0 00		
		Common Stock			6 0 0 0 00	

Situation 6: Selling No-Par Common Stock with a Stated Value

Reese Co. sells 200 shares of no-par common stock with a stated value of $40 for $50 per share on June 19, 20XX.

The Analysis: An excess over the stated value will be recorded in a stockholders' equity account called **Paid-in Capital in Excess of Stated Value — Common.**

Accounts Affected	Category	↑ ↓	Rules	
Cash	Asset	↑	Dr. $10,000	→ 200 shares × $50
Common Stock	SE	↑	Cr. $8,000	→ 200 shares × $40
Paid-in Capital in Excess of Stated Value — Common	SE	↑	Cr. $2,000	→ 200 shares × $10 ($50 − $40)

The journal entry will be as follows:

20XX July	19	Cash		10 000 00		
		Common Stock			8 000 00	
		Paid-in Capital in Excess of				
		Stated Value—Common			2 000 00	

RECORDING TRANSACTIONS IN WHICH STOCK IS EXCHANGED FOR NONCASH ASSETS

Situation 7: Exchanging Stock for Noncash Assets

On July 8, Moss Corporation exchanged 3,000 shares of $10 par-value common stock for machinery, buildings, and land. The assets had fair market value of $5,000, $10,000, and $20,000, respectively.

The Analysis: Assets are recorded at fair market value; common stock is recorded at par value. If fair market value is not available for assets, one can try to find the market (not par) value of the stock. In this chapter we assume fair market value of assets is available. The difference between fair market value and par is recorded in the account Paid-in Capital in Excess of Par. Par value is *never* used to measure the selling price of the assets.

Accounts Affected	Category	↑ ↓	Rules	
Machinery	Asset	↑	Dr. $5,000	⎫
Buildings	Asset	↑	Dr. $10,000	⎬ Fair market value
Land	Asset	↑	Dr. $20,000	⎭
Common Stock	SE	↑	Cr. $30,000	→ 300 shares × $10 par
Paid-in Capital in Excess of Par—Common	SE	↑	Cr. $5,000	→ ($35,000 − $30,000)

The journal entry will be as follows:

	20XX July	8	Machinery		5 0 0 0 00		
			Buildings		1 0 0 0 0 00		
			Land		2 0 0 0 0 00		
			Common Stock			3 0 0 0 0 00	
			Paid-in Capital in				
			Excess of Par—Common			5 0 0 0 00	

Situation 8:* Issuing Stock to Organizers of a Business for Services Performed

On June 8, Rose Corporation issued 2,000 shares of $10 par common stock to the organizers of the business for services performed.

The Analysis: Organization Cost in the formation of a corporation (legal fees, printing of stock certificates, etc.) is an intangible asset on the balance sheet. It is usually amortized over five years (can be up to 40 years) because that life is used for income tax returns.

Accounts Affected	Category	↑ ↓	Rules
Organization Cost	Asset*	↑	Dr. $20,000
Common Stock	SE	↑	Cr. $20,000

*Now being expensed

The journal entry will be as follows:

	20XX June	8	Organization Cost		2 0 0 0 0 00		
			Common Stock			2 0 0 0 0 00	

HOW TO CALCULATE DIVIDENDS

Table 19-1 summarizes the process, which is divided into four steps. For our calculation we use these basic facts:

▼ $150,000 dividend declared.
▼ Preferred stock is 6 percent and fully participating.
▼ Preferred stock: 1,000 shares, $200 par.
▼ Common stock: 6,000 shares, $100 par.

Step 1: To calculate preferred dividends, you multiply the number of shares (1,000) times the par value ($200) per share times the rate of dividend (6 percent). The result is a $12,000 dividend to preferred.

Step 2: To calculate the common stock dividend, you multiply the number of shares (6,000) times the par value per share ($100) times the same rate of dividend (6 percent). The result is a dividend of $36,000.

---

*At time of writing amortization cost is now expensed rather than an asset. For our discussion it is an asset that will be amortized.

TABLE 19-1 FOUR-STEP PROCEDURE FOR CALCULATING DIVIDENDS

The Formula	The Calculation	Preferred Stock	Common Stock	Total Dividends
Step 1: Dividend for preferred Number of shares × par value per share × rate of dividend	1,000 shares × $200 × .06 = $12,000	$12,000		$12,000
Step 2: Dividend for common Number of shares × par value per share × rate of dividend	6,000 shares × $100 × .06 = $36,000		$36,000	36,000
Step 3: Find total par value Number of shares × par value per share (preferred) *plus*	1,000 shares × $200 = $200,000			
Number of shares × par value per share (common)	6,000 shares × $100 = 600,000			
	Total par = $800,000			
Step 4: Allocate remainder of dividend based on par value Preferred = $\dfrac{\text{Par Value of Preferred}}{\text{Total Par Value}}$ × Remainder of Dividend	$\dfrac{\$200,000}{\$800,000}$ × $102,000* = $25,500	25,500		25,500
Common = $\dfrac{\text{Par Value of Common}}{\text{Total Par Value}}$ × Remainder of Dividend	$\dfrac{\$600,000}{\$800,000}$ × $102,000* = $76,500		76,500	76,500
		$37,500	$112,500	$150,000

*$150,000 − $48,000 = $102,000.

Step 3: At this point $48,000 of the $150,000 of dividends has been apportioned. Because the preferred is participating—which means it can share in additional dividends beyond the 6 percent dividend—the next step is to find the total par value and allocate the remainder of the dividend based on the total par.

Note in step 3 how the number of shares of preferred is multiplied by the $200 par and the number of common shares is multiplied by the $100 par. Thus total par is $800,000.

Step 4: Because preferred is one-fourth of the total par, preferred is allocated $25,500 ($\frac{1}{4}$ × $102,000) and common is allocated three-fourths of the $102,000 or $76,500.

We can see that both were paid the same percent on par by the following calculations:

PREFERRED:

$$\frac{\text{Total Dividends}}{\text{Total Par Value of Preferred}} = \frac{\$37,500}{\$200,000} = 18.75 \text{ Percent}$$

COMMON:

$$\frac{\text{Total Dividends}}{\text{Total Par Value of Common}} = \frac{\$112,500}{\$600,000} = 18.75 \text{ Percent}$$

The end result is that the dividends were equally divided in terms of percentage, because preferred was fully participating.

LEARNING UNIT 19-3 REVIEW

AT THIS POINT you should be able to

▼ Record transactions that issue stock with or without par value. (p. 679)
▼ Explain the account called Paid-in Capital in Excess of Par Value. (p. 680)
▼ Tell what the normal balance is for the account Discount on Common Stock. (p. 681)
▼ Explain when the account Paid-in Capital in Excess of Stated Value is used. (p. 682)
▼ Calculate capital in excess of par value when stock is exchanged for non-cash assets. (p. 682)
▼ Explain when one uses the account called Organization Cost. (p. 683)
▼ Calculate dividends on common and preferred stock. (p. 683)

SELF-REVIEW QUIZ 19-3

(The forms you need are on pages 67–68 of the *Study Guide and Working Papers.*)

1. Journalize the following transactions:

20XX

July	5	Boston Company sells 200 shares of $20 par-value common stock at $20.
Aug.	8	Jess Company sells 100 shares of $10 par-value common stock at $25.
Oct.	9	Mellisa Company sells 300 shares of no-par common stock with a stated value of $30 for $50 per share.
Nov.	12	Moss Company issued 1,000 shares of $25 par-value common stock to the organizers of the firm for services rendered costing $30,000.

2. From the following, calculate the dividends for common and preferred stock.

▼ Fourteen percent fully participating preferred stock.
▼ Board declared a $210,000 dividend.
▼ Preferred stock: 3,000 shares, $100 par.
▼ Common stock: 7,000 shares, $100 par.

Solutions to Self-Review Quiz 19-3

1.

				Dr.	Cr.
20XX July	5	Cash		4 0 0 0 00	
		Common Stock			4 0 0 0 00
Aug.	8	Cash		2 5 0 0 00	
		Common Stock			1 0 0 0 00
		Paid-in Capital in Excess			
		of Par Value—Common			1 5 0 0 00
Oct.	9	Cash		15 0 0 0 00	
		Common Stock			9 0 0 0 00
		Paid-in Capital in Excess			
		of Stated Value—Common			6 0 0 0 00
Nov.	12	Organization Cost		3 0 0 0 00	
		Common Stock			2 5 0 0 00
		Paid-in Capital in Excess			
		of Par Value—Common			5 0 0 00

2.

	PREFERRED	COMMON
Dividends for preferred:		
(3,000 shares × $100 par) × .14 =	$42,000	
Dividends for common:		
(7,000 shares × $100 par) × .14 =		$ 98,000
Amount to be divided based on total par value:		
($210,000 − $140,000) = $70,000		

Total Par:

Preferred: 3,000 shares × $100 par = $ 300,000
Common: 7,000 shares × $100 par = _700,000_
Total $1,000,000

Preferred: $\dfrac{\$300,000}{\$1,000,000} \times \$70,000 = \$21,000$ 21,000

Common: $\dfrac{\$700,000}{\$1,000,000} \times \$70,000 = \$49,000$ 49,000

Totals $63,000 $147,000

Proof:

Preferred: $\dfrac{\$63,000}{\$300,000} = 21\%$ Common: $\dfrac{\$147,000}{\$700,000} = 21\%$

LEARNING UNIT 19-4

RECORDING CAPITAL STOCK TRANSACTIONS UNDER A STOCK SUBSCRIPTION PLAN

In the last unit we assumed that stocks were immediately issued and full payment or cash or other assets were received. In this unit we examine stock transactions under **stock subscription** plans. Under such plans, buyers pledge to buy certain stocks but pay in installments or in a later lump sum. In most cases companies will not issue the actual stock certificates to these buyers until payment is complete.

Let's look at how Krump Corporation receives subscriptions for 1,000 shares of $100 par-value common stock at $160 per share on April 1, 20XX. Two equal installments will be paid on August 1 and November 1 by the buyer.

April 1: Accepted Subscription for 1,000 Shares at $160 per Share

Because the stock certificates will not be issued until paid in full, Krump Corporation records the ownership at par value in a temporary stockholders' equity account called **Common Stock Subscribed.** This account is shown in the paid-in capital section below the issue of the common stock. The amount due is recorded in an account called **Subscriptions Receivable — Common Stock.** The difference between the par value and the issue price is accumulated in a permanent account called Paid-in Capital in Excess of Par Value — Common.

Here is an analysis of the transaction:

Represents amount due on stock subscription. It is a current asset on the balance sheet.

Stock reserved but not fully paid. (1,000 shares × $100 par)

Accounts Affected	Category	↑ ↓	Rules
Subscriptions Receivable— Common Stock	Asset	↑	Dr. $160,000
Common Stock Subscribed	SE	↑	Cr. $100,000
Paid-in Capital in Excess of Par Value—Common	SE	↑	Cr. $60,000

1,000 shares × $160

1,000 shares × $60 par

The journal entry will be as follows:

20XX Apr.	1	Subscriptions Receivable—				
		Common Stock	160 0 0 0 00			
		Common Stock Subscribed			100 0 0 0 00	
		Paid-in Capital in Excess of Par			60 0 0 0 00	

August 1: Received First Installment on Common Stock Subscription

Accounts Affected	Category	↑ ↓	Rules
Cash	Asset	↑	Dr. $80,000
Subscriptions Receivable— Common Stock	Asset	↓	Cr. $80,000

The journal entry will be as follows:

20XX Aug.	1	Cash	80 0 0 0 00		
		Subscriptions Receivable—			
		Common Stock		80 0 0 0 00	

November 1: Received Final Installment on Common Stock Subscription

Accounts Affected	Category	↑ ↓	Rules
Cash	Asset	↑	Dr. $80,000
Subscriptions Receivable—Common Stock	Asset	↓	Cr. $80,000

The journal entry will be as follows:

20XX							
Nov.	1	Cash		80 0 0 0 00			
		Subscriptions Receivable—					
		Common Stock				80 0 0 0 00	

November 1: Issued 1,000 Shares of Fully Paid Common Stock

Accounts Affected	Category	↑ ↓	Rules
Common Stock Subscribed	SE	↓	Dr. $100,000
Common Stock	SE	↑	Cr. $100,000

The journal entry will be as follows:

20XX					
Nov.	1	Common Stock Subscribed	100 0 0 0 00		
		Common Stock		100 0 0 0 00	

Remember that stock is recorded at par value. At this point the Common Stock Subscribed account in the ledger (when posted) is reduced to a zero balance, and the Common Stock account records the issued stock (which has been paid for).

STOCKHOLDERS' EQUITY

The names and addresses of each stockholder are kept in a subsidiary ledger. The Stock account is the controlling account.

Before concluding this chapter, let's take a moment to set up a simplified stockholders' equity section of a balance sheet. The numbers in the following illustration are not related to the previous situations. The goal here is to show you the structure of paid-in capital and retained earnings. In the blueprint on page 693, the complete layout of stockholders' equity is illustrated by the **source-of-capital approach,** which lists classes of stockholders first. An alternative way, called the **legal capital approach,** lists all legal capital first and is illustrated in the next chapter. Both approaches are acceptable.

Stockholders' Equity			
Paid in Capital:			
Common Stock, $100 par value; authorized 10,000 shares, 7,000 issued and outstanding	$ 700 0 0 0 00		
Common Stock Subscribed, 2,000 shares at par	200 0 0 0 00		
Paid-in Capital in Excess of Par Value—Common	300 0 0 0 00		
Total Paid-in Capital	$1200 0 0 0 00		
Retained Earnings	400 0 0 0 00		
Total Stockholders' Equity	$1600 0 0 0 00		

LEARNING UNIT 19-4 REVIEW

AT THIS POINT you should be able to

- ▼ Journalize the entries in a stock subscription plan. (p. 687)
- ▼ Explain the purpose of Common Stock Subscribed. (p. 687)
- ▼ Prepare a simplified stockholders' section. (p. 689)

SELF-REVIEW QUIZ 19-4

(The forms you need are on page 69 of the *Study Guide and Working Papers*.)

Journalize the entries to record the stock subscription plan for Moose Corp. On October 1 Moose Corp. received subscriptions for 500 shares of $50 par-value common stock at $80 per share. The buyer will pay two equal installments on December 31 and March 31.

Solutions to Self-Review Quiz 19-4

Oct.	1	Subscriptions Receivable—		
		Common Stock	4 0 0 0 0 00	
		Common Stock Subscribed		2 5 0 0 0 00
		Paid-in Capital in Excess of Par		
		Value—Common		1 5 0 0 0 00
Dec.	31	Cash	2 0 0 0 0 00	
		Subscriptions Receivable—		
		Common Stock		2 0 0 0 0 00
Mar.	31	Cash	2 0 0 0 0 00	
		Subscriptions Receivable—		
		Common Stock		2 0 0 0 0 00
	31	Common Stock Subscribed	2 5 0 0 0 00	
		Common Stock		2 5 0 0 0 00

SUMMARY OF KEY POINTS

Learning Unit 19-1

1. The articles of incorporation is submitted to the state when one wants to form a corporation. It contains all the specifics of the proposed corporation. If approved, a charter (certificate of incorporation) is issued to incorporators.

2. Advantages of a corporation include limited liability, a separate legal entity, unlimited life, ease of transferring ownership interest, no mutual agency, and ease in raising capital. Disadvantages include difficulties in forming a corporation, government regulations, and double taxation.

Learning Unit 19-2

1. Stockholders' equity is broken down in Paid-in Capital and Retained Earnings.

2. Retained Earnings records the accumulated profits that are retained or kept in the corporation.

3. Authorized stock represents the total amount of stock that can be legally issued. Outstanding stock represents the amount of stock issued.

4. Common stockholders have the right to vote, share in profits, sell their ownership, and receive assets at liquidation if available; they also have preemptive rights (the right to maintain their proportionate ownership interest in the company).

5. Buyers of preferred stock, to gain stability of earnings, may give up voting rights, preemptive rights, and so forth. Preferred stock can be cumulative, noncumulative, participating, nonparticipating, or a combination.

6. Par value is an arbitrary value. It doesn't mean market value. Stocks may have a par value, no par, or no par with a stated value.

7. Legal capital is the amount that a corporation must retain in the business for the protection of the creditors. It may be based on par value, no par value, or stated value.

Learning Unit 19-3

1. Common stock or preferred stock with par value is recorded by number of shares times par value. If stock is sold for more than par, the difference is recorded in a stockholders' equity account called Paid-in Capital in Excess of Par Value. If a stock is sold below par, the difference is recorded in a contra-stockholders' equity account called Discount on Common Stock.

2. If no-par stock with a stated value is sold at a price higher than stated value, the difference is recorded in a stockholders' equity account called Paid-in Capital in Excess of Stated Value.

3. Assets are recorded at fair market value when exchanged for stock. Any difference between par value of stock and fair market value is recorded in a stockholders' equity account called Capital in Excess of Par.

4. Organization Cost is an intangible asset on the balance sheet. Today it is being expensed.

5. The calculation for a dividend to common or preferred with par value is (number of shares × par) × rate. If preferred is fully participating, the allocation of the remainder is based on par value of each class of stock over the total par value. This fraction is multiplied times remainder of dividend.

1. The source-of-capital approach will present the paid-in capital component of stockholders' equity by classes of stockholders. There is no attempt to list legal capital first.

2. Subscriptions Receivable is an asset representing amounts due on stock that has been subscribed to. It is a current asset on the balance sheet.

3. Common Stock Subscribed is a stockholders' equity account that acts as a temporary account until a subscription is paid for. When paid, the Common Stock Subscribed account is reduced and the Common Stock account is increased.

KEY TERMS

Articles of incorporation   Document submitted by incorporators when applying for a charter.

Authorized capital stock   As stated in its charter, the number of shares of capital stock (common and preferred) that a corporation can sell.

Capital stock   Classes of stock that represent the fractional elements of ownership of a corporation.

Certificate of incorporation   Document granted by the state authorizing the creation of a corporation.

Charter   Document issued to a corporation by the state that includes certificate of incorporation along with articles of incorporation.

Common stock   Part of paid-in capital representing the basic ownership equity of the corporation. If the corporation has only one class of stock, it will be common stock.

Common Stock Subscribed   Temporary stockholders' equity account that records at par value stock that has been subscribed to but not fully paid for.

Corporation   Business organization that is both a legal and accounting entity.

Cumulative preferred stock   Stock that entitles its holders to any undeclared dividends that have accumulated before common stockholders receive their dividends.

Directors   Officers elected by stockholders to represent the company and establish policies for the company.

Discount on stock   The difference between the par value of the stock and an amount less than the par value that the stockholders have contributed. Discounts do not happen very often.

Dividend   Cash, other assets, or shares of stock that a corporation issues to the stockholders.

Dividends in arrears   Dividends owed to preferred stockholders that must be paid before common stockholders can receive their dividends.

Incorporators   Persons responsible for getting the corporation formed.

Issued capital stock   Stock that the corporation issues for assets or services contributed by the stockholders.

Legal capital   Minimum amount of capital that a corporation must leave in the company (cannot be withdrawn by stockholders) for protection of the creditors.

Legal capital approach   Method of preparing paid-in capital by listing the legal section first. (See blueprint at end of Chapter 20.)

Limited liability   Freedom of stockholders from *personal* liability for the debts of the corporation.

Minute book   Book that records meetings of board of directors or stockholders.

Noncumulative preferred stock   Preferred stock that does not entitle its holders to a dividend for any year in which a dividend is not declared.

Nonparticipating preferred stock   Preferred stock that entitles its holders only to a certain percent dividend, the remainder going to holders of common stock.

No-par stock   Stock with no par value. A stated value could be placed on it.

Organization Cost   An intangible asset that records the initial cost of forming the corporation, such as legal and incorporating fees. Today it is now being expensed.

Outstanding capital stock   Stock that is held and owned by stockholders.

Paid-in Capital   Section of stockholders' equity representing what stockholders have invested into the corporation.

Paid-in Capital in Excess of Par Value—Common   Difference between what stockholders invest and par value. This amount is not credited to the Stock account.

Paid-in Capital in Excess of Stated Value—Common   Difference between what stockholders invest and the stated value placed on stock by the board of directors. This amount is not credited to the Stock account.

Participating preferred stock Stock that entitles its holders not only to a fixed dividend but also to an opportunity to share in additional dividends with common stockholders.

Par value An arbitrary value that is placed on each share of stock. Par value represents legal capital and not market value.

Preemptive right The right of the stockholder to purchase additional shares of stock to maintain his or her proportionate interest when the corporation issues additional stock.

Preferred stock Class of capital stock that has preference to a corporation's profits and assets.

Premium A term that records the sale of stock at more than par value. In this book we use the account "Paid-in Capital in Excess of Par" to record the premium received.

Retained earnings Accumulated profits of a corporation that have been kept in the business and not paid out as dividends. Retained Earnings is part of stockholders' equity.

Source-of-capital approach Method of preparing paid-in capital by listing classes of stockholder sources of capital (see p. 693 for example).

Stated value Arbitrary value placed by the board of directors on each share of no-par stock to fulfill legal capital requirements.

Stock certificate Formal document issued to investors in a corporation that shows the number of shares purchased.

Stockholders Owners of the stock of the corporation.

Stock subscription A contractual agreement to buy a certain number of shares of stock from a corporation at a specific price.

Subscriptions Receivable—Common Stock Current asset on balance sheet that represents amount due on stock subscriptions.

QUESTIONS, MINI EXERCISES, EXERCISES, AND PROBLEMS

Discussion Questions

1. What is the difference between the articles of incorporation and a charter?
2. Who elects the board of directors?
3. List the advantages of the corporate form of organization.
4. Explain the difference between paid-in capital and retained earnings.
5. Why can't a company issue more stock than is authorized?
6. What does preemptive right mean?
7. Distinguish between legal capital, par value, no par value, and no par value with a stated value.
8. Preferred stock can never be cumulative *and* nonparticipating. True or false? Support your answer.
9. What is the normal balance and the category of the account Discount on Common Stock?
10. How does one calculate Paid-in Capital in Excess of Par Value or Stated Value?
11. Explain the account Paid-in Capital in Excess of Par Value as it relates to exchange of stock for noncash assets.
12. What is the purpose of the account Organization Costs?
13. In stock subscriptions why does one credit Common Stock Subscribed?

Mini Exercises

(The forms you need are on pages 71 – 72 of the *Study Guide and Working Papers*.)

Stockholders' Equity

1. Marci Corporation has capital stock of $5,000. Its retained earnings account has a $12,000 balance. Cash has a balance of $10,000. What is the total of stockholders' equity for Marci Corporation?

Cumulative Preferred

2. Moore Co. owed $10,000 each year for three years to holders of cumulative preferred stock. This year Moore pays out $100,000 in dividends to preferred and common. How much did each class of stock receive?

Journalizing Sales of Stock

3. Journalize the following (p. 694):

BLUEPRINT: SOURCE OF CAPITAL APPROACH

VALLEY CO. PARTIAL BALANCE SHEET			
Assets			
Current Assets:			
Subscriptions Receivable, Common 8% Stock	XXX		
Intangible Assets:			
Organization Cost		XXX	
Total Assets			XXX
Liabilities			

Note that preferred stock is listed before common stock.

Stockholders' Equity			
Paid-in Capital:			
Preferred 12% stock, $10 par value, authorized 20,000 shares, 8,000 shares issued	XXX		
Paid-in Capital in Excess of Par Value—preferred	XXX		
Total Paid-in Capital by preferred stockholders		XXX	
Common Stock, no par value, stated value $10 per share, authorized 100,000 shares, 30,000 issued and outstanding	XXX		
Common Stock Subscribed, 1,000 shares at par	XXX		
Paid-in Capital in Excess of Stated Value—Common	XXX		
Total Paid-in Capital by common stockholders		XXX	
Total Paid-in Capital		XXX	
Retained Earnings		XXX	
Total Stockholders' Equity			XXX

20XX

July	8	Pete Co. sells 300 shares of $10 par-value common stock at $10.
Oct.	15	Jon Co. sells 200 shares of $10 par-value common stock at $15.
Nov.	28	Angel Co. sells 200 shares of no-par common stock with a stated value $20 for $30 per share.
Dec.	30	Lowe Co. issues 500 shares of $10 par-value common stock to organizers of the firm for services rendered costing $7,500.

Cumulative and Participating Preferred

4. From the following calculate the dividends for common and preferred stock:

   ▼ 7 percent fully participating preferred stock.
   ▼ The board declared a $150,000 dividend.
   ▼ Preferred stock 2,000 shares, $100 par value; common stock 8,000 shares, $100 par.

Stock Subscriptions

5. Journalize the entries to record the stock subscription plan for Blue Co. On October 1, Blue received subscriptions for 200 shares of $25 par-value common stock at $40 per share. The buyer will pay two equal installments on December 31 and March 31.

Exercises

(The forms you need are on pages 73–74 of the *Study Guide and Working Papers*.)

Journalizing transactions for sale of stock.

19-1. Val Corporation was authorized to issue 30,000 shares of common stock. Record the journal entry for each of the following independent situations, assuming Val issues 6,000 shares at $11 on July 20, 20XX:

   a. Common stock has a $10 par value.
   b. Common stock has no par and no stated value.
   c. Common stock is no-par stock with a stated value of $8.

Exchange of stock for noncash assets.

19-2. On July 10, 20XX, Zeron Corporation issued 3,000 shares of common stock with a par value of $100 in exchange for equipment with a fair market value of $320,000. Journalize the appropriate entry.

Calculating dividends to preferred and common.

19-3. Vetco Corporation in its first three years of operation paid out the following dividends:

   ▼ Year 1: 0
   ▼ Year 2: $30,000
   ▼ Year 3: $90,000

   Given that Vetco has 3,000 shares of $100 par 9 percent cumulative, non-participating preferred stock and 15,000 shares of $25 par value common stock, what would be the total dividends paid each year to holders of common and preferred?

Stock subscription.

19-4. On January 1, 20XX, Lavrel Corporation issued on a subscription basis 1,000 shares of $50 par-value common stock at $90 per share. Two equal installments were to be made on July 1 and December 31. Prepare the appropriate journal entries on January 1, July 1, and December 31 to record this stock subscription for Lavrel Corporation.

Stockholders' equity.

19-5. Scupper Corporation began its business on January 1, 20XX. It sold at $30 per share 6,000 shares of no-par common stock with a stated value of $20 per share. The charter of Scupper indicated 40,000 shares were authorized. Retained earnings were $60,000 on December 31. Prepare the stockholders' equity section for Scupper on December 31, 20XX, using page 689 as a guide.

694

CHAPTER 19 ...CORPORATIONS: ORGANIZATION AND CAPITAL STOCK

(The forms you need are on pages 76–83 of the *Study Guide and Working Papers*.)

19A-1. The following is the Paid-in Capital section of stockholders' equity for the Larson Corporation on June 1, 20XX:

Recording capital stock transactions; preparing Paid-in Capital section of stockholders' equity.

Paid-in Capital:

Preferred Stock, $100 par, authorized 20,000 shares, 4,000 shares issued	$ 400,000
Paid-in Capital in Excess of Par Value — Preferred Stock	120,000
Common Stock, $25 par, authorized 50,000 shares, 20,000 shares issued	500,000
Paid-in Capital in Excess of Par Value — Common Stock	160,000
Total Paid-in Capital	$1,180,000

Check Figure:
(2) Paid-in capital
$2,732,000

The following transactions occurred in the months of June and July:

20XX

June	1	Issued 3,000 shares of preferred stock at $102 per share.
	2	Issued 7,000 shares of common stock at $40 per share.
	15	Issued 8,000 shares of common stock at $42 per share.
July	2	Issued 5,000 shares of preferred stock at $104 per share.
	18	Issued 2,000 shares of common stock in exchange for building and land with a fair market value of $60,000 and $50,000, respectively.

1. Journalize the above entries and update the stockholders' equity ledger. Accounts are provided in the workbook.

2. Prepare a new Paid-in Capital section of stockholders' equity as of July 31, 20XX.

19A-2. Katie Corporation has 20,000 shares outstanding of $10 par value 8 percent preferred stock and 40,000 shares outstanding of $10 par-value common stock. In its first five years of operation, the company paid the following dividends: 20X1, 0; 20X2, $16,000; 20X3, $48,000; 20X4, 0; 20X5, $82,000. Calculate the dividends paid to preferred and common stockholders under the following three independent situations:

Calculating dividends for preferred and common stock.

a. Preferred stock is noncumulative and nonparticipating.
b. Preferred stock is cumulative and nonparticipating.
c. Preferred stock is cumulative and fully participating.

Check Figure:
(b) Pref: $ 16,000   20X2
          32,000   20X3
          32,000   20X5

19A-3. From the following partial mixed list, select the appropriate titles and prepare a stockholders' equity section using the source-of-capital approach as shown on the blueprint on p. 693 for Xenon Corporation on July 31, 20XX.

Preparing a stockholders' equity section of a balance sheet.

Office Equipment	$100,000
Land	200,000
Paid-in Capital in Excess of Par Value — Preferred Stock	100,000
Building	80,000
Accounts Receivable	120,000
Notes Receivable	40,000
Organization Costs	10,000
Common Stock, $10 Par Value (60,000 shares issued and outstanding; 80,000 shares authorized)	600,000
Retained Earnings	200,000
Subscriptions Receivable — Common Stock	80,000
Patents	10,000
Preferred 14 percent Stock, $50 Par (6,000 shares issued; 7,000 shares authorized)	300,000
Common Stock Subscribed at Par	225,000
Paid-in Capital in Excess of Par Value — Common Stock	20,000

Check Figure:
Stockholders' equity
$1,445,000

19-A4. Joilet Corporation has just been issued a charter by the state of New York. This charter gives Joilet the authority to issue 400,000 shares of $10 par-value common stock. From the following transactions,

1. Prepare journal entries to record the transactions of Joilet Corp. for the month of August.
2. Prepare the Paid-in Capital section of Joilet's balance sheet at the end of the month.

Stock subscriptions and exchange of stock for non-cash assets.

Check Figure:
Total paid-in capital
$368,500

20XX
Aug. 11 Issued 1,800 shares of stock for land and building with a fair market value of $13,000 and $17,500, respectively.
16 Accepted subscriptions to 20,000 shares of stock for $250,000 to be paid in two equal installments.
22 Collected first installment on 10,000 shares of the common stock subscribed on August 16.
28 Sold 7,000 shares of stock for $88,000.
30 Collected last installment on 10,000 shares of the common stock subscribed on August 16 and issued the shares.

Group B Problems

(The forms you need are on pages 76–83 of the *Study Guide and Working Papers*.)

19B-1. The following is the Paid-in Capital section of stockholders' equity for the Larson Corporation on June 1, 20XX:

Recording capital stock transactions; preparing Paid-in Capital section of stockholders' equity.

Check Figure:
Total paid-in capital
$678,500

Paid-in Capital:	
Preferred Stock, $25, par, authorized 20,000 shares, 5,000 shares issued	$125,000
Paid-in Capital in Excess of Par Value — Preferred Stock	37,500
Common Stock, $10 par, authorized 100,000 shares, 20,000 shares issued	200,000
Paid-in Capital in Excess of Par Value — Common Stock	45,000
Total Paid-in Capital	$407,500

The following transactions occurred in the months of June and July:

20XX
June 1 Issued 2,000 shares of preferred stock at $28 per share.
4 Issued 4,000 shares of common stock at $13 per share.
15 Issued 5,000 shares of common stock at $16 per share.
July 2 Issued 1,000 shares of preferred stock at $29 per share.
18 Issued 2,000 shares of common stock in exchange for building and land with a fair market value of $25,000 and $29,000, respectively.

1. Journalize and post the above entries and update the stockholders' equity ledger accounts provided in the workbook.
2. Prepare a new Paid-in Capital section of stockholders' equity as of July 31, 20XX.

Calculating dividends for preferred and common stock.

Check Figure:
(b) Pref: 20X2 $16,000
     20X5 $20,000

19B-2. Katie Corporation has 10,000 shares outstanding of $20 par-value 10 percent preferred stock and 120,000 shares outstanding of $5 par-value common stock. In its first five years of operation, the company paid the following dividends: 20X1, 0; 20X2, $16,000; 20X3, $80,000; 20X4, $84,000; 20X5, $120,000. Calculate the dividends paid to preferred and common stockholders under the following three independent situations:

a. Preferred stock is noncumulative and nonparticipating.
b. Preferred stock is cumulative and nonparticipating.
c. Preferred stock is cumulative and fully participating.

19B-3. From the following partial mixed list, select the appropriate titles and prepare a stockholders' equity section using the source-of-capital approach as shown in the blueprint on page 693 for Xenon Corporation on July 31, 20XX.

as shown in the blueprint on page 693

Paid-in Capital in Excess of Par Value — Common Stock	$ 1,400
Common Stock Subscribed at Par	8,800
Paid-in Capital in Excess of Par Value — Preferred Stock	12,000
Land	15,000
Office Equipment	7,600
Preferred 14 percent Stock, $50 Par (400 shares issued; 8,000 shares authorized)	20,000
Patents	1,600
Subscriptions Receivable — Common Stock	12,000
Retained Earnings	28,000
Common Stock $10 Par Value (8,000 shares issued; and outstanding; 50,000 shares authorized)	80,000
Organization Costs	1,200
Notes Receivable	5,000
Accounts Receivable	18,000
Building	5,000

> Preparing a stockholders' equity section of a balance sheet.

> Check Figure:
> Total stockholders' equity
> $150,200

19B-4. The state of New York has issued a charter to Joilet Corporation with the authorization to issue 10,000 shares of $100 par-value common stock. From the following transactions,

1. Journalize the transactions for Joilet for the month of September.
2. Prepare the Paid-in Capital section of Joilet Corporation's balance sheet at the end of the month.

> Stock subscriptions and exchange of stock for non-cash assets.

> Check Figure:
> Total paid-in capital
> $151,000

20XX

Sept. 8   Issued 500 shares of stock for land and building with a fair market value of $29,000 and $24,000, respectively.

         14   Accepted subscriptions to 300 shares of its stock for $39,000 to be paid in two equal installments.

         22   Collected first installment on 150 shares of the common stock subscribed on September 14.

         24   Sold 500 shares of stock for $59,000.

         30   Collected last installment on 150 shares of the common stock subscribed on September 14 and issued the shares.

REAL-WORLD APPLICATIONS

19R-1.

The partial balance sheet of Freedom Corporation had as of July 31, 20XX, the following balances:

Preferred Stock, $10 Par	$ 95,000
Paid-in Capital in Excess of Par — Preferred	65,000
Common Stock, $100 Par	180,000
Paid-in Capital in Excess of Par — Common	220,000
Common Stock Subscribed	10,000
Retained Earnings	520,000
Subscriptions Receivable	60,000
Bonds Payable	$300,000

The bookkeeper, Alice Fall, is quite concerned that the company has not kept enough legal capital in the business. She wants the board of directors to immediately change the par value, because the market value of the stock has increased. She believes it is only fair to protect the rights of the creditors.

Support or rebut Alice Fall's position in writing.

19R-2.

Bill Murray and Jim Smith, full-time high school teachers, had worked together in overnight camping for years. They both felt it was time to start their own overnight camp. Bill estimated he would be able to invest $30,000 and Jim could invest $2,000. Both agreed that they would need at least $200,000 to finance the purchase of land as well as the building of bunks and administrative offices.

Jim felt that forming a corporation was too involved and wanted to form a partnership. Bill, on the other hand, who trusted no one, felt that the corporate structure was best.

Jim and Bill have come to you to recommend what form of organization is best for them and how they can or should raise the money. Please write them a recommendation.

YOU make the call

Critical Thinking/Ethical Case

19R-3.

Avan Corporation just published its financial statements. The president of Avan told the accountants not to include in the annual report any information about a pending lawsuit. The president thought it would only worry the stockholders. Do you think the president is correct in not including any information about the pending lawsuit in the annual report? You make the call. Write down your recommendations to the president.

INTERNET EXERCISES

EX-1. [mosl.sos.state.mo.us/sos-sec/prospec.html] Before a company can offer its stock to the public it must publish a prospectus. The prospectus contains a myriad of information about the company, about its officers, about who its accountants are, along with much more statistical information. Most states offer online information about the requirements for a stock to be offered in that state. This site, presented by the State of Missouri, provides information on how to read a prospectus. The state you are in probably offers a similar site or a document similar to this one.

Within this document, find the answers to these questions:

1. What is the "legal status" of a prospectus?

2. When will you receive a prospectus of a company in which you may invest?

3. Why is it important for you to read the "use of proceeds" section?

4. What can you learn about the investment policy of the company from the dividend section?

EX-2. [www.nyse.com/members/members.html] The world's best known stock exchange is the New York Stock Exchange (NYSE). Many people look at the NYSE as a huge auction, which is an accurate portrayal of what occurs on the floor of the exchange. Stock brokers around the world are connected with NYSE, offering a way for buyers and sellers of stock to come together to transact their exchange.

1. Read "the role of the specialist" and briefly state what that role is.

2. Read "the role of the floor broker" and briefly state what that role is.

3. How do these two positions interact at the NYSE?

PART

6

Corporations

CHAPTER 20

Corporations

STOCK VALUES, DIVIDENDS, TREASURY STOCK, AND RETAINED EARNINGS

From its founding in 1875 to 1984, the American Telephone and Telegraph company (AT&T) was affectionately known to Americans as "Ma Bell." The name, in honor of Alexander Graham Bell, the inventor of the telephone, conjured an image of a reliable and sensible grandma, taking good care of her brood. And that's just what Ma Bell did for her investors. For 125 years the company enjoyed a monopoly on the nation's phone service and was the most widely held stock in the country. In fact, Ma Bell was the epitome of a "widows and orphans stock," a stock known for paying out reliable and sizeable quarterly **dividends.** Dividends are the portion of profits that corporations pay out to stockholders either as stock or as cash.

Yet, with the company's announcement on February 1, 2001, widows, orphans, retirees and others on fixed incomes will no longer be able to rely on the company's dividends for sustenance. As a sign of AT&T's mounting financial troubles, the dividends were slashed by 83% to only 15 cents a share, the first such decrease in the company's 125-year history. Like other troubled companies including Xerox, J.C. Penney, and Pacific Gas & Electric, AT&T is reinvesting money it would have paid out as dividends into activities that boost its market share. These "retained earnings" can be an important source of capital to help the business grow.

Insulated for years against market pressures, AT&T faces intense competition in the long-distance telephone market. A dozen years after the government broke up Ma Bell's monopoly in 1984, AT&T's market share had dropped to 50% from over 90%. Advances in technology have also created huge challenges. Voice telephone calls are only one way to connect people to information. The company is in the process of evolving from a "long-distance telecommunications company" to an "any-distance" company that uses Internet, broadband, data networking and video technologies. And they need cash, which would have gone into dividends, to do that successfully.

Every corporation has to decide how much of its profits to pay out to stockholders as dividends, and how much to reinvest in its operations. In this chapter, you will learn how dividends are paid to stockholders and why it is sometimes necessary to restrict part of the retained earnings to finance a special project. In addition, you'll learn about the differences among common, preferred and treasury stock and how to calculate the book value of each.

Based on: Dolores Kong, "The End Of A Sure Thing in Change of Policy, AT&T Cuts Dividend–And More Firms Are Following Suit," *Boston Globe,* February 1, 2001, p. D1. Gary Strauss, "More companies whittle dividends Cuts especially hurt investors who depend upon on regular income," *USA Today,* December 22, 2000. p. B1. Information on AT&T history from www.att.com/history/.

LEARNING OBJECTIVES

▼ Calculating the book value of preferred and common stock. (p. 702)

▼ Journalizing entries to record issuance of a cash dividend and a stock dividend. (p. 706)

▼ Journalizing the purchase and sale of treasury stock. (p. 711)

▼ Preparing a statement of retained earnings. (p. 715)

In this chapter we continue the study of aspects of corporate equity that we began in the last chapter. We discuss a number of topics, including stock values, how and why dividends are declared and paid, why a corporation buys back its own stock, and the restrictions on retained earnings.

In Chapter 19 we discussed two types of stock value: par value and stated value. In Learning Unit 20-1 we turn our attention to other stock values.

LEARNING UNIT 20-1

UNDERSTANDING STOCK VALUES: REDEMPTION, MARKET, AND BOOK VALUE

REDEMPTION VALUE

When a corporation issues preferred stock, it often reserves the right to retire or redeem that stock for a specific price. At the time the stock is issued, this price per share, called **redemption value,** is determined, and people buy the stock knowing that the corporation can redeem it at this price.

MARKET VALUE

Stocks are traded in decimals today. They used to be traded in fractional amounts.

The price at which shares of capital stock are bought and sold in the open market is called the **market value.** Economic conditions, a company's earnings, and investors' expectations all play a factor in determining the market price.

BOOK VALUE PER SHARE

Book value per share is, in general, the total of stockholders' equity (assets minus liabilities) divided by the number of shares issued.

Why is book value used? For several reasons:

1. When a company seeks a loan, banks may specify a minimum book value for a loan to be approved.
2. If a merger is being negotiated, book value may be used as a factor in setting an exchange ratio of stock. For example, based on book value, 1 share of Octon Co. stock could fairly be issued for 3 shares of Xeron Co. stock, if book value of Octon stock is $30 and book value of Xeron stock is $10.
3. Book value may be used when contracts are made. For example, an individual may receive in the future an option to buy or sell stock based on future book value. (That value is *not* market value, which is based on current prices.)

It is important to emphasize that book value doesn't represent what an owner might receive if the assets of a company were *liquidated*. At the time of liquidation the assets may be sold at prices quite different from the values on the books, which are based on cost and not current market prices.

CALCULATING BOOK VALUE WITH ONLY ONE CLASS OF STOCK

When a corporation has only common stock, book value is calculated using the following equation:

$$\text{Book Value per Share} = \frac{\text{Total Stockholders' Equity}}{\text{Total Shares Outstanding}}$$

As an example, we use the stockholders' equity shown below for Jones Corporation and calculate book value per share of common stock.

The book value is $45 per share ($450,000/10,000 shares). Thus for each share of stock owned, $45 would be received *if* the corporation were liquidated without any losses from disposing of assets. By the time assets are disposed of, the owner might get much less than book value.

JONES CORPORATION STOCKHOLDERS' EQUITY	
Paid-in Capital:	
Common Stock, $25 par value; 10,000 shares authorized, issued, and outstanding	$250 0 0 0 00
Paid-in Capital in Excess of Par Value—Common	110 0 0 0 00
Total Paid-in Capital	$360 0 0 0 00
Retained Earnings	90 0 0 0 00
Total Stockholders' Equity	$450 0 0 0 00

CALCULATING BOOK VALUE WITH BOTH PREFERRED AND COMMON STOCK

When there are two classes of stock, before book value can be calculated the stockholders' equity must be allocated (divided up) for each class of stock. First, for preferred stock, a corporation assigns the redemption value (or par value if there is no redemption value) of the stock along with any dividends in arrears (any dividends that are owed to holders of preferred stock but have not yet been paid out). This total of redemption value plus dividends in arrears is divided by the number of preferred shares outstanding. The *remainder* of stockholders' equity is assigned to the common stockholders, and the book value of the common stock is calculated by that amount divided by the number of common stock shares outstanding. Book value can be shown in the following formulas:

$$\text{Book Value Preferred} = \frac{\text{Redemption Value} + \text{Dividends in Arrears}}{\text{Number of Shares of Preferred Stock Outstanding}}$$

$$\text{Book Value Common} = \frac{\text{Stockholders' Equity} - \text{Amount Assigned to Preferred}}{\text{Number of Shares of Common Stock Outstanding}}$$

Let's illustrate this situation by looking at the stockholders' equity of Ryan Corporation and performing the necessary calculations.

RYAN CORPORATION STOCKHOLDERS' EQUITY			
Paid-in Capital:			
Preferred 7% Stock, $100 per value, authorized			
3,000 shares cumulative and nonparticipating,			
2,000 shares issued and outstanding	$200 000 00		
Paid-in Capital in Excess of Par Value—Preferred	10 000 00		
Total Paid-in Capital by Preferred Stockholders		$210 000 00	
Common Stock, $50 par value, authorized 12,000			
shares, 10,000 shares issued and outstanding	500 000 00		
Paid-in Capital in Excess of Par Value—Common	20 000 00		
Total Paid-in Capital by Common Stockholders		520 000 00	
Total Paid-in Capital		$730 000 00	
Retained Earnings		164 000 00	
Total Stockholders' Equity		$894 000 00	

Redemption value
$103 × 2,000 shares

Total Stockholders' Equity		$894 000 00	
Less: Equity Applicable to Preferred Stock:			
Redemption Value	$206 000 00		
Dividends in Arrears	14 000 00	(220 000 00)	
Equity Allocated to Common Stock			$674 000 00

Given: Redemption value of preferred is $103; there are $14,000 worth of dividends in arrears.

Thus

$$\text{Book Value Preferred} = \frac{\$206,000 + \$14,000}{2,000 \text{ Shares}}$$

$$= \frac{\$220,000}{2,000 \text{ Shares}} = \$110 \text{ per Share}$$

and

$$\text{Book Value Common} = \frac{\$894{,}000 - \$220{,}000}{10{,}000 \text{ Shares}}$$

$$= \frac{\$674{,}000}{10{,}000 \text{ Shares}} = \$67.40 \text{ per Share}$$

Note: When preferred stock is redeemed, the paid-in capital in excess of par is *not* returned and thus is *not* included as part of the preferred equity in the book-value calculation.

LEARNING UNIT 20-1 REVIEW

AT THIS POINT you should be able to

▼ List and define other stock values besides par value. (p. 702)
▼ Explain the purpose of book value. (p. 703)
▼ Calculate the book value of preferred and common stock. (p. 704)

SELF-REVIEW QUIZ 20-1

(The forms you need are on page 89 of the *Study Guide and Working Papers*.)

From the following information calculate the book value for preferred and common stock:

(4,000 shares issued) Preferred Stock	Paid-in Capital in Excess of Par—Preferred	(3,000 shares issued) Common Stock
300,000	20,000	600,000

Paid-in Capital in Excess of Par—Common	Retained Earnings
30,000	25,000

Dividends in arrears amount to $15,000. Assume a redemption value on preferred stock of $90 per share.

Solution to Self-Review Quiz 20-1

$90 per share × 4,000 shares redemption value

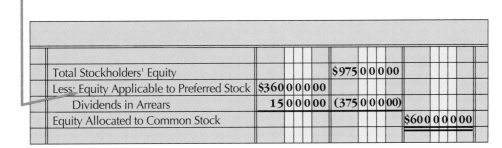

Total Stockholders' Equity		$975 00 0 00	
Less: Equity Applicable to Preferred Stock	$360 00 0 00		
Dividends in Arrears	15 0 0 00	(375 0 0 0 00)	
Equity Allocated to Common Stock			$600 00 0 00

PREFERRED STOCK	COMMON STOCK
Book Value per Share	Book Value per Share
$\dfrac{\$375{,}000}{4{,}000 \text{ shares}} = \$93.75$	$\dfrac{\$600{,}000}{3{,}000 \text{ shares}} = \$200$

In this unit we discuss the distribution of cash, stock, or other assets that the board of directors declares as dividends. **Dividends,** as we have seen, are the distribution of earnings of the corporation. It is important to realize that only the board of directors of a corporation has the authority to determine whether a dividend is to be paid, how much it will be, who receives it, and when and how it will be paid.

Three important dates are associated with the dividend process.

1. **Date of declaration:** The day the board of directors announces its decision to pay a dividend. This date creates a liability to the company called **Dividend Payable.**

2. **Date of record:** The date established by the board of directors that determines which stockholders will receive the dividend. These stockholders can be identified in the corporation's subsidiary stockholders' ledger at this date of record.

3. **Date of payment:** The date that the dividend is actually paid to stockholders of record.

> The board of directors declares the dividend.

> Date of record is usually two to four weeks after date of declaration.

> There must be a sufficient balance in retained earnings and cash to pay the dividend.

CASH DIVIDENDS

The distribution of earnings of a corporation in the form of cash to its stockholders is called a **cash dividend.** For example, on March 8, 20XX, the board of directors of Tell Corporation declares a $2 cash dividend per share on the 5,000 shares issued and outstanding. The dividend will be paid on April 16, 20XX, to stockholders of record on March 25, 20XX. Let's look at how to analyze as well as record this cash dividend.

Date of Declaration: March 8, 20XX: The following chart analyzes this transaction.

Declaration of dividends reduces Retained Earnings.
A legally declared dividend is a current liability on the balance sheet.

Accounts Affected	Category	↑ ↓	Rules
Retained Earnings	SE	↓	Dr. $10,000
Dividends Payable	Liability	↑	Cr. $10,000

The journal entry will look like the following:

> Note that no entry is made on date of record.

Mar.	8	Retained Earnings	1 0 0 0 0 00		
		Dividends Payable			1 0 0 0 0 00
		Dividends declared of $2 to stockholders			
		of record Mar. 25, 20XX: payable on			
		Apr. 16, 20XX, as declared by board			
		of directors.			

Date of Payment: April 16, 20XX: Here is an analysis of the dividend payment.

Accounts Affected	Category	↑ ↓	Rules
Dividends Payable	Liability	↓	Dr. $10,000
Cash	Asset	↓	Cr. $10,000

The journal entry will look like the following:

Apr.	16	Dividends Payable	10 0 0 0 00	
		Cash		10 0 0 0 00
		Payment of dividend to stockholders of		
		record on Mar. 25, 20XX		

The end result of these transactions is to reduce Cash and Retained Earnings. (*Remember: Retained Earnings doesn't mean Cash.* Cash is an asset, whereas Retained Earnings is part of stockholders' equity.) In effect, the company is distributing part of its accumulated income to stockholders.

THE STOCK DIVIDEND

A **stock dividend** occurs when a corporation issues its own stock instead of a distribution of assets to its stockholders. There are a number of reasons why a stock dividend is declared instead of a cash dividend:

> A stock dividend doesn't reduce cash or the total of stockholders' equity.

1. To satisfy stockholders' expectations. The corporation doesn't have enough cash to pay a cash dividend and offers the stock dividend instead. The stockholders make no new investment to receive this type of dividend.

2. To increase permanent capital in the business (because more stock is issued).

3. To reduce the market value of the stock, because the price may be too high in the trading on the open market. When more stock is supplied with no demand for it, stock prices go down.

4. Because income tax is avoided until the stock received is sold.

RECORDING A STOCK DIVIDEND

A stock dividend will *not* reduce total stockholders' equity the way a cash dividend does. The end result of a stock dividend is to transfer an amount based on market value from Retained Earnings to Paid-in Capital.* After a stock dividend a stockholder will own a larger number of shares, but the *total* ownership equity stays the same. Let's look at Jesse Corporation to illustrate recording a stock dividend.

On December 27, 20XX, Jesse Corporation declared a 10 percent stock dividend distributable January 27 to stockholders of record on January 13. Page 708 shows the stockholders' equity of Jesse Corporation before the dividend was declared. The current fair market value of the stock is $30 per share.

---

*For larger stock dividends (over 25 percent of the outstanding stock) the amount is based on par. We look at small stock dividends later.

Stockholders' Equity			
Paid-in Capital:			
Common Stock, $20 par value,			
15,000 shares authorized, 10,000 shares issued			
and outstanding	$200 000 00		
Paid-in Capital in Excess of Par, Common	24 000 00		
Total Paid-in Capital by Common Stockholders	224 000 00		
Retained Earnings	62 000 00		
Total Stockholders' Equity		$286 000 00	

Recording the Declaration of the Dividend: The following chart is an analysis of this transaction.

Accounts Affected	Category	↑ ↓	Rules
Retained Earnings	SE	↓	Dr. $30,000
Common Stock Dividend Distributable	SE	↑	Cr. $20,000
Paid-in Capital in Excess of Par Value—Stock Dividend	SE	↑	Cr. $10,000

Retained Earnings is decreased by $30,000. To arrive at that figure we multiply the market value of the stock ($30) times the number of shares issued in the dividend (1,000). The number of shares issued in the dividend is the number of shares issued and outstanding (10,000) times the percent of dividend declared (10 percent). The Common Stock Dividend Distributable is 1,000 shares times the par value of the common stock ($20).

The journal entry will look like the following:

20XX					
Dec.	27	Retained Earnings	30 000 00		
		Common Stock Dividend Distributable		20 000 00	
		Paid-in Capital in Excess of Par			
		Value—Stock Dividend		10 000 00	
		Records declaration of a 10% stock			
		dividend to stockholders of record			
		as of Jan. 13; payable Jan. 27 as			
		declared by the board of directors.			

Note that the **Common Stock Dividend Distributable** account, which records the par value of the stock, is *not* a liability; it is not payable with assets. It is part of stockholders' equity. When the stock is issued, this account will be reduced and transferred into Common Stock.

Let's first see what the stockholders' equity would look like if it were prepared between the declaration and the payment date. Note in the layout to follow that the stocks are listed first, followed by all the additional paid-in capital.

This type of layout is called the *legal approach;* earlier we showed the *source-of-capital* approach. Both ways are acceptable.

Stockholders' Equity			
Paid-in Capital:			
Common Stock, $20 par value,			
15,000 shares authorized, 10,000 shares issued			
and outstanding	$200 000 00		
Common Stock Dividend Distributable,			
1,000 shares	20 000 00		
Total Common Stock issued and			
to be issued		$220 000 00	
Additional Paid-in Capital:			
Paid-in Capital in Excess of Par			
Value—Common	24 000 00		
Paid-in Capital in Excess of Par			
Value—Stock Dividend	10 000 00		
Total Additional Paid-in Capital		34 000 00	
Total Paid-in Capital		$254 000 00	
Retained Earnings		32 000 00	
Total Stockholders' Equity		$286 000 00	

Recording the Issuance of the Stock Dividend: Let us first analyze.

Accounts Affected	Category	↑ ↓	Rules
Common Stock Dividend Distributable	SE	↓	Dr. $20,000
Common Stock	SE	↑	Cr. $20,000

Then the journal entry would look like the following:

Jan.	27	Common Stock Dividend Distributable	20 000 00	
		Common Stock		20 000 00
		Issuance of stock dividend declared		
		on Dec. 27 to stockholders of record		
		as of Jan. 13		

The Stock Split

A **stock split** is when a corporation issues additional stock to cause a large drop in the market price of the outstanding stock and receives no assets in return. The corporation reduces the par value or stated value of the authorized stock with an increase in the number of shares authorized, issued, and outstanding. The stock split, however, doesn't change the Retained Earnings account as a stock dividend did. To repeat, the stock split will

1. Increase the number of shares outstanding.
2. Reduce the par or stated value in proportion.

For example, a two-for-one split on 10,000 shares of $20 par would result in 20,000 shares with a $10 par value. The total equity remains the same. Because the stock split doesn't change the balance of any ledger account, only a *memorandum notation** in the journal, as well as in the Stock account, would be needed to update the accounting record. The number of shares in this transaction has doubled, but the corporation total equity has not changed; thus the market price of $80 per share would drop to approximately $40. If Jay Owen owned 100 shares before the split, he would own 200 now, but his market value would be the same.

Rock Around the Clock

The American group of companies, Allied Domecq Retailing USA, pays dividends to Allied Domecq in England.

To keep profits high for both shop owners and its parent, Allied Domecq Retailing USA has established a long-term goal for its three companies: Dunkin' Donuts, Baskin-Robbins, and Togos. They want to create a "multibrand environment." That means that they are encouraging shop owners to combine a Dunkin' Donuts shop with a Baskin-Robbins shop or even to combine them with Togos, and put all three shops under one roof. In this way, Allied Domecq Retailing USA hopes to maximize traffic to the shops by combining what had been businesses with three different peak traffic periods:

▼ Dunkin' Donuts = morning
▼ Togos = lunchtime
▼ Baskin-Robbins = afternoons and evenings
▼ Under one roof, these businesses could probably stay open 12 to 24 hours. Because the real estate investment in each shop is so large, it makes sense

to use the shop to full capacity around the clock, or as close to it as practical, depending on the location and the traffic.

This combination plan also helps even out the seasonal demand for ice cream, which peaks in the summer months. To a lesser extent, the demand for donuts and muffins peaks in the fall and winter. This means that sales—and cash flow and profits—are also seasonal. Uneven cash flow can create a huge problem for a small business. Recognizing this problem, Allied Domecq Retailing USA aims to use the owner's investment dollars to best advantage, all day, all year. Or, as Fred says, "This combo will keep us rockin' around the clock!"

Discussion Questions

1. How might combining two or three retail food outlets into a single shop reduce expenses?
2. How might this combination increase sales?
3. Like all corporations, Allied Domecq's goal is to increase value to its stockholders. How could the plan to combine stores help achieve this goal?

	BEFORE	AFTER
	100 shares × $80 = $8,000	200 shares × $40 = $8,000

Jay will benefit from the stock split if

1. The stock price rises on the market.
2. Dividends per share are increased.

LEARNING UNIT 20-2 REVIEW

AT THIS POINT you should be able to

▼ List as well as explain the three important dates associated with the dividend process. (p. 706)

---

*An example of such a notation is, "Called in the outstanding $20 par value 10,000 shares of common stock and issued 20,000 shares of $10 par-value common stock for old shares previously outstanding."

- ▼ Journalize the appropriate entries for a cash dividend. (p. 706)
- ▼ List possible reasons for a stock dividend. (p. 707)
- ▼ Journalize appropriate entries for a stock dividend. (p. 708)
- ▼ Compare and contrast a stock split to a stock dividend. (p. 709)

SELF-REVIEW QUIZ 20-2

(The forms you need are on page 90 of the *Study Guide and Working Papers.*)

Journalize the appropriate entries from the following facts. On September 24, 20XX, the Directors of Movy Co. declared a 5 percent stock dividend to be issued on November 8 to stockholders of record on October 10. There are 20,000 shares outstanding. The stock has a par value of $10 and a current market value of $15 per share.

Solution to Self-Review Quiz 20-2

($15 × 1,000 shares)
($10 par × 1,000 shares)

20XX Sept.	24	Retained Earnings	15 0 0 0 00		
		Common Stock Dividend Distributable		10 0 0 0 00	
		Paid-in Capital in Excess of Par			
		Value—Stock Dividend		5 0 0 0 00	
Nov.	8	Common Stock Dividend Distributable	10 0 0 0 00		
		Common Stock		10 0 0 0 00	

LEARNING UNIT 20-3   TREASURY STOCK

Previously issued preferred or common stock that has been reacquired by the corporation (or given as a gift to the corporation) is known as **treasury stock.** Why would a corporation reacquire previously issued stock? Some reasons include the following:

1. A need to issue more stock for stock option plans or for use in acquiring other corporations.
2. A desire to reduce the number of shares of stock outstanding, which might be done to create a favorable market for the sale of the stock.
3. Anticipation of an opportunity at a later date to reissue stock at a higher price.

The following are some of the characteristics of treasury stock:

1. The purchase of treasury stock does not change the amount of issued stock.
2. The purchase of treasury stock does reduce outstanding stock. Remember that stock can be issued but not outstanding.
3. Treasury stock does not have rights to dividends or voting situations (because it is not outstanding).

4. Treasury stock is a contra-stockholders' equity account.

5. When treasury stock is bought, it is recorded at the purchase price. This purchase of treasury stock does not reduce the balance in the Retained Earnings account.

6. Many state laws will restrict the amount of retained earnings available for dividends if treasury stock exists, because the purchase of treasury stock reduces assets and stockholders' equity (like a cash dividend). This restriction is commonly shown on a footnote on the balance sheet.

Let's look now at how to record the purchase of treasury stock.

PURCHASE OF TREASURY STOCK

On June 1, 20XX, Ashly Corporation has 5,000 shares of $10 par-value common stock and 2,000 shares of preferred stock outstanding. The corporation on June 1 purchases 1,000 shares of its own common stock at a price of $12 per share. The following is the analysis as well as journal entry to record the purchase:

	Accounts Affected	Category	↑ ↓	Rules
(1,000 shares × $12) →	Treasury Stock—Common	Contra SE	↑	Dr. $12,000
	Cash	Asset	↓	Cr. $12,000

Record treasury stock at the purchase price of $12. Note that the par value of common is not affected. Think of an *increase* in treasury stock as a reduction to stockholders' equity.

June	1	Treasury Stock—Common		12 0 0 0 00		
		Cash			12 0 0 0 00	
		Purchase at $12 per share of				
		1,000 shares of previously				
		issued stock.				

SALE OF TREASURY STOCK

Treasury stock can be reissued at a price above or below the cost of reacquiring the stock. Let's look at how Ashly Company could on July 8 sell 100 shares of the treasury stock at $15 per share that was reacquired on June 1 for $12 per share.
This chart analyzes the transaction:

	Accounts Affected	Category	↑ ↓	Rules
(100 shares × $15) →	Cash	Asset	↑	Dr. $1,500
(100 shares × $12) →	Treasury Stock—Common	Contra SE	↓	Cr. $1,200
(100 shares × $3) →	Paid-in Capital from Treasury Stock	SE	↑	Cr. $300

Think of a *decrease* in treasury stock resulting in an increase to stockholders' equity.

The journal entry looks like the following:

July	8	Cash	1 5 0 0 00			
		Treasury Stock—Common		1 2 0 0 00	
		Paid-in Capital from Treasury Stock		3 0 0 00	
		Sold 100 shares of Treasury stock			
		purchased at $12			

The Treasury Stock account is decreased by the number of shares reissued times the *cost* when the stock was reacquired by the company. The credit to **Paid-in Capital from Treasury Stock** represents the amount over what was paid for acquiring the treasury stock.

If a corporation sells treasury stock for less than cost, the result is a decrease in stockholders' equity that is recorded in Paid-in Capital from Treasury Stock until the balance of the account is 0. Any further decrease in this account will directly reduce Retained Earnings, because Paid-in Capital from Treasury Stock will not be a negative balance.

EXAMPLE OF STOCKHOLDERS' EQUITY WITH TREASURY STOCK

Now let's see what stockholders' equity will look like with the accounts Treasury Stock and Paid-in Capital from Treasury Stock.

> The 900 shares of treasury stock don't reduce the number of shares issued; they reduce the number of shares outstanding.

Paid-in Capital:			
Preferred Stock, 14/%, $100 par value,			
authorized 6,000 shares, 2,000 shares			
issued and outstanding		$200 0 0 0 00	
Common Stock $10 par, authorized 9,000			
shares, 5,000 shares issued and 4,100			
outstanding, 900 shares in treasury		50 0 0 0 00*	
Additional Paid-in Capital:			
Paid-in Capital in Excess of Par			
Value—Preferred	10 0 0 0 00		
Paid-in Capital in Excess of Par			
Value—Common	30 0 0 0 00		
Paid-in Capital from Treasury Stock	3 0 0 00		
Total Additional Paid-in Capital		40 3 0 0 00	
Total Paid-in Capital		$290 3 0 0 00	
Retained Earnings		60 0 0 0 00	
		$350 3 0 0 00	
Deduct: Treasury Stock—Common			
(900 shares at cost)		10 8 0 0 00	
Total Stockholders' Equity		$339 5 0 0 00	

* $50,000 = shares issued (5,000) x par ($10)

LEARNING UNIT 20-3 REVIEW

AT THIS POINT you should be able to

▼ Define and explain the characteristics of treasury stock (p. 712)
▼ Journalize the purchase as well as sale of treasury stock. (p. 712)
▼ Explain why treasury stock is a contra-stockholders' equity account. (p.713)

SELF-REVIEW QUIZ 20-3

(The forms you need are on page 90 of the *Study Guide and Working Papers*.)
Record the following transactions in general journal form (no explanation needed):

1. Also Company acquired 100 shares of its own $10 par common stock at $15 per share.
2. Fifty of the treasury shares are reissued at $18 per share.
3. Forty of the treasury shares are reissued at $6 per share.

Solution to Self-Review Quiz 20-3

❶	Treasury Stock (100 × $15)	1 5 0 0 00	
	Cash		1 5 0 0 00
❷	Cash ($18 × 50)	9 0 0 00	
	Treasury Stock (50 × $15)		7 5 0 00
❸	Paid-in Capital from Treasury		
	Stock (50 × $3)		1 5 0 00
	Cash ($6 × 40)	2 4 0 00	
	Paid-in Capital from Treasury Stock	1 5 0 00	
	Retained Earnings	2 1 0 00	
	Treasury Stock (40 × $15)		6 0 0 00

Note that Retained Earnings is reduced by $210, because Paid-in Capital is down to a zero balance:

$$\begin{array}{ll} \$150 & (50 \times \$3) \\ -\ 360 & (40 \times \$9) \\ \hline \$<210> & \end{array}$$

LEARNING UNIT 20-4

APPROPRIATION OF RETAINED EARNINGS AND THE STATEMENT OF RETAINED EARNINGS

In the first three units of this chapter we saw that cash dividends as well as stock dividends reduce the amount of Retained Earnings. Now we look at how companies indicate to those reading their financial reports that some of the Retained Earnings are not available for declaration of dividends; they are **Appropriated (Restricted) Retained Earnings.**

Restrictions on Retained Earnings limit the amount that is available to declare dividends.

This *appropriating* of retained earnings could be either voluntary or contractual. For example, the board of directors could voluntarily decide that a portion of earnings should be used for plant expansion instead of for dividends. If a company enters into a loan with a bank, the bank may require the company to keep a minimum balance in Retained Earnings to protect their rights until the loan is repaid. Companies in many states are required to keep a minimum in the Retained Earnings account at the level of legal capital. We saw in the last unit that treasury stock could result in Retained Earnings being restricted to the cost of the treasury stock.

In years past these special appropriations were recorded by transferring portions of the Retained Earnings account to accounts such as Retained Earnings Appropriated for Plant Expansion or Retained Earnings Appropriated for Contra Obligations. In reality, these appropriations didn't reduce total Retained Earnings; they just *shifted* a portion into an account that revealed its special purpose. For example, an entry to restrict $20,000 for plant expansion would be as follows:

No actual cash is involved in the appropriation of Retained Earnings.

Retained Earnings	20 00 00	
Appropriation for Plant Expansion		20 00 00

After the appropriation or restriction has passed (the loan has been paid off, or whatever), the balance is transferred back to the Retained Earnings account. No cash is involved in the appropriation.

Today, to make things clear to investors, most companies report restrictions by using a footnote to the Retained Earnings account. Restrictions about Retained Earnings do not have to be updated in the ledger; thus the use of a footnote is a common practice. (It is good practice to write a memo in the Retained Earnings account to identify each appropriation.) A footnote to announce such restrictions would look like the following:

> The loan agreement with Jones Bank contains a restriction on the payment of cash dividends. Approximately $600,000 of retained earnings was free of such a restriction as of June 30, 20XX.

PREPARING THE STATEMENT OF RETAINED EARNINGS

In past chapters we discussed the income statement, balance sheet, statement of owners' equity, and statement of partners' equity. We now turn our attention to a **statement of retained earnings** that will reveal the changes of retained earnings over a period of time. The changes in retained earnings result from the following:

1. Net income or loss.
2. Dividends declared.
3. Effects of prior period adjustments.

Often an error in a financial report of a company from a prior period may not be discovered until a later period. If the error is considered *material,* a **prior period adjustment** should be made to the beginning balance of Retained Earnings. Let's look at a specific example.

Eight months after the close of its books Ralston Company discovered that depreciation was understated by $12,000, which meant in the old period that Depreciation Expense was understated by $12,000 and Net Income was overstated by $12,000. If Net Income was overstated, Retained Earnings also was overstated, because Net Income is closed into Retained Earnings. Thus the following entry is recorded in the *new* year to adjust the prior period error (we ignore tax effect here):

Retained Earnings	12 0 0 0 00	
Accumulated Depreciation, Equipment		12 0 0 0 00

A statement of retained earnings for the Ralston Company would look like the following:

RALSTON COMPANY
STATEMENT OF RETAINED EARNINGS
YEAR ENDED DECEMBER 31, 20X2

Retained Earnings, Jan. 1, 20X2	$350 0 0 0 00
Less: Prior Period Adjustment:	
Correction of 20X1 error	12 0 0 0 00
Retained Earnings, Jan. 20X2, corrected	$338 0 0 0 00
Add: Net Income for 20X2	40 0 0 0 00
Total	$378 0 0 0 00
Deduct: Dividends declared in 20X2	28 0 0 0 00
Retained Earnings, Dec. 31, 20X2	$350 0 0 0 00

This ending figure of $350,000 will appear in the stockholders' equity section of the balance sheet.

ACCOUNTING CYCLE FOR A CORPORATION

Before we conclude our discussion of corporations, page 717 provides a simplified sample of a worksheet for a corporation. This worksheet will give you a better idea of what titles such as Subscriptions Receivable, Common Stock, Paid-in Capital, and Retained Earnings look like when all combined on one worksheet.

The cycle is then to prepare financial reports as well as journalize and post the adjusting and closing entries. We use Retained Earnings instead of Capital in the closing process. Also in the adjusting process we adjust the income tax owed. The Income Tax account is closed to Income Summary. The steps are quite similar to those discussed for a merchandise company.

A key point is that the net income shown on the income statement could be substantially different from that reported for tax purposes; certain deductions on the tax return will differ from the expenses on the corporation's books.

JANE CORPORATION
WORKSHEET
FOR YEAR ENDED DECEMBER 31, 20X3

Account Name	Trial Balance Dr.	Trial Balance Cr.	Adjustments Dr.	Adjustments Cr.	Adjusted Trial Balance Dr.	Adjusted Trial Balance Cr.	Income Statement Dr.	Income Statement Cr.	Balance Sheet Dr.	Balance Sheet Cr.
Cash	X				X				X	
Notes Receivable	X				X				X	
Accounts Receivable	X				X				X	
Subscriptions Rec., Com. Stock	X				X				X	
Merch. Inventory	X		O	X	O				O	
Prepaid Rent	X			X	X				X	
Office Equipment	X				X				X	
Acc. Dep., Office Equip.		X		X		X				X
Organization Costs	X				X				X	
Notes Payable		X				X				X
Accounts Payable		X				X				X
Dividends Payable, Com.		X				X				X
Common Stock		X				X				X
Common Stock Div. Dist.		X				X				X
Paid-in Capital in Excess of Par—Common Stock		X				X				X
Common Stock Subscribed		X				X				X
Paid-in Capital from Treasury Stock		X				X				X
Retained Earnings		X				X				X
Income Summary			X	O	X	O	X	O		
Sales (totals)		X				X		X		
Purchases	X				X		X			
Purch. Ret. and Allow.		X				X		X		
Expenses (totals)	X				X		X			
Expenses (Adj.)			X		X		X			
Income Tax	X		X		X		X			
Income Tax Payable				X		X				X

O = Ending inventory

AT THIS POINT you should be able to

▼ Explain what could lead to appropriations of Retained Earnings. (p. 715)
▼ Explain why footnotes are used on financial reports instead of appropriation accounts to report restrictions to Retained Earnings. (p. 715)
▼ Prepare a statement of retained earnings. (p. 715)

SELF-REVIEW QUIZ 20-4

(The forms you need are on page 91 of the *Study Guide and Working Papers*.)
From the following data prepare a statement of retained earnings for Janet Corporation for the year ended December 31, 20X3:

▼ Retained Earnings, January 1, 20X3, $650,000.
▼ Dividends, 20X3, $50,000.
▼ Correction of error from 20X1, $50,000 for Net Income that was discovered to be understated.
▼ Net Income, 20X3, $80,000

Solution to Self-Review Quiz 20-4

JANET CORPORATION STATEMENT OF RETAINED EARNINGS YEAR ENDED DECEMBER 31, 20X3	
Retained Earnings, Jan. 1, 20X3	$650 000 00
Add: Prior Period Adjustment,	
Correction of 20X1 error	50 000 00
Retained Earnings, Jan. 20X3, corrected	$700 000 00
Add: Net Income for 20X3	80 000 00
Total	$780 000 00
Deduct: Dividends declared in 20X3	50 000 00
Retained Earnings, Dec. 31, 20X3	$730 000 00

SUMMARY OF KEY POINTS

Learning Unit 20-1

1. Redemption value is the price per share a corporation pays to holders of preferred stock when the stock is retired or redeemed.

2. Market value represents the open-market price of stock bought and sold. Market value doesn't mean the same thing as book value.

3. Book value per share is the amount or value of net assets on a company's books for each share of stockholders' stock in the equity of the corporation. Book value is calculated for preferred and common separately.

Learning Unit 20-2

1. Dividends represent cash, stock, or other assets distributed to stockholders. The board of directors has the authority to declare dividends.

2. Three important dates associated with the dividend process are date of declaration, date of record, and date of payment.

3. A cash dividend results in a reduction of Retained Earnings and an eventual reduction in Cash.

4. Retained earnings doesn't mean cash.

5. A stock dividend will not reduce stockholders' equity like a cash dividend will. The end result is a transfer of retained earnings to Paid-in Capital.

6. Common Stock Dividend Distributable is a stockholders' equity account that is recorded at par value. It is not a liability account.

7. A stock split has no effect on Retained Earnings or any other ledger account. It increases the number of shares outstanding as well as reducing par or stated value.

Learning Unit 20-3

1. Treasury Stock is a contra-stockholders' equity account that is recorded at cost. It represents stock that was previously issued and is now reacquired or received as a gift by a corporation.

2. Treasury stock is recognized as issued but not outstanding for dividends or voting situations.

3. Paid-in Capital from Treasury Stock can never have a negative balance. Any additional "loss" is reduced in Retained Earnings.

Learning Unit 20-4

1. Appropriations of Retained Earnings can be contractual or voluntary.

2. Appropriations restrict the amount of Retained Earnings available for dividends.

3. Common practice today is to use footnotes on the balance sheet to reveal any appropriations of Retained Earnings.

4. The statement of retained earnings is made up of (1) beginning balance, (2) corrections of prior periods, (3) net income, and (4) dividends.

KEY TERMS

Appropriated (Restricted) Retained Earnings That portion of Retained Earnings that is not available for dividends.

Book value per share Amount of net assets that a stockholder would receive on a per-share basis, assuming no gain or loss on the sale of the assets.

Cash dividend   Dividend that is paid in cash.

Common Stock Dividend Distributable   Stockholders' equity account that accumulates stock dividend that has been declared but not yet issued and distributed.

Date of declaration   The date upon which the board of directors of a corporation formally declares a dividend.

Date of payment   The date the dividend is paid.

Date of record   The date of ownership that determines which stockholders will receive the dividend.

Dividend   Cash or other assets that a corporation distributes as earnings to stockholders.

Dividend Payable   Liability showing amount of cash dividend owed.

Market value   The price that a buyer pays to purchase shares of capital stock in the open market. Of course for every buyer there is a seller.

Paid-in Capital from Treasury Stock   Stockholders' equity account that records amounts more or less than par value of treasury stock sold. The balance of this account can never be negative.

Prior period adjustment   Correction made in the current year of a mistake made in previous years. The adjustment is updated on the statement of retained earnings.

Redemption value   The price per share a corporation pays to redeem or retire capital stock.

Statement of retained earnings   A financial report that reveals the changes in retained earnings for a particular period of time.

Stock dividend   Stock that is distributed to stockholders instead of cash or other assets.

Stock split   Issuing of additional shares of stock to stockholders; total par or stated value remains the same.

Treasury stock   Stock that has been issued but has been bought back by the corporation or received as a gift.

QUESTIONS, MINI EXERCISES, EXERCISES, AND PROBLEMS

Discussion Questions

1. What is the difference between market value and book value?
2. List the three important dates that are associated with the dividend process.
3. Why is no journal entry needed at the date of record?
4. Explain some possible reasons a company may declare a stock dividend instead of a cash dividend.
5. Explain why stock dividends will not reduce total stockholders' equity.
6. Common Stock Dividend Distributable is a liability. Accept or reject. Defend your position.
7. Explain the difference between a stock dividend and a stock split.
8. Treasury stock is really an asset. Defend or reject. Support your argument.
9. All treasury stock is recognized as issued and outstanding for dividends. True or false? Please explain.
10. Explain the purpose of the account Paid-in Capital from Treasury Stock.
11. Appropriation of retained earnings is always done for a contractual reason. Accept or reject. Defend your position.
12. Restrictions on retained earnings have to be updated in the ledger. Agree or disagree. Why?
13. What elements make up the statement of retained earnings?

Mini Exercises

(The forms you need are on page 93 of the *Study Guide and Working Papers*.)

Book Value per Share for Preferred and Common

1. Given the following prepare the book value per share for preferred and common stock:

BLUEPRINT: LEGAL CAPITAL APPROACH

MOOSE COMPANY PARTIAL BALANCE SHEET			
Stockholders' Equity			
Paid-in Capital:			
Preferred Stock 12%, $10 par value, authorized 30,000 shares, 9,000 shares issued and outstanding		XX	
Common Stock, $10 par value, authorized 100,000 shares, 40,000 shares issued and 29,000 shares outstanding, 11,000 shares in treasury	XX		
Common Stock Dividend Distributable	XX	XX	
Additional Paid-in Capital:			
Paid-in Capital in Excess of Par Value—Preferred	XX		
Paid-in Capital in Excess of Par Value—Common	XX		
Paid-in Capital in Excess of Par Value—Stock Dividend	XX		
Paid-in Capital from Treasury Stock	XX		
Total Additional Paid-in Capital		XX	
Total Paid-in Capital		XX	
Retained Earnings		XX	
Deduct: Treasury Stock		XX	
Total Stockholders' Equity			XX

Note that legal capital is listed first. See page 000 for blueprint example of the source-of-capital approach. Both approaches are acceptable, and in the real world both are used.

- ▼ Preferred Stock $80,000; 1,000 shares issued.
- ▼ Common Stock $150,000; 800 shares issued.
- ▼ Retained Earnings, $8,500.
- ▼ Dividend in Arrears, $4,000.
- ▼ Paid-in capital in excess of par: preferred, $5,000.
- ▼ Paid-in capital in excess of par: common, $6,000.
- ▼ Redemption value on preferred stock, $16.

Cash Dividend

2. On March 15, 20XX, the board of directors of Vision Corporation declared $3 cash dividend per share on the 6,000 shares issued and outstanding. The dividend will be paid on April 18, 20XX, to stockholders of record on March 19, 20XX. Record journal entries for date of declaration and date of payment.

Stock Dividend

3. On December 24, 20XX, Fress Corporation declared a 5 percent stock dividend distributable January 18 to stockholders of record on January 8. Currently Fress has 5,000 shares of common stock issued and outstanding.

The stock has a par value of $20. The current fair market value of the stock is $35. Journalize (a) the declaration of the dividend and (b) the issuance of the stock dividend.

Treasury Stock

4. Journalize the following transactions:

   a. Janson Co. acquired 50 shares of its own $5 par-value common stock at $10 per share.

   b. Twenty-five of the Treasury shares are reissued at $13 per share.

   c. Twenty of the Treasury shares are reissued at $4 per share.

Prior Period Adjustment

5. Seven months after its closing, Brooks Co. discovered that depreciation was understated by $8,000. Provide the journal entry to adjust the prior period error (ignore any tax effects).

Exercises

(The forms you need are on pages 94–95 of the *Study Guide and Working Papers*.)

20-1. From the following information determine the book value for preferred and common stocks assuming $15,000 of dividends are in arrears on the preferred stock.

Calculating book value of preferred and common.

STOCKHOLDERS' EQUITY

Preferred Stock 12 percent cumulative and non-participating, $20 par value, $19 redemption value, 10,000 shares issued and outstanding	$200,000
Common Stock, $10 par value, 40,000 shares issued and outstanding	400,000
Retained Earnings	80,000
Total Stockholders' Equity	$680,000

Cash dividend.

20-2. Poole Corporation has 300,000 shares of common stock issued and outstanding. On June 9, 20X6, the board of directors declared a $.50 per share dividend, payable on July 16, 20X6, to stockholders of record on June 29, 20X6. Record the appropriate journal entries on June 9 and July 16.

Stock dividend.

20-3. On July 31, 20X1, Harvey Corporation had the following stockholders' equity:

Common Stock, $10 par value, authorized 90,000 shares, 60,000 shares issued and outstanding	$600,000
Retained Earnings	200,000
Total Stockholders' Equity	$800,000

On August 5, 20X1, the board of directors declared a 10 percent stock dividend to be issued on September 6, 20X1, to the stockholders of record on August 19, 20X1. At time of declaration the market price was $17 per share. Prepare the appropriate journal entries for this stock dividend.

20-4. Given the following stockholders' equity:

Common Stock, $7 par value, authorized 100,000 shares, 80,000 shares issued and outstanding	$ 560,000
Retained Earnings	500,000
Total Stockholders' Equity	$1,060,000

Journalize the following entries:

20XX

Apr.
3 Issued 5,000 shares at $12 per share.
9 Reacquired 200 shares at $8 per share.
15 Reissued 100 shares of treasury stock at $10 per share.
17 Reissued 50 shares of treasury stock at $7 per share.

Treasury stock.

20-5. From the following, prepare in proper form a statement of retained earnings for Williams Company for the year ended December 31, 20X4.

Statement of retained earnings.

Retained Earnings, January 20X4	$40,000	Prior period adjustment increase in recording expense for Land in 20X2 (disregard taxes)	$14,000
Net Income, 20X4	$60,000	Dividends Paid, 20X4	$20,000

Group A Problems

(The forms you need are on pages 96–106 of the *Study Guide and Working Papers.*)

20A-1. The stockholders' equity of Oscar Company is as follows:

STOCKHOLDERS' EQUITY

Paid-in Capital:
   Preferred 10 percent Stock, $100 par value, authorized 5,000 shares, cumulative and nonparticipating, 4,000 shares issued
   and outstanding $400,000
   Paid-in Capital in Excess of Par Value—Preferred   50,000

Total Preferred Paid-in Capital by
Preferred Stockholders $450,000
Common Stock, $50 par value, authorized 15,000 shares, 6,000 shares issued and
outstanding $300,000
Paid-in Capital in Excess of Par Value—
Common   60,000

Total Paid-in Capital by Common
Stockholders   360,000
Total Paid-in Capital $810,000
Retained Earnings   160,000
    Total Stockholders' Equity $970,000

Calculating book value with and without dividends in arrears.

Check Figure:
Book value preferred $108

Given a redemption value of $108, calculate the book value of preferred and common stock, assuming

a. No dividends in arrears.

b. Two years' dividends in arrears.

20A-2. Lance Corporation has 400,000 shares of $7 par-value common stock issued and outstanding. Record the following entries into the general journal for Lance:

Cash and stock dividends.

20XX

July 2 Declared a cash dividend of $.60 per share.
Aug. 1 Paid the $.60 cash dividend to the stockholders.
Aug. 4 Declared a 4 percent stock dividend. The current market price is $12 per share.
Sept. 12 Issued the stock dividend declared on August 4.
Oct. 1 Declared an 8 percent stock dividend. The current market price is $17 per share.
Nov. 2 Issued the stock dividend on October 1.

Check Figure:
Aug. 4 Paid-in capital in excess of par value—stock dividend $80,000 Cr.

20A-3. At the beginning of January 20XX, the stockholders' equity of Long View
Corporation consisted of the following:

Paid-in Capital:

Common Stock, $25 par value, authorized 50,000 shares, 13,000 shares issued and outstanding	$325,000	
Paid-in Capital in Excess of Par Value — Common	70,000	
Total Paid-in Capital by Common Stockholders	$395,000	
Retained Earnings	160,000	
Total Stockholders' Equity		$555,000

1. Record the following transactions in general journal form.
2. Prepare the stockholders' equity section at year-end using the blue-print on page 721 as a guide.
3. Prepare a statement of retained earnings at December 31, 20XX.

Accounts are provided in the *Study Guide and Working Papers*. Be sure to put in the beginning balances.

20XX

June	4	Long View Corporation purchased 1,000 shares of treasury stock at $28.
	20	The board of directors voted a $.20 per share cash dividend payable on July 15 to stockholders of record on July 2.
July	15	Cash dividend declared on June 20 is paid.
Sept.	5	Sold 300 shares of the treasury stock at $36 per share.
	29	Sold 700 shares of the treasury stock at $27 per share.
Oct.	10	The board of directors declared a 6 percent stock dividend distributable on January 2 to stockholders of record on November 2. The market value of the stock is currently $38 per share.
Dec.	31	Closed the net income of $60,000 in the Income Summary account to Retained Earnings.

20A-4. The following is the stockholders' equity of Piersal Corporation on October 1, 20XX:

Paid-in Capital:

Preferred 14 percent Stock, $10 par value, authorized 6,000 shares, 3,000 shares issued and outstanding		$ 30,000
Common Stock, $10 par value, authorized 20,000 shares, 10,000 shares issued and outstanding		100,000

Additional Paid-in Capital:

Paid-in Capital in Excess of Par Value — Preferred	$10,000	
Paid-in Capital in Excess of Par Value — Common	5,000	
Paid-in Capital in Excess of Par Value — Stock Dividend	4,000	
Total Additional Paid-in Capital		19,000
Total Paid-in Capital		$149,000
Retained Earnings		200,000
Total Stockholders' Equity		$349,000

Sidebar notes:

Cash and stock dividend; treasury stock; preparation of stockholders' equity section and statement of retained earnings.

Check Figure:
Total stockholders' equity
$614,300

Journalizing and Posting various stockholders' equity situations and preparing stockholders' equity section by a legal capital approach.

Check Figure:
Total stockholders' equity
$419,500

1. Journalize the following transactions in general journal form.

2. Prepare the stockholders' equity section of the balance sheet using the legal capital approach as of December 31, 20XX.

Your *Study Guide and Working Papers* has accounts to update ledger balances. Be sure to put in the beginning balances. Use the blueprint on page 721 as a guide to the setup of stockholders' equity.

20XX

Oct.	3	Declared a $.40 per share dividend on the common stock and a $1.20 per share dividend on the preferred. (The Dividends Payable account will record amounts for both common and preferred, although companies could set up Common Dividend Payable and Preferred Dividend Payable accounts.)
Nov.	15	Dividends were paid that were declared on October 3.
	18	Purchased 300 shares of its own common stock at $13 per share.
	25	Reissued 50 shares at $16 per share.
	26	Declared a 20 percent stock dividend on common. Market value of stock is $40 per share.
Dec.	29	Distributed stock dividend declared on November 26.
	30	Reissued 100 shares of treasury stock at $12 per share.
	31	Closed the Income Summary account, which had net income of $80,000, to Retained Earnings.

Group B Problems

(The forms you need are on pages 96–106 of the *Study Guide and Working Papers.*)

20B-1. Given a redemption value of $105, calculate the book value of preferred and common stock, assuming (1) no dividends in arrears and (2) two years' dividends in arrears from the following stockholders' equity of Oscar Company:

> Calculating book value with and without dividends in arrears.

> Check Figure:
> (a) Book value preferred
> $105

STOCKHOLDERS' EQUITY

Paid-in Capital:		
Preferred 12 percent Stock, $100 par value, authorized 3,000 shares, cumulative and nonparticipating, 1,000 shares issued and outstanding	$100,000	
Paid-in Capital in Excess of Par Value — Preferred	80,000	
Total Paid-in Capital by Preferred Stockholders		$ 180,000
Common Stock, $75 par value, authorized 12,000 shares, 8,000 shares issued and outstanding	$600,000	
Paid-in Capital in Excess of Par Value — Common	70,000	
Total Paid-in Capital by Common Stockholders		670,000
Total Paid-in Capital		$ 850,000
Retained Earnings		300,000
Total Stockholders' Equity		$1,150,000

20B-2. Lance Corporation has 200,000 shares of $10 par value common stock issued and outstanding. Record the following entries into the general journal for Lance:

Check Figure:
Sept. 6   Paid-in capital in
excess of par value—stock
dividend $40,000 Cr.

20XX

Aug.	3	Declared a cash dividend of $.30 per share.
Sept.	4	Paid the $.30 cash dividend to the stockholders.
	6	Declared a 5 percent stock dividend. The current market price is $14 per share.
	29	Issued the stock dividend declared on September 6.
Nov.	1	Declared a 10 percent stock dividend. The current market price is $17 per share.
	29	Issued the stock dividend declared on November 1.

Cash and stock dividend;
treasury stock; preparation
of stockholders' equity
and statement of retained
earnings.

20B-3. At the beginning of January 20XX, the stockholders' equity of Long View Corporation consisted of the following:

Paid-in Capital:

Common Stock, $30 par value, authorized 70,000 shares, 15,000 shares issued and outstanding	$450,000
Paid-in Capital in Excess of Par Value — Common	60,000
Total Paid-in Capital by Common Stockholders	510,000
Retained Earnings	300,000
Total Stockholders' Equity	$810,000

1. Record the following transactions in general journal form.

2. Prepare a stockholders' equity section, using the blueprint on page 721.

3. Prepare a statement of retained earnings at December 31, 20XX.

Accounts are provided in *Study Guide and Working Papers*. Be sure to put in the beginning balances.

20XX

May	3	Long View Corporation purchased 2,000 shares of treasury stock at $40.
	15	The board of directors voted a $.70 per share cash dividend payable on July 9 to stockholders of record on June 13.
July	9	Cash dividend declared on May 15 is paid.
Sept.	15	Sold 200 shares of treasury stock at $50 per share.
Oct.	10	Sold 300 shares of treasury stock at $38 per share.
Nov.	1	The board of directors declared a 20 percent stock dividend distributable on January 2 to stockholders of record on November 17. The market value of the stock is $60 per share.
Dec.	31	Closed the net income of $75,000 in the Income Summary account to Retained Earnings.

Journalizing and posting
various stockholders' equity
situations and preparing
stockholders' equity section
by a legal capital approach.

20B-4. The following is the stockholders' equity of Piersal Corporation on November 1, 20XX:

Paid-in Capital:

Preferred 12 percent Stock, $10 par value, authorized 8,000 shares, 2,000 shares issued and outstanding		$ 20,000
Common Stock, $10 par value, authorized 15,000 shares, 10,000 shares issued and outstanding		100,000
Additional Paid-in Capital:		
Paid-in Capital in Excess of Par Value — Preferred	$30,000	
Paid-in Capital in Excess of Par Value — Common	10,000	
Paid-in Capital in Excess of Par Value — Stock Dividend	7,000	

	Total Additional Paid-in Capital	47,000
	Total Paid-in Capital	$167,000
	Retained Earnings	86,000
	Total Stockholders' Equity	$253,000

1. Journalize the following transactions in general journal form.
2. Prepare the stockholders' equity section of the balance sheet using the legal capital approach (see the blueprint on p. 721) as of December 31, 20XX.

Your *Study Guide and Working Papers* has accounts to update ledger balances. Be sure to put in beginning balances.

20XX

Nov.	3	Due to increased sales, the board of directors of Piersal declared a $3 per share dividend on the common stock and a $1.50 per share dividend on the preferred. (The Dividends Payable account records both common and preferred.)
	8	Purchased 500 shares of its own common stock at $16 per share.
	15	Reissued 200 shares at $18 per share.
	16	Declared a 10 percent stock dividend on common. Market value is $25 per share.
Dec.	15	Dividends were paid that were declared on November 3.
	28	Distributed stock dividend declared on November 16.
	30	Reissued 200 shares at $15 per share.
	31	Closed the Income Summary account, which had net income of $55,000, to Retained Earnings.

REAL-WORLD APPLICATIONS

20R-1.

Moose Corporation has the following stockholders' equity prepared by Jesse Ross, head bookkeeper:

Paid-in Capital:		
	Common Stock, $5 par, 3000 shares authorized, 1,600 shares issued, of which 900 shares are in the treasury	$ 4,500
	Paid-in Capital in Excess of Par Value — Common	2,000
	Total Paid-in Capital	5,500
	Retained Earnings	2,000
	Total	7,500
	Add: Cost of Treasury Stock	7,000
	Total Stockholders' Equity	$14,500

Explain what error(s) Jesse has made in the preparation of stockholders' equity. Also, Moose Corporation wants to declare a cash dividend of $3 per share. Is it feasible? Show your calculations along with a written explanation.

20R-2.

Margaret Jones owns 100 shares of Johnson Corporation. She receives in the mail a notice that a two-for-one stock split is being declared. Currently the stock is trading on the open market at $120 per share. After the split 600,000 shares will be outstanding. Margaret is very worried that this split will reduce her book value, resulting in a loss of market value. She feels her preemptive right has been ignored. She believes that a stock dividend is the best way for the corporation to go. Respond in writing specifically to Margaret's concerns.

YOU make the call

Critical Thinking/Ethical Case

20R-3.

Alan Homes serves on the Board of Directors of Flynn Company. The president of Flynn told him that in three weeks the corporation would announce a 25 percent increase in dividends. Alan called his neighbor to tell him to buy some stock. The neighbor told his friend about the stock and the friend told him that Alan was acting unethically. The neighbor called Alan back and Alan told him that no one will know the difference, that in business this happens all the time, and that he shouldn't be left out. Do you think Alan's behavior is appropriate? You make the call. Write down your recommendation to Alan's neighbor.

INTERNET EXERCISES

EX-1. [averages.dowjones.com/dija_cos.html#top]   Daily one hears news of the Dow Jones Industrial Averages (DJIA). Additionally, Dow Jones tracks selected utility stocks and transportation stocks. These stocks make up the equally important but less publicized Dow Jones Utilities Averages and the Dow Jones Transportation Averages.

The DJIA consists of 30 industrial stocks. The list is not a static one and does periodically add and delete component stocks from its listing. Glancing down the list at this site you can see the names of companies you probably recognize, but you might not have realized that those companies were components of the DJIA.

Select a stock from the list and do some stock research on that company by finding its website. Determine the following information about the stock:

1. What is the 52 week high/low price range of the stock?
2. What is the dividend paying history of the stock?
3. What is the company's earnings per share?
4. What was the closing price of that stock in yesterday's trading?
5. Look under "news" on the company's website. Summarize one of the news stories.

EX-2. [www.hillenbrand.com/press/press_01-18-00.htm]   Treasury Stock arises when a company acquires its own stock in an open market. Companies acquire stock for various reasons. One of these is to influence the market price of its publicly traded stock. If the stock price is declining the company may withdraw its stock from the market, or if the price is rising faster than the company wishes, it may sell some of it's treasury stock to slow the price rise. Essentially, it will follow the laws of supply and demand.

In the article you will view at this site the company is purchasing treasury stock for yet another reason. Read the article and state the purpose of acquiring the treasury stock. What does the statement "for other corporate purposes" imply as you read the article?

Corporations and Bonds Payable

In the opening of the previous chapter, we discussed the troubles of Xerox Corp. and mentioned two ways it was going to raise additional cash — by slashing dividends and selling assets. Companies also raise cash by selling **bonds.** A bond is a form of long-term debt, which must be repaid. Bondholders are people or businesses that have a claim against the business until the bond is repaid. Their claim against the business takes priority over the stockholders of a business.

Compared to stocks, bonds are not considered "sexy" by investors. As you've seen in the past few years, stocks can fluctuate wildly in value. An investment of $1,000 can turn into $5,000 or $500 in the course of a few months. In contrast, when an investor buys a bond certificate, she knows what she will get back at the **maturity date,** the date the company is due to repay the bond: the bond's **principal,** or face value, plus the **interest** that accrues on the principal.

Bonds have also had a more limited pool of investors than stocks. Bond issuers traditionally approach mainly the big institutional investors. However, the Internet is changing that. Companies in need of cash are stepping into e-commerce and borrowing money online from a wider array of lenders.

Bonds debuted in cyberspace shortly after the new millennium. The U.S. Government went online first: on January 5, its mortgage agency, Freddie

Mac, kicked off a $6 billion bond issue. Ford Motor took the lead among corporate borrowers: Five days later Ford announced a three-year bond issue to borrow $1 billion.

Online bond trading offers some real advantages. Over the Internet, bond issuers can reach medium-sized institutions and individual investors instantly—not just the big institutional investors. Giving and getting the latest marketing information about a company's products is another big advantage of Internet trading. And online trading lets issuers see their orders filling up in real-time. For all these reasons, there has been a frenzy of activity in online borrowing in the past year.

In this chapter, you will explore the different ways to raise capital and the detail involved in issuing, amortizing, and discounting a bond.

Based on: Chris Wright, "Cutting through the hype of Internet bond issuance," *Corporate Finance,* April 2000, pp. 5–6. Fiona Haddock, "The seduction of on-line debt," *Global Finance,* April 2000, pp. 30–33. Antony Currie, "Bonding on the Internet," *Euromoney,* February 2000, pp. 43–50.

LEARNING OBJECTIVES

▼ Journalizing the recording of bonds as well as interest payments. (p. 733)

▼ Amortizing bond discounts and bond premiums by the straight-line method and by the interest method. (p. 735)

▼ Journalizing year-end adjusting entries for bonds. (p. 740)

▼ Journalizing entries related to retirement of bonds and to sinking funds. (p. 744)

A corporation can raise funds by issuing stock or long-term notes payable. Notes or stock are good sources of funds when a company borrows from only one bank or other type of lending institution, but they may not provide the total amount of funds needed. In the last two chapters we saw how companies issue stock. Now our attention shifts to notes. After all, businesses like Dell Computer and General Motors may need to borrow millions of dollars. This chapter looks at how corporations can raise large amounts of money from groups of lenders by issuing a type of long-term interest-bearing note payable called a **bond.**

LEARNING UNIT 21-1

STRUCTURE AND CHARACTERISTICS OF A BOND

Each **bond certificate,** usually issued in denominations of $1,000, contains the following:

1. **Face value** (principal): the amount that the corporation must repay to the lender at maturity date.

2. **Contract rate** (stated interest rate): the annual interest rate, which is based on face value. Usually this interest is paid *semi*annually. The dates of interest payment are also printed on the certificate.

For example, if Joe Rosse owns a $1,000, 12 percent, 20-year bond that is issued by Von Corporation, it means the following:

1. At end of 20 years Joe will receive the $1,000.
2. Every six months Joe will receive an interest check for $60 ($1,000 × .12 × $\frac{6}{12}$).

There is also another way to calculate semiannual interest:

$$\frac{12\%}{2} = \text{Semiannual Rate of } 6\%$$

$$.06 \times \$1,000 = \$60$$

The information on the bond certificate is written by the corporation into a more formal agreement called the **bond indenture.** This agreement is usually monitored by a **trustee** (often a bank), who represents the group of bondholders.

> Trustee (usually a bank) monitors bondholders' interest as stipulated in the bond indenture.

If, before the 20 years have passed, Joe wants to cash in the bond, he can sell it on the securities exchange (like the stock exchange, but dealing in the buying and selling of bonds rather than stock). Bonds are negotiable and generally transferable. Let's assume Joe calls his broker, who indicates that the current market price of the bond is quoted at 94, a percentage (94 percent) of the bond's face value. This price can be higher or lower than the face amount (100, or 100 percent), depending on current rates of interest as well as other market factors. If market interest rates are high compared with the current bond's interest rate, the percentage would be lower. Why? The reason is that the bond's interest is not as attractive as current rates. The 94 means that a buyer is willing to pay $940 (.94 × $1,000) for the bond. If the quote were 104, then Joe could receive $1,040 (1.04 × $1,000) for the bond.

> A bond quote of 70 would mean that a bond with a face value of $1,000 is selling for $700 (.70 × $1,000).

The following is a list of different types of bonds. Keep in mind that each bond issue may have special arrangements besides the customary repayment plans. Don't memorize this list; use it as a reference.

TYPES OF BONDS

Corporations can offer many types of bonds. The following are some examples.

Secured Bonds: The corporation issuing the bonds pledges specific assets such as equipment or property as security for meeting the terms of the bond agreement.

> Assets are pledged as security for debt.

Debenture Bonds: The issuing corporation pledges no specific assets as collateral; thus the bonds are unsecured. Risk is higher than with secured bonds; these bonds will generally require a higher rate of interest to make them attractive to the investor.

> General credit rating of company is the only security the lender receives.

Serial Bonds: These bonds are made up of a series, each having its own maturity date. For example, a bond issue of $2,000,000 could be made up of a series of twenty $100,000 bonds, one series maturing at the end of each year for a period of 20 years.

> Different maturity dates of serial bonds lend flexibility to investors.

Registered Bonds: Owners of bonds are registered with the issuing company, and interest is mailed to the owners of record.

> Only the registered owner can sell a registered bond.

Callable Bonds: These bonds have a provision stating that they can be called in by a corporation after a certain date. When a bond issue is called in, the corporation has to pay a price above the face value of the bond.

> Callability gives more flexibility to the corporation as interest rates change.

Convertible Bonds: The bondholder may be allowed to convert bonds into shares of stock. For this right, the bondholder gives up fixed interest payments for what he or she hopes will be higher stock prices.

> Convertibility gives the bond buyer the option of becoming a stockholder.

STOCKS VERSUS BONDS

Why would a corporation prefer to raise money by selling bonds rather than by issuing and selling stock? Let's look at an example. Should Rojer Corporation obtain long-term funds by selling $500,000 worth of 12 percent bonds, or issue 12 percent preferred stock for $500,000? Rojer Corporation wants to make the most of its tax savings as well as earnings per share (EPS) of common stock:

$$EPS = \frac{\text{After-Tax Earnings} - \text{Dividends for Preferred}}{\text{Number of Shares of Common Stock Outstanding}}$$

We are assuming Rojer Corporation has earnings of $700,000 and we assumed a tax rate of 40 percent. The table below is a worked-out solution to this problem by the corporation's accountant.

Looking just at the numbers, Rojer Corporation would be better off issuing *bonds*, because the $60,000 of bond interest that the corporation would pay to bondholders would serve to reduce earnings on which the corporation would have to pay tax. On the other hand, *dividends* paid to stockholders would not reduce earnings on which the corporation would pay taxes (the dividend for preferred stock is not an expense, as bond interest is, but a distribution of net income *after* tax). With bonds the common stockholders have an earnings per share of $4.80 versus $4.50.

Note bond interest of $60,000 lowers earnings subject to tax. Bond interest is deductible for federal income tax purposes.

Dividend is a distribution of net income after tax. It is not deductible for federal income tax purposes.

Other factors, however, should be considered when deciding whether to issue stocks or bonds to raise money, such as how interest rates are moving in the economy or whether the corporation can meet the bond interest payments each period for 10 years. If interest rates are high, it may be that the bond issue should be delayed to get more favorable interest rates.

For a comparison of stocks and bonds, see the blueprint on page 749.

Before concluding this unit, let's see how Rojer Corporation would record the sale and pay interest on the 12 percent, $500,000 bonds.

On January 1, Rojer Corporation issued its bonds:

Bonds Payable is a long-term liability on the balance sheet.

Jan.	1	Cash	500 00 0 00		
		Bonds Payable		500 00 0 00	
		Records issuance of bonds			

STOCKS VERSUS BONDS (STOCK DIVIDENDS VERSUS BOND INTEREST)

	$500,000 12 Percent Preferred Stock Issued	$500,000 12 Percent Bond (10-Year) Issued
Earnings before Taxes or Finance Costs	$700,000	$700,000
Less: Bond Interest	—0—	60,000 (.12 × $500,000)
Earnings Subject to Income Tax	$700,000	$640,000
Less: Income Tax (40%)	280,000	256,000
Net Income	420,000	384,000
Less: Preferred Dividend	60,000 (.12 × $500,000)	—0—
Earnings Available to Common Stockholders	360,000	384,000
Number of Common Stock Shares Outstanding	80,000	80,000
Earnings per Share	$4.50 $\left(\dfrac{\$360,000}{80,000}\right)$	$4.80 $\left(\dfrac{\$384,000}{80,000}\right)$

It then made semiannual interest payments to its bondholders:

June	30	Bond Interest Expense	30 0 0 0 00		
		Cash			30 0 0 0 00
		Paid semiannual interest expense			

$$\$500{,}000 \times .12 \times \tfrac{6}{12} = \$30{,}000, \text{ or } 12\%/2 = .06 \times \$500{,}000 = \$30{,}000.$$

This entry will be recorded twice a year for 10 years. At end of 10 years Rojer will record the bond maturity.

On the year of retirement, the journal entry would look like the following:

Dec.	31	Bonds Payable	500 0 0 0 00		
		Cash			500 0 0 0 00
		Retired bonds			

The face value of the bond, $500,000 has been repaid on maturity date.

BONDS SOLD BETWEEN INTEREST DATES

What would happen if Rojer Corporation issued the bonds on January 1 but did not actually sell them until March 1? Interest would have to be paid for January and February; how is that handled? And what happens if a person buys a bond that was issued in August, but the person buys it in November? As stated earlier, bond issuers only pay interest every six months. So, when a buyer purchases a bond between the six-month interest dates, the buyer pays the purchase price of the bond *plus* the interest that has built up since the last interest payment date. Keep in mind interest is being paid only twice a year. Think of it as an adjustment as the interest accrues. On the next payment, the buyer will receive the full interest payment for the six-month period. Let's show this by seeing how Rojer Corporation records the sale of bonds on March 1 that were issued on January 1:

Mar.	1	Cash	510 0 0 0 00		
		Bonds Payable			500 0 0 0 00
		Bond Interest Payable			10 0 0 0 00
		Bond issue plus 2 months' accrued interest			

Accrued Interest

$(\$500{,}000 \times .12 \times \tfrac{2}{12} = \$10{,}000)$ or $\$500{,}000 \times \underset{\text{semiannual rate}}{\underset{\uparrow}{.06}} \times \left(\dfrac{2 \text{ months}}{6 \text{ months}} \right)$

Note the buyer pays $510,000 instead of $500,000, because $10,000 of the accrued interest has been accumulated. On June 30, the $10,000 is repaid along with interest earned for four months.

Accrued interest originally collected is returned to investor.

June	30	Bond Interest Payable	10 0 0 0 00		
		Bond Interest Expense	20 0 0 0 00		
		Cash			30 0 0 0 00
		Record semiannual interest payment			

$(\$500{,}000 \times .12 \times \tfrac{4}{12} = \$20{,}000)$ or $\$500{,}000 \times \underset{\text{semiannual rate}}{\underset{\uparrow}{.06}} \times \left(\dfrac{4 \text{ months}}{6 \text{ months}} \right)$

In the next unit we look at how to record bond issues when the selling price is less or more than the face value.

LEARNING UNIT 21-1 REVIEW

AT THIS POINT you should be able to

▼ Explain face value and contract interest rate. (p. 730)
▼ Calculate the cost of a bond from a bond quote. (p. 731)
▼ Explain the different classifications of bonds. (p. 731)
▼ Explain the pros and cons of financing with preferred stock versus bonds. (p. 732)
▼ Record accounting entries to record issuing of bonds at par as well as semi-annual interest payment. (p. 733)
▼ Explain and record an accounting entry for accrued bond interest. (p. 733)

SELF-REVIEW QUIZ 21-1

(The forms you need are on page 111 of the *Study Guide and Working Papers.*)
    Prepare general journal entries to record the following (treat items 4 and 5 as a separate situation from items 1 through 3):

1. Issued 20 $10,000 12 percent bonds that mature in 10 years at face value on January 1.
2. Paid semiannual interest on June 30.
3. Bonds retired at end of tenth year.
4. Bonds sold on May 1 instead of January 1 due to poor market conditions.
5. Paid semiannual interest on June 30 from bonds issued on May 1.

Solution to Self-Review Quiz 21-1

❶	Cash	200 0 0 0 00	
	Bonds Payable		200 0 0 0 00
❷	Bond Interest Expense	12 0 0 0 00	
	Cash		12 0 0 0 00
	(I = $200,000 x .12 x $\frac{6}{12}$		
	or $200,000 x .06 semiannual rate)		
❸	Bonds Payable	200 0 0 0 00	
	Cash		200 0 0 0 00
❹	Cash	208 0 0 0 00	
	Bonds Payable		200 0 0 0 00
	Bond Interest Payable		8 0 0 0 00
	(Accrued interest = $200,000 x .12 x $\frac{4}{12}$		
	or $200,000 x .06 x $\frac{4}{6}$ = $8,000)		
❺	Bond Interest Payable	8 0 0 0 00	
	Bond Interest Expense	4 0 0 0 00	
	Cash		12 0 0 0 00
	(Bond Interest Expense = $200,000 x .12 x $\frac{2}{12}$		
	or $200,000 x .06 x $\frac{2}{6}$ = $4,000)		

LEARNING UNIT 21-2

BONDS ISSUED
AT A DISCOUNT
OR PREMIUM;
AMORTIZATION
BY THE STRAIGHT-LINE
METHOD

When a corporation issues bonds, it must

1. Receive approval from the board of directors of the corporation as well as from a governmental regulatory agency, the Securities and Exchange Commission.
2. Print the bonds.
3. Advertise the bond issue.

> On a given day the market rate for bond interest will vary from corporation to corporation: "supply versus demand."

The problem is that by the time these steps have been done, the rate of interest stated on the bond, the *contract* rate, may be lower or higher than the current *market* rate of interest. Investors may require higher rates of interest if the bond issue appears to be different than others offered by companies that may have had fewer financial difficulties.

For example, let's assume that Jossy Corporation is attempting to sell its 12 percent bond issue. The current market rate is 13 percent. To make its bonds more attractive (investors are looking for best return on their investment), Jossy decides to sell the bonds for less than face value (91, or 91 percent of the face value of $1,000). The bondholder will still receive yearly interest of $120 per bond (.12 × $1,000) but will only pay $910 (.91 × $1,000) per bond. Thus investors' annual or **effective rate** of interest is 13.2 percent ($120/$910). The difference between the *issue price* ($910) and the face value ($1,000) is called the *discount*.

Conversely, if Jossy Corporation sells the bond for *more* than the face value (if its contract rate is higher than the market rate), the difference between issue price and face value is called a *premium*.

> Remember: Interest rate is only one factor that determines the bond issue price. A company's past earnings record, along with other factors, must be considered.

> Investors being willing to pay more than face value means a premium for the corporation. Such willingness could result from the bond interest rate being more attractive than market rate.

RECORDING AND AMORTIZING BONDS ISSUED AT A DISCOUNT

To illustrate how to record a bond discount, let's look at the Ronson Corporation, which on January 1, 20XX, issued 200, 12 percent, $1,000, 10-year bonds at 97 (97 percent of face value). The discount is used because the current market rate is 12.4 percent, and Ronson has to be competitive to make its bond attractive to investors. Bondholders will receive a yearly dividend of $120, with an effective rate of 12.4 percent ($120/$970). The accounts that will make up the journal entry include the following:

> A discount means that the contract rate is less than the market rate.

> .97 × $1,000 = $970 paid for each bond.

.97 × $200,000

Cash	Asset	↑	Dr. $194,000
Discount on Bonds Payable	Contra-Liability	↑	Dr. $6,000
Bonds Payable	Liability	↑	Cr. $200,000

($200,000 − $194,000)

Face value

CHAPTER 21 ... CORPORATIONS AND BONDS PAYABLE   735

The journal entry will look like the following:

<table>
<tr><td></td><td>Jan.</td><td>1</td><td>Cash</td><td>194 00 0 00</td><td></td></tr>
<tr><td></td><td></td><td></td><td>Discount on Bonds Payable</td><td>6 0 0 0 00</td><td></td></tr>
<tr><td></td><td></td><td></td><td>Bonds Payable</td><td></td><td>200 0 0 0 00</td></tr>
<tr><td></td><td></td><td></td><td>Record Bond Issue</td><td></td><td></td></tr>
<tr><td></td><td></td><td></td><td></td><td></td><td></td></tr>
</table>

> **Not an immediate expense.** It will be an adjustment to increase interest expense over life of bond.

Let's look at how the Discount on Bonds Payable would look on the balance sheet.

Long-Term Liabilities:

12 percent Bonds Payable	$200,000	
Less: Discount on Bonds Payable	6,000	$194,000

> **Carrying value = face value − discount on bonds payable.**

For bonds sold at a discount, the **carrying value** (also called **book value**) of $194,000 is the face value of $200,000 minus the discount on bonds payable of $6,000. At maturity (after 10 years), the carrying value will be the same as face value ($200,000).

When each interest payment is made, a portion of the **Discount on Bonds Payable** is transferred to increase Interest Expense. This portion is called **Amortization of Discount on Bonds Payable.** Bond discount causes the total interest expense to increase, because the bond is sold for less than face value, resulting in higher costs of borrowing.

Before looking at how to amortize the discount, let's prove that the interest expense will be more than the contract amount of interest of $240,000 (.12 × $200,000 × 10 years) for 10 years.

Total amount to be paid to bondholder	$440,000	($200,000 bonds + $240,000 interest)
Total amount to be received from sale of bond	−$194,000	
Interest to be paid over life of bond	$246,000	
Average interest expense per year	$24,600	($246,000 ÷ 10 years)
Semiannual interest expense	$12,300	

If no discount has been made, the semiannual payment will be $12,000 ($200,000 × .12 × $\frac{6}{12}$ or $200,000 × .06). Now the discount results in an additional $300 of interest expense *each* semiannual payment $6,000 ÷ 20 periods).

The journal entry for each semiannual payment and amortization of discount will be as follows:

<table>
<tr><td></td><td>June</td><td>30</td><td>Bond Interest Expense</td><td>12 3 0 0 00</td><td></td></tr>
<tr><td></td><td></td><td></td><td>Discount on Bonds Payable</td><td></td><td>3 0 0 00</td></tr>
<tr><td></td><td></td><td></td><td>Cash</td><td></td><td>12 0 0 0 00</td></tr>
<tr><td></td><td></td><td></td><td>Semiannual interest and amortization of</td><td></td><td></td></tr>
<tr><td></td><td></td><td></td><td>discount</td><td></td><td></td></tr>
<tr><td></td><td></td><td></td><td></td><td></td><td></td></tr>
</table>

> **If there were no discount or premium, the semiannual interest payment would be $12,000.**

After posting, the ledger would look as follows:

Discount on Bonds Payable		Bond Interest Expense
6,000	300	12,300
5,700		

TABLE 21-1 AMORTIZATION SCHEDULE FOR BOND DISCOUNT USING THE STRAIGHT-LINE METHOD FOR EACH SEMIANNUAL PERIOD

Period	Carrying Value, Beg. of Period	Total Interest Expense	Interest to Be Paid Bondholders (.06 × Face Value)*	Amortized Discount Transferred to Increase Interest Expense	Carrying Value, End of Period
1	$194,000 (200,000 − 6,000)	$12,300	$12,000 (200,000 × .06)	$300 (6,000 ÷ 20 periods)	$194,300 (194,000 + 300)
2	194,300	12,300	12,000	300	194,600
3	194,600	12,300	12,000	300	194,900
4	194,900	12,300	12,000	300	195,200
19	199,400	12,300	12,000	300	199,700
20	199,700	12,300	12,000	300	200,000

The balance in the Discount on Bonds Payable account should be equal to zero at the end of the 20 periods.

*Half of annual rate of 12% = 6% semiannual rate.

After this amortization the carrying value (book value) of the bond has increased from $194,000 to $194,300. By the end of 10 years the carrying value will be back to $200,000, or the amount due at maturity.

In this unit we calculate amortization of the bond's discount by the **straight-line method;** in the next unit we use the *interest* method. The straight-line method transfers an equal amount of bond discount to interest expense over equal periods of time.

Table 21-1 shows the straight-line method of amortizing a bond discount over the life of the bond for each semiannual period. At the end of the life of the bond, the Discount on Bonds Payable has a zero balance, and the original $6,000 has been transferred to Interest Expense. At this point, the book value or carrying value of a bond ($200,000) is what is paid at maturity.

Year-End Adjusting Entry: Accrued Interest and Amortization of Discount on Bonds Payable.
Let's consider what would happen if the semiannual interest payment were on April 1 and October 1. On December 31, $6,000, three months' interest would be accrued ($12,000 × $\frac{3}{6}$). The amount of discount to be amortized would be $150 ($300 × $\frac{3}{6}$). The journal entry would be recorded as follows:

Dec.	31	Bond Interest Expense	6 1 5 0 00		
		Discount on Bonds Payable		1 5 0 00	
		Bond Interest Payable		6 0 0 0 00	
		Accrued interest and amortization			

Note that the Discount on Bonds Payable does indeed increase total bond interest expense from $6,000 to $6,150. This adjusting entry would then be reversed on January 1, as follows:

Jan.	1	Bond Interest Payable	6 0 0 0 00		
		Discount on Bonds Payable	1 5 0 00		
		Bond Interest Expense		6 1 5 0 00	
		Reversing entry			

$200,000   Face value of bond
5,700   Bond discount
$194,300   New carrying value

After 10 years, the balance on Discount on Bonds Payable will be zero.

Straight-line allocates equal amount of discount to Interest Expense each period.

Note: Ten years with interest semiannually means 20 periods (10 years × 2).

Bond Interest Expense: $12,300 × $\frac{3}{6}$ = $6,150

Bond Interest Payable: $12,000 × $\frac{3}{6}$ = $6,000

Bond Discount Adjustment: $300 × $\frac{3}{6}$ = $150

The regular payment made on April 1 would look like the following:

Apr.	1	Bond Interest Expense	12 3 0 0 00			
		Discount on Bonds Payable			3 0 0 00	
		Cash			12 0 0 0 00	
		Semiannual interest and amortizaton of				
		discount				

RECORDING AND AMORTIZING BONDS ISSUED AT A PREMIUM

> Bonds are issued at a premium if the contract rate is greater than the market rate.

> The Premium on Bonds Payable is added to the face value of the bond.

To illustrate bonds issued at a premium, let's look at Ronson Corporation again, but assume on January 1 it issued its 200, 12 percent bonds at 102 (102 percent of face value). This premium occurred because the current market rate was 11.8 percent and Ronson's bonds were thus very attractive to investors. The bondholders would receive per bond the yearly interest payment of $120 (.12 × $1,000 bond) with an effective rate of 11.8 percent ($120/$1,020). The accounts that will make up the journal entry include the following:

1.02 × $200,000

Cash	Asset	↑	**Dr. $204,000**
Premium on Bonds Payable	Liability	↑	**Cr. $4,000**
Bonds Payable	Liability	↑	**Cr. $200,000**

$\left(\begin{array}{c}\$204,000 \\ - \$200,000\end{array}\right)$

Face value

The journal entry will look like the following:

Jan.	1	Cash	204 0 0 0 00			
		Premium on Bonds Payable			4 0 0 0 00	
		Bonds Payable			200 0 0 0 00	
		Issued bond at premium				

> Note that the Premium on Bonds Payable is *added* to Bonds Payable to arrive at the carrying value of $204,000.

Let's see how the Premium on Bonds Payable would look on the balance sheet:

Long-Term Liabilities:

12 percent Bonds Payable	$200,000	
Add: Premium on Bonds Payable	4,000	$204,000

When each interest payment is made, a portion of the **Premium on Bonds Payable** is transferred to *reduce* Interest Expense. This portion is called **Amortization of Premium on Bonds Payable.** Let's prove that the interest expense will be less than the contractual amount of $240,000 for 10 years.

> If there were no discount or premium, the semiannual interest would be $12,000.

Total amount to be paid to bondholders	$440,000	$\left(\begin{array}{l}\$200,000 \text{ bonds } + \\ \$240,000 \text{ interest}\end{array}\right)$
Total amount to be received from sale of bonds	− 204,000	
Interest to be paid over life of bond	$236,000	
Average interest expense per year	$ 23,600	($236,000 ÷ 10 years)
Semiannual interest expense	$ 11,800	

TABLE 21-2 AMORTIZATION SCHEDULE FOR BOND PREMIUM USING THE STRAIGHT-LINE METHOD FOR EACH SEMIANNUAL PERIOD

Period	Carrying Value, Beg. of Period	Total Interest Expense	Interest to Be Paid to Bondholder (.06 × Face Value)	Amortized Premium to Decrease Interest Expense	Carrying Value, End of Period
1	$204,000 (200,000 + 4,000)	$11,800	$12,000 (.06 × 200,000)	$200	$203,800 (204,000 − 200)
2	203,800	11,800	12,000	200	203,600
3	203,600	11,800	12,000	200	203,400
4	203,400	11,800	12,000	200	203,200
19	200,400	11,800	12,000	200	200,200
20	200,200	11,800	12,000	200	200,000

The balance in the Premium on Bonds Payable account should be equal to zero at the end of the 20 periods.

If no premium were made, the semiannual interest expense would be $12,000 ($200,000 × .12 × $\frac{6}{12}$ or $200,000 × .06). Now the premium results in *reducing* the interest expense for each semiannual payment by $200 ($4,000 premium ÷ 20 periods).

The journal entry for semiannual payment will look like the following:

June	30	Bond Interest Expense	11 8 0 0 00		
		Premium on Bonds Payable	2 0 0 00		
		Cash		12 0 0 0 00	
		Semiannual payment and premium			
		amortization			

After posting, the ledger will look like the following:

Premium on Bonds Payable	Bond Interest Expense
200 | 4,000	11,800 |
| 3,800	

We're using the straight-line method of amortizing the bond premium over the life of the bond for each semiannual period. This method is shown in Table 21-2. Note that at the end of the schedule, the carrying value is reduced to $200,000 and the balance in the premium account is zero.

LEARNING UNIT 21-2 REVIEW

AT THIS POINT you should be able to

▼ Calculate effective rate. (p. 735)
▼ Explain why a bond will sell at a discount or premium. (p. 735)
▼ Define and explain Discount on Bonds Payable. (p. 736)
▼ Explain why a discount will increase interest expense when semiannual interest is paid. (p. 736)
▼ Journalize the recording of bonds issued at a discount. (p. 736)

- ▼ Journalize year-end adjusting entries. (p. 737)
- ▼ Prepare an amortization schedule of bond discount by the straight-line method. (p. 737)
- ▼ Define and explain Premium on Bonds Payable. (p. 738)
- ▼ Explain why a premium on bonds payable will decrease interest expense when semiannual interest is paid. (p. 738)
- ▼ Journalize the recording of bonds issued at a premium. (p. 738)
- ▼ Prepare an amortization schedule of bond premium by straight-line method. (p. 739)

SELF-REVIEW QUIZ 21-2

(The forms you need are on page 112 in the *Study Guide and Working Papers*.)

Prepare a partial amortization schedule as on page 739 using the straight-line method for the first three semiannual periods based on the following facts: 100, 14 percent, 10-year bonds issued at 98. Each bond has a $1,000 face value.

Solution to Self-Review Quiz 21-2

Period	Carrying Value, Beg. of Period	Total Interest Expense	Interest Paid to Bondholders (.07 × Face Value)	Amortized Discount Transferred to Increase Interest Expense	Carrying Value, End of Period
1	$98,000	$7,100	$7,000	$100 (2,000 ÷ 20 periods)	$98,100 (98,000 + 100)
2	98,100	7,100	7,000	100	98,200
3	98,200	7,100	7,000	100	98,300

LEARNING UNIT 21-3

AMORTIZATION OF BOND DISCOUNTS AND PREMIUMS BY THE INTEREST METHOD

In the last unit we amortized the discount or premium by the straight-line method. The problem with this method is that it recognizes an equal amount of interest expense each period, even though the bond's carrying value changes. Accountants think that it is inconsistent for interest expense to stay the same while the amount owed changes. They think interest should be a *constant percentage of the carrying value.* For this reason, another method, called the interest method, is used in amortizing bond discounts and premiums. The Accounting Principles Board has ruled that the straight-line method be used only if the results do not materially differ from those of the interest method.

AMORTIZING THE BOND DISCOUNT BY THE INTEREST METHOD

The **interest method of amortization** makes interest expense a constant percentage of the bond carrying value.

The goal of the interest method is to calculate the interest expense to be recorded each year as a constant percentage of the carrying value of the bonds.

Period	(1) Carrying Value, Beginning of Period	(2) Interest Paid to Bondholders (.06 × Face Value)*	(3) Interest Expense to Be Recorded (.07 × Carrying Value)	(4) Discount to Be Amortized	(5) Carrying Value, End of Period
1	$178,808 (200,000 − 21,192)	$12,000	$12,517 (.07 × 178,808)	$517	$179,325 (178,808 + 517)
2	179,325	12,000	12,553	553	179,878
3	179,878	12,000	12,591	591	180,469
19	196,373	12,000	13,746	1,746	198,119
20	198,119	12,000	13,881	1,881	200,000

Adjusted for rounding

*Use 6 percent, because 12 percent is for the whole year and the calculations are made semiannually.

Note: Column 4 is the difference between columns 2 and 3.

The interest amount will thus not be the same each period. There are two formulas to use to reach this goal:

a. Carrying value of bonds at beginning of period × market interest rate = interest expense of carrying value to be recorded.

b. Face value × contract rate = interest expense to bondholders. The discount to be amortized is the difference between a and b.

To illustrate this method, let's assume Yang Corporation is issuing $200,000 of 12 percent, 10-year bonds on April 1. Interest is to be paid on October 1 and April 1. The selling price of the bonds is $178,808. The market rate is 14 percent.

> Discount on bond:
> $200,000 − $178,808 = $21,192.

Look at the amortization schedule shown in Table 21-3. Note that the discount amount to be amortized is not constant, as it is in the straight-line method. As a matter of fact, to prove that the interest expense is a constant percentage of the carrying value, let's look at semiannual periods 2 and 19.

$$\text{Period 2: } \frac{\$12,553}{\$179,325} = .07 \qquad \text{Period 19: } \frac{\$13,746}{\$196,373} = .07$$

On October 1, the date of the first semiannual interest payment, the following entry would occur:

Oct.	1	Bond Interest Expense	12517 00	
		Discount on Bonds Payable		517 00
		Cash		12000 00
		Semiannual payment and amortization		

> Bond Interest Expense:
> $12,553 × $\frac{3}{6}$ = $6,276.50

YEAR-END ADJUSTMENT

On December 31, three months' interest of $6,000 ($\frac{3}{6}$ × $12,000) has accrued, as well as $276.50 ($\frac{3}{6}$ of $553), the second-period discount shown on the amortization schedule. The following adjusting year-end entry is prepared:

> Bond Interest Payable:
> $12,000 × $\frac{3}{6}$ = $6,000

Dec.	31	Bond Interest Expense	6 2 7 6 50		
		Discount on Bonds Payable		2 7 6 50
		Bond Interest Payable		6 0 0 0 00
		Year-end adjustment		

The reversing entry on January 1 and the entry to record payment of interest on April 1 would look like the following:

Jan.	1	Bond Interest Payable	6 0 0 0 00		
		Discount on Bonds Payable	2 7 6 50	
		Bond Interest Expense		6 2 7 6 50
		Reversing entry		
Apr.	1	Bond Interest Expense	12 5 1 7 00	
		Discount on Bonds Payable		5 1 7 00
		Cash		12 0 0 0 00
		Semiannual interest and amortization of		
		discount		

AMORTIZING THE BOND PREMIUM BY THE INTEREST METHOD

Yang Corporation issues on April 1 $200,000 of 12 percent bonds with interest paid on October 1 and April 1. The selling price of the bonds is $224,926. Marked interest rate is 10 percent. The amortization schedule is shown in Table 21-4.

On April 1 the following entry records the semiannual payment:

Oct.	1	Bond Interest Expense	11 2 4 6 00	
		Premium on Bonds Payable	7 5 4 00	
		Cash		12 0 0 0 00
		Semiannual interest and premium		
		amortization		

YEAR-END ADJUSTMENT

Bond Interest Expense:
$\frac{3}{6} \times \$11,209 = \$5,604.50$

Premium on Bonds Payable:
$\frac{3}{6} \times \$791 = \$395.50$

Bond Interest Payable:
$\frac{3}{6} \times \$12,000 = \$6,000$

It should be noted that on December 31, three months' interest accrues as well as the need to amortize half the premium (for the second period). The following journal entry records this year-end adjustment:

Dec.	31	Bond Interest Expense	5 6 0 4 50	
		Premium on Bonds Payable	3 9 5 50	
		Bond Interest Payable		6 0 0 0 00
		Year-end adjustment		

Period	(1) Carrying Value, Beg. of Period	(2) Interest Paid to Bondholder (.06 × Face Value)	(3) Interest Expense to Be Recorded, (.05 × Carrying Value)	(4) Premium to Be Amortized	(5) Carrying Value, End of Period
1	$224,926	$12,000	$11,246	$754	$224,172 ($224,926 − $754)
2	224,172	12,000	11,209	791	223,381
19	203,726	12,000	10,186	1,814	201,912
20	201,912	12,000	10,088	1,912	200,000

Note: Column 4 is the difference between columns 2 and 3. Column 5 is column 1 minus column 4.

The reversing entry on January 1 and the payment of interest in April would look like the following:

Jan.	1	Bond Interest Payable	6 0 0 0 00		
		Premium on Bonds Payable		3 9 5 50	
		Bond Interest Expense		5 6 0 4 50	
		Reversing entry			
Apr.	1	Bond Interest Expense	11 2 0 9 00		
		Premium on Bonds Payable	7 9 1 00		
		Cash		12 0 0 0 00	
		Semiannual interest and amortization of			
		premium			

LEARNING UNIT 21-3 REVIEW

AT THIS POINT you should be able to

▼ Prepare an amortization schedule for bond discounts using the interest method. (p. 741)
▼ Prepare an amortization schedule for bond premiums using the interest method. (p. 742)
▼ Journalize year-end adjustments. (p. 742)

SELF-REVIEW QUIZ 21-3

(The forms you need are on page 112 of the *Study Guide and Working Papers.*)

Prepare a partial amortization schedule like the one above using the interest method for the first three periods based on the following facts: 100, 12 percent 10-year bonds issued at a selling price of $89,404. Assume a market rate of 14 percent.

Period	(1) Carrying Amount, Beg. of Period	(2) Interest Paid to Bondholders (.06 × Face Value)	(3) Interest Expense to Be Recorded, (.07 × Carrying Value)	(4) Discount to Be Amortized	(5) Carrying Amounts, End of Period
1	$89,404	$6,000	$6,258	$258	$89,662
2	89,662	6,000	6,276	276	89,938
3	89,938	6,000	6,296	296	90,234

LEARNING UNIT 21-4

RETIREMENT OF BONDS AND BOND SINKING FUNDS

In the first unit of this chapter we mentioned callable bonds, which permit the corporation to reacquire bonds at a price based on a percentage of face value. Some corporations retire them and issue new bonds (called *bond refunding*) to take their place paying a lower rate of interest. If this call provision doesn't exist, a company can repurchase its bonds in the open market and then retire them. By retiring bonds, companies can decrease the amount of debt they owe. If interest rates are high, the retirement of bonds could result in substantial cash savings, even if new bonds are issued at lower rates.

When the bonds are retired before they reach maturity, the following points have to be recognized:

1. Any amortization of discount or premium must be brought up to date at the time of retirement.
2. The premium or discount as well as the bond liability account must be removed.
3. Any gain or loss is recognized on the retirement of the bonds as an extraordinary item that will be shown on the income statement.

Let's use Roberts Corporation as an example. On June 30 the corporation retired a $500,000, 10 percent bond issue that had an unamortized premium of $19,000. The bonds were called in at 105 (105 percent of face value). All journal entries relating to interest payments and premium amortization were completed before the bonds' retirement. The entry to record the retirement of the bonds by Roberts Corporation would look like the following:

Bonds Payable	500 000 00	
Premium on Bonds Payable	19 000 00	
Loss on Bond Retirement	6 000 00	
Cash		525 000 00
Retirement of bond		

Note that the difference between the bond carrying value of $519,000 ($500,000 + $19,000) and actual cash paid results in the loss of $6,000. Of course, if the carrying value were greater than the cash paid, a gain would be realized.

THE BOND SINKING FUND

Often a corporation will agree to establish a fund that will accumulate assets over the life of the bond so as to pay off the bondholders at maturity. In fact, such a fund is often a requirement stated in the bond indentures. This fund is called a **sinking fund.**

For example, Morrel Corporation issued 8 percent, 15-year bonds for $80,000, agreeing to deposit $2946.40 at the end of the year, so that by the end of the fifteenth year the fund would contain $80,000 to pay off bondholders. Sinking fund tables are available that make these periodic deposits easy to calculate. For example, Morrel's accountant would go to a sinking fund table and look up 8 percent for 15 periods and find a table factor of .0368295. By multiplying the $80,000 × .0368295, one comes up with a yearly deposit of $2,946.40, which, at this rate of interest compounded annually, will at the end of 15 years bring a total of $80,000.

The following would be the journal entries for Morrel Corporation for establishing the sinking fund:

$500,000 × 1.05 = $525,000.
Sinking fund table, 8 percent

15 ⟶ .0368295

The Analysis:

Long-term investment ⟶

Sinking Fund	Asset	↑	Dr.
Cash	Asset	↓	Cr.

The Journal Entry:

	Debit	Credit
Sinking Fund	2946 40	
Cash		2946 40
Establishing sinking fund		

When interest is earned on the balance in the sinking fund, the following entry results:

The Analysis:

Sinking Fund	Asset	↑	Dr.
Sinking Fund Earned	Other Revenue	↑	Cr.

The Journal Entry:

	Debit	Credit
Sinking Fund	235 00	
Sinking Fund Earned ($2,946 x .08)		235 00
Interest earned		

When the bonds are paid off, there may be a little more or less cash than is needed in the sinking fund. The entry to record the payment of the bonds by Morrel is as follows (assume $50 extra in the sinking fund):

Cash		5000			
Bonds Payable	800000				
Bond Sinking Fund				805000	
Payment of bonds					

Keep in mind that the money in the sinking fund cannot be used to meet other current expenses or liabilities. Thus the sinking fund is recorded in the long-term investment section of the balance sheet. Any cash left over is returned to the Cash account.

LEARNING UNIT 21-4 REVIEW

AT THIS POINT you should be able to

- ▼ Journalize the gain or loss on retirement of bonds. (p. 744)
- ▼ Explain as well as journalize entries relating to sinking funds. (p. 745)

SELF-REVIEW QUIZ 21-4

(The forms you need are on page 113 of the *Study Guide and Working Papers*.) Journalize the following transactions:

A. Retired $300,000 of bonds that had a $20,000 premium for 106.
B. Set up a sinking fund account with an initial deposit of $3,000.
C. Earned $325 interest on sinking fund balance.
D. Sinking fund of $90,000 was used to retire bond holders amount to $89,900.

Solution to Self-Review Quiz 21-4

(A)	Bonds Payable	3000000	
	Premium on Bonds	200000	
	Cash		3180000
	Gain on Retirement		20000
(B)	Sinking Fund	300000	
	Cash		300000
(C)	Sinking Fund	32500	
	Sinking Fund Earned		32500
(D)	Bonds Payable	900000	
	Sinking Fund		900000

SUMMARY OF KEY POINTS

Learning Unit 21-1

1. Bond certificates state face value and contract rate of interest.

2. A bond indenture is a formal agreement that spells out specifics of the bond issue. The trustee, usually a bank, makes sure the bond indenture is fulfilled.

3. Bonds are negotiable and are quoted in the marketplace as a percentage of the face value. For example, 95 means 95 percent of a $1,000 bond, or $950.

4. There are many types of bonds. In this chapter we discuss secured, debenture, serial, registered, callable, and convertible bonds.

5. To a corporation trying to decide whether to issue stocks or bonds to raise money, an important difference between stocks and bonds is that stock dividends are a distribution of net income *after* tax, whereas bond interest expense is deductible from earnings *before* tax.

6. If bonds are sold between interest dates, the buyer pays the price of the bond plus accrued interest. This accrued interest is paid back when the semiannual interest payment is made.

Learning Unit 21-2

1. By the time a bond is actually issued, the contract rate of interest may be lower or higher than the effective or actual market rate.

2. A bond discount means that the issue price of bonds is less than the face value.

3. A bond premium means that the issue price of bonds is greater than the face value.

4. Discount on Notes Payable is a contra-liability found on the balance sheet. It is not an immediate expense. It will be amortized at the time of the interest payment and thus will increase the total interest expense.

5. The straight-line method of amortizing bond discounts transfers an equal amount of bond discount to interest expense over equal periods of time.

6. Premium on Bonds Payable is a liability found on the balance sheet. It will be amortized at each semiannual payment to decrease interest expense over the life of the bond.

Learning Unit 21-3

1. In the interest method of amortizing a bond discount or premium, interest expense is a constant *percentage* of the carrying value of the bonds. Thus interest amount will *not* be constant each period.

2. The amortization of the period is the difference between interest expense to be recorded and interest expense paid to bondholders.

Learning Unit 21-4

1. When bonds are retired before their maturity date:

   a. Amortization of bond discount must be up to date.

   b. The bond liability and either the discount or the premium must be removed.

   c. A gain or loss is recognized as an extraordinary item on the income statement.

2. A bond sinking fund is set up by a corporation to pay bondholders at maturity.

3. The sinking fund is an asset on the balance sheet under long-term investments.

KEY TERMS

Amortization of Discount on Bonds Payable, Amortization of Premium on Bonds Payable Writing off the bond premium or discount as a decrease or increase to interest expense for each interest period.

Bond An interest-bearing note payable usually in $1,000 denominations issued by a corporation to a large group of lenders.

Bond certificate A piece of paper held by bondholder showing evidence of a bond(s) issued by a corporation to be payable on a specified date for a specific sum to the order of the person named in the bond certificate or to the bearer.

Bond indenture A contract that spells out the provisions of the contract between the corporation and bondholder.

Callable bond Bond with a provision that it can be called in by a corporation after a certain date.

Carrying value (book value) Face value of bond less bond discount or plus bond premium.

Contract rate Rate of interest (based on face value) stated on bond certificate and bond indenture.

Convertible bond Bondholders have the option of converting bonds into stock at a specified exchange rate.

Debenture bonds Bonds that are unsecured and are issued only on the general credit of a corporation.

Discount on Bonds Payable Account used when bonds are issued below face value; indicated market rate of interest is higher than contract rate. This account is a contra-liability account.

Effective rate The real or actual rate of interest to the borrowing corporation, which affects interest payment and the bond premium or discount to be amortized.

Face value The amount the corporation must repay to the bondholder at the maturity date.

Interest method of amortization This method amortizes the premium or discount to *record* interest expense, being equal to the carrying value of the bond times the market rate. The interest expense is a constant percentage of the carrying value. The discount or premium to be amortized is the difference between the interest to be recorded and the interest paid to bondholders.

Premium on Bonds Payable Account used when bonds are issued above face value; indicated market rate is below contract rate. This account is a liability account.

Registered bond Bondholders of record are registered with the corporation, and interest checks are sent directly to them.

Secured bond Bond issued by a corporation that pledges specific assets as security to meet the terms of the bond agreement.

Serial bonds Bonds issued in a series, each one of which has a different maturity date and thus comes due at a different time.

Sinking fund A fund that accumulates cash to pay off bonds when they are retired.

Sinking Fund Earned Other revenue account used to record earnings on sinking fund balance.

Straight-line method A method recognizing equal amount of interest expense for each period when amortizing a bond discount or premium.

Trustee Organization (usually a bank) or person who monitors a bond indenture for the protection of bondholders.

BLUEPRINT: STOCKS VS. BONDS

STOCKS	BONDS
1. Stockholders are owners of corporation.	1. Bondholders are creditors to a corporation.
2. Stockholders are paid off in liquidation only after claims of creditors are satisfied.	2. Bondholders, in liquidation, have claims on assets (along with other creditors) before stockholders.
3. Dividends are paid only if earnings are sufficient; there is no fixed charge as there is with bond interest. Dividends are not an expense; they are a distribution of income.	3. Interest expense is a fixed charge. Failure to pay could result in creditors bringing bankruptcy proceedings against the corporation.
4. Stockholders have voting rights except with preferred stock.	4. Bondholders have no voting rights.
5. Dividends are deducted *after* tax on earnings.	5. Interest is deductible from earnings *before* tax.
6. Stockholders continue to receive dividends; they are not "paid off."	6. Bondholders are eventually repaid the principal.

QUESTIONS, MINI EXERCISES, EXERCISES, AND PROBLEMS

Discussion Questions

1. Explain the selling price of a bond quoted at 88.
2. What is the difference between a secured bond and a debenture bond?
3. Dividends reduce earnings before taxes. True or false? Explain.
4. Accrued interest results in seller paying extra for bonds. True or false? Explain.
5. Explain why a bond may sell at a premium.
6. Why isn't Discount on Bonds Payable an immediate expense?
7. Premium on Bonds Payable will cause total interest expense to be reduced. True or false?
8. The straight-line method of amortizing a bond discount or premium will result in an uneven amount of discount or premium that increases or decreases expense each period. Accept or reject. Why?
9. What is the carrying value of a bond?
10. Why does the interest method of amortizing a discount or premium use the market rate in calculating interest expense to be recorded?
11. Explain how a gain or loss on retirement of bonds before the maturity date is recorded.
12. What is the purpose of a bond sinking fund?

Mini Exercises

(The forms you need are on pages 115–116 of the *Study Guide and Working Papers*.)

Bond Journal Entries

1. Journalize the following transactions:
   a. Issued five $10,000, 6 percent bonds that mature in 20 years at face value on January 1.

b. Paid semiannual interest on June 30.

c. Bonds retired at end of 20 years.

Bond Issued at a Discount

2. On January 1, Borg Co. issued ten $1,000, 6 percent 10-year bonds at 96. Record the journal entry.

Interest and Amortization of Discount

3. From Mini Exercise 2, record on June 30 the semiannual payment and amortization of the discount.

Bond Issued at Premium

4. Redo Mini Exercise 2 with straight-line assuming the bond sells for 105.

Interest and Amortization of Premium with Straight-Line

5. From Mini Exercise 4, record on June 30 the semiannual payment and amortization of premium on bonds payable.

Amortization of Bond Discount by Interest Method

6. *Facts:* Bond issue: $100,000, 6 percent, 10-year bonds; selling price of bonds $78,000. Market rate 8 percent. Calculate the following:

   a. Carrying value beginning of period.

   b. Interest paid to bondholders every six months.

   c. Interest expense each six-month period to be recorded.

   d. Discount to be amortized.

   e. Carrying value end of the period.

Journalizing the Semiannual Payment of Amortization of Discount

7. For Mini Exercise 6, record a journal entry for the first semiannual interest payment on October 1.

Amortization of Bond Premium by Interest Method

8. *Facts:* Bond issue: $100,000, 6 percent, 10-year bonds; selling price of bonds, $120,000; market rate, 4 percent. Calculate the following:

   a. Carrying value at the beginning of the period.

   b. Interest paid to bondholder each six months.

   c. Interest Expense each six-month period.

   d. Premium to be amortized.

   e. Carrying value at the end of the period.

Journalizing the Semiannual Payment and Amortization of Bond Premium

9. For Mini Exercise 8, record the journal entry for the first semiannual interest payment on October 1.

Sinking Fund

10. Journalize the following transactions:

    a. Set up a sinking fund with an initial deposit of $5,000.

    b. Earned $110 interest on sinking fund balance.

    c. Sinking fund of $15,000 was used to pay off bondholders in the amount of $15,000.

Exercises

(The forms you need are on pages 117–119 in the *Study Guide and Working Papers.*)

21-1. Heller Corporation and Langle Corporation have both earned $100,000 before bond interest and taxes. The companies have the same number of outstanding shares but different capital structures. Calculate the earnings per share of common stock for both companies from the following:

Calculating earnings per share.

	HELLER	LANGLE
10 percent bond payable	200,000	—0—
10 percent preferred stock	—0—	200,000
Common stock $10 par 30,000 shares outstanding	300,000	300,000
Operating income before interest and income taxes (assume a 30 percent tax rate)	100,000	100,000

21-2. On January 1, 20XX, Alpha Corporation issued $800,000 of 10 percent, 30-year bonds to lenders at par (100). Interest is to be paid semiannually on July 1 and January 1. Journalize the following entries:

Recording sale of bonds at par, paying interest, and retirement of issue.

  a. Issued the bonds.

  b. Paid semiannual interest payment.

  c. Retirement of bonds, assuming interest expense is up to date.

21-3. Quick Corporation issued $300,000 of 10 percent, 10-year bonds at 98 on May 1, 20XX, with semiannual interest payable on May 1 and November 1. Amortization of discount is by the straight-line method. Record the journal entries for the following:

Bond sold at discount; straight-line method to amortize discount.

  a. Issuance of bonds.

  b. Semiannual interest payment on November 1 and amortization of discount.

  c. Retirement of bonds at maturity.

21-4. Redo the journal entries for Exercise 21-3 assuming bonds sold at 102.

Bonds sold at discount; straight-line method to amortize discount.

21-5. On July 1 Jonald Corporation issued 10 percent, 10-year bonds with a face value of $100,000 for $90,000, because the current market rate is 12 percent. Record the following entries, assuming the *interest method* is used to amortize the discount on bonds. Round discount to nearest dollar.

Bonds sold at discount; interest method to amortize discount.

  a. Issuance of bonds.

  b. Semiannual interest payment on December 31 and amortization of discount.

  c. Semiannual interest payment on June 30 and amortization of discount.

21-6. On January 1 Last Corporation sold $350,000 of 10-year sinking fund bonds. The corporation expects to earn 10 percent on the sinking fund balance and is required to deposit $23,609 at the end of each year with the trustee. Record the following entries:

Sinking funds.

  a. The first deposit.

  b. Earnings of $2,361 at end of first period.

  c. Payment of bondholders with sinking fund having a balance of $350,500.

21-7. From the following prepare the long-term liabilities section of a balance sheet:

Preparing a long-term liabilities section on the balance sheet.

Sinking fund	$300,000
Premium on 10 percent bonds	3,000
Discount on 12 percent bonds	5,000
10 percent Bonds Payable	500,000
12 percent Bonds Payable	200,000

(The forms you need are on pages 120–124 of the *Study Guide and Working Papers.*)

21A-1. On January 1, 20X5, Angel Corporation sold $400,000 of 8 percent, 10-year bonds at 97. Interest is to be paid on June 30 and December 31. The straight-line method of amortizing the discount is used. Prepare (1) an amortization schedule for the first three semiannual periods and (2) journal entries to record the following:

a. Bond issue on January 1.

b. Semiannual interest payments on June 30 and December 31 for interest and amortization of discount.

c. If the bonds were issued on March 1 and interest was paid on September 1 and March 1, what would be the year-end adjusting entry on December 31 to record accrued interest and amortization of discount?

21A-2. On May 1, 20X5, Deever Corporation issued $500,000 of 10 percent, 20-year bonds at 102. The interest is payable on November 1 and May 1. The premium is amortized by the straight-line method. Prepare an amortization schedule for the first three semiannual periods and journalize the following transactions:

20X5

May	1	Bonds issued.
Nov.	1	Paid semiannual interest and amortized premium.
Dec.	31	Accrued bond interest and amortized premium.

21A-3. On January 1, 20X7, Vex Corporation issued $300,000 of 10 percent, 10-year bonds for $257,616, yielding a market rate of 12 percent. Interest is paid on July 1 and December 31. Vex uses the interest method to amortize the discount.

1. Prepare an amortization schedule for first three semiannual periods.

2. Prepare journal entries to record:

a. Bond issuance on January 1.

b. Semiannual interest payments on July 1 and December 31 as well as amortization of discount.

3. If the bond were issued on March 1 and interest was paid on September 1 and March 1, what would be the year-end adjusting entry on December 31, 20X7, to record accrued interest and amortization of discount?

21A-4. On April 1, 20X6, Potter Corporation issued $200,000 of 10 percent, five-year bonds for $204,100, yielding a market rate of 9 percent. Interest is paid on October 1 and April 1. Potter Corporation uses the interest method to amortize the premium.

1. Prepare an amortization schedule for the first three semiannual periods.

2. Prepare journal entries to record the following:

a. Bond issuance on April 1.

b. Semiannual interest payment and amortization of premium on October 1.

c. The year-end adjusting entry to record expense and premium amortization.

Group B Problems

(The forms you need are on pages 120–124 in the *Study Guide and Working Papers.*)

21B-1. On January 1, 20X6, Angel Corporation sold $300,000 of 12 percent, 10-year bonds at 92. Interest is to be paid on June 30 and December 31. The straight-line method of amortizing the discount is used. Prepare (1) an amortization schedule for the first three semiannual periods and (2) journal entries to record (a) the bond issue on January 1 and (b) semiannual interest payments on June 30 and December 31 for interest and amortization of discount. (c) If the bonds were issued on March 1 and interest was paid on September 1 and March 1, what would be the year-end adjusting entry on December 31 to record interest payment and amortization of discount?

Amortization schedule; bond issue, straight-line amortization of discount.

Check Figure:
Amortized discount $1,200

21B-2. On April 1, 20X6, Deever Corporation issued $600,000 of 6 percent, 10-year bonds at 104. The interest is payable on October 1 and April 1. The premium is amortized by the straight-line method. Prepare an amortization schedule for the first three semiannual periods and journalize the following transactions:

20X6

Apr.	1	Bonds issued.
Oct.	1	Paid semiannual interest and amortization of premium.
Dec.	31	Accrued bond interest and amortization premium.

Amortizaton schedule; bond issue; accrued interest; straight-line amortization of premium; year-end adjusting entry.

Check Figure:
Amortized premium $1,200

21B-3. On January 1, 20X8, Vex Corporation issued $400,000 of 12 percent, 10-year bonds for $350,937, yielding a market rate of 14 percent. Interest is paid on July 1 and December 31. Vex uses the interest method to amortize the discount. Prepare an amortization schedule for the first three semiannual periods and prepare journal entries to record the following:

a. Bond issuance on January 1.

b. Semiannual interest payment on July 1 and December 31 as well as amortization of discount.

If the bonds were issued on March 1 and interest was paid on September 1 and March 1, what would be the year-end adjusting entry on December 31, 20X7, to record accrued interest and amortization of discount?

Amortization schedule; interest method of amortization of premium; year-end adjusting entry.

Check Figure:
Discount to be amortized $565.59

21B-4. On March 1, 20X7, Potter Corporation issued $100,000 of 12 percent, 10-year bonds for $104,408, yielding a market rate of 10 percent. Interest is paid on September 1 and March 1. Potter Corporation uses the interest method to amortize the premium.

1. Prepare an amortization schedule for the first three semiannual periods.
2. Prepare journal entries to record the following:
   a. Bond issuance on March 1.
   b. Semiannual interest payment and amortization of premium on September 1.
   c. The year-end adjusting entry to record interest expense and premium amortization.

Amortization schedule; interest method of amortization of discount; year-end adjusting entry.

Check Figure:
Premium to be amortized period 1 $779.60

REAL-WORLD APPLICATIONS

21R-1.
Ryan Small, president of Janis Corporation, has hired you as a financial consultant to analyze three proposals made by the Board of Directors to raise additional funds of $3,000,000.

The Plans

1. Issued 12 percent preferred stock.
2. Issued additional common stock at $10 par.
3. Issue 14 percent, 20-year bonds.

Given

▼ Tax rate, 48 percent.

▼ Estimated corporation earnings, $1,800,000 annually before bond interest.

Assume

▼ Before plan, 300,000 shares of $10 par outstanding all new stock would be issued at par.

Please submit a written recommendation with supporting data to Mr. Small as soon as possible.

21R-2.

The Board of Directors of French Corporation are planning to announce a new 10-year bond issue of $300,000. The contract rate of the bonds is 12 percent. Owing to several delays, the bonds in the marketplace are now 14 percent.

The directors think this bond issue has to raise at least $280,000 in cash to meet its financial needs. As the company's financial consultant, calculate the actual selling price of the bonds and make appropriate written recommendations to the Board of Directors of French regarding the pros and cons of the bond issue.

Given

1. Present value of $1.00 at compound interest for 20 periods at 7 percent equals .2584.

2. Present value of $1.00 received periodically for 20 periods at 7 percent equals 10.5940.

YOU make the call

Critical Thinking/Ethical Case

21R-3.

Alice wants to buy bonds, but her husband, Pete, thinks stocks would be a better deal. Pete was watching a finance show on TV that said stocks would be going up and that now is the time to buy stock. He called Alice over and said, "I told you so." Alice told her husband that it was no time to take a risk with their money. Do you think Pete is correct in his thinking? You make the call. Write down your recommendations to Alice and her husband.

EX-1. [www.moodys.com/moodys/cust/staticcontent/200020000265736. asp?section = rdef] Bonds represent indebtedness of a corporation and are reported on the balance sheet as liabilities. Bonds are usually issued in minimum amounts of $5,000 and may range much higher than that. A bond gets a "rating", similar to a credit rating. This "bond rating" is done by commercial companies like Moody's. You are able to borrow money more easily when you have an excellent credit rating. Companies who rely on bonds as a source of capital are able to borrow more and at more favorable rates when their credit standing is high.

Here you can view the rating codes by which bond issues are assessed. After reviewing these categories. The codes go from Aaa down to C, with Aaa being the highest grade available to the most creditworthy companies. Just as an individual's credit rating may go up or down, corporate credit ratings may also fluctuate. Bond ratings change subject to changes in markets, changing circumstances within a company.

1. Where in the Moody's rating system do bonds begin to become speculative?

2. What are some reasons for the transition to speculative status?

3. What effect does a decreasing rating have on the interest of new issues of bonds from that company?

EX-2. **[http://averages.dowjones.com/djia_cos.html#top]**   In Chapter 20 you became familiar with the companies which comprise the Dow Jones Industrial Averages. Now revisit that site and select a company different from the one you selected before. Go to that company's home page and determine what its bond rating is. Most of the companies will have been rated by Moody's. Some will have been rated by other rating services. Compare the ratings of the different services when this occurs.

CHAPTER 22

Statement of Cash Flows

In January 1999, Jason and Matthew Olim, the two brothers who founded online music store CDNow, published a book entitled "The CDNow Story: Rags to Riches on the Internet." Just a little over one year later, the Olim brothers' saga would be more aptly subtitled "Riches to Rags on the Internet." While it is one of the top five Web sites, with 800,000 daily visitors and almost 4 million customers, CDNow cannot seem to turn customers into cash. Quarterly losses, mainly due to heavy spending on advertising and marketing, steadily outpace revenue and eat into the company's cash. In April 2000, CDNow's shortage of working capital, losses from operations and significant payments due for marketing agreements raised a red flag with their accounting firm, Arthur Anderson. The firm expressed "substantial doubt" about CDNow's survival, and the company's shares tumbled by over 80% to a record low of $3.41 a share.

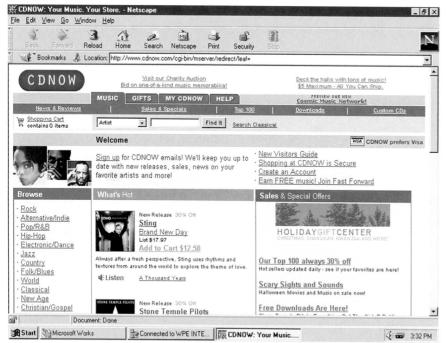

Companies closely monitor **working capital,** the total of current assets that exceed the total of current liabilities. Cash is a significant part of working capital, and positive cash flow is when there is enough cash flowing into a business to meet or exceed all of its expenses, both normal and unexpected. A positive cash flow is as vital to a business's survival as the blood pumping into your heart.

In this chapter you will learn how to prepare a cash flow statement and understand what causes a business's working capital to increase or decrease. Owners, creditors and investors always want to know a company's cash position. Measuring profit is meaningless if you do not have cash flowing into the business.

But what will CDNow do to ease their cash crunch? Unlike traditional companies, dot coms don't usually issue bonds or hit up the bank for a loan. They issue stocks to get the cash they need. At $3.00 a share, CDNow's stock is a bargain for a potential investor. Indeed, Bertelsmann, the German media giant, has stepped in to buy the company for $117 million, or $3.00 a share, plus the assumption of CDNow's 40 million in debt. That should keep the music going for now.

Based on: Anonymous, "Waiting Period on CDNow Ends," *Wall Street Journal,* August 21, 2000, p. A8. Frances Katz, "Cash-Strapped CDNow deserves helping hand," The *Atlanta Journal/the Atlanta Constitution,* April 9, 2000, p. F2. Charles Piller, "CDNow Shares Plummet on Survival 'doubt'; E-commerce: Accountants cite cash crunch at one of Web's most visited sites. Observers see signal of impending shakeout," *The Los Angeles Times,* March 30, 2000, p. C1. Matt Krantz, "E-retailers run low on fuel. Exclusive analysis: Turn profit soon or else," *USA Today,* April 26, 2000, p. 01B.

LEARNING OBJECTIVES

▼ Understanding the purpose of a statement of cash flows. (p. 757)
▼ Preparing the Operating Activities section of the statement of cash flow using the indirect method. (p. 762)
▼ Preparing the Operating Activities section of the statement of cash flow using the direct method. (p. 764)
▼ Preparing a statement of cash flows. (p. 766)

In preceding chapters we analyzed as well as prepared three financial statements. Let's quickly review the purposes of each statement.

▼ Income Statement: For a given period shows the results of the company's operations. The net income or loss results in an increase or decrease to retained earnings.
▼ Statement of retained earnings: Summarizes the changes in retained earnings of a company during a period of time.
▼ Balance sheet: Shows the end-of-period financial position of a company at a particular date.

In this chapter we turn our attention to a fourth major financial statement that is used to better understand the operating, investing, and financing activities of a company. It is called the **statement of cash flows,** and it summarizes the sources and uses of cash by a company during an accounting period. It is easy to compute the change in cash balance by looking at the comparative balance sheet, but just the change in total cash tells us nothing about specific cash transactions. The statement of cash flows not only shows in detail the sources and uses of cash; it also gives readers of the financial statements a good basis for judging the possible future cash flows. Internal users of the financial statements (such as management) can also benefit by understanding how to read the statement of cash flows.

LEARNING UNIT 22-1

STATEMENT OF CASH FLOWS: INDIRECT METHOD

We use as our example in this chapter the Zabel Company, which sells soccer equipment and supplies. To prepare a statement of cash flows, we need to obtain information from the other financial statements prepared for the company: the income statement, the statement of retained earnings and the balance sheet. These statements are shown in Figures 22-1 (p. 758), 22-2 (p. 758), and 22-3 (p. 759). Note that the balance sheet shown in Figure 22-3 is slightly different from the ones we have shown in the past. This one is a **comparative balance sheet,** which shows figures from two separate years side by side. We discuss this type of statement in more detail in Chapter 23.

FIGURE 22-1. Financial
Statement of Zabel

ZABEL COMPANY INCOME STATEMENT FOR YEAR ENDED DECEMBER 31, 2001		
Sales		$190 000 00
Cost of Goods Sold		106 000 00
Gross Profit		$ 84 000 00
Operating Expenses:		
Salaries Expense	$ 51 040 00	
Insurance Expense	7 200 00	
Rent Expense	3 600 00	
Depreciation Expense	11 000 00	
Miscellaneous Expense	1 200 00	
Total Operating Expenses		74 040 00
Net Income		$ 9 960 00

A short way to
remember the activity
classifications

Transactions with cus-
tomers, vendors and employees are operating activities.

Transactions involving the
purchase or sale of plant
assets are investing
activities.

Transactions involving the
creditors or stockholders
are financing activities.

The statement of cash flows consists of three main sections: (1) net cash flows from operating activities, (2) cash flows from investing activities, and (3) cash flows from financing activities. Some of the complexities of this statement are beyond the scope of this text, but the following paragraphs contain a few examples of transactions reported in each of the three sections mentioned above.

Operating activities include selling products or services to customers. **Cash inflows** from operating activities include cash collected from customers. **Cash outflows** from operating activities include paying for merchandise inventory, salaries, rent, and other such expenses.

Investing activities include such things as purchase or sale of plant and equipment, buying stocks and bonds (of other companies), and making loans to other businesses or individuals.

Financing activities include raising money by issuing stocks and bonds, repurchasing of the company's stock, and paying cash dividends to the stockholders.

A fourth classification reported on the statement of cash flows is called **noncash investing and financing activities,** which includes such transactions as issuing shares of stock in exchange for assets such as land and buildings. Although cash is not involved, the event is reported because no other financial statement specifically discloses the transaction. If the stock in the above example was issued for cash (financing activity, a cash increase) and if we used the cash proceeds to purchase land and a building (investing activity, a cash decrease), the event would be disclosed on the statement of cash flows in two separate sections. Because our example is a noncash transaction, it can be reported on the statement of cash flow as a footnote or on a separate schedule listing such transactions.

FIGURE 22-2. Financial
Statement of Zabel

ZABEL COMPANY STATEMENT OF RETAINED EARNINGS FOR YEAR ENDED DECEMBER 31, 2001		
Retained Earnings, January 1, 2001		$ 38 140 00
Net Income for the Year	$ 9 960 00	
Less: Cash Dividends	8 000 00	
Increase in Retained Earnings		1 960 00
Retained Earnings, December 31, 2001		$ 40 100 00

ZABEL COMPANY
COMPARATIVE BALANCE SHEET
AS OF DECEMBER 31, 2000, AND DECEMBER 31, 2001

FIGURE 22-3. Comparative Balance Sheet for Zabel

Assets	2001	2000	Increase (Decrease)
Current Assets:			
Cash	$ 2 900 00	$ 2 480 00	$ 420 00
Accounts Receivable	19 560 00	14 720 00	4 840 00
Merchandise Inventory	30 000 00	32 000 00	(2 000 00)
Prepaid Insurance	600 00	400 00	200 00
Total Current Assets	$ 53 060 00	$ 49 600 00	$ 3 460 00
Plant and Equipment:			
Office Equipment	$ 96 000 00	$ 66 000 00	$ 30 000 00
Accum. Dep., Office Equipment	(37 200 00)	(26 200 00)	(11 000 00)
Total Plant and Equipment	$ 58 800 00	$ 39 800 00	$ 19 000 00
Total Assets	$111 860 00	$ 89 400 00	$ 22 460 00
Liabilities			
Current Liabilities:			
Notes Payable—Short Term (used to purchase inventory)	$ 17 400 00	$ 14 800 00	$ 2 600 00
Accounts Payable	360 00	460 00	(100 00)
Total Current Liabilities	$ 17 760 00	$ 15 260 00	$ 2 500 00
Long-Term Liabilities:			
Long-Term Note Payable	$ 28 000 00	$ 20 000 00	$ 8 000 00
Total Liabilities	$ 45 760 00	$ 35 260 00	$ 10 500 00
Stockholders' Equity			
Common Stock, $10 par	$ 11 000 00	$ 10 000 00	$ 1 000 00
Paid-in Capital in Excess of Par	15 000 00	6 000 00	9 000 00
Retained Earnings	40 100 00	38 140 00	1 960 00
Total Stockholders' Equity	$ 66 100 00	54 140 00	$ 11 960 00
Total Liabilities and Stockholders' Equity	$111 860 00	$ 89 400 00	$ 22 460 00

CASH FLOWS FROM OPERATING ACTIVITIES: INDIRECT METHOD

A business needs a positive cash flow to survive. A company's ability to raise money from financing activities (issue stocks, bonds, or long-term notes) is often tied to its success in generating cash flow from its operations. The operating activities section of the statement of cash flows is therefore of great importance to potential investors and creditors.

This section introduces a procedure known as the **indirect method** of reporting cash flows from operating activities. Note that the distinction between the indirect method and the direct method (discussed in the next learning unit) only applies to the operating activities section of the statement of cash flows.

In the indirect method we are converting the net income on the income statement from the accrual basis to the cash basis. As we have been learning throughout this text, businesses normally usually report their net income on the accrual basis, which places the primary emphasis on *when* the revenues are earned and *when* the expenses are incurred.

The indirect method's name comes from the way we view the income statement. We begin with the bottom line of the income statement and work backwards until we have computed net cash flow from operating activities. We begin the operating activities section with the net income as reported on the income statement (see Figure 22-2) and convert it from the accrual basis to the cash basis. The following illustration shows how the net cash flows from operating activities is computed for the Zabel Company using the indirect method.

ZABEL COMPANY STATEMENT OF CASH FLOW (INDIRECT METHOD) FOR YEAR ENDED DECEMBER 31, 2001		
Cash Flows from Operating Activities:		
Net Income from Operations	$ 9 960 00	
Add (deduct) items to Convert Net Income from		
Accrual Basis to Cash Basis:		
Depreciation Expense	1 100 000	
Increase in Accounts Receivable	(4 840 00)	
Decrease in Merchandise Inventory	2 000 00	
Increase in Prepaid Insurance	(200 00)	
Increase in Notes Payable (Short Term)	2 600 00	
Decrease in Accounts Payable	(100 00)	
Net Cash Provided by Operating Activities		$ 20 420 00

In this example, the first item to be added to the net income is depreciation expense. The depreciation is *added back* to net income because it was subtracted out as an expense on the income statement to derive the $9,960 net income. You will recall that when depreciation is recorded, the entry involves a debit to depreciation expense and a credit to accumulated depreciation. Neither of these accounts involves cash. Because depreciation is therefore a "noncash" expense, it is added back to net income when using the indirect method. Next, each of the current assets and current liabilities are examined to determine their effect on cash flow.

The aid sheet shown in Figure 22-4 is useful for remembering whether to add or subtract a given item on the statement of cash flow. Alternatively, some instructors prefer the simple opposite effect/same effect approach. For current assets, cash flow has the *opposite effect,* whereas for current liabilities, the cash flow has the *same effect.* For example, the increase in accounts receivable (a current asset) must be subtracted whereas the increase in Short-Term Notes Payable (a current liability) would be added.

After each of the above items is listed with its proper sign, the entire list is combined with net income to compute the net cash provided by operating activities of $20,420. The term *net cash provided* by operating activities is commonly used if the result is positive, whereas *net cash used* in operating activities indicates that the result is negative. As you might imagine, the goal is to have a strong posi-

FIGURE 22-4. Aid Sheet for Converting from Accrual Basis to Cash Basis	Add to Net Income If This Account Has:	Deduct from Net Income If This Account Has:
Current Assets	DECREASED	INCREASED
Current Liabilities	INCREASED	DECREASED

tive cash flow from operating activities. A negative operating cash flow cannot be tolerated for very long. Investors and creditors would hesitate to provide funds to a firm that cannot generate a positive cash flow from its operating activities.

CASH FLOWS FROM INVESTING ACTIVITIES

The cash flows from investing activities section of the statement of cash flows includes (1) the purchase and sale of other companies' stocks and bonds, (2) the buying and disposal of plant assets, and (3) making loans to other parties. We analyze the noncurrent accounts to find these activities. For example, the following transactions would be recorded in this section:

1. Sale or purchase of equipment.
2. Sale or purchase of land.
3. Cash spent to invest in other companies' stocks and bonds.
4. Cash received from sales of stock or bond investments.
5. Loaning cash to borrowers.

On the balance sheet for Zabel Company, we see an increase in plant and equipment from 2000 to 2001 of $30,000. Thus the cash outflow for equipment would be reported as follows:

Cash Flows from Investing Activities		
Purchase of Plant Asset	$ (30 0 0 0 00)	
Net Cash Flows Used in Investing Activities		$ (30 0 0 0 00)

CASH FLOWS FROM FINANCING ACTIVITIES

The cash flows from financing activities section of the statement of cash flows records transactions such as the following:

1. Issuance of long-term notes and bonds.
2. Issuance of common stock.
3. Purchasing and reissuing treasury stock.
4. Payment of cash dividends.
5. Retirement of bonds.

From the comparative balance sheet for Zabel Company, we see that the Long-Term Notes Payable account increased by $8,000. This increase is shown as a source (increase) of cash, because an increase in Long-Term Notes Payable means that more cash has been borrowed and therefore has been received by the business. Also, note that the issuance of $10,000 of common stock has *increased* the cash flows, whereas the payment of $8,000 in dividends results in a *decrease* in cash flows. The end result is that net cash provided by financing activities has increased by $10,000, as shown:

Cash Flows from Financing Activities		
Issuance of Long-Term Note	$ 8 0 0 0 00	
Issuance of Common Stock	10 0 0 0 00	
Payment of Dividends	(8 0 0 0 00)	
Net Cash Flows Provided by Financing Activities		$ 10 0 0 0 00

To arrive at net change in cash for the overall statement, we perform the following calculation:

Net Cash Provided by Operating Activities	$ 20,420
− Cash Flow Used by Investing Activities	(30,000)
+ Net Cash Provided by Financing Activities	10,000
= Net Increase in Cash	$ 420

Figure 22-5 shows all three sections together in the statement of cash flows.

Note that at the bottom of the statement of cash flows the cash has increased by $420 (just as shown for cash on the comparative balance sheet), but this report gives us a complete breakdown of just what caused the cash to increase by $420.

The statement of cash flows is helpful in evaluating, comparing, and predicting future cash flows. By dividing this report into three sections, creditors as well as investors can judge how cash flows from operations compared with those from investing or financing activities. For example, in the case of Zabel Company, an investor or a creditor can see that there has been a substantial reduction in cash in one area (investing), only to be offset by an increase in cash from the other areas (operating and financing).

A second approach, known as the direct method, gives a more useful presentation of cash flows from operating activities. Although this method gives more understandable data, many firms think it much easier to use the indirect method to prepare the reports. Regardless of method used, the cash flows from operating activities will be the same. The direct method is illustrated in Learning Unit 22-2.

FIGURE 22-5. Statement of Cash Flow–Indirect Method

ZABEL COMPANY STATEMENT OF CASH FLOWS—INDIRECT METHOD FOR YEAR ENDED DECEMBER 31, 2001		
Net Cash Flows from Operating Activities		
Net Income	$ 9 960 00	
Add (Deduct) Items to Convert Net Income		
from Accrual Basis to Cash Basis:		
Depreciation Expense	11 000 00	
Increase in Accounts Receivable	(4 840 00)	
Decrease in Merchandise Inventory	2 000 00	
Increase in Prepaid Insurance	(200 00)	
Increase in Short-Term Notes Payable	2 600 00	
Decrease in Accounts Payable	(100 00)	
Net Cash Flows from Operating Activities		$ 20 420 00
Cash Flows from Investing Activities		
Purchase of Plant Asset	$(30 000 00)	
Net Cash Flows Used by Investing Activities		(30 000 00)
Cash Flows from Financing Activities		
Issuance of Long-Term Note	$ 8 000 00	
Issuance of Common Stock	10 000 00	
Payment of Dividends	(8 000 00)	
Net Cash Provided by Financing Activities		10 000 00
Net Increase in Cash		$ 420 00
Beginning Balance of Cash		2 480 00
Ending Balance of Cash		$ 2 900 00

LEARNING UNIT 22-1 REVIEW

AT THIS POINT you should be able to

- ▼ Explain the components of a statement of cash flows. (p. 757)
- ▼ Calculate net cash flows from operating activities using the indirect method. (p. 759)
- ▼ Calculate net cash flows from investing activities. (p. 761)
- ▼ Calculate net cash flows from financing activities. (p. 761)
- ▼ Prepare a complete statement of cash flows using the indirect method. (p. 762)

SELF REVIEW QUIZ 22-1

(The forms you need are on page 130 of the *Study Guide and Working Papers*.)
From the following, calculate net cash flows from operating activities.

JOHNSON COMPANY INCOME STATEMENT FOR YEAR ENDED DECEMBER 31, 2001		
Sales		$150 000 00
Cost of Goods Sold		90 000 00
Gross Profit		$ 60 000 00
Operating Expenses:		
Salaries Expense	$40 000 00	
Depreciation Expense	3 000 00	
Advertising Expense	8 000 00	
Total Operating Expenses:		51 000 00
Net Income		$ 9 000 00

Additional Data	2001	2000
Accounts Receivable	$ 10 600 00	$ 4 000 00
Merchandise Inventory	10 000 00	12 000 00
Prepaid Advertising	1 400 00	3 000 00
Accounts Payable	18 000 00	15 000 00
Salaries Payable	1 800 00	1 900 00

Solution to Self-Review Quiz 22-1

Net Cash Flow from Operating Activities:	
Net Income	
Add (deduct) Items to Convert Net Income to Cash	$ 9 000 00
Basis from the Accrual Basis:	
Depreciation Expense	3 000 00
Increase in Accounts Receivable	(6 600 00)
Decrease in Merchandise Inventory	2 000 00
Decrease in Prepaid Advertising	$ 1 600 00
Increase in Accounts Payable	3 000 00
Decrease in Salaries Payable	(1 00 00)
Net Cash Flow from Operating Activities:	$ 11 900 00

A simple way to identify whether a particular change has a positive or negative cash effect:

Current Asset Increase: Negative effect on cash because more of your cash has been spent on that asset compared with the previous balance sheet date. Example: Inventory increasing means that more of our dollars are tied up in the inventory.

Current Asset Decrease: Positive effect on cash because less of your cash has been spent on that asset compared with the previous balance sheet date. Example: Inventory decreasing means that fewer of our dollars are tied up in the inventory.

Current Liability Increase: Positive effect on cash because compared with a year ago, less of the liability has been paid off (leaving more cash in our pockets).

Current Liability Decrease: Negative effect on cash because although we do not owe as much as we did a year ago, we have paid more of it off (and have less cash still in our pockets).

As indicated in Learning Unit 22-1, cash flows from operating activities include the cash effects of transactions such as selling goods or services to customers and paying for merchandise inventory and operating expenses. Many accountants prefer the **direct method** of reporting the cash flows from operating activities. This approach provides useful information and is easily understood by the users of the financial statements.

The direct method requires listing major groups of operating cash receipts and cash payments. We first compute cash receipts from customers. Because most firms sell products or services on account as well as for cash, the sales figure on the income statement is not the same as total cash received. We analyze accounts receivable and combine its change (increase or decrease) with the sales figure from the income statement. If accounts receivable has *increased,* there is a negative impact on cash, so the amount of the increase is *subtracted* from sales. If accounts receivable has *decreased,* there is a positive effect on cash, so the amount of the decrease is *added* to sales. Thus for computing cash received from customers, we can treat accounts receivable as we did in the indirect method by using the *opposite effect.*

The same reasoning applies to cash payments, except that because these are outflows of cash, any change with a *positive* cash effect is *subtracted* (because a positive effect means less cash to pay out). Any change with a *negative* cash effect is *added* (because a negative effect means more cash to pay out).

Our first example of an operating **cash outflow** is cash paid for merchandise inventory. We begin the computation with cost of goods sold and then adjust by the change in the merchandise inventory account. A further adjustment is necessary to account for changes in accounts payable and short-term notes payable (if notes were used to pay for inventory, as in our example). Specifically, if the balance of merchandise inventory has increased, there would be a *negative* cash effect that would be *added* in the computation of cash paid for merchandise. If merchandise inventory has decreased, it is a *positive* cash effect that is *subtracted* to compute cash paid for merchandise. After adjusting for inventory changes, if accounts payable has increased, the cash effect is positive and thus would be subtracted from the computation. If accounts payable has decreased, the cash effect is negative and thus would be added to the calculation. The changes in short-term notes payable (assuming notes were used to pay for inventory) would be analyzed in the same way as accounts payable.

Cash paid for operating expenses is handled in much the same way as cash paid for merchandise inventory. Cash paid for salaries, for instance, is computed by combining the change in salaries payable with the amount of salary expense from the income statement. If salaries payable has increased (positive cash effect), the amount of increase is subtracted from salary expense. If this account has decreased (negative cash effect), the amount of the decrease would be added to the salary expense.

For expenses involving a prepayment (such as prepaid insurance), the insurance expense balance would be combined with the change in prepaid insurance. If prepaid insurance had increased (negative cash effect), the amount of the change would be added to insurance expense to compute

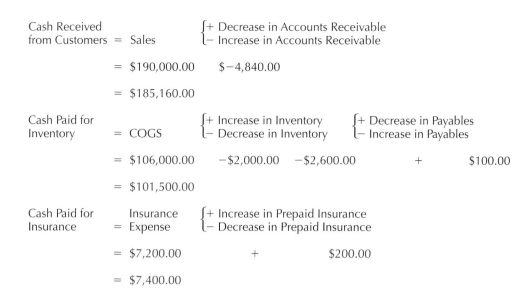

Cash Received
from Customers = Sales { + Decrease in Accounts Receivable
{ − Increase in Accounts Receivable

= $190,000.00 $−4,840.00

= $185,160.00

Cash Paid for
Inventory = COGS { + Increase in Inventory { + Decrease in Payables
{ − Decrease in Inventory { − Increase in Payables

= $106,000.00 −$2,000.00 −$2,600.00 + $100.00

= $101,500.00

Cash Paid for
Insurance = Insurance
Expense { + Increase in Prepaid Insurance
{ − Decrease in Prepaid Insurance

= $7,200.00 + $200.00

= $7,400.00

Note: The other items on Zabel's Net Cash Flows from Operating Activities section do not require any adjustment, because there were no current asset or current liability changes from the income statement figures for such items salaries, rent, and miscellaneous expenses.

cash paid for insurance. If prepaid insurance had decreased (positive cash effect), the amount of the change would be subtracted from insurance expense.

We now look at an example of the computation of net cash flow from operating activities. The Zabel Company computes cash received from customers by combining the sales figure from the income statement with the change in accounts receivable from the comparative balance sheet (see Figures 22-1 and 22-3). Sales is $190,000, and accounts receivable has *increased* by $4,840. Because the increase in accounts receivable means a negative cash effect (more of our money is currently in the pockets of our customers!), it is *subtracted* from sales to arrive at the cash collected from customers figure of $185,160. This computation is illustrated in Figure 22-6.

A second computation in Figure 22-6 shows cash paid for inventory. The cost of goods sold figure is adjusted for changes in merchandise inventory, accounts payable, and short-term notes payable (if such notes are used to finance inventory). In our example, cost of goods sold of $106,000 is adjusted by subtracting the decrease in inventory, subtracting the increase in short-term notes payable, and adding the decrease in accounts payable to arrive at the cash paid for inventory figure of $101,500.

Cash paid for insurance is also illustrated in Figure 22-6 by adding the decrease in prepaid insurance to the insurance expense to yield $7,400 for cash paid for insurance.

Figure 22-7 (p. 766) shows the complete statement of cash flows for the Zabel Company using the direct method. Note that the investing activities and financing activities sections are the same as Figure 22-5, because the distinction between the indirect and direct methods only applies to the cash flows from operating activities section.

To summarize, we can still use the "same effect/opposite effect" reasoning mentioned in the previous learning unit. Current asset cash effects are always the opposite effect, whereas current liability cash effects are always the same effect.

FIGURE 22-7. Statement of
Cash Flows–Direct Method

ZABEL COMPANY STATEMENT OF CASH FLOWS—DIRECT METHOD FOR YEAR ENDED DECEMBER 31, 2001			
Net Cash Flows from Operating Activities			
Cash Received from Customers			$185 160 00
Cash Paid for Merchandise Inventory	$(101 500 00)		
Cash Paid for Salaries	51 040 00		
Cash Paid for Insurance	(7 400 00)		
Cash Paid for Rent	(3 600 00)		
Cash Paid for Miscellaneous Expenses	(1 200 00)		
Total Cash Paid for Operating Activities			(164 740 00)
Net Cash Flows from Operating Activities			$ 20 420 00
Cash Flows from Investing Activities			
Purchase of Plant Asset	$(30 000 00)		
Net Cash Used by Investing Activities			(30 000 00)
Cash Flows from Financing Activities			
Issuance of Long-Term Note	$ 8 000 00		
Issuance of Common Stock	10 000 00		
Payment of Dividends	(8 000 00)		
Net Cash Provided by Financing Activities			10 000 00
Net Increase in Cash			$ 420 00
Beginning Balance of Cash			2 480 00
Ending Balance of Cash			$ 2 900 00

LEARNING UNIT 22-2 REVIEW

AT THIS POINT you should be able to

▼ Explain the difference between the direct method and the indirect method. (p. 764)
▼ Compute the net cash flows from operating activities section of the statement of cash flow. (p. 766)

SELF REVIEW QUIZ 22-2

(The forms you need are on page 131 of the *Study Guide and Working Papers.*)
   Using the data from Self-Review Quiz 22-1 on page 763, show in good form the cash flows from operating activities section of the statement of cash flows for the Johnson Company using the direct method.

Solution to Self-Review Quiz 22-2

Net Cash Flow from Operating Activities:		
Cash Received from Customers		$143 40 0 00
Cash Paid for Merchandise Inventory	$ 85 0 0 0 00	
Cash Paid for Salaries	40 1 0 0 00	
Cash Paid for Advertising	6 4 0 0 00	
Total Cash Paid for Operating Activities		131 5 0 0 00
Net Cash Flows from Operating Activities:		$ 11 9 0 0 00

Explanations of above computations:

Cash from Customer = Sales − Increase in Accounts Receivable

Cash Paid for Inventory = CGS − Decrease in Inventory − Increase in Accounts Payable

Cash Paid for Salaries = Salary Expense + Decrease in Salaries Payable

Cash Paid for Advertising = Advertising Expense − Decrease in Prepaid Advertising

SUMMARY OF KEY POINTS

Learning Unit 22-1

1. In the statement of cash flows, net change in cash equals net cash from operating activities plus or minus cash from investing activities plus or minus cash from financing activities.

2. In figuring the net cash from operating activities section of the statement, it is necessary to convert the net income from the income statement from the accrual basis to the cash basis. This change affects the following accounts: Depreciation Expense, Accounts Receivable, Inventory, Prepaid Expenses, Accounts Payable, and Short-Term Notes Payable. Note that we are analyzing current assets and current liabilities to see their effect on net income. This approach to computing cash flows from operating activities is known as the indirect method.

3. Cash flows from investing activities include such things as purchase and sale of stocks and bonds (of other companies), buying and selling plant assets, and lending money to other parties.

4. Cash flows from financing activities include such things as issuing and repaying long-term notes and bonds, issuing common stock, buying back common stock (treasury stock), and paying dividends.

Learning Unit 22-2

1. An alternative way of preparing the net cash from operating activities section of the statement is called the direct method.

2. The direct method requires listing separately the major categories of cash inflows and outflows. The major cash inflow for most firms is the cash received from customers, which is computed by adjusting the sales figure by the change in accounts receivable.

3. Cash outflows under the operating activities section include cash paid for inventory, cash paid for salaries, and cash paid for other operating expenses. In each case, the appropriate income statement figure is adjusted by the changes in one or more current asset or current liability accounts.

4. Regardless of the method selected, the net cash from operating activities will be the same. Also, the distinction between the direct and indirect methods only applies to net cash from operating activities. The investing and financing sections remain the same.

KEY TERMS

Cash inflow Any increase in cash is called a cash inflow or a source of cash. When listing the total for a major section of the statement of cash flows, if cash is increased, the figure is often described as "cash provided" by operating activities (or by investing activities or financing activities).

Cash outflow A decrease in cash is called a cash outflow or a use of cash. When listing a total for a major section of the statement of cash flows, if cash has decreased, the figure is often described as "cash used" in operating activities (or in investing activities or financing activities).

Comparative balance sheet A balance sheet listing financial condition for two or more years in a side-by-side manner. This format allows the reader to make quick comparisons between the two balance sheet dates.

Direct method One of two methods of preparing the net cash flow from operating activities section of the statement of cash flows. Each of the major areas of sources and uses of cash for operations is detailed separately.

Financing activities   Activities relating to raising money from investors and creditors such as the issuance of stocks and bonds and long-term notes. Also, repurchase of outstanding stock and retiring bonds and notes as well as paying dividends.

Indirect method   One of two methods of preparing the net cash flow from the operating activities section of the statement of cash flows. Involves converting the accrual basis net income figure from the income statement to the cash basis net income.

Investing activities   Activities such as purchase and sale of plant and equipment and placing excess cash in stocks, bonds, and notes of other companies.

Noncash investing and financing activities   Transactions such as the issuance of stock in exchange for land would be listed in a footnote or a separate schedule to the statement of cash flow, because such transactions would not be separately reported on any other financial statement.

Operating activities   Those activities most closely related to conducting the business for which the enterprise was established. Activities such as selling merchandise and services to customers and paying salaries and other expenses needed to continue earning the operating revenue are classified as operating activities.

Statement of cash flows   A financial report that provides a detailed breakdown of the specific increases and decreases in cash during an accounting period. It helps readers of the statement evaluate past performance as well as predict future cash flows of the business.

BLUEPRINT: STATEMENT OF CASH FLOWS

Indirect Method

Net Cash Flows from Operating Activities		
Net Income		XXX
Add (Deduct) Items to Convert Net		
Income to Cash Basis:		
Depreciation Expense		XX
Increase in Accounts Receivable		(XX)
Decrease in Inventory		XX
Increase in Prepaid Expenses		(XX)
Increase in Accounts Payable		XX
Decrease in Salaries Payable		(XX)
Net Cash Flows from Operating Activities		XXX
Cash Flows from Investing Activities		
Purchase of Investment Securities	(XXX)	
Purchase of Equipment	(XXX)	
Sale of Land	XXX	
Cash Used by Investing Activities		(XXX)
Cash Flows from Financing Activities		
Issuance of Common Stock	XX	
Payment of Dividends	(X)	
Cash Provided by Financing Activities		XX
Net Increase in Cash		XXX
Beginning Balance of Cash		XXX
Ending Balance of Cash		XXX

Direct Method

Net Cash Flows from Operating Activities		
Cash Received from Customers		XXX
Cash Paid for Inventory	XXX	
Cash Paid for Salaries	XX	
Cash Paid for Insurance	X	
Cash Paid for Rent	X	
Cash Paid for Other Expenses	XX	
Total Cash Paid for Operations		XX
Net Cash Flows from Operating Activities		XXX

QUESTIONS, MINI EXERCISES, EXERCISES, AND PROBLEMS

Discussion Questions

1. List the three main sections of the statement of cash flows.
2. Explain how net cash flows from operating activities is calculated using the indirect method.
3. Explain how net cash flows from operating activities is calculated using the direct method.
4. The issuance of stock is an investing activity. Agree or disagree. Why?
5. Explain how a creditor might analyze a statement of cash flows.
6. Explain what is meant by financing activities.
7. Explain why depreciation is *added* to net income when using the indirect method.

Mini Exercises

(The forms you need are on page 132 of the *Study Guide and Working Papers*).

Calculating Net Cash Flows from Operating Activities: Indirect Method

1. The following accounts showed an increase or a decrease from the comparative balance sheet. Explain which account will be added to net income and which will be subtracted in calculating net cash flows for operating activities.

   a. Accounts Receivable: increase.
   b. Inventory: decrease.
   c. Short-Term Notes Payable: increase.
   d. Accounts Payable: decrease.

2. From the following, calculate the net cash flow from operating activities:

	2000	2001
Merchandise Inventory	$2,000	$2,500
Accounts Receivable	500	700
Prepaid Insurance	400	300
Accounts Payable	1,000	600
Salaries Payable	500	700

For the year ended 2001:
Net Income $1,900
Depreciation Expense   500

Calculating Net Cash Flows from Operating Activities: Direct Method

3. Using the data from Mini Exercise 2 plus the following additional information, compute net cash flows from operating activities using the direct method.

Sales			$ 800000
Cost of Goods Sold			240000
Gross Profit			$ 560000
Expenses:			
Depreciation Expense	$ 50000		
Salary Expense	220000		
Insurance Expense	70000		
Miscellaneous Expense	30000		
Total Expenses		370000	
Net Income		$ 190000	

Calculating Cash Flows from Financing Activities

4. From the following, calculate net cash flows from financing activities:

Payments of Dividends $ 6,000
Issuance of Common Stock   2,000
Issuance of Long-Term Note   14,000

Calculating Change in Cash

5. Given the following, calculate net change in cash:

Net Cash Flows from Operating Activities $3,000
Net Cash Used by Investing Activities   (1,000)
Net Cash Provided by Financing Activities   600

Exercises

(The forms you need are on page 133 of the *Study Guide and Working Papers*).

22-1. Complete the following chart regarding the indirect method.

Add to Net Income		Subtract from Net Income
?	Decrease	Increase
?	Increase	Decrease

Converting to Cash Basis:
Indirect Method.

22-2. From the following, calculate the net cash flow from operating activities (use the indirect method):

Net Cash Flow from
Operating Activities: Indirect
Method.

	2000	2001
Accounts Receivable	$5,900	$7,900
Prepaid Insurance	900	850
Accounts Payable	4,000	4,600
Salaries Payable	1,200	2,200

For the year ended 2001:
Net Income $17,000
Depreciation Exp: 4,000

22-3. From the following, calculate the net cash flow from operating activities (use the direct method):

Sales	$9,000
Cost of Goods Sold	4,400
Salary Expense	1,600
Insurance Expense	800
Other Expenses (all cash)	1,000

Changes in current assets and liabilities:

Accounts Receivable increased by $600.
Inventory increased by $500.
Accounts Payable increased by $100.
Salaries Payable decreased by $200.
Prepaid Insurance decreased by $150.

2-4. For each of the following transactions, identify the appropriate section of the statement of cash flows (OA = Operating, IA = Investing, FA = Financing, and NC = Noncash).

_____ **a.** Sold merchandise to customers.

_____ **b.** Purchase of equipment.

_____ **c.** Buy stocks of another corporation.

_____ **d.** Pay dividends to stockholders.

_____ **e.** Paid salaries to employees.

_____ **f.** Issue stock in exchange for equipment.

Group A Problems

(The forms you need are on pages 134–135 of the *Study Guide and Working Papers*.)

22A-1. From the following income statement, balance sheet, and additional data for Dent Company, prepare a statement of cash flows using the indirect method.

DENT COMPANY INCOME STATEMENT FOR THE YEAR ENDED DECEMBER 31, 2001		
Sales		$ 95 5 0 0 00
Cost of Goods Sold		69 1 0 0 00
Gross Profit		$ 27 4 0 0 00
Operating Expenses:		
Rent Expense	$ 7 5 0 0 00	
Depreciation Expense	7 0 0 0 00	
Salaries Expense	6 6 0 0 00	
Miscellaneous Expense	3 2 0 0 00	
Total Operating Expenses		24 3 0 0 00
Net Income		$ 3 1 0 0 00

DENT COMPANY BALANCE SHEET DECEMBER 31, 2001		
Assets	2001	2000
Current Assets:		
Cash	$ 3 4 0 0 00	$ 2 6 0 0 00
Accounts Receivable, Net	5 6 0 0 00	4 5 0 0 00
Merchandise Inventory	2 2 0 0 00	2 0 0 0 00
Prepaid Rent	1 0 0 0 00	1 2 0 0 00
Total Current Assets	$ 12 2 0 0 00	$ 10 3 0 0 00
Plant and Equipment:		
Store Equipment	$ 58 0 0 0 00	$ 50 0 0 0 00
Accum. Dep., Store Equipment	(12 0 0 0 00)	(5 0 0 0 00)
Total Plant and Equipment	$ 46 0 0 0 00	$ 45 0 0 0 00
Total Assets	$ 58 2 0 0 00	$ 55 3 0 0 00
Liabilities		
Current Liabilities:		
Notes Payable—Short Term	$ 6 8 0 0 00	$ 5 2 0 0 00
Accounts Payable	4 4 0 0 00	4 8 0 0 00
Total Current Liabilities	$ 11 2 0 0 00	$ 10 0 0 0 00
Long-Term Liabilities:		
Bonds Payable	$ 12 5 0 0 00	$ 15 0 0 0 00
Total Liabilities	$ 23 7 0 0 00	$ 25 0 0 0 00
Stockholders' Equity		
Common Stock, $1 par	$ 22 5 0 0 00	$ 20 0 0 0 00
Retained Earnings	12 0 0 0 00	10 3 0 0 00
Total Stockholders' Equity	$ 34 5 0 0 00	$ 30 3 0 0 00
Total Liabilities and Stockholders' Equity	$ 58 2 0 0 00	$ 55 3 0 0 00

Additional Data:

1. All Plant and Equipment was purchased in cash.
2. Sold additional 2,500 shares of stock for cash at par.
3. A $1,400 dividend was declared and paid.
4. Short-term notes used to finance inventory.

22A-2. From the financial statements and additional information provided in Problem 22A-1 for the Dent Company, prepare a statement of cash flows using the direct method.

> Statement of cash flows: direct method.

Group B Problems

(The forms you need are on pages 134–135 of the *Study Guide and Working Papers*.)

22B-1. From the following income statement, balance sheet, and additional data for Blumer Company (p. 774), prepare a statement of cash flows using the indirect method.

> Statement of cash flows: indirect method.

BLUMER COMPANY
INCOME STATEMENT
FOR THE YEAR ENDED DECEMBER 31, 2001

Sales			$ 36 000 00
Cost of Goods Sold			25 000 00
Gross Profit			$ 11 000 00
Operating Expenses:			
Depreciation Expense—Equipment	$	80 000	
Depreciation Expense—Machinery		50 000	
Advertising Expense		66 000	
Salaries Expense		1 80 000	
Miscellaneous Expense		3 60 000	
Total Operating Expenses			7 36 000
Net Income			$ 3 64 000

BLUMER COMPANY
BALANCE SHEET
DECEMBER 31, 2001

Assets	2001	2000
Current Assets:		
Cash	$ 2 04 000	$ 54 000
Accounts Receivable, Net	2 68 000	2 91 000
Merchandise Inventory	3 20 000	2 43 000
Total Current Assets	$ 7 92 000	$ 5 88 000
Plant and Equipment:		
Office Equipment, Net	$ 6 03 000	$ 4 53 000
Machinery, Net	4 83 000	3 03 000
Land	1 18 000	48 000
Total Plant and Equipment	$ 12 04 000	$ 8 04 000
Total Assets	$ 19 96 000	$ 13 92 000
Liabilities		
Current Liabilities:		
Notes Payable—Short Term	$ 2 08 000	$ 1 98 000
Accounts Payable	10 000	15 000
Total Current Liabilities	$ 2 18 000	$ 2 13 000
Long-Term Liabilities:		
Mortgage Payable	$ 2 12 000	$ 1 77 000
Total Liabilities	$ 4 30 000	$ 3 90 000
Stockholders' Equity		
Common Stock, $1 par	$ 9 53 000	$ 7 53 000
Retained Earnings	6 13 000	2 49 000
Total Stockholders' Equity	$ 15 66 000	$ 10 02 000
Total Liabilities and Stockholders' Equity	$ 19 96 000	$ 13 92 000

Additional Data:

1. All increases in Plant and Equipment were paid for in cash.
2. No dividend was declared in 2001.
3. Sold 2,000 shares of stock for cash at par value.

Hint: Office Equipment and Machinery are recorded at *net* on the balance sheet. Be sure to add back depreciation expense to the cost of the assets in 2001 to compute the actual cost of the additional assets purchased.

22B-2. From the financial statements and additional information provided in Problem 22B-1 for the Blumer Company, prepare a statement of cash flows using the direct method.

> Statement of cash flows: direct method.

REAL-WORLD APPLICATIONS

22R-1.

Diane Clubb is trying to convert income statement items from an accrual basis to a cash basis. Accounts receivable at the beginning of the year totaled $205,000. At the end of the year accounts receivable amounted to $240,000. On the income statement using accrual accounting, sales were $360,000. Depreciation expense is $18,000 on the accrual income statement.

Diane calculates her cash received from customers to be $305,000. Do you accept her calculation? What written recommendations could you suggest to Diane? How would she calculate the amount of cash paid for advertising if advertising expense was listed as $6,000 and the prepaid advertising account showed a decrease of $400?

22R-2.

Pat Kinne is trying to calculate how much cash is being paid to suppliers of her firm's inventory during 2001. Cost of goods sold was reported at $190,500. Pat thinks she needs more data than are provided. From the following facts, could you show Pat how to calculate cash paid to suppliers as well as explain whether this method of computation is a part of the direct method or the indirect method?

	12/31/2001	12/31/2000
Accounts Receivable	$39,000	$37,000
Merchandise Inventory	50,400	53,000
Accounts Payable	28,500	30,700
Notes Payable (used to buy Merchandise Inventory)	17,000	15,000
Salaries Payable	11,000	11,200

YOU make the call

Critical Thinking/Ethics Case

22R-3.

Risch Company each year prepares an income statement and balance sheet. Tom Martin, the controller, issued a memo to Debbie Kreiger, vice president, that the company should prepare a statement of cash flows. Debbie called the controller and told him that there is no way she will let a cash flow statement be published, that this type of information is for internal purposes only, and that the public has no right to these data. She said that the competition would kill them if they got this information. Do you agree with Debbie's position or with Tom's? Write your recommendation to Dave Risch, the chief executive officer.

INTERNET EXERCISES

EX-1. **[www.hp.com/hpinfo/investor/99annrep/financialstatements/ccscf/htm]**
Here is a typical Statement of Cash Flows. It is important in the study of accounting and in preparation of financial statements to understand the uniformity that goes into them. This makes the reading and analysis by knowledgeable users much easier. Imagine how confusing it would be if HP had one way to prepare the statement, Microsoft had another, and Apple had yet another way.

This uniformity of format and content also is a good indicator that textbooks do approach the "real world" of accounting! The only difference is the complexity of the statements that are published in the "real world".

The HP Statement of Cash Flows has two significant items in it that are not in the examples in your text. What are they?

EX-2. **[http://www.hp.com/hpinfo/investor/99annrep/financialstatements/ ccscf/htm]** In a Statement of Cash Flows the amounts invested in equity securities (stocks) are shown as investing activities. The amounts received as from the investments of others into our company's stock is a financing activity.

In the operating section of the HP Statement of Cash Flows is a category entitled "Other, Net" which provided $213,000,000 to HP's operating cash. Frequently this amount includes the Interest Earned on receivables and the Dividend Income. At first glance this seems inconsistent with the idea of investing and financing activities. The difference is subtle. Why do you think the earnings on investments are lumped into operating cash?

CHAPTER 23

Analyzing Financial Statements

It's the newest self-indulgence spurred by the booming economy, the increasing sophistication of America's palate, and the New Age quest for serenity: a perfectly brewed pot of tea, preferably a premium tea like Tealuxe's Blue Flower Earl Grey or Blood Orange Sencha.

In 1996 Bostonians Bruce Fernie and his wife, Katherine Walsh, founded Tealuxe-A Tea Bar in Harvard Square. Their mission — to remove tea's sick room and hoity-toity connotations and bring it to the masses, much the

way Starbucks brought premium coffee to every corner. And, in fulfilling this mission Fernie and Walsh are brewing up some handsome profits. According to the Tea Council, the business of tea has doubled in the last decade from $2 billion to $4 billion, and sales of premium teas, such as those sold by Tealuxe, are growing at an annual rate of 30–50%. "Sales were immediately double and triple what we had anticipated," says Fernie, of Tealuxe's success. In 1999 the company expanded from a 600 sq. foot warehouse to 6,000 feet for storing all their teas and tea paraphernalia. In 2000, Tealuxe expanded to four New York City locations and plan to bring the grand total of their tea bars to 30 in the next two years.

How does Tealuxe make business decisions, such as where to open new tea bars and how many new ones to open? Fernie and Walsh need to take a detailed look at the company. They will do this by having their Corporate Financial Officer or outside accountants interpret the year end financial statements. Fernie and Walsh will then use the financial statements to provide answers to several key questions.

- ▼ Are we effectively using the resources of the firm?
- ▼ How does our debt to equity position compare across the years, and to other similar companies (tea salons and upscale coffee lounges, like Starbucks)?
- ▼ Can the company expand to ten more cities with adequate financing?
- ▼ Should we go public and issue shares of stock?

As you will learn in this chapter, the accountant's responsibility is to provide a financial interpretation by analyzing the financial statements. This is done through calculating ratios, by providing a horizontal and vertical analysis of the statements, and by preparing comparative balance sheets. Tealuxe uses this information as a basis for making decisions. The comparisons to industry standards give them an idea of how they are doing within the industry. Comparisons can also be used to determine patterns or trends. Will tea bars do best in student enclaves or in a business center? How much space should be devoted to tea paraphernalia, like teapots and infusers, and how much to seating customers? How do merchandise sales from our Web site compare to sales on those other premium tea or coffee chains?

Based on: Susanna Meadows, "The temptations of tea," *Newsweek*, October 23, 2000, p. 58. Karyn Strauss, "Specialty tea bars stir up beverage segment, brew big profits," Nation's Restaurant News, June 21, 1999, pp. 8, 73. Naomi R. Kooker, "His Cuppa Runneth Over Founder of Tealuxe Looks at Expansion," *Boston Globe*, July 23, 2000, p. 7. Kelly Crow, "Selling Tea as Serenity, Not Snobbery," *New York Times*, October 1, 2000, City section, p. 4.

LEARNING OBJECTIVES

- ▼ Preparing comparative balance sheets. (p. 779)
- ▼ Using horizontal and vertical analysis techniques. (p. 784)
- ▼ Calculating the four different types of ratios: liquidity ratios, asset management ratios, debt management ratios, and profitability ratios. (p. 787)

Financial reports are used by investors, creditors, and management to assist in making business decisions. Typical business decisions might involve such questions as the following:

- ▼ *For investors:* How profitable is the company when compared with competing companies? Will dividends be paid? Can the company expand with adequate financing?
- ▼ *For creditors:* Does the company have enough cash to pay back periodic interest payments as well as balance on maturity?
- ▼ *For management:* Is the company operating as efficiently as possible? How can we do better?

The four financial statements that we have discussed in earlier chapters—the balance sheet, the income statement, the statement of retained earnings, and the statement of cash flows—help provide the answers to these questions. In this chapter we discuss how to analyze the numbers that appear on these statements.

Numbers on a financial statement may not have meaning in and of themselves; they must be placed in a context. This context may be a comparison with last year's figures, a comparison with other companies in the same industry, or even a comparison with other figures on the same report.

In the following units we look at what the numbers mean as well as how to apply that meaning toward making useful business decisions.

LEARNING UNIT 23-1

HORIZONTAL AND VERTICAL ANALYSIS OF BALANCE SHEETS

In the **comparative balance sheet,** a statement showing data from two or more periods side by side, shown in Figure 23-1, the accountant has placed the current year's balance sheet figures next to figures from the preceding year's

FIGURE 23-1. Comparative Balance Sheet

SCRUPPER SUPPLY COMPANY COMPARATIVE BALANCE SHEET AS OF DECEMBER 31, 20X8, AND DECEMBER 31, 20X7				
Note: Most recent year is shown first.	December 31		Amount of Increase or Decrease	Percent Increase or Decrease
Assets	20X8	20X7	During 20X8	During 20X8
Current Assets:				
Cash	$ 3 040 00	$ 4 080 00	$ (1 040 00)	(25.5)
Accounts Receivable, Net	2 000 00	1 600 00	400 00	25
Merchandise Inventory	24 16 00	26 12 00	(1 96 00)	(7.5)
Prepaid Expenses	800 00	600 00	200 00	33.3
Total Current Assets	$ 48 000 00	$ 46 800 00	$ 1 200 00	2.6
Plant and Equipment:				
Office Equipment, Net	$125 200 00	$116 800 00	$ 8 400 00	7.2
Total Assets	$173 200 00	$163 600 00	$ 9 600 00	5.9
Liabilities				
Current Liabilities:				
Notes Payable	$ 20 960 00	$ 17 320 00	$ 3 640 00	21
Accounts Payable	240 00	280 00	(40 00)	(14.3)
Total Current Liabilities	$ 21 200 00	$ 17 600 00	$ 3 600 00	20.5
Long-Term Liabilities:				
Mortgage Payable	60 000 00	60 000 00	–0–	–0–
Total Liabilities	$ 81 200 00	$ 77 600 00	$ 3 600 00	4.6
Stockholders' Equity				
Common Stock, $10 par value	$ 60 000 00	$ 60 000 00	–0–	–0–
Retained Earnings	32 000 00	26 000 00	6 000 00	23.1
Total Stockholders' Equity	$ 92 000 00	$ 86 000 00	$ 6 000 00	7.0
Total Liabilities and Stockholders' Equity	$173 200 00	$163 600 00	$ 9 600 00	5.9

Comparison Time

"FRED DID IT!" shouted the business consultant. "Number 1 in sales this month!" He was busy at his desk, pouring over Fred's monthly report. He was smiling broadly as he announced Fred's success to the world.

Fred does a monthly management report to the business consultant, consisting of an Income Statement. A Balance Sheet is done quarterly. The business consultant does a horizontal analysis of Fred's Balance Sheet, comparing each line to its budget and to last year. That tells him if Fred is on target and points up any weak areas in the business. Then he does a vertical analysis of Fred's Balance Sheet to arrive at percents of the totals.

The business consultant compares Fred's results (in percentages) with each of the other shops in his zone, using a common-size statement. This exercise is useful because, although each shop is different in size, a common-size statement deals only in percentages. This comparison quickly points up exceptions, which may be good or bad. In either case, he then has the clues he needs to discover a strength other shops can copy or a weakness Fred can fix.

Everyone in the zone looks forward to seeing how they are doing in comparison to the others in their zone. There is a good deal of friendly rivalry and a good deal of mutual help. Owners regularly share successful strategies as well as news about the competition.

The business consultant also does a quarterly report for Dunkin' Donuts Inc. on all the shops he supervises. These reports are then folded into Dunkin' Donuts Inc.'s internal management reports to Allied Domeq Retailing USA. They, in turn, report to Allied Domeq headquarters in England. As the financial picture grows more inclusive, it is less detailed. So, although Fred's shop is unknown outside his zone, his success is reflected all the way up the line.

Discussion Questions

1. Why does the business consultant use a common-size statement to compare shops in his zone?
2. Why does he use both horizontal and vertical analyses of the Balance Sheets for the shops in his zone?
3. As the financial statements at the various levels of Dunkin' Donuts and Allied Domeq include more shops, they become less detailed. Why?

---

balance sheet. The third column shows the amount of increase or decrease in the 20X8 figures over the 20X7 figures, and the last column shows the percentage of decrease or increase of 20X8 over 20X7. This type of analysis, in which each item on the report is compared with the same item in other periods, is called **horizontal analysis.**

HORIZONTAL ANALYSIS OF THE BALANCE SHEET

Let's perform a sample horizontal analysis on one of the items on Scrupper Supply Company's comparative balance sheet. Look at the entry for Cash in Figure 23-1. In 20X8 it is $3,040 and in 20X7 it was $4,080, for a decrease of $1,040. This decrease is placed in parentheses on the report to show that it is a decrease and not an increase. To figure the percentage that this decrease represents, you use the equation

$$\text{Percent} = \frac{\text{Amount of Change}}{\text{Base (Old Year)}}$$

In this case it would be

$$\frac{\$1,040}{\$4,080} = 25.5 \text{ Percent}$$

This type of analysis is called horizontal analysis because in each case you are comparing two figures across columns, from one period to another, rather than comparing figures within a column. Although cash decreased by 25.5 percent, Scrupper's retained earnings increased by 23.1 percent. You can see that the percentages in the last column in Figure 23-1 cannot be added down the column to total 100 percent; each figure relates only to the figures for the same

FIGURE 23-2. Vertical
Analysis of a Comparative
Balance Sheet

SCRUPPER SUPPLY COMPANY
COMPARATIVE BALANCE SHEET
DECEMBER 31, 20X8, AND DECEMBER 31, 20X7

Assets	20X8		20X7	
Current Assets:				
Cash	$ 3 0 4 0 00	1.8%	$ 4 0 8 0 00	2.5%
Accounts Receivable, Net	20 0 0 0 00	11.5	16 0 0 0 00	9.8
Merchandise Inventory	24 1 6 0 00	13.9	26 1 2 0 00	16.0
Prepaid Expenses	8 0 0 00	.5	6 0 0 00	.4
Total Current Assets	$ 48 0 0 0 00	27.7%	$ 46 8 0 0 00	28.7%
Plant and Equipment:				
Office Equipment, Net	125 2 0 0 00	72.3%	116 8 0 0 00	71.4%
Total Assets	$173 2 0 0 00	100.0%	$163 6 0 0 00	100.0%
Liabilities				
Current Liabilities:				
Notes Payable	$ 20 9 6 0 00	12.1%	$ 17 3 2 0 00	10.6%
Accounts Payable	2 4 0 00	.1	2 8 0 00	.2
Total Current Liabilities	$ 21 2 0 0 00	12.2%	$ 17 6 0 0 00	10.8%
Long-Term Liabilities:				
Mortgage Payable	60 0 0 0 00	34.6%	60 0 0 0 00	36.7%
Total Liabilities	$ 81 2 0 0 00	46.9%	$ 77 6 0 0 00	47.5%
Stockholders' Equity				
Common Stock, $10 par value	$ 60 0 0 0 00	34.6%	$ 60 0 0 0 00	36.7%
Retained Earnings	32 0 0 0 00	18.5	26 0 0 0 00	15.9
Total Stockholders' Equity	$ 92 0 0 0 00	53.1%	$ 86 0 0 0 00	52.6%
Total Liabilities and Stockholders' Equity	$173 2 0 0 00	100.0%	$163 6 0 0 00	100.0% *

* Total equals 100% due to rounding.

item across the other columns. These percentages provide us with a quick way of monitoring specific accounts.

VERTICAL ANALYSIS OF THE BALANCE SHEET

In **vertical analysis,** each item on a report is shown as a percent of a total base. The base will be either total assets or total liabilities and stockholders' equity on a balance sheet, and it can be total sales on an income statement. Look at the comparative balance sheet in Figure 23-2. Each item is listed for 20X8, and next to it is a percentage, which is that item's percentage of total assets or total liabilities and stockholders' equity. In the next column each item is listed for the preceding year, 20X7, and then the item is listed as a percentage of total assets or total liabilities and stockholders' equity.

Take the item Cash as an example again. In 20X8, Cash is $3,040 and total assets $173,200; thus Cash represents 1.8 percent of total assets for this year.

FIGURE 23-3. Common-Size
Comparative Balance Sheet

SCRUPPER SUPPLY COMPANY COMMON-SIZE COMPARATIVE BALANCE SHEET DECEMBER 31, 20X8, AND DECEMBER 31, 20X7		
	December 31	
Assets	20X8	20X7
Current Assets:		
Cash	1.8%	2.5%
Accounts Receivable, Net	11.5	9.8
Merchandise Inventory	13.9	16.0
Prepaid Expenses	.5	.4
Total Current Assets	27.7%	28.7%*
Plant and Equipment:		
Office Equipment, Net	72.3%	71.4%
Total Assets	100.0%	100.0%
Liabilities		
Current Liabilities:		
Notes Payable	12.1%	10.6%
Accounts Payable	.1	.2
Total Current Liabilities	12.2%	10.8%
Long-Term Liabilities:		
Mortgage Payable	34.6%	36.7%
Total Liabilities	46.9%	47.5%
Stockholders' Equity		
Common Stock, $10 par value	34.6%	36.7%
Retained Earnings	18.5	15.9
Total Stockholders' Equity	53.1%	52.6%
Total Liabilities and Stockholders' Equity	100.0%	100.0%*

* Total equals 100% due to rounding.

In 20X7, Cash was $4,080 and total assets $163,600; thus Cash was 2.5 percent of total assets in that year.

Note how in this type of analysis you do add down the columns to total 100 percent, unlike horizontal analysis. Keep in mind that vertical analysis provides us with *another* way of analyzing financial reports that contain data for two or more successive accounting periods.

A shorter version of this report can be seen in Figure 23-3, in which are listed just the percentages of two columns that have been analyzed. Such a report in general is called a **common-size statement;** this particular one is a common-size comparative balance sheet.

The common-size statement makes it easy to see, for example, that from 20X7 to 20X8 there was a drop in inventory (it went from 16 percent to 13.9 percent as a percent of total assets) and an increase in accounts receivable (from 9.8 percent to 11.5 percent). The common-size statement is often used to compare companies of different sizes; that way the dollar amounts do not get in the way and it is easier to see each item as a percent of the base in each company.

LEARNING UNIT 23-1 REVIEW

AT THIS POINT you should be able to

▼ Explain the items making up a comparative balance sheet. (p. 779)
▼ Compare and contrast vertical and horizontal analysis. (p. 780)
▼ Explain the advantage of a common-size statement. (p. 782)

SELF-REVIEW QUIZ 23-1

(The blank forms you need are on page 138 of the *Study Guide and Working Papers.*)

Complete the following Comparative Balance Sheet:

Assets	December 31 20X5	December 31 20X4	Amount of Increase or Decrease during 20X5	Percent Increase or Decrease during 20X5
Current Assets:				
Cash	$ 5 000 00	$ 4 000 00		
Accounts Receivable, Net	4 000 00	2 500 00		
Merchandise Inventory	6 000 00	5 600 00		
Prepaid Expenses	2 000 00	400 00		
Total Current Assets				
Plant and Equipment:				
Store Equipment, Net	146 000 00	125 000 00		
Total Assets				

Solution to Self-Review Quiz 23-1

Assets	December 31 20X5	December 31 20X4	Amount of Increase or Decrease during 20X5	Percent Increase or Decrease during 20X5
Current Assets:				
Cash	$ 5 000 00	$ 4 000 00	$ 1 000 00	25 ($1,000 / $4,000)
Accounts Receivable, Net	4 000 00	2 500 00	1 500 00	60
Merchandise Inventory	6 000 00	5 600 00	40 00	7.1
Prepaid Expenses	2 000 00	400 00	1 600 00	400
Total Current Assets	$ 17 000 00	$ 12 500 00	$ 4 500 00	36
Plant and Equipment:				
Store Equipment, Net	146 000 00	125 000 00	21 000 00	16.8
Total Assets	$163 000 00	$137 500 00	$ 25 500 00	18.5

LEARNING UNIT 23-2

HORIZONTAL AND VERTICAL ANALYSIS OF INCOME STATEMENTS; TREND ANALYSIS

In the last unit we showed how to perform a horizontal and a vertical analysis of the balance sheet for Scrupper Supply Company. We now show how to perform the same two types of analysis on the income statement for Scrupper Supply Company.

HORIZONTAL ANALYSIS OF THE INCOME STATEMENT

Figure 23-4 shows a comparative income statement for Scrupper Supply Company using horizontal analysis. As in horizontal analysis for the balance sheet, each item on the income statement is compared with the same item for the preceding year; the amount of increase or decrease is recorded and then shown as a percent. For net sales, the amount was $302,000 in 20X7 compared with $317,600 in 20X8; that is an increase of $15,600, which comes out to a 5.2 percent increase ($15,600/$302,000). The percent increase or decrease is the amount of increase or decrease divided by the figure for the base year of 20X7.

VERTICAL ANALYSIS OF THE INCOME STATEMENT

Figure 23-5 shows the vertical analysis of a comparative income statement for Scrupper Supply Company. In the case of an income statement, the base used is net sales. (On a balance sheet, it is assets or total liabilities and stockholders' equity.) Thus on the vertical analysis of an income statement, each item is calculated as a percentage of net sales.

FIGURE 23-4. Horizontal Analysis of a Comparative Income Statement

SCRUPPER SUPPLY COMPANY COMPARATIVE INCOME STATEMENT FOR YEARS ENDED DECEMBER 31, 20X8, AND 20X7				
	December 31		Amount of Increase or Decrease During 20X8	Percent of Increase or Decrease During 20X8
	20X8	20X7		
Net Sales	$317 600 00	$302 000 00	$ 15 600 00	5.2
Cost of Goods Sold	198 000 00	194 000 00	4 000 00	2.1
Gross Profit from Sales	$119 600 00	108 000 00	11 600 00	10.7
Operating Expenses:				
Selling	$ 63 600 00	$ 55 000 00	8 600 00	15.6
General and Administrative	20 000 00	26 000 00	(6 000 00)	(23.1)
Total Operating Expenses	$ 83 600 00	$ 81 000 00	$ 2 600 00	3.2
Operating Income	$ 36 000 00	$ 27 000 00	9 000 00	33.3
Less Interest Expense	4 200 00	4 300 00	(1 000 00)	(2.3)
Income before Taxes	$ 31 800 00	$ 22 700 00	$ 9 100 00	40.1
Income Taxes	15 900 00	11 350 00	4 550 00	40.1
Net Income	$ 15 900 00	$ 11 350 00	$ 4 550 00	40.1

FIGURE 23-5. Vertical
Analysis of a Comparative
Income Statement

Assets	20X8		20X7	
	SCRUPPER SUPPLY COMPANY COMPARATIVE INCOME STATEMENT FOR YEARS ENDED DECEMBER 31, 20X8, AND DECEMBER 31, 20X7			
Net Sales	$317 6 0 0 00	100 %	$302 0 0 0 00	100 %
Cost of Goods Sold	198 0 0 0 00	62.3	194 0 0 0 00	64.2
Gross Profit from Sales	$119 6 0 0 00	37.7%	108 0 0 0 00	35.8%
Operating Expenses:				
Selling	$ 63 6 0 0 00	20.0%	$ 55 0 0 0 00	18.2 %
General and Administrative	20 0 0 0 00	6.3	26 0 0 0 00	8.6
Total Operating Expenses	$ 83 6 0 0 00	26.3%	$ 81 0 0 0 00	26.8 %
Operating Income	$ 36 0 0 0 00	11.3%	27 0 0 0 00	8.9
Less Interest Expense	4 2 0 0 00	1.3	4 3 0 0 00	1.4
Income before Taxes	$ 31 8 0 0 00	10.0%	$ 22 7 0 0 00	7.5 %
Income Taxes	15 9 0 0 00	5.0%	11 35 0 00	3.75
Net Income	$ 15 9 0 0 00	5.0%	$ 11 35 0 00	3.75%

From such an analysis of a comparative income statement we can easily see that cost of goods sold decreased (from 64.2 to 62.3 percent) from 20X7 to 20X8, selling expenses increased (from 18.2 to 20.0 percent), and profit before tax was up (7.5 to 10.0 percent). If we had listed just the percentages (each item as percentage of net sales) and left out the dollar amounts, we would have produced a common-size comparative income statement.

TREND ANALYSIS

A special type of horizontal analysis, called **trend analysis,** deals with the percentage of changes in a certain item over several years. For example, if we want to understand why sales in 20X8 are 118 percent of 20X5 of Scrupper Supply Company, we have to look at figures for several years. Following are listed figures for sales, cost of goods sold, and gross profit for 20X5 to 20X8:

	20X8	20X7	20X6	20X5
Sales	$317,600	$302,000	$290,000	$270,000
Cost of Goods Sold	198,000	194,000	184,000	142,000
Gross Profit	$119,600	$108,000	$106,000	$128,000

When the trend analysis is developed, a base year is chosen. We will choose 20X5 (the base year is usually the earliest year listed). For each of the following years, each item is stated as a percentage of the amount of the base year. For example, sales in 20X8 as a percentage of the base year equal 118 percent. The calculation is as follows:

$$\text{Base} \longrightarrow \frac{\$317,600}{\$270,000} = 118 \text{ Percent}$$

Thus sales in 20X8 have increased by 18 percent since 20X5. Over a period of years these percentages are analyzed in relation to a company's history as well as to industry averages that are supplied by companies like Robert Morse Associates and Dun & Bradstreet.

The following is the trend analysis for Scrupper Supply Company for sales, cost of goods sold, and gross profit.

	20X8	20X7	20X6	20X5
Sales	118%	112%	107%	100%
Cost of Goods Sold	139	137	130	100
Gross Profit	93	84	83	100

Note that in 20X6 sales increased 7 percent from 20X5, but cost of goods sold was up 30 percent, resulting in gross profit being down 17 percent. Such analysis can reveal internal problems in Scrupper Supply Company or industrywide problems in a certain year. For example, Scrupper might want to investigate why cost of goods sold has risen 39 percent in the last three years.

LEARNING UNIT 23-2 REVIEW

AT THIS POINT you should be able to

▼ Analyze income statement items by vertical and horizontal analysis. (p. 784)
▼ Prepare a trend analysis. (p. 785)

SELF-REVIEW QUIZ 23-2

(The blank forms you need are on page 138 of the *Study Guide and Working Papers.*)

From the following prepare a trend analysis (round to nearest whole percent using 20X3 as the base year).

	20X6	20X5	20X4	20X3
Sales	$189,000	$165,000	$142,000	$130,000
Cost of Goods Sold	85,000	124,000	99,000	88,000
Gross Profit	$104,000	$ 41,000	$ 43,000	$ 42,000

Solution to Self-Review Quiz 23-2

	20X6	20X5	20X4	20X3
Sales	145%	127%	109%*	100%
Cost of Goods Sold	97	141	113	100
Gross Profit	248	98	102	100

LEARNING UNIT 23-3   RATIO ANALYSIS

Another method for understanding the numbers on the financial statement is the use of ratio analysis.

A **ratio** is the relationship of two quantities or numbers, one divided by the other. **Ratio analysis** looks at the relationship of figures on the financial

---

*$142,000/$130,000.

statement. For example, if Broome Company's net income is $10,000 and sales are $100,000, the ratio of sales to net income may be expressed as follows:

a. Net income is $\frac{1}{10}$ or 10 percent of sales ($10,000/$100,000 = .1 = $\frac{1}{10}$ = 10 percent).

b. Ratio of sales to net income is 10 to 1 or 10 times net income (10:1).

c. For every $10 of sales, Broome Company earns $1.00 of net income.

In this unit we look at a number of different ratios that are used to analyze different aspects of a business. To be meaningful, ratios are often compared with other standards, such as past company ratios or industrywide ratios. The ratios we discuss fall into four general categories:

▼ **Liquidity ratios** measure a company's ability to meet short-term obligations.

▼ **Asset management ratios** measure how effectively a company is using its assets.

▼ **Debt management ratios** measure how well a company is using debt versus its equity position.

▼ **Profitability ratios** measure a company's ability to earn profits.

Let's now do the calculations as well as provide an explanation of each ratio. All calculations for the ratios come from the financial reports of Scrupper Supply Company presented in the last two units.

LIQUIDITY RATIOS

Current Ratio

The **current ratio** expresses the relationship of Scrupper's current assets to its current liabilities, as follows:

20X8

▼ Total current assets, $48,000.
▼ Total current liabilities, $21,200.

$$\text{Current Ratio} = \frac{\text{Current Assets}}{\text{Current Liabilities}} = \frac{\$48,000}{\$21,200} = 2.26:1$$

Thus for each $1 of debt, Scrupper has $2.26 of current assets to meet its short-term debt obligations.

It is important to note that this ratio should be evaluated in terms of (1) the type of business Scrupper is in, (2) the composition of current assets, and (3) the type of credit terms Scrupper extends. Ratios can also be compared from year to year to spot trends in a company or in an industry. For example, in 20X7 the current ratio for Scrupper Supply Company (p. 781) was 2.66 ($46,800/$17,600). This year's current ratio is 2.26, which means that Scrupper's ability to pay off short-term debts has decreased from last year to this year. The ratio is something creditors and investors, as well as the management of Scrupper Corporation, will be interested in.

Depending on the inventory or prepaid expenses, the current assets might not be worth what is shown on the balance sheet. For example, if Scrupper Supply Company has overstocked amounts of inventory, a high current ratio could occur. If Scrupper has a large amount of prepaid insurance or rent, it will not be possible to convert these assets into cash, because they have already been paid for. Thus current ratio is not a very rigorous test of Scrupper's ability to pay its short-term debts. The next ratio we discuss shows that more clearly.

Acid Test Ratio (Quick Ratio)

The **acid test ratio** divides those assets that are most easily converted into cash (called **quick assets**) by the current liabilities. To determine quick assets, we subtract Merchandise Inventory and Prepaid Expenses from current assets (which usually leaves Cash, Notes Receivable, and Accounts Receivable). Thus the acid test ratio would look like this equation:

Acid Test Ratio =

$$\frac{\text{Current Assets} - \text{Merchandise Inventory} - \text{Prepaid Expenses}}{\text{Current Liabilities}}$$

$$= \frac{\$23,040}{\$21,200} = 1.09 : 1$$

Thus for each $1 of short-term debt there is $1.09 of current or quick assets to meet them. This ratio should be at least 1 : 1 to pass the acid test or be acceptable. If you compare this 1.09 : 1 ratio with the current ratio figure of 2.26 : 1, you will see what a difference the inclusion of Merchandise Inventory and Prepaid Expenses makes.

ASSET MANAGEMENT RATIOS

Accounts Receivable Turnover

The **accounts receivable turnover ratio** shows how many times in a year Scrupper is able to convert its accounts receivables into cash. Usually, the higher the turnover, the better, because a company does not want its money tied up in something that is not yielding any revenue. The turnover rate depends on the length of the credit period Scrupper gives its customers (for Scrupper, all sales are on credit). Scrupper's income statement is on page 784.

$$\text{Accounts Receivable Turnover} = \frac{\text{Net Credit Sales}}{\text{Average Accounts Receivable}}$$

At the end of 20X7 Accounts Receivable was $16,000; at the end of 20X8 it was $20,000. We thus take $18,000 as a figure for *average* accounts receivable.

$$\text{Accounts Receivable Turnover} = \frac{\$317,600}{\$18,000} = 17.6$$

Thus Scrupper is able to turn over its accounts receivable 17.6 times a year. Of course, this turnover rate has to be compared with industry standards and must be seen in the context of how aggressive Scrupper is in its attempts to collect the accounts receivable. The next ratio breaks these steps into the number of days per collection period for accounts receivable.

Average Collection Period

In 20X8, Scrupper Supply Company turns its accounts receivable into cash every 20.7 days:

$$\text{Average Collection Period} = \frac{365 \text{ days}}{\text{Accounts Receivable Turnover}} = \frac{365}{17.6}$$
$$= 20.7$$

If Scrupper's **average collection period** increases, although its credit terms have not changed, it may necessitate a greater emphasis on collecting outstanding accounts receivable.

Inventory Turnover

The **inventory turnover ratio** calculates the number of times the *inventory* turns over in one period. Usually, a high inventory turnover means that the company has tied up less cash in inventory. Scrupper calculates its inventory turnover for 20X8 as follows:

$$\text{Inventory Turnover} = \frac{\text{Cost of Goods Sold}}{\text{Average Inventory}}$$

$$= \frac{\$198,000}{\$25,140} = 7.9$$

$$\left(\frac{\$24,160 + \$26,120}{2} \right)$$

A high inventory turnover means that there is less inventory obsolescence. If inventory turnover is slow, it could mean that Scrupper's sales are not keeping pace with the purchasing department.

Asset Turnover

The **asset turnover ratio** shows whether Scrupper Supply Company is using its assets effectively to generate sales. Scrupper calculates this ratio as follows for 20X8:

$$\text{Asset Turnover} = \frac{\text{Net Sales}}{\text{Total Assets}} = \frac{\$317,600}{\$173,200} = 1.8 \text{ Times}$$

(*Note:* Assets that are not used in producing sales, such as investments, are subtracted from total assets.) In general, the higher the asset turnover rate, the better. A low asset turnover rate compared with industry standards could mean that the company is not generating enough sales for its investment in its assets.

DEBT MANAGEMENT RATIOS

Debt to Total Assets

The **debt to total assets ratio** indicates the amount of assets that are financed by creditors. A low ratio would be favorable to creditors, because in liquidation they would be more likely to be paid. On the other hand, stockholders like to see a higher ratio so as to attempt to maximize their return. The following is Scrupper's debt to total assets ratio for 20X8:

$$\text{Debt to Total Assets} = \frac{\text{Total Liabilities}}{\text{Total Assets}} = \frac{\$81,200}{\$173,200} = 46.9 \text{ Percent}$$

A low percentage (if that were the case for Scrupper) could possibly mean that more financing by bonds, and so forth may be in order.

Debt to Stockholders' Equity

The **debt to stockholders' equity ratio** attempts to measure the risk of the creditors in relation to the risk taken by the stockholders. For example, for 20X8 the ratio of debt to stockholders' equity for Scrupper Supply Company is as follows:

$$\text{Debt to Stockholders' Equity} = \frac{\text{Total Liabilities}}{\text{Stockholders' Equity}}$$

$$= \frac{\$81,200}{\$92,000} = 88.3 \text{ Percent}$$

If the industry norm is 60 percent, Scrupper's ratio could mean that the company has too much debt financing. In general there is no guideline as to what the ratio of debt to stockholders' equity should be.

Times Interest Earned (Interest Coverage Ratio)

The **times interest earned ratio** is of interest to creditors, because it indicates the degree of risk to creditors from a company defaulting on interest payments. For example, for 20X8 Scrupper Supply Company calculates its times interest earned ratio as follows:

$$\text{Times Interest Earned} = \frac{\text{Income before Taxes and Interest Expense}}{\text{Interest Expense}}$$

$$= \frac{\$36,000}{\$4,200} = 8.6 \text{ Times}$$

The 8.6 means that the income of Scrupper could be reduced to approximately $\frac{1}{9}$ its current amount (before taxes and interest) and Scrupper would still have income that is equivalent to its interest charges. Thus the higher the times interest earned ratio is, the more likely it is that the interest payment will be made, even if earnings start to decline.

Now let's turn our attention to calculating ratios involving the profitability of the company.

> Remember: Debt is not bad. It provides a company with flexible financing plans.

PROFITABILITY RATIOS

Gross Profit Rate

The **gross profit rate** reveals how much profit from each sales dollar is generated to cover administrative and selling expenses. For example, for Scrupper Supply Company in 20X8, $.38 of each $1 resulted in profit *before* selling and general administrative expenses. This ratio was calculated as follows:

> If this rate goes down, it could mean price cutting between competitors.

$$\text{Gross Profit Rate} = \frac{\text{Gross Profit}}{\text{Net Sales}} = \frac{\$119,600}{\$317,600} = 37.7 \text{ Percent}$$

Return on Sales

In 20X8 Scrupper Supply Company earned 10 cents for each sales dollar. This **return on sales ratio** is calculated as follows:

$$\text{Return on Sales} = \frac{\text{Net Income before Taxes}}{\text{Net Sales}} = \frac{\$31,800}{\$317,600} = 10 \text{ Percent}$$

> Some firms use after-tax figures in calculation. When making comparisons, be sure to check which method is used. They are both acceptable.

Stores that have a low inventory turnover (furniture, autos) will have a high return on sales because the goods are priced high. On the other hand, a store that has a high inventory turnover (like a grocery store) will price its goods lower, resulting in a lower return per dollar of sales. If the 10 cents is low compared with its competitors, Scrupper should try to lower its cost and expenses as a percentage of its total sales.

Rate of Return on Total Assets

> As with other ratios, an individual company's performance should be compared with industry standards.

Scrupper Supply Company wishes to measure the amount of profitability it has earned in 20X8 on each dollar it has invested in assets. This figure can be calculated by the rate of **return on total assets ratio**, as follows:

> This ratio shows the earnings power of Scrupper Supply.

$$\text{Rate of Return on Total Assets} = \frac{\text{Net Income before Interest and Taxes}}{\text{Total Assets}}$$

$$= \frac{\$36,000}{\$173,200} = 20.8 \text{ Percent}$$

If the 20.8 percent rate is lower than Scrupper's competitors, it could be the result of decreases in return on sales or asset turnover (or a combination of both), which can be seen from the following alternative calculation:

$$\left(\begin{array}{c}\text{Return on}\\\text{Sales}\end{array}\right) \times \left(\begin{array}{c}\text{Total Asset}\\\text{Turnover}\end{array}\right) = \left(\begin{array}{c}\text{Rate of Return on}\\\text{Total Assets}\end{array}\right)$$

$$\frac{\$36{,}000^*}{\$317{,}600} \times \frac{\$317{,}600}{\$173{,}200} = \quad 20.8 \text{ Percent}$$

Rate of Return on Common Stockholders' Equity

The **return on common stockholders' equity ratio** aids Scrupper in evaluating how well it is earning profit for its common stockholders. The rate of return on common stockholders' equity is calculated as follows:

$$\left(\begin{array}{c}\text{Rate of Return}\\\text{on Common}\\\text{Stockholders'}\\\text{Equity}\end{array}\right) = \frac{(\text{Net Income Before Taxes}) - (\text{Preferred Dividends})}{(\text{Common Stockholders' Equity})}$$

$$= \frac{\$31{,}800 - 0}{\$92{,}000} = 34.6 \text{ Percent}$$

This return has to be compared with Scrupper's competitors. If the rate is higher than the industry standards, Scrupper is using debt financing wisely.

LEARNING UNIT 23-3 REVIEW

AT THIS POINT you should be able to

▼ Define, compare, and contrast the following four types of ratios: liquidity ratios, asset management ratios, debt management ratios, and profitability ratios. (p. 787)
▼ Explain and show the calculations for the following: current ratio, acid test ratio, accounts receivable turnover, average collection period, inventory turnover, asset turnover, debt to total assets, debt to stockholders' equity, times interest earned, gross profit rate, return on sales, rate of return on total assets, and rate of return on common stockholders' equity. (p. 787)

SELF-REVIEW QUIZ 23-3

(The blank forms you need are on page 139 of the *Study Guide and Working Papers.*)

From Scrupper's balance sheet and income statement, calculate the 13 ratios presented in this unit for 20X7. Assume the following: Accounts Receivable at the end of 20X6 was $18,000; Merchandise Inventory at the end of 20X6 was $26,000.

Solution to Self-Review Quiz 23-3

1. Current ratio:

$$\frac{\text{Current Assets}}{\text{Current Liabilities}} = \frac{\$46{,}800}{\$17{,}600} = 2.66$$

---

*The $36,000 is before interest and taxes.

2. Acid test:

$$\frac{\text{Current Assets} - \text{Merchandise Inv.} - \text{Prepaid Expenses}}{\text{Current Liabilities}}$$

$$= \frac{\$20,080}{\$17,600} = 1.14$$

3. Accounts receivable turnover:

$$\frac{\text{Net Credit Sales}}{\text{Average Accounts Receivable}} = \frac{\$302,000}{\$17,000} = 17.8$$

4. Average collection period:

$$\frac{365 \text{ Days}}{\text{Accounts Receivable Turnover}} = \frac{365}{17.8} = 20.5 \text{ Days}$$

5. Inventory turnover:

$$\frac{\text{Cost of Goods Sold}}{\text{Average Inventory}} = \frac{\$194,000}{\$26,060} = 7.4$$

6. Asset turnover:

$$\frac{\text{Net Sales}}{\text{Total Assets}} = \frac{\$302,000}{\$163,600} = 1.8 \text{ Times}$$

7. Debt to total assets:

$$\frac{\text{Total Liabilities}}{\text{Total Assets}} = \frac{\$77,600}{\$163,600} = 47.4 \text{ Percent}$$

8. Debt to stockholders' equity:

$$\frac{\text{Total Liabilities}}{\text{Stockholders' Equity}} = \frac{\$77,600}{\$86,000} = 90.2 \text{ Percent}$$

9. Times interest earned:

$$\frac{\text{Income before Taxes and Interest Expense}}{\text{Interest Expense}} = \frac{\$27,000}{\$4,300} = 6.3 \text{ Times}$$

10. Gross profit rate:

$$\frac{\text{Gross Profit}}{\text{Net Sales}} = \frac{\$108,000}{\$302,000} = 36 \text{ Percent}$$

11. Return on sales:

$$\frac{\text{Net Income before Taxes}}{\text{Net Sales}} = \frac{\$22,700}{\$302,000} = 7.5 \text{ Percent}$$

12. Rate of return on total assets:

$$\frac{\text{Net Income before Interest and Taxes}}{\text{Total Assets}} = \frac{\$27,000}{\$163,600} = 16.5 \text{ Percent}$$

13. Rate of return on common stockholders' equity:

$$\frac{\text{Net Income before Taxes} - \text{Preferred Dividends}}{\text{Common Stockholders' Equity}} = \frac{\$22,700 - 0}{\$86,000}$$

$$= 26.4 \text{ Percent}$$

SUMMARY OF KEY POINTS

Learning Unit 23-1

1. Investors, creditors, and management need to analyze financial statements.
2. Horizontal analysis compares each item in a financial statement with the same item from another period.
3. Vertical analysis compares each item in a financial statement as a percentage of a certain base (usually net sales on an income statement and total assets or total liabilities and stockholders' equity on the balance sheet).
4. A common-size statement shows two or more vertically analyzed columns, usually with the dollar figures deleted and replaced by percentages.

Learning Unit 23-2

1. Vertical and horizontal analysis can be used to analyze income statements as well as balance sheets.
2. In a vertical analysis of an income statement, items are given as a percentage of net sales (as the base).
3. Trend analysis provides a financial picture of how accounts change over the years.

Learning Unit 23-3

1. Ratio analysis shows relationships between two figures, such as ratio of sales to net income or of current assets to current liabilities. These ratios can then be compared with ratios from other years, other companies, or industry standards as a means of analysis.
2. Liquidity ratios measure the ability of a company to meet its short-term obligations.
3. Asset management ratios measure how effectively a company is using its assets.
4. Debt management ratios measure if there is an appropriate mix of debt versus equity financing.
5. Profitability ratios measure the company's ability to earn profits.
6. All ratios should be analyzed in relation to industry standards as well as economic conditions prevailing in the marketplace.

KEY TERMS

Accounts receivable turnover ratio A ratio that indicates the number of times accounts receivables are converted to cash within a given period and the effectiveness of a company's credit policy.

Acid test ratio A liquidity ratio; those assets that are most easily converted to cash are divided by current liabilities to indicate ability to pay off short-term debt. Also called *quick ratio*.

Asset management ratios Those ratios—accounts receivable turnover, average collection period, inventory turnover, and asset turnover—that measure how effectively a company uses its assets.

Asset turnover ratio A ratio that indicates how efficiently a company uses its assets to generate sales and thus helps measure the overall efficiency of the company.

Average collection period A ratio that shows how quickly moneys owed are received from customers and thereby measures how effectively a company collects its accounts receivables.

Common-size statements Comparative reports in which each item is expressed as a percentage of a base amount without dollar amounts.

Comparative balance sheets Current and past financial reports covering two or more successive periods that place data in single columns side by side.

Current ratio A liquidity ratio; current assets are divided by current liabilities to indicate a company's ability to pay its short-term debt. This ratio does not provide as much certainty as the acid test ratio.

Debt management ratios Those ratios—debt to total assets, debt to stockholders' equity, and times interest earned—that measure a company's mix of debt and equity financing.

Debt to stockholders' equity ratio A ratio in which total liabilities are divided by the amount of stock that is owned to measure the risk creditors run in comparison with stockholders.

Debt to total assets ratio A ratio that shows how much of a company's assets are financed by creditors.

Gross profit rate A profitability ratio that indicates how well net sales cover administrative and selling expenses.

Horizontal analysis Amounts of items compared on the same line of comparative financial reports. Horizontal analysis can also be in the form of a trend analysis.

Inventory turnover ratio An asset management ratio that indicates how quickly inventory moves off the shelf and therefore how well a company sells its product.

Liquidity ratios The two ratios—current ratio and acid test ratio—that measure a company's ability to pay off short-term debts.

Profitability ratios Those ratios—gross profit rate, return on sales, return on total assets, and return on common stockholders' equity—that measure a company's ability to earn a profit.

Quick assets Those assets—mainly cash, accounts receivable, and notes receivable—that can be easily turned into money.

Ratio A relationship of two quantities or numbers, one divided by the other. See the blueprint on pages 796–797.

Ratio analysis An examination of the relationship between two numbers or sets of numbers on financial reports. Analyses of ratios, especially over time, can give a fairly clear picture of how well a company conducts its business.

Return on common stockholders' equity ratio A profitability ratio that indicates how well a company is managing debt financing to earn a profit for holders of common stock.

Return on sales ratio A profitability ratio that shows the relationship of net income before taxes to net sales and thereby the effectiveness of a company's pricing policy.

Return on total assets ratio A profitability ratio that measures how wisely a company has invested in and managed its assets. This ratio can be arrived at in two ways: (1) net income before interest and taxes divided by total assets and (2) return on sales multiplied by asset turnover.

Times interest earned ratio A debt management ratio indicating the degree of risk to lenders that a company will default on its interest payments. Also called *interest coverage ratio*.

Trend analysis A type of horizontal analysis that deals with percentage changes in items on the financial reports for several years. This analysis uses a base year to calculate the percentage change of each item.

Vertical analysis Comparing items in a financial report by expressing each item as a percentage of a certain base total.

QUESTIONS, MINI EXERCISES, EXERCISES, AND PROBLEMS

Discussion Questions

1. Compare and contrast the needs of investors, creditors, and management as they relate to financial statement analysis.
2. Horizontal analysis cannot be presented on comparative financial statements. True or false? Please explain.
3. What is meant by vertical analysis?
4. Common-size statements use horizontal analysis. True or false? Please explain.
5. Why is a base year chosen in trend analysis?

6. How can ratios be expressed?

7. Explain the following types of ratios:

    a. Liquidity.

    b. Asset management.

    c. Debt management.

    d. Profitability.

8. What current asset accounts are deleted in the calculation of the acid test ratio? Why?

9. What could a low accounts receivable turnover rate indicate?

10. Stockouts could easily result if inventory is higher than it should be. True or false? Please explain.

11. What does possible liquidation have to do with the ratio of debt to total assets?

12. Rate of return on assets is affected by return on sales and asset turnover. Agree or disagree.

Mini Exercises

(The blank forms you need are on page 141 of the *Study Guide and Working Papers*.)

Horizontal Analysis Balance Sheet

1. Calculate the amount of increase or decrease as well as the percentage of increase or decrease. (Round to the nearest tenth of a percent.)

	20X8	20X7	Amount	%
a. Accounts Receivable	$600	$500		
b. Accounts Payable	400	600		

Vertical Analysis Balance Sheet

2. Complete a vertical analysis of the assets. (Round to the nearest tenth of a percent as needed.)

a. Cash	$ 500
b. Accounts Receivable	600
c. Merchandise Inventory	900
d. Office Equipment	1,000
Total Assets	$3,000

BLUEPRINT: RATIOS

Ratio	Formula	What Calculation Says	Key Points
1. Current ratio	$\dfrac{\text{Current Assets}}{\text{Current Liabilities}}$	For each $1 of current liabilities, how many dollars of current assets are available to meet the current debt.	The ratio should be evaluated based on the type of business credit terms, along with the composition of the current assets.
2. Acid test ratio	$\dfrac{\text{Current} \_ \text{Merchandise} \_ \text{Prepaid}}{\text{Assets} \quad \text{Inventory} \quad \text{Expenses}}$ over $\text{Current Liabilities}$	For each $1 of current liabilities, how many dollars of cash and near-cash assets are available to meet the current debt.	Because inventory and prepaid expenses may not be easily converted into cash, they are not used in the calculation.
3. Accounts receivable turnover	$\dfrac{\text{Net Credit Sales}}{\text{Average Accounts Receivable}}$	How many times accounts receivable is collected and turned into cash.	Cash sales are not included in the calculation. High turnover is often the best unless the credit terms cause a reduction in sales.
4. Average collection period	$\dfrac{\text{365 Days}}{\text{Accounts Receivable Turnover}}$	The number of days that it takes a business to collect its accounts receivable.	If the average collection period goes up and the credit terms remain the same, increased collection attempts should be emphsized.
5. Inventory turnover	$\dfrac{\text{Cost of Goods Sold}}{\text{Average Inventory}}$	The time period it takes from the purchase of inventory until its sale.	High turnover indicates low amounts of inventory. Care must be taken if frequent stockouts occur.
6. Asset turnover	$\dfrac{\text{Net Sales}}{\text{Total Assets}}$	How effectively the company is using its assets to generate sales.	A low turnover could mean excessive investment in assets or that the sales volume is too low.
7. Debt to total assets	$\dfrac{\text{Total Liabilities}}{\text{Total Assets}}$	Amount of assets financed by the creditors.	Low percent, reduces creditors' risk if liquidation occurs. The higher the percentage, the more coverage a company is using.

Common-Size Income Statement

3. Prepare a common-size income statement from the following (use net sales as 100 percent):

Net Sales	$500
Cost of Goods Sold	300
Gross Profit from Sales	200
Operating Expenses	60
Net Income	$140

Ratio	Formula	What Calculation Says	Key Points
8. Debt to stockholders' equity	$\dfrac{\text{Total Liabilities}}{\text{Stockholders' Equity}}$	Amount of Debt in relation to total stockholders' equity.	The higher the percentage, the more interest cost result for stockholders.
9. Times interest earned	$\dfrac{\text{Income before Taxes and Interest Expense}}{\text{Interest Expense}}$	Degree of risk to creditors if a company defaults on interest payments.	A high times interest earned means a company can have declines in earnings but have the ability to meet its annual interest obligations.
10. Gross profit rate	$\dfrac{\text{Gross Profit}}{\text{Net Sales}}$	Profit from a sales dollar that will be used to cover expenses (general, selling, etc.)	This rate could drop if stiff competition results in price cuts.
11. Return on sales	$\dfrac{\text{Net Income before Taxes}}{\text{Net Sales}}$	How much a company earns on each sales dollar.	A company with a low inventory turnover rate usually prices goods with a high return on sales.
12. Rate of return on total assets	$\dfrac{\text{Net Income before Interest and Taxes}}{\text{Total Assets}}$	Without looking at how assets are financed, this ratio measures how productively total assets have been used.	The rate of return can be increased by controlling costs and expenses as well as increasing asset turnover.
13. Rate of return on common stockholders' equity	$\dfrac{\text{Net Income before Taxes} - \text{Preferred Dividends}}{\text{Common Stockholders' Equity}}$	Measures a company's ability to earn profits for the common stockholder.	If this rate is higher than a return on total assets, the company is using financial leverage to its benefit.

Trend Analysis

4. Complete a trend analysis from the following data of Blue Corporation using 20X5 as the base year. (Round to nearest percent.)

	20X8	20X7	20X6	20X5
Sales	$800	$700	$600	$500
Gross Profit	600	200	500	300
Net Income	100	60	25	50

Ratios

5. From the data given calculate the following. (Round to the nearest hundredth or hundredth of a percent as needed.)

- **a.** Current ratio.
- **b.** Acid test ratio.
- **c.** Asset turnover ratio.
- **d.** Gross profit rate.

Net Sales	$300,000
Current Assets	42,000
Gross Profit	104,000
Current Liabilities	17,000
Total Assets	149,000
Merchandise Inventory	5,000
Prepaid Expenses	3,000

Exercises

(The blank forms you need are on pages 142–143 of the *Study Guide and Working Papers.*)

Comparative income statement.

23-1. From the following complete a comparative income statement for Auster Co. for December 31, 20X8, and December 31, 20X9. (Round to the nearest hundredth of a percent as needed.)

	20X9	20X8
Net Sales	$70,000	$40,000
Cost of Goods Sold	30,000	20,000
Operating Expenses	17,000	12,000
Interest Expense	5,000	4,000
Net Income (loss)	18,000	4,000

Common-size income statement.

23-2. From the following, prepare a common-size income statement for Ted Co. by converting the dollar amounts into percentages. (Round to the nearest tenth of a percent.) Use net sales as 100 percent.

	20X9	20X8
Net Sales	$500,000	$400,000
Cost of Goods Sold	400,000	355,000
Gross Profit from Sales	100,000	45,000
Operating Expenses	60,000	30,000
Net Income	$ 40,000	$ 15,000

Common-size comparative balance sheet.

23-3. From the following comparative balance sheet of Hoster Co., prepare a common-size comparative balance sheet. (Round all percentages to the nearest tenth of a percent.)

	DECEMBER	
	20X9	20X8
Current Assets	$ 90,000	$ 50,000
Plant and Equipment	450,000	310,000
Total Assets	$540,000	$360,000
Current Liabilities	$ 10,000	$ 30,000
Long-Term Liabilities	30,000	100,000
Common Stock	300,000	200,000
Retained Earnings	200,000	30,000
Total Liabilities and Stockholders' Equity	$540,000	$360,000

Trend analysis.

23-4. Complete a trend analysis from the following data of Band Corporation using 20X5 as the base year. (Round to the nearest percent.)

	20X8	20X7	20X6	20X5
Sales	$600,000	$500,000	$400,000	$300,000
Gross Profit	166,000	141,000	112,000	124,000
Net Income	48,000	41,000	22,000	38,000

Asset turnover; inventory turnover; accounts receivable turnover.

23-5. From the given income statement of Canry Co. as well as from the additional data, compute the following:

a. Asset turnover for 20X7.

b. Inventory turnover for 20X7.

c. Accounts receivable turnover for 20X7.

	20X7	20X6
Net Sales	$800,000	$700,000
Cost of Goods Sold	710,000	490,000
Gross Profit	$ 90,000	$210,000
Operating Expenses (includes taxes)	70,000	160,000
Net Income	$ 20,000	$ 50,000

Additional data

	20X7	20X6
Year-End Accounts Receivable	$ 60,000	$ 50,000
Year-End Inventory	90,000	70,000
All sales were on credit		
Total Assets	230,000	160,000

Group A Problems

(The blank forms you need are on pages 144–153 of the *Study Guide and Working Papers*.)

23A-1. From the following comparative balance sheet of Hesler Corporation (p. 800): (a) Prepare a horizontal analysis of each item for the amount of increase or decrease as well as the percent increase or decrease (to the nearest tenth of a percent). (b) Vertically analyze the 20X8 column of the balance sheet (to the nearest tenth of a percent).

> Horizontal and vertical analysis of a balance sheet.

HESLER CORPORATION
COMPARATIVE BALANCE SHEET
DECEMBER 31, 20X8, AND DECEMBER 31, 20X7

Assets	December 31 20X8	December 31 20X7
Current Assets:		
Cash	$ 3 9 0 0 00	$ 3 7 0 0 00
Accounts Receivable, Net	28 0 0 0 00	16 1 0 0 00
Merchandise Inventory	47 0 0 0 00	15 0 0 0 00
Prepaid Expenses	1 6 0 0 00	1 3 0 0 00
Total Current Assets	$ 80 5 0 0 00	$ 36 1 0 0 00
Plant and Equipment:		
Office Equipment, Net	$115 0 0 0 00	$110 0 0 0 00
Total Assets	$195 5 0 0 00	$146 1 0 0 00
Liabilities		
Current Liabilities:		
Notes Payable	$ 20 0 0 0 00	$ 26 0 0 0 00
Accounts Payable	21 2 0 0 00	24 0 0 0 00
Total Current Liabilities	$ 41 2 0 0 00	$ 50 0 0 0 00
Long-Term Liabilities:		
Mortgage Payable	$ 50 0 0 0 00	$ 40 0 0 0 00
Total Liabilities	91 2 0 0 00	90 0 0 0 00
Stockholders' Equity		
Common Stock, $10 par value	$ 50 0 0 0 00	$ 30 0 0 0 00
Retained Earnings	54 3 0 0 00	26 1 0 0 00
Total Stockholders' Equity	$104 3 0 0 00	$ 56 1 0 0 00
Total Liabilities and Stockholders' Equity	$195 5 0 0 00	$146 1 0 0 00

23A-2. From the accompanying comparative income statement of Oper Company:

a. Prepare a horizontal analysis with the amount of increase or decrease during 20X8 along with the percent increase or decrease during 20X7 (to the nearest tenth of a percent).

b. Vertically analyze the 20X8 column of the income statement (to the nearest tenth of a percent).

c. Prepare a common-size comparative income statement (to the nearest tenth of a percent).

OPER COMPANY
COMPARATIVE INCOME STATEMENT
FOR YEARS ENDED DECEMBER 31, 20X8, AND DECEMBER 31, 20X7

	Years Ended December 31	
	20X8	20X7
Net Sales	$288 0 0 0 00	$275 0 0 0 00
Cost of Goods Sold	197 0 0 0 00	170 0 0 0 00
Gross Profit from Sales	$ 91 0 0 0 00	$105 0 0 0 00
Operating Expenses:		
Selling	$ 50 0 0 0 00	$ 51 0 0 0 00
General and Administrative	21 0 0 0 00	23 0 0 0 00
Total Operating Expenses	$ 71 0 0 0 00	$ 74 0 0 0 00
Operating Income	$ 20 0 0 0 00	$ 31 0 0 0 00
Less Interest Expense	6 0 0 0 00	8 0 0 0 00
Income before Taxes	14 0 0 0 00	23 0 0 0 00
Income Taxes	5 6 0 0 00	9 2 0 0 00
Net Income	$ 8 4 0 0 00	$ 13 8 0 0 00

23A-3. From the accompanying income statement and balance sheet of Austin Company, compute for 20X8: (a) current ratio, (b) acid test ratio, (c) accounts receivable turnover, (d) average collection period, (e) inventory turnover, (f) asset turnover, (g) debt to total assets, (h) debt to stock-holders' equity, (i) times interest earned, (j) gross profit rate, (k) return on sales, (l) return on total assets, and (m) return on common stockholders' equity.

> Calculating ratios from financial reports.

> *Check Figure:*
> Current ratio   2.22

AUSTIN COMPANY
COMPARATIVE INCOME STATEMENT
FOR YEARS ENDED DECEMBER 31, 20X8, AND 20X7

	Years Ended December 31	
	20X8	20X7
Net Sales	$430 0 0 0 00	$376 0 0 0 00
Cost of Goods Sold	238 0 0 0 00	221 0 0 0 00
Gross Profit from Sales	$192 0 0 0 00	$155 0 0 0 00
Operating Expenses:		
Selling	$ 120 4 0 0 00	$110 0 0 0 00
General and Administrative	21 6 0 0 00	22 4 0 0 00
Total Operating Expenses	$ 142 0 0 0 00	$132 4 0 0 00
Operating Income	$ 50 0 0 0 00	$ 22 6 0 0 00
Less Interest Expense	8 2 0 0 00	8 6 0 0 00
Income before Taxes	$ 41 8 0 0 00	$ 14 0 0 0 00
Income Taxes	12 5 4 0 00	5 6 0 0 00
Net Income	$ 29 2 6 0 00	$ 8 4 0 0 00

AUSTIN COMPANY
COMPARATIVE BALANCE SHEET
DECEMBER 31, 20X8, AND DECEMBER 31, 20X7

Assets	December 31 20X8	December 31 20X7
Current Assets:		
Cash	$ 11 000 00	$ 24 400 00
Accounts Receivable, Net	416 000 00	362 000 00
Merchandise Inventory	612 000 00	624 000 00
Prepaid Expenses	56 000 00	32 000 00
Total Current Assets	$1194 000 00	$1262 000 00
Plant and Equipment:		
Office Equipment, Net	$ 656 000 00	$63 000 00
Total Assets	$185 000 00	$189 200 00
Liabilities		
Current Liabilities:		
Notes Payable	$ 36 800 00	$ 35 200 00
Accounts Payable	17 000 00	15 800 00
Total Current Liabilities	$ 53 800 00	$ 51 000 00
Long-Term Liabilities:		
Mortgage Payable	$ 39 600 00	$ 30 000 00
Total Liabilities	$ 93 400 00	$ 81 000 00
Stockholders' Equity		
Common Stock, $10 par value	$ 56 000 00	$51 000 00
Retained Earnings	35 600 00	57 200 00
Total Stockholders' Equity	$ 916 000 00	$108 200 00
Total Liabilities and Stockholders' Equity	$185 000 00	$189 200 00

Ratio calculations; common-size percentages; and trend analysis.

Check Figure:
20X8   Current assets
72%

23A-4. From the accompanying information about Vargo Corporation:

    a. For each year calculate its current ratio and acid test ratio.

    b. For each year prepare the income statement in common-size percentages. (Round to the nearest tenth of a percent).

    c. Prepare a trend analysis of the balance sheet using 20X6 as the base year (Round to the nearest percent.)

VARGO CORPORATION
COMPARATIVE INCOME STATEMENT
FOR YEARS ENDED DECEMBER 31, 20X8, 20X7, 20X6

	20X8	20X7	20X6
Net Sales	$ 32 000 00	$ 28 000 00	$ 24 400 00
Cost of Goods Sold	23 450 00	19 600 00	17 200 00
Gross Profit from Sales	$ 8 550 00	$ 8 400 00	$ 7 200 00
Operating Expenses:			
Selling	$ 4 600 00	$ 4 820 00	$ 3 456 00
General and Administrative	2 400 00	2 280 00	2 482 00
Total Operating Expenses	$ 7 000 00	$ 7 100 00	$ 5 938 00
Operating Income before Taxes	$ 1 550 00	$ 1 300 00	$ 1 262 00
Income Taxes	620 00	520 00	504 00
Net Income	$ 930 00	780 00	$ 758 00

VARGO CORPORATION
COMPARATIVE BALANCE SHEET
FOR YEARS ENDED DECEMBER 31, 20X8, 20X7, 20X6

Assets	20X8	20X7	20X6
Current Assets*	$ 2 046 00	$ 1 782 00	$ 2 842 00
Plant and Equipment	10 000 00	9 000 00	8 400 00
Total Assets	$ 12 046 00	$ 10 782 00	$ 11 242 00
Liabilities and Stockholder's Equity			
Current Liabilities	$ 1 000 00	$ 960 00	$ 920 00
Common Stock	7 000 00	6 200 00	6 400 00
Retained Earnings	4 046 00	3 622 00	3 922 00
Total Liabilities and Stockholders' Equity	$ 12 046 00	$ 10 782 00	$ 11 242 00

*20X8 Inventory $484; 20X7 $310; 20X6 $600.

Group B Problems

(The blank forms you need are on pages 144–153 of the *Study Guide and Working Papers*.)

23B-1. From the following comparative balance sheet of Hesler Corporation (p. 804):

    a. Prepare a horizontal analysis of each item for the amount of increase or decrease as well as the percent increase or decrease (to the nearest tenth of a percent).

    b. Vertically analyze the 20X8 column of the balance sheet (to the nearest tenth of a percent).

> Horizontal analysis, vertical analysis, and common-size preparation of a balance sheet.

> *Check Figure:*
> Cash 3.3%

HESLER CORPORATION
COMPARATIVE BALANCE SHEET
DECEMBER 31, 20X8, AND DECEMBER 31, 20X7

Assets	December 31 20X8	December 31 20X7
Current Assets:		
Cash	$ 16 500 00	$ 12 300 00
Accounts Receivable, Net	525 00 00	44 700 00
Merchandise Inventory	660 00 00	78 000 00
Prepaid Expenses	9 300 00	5 700 00
Total Current Assets	$144 300 00	$140 700 00
Plant and Equipment:		
Office Equipment, Net	$351 600 00	$330 000 00
Total Assets	$495 900 00	$470 700 00
Liabilities		
Current Liabilities:		
Notes Payable	$ 72 000 00	$ 54 000 00
Accounts Payable	45 000 00	28 500 00
Total Current Liabilities	$117 000 00	$82 500 00
Stockholders' Equity		
Common Stock, $10 par value	$300 000 00	$300 000 00
Retained Earnings	78 900 00	88 200 00
Total Stockholders' Equity	$378 900 00	$388 200 00
Total Liabilities and Stockholders' Equity	$495 900 00	$470 700 00

Horizontal analysis, vertical analysis, and common-size preparation of an income statement.

23B-2. From the accompanying comparative income statement of Oper Company:

a. Prepare a horizontal analysis with the amount of increase or decrease during 20X8 along with the percent increase or decrease during 20X7 (to the nearest tenth of a percent).

b. Vertically analyze the 20X8 column of the income statement (to the nearest tenth of a percent).

c. Prepare a common-size comparative income statement (to the nearest tenth of a percent).

OPER COMPANY
COMPARATIVE INCOME STATEMENT
FOR YEARS ENDED DECEMBER 31, 20X8, AND DECEMBER 31, 20X7

	Year Ended December 31	
	20X8	20X7
Net Sales	$ 1225000	$ 888000
Cost of Goods Sold	605000	424000
Gross Profit from Sales	620000	464000
Operating Expenses:		
Selling	270000	192000
General and Administrative	105000	96000
Total Operating Expenses	375000	288000
Operating Income	245000	176000
Less Interest Expense	22500	22000
Income before Taxes	222500	154000
Income Taxes	89000	61600
Net Income	$ 133500	$ 92400

Check Figure:
20X8 Net sales increase 38%

23B-3. From the accompanying income statement and balance sheet of Austin Company, compute for 20X8: (a) current ratio, (b) acid test ratio, (c) accounts receivable turnover, (d) average collection period, (e) inventory turnover, (f) asset turnover, (g) debt to total assets, (h) debt to stockholders' equity, (i) times interest earned, (j) gross profit rate, (k) return on sales, (l) return on total assets, and (m) return on stockholders' equity.

Calculating ratios from financial reports.

Check Figure:
Current ratio 2.12

AUSTIN COMPANY
COMPARATIVE INCOME STATEMENT
FOR YEARS ENDED DECEMBER 31, 20X8 AND DECEMBER 31, 20X7

	Years Ended December 31	
	20X8	20X7
Net Sales	$ 9900000	$ 8925000
Cost of Goods Sold	5050000	5500000
Gross Profit from Sales	4850000	3425000
Operating Expenses:		
Selling	2705000	2590000
General and Administrative	355000	400000
Total Operating Expenses	3060000	2990000
Operating Income	1790000	435000
Less Interest Expense	455000	225000
Income before Taxes	1335000	210000
Income Taxes	534000	84000
Net Income	$ 801000	$ 126000

AUSTIN COMPANY
COMPARATIVE BALANCE SHEET
DECEMBER 31, 20X8, AND DECEMBER 31, 20X7

	December 31	
Assets	20X8	20X7
Current Assets:		
Cash	$ 3 40 0 00	$ 5 40 0 00
Accounts Receivable, Net	9 75 0 00	8 70 0 00
Merchandise Inventory	14 50 0 00	14 90 0 00
Prepaid Expenses	1 20 0 00	85 0 00
Total Current Assets	$ 28 85 0 00	$29 85 0 00
Plant and Equipment:		
Office Equipment, Net	$ 14 90 0 00	$ 11 00 0 00
Total Assets	$ 43 75 0 00	$40 85 0 00
Liabilities		
Current Liabilities:		
Notes Payable	$ 9 75 0 00	$ 9 05 0 00
Accounts Payable	3 85 0 00	3 40 0 00
Total Current Liabilities	$ 13 60 0 00	$ 12 45 0 00
Long-Term Liabilities:		
Mortgage Payable	$ 10 00 0 00	$ 7 50 0 00
Total Liabilities	$ 23 60 0 00	$19 95 0 00
Stockholders' Equity		
Common Stock, $10 par value	$ 14 05 0 00	$12 00 0 00
Retained Earnings	6 10 0 00	8 90 0 00
Total Stockholders' Equity	$ 20 15 0 00	$20 90 0 00
Total Liabilities and Stockholders' Equity	$ 43 75 0 00	$40 85 0 00

Ratio calculations; common-size percentages; trend analysis.

Check Figure:
20X8   Current assets
136%

23B-4. From the accompanying information about Vargo Corporation:

  a. For each year calculate its current and acid test ratios.
  b. For each year prepare the income statement in common-size percentages. (Round to the nearest tenth of a percent.)
  c. Prepare a trend analysis of the balance sheet using 20X6 as the base year. (Round to the nearest percent.)

VARGO CORPORATION COMPARATIVE INCOME STATEMENT FOR YEARS ENDED DECEMBER 31, 20X8, 20X7, 20X6,	20X8	20X7	20X6
Net Sales	$ 55 500 00	$ 50 400 00	$ 38 700 00
Cost of Goods Sold	40 200 00	37 200 00	23 700 00
Gross Profit from Sales	$ 15 300 00	$ 13 200 00	$ 15 000 00
Operating Expenses:			
Selling	$ 7 200 00	$ 4 800 00	$ 5 400 00
General and Administrative	5 700 00	2 730 00	3 750 00
Total Operating Expenses	$ 12 900 00	$ 7 530 00	$ 9 150 00
Operating Income before Taxes	2 400 00	5 670 00	5 850 00
Income Taxes	960 00	2 268 00	2 340 00
Net Income	$ 1 440 00	$ 3 402 00	$ 3 510 00

VARGO CORPORATION COMPARATIVE BALANCE SHEET DECEMBER 31, 20X8, 20X7, 20X6	20X8	20X7	20X6
Assets			
Current Assets*	$ 6 720 00	$ 5 550 00	$ 4 950 00
Plant and Equipment	18 000 00	12 000 00	10 500 00
Total Assets	$ 24 720 00	$ 17 550 00	$ 15 450 00
Liabilities and Stockholders' Equity			
Current Liabilities	$ 2 400 00	$ 1 800 00	$ 1 560 00
Common Stock	11 700 00	10 800 00	7 500 00
Retained Earnings	10 620 00	4 950 00	6 390 00
Total Liabilities and Stockholder's Equity	$ 24 720 00	$ 17 550 00	$ 15 450 00

* Inventory: 20X8, $1,350; 20X7, $1,800; 20X6, $1,200.

REAL-WORLD APPLICATIONS

23R-1.

You have been hired as a consultant to determine which of the two following companies is in overall better shape. From the accompanying information, prepare a schedule of ratio calculations that can be derived from the facts along with your recommendations. Both companies are in the same industry.

	Joyne Co.	Smokey Co.
Cash	$ 17,000	$ 28,000
Accounts Receivable, Net	18,000	55,000
Inventory	80,000	96,000
Plant and Equipment, Net	90,000	170,000
	$205,000	$349,000
Current Liabilities	$ 58,000	$ 89,000
Mortgage Payable	40,000	60,000
Common Stock	79,000	175,000
Retained Earnings	28,000	25,000
	$205,000	$349,000
Sales (all credit)	$230,000	$380,000
Cost of Goods Sold	160,000	275,000
Interest Expense	8,000	12,000
Income Taxes	10,000	16,000
Net Income	24,000	40,000

23R-2.

The bookkeeper of Blue Co. is trying to determine (a) the amount of average inventory, (b) the accounts receivable average balance, and (c) the balance of cash from the following information:

Prepaid Rent	$ 16,000
Accounts Receivable Turnover	9 times
Cost of Goods Sold	$270,000
Inventory Turnover	27
Current Liabilities	$ 90,000
Credit Sales	$270,000

The bookkeeper's assistant thinks there is not enough information available to complete the calculations. Accept or reject the assistant's remarks. Please provide a written response.

YOU make the call

Critical Thinking/Ethical Case

23R-3.

Jill Land, President of Loon Co., is happy to report to the company's stockholders that the company has increased its cash position by 20 percent from last year. Its average collection period has decreased by 12 days. Jill knows some customers are unhappy about the new credit terms, but believes that you cannot please everyone; that's part of business. Do you think Loon Co. is on the right track? One shareholder is quite upset to learn that the company is holding so much cash. Do you agree with the company's belief that increasing the cash position by 20 percent is sound? You make the call. Write down your recommendation to Jill.

INTERNET EXERCISES

EX-1. [www.delta.com/inside/investors/annual_reports/2000_annual/ ar_frameset.html]   Welcome back to Delta Airlines' website for another look at their financial statements. For this exercise make a "common size" balance sheet using the numbers in the "2000" column. The key to this is knowing that in a common size balance the "100%" figure is Total Assets.

EX-2. [www.delta.com/inside/investors/annual_reports/2000_annual/ ar_frameset.html]   Calculate the following ratios using the 2000 financial statements:

1. Current Ratio
2. Accounts Receivable Turnover
3. Asset Turnover
4. Debt to Total Assets
5. Debt to Stockholders' Equity

CHAPTER 24

The Voucher System

The cost of processing a single purchase order is about $175. General Motors issues over 100,000 purchase orders per year. By purchasing online, the cost of a purchase order drops to as little as $10. Do the math, and you'll see why GM is keen to use the Internet to streamline the purchasing process.

The Big Three automakers (Ford, General Motors and Daimler-Chrysler) are in the process of moving all business—more than $250 billion and 60,000 suppliers—to the Internet. The business-to-business exchange is called Covisint, and it will replace a bloated procurement system built on phone calls and faxes.

And the automakers are not alone. Competitors in industries ranging from pharmaceuticals and aerospace to retailing and railroads are joining forces to move mundane but essential tasks, such as purchasing and order fulfillment, to cyberspace. For sellers, mouse clicks replace costly sales visits and allow them to connect with customers across the globe. For buyers, the Internet allows them to scan an entire universe of suppliers for the best price on what they want. This incredible potential for wringing excess costs from supply chains is making business-to-business (B2B) e-commerce "the next big killer app" of the World Wide Web. Analysts estimate the B2B e-commerce market will soar to $6.4 trillion in 2004.

Whether businesses purchase materials and parts via online exchanges or via paper invoices, **internal control** is extremely important. Internal control is the set of rules and procedures governing business transactions. One such rule might be that all purchases must be authorized and backed up by documentation. Another rule would require that the person who approves a purchase cannot also do the accounting for it. In this chapter, you will learn how to accomplish internal control over purchasing transactions by using a voucher system. You'll learn how to prepare vouchers, record them in a voucher register, and take advantage of your discounts when paying your invoices.

Based on: Mark McLaughlin, "The winners in B2B commerce," Kiplinger's Personal Finance Magazine, September 2000, pp. 48–50. Anonymous, "For aiming to lead its industry in online consumer services THE PROMISE OF THE INTERNET," The Atlanta Constitution, September 20, 2000, p. H7. Russ Banham, "The B-to-B Virtual Bazaar," Journal of Accountancy, July 2000, pp. 26–30. Don Tapscot, "Manager's Journal: Virtual Webs Will Revolutionize Business," Wall Street Journal, April 24, 2000, P. A38. Kevin P. O'Brien, "Value-Chain report: Should Your Firm Be Using E-Procurement?" June 12, 2000, http://www.iwvaluechain.com.

LEARNING OBJECTIVES

▼   Preparing vouchers, recording them in a voucher register, and recording payment of vouchers in a check register. (p. 812)

▼   Recording revised vouchers to handle nonroutine transactions in a voucher system. (p. 818)

▼   Using the net amount method to record invoices and payment. (p. 819)

In small companies owners may be able to do or look at every step of their business themselves. As such companies grow larger and as the sheer number of business transactions multiplies, however, that becomes impossible. How, then, do owners or managers keep control over the activities of a company? If they don't sign every check themselves or approve every purchase themselves, how do they know if money is being spent in approved ways, or even where it's going? Some rules have to be formulated for employees to impose order; such rules and procedures are referred to as *internal control*. One type of system used to implement this internal control is called a *voucher system*.

In Chapter 10 we discussed the steps taken when a company purchases goods. You might take a moment to look back at those pages (pp. 370–371), because we use these steps in this chapter to explain how a voucher system works. The steps include the following:

1. Preparing a purchase requisition and getting it authorized.

2. Preparing a purchase order, which specifies details such as company, number of items, and so forth, and getting it authorized.

3. Company receiving the purchase order prepares a sales invoice specifying number and type of goods and price.

4. Company receiving the goods inspects the shipment, checks it against the purchase order and the sales invoice, and completes a receiving report.

5. Someone in the accounting department verifying the numbers (checks the purchase order, the invoice, and the receiving report to make sure the numbers are in agreement and no steps are left out). This person then issues a voucher for payment, which is authorized.

6. Issuing payment in the form of a check.

These steps show internal control, in the form of a voucher system, at work. Other procedures discussed in other chapters of this text also are part of internal control, including banking procedures and petty cash and change funds.

What is a voucher? A **voucher** (see the sample shown later) is a written authorization form that is used for every cash payment the company makes. It contains all the details of the transaction in question along with the signatures of appropriate employees as authorization. A **voucher system,** then, is a system in which no payment is made without an approved voucher.

CHARACTERISTICS OF A VOUCHER SYSTEM

A number of principles of internal control are embedded in the voucher system. Perhaps the most important is the separation of duties. In a voucher system no one person in a company is in control of all transactions or of everything to do with one transaction. The person who approves purchase and payment is different from the person who makes the accounting entries related to these functions, and that person is different from the person who signs and mails the checks. In this way no one can do anything without other people supplying approval.

A second important principle, perhaps the backbone of a voucher system, is the rule that no purchases are made without an approved voucher backed up by documentation. There are several layers of documentation and authorization here, beginning with a purchase requisition, moving on to a purchase order, and ending up with actual payment by a check. At every layer and step the appropriate documents are presented, checked, and approved before going further.

There is a lot of cross-referencing and cross-checking in a voucher system. Every document is numbered; transactions are recorded in different places by different people and backed up by reference to numbers of other documents. In this way it is always possible to trace one transaction all the way through the system. After a purchase is made and paid for, the documents and forms are kept on file for a certain period of time to allow such checks to be made.

In the next two learning units we show how a voucher system works in a specific company and then how certain transactions are handled that don't fit into the voucher system. The specific company we use is Jones Company.

LEARNING UNIT 24-1

HANDLING TRANSACTIONS IN A VOUCHER SYSTEM

Jones Company is a medium-sized merchandise business that believes in strong internal control practices and procedures. It uses the voucher system to control all cash payments except payments out of the petty cash fund. Company rules state that all invoices must be compared with purchase requisitions, purchase orders, and receiving reports before payment and that all payments must, of course, be supported by appropriate documents and authorizations.

Jones Company's voucher system is made up of the following elements:

1. Vouchers.
2. Voucher register.
3. Unpaid voucher file.
4. Check register.
5. Paid voucher file.

To see this system in action, let's follow one transaction all the way through. To begin with, Jones Company decides to buy $4,500 worth of merchandise from Beam Enterprise. The purchase order is shown in Figure 24-1. When the merchandise is received, along with an invoice (Figure 24-2), a special serially numbered form called a voucher is prepared (Figure 24-3).

Jones Supply Co.
1818 Roger Road
Small, PA 19108

Purchase Order
0732

Date November 3, 20X8

Ordered from:
Beam Enterprise
9 Lowell St.
Swampscott, Mass. 01907

Ship to:
Same as Above

Date Needed		Ship via	F.O.B	Terms
November 28, 20X8		Rail	Destination	2/10, n/30
Quantity			Unit	
Ordered	Received	Description	Price	Amount
100		V1342 Staplers	$5.00	$ 500
200		V3918 Calculators	20.00	4,000
		Total.......................		$4,500

By: *Bill Small*
Authorized Signature

Original Purchase Order

FIGURE 24-1. Purchase Order

THE VOUCHER

In preparing the voucher the invoice from Beam Enterprise is compared with the purchase requisition, purchase order, and receiving report to be sure that it matches the specific requirements and prices of the order. For example, the information in Figure 24-1, the purchase order, does indeed match the information on the invoice shown in Figure 24-2. The original supporting documents (purchase orders, etc.) are attached to the voucher. Note that there is a front and back side to the voucher. The front side indicates the voucher number, invoice number and date, purchase order number, to whom amount will be paid, and verification

Invoice
Invoice Number: B20
Date: November 28, 20X8

Beam Enterprise
9 Lowell St.
Swampscott, Mass. 01907

Sold to: Jones Supply Co.
1818 Roger Road
Small, PA 19108

Ship to: Same

Your Purchase Order Number	Invoice Number	Salesman	Terms	Shipped via:
0732	B20	Munroe	2/10, n/30	Rail (PPD) F.O.B. Destination

Quantity			Unit	
Ordered	Received	Description	Price	Amount
100	100	V1342 Staplers	$5.00	$ 500
200	200	V3918 Calculators	20.00	4,000
		Total.......................		$4,500

Original Invoice

FIGURE 24-2. Invoice

FIGURE 24-3. Voucher, front

```
                              VOUCHER

  Jones Supply Co.                    Voucher No. 23
  1818 Roger Road
  Small, PA 19108                     Date check needed:
                                      December 5, 20X8
  Invoice
  Number and Date:                    Payable to:   Beam Enterprise
  B20 November 28, 20X8                             9 Lowell Street
                                                    Swampscott, MA 01907
  Purchase
  Order Number:  0732                 Invoice Amount      $4,500
                                      Less: Discount          90
                                      Net Amount Due      $4,410
 ─────────────────────────────────────────────────────────────────────
  Verification Steps:                 Approved by:         Date

  (1) Invoice compared with purchase
      requisition and purchase order       JS             12/1/X8
  (2) Invoice compared with receiving
      report                                BM             12/1/X8
  (3) Extensions and footings done          BJ             12/1/X8
  (4) Approved for payment                  PS             12/3/X8
```

```
  ┌──────────────────────────┬──────────────────────────────────────┐
  │   Account Distributory   │   Voucher No. 23                      │
  ├──────────────┬───────────┤                                       │
  │ Debit        │  Amount   │   Date check needed:  12/5/X8         │
  │              │           │                                       │
  │ Purchases    │  $4,500   │   Payable to:                         │
  │ Supplies     │           │                                       │
  │ Salaries Expense         │   Beam Enterprise                     │
  │ Repair Expense           │   9 Lowell Street                     │
  │ Sundry       │           │   Swampscot, MA 01907                 │
  │              │           │                                       │
  │ ──────────   │           │   Summary of Voucher                  │
  │              │           │                                       │
  │              │           │   Invoice Amount   $4,500             │
  │ ──────────   │           │   Less: Discount       90             │
  │              │           │   Net Amount Due   $4,410             │
  │              │           │                                       │
  │ ──────────   │           │   Payment Summary of Voucher          │
  │              │           │                                       │
  │              │           │   Date:  12/5/X8                      │
  │ ──────────   │           │   Amount:  $4,410                     │
  │              │           │   Check No.:  55                      │
  │ ──────────   │           │                                       │
  │              │           │   Recorded in Voucher                 │
  │ Credit Vouchers          │   Register by:  ____PM____            │
  │ Payable for Total │ $4,500│                                      │
  ├──────────────┴───────────┤                                       │
  │ Distribution approved by: ____JS____                             │
  │ (Accounting Department)                                          │
  └──────────────────────────────────────────────────────────────────┘
```

steps. For Jones Company, all supporting documents are attached to the front of the voucher and folded. The back side shows the account distribution along with space to complete the payment summary and final approvals as needed.

THE VOUCHER REGISTER

Using the approved account distributions, the voucher is recorded in a special journal called the **voucher register** (Figure 24-4). This journal replaces the purchases journal. Note that the vouchers are entered in the voucher register in

FIGURE 24-4. Voucher Register

VOUCHER REGISTER

Date		Voucher Number	Payable to	Date of Payment	Check Number	Voucher Payable Cr.	Purchases Dr.	Supplies Dr.	Repair Expense Dr.	Sundry Accounts Account	Sundry Accounts PR	Sundry Accounts Dr.	Sundry Accounts Cr.
20X8 Dec.	2	22	Petty Cash	12/4	53	50 00				Petty Cash	114	50 00	
	3	23	Beam	12/5	55	4,500 00	4,500 00						
			Enterprise										
	3	24	Ron Co.	12/4	54	425 00		425 00					
	7	25	Rose Co.	12/9	56	28 00			28 00				
	9	26	Blew Co.	12/30	67	1,000 00				Equip.	121	1,000 00	
	15	27	Security	12/27	58	5,150 00				Note Payable	211	5,000 00	
			Bank										
										Int. Exp.	531	150 00	
										FICA Tax*			
	28	42	Internal	12/28	65	900 00				Payable	212	250 00	
			Revenue										
			Service										
										FIT Tax			
										Payable	216	650 00	
										Salary and			
	9	43	Payroll	12/29	66	4,000 00				Wages Payable	210	4,000 00	
						20,665 00	7,950 00	600 00	1,015 00			11,100 00	
						(212)	(513)	(116)	(562)			(X)	

* Includes Medicare and Social Security.

numerical order at the time the liability is *incurred*. For Jones, the **Vouchers Payable** credit column records the amount due on each voucher (before any discounts) for purchases of merchandise, services, or other assets. Special debit columns have been set up for Jones's accountant based on how often they're used. The sundry column, as in other special journals, records amounts that do not have special columns set up. The posting rules are the same as we covered in the past for special journals. Keep in mind that the columns for date of payment and check number are *not* filled in until *time of payment*.

When a balance sheet is prepared, the term *Accounts Payable* is used instead of Vouchers Payable, because users of financial reports are more used to that wording.

UNPAID FILE VOUCHER

> The voucher remains in the unpaid file until paid.

Each voucher, once it has been recorded in the voucher register, is filed in an **unpaid voucher file** according to due date. This file is often referred to as a **tickler file**. Although the amount owed Beam is $4,500, there is a $90 cash discount available if Beam receives payment by December 8, 20X8. Thus the voucher is filed on a *December 5 due date,* anticipating that it will take three days in the mail for Beam to receive it.

In the voucher system, the accounts payable ledger is not used; for Jones, the unpaid file is its subsidiary ledger for the controlling account Vouchers Payable in the general ledger. At the end of the month Jones Company will prepare a schedule of vouchers payable, just as we discussed in Chapter 7 for the schedule of accounts payable, with the total of all unpaid vouchers being equal to the ending balance in Vouchers Payable in the general ledger.

CHECK REGISTER

> Payment requires notation in three places:
> 1. Check register.
> 2. Voucher register payment column.
> 3. Back of voucher.

On December 5, Jones Company records the payment to Beam in a special journal called a **check register**. The check register replaces the cash payments journal in recording the payment of vouchers payable. Note in Figure 24-5 that the

Date		Check Number	Payable to	Voucher Number	Vouchers Payable Dr.	Purchases Discount Cr.	Cash in Bank Cr.	Bank	
								Deposits	Bal.
20X8 Dec.	1	52	Broom Co.	21	460 00		460 00		1 200 00
									740 00
	2	53	Moore Co.	22	600 00	12 00	588 00	400 00	552 00
	4	54	Ron Co.	24	425 00		425 00	100 00	1 127 00
	5	55	Beam Ent.	23	4 500 00	90 00	4 410 00	400 00	717 00
	28	65	Internal Revenue	42	900 00		900 00		8 200 00
	29	66	Payroll	43	4 000 00		4 000 00		4 200 00
					(212)	(514)	(111)		

FIGURE 24-5. Check Register

Vouchers Payable account is debited for $4,500, whereas Purchases Discount is credited for $90 and Cash in Bank for $4,410. The date of payment, along with check number, is updated in the voucher register. Posting of the check register follows the same rules as other special journals. (*Note:* Once the voucher has been paid, it should be marked "Paid" so as to avoid duplication of payments.)

PAID VOUCHER FILE

After Beam's voucher is paid, it is filed by Jones in a **paid voucher file.** The voucher is filed in sequential order according to the voucher numbers. Some companies will file the voucher alphabetically based on the creditor's name. Jones keeps all paid vouchers for six years. This amount of time will vary from company to company.

LEARNING UNIT 24-1 REVIEW

AT THIS POINT you should be able to

▼ List and define the components of a voucher system. (p. 812)
▼ Explain the steps to record and pay a voucher. (p. 814)
▼ Discuss why the unpaid file voucher is recorded by due dates. (p. 816)

SELF-REVIEW QUIZ 24-1

(The blank forms you need are on page 158 of the *Study Guide and Working Papers.*)

Respond true or false to the following:

1. All companies use the same voucher system.
2. Supporting documents are attached to a voucher.
3. The account distribution is used to record the voucher in the voucher register.
4. Vouchers are recorded in the voucher register in alphabetical order.
5. A schedule of vouchers payable can be prepared from the unpaid voucher file at end of month.

Solutions to Self-Review Quiz 24-1

1. False   **2.** True   **3.** True   **4.** False   **5.** True

LEARNING UNIT 24-2

RECORDING ADDITIONAL TRANSACTIONS IN JONES'S VOUCHER SYSTEM

SITUATION 1: PURCHASES RETURNS AND ALLOWANCES AFTER VOUCHER HAS BEEN RECORDED

On December 26, Jones Company prepared voucher no. 32 for merchandise that was bought from Booth Company for $400. The accountant records the voucher in the voucher register as a debit to Purchases and a credit to Vouchers

FIGURE 24-6. Voucher Register with Purchases, Returns, and Allowances

VOUCHER REGISTER

Date	Voucher Number	Payable to	Date of Payment	Check Number	Voucher Payable Cr.	Purchases Dr.	Account	PR	Sundry Accounts Dr.	Sundry Accounts Cr.
Dec.	32	Booth Co.	Cancelled Voucher	See No. 39	40000	40000				
28	39	Booth Co.			30000		Voucher Payable	212	40000	
							Purchases Returns and Allowances	515		10000

FIGURE 24-7. Voucher Register with Partial Payments

VOUCHER REGISTER

Date	Voucher Number	Payable to	Date of Payment	Check Number	Vouchers Payable Cr.	Account	PR	Sundry Accounts Dr.	Sundry Accounts Cr.
Jan. 18	64	Ron Co.	Cancelled 1/29	V69-71	15000000	Office Equip.	121	15000000	
29	69	Ron Co.			500000	Vouchers Payable	212	500000	
29	70	Ron Co.			500000	Vouchers Payable	212	500000	
29	71	Ron Co.			500000	Vouchers Payable	212	500000	

Payable for $400. On December 28, $100 of the merchandise is found to be defective and is returned to Booth Company. The procedure that Jones Company uses is to cancel the original voucher and prepare a new voucher for $300. Figure 24-6 shows how Jones Company records the cancellation of voucher 32 and the recording of the revised voucher no. 39. The end result is a debit to purchases of $400, a credit of $300 to Vouchers Payable, and a credit to Purchases Returns and Allowances of $100. Another way of handling this transaction is to modify the original voucher and make a *general journal* entry that debits Vouchers Payable $100 and credits Purchases Returns and Allowances $100.

SITUATION 2: PARTIAL PAYMENTS PLANNED AFTER VOUCHER PREPARED FOR FULL AMOUNT

On January 18, voucher no. 64 was prepared by Jones Company on the assumption they would pay Ron Co. $15,000 for office equipment in one payment. The top section of Figure 24-7 shows a debit to Office Equipment and a credit to Vouchers Payable for $15,000.

Owing to a cash shortage, on January 29 it was decided by Jones Company to pay Ron Company in three equal installments on February 8, 19, and 21. Thus the original voucher on January 18 is canceled and a *new* voucher is prepared for each installment. Note in Figure 24-7 how the old voucher is canceled and the new vouchers are prepared. In the date of payment column, the January 18 line shows the cancellation along with the new date recording the new voucher (1/29). The check number column indicates which new vouchers are replacing the canceled voucher. Note in the sundry column how Vouchers Payable is debited three times to cancel the original voucher.

RECORDING PURCHASES AT NET AMOUNT

In this chapter Jones Company recorded all invoices at the gross amount, although the check register did show a Purchases Discount column. Many companies, on the other hand, record purchases at net. When a discount is missed using the net approach, a title called Discount Lost is shown in the payment column of the voucher register.

> The net approach means that a Purchases Discount account is not needed.

Let's look at journal entries showing the same purchase recorded at gross and at net.

(A) Mill Company Buys merchandise on account from Ryan Company for $8,000. Terms are 2/10, n/30. Mill Company issues voucher no. 299.

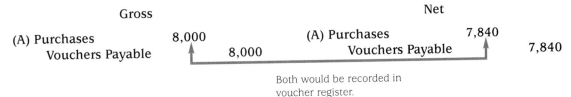

Gross		Net	
(A) Purchases	8,000	(A) Purchases	7,840
Vouchers Payable	8,000	Vouchers Payable	7,840

Both would be recorded in voucher register.

If Discount Is Taken on Time

(B) Mill Company issues check no. 531 in payment of voucher no. 299 less the cash discount.

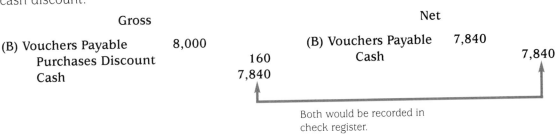

Gross			Net	
(B) Vouchers Payable	8,000		(B) Vouchers Payable	7,840
Purchases Discount		160	Cash	7,840
Cash		7,840		

Both would be recorded in check register.

If Discount Is Missed

(C) Mill Company issues check no. 531 in payment of voucher no. 299. The discount date has passed.

	Gross				Net		
(C) Vouchers Payable	8,000			(C) Vouchers Payable	7,840	
Cash		8,000		Discount Lost	160	
				Cash		8,000

Note that when the discount is missed in the net method, the Purchases Discount Loss account is used. (The end-of-chapter problems and exercises record all vouchers at gross unless otherwise stated.)

LEARNING UNIT 24-2 REVIEW

AT THIS POINT you should be able to

▼ Record transactions in a voucher system involving purchases returns and allowances and/or partial payments. (p. 818)
▼ Explain how the Discount Lost account could be used in a voucher system. (p. 819)

SELF-REVIEW QUIZ 24-2

(The blank forms you need are on page 159 of the *Study Guide and Working Papers*.)

Record the following entries in the voucher register for Joe Corporation:

20X8
Oct. 10 Prepared voucher no. 82 for purchase of merchandise for $3,000 from Rose Co.
Oct. 15 Returned $400 of the merchandise purchased from Rose Co. on October 10 due to poor workmanship. Joe Corp. canceled voucher no. 82 and replaced it with voucher no. 95.

Solution to Self-Review Quiz 24-2

						Voucher	Purchases	Sundry Accounts			
Date		Voucher Number	Payable to	Date of Payment	Check Number	Payable Cr.	Dr.	Account	PR	Dr.	Cr.
20X8 Oct.	10	82	Rose Co.	Cancelled Voucher	See No. 95	3 0 0 0 00	3 0 0 0 00				
	15	95	Rose Co.			2 6 0 0 00		Vouchers Payable		3 0 0 0 00	
								Purchases Returns			
								and Allowances			4 0 0 00

SUMMARY OF KEY POINTS

Learning Unit 24-1

1. In a voucher system, no payment is made without an approved form called a voucher. The voucher system consists of these elements: vouchers, voucher register, unpaid voucher file, check register, and paid voucher file.

2. Supporting documents are attached to a voucher.

3. The distribution of accounts when approved is the basis for the entry into the voucher register.

4. The voucher register, a special journal, replaces the purchases journal.

5. Cash discounts can be taken advantage of by filing vouchers in an unpaid voucher file (tickler file) by due dates.

6. A schedule of vouchers payable can be prepared at the end of the month. The accounts payable subsidiary ledger in a voucher system is eliminated.

7. The check register is a special journal that replaces the cash payments journal.

Learning Unit 24-2

1. After a voucher is recorded, a purchases return can be recorded by canceling the original voucher and debiting Vouchers Payable and crediting Vouchers Payable and Purchases Returns and Allowances.

2. For partial payments after a voucher has been prepared, the old voucher is canceled and a new voucher is prepared for each installment.

3. Companies recording invoices at the net amount would record any discounts missed in the Discount Loss account.

KEY TERMS

Check register A special journal that replaces the cash payments journal in recording payments of vouchers.

Paid voucher file Holds paid vouchers filed either in sequential order by voucher number or alphabetically by creditor's name.

Unpaid voucher file (tickler file) The file containing unpaid vouchers; arranged by due dates to take advantage of cash discounts.

Voucher A written authorization form containing data about a transaction along with proper authorizations for payment, account distributions, and so forth.

Voucher register A special journal replacing the purchases journal; records prenumbered vouchers at the time the liabilities are incurred.

Vouchers Payable A liability account in the general ledger that represents the controlling account for the sum of individual vouchers.

Voucher system An internal control system designed to control a company's cash payments.

BLUEPRINT: STEPS TO RECORD AND PAY A LIABILITY USING THE VOUCHER SYSTEM

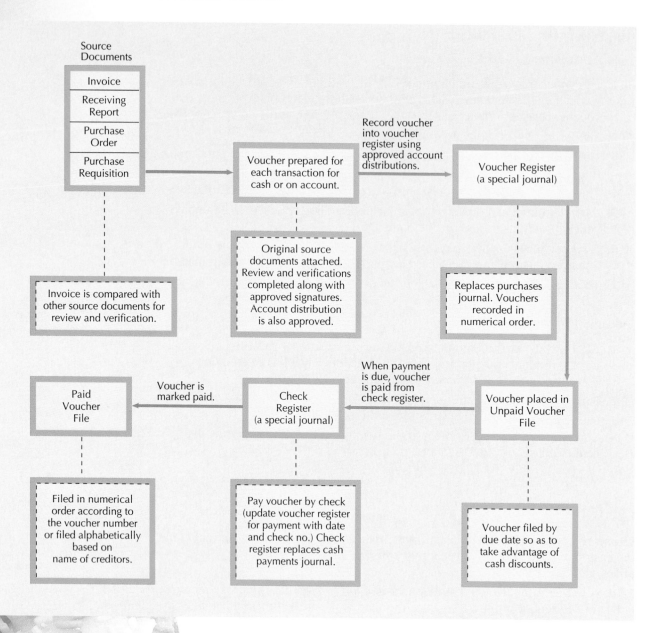

QUESTIONS, MINI EXERCISES, EXERCISES, AND PROBLEMS

Discussion Questions

1. What is the structure of a voucher?
2. List the five components of a voucher system.
3. What source documents are attached to a voucher?
4. Compare a voucher register to a purchases journal.
5. Why are vouchers filed by due dates?
6. Posting to a voucher register is quite different from posting to other special journals. Agree or disagree. Why?
7. Why is an accounts payable ledger eliminated in the voucher system?
8. Once a voucher is recorded, it cannot be canceled. True or false? Why?
9. Explain how partial payments would be recorded in the voucher register.

Mini Exercises

(The blank forms you need are on page 161 of the *Study Guide and Working Papers*.)

Journal Entries to Record and Pay Vouchers

1. Record the following transactions into the general journal:

20XX
June 9   Voucher no. 8 was prepared for the purchase of $500 of merchandise from Reel Co.; terms 2/10, n/30.

    12   Voucher no. 9 was prepared for $1,000 of equipment; terms 2/10, n/30.

    16   Check no. 15 was issued in payment of voucher no. 8.

Petty Cash

2. Record the following transactions into the general journal. The company uses a voucher system along with a petty cash fund.

20XX
Sept. 9   Voucher no. 18 was prepared to establish petty cash for $90.

    28   Voucher no. 42 was prepared to replenish the petty cash fund from the following receipts: Supplies $15; Delivery $18.

Purchases Returns and Allowances

3. On November 15, Pete Co. prepared a voucher for $500 for merchandise purchased from Pool Co. on November 19. Pete Co. decided to return the merchandise due to poor workmanship for $200. Record the general journal entries.

Equal Installments

4. On April 8, Pete Co. prepared voucher no. 18 to record purchases of equipment for $1,200. On April 16, Pete Co. decided to pay $1,200 in two equal installments (voucher nos. 21 and 22). Record the general journal entries.

Gross Versus Net

5. Record the following transactions at (a) gross and (b) net:

20XX
Dec. 8   Bought merchandise on account from Pill Co.; terms 2/10, n/30, $6,000. Voucher no. 31 was prepared.

    20   Issued check no. 480 in payment of voucher no. 31.

Exercises

(The blank forms you need are on pages 162–163 of the *Study Guide and Working Papers*.)

24-1. Agnes Company, which is a medium-sized firm, uses a voucher system. Record each of the following entries in general journal form (explanations can be omitted).

20X9
July 6   Voucher no. 50 was prepared for the purchase of $7,000 of merchandise from Loop Company; terms 2/10, n/30.

    9   Voucher no. 51 was prepared for the purchase of $4,000 of equipment; terms 2/10, n/30.

    15   Check no. 55 was issued in payment of voucher no. 51.

    16   Check no. 56 was issued in payment of voucher no. 50.

24-2. Dan Company uses a voucher system along with a petty cash fund. Record each of the following entries in general journal form (explanations can be omitted):

> General journal entries to record and pay vouchers.

> General journal entries to record and pay vouchers; includes establishment and replenishment of petty cash.

20X9

Aug.

10 Purchased $500 of merchandise from Glow Company; voucher no. 150 was prepared; terms 2/10, n/30.

14 Voucher no. 151 was prepared to establish petty cash for $70.

16 Issued check no. 60 in payment of voucher no. 150.

17 Check was issued to pay voucher no. 151.

28 Voucher no. 152 was prepared to replenish the petty cash fund from the following receipts: supplies, $17; delivery, $19.

Recording purchases returns and allowances.

24-3. On November 10, 20X9, a voucher for $1,000 for merchandise purchased from Gurn Company was prepared by Doll Corporation. On November 14, Doll decided to return the merchandise due to poor workmanship. The price of the merchandise was $600. Record the entries in general journal form for November 10 and 14 (explanations can be omitted).

Recording partial payments.

24-4. On March 15, 20X9, Lori Company prepared voucher no. 89 to record the purchase of equipment for $900. On March 18, Lori Company decided to pay $900 in two equal installments. (Voucher nos. 90 and 91 were prepared.) Prepare the appropriate journal entries in general journal form for March 15 and 18.

Gross versus net in recording invoices.

24-5. Marvin Company records invoices at gross in its voucher system. From the following transactions, (a) record in general journal form the appropriate entries at gross and (b) record the entries as if Marvin Company recorded invoices at net.

20X9

Dec.

15 Bought merchandise on account from Levron Corporation; terms 2/10, n/30; $9,000 voucher no. 300 was prepared.

29 Issued check no. 600 in payment of voucher no. 300.

Group A Problems

(The forms you need are on pages 164–170 of the *Study Guide and Working Papers.*)

Recording entries in the voucher register.

24A-1. Rowley Corporation uses a voucher system. Record the following transactions into the voucher register:

20X9

June

8 Purchased office equipment from Tam Corporation, $900; voucher no. 300 was prepared.

12 Established a petty cash fund of $70; voucher no. 301 was prepared.

14 Purchased merchandise from Screen Corporation, $800; voucher no. 302 was prepared.

15 Purchased office supplies from Longview Corp., $900; voucher no. 303 was prepared.

29 Voucher no. 304 was prepared to replenish the petty cash fund based on the following receipts: supplies, $34; postage, $16.

Check Figure:
June 12
Dr. Petty cash (sundry)
$70
Cr. Voucher payable $70

Voucher and check register: routine transactions.

24A-2. Skippy Corporation uses a voucher system. Record the following transactions into the voucher register and/or check register as appropriate:

20X9

July

5 Purchased merchandise for $2,000 from Dork Company; terms 2/10, n/30; voucher no. 280 was prepared authorizing payment on July 15.

8 Purchased merchandise for $6,000 from Hornet Company; terms 2/10, n/30; voucher no. 281 was prepared authorizing payment on July 18.

15 Paid amount due Dork from voucher no. 280; check no. 91.

18 Paid amount due Hornet from voucher no. 281; check no. 92.

Check Figure:
July 18
Dr. Voucher payable
$6,000
Cr. Purchases discount
$120
Cr. Cash $5,880

29 Voucher no. 282 was prepared from July rent to be paid to Loy Realty, $2,500.

30 Purchased office equipment for $2,900 from Lyle Company; voucher no. 283 was prepared.

30 Paid amount due Loy Realty from voucher no. 282; check no. 93.

24A-3. Jona Corporation has been using a voucher system for several years. Prepare entries in the voucher register and check register for the following transactions:

20X8
Sept.

1 Purchased merchandise inventory from Ricardo Corporation for $6,000; terms 2/10, n/30; voucher no. 68 was prepared.

5 Purchased merchandise inventory from Ree Corporation for $7,000; terms 2/10, n/30; voucher no. 69 was prepared.

8 Issued check no. 75 to pay for voucher no. 69.

10 Issued check no. 76 to pay for voucher no. 68.

14 Purchased merchandise inventory from Langle Corporation for $9,000; terms 2/10, n/30; voucher no. 70 was prepared.

17 Returned $3,000 of the merchandise to Langle Corporation due to poor workmanship; voucher no. 71 was prepared to replace voucher no. 70.

20 Issued check no. 77 to pay for voucher 71.

24A-4. The Swellon Company uses a voucher system. Record the following transactions:

20X9
Mar.

1 Voucher no. 200 was prepared for the purchase of $4,000 worth of merchandise inventory from Rolo Company; terms 2/10, n/30.

2 Voucher no. 201 was prepared for freight-in that was to be paid to Lance Company, $300.

3 Office supplies were purchased from Marge Company for $400; terms 2/10, n/30; voucher no. 202 was prepared.

8 Check no. 150 was issued in payment of voucher no. 200.

10 Purchased office equipment from Hal's Company for $10,000; payment is to be in two equal installments. Vouchers nos. 203 and 204 were prepared to cover these payments.

12 Check no. 151 was issued to pay voucher no. 203.

12 Check no. 152 was issued to pay voucher no. 201.

18 Purchased $6,000 of merchandise from Lowe Corporation; terms 2/10, n/30; voucher no. 205 was prepared.

20 Purchased $3,000 of merchandise from Ken Company; terms 2/10, n/30; voucher no. 206 was prepared.

25 Check no. 153 was issued to pay voucher no. 205.

27 Returned $1,000 of merchandise bought from Ken Company; voucher no. 206 was canceled and voucher no. 207 was prepared.

29 Issued check no. 154 to pay voucher no. 207.

Group B Problems

(The blank forms you need are on pages 164–170 of the *Study Guide and Working Papers*.)

24B-1. Daper Company uses a voucher system. Record the following transactions into the voucher register:

20X8
July

10 Purchased office equipment from Smooth Company, $1,600; voucher no. 400 was prepared.

13 Established a petty cash fund of $60; voucher no. 401 was prepared.

14 Purchased merchandise from Roy Corporation, $650; voucher no. 402 was prepared.

Voucher and check register with cancellation due to purchases returns and allowances.

Check Figure:
Sept 8
Dr. Voucher payable
$7,000
Cr. Purchases discount
$140
Cr. Cash $6,860

Voucher and check register with cancellation and partial payments.

Check Figure:
Mar. 25
Dr. Voucher payable
$6,000
Cr. Purchases discount
$120
Cr. Cash $5,880

Recording entries in the voucher register.

Check Figure:
July 13
Dr. Petty cash (sundry)
$60
Cr. Voucher payable $60

15 Purchased office supplies from Kendall Corporation, $600; voucher no. 403 was prepared.

29 Voucher no. 404 was prepared to replenish the petty cash fund based on the following receipts: supplies, $28; postage, $14.

24B-2. Caven Company uses a voucher system. Record the following transactions into the voucher register and/or check register as appropriate:

20X9

May

6 Purchased merchandise for $2,000 from Hall Company; terms 2/10, n/30; voucher no. 600 was prepared authorizing payment on May 14.

8 Purchased merchandise for $8,000 from Ryan Company; terms 2/10, n/30; voucher no. 601 was prepared authorizing payment on May 17.

14 Paid amount due Hall Company from voucher no. 600; check no. 300.

17 Paid amount due Ryan Company from voucher no. 601; check no. 301.

25 Voucher no. 602 was prepared for June rent to be paid to Paul Realty, $800.

30 June rent was paid by check no. 302.

30 Purchased office equipment for $3,000 from Kline Company; voucher no. 603 was prepared.

24B-3. Lava Company has been using a voucher system for several years. Prepare entries in the voucher register and check register for the following transactions:

20X8

Nov.

1 Purchased merchandise inventory from Lester Corporation for $9,000; terms 2/10, n/30; voucher no. 52 was prepared.

6 Purchased merchandise inventory from Jungle Corporation for $7,000; terms 2/10, n/30; voucher no. 53 was prepared.

8 Issued check no. 50 to pay for voucher no. 53.

10 Issued check no. 51 to pay for voucher no. 52.

14 Purchased merchandise inventory from Horv Corporation for $11,000; terms 2/10, n/30; voucher no. 54 was prepared.

17 Returned $2,000 of the merchandise to Horv Corporation due to poor workmanship; voucher no. 55 was prepared to replace voucher no. 54.

19 Issued check no. 52 to pay for voucher no. 55.

24B-4. Krown Corporation uses a voucher system. Record the following transactions:

20X9

June

1 Voucher no. 100 was prepared for the purchase of $6,000 worth of merchandise inventory from Langley Corporation; terms 2/10, n/30.

2 Voucher no. 101 was prepared for freight-in that was to be paid to J. Kane Company, $400.

3 Office supplies were purchased from Harold Company for $600; terms 2/10, n/30; voucher no. 102 was prepared.

8 Check no. 150 was issued in payment of voucher no. 100.

10 Purchased office equipment from Lyon Company for $7,000; payment is to be in two equal installments. Vouchers nos. 103 and 104 were prepared to cover these payments.

12 Check no. 151 was issued to pay voucher no. 103.

12 Check no. 152 was issued to pay voucher no. 101.

18 Purchased $5,000 of merchandise from Von Company; terms 2/10, n/30; voucher no. 105 was prepared.

20 Purchased $5,000 of merchandise from Lallan Company; terms 2/10, n/30; voucher no. 106 was prepared.

25 Check no. 153 was issued to pay voucher 105.

26 Returned $200 of merchandise bought from Lallan Company; voucher no. 106 was canceled and voucher no. 107 was prepared.

27 Issued check no. 154 to pay voucher no. 107.

Voucher and check register: routine transactions.

Check Figure:
May 17
Dr. Voucher payable
            $8,000
Cr. Purchases discount
            $160
Cr. Cash $2,840

Voucher and check register with cancellation due to purchases returns and allowances.

Check Figure:
Nov. 8
Dr. Voucher payable
            $7,000
Cr. Purchases discount
            $140
Cr. Cash $6,860

Voucher and check register with cancellation and partial payments.

Check Figure:
June 8
Dr. Voucher payable
            $6,000
Cr. Purchases discount
            $120
Cr. Cash $5,880

REAL-WORLD APPLICATIONS

24R-1.
Mel Ring has recently opened a pizza shop. Over lunch, a salesman told Mel that to control his operation he should set up a voucher system so that all bills would be paid on time and properly approved. Mel thinks that in 10 years he will probably franchise his pizza operation. As his accountant, do you think the voucher system is the best way to go? Why? Please respond in writing.

24R-2.
Morris Company uses a voucher system. For the past two years the bookkeeper has recorded installment purchases as a lump-sum payment in the voucher register. The bookkeeper thinks an unpaid voucher file is not needed, because cash discounts are minimal compared with total dollar sales. When his supervisor is out to dinner, the bookkeeper will sign her name to the distribution accounts authorization. His supervisor has told him not to worry, because she can adjust "any mistakes" later on.

After two weeks from the date a voucher is paid, the bookkeeper destroys all pertinent data about the transaction. May Weston, an accounting intern, is quite upset about what's going on at Morris Company. Her textbook theory is not being followed, but her supervisor has told her that textbook principles are not always followed in the real world. Are May's concerns justified? State in writing your reasons.

YOU make the call

Critical Thinking/Ethical Case

24R-3.
Most Companies use the voucher system. Due to poor profitability, several employees in the accounting office were let go. Joe Rose, who handled the verification of the vouchers in the voucher register, was now given the responsibility of writing the checks from the check register. The head of accounting thought Joe was the most honest person in the company and that all would be fine. Do you agree with this move? What would you recommend? You make the call. Write down your recommendation to Jay Flynn, head of accounting.

INTERNET EXERCISES

EX-1. [www.generaldynamics.com/]   Voucher systems provide high degrees of internal control in acquiring inventory and in controlling cash payments. Your text has also emphasized the assistance a voucher system provides in assuring that all purchases discounts earned are taken. Missing a purchase discount is a costly event. The person responsible for ascertaining that all of them are taken will quickly fall from grace if discounts are not taken. Here is an example of how important discounts are. For this exercise you are the person who is responsible for this important step.

You have an invoice due for $100,000. You also have the authority to borrow money on a 30 day basis if it is necessary. The interest rate you would borrow the money at is 12%. This invoice has a discount of 3% if paid within the next ten days. Today, you don't have the cash but you know you will in 30 days. What you must determine is should you borrow the money to pay the invoice. These are the decisions money managers at companies like General Dynamics face routinely.

What is your recommendation in this case?

EX-2. [www.ge.com/] This is an excellent website for many reasons. Pay attention while here on the tabs on personal finance. You will find them both helpful and enlightening in working with your own cash and investments.

A large business protects its assets with good internal controls. One internal control measure that large companies employ is that of using vouchers. As this chapter explained, vouchers are in place for every payment of cash, from the highest expenditure to the lowest petty cash reimbursement.

General Electric uses vouchers to control its cash and to centralize its payment system. Not every GE branch operation maintains its own accounting records. Purchases and payments are centralized as an additional method of internal control.

Discuss how you believe this helps or hinders their day to day cash operation.

Departmental Accounting

Founded in Chicago in 1886, Sears Roebuck & Co. was the nation's first department store. Sears came into its own in the prosperous years after WWII, putting washing machines and other appliances in the homes of America's burgeoning middle class. Now, in the new millennium, Sears is having a tough time trying to find its market. The baby boomers who built Sears' business have made all their hard goods purchasers and are more concerned with travel and other indulgences. More importantly, retailers that offer mid-prices and which appeal to middle America tastes are now getting caught in the middle. Sears is being squeezed on one hand by discounters (Wal-Mart, Kmart & Target) and "big box" retailers (Home Depot) and, on the other hand, by high-end service-oriented stores (Nordstrom, Neiman Marcus).

Analysts and investors are looking to Sears' new CEO, Alan Lacy, to turn the ailing company around. Most industry watchers agree that the company needs to focus on these five key areas of operation: apparel, appliances, credit operations, e-commerce, and "The Great Indoors," Sears' new home design centers. Apparel will most certainly be Lacy's top priority. Clothing takes up a lot of retailing floor space and if a department store becomes known for fashion misses, as Sears has, then apparel becomes a drag on the entire company's bottom line.

Alan Lacy needs to have an accurate financial portrait of each of Sears' departments if he is to formulate a winning strategy for the company. Tracking purchases, sales, and operating expenses by department allows managers to see what segments of the business are succeeding. For instance, with sales of about $50 million per unit for The Great Indoors, Sears plans to open 50 more of these envelope-pushing home design stores by 2005, bringing the total count to 150. Only by doing departmental accounting can Sears control expenses and determine which departments need to be improved or even eliminated. In this chapter you will learn how to address the accounting needs of a merchandise company with many departments, like Sears. You'll see how to prepare income statements that focus on departmental gross profit, net income and contribution margin.

Based on: Peter J. Gallanis, "Lacy identifies agenda as new CEO of Sears," *Dsn Retailing Today,* October 2, 2000, pp. 3, 57. Sandra Dolbow, "Mid-tier muddle," *Brandweek,* April 10, 2000, pp. 36–48. Calmetta Coleman, "Sears' New CEO Has Handle on Finance, But May Need to Master Merchandising," *Wall Street Journal,* September 12, 2000, p. B14. Alec Appelbaum, "The softer side of Sears," *Money,* November 2000, pp. 44–46.

LEARNING OBJECTIVES

▼ Preparing income statements focusing on gross profit by departments. (p. 830)

▼ Preparing income statements focusing on departmental net income. (p. 833)

▼ Preparing income statements focusing on departmental contribution margin. (p. 837)

Many large companies find it necessary to keep separate accounting records for their various departments so that management can see how efficient each department is and how each contributes to overall performance. This chapter focuses on various accounting and reporting aids that allow management to do so.

We use as our example Catlin's Department Store, which sells mainly clothing. The manager of the Adult Clothes Department at the store is quite concerned about the department's performance; there has been talk by upper management of the possibility of reducing the space of the Adult Department in favor of expanding the Children's Department.

LEARNING UNIT 25-1

THE INCOME STATEMENT: FOCUS ON GROSS PROFIT BY DEPARTMENT

Each department of Catlin's Department Store is a unit in which the manager has the responsibility for controlling and incurring certain costs as well as generating revenue. Each unit, or department, is known as a **profit center.** If a manager had the responsibility for controlling costs, but not that for directly generating revenue, the unit would be called a **cost center** (an example is the office maintenance department at Catlin's).

Figure 25-1 shows the income statement for Catlin's Department Store. As you can see from this figure, the total gross profit of the company is $373,800 ($841,300 − $467,500), and the operating expenses are $170,000.

To break down the gross profit figure by department, a company must gather information about each department. It does so by setting up separate accounting records for each department, with separate accounts for Sales, Sales Returns and Allowances, Sales Discount, Merchandise Inventory, Purchases, Purchases Returns and Allowances, and Purchases

CATLIN'S DEPARTMENT STORE
INCOME STATEMENT
FOR YEAR ENDED DECEMBER 31, 20X8

Revenue from Sales:			
Sales		$870 0 0 0 00	
Less: Sales Returns and Allowances	$14 7 0 0 00		
Sales Discount	14 0 0 0 00	28 7 0 0 00	
Net Sales			$841 3 0 0 00
Cost of Goods Sold:			
Merchandise Inventory, Jan. 1, 20X8		$143 0 0 0 00	
Purchases	$499 0 0 0 00		
Less: Purchases Returns and			
Allowances	15 4 0 0 00		
Purchases Discount	16 1 0 0 00	467 5 0 0 00	
Cost of Goods Available for Sale		610 5 0 0 00	
Less: Merchandise Inventory,			
Dec. 31, 20X8		143 0 0 0 00	
Cost of Goods Sold			$467 5 0 0 00
Gross Profit on Sales			373 8 0 0 00
Operating Expenses			170 0 0 0 00
Income before Taxes			203 8 0 0 00
Income Tax Expense			89 5 2 0 00
Net Income			$114 2 8 0 00

FIGURE 25-1. Income Statement for Catlin's Department Store

Discount. Once this information has been separated by department, we can calculate the gross profit of each department. The use of a computer makes it possible to record and gather information for many departments easily and quickly.

Let's look at an example. Figure 25-2 shows how in the sales journal of Catlin's Department Store there is a Sales account for the Children's Department and one for the Adult Department.

Figure 25-3 (p. 832) is an income statement showing the gross profit for each department and the combined totals. You would not see a balance sheet prepared in this way, broken down by department; only an income statement is done this way. Keep in mind that an income statement indicates how well a business or department is performing.

> Income statements can be broken down by departments; balance sheets are not.

CATLIN'S DEPARTMENT STORE
SALES JOURNAL

Date		Account Debited	Invoice Number	Post. Ref.	Accounts Receivable Dr.	Children's Sales Cr.	Adult Sales Cr.
Nov.	3	Marsie Rose	325	✔	1 9 0 00	1 0 0 00	9 0 00
	8	Bill Stone	326	✔	1 8 5 00	1 7 5 00	1 0 00
					(115)	(411)	(412)

FIGURE 25-2. Sales Journal of Catlin's Department Store

FIGURE 25-3. Income Statement with Gross Profit Broken Down by Department

CATLIN'S DEPARTMENT STORE
INCOME STATEMENT SHOWING DEPARTMENTAL GROSS PROFIT
FOR YEAR ENDED DECEMBER 31, 20X8

	Children's		Adult		Total	
Revenue from Sales:						
Sales		$580 000 00		$290 000 00		$870 000 00
Less: Sales Returns and Allowances	$ 6 500 00		$ 8 200 00		$ 14 700 00	
Sales Discounts	8 000 00	14 500 00	6 000 00	14 200 00	14 000 00	28 700 00
Net Sales		$565 500 00		$275 800 00		$841 300 00
Cost of Goods Sold:						
Merchandise Inventory, Jan. 1, 20X8		75 000 00		$ 68 000 00		$143 000 00
Purchases	$289 000 00		$210 000 00		$499 000 00	
Less: Purchases Returns and Allowances	6 900 00		8 500 00		15 400 00	
Purchases Discounts	8 200 00	273 900 00	7 900 00	193 600 00	16 100 00	467 500 00
Cost of Goods Available for Sale		$348 900 00		$261 600 00		$610 500 00
Less: Merchandise Inventory, Dec. 31, 20X8		79 000 00		64 000 00		143 000 00
Cost of Goods Sold		$269 900 00		$197 600 00		467 500 00
Gross Profit on Sales		$295 600 00		$ 78 200 00		$373 800 00
Operating Expenses						170 000 00
Income before Taxes						203 800 00
Income Tax Expense						89 520 00
Net Income						$114 280 00

LEARNING UNIT 25-1 REVIEW

AT THIS POINT you should be able to

▼ Explain the difference between a cost center and a profit center. (p. 830)

▼ Prepare an income statement focusing on gross profit by department. (p. 831)

SELF-REVIEW QUIZ 25-1

(The blank forms you need are on page 174 of the *Study Guide and Working Papers.*)

Respond true or false to the following:

1. In a cost center a manager directly generates revenue.

2. Each department can have its own separate accounts for Sales, Sales Returns and Allowances, and so forth, to record information for the income statement.

3. A balance sheet is always separated by departments.

Solutions to Self-Review Quiz 25-1

1. False   2. True   3. False

LEARNING UNIT 25-2

THE INCOME STATEMENT: FOCUS ON DEPARTMENTAL NET INCOME

DEPARTMENTAL INCOME FROM OPERATIONS

So far we have shown how gross profit has been accumulated by departments. In this unit we look at how the $170,000 of operating expenses can be allocated by departments if we want to extend departmental reporting beyond gross profit.

The operating expenses of Catlin's Department Store that can be traced and identified directly to a separate department are called **direct expenses.** An example is the salaries of the salespeople who work only for the Children's Department at Catlin's. The operating expenses that cannot be identified with a specific department but are incurred on behalf of the company are called **indirect expenses.** An example is the expense incurred in the upkeep of the building in which Catlin's is located.

In Figure 25-4 (p. 834) we can see a sample of operating expenses that can now be apportioned to the Children's and Adult Departments. Note that the total is still $170,000. Now let's see how these calculations for operating expenses were arrived at. Figure 25-5 (p. 834) is a summary of how the expenses were apportioned. Following that is a detailed explanation. Use Figure 25-5 as a reference sheet as you read the explanation that follows.

FIGURE 25-4. Operating Expenses Apportioned by Department

CATLIN'S DEPARTMENT STORE
INCOME STATEMENT SHOWING DEPARTMENTAL INCOME BEFORE TAX
FOR YEAR ENDED DECEMBER 31, 20X8

	Children's	Adult	Totals
Net Sales	$565,500.00	$275,800.00	$841,300.00
Cost of Goods Sold	269,900.00	197,600.00	467,500.00
Gross Profit on Sales	$295,600.00	$ 78,200.00	$373,800.00
Operating Expenses:			
Sales Salaries	$ 25,000.00	$ 15,000.00	$ 40,000.00
Building Expense	12,000.00	4,000.00	16,000.00
Delivery Expense	6,000.00	4,000.00	10,000.00
Advertising Expense	9,000.00	5,000.00	14,000.00
Depreciation Expense	22,500.00	7,500.00	30,000.00
Administrative Expense	40,000.00	20,000.00	60,000.00
Total Operating Expenses	$114,500.00	$ 55,500.00	$170,000.00
Income before Taxes	$181,100.00	$ 22,700.00	$203,800.00
Income Tax Expense			89,520.00
Net Income			$114,280.00

1. Sales Salaries

The payroll records of Catlin's show that salespeople in the Children's Department were paid $25,000 and salespeople in the Adult Department were paid $15,000. These expenses can be identified with specific departments, so they are considered direct expenses.

2. Building Expense

The costs relating to the occupancy of Catlin's building are lumped into an account called Building Expense. Building Expense is an indirect expense, apportioned on the basis of square footage. Catlin's allocates the total cost of Building Expense of $16,000 on the basis of the number of square feet that each department occupies. Catlin's total space is 40,000 square feet, with the Children's Department occupying 30,000 square feet and the Adult Department

	Children's		Adult		Total Operating Expense	
	Direct	Indirect	Direct	Indirect	Direct	Indirect
(1) Sales Salaries	$25,000.00		$15,000.00		$40,000.00	
(2) Building Expense		$12,000.00		$4,000.00		$16,000.00
(3) Delivery Expense	6,000.00		4,000.00		10,000.00	
(4) Advertising Expense	7,000.00	2,000.00	4,000.00	1,000.00	11,000.00	3,000.00
(5) Depreciation Expense		22,500.00		7,500.00		30,000.00
(6) Administrative Expense		40,000.00		20,000.00		60,000.00
	$38,000.00	$76,500.00	$23,000.00	$32,500.00	$61,000.00	$109,000.00
						$170,000

FIGURE 25-5. Direct and Indirect Operating Expenses by Department

CHAPTER 25 ... DEPARTMENTAL ACCOUNTING

10,000 square feet. Building Expense is allocated to each department as follows:

Children's	Adult
$\dfrac{30,000 \text{ ft}^2}{40,000 \text{ ft}^2} = .75 = 75 \text{ percent}$	$\dfrac{10,000 \text{ ft}^2}{40,000 \text{ ft}^2} = .25 = 25 \text{ percent}$
$.75 \times \$16,000 = \$12,000$	$.25 \times \$16,000 = \$4,000$

Thus of the $16,000 in Building Expense, the Children's Department is allocated $12,000 and the Adult Department $4,000.

3. Delivery Expense

The Children's Department shipped 60 percent of all merchandise, and the Adult Department shipped 40 percent of the merchandise. The total cost of Delivery Expense is $10,000. Because the exact amount of Delivery Expense is traceable to each department, it is considered a direct expense. If the cost of delivery is *not* specifically traceable to each department, it is considered an indirect expense and can be charged to departments based on past delivery records. Delivery Expense is calculated as follows:

Children's	Adult
$.60 \times \$10,000 = \$6,000$	$.40 \times \$10,000 = \$4,000$

4. Advertising Expense

Advertising Expense for Catlin's totaled $14,000. Of that total, $4,000 was spent on advertising adult clothes and $7,000 on advertising children's clothes. The remaining $3,000 ($14,000 − $11,000) was spent on advertising the store's image in general. Thus this $3,000 is an indirect expense. How would you divide this expense by department? One common way is to apportion it based on gross sales of each department, as follows:

Gross Sales:	$580,000	Children's
	290,000	Adult
	$870,000	Total Gross Sales

Children's	Adult
$\dfrac{\$580,000}{\$870,000} \times \$3,000$	$\dfrac{\$290,000}{\$870,000} \times \$3,000$
$= \frac{2}{3} \times \$3,000 = \$2,000$	$= \frac{1}{3} \times \$3,000 = \$1,000$

Thus of the $3,000 of indirect expenses, $2,000 is charged to the Children's Department and $1,000 to the Adult Department.

5. Depreciation Expense

Catlin's Department Store apportions depreciation on its building based on the square footage each department occupies. (Some companies apportion depreciation based on the average cost of the equipment in each department.) Catlin's has 40,000 square feet, of which the Children's Department takes up 30,000 (3/4) and the Adult Department takes up 10,000 (1/4). The amount of Depreciation Expense charged to each department is calculated as follows:

> Depreciation Expense is an indirect expense.

Children's	Adult
$\frac{3}{4} \times \$30,000 = \$22,500$	$\frac{1}{4} \times \$30,000 = \$7,500$

6. Administrative Expense

Administrative expenses are incurred for the company as a whole and are not broken down by department; they are thus indirect expenses. In the case of Catlin's it was decided that the Administrative Expense of $60,000 would be divided on the basis of each department's gross sales. We saw this method of alteration used in Advertising Expense. The calculation for indirect expenses charged to each department is as follows:

$580,000	Children's
290,000	Adult
$870,000	Total Gross Sales

Children's	Adult
$\frac{\$580,000}{\$870,000} = \frac{2}{3}$	$\frac{\$290,000}{\$870,000} = \frac{1}{3}$
$\frac{2}{3} \times \$60,000 = \$40,000$	$\frac{1}{3} \times \$60,000 = \$20,000$

Now take a moment to review Figure 25-4 to make sure you understand how we arrived at the total operating expenses of $170,000.

LEARNING UNIT 25-2 REVIEW

AT THIS POINT you should be able to

▼ Explain the difference between direct and indirect expenses. (p. 833)
▼ Explain how operating expenses are allocated to specific departments. (p. 834)
▼ Prepare, in proper form, an income statement showing departmental income before tax. (p. 834)

SELF-REVIEW QUIZ 25-2

(The blank forms you need are on page 175 of the *Study Guide and Working Papers.*)

Given the following, apportion the Rent Expense on the basis of floor space:

	Dept. A	Dept. B	Total
Floor space	208,000	112,000	320,000
Rent expense			$ 30,800

Solution to Self-Review Quiz 25-2

Apportionment of Rent Expense:

Dept. A	Dept. B
$\frac{208,000}{320,000} \times \$30,800 = \$20,020$	$\frac{112,000}{320,000} \times \$30,800 = \$10,780$

THE INCOME STATEMENT
SHOWING DEPARTMENTAL
CONTRIBUTION MARGIN

Referring back to Figure 25-4 (p. 834), income before taxes for the Children's Department equaled $181,100 and the Adult Department showed $22,700. Some accountants think these figures are misleading, because the indirect expenses in Figure 25-5 were apportioned to the total operating expenses of each department. An alternative to this approach to indirect expense allocation is shown in Figure 25-6, which lists direct departmental expenses and the contribution each department makes to cover indirect expenses. This breakdown is called the **contribution margin,** which can also be defined as the gross profit of a department minus its direct expenses. This approach charges to a department only those expenses that are directly traceable to it. Note in Figure 25-6 that the Children's Department contributes $257,600 to cover indirect expenses and net income. This figure is quite different from the $181,100 listed in Figure 25-4.

> In this approach indirect expenses are separated from direct expenses.

Supporters of this approach think indirect expenses are not controlled by the department manager and thus should not be used in evaluating departmental performance. Some accountants contend that even if a department is eliminated, the indirect expenses would not be decreased. For example, Catlin spends $3,000 in advertising that is basically aimed at advertising the store's overall image, and that expense would still remain if the Adult Department or the Children's Department were eliminated.

CATLIN'S DEPARTMENT STORE
INCOME STATEMENT SHOWING DEPARTMENTAL CONTRIBUTION MARGIN
FOR YEAR ENDED DECEMBER 31, 20X8

	Children's	Adult	Totals
Net Sales	$565 500 00	$275 800 00	$841 300 00
Cost of Goods Sold	269 900 00	197 600 00	467 500 00
Gross Profit on Sales	$295 600 00	$ 78 200 00	373 800 00
Direct Departmental Expenses			
Sales Salaries	$ 25 000 00	$ 15 000 00	$ 40 000 00
Advertising Expense	7 000 00	4 000 00	11 000 00
Delivery Expense	6 000 00	4 000 00	10 000 00
Total Direct Departmental Expenses	$ 38 000 00	$ 23 000 00	$ 61 000 00
Contribution Margin	$257 600 00	$ 55 200 00	$312 800 00
Indirect Departmental Expenses			
Building Expense			$ 16 000 00
Advertising Expense			3 000 00
Depreciation Expense			30 000 00
Administrative Expense			60 000 00
Total Indirect Expenses			$109 000 00
Income before Taxes			$203 800 00
Income Tax Expense			89 520 00
Net Income			$114 280 00

FIGURE 25-6. Income Statement Showing Department Contribution Margin

Determining whether certain departments at Catlin's should be expanded or reduced would involve investigation of the financial reports presented in the chapter along with topics such as the following:

1. The effect that dropping a department would have in terms of loss of its contribution margin. For example, would closing a jewelry department in a clothing store reduce the store's total administrative expenses?

2. The effect one department has in drawing customers to other departments. Do customers who come into the store to look at jewelry go on to look at dresses in another department?

3. Trends in the industry. Even though a certain department is not doing well, all the competing stores have such a department; the answer may be to cut down the size of the department rather than eliminate it.

4. Ability of suppliers to meet increasing demand for items. For example, it would not be a good idea to open a pastry shop in Catlin's until one had lined up a number of good, reliable suppliers.

We conclude this unit with an example that shows how eliminating a department that has a net loss may in fact cause an even greater loss in the overall net income for the company. The situation is as follows:

	Depts. A, B, C,	Dept. D Only	Totals for Depts. A – D	Totals if Dept. D Is Eliminated
Sales	$1,469,000	$130,000	$1,599,000	$1,469,000
Cost of Goods Sold	869,000	82,000	951,000	869,000
Gross Profit	600,000	48,000	648,000	600,000
Direct Expenses	340,000	31,000	371,000	340,000
Contribution Margin	260,000	17,000	277,000	260,000
Indirect Expenses	130,000	26,000	156,000	156,000
Net Income (Loss)	$ 130,000	$ (9,000)	$ 121,000	$ 104,000

Note that if Department D is eliminated, net income of the other departments is reduced by $17,000, from $121,000 to $104,000. This change is the result of losing the contribution margin of $17,000 from Department D.

LEARNING UNIT 25-3 REVIEW

AT THIS POINT you should be able to

▼ Explain why an income statement might report departmental contribution margin rather than listing all direct and indirect expenses under total operating expenses. (p. 837)
▼ Prepare an income statement showing the contribution margin. (p. 837)

SELF-REVIEW QUIZ 25-3

(The blank forms you need are on page 175 of the *Study Guide and Working Papers.*)

Respond true or false to the following:

1. Allocating indirect expenses will never be subjective.
2. A direct expense is traceable to a respective department.

3. Direct expenses of a department in the contribution margin approach are combined with indirect expenses.

4. Eliminating one department could reduce sales of another department.

5. Contribution margin equals gross profit on sales plus direct department expenses.

Solutions to Self-Review Quiz 25-3

1. False   **2.** True   **3.** False   **4.** True   **5.** False

SUMMARY OF KEY POINTS

Learning Unit 25-1

1. A profit center means that a manager is responsible for controlling certain costs as well as generating revenues.
2. Separate accounts for Sales, Purchases, and so forth, can be set up for each department so as to calculate departmental gross profit.
3. Income statements can be broken down by departments; balance sheets are not.

Learning Unit 25-2

1. Direct expenses can be directly identified with a specific department.
2. The method used to apportion indirect expenses to departments may vary from company to company; there is no one absolute method.
3. One department's direct expense may be another department's indirect expense.
4. One way to apportion indirect expenses such as Advertising Expense or Administrative Expense by department is on the basis of each department's gross sales.

Learning Unit 25-3

1. Indirect expenses are *not* combined with direct expenses when preparing an income statement showing departmental contribution margin.
2. Gross profit on sales minus direct departmental expenses equals contribution margin.

KEY TERMS

Contribution margin   A department's net profit used to cover indirect expenses.

Cost center   A unit or department that incurs costs but does not generate revenues.

Direct expenses   Expenses that can be traced directly to a specific department.

Indirect expenses   Expenses that cannot be traced directly to one department.

Profit center   A unit or department that incurs costs and generates revenues.

BLUEPRINT: DEPARTMENTAL ACCOUNTING

Situation 1:
Income statement showing departmental gross profit

	DEPT. A	DEPT. B	TOTAL	
Net Sales	1	2	3	(1 + 2)
− Cost of Goods Sold	4	5	6	(4 + 5)
= Gross Profit on Sales	7 (1 − 4)	8 (2 − 5)	9	(3 − 6)
− Operating Expenses			10	
= Income before Taxes			11	(9 − 10)
− Income Tax Expense			−12	
= Net Income			13	

Situation 2:
Income statement showing departmental income before tax

Direct and indirect expenses → allocated

	DEPT. A	DEPT. B	TOTAL	
Net Sales	1	2	3	(1 + 2)
Cost of Goods Sold	4	5	6	(4 + 5)
Gross Profit on Sales	7 (1 − 4)	8 (2 − 5)	9	(3 − 6)
Operating Expenses				
Salaries Expense	10	11	12	(10 + 11)
Delivery Expense	13	14	15	(13 + 14)
Depreciation Expense	16	17	18	(16 + 17)
Administrative Expense	19	20	21	(19 + 20)
Total Operating Expenses	22 (10 + 13 + 16 + 19)	23 (11 + 14 + 17 + 20)	24	(12 + 15 + 18 + 21)
Income before Taxes	25 (7 − 22)	26 (8 − 23)	27	(9 − 24)
Income Tax Expense			28	
Net Income			29	(27 − 28)

Situation 3:
Income statement showing departmental contributions to indirect expenses

	DEPT. A	DEPT. B	TOTAL	
Net Sales	1	2	3	(1 + 2)
Cost of Goods Sold	4	5	6	(4 + 5)
Gross Profit on Sales	7 (1 − 4)	8 (2 − 5)	9	(3 − 6)
Direct Departmental Expenses			10	
Sales Salaries	10	11	12	(10 + 11)
Advertising Expenses	13	14	15	(13 + 14)
Delivery Expenses	16	17	18	(16 + 17)
Total Direct Expenses	19 (10 + 13 + 16)	20 (11 + 14 + 17)	21	(12 + 15 + 18)
Contribution to Indirect Expenses	22 (7 − 19)	23 (8 − 20)	24	(9 − 21)
Indirect Departmental Expenses				
Building Expense			25	
Advertising Expenses			26	
Depreciation Expenses			27	
Total Indirect Expenses			28	(25 + 26 + 27)
Income before Taxes			29	(24 − 28)
Income Tax Expense			30	
Net Income			31	(29 − 30)

QUESTIONS, MINI EXERCISES, EXERCISES, AND PROBLEMS

Discussion Questions

1. What is the difference between a cost center and a profit center?

2. Explain how gross profit is calculated.

3. Special journals are not used in departmental accounting. True or false? Please explain.

4. Compare and contrast indirect expenses and direct expenses.

5. Explain how advertising expense could be both a direct cost and an indirect cost for a company.

6. Square footage is often used to allocate indirect costs to various departments within a company. True or false?

7. An income statement showing departmental income before tax does not list individual operating expenses for each department. True or false? Please explain.

8. Explain why a company might prepare an income statement showing each department's contribution margin.

Mini Exercises

(The blank forms you need are on pages 177–178 of the *Study Guide and Working Papers*.)

Appropriating Rent to Departments Based on Sales

1. The cost of rent of $6,000 for Moore Co. is appropriated to each department based on sales. Given the following, assign the cost of rent to each department.

Rent	Toys	Clothing
$6,000	$20,000	$40,000

Appropriating Fire Insurance Based on Square Footage

2. Calculate the assignment of fire insurance of $16,000 to each department:

INDIRECT EXPENSE	BASIS OF ASSIGNMENT	BAKERY	GROCERY
Fire Insurance	4,000 ft² total	1,000 ft²	3,000 ft²

Calculating Net Income from Total Operating Expenses

3. Given the following, calculate net income.

	Dept. 1	Dept. 2
Net Sales	$4,000	$6,000
Cost of Goods Sold	1,000	2,000
Operating Expenses		$2,500
Income Tax Expense, 40 percent rate		

Calculating Departmental Net Income

4. From the following, calculate departmental income before tax. Assume a tax rate of 40 percent.

	Dept. A	Dept. B
Net Sales	$3,000	$4,000
Cost of Goods Sold	1,000	1,200
Delivery Expense	500	700
Advertising Expense	400	500
Depreciation Expense	200	300

Calculating Contribution Margin

5. Calculate the contribution margin for each department and income before taxes, based on the following:

	Dept. A 1,000 Ft^2	Dept. B 2,000 Ft^2
Net Sales	$5,000	$10,000
Cost of Goods Sold	2,000	6,000
Sales Salaries	$800 (30 percent directly related to Dept. A and 70 percent related to Dept. B)	
Rent Expense	$400	
Advertising Expense	900 ($400 directly related to Dept. A and $200 related to Dept. B)	

Exercises

(The blank forms you need are on pages 179–180 of the *Study Guide and Working Papers*.)

25-1. The cost of rent of $8,000 for Poller Company is appropriated to each department based on its sales. Given the following, assign the cost of rent to each department.

> Appropriating rent to departments based on sales.

	Jewelry	Hardware	Automotive
Sales	$30,000	$50,000	$20,000

25-2. Complete the assignment of fire insurance to each department.

> Appropriating fire insurance based on square footage.

Indirect Expense	Amount	Basis of Assignment	Candy Sales		Ice Cream Sales		Pizza Sales	
Fire Insurance	$90,000	30,000 ft^2 total	18,000 ft^2	A	7,500 ft^2	B	4,500 ft^2	C

25-3. Given the following, calculate net income.

> Calculating net income from total operating expenses.

	Dept. 1	Dept. 2
Net Sales	$30,000	$40,000
Cost of Goods Sold	14,000	26,000
Operating Expenses		$16,000
Income Tax Expense, 30 percent rate		

25-4. From the following, calculate departmental income before tax. Assume a tax rate of 30 percent.

> Calculating departmental income.

	Dept. A	Dept. B
Net Sales	$200,000	$250,000
Cost of Goods Sold	100,000	125,000
Delivery Expense	24,000	28,000
Advertising Expense	23,000	22,000
Depreciation Expense	25,000	24,000

25-5. Calculate the contribution margin for each department and income before taxes, based on the following:

	Dept. A 10,000 Ft^2	Dept. B 20,000 Ft^2
Net Sales	$60,000	$90,000
Cost of Goods Sold	25,000	50,000
Sales Salaries	8,000 (40 percent directly related to Dept. A and 60 percent to Dept. B)	
Rent Expense	5,000	
Advertising Expense	18,000 ($3,000 directly related to Dept. A and $9,000 to Dept. B)	

Group A Problems

(The blank forms you need are on pages 181–187 of the *Study Guide and Working Papers*.)

Preparing an income statement showing departmental gross profit.

Check Figure:
Total net income $4,950

25A-1. From the following data, prepare in proper form an income statement showing departmental gross profit (assume a 25 percent tax rate) for Bill's Variety for the year ended December 31, 20X9.

Cash	$12,000
Accounts Receivable	6,000
Allowance for Doubtful Accounts	1,500
Merchandise Inventory, January 1, 20X9, Grocery	7,000
Merchandise Inventory, January 1, 20X9, Pizza	5,000
Merchandise Inventory, December 31, 20X9, Grocery	19,000
Merchandise Inventory, December 31, 20X9, Pizza	7,000
Equipment	15,000
Acc. Depreciation, Equipment	9,100
Accounts Payable	10,200
B. Smith, Capital	10,500
B. Smith, Withdrawals	3,100
Sales, Grocery	20,000
Sales, Pizza	18,000
Sales Returns and Allowances, Grocery	2,000
Sales Returns and Allowances, Pizza	3,000
Purchases, Grocery	22,400
Purchases, Pizza	14,500
Purchases Returns and Allowances, Grocery	800
Purchases Returns and Allowances, Pizza	400
Total Operating Expenses	4,700

Constructing a departmental expense sheet.

Check Figure:
Total indirect expenses $32,400

25A-2. Given the following information about the clothing and hardware departments of Sally Company, prepare a Departmental Expense Allocation sheet showing expenses by department.

Account	Indirect	Direct	
		Clothing	Hardware
1. Rent Expense	$14,000		
2. Insurance Expense	7,000	$1,400	$2,600
3. Depreciation Expense		300	700
4. Advertising Expense	2,000		
5. Supplies Expense	3,000		
6. Salaries Expense	6,400		

Additional Facts

	Clothing	Hardware
Net sales	$70,000	$30,000
Cost of goods sold	50,000	18,000
Floor space	200 ft^2	500 ft^2

Appropriation Basis

Rent and Insurance:	Floor space
Advertising and Supplies:	Net sales
Salaries:	Gross profit of clothing and hardware departments

25A-3. From the following partial data, prepare an income statement showing departmental income before tax along with net income for Pete's Corporation for the year ended December 31, 20X9.

Net Sales, TV's	$60,000
Net Sales, Washers	30,000
Cost of Goods Sold, TV's	39,000
Cost of Goods Sold, Washers	18,000
Income tax rate 30 percent	
TV Dept., 5,000 sq. ft.	
Washers, 3,000 sq. ft.	

Assigning direct expenses and preparing an income statement showing departmental income before tax.

Check Figure:
Net income $14,140

Basis of Appropriation

Sales Salary Expense	$4,500	Net sales
Building Expense	4,800	Square footage
Delivery Expense	2,700	Net sales
Depreciation Expense	800	Square footage

25A-4. Educator Company has requested that you (1) assign indirect expenses to its jewelry and fur departments as appropriate and (2) prepare an income statement for November 20X9 showing departmental contribution margins along with net income. Assume a 30 percent tax rate.

Appropriating indirect expenses and preparing an income statement showing departmental contribution margin.

Check Figure:
Total indirect expenses $20,400

	Jewelry: 30,000 Ft^2	Fur: 10,000 Ft^2	Indirect Cost
Net Sales	$280,000	$220,000	
Merchandise Inventory (Nov. 1)	50,000	70,000	
Merchandise Inventory (Nov. 30)	35,000	30,000	
Purchases	200,000	100,000	
Purchases Discount	10,000	20,000	
Salaries	2,900	2,100	$10,000
Depreciation	25,000	21,300	
Advertising	1,000	2,000	20,000
Administrative			32,000
Rent Expense			12,000

Appropriations of Indirect Expenses

Salaries are based on net sales. All other indirect expenses are based on square footage.

Group B Problems

(The blank forms you need are on pages 181–187 of the *Study Guide and Working Papers*.)

25B-1. From the following data, prepare in proper form an income statement showing departmental gross profit (assume a 25 percent tax rate) for Randy Company for the year ended December 31, 20X9.

Cash	$13,100
Accounts Receivable	6,200
Allowance for Doubtful Accounts	2,400
Merchandise Inventory, January 1, 20X9, Cosmetics	8,000
Merchandise Inventory, January 1, 20X9, Jewelry	6,000
Merchandise Inventory, December 31, 20X9, Cosmetics	19,000
Merchandise Inventory, December 31, 20X9, Jewelry	8,000
Equipment	19,000
Acc. Depreciation, Equipment	9,200
Accounts Payable	13,500
R. Glade, Capital	14,000
R. Glade, Withdrawals	5,000
Sales, Cosmetics	20,000
Sales, Jewelry	18,000
Sales Returns and Allowances, Cosmetics	2,000
Sales Returns and Allowances, Jewelry	1,500
Purchases, Cosmetics	24,800
Purchases, Jewelry	15,100
Purchases Returns and Allowances, Cosmetics	900
Purchases Returns and Allowances, Jewelry	500
Total Operating Expenses	5,500

25B-2. Given the following information about the toys and clothing departments of Avery Company, prepare a Departmental Expense Allocation sheet showing expenses by department.

Account	Indirect	Direct	
		Toys	Clothing
1. Rent Expense	$15,000		
2. Insurance Expense	21,000	$1,900	$1,700
3. Depreciation Expense		1,000	700
4. Advertising Expense	3,000		
5. Supplies Expense	10,000		
6. Salaries Expense	30,000		

Additional Facts

	Toys	Clothing
Net sales	$20,000	$30,000
Cost of goods sold	10,000	20,000
Floor space	1,000 ft^2	2,000 ft^2

Allocation Basis

Rent and Insurance:	Floor space
Advertising and Supplies:	Net sales
Salaries:	Gross profit of toys and clothing departments

25B-3. From the following partial data, prepare an income statement showing departmental income before tax along with net income for Logan Corporation for year ended December 31, 20X9.

Net Sales, Rugs (10,000 ft^2)	$180,000
Net Sales, Furniture (30,000 ft^2)	220,000
Cost of Goods Sold, Rugs	55,000
Cost of Goods Sold, Furniture	69,000
Income tax rate, 30 percent	

		Basis of Appropriation
Sales Salary Expense	$60,000	Net Sales
Building Expense	20,000	Square footage
Delivery Expense	80,000	Net sales
Depreciation Expense	16,000	Square footage

Check Figure:
Net income $70,000

25B-4. Lonestar Company has requested that you (1) assign indirect expenses to its candy and grocery departments as appropriate and (2) prepare an income statement for November 20X9 showing departmental contribution margins along with net income. Assume a 30 percent tax rate.

Assigning indirect expenses and preparing an income statement showing departmental contributions to indirect expenses.

	Candy: 20,000 Ft²	Grocery: 30,000 Ft²	Indirect Cost
Net Sales	$18,000	$22,000	
Merchandise Inventory (November 1)	1,000	1,500	
Merchandise Inventory (November 30)	2,000	2,500	
Purchases	9,250	8,450	
Purchases Discount	250	450	
Salaries	750	1,500	$2,500
Depreciation	1,250	250	
Advertising	250	1,500	
Administrative			7,500
Rent Expense			2,000

Check Figure:
Total indirect expenses $7,075

Appropriations of Indirect Expenses

Salaries are based on net sales. All other indirect expenses are based on square footage.

REAL-WORLD APPLICATIONS

25R-1.
Dot Jenson received the following memorandum:

	MEMO
To:	Dot Jensen, Manager of Children's Clothing
From:	Bill Barnes
Re:	Annual evaluation

Based on the following data (attached), I am sorry to inform you that you will not be rehired at the end of your current contract. Your department's performance was far below the budgeted level we had projected for this period.

Dot is quite upset and thinks her evaluation is not justified. Analyze the data to see whether Dot's evaluation is indeed not justifiable. What additional factors might be considered? Please respond in writing.

Clothing Sales		$320,000
Cost of Goods Sold		170,000
Gross Profit		$150,000
Operating Expenses:		
Hourly Wages	$75,000	
Manager's Salary	40,000	
Depreciation of Building	15,000	
Interest on Long-Term Bonds	12,000	
Payroll Taxes	16,000	
Total Operating Expenses		158,000
Departmental Loss		(8,000)

25R-2.

Moore Markets is considering the elimination of the Bakery Shop. Based on the following data, make your written recommendations to Jim Moore, president of Moore Markets.

	Produce	Dairy	Bakery
Sales	$60,000	$90,000	$82,000
Cost of Goods Sold	19,000	58,000	67,000
Gross Profit	$41,000	$32,000	$15,000
Direct Expenses	12,000	6,000	8,000
Indirect Expenses	6,000	12,000	4,000
Total Operating Expenses	18,000	18,000	12,000
Net Income before Tax	$23,000	$14,000	$ 3,000

YOU make the call

Critical Thinking/Ethical Case

25R-3.

Hernando Favor had been working in the bakery department of Long Company for four years when he was promoted to the accounting department. Since his promotion, sales in the bakery department have slipped and management is considering cutting the department in half. Hal Moore, who works in the bakery, will be laid off. Hernando has thought about shifting some of his sales figures in his accounting records to the bakery department from other departments so as to save his friend Hal from losing his job. Hernando thinks no one will find out in the long run, because he knows the bakery can increase sales. Do you feel Hernando has clear justification for his actions? You make the call. Write down your recommendation to Hernando.

INTERNET EXERCISES

EX-1. [www.caesars.com]   From the website you can visualize that Caesar's World has several profit centers. The obvious profit centers are the casino and gaming operations, Caesar's Palace Hotels in Nevada, New Jersey, and Indiana, and an online shopping mall.

If you have ever visited Caesar's Palace you know that they have an extensive shopping mall within the hotel and casino operation. It is also among the "showiest" of the show place hotels in Las Vegas.

1. Can you name at least two additional departments not mentioned on the website? Think of what is available in a hotel but is not specifically mentioned in the website.

2. How do you believe that Caesar's evaluates its overall operation with "departmental" accounting? In your answer to this question mention profit centers and cost centers and connect them to Caesar's operations.

EX-2. [http://www.k2sports.com] This site is an excellent of a departmentalized operation. The main page shows operations in four areas: ski, snowboards, skates, and bikes. After you browse through the website answer these questions based upon your impressions of the company:

1. Are these four areas "profit centers" or "cost centers"?

2. Does each of these generate "gross profit"?

3. From the chapter's discussion of "contribution margin", what kind of costs would go into a "contribution margin" income statement?

4. What kind of fixed costs or common costs do you believe K2 would have, and how would you incorporate them into a departmental statement?

CHAPTER **26**

Manufacturing Accounting

Raw material . . . direct labor . . . maintenance . . . engineering . . . rent . . . machinery . . . insurance . . . and the list could go on and on. There is a more daunting array of costs associated with making a product than with selling goods that are already made or selling a service. Hence, financial managers of manufacturing companies are in a constant quest to lower the **cost of goods manufactured.** One of the best ways to do that? Simply, to let someone *else* do the manufacturing.

Increasingly, companies are handing over their entire manufacturing process — not just parts — to contract manufacturers. After all, the manufacturing process is now viewed as a commodity, something any number of companies can do well. Original equipment manufacturers (OEMs) would rather put their resources into activities that add value: product development, marketing, and customer support are all areas in which OEMs can gain a competitive edge.

Motorola, the Schaumburg-IL based electronics company, is one of the leaders in the outsourcing trend. While your cell phone may sport the Motorola, Inc. logo, there's a good chance it was actually made by a little-known company based in Singapore, Flextronics International Ltd. In May 2000 Motorola announced that it expects to outsource over $30 billion of consumer-electronics production to Flextronics. It was the largest outsourcing agreement to date between a name-brand electronics company and a contract manufacturer. In 1998 contract manufacturing was a $60 billion industry. By 2003 it will grow to nearly $150 billion.

How does Flextronics do the job more cheaply than Motorola? Flextronics doesn't pay for idle machines and empty factory floors. Orders from multiple clients keep its plants busy around the clock and cover overhead costs. **Manufacturing overhead** is one of the key elements of manufacturing costs. It consists of all the other manufacturing costs not included in **raw material** and **direct labor** — such as the maintenance of Motorola's or Flextronics' equipment.

This chapter will give you an overview of **cost accounting,** the methods manufacturing companies use to track and compile cost flows associated with goods sold and goods on hand. A cost must be determined for each product manufactured. Because there are so many details involved in tracking this type of accounting, most companies now use computer accounting software to do the tracking.

Based on: Scott Thurm, "Motorola Plans to Outsource Production To Flextronics in $30 Billion Agreement," *Wall Street Journal,* May 31, 2000, p. A3. Paul Gibson, "The asset paradox," *Electronic Business,* April 2000, pp. 120–126. James Carbone, "What buyers look for in contract manufacturers," *Purchasing,* March 23, 2000, pp. 32–38. John Teresko, "E-collaboration," *Industry Week,* June 12, 2000, pp. 31–36.

LEARNING OBJECTIVES

▼ Preparing a cost of goods manufacturing schedule. (p. 851)

▼ Journalizing transactions recording the manufacturing process. (p. 856)

▼ Preparing a worksheet for a manufacturing company. (p. 862)

Manufacturing accounting refers to the specialized accounting concepts and techniques that are required to record, report, and control the operations of a manufacturing company properly. The financial accounting procedures discussed in the previous merchandising chapters are all still valid in a manufacturing firm, but they are supplemented by the manufacturing accounting to be presented in this chapter, including some new terms and techniques that were not considered or required in the accounting for merchandising operations.

LEARNING UNIT 26-1

COST OF GOODS MANUFACTURED AND THE INCOME STATEMENT

In a manufacturing company it is necessary to separate the manufacturing costs from all other selling and administrative expenses, because product costs, inventory costs, and even gross profit come from the manufacturing process. One way of thinking about it is to imagine manufacturing costs being incurred in one building and the other costs in another building as shown:

MANUFACTURING	ADMINISTRATIVE
Raw Material	Selling
Direct Labor	Administrative
Overhead	

All the costs incurred in the manufacturing building are manufacturing costs, including the managers' salaries, maintenance, all the labor, all materials, supplies, electricity, rent, and the depreciation of manufacturing property and machinery. In addition, it is necessary to allocate a portion of the accounting, personnel, purchasing, and data-processing departments each month based on their contribution to manufacturing.

The administrative building would house top management, sales personnel, and other administrative personnel and their supplies and expenses.

ELEMENTS OF MANUFACTURING COST

Once we have determined which are administrative and which are manufacturing costs, we can break the manufacturing costs into three elements: raw material, direct labor, and manufacturing overhead.

Raw material (or direct material) consists of all the items of material that will become a part of the product or will change the quality or characteristics of the product. For example, for a furniture manufacturer, the raw material includes lumber, metal parts, fabric, epoxy, finishing material, and even nuts and bolts. In a company that manufactures aluminum products, raw material includes the pure aluminum and the additives that are inserted to make the aluminum shiny or dull, or rigid or flexible.

Direct labor includes the wages of those *personnel* whose efforts directly change the quality or characteristics of the products. In a furniture manufacturing company, the direct labor includes the person who saws the table top, the person who paints the furniture, the person who attaches the handles to the drawers, and so on. In that same company, however, the supervisor, the maintenance person, and the forklift driver are *not* direct labor.

Manufacturing overhead consists of all other manufacturing costs not included in raw material or direct labor. Manufacturing overhead includes many diverse items such as indirect labor, maintenance, engineering, manufacturing supervision, and supplies. Some of the most common items of manufacturing overhead are as follows:

- ▽ Maintenance wages and supplies.
- ▽ Production supervision and expenses.
- ▽ Depreciation expense of manufacturing assets.
- ▽ Rent expense for buildings or machinery.
- ▽ Electricity for manufacturing.
- ▽ Insurance expense for manufacturing.
- ▽ Indirect labor: material handlers.
- ▽ Manufacturing clerical wages

MANUFACTURING INVENTORIES

In a merchandise firm there is one inventory made up of goods for sale. In a manufacturing firm there are *three* major inventories: raw material, work-in-process, and finished goods. (In addition, there are other minor inventories for such things as maintenance supplies and operating supplies.)

The *raw material inventory* consists only of the cost of the items of raw material being held for production plus the freight cost to bring the material in. The acquisition of raw material is recorded as Purchases, the account reserved for the purchase of raw material.

The *work-in-process inventory* represents the cost of the products being processed (the step before becoming finished goods) and includes the raw material, direct labor, and the manufacturing overhead costs incurred at the time of the inventory.

The *finished goods inventory* consists of the manufacturing cost of the products that have been completed and are awaiting shipment to customers.

COST OF GOODS SOLD

To prepare an income statement for a manufacturing company, we first must figure the cost of goods sold. This section of the income statement for a manufacturing company is somewhat different from that of a merchandise company. The following diagram shows how cost of goods sold is calculated for a merchandise firm and for a manufacturing company.

LAYOUT TO CALCULATE COST OF GOODS SOLD

Merchandising Company	Manufacturing Company
Beginning Merchandise Inventory + Net Purchases	Beginning Finished Goods Inventory + Cost of Goods Manufactured
= Cost of Merchandise Available for Sale − Ending Merchandise Inventory	= Cost of Goods Available for Sale − Ending Finished Goods Inventory
= Cost of Goods Sold	= Cost of Goods Sold

As you can see in the diagram, the cost of goods manufactured replaces the purchases of the merchandise company statement. The purpose of the cost of goods sold section is to properly match the manufacturing costs with the sales, and for this reason it is necessary to include the beginning and ending finished goods inventories so as to calculate the cost. For example, the sales may have been for 500 units of product, whereas the company manufactured only 400 units this month. In this case there would be a 100-unit reduction in inventory. Thus, by adding the cost of goods manufactured to the beginning inventory and subtracting the ending inventory, the result will be the cost of 500 units of product. Similar reasoning is applied if the units manufactured for the month exceed the units sold.

The cost of goods manufactured is figured on a separate form or schedule. This statement is shown in Figure 26-1. There are a few key points to be remembered when preparing this figure:

FIGURE 26-1. Statement of Cost of Goods Manufactured

DUKE MANUFACTURING COMPANY
STATEMENT OF COST OF GOODS MANUFACTURED
FOR MONTH ENDED 6/30/X8

Direct Materials:			
Raw Material Inventory, 6/1/X8		$ 5 000 00	
Plus: Net Purchases	55 000 00		
Less: Raw Material Inventory, 6/30/X8	8 000 00	47 000 00	
Raw Material Cost			$ 52 000 00
Direct Labor			90 000 00
Overhead:			
Factory Supervision	$ 37 000 00		
Maintenance Labor	37 000 00		
Electricity	15 000 00		
Maintenance Supplies	6 000 00		
Operating Supplies	5 000 00		
Depreciation of Machinery	3 000 00		
Total Overhead	4 000 00		70 000 00
Total Manufacturing Costs			212 000 00
+ Work-in-Process Inventory, 6/1/X8			7 000 00
− Work-in-Process Inventory, 6/30/X8			9 000 00
Total Cost of Goods Manufactured			$210 000 00

FIGURE 26-2. Income Statement for a Manufacturing Firm

DUKE MANUFACTURING COMPANY INCOME STATEMENT FOR MONTH ENDED 6/30/X8		
Sales		$400 0 0 0 00
Cost of Goods Sold:		
Finished Goods Inventory 6/1/X8	$ 25 0 0 0 00	
Plus: Cost of Goods Manufactured	210 0 0 0 00	
Cost of Goods Available for Sale	235 0 0 0 00	
Less: Finished Goods Inventory 6/30/X8	15 0 0 0 00	
Cost of Goods Sold		220 0 0 0 00
Gross Profit		180 0 0 0 00
Operating Expenses:		
Selling Expenses	$ 55 0 0 0 00	
Administrative Expense	65 0 0 0 00	120 0 0 0 00
Net Income (before taxes)		$ 60 0 0 0 00

1. Cost of raw materials equals beginning raw materials inventory plus purchases less ending inventory of raw materials.
2. Total manufacturing costs incurred equals the following:

   Cost of Raw Material Used

   + Direct Labor

   + Factory Overhead
3. Cost of goods manufactured equals the following:

   Total Manufacturing Costs

   + Beginning Work-in-Process

   − Ending Work-in-Process

The first step in preparing the cost of goods manufactured is the calculation of the raw material cost for the month. If the accounting department has its records on a computer, the raw material cost may be readily available. If it is not, the cost must be calculated as shown by adding purchases to the beginning raw material inventory and then subtracting the ending inventory. The direct labor cost is usually a single figure found on the payroll or the labor distribution report. The overhead costs are then totaled and added to the raw material and direct labor to arrive at the total costs for the month. *The final step is to add the beginning work-in-process inventory and subtract the ending inventory.* Keep in mind that we subtract ending inventory, because it is not part of the cost of goods manufactured (yet).

Let's see how this figure is then used in preparing the income statement, shown in Figure 26-2.

LEARNING UNIT 26-1 REVIEW

AT THIS POINT you should be able to

▼ Define and explain the three elements of manufacturing costs: raw material, direct labor, and manufacturing overhead. (p. 852)

- ▼ Define and explain the three major inventories in a manufacturing company: raw material, work-in-process, and finished goods. (p. 852)
- ▼ Compare the cost of goods sold section on an income statement for a merchandising company with the cost of goods manufactured section for a manufacturing company. (p. 853)
- ▼ Prepare a cost of goods manufactured schedule. (p. 853)

SELF-REVIEW QUIZ 26-1

(The blank forms you need are on page 193 of the *Study Guide and Working Papers*.)

Using the accounts and amounts below, prepare a separate statement of cost of goods manufactured and a cost of goods sold section of the income statement:

Finished Goods Inventory, June 1	$ 45,000
Depreciation of Machinery	15,000
Purchases (Net)	250,000
Maintenance Labor	15,000
Raw Material Inventory, June 1	15,000
Direct Labor	320,000
Work-in-Process Inventory, June 1	30,000
Factory Supervision Salaries	45,000
Finished Goods Inventory, June 30	60,000
Raw Material Inventory, June 30	20,000
Indirect Factory Labor	120,000
Work-in-Process Inventory, June 30	40,000
Factory Electricity Expense	15,000

Solution to Self-Review Quiz 26-1

Statement of Cost of Goods Manufactured

Raw Material Inventory, June 1	$ 15,000	
Plus: Net Purchases	250,000	
Less: Raw Material Inventory, June 30	20,000	
Raw Material Cost		$245,000
Direct Labor		320,000
Overhead:		
Depreciation	$ 15,000	
Maintenance Labor	15,000	
Factory Supervision Salaries	45,000	
Indirect Labor	120,000	
Electricity Expense	15,000	210,000
Total Manufacturing Costs		$775,000
Plus: Work-in-Process Inventory, June 1		30,000
Less: Work-in-Process Inventory, June 30		40,000
Total Cost of Goods Manufactured		$765,000

Cost of Goods Sold

Finished Goods Inventory, June 1	$ 45,000
Plus: Cost of Goods Manufactured	765,000
Cost of Goods Available for Sale	810,000
Less: Finished Goods Inventory, June 30	60,000
Cost of Goods Sold	$750,000

THE ACCUMULATION OF MANUFACTURING COSTS

As the raw material, direct labor, and overhead are charged into the manufacturing process, they must be recorded. The issuance of material from the warehouse, the assignment of labor to departments, and the movement of the products through the process must be provided to the cost accountants as the basis for journal entries.

Source Documents: The required data are submitted to the cost accountants through various source documents. The timely receipt of legible documents is often a problem in some companies, and employees must be made aware of their importance.

Receiving reports are prepared by the receiving department to acknowledge receipt of all material and supplies from vendors. A typical receiving report is shown in Figure 26-3. The accounting copy becomes a part of the vendor payment voucher, along with the purchase order and the vendor invoice.

Material requisitions are the documents initiated by the manufacturing personnel, or other users, to request material from the inventory warehouse. The requisition (Figure 26-4) is presented to the storekeeper as the materials are issued. Copies of the requisitions are kept in accounting as a basis for charging material into production.

A **clock card** is a card used by each hourly based employee to clock in and out of the factory each day. A typical clock card is shown in Figure 26-5. The cards are collected each week by the payroll department and become a basis for the payroll check and for charging labor into production.

FIGURE 26-3. Receiving Report

RECEIVING REPORT			
Received from: Adams Company		Receiving Report No. __1031__ Date: 6/20/X8	
Quantity	Description	Unit Price	Total Price
50 Gals.	Paint	$6.50/Gal.	$325.00
Revilo Manufacturing Co. Inspected By __MS__ Received By __BJ__			

FIGURE 26-4. Material Requisition

MATERIAL REQUISITION			
Department Finishing		Requisition No. __3648__ Date: 6/20/X8	
Quantity	Description	Unit Price	Total Price
8 Gals.	White Paint	$6.50	$52.00
Revilo Manufacturing Co. Inspected By __CY__ Received By __FU__			

CLOCK CARD

Name: David Ross
Social Sec. No. 420-80-5178
Department: Cutting
Clock No. 1432

Day	In	Out	In	Out	Hours
Mon	7:58			4:03	8
Tue	7:57			4:01	8
Wed	8:00			4:02	8
Thu	7:59			5:02	9
Fri	7:57			4:03	8
Sat					
Sun					
		Total Hours			41

FIGURE 26-5. Clock Card

Lot tickets, or move tickets, are documents that are written by departmental managers to reflect the movement of products, or parts of products, from one department to another. The department receiving the products must verify the quantity and quality of the products. These tickets become the basis for transferring costs between departments and to finished goods inventory. An example of a lot ticket is shown in Figure 26-6.

A **labor distribution report** is a byproduct of the payroll that has been reassembled into the categories of direct labor, maintenance labor, and so forth. Based on this report the cost accountants charge labor into departments. An example of a typical labor distribution report is shown in Figure 26-7.

Bills of lading are documents that are used to show the shipment of products to customers. The cost accounting copies of the bills become the basis for recording the transfer of the cost of the products from the finished

LOT TICKET

Date
Transferred from: Assembling
Transferred To: Finishing

Quantity	Description
20 Tables	36" Oak
20 Tables	36" Pine

Received By MB

FIGURE 26-6. Lot Ticket

LABOR DISTRIBUTION REPORT
WEEK ENDING 9/10/X8

Employee	Department	Hours	Rate	Total
Direct Labor:				
James Amos	Cutting	42	$6.20	$260.40
Andrew Brown	Cutting	39	6.00	234.00
—				
Indirect Labor:				
Don Able	Cutting	40	7.20	280.00
Carl Baker	Cutting	40	7.50	300.00
—				

FIGURE 26-7. Labor Distribution Report

FIGURE 26-8. Bill of Lading

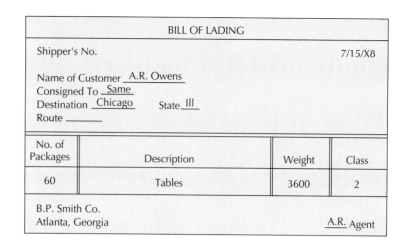

BILL OF LADING			
Shipper's No.			7/15/X8

Name of Customer __A.R. Owens__
Consigned To __Same__
Destination __Chicago__   State __Ill__
Route _____

No. of Packages	Description	Weight	Class
60	Tables	3600	2

B.P. Smith Co.
Atlanta, Georgia   __A.R.__ Agent

goods inventory to the cost of goods sold. A typical bill of lading is shown in Figure 26-8.

> More explanations, along with an extra demonstration problem, follow the journal entries.

THE FLOW OF MANUFACTURING COSTS

To record and control manufacturing costs as the products move through the manufacturing process properly, it is necessary to establish the pattern of the flow of the costs. To do so, we use a flowchart.

FIGURE 26-9. Flow of Costs

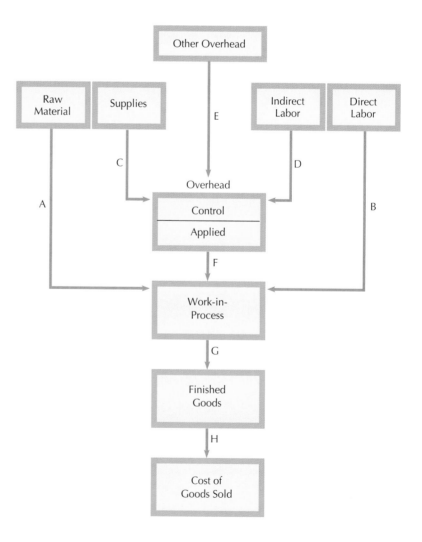

The Flowchart: Figure 26-9 illustrates the movement of the material, labor, and overhead through the operation. Each step of the flow, from A to H, is illustrated and is followed by an example of the journal entries and the source documents for each step. *It should be noted that the journal entries reflect a debit to the destination and a credit to the source.*

This process may seem overwhelming, so take the time to match each step in Figure 26-10 with its corresponding journal entry. Remember that the debit is to the destination and the credit is to the source. See the blueprint on page 868 for samples involving T accounts.

Overhead Application: As shown in the flow of cost journal entries C, D, and E, the debit is to an account called Overhead—Control and in F the credit is to the account Overhead—Applied. It is desirable to maintain both these overhead accounts to avoid errors and confusion. Overhead—Control is used for the accumulation of all actual overhead costs as debits, and the Overhead—Applied is credited for the application of overhead to production.

It is necessary to apply overhead each week to determine the total costs for that week. Some overhead accounts, however, such as electricity, supervision, and depreciation, are not known until the end of the month. For this reason, an overhead rate must be established as a basis for applying the overhead. There are several methods of determining a rate, depending on the type of operation of the company.

		Debit	Credit	SOURCE DOCUMENTS
(A)	Work-in-Process Inventory	2 00 00 00		Material requisitions
	Raw Material Inventory		2 00 00 00	
(B)	Work-in-Process Inventory	18 00 00 00		Labor distribution report
	Payroll		18 00 00 00	
(C)	Overhead—Control	4 00 00 00		Material requisitions
	Supplies Inventory		4 00 00 00	
(D)	Overhead—Control	10 00 00 00		Labor distribution report
	Payroll		10 00 00 00	
(E)	Overhead—Control	10 00 00 00		Various
	Supervision Salaries		6 00 00 00	
	Rent Expense		1 00 00 00	
	Depreciation Expense		2 00 00 00	
	Electricity Expense		1 00 00 00	
(F)	Work-in-Process Inventory	25 00 00 00		None
	Overhead—Applied		25 00 00 00	
(G)	Finished Goods Inventory	22 00 00 00		Lot tickets
	Work-in-Process Inventory		22 00 00 00	
(H)	Cost of Goods Sold	24 00 00 00		Bills of lading
	Finished Goods Inventory		24 00 00 00	

FIGURE 26-10. Journal Entries

The most common and practical methods are based on direct labor or machine hours. A rate can be developed from the annual budget of the overhead costs and the *direct labor dollars* (wages of those persons whose efforts *directly* affect the characteristics of the products manufactured) as follows:

Annual Overhead ÷ Annual Direct Labor Dollars
$500,000 ÷ $1,000,000 = 50 Percent

Based on this calculation, overhead can be applied to production each week or month at a rate of 50 percent of the direct labor cost charged to production. For example, if the direct labor this month is $20,000, overhead would be applied at $10,000, as follows:

Work-in-Process Inventory	10 0 0 0 00	
Overhead—Applied		10 0 0 0 00

Another much-used rate is based on *direct labor hours:*

Annual Overhead ÷ Annual Direct Labor Hours
$500,000 ÷ 200,000 Hours = $2.50/Hour

In this case, the rate of $2.50 per direct labor hour would be applied as overhead. If direct labor hours this month were 2,000 hours, the applied overhead would be $5,000, as follows:

Work-in-Process Inventory	5 0 0 0 00	
Overhead—Applied		5 0 0 0 00

Still another method that is convenient in some companies is based on *machine hours,* as follows:

Annual Overhead ÷ Annual Machine Hours
$500,000 ÷ 100,000 Machine Hours = $5.00/Hour

Using the $5.00 per machine hour rate, if the machine ran 3,000 hours, the overhead applied would be $15,000.

DEMONSTRATION PROBLEM

To further illustrate the journal entries and overhead application, consider the following transactions and the resulting journal entries for the month of August:

A. Issued raw material from the storeroom costing $69,000.

B. Charged direct labor into production, $60,000.

C. Issued supplies from the storeroom costing $6,000.

D. Incurred indirect labor costs of $15,000.

E. Charged the following expenses to overhead: rent, $3,000; supervision, $12,000; depreciation, $4,000; electricity, $6,000.

F. Applied overhead at 85 percent of direct labor dollars.

G. Transferred completed products costing $200,000 to finished goods.

H. Sold products costing $208,000.

Journal Entries

(A)	Work-in-Process Inventory	69 00 0 00			
	Raw Material Inventory		69 00 0 00		
(B)	Work-in-Process Inventory	60 00 0 00			
	Payroll		60 00 0 00		
(C)	Overhead—Control	6 00 0 00			
	Supplies Inventory		6 00 0 00		
(D)	Overhead—Control	15 00 0 00			
	Payroll		15 00 0 00		
(E)	Overhead—Control	25 00 0 00			
	Rent Expense		3 00 0 00		
	Supervision Expense		12 00 0 00		
	Depreciation Expense		4 00 0 00		
	Electricity Expense		6 00 0 00		
(F)	Work-in-Process Inventory	51 00 0 00			
	Overhead—Applied		51 00 0 00		
(G)	Finished Goods Inventory	200 00 0 00			
	Work-in-Process Inventory		200 00 0 00		
(H)	Cost of Goods Sold	208 00 0 00			
	Finished Goods Inventory		208 00 0 00		

LEARNING UNIT 26-2 REVIEW

AT THIS POINT you should be able to

▼ List the six source documents covered in this unit and explain the function of each in the accounting process. (p. 856)
▼ List the steps of the flowchart showing the movement of raw materials through the manufacturing process. (p. 858)
▼ Explain the difference between Overhead—Control and Overhead—Applied. (p. 860)

SELF-REVIEW QUIZ 26-2

(The blank forms you need are on page 194 of the *Study Guide and Working Papers*.)

Prepare the general journal entries required to record the following transactions (omit explanations):

A. Charged raw material into production, $6,000.

B. Charged direct labor into production, $8,000.

C. Issued operating supplies, $2,000.

D. Charged indirect labor into production, $5,000.

E. Incurred the following overhead: supervision, $4,500; rent, $1,000; depreciation, $500; electricity, $1,500; maintenance, $2,500.

F. Applied overhead to production at 180 percent of direct labor dollars.

G. Transferred products to finished goods, $9,000.

H. Sold products costing $10,000.

Solution to Self-Review Quiz 26-2

(A)	Work-in-Process	6 0 0 0 00	
	Raw Material		6 0 0 0 00
(B)	Work-in-Process	8 0 0 0 00	
	Payroll		8 0 0 0 00
(C)	Overhead—Control	2 0 0 0 00	
	Supplies Inventory		2 0 0 0 00
(D)	Overhead—Control	5 0 0 0 00	
	Payroll		5 0 0 0 00
(E)	Overhead—Control	10 0 0 0 00	
	Supervision		4 5 0 0 00
	Rent		1 0 0 0 00
	Depreciation		5 0 0 00
	Electricity		1 5 0 0 00
	Maintenance		2 5 0 0 00
(F)	Work-in-Process	14 4 0 0 00	
	Overhead—Applied		14 4 0 0 00
(G)	Finished Goods Inventory	9 0 0 0 00	
	Work-in-Process		9 0 0 0 00
(H)	Cost of Goods Sold	10 0 0 0 00	
	Finished Goods		10 0 0 0 00

LEARNING UNIT 26-3

WORKSHEET FOR A MANUFACTURING COMPANY

In past chapters we viewed worksheets for a service company as well as a merchandise company. We now examine and explain the preparation of a worksheet for a manufacturing company. Figure 26-11 shows a worksheet for Roe Corporation. We have changed companies to provide you with more insight into other account titles used by different companies. The theory is the same. We then see how reports are prepared from the worksheet. Let's first look at some key points to remember when a worksheet is prepared. Keep in mind that the steps of the accounting cycle for a manufacturing company are the same as those used for a merchandise company.

FIGURE 26-11. Worksheet for a Manufacturing Company

Account Titles	Trial Balance Dr.	Trial Balance Cr.	Adjustments Dr.	Adjustments Cr.	① Statement of Cost of Goods Manufactured Dr.	① Statement of Cost of Goods Manufactured Cr.	Income Statement Dr.	Income Statement Cr.	Balance Sheet Dr.	Balance Sheet Cr.
Cash	135000								135000	
Accounts Receivable	153000								153000	
Allowance for Doubtful Accounts		48000		(B)66000						114000
Raw Materials Inventory	57000				②57000	②96000			②96000	
Work-in-Process Inventory	123000				②123000	②159000			②159000	
Finished Goods Inventory	75000						③75000	54000	54000	
Factory Supplies	99000			(A)78000					21000	
Prepaid Factory Insurance	105000			(D)75000					30000	
Factory Machinery	648000								648000	
Acc. Dep., Factory Mach.		120000		(C)84000						204000
Note Payable (due within 30 days)		225000								225000
Common Stock $10		225000								225000
Retained Earnings		180000								180000
Sales (Net)		2430000						2430000		
Raw Material Purchases (Net)	540000				540000					
Direct Labor	330000		(E)132000		462000					
Indirect Labor	102000		(E)48000		150000					
Heat, Light and Power	174000				174000					
Machinery Repairs	45000				45000					
Rent Expense—Factory	180000				180000					
Selling Expense—Control	261000						261000			
Administrative Expenses (Control)	201000		(E)33000				234000			
	3228000	3228000								
Factory Supplies Expense			(A)78000		78000					
Bad Debts Expense			(B)66000				66000			
Dep. Expense—Factory Mach.			(C)84000		84000					
Factory Insurance Expense			(D)75000		75000					
Accrued Payroll Payable				(E)213000		④				213000
			516000	516000	1968000	255000				
Cost of Goods Manufactured						1713000	1713000			
					1968000	1968000	2349000	2484000	1296000	1161000
Net Income							135000			135000
							2484000	2484000	1296000	1296000

KEY POINTS TO LOOK AT ON THE WORKSHEET

Key points on the worksheet include the following:

See number of key points circled on the worksheet (Fig. 26-11).

1. New set of columns for statement of cost of goods manufactured.

2. Beginning balances of raw materials inventory, $570, and work-in-process, $1,230, are listed in debit column of statement of cost of goods manufactured. Ending balances of $960 and $1,590 are entered in the credit column.

3. Finished goods inventory is not listed on statement of cost of goods manufactured. The beginning figure of finished goods, $750, is listed in the debit column of the income statement, whereas the ending balance of finished goods, $540, is listed on the credit column of the income statement and debit column of the balance sheet.

4. These are expenses that are not part of the cost of manufacturing and thus are not listed on the statement of cost of goods manufactured.

REPORTS PREPARED FROM THE WORKSHEET

The following reports can be prepared from the worksheet:

ROE CORPORATION STATEMENT OF COST OF GOODS MANUFACTURED FOR YEAR ENDED DECEMBER 31, 20XX		
Direct Materials:		
Raw Materials Inventory (Beg.)	$ 570 00	
Raw Materials Purchased (Net)	5 400 00	
Cost of Available Raw Materials	5 970 00	
Less: Raw Materials Inventory (End.)	960 00	
Cost of Raw Materials Used		$ 5 010 00
Direct Labor		4 620 00
Factory Overhead:		
Indirect Labor	$ 1 500 00	
Heat, Light, and Power	1 740 00	
Rent Expense	1 800 00	
Machinery Repairs	450 00	
Factory Supplies Expense	780 00	
Dep. Exp., Factory Machinery	840 00	
Factory Insurance Expense	750 00	
Total Factory Overhead		$ 7 860 00
Total Manufacturing Cost Incurred		17 490 00
Plus: Work-in-Process (Beg.)		1 230 00
Less: Work-in-Process (End.)		1 590 00
Cost of Goods Manufactured*		$ 17 130 00

*This amount will go on the cost of goods sold section of the income statement, as shown on page 865.

THE INCOME STATEMENT

Figure 26-12 is the income statement for Roe Corporation. Note how the $17,130 from the statement of cost of goods manufactured is listed below the beginning finished goods inventory. Note that the operating expenses, which were not part of the cost of the goods sold, are listed below gross profit. For example, Bad Debts Expense, a selling expense, had no part in the production of bean bag chairs for Roe. Remember that the cost of goods manufactured is not the same as the cost of goods sold.

ROE CORPORATION INCOME STATEMENT FOR YEAR ENDED DECEMBER 31, 20XX			
Net Sales			$24 30 0 00
Cost of Goods Sold:			
Finished Goods Inventory (Beg.)	$ 75 0 00		
Cost of Goods Manufactured	17 13 0 00		
Cost of Goods Available for Sale	$17 88 0 00		
Less: Finished Goods Inventory (End.)	54 0 00		
Cost of Goods Sold:		$17 34 0 00	
Gross Profit on Sales		$ 6 96 0 00	
Operating Expenses:			
Selling Expense*	$ 3 27 0 00		
Administrative Expense	2 34 0 00		
Total Operating Expenses		$ 5 61 0 00	
Net Income (before taxes)		$ 1 35 0 00	

FIGURE 26-12. Income Statement

* Includes the $660 of bad debt expense.

THE BALANCE SHEET

Figure 26-13 is the completed Balance Sheet of Roe Corporation. The net income of $1,350 in Figure 26-12 helps update retained earnings in Figure 26-13. Note how under current assets the manufacturing company lists its raw materials and work-in-process as well as finished goods.

ROE CORPORATION BALANCE SHEET DECEMBER 31, 20XX			
Assets			
Current Assets:			
Cash			$ 1 35 0 00
Accounts Receivable	$ 1 53 0 00		
Less: Allowance for Doubtful Accounts	1 14 0 00	$ 39 0 00	
Inventories			
Raw Materials	$ 96 0 00		
Work-in-Process	1 59 0 00		
Finished Goods	54 0 00	$ 3 09 0 00	
Prepaid Expenses:			
Factory Supplies	$ 21 0 00		
Prepaid Factory Insurance	30 0 00	$ 51 0 00	
Total Current Assets		$ 5 34 0 00	
Plant and Equipment			
Factory Machinery	$ 6 48 0 00		
Less: Accum. Depreciation, Factory Machinery	2 04 0 00	$ 4 44 0 00	
Total Assets		$ 9 78 0 00	

FIGURE 26-13. Balance Sheet

(cont. at top of p. 866)

FIGURE 26-13. continued

Liabilities and Stockholders' Equity			
Current Liabilities:			
Notes Payable	$ 2 2 5 0 00		
Accrued Payroll Payable	2 1 3 0 00	$ 4 3 8 0 00	
Stockholders' Equity			
Common Stock, $10 par 225 shares	$ 2 2 5 0 00		
Retained Earnings*	3 1 5 0 00	$ 5 4 0 0 00	
Total Liabilities and Stockholders' Equity		$ 9 7 8 0 00	

* Beginning Retained Earnings + Net Income.

LEARNING UNIT 26-3 REVIEW

AT THIS POINT you should be able to

▼ Explain the key points to consider of a worksheet for a manufacturing company. (p. 864)
▼ From the worksheet, prepare a statement of cost of goods manufactured along with the income statement and balance sheet. (p. 864)

SELF-REVIEW QUIZ 26-3

(The blank forms you need are on page 194 of the *Study Guide and Working Papers*.)

Respond true or false to the following:

1. The figure for cost of goods manufactured is always placed on the credit column of the income statement on the worksheet.
2. Finished goods are not listed on the statement of cost of goods manufactured.
3. All expenses are listed on the cost of goods manufactured.
4. The ending balances of raw materials inventory and work-in-process are entered in the debit columns of cost of goods manufactured.

Solutions to Self-Review Quiz 26-3

1. False   2. True   3. False   4. False

SUMMARY OF KEY POINTS

Learning Unit 26-1

1. Manufacturing costs are broken into raw materials, direct labor, and manufacturing overhead.

2. A manufacturing firm has three major inventories: raw materials, work-in-process, and finished goods.

3. Cost of goods manufactured is prepared first, before the income statement is completed.

Learning Unit 26-2

1. When journal entries are prepared to record the movement of material, labor, and overhead through the operation of a company, each debit is the destination and each credit is the source.

2. Overhead may be applied based on direct labor hours, direct labor dollars, or machine hours.

Learning Unit 26-3

1. The steps of the accounting cycle for a manufacturing company are the same as those used for a merchandise company.

2. The worksheet for a manufacturing company has columns for items used to calculate the statement of cost of goods manufactured. This figure is then updated on the income statement debit column of the worksheet.

KEY TERMS

Bill of lading A formal document issued to the carrier of the finished product. It is the basis for charging the cost of goods sold.

Clock card A card used by employees when clocking in and out for the factory; it becomes the basis for the payroll.

Direct labor The wages of those persons whose efforts directly affect the quality or other characteristics of the products manufactured.

Labor distribution report A report issued by the payroll department to categorize all the types of labor incurred during the week.

Lot ticket A document prepared to show the movement of materials or products between departments. Also called *move ticket*.

Manufacturing overhead All the manufacturing costs except raw material and direct labor.

Material requisition A document used to order material or supplies from the storeroom that is the basis for charging material into production.

Raw material Material that is to be processed into a finished product or that changes the quality or characteristics of the product.

Receiving report A document prepared by the receiving department to evidence the receipt of material or supplies that were ordered.

BLUEPRINT: MANUFACTURING ELEMENTS

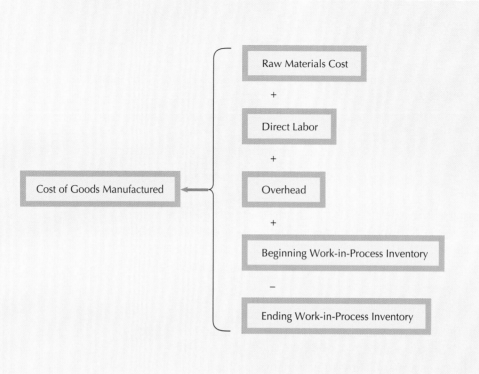

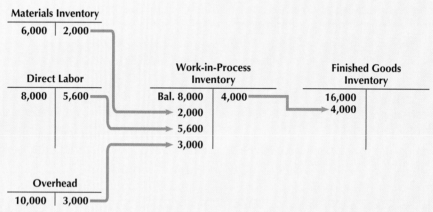

QUESTIONS, MINI EXERCISES, EXERCISES, AND PROBLEMS

1. Into what three elements can manufacturing costs be broken?

2. Direct labor includes the wages of those personnel whose efforts indirectly change the quality or characteristics of the product. True or false? Please explain.

3. What are the three major inventories of a manufacturing firm?

4. Explain how to calculate the total cost of goods manufactured.

5. Explain the purpose of receiving reports as well as materials requisitions.

6. What tickets become the basis for transferring costs between departments to finished goods inventory?

7. What is the purpose of a bill of lading?

8. Draw a diagram to show the flow of manufacturing costs.

9. Explain how overhead may be applied.

10. Compare and contrast the structure of a worksheet for a merchandise company and a manufacturing company.

Mini Exercises

(The blank forms you need are on page 196 of the *Study Guide and Working Papers.*)

Classifications of Raw Material, Direct Labor, and Overhead

1. Classify each of the following as raw material, direct labor, or overhead:

    a. Finishing material for a furniture manufacturer.

    b. Depreciation expense of manufacturing assets.

    c. Labor of a person who paints furniture for a furniture manufacturer.

    d. Pure aluminum in a company that manufactures aluminum products.

Calculating Cost of Raw Materials

2. From the following, calculate the cost of raw materials used.

Raw materials Inventory, January 1	$ 5,000
Raw materials Inventory, December 31	12,000
Purchases of raw materials	70,000

Calculating Total Manufacturing Costs

3. From the following, calculate total manufacturing costs.

Direct labor	$ 7,000
Raw materials inventory, June 30	4,500
Raw materials purchases	15,000
Raw materials inventory, June 1	3,000
Overhead	4,000
Finished goods	8,000

Journal Entries to Record Manufacturing Costs

4. Journalize the following transactions:

    a. Storeroom issued raw materials costing $5,000.

    b. Direct labor of $3,000 was charged into production.

    c. Supplies costing $2,000 were issued by the storeroom.

    d. Indirect labor cost of $4,000 was incurred.

    e. Rent of $1,000 and Depreciation of $400 was charged to overhead.

5. Identify where each title is placed on the worksheet.

    1. Cost of goods manufactured column.

    2. Income Statement column.

    3. Balance Sheet.

    _____ a. Raw materials purchases.
    _____ b. Ending finished goods inventory.
    _____ c. Ending raw materials inventory.
    _____ d. Sales.

Exercises

(The blank forms you need are on page 197 of the *Study Guide and Working Papers.*)

26-1. Classify each of the following as raw material, direct labor, or overhead:

    a. The lumber in making furniture.

    b. The insurance for a factory.

> Classifications of raw material, direct labor, and overhead.

c. The wages of a forklift driver.

d. A manufacturing foreman's salary.

Calculating raw materials costs.

26-2. From the following balances, calculate the cost of raw material used.

Raw materials inventory, January 1	$ 60,000
Raw materials inventory, December 31	90,000
Purchases of raw materials	800,000

Calculating total manufacturing costs.

26-3. From the following, calculate total manufacturing costs.

Direct labor	$ 80,000
Raw materials inventory, May 30	9,600
Raw materials purchases	70,000
Raw materials inventory, May 1	9,000
Overhead	75,000
Finished goods	120,000

Journal entries to record flow of manufacturing costs and the application of overhead.

26-4. From the following transactions, prepare the appropriate general journal entries for the month of May:

a. Raw materials costing $75,000 were issued from the storeroom.

b. Direct labor of $65,000 was charged into production.

c. Supplies costing $7,000 were issued from the storeroom.

d. Indirect labor costs of $18,000 were incurred.

e. Rent of $3,000 and depreciation of $500 were charged to overhead.

f. Eighty percent of the direct labor dollars used were applied to overhead.

g. Completed products costing $70,000 were transferred to finished goods.

h. Products costing $39,000 were sold.

Placement of data on a worksheet for a manufacturing company.

26-5. a. In which columns on the worksheet would the following additional data be placed?

	Year-End Figures	Column
Raw materials	$34,000	
Goods-in-process	19,500	
Finished goods	30,000	

b. In which columns would the beginning-of-year figures be placed?

Group A Problems

(The blank forms you need are on pages 198 – 199 of the *Study Guide and Working Papers*.)

Preparing a cost of goods manufactured schedule.

26A-1. An analysis of the accounts of Harwood Manufacturing reveals the following data for the month ended July 31, 20XX:

Inventories	Beginning	Ending
Raw materials	$18,000	$19,000
Work-in-process	13,000	17,000
Finished goods	15,000	14,000

Check Figure:
Total cost of goods manufactured $307,000

Costs Incurred

Raw materials purchased, $130,000; direct labor, $130,000; manufacturing overhead, $52,000. These specific overheads included indirect labor, $20,000; factory insurance, $9,000; depreciation on machinery, $10,000; machinery repairs, $4,000; factory utilities, $6,000; and miscellaneous factory costs, $3,000.

Instructions

Prepare a cost of goods manufactured statement.

26A-2. As the bookkeeper of Ace Manufacturing, you are to record the following transactions in the general journal for the month of November:

Check Figure:
(D) Dr. Overhead control $15,000
Cr. Payroll $15,000

a. Raw materials of $80,000 were issued from the storeroom.

b. Charged $60,000 of direct labor to production.

c. Supplies costing $7,000 were issued from the storeroom.

d. Incurred indirect labor costs of $15,000.

e. The following expenses were charged to overhead: rent, $3,000; supervision, $8,000; depreciation, $4,000; electricity, $6,500.

f. Overhead was applied at 90 percent of direct labor dollars.

g. Transferred completed products costing $160,000 to finished goods.

h. Sold products costing $198,000.

26A-3. From the following information, prepare a worksheet for Keep Corporation (assume no adjustments).

	TRIAL BALANCE	
	Cr.	Dr.
Cash	6 2 4 0 00	
Raw Materials Inventory	8 8 8 0 00	
Goods-in-Process Inventory	7 4 4 0 00	
Finished Goods Inventory	10 3 2 0 00	
Factory Supplies	3 2 4 0 00	
Prepaid Factory Supplies	3 6 0 00	
Desks	9 6 0 00	
Machinery	57 2 4 0 00	
Acc. Depreciation, Machinery		8 2 8 0 00
Accounts Payable		3 1 2 0 00
Common Stock $10 Par		60 0 0 0 00
Retained Earnings		8 0 4 0 00
Sales		115 6 8 0 00
Raw Materials Purchases	38 4 0 0 00	
Direct Labor	22 3 2 0 00	
Indirect Labor	9 9 6 0 00	
Machinery Repairs	7 2 0 00	
Selling Expenses	14 7 6 0 00	
Administrative Expense	10 0 8 0 00	
Factory Supplies Expense	1 3 2 0 00	
Depreciation of Machinery	2 8 8 0 00	
	195 1 2 0 00	195 1 2 0 00

Additional data

Year-End Figures

Raw materials	$11,400
Goods-in-process	8,280
Finished goods	10,200

Check Figure:
Net income $18,480

Group B Problems

(The blank forms you need are on pages 198–199 of the *Study Guide and Working Papers.*)

26B-1. An analysis of the accounts of Harwood Manufacturing reveals the following data for the month ended July 31, 20XX.

Preparing a cost of goods manufactured schedule.

Inventories	Beginning	Ending
Raw materials	$16,000	$22,000
Work-in-process	12,000	16,000
Finished goods	16,000	14,000

Costs Incurred

Raw materials purchased, $130,000; direct labor, $90,000; manufacturing overhead, $39,000. These specific overheads included indirect labor, $9,600; factory insurance, $8,000; depreciation on machinery, $7,600; machinery repairs, $6,000; factory utilities, $6,300; and miscellaneous factory costs, $1,500.

Instructions

Prepare a cost of goods manufactured statement.

26B-2. From the following transactions for May for Ace Manufacturing, record the appropriate general journal entries.

   a. Raw materials of $70,000 were issued from Ace's storeroom.

   b. Charged $75,000 of direct labor to production.

   c. Supplies of $4,000 were issued from the storeroom.

   d. Indirect labor costs were incurred for $20,000.

   e. The following expenses were charged to overhead: rent, $5,000; supervision, $9,000; depreciation, $6,200; electricity, $9,000.

   f. Overhead was applied at 80 percent of direct labor dollars.

   g. Completed products costing $180,000 were transferred to finished goods.

   h. Sold products costing $208,000.

26B-3. From the following information, prepare a worksheet for Keep Corporation (assume no adjustments).

	TRIAL BALANCE	
	Cr.	Dr.
Cash	1 3 1 0 00	
Raw Materials Inventory	2 2 2 0 00	
Goods-in-Process Inventory	1 8 6 0 00	
Finished Goods Inventory	2 5 8 0 00	
Factory Supplies	5 6 0 00	
Prepaid Factory Insurance	5 9 0 00	
Desks	2 4 0 00	
Machinery	14 3 1 0 00	
Acc. Depreciation, Machinery		2 0 7 0 00
Accounts Payable		7 8 0 00
Common Stock $10 Par		15 0 0 0 00
Retained Earnings		2 0 1 0 00
Sales		28 9 2 0 00
Raw Materials Purchases	9 6 0 0 00	
Direct Labor	5 5 8 0 00	
Indirect Labor	2 4 9 0 00	
Machinery Repairs	1 8 0 00	
Selling Expenses	3 6 9 0 00	
Administrative Expense	2 5 2 0 00	
Factory Supplies Expense	3 3 0 00	
Depreciation of Machinery	7 2 0 00	
	48 7 8 0 00	48 7 8 0 00

Additional data

Year-End Figures

Raw materials	$ 285
Goods-in-process	2,070
Finished goods	2,550

REAL-WORLD APPLICATIONS

26R-1.

Peter Roel had to leave the office on urgent business and has asked you to close the costs into the manufacturing summary account. Please do so. Why do you think Peter forgot to close the accounts? Provide a written response.

MEMO

To: Peter Roel, Bookkeeper

From: M. V. Rooy, Vice President

Re: Closing Entries

I notice that you forgot to close the costs that appeared in the statement of cost of goods manufactured into the manufacturing summary account. Here is a blueprint of the form. Please provide them to me as soon as possible.

Manufacturing Summary	XXX	
Raw Materials Inventory		XXX
Raw Materials Inventory	XXX	
Manufacturing Summary		XXX
Manufacturing Summary	XXX	
Work-in-Process Inventory		XXX
Work-in-Process Inventory	XXX	
Manufacturing Summary		XXX

YOU make the call

Critical Thinking/Ethical Case

26R-2.

Dot Lovet works in the receiving department of a leading publishing company. She has become good friends with many of the suppliers. At 4 P.M., Joe Andrews delivered a truckload of art supplies. Joe was in a hurry and asked Dot to accept the order. He promised that everything was there. Dot signed the receiving report without verifying the specifics of the order. Two weeks later the art department called complaining that their department was being charged for items they never received. The accounting department has already processed the payment to this vendor. If you were Dot's supervisor, what would you do in this situation? You make the call. Write down your recommendation to Dot.

INTERNET EXERCISES

EX-1. [http://www.papajohns.com/]   Papa Johns is the third largest pizza retailer in the United States. Believe it or not, we can consider them as

"manufacturers" of pizza! The "direct" costs of the pizza include the dough, the sauces, the toppings (raw materials) and the labor of those who work in the kitchen baking the pizzas (direct labor).

Let's take a look at the "factory overhead" or "indirect costs" that go into a pizza. What are 5 examples of "indirect costs" that go into consumption of a pizza?

EX-2. [www.ford.com]   In manufacturing accounting three major categories of costs are considered—Raw or Direct Materials, Direct Labor, and Factory Overhead. In a manufacturing process the "direct" costs are usually easily identified. The area of Factory Overhead is the most difficult area of costs to identify.

In a large manufacturing environment such as Ford has there are literally hundreds of indirect costs to account for in the production process. List five of the indirect assembly personnel costs that would go into Factory Overhead.

How Companies Record Credit Card Sales in Their Special Journals

RECORDING BANK CREDIT CARDS

Example: Credit Card Sale of $100, MasterCard: It is interesting to note that for bank credit cards (MasterCard, Visa), the sales are recorded in the seller's Cash Receipts Journal, because the slips are converted into cash immediately. Bank credit cards are not treated as accounts receivable. The fee the bank charges, $2\frac{1}{2}$ to 6 percent, is usually deducted, and the bank credits the depositor's account immediately for the net. The end result for the seller is as follows:

Accounts Affected	Category	↑ ↓	Rules
Cash	Asset	↑	Dr. $94
Credit Card Expense	Expense	↑	Dr. 6
Sales	Revenue	↑	Cr. 100

		CASH RECEIPTS JOURNAL						
Date	Cash Dr.	Credit Card Expense Dr.	Accounts Receivable Cr.	Sales Credited	Sales Tax Payable Cr.	Account Name	Amount Cr.	
	94 00	6 00		100 00				

It is the responsibility of the credit card company to sustain any losses (bad debts) from customers' nonpayment. If the bank waits to take the discount until the end of the month, the seller makes a nonpayment entry in the cash payment journal to record the credit card expense; the end result would be credit card expense up and cash balance down. Usually, the bank sends the charge on the monthly statement. *Remember: Bank credit cards are not treated as accounts receivable.*

RECORDING PRIVATE COMPANY CREDIT CARDS

Private companies such as American Express are considered by sellers as accounts receivable. The seller periodically summarizes the sales slips and submits them to the private credit card company for payment (which the company will pay quickly). Let's look at two situations to show how a company would handle its accounting procedures for these credit sales transactions.

Situation 1: On May 4, Morris Company sold merchandise on account of $53 to Bill Blank. Bill used American Express. Assume Morris Company has a low dollar volume and few transactions.

Note in Figure A-1 how the sale of $53 is recorded in the sales journal. Keep in mind that Morris is treating American Express, not Bill Blank, as the accounts receivable. In Figure A-2 we see on June 8 payment is received from American Express and results in the following:

1. Cash increasing by $50.35.
2. Credit card expense rising by $2.65.
3. Accounts receivable being reduced by the $53 originally owed by American Express.

Situation 2: On March 31, Blue Company summarized its credit card sales for American Express. Payment was received on April 13 from American Express. Assume Blue Company has a high dollar volume and many transactions.

Note in Figure A-3 how each credit company has its own column set up. In the ledger there is an account set up for each as well; the posting to the ledger would be done at the end of the month. With high volume and the need to record many transactions, the use of these additional columns (versus Figure A-1) will result in increased efficiency. Figure A-4 shows the receipt of money from American Express less the credit card expense charge.

FIGURE A-1. Sales Journal

				Description of Accounts Receivable	PR	Accounts Receivable Dr.	Sales Tax* Payable Cr.	Sales Cr.	
	Date	Invoice							
	May 4	692		American Express		53 00	3 00	50 00	
				(Bill Blank)					

SALES JOURNAL

* Assume a 6% sales tax.

FIGURE A-2. Cash Receipts Journal

CASH RECEIPTS JOURNAL

		Cash Dr.		Sales Discount Dr.	Credit Card Expense Dr.	Accounts Receivable Cr.	Sales Tax Payable Cr.	Sundry		
	Date							Account Name	PR	Amount Cr.
	June 8	50 35			2 65*	53 00		American Express		
								(Bill Blank)		

* Assume credit card expense of 5%. Note that the $2.56 is 5% × $53.

APPENDIX A ... HOW COMPANIES RECORD CREDIT CARD SALES IN THEIR SPECIAL JOURNALS

FIGURE A-3. Blue Co. Sales Journal

BLUE COMPANY SALES JOURNAL

Date	Invoice Number	Description of Accounts Receivable	PR	Accounts Receivable Dr.	Credit Cards — American Express Dr.	Credit Cards — Diners Club Dr.	Sales Tax Payable Cr.	Credit Card Sales Cr.	Sales Cr.
Mar. 31		Summary of American Express			11970|00		570|00	11400|00	
					(112)			**(401)**	

FIGURE A-4. Blue Co. Cash Receipts Journal

BLUE COMPANY CASH RECEIPTS JOURNAL

Date	Cash Dr.	Sales Discount Dr.	Credit Card Expense Dr.	Accounts Receivable Cr.	Credit Card Accounts Rec. — American Express Cr.	Credit Card Accounts Rec. — Diners Club Cr.	Sales Cr.	Sales Tax Payable Cr.	Sundry — Account Name	Sundry — PR	Sundry — Amount Cr.
Apr. 13	11251|80		718|20		11970|00				Summary of American Express payments		

Computerized Accounting

PART A

Accounting procedures are essentially the same whether they are performed manually or on a computer. The following is a list of the accounting cycle steps in a manual accounting system as compared to the steps in a computerized accounting system.

STEPS OF THE ACCOUNTING CYCLE

Manual Accounting System	Computerized Accounting System
1. Business transactions occur and generate source documents.	1. Business transactions occur and generate source documents.
2. Analyze and record business transactions in a manual journal.	2. Analyze and record business transactions in a computerized journal.
3. Post or transfer information from journal to ledger.	3. Computer automatically posts information from journal to ledger.
4. Prepare a trial balance.	4. Trial balance is prepared automatically.
5. Prepare a worksheet.	5. Enter necessary adjustments directly.
6. Prepare financial statements.	6. Financial statements are prepared automatically.
7. Journalize and post adjusting entries.	7. Completed prior to preparation of financial statements.
8. Journalize and post closing entries.	8. Closing procedures are completed automatically.
9. Prepare a post-closing trial balance.	9. Trial balance is automatically prepared as needed.

The accounting cycle comparison shows that the accountant's task of initially analyzing business transactions in terms of debits and credits (both routine business transactions and adjusting entries) is required in both manual and computerized accounting systems. However, in a computerized accounting system, the "drudge" work of posting transactions, creating and completing worksheets and financial statements, and performing the closing procedures is all handled automatically by the computerized accounting system.

In addition, computerized accounting systems can perform accounting procedures at greater speeds and with greater accuracy than can be achieved in a manual accounting system. It is important to recognize, however, that the computer is only a tool that can accept and process information supplied by the accountant. Each business transaction and adjusting entry must first be analyzed and recorded in a computerized journal correctly; otherwise, the financial statements generated by the computerized accounting system will contain errors and will not be useful to the business.

Before a business can begin to use a computerized accounting system, and specifically the Peachtree Complete Accounting system, it must have the following items in place:

1. A computer system
2. Computer software
    a. Operating system software
    b. Peachtree Complete Accounting (any version)

COMPUTER SYSTEM

A computer system consists of several electronic components that together have the ability to accept user-supplied data; input, store, and execute programmed instructions; and output results according to user specifications. The physical computer and its related devices are the hardware, while the stored program that supplies the instructions is called the software.

To understand how a computer system works, we must first look at a conceptual computer that demonstrates the major components and functions of a computer system. The conceptual computer shown in Figure A-1 has four major elements—input devices, processing/internal memory unit, secondary storage devices, and output devices. The illustration also shows the flow of data into the computer and of processed information out of the computer.

FIGURE A-1. Conceptual Computer

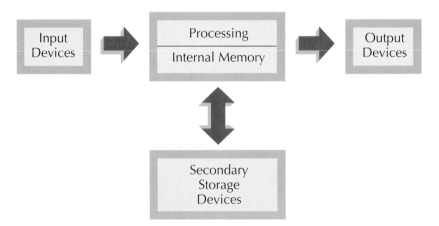

Input devices are used to feed data and instructions into the computer. Once the data and instructions are entered, the computer must be able to store them internally and then process the data based on the instructions. Storage and processing occur in the processing/internal memory unit.

There are two types of internal computer memory: random-access memory (RAM) and read-only memory (ROM). RAM is the largest portion of the memory but still has limited capacity; consequently, secondary storage devices are needed. In addition, RAM is temporary—anything stored in RAM is erased when power to the computer is interrupted. Therefore, data stored in RAM must be saved to a secondary storage medium through the use of a secondary storage device before the power is turned off. ROM is permanent memory and consists of those instruction sets necessary to start the computer and receive initial messages from input devices. ROM takes up only a small portion of the total internal memory capacity of a computer system.

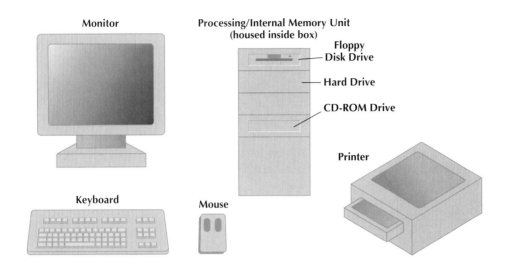

FIGURE A-2. Typical Configuration of a Microcomputer System

Finally, the results of processing must be made available to computer users through output devices. These components form a collection of devices referred to as computer hardware because they have physical substance. In a typical microcomputer system (see Figure A-2) a keyboard and mouse are used for input and a printer and monitor are used for output. The processing/internal memory unit is housed inside a box along with secondary storage devices consisting of a hard drive unit, one or more floppy disk drives, and a CD-ROM drive.

Computer hardware can do nothing without a computer program. Computer programs are supplied on floppy disks or CD-ROMs, which are secondary storage media used in floppy disk or CD-ROM drives. Figure A-3 shows an example of a floppy disk and of a CD-ROM.

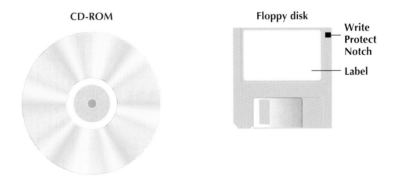

FIGURE A-3. Storage Media

To operate a particular computer program you must first load the program into the system's internal memory (RAM) through the use of a floppy disk or CD-ROM drive or by accessing the program that has been installed and stored on the system's hard drive. Once RAM accesses a program, the computer can execute the program instructions and process data as directed by the user through the keyboard or mouse. At the end of a processing session, the results may be viewed on the monitor, printed on the printer, and/or stored permanently on a floppy disk or hard drive.

COMPUTER SOFTWARE

The computer can do nothing without a computer program. Computer programs control the input, processing, storage, and output operations of a computer. Computer programmers write the instructions that tell the computer to execute certain procedures and process data. There are two broad categories of computer software; operating system software and applications software.

Operating System Software

Operating system software provides the link between the computer hardware, applications software, and the computer user. It consists of programs that start up the computer, retrieve applications programs, and allow the computer operator to store and retrieve data. Operating system software controls access to input and output devices and access to applications programs. There are several popular operating systems for microcomputers. They include Windows 95/98/2000, DOS, DOS combined with Windows 3.XX, OS/2, the Macintosh operating system, and UNIX.

Applications Software

Applications software refers to programs designed for a specific use. The five most common types of business applications software are database management, spreadsheet, work processing, communications, and graphics. Spreadsheet software allows the manipulation of data and has the ability to project answers to "what if" questions. For example, a spreadsheet program could project a company's profit next year if sales increased by 10 percent and expenses increased by 6 percent. Word processing software enables the user to write and print letters, memos, and other documents. Graphic software display data visually in the form of graphic images, and communications software allows your computer to "talk" to other computers. But to accomplish communications you need additional hardware: a modem to transmit and receive data over telephone lines. Database management software stores, retrieves, sorts, and updates an organized body of information. Most computerized accounting systems are designed as database management software. Accounting information is data that must be organized and stored in a common base of data. This allows the entry of data and the retrieval of information in an organized and systematic way.

Applications software is frequently linked with a particular operating system. Database management, spreadsheet, word processing graphics, communication, accounting, and other software applications are available in versions that work with most of the popular operating systems. For example, if your computer system is using Windows 98 you would purchase the Windows 98 version of a word processing program. If you were using a Macintosh computer and operating system you would purchase the Macintosh version of a spreadsheet program.

Accounting Applications Software Most computerized accounting software is organized into modules. Each module is designed to process a particular type of accounting data such as accounts receivable, accounts payable, or payroll. Each module is also designed to work in conjunction with the other modules. When modules are designed to work together in this manner, they are referred to as integrated software. In an integrated accounting system each module handles a different function but also communicates with the other modules. For example, to record a sale on account, you would make an entry into the accounts receivable module. The integration feature automatically records this entry in the sales journal, updates the customer's account in the accounts receivable subsidiary ledger, and posts all accounts affected in the general ledger. Thus in an integrated accounting system, transaction data are only entered once. All of the other accounting procedures required to bring the accounting records up-to-date are performed automatically through the integration function.

Peachtree Complete Accounting   The most current version of Peachtree Complete Accounting has been selected for use in this text to demonstrate and help you learn how to use a computerized accounting system. It is easy to use, fully integrated, and is also available in versions that work with several different operating systems. The program can be used to maintain the accounting data for a sole proprietorship, a partnership or a corporation. It will accommodate service, merchandising and manufacturing businesses. The payroll functions in this version are based on the federal and state tax laws in effect in 2000 and contain tax tables for 1999 and 2000. Tax tables for subsequent years can be obtained from Peachtree. The workshops contained in this text are designed to illustrate how manual accounting concepts will be handled by a computerized accounting system. They are not intended to provide a comprehensive course of study for a computerized accounting system.

WORKING WITH PEACHTREE COMPLETE ACCOUNTING

Before you begin to work with Peachtree Complete Accounting you need to be familiar with your computer hardware and the Windows operating system. When you are running Windows, your work takes place on the desktop. Think of this area as resembling the surface of a desk. There are physical objects on your real desk and there are windows and icons on the Windows desktop. There are minor differences between the various versions of Windows. The figures will reflect a typical Windows 98 Desktop. Other Windows versions will have small differences but will be essentially the same.

A mouse is an essential input device for all Windows applications. A mouse is a pointing device that assumes different shapes on your monitor as you move the mouse on your desk. According to the nature of the current action, the mouse pointer may appear as a small arrowhead, an hourglass, or a hand. There are five basic mouse techniques:

▼ Click   To quickly press and release the left mouse button.

▼ Double-click   To click the left mouse button twice in rapid succession.

▼ Drag   To hold down the left mouse button while you move the mouse.

▼ Point   To position the mouse pointer over an object without clicking a button.

▼ Right-click   To quickly press and release the right mouse button.

The Windows 98 Desktop

Figure A-4 shows a typical opening Windows 98 screen. Your desktop may be different, just as your real desk is arranged differently from those of your colleagues.

▼ **Desktop icons:** Graphic representations of drives, files, and other resources. The desktop icons that display will vary depending on your computer setup.

▼ **Start button:** Clicking on the Start button displays the start menu and lets you start applications.

▼ **Task bar:** Contains the Start button and other buttons representing open applications.

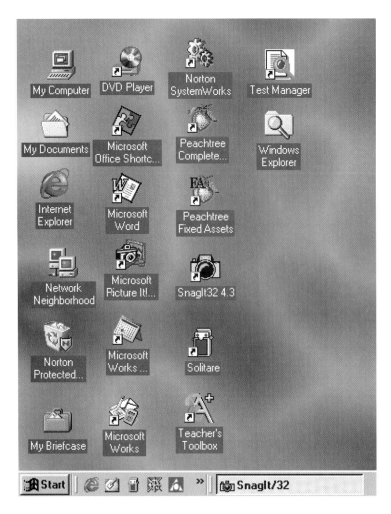

Applications Window

As you work with Peachtree Complete Accounting two kinds of windows will appear on your desktop. The Main Menu window is where all activities in Peachtree will begin. An application window contains a running application. The name of the applications and the application's menu bar will appear at the top of the application window. Regardless of the windows that are open on your desktop, most windows have certain elements in common.

FIGURE A-5. Peachtree Main Menu Applications Window

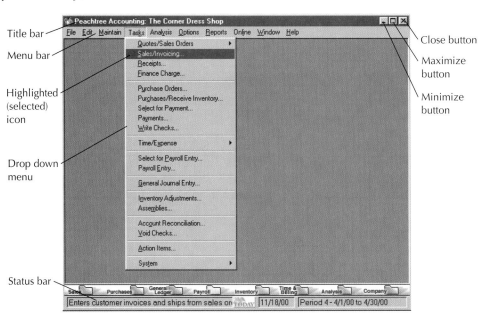

- ▼ **Minimize button:** Clicking on this button minimizes a window and displays it as a task button on the taskbar.

- ▼ **Maximize button:** Clicking on this button enlarges the window so that it fills the entire desktop. After you enlarge a window, the maximize button is replaced by a Restore button (a double box, not shown) that returns the window to the size it was before it was maximized.

- ▼ **Close button:** Clicking on this button will close the window.

- ▼ **Title bar:** Displays the name of the application.

- ▼ **Menu bar:** This window element lists the available menus for the window.

- ▼ **Drop down menu:** Shows the options available under each menu option.

- ▼ **Highlighted (selected) item:** The active selection in a Drop Down Menu.

- ▼ **Status bar:** A line of text at the bottom of many windows that gives more information about a field. If you are unsure of what to enter in a field, select it with your mouse and read the status bar.

Dialog Boxes

A dialog box appears when additional information is needed to execute a command. There are different ways to supply that information; consequently, there are different types of dialog boxes. Most dialog boxes (see Fig. A-6) are for specific functions and tasks and require you to supply the data for that task. After you supply the needed information, you can choose a command button to carry out a command such as to Post or Print.

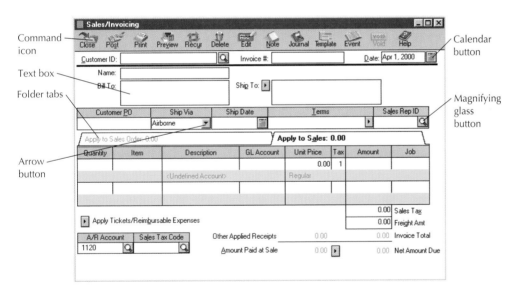

FIGURE A-6. Peachtree Sales/Invoicing Dialog Box

- ▼ **Folder tabs:** Some dialog boxes have multiple pages of entry fields available to them. These tabs allow you to switch between available screens.

- ▼ **Arrow button:** A button with an arrow will generally bring up a pull down menu of options for that field.

- ▼ **Text box:** When you move to an empty text box, an insertion point appears at the far left-hand side of the box. The text you type starts at the insertion point. If the box you move to already contains text, this text is selected (highlighted), and any text you type replaces it. You can also delete the selected text by pressing the DELETE or BACKSPACE key.

- ▼ **Command icons:** Choose (click) on a command button to initiate an immediate action such as carrying out or canceling a command. The Close, Print and Post buttons are common command buttons.

▼ **Magnifying glass button:** Click on this button to pull down a list of choices. Some fields will not show the magnifying glass until the field has been selected.

▼ **Calendar button:** Click on this button to bring up a calendar in order to select the date to be inserted in the field next to the button.

Other dialog boxes (see Fig. A-7) may require that choices be made, request additional information, provide warnings, or give messages indicating why a requested task cannot be accomplished.

FIGURE A-7. Peachtree
Select a Report Dialog Box

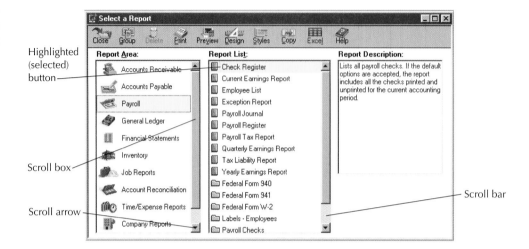

▼ **Highlighted (selected) item:** To highlight or select an item in a displayed list, click on the item. Some may require a double click to select. In Figure A-7, highlighting an item in the Report Area will bring up a list associated with that item in the Report List box. Highlighting an item in the Report List box will bring up a description in the Report Description box.

▼ **Scroll bar:** A bar that may appear at the bottom and/or right side of a window or dialog box if there is more text than can be displayed at one time within the window.

▼ **Scroll arrow:** A small arrow at the end of a scroll bar that you click on to move to the next item in the list. The top and left arrow scroll to the previous item; the bottom and right arrows scroll to the next item.

▼ **Scroll box:** A small box in a scroll bar. You can use the mouse to drag the scroll box left or right, or up or down. The scroll box indicates the relative position in the list.

Using Menus

Commands are listed on menus, as shown in Figure A-8. Each item on the **Main Menu Bar** has its own menus, which are listed by selecting the menu. When a menu is displayed, choose a command by clicking on it or by typing the **Underlined letter** to execute the command. You can also bypass the menu entirely if you know the **Keyboard equivalent** shown to the right of the command when the menu is displayed.

A **Dimmed command** indicates that a command is not currently executable; some additional action has to be taken for the command to become available. Some commands are followed by **Ellipses** (...) to indicate that more information is required to execute the command. The additional information can be entered into a dialog box, which will appear immediately after the command has been selected.

Although Peachtree has 10 menu options available on the **Main Menu Bar,** most of your activities will involve the **Maintain, Tasks,** or **Reports** menus. The **Tasks** menu contains all of our routine, day to day activities such as invoicing customers, paying vendors, generating payroll, et al. The **Maintain** menu allows us to add, delete and edit customers, vendors, employees and default options, et al. The **Reports** menu allows us to generate the information contained in Peachtree in a variety of formats including custom designed ones.

Working in the Windows 98 Environment

You can use a combination of mouse and keyboard techniques to navigate within the Windows 98 environment. For example, you can click on an item to select it, and then press the ENTER key to choose it, or you can just double-click on the item. Peachtree Complete Accounting is designed for a mouse, but it also provides keyboard equivalents for almost every command. It may seem confusing at first that there are several different ways to do the same thing. You will find this flexibility useful. For example, if your hands are already on the keyboard, it may be faster to use the keyboard equivalent of a mouse command. Alternatively, if your hand is already on the mouse, it may be faster to use a mouse technique to carry out a command. When a procedure in an assignment says to select or choose an item, generally use whichever method you prefer. Alternative procedures are often provided as well. It is not necessary to memorize any particular technique, just be flexible and willing to experiment. As you gain experience with the program, you will develop personal preferences, and the various techniques will become second nature.

Opening a File in Peachtree Complete

As with any other Windows program, files in Peachtree are opened by using the **Open Company** option from the **File** menu. Peachtree will then open up an Open Company dialog box where you can tell Peachtree where to find the files you need. The files that have been supplied with this text for the sample companies should reside in the same directory as the Peachtree program files, generally "Peachw". Each company will have its own folder that can be read by the Open Company dialog box. If you do not see these files when you first open the box, you may need to change the directory or drive to one your instructor will specify.

Before starting any assignment, it is suggested that you create a backup of the files for that sample company in the event you need to restore back to the beginning of the assignment.

Backing up a File in Peachtree Complete

Peachtree has the capability to quickly and easily back up your data to protect against accidental loss.

1. You must open the files of the company you wish to back up. Let's say we wish to backup The Zell Company. We would open that company using the **Open** feature from the **File** menu option.

2. While in the Menu Window, select **Back Up** from the **File** menu option. This will bring up the Back Up Company dialogue box as follows:

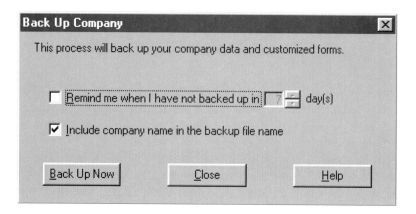

3. Click in the box next to **Include company name in the backup file name.** This will make Peachtree use Zell in the filename it selects for the backup. You could also use this dialogue box to have Peacthree provide a reminder at periodic intervals but we will leave this option alone for now. Press **Back Up Now** to continue.

4. You are now presented with a Save Back Up for the Zell Company as: dialog box as follows:

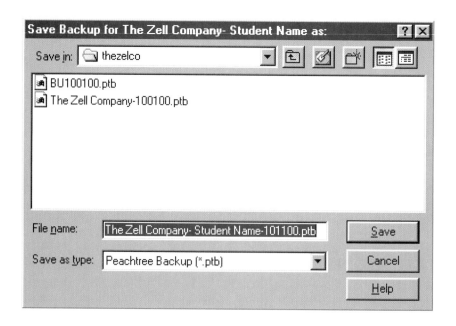

5. Peachtree will save your data files into one compressed .ptb file to any drive or path you specify including a floppy drive. It defaults to the location where the program files are stored and specifically to the folder where the company files are kept. Use the **Save in** pull down menu to save the files to a location specified by your instructor. This could be a

network drive. a student floppy disk or even the local hard drive. Click **Save** and then **Ok** to complete the process. You now have a back up of your data. You should consider saving each and every day to protect yourself against possible loss. Peachtree will use the date as part of the backup's name so you could have a separate backup for each day. You do not have to accept the name Peachtree assigns and you can use a name with more meaning to you. You should be able to fit about 5 different backups on a floppy disk.

See parts C and D of this appendix for information on using these backups.

PART B

INSTALLING PEACHTREE COMPLETE ACCOUNTING/ STUDENT DATA FILES

This section of the appendix discusses several basic operations that you need to complete to install the Peachtree Complete Accounting program and the student data files disk for use in completing the computer Workshop assignments in this text.

SYSTEM REQUIREMENTS

The recommended minimum software and hardware requirements your computer system needs to run both Windows and Peachtree Complete Accounting successfully are:

  ▼ Microsoft Windows 2000, 98, 95 or Windows NT 4.0 with Service Pack 3.
  ▼ A personal computer with a Pentium 150 MHz or higher processor.
  ▼ A hard disk with a minimum of 60MB free disk space.
  ▼ One 3.5 inch high-density floppy disk drive (if student floppy backups are desired).
  ▼ A CD-ROM drive (optional if installed on a Network).
  ▼ 32MB of RAM minimum (64MB recommended).
  ▼ A 256 color SVGA, or similar high-resolution monitor that is supported by Windows.
  ▼ A printer that is supported by Windows.
  ▼ A mouse that is supported by Windows.

CD-ROM CONTENTS

The Peachtree Complete Accounting installation and program files (in condensed form) and the Student Data Files for use in completing the Computer Workshops are on the CD-ROM that accompanies this text.

Installation Procedures

To install Peachtree Complete Accounting on your hard disk, follow these instructions:

  1. Start Windows.
  2. Make sure that no other programs are running on your system.
  3. Insert the CD-ROM in your CD-ROM drive.

4. Click on the Start button; then click on Run.
5. Type d:setup and press the ENTER key. For d, substitute the letter of your CD-ROM drive.
6. Put your CD-ROM away for safekeeping.

Installing Peachtree Complete Accounting on a Network

Peachtree Complete Accounting can be used in a network environment as long as each student uses a separate Student Data Files disk to store his or her data files. Refer to the *Instructor's Resource and Solutions Manual for College Accounting,* eighth edition, for specific network installation instructions.

Students should consult with their instructor and/or network administrator for specific procedures regarding program installation and any special printing procedures required for proper network operation.

Student Data File Integrity

Peachtree will run most efficiently if the student data files are installed on a hard drive. This can occur on the local hard drive or in a student folder on a network drive. Since it is possible that student files may be tampered with between class sessions, it is recommended that students back up and restore their files with a floppy disk each class day. Peachtree's back up and restore functions are quick and easy. The specific procedures will be discussed in Part E of this appendix.

PART C   CORRECTING TRANSACTIONS

Once a transaction is posted in Peachtree Complete Accounting, the journal entry will be reflected in the accounting records. You will however, be allowed to freely edit transactions due to the way the program has been configured for you. Peachtree does have an electronic audit feature that would not allow you to make corrections without creating an audit trail of all such changes. This feature of Peachtree Complete Accounting is designed to ensure that a good audit trail of all transactions is constantly maintained within the program. This feature is turned on and off in the **Company Information** of the **Maintain** menu option. In a real world working situation, this feature would be turned on. Unless your instructor has you turn this feature on, you will be able to correct errors quickly and easily without creating a record of those corrections.

Correcting Unposted Errors.

If you should detect an error while in any of Peachtree's input screens prior to posting or printing, you can quickly and easily correct the error prior to continuing with the transaction.

1. Using your mouse, click in the field that contains the error. This will highlight the selected text box information so that you can change it.
2. Type the correct information; then pres the TAB key to enter it. You may then either TAB to other fields needing corrections or again use the mouse to click in the proper field.
3. If you have selected an incorrect account or any other type of look up information, use the pull down menu to select the correct account or information. This will replace the incorrect account with the correct account.
4. To discard an entry and start over, click on the Delete icon. You will not be given the opportunity to verify this step so be sure you want to

delete the transaction before selecting this option. This option may not be available on every input screen.

5. Review the entry for accuracy after any editing corrections.
6. Complete the transaction by posting or printing.

Should you detect an error after you have posted the transaction, it can still be quickly and easily corrected. The only additional step needed to correct a posted transaction is to find it and bring it up on your screen.

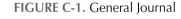

Correcting Posted Errors.

Generate an on-screen report which will contain the document needing correction. As an example, a sales invoice can be found in an Aged Receivables Report, an Invoice Register or a Sales Journal. A General Journal entry can be found in a General Journal or a General Ledger report.

Select the line containing the item needing correction by single clicking the mouse cursor. This will place a blue box around the line and the cursor will turn into a magnifying glass with a Z in the center. Peachtree Complete 8.0 comes packaged with a sample company called Bellwether Garden Supply. Looking at a General Journal report under the Reports menu your screen will look like this:

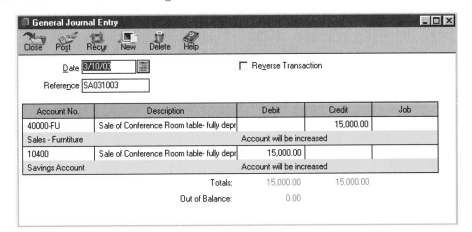

FIGURE C-1. General Journal

By double clicking on any selected line, you can bring up that particular transaction. If for example, we double click the selection from Figure C-1, we are presented with the following:

FIGURE C-2. General Journal Entry

We could now edit any field of this entry and **Post** it again. The procedures that were presented for correcting an unposted transaction can now be applied. You can experiment with this feature in the sample company if your program has Bellwether installed.

PART D

**HOW TO REPEAT OR RESTART
AN ASSIGNMENT**

You always have the option to repeat an assignment for additional practice or start over on an assignment. You simply restore the sample company files back to their original state using the Backup created at the start of the assignment. (See Part A). The procedure for restoring a file is very similar:

1. Open the company whose files you wish to restore. Let's say we wish to restore Bellwether Garden Supply. We would open that company using the **Open** feature from the **File** menu option.

2. While in the Menu Window, select **Restore** from the **File** menu option. This will bring up the Open Backup File dialogue box as follows:

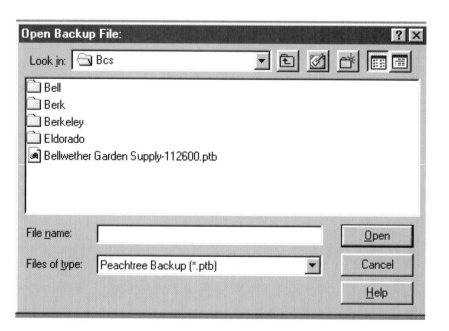

3. Peachtree will default to the folder where the regular company files are kept. If you are keeping your backups on a floppy or on a drive/path other than the one Peachtree is defaulting to, you must use the **Look in** option to change the drive and select the correct path from the options given. You may have several backups made at different points in time so be sure to select the correct one. In the example above, there is only one backup so we would select Bellwether Garden Supply-112600.ptb. This was a backup made on November 26, 2000. After you have selected the correct filename, click on **Open**.

PART E

At certain times in the assignments you are asked to make a backup copy of a company's data files. There are several reasons why you might wish to access the backup copy of a company's data files. For example, you may not have printed a required report in an assignment before advancing the period to a new month or before adding additional transactions. You may have several errors and simply want to start an assignment over or to a point prior to the errors rather than correct the many mistakes.

If you backup your data using a different filename each day, you will have the option of restoring from any of these files. It would be wise to indicate in your text the point at which you created each backup so you will know what transactions have been completed at each of the backup's dates.

PART F

When you install Peachtree Complete Accounting, the program automatically installs the printer established as the default Windows printer as the default printer for Peachtree Accounting. If you have not yet installed a default printer in Windows, you will need to do so prior to attempting to print any reports from the Peachtree Accounting program. Refer to your Windows manual for information on installing a printer.

The installation process for the Windows default printer does not ensure that the default printer and display settings within Peachtree Accounting will work to your satisfaction; consequently, you must test and if necessary adjust your printer and display settings before you complete any of the assignments in the text. Once the print and display settings are adjusted, they will become the default printer and display settings for each set of company data files. You need only make these adjustments once.

If you need to change the font sizes or typefaces on your reports, you can do that from within Peachtree. Each report that you select will have an **Options** button as illustrated in Figure F-1.

FIGURE F-1. Options Button

Selecting **Options** will bring up a dialog box with multiple tabs containing various parameters that can be changed for the report. One of these tabs is **Fonts** from which you can change the typeface and font for each item on the report. See Figure F-2.

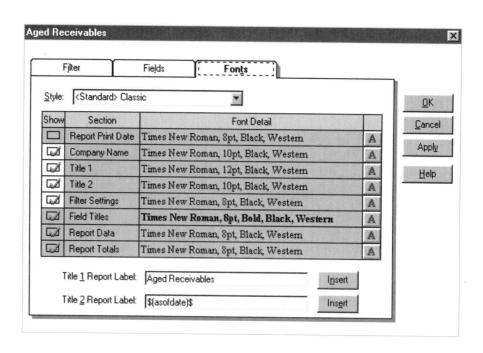

PHOTO CREDITS

Account Title	Normal Balance	Financial Report Found On	Category	Permanent or Temporary
Accounts Payable	Credit	Balance Sheet	Current Liability	Permanent
Accounts Receivable	Debit	Balance Sheet	Current Asset	Permanent
Accumulated Depreciation	Credit	Balance Sheet	Contra Plant & Equipment	Permanent
Advertising Expense	Debit	Income Statement	Operating Expense	Temporary
Allowance for Doubtful Accounts	Credit	Balance Sheet	Contra Current Asset	Permanent
Bad Debts Recovered	Credit	Income Statement	Other Income	Temporary
Bad Debts Expense	Debit	Income Statement	Operating Expense	Temporary
Bond Interest Expense	Debit	Income Statement	Operating Expense	Temporary
Bond Interest Payable	Credit	Balance Sheet	Current Liability	Permanent
Bonds Payable	Credit	Balance Sheet	Long-Term Liability	Permanent
Building	Debit	Balance Sheet	Plant & Equipment	Permanent
Capital	Credit	Statement of Owner's Equity; Balance Sheet	Owner's Equity	Permanent
Cash	Debit	Balance Sheet	Current Asset	Permanent
Cash Short and Over (Assume Short)	Debit	Income Statement	Miscellaneous Expense	Temporary
(Assume Over)	Credit	Income Statement	Other Income	Temporary
Change Fund	Debit	Balance Sheet	Current Asset	Permanent
Commissions Earned	Credit	Income Statement	Revenue	Temporary
Common Stock	Credit	Balance Sheet	Stockholders' Equity	Permanent
Common Stock Subscribed	Credit	Balance Sheet	Stockholders' Equity	Permanent
Common Stock Dividend Distributable	Credit	Balance Sheet	Stockholders' Equity	Permanent
Copyright	Debit	Balance Sheet	Intangible Asset	Permanent
Cost of Goods Sold	Debit	Income Statement	Cost	Temporary
Credit Card Expense	Debit	Income Statement	Other Expense	Temporary
Depletion Expense	Debit	Income Statement	Operating Expense	Temporary
Depreciation Expense	Debit	Income Statement	Operating Expense	Temporary
Discount on Bonds Payable	Debit	Balance Sheet	Contra Long-Term Liability	Permanent
Discount on Notes Payable	Debit	Balance Sheet	Contra Current Liability	Permanent
Dividends Payable	Credit	Balance Sheet	Current Liability	Permanent
Equipment	Debit	Balance Sheet	Plant & Equipment	Permanent
Federal Income Tax Payable	Credit	Balance Sheet	Current Liability	Permanent
FICA Tax Payable	Credit	Balance Sheet	Current Liability	Permanent
Freight-In	Debit	Income Statement	Cost of Goods Sold	Temporary
FUTA Tax Payable	Credit	Balance Sheet	Current Liability	Permanent
Gain on Sale of Asset	Credit	Income Statement	Other Income	Temporary
Goodwill	Debit	Balance Sheet	Intangible Asset	Permanent
Income Summary	—	—	Owner's Equity	Temporary
Insurance Expense	Debit	Income Statement	Operating Expense	Temporary
Interest Earned	Credit	Income Statement	Other Income	Temporary
Interest Expense	Debit	Income Statement	Other Expense	Temporary
Interest Payable	Credit	Balance Sheet	Current Liability	Permanent
Land	Debit	Balance Sheet	Plant & Equipment	Permanent
Land Improvement	Debit	Balance Sheet	Plant & Equipment	Permanent
Loss from Fire	Debit	Income Statement	Other Expense	Temporary
Loss on Sale of (Asset)	Debit	Income Statement	Other Expense	Temporary
Loss or Gain from Realization (Assume Loss)	Debit	Income Statement	Other Expense	Temporary
(Assume Gain)	Credit	Income Statement	Other Income	Temporary
Machinery	Debit	Balance Sheet	Plant & Equipment	Permanent